HANDBOOK
TO THE ENVIRO
OF LONDON

alphabetically arranged

HANDBOOK

TO THE ENVIRONS

OF LONDON

containing an account of every town and village
and of all places of interest
within a circle of twenty miles round London

by JAMES THORNE, F S A
with 35 engravings

GODFREY CAVE ASSOCIATES

The original edition, which was not illustrated,
was published in two volumes in 1876

This edition published 1983
by Godfrey Cave Associates Ltd.
ISBN 0-906223-90-3

Printed and bound by R. J. Acford, Chichester, Sussex, England.

PREFACE.

THE HANDBOOK OF THE ENVIRONS OF LONDON contains an account—written in every instance from personal examination and inquiry—of every town and village, and all places of historical, antiquarian, and artistic interest, within a circuit of twenty miles round London, and of the more important places lying four or five miles beyond that boundary. For the Metropolis an inner circle of four miles has been taken, and places within that circle are not included in the Environs. These limits comprise the whole of Middlesex outside the capital, a large part of Surrey, Kent, Essex, and Hertfordshire, and smaller portions of Berkshire and Buckinghamshire.

The district thus marked out is probably unrivalled in scenes of historical interest and personal and literary associations; in existing palaces, manor-houses, and mansions, and the sites of those which have been swept away; in abbeys and churches; the homes and graves of remarkable men; in beautiful and characteristic scenery; in collections of pictures and works of art; in national workshops and arsenals, and places of popular amusement and resort. How rich and varied are the subjects and associations, the lightest draft on the memory will determine. Runnimede and the Great Charter, Tilbury Fort and the Armada, Uxbridge and its abortive Treaty, the Rye House and its Plot, at once recur to every one's recollection. We think of Windsor Castle, glorious in itself and its surroundings, and the residence of the long line of British monarchs from the Conqueror to Victoria; of Hampton Court, witness of the grandeur and the fall of Wolsey, the abode of his imperious master, of William III. and Mary, of Anne and the early Georges; the Richmond of Henry VII. and James I., of George II. and Queen Caroline, and Merlin's Cave, Lord Hervey and Stephen Duck; of Greenwich, the birthplace and the favourite seat of Elizabeth, its Hospital and Observatory; the sites of the royal palaces of Eltham, Havering-atte-Bower, Oatlands, and Nonsuch; the Theobalds and

Hatfield of James I. and Cecil; the Gorhambury of the Bacons; the Ham House of the Lauderdales and Dysarts; the Claremont of Clive, of the Princess Charlotte, and of Louis Philippe; the Beddington of the Carews; Panshanger with its Raphaels and matchless Bartolommeo; the Grove and the Clarendon portraits; Cassiobury, Osterley, Chevening, and Knole; Gobions and Sir Thomas More; Barn-Elms and Bayfordbury, the Kit-Cat Club and the Tonson relics; Syon House and Monastery, and wandering nuns; Kew with its unequalled Botanic Gardens, and courtly recollections; Burnham Beeches and Epping Forest; Blackheath with its Jack Cade gatherings and royal pageants and cavalcades; Putney Heath and its duels, Wimbledon with its Common and camp; Cooper's Hill and St. George's; Hayes, Holwood, and St. Anne's Hill, the cherished retreats of Chatham, Pitt, and Fox; Chertsey, where "the last accents flow'd from Cowley's tongue;" Chalfont St. Giles and Horton, Milton's "daily walks and ancient neighbourhood;" and Stoke Poges, the ivy-mantled tower and tomb of Gray; Eton and Harrow, with their long roll of scholars, poets, statesmen; the sister heights of Highgate and Hampstead, the former with its oath and horns, the latter with old memories of its wells and flask, its assemblies, bowling greens, and fleet marriages, Clarissa Harlowe and Evelina, Akenside and Steele, Erskine, Mansfield, and Romney; Hounslow with its highwaymen; St. Albans with its abbey, battle-fields, the grave of Bacon, and the buried Verulamium; Chertsey and Barking Abbeys; Waltham Abbey, Cross, and powder-mills; the lost palaces of Canons and Wanstead; Fulham, the palace and tombs of the Bishops of London; and Croydon, where were the palace and monuments of the Archbishops of Canterbury; the old medicinal wells of Epsom, Hampstead, Richmond, Acton, Barnet, with their assemblies, raffling-shops, card-rooms, and concerts; Deptford with its Royal Dockyard; Woolwich with Dockyard, Arsenals, and Gun Factory, and all the marvels of the heavy ordnance manufacture; and Enfield and its Small-Arms Factory, the triumph of modern mechanism, contrasting with its ancient chase and palace; Horace Walpole's Strawberry Hill, and Pope's Villa and Grotto; and the homes and groves of Evelyn and Temple, of Bolingbroke, Swift, and Gay, of Thomson, Hogarth, Johnson, and Charles Lamb.

The list might be extended almost indefinitely, and every item in it would suggest some memorable name or animating association. Yet for the illustration of this rich tract comparatively little has been done. Lysons' 'Environs' is a painstaking and thoroughly trustworthy "history of the parishes within twelve miles of the capital;" but it is a parish history, loaded with all local details, admirable in its way, but limited in interest, and wearisome from its extent. The first edition of Lysons' Environs was published in 1791-96; and nearly seventy years have passed since the last edition was issued, its bulk—it is in five parts equal to five large quarto volumes—probably deterring republication; and no other book has taken its place. Earlier than Lysons was ' The Ambulator, or Stranger's Companion—(in later editions altered to the ' Pocket Companion') —in a Tour Round London.' The Ambulator professed to describe, under an alphabetical arrangement, " whatever is remarkable either for Grandeur, Elegancy, Use, or Curiosity, within the circuit of twenty-five miles." The materials were " collected by a gentleman for his amusement," and the work was comprised in one thin pocket volume. The Ambulator was as meagre as Lysons was diffuse, and as negligent and inexact as he was careful and accurate. But the book supplied a want, and was several times reprinted at intervals of a few years.* The Environs were also included in Dr. Hunter's ' London and its Environs,' two vols., quarto, 1803—1811; in Lambert's tedious ' History and Survey of London and its Environs,' four vols., quarto, 1806; in the still more tedious ' History and Description of London and its Neighbourhood,' by David Hughson, LL.D., six thick vols., octavo, 1805, etc., and in other books of a like kind which appeared in curious abundance in the early years of the present century. But in all these the Environs are treated by way of appendage to the Capital, and the descriptions are poor and perfunctory, showing not a trace of original research or personal examination.

The present volume has the alphabetical arrangement of the Ambulator, and somewhat of the fulness of Lysons, whilst it takes a wider range than either. Leaving to Lysons and the county historians family annals, genealogies, the descent of properties, parish registers, the bills of mortality, and cases of longevity, it yet aims to serve as a book of reference as well as a guide. Without dwelling on historical, biographical, antiquarian, or architectural details, a broad outline is sketched of the history of remarkable places and objects. The descent of manors is traced where of more than local interest. Important buildings are described, and their owners and occupants mentioned. In passing through galleries, attention is directed

* The second edition was published in 1782; the twelfth, and we believe the last, in 1820.

to the more noteworthy pictures. Literary and personal associations are recalled, and matters of general or permanent interest are recorded, and illustrated by quotations from contemporary authors, or writers who have made the subject a special study, where such extracts promised to throw a clearer light on the circumstances, or to brighten the page. And while the past is thus illustrated, existing houses, churches, and objects of interest are described at sufficient length to mark their present condition and character. The physical features of the country, and the geology, where distinctive or exceptional, are noted, the leading occupations pointed out, and special processes, as at Enfield and Woolwich, briefly described.

As far as it goes, and bearing in mind its limits, the book claims to be comprehensive, full, and fairly complete. No pretence is made of exhaustive treatment : rather, it is offered as a series of rapid though faithful sketches, to serve for indication and suggestion. To ensure accuracy, every place has been visited, and most places several times. The descriptions are written from personal observation, but much assistance has been derived from residents, owners or occupiers of houses, directors of works, architects of buildings, etc.

The work has been several years on hand, and no available source of information has been intentionally neglected. The authorities used are referred to as they occur. Private communications and official and local replies to inquiries have been liberally furnished, and are gratefully acknowledged. But with all possible care and diligence, there must, in a work of such extent, and embracing so many facts, names, and dates, be many omissions, oversights, and mistakes ; and, while asking indulgence for them, the writer earnestly requests that, where detected, information of them will be kindly communicated to the Publisher, that thus the next edition may be rendered as correct and useful as possible.

It only remains to point out that, in order to interfere as little as may be with the narrative, the situation, access by railway, and population of each place are given in an opening paragraph. The population is in all cases that of 1871. A full Index has been added of names and things not expressed in the alphabetical arrangement of the headings.

HANDBOOK OF THE ENVIRONS OF LONDON.

ABBEY WOOD, KENT, a station on the North Kent Rly., 12 m. from London, and midway between Plumstead and Erith, but in the latter parish, occupies part of the site of Lesness Abbey Wood, which reached E. to Erith and back to Lesness Heath. Inn, the *Harrow*.

The district of *Lesness* or Lesnes (*Loisnes* in Domesday) was of considerable extent, and gave its name to the hundred. *Lesness Abbey* was founded in 1178, by Richard de Lucy, Justiciary of England, at West Wood in his village of Lesness, " on rising ground at the edge of the marshes," for canons regular of the order of St. Augustine, and dedicated to St. Mary and Thomas the Martyr. In 1279 "the Abbat and Covent of *Lyesnes* inclosed a great part of their marshe in Plumsted, and within 12 yeeres after they inned the rest also to their great benefite."* The breach of the embankment and "drowning" of the lands of Lesness in 1527, with their subsequent recovery under the direction of the theologian Jacobus Acontius (Giacomo Aconzio) are more particularly noticed under PLUMSTEAD. The abbey was granted various privileges, among others that of holding a fair here (*temp.* Henry III.) on the eve of SS. Simon and Jude and three days after; and at the beginning of the 14th cent. we find Pope Boniface VIII. writing to the abbot † to use his influence for the preservation of the rights and privileges of the

* Perambulation of Kent, Lambarde, p. 440, ed. 1596.
† Brit. Mus. MSS., Faust, A. VIII.

monastery of Southwark; but the house was always poor, and in 1524 Wolsey procured a bull from Pope Clement VII. for the suppression of this and three other small monasteries, and the appropriation of their revenues to his new colleges at Oxford and Ipswich. On Wolsey's fall, Lesness was seized by Henry VIII., who sometime after granted it to William Brereton, on whose execution it reverted to the Crown; it was given to Sir Ralph Sadler in 1546, and, after passing through various hands, was towards the end of the 17th cent. settled on Christ's Hospital.

Of the outer walls of the *Abbey* a few fragments may be seen on the hillside immediately S.E. of the station: an open path leads up to them. They are of flint, and of no architectural or picturesque value. The walls of the convent garden, the most perfect relic, still enclose a vegetable garden and orchard. The cloisters are said to be traceable, but the ground is too fully cropped to allow the assertion to be readily tested. The site of the Abbey Grange is marked by *Abbey Farm* (the farm-house on the hillside facing the marsh), a tasteless modern house raised on the old foundations. Stone coffins and other vestigia were exhumed in the last century.

A few years ago Abbey Wood was much in favour with sketchers, botanists, gipsy parties, and holiday-makers generally. There was the wood to ramble over at will; the hillside furnished wide prospects across the broad expanse of level marsh and the Thames beyond—here always alive with every kind of craft,—

whilst Abbey Farm and the Harrow Inn were almost the only houses. Now the Wood is in part built over; the upper part is "to let on building leases," and the rest is close fenced in, whilst notices at every turn convey the information and warning that "These Woods are the private property of the Governors of Christ's Hospital," and that "all persons trespassing in them will be prosecuted." In early summer the wood is resplendent with foxgloves—literally acres of them may be seen in flower.

About the Rly. Stat. a railway village is growing up, which has assumed the name of *Abbey Wood*. From it little is to be seen but the flat marsh, the river wall shutting out the Thames. The large noticeable building by the river side, at *Crossness* (1¼ m. across Plumstead Marsh) marks the *Southern Outfall Station* of the Metropolitan Main Drainage, where an average of 50 million gallons of sewage is pumped daily into the Thames. (*See* ERITH.) There are many pleasant strolls from Abbey Wood. *Bostall Heath*, within very easy distance—go up the lane by the Harrow, noting the dells on either side—is a charming bit of still open heath, and now (1874) happily secured from enclosure, with wide views across the Thames valley; farther S. is East Wickham; S.E. is a pleasant way from Bostall Heath to Bexley or Crayford. Bostall or Borstall is a hamlet of Plumstead; the manor belongs to the Clothworkers' Company, London.

ABBOT'S LANGLEY (Dom. *Langelai*), HERTS, 20 m. N.W. from London, and about 1½ m. S.E. (by field and lane) from the King's Langley Stat. of the North-Western Rly., pop. 2638. In the time of Edward the Confessor, "Egelwine the Black, and Winefled his wife, gave the vill. to the abbots of St. Albans, from whence it had the adjunct of Abbot to distinguish it from the neighbouring vill [of King's Langley], and was denominated *Langley* from the length of the vill., for the name signifies a long land."[*]

On the E. the parish is hilly and broken, with pretty lanes and good views; along the W. side is the broad valley of the

[*] Chauncy, Hist. Antiquities of Hertfordshire, reprint, vol. ii., p. 336.

Gade, through which also run the Grand Junction Canal and the North-Western Rly. The village stands on high ground in a richly wooded neighbourhood, and is famous as the birthplace of the only Englishman who ever became Pope (Adrian IV.) Nicholas Breakspeare was the son of a servant in the abbey of St. Albans, where he himself for some time filled a menial post, but asking to be admitted a monk, he was driven from the convent for his presumption—which proved, quoth Fuller, "no mishap, but a happy miss unto him." Born towards the end of the 11th cent., he was elected Pope in 1154, and died in 1159.

The *Church* (St. Lawrence) is in part as old as Breakspeare's time, but the greater part is later. It consists of nave and aisles with clerestorey; chancel with S. aisle; and at the W. end a square embattled tower, in which is a peal of 6 bells. The nave and tower are rough-cast, the chancel of flint and stone set in alternate squares. The two west bays of the nave have round-headed arches, with nail-head mouldings (re-chiselled in restorations, the last in 1866), borne on thick cylindrical piers; the arches of the other three bays are pointed. The windows of the S. aisle are Dec., the others mostly Perp. They contain some poor modern painted glass by Laurent of Paris. The font is of the early part of the 15th cent. *Brasses*, in centre aisle of nave: half-size to Thos. Cogwell and his two wives, 1607; and an older, but very small and much worn one, without inscription. The principal *Mont.* is of Lord Chief Justice Raymond, Lord Abbot of Abbot's Langley (d. 1732), best known by his 'Reports.' The mont. represents Raymond in his official robes, in a reclining position, attended by an allegorical female; above are the family arms. It is a good example of the art and taste of the time, and interesting from the sculptor, Westley Gill, having inscribed his name upon it. S. of the chancel aisle is a small mural mont. with well-executed kneeling effigy, coloured and gilt, of Mrs. Anne Combe, d. 1640. On one side is a statuette of Time, with his scythe; on the other Death, with dart and hour-glass.

Near the ch. is *Cecil Lodge* (W. H. Smith, Esq., M.P.), formerly a seat of the Marquis of Salisbury. *Hazlewood* (Lord

Rokeby) is a little S. Other seats are— *Abbot's Hill House* (J. Dickinson, Esq.); *Nash Mill* (John Evans, Esq., F.R.S., F.S.A.), containing fine collections of stone and bronze implements and British coins; and the *Manor House* (Sir Samuel Canning, Bart.) On the rt. of and close to the N.W. Rly., just before reaching King's Langley Stat., is the *Booksellers' Provident Retreat*, a neat red brick Tudor building, erected in 1849. It comprises 7 houses for aged members of the Booksellers' Provident Institution and their widows, who, besides residence, receive annuities of from 20 to 50 guineas.

At *Hunton Bridge*, a large hamlet on the N.W. Rly. and Grand Junction Canal, 1½ m. S.W. from Abbot's Langley vill., is a remarkably good Dec. ch., *St. Paul's, Langley Bury*, built and endowed in 1864 at the cost of W. Jones Loyd, Esq., from the designs of Mr. H. Woodyer. It is of squared flint with Bath stone dressings, and has at the W. a tower and tall shingled spire 130 feet high. The projection on the S.E. is a mortuary chapel for the family of the founder. The interior is very chastely fitted, and has some good carving. A little S.W. of the ch. is *Langley Bury* (W. Jones Loyd, Esq.), built by Chief Justice Raymond, and a good building of its time, but enlarged and improved of late.

At *Laverstock Green*, another hamlet (the eccl. district, with 263 inhabitants, being partly formed out of Abbot's Langley, Hemel Hempstead, and St. Michael's parish, St. Albans), about 3 m. N. on the road to Harpenden, is a neat little Gothic ch. (Holy Trinity) of flint and stone, built in 1858.

Nash Mill, on the Grand Junction Canal, where are the extensive paper mills of Messrs. Dickinson and Evans, is in Abbot's Langley parish, but is much nearer to the vill. of King's Langley, from which it is 1 m. N. It was in a field at *Bedmont*, 1 m. N. of Abbot's Langley, that Mr. Evans found, in 1862, the first two flint implements discovered in the drift of the Thames Valley.

ABRIDGE, Essex (anc. *Affebrugge*, or *Affebridge*), so called from its position by the bridge over the Roding; *

on the Ongar road, 13 m. from Whitechapel, 1½ m. S.E., down a pretty country lane, from Theydon Stat. (15½ m.) of the Grt. E. Rly. (Ongar branch). In coaching days the *White Hart* was a busy posting house; it is now a country inn, where the tourist will find reasonable accommodation and great civility. The vill. consists of a single street of old-fashioned shops and private houses,—in appearance a compound of a country village and a small roadside town. Abridge is a hamlet of Lambourne par. Lambourne ch. is about 1 m. S.E., by a pleasant walk across the fields; Abridge has a small chapel of ease served by a curate. The manor of Affebrugge was given to the Knights Hospitallers by Peter de Voisnes and William de Blois. Abridge stands in the midst of pleasing scenery: the low hills of Theydon on one side, and Lambourne on the other, command wide views over Epping Forest (about 2½ m. W.), and the hills of Kent.

ACTON, Middx. (A.-S. *Ac.*, oak, *tun*, town), sometimes called West Acton, to distinguish it from the neighbouring hamlet of East Acton, a vill. on the Uxbridge rd., 5 m. W. of the Marble Arch; and a Stat. on the N. and S.W. Junction Rly., 10 m. from the Euston terminus; pop. 8306. The manor has belonged to the see of London from time immemorial. There is little to be seen in the village; and the immediate vicinity, never very interesting, has been rendered less so by building operations. On the W. are some pleasant lanes; the S., towards the Thames, is level, and laid out in market gardens and orchards, with a few wheat fields.

The *Church* was, except the tower, rebuilt in 1865. It is of red and black bricks, Dec. in style, with gables to the bays of the aisles, a deep chancel, and a large E. window of 5 lights filled with painted glass, a memorial to Earl Howe: archi-

---

At the bridge," from the A.-S. *æt*, at, and bridge. (Words and Places, p. 384, n. 3, and 463.) But the oldest form, *Affebrugge*, hardly agrees with this derivation. May it not rather come from Celtic *Aff* or *Avon*, water, and bridge? The valley of the Roding here broadens out into level meadows, which are even now flooded in wet seasons, and may in early times have been permanently under water, so as to form a sort of lake along which the road ran.

tects, Messrs. Francis. The massive-looking tower is the ancient one "cased with brick in 1766." The place of the "convenient conduit at the entrance to Acton on the London side," made and endowed for the public benefit by Thomas Thorney in 1612, and recovered to the public use at a heavy cost by means of a Chancery suit instituted by Samuel Wegg in 1755, is marked by a pump "erected by the Rev. Wm. Antrobus in 1819." Acton has of late so increased in size and population that pump or conduit would be a very inconvenient medium for its water supply. Such matters are now looked after by the Local Board of Health, whose office is the handsome new Gothic building at the corner of the road leading to the Steyne.

During the Commonwealth period Acton seems to have been quite a Puritan stronghold. Philip Nye, whose "thanksgiving beard" Butler has immortalized, held the living. Nye was at this time one of the most prominent of the Puritan ministers, and filled several government offices; in a pamphlet, entitled 'The Levite's Scourge,' quoted in the Notes to Gray's Hudibras, it is said that "he rode to London every Lord's day in triumph, in a coach drawn by four horses, to exercise them." Francis Rous, Speaker of the Little Parliament, one of Cromwell's peers, provost of Eton, benefactor of Pembroke College, Oxford, and author of several Puritan books, resided for some years at Acton, where he died in 1659; he was carried in great state to be buried at Eton. Sir Matthew Hale, the celebrated Lord Chief Justice, and Richard Baxter, the eminent Nonconformist divine, were also contemporary residents here. Their houses, and that of General Skippon, were near the ch.; but some have been pulled down, and others are difficult to identify. On the Restoration, Nye was ejected, and the living given to Bruno Ryves, chaplain to Charles II., and author of the 'Mercurius Rusticus,' as bitter an enemy to Puritans as Nye had been to Churchmen. In the ch. register are entries of the marriage of the daughter "of the Right Honble. Major-General Philip Skippon," and the burial of his wife, in which Skippon's titles have been struck out, and the word "traytor" written over; Lysons conjectures by Ryves. William Lloyd,

the nonjuring Bishop of Norwich, lived here in 1682. Mrs. Barry, the noted tragedy actress, and pupil of Charles II.'s Earl of Rochester, resided at Acton after her retirement from the stage in 1706 to her death, Nov. 13, 1713. A tablet to her memory was attached to a pillar in the S. aisle of the old ch. In 1750 the name of Capt. Philip Thicknesse occurs in the register. In the house formerly Gen. Skippon's, Lady Derwentwater was living at the time of her husband's execution. Cromwell, on his return from the battle of Worcester, was met at Acton by the Council of State, the House of Commons, the Lord Mayor, Aldermen, and Common Council, and escorted in triumph to London.

Berrymeade Priory (J. Dawson, Esq.), a stuccoed Gothic building of the Strawberry-Hill type, at the entrance to Acton on the l., is said to occupy the site of a convent of 40 nuns. *Fordhook* (Capt. G. Tyrrel, R.N.), once the residence of Fielding the novelist, is a good mansion at the W. extremity of the vill. : from the W. side of it a series of country lanes and field paths (the pleasantest stroll out of Acton) leads to Twyford Abbey. (*See* TWYFORD).

At *East Acton*, on the rt. of the Uxbridge rd., and close to the rly. stat., are the *Goldsmiths' Almshouses* for 10 poor men and as many poor women.

At the S.W. corner of *Old Oak Common*, by Wormwood Scrubs, in the angle between the Grt. W., and the N. and S.W. Jn. Rlys., stood *Acton Wells House*, in the garden of which are springs that early attracted attention as "purging waters"* and later were reputed to have medicinal qualities similar to the Cheltenham waters. About the middle of the last century the Acton Wells were in great repute. "The Assembly Room was a place of fashionable resort, and the neighbouring hamlets of East and West Acton, and Friars' Place, were filled with persons of all ranks who came to reside here during the summer season."† The wells are in the garden, and what remains of the Wells House now forms part of the outbuildings of a farmhouse, which stands on the W. side of the Grt. W. Rly. The farmhouse itself is recent. On the adjacent portion of Old Oak Common was formed in 1870

---

* Boyle's Works, vol. iv., p. 246. † Lysons.

the so-called *People's Garden,* now held by the German Club, Foley Street, London, and transformed into a veritable summer *Biergarten,* with the biggest dancing platform in this country, and where German is chiefly spoken.

In Nov. 1642 there was an encounter at *Acton Back,* near Turnham Green, between the army of Charles I. and that of the Parliament under the Earl of Essex. This part, now better known as *Acton Green,* has some pleasant villa residences, among others *Fairlawn* (R. Attenborough, Esq.) Here dwelt till his death, Oct. 19, 1863, *æt.* 84, John Bowyer Nichols, F.S.A., the well-known printer and antiquary ; also Prof. Lindley, F.R.S., the distinguished botanist, d. Nov. 1, 1865.

ADDINGTON, SURREY (Dom.

Edintone, perhaps the *Town of the Edings*), lies at the foot of a range of hills called Addington Common, about 3 m. S. by E. of the East, or New Croydon Stat. of the L. B. and S. C., and the S E. Rlys. The road to it is by Addiscombe and Shirley, but a pleasanter way is by the fields, a little E. of the stat., to Addington Common, whence you descend by a pretty lane to the village.

Addington, now a rural vill. of 607 inhab., is a place of considerable antiquity. At the Domesday Survey the manor belonged to Tezelin, the king's cook. It afterwards reverted to the Crown, passed to the Ailwyns, Aguillons, and (temp. Henry III.) to the Bardolfs, being still held by " the serjeanty of making *hastias* in the king's kitchen on the day of his coronation ; or providing some one, as his deputy, to make a dish called *girunt,* and if suet [*seym*] was added, it was called *malpigernoun.*" * " At the coronation of James II. the lord of the manor of Bardolf claimed to find a man to make a mess of *grout* in the king's kitchen, and prayed that the king's cook might perform that service," † which was allowed, and the lord of the manor, according to ancient custom, was knighted. At the coronation of George III., Mr. Spencer, as lord of the manor of Addington, presented a dish of pottage to the king : this was the last occasion on which the custom was observed. Mr. Lysons

quotes from the vol. on the Government of Royal Households, published by the Soc. of Antiquaries, a recipe of the 14th cent. to make a pottage called Bardolf, which he not unreasonably conjectures may be the dish in question; " it consisted of almond milk, the brawn of capons, sugar and spices, chicken parboiled and chopped, etc." * There was a second manor in Addington, which in the reign of Edward I. was given by William de Merton to the Knights Templars, and, on the dissolution of that order in 1311, passed with their other possessions in England to the Knights of St. John of Jerusalem. After the suppression of monasteries the two manors were united. In 1807 the manor, park, and advowson were purchased by Abp. Sutton, under powers granted by an Act of Parliament, as a summer residence for the Archbishops of Canterbury, instead of the former palace of the archbishops at Croydon. The ancient manor house of the Aiguillons and Bardolfs—an embattled mansion of stone and flint—stood near the church. It was erected in 1400, and pulled down on the completion of the present mansion in 1780 : the site is still known as Castle Hill.

Addington Place, the country seat of the archbishops of Canterbury, was begun by Alderman Trecothick in 1772, and finished by his nephew. It was merely an ordinary mansion in the style common at that time, but in 1829-30 a chapel, library, and several rooms were added by Abp. Howley, from the designs of Mr. H. Harrison. It is now a spacious and convenient residence, though little palatial, and nothing ecclesiastical, in character. The archbishops usually reside here the last half of the year. The park, to which Abp. Howley made considerable additions, is extensive, varied in surface, very beautiful, with romantic dells filled with noble trees and an undergrowth of rhododendrons, while the heights afford fine views : it is not open to the public.

Addington *Church* (St. Mary's) is small and plain : it consists of a Norman chancel, an E.E. nave, with a south aisle divided from it by four massive piers, and a low embattled tower at the W. end. In the chancel are three narrow round-

---

arched windows, very deeply splayed : the outline of a fourth may be traced in the wall above. The exterior is chiefly modern : it was faced with brick by Alderman Trecothick in 1773, but refaced in flint and stone by Abp. Howley in 1843, when a new porch was erected, and the interior restored. Observe in the chancel undersized *brasses* of John Leigh (1509), and his wife Isabel (1544) ; and, S. side, Thos. Hatteclyff, " one of the fowre Masters of the Howsholde " of Henry VIII., and Anne his wife (1540). *Monts.*—On N. side of chancel, a large one, with kneeling effigies to Nicholas Leigh (d. 1565) and his wife Ann, his son John Leigh (d. 1576) and his wife Joan, his grandson Sir Oliph Leigh (d. 1611), who erected the mont., and his wife Jane. A large and tasteless mont. to Alderman Trecothick, d. 1775. Three of the four archbishops buried here have —Abp. Sutton, d. 1828, a mural tablet; Abp. Howley, d. 1848, an altar-tomb in the chancel, with a Bible on a cushion and a crosier laid upon it; and Abp. Sumner, d. 1862, a small and plain mural slab. Abp. Longley, d. Oct. 27, 1868, lies in a plain grave at the S.W. angle of the churchyard. The last Archbishop of Canterbury buried at Croydon was Herring, in 1757; the last at Lambeth was Moore, in 1805. S. of the nave is a plain mural slab to Manners Sutton, Viscount Canterbury (d. 1848), Speaker of the House of Commons from 1817 to 1835. In the ch.-yd. is a large yew, but the trunk is a mere shell.

The village is clean, quiet, and rather picturesque : observe the fine flowers in the cottage gardens. Opposite the church is a neat country inn, the *Cricketers.* Seats : *Heathfield Lodge* (J. C. Cowley, Esq.) ; *Spring Park*, between Addington and Wickham Street (J. Tillett, Esq.) ; and *Ballards*, 1½ m. W. (A. Hoffman, Esq.) On Addington Common are vestiges of a group of 25 barrows, mostly small, but one nearly 40 ft. in diameter. All of them have been opened. Here and on *Shirley Common* are extensive views. The walks hence, S. along the hills to Sanderstead, and N.E. by the ' bottoms ' to Wickham and Hayes, are charming : the ' bottoms ' are a favourite resort of the botanist.*

* Lysons, Brayley, R. Symmes, Collections for the History of Addington, Brit. Mus. MSS., 6167.

ADDISCOMBE (formerly *Adgecombe*), SURREY, ½ m. E. of the East or New Croydon Stat. of the Brighton and S.E. Rlys., was a seat of the Heron family in the early part of the 16th cent. The once famous mansion was built in 1702 for Wm. Draper, Esq., the son-in-law of John Evelyn. In his Diary (July 11, 1703,) Evelyn records having visited the new house, and adds : " The outside to the coveing being such excellent brickwork, based with Portland stone, with the pilasters, windows and within, that I pronounced it, in all the points of good and solid architecture, to be one of the very best gentleman's houses in Surrey, when finished." The archt. was, it is said, Vanbrugh ; the walls and ceilings of the staircase and saloon were painted by Sir James Thornhill. Addiscombe was successively the residence of Lord Chancellor Talbot, who died here in 1737 ; Lord Grantham, and Charles Jenkinson, 1st Earl of Liverpool. It was sold in 1809 to the East India Company, who added to the buildings, and established here a *Military College*, at first only for cadets of the engineers and artillery, but afterwards of the whole service. On the transfer of the government of India to the Crown, the institution, which had acquired a high reputation, became the *Royal Military College for the East Indian Army*, but was closed in June 1862, on the amalgamation of the Indian with the British service, the cadets being transferred to the Woolwich Academy. In 1863 the estate was sold by auction for about £30,000 ; the house was pulled down, and the site became a nest of ' villas,' with a short branch from the North Kent Rly. (the Stat. is at the bottom of *Clyde Road*). A neat ch. (St. Matthew's) E.E. in style, was built in 1865, in the Addiscombe Road, but not on the old Addiscombe estate.

ADDLESTONE (anc. *Atlesdon*), SURREY, a long scattered vill., and a stat. on the Weybridge and Virginia Water br. of the L. and S.W. Rly., 19 m. from London by road, 20½ m. by rly., and 1½ m. S. by E. from Chertsey, of which it is a tithing ; pop. of the eccl. dist. 2894.

The neat E.E. *Church* (St. Paul) was erected in 1837, from the designs of Mr. J. Savage. In the ch.-yd. is the tomb of Mrs. Charles Kemble, d. 1838, as an actress known as Miss De Camp. She resided here some years with her son, John Mitchell Kemble, the eminent Anglo-Saxon scholar (whose 'Codex Diplomaticus Ævi Saxonici' and 'Saxons in England' are known to every student of English history), in a pretty rural villa known as Chapel Fields. An object of general interest is the *Crouch Oak*, a most venerable tree, 24 ft. in girth at 3 ft. from the ground. It has lost its head, but is still vigorous, and at 9 ft. from the ground, its main branch, a large tree in itself, extends horizontally from the trunk a distance of 48 ft. The tradition is that the Crouch Oak was a boundary of Windsor Forest, whence its name, from the *crouch*, or cross, cut upon it.* Such boundary oaks, as Mr. Kemble observes, are frequently referred to in ancient charters; a very remarkable one, a boundary of the lands of Waverley Abbey, and now known as the King's Oak, may be seen at Tilford Green, near Farnham.† Tradition says that Wycliffe preached under the Crouch Oak, and that Queen Elizabeth dined beneath its branches. In July 1872, Mr. Spurgeon, after presiding at a tea-meeting held in the meadow by which the oak stands, on the occasion of laying the memorial stone of a new Baptist chapel to replace the old one close by, preached to a congregation that spread far beyond the old oak's branches. When the Act was obtained (1808) for enclosing the waste Crown lands in the manor of Chertsey Beamond, the Crouch Oak was sold by the Commissioners of Woods and Forests for timber; but the purchaser, the late Colonel de Visme, a resident in the neighbourhood, instead of cutting it down, had the good taste to fence it round, and thus ensure its protection. Another source of danger to the tree was the belief of the damsels of the locality that a piece of its bark taken internally acted as a love-charm. The oak stands just within the entrance gateway of *Crouch Oak House* (W. Hudson, Esq.), in a lane N. of the main street.

Within a stone's throw of Crouch Oak are *Princess Mary's Village Homes*, a group of 10 neat model cottages, with an excellent schoolroom, erected in 1871, under the patronage of the Princess Mary of Teck, by voluntary subscriptions, to provide 'homes' for the daughters of convict mothers, and girls selected from Industrial Schools. Each home, with its little family of 10 children, is under the care of a resident 'mother,' who seeks to train her charge in household duties, so as to fit them for industrial life. Ten of these cottage homes have been erected in a field of about three acres, presented by Miss Cavendish, of Lyne Grove, Chertsey, and it is intended to increase their number so as to provide for 300 children.

Addlestone has become a village of numerous comfortable villas, and is steadily increasing in population. In the neighbourhood are some houses of mark. *Woburn Park* (W. J. Alt, Esq.), under a somewhat different name, has a place in our literature. About 1735 Philip Southcote designed it as a sort of garden farm, calling it Woburn Farm, but eventually building a better house and adding 150 acres to the grounds, he converted it into an ornamental demesne which attracted general notice both for its novelty and elegance. Gray visited and praised it. Horace Walpole, who more than once refers to it in his Letters, says in his 'Essay on Gardening' that in Woburn Farm "Mr. Philip Southcote founded the *ferme ornée*;" Whateley* gives an elaborate and laudatory description of it; and Mason, in his 'English Garden,' writes—

> "On thee too, SOUTHCOTE, shall the Muse bestow
> No vulgar praise; for thou to humblest things
> Couldst give ennobling beauties; deck'd by thee,
> The simple Farm eclipsed the Garden's pride,
> Ev'n as the virgin blush of innocence,
> The harlotry of art."

After a while the house was eclipsed by the greater novelty of Walpole's Gothic, as Lord Bath notes in his verses on Strawberry Hill:—

> "Though Surrey boasts its Oatlands,
> And Claremont kept so jim,
> And though they talk of Southcotes,
> 'Tis but a dainty whim;
> For ask the gallant Bristow,
> Who does in taste excel,
> If Strawberry Hill, if Strawberry
> Don't bear away the bell."

Mr. Southcote died here Sept. 25th, 1758. Little is left of the *ferme ornée* now. The house, which was successively the residence of Admiral Stirling, and for more than a quarter of a century of the Rt.

---

* Kemble, Saxons in England, vol. i., p. 59, n.
† See Handbook for Surrey, p. 89, ed. 1865.

* Observations on Modern Gardening.

Hon. the Dowager Lady King, widow of the 7th Baron King, father of the present Earl of Lovelace, was enlarged a few years ago by the Earl of Kilmorey, and a chapel, semi-Byzantine in style, added, but not consecrated. The grounds were also entirely rearranged; but many of the trees planted by Mr. Southcote still remain. From the summit of Woburn Hill the views are very beautiful.

Sayes Court (the property of Mr. Rastrick), in the centre of the village, was the residence of James Payne, the architect, and afterwards of Sir Charles Wetherell. *Ongar Hill*, ½ m. S.W. (B. L. Lewis, Esq.), once the residence of Admiral Sir Hyde Parker, and afterwards of Sir Fred. Morton Eden, Bart., was built about a century back, and, working at it as a bricklayer's boy under his brother, an illiterate petty bricklayer, was a lad named John Swan, who afterwards made some figure in the world as Sir John Soane, R.A., the architect of the Bank of England, Professor of Architecture in the Royal Academy, and founder of the Soane Museum.

Anningsley Park, the seat of the Hon. Mrs. James Norton, about 2 m. S.W. from Addlestone, was the property of Thomas Day, the author of 'Sandford and Merton.' He purchased it on coming of age (1770), and here endeavoured to work out his educational, matrimonial, and philanthropic speculations, wrote his well-known book, and cultivated the land, which was a desolate heathy track when he obtained possession of it. He resided here till his death, which occurred near his mother's house, Bear Wood, Berks, from the kick of a colt he was training, Sept. 28th, 1789. The wild bit of woodland beyond the lodge, chiefly Scotch fir, was planted by Mr. Day; a short drive through highly cultivated grounds beyond leads to the old-fashioned but thoroughly comfortable looking house.

Ottershaw Park, the seat of Sir T. R. Colebrooke, Bart., M.P., about a mile from Anningsley, is a stately Italian structure; the park is very extensive, greatly diversified in surface, richly wooded, contains some broad sheets of water, and from various points commands wide and charming prospects. *Coombelands* (J. M. Paine, Esq.), *Fan Court* (R. Innes Noad, Esq.), and *Potters Park* (Albert Savory, Esq.),

are other good seats. It was at Addlestone (*Grove End*) that Charles Knight, the well-known publisher and author, died March 9th, 1873, within a few days of the completion of his 82nd year. At Fifield, in this village, Mr. and Mrs. S. C. Hall lived and wrote for many years; and here also, in an old-fashioned looking cottage in the heart of the village, built by the late Daniel Thorne, dealer in Wardour Street antiquities, reside the Misses Catlow, whose books on natural history and botany are widely known.

ALBANS, ST. (*see* St. Albans).

ALBYNS, or ALBINS, Essex, the seat of W. C. Gellibrand, Esq., in the parish of Stapleford Abbots, and about ½ m. N. of the ch. Albyns manor passed by marriage to Sir Thomas Edmondes,—a distinguished diplomatist in the reign of Elizabeth, and treasurer of the household of James I., whose letters and state papers, published with a Life by Birch ('An Historical View,' etc., 8vo, 1749,) have been of much service to historians,—and the house was probably erected by him. The design is ascribed to Inigo Jones. Walpole says,[*] "If he had any hand in it, it must have been during his first profession, and before he had seen any good buildings," but he admits that "the house is handsome . . . though all entirely of the King James's Gothic." About 1640 the estate was purchased by Ald. Antony Abdy, and a century later the house was restored by Sir John Abdy. It is a good and picturesque Jacobean brick and stone structure, and stands in a fine park.

ALDBOROUGH (or ALDBURY)

HATCH, Essex, 2 m. N. by E. from the Ilford Stat. of the Grt. E. Rly., a hamlet and eccl. dist. of Barking: pop. 430. It is called Aldbury Hatch, says Morant, "as denoting an old seat, near a *hatch*, or low gate, belonging to the forest." Lysons (1810) describes it as "a capital mansion situated in the forest." But all is changed now. Of the mansion little if anything remains, and though the name of *Aldborough Gate* is retained, the forest has receded to a considerable distance,

---

* Anecdotes, vol. ii., p. 273, ed. 1786.

and promises soon to disappear altogether. In 1852 Hainault Forest was disafforested, and an area of 1870 acres at Aldborough was allotted to the Crown. This was converted into a farm. "Upwards of 100,000 trees, oak, hornbeam, and the like," were cut down, the land was drained and made arable, model buildings of the most formal type were erected, and long rigid rectangular roads formed, without a field-path, and with scarcely a tree to relieve the dreary uniformity: and thus what, though level, was a wild and matchless woodland waste, has been transformed into one of the most uninviting and wearisome tracts around London. The sum of £42,000 was expended, and the farm is let at a rental of £4000; the annual product of the trees, etc., before the ground was disafforested, was about £500.* For the use of the inhabitants of the reclaimed forest land, the Government built in 1863, a little S. of Aldborough Gate, an elegant little ch., St. Peter's, Dec. in character: archt., Mr. A. Ashpitel.

ALDENHAM, HERTS, (Dom.

Eldenham,) pop. 1929, 15 m. from London by road, 2½ m. N. by E. from Bushey Stat. the L. and N.W. Rly., through charming of lanes, by *Bushey Grove, Bushey Mill,* and *Berry Wood,* and about 2 m. S.W. across a pleasant country, from the Radlett Stat. of the Midland Rly.

Aldenham was given to St. Albans Abbey by Offa, king of the Mercians. Shortly after the Conquest it was demised by the Abbot of St. Albans for 20 years to the Abbot of Westminster, on condition that he so kept the woods here that persons journeying from St. Albans to London might be safe from the robbers who infested the neighbourhood. But the Abbot of Westminster, strong in favour of the Conquerer, would neither carry out the conditions of his tenure, nor give up possession, and the Abbot of St. Albans did not recover the land till long after the expiration of the term. At the Dissolution the manor reverted to the Crown, but was soon after granted to Henry Stepney, whose heir sold it to Sir Edward Carey, father of Henry Visct.

* Evidence of the Hon. C. A. Gore, Com. of Woods and Forests, 1863.

Falkland, the celebrated Lord Deputy of Ireland. In the reign of Charles II. the manor was held by Denzil, Lord Hollis, the famous plenipotentiary. It now belongs to Lord Rendlesham.

Aldenham Church (St. John the Baptist) stands on high ground near the centre of the vill., and is worth visiting. It is of flint and stone, chiefly Perp. in character, but with portions of earlier date, and consists of a nave and aisles, a long chancel, and a large and lofty embattled tower, having a stair turret at the N.W. angle, and surmounted with a thin shingled spire. The interior is unusually good. The nave is separated from the aisles by three octagonal piers on each side, carrying tall pointed arches, and a clerestorey. Over the nave is the original and untouched chesnut roof, the tie-beams of which have angels supporting shields, carved and coloured, and the principal rafters are painted in pattern-work. The roof is borne on timber wall-shafts which rest on grotesque stone corbels. The chancel has a timber roof added by Sir C. Barry when he restored the church about 1846. At the same time a large five-light Dec. east window was inserted, but showing marks of settlement, it was repaired and some alterations made two or three years back. Memorial painted glass of fair character by Howes, of Durham, fills the great E. window; the W. window by O'Connor, one in the chancel aisle by Wailes, of Newcastle, another by Warrington, and one on the N. of the nave by Clayton and Bell. At the end of the N. aisle is a modern open oak screen. S. of the chancel are a piscina and (modern) sedilia. The font is E.E., of Purbeck marble; octagonal, with a thick central shaft and four thin ones. It had been entirely plastered over, but, when the ch. was repaired, was carefully restored by Richardson. At the same time a painting was uncovered at the E. end of the N. aisle, but it had been so much mutilated that it is only possible to guess that the subject was the Trinity.

The *Monts.* are interesting. In the chancel are six small 16th century *brasses,* in fair preservation, though the inscriptions are gone. Against the wall of the S. aisle of the chancel, under flat arched canopies of rather rich details, are two recumbent effigies of females, with small figures of angels at the heads, and hounds at the feet. The two form in effect a single mont.; it is not known whom they represent, but Chauncy (1720) says, "I have it by relation, they were two sisters here entombed, the founders of this church and coheirs to this lordship," a sort of tradition not uncommon in connection with country churches. There are good engravings of the mont. by Byrne, and of the effigies by C. Stothard, after drawings by Mr. Blore, in Clutterbuck's, 'Hertfordshire,' i., 139. S. of the chancel is a large altar tomb to John Coghill of Berry, d. 1714. Coghill is represented reclining in the full dress of his day, and his wife, Deborah, leaning on her elbow and contemplating him. *Obs.* at E. end of the S. aisle an ancient *church chest :* it is 10 ft. long. hewn out of a single block of oak, and everywhere bound and clamped with iron. In its S. end, as it stands, is a secret chamber, with its distinct locks and fastenings : although not among the handsomest, it is one of the most massive and remarkable of these chests remaining. In it were kept the church registers to the reign of Elizabeth, but becoming mildewed they have been removed to a dryer depository. In the vestry are suspended two helmets; both are rusty, but on the vizor of one the gilding is still bright. In the ch.-yard *obs.* the fine group of tall sycamores, and the tomb (crowned with an urn) of Lt.-Gen. Robert Burne, d. 1825, an officer who commanded a division of the British army under Wellington in the Peninsula, and served with great distinction in India.

Aldenham Grammar School, on Boydon's Hill, 1½ m. S.E. of Aldenham ch., was founded and endowed, with 6 almshouses, in 1599, by Richard Platt, of London, brewer, the government of both institutions being entrusted to the Brewers' Company. Within the last few years a new scheme has been sanctioned by which the Grammar School has been made a strictly classical school, and 2 lower schools erected out of the endowment for the use of parishioners, one near Aldenham, the other at Medbourne, at the eastern extremity of the par. near Elstree : both are good Elizabethan red brick buildings.

Altogether Aldenham is an interesting place to visit. About the cottage doors, in summer, straw-plaiters may be seen plying their nimble fingers. Almost all the lanes are picturesque; and the stranger, if at Aldenham in the early summer, should not fail to stroll through *Berry Wood* down to the river Colne, which skirts its western boundary. The wood is a remnant of that which gave the Abbot of St. Albans so much trouble, but is safe enough now, and is one it is a joy to come upon in these days of enclosures. It has wild walks, abounds in flowers,—the rare yellow pimpernel and the tall yellow iris are in profusion,— and the birds answer each other from every spray. A chalk pit in it will reward the geologist with an abundance of sponges, *foraminifera*, and perchance " beautifully preserved *polyzoa*."* Along the river there are two or three level reaches that would have delighted the hearts, and defied the pencils, of the best of the old Dutch river painters. *Aldenham Abbey* is the seat of W. Stuart, Esq.; *Aldenham House*, near Elstree, of H. Gibbs, Esq.; *Otters' Pool* was that of the late Hon. Sir J. S. Willes. Aldenham has several outlying hamlets—as *Letchmoor Heath* and *Four Ways*, 1 m. E. by S. from the vill.; *Patchett's Green*, 1 m. S.E., near which is *Delrow* (Vice-Admiral E. G. Fanshawe, C.B.); *Radlett*, 2 m. N.E., on the St. Albans road; and *Theobalds*, 3½ m. E.—all fair samples of the rural Hertfordshire hamlet. (*See* RADLETT.)

ALEXANDRA PARK AND PALACE (*see* MUSWELL HILL).

ALPERTON, or APPERTON,

MIDDX., a hamlet of Harrow-on-the-Hill, but nearly 3 m. S. of the town. From the Sudbury Stat. of the L. and N. W. Rly. it is ¾ m. S. by W. Besides the farmhouses, it comprises a few straggling cottages, with a ' public ' (the *Chequers*), and two or three beershops, along the road by the Grand Junction Canal, and between the canal and the little river Brent. It is a pretty summer evening stroll from Sudbury to Twyford and Hanger Hill, across

---

* See Proc. Geologists' Association, vol. ii., p. 45.

the Alperton meadows, but the brick-maker and the builder threaten a descent upon them.

ALVELEY, Essex (see Aveley).

AMBRESBURY (or AMBREYS) BANKS, an ancient earthwork, fortified station, or camp, in Epping Forest, about 100 yds. to the right or E. of the Epping road, and 1½ m. S.W. of that town : you reach it by a forest track which leaves the road nearly opposite the 14 mile-stone. The entrenchment consists of a broad and high bank or earthen wall with a deep outer ditch ; the figure is an irregular square or oblong, having the longest side, from S.W. to N.E., about 230 yards, parallel with the highroad. The work is very difficult to trace satisfactorily, from the bank being in many places entirely broken down and the ditch levelled, whilst ditch, wall, and area are, equally with the adjacent land, overgrown with hornbeam, oak, beech, and hawthorn, with a few hollies, sloes, and crabs, a dense tangle of brambles, and an exuberant growth of ferns ; still it is possible to make out its form and measure its dimensions, as we ascertained quite recently (Oct. 1873). Our measurement corresponded very nearly with that of the Ordnance Map, though the lines are less regular, and the angles more rounded than there laid down. It is about 850 yards, or nearly half a mile, in circuit ; the area enclosed about 9 acres—not 12, as in the books. It has been generally assumed to be a British work, though British works are not usually rectangular. Some early antiquaries, like Stukely, have even imagined it to be the last stronghold held by Cassivelaunus before retreating to his oppidum at St. Albans ; others, that it was the fortress of Boadicea.* Its name has been supposed to be a corrupted form of the British emrys, an enclosure ; but it is noteworthy that Ambresbury was the ancient form of Amesbury, near Stonehenge, the asserted burial-place of Ambrosius, the successor of Vortigern.† To us, Ambresbury Banks has much more the appearance of a small Roman than a British camp, though of course it may have been occupied by the Britons after the departure of the Romans.

AMWELL (Dom. *Emmewell*), one of the prettiest villages in Hertfordshire, and closely associated with the kindly Quaker poet (the first of his creed), John Scott, generally known as Scott of Amwell. Amwell (pop. of the parish 2245), or GREAT AMWELL, to distinguish it from the hamlet of *Little Amwell*, stands on the rt. bank of the Lea (but separated from it by the Lea Navigation, the Grt. E. Rly., and the New River, which here run side by side), and is 19 m. from London by rd. and 1½ m. S. by E. from the Ware Stat. of the Grt. E. Rly. (Hertford Branch). It is best reached, however, from the St. Margaret's Stat., from which it is 1 m. N. On leaving St. Margaret's Stat., take the first gate-path on the rt., then almost immediately turn up the slope on the l. The path, by the New River, leads direct to the bridge, above which rises the hillside, crowned by the old church. Here, as Scott sings,

> "The pleased eye
> On Amwell rests at last, its favourite scene.
> How picturesque the view ! where up the side
> Of that steep bank her roofs of russet thatch
> Rise mixed with trees, above whose swelling tops
> Ascends the tall church tower, and loftier still
> The hill's extended ridge."

You have indeed from the bridge a charming little landscape of the kind here painted, though more dressed than when Scott sketched it. Scott's poetry abounds with like descriptions of the scenery of the neighbourhood. From the bridge *obs.* on the trim lawn of the little island, a stone inscribed with some of his lines, which tell that here issues one of the head springs of the New River :—

> " Amwell, perpetual be thy stream,
> Nor e'er thy spring be less,
> Which thousands drink who never dream
> Whence flows the boon they bless."

The Amwell springs do, in fact, supply the New River Company with about 4,000,000 gallons of water daily.

From the bridge a path past the *George IV.*—a country inn with a large ash-tree in front of it—leads to the churchyard, which you enter between a couple of lofty limes, with, at their feet, a little rustic fernery planted by the vicar's wife,

---

* Morant's Essex.
† Taylor, Words and Places, 2nd ed., p. 315.

by way of impressing a lesson in taste and the love of nature on the children who have to pass daily to and fro to the school-house. The *Church* (St. John the Baptist) is small, comprising nave, apsidal chancel, and massive W. tower ; is of flint and stone, covered with rough-cast ; was partially restored about 1843, and more thoroughly in 1866, and has lost thereby something of its old rude, weather-beaten venerableness of aspect. It is in part E.E., but the lancets in the apse are recent. In the nave are windows with old Dec. tracery. Note on the S. a window of painted glass, " the offering of Amwell children, 1857." The interior is plain, but admirably kept. *Obs.* the small low round-headed chancel arch, with smaller arches on each side. At the end of the S. wall is an ambry ; S. of the altar a piscina, and on each side sedilia. William Warner, the author of 'England's Albion' (1586), was buried in Amwell ch., March 1609. Isaac Reed, the Shakspeare commentator, was also interred here, Jan. 1807, "near the spot he loved," as the insc. on his mont.—an altar tomb in the ch.-yd.—records. Here, too, is a showy mont. erected over his wife (1797), by Mylne, the archt. of the old Blackfriars Bridge, and engineer to the New River Company, and there is an inscription to Mylne himself, though he lies in St. Paul's Cathedral, close by Sir Christopher Wren. In the ch. is a mural tablet to Wm. Empson, D.C.L. (d. 1853), and in the ch.-yd., by the path leading up to the school, an altar-tomb to the Rev. Richard Jones (d. 1854), the former the well-known professor of law, the latter for 20 years the accomplished professor of political economy in Haileybury College. The ch.-yd., on the slope of the hill, is one of the most picturesque of village ch.-yds., is kept in excellent order, and affords from many points fine views across the valley of the Lea and over Ware Park, though still finer are obtained from the higher part of the hill. The thatched school-house above the ch.-yd. is in admirable keeping with its trim rusticity.

Izaak Walton, in the opening of the 'Complete Angler,' agrees with Venator "to meet, to-morrow morning, a pack of otter dogs of noble Mr. Sadler's, upon Amwell Hill, who will be there so early that they intend to prevent the sun rising ; " and in the morning we find him there (chap. ii.), looking at them, " men and dogs, dogs and men, all busy at the bottom of the hill there, in that meadow, checquered with water-lilies and lady-smocks." That sight would not be seen there now on a " fine fresh May morning," but a visitor, "just as the sun is rising," would probably be rewarded with one hardly less pleasant. Here may still be traced vestiges of earthworks which local antiquaries associate, and perhaps correctly, with the Danes and Saxons of the time of Alfred.

Scott's residence, *Amwell House*, is at *Amwell End*, close to Ware. It is a large, comfortable, 18th cent., red-brick building with projecting wings, and stood within what the auctioneer described as " beautiful and park-like pleasure-grounds of about 25 acres." What made the grounds a local celebrity was " an exceedingly curious grotto," constructed with infinite patience by Scott and an ingenious native of Ware named Frogley. In Scott's day, when the fame of Pope's grotto had rendered this sort of folly fashionable, the Amwell grotto had more than local notoriety. Beattie mentions it in a letter to the Duchess of Gordon as " one of the most curious grottoes he has ever seen," and recommends her Grace to visit it ; whilst Samuel Johnson, who had a great liking for Scott, though he spoke superciliously of Pope's grotto, was moved to unwonted admiration of this one. He writes to Scott (May 24, 1774) : " I have excited in Mr. Thrale and his lady the curiosity to see your gardens and grotto," and apprises him that they will "visit his Dryads and Fairies on Tuesday, the 31st of May, if it will not be inconvenient." Again the Doctor writes the following June, that he " hopes to have the pleasure of introducing some very judicious spectators to your gardens and subterranean retirements." The house and grounds remained in the hands of Scott's descendants till June 1864, when they were sold by auction, the purchasers being the 'British Land Company,' who divided the estate for building villas. The house was, however, preserved ; and the grotto, kept intact, is, with a very pretty fragment of the garden, rented by a nurseryman, who " provides tea in the grounds," and admits visitors to the grotto on payment of 6d. each. The grotto is really curious in its way, and perhaps the best preserved specimen of its class remaining. It is excavated in the side of a chalk hill, and comprises 7 chambers (now bearing such titles as the Palm Pillar Room, the Hermit's Cave, and the Quaker's Room), connected by subterranean passages, and very skilfully and ingeniously inlaid with flints, shells, spar, and fossils. It is a pity the townspeople of Ware did not secure the house and grounds—the former for a local museum, the latter for a public garden or recreation ground.

The hamlet of *Little Amwell* (Inns: *Townshend Arms, College Arms*, about 1½ m. S.W. of Great Amwell, is pleasantly situated on high ground, but has little to attract a stranger. The small red-brick, rather fanciful E.E. ch. (Holy Trinity), was built in 1863, from the designs of Mr. E. Christian. The interior is lined with variegated bricks, and has shafts of Devonshire marbles and red Mansfield stone. About ¾ m. S., by *Hertford Heath*, is *Haileybury College*, erected in 1806, from the designs of W. Wilkins, R.A., for the East India Company, and here Malthus, Mackintosh, and Jones were professors, and many of the eminent members of the E. I. civil service received their education. The building, large and coldly classic, is a bald copy of Downing College, Cambridge, erected by Wilkins a few years earlier. It is now a proprietary college, incorporated by royal charter in 1864, for the education of 500 youths. It has at present a head master, 15 assistant masters, and over 300 scholars.

ANERLEY, SURREY, on the Croydon Rly., 7½ m. from London Bridge, owes its name to a Mr. Anerley who once owned the estate. From a pleasant rural hamlet of hardly half a dozen houses fringing the skirts of Penge Wood, it has grown into a populous vill. of streets, terraces, semi-detached cottages, shops, and inns, mainly no doubt on account of the railway facilities and the proximity of the Crystal Palace. Close by the stat. was *Anerley Gardens*, long a popular place of entertainment, in its later years a sort of minor Vauxhall or Cremorne. The house and gardens were dismantled and built over in 1867-69. The ornamental water, a chief attraction of the gardens, and of which a fragment is left, was a portion of the old Croydon Canal, broken up to form the Croydon Rly. At Anerley is an entrance to the Crystal Palace grounds. The great pile of red-brick buildings beyond the stat., rt. of the rly., is the *North Surrey Industrial School*, built in 1852, and since enlarged—the archt., Mr. C. Lee, taking Wren's Chelsea Hospital as his model. It now (1874) contains about 950 pauper children, who are trained on the 'half-time' system,—alternate days being devoted to the school and to the workshops or farm by the boys, to household work by the girls.

ANKERWYKE, BUCKS, on the Thames, opposite Runnimede, and about 1 m. S. from the Wraysbury Stat. of the L. and S.W. Rly. (Windsor br.), occupies the site of a Priory of Benedictine nuns, founded (temp. Henry II.) by Gilbert Montfichet, in honour of St. Mary Magdalen. Edward VI. gave the manor to Sir Thomas Smith, the distinguished statesman, and provost of Eton, who built himself a mansion here, which was pulled down in 1805. The present *Ankerwyke House* is a plain stucco-fronted mansion with a portico. The grounds, which extend for some distance along the Thames, though level, are very beautiful. But the glory of the place is the great *Yew*, one of the most famous trees in the kingdom. It is on the l. side of the main drive, about 200 yards beyond the house. It stood here, as is believed, when King John and the Barons met in the opposite meadows, and was already celebrated for its size when Leland wrote.* It is one of the many trysting-places assigned by local traditions to Henry VIII. and Anna Boleyn.† At 4 ft. from the ground the trunk is 30 ft. in girth. The trunk is hollow, but many young stems have grown up within it, and the tree is full of leaves and quite vigorous. Close against, and indeed overshadowing, the yew, stands a cedar of great size and fine form : a companion cedar on the rt. of the path, is somewhat smaller, but a noble tree. A little beyond

---

* Itinerary, vol. i., p. 118.
+ Strutt, Sylva Britt., p. 8.

the cedars is a fragment of the old priory. The grounds are strictly private, but permission to see the yew and cedars is readily accorded. (*See* WRAYSBURY.)

ANNE'S HILL, ST., famous for the view and as the residence of Charles Fox, is 1 m. N.W. from Chertsey Stat. of the L. and S.W. Rly. Take the road W. (the first on the l.) from the stat. to *Golden Grove*, where the road divides: here ascend the rt.-hand road, and ¼ m. up on the l. is Fox's house, and opposite to it, on the rt., the wicket which gives access to the summit of the hill. *Golden Grove* is a little country inn, to be known by the grand old elm standing in front of it, with a sort of summer-house among the branches, in which a group of ruralizing wayfarers may ordinarily be seen on a fine afternoon, enjoying the shade and whiling away an hour, like Izaak Walton and his Scholar, with a glass of ale and pipe of tobacco.

St. Anne's Hill is a long insulated mass, or ridge, of Lower Bagshot Sand, rising 240 ft. from the river plain. The hill is enclosed, wooded to the summit, and the walks are carefully kept; but every part is open to the public, and seats are placed at the best points of view. The prospects from the summit and sides are varied and beautiful. The range reaches along the Surrey heaths and downs from Bagshot, by Pirbright, St. George's Hill, Richmond, and the valley of the Thames, over London, the rival heights of Highgate, Hampstead, and Harrow, to the beech-crowned hills of Hertford and Buckinghamshire. Windsor Castle is just shut out by Cooper's Hill (though Mrs. S. C. Hall says you may see the towers "in the bend just where Cooper's Hill meets the plain"). The hill was anciently called *Eldebury Hill*, from an earthwork which crowned its summit. Remains of the fosse may still be traced; and in the meadows below are two small rectangular camps, probably Roman. (*A. Way.*) The present name is derived from a chapel dedicated to St. Anne, erected on the hill by the monks of Chertsey Abbey about 1334, in which year Oreton, Bishop of Winchester, licensed the chapel for divine worship, and granted an indulgence of forty days to all who should repair to it or contribute towards its decoration. A fragment

of wall, near the house built for the accommodation of visitors, is all now left of the chapel. In 1440 Henry VI. granted the Abbot of Chertsey the privilege of holding a fair upon the hill on St. Anne's day: the fair, now known as Black Cherry Fair, is still held in Chertsey on the 6th of August, the tolls being taken by the proprietor of the Abbey lands. On the hill top is a spring, formerly held to possess some remarkable virtues. Near it, in Aubrey's time, was "a huge stone (a conglobation of gravel and sand), which they call the *Devil's Stone*, and believe it cannot be mov'd, and that treasure is hid underneath." Long after, the stone was moved and broken up, but no treasure rewarded the exploit. Another medicinal spring, known as *Nun's Well*, rises in *Monk's Grove* (Miss St. Aubyn's), on the N.E. side of the hill.

St. Anne's Hill appears to have been a favourite resort of the poet Cowley when he resided at Chertsey. In the somewhat lugubrious letter which he wrote to Dr. (afterwards Bishop) Sprat a few months before his death, he says that if he recovers so as to walk about again, "then methinks you and I and the Dean might be very merry upon St. Anne's Hill." But St. Anne's Hill has acquired more celebrity from Charles James Fox, who spent his last years chiefly in the house already noticed, opposite the entrance to the enclosure. The house is an unpretending country seat, "comfortable and convenient," with a few good rooms, and some charming prospects—that from the balcony, with the Thames flowing beneath the hill, being especially famous. The grounds are very pretty in themselves, and Fox indulged his own taste and that of the time by erecting in them a small temple as a memorial of Henry Lord Holland attaining his majority (1794), a grotto, and several vases and poetical inscriptions. "Fox," says Earl Russell,[*] "loved the place with a passionate fondness." Here the veteran statesman gave free scope to his love of a country life, loitering about his fields or watching the growth of his fruits and vegetables. ("I dare say," said General Fitzpatrick, when one asked him at an important epoch in the French Revolution, "Where is Fox

* Life and Times of C. J. Fox, vol. iii., p. 143.

now?'" "I dare say he is at home sitting on a haycock, reading novels, and watching the jays steal his cherries.") But as Lord Holland observed, and as Mr. Trotter and Earl Russell in their biographies of Fox have shown more in detail, at the same time prosecuting with zeal his "historical researches, critical inquiries, the study of the classics and works of imagination and poetry." It was here he composed his abortive 'History of the early part of the Reign of James II.' and here, in the very paradise of nightingales, that he wrote that pleasant, oft-printed letter to Lord Grey in which, from the authority of the classic writers as well as his own observation, he defends the note of the nightingale from the charge of melancholy. Lord Albemarle in his 'Memoirs of the Marquis of Rockingham' (ii., 292), describing a visit he paid with his brother to St. Anne's Hill when a boy, relates that their dinner "was no sooner despatched than the Prime Minister and his youthful guests would adjourn to the lawn before the house, and devote the remainder of the evening to trap-ball, Mr. Fox having always the innings and the boys the bowling and fagging out." At this time (the spring of 1806) Fox always wore at St. Anne's "a light grey single-breasted coat, with large white metal buttons, a thick woollen waistcoat, dark worsted stockings, and shoes coming up to the ancles." A graver memorial of a visit to Fox at St. Anne's Hill will be found in Rogers's 'Human Life;' and the scandal that was afloat about Fox's acquisition of some land here in Cobbett's 'Rural Rides' (p. 3); but the scandal was mere hearsay and apparently without foundation. St. Anne's Hill was purchased by Mrs. Fox before her marriage with Fox, and she continued to reside there till her death in 1842, some 36 years after that of her husband. A large cedar, that will be noticed by the house, was planted by Mrs. Fox "when the size of a mere wand." St. Anne's Hill is now the seat of Lady Holland.

ANNINGSLEY PARK (see ADDLE-STONE, p. 8).

APPS COURT, or ABB'S COURT
(Dom. *Ebsa*), SURREY, a manor and seat,

1½. m. N.E. from Walton-on-Thames, on the road to Molesey. Pope says,*—

> "If there be truth in law, and use can give
> A property, that's yours on which you live:
> Delightful Ab's Court, if its fields afford
> Their fruit to you, confesses you its lord."

The manor was inherited by Charles Montague, Earl of Halifax, who, by a codicil of his will, dated Feb. 1, 1712, bequeathed it to "Mrs. Catherine Barton, during her life," together with the rangership, house, and lodge of Bushey Park. Mrs. (or Miss) Catherine Barton was the daughter of Sir Isaac Newton's half-sister, and for 20 years lived in Sir Isaac's house; yet for a century and a half, by writers grave as well as scurrilous, from Mrs. Manley (1711) to Sir David Brewster (1855), she has been spoken of as Lord Halifax's mistress. Prof. De Morgan seems, however, after careful investigation, to have fairly re-established the lady's reputation. His conclusion is that "she was privately married to Lord Halifax, probably before his elevation to the peerage, and that the marriage was no very great secret among their friends," though not publicly acknowledged.† Mrs. Barton was a famous beauty, and is celebrated as a toast in Dryden's 'Miscellanies' Her name occurs several times in Swift's Journal to Stella. After Halifax's death she married Mr. Conduitt, Newton's successor as Master of the Mint, and died in 1739. The "capital mansion of Apps Court" has long since disappeared. The present house (R. Gill, Esq.), a large plain brick building, was erected by J. Hamborough, Esq., in the early part of the present century. The grounds are level, but contain some noble elms and oaks, and have a pretty look-out towards Walton and across the Thames to Hampton.

ARKLEY, HERTS (*see* BARNET).

ARLINGTON, MIDDLESEX. Sir
Henry Bennett, Secretary of State to Charles II., and one of the members of the Cabal, was in 1644 raised to the

---

* Imitations of Horace, 2nd Ep., addressed to Colonel Cotterell.
† Notes and Queries, S. 1, vol. viii., p. 429, and S. 2, vol. ii., p. 161.

peerage by the title of Baron Arlington *of Arlington in the county of Middlesex.* The place intended was Harlington, a place never before (nor in any other connection since) written without the aspirate, though, considering its nearness to London, it may possibly have been sometimes so pronounced. Baron Arlington was made Earl of Arlington in 1672. The title merged in that of Grafton by the marriage of his only daughter and heir with the Duke of Grafton. (*See* HARLINGTON.)

ASHE, or ASH, KENT, 4½ m. S.E. from the Farningham Road Stat. (23½ m.) of the L. C. and D. Rly., (by way of Horton Kirby, across the hills eastward and through *Fawkham Green*,) is an out-of-the-way agric. vill. of 655 inh. Along the road you have extensive views, particularly northwards, over the valley of the Thames to the low Essex hills. The immediate neighbourhood is undulating, wooded, and in places picturesque, with hop-gardens all around; and the little village has its general and butcher's shop, post-office, smithy, and a decent inn, the *White Swan* (the landlord a farmer), at the parting of the roads to Farningham and Hartley. The *Church* (St. Peter and St. Paul) stands a little N. of the vill., up a lane bordered with tall elms, close by a fine old red-brick many-gabled mansion, half farmhouse, half parsonage. The ch. is rather large; has nave with aisles, chancel, a tall sq. tower at the W. end with a stair turret and a peal of 6 bells, and a porch on the S.W. with a stoup on rt. of the ch. door. It is of flint and stone, but the tower is covered with plaster. Style, late Dec. and Perp.: *obs.* the tracery of the E. window of the N. aisle, in which is a small figure of the Madonna with other fragments of old painted glass. *Interior* plain, pewed, and whitewashed; has no monts. of interest. W. of the ch. stands an old battered yew.

ASHFORD, MIDDX., an agric. par. and vill. on the Richmond and Staines branch of the L. and S.W. Rly., 15 m. W.S.W. of London, and 2 m. E. of Staines: pop. 1019. In Domesday the name is written *Exeforde*, in documents of the 13th and 14th cents. *Echelesford*, or *Ec-*

hoalford, the name being derived from the ford over the little river Exe or Echel, which, however, is ½ m. W. of the vill. On leaving the stat. turn l.; the ch. will soon be seen peering from among the trees on the l.; beyond it is the vill., stretching, horseshoe shape, right and left.

The old *Church*, St. Matthew, a small Norman edifice, was pulled down in 1796, and a mean brick building erected in its place. In 1858 this, in its turn, made way for a handsome structure of hammered stone, designed by Mr. Butterfield. It consists of a nave with aisles and clerestorey, chancel, and tower at the S.W., added in 1865. The interior is striking from its unusual altitude. On the floor, by the font, is a *brass*, small, but good of its kind, with effigies of Edward Woode, d. 1525, his wife, 6 sons and 2 daughters. In the ch.-yard is a tall and well-shaped yew. The vill. is clean and pleasant; the neighbourhood well wooded, well cultivated, and, though level, affords some agreeable strolls.

Among the seats are *Echoalford* or *Ecclesfield* (R. Gosling, Esq.), by the ch.; and *Ashford House* (F. H. Dyke, Esq.) Rt. of the rly., close by the stat., is the *Welsh Charity School*, of the Society of Ancient Britons, founded in 1714. The school is a noticeable and pict. building of a modified Elizabethan character, white brick with tall dormer gables, clock tower, and high red-tiled roof, designed by Mr. H. Clutton, and formally opened July 13, 1857, by the Prince Consort and the Prince of Wales. It is intended for 200 children of Welsh parents, born within 12 m. of the Royal Exchange. At the census of 1871 it contained 110 boys and 84 girls. The large red brick and stone building seen from the rly., midway between Ashford and Staines, is the *West London District School*, completed at the end of 1872 at a cost of over £50,000, from the designs of Mr. H. H. Collins, for 800 children.

ASHLEY PARK (*see* WALTON-ON-THAMES).

ASHTEAD, SURREY (Dom. *Stede*), 2 m. S.W. from Epsom on the road to Leatherhead, and ½ m. S. from the Ashtead Stat. (16 m.) of the Epsom and Leatherhead Rly., L. Br. and S. C., and L. and S.W. lines : pop. 906.

The manor has belonged successively to the De Montforts, Frevilles, Astons, Howards (first the Arundel and afterwards the Berkshire families), and then, by heiresses, to the Bagots and Uptons, who respectively assumed the name of Howard. The vill. has little to detain a visitor : the objects of interest are the church and park. *Ashtead Park* (Hon. Mrs. Howard) lies E. of the vill. The house, erected towards the end of the last century, by R. Bagot Howard, Esq. (at a cost of nearly £100,000), is one of those great formal square white brick country mansions, with a portico entrance, which were at that time everywhere regarded as the perfection of dignity and good taste. Its predecessor was built 100 years earlier by Sir Robert Howard, famous alike as rhymester, dramatist, historian, privy councillor, and politician,—the Sir Positive Atall of Shadwell's 'Sullen Lovers,' —who is said to have entertained here as guests Charles II., James II., and William III.

"Went to visite my brother in Surrey. Call'd by the way at Ashted, where Sir Robert Howard entertain'd me very civilly at his new built house, which stands in a Park on the Downe, the avenue South, tho' downe hill to the house—which is not greate, but with the outhouses very convenient. The staire-case is painted by Verrio with the story of Astrea ; amongst other figures is the Picture of the Painter himself, and not unlike him ; the rest is well done, onely the columns did not at all please me ; there is also Sir Robert's own picture in an oval ; the whole in *fresca*. The place has this greate defect, that there is no water but what is drawn up by horses from a very deepe well." *

A fine avenue of limes leads to the house. The park is greatly varied in surface, contains many noble old oaks and elms, and a herd of deer. In the house is a good collection of pictures, including several by the old masters, some Howard family portraits by Kneller, and Reynolds's 'Fortune Teller' and 'Little Shepherdess.' The house is not shown, but there are public paths across the park.

The *Church* (St. Giles), within the park, and some distance from the vill., is most picturesquely situated on the site of a Roman villa, part of the outer trench remaining, and some of the Roman bricks

being worked up in the building. It is large, handsome, of various dates; was restored about 1835, and enlarged in 1862. The interior should be seen. It has been modernized in the restoration, but has a noble appearance. The carved roof is of cedar, but new. There are numerous *monts.* to members of the Howard family, the most noteworthy perhaps being that of Lady Diana Fielding. *Obs.* the painted glass of the E. window—a fair specimen of late 15th cent. Flemish work, brought from a convent at Herck, near Maestricht. There are other painted glass windows by Wailes, of Newcastle, and Powell. The richly carved reredos was one of the last works of Mr. J. Thomas. In the ch.-yard is a fine yew. There are almshouses in the village for 8 poor widows, founded by Lady Diana Fielding in 1736, and rebuilt in 1856 by the Hon. Mrs. Howard, who also erected the schoolhouse in 1852.

Dr. Johnson's friend Tom Tyers, the Tom Restless of the 47th 'Idler,' and the author of some amusing pages of biography, died at his house at Ashtead in 1787. When Pepys went, July 25, 1663, "to see a famous race on Banstead Downs," the Derby of his day, he was unable at night to procure a lodging at Epsom, "the town was so full," and so, "which was better, went towards Ashtead, where we got a lodging in a little hole we could not stand upright in. While supper was getting," he continues, "I walked up and down behind my cousin Pepys's house that was, which I find comes little short of what I took it to be, when I was a little boy." Pepys had pleasant recollections of his boyish days at his cousin's house, for it was there he eat mulberries, "a thing," as he carefully records, he "did not eat of again for many years," a proof, perhaps, that the fruit was then rare. A mile N. of Ashtead is *Ashtead Common*, despite of Enclosure Acts, a still wild forest-like track abounding in oaks, and affording many picturesque peeps across the country. At *Newton Wood*, in the closer part of the common, N.E., may still be traced, though with some difficulty, an oblong entrenchment enclosing an area of above 2 acres.

AVELEY, or ALVELEY, ESSEX
(Dom. *Alvithelea*), 2 m. N.E. from the

2

Purfleet Stat. of the Tilbury and Southend Rly. The shortest route is by the Wennington road and Aveley Lane; a pleasanter but somewhat longer way is by the river road to Stone House—a large flint and brick house of good plain form, having a stone on the front inscribed " built 1683, repaired 1856 "—and then to take the lane opposite, a very pretty one running over the hill and by Aveley Bridge, and affording some pleasant peeps across the Thames.

According to Morant, Aveley was once a market town : it is now a quiet agricultural village of 892 inhab., and consists of a long street of small houses and cottages, some of which are of timber framing filled in with plaster, with a decent inn, the *Old Ship*.

The *Church*, St. Michael, lies back at the E. end of the vill. It should be examined : the keys are kept by the clerk, Izaac Finch, at the other end of the street. The exterior, of flint and stone, much patched, and bolstered by ugly brick buttresses, has a venerable weather-beaten aspect. It had formerly a tall spire, but it was blown down in the storm of 1703. The interior is of greater interest. It has a long chancel, and a nave of 3 bays, divided from the aisles, on the S. by square piers supporting round arches, and on the N. by cylindrical piers bearing early pointed arches. The clerestorey windows are also E.E. Some Vandal churchwarden has had the piers painted and splashed to imitate granite, the old open-timber roof whitewashed, and a late oak chancel-screen modernized and painted. S. of the altar is a piscina. The font, of Purbeck marble, is of a common Norman type, having a thick central shaft with four thinner ones at the angles, and a very large basin with plain arcade panelling. A small but well-executed *brass* of Radulphus de Knevynton is noteworthy, not only for the costume, but as giving, besides the day of the week, and the festival of the saint, the dominical letter of the year in which the good knight died : "die jovis ante festū sͨi Nicholai Episcopi, MCCCLXX. lͬa dͦnical. f." The effigy is in full armour, with a two-handed sword on the left side, and a short sword or dagger on the right ; under a cusped arch : *obs.* the chains fastening the helmet to the breast, and the sword and dagger to the girdle. A smaller mutilated mural

brass is of an infant in swaddling-clothes, Elizabeth daughter of Edw. Bacon, Esq., d. 1583, aged 13 weeks. At the entrance to the chancel is a coffin-shaped Purbeck marble slab, the mont. of an unnamed ecclesiastic, having on it a cross of good form. There are also several monts. of the Barrett family. In the tower are five bells, two of which are cracked, while one, sound, bears the date 1400, and the legend " S. Pet. ora pro nobis."

Belhus, ½ m. N., the seat of Sir Thos. Barrett Lennard, Bart., is a large and, though much altered, still characteristic Tudor mansion. It was built by John Barrett, a distinguished lawyer, who died in 1526 ; is castellated, with projecting tower and bays ; the basement brick, the rest rough-cast. The house has its ghost : " At the ancient and interesting seat of my friend Sir Thos. Barrett Lennard, at Belhus in Essex, the form of an old female domestic is reputed there as occasionally seen haunting the galleries and stairs between the rooms."[*] It was last (and very lately) seen, according to the same authority, seated " by the fire in the bedroom in which more recently I slept, the old shrivelled hands resting on the knees." The house was new fronted and otherwise altered by Mr. Lennard Barrett, afterwards Lord Dacre, about 1750. Horace Walpole visited it in 1754, and wrote (to Bentley, Nov. 3) : " I never saw a place for which one did not wish, so totally devoid of faults. What he has done is in Gothic, and very true. The hall is pretty ; the great dining-room hung with good family pictures ; among which is his ancestor, the Lord Dacre who was hanged [for the murder of a keeper in a fray at Lawton Park, by Hurstmonceaux, 1547]. The chimney pieces, except one little miscarriage into total Ionic (he could not resist statuary and Siena marble), are all of a good King James the First Gothic." The house contains several old family portraits of the Dacres of the south, including one of Thomas Dacre attributed to *Holbein*, and another of Richard Lennard Lord Dacre, by *Vandyck.*

" At Lord Dacres at Belhouse in Essex is one of the best works of this master [Lucas de Heere] it always passed for Holbein's but Vertue discovered

* Hon. Grantley Berkeley, Life and Recollections, 1866, vol. iv., p. 233.

it to be of De Heere, whose mark is still discernible. It is the portrait of Mary Neville, daughter of George, Lord Abergavenny, and widow of Thomas Fiennes, Lord Dacre, executed for an accidental murder in the reign of Henry VIII. . . . Her head is finely coloured." *

Some of the rooms still retain the curious old tapestry hangings. The park is large and finely timbered. Here was formerly a heronry, carefully kept long after hawking was out of fashion. Walpole saw it in 1754 ; " but of late years," says Morant (writing in 1768), " not thought to ballance the inconveniences attending it, and the herons therefore not suffered to build longer." The estate was originally called *Keliton* — a name still preserved, but corrupted into *Kennington*, in a large farm adjoining Belhus on the W. The name Belhus, or as it used to be written Belhouse, was derived from a family who inherited the estate in the 14th cent. At the end of that century it passed to the Barrett family, the last of whom, Edward Baron Newburgh, bequeathed it to his cousin Richard Lennard, subsequently Lord Dacre, who assumed the name and arms of Barrett. A little W. of Kennington is *Bretts*, now a farmhouse, but formerly a moated mansion.

* Walpole, Anecdotes of Painting, vol. i., p. 229.

BALL'S PARK (*see* HERTFORD).

BANSTEAD, SURREY (Dom. *Benestede*), 15 m. from London by road, 3½ m. E. of Epsom, and a Stat. of the Banstead and Epsom Downs branch of the L. Br. and S. C. Rly. ; pop. 1668.

Banstead is delightfully situated on the Surrey Downs, the vill. itself standing at a height of 556 ft. above the sea-level on a little patch of Thanet sand, which here overlies the chalk : Banstead Court and Parsonage, and Banstead Heath, about 1½ m. S., occupy similar insulated patches of the sand.

The manor of Banstead belonged to Hubert de Burgh, who, after the restoration of his estates in 1233, retired here and built himself a castellated mansion E. of the ch. Every trace of the building has long disappeared ; but a hollow used to be shown as marking the site. From the reign of Edward I. to that of Henry VIII. the manor was held by the Queens of England. It was then transferred to the Carews, from whom it passed in 1762. Banstead comprises several clusters of houses : its title is Banstead cum Membris.

The vill. proper is of moderate size, and looks neat, clean, and prosperous. Inn, the *Woolpack*, a good house. As in so many of the Down villages, good water has to be procured from a great depth : the well at Canons is 360 ft. deep, that for general use in the village of Banstead 296 ft.* The *Church* (All Saints), at the W. extremity of the vill., is rather large ; Perp. ; of flint and stone ; and consists of nave, aisles, chancel, and at the W. a low square tower with double buttresses, and a small shingled spire, which from the loftiness of the site serves as a landmark for miles around. The S. aisle and porch were restored, or rebuilt, some years back ; the N. aisle and chancel in 1866. The interior has good nave arches. There are mural monts. both old and modern, but none of consequence. *Obs.* the large ash in the churchyard.

Banstead parish contains several good seats : *Nork Park* (Earl of Egmont), a large mansion with projecting wings, erected about 1750, but since much altered, stands on a finely wooded height about a mile W. of the ch. ; *Banstead House* (B. Lambert, Esq.), altered to its present formal appearance by the eminent engineer Thomas Maudesley, who died here May 26, 1864, is a mile S.E. of the ch. ; *Court House* (C. W. Johnson, Esq.), etc.

Banstead Downs have always been famous for their fine views, pure air, and the short, close, thymey turf with which they are covered. Dyer in his 'Fleece' (B. i.) did his best to immortalize among sheep pastures

" The Downs of Banstead, edg'd with woods,
    And towery villas."

* Brayley, Hist. of Surrey, vol. iv., p. 338.

So Pope :—

"To Hounslow Heath I point, and Banstead Down :
  Thence comes your mutton, and these chicks
  my own."

Much of Banstead Down has been enclosed, and what is left has been marred by rly. works, but a beautiful tract remains, and this, about 1400 acres in extent, the late lord of the manor, Thos. Alcock, Esq., offered to make over as a free gift to a duly constituted public trust, that the Downs "might be dedicated to the public as open land for ever." * About 750 acres are included in the provisions of the Metropolitan Commons Act, 29 and 30 Vict., cap. 122 (1866). From the nearest height, just over the railway bridge, ½ m. W. of Banstead ch., the eye embraces a wide panorama, with such landmarks as Windsor Castle, Westminster Abbey and the lofty Victoria Tower, the dome of St. Paul's, and the rival heights of Highgate, Hampstead, and Harrow, distinctly visible, whilst the Crystal Palace looks close at hand.

In reading the older references to Banstead Downs, it must be borne in mind that much of what are now called the Epsom Downs were then included under that designation. Thus Pepys speaks of the "famous race on Banstead Downs," in the extract given under ASHTEAD ; and again (July 30, 1663), "The town-talk this day is of nothing but the great foot-race run this day on Banstead Downs, between Lee, the Duke of Richmond's footman, and a tyler, a famous runner. And Lee hath beat him ; though the King and Duke of York, and all the men almost, did bet three or four to one upon the tyler's head." In the *London Gazette*, No. 3414, (1698) occurs the following advertisement: "Banstead Downs Plate of £20 value, will be run for on the 24th inst. [August] being Bartholomew Day ; any Horse may run for the said Plate that shall be at Carshalton, Barrowes-hedges, or some of the Contributors' Stables 14 days before the Plate day. . . . The Weight 10 stone." A century later † we find it noted under Banstead, "In these Downs there is a 4 mile course for horse-races, which is much frequented :" this is the Epsom course.

Besides the open Downs there are charming walks on all sides of Banstead. One of

* H. of Commons Report on Open Spaces, 1865.
† Ambulator, 1782, and 4th ed., 1792.

the pleasantest is by the lane or footpath, beyond the ch. to *Chipstead*, by way of Banstead or Perrott's Park, past the White Hart Inn, Yew Pond Farm, and Shabdon.

BARKING, ESSEX ; pop. of the town-ward 5766 (the entire par. contains 12,523 inhab.) ; is 7 m. from Whitechapel ch. by road ; 7½ m. by Grt. E. Rly. (Southend line) : the rly. stat. is just outside the town on the E., and a rd. leads direct from it to the ch. Inn, the *Bull*. Barking stretches for a mile along the l. bank of the Roding, but at a little distance from the river, which falls into the Thames about 1½ m. below the town, widening towards its mouth into what is known as *Barking Creek*. The name (anc. *Bereching* and *Berching*, Dom. *Berchingæ*), derived by Morant from *beorce* and *ing*, a meadow of birch trees ; by other antiquaries from *Burgh-ing*, the fortification in the meadow,—referring to the earthwork N. of the town ;—is by Kemble regarded as designating the mark of the *Beorcingas*.

Barking Abbey, at first no doubt a modest house on the upland bordering the broad and dreary marsh, with the wide Forest of Essex stretching inland, was probably the nucleus of the town. Its reputed founder was Erkenwald, afterwards Bishop of London, who founded Chertsey Abbey for monks, with himself as abbot, and Barking Abbey (about 670, but 675 according to Harl. MS. 261, f. 107), for nuns, with his sister Ethelberga as first abbess. Erkenwald died when on a visit to his sister at Barking, about 685. The monks of Chertsey claimed the body as that of their abbot ; the nuns of Barking held it by right of possession ; but the dispute was terminated by the chapter of London, backed by the citizens, carrying off the corpse in triumph to St. Paul's, where, after his formal canonization, the shrine of St. Erkenwald was long the chief glory of the cathedral. Ethelberga died and was buried at Barking. Like her brother, she was in due time canonized, and her shrine was conspicuous in the abbey ch. After her, several of the abbesses were of royal blood, and three of them received the honour of canonization. The abbey was burned by the Danes in 870, and the nuns dispersed. It lay desolate for nearly a century, when it was rebuilt by King Edgar in expiation of violence offered to Wulfhilda, a nun of Wilton. Wulfhilda was made abbess of the restored convent; some years after ejected to make way for Elfrida, widow of Edgar; but at the end of 20 years, on the queen repenting of her injustice, resumed her office, and 7 years later died in the odour of sanctity, being the fifth abbess of Barking who was canonized. Under these holy women Barking Abbey became famous for the miracles wrought in it, and Bede devotes 5 chapters (7—11) of his 'Ecc. Hist.' to an account of the more remarkable of the earlier ones,—chiefly those in connection with St. Ethelberga. Alfgiva, who was abbess at the Conquest,* was succeeded by Maud, queen of Henry I. Later, Maud, queen of Stephen, was for awhile abbess, but resigned the dignity to Adeliza, the sister of a powerful baron, who entertained Stephen, Maud, and the whole court for several days at the abbey. Her successor was Mary, sister of Thomas à Becket. Till now the abbess had been nominated by the king, but in 1200 the election was, by a papal rescript, vested in the nuns. The abbesses appear, however, to have been still mostly of noble families. The convent was celebrated as a place of education. Among children of high rank placed here were the two sons of Catherine Tudor, widow of Henry V., whose school fees were very irregularly paid. Eleanor, Duchess of Gloucester, withdrew to Barking Abbey after the murder of her husband, and died here in 1399: on her brass in Westminster Abbey she is represented as a nun of Barking. The nuns were of the Benedictine order. The abbess was one of the four who were baronesses in right of their station and estates. The monastery, however, became much impoverished by the bursting of the river wall at Dagenham in 1376, and the consequent inundation of the lands, and does not seem ever to have regained its original

prosperity. In the reign of Richard III. a royal licence was issued "to the prior and convent of the Holy Trinite in Londone to graunt unto th' Abbesse of Berking an annuytie of 20l."* probably to assist her in her efforts to reclaim the drowned lands. At the Dissolution the income was valued at £1084. The abbess, Dorothy Barley, on executing the surrender, Nov. 14, 1539, received a pension of 200 marks. Henry leased the abbey and grounds to Sir Thomas Denny. It was granted by Edward VI. to Edward Fynes, Lord Clinton, who conveyed it next day to Sir Richard Sackville. It has since passed through many hands, and is now the property of Mr. W. Thompson of Ilford. Barking Manor, also the property of the Abbey, was sold by Charles I. to Sir Thomas Fanshawe: it is now the property of Sir Edward Hulse, Bart.

The site of the abbey is immediately N. of the ch. It is now a market garden, entered by a dilapidated E.E. gateway. Inside, not a vestige of the conventual buildings is visible. Lysons gives a ground-plan of the ch., "taken from the ruins of the foundations in 1724," by Mr. Lethieullier, then lord of the manor; but its accuracy is open to question. According to it, the ch. (erected 1215-47) was cruciform, 170 ft. long and 33 wide, and the transept 150 ft. across. There can be little doubt that the ch. was a noble one, and the conventual buildings of corresponding extent and splendour. The library of Magdalen College, Oxford, possesses a relic of Barking Abbey in the shape of a beautiful French MS. containing the Lamentations of St. Bernard, the Meditations of St. Augustine, and a Life of St. Louis, presented to the convent by the Countess of Oxford (wife of the 12th earl).

The entrance to Barking Churchyard is by a square embattled gateway with an octagonal angle-turret, of the Dec. period, known as *Fire-Bell Gate*, from a tradition that the curfew-bell was suspended in it. It is much dilapidated, but picturesque, and should be visited. In an old record, quoted by Lysons, it is called "the chapel of the Holy Rood Loft atte Gate." The chapel is the room over the gate, and in it is still a rilievo of the Cru-

---

* Some early authorities make William I. to have received here the formal submission of the citizens of London. That act, however, undoubtedly occurred at Berkhamstead; but William appears to have been at Barking, and perhaps, as Mr. Freeman supposes ('Norman Conquest,' App., Note PP, vol., iii., p. 767) he may have come here from Berkhampstead, as he would not enter London till the Tower, or some fortress on its site, was made ready.

---

* Harl. MSS., 433.

cifixion, but terribly injured, the faces of the Virgin and St. John having been knocked off, and the figure of Christ much mutilated. One of the windows (good Dec.) is in tolerable preservation ; the others have been built up and the tracery destroyed. If there was ever a bell, there must have been a roof spire to the building : it has now a flat roof and leads, from which there is a wide view over the marshes and the Thames. But a still wider view is obtained from the ch. tower, access to which it may be worth trying to obtain if the day be clear.

Barking *Church* (St. Margaret) is large, and of different dates, and consists of nave and chancel, S. aisle, and two N. aisles, and an embattled tower at the W. end. The exterior is of stone, much patched, with brick buttresses. The windows are modern and common. The tower (which is shut off from the ch.) is 72 ft. high, and is a landmark for miles in the surrounding flat country. The interior has been so often repaired, the last time in 1837, as to retain little of its early character. All the columns are whitewashed, but before the last repairs were cased in plaster. At the W. end of the nave, N. side, are 3 Norm. piers. The roof is semicircular, of plaster in pattern-work of fair 18th cent. design. *Brasses*: A priest holding a chalice, small, probably Flemish, about 1480. Thomas Broke, d. 1493, wife and 2 children, sm. John Tedcastell, d. 1596, and wife (with labels), 4 children, and 5 infants in swaddling-clothes. Some others formerly here were stolen whilst the ch. was being repaired. *Monts.* S. of chancel : Sir Charles Montague of Cranbrook (brother of the 1st Earl of Manchester), d. 1625 ; marble relief of Montague on a battle-field, seated in his tent, a sentinel with matchlock on each side of the door, by it a page holding a horse. N. of chancel : Francis Fuller, of Beehive, clerk of the estreats, d. 1636 : a good coloured bust. Under it is an ambry ; another is behind a pier. N. chancel aisle, Captain John Bennett, d. 1706 ; bust between stem and stern of a ship. N. aisle of nave, John Bamber, M.D., d. 1752, a well-modelled and characteristic bust. Opposite, in S. aisle, Sir Orlando Humfreys, of Jedkins, d. 1736, bust and weeping cherubs.

In early times the vicar of Barking drew his income from the abbey, with a hog, a goose, a cheese, and a lamb for diet ; but after many disputes it was settled in 1437, between Catherine de la Pole, the abbess, and Sir John Greening, the vicar, that in future the vicar should have provision every day in the convent, so long as he should not be of a litigious disposition, he sitting at the chaplain's table, his servant with the domestics ; but if he should, without licence of the abbess, have any familiarity or discourse with any of the nuns, he should, for the first offence, lose his diet for a week ; for the second, for a month ; and for the third be excluded the convent for life. In the time of the last abbess the diet was commuted for an annual payment of £10, which is still paid to the vicar by the Exchequer.* The living is now a valuable one. The parish is said to embrace a circuit of 30 miles, and includes Ilford, Chadwell, Rippleside, Barkingside, and Aldborough Hatch. That part of Hainault Forest called the King's Forest was also in Barking parish.

The *Town* has little to show besides what has been described. As late as Fuller's time Barking had "no mean market." But the market has been long given up, though a few stalls and country people still collect in the streets on Saturdays. The old market-house is standing, but is a mean building. The visitor should stroll down the narrow street (which has "a most ancient and fish-like smell," the side streets and lower part have often worse odours from insufficient drainage), to the *Wharf* at the bottom of the town. Here is a large corn mill, on the site of the old abbey mill, and immediately below it, where the river suddenly widens, are barges lading, fishing smacks beached or lying at anchor, and two or three new ones building, fishermen lolling over the bridge, and, if the tide is up, perhaps a yacht or two tacking up or down the creek : in its way by no means an unpicturesque or uninteresting scene. When Hainault and Epping forests used to supply timber for the navy, it was shipped from Barking Wharf for Woolwich.† A few years back, Barking owned about 150 smacks of 60 or 70 tons each, but the fishing trade has decreased of late.

---

* Lysons.
† Pepys, Diary, Aug. 18, 1662.

Many barges are still employed in carrying to London the potatoes and onions so largely grown in the neighbourhood.

From the Wharf there is a path along the artificial bank on either side of the Roding to the Thames, but, following the windings of the river, it is a long, tedious, and far from odorous walk. At the mouth on the E. side of the creek, are a magazine, a coastguard station, and some factories; on the W. is the *Outfall of the Northern Main Drainage.* Ten million cubic feet of sewage are brought daily across the marshes in a concrete embankment to Barking Creek, and deposited in a reservoir, to be discharged into the Thames "at or about high water." The reservoir, an immense work, covers an area of 9½ acres, is divided into four compartments, with an average depth of 16½ ft., and will hold 39 million gallons of sewage. The walls are of brick, the floor of stone, supported on brick arches; the foundations are carried down in concrete to a depth of 20 ft. The pumping machinery is perfect of its kind, and beautifully kept. 'The Metropolitan Sewage and Essex Reclamation Company' was formed with the view of conveying the sewage to the Maplin Sands, to reclaim a part of the foreshore and apply the sewage. Experiments made by the company at Barking Creek, on soil composed of Maplin sand, spread 30 in. deep, and at the Lodge Farm, Barking, 2 m. from the outfall, are described as remarkably successful; but the company seems to have failed in obtaining sufficient pecuniary support. Lodge Farm is, however, still in full operation as an experimental farm for the application of town sewage to agricultural purposes, and immense crops of Italian rye grass, with smaller crops of mangel-wurzel and grain, have been obtained in each successive year. Here also are carried on the experimental works of the 'Phosphate Sewage Company,' who propose by the application of phosphate of alumina to defecate the sewage, form a dry manure from the solid matter, and employ the liquid effluent for irrigating the land, or, after filtration, discharge it as clear innocuous water.

The long stretch of marsh land W. of Barking Creek is called *East Ham Level*, that to the E., *Barking Level*. The bend, or reach of the Thames off here, is known as *Barking Reach:* it extends "from Maggott's Ness to Cross Ness," the points on the opposite bank above and below Barking Creek, and is 1·7017 m. long.* Pepys records that when the Dutch fleet sailed up the Thames, and burned the men-of-war lying at Chatham (1667), ships were sunk "at Barking Creek and other places, to stop their coming up higher."

Of old there were several manor-houses in the parish, but they have mostly been pulled down or transformed. One, however, is still standing, and worth visiting. *Eastbury House* is a short mile E. of Barking ch. on the Rainham rd. A lane on rt. of the rd. by the 8 m. stone leads down to it. It is a large 16th cent. red brick building, with cement quoins; has a commanding principal front, and a more broken and picturesque back, with octagonal turrets, many gables, and ornamental chimney stacks. In the rooms were some curious chimneypieces, and on some of the walls were pictures in fresco, or tempera, Falstaff's "water-work." Altogether, the house is a very interesting example of Elizabethan domestic architecture. It had become almost a ruin, but has been restored by the present owner. According to a tradition, of long standing when Lysons wrote, it was here that Lord Mounteagle received the letter which led to the discovery of the Gunpowder Plot. But the facts hardly bear out the story. Lord Mounteagle appears from the baptismal register to have been resident at Barking about the time, or a little later ("William, son of Sir Wm. Parker, knt., Lord Mounteagle, baptized Dec. 3, 1607"); but according to his 'deposition,' he was at his house at Hoxton when the letter was put into the hands of his footman, "whom he had sent of an errand over the street." Eastbury House was in 1605 the property of Thomas Sisley.

The *Roman Encampment* referred to above is by *Uphall*, now a farmhouse, on the N. of the town between the Roding and the road to Ilford. It is nearly quadrangular, about a mile in circuit, and encloses an area of 40 acres. The bank is tolerably perfect, but the trench, which Lysons describes as double on the river side, is for the most part filled up, the land

---

having been for more than a century under cultivation. At the N.W. angle " was an outlet to a very fine spring of water, which was guarded by an inner work, and a high keep or mound of earth;" and though much else is changed, the spring still flows and the mound is yet standing. The camp is unusually large, and must have been an important work. Whether any traditions still lurk in the neighbourhood respecting it we do not know ; but some 30 years since, talking with the then sexton of Barking ch. about the local antiquities, he asked if we had been to " the battle-field by Uphall?" On inquiring what battle was fought there, he replied, " Why the last battle, when Oliver Cromwell *druv* the Romans out of England ; " but noticing perhaps a look of incredulity, he cautiously added—" so at least ould histories tell us." His chronology was, however, altogether somewhat entangled, for he also mixed up Oliver Cromwell (a great hero in his estimation), the Romans, and " the two-penny post," with Lord Mounteagle's letter, Gunpowder Plot, and Eastbury House.

BARKING SIDE, Essex ; pop. 1828 ; 9 m. from London by rd., 2½ m. N. by E. from Ilford Stat. of the Grt. E. Rly.

The vill. is merely a gathering of a few small houses along a cross road, and a few others by a scrubby green; the inhabitants are chiefly engaged in agriculture. Barking Side is in Barking par., though 5 m. from the town. In 1841 it was divided from Ilford, and is now an eccl. district. The *Church*, small and neat, is of brick, transition Norm. to E.E. There are still green lanes and walks, but the place has now little to interest a stranger. Formerly the road skirted the pleasantest part of Hainault Forest, and here was the site of the famous East End saturnalia, *Fairlop Fair*. The fair was held originally under the spreading branches of a great oak, about a mile E. of the *Maypole* Inn. Its reputed founder was a Mr. Daniel Day, an opulent block-maker of Wapping, who about 1725 commenced to give an entertainment, under the great oak, to his tenants and friends, at his midsummer rent collection. Day was a local celebrity, and the gathering seems to have grown into a fair before his death

in 1767. After that, the mast and block-makers of Wapping regularly visited the fair, which was held " on the first Friday in July," riding there in two or three fully rigged model ships, mounted on carriage-frames, each drawn by 6 horses, with postilions and outriders, and attended by music. The Fairlop Oak was famous long before Day's time. Gilpin, in his ' Forest Scenery ' (1791), writes : " The tradition of the country traces it half-way up the Christian era. It is still a noble tree, though it has suffered greatly from the depredations of time. About a yard from the ground, where its rough fluted stem is 36 ft. in circumference, it divides into 11 vast arms ; yet not in the horizontal manner of an oak, but rather in that of a beech." The once popular ' Fairlop Fair Song,' accounts in a very prosaic manner for the name :—

" To Hainault Forest Queen Anne she did ride
 And beheld the beautiful Oak by her side;
 And, after viewing it from the bottom to the top,
 She said to her Court, ' It is a Fair-lop !' "

According to the same poetic chronicle,

" It was eight fathoms round,
 Spread an acre of ground."

Gilpin describes it as " overspreading an area of 300 ft. in circumference." It had lost some of its great branches (said to have been 12 ft. in girth), been injured by a fire kindled by a pleasure-party, June 25th, 1805, and was altogether much dilapidated when it was blown down in a gale in Feb. 1820. Fragments were wrought into various articles, but the most important relics are the pulpit and reading-desk of St. Pancras Church, Euston Road (at that time in course of erection), which were made out of the branches of the fallen monarch. Though Fairlop Fair was popularly supposed to be held by charter " under the shadow of the great oak," the fall of the tree did not put an end to it. The power of holding it was taken away by the Disafforesting Act of 1852, which allotted the site to the Crown. The fair, however, lingered on till the ground was actually enclosed, four or five years later. Even now, on " the first Friday in July," the block-makers of Wapping visit Barking Side in their ships, drawn by six horses, and after skirting the scenes of their old revels, dine at the Maypole or one of the neighbouring inns.

A sort of fair continues to be held on the unenclosed wastes, but it is a fragmentary, disreputable mockery. The site of Fairlop Fair is now a part of Crown Farm. (*See* ALDBOROUGH HATCH, and HAINAULT FOREST.) It may be noticed as illustrating the tenacity with which the memory of Fairlop is held, that the London Foresters named the lifeboat which they presented to the Lifeboat Society in 1865, 'The Fairlop.'

BARN-ELMS, SURREY, on the Thames, ½ m. E. of Barnes ch.: the way to it is by the private road rt. of the Red Lion, at the angle formed by the meeting of the Richmond and Hammersmith roads. The manor of Barn-Elms was given by Athelstane to the canons of St. Paul's, and is still held by them. The name, according to Lysons, is the Saxon *berne*, a barn; and it has been suggested that the canons may have had a *spicarium*, or great barn, here; but others think that Barn was the patronymic of a family or tribe, as in *Barnsbury*, etc. The addition, *elms*, seems to point to the trees which have always been a distinctive feature of the place.

Barn-Elms consists of a mansion and one or two smaller houses standing in park-like grounds which extend from Barnes Common to the river. It has had many distinguished occupants. In 1579 it was leased to Sir Francis Walsingham, who entertained Queen Elizabeth here in 1585, 1588, and 1589. On the last of these visits, Lord Talbot, who was appointed to attend the Queen at Barn-Elms, wrote to his father, the Earl of Shrewsbury (May 26th, 1589):—

"I pray God my diligent attendance there, may procure me a gracious answere in my suite at her return; for while she is ther nothing may be moved but matter of delyghte, and to content her; which is the only cause of her going thither."

Walsingham died poor at his house in Seething Lane in 1590; his widow resided at Barn-Elms till her death, 12 years later. The manor passed to their daughter, who, as Lysons observes, " had the singular good fortune of being wife to three of the most accomplished men of the age, Sir Philip Sidney, the Earl of Essex, and the Earl of Clanricarde," (i., 8), but only her second husband, the Earl of Essex, is known to have made Barn-Elms his resi-

dence. Abraham Cowley came here, probably to the smaller house, "for solitude," but, says his biographer, Bishop Spratt, it did not

"agree so well with his body as his mind. The chief cause of it was, that out of haste to be gone away from the tumult and noise of the city, he had not prepared so healthful a situation in the country as he might have done. Of this he soon began to find the inconvenience at Barn-Elms, where he was afflicted with a dangerous and lingering fever. After that he scarce ever recovered his former health."　*

Evelyn records two visits to Cowley here:—

"14*th May*, 1663.—Went to Barnes to visit my excellent and ingenious friend, Abraham Cowley."
"*June* 2, 1664.—To Barne-Elms, to see Abraham Cowley after his sickness."

In 1665 Cowley removed to Chertsey, where he died two years later, 1667. But though Cowley sought solitude, others came here about this time with very different intent:—

"After dinner I by water alone to Westminster to the parish church, and there did entertain myself with my perspective glass up and down the church, by which I had the great pleasure of seeing and gazing at a great many very fine women; and what with that and sleeping, I passed away the time till sermon was done. Then away to my boat, and up with it as far as *Barn-Elms*, reading of Mr. Evelyn's late new book against Solitude, in which I do not find much excess of good matter, though it be pretty for a bye discourse. I walked the length of the Elms, and with great pleasure saw some gallant ladies and people come with their bottles, and basket, and chairs, and form, to sup under the trees, by the water-side, which was mighty pleasant: so home."　†

Pepys several times notes in his diary that he went on the

"Lorde's-day" afternoon up the river in his boat, "to Barn-Elms, and there took a turn," alone, or "with my wife and Mercer up by water to Barn-Elms, where we walked by moonlight." But on one occasion, after "an extraordinary good dinner," which he gave to "Mrs. Pierce and Mrs. Manuel the Jew's wife, and Mrs. Corbet, and Mrs. Pierce's boy and girl . . . . I had a barge ready at the Tower wharf, to take us in, and so went, all of us, up as high as Barn-Elms, a very fine day, and all the way sang; amd Mrs. Manuel sings very finely, and is a mighty-discreet sober-carriaged woman, that both my wife and I are mightily taken with her. At Barn-Elms we walked round, and then to the barge again, and had much merry talk, and good singing."　‡

---

* Account of the Life of Abraham Cowley prefixed to his Works, 1688.
† Pepys. Diary, May 26, 1667.
‡ Diary, March 23, 1668.

The velvet lawns of Barn-Elms seem about this time to have been very attractive to pleasure-seekers; even the Lord Mayor and other civic magnates, when they went up the river in their barges, usually halted at Barn-Elms to indulge in music, feast, and dance. It was at Barn-Elms that the duel was fought, January 16, 1678, between the Earl of Shrewsbury and the Duke of Buckingham, respecting the wife of the former, which caused so much scandal even in the licentious court of Charles II.

"Much discourse of the duel yesterday between the Duke of Buckingham, [Sir Robert] Holmes, and one [Capt. William] Jenkins, on one side, and my Lord of Shrewsbury, Sir John Talbot, and one Bernard Howard [son of the Earl of Arundel], on the other side; and all about my Lady Shrewsbury, who is at this time, and hath for a great while been, a mistress to the Duke of Buckingham. And so her husband challenged him, and they met yesterday in a close near Barn-Elms, and there fought; and my Lord Shrewsbury is run through the body, from the right breast through the shoulder; and Sir John Talbot all along up one of his arms; and Jenkins killed upon the place, and the rest all, in a little measure, wounded." *

The Earl of Shrewsbury died of his wounds two months later, but a pardon had meantime been granted under the great seal to all persons concerned in the duel. It was said that the Countess, habited as a page, held the Duke's horse whilst he was fighting her husband, and went home with him afterwards.

In the reign of George II., the Swiss Count Heidegger, the master of the revels, rented the manor-house. Heidegger was noted at court for his skill in arranging entertainments (as he was among the wits for his ugliness —"Something betwixt Heidegger and an owl") and the King invited himself one evening to sup with him. His Majesty came by boat from his palace at Richmond, and it was dark when he reached Barn-Elms. There were no lights, and he made his way with some difficulty along the avenue to the house. That was dark also, and the King grew angry at the absence of preparation, when in an instant house, avenue, and grounds became brilliantly illuminated by innumerable lamps, which had been so arranged as to be lighted simultaneously. The King greatly enjoyed the surprise, and as the rest of

the entertainment was equally successful Heidegger was abundantly complimented for his device. Heidegger was for many years lessee of the King's Theatre, and during the years 1728-34 Handel was his partner, and produced there his oratorio of 'Esther' and operas of 'Orlando' and 'Deborah'; but their friendship was of earlier date, and Handel when he first came to England resided for some time at Barn-Elms. The house was afterwards leased by Sir Richard Hoare the banker, who in 1771 added new wings, and modernized it. His son, Sir Richard Colt Hoare, the antiquary, afterwards occupied it; later it became the residence of Vice-Chancellor Sir Lancelot Shadwell; and is now that of H. D. Pochin, Esq.

The other house, known in the last century as *Queen Elizabeth's Dairy*, was the residence of Jacob Tonson, the bookseller, who died here Nov. 25, 1735. Tonson built a room adjoining the house for the meetings of the Kit-Cat Club, and hung the room with the portraits of the members, painted for him by Sir Godfrey Kneller. Here met the leading Whigs, and wits, the 'proud Duke of Somerset,' Dorset, Somers, Walpole, Charles Montague, Dryden (at least his portrait was here), Congreve, Vanbrugh, Walpole, Addison, Steele, and others of not unworthy companionship. After Tonson's death, the portraits, 48 in number, and with the exception of Tonson's of uniform size (36 inches by 28)—perhaps the most remarkable series of English male portraits extant—were removed to Water-Oakley, by Windsor, where a room was built for their reception by Richard Tonson, grandson of 'Old Jacob.' They are happily still preserved intact at Bayfordbury, Herts, the seat of R. W. Baker, Esq., the present representative of the Tonson family.* (*See* BAYFORD.) When Sir Richard Phillips visited Barn-Elms in 1817, he found the place

"a handsome structure in the architectural style of the last century," in a semi-ruinous condition: "the once elegant hall filled with cobwebs, a fallen ceiling, and accumulating rubbish . . . one of the parlours converted into a wash-house, . . . and the entire building, for want of ventilation become

* Pepys, Diary, Jan. 17, 1667-8.

* Sir Wm. Baker, M.P. for Plympton, and alderman of London, married young Jacob Tonson's eldest daughter.

food for the fungus called dry-rot." But the *Kit-Cat Room* was nearly as it existed in its glory. "It is 18 ft. high, and 40 long, by 20 wide. The mouldings and ornaments were in the most superb fashion of its age; but the whole was falling to pieces from the effects of the dry-rot. My attention was chiefly attracted by the faded cloth-hanging of the room, whose red colour once set off the famous portraits of the Club that hung around it. Their marks and sizes were still visible, and the numbers and names remained as written in chalk for the guidance of the hanger." On "expressing his grief that so interesting a building should be suffered to go to decay for want of attention," he was told that the owner "intended to pull it down and unite it to an adjoining barn, so as to form of the two a riding house : and I learn," he adds, "that this design has since been executed." *

The portraits were engraved in mezzotint by Faber, and published the year before Tonson's death ; and re-engraved by Cooper, and published, accompanied with flimsy ill-written 'Memoirs,' in 1821. There is yet another association connected with Barn-Elms. Cobbett for awhile rented the farm in order to grow his favourite dwarf maize, 'Cobbett's Corn,' and show how *he* could farm.

BARNES, SURREY (Dom. *Berne*),

by the Thames, between Mortlake and Putney, pop. 4197 : the Barnes Stat. of the Richmond (L. and S.W.) Rly. (7 m.) is on Barnes Common, ¾ m. S. of the vill.

Barnes is a long and straggling place, very pleasant in parts, and has some good residences, among others, *St. Anne's House* (the Earl of Lonsdale), *Mill Hill* (H. Scarth, Esq.), *Mill Hill Lodge* (W. Tayler, Esq.), and *The Laurels* (H. B. Alexander, Esq.) Barnes has lost much of its rural character by the inroads of the builder, and has nearly doubled in population during the last ten or twelve years. Barnes *Church* (St. Mary) is of flint and stone, rough-cast, with a tall red brick tower. The chancel at least is E.E.; the three lancet windows were opened in 1852, when, after having been many times altered and enlarged, the church was restored throughout. The exterior was whitewashed in 1866; it now possesses little architectural character or antiquarian interest. *Obs.* between two buttresses on the S. a tablet to Edward Rose, citizen of London, d. 1653, who left £20 to purchase an acre of land, the proceeds of which were to be given to the poor, but

first, to keep his name and memory fragrant, *rose bushes* were to be planted on his grave between the buttresses, and protected by a wooden paling. The bushes are still to be seen, but their condition does little credit to the gratitude or gardening of the parochial authorities. Less fortunate has been Mrs. Anne Baynard (d. 1697, at the age of 25), whose tomb is no longer to be seen, but whose life has been written by Ballard in his 'Memoirs of Learned Ladies.' She made herself a proficient in Greek for the sake of reading St. Chrysostom in the original.

Inside the ch. observe by the communion table a *brass* of Wm. Millebourne, d. 1415 ; and on N. wall a mural mont., by Hickey, to Sir R. Hoare, Bart. The rectory was held by Hezekiah Burton, d. 1681, whose 'Sermons' in 2 vols. 8vo were published, with a biographical preface, by Archbp. Tillotson ; and by Francis Hare (d. 1717) successively Bp. of St. Asaph, and of Chichester, but best known by the prominent part he took against Bp. Hoadley in the Bangorian Controversy.

Barnes Common, originally of 135 acres, but reduced to 120 by encroachments of the Richmond Rly., and the loop line diverging from it, as well as by a cemetery, is among the best kept, and pleasantest, of the commons round London ; its pleasantness being increased by its contiguity to Putney Heath and Wimbledon Common, of which it is in effect an extension. Barnes Common is a favourite haunt of microscopists and moss-hunters. *Barnes Green* is a detached fragment of the common at its lower or N.W. angle, close to the village.

Barnes Terrace is a line of good houses facing the Thames, ½ m. W. of the ch. Here settled in the early part of the century a little colony of French *émigrés*. Among them were the Count and Countess D'Antraigues, noted for the activity of their partizanship, who occupied a small house near the upper end of the terrace. One morning, in 1812, they were about to proceed to London, and the Count was following his lady downstairs towards the coach, when his valet, an Italian, fired a pistol at him, and then struck him between the shoulders with a dagger. The Count made towards his room, but fell dead on the floor. The Countess, unconscious of what had occurred, turned back to see why she was not followed, when the assassin plunged his dagger into her breast. She shrieked, reeled forward, and fell dead on the pavement. The murderer fled upstairs, and before any one could reach him had killed himself. It was said that he was led to the deed from having on the previous evening over-heard the Count and Countess, as they were watching the moonlight on the river, speak of dismissing him from their service. Besides the persons mentioned under *Barn-Elms*, the more eminent residents at Barnes include Henry Fielding, the novelist, who inhabited an old house on the common known as *Milbourne House;* Monk Lewis, who wrote in a cottage here his ' Crazy Jane,' and other pieces ; and Edw. W. Cooke, R.A., who resided for several years at Barnes Terrace, and there painted many of his most successful pictures.

Castlenau, villas and shops which line the road to the foot of Hammersmith Bridge, is a hamlet of Barnes, with a little ch., Holy Trinity, for a congregation of 250 persons. The extensive reservoirs along the Thames, W. of Castlenau, are the store and filtering beds of the West Middlesex Water Works Company. They have an area of 16 acres, and receive water from the company's works at Hampton, when the machinery is in full operation, at the rate of 14,000 gallons a minute. From these reservoirs the water, after filtration, passes under the Thames to the works at Hammersmith, whence it is pumped to the covered reservoir at Primrose Hill for distribution.

BARNET, CHIPPING BARNET,

or HIGH BARNET, HERTS : pop. of par. 3375, of Local Board district 3720 ; a market town situated on the Great North Road, 11 m. from London : High Barnet Stat., Gt. N. Rly. (Edgware and High Barnet branch), is at the London end of the town (*obs.* the fine view S. on reaching the road from the stat.) ; the Barnet Stat. of the Gt. N. Rly. (main line) is at New Barnet, 1½ m. S.E. of High Barnet.

In Saxon times the site was part of an extensive wood called *Southaw*, belonging to the Abbey of St. Albans. The name of the town appears in early deeds as *Berg-net,* "from the high situation hereof, for the word Bergnet in the Saxon language

signifies *monticulus*, a little hill."* Its elevated position is also indicated in the appellation *High Barnet*, which it bears in many old books and maps, and which the rly. company has restored. It is the belief of the older natives that " Barnet stands on the highest ground betwixt London and York." " It had the adjunct *Chipping Barnet* from the market, which King Henry II. granted to the Abbots of St. Albans to be kept in this town ; it was famous for cattle, and was held on every Monday." †

The market is still held, but on Wednesday instead of Monday, and its fame as a mart for cattle is transferred to the *Great Fair* held Sept. 4th to 6th, to which cattle and horses, and particularly young stock, are brought from all parts of the kingdom. The horses, cattle, and sheep are shown in different fields, stretching from the meadows on the S., or London side of the town, to the commons on the W. and N. of it, so as to form in effect half a dozen distinct fairs. The horse fair always attracts numerous herds of Welsh ponies and Irish colts ; the cattle, great droves of Devons and Herefords, Welsh and Scotch cattle, and there is generally a large show of sheep. The unsold stock are mostly driven to Harlow Bush Fair, held Sept. 9th and 10th. The horse and cattle fair used to be wound up by a pleasure fair and races, which were very popular with the costermongers and roughs of the N. and N.E. of London. On the evening of the races the Barnet road used to present a coarse copy, on a smaller scale, of the Epsom road on the evening of the Derby. The race-ground was, however, broken up in forming the new (High Barnet) rly., in 1871, and the races were then of necessity abandoned. The pleasure fair is, however, continued, but it has become such a scene of ruffianism that its early suppression may be anticipated.

The town consists of a straggling street over a mile long, chiefly of small commonplace houses, with two or three shorter streets diverging from it. From its situation on the main road, as the centre of an agricultural district, the seat of a county court and petty sessions, and having a

---

* Chauncy, Hist. Antiq. of Hertfordshire.
† *Ibid.*, vol. ii., p. 374 (reprint).

barracks close at hand, Barnet is a busy-looking place, and has some good shops; one or two excellent inns (*Red Lion*, the principal, *Old Salisbury Arms*,) and an undue proportion of public-houses; but on the whole it has rather a shabby and not a very picturesque appearance: it is, however, improving. In coaching days, 150 stage coaches passed through it daily. Since the opening of the rly., the town has increased considerably, especially on the W. about the Common; or, as it is now called, Arkley.

Barnet *Church* (St. John the Baptist), which stands in what was the centre of the town, was erected by John de la Moote, abbot of St. Albans, about 1400, the architect being one Beauchamp. * It consisted of a nave and aisles, separated by clustered columns which supported 4 pointed arches; a chancel with an east window of good Perp. tracery; a vestry, built in the reign of James I. by Thomas Ravenscroft; and, at the west end, a low, square embattled tower. In 1839 the church was enlarged, but not improved: it is now (June 1874) far advanced in the process of restoration, or reconstruction, under the direction of Mr. Butterfield. The S. aisle, transept, and chancel are entirely new. The old tower has been lowered, thrown into the nave, and received a new W. window. A new tower of flint and stone, in squares, is being built on the S.W. In the chancel were several monuments of the Ravenscroft family, the most noteworthy being an altar-tomb with a recumbent statue of Thomas Ravenscroft, Esq., who died Feb. 12th, 1630. A mural monument erected by him in memory of his wife, Tomasin Ravenscroft, who died in 1611, has an inscription in verse, the first stanza of which may be quoted as illustrating the curious mingling of classic with Christian sentiment current in the early part of the 17th cent. :—

" Whom Nature made a lovely modest Maid,
　And Marriage made a loving virtuous Wife,
　Her Death hath made a Corps, and here hath laid
　A Goddess-saint in everlasting life."

The living of Barnet is a curacy, held with the rectory of EAST BARNET till

* Newcome, Hist. of the Abbey of St. Albans, p. 279.

the death of the late incumbent in 1866, when the livings were separated. The town also includes parts of the parishes of Monken Hadley and South Mimms. Barnet *Christ Church*, a neat Gothic building, N.W. of the town, but in the par. of South Mimms, Middx., consecrated 1852, was built in 1845 at the cost of Capt. Trotter of Dyrham Park, South Mimms.

There are several almshouses in the town. The oldest, called *Jesus' Hospital*, on the rt. in Wood Street, was built and endowed by James Ravenscroft, in 1672, for 6 poor ancient women of Barnet, who are to be "neither common beggars, common drunkards, backbiters, tale-bearers, common scolds, thieves, or other like persons of infamous life, or evil name or repute; or *vehemently suspected* of *sorcery, witchcraft, or charming*, or guilty of perjury; nor any idiot or lunatic." These " Sisters of Jesus " have each an apartment furnished with " a table, a bedstead, and a chair." The trustees are understood to have large funds in hand. Another almshouse in Wood Street was founded by John Garrett in 1729, for 6 old spinsters or widows, who each receive a weekly stipend of 2s. 6d., besides lodging and maintenance. *The Leathersellers' Almshouses*, standing at the junction of Union Street and Wood Street, were erected in 1843 by Richard Thornton, Esq., for 6 poor freemen of the Leathersellers' Company, London, and 6 freemen's widows, who have lodging, 2 tons of coals yearly, and 10s. a week each: the buildings, Domestic Gothic, of white brick, were enlarged in 1865 by the addition of 8 new houses: Mr. S. Hills, archt. One erected on Barnet Common by Mr. Palmer in 1823, for 6 aged townsmen and 6 aged women, who have each 6s. a week, besides lodging. The *Free Grammar School*, in Wood Street, was founded and endowed with a rental of £7 by Queen Elizabeth, in 1573. It is now, 1874, closed for reconstruction. There are schools and an infirmary here, supported out of the Patriotic Fund, for children of soldiers and sailors who died in the Crimean war.

The BATTLE OF BARNET was fought on Easter Sunday, April 14, 1471, between the Yorkists and Lancastrians, commanded respectively by the King,

Edward IV., and the King-maker, Warwick, when the latter was slain and his army defeated. The battle-field is believed to have been the heath, now called *Hadley Green*, about half a mile N. of the town. The site is marked by an obelisk, erected in 1740 by Sir Jeremy Sambrook, which stands at the division of the St. Albans and Hatfield roads, but originally stood about 30 yards S., close to the *Two Brewers*. It was removed to where it now stands about 1840. Some antiquaries are of opinion that the battle was fought on Gladmore Heath, or Monkey Mead Plain, more to the E., and within Enfield Chase; but the elevated site, marked by the obelisk, with the sudden fall of the ground to the E., seems to agree better with contemporary accounts of the battle. Immediately beyond the obelisk (but in South Mimms, Middlesex) is *Wrotham Park*, the seat of George Stevens Byng, Earl of Strafford. The house was built by Ware in 1754, for the unfortunate Admiral John Byng.

At *Barnet Common*, nearly a mile to the W. of the town, is a medicinal spring, once in great repute as *Barnet Wells*. Its discovery was announced in the 'Perfect Diurnal' of June 5, 1652. Fuller, in his 'Worthies' (Hertfordshire), ranks it with the wells of Tunbridge and Epsom, and says that already (1662) "the catalogue of the cures done by this spring amounteth to a great number; insomuch that there is hope, in process of time, the water rising here will repair the blood shed hard by, and save as many lives as were lost in the fatal battle at Barnet." That insatiable gobemouche Pepys, notes in his Diary, under July 11, 1664, "I and my man Will on horseback by my wife to Barnet: a very pleasant day." Having dined with his wife, and despatched her on her journey, he adds: "I and Will to see the Wells, and there I drunk three glasses, and walked, and come back and drunk two more; and so we rode home, round by Kingsland, Hackney, and Mile End." Either the ride or the water—which was considered to be twice as potent as that of the Epsom Wells—made him feel "not very well," and so he went "betimes to bed." But not to sleep: "About eleven o'clock, knowing what money I have in the house, and hearing a noise, I begun to

sweat worse and worse, till I melted almost to water." Three years later (Aug. 11, 1667) he journeyed down to Barnet Wells on a " Lord's Day " morning. He arrived there by " seven o'clock and found many people a drinking; but the morning was a very cold morning," and so he contented himself with drinking three glasses, and then hied by coach to the Red Lion (his usual inn) at Barnet, where he "did eat some of the best cheese cakes [a commodity for which Barnet seems to have been noted] that ever I eat in my life." In 1667 Alderman Owen left £1 per annum to keep the well in repair. Chauncy, in 1700, describes the water as an " excellent safe purger," and "of great use in most weakly bodies, especially those that are hypocondriacal or hysterical."[*] It is mentioned by Boyle;[†] and Campbell speaks of it as a "purging water, formerly, when fewer of these salubrious springs were known, as a very gentle and safe chalybeate, deservedly in great esteem." [‡] As late as 1800 a pamphlet was published on ' The Barnet Well Water,' by the Rev. W. M. Trinder, M.D.

The old well-house was pulled down, and a small farmhouse erected on the foundations, about 1840. The well is now covered over, and the water is obtained from it by a small iron pump. To reach it you go along Wood Street (by Barnet ch.) for $\frac{1}{4}$ m., and down the lane on the l. in front of the Union Workhouse to where the lane is crossed by a light iron gate. Here turn through a small clap-gate on the l. into a field path, which presently passes through a gap in the hedge, on the rt., into a field, in the midst of which the pump will be seen, and above it the Well House. The well is quite open to every one, and is still occasionally resorted to by invalids. The visitor who is disposed to test the efficacy of the water will remember Pepys's experience.

Around Barnet Common, N. of the well-house (a field path connects them), has grown up a little settlement of neat residences and newer 'villas,' which has received the name of *Arkley*, and for

* Hist. Antiquities of Hertfordshire, vol. i., p. 11.
† Works, vol. iv., p. 247.
‡ Political Survey of Great Britain (1784), vol. i., p. 79.

which an episcopal chapel—a sham Gothic structure covered with plaster—was built in 1840 at the cost of Mr. Enoch Durant. Arkley is on the Elstree road, and a very pleasant, little-frequented, country road it is. *Barnet Gate*, ½ m. beyond Arkley, affords a picturesque turn; along the Woodcock and Deacon's Hills you have wide views; and the heights continue, with bosky dips between, all the way to Elstree: from Barnet to Elstree is about 4½ m.

The stranger at Barnet should not fail to visit *Hadley*, immediately N.E. of the town (on the rt. of the Green where stands the battle obelisk, locally known as *Hadley High Stone*,) for the sake of the interesting old ch., and the Green beyond it—a goodly avenue on one side and a picturesque fragment of wild wood on the other: a path from the bottom of the wood leads direct to the Barnet Rly. Stat. of the Grt. N. main line. (*See* HADLEY, MONKEN.) About the Barnet Stat. has sprung up, within the last few years, one of those new, half-finished rly. villages which we have come to look on as almost a necessary adjunct to every stat. within a moderate distance of London. This is known as *New Barnet*, but the ecclesiastical district, formed out of the parishes of Chipping Barnet and East Barnet, is named *Lyonsdown*: it had 2340 inhab. in 1871. Close against the stat. are shops, a Baptist chapel, public-houses, and a Rly. Hotel. Farther off are terraces and villas; and on the higher ground is a belt of more pretentious detached residences. In 1865 was added a Gothic ch., Holy Trinity, designed by Mr. E. Christian. It is of parti-coloured bricks, Early Dec. in style, and somewhat quaint in character; has an apsidal chancel, and a thin bell-spire.

BARNET, EAST, HERTS, a pleasant village 10 m. N. from London, 2 m. S.E. from Barnet, and ½ m. from the Barnet Stat. of the Grt. Northern Rly.: pop. 992 (exclusive of 2,003 in the eccl. district of Lyonsdown or New Barnet). Inn, the *Cat*. It is called East Barnet to distinguish it from Chipping Barnet and Friern Barnet immediately adjoining. Since the Conquest, East Barnet has been a part of the manor of Chipping Barnet. The *Church* (St. Mary the Vir-

gin) consists of a nave, built by an Abbot of St. Albans early in the 12th cent.; a chancel built in 1663 by Sir Robert Bartlet, and a modern brick tower at the W. end; to which was added in 1868 a S. aisle of Kentish rag with Bath-stone dressings, and at the same time the int. was restored and refitted. There are no monts. of mark in the ch. *Obs.* in the ch.-yd. the tomb of Major-Gen. Augustin Prevost, d. 1786, " by birth a native and citizen of Geneva," but who served with great distinction, and rose to high rank, in the British army. His last and most eminent service was the defence of Savannah (1779) "against the combined armies of France and America, supported by a powerful fleet." A painted glass window was erected in the ch. in 1840, as a memorial to the Wyatt family. Gilbert Burnet, son of the Bishop, was rector of East Barnet from 1719 to 1726. Dr. Richard Bundy, author, among other works, of a long forgotten but very voluminous Roman History, was rector from 1733 to 1739.

It was from East Barnet, where she had been taken April 1, 1611, to the house of Thomas Conyers, Esq., (who received "20s. the week, houserent,") that the beautiful and unhappy Lady Arabella Stuart escaped disguised in male apparel, June 3, 1611. The admirable Lady Fanshawe lived for awhile at East Barnet. Thomson's patron, Lord Binning, occupied the Manor House, and the poet was, as Johnson expresses it, " for some time entertained in the family;" but while here (1725) he had to teach Lord Binning's son (the future 7th Earl of Haddington) to read. Unfortunately he did not find it the " delightful task " he describes in his ' Spring.' In one of his letters he speaks of it as " a low task, but so suitable to the temper—and I must learn that necessary lesson of suiting my mind and my temper to my state." The publication of ' Winter ' (1726) happily released him from the necessity of such drudgery.

The scenery around East Barnet is pleasing, but the place has lost somewhat of its rural quiet since the opening of the rly. Between the village of East Barnet and the stat. many small houses have been built. By the ch. is *Church Farm*, " The Country Home," Industrial Schools for about 100 destitute boys, between the ages of 6 and 13, not convicted of crime. The farm of 50 acres is cultivated by the boys. It is an excellent and well-managed establishment, and has been productive of much good. "Visitors are always welcome." (London office, The Boys' Home, Regent's Park Road, of which it is a branch.) *Oak Hill Park*, E. of the vill. (C. Baring Young, Esq.), is a fine mansion standing on an eminence, and commanding extensive views. *Belmont* (C. A. Hanbury, Esq.), on the N. of it, was formerly called *Mount Pleasant*, and was the residence of Elias Ashmole, founder of the Ashmolean Museum. *Trent Park* (R. C. L. Bevan, Esq.), and *Beech Hill Park* (Chas. Jack, Esq.), though close to Oak Hill, belong to Enfield Chase.

BARNET, FRIERN, (or FRY-ERN,) lies S. of East Barnet, ½ m. E. of the Barnet road; 8 m. from London, and 1 m. N.W. from the Southgate Stat. of the Grt. Northern Rly. The par. includes the hamlet of COLNEY HATCH and the E. side of WHETSTONE (*see* those places), and the pop. (exclusive of 2117 inmates of the County Lunatic Asylum, Colney Hatch,) was 2230 in 1871. Friern Barnet itself is a quiet, retired, and very pretty place, hardly to be called a vill., the houses lying dispersed between the Barnet road and Colney Hatch. Many are the residences of wealthy citizens, stand in spacious grounds, and are embowered among old elms and limes, and altogether the aspect of the place is verdurous and flourishing. But here as elsewhere the builder is making inroads.

The manor of Friern Barnet belonged to the Knights of St. John of Jerusalem; on the suppression of monasteries it was assigned to the Dean and Chapter of St. Paul's, and now belongs to J. Miles, Esq. The *Manor House* (John Miles, Esq.), close by the ch., retains few vestiges of antiquity. When Norden wrote his 'Survey of Middlesex,' (1592), Lord Chief Justice Popham resided here.

The *Church* (St. James) has a Norm. doorway; nave chiefly E.E. in character, and Dec. E. and W. windows—all filled with painted glass. It is of flint and stone; small but picturesque; and was restored, somewhat enlarged, and had a tower and square pyramidal shingled

spire and glazed porch on the S.W. added in 1853. *Obs.* the fine elm at entrance of the ch.-yd., and the yew by the E. end of the ch.

Beyond the ch. (towards Whetstone) is a range of *Almshouses*, founded in 1612 by Lawrence Campe for 12 aged persons, who besides lodging, receive 2s. a week each. It is the original building, but repaired and stucco-fronted in 1843. *Obs.* the three grand old elms standing in the front garden; and note directly E. of the almshouses, the pretty Gothic school-house built by Mr. Miles of the Manor House. On the E. side of the parish, by the rly., is the *Great Northern Cemetery*. In olden times the Great North Road passed through Friern Barnet by way of Colney Hatch, but becoming inconvenient "by reason of the deepness and dirty passage in the winter season," the Bishop of London undertook to make a new and more direct road to Whetstone through his park at Highgate (*see* HIGHGATE); and to compensate the inhabitants of Friern Barnet for loss of the traffic on their road, they were made free of the toll levied at the Bishop's Gate.

BARNET, NEW (*see* BARNET, p. 30).

BAYFORD, HERTS (Dom. *Begesford*, i.e., By the Ford), an agricultural parish; there is no proper vill.; about 3 m. S. of Hertford: pop. 352. A quiet, secluded place, reached by winding lanes bordered by hedge-row elms and oaks. The only noticeable objects besides the pleasant walks are the ch., and Bayfordbury, the seat of W. R. Baker, Esq.

The manor of Bayford belonged in the reign of Edward the Confessor to Tosti, son of the famous Earl Godwin. From the Conquest it was held by the Crown till given by Henry I. for life to William de Valence. On the death of William de Valence, *t.* Edward I., it reverted to the Crown. In the 24th Edward III. (1350), William de Scrope was lord of the manor, and held the demesne lands of the king " *in capite* by knight's service, and 2d. to be paid at the feast of St. Michael." In the reign of Edward IV. the manor was in the possession of John Knighton, Esq., and afterwards successively in the families of Ferrers, Fanshawe, and Mayo, and is now held by R. W. Baker, Esq., of Bayfordbury.

Bayford was formerly a part of the rectory of Essendon, but is now a separate parish. The *Church*, of plain brick, of the year 1802, with a battlemented tower at the W. end, its meanness partially concealed by a luxuriant covering of ivy, has been replaced by a handsome cruciform building, E.E. in style, with a tall flèche at the intersection, and an apsidal chancel, designed by Mr. H. Woodyer. The interior is elegant and well finished. The lancets in the apse are filled with painted glass. Under an arch in the chancel is a recumbent alabaster effigy of Sir George Knighton, d. 1613, in short armour and puffed breeches ; a good example of the monumental sculpture of the time. There are also two *brasses* of knights in armour; one (with wife) imperfect, of the 16th, the other of the 17th cent.

In the ch.-yd., by the S.E. angle of the ch., is the burial-place (enclosed within a tall railing) of the Yarrell family. Here was interred, in Sept. 1856, that admirable naturalist William Yarrell, author of the ' History of British Birds,' and ' British Fishes.' As his tombstone records, " He was the survivor of 12 brothers and sisters, who with their father and mother are all placed close to this spot ; " and he left to the parish the interest of £500, to be applied in keeping the family grave in repair, the surplus to be annually distributed among the poor. The ch. stands high, and there are extensive views from the ch.-yd.

Bayfordbury lies ½ m. nearer Hertford. The park is large, undulating, wild, and pleasantly watered and wooded. The grounds by the house are rich and interesting. *Obs.* the large cedars planted in 1763. The house is modern and spacious, but cold and poor in style. In it are the famous portraits, forty-six in number, of the members of the Kit-Cat Club, painted by Sir Godfrey Kneller to be presented by the several members to their secretary, Jacob Tonson, and hung in a room built for them at Barn-Elms. The heads are for the most part good, manly likenesses, a little monotonous perhaps, and as pictures somewhat slight, whilst the costume is that curious mingling of stiff curled and powdered full-bottomed

perukes, lace cravats and ruffles, or open necks and loosely flowing robes, usual in Kneller's male portraits. They are of the size (36 by 28 in.), called from them ' kit-cat.' (*See* BARN-ELMS.)

As perhaps the most remarkable series of portraits of distinguished Englishmen painted from the life by the most eminent portrait painter of the time, it may be well to give a list of them—placing first the secretary of the club, for whom they were painted. *Jacob Tonson* is represented in green dressing gown, with red velvet cap instead of wig : portly, keen, and clubable. *Sir Godfrey Kneller* in a rich dress and flowing robe, with peruke of moderate dimensions, sword by his side ; wears the massive gold chain and medal given him when he was knighted (1692) by William III., in acknowledgment of the skill with which he had executed the royal commission to paint the portraits of the Plenipotentiaries of Ryswick. The face is plump, but bright and intelligent. *Dryden's* head is well known by the engravings. *Congreve*, in a slate-coloured coat, with curls flowing half-way down his back ; face self-satisfied rather than intellectual, and the easy, unembarrassed air of a somewhat foppish man of the world. It was painted in 1709, when Congreve was 49 years old, and the beauty for which in early manhood he was celebrated was passing away. It is very well painted, but still better is that of *Vanbrugh*, which is among the best of Kneller's male heads. Vanbrugh, in a brown dress, is seated at a table holding a pair of compasses carelessly between his fingers, as though engaged in conversation : with its clear open expression, large frank eyes, and full lips, it looks, however, rather the likeness of a clever social professional or business man than one of much original power. *Addison*, in bright blue coat and stupendous peruke, with large, clear, bluish-grey eyes, and bright and sharp expression tinged with the faintest suspicion of self-complacency, is here, as in life, in delightful companionship and contrast with one whose name always recurs to the memory when that of the other is mentioned—*Sir Richard Steele*—the Honest Dick of those who knew him, and the prototype of his countryman Goldsmith. It is a capitally painted portrait, and brings out well the distinctive Irish character and lurking humour somewhat slurred over in the engravings. *George Stepney*, diplomatist, small politician, and smaller poet, commissioner of stamps, and the husband of Vandyck's daughter, will be remembered longer by this portrait and Johnson's memoir than by his own productions—as in life he owed more to the patronage of Halifax and Dorset than to his own merits. An equally small, but still more bepraised, poet and critic, *William Walsh*, is shown here in a well-painted face, the portentous peruke and flowing wig having only their outlines roughly indicated—a picture chiefly interesting for the opportunity it affords for observing the painter's manner of working. *Sir Samuel Garth*, of 'The Dispensary,' like many of these portraits, a side view, with the head looking over the shoulder towards the spectator. *Charles Dartiquenave*, wit, punster, epicure,— the Dartineuf, or Darty, of Swift, Pope, Steele, and Addison,—"the man that knows everything and everybody,"—is here, the well-dressed careless man of the world, who might easily develop into the epicure or the voluptuary, but as yet is certainly neither the one nor the other. *Arthur Maynwaring*, the wit of the club, pamphleteer, politician, and, through the good services of the Treasurer Godolphin, Auditor of the Imprests,from which he drew the comfortable salary of £2000 a year ; in loose blue dress, left hand in vest. *Lord Mohun*, the duellist, twice tried for murder and acquitted, and again engaging in a duel, fell, like his opponent, the Duke of Hamilton, mortally wounded. Mohun forced his way into the club in spite of Tonson, and on the night of his admission disturbed the proceedings by breaking off the gilt ornament at the back of his chair. Kneller, detesting the man, painted him with sharpened appreciation of character—a coarse, bloated, brutal face, sensual lips and lower jaw. He is dressed in a rich blue coat and embroidered waistcoat, and holds a snuff-box in his left hand, the lid open to show the miniature of a lady, apparently an actress. Very different is the bright open countenance of *Robert Walpole, Earl of Orford*, the famous Minister of the first two Georges. He wears a brown coat,

flowing peruke, and the star and ribbon of the Order of the Garter. His persistent opponent, *William Pulteney, Earl of Bath*, in a blue coat, is standing with a scroll of paper in his right hand, as though about to commence a speech : a frank, manly, cheerful face, such as might be looked for in the friend and companion of Bolinbroke, Swift, Pope, and half the wits and politicians of his day. *Charles Lenox, Duke of Richmond*, son of Charles II. by the Duchess of Portsmouth—a somewhat effeminate likeness of his father mingling with the French features of his mother : in a magnificent wig and coat, on which are the ribbon and star of the Garter, yet has a loose shirt, rumpled and open at the neck. Another of King Charles's descendants in the natural line, *Charles Fitzroy*, 2nd *Duke of Grafton*, a smooth-faced, languid-looking creature, is represented in loose coat, shirt open to the chest, and velvet cap in place of wig. On his breast is the star, and his fingers are playing with the ribbon and George which lie on the table before him. Beside him may be set the sterner head of *Charles Seymour*, (the proud) *Duke of Somerset*. It was Somerset who proposed that the members of the Kit-Cat Club should have their portraits painted by Kneller and present them to Tonson, and he set the example by presenting his own ; in consequence of which, when Faber published his engravings from them, he dedicated the series to the Duke. *William Cavendish*, 2nd *Duke of Devonshire*, in full dress, holding in his right hand his wand of office as Lord Steward of the Household. *Thomas Holles Pelham, Duke of Newcastle*, for 30 years Secretary of State, and for 10 years Prime Minister, and who during the time did nothing with infinite bustle, is in a rich laced coat, and full wig, seated in his coroneted chair, proper, pouring wine into a glass he holds in his right hand ; and with him, behind the table, *Henry Clinton*, 7th *Earl of Lincoln*, wine glass in hand. *John*, 2nd and last *Duke of Montague*, in military costume, youthful, amiable, and intelligent. *Charles Montague*, 1st *Duke of Manchester*, diplomatist and Minister in the reigns of William, Anne, and George, in full court suit and peruke of largest size. *Charles*

Sackville, Earl of Dorset, the famous wit and munificent patron of wits and poets from Dryden to Shadwell, Durfey, and Tom Brown, the friend of Prior, Addison, and a host of lesser luminaries—himself a writer of verses of which one alone, 'To all you ladies now on land,' is remembered ; though Dryden, in dedicating his Translation of Juvenal to the Earl, says, in speaking of our English poets, " I would instance your Lordship in satire and Shakspeare in tragedy," Pope's " Dorset the grace of Courts, the Muse's pride," the "intellectual voluptuary " of Macaulay,—is here depicted by Kneller as a staid and sober-looking elderly gentleman, carrying his Chamberlain's wand with all the indifference of one whose thoughts had never risen above the level of court suits and court ceremonies. His only son, the 1st *Duke of Dorset*, the successful courtier of Anne and the first three Georges, figures in a well-painted rich court dress. A better head, masterly and well painted, is that of *Thomas*, 1st *Marquis of Wharton*, a prominent partizan of the Prince of Orange, a trusted Minister of William III., under Anne, Commissioner for the Union with Scotland, Lord Lieutenant of Ireland (where he had Addison for his secretary, and was bitterly abused by Swift), Lord Privy Seal to George I., and author of 'Lillebullero.' *Charles Montague*, 1st *Earl of Halifax*—the author, with Prior, of 'The City Mouse and Country Mouse,' and of the verses inscribed on the drinking glasses of the Kit-Cat Club, and to whom we owe the purchase of the Cotton MSS. and the foundation of the British Museum—a stately looking personage in loose robe and lofty peruque, very like one of Louis XIV.'s courtiers. *James*, 1st *Earl of Stanhope*, whose character and public services have been so well set forth by his descendant,[*] is painted, in early middle age, in a general's uniform, baton in hand, and is a better portrait than the larger one, also by Kneller, in the National Portrait Gallery. *Richard Boyle*, the architect *Earl of Burlington*, the princely patron of art and artists, and builder of Burlington House and the much-lauded villa at Chiswick, whose name is so familiar

to the reader of the poets and memoir writers of the first half of the 18th cent., is here, a young, handsome, and richly dressed man—the very model in aspect and bearing of an English nobleman. *Theophilus Hastings*, 9th *Earl of Huntingdon*, the somewhat free-living and indolent husband of the pious and imperious Countess of that name, is only shown in a smooth and sleepy head—the dress being but roughly outlined. *Francis, Earl of Godolphin*, in buff dressing gown, a commonplace portrait of the commonplace son of Sydney Godolphin, by no means a commonplace man. *James*, 7th *Earl of Berkeley*, a youthful face and figure, in vice-admiral's uniform, holding in his right hand a baton. *Charles Howard*, 3rd *Earl of Carlisle*, holder of many offices under Anne and George I.,—young, chubby, fair-faced, with ample wig ; in his right hand his official staff. *John Vaughan*, 3rd and last *Earl of Carberry*, hard-featured, with ruffled robe and wig. *Henry Lumley*, 3rd *Earl of Scarborough*, in military costume and full wig, ribbon of the Garter across his breast, three-cornered cocked-hat under his left arm. *Algernon Capel*, 2nd *Earl of Essex*, son of Arthur, 1st Earl, who committed suicide in the Tower while under arrest with Lord William Russell ; looks the cheerful, genial man he was reported to be. *Spencer Compton, Earl of Wilmington*, K.G., successively Speaker of the House of Commons, Paymaster-General, Lord Privy Seal and President of the Council, Chancellor of the Exchequer, and Prime Minister after Walpole—a dwarf following a giant. *Charles, Lord Cornwallis*, successor of Sir Robert Walpole as Postmaster-General, afterwards Paymaster of the Forces ; portly, self-satisfied, but affable : not among the best as a work of art. *Richard Boyle*, 3rd and last *Viscount Stannon*, a pleasant, nicely painted head ; the rest untouched. *John, Lord Somers*, the illustrious Whig lawyer and statesman of the reigns of James II., William, and Anne ; painted in his declining years, and showing little brilliancy or intellectual power. Field Marshal *Richard Temple*, 1st *Viscount Cobham*, a well though slightly painted portrait of a slim, handsome, soldierly man. *Edmund Dunch*, Gentleman of the Horse to Queen Anne and George I.

---

[*] History of England, vols. i.—iii.

General Dormer; Abraham Stanyan, Commissioner of the Admiralty, and an author of some repute in his day ; and *Brigadier-General John Tidcombe*, it will be enough to name : nor need we linger over *Thomas Hopkins* and his son *Edward*, near relatives to Vulture Hopkins, and possessing the distinctive family character ; though they must have had other and better qualities, in addition to their wealth, to obtain admission to the Kit-Cat Club. Both the heads are lifelike and effective.

The portraits were inherited by an ancestor of the present owner of Bayfordbury, Alderman Sir William Baker, M.P., who married the eldest daughter of young Jacob Tonson. Among other Tonson relics preserved here, is a large volume of letters from Dryden, Congreve, Addison, and other distinguished correspondents of Old Jacob. In one, the famous Sarah Duchess of Marlborough offers any one of her Vandycks in exchange for Tonson's portrait of the Duke : Tonson refused to exchange, but the portrait of the Duke was not at Water Oakley (whither the portraits were removed from Barn-Elms), and has somehow escaped from the collection. Among the papers is Dryden's receipt of £10 for " My trajady of Cleomenes." Mr. Baker also possesses a contemporary MS. of the first book of ' Paradise Lost ' : apparently the copy prepared for the press.

BAYFORDBURY (*see* BAYFORD).

BECKENHAM, KENT (*Beckham*, the home by the brook), situated on a little feeder of the Ravensbourne, midway between Sydenham and Bromley ; 10 m. S.E from London by road, 9 m. by S.E. Rly. (Mid-Kent line), 11¾ m. by L. C. and D. Rly.; pop. of par. 6090 ; is a pleasant suburban vill., but has lost much of its old-fashioned rusticity and seclusion since the opening of the rlys. The neighbourhood is, however, still agreeable : it abounds in trees, the surface is undulating, and there are tempting field and lane walks to Bromley, Hayes, and Wickham.

Beckenham *Church* (St. George) stands high, and with its tall white spire rising from among the thick trees, looks at a little distance the very ideal of a village ch. Close at hand it suffers somewhat. The nave and chancel are old ; but the aisles were added in the 17th cent. The whole has been covered with rough-cast. Some of the modern work and churchwardens' beautifyings were, however, removed when the ch. was restored two or three years ago. Inside there are a few old and one or two modern *monts.* of some interest. N. of the chancel is an altar tomb of Sir Humphrey Style (d. 1552), with mural brasses of Sir Humphrey in a tabard, and his two wives in heraldic mantles, Bridgett (d. 1548), with 6 sons and 3 daughters, and Elizabeth, who survived him, with 1 son and 1 daughter. There is another brass of Dame Margarett, wife of Sir Wm. Dansell (d. 1563). On the walls are other monts. to the Styles, Burrells, etc. Among the modern monts. *observe* those of Lady Hoare, d. 1800 (S. of chancel) with a bas-relief by Flaxman ; Mrs. Jane Clarke, d. 1757 (N. wall), with a poetic epitaph by Gray ; and tablet to Capt. Hedley Vicars, 97th Regt., who fell at Sebastopol. In the ch.-yd., under a sarcophagus, lies Edw. King (d. 1807), author of the ' Monumenta Antiqua.' King resided for many years at Clay Hill. The entrance to the ch.-yd. is by a lich gate (old and unrestored), from which an avenue of clipped yews leads to the S. porch.

Beckenham was one of the many manors granted by the Conqueror to his brother Odo, Bishop of Bayeux. In the 15th cent. it belonged to the Bruyns, and in the manor-house, *Beckenham Place*, Charles Brandon, Duke of Suffolk, (son of Eliz. Bruyn by her second husband) entertained Henry VIII. " with all the cunning pomp of magnificence, as he went to bestow a visit at Hever, on his discarded and repudiated wife, Anne of Cleve."[*] From 1650 the manor belonged to the St. John's till 1773, when it was sold by Viscount Bolingbroke to John Cator, Esq., in whose descendant it remains. The house, *Beckenham Place*, stands in a fine park ½ m. N. from the ch. *Eden Park* (F. Harrison, Esq.), 1 m. S., was built about 1790, by Eden, Lord Auckland, and here (it was then called *Eden Farm*) the historian Gibbon was accustomed to pass a night

[*] Philipott, Villare Cantianum, p. 63.

or two on his way to Sheffield Place. His last visit was in Nov. 1790, about six weeks before his death; and "he was much gratified by the opportunity of again seeing during a whole day, Mr. Pitt, who passed the night there."* The house stands in a finely timbered park of 130 acres.

Shortlands, the birthplace of George Grote, the author of the 'History of Greece,' now the seat of Conrade Wilkinson, Esq., is 1½ m. E. of Beckenham ch.; *Langley Park* (C. E. Goodhart, Esq.), of old the seat of the Styles family, is nearly 2 m. S.E. towards Hayes; *Kelsey Park* (P. Hoare, Esq.) is on the S.W., and other seats are in the neighbourhood. *Kent House*, a fine old brick mansion, 1 m. N.W. of Beckenham ch., by the field path to Sydenham, for generations the seat of the Lethieulliers, is now a farmhouse.

New Beckenham, about ½ m. N.W. of old Beckenham ch., is a village of villas, many of a superior class, which have sprung up in proximity to the New Beckenham Stat. of the Mid-Kent line. A district ch. (St. Paul's) was erected here some years back, but proving insufficient, has been altered and enlarged.

A portion of the *Shortlands* estate, 1½ m. E. from old Beckenham ch., has also been built over, and a railway stat. and railway hotel opened. Shortlands has been formed into an ecclesiastical district, and a handsome Dec. *Church* (St. Mary), consisting of nave and S. aisle, short transepts and chancel, with a good tower and tall stone spire on the N.W., erected at the cost of C. Wilkinson, Esq., of Shortlands. The entrance to the ch.-yd. is by a lich-gate imitated from that at Beckenham. On the high ground by the ch. several good villas have been built. Near the rly. stat. will be observed the engine-house of the West Kent Water Works. The water, of perfect purity, is obtained from a well sunk to a great depth; the resident engineer, Mr. Morris, has a capital section of the well which will interest the geologist.

The quiet hamlet of *Clay Hill* lies midway between Shortlands and Beckenham.

At the little hamlet of *Elmers* (or *Elms*) *End*, 1½ m. S.W. of Beckenham, by Eden Park, is a stat. of the Addiscombe Br. Rly.

BEDDINGTON, Surrey (the mark of the *Beadingas*, Kemble; Dom. *Beddingtone*); pop. 1499; of the entire par., which includes Wallington, 2834. The vill., situated chiefly on the l. bank of the Wandle, on an outlying patch of Thanet Sand, is 11 m. from London by rd.: *Waddon* Stat. of the Croydon and Epsom br. of the L., Br. and S. C. Rly., is 1 m. S. of the ch.; but there is a pleasanter walk of 2 m. to it from the more convenient *W. Croydon* Stat. by the river Wandle, past *Waddon Mill*. The Beddington Stat. of the L. and S.W. Rly. (Wimbledon and C. Pal. br.) is 1½ m. N. of the vill.

Beddington appears to have been a Roman station; the ancient Stone Street passed by *Woodcote* on the S. side of the par., and there, at Beddington, and at *Wallington*, a hamlet of Beddington, but nearer Carshalton, foundations of buildings, urns, spear-heads, and other Roman remains have been found. In Beddington Park Mr. Wickham Flower found a number of broken and imperfect castings of bronze spear-heads and other implements, an ingot of metal, part of a mould, and other objects which clearly showed that this was the site of the foundry where the articles were manufactured.* A later and in some respects more important discovery was made in Feb. 1871, in carrying out some engineering works for the Croydon sewage irrigation at Park Farm, on the N. side of the Wandle, between Beddington Lane and the Hackbridge Rly. Stat., when a Roman villa of considerable pretensions, with its detached outhouses, was laid open. The remains were about 2 ft. below the surface; the foundations, of Roman bricks, being laid on the natural bed of drift gravel. The outer walls, 6 to 21 in. high, were composed of large flints and mortar, flat Roman bricks being used as bonding-courses only in the inner walls. The interior was a mass of rubbish, in which were found fragments of Samean ware, a bronze head, and a few coins of the times of Commodus, Constantine, and Claudius. The building extended E. and W. from a central chamber, 16 ft. by 10 ft.; south of it was a pavement of square tiles, which appeared to have been subjected to great heat, and which was thought to have

---

* Life, by Lord Sheffield.

† Archæol. Journal vol. xxx. p. 283

been the floor on which the fire of the hypocaust was made. About 500 yds, S. of the villa, two or three skeletons, some sepulchral urns, a spear-head, iron knives, and the boss of a shield, were exhumed, marking, as is believed, the site of an Anglo-Saxon burial-ground; but the works were not carried farther in that direction, and the remains are again hidden from sight.* In March 1874 the "remains of a Roman warrior, who had evidently been buried in his armour, together with some arms," were found by labourers while digging gravel on the irrigation farm. Camden, Leland, Talbot, and other early antiquaries, placed the station *Noviomagus* at Beddington, but its site is now more generally assigned to Holwood Hill. (*See* KESTON.)

Beddington is chiefly remarkable from its connection with the Carew family. The manor came into the possession of Sir Nicholas Carew (or De Carrew, Keeper of the Privy Seal and executor to Edward III.) by his marriage with Lucy, widow of Sir Thomas Huscarle, about 1360, and, with a brief interval, it belonged to a Carew for five centuries. Another, Sir Nicholas Carew, was for awhile one of the favourites of Henry VIII., who made him Master of the Horse, and a Knight of the Garter; but falling into disgrace, (Fuller, on the authority of a family tradition, says in consequence of returning a sharp answer to some opprobrious language of the king, with whom he was playing at bowls,) he was charged with engaging in the conspiracy to seat Cardinal Pole on the throne, and beheaded on Tower Hill, March 3, 1539. His estates were forfeited, but the attainder was reversed by Elizabeth in 1554, and the estates restored to Sir Francis Carew, only son of Sir Nicholas. Sir Francis built a new manor house on a splendid scale, and in it he on two occasions (August 1599 and 1600) entertained Queen Elizabeth at great cost, and with "many curiosities." One of these curiosities is thus described by Sir Hugh Platt: †

"Here I will conclude with a conceit of that delicate knight Sir Francis Carew, who, for the better accomplishment of his royal entertainment of our late Queen Elizabeth, of happy memory, at

his house at Beddington, led her Majesty to a cherry-tree, whose fruit he had of purpose kept back from ripening at the least one month after all cherries had taken their farewell of England. This secret he performed by straining a tent, or cover of canvas, over the whole tree, and wetting the same now and then with a scoop or horn, as the heat of the weather required; and so, by withholding the sunbeams from reflecting upon the berries, they grew both great and were very long before they had gotten their perfect cherry colour; and when he was assured of her Majesty's coming, he removed the tent, and a few sunny days brought them to their full maturity."

In the garden Sir Francis had built the queen a summer-house, with the Spanish Invasion painted on the top. The Queen's Walk, and her favourite oak, are still pointed out. In 1603 James I. visited Beddington Park, and here occurred Sir Walter Raleigh's last formal interview with the new king,* whom Raleigh deeply offended by his earnest advocacy of war with Spain.

Sir Francis's gardens acquired great celebrity. Edw. Sackville, Earl of Dorset, wrote to beg some asparagus of him, "for I am sure you are master of some excellent good ones," and at the same time asks for "myrtle and orange trees." Sir Francis's orange trees were the first seen in England. According to Aubrey, they "were brought from Italy by Sir Francis Carew, Knt. (who built the old mansion house);" but the tradition preserved in the family was that they were raised from seeds brought to England by Sir Walter Raleigh. Sir Walter's wife, the daughter of Sir Francis Throckmorton, of Carshalton, was niece to Sir Francis Carew, and Raleigh was himself a frequent visitor at Beddington: his son, who was born in the Tower, it will be remembered was named Carew Raleigh. Sir Francis Carew, who d. unmarried in 1611, bequeathed his estates to his nephew, Sir Nicholas Throckmorton, who took the name of Carew, and in whose line the estate continued till 1772. Evelyn records in his Diary a visit he made to Beddington in 1658, and his admiration of the "fine old hall," and again,

"20 *Sept.* 1700.—I went to Beddington, the ancient seat of the Carews, in my remembrance a noble old structure, capacious and in form of the buildings of the age of Henry VIII. and Queen Elizabeth, and proper for the old English hospitality, but now decaying with the house itself, heretofore adorned

* Proc. of Soc. of Antiquaries, 2nd Series, vol. v., pp. 149—155.
† The Garden of Eden, 12mo, 1653.

* Edwards, Life of Raleigh, vol. i., p. 364.

with ample gardens, and the first orange trees that had been seen in England, planted in the open ground, and secured in winter only by a tabernacle of boards, and stoves, removeable in summer, that standing 120 years, large and goodly trees, and laden with fruit, were now in decay, as well as the grotto, fountains, cabinets and other curiosities in the house and abroad, it being now fallen to a child under age, and only kept by a servant or two from utter dilapidation. The estate and park about it also in decay."

Evelyn's statement, however, does not agree very well with an Account of several Gardens near London, written in 1691, by J. Gibson, and printed in vol. xii. of the 'Archæologia,' in which it is said that " *the house* in which these orange-trees grew was above 200 ft. long; that most of the trees were 13 ft. high, and that the gardener had the year before gathered off them at least 10,000 oranges." The trees were destroyed by the hard frost in 1739-40.*

The old mansion, with the exception of the hall, was pulled down, and a new one erected on its site, by Sir Nicholas Carew, about 1709. In 1780 the estate, in default of direct issue, passed by will to the descendant of a female branch of the Throckmorton-Carews, Richard Gee, Esq., who took the name of Carew. Dying unmarried (1816), he bequeathed the estate to his brother's widow, who left it (1828) to her cousin, Admiral Sir Benj. Hallowell—the gallant Capt. Hallowell who commanded the 'Swiftsure' at the Nile, and afterwards presented Nelson with a coffin made from the mainmast of 'L'Orient,' which Nelson annoyed his visitors by having set up behind his chair in his state cabin. The admiral, who assumed the name and arms of Carew, died in 1834.

In passing to Mrs. Gee, Beddington became disconnected from the Carew family ; a brief note from a Chancery Report will record its severance from the Carew name. The Mr. Carew who had succeeded to the estates having contracted debts "to the extent apparently of £350,000," and executed disentailing deeds and mortgages, and a settlement that was disputed, an Act of Parliament was obtained in 1857 vesting the property in trustees, who under its powers have sold the greater part of the estates and discharged the debts. Beddington House,

with about 22 acres of ground, was purchased by the Corporation of the Asylum for Female Orphans, Westminster Bridge Road, for £14,500.

The park with its stately avenues now looks decayed and desolate. Part of it is built upon; as much as is available of the remainder is " to let for building on." The *Beddington House* of 1709 seems to have been built on the lines of the Elizabethan mansion, the noble old hall being incorporated in the new house. As it stood in 1865, Beddington House, though dismantled, was a good example of the domestic architecture of the reign of Anne. It was of red brick with stone pilasters, having Corinthian capitals, and consisted of a centre with very projecting wings. With the church which adjoined it, backed by the majestic elms in the ch.-yard, it was one of the most picturesque as well as one of the stateliest mansions of the old English gentry in the home counties. Of the interior, the finest feature was the great hall, 61 ft. long, 32 wide, and 46 to the crown of the rich original open timber roof—" a brave old hall," Horace Walpole termed it,* " with a pendent roof copied by Wolsey at Hampton Court, a vast shield of arms and quarterings over the chimney, and two clumsy brazen and-irons, which they told us had served Queen Elizabeth in the Tower, but look more as if they had served her for cannon to defend it." The lower part was re-panelled when the house was rebuilt, but the roof remained unaltered. The hall is well represented in Nash's 'Mansions.'

The house was in the main pulled down in 1865, but happily the great hall was preserved, restored, and incorporated in the new building. The present structure, *The Female Orphan Asylum*, is a dull, heavy-looking example of Secular Gothic, but is stated to be well adapted to its purpose. It will accommodate 200 children, and in 1873 contained 160. It was formally opened by the Duke of Cambridge, June 27, 1866.

Beddington *Church* is good Early Perp. Towards its erection the first Carew bequeathed £20 in 1390. It is of flint and stone, and consists of nave, aisles, chancel,

---

* Lysons, Environs, vol. i., p. 39.

* Letter to the Countess of Ossory, July 14, 1779.

massive W. tower, in which is a peal of 10 bells, and good stone porch. It was restored in 1852, a new north aisle erected, and the old carving generally re-chiselled. In 1869 it underwent further 'restoration' and enlargement, and received much internal decoration, the outlay (including the purchase of a new organ) exceeding £10,000. The outside is noble, impressive, and picturesque among the grand old elms which surround it. The interior is lofty and effective. The large E. window, of 5 lights, has flowing tracery; the W. window is a large and handsome Perp. one, also of 5 lights. In the chancel are 10 carved misereres. *Brasses* in chancel—Nicholas Carew (the 2nd of that name), d. 1432; an excellent full-length with effigies of Carew and his wife Isabella, under a rich double canopy. A smaller brass on rt. of a lady and her 13 children (the heads only remaining: it is noteworthy that four of the sons were named John and two of the daughters Agnes). *Monts.*—In the Carew Chapel—Sir Richard Carew, governor of Calais, d. 1520, and wife; the brasses gone. Sir Walter Carew (" servant to Henry VIII.," the host of Elizabeth, and the builder of the great hall), d. 1611, an exceedingly rich example of the monumental art of the time of James I., of coloured marbles, with a recumbent statue in alabaster of the knight in complete armour, and below kneeling figures of Sir Nicholas Throckmorton (Carew's nephew and heir), his wife and their 5 children : obelisks, helmets, and shields of arms complete the design. This Sir Nicholas Throckmorton was, as mentioned above, the nephew of Sir Francis Carew, and succeeded to his name and estate. His sister married Sir Walter Raleigh, on whose execution she wrote to her brother that he " would be pleased to let me bury the worthy body of my noble husband Sir Walter Raleigh in your church at Beddington." As Lysons observes, it is scarcely to be supposed such a request could have been refused; but it is certain the body was not buried at Beddington, but in St. Margaret's church, Westminster, whilst according to tradition the head was carried to West Horsley. Below the E. window is the tomb, a sarcophagus, of Sir B. Hallowell Carew, of the Nile, d. 1831.

Obs. on the N. wall a brass plate, with punning verses, to the memory of Thos. Greenhill, steward to Sir N. Carew, d. 1634 :—

" Hee once a *Hill* was, fresh and *Greene*,
Now wither'd is not to bee seene.
Earth in earth shovel'd up is shut
A *Hill* into a *Hole* is put."

The *Hospital of St. Mary, Beddington*, comprises a central hall and half a dozen almshouses, erected by the parishioners in 1862 as a memorial of their late rector (1841-60), the Rev. Jas. Hamilton. It is a neat collegiate Gothic building of flint and stone, designed by Mr. J. Clarke, and, as well as the pretty school-rooms erected by Mr. Hamilton's exertion, deserves notice. On the Wandle is a large snuff mill.

When at Beddington the visitor should extend his walk through the park to *Carshalton*, 1 m. *Wallington*, a hamlet of Beddington, adjoins Carshalton. The Warehousemen and Clerks Schools, for 200 orphans, on Russell Hill, which form a conspicuous object from Caterham Junction, are in Beddington parish.

BEDFONT, EAST, MIDDX. (Dom. *Bedefunte ;* vulg. *Bedfound*), pop., with hamlet of Hatton, 1288, is on the Staines rd., 3 m. beyond Hounslow, 13 m. from London, 1½ m. N.W. from the Feltham Stat. of the L. and S.W. Rly., *Windsor* line. Inn, the *Black Dog*, a late landlord of which is celebrated by George Colman, in his Random Recollections, for his dinners, and especially for his fish sauce :—

"Harvey, whose inn commands a view
Of Bedfont's church, and churchyard, too,
Where yew trees into peacocks shorn,
In vegetable torture mourn."

The village is always called Bedfont, without the prefix East, which is added to distinguish it from *West Bedfont*, a hamlet of Stanwell, 1½ m. N.W. The country hereabout is level and highly cultivated. The *Church*, the only object of interest, stands back from the road, at the N.W. corner of a large green, bordered with noble elms. At the entrance to the ch.-yard are two good-sized yews, which have been clipped and trained (the boughs being tied in their places by wire) so as to form a kind of table, with the letters J. H., J. G., R. T., and the date 1704 ; above are arches, and at the top, as the crown of each tree, a peacock. This odd piece of topiary, which for above a century has been one of the lions of cockney holiday-makers, has often been engraved, and is celebrated in one of Hood's poems, had become dilapidated and appeared to be moulder-ing away, but since 1865 has been care-fully attended to, and seems likely to renew its youth. Bedfont *Church* (of the Virgin Mary) is sm., but very ancient and interesting. It consists of nave, chancel, and a tower at the S.W. (new ; till 1865 there was a wooden bell turret, with a short spire, at the W.) The walls are of soft rubble, with blocks of conglome-rate (pudding-stone) and some tiles, ap-parently Roman, worked up. The S. door is Norm., with a plain chevron ornament. Under the window at the W. end is an early holy-water stoup. In the chancel are some original lancet windows, but the E. end is an extension made in 1866. The low chancel arch is Norm., with moulding all round. The windows at the W. and S. of the nave are Perp. On the N. is an ugly brick addition made in 1829. The ch. had, with its yew-trees in front, a quaint, old-fashioned, weather-beaten appearance, but was very much out of repair ; and in 1865-66 it was restored and somewhat enlarged. It is undoubtedly improved in appearance, especially inside, as well as strengthened, but it has lost something of its unpre-tending air of quaint rusticity. In re-moving the plaster from the nave (Sept. 1865), two curious wall paintings were discovered. One (4 ft. 6 in. by 4 ft.) in a recess in the N. wall, represents, within a quatrefoil, the Saviour enthroned, with His hands lifted up, and feet uncovered (in the language of the Roman ecclesiolo-gists, displaying the Five Wells of Mercy, *i.e.*, the wounds in the hands, feet, and side). Below on each side is an angel sounding a trumpet, and between them are the tombs giving forth their dead. It is remarkably perfect, and rich in colour. The other, less well-preserved, represents the Crucifixion. They appear to be late 13th cent. work ; are for the time and place well designed ; and should be seen. Traces were found of a third painting,

which had been cut through in forming a hagioscope.

The large old red brick house by the ch. is the seat of Major W. Reed. *Temple Hatton*, the seat of the late Sir F. Pollock, Bart., Chief Baron of the Exchequer, and now the residence of Lady Pollock, lies between Bedfont and the hamlet of *Hatton*, where are a neat new district ch. and schools. On the Sion Brook in this par. are the powder mills of Messrs. Curtis and Harvey.

BEDWELL PARK, HERTS (*see* ESSENDON).

BELHUS, ESSEX (*see* AVELEY).

BELSIZE, MIDDX. (*see* HAMP-STEAD).

BELVEDERE, KENT, on the Thames, immediately below Erith, a vill. and stat. on the North Kent Rly., 14 m. from London Bridge. Belvedere is an ec-clesiastical district of 2868 inhabitants, formed out of Erith parish. The place owes its name to the mansion on the brow of the hill, 1 m. W. of Erith, erected in 1764 by Sir Sampson Gideon, after-wards Lord Eardley. The house, a good example of the classic Italian of a cen-tury back, has always been famous for the wide and striking prospect it affords of the Thames with its shipping, and the green meadows and low hills of Essex beyond : a still wider view is obtained from the lofty prospect tower (*Belvedere*) in the grounds nearer Erith ch. While the residence of Lord Eardley, and of Lord Saye and Sele, Belvedere was equally celebrated for its fine collection of pic-tures, including one of the most famous of Murillo's *Assumptions*, and several other works of the highest class. The collection was dispersed in 1859 by the late Sir Culling Eardley, with the excep-tion of the Murillo and a few others which are now at Bedwell Park, Essendon. About the same time Sir Culling sold a large portion of the grounds for building on. Many good houses were erected, and there has grown up quite a village of 'villas,' with a ch. (All Saints, a Dec. cruciform structure of black flint and stone, with a W. tower and spire), chapels, public rooms, a club, shops, inns, and a rly. stat., all bearing the name of *Belvedere*. The mansion, with the reserved grounds, about 24 acres, was purchased for £12,148 to convert into the *Royal Alfred Institution for Aged Merchant Seamen*—so named after its president, the Duke of Edinburgh. The house, it has been officially reported, will accommodate 500 inmates: 20 were received "as a first instalment," Jan. 1st, 1867, and the number is now over 100. The prospect tower stands within the hospital grounds.

BENGEO, Herts (Dom. *Bellingehou*, qy. *Bælingas*), ½ m. N. of Hertford, pop. 2044, is pleasantly situated on high ground, with the Lea river below it on the S., and on either side its tributaries, the Bene on the W. and the Rib on the E. Ware Park is immediately N.E.

The old *Church* (St. Leonard's) is reached from Hertford by a pretty walk of ½ m. having the Lea on the rt. and on the l. a high sandy bank, wood, and rabbit warren. It stands in the lower part of the vill., just above the Lea, and is now only used when there is a burial in the ch.-yd. It is small, with an apsidal chancel divided from the nave by a small semicircular arch. The apse is lighted by altered lancets and a two-light Perp. window. The nave is Perp., has a stuccoed porch on the S.W., and a recent wooden bell-cote. S. of the chancel arch are some faint vestiges of a fresco. The old monts. remain on the walls inside, but are of no interest.

The new *Church* (Holy Trinity), erected in 1855, near the summit of the hill, ¼ m. farther N., is of Kentish rag, has nave, aisles, chancel, and W. tower, with a stone spire, conspicuous for miles around. From the hill just behind the ch. is a fine view over three points of the compass.

Sir Richard Fanshawe and his admirable wife retired for awhile to Bengeo after his release from the Commonwealth prison. "My husband, weary of the town, and being advised to go into the country for his health, procured leave to go in September [1656] to Bengy, in Hertford, to a little house lent us by my brother Fanshawe."*

---

* Lady Fanshawe's Memoirs, p. 124.

At the hamlet of *Tonwell*, 2 m. N., is a neat little chapel of ease erected by Mr. Abel Smith in 1859. The large building seen at *Chapmore End*, on the road to Tonwell, is the *County Reformatory*, opened in 1858 for 50 boys convicted of felony, who, during the week, cultivate the 40 acres of arable land attached to the building, and attend Tonwell chapel on the Sunday.

In the hamlet of *Waterford*, 1½ N.W. of Bengeo, a very pretty little cruciform E.E. *Church* (St. Michael and All Angels), designed by Mr. H. Woodyer, was erected at the cost of Mr. R. Smith, of Goldings, in 1872. The quaint little half timber gable fronted houses close by were also built at the same time by Mr. Smith as dwellings for poor widows.

From Bengeo old ch. there is a charming walk (2 m.) across the Rib and through Ware Park to Ware. Bengeo now forms part of the borough of Hertford. For the portion of the par. next Hertford, a neat cruciform ch. designed by Mr. T. Smith of Hertford, was erected at *Port Vale* in 1869.

BENHILTON, Surrey (*see* Sutton).

BENTLEY HEATH, Middx. (*see* Potter's Bar).

BENTLEY PRIORY (*see* Stanmore).

BERKHAMSTEAD, LITTLE, Herts (Dom. *Berchehamsted*), 17 m. from London, and 4½ m. S.W. from the Hertford stat. of the Gt. Eastern Rly., through Bayford; pop. 408; a small, secluded agricultural village in the midst of very pleasant scenery.

The manor of Berkhamstead was granted by King John to Fulke de Brent, on service of a pair of gilt spurs, or 6*d*. in money. After passing through many hands, it reverted to the Crown, and in 1539, Henry VIII. granted to Anthony Denny the stewardship of the manors of Bedwell and Berkhamstead. In 1600, Elizabeth assigned the manor to Sir Edward Denny, who the same year sold it to Alderman Humphrey Welt. It is now held by Baron Dimsdale.

The *Church* (St. Mary), which stands on high ground, is E.E., but was restored and refaced with stone in 1856, and is of little interest. It has nave with short N. aisle, chancel, and at the W. end a wooden belfry (in which are 3 old bells) surmounted by a short spire.

A short distance N.E. of the ch. is the *Observatory*, a lofty and massive brick tower, from the summit of which a splendid view is obtained : the vill. tradition is that it was built by a rich shipowner, who resided at Berkhamstead House, that he might watch his ships enter the Thames. It is now in a neglected condition : the key is kept in a neighbouring cottage. Bishop Ken was born at Little Berkhamstead in 1637. *Berkhamstead House* (E. T. Daniell, Esq.), is N. of the ch. ; *Woodcock Lodge* (E. Dewey, Esq.) ¾ m. S. ; *Bedwell Park* adjoins the vill. on the W., and there is a pleasant walk across it to *Essendon* (which *see*).

BETCHWORTH, SURREY (Dom.

Becesworde), pop. 635 ; of the entire par., including Brockham Green, 1558 ; is situated on the Mole, in the midst of delightful scenery, midway between Reigate and Dorking, and 26 m. from London by the Dorking branch of the S.E. Rly. ; the ch. is nearly a mile S. of Betchworth Stat.

Betchworth *Church* (St. Michael) is spacious, of stone, in part E.E., with windows of the Dec. and Perp. periods. It was restored and in a measure rebuilt (E. C. Hakewill, archt.) in 1851. Further restoration, alteration, and decoration were effected in 1870. A new tower was erected in 1851 on the S.; the old one (basement Norm.) stood between the nave and chancel. The windows are filled with painted glass. On the chancel floor is the brass of Wm. Wardysworth, vicar of Betchworth, d. 1533 : he is holding a chalice in both hands. Near it is a huge chest rudely hewn out of a noble oak. *Obs.* in the ch.-yd., E. of the ch., the grave of the noted convivial song writer of the Regency, Capt. Charles Morris, d. July 11, 1838, aged 93. Capt. Morris resided at *Brockham Green* in this par. (*see* BROCKHAM GREEN). Note the picturesque appearance of the ch. backed by the tall elms of Betchworth House, from the ch.-yd. stile.

Betchworth House (formerly *B. Place*), a fine mansion built by Sir Ralph Freeman, temp. James I., close by the ch., contains some noble rooms, and stands in a well-timbered park. It is the manor house of East Betchworth (so called to distinguish it from West Betchworth in Dorking par.), and from the death of Sir Ralph Freeman belonged to the Bouveries till 1817, when it was purchased by the Rt. Hon. Henry Goulburn, Chancellor of the Exchequer in the Wellington and Peel ministries, who died here in 1856. It is now the property of Col. Edward Goulburn. E. of the ch. is *Moor Place* (J. R. Corbet, Esq.), the oldest example of domestic architecture remaining in these parts : it is of the time of Henry VI., but restorations and improvements have disguised its antiquity. In it is some curious old furniture. Immediately E. of this is *Wonham Manor House*, the pleasant seat of the late Albert Way, the distinguished antiquary. The Mole skirts the grounds of these three mansions, and adds greatly to their beauty. *Broome Park* (C. Dobson, Esq.), close to the rly. stat., was purchased by Sir Benjamin Brodie, the eminent surgeon, in 1837, and continued his favourite residence till his death in 1862. In the older books Broome Park will be found described in somewhat romantic language as *Tranquil Dale*. Obs. the fine cedars in front of the house. *Snower Hill* (J. Gibson, Esq.), ½ m. S. ; and beyond it *Gadbrook House* (J. Wratten, Esq.), by *Gadbrook Common*, a very pleasant place. Under the high chalk ledge will be observed extensive lime works ; the lime is prepared from 'the Dorking greystone,' largely quarried hereabouts.

From the Stat. a path leads up to *Betchworth Clump*, the grove of beech trees that crowns the summit of the ridge. From it you have a splendid prospect southwards across the broken and verdant sand-hills, Holmsdale, and the Weald, to the distant South Downs of Sussex ; far away northwards, over a rich country, with Windsor Castle on one side and the Crystal Palace on the other as landmarks ; on the east over Reigate, whilst west are the woods and hills of Betchworth and Deepdene, backed by the giant mass of Leith Hill. The visitor should not fail to mount to Betchworth Clump ; and from it, when satisfied with the prospect, he will find a fine breezy walk along the ridge (though unhappily not so free and unobstructed as it used to be), with frequent views over a beautiful country, E. to Reigate; W. to the summit of Box Hill ; forwards to Walton-on-the-Hill. Along the ridge, *obs.* the yew trees as marking the line of the old Pilgrim's Road. From the vill. there is a delightful walk by Brockham Green and through Betchworth Park to Dorking (*see* those places). Another, in its way equally pleasant, and of about the same length, to Reigate, is to go from Betchworth ch. past Wonham, where take the lane on l. just beyond *Wonham Mill*, over Trumpet Hill, and thence direct across Reigate Heath.

BETCHWORTH PARK is about

1 m. W. of Betchworth vill., and immediately W. of Brockham Green. At the Domesday Survey *Becesworde* appears to have been a single manor. It was afterwards divided into the manors of *East Betchworth*, described in the preceding article. *West Betchworth*, the subject of the present notice, which is in Dorking par., and *Brockham*, which lies between the two Betchworths. In 1373 West B. manor was transferred to Richard Earl of Arundel, with remainder to his 2nd son, John Fitz-Alan. The earl died in 1376, and in the following year his son (soon after created Baron Maltravers and Marshal of England) obtained licence to embattle his house at Betchworth. In 1437 the manor passed by marriage to Thomas (afterwards Sir Thomas) Brown, who procured licence not only to fortify the house, but to empark the manor. Being attainted on the accession of Edward IV., his estates were forfeited to the Crown. A few years later they were restored to his son, Sir George, but he being executed for participation in Buckingham's conspiracy against Richard III., they were again forfeited, but once more restored on the accession of Henry VII. From Mrs. Fenwick, the last representative of the Browns, the manor was purchased, in 1727, by Abraham Tucker, who wrote his 'Light of Nature Pursued' in Betchworth Castle, where

he died in 1774. A century earlier, William Browne, the author of 'Britannia's Pastorals,' lived here, but none of his poetry is associated with the place. In 1798 Betchworth Park was bought by Mr. H. Peters, the banker, who spent a considerable sum on the house and grounds. It was purchased in 1834 by Henry Thomas (*Anastasius*) Hope, who dismantled the house, and united the park with that of Deepdene.

Long before this Betchworth Castle had lost its military character, part having been pulled down in the reign of Anne, and the rest converted into an ordinary mansion. The *ruins* stand on a gentle eminence on the l. bank of the Mole. The walls are covered with ivy : trees and underwood grow thick within ; it looks picturesque, but is of no architectural interest. The *Park* is varied in surface and very beautiful. It contains an almost matchless triple avenue, nearly 1000 ft. long, of lime trees and magnificent chesnuts. Some of the chesnuts are 20 ft. in girth, and in the late autumn are resplendent in their rich golden foliage. The park is open ; there are entrances by Brockham Green and in the Dorking road, near Box Hill Stat., or, keeping the upper road across the bridge to Deepdene, the visitor may return to Dorking by Cotmandene.

BEXLEY, KENT (anc. *Bekesley*),

13 m. from London by road, and by the Loop line of the N. Kent Rly. ; and 1¼ S.W. of Crayford. Bexley is an old-fashioned quiet village, with the little Cray river running through it, and standing in the midst of pleasant sylvan scenery. The parish has 6448 inhab., but it includes Bexley Heath, Blendon, Bridgend, and Upton. Bexley itself has 1479 inhab.

Bexley manor belonged to the see of Canterbury, and Abp. Walter Reynolds obtained a grant of a market from Edward II. in 1315. Cranmer, in 1537, alienated the manor to Henry VIII. By James I. it was granted to Sir John Spielman, who established the first paper-mills at Dartford. Spielman sold it to Camden the antiquary ; and he bequeathed it (March 5, 1622) to Oxford University, " to the end and purpose to maintain within the University one Reader, who shall be called the *Reader of Histories*."

This "end and purpose" the rental of the manor still serves, but the reader now bears the more sounding title of Professor of Ancient History.

Bexley *Church* is of E.E. date, and on the N. side are traces of an orig. E.E. doorway, but the windows are Dec. and Perp. insertions. The ch. consists of a nave and Dec. N. aisle, chancel, tower at the W. end, with a low shingle spire, and at the S.W. a modern porch with vestry over. The int. has been much altered and is of little interest. In the chancel is some old stall-work, the ch. having been of old attached to the Priory of the Holy Trinity, London. In the N. aisle is a mural *mont.* to Sir John Champneys (1556) and wife, with two small well-carved kneeling effigies. In the chancel is a small *brass* to Thomas Warrow, 1513; also the place of a hunting-horn with insc., the brass of which is lost. N. of the ch. is a fair-sized yew. The entrance to the ch.-yd. is by a lich-gate (renewed). The old-fashioned almshouses W. of the ch. were founded by John Styleman, Esq., in 1755, for 12 poor persons. On the Cray is a not very picturesque corn-mill.

Hall Place (Maitland Dashwood, Esq.), on the rt. of the road to Crayford, according to Hasted gave their name (At-Hall) to the family who originally owned it : the last of them, Sir Thomas At-Hall, conveyed it in 1366 to Sir Thos. Shelley ; in 1537 it passed to Sir John Champneys ; in 1660 to the Austens, and in 1743 to Lord Le Despencer. The present Hall Place is a good 17th cent. mansion, of stone, with projecting wings. It was restored in 1865-6.

Lamorbey (R. Bousfield, Esq.), "Lamienby, now corruptly Lamaby," according to Hasted, and in maps, *Lamb Abbey*, rebuilt in 1744, is about 2 m. W. by S. of Bexley ; immediately beyond it is *Halfway Street* (F. M. Lewin, Esq.) By these mansions on the Eltham Road is the hamlet of *Halfway Street*, or *Lamorbey* (pop. 361), with a neat district ch., built and endowed by John Malcolm, Esq., who also built the National School. Here, as well as at Bexley, is a stat. of the N. Kent Rly.

BEXLEY HEATH, or BEXLEY NEW TOWN, 1½ m. N. of Bexley (by a

very pretty lane which leaves the road to Crayford nearly opposite the National School and Hall Place), is a long unattractive street of small new shops and dwellings, on the main Dartford road, with, at the W. end, a modern E.E. district ch. (Christ Church), of which the best part is the tall spire. Bexley Heath itself is enclosed, and in good part built over. The eccl. district of Bexley Heath had 4608 inhab. in 1871.

BICKLEY, Kent, a hamlet and eccl. dist. (pop. 623) of Bromley, from which it is 1½ m. E. From London it is 12 m. by the L. C. and D., or Mid-Kent br. of the S.-Eastern Rly. It is pleasantly situated between Bromley and Chiselhurst, and the country around is hilly, well-wooded, and picturesque, though a good deal changed by building operations —the inevitable result of railway facilities. The more conspicuous new houses —those on the higher grounds—have however been built with an eye to their appearance in the landscape, and as they are set wide apart, and in spacious grounds, when toned down by time or half-hidden by foliage, the village will bear a favourable comparison even in this respect with most of like character round London. The principal seat is *Bickley Hall*, the residence of George Wythes, Esq., to whom most of the recent improvements in Bickley are due. The house is large but plain ; the park is richly wooded and affords some good views.

Close by the Hall is *Bickley Church* (St. George's), erected in 1865 from the designs of Mr. Barnes, at a cost of £10,000 defrayed by Mr. G. Wythes, Mr. J. Tredwell, and Mr. W. Dent (the former proprietor of Bickley Hall). The ch. is spacious, Dec. in style, cruciform, with a deep apsidal chancel, and, at the W., a lofty tower and stone spire, conspicuous for many a mile. On the hill, half a mile E., at the edge of Chiselhurst Common, is rather a novel building—a quaint red brick and half-timber framed gate-house, carried across the main road. With the windmill on the rt. (now about to be removed, April 1874, to make way for a large hotel), and the other adjuncts, it forms a piquant group ; but its use would hardly be guessed. It was constructed by Mr. Wythes as the eastern entrance to his property, but also as a water tower—the central portion over the road arch containing a great tank into which water was intended to be pumped from the springs at the foot of the hill, for the supply of the Bickley estate. The building and works have, however, been purchased by the Kent Water Company, and the Bickley tank is empty.

BISHOP'S HATFIELD (*see* HATFIELD).

BISHOP'S WOOD (*see* CAEN WOOD).

BLACKHEATH, KENT, 6 m. from

London by rd., or by the S.E. Rly. (N. Kent line); pop. 1827. The Rly. Stat. is at Tranquil Vale, S. of the Heath. The two Gothic buildings seen on the rt. before reaching it are the Blackheath Congregational Church and School, and (red brick) the School for Sons of Missionaries; close by the latter is the Blackheath Proprietary School.

Blackheath lies S. of Greenwich Park. It is chiefly in the parishes of Greenwich and Lewisham, but extends into Charlton and Lee. The name is variously derived from its *bleak* site, or its *black* appearance. Across the heath, nearly in the line of the present Dover road, ran the ancient Watling Street. Along this were numerous tumuli. Many of them, including 50 which stood within the pale of Greenwich Park, by Croom's Hill Gate, were opened by the Rev. Jas. Douglas, Jan. 1784, and described in his 'Nenia Britannica,' p. 89. They were mostly small, conical, with a circular trench at the base, and appear to have been Romano-British. No skeletons remained in them, but there were some locks of hair, and one fine braid of an auburn hue was "tenacious and very distinct," and "contained its natural phlogiston." The spolia were chiefly iron spear-heads (one 15 in. long and 2 in. broad, was found "in the native gravel"), knives, and nails, glass beads, and woollen and linen cloth. At the S.W. corner of the heath, by Blackheath Hill, urns (some of which are in the British

Museum) and other Roman remains have been found.* Near the summit of the hill, at a spot called *the Point*, is a *Cavern* cut in the chalk, which has been by some ascribed to the Danes, and by others to the Saxons. It resembles the *Dane-holes* found about Crayford and Tilbury, and described under CHADWELL. It extends 127 ft., and consists of 4 chambers, connected by narrow passages. In the farthest is a well 27 ft. deep. When discovered, about 1780, the only entrance was by a narrow shaft, but a flight of steps has since been cut for the convenience of visitors. It may be seen upon payment of a small fee.

Lying at an easy distance from London on the great road from Dover and Canterbury, Blackheath was a favourite theatre for military gatherings and state receptions. Whilst the Danish fleet was moored at Greenwich, 1011-13, their army was encamped on the heath—probably on the high ground at East and West Coombe, where extensive earthworks were traceable at the beginning of the present century. Wat Tyler with his followers lay at Blackheath for several days in June 1381. In the autumn of 1400, Manuel Palæologus, Emperor of the East, who had come to solicit aid against Bajazet, was met at Blackheath by Henry IV. and his court, and escorted with great pomp into London. On Nov. 3, 1415, Henry V., on his return from Agincourt, was met here by the mayor, aldermen and sheriffs, attended by 300 of the principal citizens, in scarlet robes, and mounted on stately horses; and 20,000 of the meaner citizens, all "with the devices of their craft," came thus far to welcome their hero. The following May a like civic cavalcade received here the Emperor Sigismund. Fifteen years later, Henry VI., after his coronation at Paris, was met at Blackheath by the Lord Mayor dressed in crimson velvet, with a girdle of gold about his waist, the aldermen in their scarlet robes, and the citizens in white gowns and scarlet hoods, and having each the badge of his company emblazoned on his sleeve.

Twice, during 1449-50, did Jack Cade encamp his "rebellious hinds, the filth and scum of Kent," upon "the plaine of Blackheath;" and here, after Cade's

* Archæologia, vol. xv., p. 392.

death, his followers (Feb. 23, 1451) "with halters on their necks," knelt to the king to receive their "doom of life or death." Next year, 1452, the Duke of York, having entrenched his forces in the neighbourhood of Dartford, Henry VI. encamped at Blackheath, where the Duke, having been induced to enter the royal tent unarmed, was seized and carried prisoner to London. In 1471, Falconbridge brought his army here. Three years later the mayor and aldermen at the head of 400 of the principal citizens assembled here to welcome Edward IV. on his return from France. Here, in June 1497, the Cornish rebels under Lord Audley and Michael Joseph the blacksmith were attacked and utterly defeated by Henry VII. Lambarde, who lived at West Coombe, and was familiar with the locality, says,* "there remaineth yet to be seen upon the heath the place of the Smith's tent, called commonly his Forge, and the grave-hills of such as were buried after the overthrow." The Smith's Forge is the mound marked with fir trees. W. of it are traces of ridges, which may be vestiges of one of the encampments mentioned above ; or possibly they may mark the graves of the Cornish rebels, for it is hardly necessary to say that Lambarde was mistaken in supposing that the barrows were their "grave-hills." In 1519 the papal legate, Cardinal Campegius, was met here by "the Duke of Norfolk, with a great number of prelates, knights, and gentlemen, all richly appareled. And in the way he was brought into a rich tent of cloth of gold, where he shifted himself into a robe of a cardinal, edged with ermines, and so took his moyle [mule] riding toward London."† A few months later, Bonevet, High Admiral of France, attended by a splendid cavalcade of 1200 lords and gentlemen, was met by the Earl of Surrey, as High Admiral of England, with a still more gorgeous retinue. "The young gallants of France had coats guarded with one colour, cut in 10 or 12 parts very richly to behold : and so all the Englishmen accoupled themselves with the Frenchmen, lovingly

together, and so rode to London."* But the most splendid of these pageants was probably the formal reception of Anne of Cleves, Jan. 3, 1540. On the eastern side of the heath "was pitched a rich cloth of gold, and divers other tents and pavilions, in the which were made fires and perfumes for her and such ladies as should receive her grace." Henry was staying at his palace at Greenwich, and

"from the tents to the park gate . . . a large and ample way was made for the shew of all persons." Along this way were ranged the mayor and aldermen, citizens and foreign merchants, all in their richest liveries, esquires, gentlemen pensioners, and serving-men, "well horsed and apparelled, that whosoever had well viewed them might say that they, for tall and comely personages, and clean of limb and body, were able to give the greatest prince in Christendom a mortal breakfast if he were the king's enemy."

About 12 o'clock Anne came down Shooter's Hill, accompanied by the Dukes of Norfolk and Suffolk, the Archbishop of Canterbury, and a large array of other noblemen and bishops, besides her own attendants, and was met and conducted to her tent by the Lord Chamberlain and other officials. With her suite Anne made a magnificent display, but it appears to have been far outshone by that of the king, with whom came all the pride of his court, and the several ambassadors. It is, however, on Henry himself that the old chronicler, who writes as though he had been a spectator of the solemnity, lavishes his choicest rhetoric :—

"The king's highness was mounted on a goodly courser, trapped in rich cloth of gold traversed lattice-wise square, all over embroidered with gold of damask, pearled on every side of the embroidery, the buckles and pendants were all of fine gold. His person was apparelled in a coat of purple velvet, somewhat made like a frock, all over embroidered with flat gold of damask with small lace mixed between of the same gold, and other laces of the same so going traverse-wise, that the ground little appeared : about which garment was a rich guard very curiously embroidered, the sleeves and breast were cut, lined with cloth of gold, and tyed together with great buttons of diamonds, rubies, and orient pearl, his sword and sword girdle adorned with stones and especial emerodes, his night cap garnished with stone, but his bonnet was so rich with jewels that few men could value them. Beside all this he ware in baudrick-wise a collar of such balystes and pearl that few men ever saw the like. . . . And notwithstanding that· this rich apparel and precious jewels were pleasant to the nobles and

---

* Perambulation of Kent, 1596, p. 392 of the reprint.
† Hall, Chronicle, p. 592.

* Hall, p. 594, reprint.

all other being present to behold, yet his princely countenance, his goodly personage and royal gesture so far exceeded all other creatures being present, that in comparison of his person, all his rich apparel was little esteemed."

Even the assembled portraits of Henry in the great Portrait Exhibition of 1866 hardly made up so gorgeous a picture of the burly monarch. The chronicler gives a minute account of the meeting and the ordering of the procession to Greenwich Palace, but it will be enough to cite one sentence, though it reads oddly by the light of what followed a few months later: " O what a sight was this to see so goodly a prince and so noble a king to ride with so fair a lady of so goodly a stature and so womanly a countenance, and in especial of so good qualities, I think no creature could see them but his heart rejoiced." * Yet we have Henry's own declaration: " When I saw her I liked her so ill, and so far contrary to that she was praised, that I was woe that ever she came into England."

The last of these meetings was, however, the most memorable,—one for which all London had made holiday, —the arrival of Charles II. on the 29th of May, 1660. Every one will remember Sir Walter Scott's account of the king's welcome " to his own again," by Sir Henry Lee of Woodstock; but Lord Macaulay's picture is even more striking :—

" Everywhere flags were flying, bells and music sounding, wine and ale flowing in rivers to the health of him whose return was the return of peace, of law, and of freedom. But in the midst of the general joy, one spot presented a dark and threatening aspect. On Blackheath the army was drawn up to welcome the sovereign. He smiled, bowed, and extended his hand graciously to the lips of the colonels and majors. But all his courtesy was vain. The countenances of the soldiers were sad and lowering; and, had they given way to their feelings, the festive pageant of which they reluctantly made a part, would have had a mournful and bloody end.+

Evelyn mentions temporary camps formed (June 1673) of the troops about to be sent to Holland; of others on their return (July 1685), and of one " of about 4000 men," formed here when London was excited by the news that the English fleet had sought refuge in the Thames

from the French fleet under De Tourville. He also records (May 1, 1683,) his visit to " Blackheath to the New Fair, being the first, procured by the Earl of Dartmouth. This was the first day, pretended for the sale of cattle, but I think, in truth, to enrich the new tavern at the Bowling Green, erected by Snape, his Majesty's farrier, a man full of projects." Evelyn thinks it " too near London to be of any great use to the country." But the fair lasted as a 'hog' and pleasure fair, being held on May 12 and October 11, till 1872, when it was suppressed by an order signed by the Home Secretary.

Since the days when the Cornish rebels were slaughtered, or Anne of Cleves was received here, the heath has been a great deal circumscribed in extent, but with the exception of a site for a ch. no new enclosure has been made for some years past. The surface of the heath had, however, been grievously disfigured owing to the Crown having let, for a rental of £56, the right to excavate an unlimited quantity of gravel. The gravel digging began in 1818, and was continued till 1865. All this, and any encroachment, is now put an end to. By the Metropolitan Commons Act, 1866, Blackheath was secured for public use in perpetuity, and placed under the management of the Metropolitan Board of Works. Its area is now about 267 acres. The heath is dry, healthy, and from parts (as *the Point* by Blackheath Hill) there are extensive prospects : but the views are inferior to those from Greenwich Park. Shooter's Hill, on the E., forms a pleasant background to the heath. During the summer the heath is greatly resorted to by holidaymakers, but, under the new bye-laws of the Board, they are no longer the noisy nuisance they — or rather, the donkeydrivers, gipseys, and cockshy men—sometimes used to be. The Royal Blackheath Golf Club use the heath as their playground, and a well-contested match may often be witnessed here. In the last century it was a notorious resort of highwaymen.

The mound, marked by a group of firs, nearly opposite the S.W. corner of Greenwich Park, is the barrow spoken of by Lambarde as the *Smith's Forge*. A few years back it used to be commonly known as *Whitefield's Mount*, it having

* Hall, reprint, pp. 833—836.
+ Hist., ch. i. (vol. i., p. 156, ed. 1858).

The 'Green Man' Blackheath

Burnham Beeches (see p.66)

served that popular preacher on more than one occasion as a pulpit : but the name seems dying out. In the 17th cent. it was used for proving mortars :—

"*March* 16th, 1687.—I saw a trial of those devilish mischief-doing engines called bombs, shot out of a mortar-piece on Blackheath. The distance that they are cast, the destruction they make where they fall is prodigious." *

Of late the heath has been built up to, wherever land was available, and new houses are still being erected on those parts of Lewisham, Lee, and Charlton which abut on Blackheath. The vill., or, as it is beginning to call itself, town of *Blackheath*, lies about *Tranquil Vale*, between the S.E. corner of the heath and the rly. stat. It has churches, schools, assembly rooms, banks, and several good shops. At the opposite end of the heath, by *Blackheath Hill*, is another collection of shops and dwellings, with ch. and schools and all the usual accompaniments of a suburban vill., and here is the principal inn, the *Green Man*, well known to holiday-makers. About the heath are some good mansions, and bordering it is a fringe of substantial old-fashioned houses, with a sprinkling of smart new villas. Blackheath has 5 churches and district chapels—all modern, and none of architectural interest. The best, perhaps, are, All Saints, on the heath by Tranquil Vale, erected 1859, B. Ferrey, F.S.A., archt.; and St. John's, Charlton Lane, built at the cost of the late W. Angerstein, Esq. Trinity Church, on Blackheath Hill, conspicuous by its two towers and spires, is in Greenwich par.: it is noteworthy as an early example of revived Gothic, having been erected in 1838 from the designs of Mr. J. W. Wild.

Of the mansions, the first place may be given to the *Ranger's Lodge*, on the S.W. side of Greenwich Park, its front facing the heath. This was the residence of Philip Earl of Chesterfield, who purchased it in 1753, and considerably enlarged and improved it. In his ' Letters ' he calls it *Babiole*, and afterwards *La Petite Chartreuse*, but it was known to the outer world as *Chesterfield House*, and his connection with it is still commemorated in the name of *Chesterfield Walk*.

In 1807 it became the residence of the Dowager Duchess of Brunswick, sister of George III., and was called *Brunswick House*. She came here in consequence of her daughter, Caroline, Princess of Wales, having had the adjoining mansion, Montague House, assigned her as a residence when appointed Ranger of Greenwich Park in 1806. Lord Malmesbury and the Speaker Abbott give some rather amusing accounts of their visits to the Dowager Duchess here.* On her death the house was purchased by the Crown, and appropriated as the residence of the Ranger of Greenwich Park. In it Princess Sophia of Gloucester lived from 1816 till her death in 1844. It is now the residence of Prince Arthur and Major H. C. Elphinstone.

Montague House stood immediately S. of the Ranger's house : it owed its name to having belonged to the Duke of Montague, who bought it in 1714. Whilst it was the residence of the Princess of Wales she enlarged the grounds by enclosing a portion of the Park called ' The Little Wilderness.' This now forms a part of the grounds of the Ranger's Lodge. Montague House was pulled down in 1815, but the name is preserved in *Montague Corner* at the S.E. end of Chesterfield Walk.† The house at the top of Chesterfield Walk (where it joins Croom's Hill) was the seat of Major-General Wolfe, and the occasional residence of his son the hero of Quebec, whose remains were brought here and interred in Greenwich Church. It was afterwards the seat of Lord Lyttelton. On Maize Hill, E. of the park (by the gate to the path from One Tree Hill) is *Vanbrugh Castle*, a large grotesque red brick castellated building with a round tower and spire. It is entered by an odd-looking embattled gateway. Vanbrugh took a lease of 12 acres of ground here in 1714, and erected on it this building which he called ' the Castle,' but which became better known as ' the *Bastille*,' and another, equally odd-looking, a short distance E., which obtained the name of *Minced Pie House*, but is now more politely

---

* See Lord Malmesbury's Memoirs, vol. iii., and Lord Colchester's Memoirs, vol. ii.
† For an account of the Princess at home there, see Miss Berry's Journal, June 9, 1811, etc.

---

* Evelyn, Diary.

entitled *Vanbrugh House*. V. Castle is now a ladies' boarding-school. V. House is of brick with raised bands, and has a round tower at each end, a central porch, and square entrance lodges : both should be seen by the architectural student.

A little N.E. is *West Combe*, where William Lambarde d. 1601. The present house was built by Capt. Galfridus Walpole, about 1720, and the design has been attributed to the Earl of Pembroke. Here the Duke of Bolton lived with Lavinia Fenton (the original Polly Peachum), whom he married after the death of his Duchess, in 1751,—23 years after he had taken her from the stage. *East Combe*, farther E., by the Charlton rd., was of old attached to the manor of Greenwich. In 1613 it was settled on Queen Anne of Denmark. It has since been in private hands, and is now the seat of C. S. Millington, Esq. *Woodlands* (Wm. Angerstein, Esq.) is in Charlton rd., between East and West Coombe. Here d., 1823, J. J. Angerstein, Esq., whose fine collection of pictures formed the nucleus of our National Gallery. Caroline Princess of Wales lived for awhile here. In a letter dated Geneva, May 25, 1820, she tells Miss Berry that she shall go to "the Maison Angerstein à Blackheath" on her return to England. During her earlier residence at Blackheath, her daughter the Princess Charlotte had a separate establishment, presided over by the Countess Dowager of Elgin, at *Shrewsbury House*, nearer Shooter's Hill. Bishop Porteus describes "a very pleasant day (Aug. 6, 1804) spent with the Princess at Shrewsbury House." *

At the S.E. extremity of Blackheath, but in Charlton par., is *Morden College*, erected 1694 by Sir John Morden, Bart., a wealthy Turkey merchant. During his life Sir John kept 12 decayed merchants here, and by will (Oct. 15, 1702) bequeathed to the college, upon the decease of his wife, all his real and copyhold estates, for the maintenance of poor and aged merchants of England, whose fortunes had been ruined by perils of the sea or other unavoidable accidents : preference being given to those who had traded with the Levant. Sir John d. 1708; his wife, 1721. The estates have since

* Works, vol. i., pp. 160—163 ; and see Lady Rose Weigall's Brief Memoir of the Princess Charlotte, p. 35, etc.

greatly increased in value, and are likely to increase much more. The original scheme of the college has been extended, but it will have to be remodelled. There are now a chaplain, richly provided for, and about 40 pensioners, who besides lodging, maintenance, and attendance, have each an annual stipend of £72. As seen through the screen of sheltering elms, the college looks a sufficiently comfortable retreat from the vicissitudes of commerce. The building is of the later collegiate type : a square, with lofty entrance gateway, enclosing a quadrangle, and having lodgings, dining hall, and chapel. It is of red brick with stone quoins and dressings (the work of Strong, the master mason of St. Paul's), and has over the entrance statues of the founder and his wife. Their portraits are also in the hall, and their arms in the chapel, where they were interred. The visitor who compares the present appearance of the college with engravings of it, will miss the 'canal' from the front. It was drained when the North Kent Rly. was carried under the grounds by a tunnel, the sand from which served to form the undulating lawn now so prettily laid out with evergreens and flowering shrubs. The grounds behind the college are also very pleasant, and afford some cheerful peeps over the country beyond. They are open to the stranger and worth seeing. From them there is a path to *Kidbrooke* new ch. (erected 1867, archts. Messrs. Newman and Billing), whence there are pleasant fieldpaths to ELTHAM, 1½ m. [From the ch. turn short to rt., and presently l. across the scrubby little green ; then take to the fields, proceeding S.E., with the roof of the great hall of Eltham Palace as a landmark the whole way.]

BLETCHINGLEY, or BLECHINGLEY, SURREY (Dom. *Blachingelei :* the mark of the *Bleccingas*, Kemble); 3 m. E. from the Redhill Stat. of the S.E. and the L., Br., and S. C. Rlys., by the road along the elevated ridge of Lower Greensand, through Nutfield,—a very pleasant walk. Inn, the *White Hart*.

Though now a quiet little townlet (the entire par. of 5585 acres had in 1871 only 1916 inhab., of whom 103 were in the Union Workhouse), Bletchingley cherishes the memory of former importance. It was a parliamentary borough returning two members till the Reform Act of 1832: though at the later elections the voters seldom exceeded 10. Lord Palmerston was one of the members when the borough was disfranchised. Further, there are traditions —but they are only traditions—that the town once possessed 7 churches; that Earl Godwin, after the sea had converted his Kentish manors into the Goodwin Sands, lived here in great state; and that Sir Thos. Cawarden entertained Henry VIII. and Anne Boleyn at the manor-house. At the Domesday Survey, the manor belonged to Richard Earl of Clare; and it continued in his family to the 9th generation, when it was conveyed by marriage to Humphrey Earl of Stafford, created in 1422 Duke of Buckingham. On its forfeiture by the conviction of Edward Duke of Buckingham for treason in 1521, it was granted by Henry VIII. to Sir Nicholas Carew; but on his meeting the fate of his predecessor, in 1539, it reverted to the Crown, and two years later Henry settled it for her life on his divorced wife, Anne of Cleves, with reversion to Sir Thos. Cawarden, who resided here and managed the estate.* The subsequent owners have been very numerous.

Bletchingley Castle, then held by Gilbert Clare, Earl of Gloucester, was destroyed by Prince Edward (afterwards Edward I.) on his return from the battle of Lewes, 1263, but was afterwards rebuilt. It stood in a field S.W. of the town, and overlooking Holmesdale and the Weald. Aubrey writes (1673), "this castle (with great graffs) is in a coppice, and was heretofore a stately fabric, and pleasantly situated, but shows now only one piece of wall 5 foot thick." This has long disappeared; but at the beginning of the present century the foundations were still traceable. Evelyn says that the remarkable carved oak chimneypiece in the hall of the Priory, Reigate, "was of Henry VIII., and was taken from a house of his in Bletchingley." This royal house, however, was probably not the castle, but the Manor House, which stood near the little

hamlet of *Brewer Street* ($\frac{1}{2}$ m. N. of the ch.), and was pulled down by the Earl of Peterborough, who held the manor, 1649—77.

Bletchingley is now little more than an old-fashioned village in appearance, but has some picturesque old houses. The *Church* (St. Mary) is large, chiefly Perp., and consists of nave, aisles, double chancel, and N. transept, or Ham Chapel, with W. tower; but the N. aisle is new, having been added when the ch. was restored in 1864. The E. window is of the same date; it is filled with painted glass representing the leading events in the history of our Lord, from the Annunciation to the Ascension. The W. window is also filled with painted glass; and there are 4 memorial windows in the N. aisle. The massive tower is older than the body of the ch., the lower part being perhaps Norman. It was formerly surmounted by a lofty wooden spire; but this was destroyed by lightning in 1606, and never rebuilt. The *Monts.* are of some interest. In the Ham Chapel is a *Brass* of Thomas Warde, d. 1541, his wife Jone and their 6 sons and 6 daughters; and in the chancel a small one without an inscription. Between the two chancels is an altar tomb from which the canopy has been removed, and which is without an inscription, but known to be that of Sir Thomas Cawarden (d. 1559), the brass plate with the inscription having been found in an old chest at Loseley, and published by Mr. Kempe in 'The Loseley Manuscripts.' Cawarden was knighted by Henry VIII. "at the seige of Bullen." Sir Thomas held the manor of Bletchingley after Anne of Cleves, and on suspicion of his complicity in the Wyatt conspiracy his armour and munition of war in his castle of Bletchingley were seized, and taken to the Tower. Five times during the reign of Mary he was indicted for heresy; but on the accession of Elizabeth he was restored to favour. In the S. chancel, and wholly blocking up one of the windows, is a prodigious mont., erected during his lifetime by Sir Robert Clayton of Marden, d. 1707; " Lord Mayor, and at his death Alderman and Father of the City of London, and near 30 years one of its representatives in Parliament." Sir Robert was a citizen of great fame in his day. He it was who

---

* Note of the manor of Bletchingele as forming part of the dower of Q. Anne of Cleves, Brit. Mus. MSS., Harg., 497, fol. 56.

at the Oxford Parliament of 1681, moved for leave to bring in the Bill of Exclusion, and was seconded by Lord William Russell. He is the "extorting Ishban . . . as good a saint as usurer ever made," of Dryden's (or rather Tate's) second part of 'Absolom and Achitophel.' Macaulay says of him,* " Sir Robert Clayton, the wealthiest merchant of London, whose palace in the Old Jewry surpassed in splendour the aristocratical mansions of Lincoln's Inn Fields and Covent Garden, whose villa among the Surrey Hills was described as a garden of Eden, whose banquets vied with those of kings, and whose judicious munificence, still attested by numerous public monuments, had obtained for him in the annals of the City a place second only to that of Gresham." Under a lofty canopy is a marble statue of Sir Robert, in his robes as Lord Mayor, with his insignia of office beneath the figure, and the words " Non vultus instantis tyranni." A corresponding statue of Lady Clayton has the motto " Quando ullam invenient parem ? " Between them, upheld by cherubs shedding marble tears, is a curtain of white marble, with an inscription of extraordinary length and panegyric, it being " but just the memory of so good and so great a man should be transmitted to after ages." The inscription placed by Sir Robert at the base of the mont. in commemoration of his wife is somewhat less long and eulogistic. The mont., which is worth examining as a good example of the costly and elaborate monumental sculpture of the time, is the work of Richard Crutchen. Obs. on S. side of this mont. a small piscina. Among the monts. in the Ham Chapel is a slab to Sir William Bensley, R.N., d. 1809, with an emblematic design by Bacon, jr. The living, a rectory valued at £1200, was held 1731-37 by Thos. Herring, D.D., afterwards Abp. of Canterbury; and his successor, Dr. Thomas, became Bp. of Rochester.

The vill. stands high, on the Folkstone beds of the Lower Greensand, but the par. stretches far down into the Weald clay. Along the heights, both towards Godstone and across the country towards Caterham, are wide and beautiful prospects, whilst there are charming lanes

* History of England, ch. x.

towards the Weald. One of the head springs of the Medway rises on the S.E. of the vill. *Pendell* or *Pendhill* (Miss Kenrick), 1 m. N.E. from the vill., was erected by J. Glyd, Esq., in 1636, the archt., it is said, being Inigo Jones. *Pendell Court* (Geo. MacLeay, Esq.) is a fine mansion, built about 1624. In a field N.E. of the house a Roman hypocaust was discovered in grubbing up a bank in the summer of 1813. The field was near the foot of White Hill, along which ran the Roman vicinal way. Many Roman coins have been found at different times in this and the adjoining parish, Nutfield; and on the *Cardinal's Cap*, the point of the hill overlooking Caterham, are remains of a Roman camp.

BOBBINGWORTH, Essex,

(locally *Bovinger*—as Bovinger Mill, etc., —pron. *Búvinger:* Dom. *Bubingeorda*, probably from the A.-S. patronymic *Bobbings*, and *reorth*, or *worth*, an enclosed place), an agric. vill. and par. of 307 inhab., 2½ m. N.W. from Ongar, and 1 m. from Blake Hall Stat. of the Epping and Ongar line of the Grt. E. Rly.

The few scattered houses lie far from a main road, and the whole neighbourhood is quiet, secluded, and pleasant to look on, but said by the natives to be " terribly dull." The *Church* (St. Germain) consists of an old nave refaced with white brick, a new chancel, and an embattled brick tower with 6 bells, erected about 1841, as a board within the ground floor, which serves as an open porch, states that on Oct. 12, 1841, "the Hornchurch Youths performed two true and complete peals on those bells, the first ever completed." The interior of the ch. is well kept, and contains mural monts. to the Chapman family, 1627, the Cowpers, 1647, Bournes, 1663, and the Capel Cures, the present lords of the manor. On the N. wall of the nave is an old ambry. The chancel windows, Dec. in style, are filled with painted glass, the east window containing the leading incidents in the life of Christ.

Bobbingworth Hall, near the ch., is now a farmhouse. *Blake Hall* (Capel Cure, Esq.), ¼ m. S.E. of the ch., is a large white-fronted mansion standing in a richly wooded park. A pleasant path across the park and onwards by the fields leads to Greenstead ch., 2 m. S.

BOOKHAM, GREAT, Surrey

(Dom. *Bocheham*, prob. fr. *Bock*, beech, *ham*, home), 2¼ m. S.W. from Leatherhead Stat. (L. and S.W. and L., Br., and S. Coast Rlys., Epsom br.), on the road to Guildford ; pop. 978, of the entire par. (including 111 in the eccl. dist. of Ranmore), 1089.

The vill. extends for the most part northwards at rt. angles to the high-road, looks clean and prosperous, and is in the midst of beautiful scenery. An annual cattle and pleasure fair formerly held here was much resorted to. Richard Flecknoe in his ' Diarium,' 1656, tells that he

> "Through Leatherhead went to Bookham Down,
>   Where fair was kept of great renown ; "

and in his coarse way describes several of the incidents.

Near the centre of the vill., at the S.W. angle of Eastwick Park, is the *Church* (St. Nicholas), a large and pict. structure of flint, chalk, and stone, with, at the W. end, a sq. tower, the lower part of stone covered with ivy, the upper part of wood, with a shingled spire. The ch. is of various dates : the nave, piers, and arches are Norm. ; the chancel was erected in 1341, by Abbot John de Rutherwyke, as is recorded by an inscription in Gothic characters on the E. wall of the chancel (engraved in facsimile in Brayley's ' Topog. Hist. of Surrey,' vol. iv., p. 492, and in Parker's ' Gloss. of Arch,' vol. iii., p. 115). Bookham, including manor, ch., and mill, belonged to the Abbot of Chertsey at the Dom. Survey, and was one of the reputed gifts of St. Erkenwald, the founder of the abbey. The ch. contains numerous costly monts., and some interesting brasses. In the chancel is a *brass* of Eliz. Slyfield, d. 1483. In the Slyfield Chapel, at the E. end of the S. aisle, are some late but well-engraved brasses of the Slyfield family. The effigies are gone from that of Edmond Slyfield, d. 1592 :

> "Of Slyfield place, in Surrey soile, here Edmond
>   Slyfield lyes,
>   A stout Esquier, who allweys sett Godes feare
>   before his eyes ; "

but a quaint rhyming inscription, of which the above are the first two lines, sets forth at length his virtues, and his wife's family connections. That of Henry Slyfield, d. 1598, has effigies of himself, his wife, and their 6 sons and 4 daughters. Robert Shiers, of the Inner Temple, d. 1668, is engraved in his student's habit, with an open book in his hand. A large and elaborate mont. to Shiers and his family formerly concealed the lower part of the E. window in this chapel, but has been removed, and the restored window filled with painted glass by Lady Farquhar, of Polesden, in 1859, as a memorial of her uncle, Earl Raglan, who died before Sebastopol. *Obs.* the piscina on N. side of this chapel. *Monts.* S. of chancel, Col. Thos. Moore, of Polesden, d. 1735, a full-sized recumbent statue in Roman military costume. By it, on one side, a mural tablet with medallion of his nephew and heir, William Moore, d. 1746 ; on the other, one to Cornet Francis Geary, "killed whilst gallantly fighting at the head of his little troop," in America, 1776, with a bas-relief of his death. The E. window is a memorial erected by Lady Farquhar to her mother, Charlotte, wife of the 6th Duke of Beaufort. On the N. wall of the nave are tablets in memory of the 3rd and 4th Viscounts Downe and various members of their families.

Immediately N. of the ch. is *Eastwick Park*, the stately Italian mansion of Hedworth D. Barclay, Esq., a lineal descendant of the famous Apologist. The park is richly wooded, and the adjoining farm is noted for its high cultivation. *Bookham Grove* (Viscountess Downe) is on the S. of the vill. The sign of the inn by the entrance to the Grove, in the Guildford road, the *Saracen and Ring*, which puzzles many people, is the Downe family crest. *Bookham Lodge* is the seat of Viscount Chewton. *Polesden* (Sir Walter Rockliff Farquhar, Bart.) stands on a ridge of high ground, 1½ m. S. of the vill., and is reached by a pleasant uphill walk. Polesden was bought in 1804 for Richard Brinsley Sheridan, whose residence it became. On his death, in 1816, it was purchased by Mr. Joseph Bonsor, who pulled down the old house and built the present more commodious structure in 1824. It is a well-built semi-classic mansion, having an Ionic portico extending along the greater part of the front. It is approached by a long beech avenue. The grounds are celebrated for their beauty, and for the views, especially those across Box Hill from the long Terrace Walk. From Polesden there is a delightful walk of about 3 m., by *Ranmore* to Dorking.

The old manor-house of *Slyfield*, the seat of the Slyfields and Shears whose monts. we have seen in the Slyfield Chapel, is about 2 m. N. from Bookham ch. To reach it keep Eastwick Park on your rt. to *Fetcham Common;* cross that, and continue due N. to the Mole, on the near bank of which is the house, now *Slyfield Farm*, and by it is *Slyfield Mill.* The house is red brick, with Corinthian pilasters between the windows, and Elizabethan in date : the Slyfield arms being over the chimneypiece of one of the lower rooms. Much of the old house has been pulled down, but a stately staircase, and some handsome rooms, having old oak panellings and elaborate plaster-work ceilings, remain. A short ½ m. N. of Slyfield House (cross the river to the ch. tower directly before you) is *Stoke D'Abernon*—famous for its brasses, the oldest and among the finest known. (*See* STOKE D'ABERNON.)

BOOKHAM, LITTLE, a charming little secluded agric. vill., of 30 houses and 146 inhab. (there are 10 more houses and 51 inhab. in the par., but assigned to the eccl. dist. of Ranmore). Little Bookham lies about ½ m. W. of Great Bookham— whence you reach it by a pleasant field-path direct to the ch.-yard.

The *Church* (dedication unknown) is of stone and rubble, and consists of a nave and chancel (60 ft. long), with wooden tower and shingled spire. Originally it had a S. aisle, the Norman piers of which are shown inside, and in the late restoration of the ch. the aisle-arches and Norman caps. on which they rested were uncovered outside, the carvings being quite sharp : they have very properly been left exposed. In 1864 the ch. was carefully restored, but much new work added. Among the additions were the porch, and the graceful three-light window in the chancel, with detached mullion shafts of Sussex marble.

In the ch.-yard is a very fine yew : at 3 ft. from the ground it measures 17 ft.

6 in., but swells out a foot higher. Near the ch. is the *Manor House*, the seat of Thos. Helme, Esq.

BOSTALL, or BORSTALL, KENT (*see* ABBEY WOOD).

BOSTON HOUSE (*see* BRENTFORD).

BOX HILL, SURREY, 1 m. N.E. of Dorking, is one of the highest points of the chalk ridge between that town and Reigate, and in the heart of the most beautiful scenery of Surrey. Its name is doubtless derived from the box trees growing on it, and which are perhaps indigenous. The name of *de Buxeto* occurs here as early as the reign of John. In 1608 " the rent for box-trees cut down upon the sheep-walk upon the hill was 50l." About the close of the 18th cent. the hill was nearly denuded of its ancient vesture ; Sir H. P. St. John Mildmay, lord of West Betchworth manor, of which it is a part, having sold " all the box upon the hill of more than 20 years growth " for £10,000. At the present time about 230 acres of the western slopes of the hill are overgrown with box. On this side the hill terminates abruptly, the chalk ridge being cut through by the Mole, Box Hill standing at the south end of the well-known *Vale of Mickleham.*

The summit of the hill is 445 ft. above the Mole ; the surface is broken, and a good part of it planted. The views are among the most famous, and the hill is perhaps the most popular with holiday-makers and picnic parties of any in Surrey at a like distance from London. For their accommodation walks have been formed through the plantations, seats have been placed at the points commanding the widest prospects, and a cottage built for the supply of hot water and simple refreshments. The views from Box Hill are less extensive and panoramic than those from Leith Hill, or perhaps from Betchworth Clump, and one or two other points between Box Hill and Reigate, but they are very beautiful, and from different points very different. To enjoy the distant prospects to the full, the visitor should stroll to Betchworth Clump from Box Hill : the country westward, the rich woods of Deepdene and Betchworth, and the more distant Leith Hill, form objects of great beauty; but these last develop themselves more fully as you proceed eastward, whilst more and more is seen of the Weald stretching away to the Sussex Downs. For the young botanist we may mention that the Green Man Orchis (*Aceras anthropophora*), as well as the Large Butterfly, Small Butterfly, Bird's Nest, Fly, Bee, and Spider, and several other varieties of the orchis, are found on Box Hill, while about the dells and hollows many varieties of ferns flourish; indeed Box Hill has the reputation of being one of the best collecting grounds for botanists around London.

On the N.W. brow of Box Hill, and "nearly in a line with the stream of the Mole as it flows towards Burford Bridge," Major Peter Labelliere, of the Marines, was buried, June 11th, 1800. In consequence of an unrequited attachment in early life he retired to Dorking, where he became known by his harmless eccentricities. He was interred at his own desire with his head downwards, in order that "as the world was turned topsy-turvy, he might be right at last." *

Box Hill is commonly ascended from the back of the *Hare and Hounds*, at *Burford Bridge*, on the Mickleham rd. The way is plain, the ascent not at all fatiguing. But a still easier route, and for the rly. visitor perhaps more convenient, is from near Box Hill Farm, nearly midway between the Betchworth and Box Hill stations of the Dorking rly. The left-hand path is the gentlest gradient. If this way be chosen for the ascent, the descent should be made by Burford Bridge. The *Hare and Hounds* is a good inn, and has fine grounds. It is a favourite house for dinners, and used to be noted for wedding guests. Among those who have stayed for awhile here are—Mrs. Barbauld, John Keats, who wrote Endymion here, and Lord Nelson, who made a brief holiday here before leaving England for Trafalgar. *Obs.* the remarkable appearance of this side of Box Hill from the valley. The Mole washes the foot of the hill from Burford Bridge to Betchworth Park, and affords some remarkably

picturesque reaches—hardly seen, however, except by the angler. The *Grove*, a little S. of Burford Bridge, has a local celebrity from having a century ago been a good deal berhymed by Mrs. Knowles and other very minor poets. It was also for awhile the residence of the Marquis of Wellesley.

BOYLE FARM (*see* THAMES DITTON).

BRANDENBURGH HOUSE (*see* HAMMERSMITH).

BRASTEAD, KENT (pop. 1130), a pleasant rural village lying along the road from Westerham to Sevenoaks, on the rt. bank of the Darenth, and surrounded by hop-gardens, parks, and woodlands; 1½ m. E. of Westerham, 3½ m. W. from the Sevenoaks Stat. of the L. C. and D. Rly.

The single street is wide and clean; the cottages stand well apart, several of the old ones have gables faced with shaped tiles, and several good and comfortably fitted new ones are built in a similar style; amidst the cottages are many houses of a better class, and by the park gates is a quaint old-fashioned hostelrie (a modern antique), the *White Hart:* altogether a pleasant as well as picturesque specimen of a Kent roadside vill. set in the midst of a singularly beautiful district.

The *Church* (St. Martin) stands a little N. of the main street (up the lane at the Westerham end). It was a cruciform structure (nave, S. aisle, transepts, chancel, and W. tower), of various dates, but chiefly Perp.; but becoming dilapidated, was pulled down, except the tower, and "restored," *i. e.*, rebuilt, and a N. aisle added, in 1865-66, under the direction of Mr. A. Waterhouse. The new ch. is a handsome E.E. building of Kentish rag. In the tower is a good peal of 6 bells. The *monts.* (with effigies of the Heath and Turton families) in the N. transept have been carefully replaced. The chief one is of Robert Heath and his wife Margaret, with recumbent effigies. *Brastead Park* (Wm. Tipping, Esq.,), on the S. side of the vill., is a plain mansion standing in a fine park. Prince Louis Napoleon resided for a year at

---

* Brayley, Hist. of Surrey, vol. iv., p. 462.

Brastead Park, and set out from there on his expedition to Boulogne, 1840. *Combe Bank*, on the opposite side of the road, conspicuous by its gables and spirelets, and spoiled by whitewash, is in Sundridge parish.

BRENTFORD, Middx., lies on

the l. bank of the Thames, 6 m. from Hyde Park Corner, and extends for nearly 1½ m. along the highroad to Staines. There are 3 Rly. stations : L. and S.W. Rly. (Windsor Loop-line), one E. of the river (*Kew Stat.*, opposite the foot of Kew Bridge, serving also for the N. Lond., and the L. C. and Dover lines), and another in Boston Lane, on the N. (*Brentford Stat.*); and the Grt. W. Rly. (B. and Thames Junction branch) one at *Brentford End*, W. of the town. The town (pop. 11,091) is divided into Old and New Brentford. *Old Brentford* (pop. 8230), really New Brentford, is the E. portion, and is a chapelry in Ealing par.; *New Brentford*, really the oldest part of the town, comprises the market and all W., and is in the par. of Hanwell (pop. 2043) as far as the bridge, and W. of it (pop. 818) in that of Isleworth.

Brentford derives its name from the ford over the little river Brent, which here falls into the Thames, and is now crossed by a bridge of a single arch. Leland * mentions the "bridge over Brent ryveret of three arches, and an hospital builded with brick on the further end of it." This may have been the bridge of which we read that—

"A toll upon all cattle and merchandize was granted anno. 9 Edw. I. in aid of the bridge at 'Braynford' : . . . all Jews and Jewesses who passed over it on horseback were to pay 1*d*., on foot ½*d*.; other passengers were exempted." †

Some centuries later the Jews seem to have had a design to toll the Christians entering Brentford, if we may credit a strange story related by Lockyer :—

"The Jews offered my Lord Godolphin to pay 500,000*l*. (and they would have made it a million), if the government wd. allow them to purchase the town of Brentford, with leave of settling there entirely, with full privileges of trade, &c. The agent from the Jews said that the affair was already concerted with the chiefs of their brethren abroad,

that it wd. bring the richest of their merchants hither, and of course an addition of above 20 millions of money to circulate in the nation. Lord Molesworth was in the room with Lord Godolphin when his proposal was made, and, as soon as the agent was gone, pressed him to close in with it. Lord Godolphin was not of his opinion. He foresaw that it would provoke two of the most powerful bodies in the nation, the clergy and the merchants ; he gave other reasons too against it, and in fine it was dropped." *

Brentford has been twice a battlefield. In 1016 the Danes were defeated here by Edmund Ironsides. At noon of the 12th of November, 1642, a couple of regiments of the Parliamentary army, who were holding Brentford as an outpost of London, were surprised, under cover of a thick mist, by a detachment of Royalists led by Prince Rupert. There was hard fighting in the streets till dusk, when the Roundheads were driven out with great loss. Among the prisoners was the querulous Puritan John Lilburne. For his share in the Fight of Brentford, Patrick Ruthen, Earl of Forth, was created Earl of Brentford, by Charles I. On his death, 1651, the title became extinct ; but it was revived in 1689 by William III. as a second title for Frederick Duke of Schomberg. The last Earl of Brentford was Schomberg's son, who died in 1719.

The town, with its long narrow High-street, back-slums, factories, and rough river-side and labouring population, has always borne an unenviable reputation for dirt and ill odours. Thus Thomson makes the "herd of prickly swine" revel in "the mire" of "Brentford town, a town of mud ; " and Gay celebrates

"Brentford, tedious town,
For dirty streets and white-legged chickens known."

It is supposed to have been this characteristic that caused the town to find so much favour with George I., as reminding him of his beloved Hanover, that, in his frequent journeys to and from Hampton Court, he always ordered his carriage to be driven slowly through Brentford. Johnson found in it a resemblance or contrast to another famous city. " When Dr. Adam Smith was expatiating on the beauty of Glasgow, Johnson cut him short by saying, 'Pray, sir, have you ever

---

* Itinerary, vol. ii., p. 1.
† Lysons, Environs, vol. iii., p. 38.

* Spence's Anecdotes, by Singer, p. 77.

seen Brentford ? ' " This, Boswell " took the liberty " of telling him was *shocking*. " Why, then, sir," he replied, " YOU have never seen Brentford."* " The Quality of Brentford " are commemorated by Goldsmith in the Citizen of the World's account of the race " run on the road from London to a village called Brentford, between a turnip cart, a dust cart, and a dung cart."†

Brentford is the county town of Middlesex, and, as the polling-place for the county elections, was the scene of serious rioting during the Wilkes and '45 agitation :—

" Now nearer town and all agog,
  They knew dear London by its fog.
  Bridges they cross, through lanes they wind,
  Leave Hounslow's dangerous heath behind,
  Through Brentford win a passage free
  By shouting Wilkes and Liberty." ‡

Perhaps it is almost as well known for " the Two Kings of Brentford," made immortal by ' The Rehearsal ' and ' The Task ' :—

So sit two kings of Brentford on one throne."

A weekly market was granted to Brentford by Edward I., and is still held every Tuesday. The old Market House, a curious picturesque structure, consisting of little more than a high-pitched roof, with central clock tower, supported on wooden columns, stood in the open space called the *Butts*, where the county elections were held. It was pulled down in 1850, and the present Town Hall erected. At the farther corner opposite the market house was an old-fashioned half-timber inn, the veritable *Three Pigeons* celebrated in many a page of our older literature. It was the scene of some of the ' Merrie Conceited Jests ' of George Poole, the early dramatic poet. On the suppression of the theatres during the Civil War, John Lowen, one of Shakspeare's " fellows," an original actor in his plays, and his successor at the Globe, Blackfriars, became landlord of the Three Pigeons. According to tradition, he was often visited by his old comrades, Ben Jonson among the number—but this the date of his death con-

tradicts. At any rate Ben has helped to preserve the memory of the hostelry.

" *Subtle*. We will turn our course
To Brainford, westward, if thou say'st the word.

     *   *   *   *   *

My fine flitter-mouse !
My bird o' the night ! we'll tickle it at the
     Pigeons." *

A large low room with carved wood fittings was shown as the scene of the " wit combats." The old inn was pulled down a few years back, and a vulgar compo-fronted gin-shop built on the site. At another noted Brentford inn, the *Lion*, Henry VI., in 1445, assembled a large party, and after supper created Alonzo d'Almada, Earl of Avranches. Next morning he held a Chapter of the Garter (the only instance of a chapter being held at an inn), at which he created two knights. The chief inns of the present day are the *Castle* in High-street, and the *Star and Garter* by Kew Bridge. There is also " the inn that goes down to the water-side," at which Pepys " eat and drank," and in the evening took boat, after going to Brentford church, " where a dull sermon and many Londoners."† At the inn, if not at the church, many Londoners may still be seen any fine Sunday evening in the summer.

Old Brentford Church (St. George) is a mean building, erected about 1770; the only thing noteworthy in it is the altarpiece, a representation of the Last Supper, presented to the ch. by the artist, J. Zoffany, R.A., who lived at Strand-on-the-Green, on the Chiswick side of Kew Bridge. St. Peter is a portrait of Zoffany himself. The heads of the Apostles were painted from Brentford fishermen. *New Brentford Church* (St. Lawrence) is at the W. end of the town. The body of the ch. was rebuilt of brick in 1774, in true churchwarden style. The tower, Perp., is of stone, but was repaired and improved when the ch. was rebuilt. The int. has large galleries, and is gaily painted. *Obs.* at E. end of S. gallery a mural mont., with two kneeling figs., alabaster, coloured and gilt. Also at E. end, one by Flaxman to W. H. Ewin, LL.D., d. 1804. Mr. Attorney-General Noy, whose name is inseparably connected

---

   * Croker's Boswell, vol. viii., p. 176.
   † Letter 86.
   ‡ Whitehead, Poems, 1788, p. 11.

   * Ben Jonson, Alchemist.
   † Diary, 20th Aug. (Lord's Day), 1665.

with Ship Money and Charles I., was buried in the chancel, Aug. 11, 1634. He lived in a half-timber house by the church. We have a note of him taken shortly before his death :—

"Mr. Noy continues ill, and is retired to his house at Brentford. Passing by with my Lord Cottington to Hanworth. I saw him, much fallen away in his face and body, but as yellow as gold, peppered mightily with the jaundice." *

Horne Tooke, but then known as the Rev. John Horne, was curate of this chapel from 1760 to 1773, in which year he resigned his gown. His father had purchased the right of presentation. "Brentford, the bishopric of Parson Horne," is a well-known line in Mason's 'Heroic Epistle.' Tooke's elder brother, Benjamin, was a market gardener "in the fruit line" at Brentford, and was celebrated among the craft as the first to introduce the pine strawberry.

Falstaff, as will be remembered, disguised himself as the old fortune-telling Fat Woman of Brentford, whom Master Ford swore was a witch. In the 4to ed. Mrs. Ford calls the fat woman "My maid's aunt, Gillian of Brentford," and Gillian was evidently a witch of fame. R. Copland wrote a now rare black-letter tract, 'Jyl of Brainfort's Testament.' Henslowe † records the payment of 6l. 10s. to Thomas Downton and Samuel Redley for a play called ' Friar Fox and Gyllen of Branforde,' which was acted shortly after. Gillian was also celebrated in Nash's ' Summer's Last Will and Testament ;' and Webster, in his ' Westward Ho ' (Act v., sc. 1, " Room in an inn at Brainford,") makes Mrs. Tenterhook say, " I doubt that old hag Gillian of Brainford has bewitched me." It would seem from an entry in the chapelwarden's books that Brentford continued to be afflicted with witches long after the days of Falstaff and Mrs. Tenterhook : " 1634. Paid Robt. Warden, the Constable, which he disbursed for conveying away the witches, 11s."

Brentford has no buildings of interest. But it is a place of a good deal of trade; has a market held every Tuesday ; a prodigious number of public-houses and beershops ; and, as has been indicated, many factories, not always of the most odoriferous kind—as gas works (in the High Street), soap works, colour, mineral oil, varnish and size factories, potteries, saw mills, malt houses, and an extensive brewery (Messrs. Gibbon and Croxford). The huge chimney, 150 ft. high, at the E. entrance of the town, belongs to the Grand Junction Waterworks. The circular iron steps (120 in number) were built into it in order that the workmen might ascend to the old standpipe which formerly stood beside it. An independent standpipe, 226 ft. high, was afterwards erected ; but being found liable to injury from frost, was in 1867 superseded by the lofty campanilelike structure that now forms so noticeable a feature on approaching the town. At the termination of the Great W. Rly. are the Great Western Docks, chiefly for barges. The Grand Junction Canal, constructed 1799—1805 to connect the Thames with the Midland Counties, terminates in the Brent above Brentford, the stream being rendered navigable thence to the Thames.

In the neighbourhood of Brentford are pleasant walks and fine buildings. The grounds of Sion House are only divided from the town by the Brent, and there is a public path across them to *Isleworth*. In Boston Lane, ½ m. N.W. of Brentford Stat., is *Boston House* (Col. E. J. S. Clitherow). The manor (*Bordeston* in old court rolls—*borde*, a boundary) belonged to the priory of St. Helen, Bishopsgate, at the Suppression; was granted by Edward VI. to Edward Duke of Somerset; on his attainder reverted to the Crown, and was given in 1572 by Elizabeth to the Earl of Leicester, who sold it the same year to Sir Thomas Gresham. After passing through several hands, it was purchased in 1670 by James Clitherow, Esq. Lysons, writing towards the close of the last century, remarks that " Such has been the fluctuating state of property in the county of Middlesex, that this family is to be mentioned as one of the very few who have been resident upon the same estate for more than a century." * Another century has passed, and Boston House is still the residence of a Clitherow. To reach it take the last broad turning on the rt. at the W. end of the town. The house, distant about ¾ m., will easily be recognized, as it stands on a slight elevation, and is of

---

* Garrard to the Earl of Strafford, June 3, 1634.
† Diary, Feb. 10, 1599.

* Environs, vol. iii., p. 30.

brick, with 3 gables in the front : the grounds slope down to the Brent. It was built by Lady Reade, 1622, and enlarged by Mr. Jas. Clitherow, 1671. The interior has some richly carved fireplaces, and several decorated plaster ceilings in high relief, of complex panelling with numerous emblematic figures—excellent examples of the serio-grotesque decoration of the later English Renaissance : the chimneypiece in the great chamber is exceptionally fine.

There is a pleasant walk, for a good distance between apple orchards, from Brentford to *Osterley Park*, the residence of the Dowager Countess of Jersey, 1½ m. N.W. over Sion Hill. (*See* HESTON). On the way observe, on l., *Wyke House*, a large old-fashioned (but modernized) stucco-fronted manor-house, with broad smooth lawn and statuary in front, skirted by large and lofty cedars : the manor belonged to Sir Thomas Gresham, and has since passed through many hands. The house is now a private lunatic asylum. A little way beyond Wyke House is the entrance to Osterley Park, through which there is a public way to Norwood.

BRENTWOOD (formerly, and still locally, *Burntwood*), ESSEX ; pop. 3285 (exclusive of 392 inmates of the Shoreditch Union Industrial School, and 60 of the Roman Catholic Orphanage. Inns, *White Hart, Chequers, Essex Arms, Lion and Lamb*. Brentwood is 18 m. from London by road, or by the Grt. E. Rly. It is supposed to owe its name to having been built on the site of a clearing made by fire in the ancient Forest of Essex ; in early documents the name occurs as *Boscus Arsus* and *Bois-ars*, clearly pointing to such an origin. It is a chapelry of South Weald ; belonged to Waltham Abbey at the death of Harold ; later to the Abbey of St. Osyth ; at the dissolution was given by Henry VIII. to Thomas Cromwell, and on his attainder was granted by Edward VI. to Sir Anthony Brown ; afterwards passed to the Smiths, and then to the Towers.

The town stands on high ground in the midst of some of the best scenery in Essex ; and consists chiefly of one long street—tolerably wide throughout, very wide at each end. Some of the houses are old, and they are planned with little regard to regularity of appear-

ance ; but the place has a clean, quiet, well-to-do, and rather more ' genteel ' look than is common in Essex towns. The suburbs are pretty and pleasant. The only public building of any pretension is the Town Hall (erected 1864), a compofronted pile, with Corinthian columns above, and shop fronts below ; the great room is 74 ft. by 37. A good many new houses have been built about the rly. stat., and towards Warley. Besides the trade incident to an agricultural district, brewing and brickmaking are the chief occupations. Brentwood had a market granted it by King Stephen, but it has long fallen into disuse. Here also at one time the county assizes were held, and the courthouse and prison were standing in the High-street till recently, though degraded to a public-house and mean shops, the tenants of which were bound by their leases to put the buildings in suitable order when the assizes were restored from Chelmsford.

On the rt. of the High-street, by the Chequers Inn and near the E. end of the town, stands the desecrated *Chapel of Brentwood*, founded in 1221 by Abbot David, for the use of the tenants of the convent of St. Osyth, the Bp. of London and the parson of Welda (S. Weald) assenting, on condition that it should not injure the mother-church of Welda, nor receive its parishioners for interment.[*] It was dedicated to St. Thomas the Martyr, and consists of a nave (39 ft. by 27), chancel (27 ft. by 17), a tower and short spire at the N.W. angle, and a N. porch ; and is partly E.E., but for the most part Perp. in style. S. of the chancel is a double piscina, and on the S. side of the nave a single one. It is a rude looking, patched and battered structure of flint and pebbles, now used as the Boys' National School, but is picturesque as well as interesting, and it is satisfactory to know that every care is taken of it compatible with the purpose to which it is applied. It is figured and described in Buckler's ' Churches of Essex,' p. 161.

The *Church*, a little farther E., is of white brick, Gothic, of the year 1835 ; but enlarged and improved of late by the addition of an apsidal chancel. In it, relics from the old chapel, are a small brass to

---

[*] Salmon's Essex, p. 260.

John Parker, 1672, and a couple of fragments of heraldic glass.

Farther E. are the buildings of the *Grammar School*, founded and endowed in 1557 by Sir Anthony Brown. In 1852, the income having largely increased, a new scheme was sanctioned by the Court of Chancery. There are now about 100 pupils. Sir Anthony Brown and his wife Joan also founded an almshouse for 5 poor persons of South Weald : under provisions of the scheme of 1852, a new building has been erected, and the number of inmates doubled. The handsome Gothic ch., nearly opposite the Grammar School, is Roman Catholic, built in 1861, from the designs of Mr. G. Blount. At the northern end of the town is a tall *Obelisk* of polished red granite, on a rough granite base, erected in 1861 in memory of William Hunter, a Protestant martyr (whose story is narrated at length by Foxe), burned near the spot in the Marian persecution, March 26th, 1555. The long red brick building, with a chapel of Kentish rag, seen on the rt. of the rly. on approaching Brentwood, is the *Essex County Lunatic Asylum*, an admirably conducted institution, erected in 1851, from the designs of Mr. H. E. Kendall, but enlarged in 1864, and which now contains about 600 patients. It is Tudor in style, occupies an area of 8 acres, and has 80 acres of ground attached, in part laid out as pleasure-grounds, in part for farming, and cultivated by the patients. The large building farther W., by the hamlet of Brook Street, is the *Agricultural Industrial School* of the Shoreditch Union.

From Brentwood there is a delightful stroll N.W. to (and through) South Weald Park. Southward, *Thorndon Park* (Lord Petre's) (*see* INGRAVE) is visible from *Brentwood Common*—a fragment of the broad *Warley Common*, now pretty well all enclosed, famous in the last century for its camps, on the S. side of which are the Warley Barracks.

BRICKENDONBURY (*see* HERTFORD).

BROCKETT HALL (*see* HATFIELD).

BROCKHAM GREEN, SURREY, an

eccl. dist. of 923 inh. ,in Betchworth par., on the Mole, 1 m. W. of Betchworth Church, and a little E. of Betchworth Park, (*See* BETCHWORTH.) The pretty rural village green is surrounded by neat country cottages, two or three old half-timber houses, a village inn, a wheelwright's shop and smithy, and a handsome cruciform ch., E.E. in style, by Mr. Benj. Ferrey, erected in 1849, as a memorial of the accomplished eldest son of the Chancellor Goulburn. On the Mole, close by the Green, is a watermill, and the river is crossed by a bridge of four arches : both the vill. and the reach of the river by it being more than commonly picturesque. Obs. *Brockham Home*, an industrial school opened in 1859 by the Hon. Mrs. Way, as an experiment, with 14 orphan girls about 12 years old, selected from parish Unions, in order to train them for domestic service. They are kept in the Home till about 16 ; and the experiment is said to have succeeded thoroughly. The Home has now 25 inmates.

Brockham Lodge, by the river, was for many years the "summer villa," and eventually the regular residence, of Capt. Morris, the noted convivial song writer of the Regency ; and here the Duke of York, and, as is said, the Prince Regent, used often to visit him. His tastes, however, if we may trust his 'Song on the Town and the Country,' would have led him to settle in quite another region :—

"Then in town let me live, and in town let me die,
  For I own I can't relish the country, not I.
  If I *must* have a villa in summer to dwell,
  Oh give me the sweet shady side of Pell Mell !"

Capt. Morris lies in Betchworth ch.-yard. The house, after being long occupied by a very different kind of local magnate, Mr. William Benett, a member of the Society of Friends, is now the abode of G. Drayson, Esq. *Brockham Warren*, on the hill above Box Hill Farm, is the pleasant residence of the present Sir Benj. Brodie, Bart. The entrance to *Betchworth Park* is close by Brockham Green, and there is a delightful walk through it to Dorking.

BROMLEY, KENT (pop. 10,674 ;

or 5783 if the eccl. districts of Bromley Common, Bickley, and Plaistow are excluded), a market town on the rt. bank of the Ravensbourne, 10 m. from London by road, 11 m. by the Mid-Kent line of the S.E., and 13 m. by the L. C. and D. Rly. Inns, *White Hart, Bell.* The name is usually derived from the A.-S. *brom-leag*, a field or heath where broom grows : and, says Lysons, "the great quantity of that plant on all the waste places near the town sufficiently justifies this etymology."* Seventy years have passed since Lysons wrote, and now there are few waste places near the town, and hardly any broom ; still the etymology might stand by its traditional justification, had not Mr. Kemble noticed that in Saxon charters the name occurs as *Brómléagingas*, which suggests an original Saxon patronymic as the more probable derivation.†

Bromley stands on high ground in the midst of a richly wooded and picturesque country ; is reputed healthy ; has good seats ; is easy of access, and consequently is in much favour with City merchants, for whom comfortable villas have been built, or are building, on every available site. The town itself has a quiet air of conscious respectability. The approach to it from the rly. stat. is between the tall walls of well-timbered domains, some of which, however, are being broken and built over. At one end of the town is what was the palace of the Bishops of Rochester ; at the other the no less stately buildings of Bromley College. On the crown of the hill, just out of the High-st., is the old weather-worn church ; and close at hand the Market Place, in the centre of which stands a showy new red brick Gothic Town Hall, emblem of prosperity and modern gentility, as the plain shed-like building, perched on wooden columns, which it has supplanted, seemed to be of old-fashioned, tradesman-like thrift and humility. By the market-place are two or three large posting-houses, vestiges of old coaching days, now transformed into hotels. The business part of the town slopes down the street towards London. Along it are still a few good old red-brick houses, but the town, as well as the vicinity, is in process of modernization.

The *Church* (St. Peter and St. Paul) is of the Perp. period, but the N. aisle was

rebuilt in 1792, and the whole repaired and large galleries added in 1830. The outside is rough-cast and patched ; the interior cumbered with galleries ; but the old tall pews have been lately removed, and low-backed benches substituted, and the whole brought into accordance with modern taste. All the old window tracery is gone, but a large W. window with new tracery has been erected, and there is a noticeable W. tower with an angle turret. Inside the ch. are some monts. of interest. The painted glass in the E. window is by Willement. The font is Norm., with rude arcading. *Obs.* the Dec. recess for an altar-tomb at the end of the S. aisle. A plain blue slab at the entrance of the centre aisle of the nave, is the gravestone of Dr. Johnson's wife (d. 1753), the 'Tetty' of his 'Prayers and Meditations.' On it is the well-known Latin inscription (printed by Boswell), in which Johnson celebrates her worth, wit, and beauty (which he seems alone to have recognized). She was brought here for interment in consequence of the doctor, finding himself unequal to the duty of arranging for her funeral, having transferred the task to his friend Dr. Hawkesworth, who resided at Bromley. Hawkesworth's own mont. will be found on the N. wall, at the E. end of the N. gallery ; it has a long inscription in English, ending with a quotation from one of Hawkesworth's papers in the 'Adventurer' (No. 140). Close by it, on the E. wall, is a mont. to Zachary Pearce, Bishop of Rochester, d. 1774. A slab on the chancel floor marks the grave of John Yonge, Bishop of Rochester, d. 1605. On the S. wall is a slab erected by the Pitt Club in memory of Pitt's biographer, John Gifford. There are two or three inscribed brasses, but none with effigies. Outside the ch., a slab by the vestry door commemorates a sort of village Henry VIII. : " Here lyeth .. Martine French of this parish, with *four of his wives.*" How many others he may have had, and where they lie, is not told. The long, inflated inscription on the mont. of Elizabeth Monk, d. 1753, æt. 101, is from the pen of Dr. Hawkesworth. *Obs.* the large old *lich-gate* at the entrance to the ch.-yard, and the yew avenue leading to the N. door of the ch. On leaving the ch.-yard go to the open space immediately W. of it, for the fine view over Beckenham, Hayes,

---

* Environs, vol. ii., p. 420.
† Codex Diplomaticus, No. 657.

and Sydenham, and the valley of the Ravensbourne.

The *Town Hall*, referred to above, is a rather fantastic specimen of modern Gothic; red brick and stone, with a tall saddle-roofed clock-tower at one corner, erected in 1864 by the late Coles Child, Esq., of Bromley Palace, from the designs of Mr. T. C. Sorby. It contains a handsome room for meetings and concerts, 60 ft. by 32, and 40 ft. high. The weekly market, long given up, has been revived. A large cattle fair is held annually in Widmore Lane, W. of the market-place.

Bromley Palace lies just outside the town, between Widmore Lane and the rly. An avenue of elms, on the rt. in Widmore Lane, leads down to it. From the time of Ethelbert, king of Kent, to our own, the manor of Bromley belonged, with temporary alienations, to the see of Rochester, and Bromley Palace was the chief residence of the bishops. Here it was that the forged Deed of Association for the Restoration of James II., which it was pretended was drawn up by Bishop Sprat and signed by Marlborough, Sancroft, and other prominent malcontents, was deposited in a flower-pot in order to be found by the Government officers. Sprat was certainly innocent of Jacobite conspiracies, if he was not free from Jacobite tendencies; but his successor, Atterbury, undoubtedly did make Bromley Palace the theatre of plots for the restoration of the ejected family. Pope and Swift often visited Atterbury here.* Horace Walpole made a journey to the palace in 1795, "for the sake of the chimney in which stood the flower-pot in which was put the counterfeit plot against Bp. Sprat;" the flower-pot itself having been secured as a precious relic by George Selwyn, for his house at Matson, in Gloucestershire. Walpole admired the bishop's grounds and fish-ponds, but pronounced the palace "a paltry parsonage."† It was pulled down by Bishop Thomas in 1776, and the present "plain brick mansion" erected in its stead. When the see of Rochester was re-arranged, the manor passed into the hands of the Ecclesiastical Commissioners, and the episcopal residence was transferred to Danbury in

Essex. The palace became the seat of the late Coles Child, Esq., lord of the manor, who enlarged it and built a new front towards the rly.; it is now the residence of his widow. The park front is nearly covered with ivy, and looks older than it is. Near the house is a spring, over which stood an oratory dedicated to St. Blaize. After the Reformation this went to ruin, and the well was filled up and forgotten, till it was rediscovered in 1756, when an account of its curative properties was published by Mr. Thomas Reynolds, surgeon.* It is now kept in excellent order. The grounds, though not extensive, are very beautiful, with an unusual display of evergreens. Just beyond them is a hop-garden, the nearest to the metropolis, and Mr. Child used to take pride in getting into the market "the first pocket of the year's growth" from it.

Bromley College, at the opposite end of the town, rt. of the road, was founded in 1666 by Bp. Warner for "Twenty poore Widowes of orthodoxe and loyall Clergymen and a Chaplin." By subsequent benefactions the number of widows has been increased to 40, and the annual stipend raised from £20 to £38; and in 1840 Mrs. Sheppard founded 5 additional houses and a stipend of £44 each for maiden ladies, daughters of clergymen, who have previously resided with their mothers in the college. The widow of Bp. Atterbury's only son died a pensioner in the college in 1789, æt. 80. The buildings are chiefly the original comfortable-looking 17th century red-brick houses, surrounded by well-stocked flower gardens set in a large, finely timbered paddock. Warner's *chapel* has, however, given place to one of more orthodox Gothic, erected by Messrs. Waring and Blake in 1865. It is of good early Dec. character, and richly furnished.

A little S. of the ch., down a narrow lane (Ringer's Lane), on the rt. of the road to the rly. stat., are a few vestiges of the old manor-house of *Simpson's;* also the N. and E. sides, 25 ft. wide, of the moat with which it was encompassed by licence of Henry V.: the W. and S. sides were filled in 50 years ago. The path past it leads by the *Water-Gate* to the Ravensbourne—still a pretty walk, though much

---

* Pope's Works, vol. vii., p. 195.
† Letters, vol. ii., p. 438.

* Lysons, vol. ii., p. 422.

injured by railways and other innovations. The new building seen in front is the engine-house of the W. Kent Waterworks.

Sundridge Park (E. J. Scott, Esq.), 1½ m. N.E. of Bromley, will afford a pleasant stroll, and has special interest for the geologist. "One of the most interesting localities I am acquainted with is Sundridge Park, where a hard conglomerate, entirely made up of oyster shells, and the shingle that formed their native bed, is quarried."* The pit in Sundridge Park, by *Elmstead Lane*, affords a fine section, rich in the fauna of the period, of what are called the Woolwich and Reading Beds, the oldest of the Tertiaries in this country except the Thanet Sands. The oysters found here occur along with *Cyrenæ* in a coarse limestone, the shells being cemented together by a calcareous base. *Obs.* the Park Lodge, which is built of stone quarried from the pit just noticed, and which is full of fossils: some remarkably fine cyrenæ may be seen in the walls. A charming walk leads from Sundridge Park to Chiselhurst, where the geologist may continue his investigations on the Woolwich Beds, study the pebble deposits from which Chiselhurst derives its name, and examine the chalk caves in Camden Park. (*See* CHISELHURST.)

By the hamlet of *Plaistow*, W. of Sundridge Park, is *Plaistow Hall* (Mrs. Shuttleworth). A Gothic ch. (St. Mary), of flint, with Bath-stone dressings, was built here a few years back. The eccl. dist. of Plaistow had 2234 inhab. in 1871, and has since increased considerably.

At *Bromley Common*, 2 m. from Bromley, on the road to Sevenoaks (pop. of eccl. dist. 2034), is a dist. ch. (Holy Trinity), Perp. Gothic, of black flint and stone, erected in 1841. In the fields behind the ch. the Bromley races and steeplechases are held three or four times a year. The hamlets of *Bromley New Town*, ½ m. E. of Bromley, and *Southborough* by Bickley, are new villages of not very attractive aspect. *Widmore*, 1¼ m. E. of Bromley, is another hamlet, with some good residences, extensive brick and tile works, and a little inn, the *Bird-in-hand*. Beyond it is BICKLEY (which *see*).

* Mantell, Medals of Creation.

BROXBOURNE, HERTS (from *Broc*, a badger, and *bourne*, = the badger's stream; Dom. *Brochesbourne*), on the Lea, 16 m. N. from London by rd., 19 m. by the Grt. E. Rly.; pop. 782. The Stat. is close by the church, the New River, and a large and rather picturesque watermill. E. is the Lea and Stour Navigation: the village lies to the W. along the Hertford road.

The *Church* (St. Augustine) stands high above the river. It is a very fine Perp. building, of flint and stone, with a large and characteristic tower with tall angle-turrets, and a porch at the S.W., with stoup for holy water on rt. of door. N. of the chancel is a chapel, of stone, with crocketed angle finials, and along the parapet, between shields of arms, the inscription in large Gothic letters, "Pray for the welfayr of Sir Wylyam Say, knygt wych fōdyd yis Chapel in honor a ye Trenete the yere of our Lord God 1522." By his will, dated 1529. Say left "a chalyce of sylver and gylte and a payre of cruettes of silver parcel gylte with the ornaments and vestementes that shall be necessary" for the use of the chapel; also his "wretched body to be buried in the new chapel which I lately edified and builded." He was buried there accordingly, and an inscription asks you "Of your cheritie pray for the sowl of Sir Wyllyam Say, Knt, dec., late Lord of the Manor of Base, his Fader and Moder, Genevese and Elizabeth his Wyffs": he d. 1529. The interior of the ch. is light and well-proportioned, and has a good panelled oak roof. It was restored, in 1857, under the care of Mr. J. Clarke. In it are several good monts. to the Monsons, Rawdons, and Skevingtons. *Obs.* altar tomb in chancel, with a double brass of Sir John Say and wife, d. 1473: they are in heraldic dresses, he having a well-designed tabard, and are among the few which retain traces of the original colours; the knight (head gone) has a collar of suns and roses, the badge of Edward IV. Marble mont. with effigies of Sir Henry Cock, Knt., d. 1609, cofferer to Q. Elizabeth, and lord of Broxbourne Manor, and his lady; beneath are figures of sons, daughters, and 4 granddaughters. There are besides two brasses of priests, one holding a chalice, 15th cent., the other beginning of 16th; and two inscribed scrolls. An old yew or group of yews, full of verdure, but with the trunks decayed, stands W. of the ch.

The manor of Broxbourne was a part of the rich possessions of the Knights Templars, transferred, on the fall of the order, to the Knights Hospitallers. Whilst Sir Henry Cock held the manor he entertained James I. on his journey from Scotland, May 2, 1603. *Broxbourne Bury* (H. J. S. Bosanquet, Esq.), 1 m. W. of the vill., is a fine house in a beautiful situation. The vill. straggles from Wormley along the highroad nearly to *Hoddesdon*, part of which is in Broxbourne par.

The *New Inn*, by the stat., with the New River at the foot, is a good house, but the stranger should go down to the *Crown*, by the Lea, and look at the gardens, which during best part of the year are crowded with the most brilliant flowers. A great floricultural authority has cited these gardens as "the finest example of flower gardening in the kingdom,"* and there can be little doubt that of their kind they are unequalled. The hollyhocks are, in their season, "a sight to see." The Crown is a fishing-house, the Lea being here strictly preserved; and along this part of the Lea occurs some of the first rural scenery now to be found on its banks. There are nearly 5 miles of water and 2 weirs : annual subs. 1 guinea, trout fishing 2 gns.; day tickets for trout 5s., for jack 2s., bottom fishing 1s. The Crown is in repute for trade and private dinners, and an excellent dinner will at any hour be extemporized for a visitor. Its rank among East-end pleasure houses is marked by the announcement that "Van-parties are not received."

BUCKHURST HILL, ESSEX

(A.-S. *Boc-hyrst*, Beech forest, Buck's forest, or, perhaps, Book-forest (comp. Boc-land), *i. e.*, a portion of the forest set apart, or severed, by royal charter from the neighbouring open forest), 10 m. from London by road or by the Epping and Ongar br. of the Grt. E. Rly.: pop. of the eccl. dist. 2520, having nearly trebled from 1861.

* Glenny, 1864.

The Stat. is at the foot of the hill, and about it a number of ugly houses have been awkwardly disposed. From the stat. a street, mostly of cottages and small 'villas,' has been carried to the top of the hill, where are some older and better houses and a *Church* (St. John's), erected when the eccl. dist. was formed (1838), but since, more than once, enlarged —the last time in 1870 : it now consists of nave, aisles, and chancel.

Buckhurst Hill was a place of great resort, as the nearest station to Epping Forest, but since the enclosures of this side of the forest, rly. visitors mostly make Loughton their starting-point.

The views are extensive, and still pleasing from the summit of the hill, and along the high ground eastwards, but the forest has been pretty well swept away, and sad havoc has been played with the scenery by the enormous enclosures made in these parts within the last few years. It was from Buckhurst Hill that the stag was started at the once famous Easter Hunt (*see* EPPING FOREST). The inns along the hill-top commemorate the former glories of the place. They are—the *Roebuck*, noted for its dinners, having a hall in which 500 persons can dine, and over 22 acres of pleasure-grounds ; the *Bald Faced Stag ;* the *Reindeer ;* and the *Warren House.* The vulgar name of the place is *Buckett's Hill*, hence poor John Clare in one of the crazy sonnets he wrote when in Fairmead Asylum (*see* HIGH BEECH), says—

"There's Buckett's Hill, a place of furze and clouds,
Which evening in a golden blaze enshrouds."

BUCKLAND, SURREY (A.-S.

Bocland, Bookland, *i. e.*, land severed from the *folc-land*, and converted by charter into a personal and heritable estate; Dom. *Bochelant*), pop. 385, 2 m. W. of Reigate, a pretty vill. on the Dorking rd., adjoining Betchworth.

The little *Church* (St. Mary) was almost entirely rebuilt in 1860, only the old wooden tower remaining unaltered. It is worth visiting. The E. window is Dec., the nave windows Perp. The interior is highly ornamented. All the windows are filled with painted glass by Hárdman; some portions of old glass, however, being carefully preserved : *obs.* particularly the St.

Paul, pronounced by Winston (who made careful drawings of it) to be unusually fine.

The *Village Green*, with its pond, old-fashioned cottages, neat modern school, and handsome ch., is very pleasant to look upon. *Obs.* the picturesque effect from the ch.-yard of the quaint brick and timber buildings, with their long sloping thatched and tiled roofs, W. of the ch. The great elms N. of the ch., which used to add so much to the rustic aspect of the vill., have been barbarously cut down to within a few feet of the ground. The large house adjoining the ch.-yard is the old manor-house, *Buckland Court* (H. Waring, Esq.); but the present seat of the lord of the manor (F. H. Beaumont, Esq.) is a more modern house, *Buckland Lodge*. The other manor-house, *Hurstwood* (Robert Clutton, Esq.), lies some distance away to the S.E. Mr. Albert Way writes, "The wild old tradition of a spectral monster at a brook in this parish, a sort of *Bar-guest*, was fully credited when I came [to Wonham]. It had been formally laid in the Red Sea by a former vicar. The blood-stained stone on which the shaggy demon sat exists, but has been moved to dispel the superstition—which has, however, been more effectually scared by the whistle of the adjacent railroad."

BULPHAN, ESSEX, 7 m. S. from the Brentwood Stat. of the Grt. E. Rly. (Colchester br.), and about the same distance N. by E. of the Grays Stat. of the Tilbury and Southend line; pop. 334; is an out-of-the-way place, hardly a vill., lying along the eastern edge of the Bulphan fen; uninviting, uninteresting, dreary to an ordinary visitor, but where a sketcher like old David Cox might find, about the outskirts of the flat and spongey fen, and among the old farm-houses, cottages, and long dykes, materials for many an effective picture; and perhaps obtain, whilst pursuing his studies, sufficient accommodation at the little inn, the *Harrow*, kept by Ezekiah Hollowbread. The name, anc. *Bulfan*, *Bulvan*, *Bulgeven*, in Morant *Bulfen*, is probably *Bull Fen*. There is still a considerable tract of fen-land here. Besides Bulphan Fen, there are the Upper and Lower Fens, Orsett Fen, Orsett Lower Fen, etc.; and Fen Gates on every side and miles apart.

Of old, Bulphan belonged to Barking Abbey. The *Church* (St. Mary) stands apart on gently rising ground, by a large farmhouse, Bulphan Hall. It is of flint, partly rough-cast, and, as Morant long ago described it, "of one pace with the chancel, tyled," with, at the W., a poor wooden tower and shingled spire; and is in bad condition, though the interior has been in part restored. The windows are mostly Perp., but the walls are older. The painted glass in the E. window is a memorial erected in 1867 of Mr. M. Gotts. On the S. wall is a terra-cotta tablet referring to a partial rebuilding in 1686. An old oak porch on the S. has, in the spandrels by the ch. door, boldly carved oak branches.

BULSTRODE (*see* GERARD'S CROSS).

BURNHAM, BUCKS (Dom. *Burneham*), a vill. on the old Bath road, 3½ m. N.W. from Slough; pop. of the par. (which is 8 m. long and 2 m. wide, has an area of 5297 acres, and includes several hamlets), 2281: Inn, the *George*.

The village extends for more than ¾ m. on both sides of the road: long, straggling, old-fashioned, drowsy; but, standing on a slope, is, in parts, not unpicturesque, though without any feature of particular interest. Of old it belonged to Burnham Abbey, and the Abbess in 1271 obtained the grant of a market, to be held on Thursdays, but it has long been discontinued. Later, three fairs were held annually: now there is only a "hiring fair," held on October 2.

The *Church* (St. Peter) is a spacious, cruciform, late Dec. building, comprising nave with aisles, chancel, transept, and tower, the upper part of which is of wood. The E. window is large, of 5 lights, with some noteworthy late Dec. tracery. The N. transept window, of 4 lights, has good Perp. tracery. The interior has been restored and reseated. It contains a few brasses, imperfect, and of little value. *Monts.*: on N. side of chancel, a large marble structure to the memory of George Evelyn of Huntercombes (d. 1657), with half-length coloured alabaster effigies of Evelyn and his wife, Dudley Evelyn (d. 1661), and beneath, smaller figures of their two sons, the one in armour, the other in an official robe. S. side of chancel, Mr. Justice Willes (d. 1787). with medallion portrait of the judge, supported by an emblematic female figure. Also various monts. to the Eyres, who held the manor of East Burnham for over 400 years, and other families of local importance.

Burnham Abbey was founded in 1265, by Richard, King of the Romans and Earl of Cornwall (brother of Edward III.), as a convent for Benedictine nuns, and endowed with several manors. It has no history, but it lasted till the Dissolution, when its revenues were returned at £51 2s. 4½d. The site was granted to William Tyldesley, but soon reverted to the Crown. In 1574 it was leased by Queen Elizabeth to Paul Wentworth; in 1623 the site and remains of the convent were demised by King James on lease to Sir Henry Vane; and in 1693 it was granted to Edward Visct. Villiers (afterwards Earl of Jersey), in whose successors it remains. In the early part of the 17th cent. the mansion house of the abbey was standing. It was in the shape of an L, and was let to a farmer, but only used for storing the farm products and implements, the farmer living with his family in a small house close by. Now all that is left of the abbey buildings is a fragment which has been converted into a barn; the mouldings, in clunch, of small windows and doorway, where not mutilated, are still perfect. The Abbey fishpond is in the garden of the vicarage. The site of the abbey is rather over a mile directly S. from Burnham vill., and ¼ m. S. of the Bath road. The house, *Burnham Abbey*, is the seat of Boyd E. Lennox, Esq.

BURNHAM BEECHES, a wild

woodland tract of almost unique beauty, in the par. of Burnham, Bucks, about 4 m. N. by W. from Slough Stat. of the G. W. Rly., by way of Farnham Royal and East Burnham; it may be reached by way of Gray's Stoke Poges, but that is a longer and less direct route.

Gray wrote to Horace Walpole from his uncle's at Burnham (Sept. 1737),

"I have at the distance of half a mile, through a green lane, a forest (the vulgar call it a common) all my own, at least as good as so, for I spy no human thing in it but myself. It is a little chaos of mountains and precipices ; mountains, it is true, that do not ascend much above the clouds, nor are the declivities quite so amazing as Dover cliff ; but

just such hills as people who love their necks as well as I do may venture to climb, and crags that give the eye as much pleasure as if they were more dangerous. Both vale and hill are covered with most venerable beeches, and other very reverend vegetables, that, like most other ancient people, are always dreaming out their old stories to the winds,

And as they bow their hoary tops relate,
In murm'ring sounds, the dark decrees of fate ;
While visions, as poetic eyes avow,
Cling to each leaf, and swarm on every bough.

At the foot of one of these squats me I (*il penseroso*) and then grow to the trunk for a whole morning. The timorous hare and sportive squirrel gambol around me, like Adam in Paradise, before he had an Eve ; but I think he did not use to read Virgil, as I commonly do there. In this situation I often converse with my Horace, aloud too, that is talk to you, but I do not remember that I ever heard you answer me."

The publication of Gray's Letters directed attention to this previously unnoticed tract, but visitors to it continued to be few till the opening of the rly. rendered it generally accessible. Now, in the summer and early autumn, it is a favourite resort of tourists, holiday-makers, and picnic parties; an inexhaustible sketching-ground for artists; whilst Vernon Heath's remarkable photographs have made the trees familiar everywhere, and sent hundreds of amateur cameras in the footsteps of the master.

The Beeches are only a fragment of the great forest which once stretched across this part of the country. On the Stoke side of East Burnham Common, the part that Gray would first reach, and which it may be he had in his eye when writing, there are scattered beeches of venerable age, picturesque aspect, and huge size, and the ground is rough and broken. The common, wild, glorious with gorse, fern, and heather, and bordered with heavy woodland masses, would be a pleasant object anywhere, but here you cross the common for the woods beyond, and plunge at once into a veritable forest, very limited, as you soon find, in area, but various in surface, and abounding in trees such as you might seek in vain elsewhere to parallel. The trees are not all beech, but beech dominate, and give character to the place. They are in aspect "most venerable," looking so old that, with Wordsworth, you'd find it hard to say how they could ever have been young, they look so old and grey. Most of the trunks are hollow, and all, or nearly all, were, long ago, pollarded. Tradition, which loves to associate Cromwell's name with any act of destruction, attributes the pollarding of these beeches to Cromwell's soldiers, but, to judge from their appearance, the decapitation must have occurred before their day. However that may be, there can be little doubt that it is to that operation the gnarled and rugged growth of the trunks is due, and that, beyond even the customary eccentricity of beeches, these "wreathe their wild fantastic roots on high." Finer single trees may be seen in Windsor Forest or at High Beech, and more superb and lofty boles in Knole Park, and there were grander and more solemn masses of umbrageous shade in the New Forest before the late worse than Vandalic clearances, but nowhere so wildly picturesque an assemblage of ever-varying giant trunks, or such striking combinations of sylvan forms and colours and endless contrast of lights and shadow, varied too, as Mr. Jesse has so happily expressed it,* "by glens and vallies interspersed with little rushy pools, the winter haunt of the snipe and woodcock, and overhung with the rich foliage of the holly, birch, juniper, and other trees, under whose shade the purple heaths flourish, and the fern and foxgloves add a charm and variety to the scene." The juniper is indeed remarkable, growing here to unwonted size and beauty; and the ferns and foxgloves seem to revel on these banks and hollows. The splendid flowering fern (*Osmunda regalis*), though sadly thinned by fern collectors, is still more abundant here than perhaps anywhere else so near to London, and the aquatic mosses and fungi are singularly rich, and add not a little to the beauty of the surface. In its kind, little is wanting in this forest fragment; and winding forest roads penetrate in all directions, rendering every part accessible, and in their picturesque combinations reminding you at every turn, and almost every step, of Ruysdael, Hobbema, Waterloo, and other cunning old forest craftsmen.

At *Crabtree Heath*, near the N.W. extremity of the Burnham Beeches, is an oblong *Encampment*, on which the antiquary may exercise his ingenuity. It is circumscribed by a vallum and ditch,

and, according to Lysons' admeasurement, is "about 130 paces long by 60 wide," but this seems to us below the actual dimensions. It is known as *Harlicot's Moat*, or, as rendered by the natives, *Harlequin's Moat*. Traces of another earthwork occur in the direction of Hedgerley Dean; and charming country lanes run out on every side.

East Burnham hamlet consists of a few poor cottages and indescribable tenements, with a little public-house, the *Crown*, a farmhouse or two, and three or four houses of a better class, scattered irregularly along the S. side of the common, and about the skirts of Burnham Beeches. The Manor House, in which the Eyres had lived for over four centuries, and the Great House, which also belonged to them, were both demolished in 1838. A smaller house, now enlarged, was the *East Burnham Cottage*, to which Richard Brinsley Sheridan brought his lovely young bride (Miss Linley) after their furtive flight to Paris, and from which several of his letters printed in Moore's 'Life of Sheridan' are addressed. This house was purchased by George Grote in the spring of 1838, with "a wood of about 11 acres," enlarged, and made "tolerably comfortable," and, other land being added to it, "called (by courtesy) East Burnham Park."* In this house Grote "laid out the scheme" of his 'History of Greece,' and wrote a large part of it. Here he resided till 1852, when, writes Mrs. Grote, "I caused a small Elizabethan house to be built in Popple's Park, and also a range of farm buildings and a labourer's cottage." The house was built with the profits accruing from the History, and hence was playfully named *History Hut*, a name by which it is constantly referred to in Mrs. Grote's memoir of her husband. Here the 'History' was continued to its conclusion, at the Christmas of 1855, when, writes Mrs. Grote, "I had a bowl of punch brewed for our little household at History Hut, in celebration of the completion of the *opus magnum;* Grote himself sipping the delicious mixture with great satisfaction, whilst manifesting little emotion outwardly, though I could detect unmistake-

---

* Favourite Haunts, p. 188.

* Some Account of the Hamlet of East Burnham, in Mrs. Grote's Collected Papers, 1862.

able signs of inward complacency as I descanted upon 'the happiness of our living to see this day,' and so forth."* Assuredly, the bowl of punch that celebrated the completion of the 'History of Greece' will be as lastingly associated with History Hut at Burnham Beeches as those "several turns in a berceau of acacias" taken by the historian of the 'Decline and Fall' when he laid down his pen after writing "the last lines of the last page, in a summer house of *his* garden" at Lausanne. Perhaps, too, it will be remembered that, among the visitors at History Hut, were such men as Hallam, Bunsen, Lewis, De Tocqueville, and others of hardly inferior fame. A visit to Burnham Beeches will, at any rate, lose none of its interest by the recollections called forth by the "Elizabethan House," or its older neighbour. The Grotes sold the property (for reasons fully set forth in the 'Collected Papers') in January 1858, "after having resided in the hamlet —with one short interval—for twenty years."

BUSHEY, HERTS, 13 m. from London, ¾ m. E. from Watford, and the Bushey Stat. (16 m.) of the L. and N.W. Rly.; pop. 4543; is a long vill. of small shops and private houses, straggling for nearly a mile along the Berkhamstead road, from Clay Hill, by Stanmore Heath to Chalk Hill, close upon Watford. Inns: the *Bell*, High Street; *Three Crowns*, Bushey Heath. About the neighbourhood are pleasant leafy lanes, with peeps of distant scenery, but bricks and mortar are spreading over many a lately verdant spot.

The only object of antiquity is the *Church* (St. James), which till 1871 was sadly patched, covered with rough-cast, and held up by clumsy brick buttresses, though not unpicturesque. In that year the church underwent a thorough renovation, under the skilful direction of Sir G. Scott, and was put into a condition to stand for centuries. The plaster was removed, all incongruities were swept away, and the exterior made to present a uniform surface of flint and stone. It now consists of nave and aisles, chancel, massive tower with stair turret at W. end, and a

good porch. The oldest portion is the chancel, which is E.E.; but the E. window, of three lancets, was inserted at the restoration; the former E. window was a large Perp. one of five lights. The lower part of the tower appears also to be of the E.E. period; the upper part is Perp. The aisles were added in 1871. The windows, late Dec. and Perp., agree in character with the old windows of the nave. The interior was thoroughly restored. The open timber roof of the nave was repaired, and the tall pews, curiously bad specimens of their class, replaced by neat open oak seats. The chancel was fitted with a similar roof, elaborately painted and decorated; the windows filled with painted glass; the floor paved with ornamental tiles; a rich reredos erected, and divided from the nave by a well-carved oak rood screen: it looks well, but requires gaslight to see it properly. Four of the aisle windows have been filled with painted glass. N. of the altar is an ambry.

The *monts.* are of little consequence. In the chancel was buried Capt. Silas Titus (d. 1667), who planned the escape of Charles I. from Carisbrooke Castle, wrote the notorious pamphlet, 'Killing no Murder,' with a view to procure the assassination of Cromwell, and has the discredit of having suggested the inhuman act of disinterring and hanging the bodies of the Protector and certain of the regicides. Outside the ch., on the S., is an altar tomb to Mrs. Catherine Titus (d. 1732). A little W. of the ch., rt. of the row of 5 slabs within a railed enclosure dedicated to the Munro family, is a rather large mont., with palette and brushes carved on one side, to Henry Edridge, A.R.A. and F.S.A. (d. 1821); and beside it a humbler upright (now, alas! leaning and dilapidated) slab, to a once well-known artist and antiquary, Thomas Hearne (not the great and irascible Thomas), "author of the 'Antiquities of Great Britain'" (d. 1817, æt. 73): both these monts. were erected by Dr. Munro, the physician of the Adelphi, a generous friend to young artists, and the early patron of Turner, Girtin, and William Hunt. Dr. Munro had a country residence here, to which he used to invite his young students, that they might sketch

---

* Personal Life of George Grote, p. 224.

in the vicinity. Turner and Girtin have left hundreds of these sketches. "Hunt often stayed with him for a month at a time, and was paid at the rate of 7s. 6d. per diem for his labours for the folio of Munro."* Observe, by entrance to ch.-yd., a magnificent elm, though it has suffered by losing some of its spreading branches.

Bushey Heath, once famous for its views, is now to a great extent enclosed and built over or cultivated. Outlying fragments of the heath towards Bentley Priory are, however, still brilliant with golden gorse, and afford wide prospects across Hertfordshire, and S. (by Harrow) over Middlesex to Surrey and Berks.

In the hamlet of *Bushey Heath* is a neat modern E.E. ch. (St. Peter's), in a well-kept enclosure, and partly covered with ivy. From it a pretty lane leads through *Little Bushey* to *Bushey Mill*, and *Bushey Hall* (E. Majoribanks, Esq.) Among the many good seats here may be mentioned *Bushey House* (Geo. Lake, Esq.), the *Manor House* (Mrs. Callard), the *Grange* (H. H. B. Herne, Esq.); *Powis Lodge* (C. Powis, Esq.), and *Hartsbourne Manor House* (J. Sladen, Esq.)

BUSHEY PARK, Middx., lies N.

of Hampton Court. The S. entrance is directly opposite the Lion Gate of Hampton Court Gardens; the N., or Teddington Gate, is ¼ m. S. of the Teddington Stat. of the L. and S.W. and the N. L. Rlys. It is a royal park; in all about 1110 acres in area. The surface is level, but richly wooded. It is said to owe its name to the thorn bushes for which it has always been famous; and which, though thinned of late years, are still numerous. But the glory of the park now is its unrivalled triple avenue of limes and horse-chesnuts, over a mile long; the horse-chesnuts forming the centre, the limes the side lines. Bushey Park is always a pleasant place to stroll through; it is especially so when the hawthorns are in flower, and the air is loaded with the perfume of the lime blossoms; but its full splendour is only seen when the horse-chesnuts are in bloom. The event is usually announced in the newspapers, and attracts numerous visitors. It is a sight worth journeying from London to witness. The avenue is said to have been planted by William III., and is now just passing, or past, its meridian. Towards the Hampton Court end it is broken by a circular sheet of water, stored with carp and gold-fish, and decorated with a bronze statue of Diana in the centre.

The park is always open to the public. A local celebrity, Timothy Bennet, shoemaker, of Hampton Wick, has the credit of having secured this privilege. According to an inscription under a mezzotint portrait of the Hampton worthy, "1752, aged 75," Bennet, "unwilling to leave the world worse than he found it, by a vigorous application of the laws of his country, obtained a free passage through Bushey Park, which had many years been withheld from the public." George I. was not, however, the first to close the park. "In 1662 the jury presented that the highway for horse and foot, leading from the Wick to Hampton Court, was stopped up by pales erected by Oliver Cromwell, and continued then stopped up."* The *Lodge*, the large sombre red brick house seen on the l. of the avenue on approaching Teddington Gate, is the residence of the ranger. Here George III.'s favourite Minister, Lord North, relaxed from his official cares. The king wrote to North, June 7, 1771, on the death of Lord Halifax, "I shall immediately appoint you Ranger of Bushey Park," but in July, *Lady* North was gazetted to the rangership. Here the Duke of Clarence dwelt till his accession to the throne as William IV. It is now occupied by Lord Alfred Paget.

BYFLEET, Surrey (Sax. *Bifleót, fleót*, a running stream, Dom. *Biflet*),

pop. 915; about 2 m. S. by W. from Weybridge Stat. of the L. and S.W. Rly. (cross the Common, due S. towards St. George's Hill, and keep the hill on your l., to Byfleet Bridge, which cross to the vill.) Inn, the *Blue Anchor*.

The village is built on the level gravel, between the main branch of the Wey, here a stream of some volume, and the artificial branch known as the Wey Navigation; but outside the narrow valley alluvium, the sandy furze-clad common, so characteristic of this part of Surrey, stretches far away on either hand. Much of this common has, however, been enclosed and planted during the present century. In Byfleet par. itself, 800 acres were enclosed in 1800, about 40 acres being left open for the cottagers. Byfleet manor passed to the Crown, temp. Edward I., and Edward II. seems to have occasionally resided here, as his warrants for the arrest of the Knights Templars, Dec. 20, 1307, and certain writs in 1308, are dated from Byfleet. Henry VIII., who according to Aubrey was nursed "by the wharf at Byfleet in a house called Dorney House," annexed the manors of Byfleet and Weybridge to the "honor of Hampton." James I. settled Byfleet on Prince Henry, and after his death on Queen Anne, who "began to build a noble house of brick, here, which was completed by Sir James Fullerton, one of the King's favourites."* The manor continued in the Crown till 1804, when an Act was passed enabling it to be purchased, together with Weybridge and Walton-on-Thames, by the Duke of York. From the Duke it passed to Ball Hughes, Esq. (Golden Ball); and it has since changed owners two or three times.

Byfleet Park, about ½ m. S.E. of the vill., stands in solitary stateliness, by the Wey (the course of which the 'Ambulator,' by some unaccountable misconception, wrote, 1783, and again, 4th ed., 1792, "is near 4 m. within the compass of the enclosure"!). It is now a farmhouse, and retains few traces of its regal origin. The older part is perhaps of the time of Anne of Denmark, the rest dates from the first years of the 18th cent. Evelyn† "went to see my Lord of St. Alban's house at Byfleet, an old large building. Thence to the paper mills, where I found them making a coarse white paper." There are no paper-mills at Byfleet now; the nearest are at Woking, some 6 or 7 miles distant.

Byfleet has about it other old-fashioned mansions sheltered by patriarchal trees, some good farmhouses, one or two large and picturesque water-mills, and many comfortable cottages, and the country is extremely pleasant. The *Church* (St. Mary) stands some way S. of the vill. It used to be both small and poor; but it was enlarged and cleverly Gothicised, by Mr. H. Woodyer, in 1865. It contains a *brass* of Thos. Teylar, rector of Byfleet, who d. about 1480; and a mural mont. of Joseph Spence, author of the once famous 'Polymetis,' and the now better known 'Anecdotes.' Spence lived here in a house given him by Lord Lincoln, afterwards Duke of Newcastle, who had been his pupil. Brayley* says that Spence "composed his Polymetis here;" but this is a mistake. The Polymetis was published in 1747, and Spence did not remove to Byfleet till 1749. It has, however, a certain connection with the place. He came here to cultivate his garden, and he expended a great part of the profits of his Polymetis in converting his fields into pleasure-grounds, and "embellishing his little seat."† Spence's garden achievements acquired considerable celebrity. Walpole was loud in their praise. But he had other visitors besides those attracted by his rural improvements. Joseph Warton came here to pick up materials for his Life of Pope. In his preface he says he is indebted to Spence "for most of the anecdotes relating to Pope, mentioned in this work, which he gave me when I was making him a visit to Byfleet in 1754." Johnson also borrowed largely from the 'Anecdotes,' the MS. of which had been lent him by the Duke of Newcastle; but enough was left to repay the curious when the work itself was printed in 1820. Spence was found drowned, Aug. 20, 1768, in a canal in his garden, into which he was supposed to have fallen whilst in a fit, as the water was only a few inches deep. Stephen Duck, 'the Poetical Thresher,' was rector of Byfleet 1752—56. The principal seats are *Westhall Lodge* (R. Hay Murray, Esq.), W. of the vill.; *Sheerwater* (Percy Ricardo, Esq.), ½ m. W., by the Rly.; and *Byfleet Lodge* (P. L. Hinds, Esq.)

.* Aubrey, Surrey, vol. iii., p. 196.
† Diary, Aug. 24, 1678.

* Hist. of Surrey, vol. ii., p. 157.
† Singer, Preface to Anecdotes.

CAEN WOOD (more correctly KEN WOOD), HAMPSTEAD, but in St. Pancras par., the seat of the Earl of Mansfield, lies between Hampstead Heath and Highgate, the principal entrance being in Hampstead Lane, opposite Bishop's Wood. Lysons thinks the wood and the neighbouring hamlet of Kentish Town (anc. *Kentestoune*) were both named after some very remote possessor. There was, he says, a Dean of St. Paul's named Reginald de Kentewode, and "the alteration from Kentwode to Ken-wood is by no means unlikely to happen." Caen Wood was at the beginning of the 18th cent. the property and seat of the Duke of Argyll. From him it passed to "one Dale an upholsterer who bought it out of the bubbles." Its next owner was the Earl of Bute, from whom it was purchased in 1755 by William Murray, afterwards Lord Chief Justice and Earl of Manfield, who died here in 1793.

The earl enlarged and new-fronted the house, Robert Adam furnishing the design. The garden front presents a stately classic elevation, the basement being rusticated, and a pediment with 6 supporting columns the central feature of the upper storeys. But the interior, and especially the library, a handsome room, 60 ft. by 21, and decorated with paintings by Zucchi, gained the warmest contemporary admiration. Adams published the ground-plans, elevations, and sections of the house and principal apartments.

Among noteworthy *pictures* here are *Reynolds'* superb portrait of the Earl of Mansfield in his scarlet and ermine robes; small-eyed and keen, but with great force of character; Pope by his friend *Jarvis;* Betterton the actor, said to be a copy by Pope of Kneller's picture; Gay's Duchess of Queensbury; two small half-length portraits of "those goddesses the Gunnings," disguised as laundresses: Elizabeth Duchess of Hamilton at the wash-tub, and Maria Countess of Coventry busy with the smoothing-iron, but the ascription of which is at least doubtful. There are also, carefully preserved in the library, the charred and stained relics saved from the fire made of Lord Mansfield's books, by the Gordon rioters, in 1780. From the house there are beautiful views; but the glory of the place lies in the grounds and woods. The grounds about the house were laid out under the great Lord Mansfield, and the cedars on the lawn were planted by his own hands. The wood is undulating, the trees are in the main oak and indigenous, but there are many fine beech and birch, and an avenue of giant limes, which according to tradition was Pope's favourite retreat for poetic composition when on a visit to the old Earl.*

"Canelond in Pancras" was a part of the property surrendered by the monks of Waltham to Henry VIII. The wood served Venner and his insurgent Fifth Monarchy men as a retreat in Jan. 1661. The head springs of the obsolete Fleet river rise in and about Caen Wood; and the large sheets of water (there are 7 in all) which form so striking a feature in the scenery, were originally formed in the 16th cent., by the Corporation of London, as reservoirs in order to secure a sufficient supply of water to the river; other springs from Hampstead Heath having been diverted so as to swell the quantity. More recently they have served as reservoirs for the Hampstead Water Works, now incorporated with the New River Company. The three outside Caen Wood are known as *the Highgate Ponds.*

Bishop's Wood, N. of Caen Wood, and divided from it by the highroad (with *Mutton Wood* farther N., and *Wild Wood* on the W.), was a portion of the great wood attached to the seat of the Bishop of London at Highgate; it was purchased by Lord Mansfield in 1755, and left as wild copse, but is now strictly preserved. When open it was a paradise for the London botanist, ornithologist, and entomologist; and equally so for the unlearned lover of song-birds, wild flowers, and rough woodland. Woodpeckers, kingfishers, and other rather rare birds may be observed in Caen and Bishop's Woods. A few years ago Bishop's Wood was a favourite haunt of nightingales, but the London bird-catchers pursued the nightingales so keenly that they almost eradicated them. Since, however, the wood has been preserved, prowling birdcatchers are themselves watched and trapped, and the nightingales are reappearing; in the spring of 1873 and 1874 their song

* Coleridge to H. Crabb Robinson, June 1817. Robinson's Diary, vol. ii., p. 57; Campbell, Lives of the Lord Chief Justices, vol. ii., p. 555.

was constantly heard on fine nights. Bishop's Wood is also still visited by many of our rarer and shyer birds, among which Mr. Harting* enumerates the Lesser Spotted and the Black Woodpecker, the Stock Dove, the Short-eared Owl, the Pied Fly-catcher, and many others. Caen Wood is "a favourite locality for Bramblings, where they resort to feed upon the fallen beech-mast."

CAMDEN HOUSE (see CHISELHURST).

CANONS, by Edgware, MIDDX.,

(in the par. of Stanmore Parva, or Whitchurch,) the site of the large and costly mansion of James Brydges, Esq., Paymaster of the Forces in the reign of Anne, created Visct. Wilton and Earl of Carnarvon 1714, and Duke of Chandos 1729. The manor of Canons accrued to him by his marriage with Mary, daughter and heir of Sir Thomas Lake, to whom it had descended from her grandfather, Sir Thos. Lake, secretary to James I. Thorpe (the architect of Holland House) erected a mansion here for the secretary : the design is among Thorpe's drawings in the Soane Museum. The Duke's house, designed by J. James, of Greenwich, was commenced in 1715, when the N. front was built by Strong, the mason of St. Paul's. The S. front, of which there is an elevation by Hulsberg, was completed in 1720.

"It stood at the end of a spacious avenue, being placed diagonally so as to show two sides of the building, which, at a distance, gave the appearance of a front of prodigious extent. Vertue describes it as 'a noble square pile, all of stone; the four sides almost alike, with statues on the front: within was a small square of brick, not handsome, the out-houses of brick and stone, very convenient and well-disposed ; the hall richly adorned with marble statues, busts, &c. ; the ceiling of the staircase by Thornhill, the grand apartments finely adorned with paintings, sculpture and furniture.' (Strawberry Hill MSS.) The columns which supported the building were all of marble, as was the great staircase, each step of which was made of an entire block, above 20 ft. in length. The whole expense of the building and furniture is said to have amounted to £200,000." †

Earlier accounts make the cost from £250,000 to £300,000. The Park and grounds were laid out by Dr. Alexander Blackwell, with "vistas, lakes, canals, and statues." The neighbouring church was

* Birds of Middlesex.
† Lysons, vol. ii., p. 671.

rebuilt to correspond with the palace, adorned with marbles, painted by Bellucci and Laguerre, and made to serve as the Chapel of Canons. The Duke's style of living was commensurate with the splendour of his house :—

"Here are continually maintained, and that in the dearest part of England, as to house expenses, not less than 120 in family, and yet a face of plenty appears in every part of it ; nothing needful is withheld, nothing pleasant is restrained ; every servant in the house is made easy and his life comfortable." *

"The chapel hath a choir of vocal and instrumental music, as in the Chapel Royal ; and when his grace goes to church, he is attended by his Swiss Guards, ranged as the yeomen of the guards ; his music also plays when he is at table ; he is served by gentlemen in the best order ; and I must say that few German sovereign princes live with that magnificence, grandeur, and good order." †

The Swiss guards, De Foe explains, were 8 old sergeants of the army, whom he took out of Chelsea Hospital, and provided "with neat lodgings at the end of each of his chief avenues;" their duty was to watch the house and park, "prevent disorders, and wait upon the duke to chapel on Sundays."

Canons was believed to have been the "Timon's villa" of the 'Epistle on False Taste' (1731),‡ addressed by Pope to the architect Earl of Burlington. Pope wrote to the Duke himself to deny the charge, and the Duke in reply said that he "took the application of the satire as a sign of the malice of the town against himself, and seemed very well satisfied it was not meant for him." § The poet repeats his denial, with some show of indignation, in a letter to Aaron Hill (Feb 5, 1732) ; and in his 'Epistle to Arbuthnot' he laughs at one

"Who to the dean and silver bell can swear,
And sees at Canons what was never there."

But the general belief has always been that Timon's Villa was the palace at Canons ; and the clamour to which the supposed allusion gave rise, occasioned Hogarth's satirical print in which Pope is seen whitewashing the great gateway of Burlington House, and at the same time bespattering the coach of the Duke of Chandos, which is passing by. Pope's verses are sufficiently biting :—

* De Foe, Tour through England, ed. 1725, vol. ii., p. 11.
† De Foe, Journey through England, 1732.
‡ Epistle iv. of the Moral Essays.
§ Spence, by Singer, p. 145.

" At Timon's Villa let us pass a day
Where all cry out, ' What sums are thrown away ! '
So proud, so grand ; of that stupendous air,
Soft and agreeable come never there.
Greatness with Timon dwells in such a draught
As brings all Brobdignag before your thought.
To compass this, his building is a town,
His pond an ocean, his parterre a down.

*   *   *   *   *

Lo, what huge heaps of littleness around !
The whole, a labour'd quarry above ground,
Two Cupids squirt before : a lake behind
Improves the keenness of the northern wind.
 His Gardens next your admiration call,
On every side you look, behold the wall !
No pleasing intricacies intervene,
No artful wildness to perplex the scene :
Grove nods at grove, each alley has a brother,
And half the platform just reflects the other.
The suffering eye inverted Nature sees,
Trees cut to statues, statues thick as trees ;
With here a fountain never to be play'd ;
And there a summer-house that knows no shade."

And so forth. From the garden and the
terrace the satirist turns to the study,
with its vellum-bound volumes (" in books,
not authors, curious is my lord "); and
thence to the chapel and the marble dining
hall, casting bitter reflections at " the
lavish cost and little skill " displayed in
each. The chapel, notwithstanding Pope's
reclaimer, there is no mistaking, as any
one may satisfy himself by entering
Little Stanmore church (*see* STANMORE
PARVA), and calling to mind De Foe's
account of the service :—

" And now the chapel's silver bell you hear,
That summons you to all the pride of prayer :
Light quirks of music, broken and uneven,
Make the soul dance upon a jig to Heaven.
On painted ceilings you devoutly stare,
Where sprawl the saints of Verrio or Laguerre,
Or gilded clouds in fair expansion lie,
And bring all Paradise before your eye.
To rest, the cushion and soft dean invite,
Who never mentions Hell to ears polite."

The service at the Duke's chapel " was
performed with all the aid of the best
vocal and instrumental music. Handel,
who resided at Canons as chapel-master
(having quitted the service of Pope's
friend, the Earl of Burlington, for the
purpose*), composed the anthems, and
Pepusch the morning and evening
services,"† but Pope, with "no ear for
his music," and more familiar with the
older and more monotonous Roman
Catholic chants, might easily regard the
compositions of Handel and Pepusch as

"broken and uneven," though 'quirks'
and 'jigs' were rather strong words.
A passage descriptive of the chapel
service in Charles Gildon's pompous but
long-forgotten 'Canons, or The Vision,
a Poem, addressed to the Right Hon. the
Earl of Carnarvon,' (fol., 1717,) would
almost seem to have suggested or pro-
voked Pope's verse :—

" Hark, hark ! what wondrous melody is this ?
See, see, what radiant scenes of opening bliss !
All Heaven descends, a thousand seraphs come,
And with a burst of glory fill the room."

The glory of Canons was of brief duration. Pope concluded his satire with a
prophecy :—

" Another age shall see the golden ear
Imbrown the slope, and nod on the parterre,
Deep harvests bury all his pride has plann'd,
And laughing Ceres reassume the land."

Warburton, in a note to this passage in
his 1st ed. of Pope, wrote, " Had the poet
lived *three years* longer he had seen this
prophecy fulfilled ;" but perceiving how
damaging it was to his friend's moral
fame, whatever it might be to his power
of vaticination, modified it in the subsequent edition. The fact, however, was so.
The Duke of Chandos had engaged largely
and unsuccessfully in the Mississippi and
South Sea schemes, and though he continued his state at Canons, on his death
in 1744, his successor found the establishment far beyond his needs or means.
After trying in vain to dispose of it entire,
the pictures and statues, furniture, and,
finally, the materials of the building, were
sold by auction in the summer of 1747 :
the building, which cost £250,000, brought
£11,000 ! The columns of the portico
were bought for the almost equally splendid and short-lived Wanstead House. The
grand staircase was bought by the witty
Earl of Chesterfield, for Chesterfield
House (now the Earl of Abercorn's, South
Audley Street), where it still is. The
equestrian statue of George I., one of the
ornaments of the grounds, was removed
to Leicester Square, where it stood till
1851, when it was taken down and buried,
but replaced in a mutilated condition in
1866, to disappear finally in 1873. Gibbon's famous carving in relief of the
Stoning of St. Stephen, went to adorn the
great hall of Bush Hill Park, Winchmore
Hill. The iron railings of the garden
(described by De Foe) were purchased

---

* Hawkins, History of Music, vol. v., p. 271.
† Lysons, and see Hawkins, History of Music,
vol. v., p. 198.

for the gardens and quadrangle of New College, Oxford. The pulpit, carved by Gibbons, altar, font, and pews of the private chapel, were bought by Mr. Freeman, of Fawley Court, and set up in Fawley Church, Buckinghamshire. The organ, by Harris and Byfield, went to the church of St. John's, Southover, by Lewes, Sussex.*

With part of the materials of the Duke's house, a villa was built on its site by Hallett, the cabinet-maker of Long Acre, who bought the estate. It was sold by Hallett's grandson to Dennis O'Kelley, celebrated as the owner of the famous racehorse Eclipse. Kelley d. in 1788, and lies in the adjoining church. Eclipse, after having had the run of the paddocks for some years, was buried in the park.

The present Canons, Hallett's villa (Mrs. Begg), is a neat though somewhat formal stone mansion, and stands in a moderate sized and tolerably well-timbered park. But there is little in the general aspect to remind a casual visitor of the palatial Canons of "the Grand Duke," though traces of the leading arrangements may easily be made out. Pope's Timon died Aug. 1747, within 3 months of his satirist. A magnificent mont. in the neighbouring ch. commemorates his greatness and his virtues. The Dukedom of Chandos became extinct in 1789, on the death of the Duke's grandson. (*See* STANMORE PARVA.)

CARSHALTON, SURREY (pronounced *Casehorton;* Dom. *Aultone,* or Old-town, afterwards written *Kersaulton, Cresalton, Carsalton:* fr. *cars,* cross), lies ½ m. N. of the Carshalton Stat. of the Croydon and Epsom branch of the London Br. and S. C. Rly. (13 m.); 11 m. from Westminster Bridge by road, and 3 m. W. of Croydon—a very pleasant walk, past Waddon Mill, and through Beddington Park: pop. 3668. Inn, the *Greyhound,* a good house, W. of the church.

The situation is agreeable, and the scenery around unusually varied. The church, Carshalton Park, Carshalton House, and the main street are on the chalk (the N. edge of the Surrey Downs); the northern part of the village is on a slip of Thanet sand, bordered by the Woolwich beds, whilst E. of the Wandle are the Drift beds of the Thames. The Wandle (of old a trouty stream) flows through the parish, and being replenished by several springs which rise here, forms a lake of over two acres in the middle of the village, and which, being bridged, and skirted with elms, cedars, and willows, imparts to the place character and beauty. Carshalton is remarkably healthy, and the air is so mild that it is said that ice has never been known to settle on the lake. By the ch.-yard is a spring arched over, called *Anna Boleyn's Well,* the local tradition being that it burst forth from a stroke of her horse's hoof. Carshalton had a weekly market (on Tuesdays) granted by Henry III. in 1258, but long lost. Walpole described it * "as rural a village as if in Northumberland, much watered with clearest streams, and buried in ancient trees of Scawen's [now Carshalton] Park, and the neighbouring Beddington."

Carshalton is now a quiet, flourishing village, dependent mainly, perhaps, on the resident gentry, but having also manufactories, herb farms, and market gardens. On the Wandle are the papermills of Messrs. Muggeridge, snuff, drug, and corn mills; and in summer the fields S. of the village fill the air for miles with the perfume of lavender, peppermint, and other 'sweet-herbs.' Still, as when Thomas Fuller wrote, though hardly perhaps to the same extent, "in Cash-Haulton there be excellent trouts; so are there plenty of the best wall-nuts, as if nature had observed the rule of physic, *Post pisces nuces.*" Evelyn (under Aug. 27, 1658) mentions the Carshalton "walnut and cherry trees, which afford a considerable rent."

The *Church,* All Saints', in the centre of the village, is large, comprises nave and aisles, a long chancel, and a low em-

---

* This is the received account, and it is so stated at p. 94 of 'The Organ,' by Hopkins and Rimbault; but at p. 91 of the same work, Dr. Rimbault states that the Canons organ, "by the Jordans, is said to be in Spa Fields Chapel." This, on the face of it, is unlikely, and appears the more so when it is remembered that Spa Fields Chapel

was not opened as a place of worship till 1776, nearly 40 years after the sale at Canons. But Jordan's organ was not the chapel organ, but that in the church, where it still remains. (*See* STANMORE PARVA.)

* Letter to Countess of Ossory, July 14th, 1779.

battled tower, rising from the intersection of the nave and chancel. Its oldest parts are of the E.E. period, but it has been at various times patched, covered with rough-cast, and altered (the upper part of the nave is brick, temp. William III.) But something has been done in the way of internal restoration : a pretty porch-like addition was made to the W. end in 1863 (Mr. H. Hall, architect) ; the original flint and stone work is in places exposed, and a luxuriant growth of ivy conceals some of the worst of the modern features. The interior should be seen, both for the architecture and the monts. Observe, on floor of the chancel, *Brass* of Thomas Ellynbridge, d. 1497, gentleman porter to Cardinal Morton ; the effigy is gone, but the canopy, with a figure of our Lady of Pity—an extremely rare device—remains. N. of chancel, an altar tomb of Purbeck marble, with brass above of Nicholas Gaynesford, "sometime esquier for the body" of Edward IV. and Henry VII., his wife Margaret, and their 8 children. This brass is noteworthy as being erected during the life of the persons commemo-rated, blanks being left for the day and year of decease ; it is remarkable also for the costumes, which are very characteristic of the period, and it retains some of the original enamelling. The lady wears a prodigious butterfly head-dress ; the four sons are in their proper habits—a knight, a tonsured priest, and two merchants. *Monts.:* S. aisle, to Sir Edmund Hoskyns, Knt., serjeant-at-law, d. 1664. E. end of S. aisle, marble effigy of Sir William Scawen, d. 1722, who, clad in loose robe and flowing peruque, is reclining on his left elbow, his hand resting on a skull. E: end of N. aisle, a pompous marble pile in honour of Sir John Fellows, d. 1724. One, by the Gaynesford mont., hardly less pompous, commemorates Henry Herring-man, d. 1703, the publisher of Davenant and Dryden, and predecessor in publish-ing popularity of Jacob Tonson. There are also two or three recent mural monts. with conventional figures in relief.

Carshalton Park (J. Colman, Esq.), S. of the ch., belonged successively to the Ellynbridge, Burton, Hoskyns, and Scawen families. About 1723, James Leoni made designs for rebuilding the house for Thomas Scawen, on a magnificent scale ; but though the materials were collected,

the house was never begun : Leoni pub-lished his designs in his ed. of 'Alberti's Architecture.' The estate was afterwards sold for, it is said, "less money than was expended on the brick wall of the park :" which wall, by the way, is two miles in circuit, lofty, and very well built, and the great iron gates are as good an example of the blacksmith's art of the reign of the first George, as the wall is of the brick-layer's. *Carshalton House*, at the W. end of the vill.—the great gates face you in going towards Sutton—was the residence of the famous physician Dr. Radcliffe, founder of the Radcliffe Library. He was here when summoned to attend the death-bed of Queen Anne (there is a Treasury entry, "Wm. Nightingale for his travel-ling charges in a journey to Carshalton to fetch Doctor Ratcliffe, 12s. 6d.") The doctor, offended as was supposed at some irregularity in the summons, pleaded gout, and declined to go. The populace were furious at his punctiliousness, and he dared not venture into town lest he should be mobbed. He died within three months of the queen ; his death, it was said, being hastened by chagrin—but the dates seem rather to confirm his own assertion that he was really unable from illness to attend her Majesty. His body lay in state for a fortnight at Carshalton, when it was re-moved for burial to St. Mary's, Oxford. The house Radcliffe built for himself here was, soon after his death, pulled down by Sir John Fellows, a South Sea director, who built a more stately one, and laid out the grounds in a manner that excited abundant admiration. It was afterwards the residence of Lord Chancellor Hard-wicke. It is now a "collegiate boarding school" for boys. Notice the lofty and peculiar summer-house (like the mansion of red brick) by the E. wall, as a relique of South-Sea garden architecture.

CASSIOBURY (or CASHIO-BURY), HERTS, the stately seat of Arthur Algernon Capel, Earl of Essex, 1 m. W. from the Watford Stat. of the N.W. Rly., and about as far from the town of Wat-ford. On leaving the stat., turn to the l. (in the St. Albans rd.), cross the main street, leaving Watford town on the l., and enter the park by the lodge on the rt., about 200 yds. up the rd. to Rick-mansworth.

Cassiobury (Dom. *Caissou*), Chauncy thinks was so called from the residence here of Cassivellaunus, chief of the Cassii, whence also the hundred of Cashio derives its name. The manor belonged to St. Albans Abbey, and at the dissolution of monasteries was given to Sir Richard Morrison (or Moryson), the friend of Ascham. From the Morrisons it passed by marriage to Arthur Lord Capel, in whose descendants it remains. The first two Capels who possessed Cassiobury were singularly unfortunate; the one losing his life for Charles I., the other his through Charles II. Lord Capel, the heroic defender of Colchester against Gen. Fairfax, was beheaded in Old Palace Yard, March 9, 1649. His son Arthur, 1st Earl of Essex of the Capel family, was committed to the Tower, July 1683, for complicity in the Rye House Plot, and found, a few days after, with his throat cut.[*]

Sir Richard Morrison " began a fair and large house in this place, sicuated upon a dry hill not far from a pleasant river in a fair park," which was finished by his son Sir Charles, who d. 1599.[†] With the exception of the N.W. wing, this house was pulled down, and a new one erected on the site by the 1st Earl of Essex, on his return from Ireland in 1677. Evelyn saw it soon after its completion :—

"*April* 18*th*, 1680.—On the earnest invitation of the Earl of Essex I went with him to his house at Cassiobury in Hertfordshire. . . . The house is new, a plain fabric, built by my friend Mr. Hugh May. There are divers fair and good rooms, and excellent carving by Gibbons, especially the chimney piece of the library. There is in the porch or entrance a painting by Verrio, of Apollo and the liberal Arts. One room pargetted with yew which I liked well. Some of the chimney mantels are of Irish marble, brought by my Lord from Ireland, when he was Lord Lieutenant, and not much inferior to Italian. The tympanum or gable at the front is a bass-relievo of Diana hunting, cut in Portland Stone, handsomely enough. I do not approve of the middle doors being round; but when the hall is finished as designed, it being an oval with a cupola, together with the other wing it will be a very noble palace. The library is large and very nobly furnished, and all the books are richly bound and gilded, but there are no MSS. except the Parliament Rolls and Journals, the transcribing and binding of which cost him, as he assured me, £500. No man has been more industrious than this noble Lord in planting about his seat,

adorned with walks, ponds and other rural elegancies; but the soil is stony, churlish and uneven, nor is the water near enough to the house, though a very swift and clear stream runs within a flight shot from it in the valley, which may fitly be called Coldbrook, it being indeed excessive cold, yet producing fair trouts. 'Tis a pity the house was not situated to more advantage, but it seems it was built just where the old one was, which I believe he only meant to repair; this leads men into irremediable errors, and saves but a very little."

May's house was pulled down in 1800 by the Earl of Essex (who married Miss Stephens), and the present mansion erected from the designs of James Wyatt, in his so-called Gothic style. As Gothic it is bad; but the house is well proportioned, and has an air of picturesque stateliness, very becoming in such a structure. It is built about an open courtyard, and has for its reception-rooms capacious cloisters, vestibule, and saloon, dining and drawing rooms overlooking the park, and a noble library, 54 ft. by 23, with three subsidiary libraries, all large and well-filled rooms, and one of them connecting the state apartments with the Winter Dining and Drawing Rooms. A portion of the N. wing of Morrison's house is still preserved, and what Britton in his sumptuous volume on 'Cassiobury' considers to be a part of the still earlier monastic edifice; also a chamber with a handsome ceiling of May's building.

The house contains some good and many interesting *portraits*. The most noteworthy are — Henry IV., with the inscription "Henry the Fourth, King of England, who layd the first stone of this hous, and left this picture in it when he gave it to Lentall, whoe sold it to Cornwall of Burford, who sold it to the Auncesters of the Lord Coningesby in the reign of King Henry the Sixth." The house referred to was Hampton Court, in Herefordshire, which passed to the Earls of Essex by marriage, but notwithstanding the pedigree and Walpole's assertion that the picture is " an undoubted original," it must be either a copy or a repetition of the portrait of Henry IV. in Windsor Castle. Arthur Lord Capel (beheaded 1649) and his family, 9 figures in all, by *C. Jansen*: the Lady Capel in this picture is the heiress of the Morrisons who brought Cassiobury to the Capels. His son, Arthur Capel, 1st Earl of Essex, $\frac{3}{4}$ by *Lely*; good. Sir Thomas Coningsby, d. 1625, and Cricket his dwarf: full lengths.

---

[*] In the collection of MSS. at the British Museum, is the Grant of the Manors of Cashiobury, Bushey, etc., by the Parliament to Lord Essex (5497, f. 133).

[†] Chauncy, Hertfordshire, vol. ii., p. 354.

Bust of the infamous Frances Howard, Countess of Essex, afterwards Somerset, in a low dress. A brilliant and untouched portrait, by *Rubens*, said to be the youthful Charlotte de la Tremouille, afterwards famous, as Countess of Derby, for her defence of Lathom House. Algernon Percy, 10th Earl of Northumberland, d. 1688, by *Vandyck:* full length, as Lord High Admiral. An inscription on the frame tells that when the picture was cleaned under the supervision of T. Phillips, R.A., it was found that the truncheon in the Earl's hand had been originally painted in a different position. Of this there is no appearance now—confirming the suspicion suggested by the look of the picture, that, besides cleaning, it was a good deal repainted. Charles II., seated, by *Lely;* good. Head of the Duke of Monmouth, in long wig and armour, oval, by *Wissing,* dated 1683. Moll Davis, the actress, by *Lely,* seated, holding a gold casket : is believed to be the portrait which Mrs. Beale saw in Bab May's lodgings at Whitehall— Bab was the brother of Hugh May, the architect of Cassiobury : the face and neck have been repainted (by Phillips ?). William, Lord Russell, the patriot, head in an oval, attributed to Kneller, but not by him. Undoubtedly by *Kneller*, however, and a charming example of his best manner, is a full length of the Countess of Ranelagh. This is the lady, and probably the picture, to which Fielding refers when he says that Sophia Western was "most like the picture of Lady Ranelagh," though there are replicas of it at Hampton Court and Hatfield. With her *comp.* two other famous (sister) beauties, Catherine Hyde, Duchess of Queensberry, d. 1777,—Prior's "Kitty beautiful and young," and the fast friend of Gay, as a shepherdess with lamb and crook ; exhibited in the Nat. Port. Exh. 1867, without the painter's name, but clearly by *Jervas;* and Jane Hyde, Countess of Essex, d. 1724, whom Swift* describes as a "top toast." Sir Charles Hanbury Williams, the poet, by *Hudson;* and his daughter Frances, Countess of Essex, a kitcat by *Reynolds,* good, and in good preservation. A still finer *Reynolds* is the picture (well known by C. Turner's capital mezzotint) of George Viscount Malden, æt. 10 (after-

* Journal to Stella.

wards 5th Earl of Essex), and his sister, æt. 13 ; *obs.* the splendid carvings by Grinling Gibbons in which it is set. Garrick as Sir John Brute, one of *Zoffany's* clever theatrical pieces. There are also some nameless but not uninteresting Morrison portraits, and several more of the Capels.

Among the general pictures are 2 or 3 attributed to Rubens, and some bearing the names of Teniers, Wouvermans, etc., but they are not of much value. By recent native painters are—a cleverly painted Farmyard by *Morland ;* three paintings by *Turner,* one, the Two Bridges at Walton-on-Thames, an exquisite specimen of his earlier manner, the others a Coast Scene, and a Sea-piece ; a View of Rotterdam by *Calcott ;* the Highland Family, by *Wilkie* (1824); Fish Auction on the Devonshire Coast, by *Collins ;* the Cat's-paw, a clever early picture, by *Landseer ;* Don Quixote and Sancho Panza with the Duchess, by *Leslie.* In the rooms are exhibited many articles of *virtù,* and some cherished memorials—as a piece of the blue ribbon worn by Charles I. on the scaffold ; and a white pocket handkerchief with which Lord Coningsby stopped the wound of William III. at the battle of the Boyne : above which hangs a painting of the event by A. Cooper, R.A. In several of the rooms are carvings by Grinling Gibbon of scrolls of flowers, fruit, with dead game, etc., exquisitely wrought, but they have suffered terribly from paint and the worm.

To see the house an introduction is required ; but the park is always open, and the *Gardens* may generally be viewed on application to the gardener. They are very beautiful, and have always been famous. E. and S. of the house the ground is laid out in lawns, interspersed with choice shrubs and trees, and opens E. into a wild-looking bit of the park rich in old timber and overgrown with furze and fern. A dell here serves as a cemetery, with monts. and monumental verses to the favourite spaniels and other canine pets of the late Countess of Essex and other fair members of the Capel family. The *Gardens* to the N., of 8 acres, are broken with terraces and dells, rock beds, etc., include a sub-tropical section, and are gorgeous with flowers. More than a century a and half ago Cassiobury was celebrated as "one of the first places in England where the polite spirit of gardening shone the brightest," * and its reputation has never faded.

The *Park* comprises nearly 700 acres, of which 127 are attached to the house; 310 form the Home Park, and 250 the Upper Park, which is separated from the Home Park by the Gade, parallel to which, and in part one with it, flows the Grand Junction Canal. The Home Park is smooth and stately, the Upper Park more hilly and wilder : both contain many grand old oak, elm, chesnut, beech, and fir trees. The park was planted by Moses Cook, author of a work on ' Forest Trees ' (1675), who was gardener to the 1st Earl of Essex, and an enthusiast in his calling. The gardens and private grounds are commonly said to have been laid out by Le Nôtre, but Clutterbuck says, by the Earl's town gardener, Rose, whilst Evelyn, remarking that "the gardens are very rare," adds, "and cannot be otherwise, having so skilful an artist to govern them as Mr. Cooke." The somewhat fanciful, but picturesque and comfortable looking ' Swiss' cottages sprinkled about the park, were designed or suggested by James Wyatt : that by the Gade is, or was, specially dedicated to picnic parties. The *Grove* (Earl Clarendon) adjoins Cassiobury on the W.

CATERHAM, Surrey, a village and terminus of the Caterham branch line of the S.E. Rly., 18 m. from London, 7 m. S. of Croydon ; pop. 3577, or, excluding the inmates of the Asylum for Imbeciles, 2250. Caterham is not mentioned in Domesday, and the origin of the name is not very clear. Mr. Taylor † thinks that " Caterham may possibly be referred" to the A.-S. root *geat*, "a pass through a line of hill or cliff;" but farther on ‡ he suggests that "it may perhaps be referred to the Celtic word *cath*, a battle." The more likely reference is to its position on the old Roman vicinal way, which passed through Caterham and under White Hill, where it is known as Stane Street.

The old vill. is on the chalk hill ; the

new part lies ½ m. E. in the valley along the Godstone rd., by the rly. stat. The manor belonged to the Abbey of Waltham, but since the Dissolution has been in private hands. The Abbey of Chertsey also possessed land here ; and in 1285 Edward I. granted a fair at Caterham to the monastery of Leeds in Kent.

Caterham *old Church* (St. Lawrence) is partly E.E., but has lost all architectural character by repeated alterations. Having fallen into disrepair, a new Early Dec. church was erected opposite it in 1866. It is of flint with stone bands, and tall red tiled roofs, and consists of nave, chancel, and N. aisle, but has no tower, and is rather conspicuously ugly, and ill-adapted for the site. *Obs.* in chancel of old ch. a good mural mont., with kneeling female figure in high relief, to Eliz. Legrew, d. 1825, wife of a former rector. *Caterham Court House*, near the ch., is the seat of J. F. Harrison, Esq.

The old vill. straggles along the high ground above the ch., and though 'improved' still retains an air of old-fashioned picturesqueness. *Obs.* on l. a cottage with yews clipped into fantastic forms. About the rly. stat. a good-sized vill., with Railway Hotel (a moderately good inn), shops, and dwellings, has grown up within the last few years, whilst the slopes on either side have been laid out in ornamental grounds, and dotted over with first-class villas, one of which is the residence of the Rt. Hon. Robert Lowe, M.P.

" In this parish," wrote Aubrey, " are many pleasant valleys, stored with wild thyme, sweet marjoram, burnell, boscage, and beeches." But the bricklayer and scientific agriculturist have changed much of that. There are, however, still bosky valleys and thymey downs about Caterham, and the whole neighbourhood remains perhaps the pleasantest of those near London which have been made the prey of the rly. engineer, speculative builder, and ' Conservative' and ' Commonwealth' building societies.

The huge building or range of buildings on the hill ½ m. away is the *Metropolitan District Imbecile Asylum*, erected in 1869-70 from the designs of Messrs. Giles and Bevan, and enlarged in 1873 by the addition of new wards and a recreation hall 120 ft. long, 35 ft. wide, and 25 ft. high. The building is a plain brick structure,

* Stephen Switzer's Nobleman, Gentleman, and Gardener's Recreation, 1715.
† Words and Places, 2nd ed., p. 252.
‡ *Ibid.*, p. 304.

remarkable chiefly for its extent and the thoroughness with which all the results of medical and hygienic science and experience have been applied. It is constructed on the pavilion system, half a dozen distinct blocks for males on one side, and as many for females on the other, being connected by covered corridors some 550 ft. long; the administrative block, chapel, recreation hall, and various offices occupying the centre, while separate houses for the medical officers, chaplain, etc., stand a little distance apart. The entire cost of the building has been little short of £200,000. There are now in the asylum 1800 pauper inmates, ranging in age from 5 years to over 80.

Caterham, and its neighbours Woldingham, Warlingham, and Chelsham, are locally known as ' the four places on the hills ;' and the hills themselves are crested with numerous camps, probably of British origin. One is on Bottle, Botley, or Battle Hill in Chelsham par.; another and much larger one, known as 'the Cardinal's Cap,' is on the top of White Hill, above Bletchingley (*see* those places). There is a delightful walk of about 2 m. from Caterham to *Woldingham* (which *see*).

CATERHAM JUNCTION, a Stat.

in the S.E. Rly., 3 m. beyond Croydon, is a convenient starting-point for a series of pleasant walks. It is situated near the N. border of the Chalk Downs; *Smitham Bottom*, the valley along which runs the Brighton coach rd., is a narrow belt of Thames alluvium; the scenery around is varied, and the country tolerably open. The old scattered oaks on l., about ½ m. before reaching the stat., mark *Purley Lodge* (W. Hunter, Esq.), once the residence of the regicide Bradshaw, and for several years of John Horne Tooke, who here wrote (as the second title indicates), his 'Επεα Πτεροεντα; or, The Diversions of Purley' (8vo, 1786). Tooke wished to be interred in a vault he had prepared in the garden, but, dying at Wimbledon in 1812, he was buried at Ealing.

The large and palace-like Italian building with a lofty central tower, and turrets at the angles, seen on the hill-side, ½ m. beyond the Rly. Stat. (in *Coulsdon* par.), is *The Asylum for Fatherless Children, Reedham*—so called in honour of the founder, the late Rev. Andrew Reed, D.D. It was erected in 1858 from the designs of Mr. W. B. Moffat; will accommodate 300 children, and in April 1874 had about 270. The conspicuous edifice, of red brick, with black and white brick in bands, tall roofs, and quaint turrets, on Russell Hill, on the opposite side of Smitham Bottom, and in Beddington par., is the *Warehousemen and Clerks' Schools*, for Orphans and Necessitous Children. The first stone was laid by the Prince of Wales, July 11, 1863, and the building was opened by H.R.H., June 18, 1866. It has a frontage of nearly 300 ft., was designed by Mr. Bland, cost £20,000, will accommodate 150 children, and had at the close of 1873 about 130, of whom two-thirds were boys.

Immediately E. of the stat. is *Riddlesdown*, along the summit of which is a delightful breezy stroll. The down is thick with gorse, heath, and the smaller wild flowers; on one side is a coppice of oak, thorn, hazel, and underwood, where on a June morning you may still hear the wood-pigeon and in the evening the nightingale, and all day long the cuckoo, lark, and blackbird. But the S. end has been spoiled by the unfinished Surrey and Sussex Rly.; cultivation is making steady progress along the N. and W. slopes, and in a few years Riddlesdown will be to the tourist only a name. Now holiday-makers from the S. of London come here in considerable numbers in vans and light carts, making the Rose and Crown, at the S.E. edge of the Down, their head-quarters. From Riddlesdown the walk may be extended to *Warlingham*.

If, instead of mounting the hill on leaving the stat., a stroll S. be preferred along the valley, *Stoats Nest*, the now disused stat. of the L. B. and S. Coast Rly., will soon be reached. *Obs.* here on l. of road an uncommonly picturesque old farmhouse of wood and rough-cast, with bay windows, tall overhanging roof, and fine clump of elms in front. With its barns, outhouses, and accessories, the young sketcher would find it an excellent study. The lane beyond, on l., (or one still farther by the Red Lion,) leads to *Coulsdon*. On the rt. is a path up the hill-side to *Woodmansterne;* whence, or from Coulsdon, you may go on to *Chip-*

stead, and return the direct way to the station.

Mantell has noticed the fine sections of chalk, with layers of flint and parallel seams of marl, which the geologist will observe here; the attention of the ordinary visitor may be called to the vast extent of the chalk-pits and lime-works. They afford excellent opportunities for observing sections and obtaining what the boys in the works call 'spozzles.' It was in the pit near Purley that the remarkable granite boulder described by Mr. Godwin-Austen* was discovered by the workmen in raising chalk for lime, and which has become the standard illustration of the movement of boulders by coast ice at the cretaceous period. Mr. Godwin-Austen, after a full consideration of all the circumstances, arrived at the conclusion that this Purley block of granite, with the associated sands, was a compact mass of Polar beach, broken off and drifted away at the annual breaking up of the coast ice, its native home being probably the line of coast "a little to the S. of the 60th degree of N. lat." The deep cuttings of the Surrey and Sussex Rly. will also supply good chalk sections: obs. the band of *Ananchytis ovata* and *Spondylus spinosus* at the S. mouth of the Riddlesdown Tunnel. The upper beds contain many specimens of *Micraster cor anguinum*, and *Inoceramus Cuvieri* in abundance. The district is well described by Mr. Caleb Evans, F.G.S., in 'Some Sections of Chalk between Croydon and Oxtead.'†

CHADWELL HEATH, Essex,

2 m. W. of Romford on the London road, and a Stat. on the Grt. E. Railway, 9½ m. from Bishopsgate St., is a collection of commonplace houses straggling along the highroad, over what was in the last century a heath noted for highwaymen. A little W. of it is another nest of similar houses, known as *Chadwell Street*. *C. Heath* is a hamlet of Dagenham; *C. Street* of Barking: both depend mainly on agriculture.

* Journal of Geol. Soc., Dec. 1858, pp. 252—266.
+ Proceedings of the Geologists' Association, 1870.

CHADWELL ST. MARY,

Essex (Dom. *Celdewella*), 2 m. N. of Tilbury Fort, is an agric. parish of 589 inhab., standing on the chalk hills which here rise steeply from the Thames marshes. The name recalls that of the famous A.-S. saint and Bishop of the Mercians, Ceadda, or Chad, which so often occurs in connection with springs (as Chadswell Springs by Amwell, the source of the New River; St. Chad's Well by Battle Bridge, London, of old renowned for its medicinal qualities; Chadwell by Rothley, Leicestershire). But St. Chad may have had a local relation to the village. St. Cedd, the apostle of the East Saxons, whilst engaged in the conversion of that people, resided at West Tilbury, where his brother was associated with him in his labours. The spring, "discovered in the year 1727," and which became celebrated in the cure of hæmorrhages, scurvy, etc., was possibly only a rediscovery of that from which the place derived its name; the Domesday *Celdewella* is however very suggestive of a cold-spring, and curiously enough the Leicester *Chadwell* has *Caldwell* as an alternative designation.

The *village* consists of two or three farm-houses and a few cottages, with a plain inn (the *Cross Keys*) by the ch. *Chadwell Marsh* extends from the foot of the hill to *Tilbury Fort*, which is partly in Chadwell parish. The marsh affords some singularly Cuyp-like views; and the dykes which drain it abound in bulrushes, sedges, and other members of the genera *Scirpus* and *Typha*.

The *Church* (St. Mary) dates from the E.E. period, but has been often altered. It was restored, and much of it rebuilt, in 1860, when several new Dec. windows were inserted. *Obs.* on S. a lancet, blocked up. By the W. door is a Dec. recess for a holy-water stoup, with places where have been the hinges and fastenings of a door. S. of the altar is a piscina. The tower, Early Dec., has an angle turret half-way up, and quaint gargoyles; the battlements are later.

In *Hanging Wood* (marked *Hangman's Wood* in the Ord. Map), on the road to Stifford, are some of those curious excavations in the chalk which have so sorely puzzled antiquaries, and are commonly known as Danes' Holes, from a tradition that they were lurking-places of

the Danes. Camden describes them, not as rude excavations, but as built-up with much care and skill. There is however no sign of building-up in the ordinary sense of the term. They consist of a central shaft of from 3 to 5 or 6 ft. in diameter, and 60 to 80 ft. deep, opening at the base into a chamber like an inverted funnel, from which passages give access to two or more oval chambers; some occur with five—3 on one side, 2 on the other. The chambers are all hewn out of the chalk, the marks of the pick being still visible. In all, there are in the neighbourhood 5 of these 'holes,' and they correspond closely in size and plan. Similar pits are found in the adjacent parishes of Grays and Little Thurrock, and in East Tilbury some not so deep, the depths evidently depending on the thickness of the chalk, and having only 2 or 3 chambers in all. Others, but with more extensive chambers, and shafts of somewhat larger diameter, occur in great numbers on the opposite side of the Thames at Crayford, Dartford, Chiselhurst, and elsewhere along the chalk hills of Kent. But they are not confined to this part of the country. They are found in the chalk districts of Berkshire, Wiltshire, Herts, and Norfolk, but not, it is said, in Sussex. Pits occur on a larger scale in France and Belgium, but they belong to a different time and class.*
Many speculations have been put forward as to the period and purpose of the Danes' Holes of Kent and Essex, but the probability is that they were originally merely shafts sunk in order to procure chalk for agricultural purposes, though they may later have been used as lurking-places, or places of refuge. Pliny seems to point to some such excavations in his statement that the finer chalk exported from Britain was obtained by means of shafts sunk to a great depth, and then extended at the bottom in the manner of mines.†
Chalk is at the present day excavated in like manner on Salisbury Plain; and even in Kent, when there are no chalk hills near, the farmer finds it less expensive to sink a shaft than to send his carts to a distance for this indispensable

material. Our earlier antiquaries saw in them the subterranean caves which Tacitus says the German tribes employed as granaries, as dwellings in winter, and as hiding-places from invaders.* They are unquestionably of an earlier date than the traditional Danish epoch, since numerous fragments of Roman-British pottery have been found alike in those opened at Grays and in Kent. (*See* CHISELHURST.) The common tradition may after all only be a perversion of the theory of some early Monkbarns. Thus Lambarde,† in speaking of the Crayford caverns, says: " *In the opinion of the inhabitants*, these were in former times digged as well for the use of the chalk towards building, or for to marle (or amend) their arable land therewith. But *I suppose* that they were made to another end also by the Saxons our ancestors, who (after the manner of their elders) used them as receptacles, and places of secret retraict, for their wives, children, and portable goods, in the time both of civil dissension and foreign invasion." Morant, in describing the Chadwell caverns, tells us that "Tradition will have it that here were King Cunobelino's gold mines;" and in the days when the South-Sea mania had set every one speculating, some bold projector acquainted with the tradition started a company "For Improving a Royalty in Essex"—in other words, to dig in the Chadwell caverns for the precious metals. The visitor who may now desire to 'prospect' here for gold, or to resolve the secret of the caves, must submit to be let down the shaft astride a stick fastened to the end of a rope.

CHALDON, SURREY (Dom. *Calvedone*), a rural vill. of 165 inhab., 17 m. from London, 1¾ m. N.E. from Merstham Stat. of the S.E. Rly. (field-path by Alderstead and A. Heath). The vill. lies on the N. of the chalk hills, away from any main road.

The *Church* (St. Peter and St. Paul) is of flint and st., with, at the S.W. angle, a sq. tower and thin shingle spire; on the S. a plain porch, and tall red-tiled roofs. It is E.E., with later insertions: *note* flamboyant window to chancel aisle. The E.

---

* See Prof. Von Benenden on the Caves of Louvain.
† Nat. Hist., Lib. xvii., ch. 8.

* Germania, xvi.
† Perambulation of Kent, 1596, reprint, p. 401.

window is a triple lancet, there is a small lancet in base of tower, and W. of the nave is a small round-arched window of what looks much like Saxon long and short work. It was restored in 1870, under the direction of Mr. R. Martin, when on removing the whitewash from the internal walls some very early and curious paintings were discovered, representing the Last Judgment; they have been described, and illustrated with chromolithographs, by Mr. Waller, in the 'Surrey Archæological Collections,' 1872. W. of the ch. is a spreading yew. By the ch.-yard is a rookery, and beyond a farmhouse named from it. Altogether the ch. and its surroundings are unusually picturesque, in a quiet rustic way. On all sides are charming strolls: N.E. through the bottom and the copse beyond, to Coulsdon Common and ch.; by the thatched wooden cottages and narrow gritty lane (the banks crowded with primroses) S.E. to Caterham; or W., over the hill, to Chipstead.

CHALFONT ST. GILES, BUCKS

(Dom. *Celfunde;* locally *Charfunt*), a quiet little out-of-the-way village, 5 m. from the nearest rly. stat., Rickmansworth (on the Watford and R. branch of the L. and N.W. line), and 7½ m. from the Uxbridge Stat. of the Grt. W. Rly.; pop. of the par. 1243; is situated on the Misbourne, a feeder of the Colne, and a little to the l. of the Amersham road, on a byroad to Beaconsfield. The interest of the place centres on its connection with Milton, but, as we shall see, it has other associations; is itself a pretty little place, stands in a pleasant country, there is a fishery on the stream, and altogether is well worth a visit.

Milton retired here in 1665, from the plague then raging in London, to "a pretty box" which his friend Thomas Elwood, the Quaker, had hired for him; and in it he finished ' Paradise Lost,' and, at Elwood's suggestion, planned, and in part wrote ' Paradise Regained.' He did not return to London till "the sickness was over and the city well cleansed, and become safely habitable."

Milton's house, on the rt. near the end of the vill., is a plain half-timber, gable-fronted cottage, with projecting brick chimney, and a little garden before it.

The house is said to have been originally much larger: the porch, shown in some engravings, and under which tradition affirmed the poet was wont to sit, was removed several years ago. Milton's name is inscribed over the door, and on a stone are carved the arms of the Fleetwood family, to whom the house belonged. The parlour, a little low room, on the rt. as you enter, with a single long, low window, is pointed out as that in which the Blind Bard dictated his second great epic, and looks as though it had been little altered, except by age, since he occupied it.

The *Church*, prettily situated just above the Misbourne, here crossed by a foot-bridge, is of flint and stone, and consists of nave and aisles with clerestorey, chancel, and Norman tower at the W. end. The style, somewhat mixed, was chiefly Dec., but in restoring it, 1862, the later portions were removed, and some E.E. features added. In the chancel is an altar-tomb of Thos. Fleetwood, Lord of the Vache, d. 1570, with brasses affixed representing Fleetwood in plate-armour, with his two wives, kneeling,—4 children kneeling behind one wife, and 14 behind the other. In marked contrast with this is the florid marble mont. with urn and flowers and weeping children, of a later Lord of the Vache, James Clayton, d. 1714. Another mural mont. is to Admiral Sir Hugh Pallisser, of the Vache, d. 1796. There are many other monts. of Chalfont families, but none worth noticing. Bp. Hare was buried in the ch., but has no mont. *Obs.* the *Lich-gate*, old and unspoiled, at the entrance to the ch.-yard.

The *Vache* (T. Newland Allen, Esq.), on an eminence about a mile N.E. from Chalfont ch., is the old manor-house, formerly a moated mansion, with a chapel; but the chapel was destroyed and the moat filled up when the house was rebuilt many years ago. The brick building, with a pedestal in front of it, is a memorial to Capt. James Cook, "the ablest and most renowned navigator this or any other country hath produced," erected by his friend Adml. Sir Hugh Pallisser, Lord of the Vache. The origin of this name has been a subject of some speculation. The manor belonged in the 14th cent. to Richard de la Veche, but whether he

Chalfont St. Giles

Chertsey Bridge (see p.92)

derived his name from, or gave it to, the place is uncertain. A local tradition makes the original Vache to have been King John's dairy. King John may be dismissed as merely one of those mythical nuclei that seem requisite to the crystallization and preservation of a tradition, but it may be worth noting, for those who think traditions "have mostly something in them," that *vachery* was a mediæval term for a dairy.* Other seats are the *Stone* (Rev. Edw. Moore); the *Grove* (Mrs. Priestley); and *Misbourne House* (A. Davis, Esq.)

Milton's House is not the only place of pilgrimage at Chalfont. At the little hamlet of *Jordans*, about 1½ m. from Chalfont ch., in a pretty secluded nook on the rt. of the road to Beaconsfield, is a small plain brick Friends' Meeting House, and at the back of it an equally modest burial-ground. Both have long ceased to be used, but they are reverentially preserved. Here, on the 5th of Aug., 1718, in the presence of a great assemblage of Friends, were deposited the remains of WILLIAM PENN, the founder of Pennsylvania ; beside him lie the remains of his two wives and five children. No stone or monumental record marks the grave of Penn, or of any of the many men of mark in the early history of the sect who were buried along with him in this the Campo Santo of Quakerdom. But whilst the sites of most have faded from the memory, tradition has preserved his. It is under the fifth mound from the chapel door that Penn lies, between his two wives. One of the graves close by is that of Milton's friend, Thomas Elwood.

CHALFONT ST. PETER'S (pop.

1459, of whom 327 belong to the eccl. dist. of Gerard's Cross) is 2 m. nearer Uxbridge than Chalfont St. Giles. The Misbourne runs through the midst of the village, uncrossed by a bridge. A market was once held here ; and formerly a large building stood in the centre of the vill., which the notorious Judge Jeffries, then a resident at the *Grange*, just outside the vill. on the road to Uxbridge, caused to be erected for a Sessions House. It was afterwards converted into a large inn,

* Promptorium parvulorum, *in loc.*

the Swan, but when railways destroyed the posting trade it was found to exceed the requirements of the locality, and was pulled down, 1837. The stables and some of the outbuildings now form part of the Swan Farm.

The *Church*, formerly a plain brick building of the reign of George I., was very ingeniously transformed and mediævalized a few years ago by Mr. E. G. Street, R.A. There are several monts. of the Bayley, Denry, Gould, and Whitchurch families : also good *brasses* of William Whapclode, 1388 ; John Whapclode, seneschal of Cardinal Beaufort, 1446 ; and Robert Hansom, the last Roman Catholic incumbent of Chalfont St. Peter's, d. 1548.

Chalfont Park (J. N. Hibbert, Esq.), S. of the vill., occupies the site of the ancient manor-house of Brudenells. The present mansion was built by General Churchill, the brother-in-law of Horace Walpole, who gave his best advice in its erection, and who thought Chute's design "the sweetest plan imaginable." The park is charming, undulatory, richly wooded, and has the Misbourne winding through it. In it is the largest ash in England : the trunk is said to be 25 ft. in circ. ; here also is the first Lombardy poplar planted in this country. *Newland Park*, the property of T. N. Allen, Esq., was, till his death in 1807, the seat of Abraham Newland, Esq., of the Bank of England, whose signature to the banknotes made his name universally familiar.

The *Obelisk* at the Crossways, ½ m. from the vill., was erected, 1770, in commemoration of George III. having been in at the death of a stag at this spot, at the close of a long run. The obelisk, which is of brick, and 50 ft. high, is a conspicuous landmark.

CHARLTON, KENT (A.-S. *Ceorle-*

ton, from *Ceorle*, a husbandman ; Dom. *Cerletone*), on the high ground between Greenwich and Woolwich, and reaching down to the Thames, 7 m. from London by rd., 8 m. by the North Kent line of the S.E. Rly. [on leaving the stat. turn rt. *up* the lane ; the ch. is ½ m. S.] Inn, the *Bugle Horn*, opposite the ch. A few years ago Charlton was a charming country vill., but, though still green and pleasant, it has pretty well lost its rural character, having been much built over, and constantly absorbing a large proportion of the redundant population of Woolwich. The pop. of Charlton *vill.* was 2444 in 1871, but the entire parish, including the eccl. district, of Old Charlton, and parts of Kidbroke, and St. Thomas, Woolwich, was 7699.

The manor of Charlton was given by William I. to his half-brother Odo, Bp. of Bayeux; from him it passed to Robert Bloet, Bp. of Lincoln, who, about 1093, gave it to the priory of St. Saviour's, Bermondsey. At the Dissolution it reverted to the Crown. James I. granted it to one of his northern followers, John Earl of Mar, who, in 1606, sold it to his countryman, Sir James Erskine, for £2000, and he, the following year, disposed of it for £4500 to another northern knight, Sir Adam Newton, tutor to Henry Prince of Wales. It was alienated in 1659 to Sir Wm. Ducie, afterwards Visct. Downe, who died here in 1679. It then passed successively to the Langhornes, Games, and Maryons, and by bequest to Lady Spencer Wilson, from whom it has descended to the present owner, Sir John Maryon Wilson, Bart.

The manor-house, *Charlton House*, immediately S. of the ch., was commenced by Sir Adam Newton in 1607, and completed in 1612. Inigo Jones is said to have been the architect. He lived at Charlton, in a house built by himself, and afterwards known as Cherry Garden Farm, and he was architect to Prince Henry. But the strongest support to the tradition is in the character of the building. It is a capital example of the florid Jacobean type—quaint, elaborately ornate, but very picturesque; and it is strikingly like Charlton in Wilts (the Earl of Suffolk's), built by Inigo Jones about the same time. It is of red brick and stone; the plan, that of a capital E, in form an oblong, with projecting wings and porch, the latter richly decorated, a sq. turret at each end, and a balustrade along the summit. The int. has a large central hall, panelled with oak, and profusely ornamented; a grand staircase of chesnut, fancifully carved; a principal dining room, with chapel adjoining; a grand saloon, with a ceiling of elaborate design, and a rich and lofty chimneypiece; and an oak gallery on the N., 76 ft. by 16, in which are some good family pictures. The grounds, of about 70 acres, are very fine, but, like the house, strictly closed against strangers. Evelyn writes, June 9th, 1653, "Went to visit my worthy neighbour, Sir Henry Newton, and consider the prospect, which is, doubtless, for city, river, ships, meadows, hills, woods, and all other amenities, one of the most noble in the world; so as had the house running water, it were a princely seat." The march of the builder has seriously curtailed these amenities, but the prospect is still "most noble."

The *Church* (St. Luke) is of red brick, and consists of nave, aisles, and tower. It was erected by Sir Adam Newton's trustees, 1630-40; the chancel in 1840. Of its architectural character the less said the better, though Hasted* declares that "when finished it surpassed in beauty most churches in the county." The int., aided by its carved pulpit, tall pews, and showy monts., furnishes a fair example of a 17th cent. ch. *Monts.*—In N. aisle of chancel, Sir Adam Newton, d. 1629, and wife; a plain work by Nicholas Stone, for which, as we learn by his pocket-book, he received £180. Near the pulpit, a life-size statue in armour with baton in rt. hand, and military trophies, of the Hon. M. Richards, Surveyor-General of the Ordnance, d. 1721. Marble statue, by Westmacott, of Sir Thos. Hislop, G.C.B., d. 1834. Sir William Congreve, d. 1828, inventor of the rockets named after him. *Obs.* also the mont. of Mrs. F. Hoare (a Dingley by birth), d. 1799, for whose portrait, by Reynolds, the Marquis of Hertford gave 2550 guineas in 1859. Some other memorials have a melancholy interest. Tablet, by Chantrey, to the Rt. Hon. Spencer Perceval, who was shot by one Bellingham in the lobby of the H. of Commons, May 11, 1812. In the ch.-yard (the gate of which is kept locked), by the porch, Mr. Edw. Drummond, who was shot at Charing Cross, Jan. 20, 1843, in mistake for another Prime Minister, Sir Robert Peel, whose private secretary he was. In the ch.-yard is the tomb of James Craggs, Esq., Postmaster-General, and father of Pope's friend, Secretary Craggs, who in consequence of the scandal created by their connection with the

---

* Hist. of Kent, vol. i., p. 39.

South Sea Bubble, destroyed himself by poison, March 28th, 1721. Henry Oldenburg, whose services as secretary to the Royal Society were of so much value to science in England, d. at his residence, Charlton, Sept. 1677, and was buried in the ch., but without a mont.

The old ch. having become insufficient for the increasing pop., another ch., St. Thomas, was erected at *New Charlton* in 1850; and in March 1867 a third ch., St. Paul, was consecrated at Old Charlton, of better design, cruciform, Mr. W. Wiggington, archt.

Besides Charlton House, there are several superior residences in the par., but none that require particularization. It was to a house at Charlton, which had some time previously been occupied by Mrs. Fitzherbert, that Caroline Princess of Wales retired in 1795, with her infant (the Princess Charlotte), of 3 months old : she retained possession of the house for about 2 years. *Morden College*, noticed under BLACKHEATH, is in Charlton par., and *Kidbrooke* is an extra-parochial hamlet of it.

In 1268 Charlton received the grant of a weekly market, to be held on Monday, and an annual fair for 3 days. The market has long ceased; and the fair became in course of time an intolerable nuisance. De Foe* wrote in 1725, " Charlton is a village famous, or rather infamous, for that yearly-collected rabble of mad people at *Horn Fair*." It was held on St. Luke's Day (Oct. 18), the proceedings being ushered in by a sermon preached in the ch. "It is said (by a vague and absurd tradition) to have owed its origin to a compulsive grant made by King John, or some other of our kings, when detected in an affair of gallantry, being then resident at Eltham Palace."† In the vulgar opinion the tradition was, even to our own day, considered to be proved by the point of land by the river-side, to which the grant was supposed to extend, being named Cuckold's Point. Philipott, writing in 1659, says "it is called Horn-fair by reason of the great plenty of all sorts of winding horns and cups, and other vessels of horn then brought to be sold." This to the last continued to be the

character of the fair; horns of all kinds decorating the booths and shows, and being worn by the rougher visitors. For many years a burlesque procession, in which every person wore horns, used to proceed from Deptford through Greenwich to Charlton fair, but in consequence of the turbulent scenes to which it gave rise, it was abolished in 1768. The fair itself, after being tolerated for another century, was finally suppressed by an order issued by the Home Secretary, in March 1872.

Charlton is of interest to the geologist as affording the best illustration near London of the junction of the chalk with the Lower Tertiary strata. This is well seen in the great pit E. of the rly. stat. The chalk with flints, of a jointed structure, is overlaid by Thanet sands 35 ft. thick, having at the base a bed of green-coated flints. Above the Thanet sands are the sands, pebble-beds, and clays of the Woolwich and Reading series. The chalk abounds in characteristic fossils, which may be procured *in situ*, or purchased of the pitmen. The sands are less prolific, but various plants, and vertebræ and teeth of the shark, *Lamna elegans*, have been found here. The sands may be more conveniently examined in the sand-pit farther E.

Lower Charlton, by the Thames, is really a part of Woolwich. Off Charlton Pier is moored the Marine Society's training ship Warspite.

CHARTER ISLAND (*see* WRAYSBURY).

CHEAM, SURREY (A.-S. *Cheyham;* Dom. *Ceiham*), is a vill. and stat. on the Epsom branch of the London, Br., and S. C. Rly., 14 m. from London, midway between Sutton and Ewell, and 3 m. N.E. from Epsom ; pop. 1629.

Cheam stands on high ground amidst pleasant and varied scenery ; the ch. and centre of the vill. on what geologists know as the Reading sand ; the rly. stat. and S. side of the vill. on the chalk, a narrow belt of Thanet sand intervening ; whilst the N. part of the par. is London clay. At the Domesday Survey the manor belonged to the see of Canterbury. It was subsequently divided into West Cheam and East Cheam, West Cheam being appropriated to the prior and convent of

---

* Tour through Great Britain, vol. i., Letter 2.
† Lysons, vol. ii., p. 431.

Christ Church; East Cheam to the archbishop. In the reign of Henry VIII. both were alienated to the Crown, and in the reign of Elizabeth became the property of Lord John Lumley. He dying without surviving issue, the united manor devolved to his nephew, Henry Lloyd, son of Humphrey Lloyd, the antiquary, whose descendant, Dr. Robert Lumley Lloyd, bequeathed the manors, 1729, to John Duke of Bedford, who, in 1755, sold them to Edw. Northey, Esq., whose descendant, E. R. Northey, Esq., is the present owner.

East Cheam manor-house (about ½ m. E., towards Sutton), of Elizabethan date, was pulled down about 1795, and the present mansion erected by J. Antrobus, Esq. It is now called *Lower Cheam Park*, and is the seat of H. Lindsay Antrobus, Esq. West Cheam manor-house has also long been pulled down. *Whitehall* (Miss Killick, whose family have held it for a century and a half), an old timber house by the ch., contains a room known as the council chamber, from a tradition that it was used by Queen Elizabeth, when at Nonsuch Palace, for state affairs. Beneath the house are large vaults excavated in the sandstone.

Cheam *Church* (St. Dunstan) was erected 1862-64, from the designs of Mr. Pownall. It is large and handsome, of hammered stone, E.E. in style, and has a massive tower at the W. The interior is of red brick, with bands of black bricks and stone; the nave and aisles are divided by shafts of Purbeck marble, which support 5 pointed arches and a clerestorey. The apse is lighted by 4 lancets, with a rose window above.

Alongside it, but detached, is the chancel of the old ch., preserved for the *Monts.*, which are of much interest. The most striking is that of John Lord Lumley (d. 1609)—the great book collector of the reign of Elizabeth, whose library was bought by James I., and became the foundation of the Royal Library now in the British Museum. The mont. is in the Lumley aisle, built for the purpose by Lord Lumley in 1592. It is a lofty mural structure of many coloured marbles; the arms of all the Lumleys are around it, and an enormously long Latin inscription traces the pedigree back through 16 generations to Liulph the Anglo-Saxon. Happily, Lord Lumley did not carry his veneration for his ancestors quite so far as he did at the ch. of Chester-le-Street, Durham, opposite Lumley Castle, where " he caused monuments to be erected for them in the order as they succeeded one another, from Liulphus down to his own time; which he had either picked out of the demolished monasteries, or made new." * S. of the chancel is a large marble mont., with kneeling effigy, of Jane Lady Lumley (d. 1577), who translated the Iphigenia of Euripides, and some of the orations of Isocrates; and on the N. one of Elizabeth, Lord Lumley's second wife, a recumbent alabaster effigy under an arch, " chequered with cinquefoils and popinjays." In the Fromond chapel were one or two brasses, and other memorials of various members of that family. The brasses have been removed, and are now in the possession of the vicar. The most interesting is a mural brass of Thos. Fremond, Esq., d. 1542, and wife Elizabeth, kneeling, their 6 sons and 4 daughters behind them; above the group was a shield of arms, long lost, and over this a rude representation of the Trinity—the Father holding a cross before Him, on which the Dove is descending. On removing the old ch. tower, a stone coffin was found *in situ*, containing the body of a priest and a pewter chalice.† It was in Cheam old ch. that Sidney Smith was married, July 2, 1800, to Miss Catherine Amelia Pybus.

It is noted that of six successive rectors of Cheam in the 16th and 17th centuries, five were created bishops. Two or three were men of fame : the learned Lancelot Andrews, Bp. of Chichester ; Richard Senhouse, Bp. of Carlisle ; and John Hacket, Bp. of Lichfield and Coventry. Hacket, then holding the living of St. Andrew's, Holborn, was presented to the rectory of Cheam by his patron, the Lord Keeper Williams, who accompanied the gift with the rhyme,

" Holborn for wealth,
And Cheam for health."

Hacket retained Holborn, accepted Cheam, and lived to a good old age. " Myself,"

* Camden, Britannia.
† Heale and Percival, ' Monumental Memoranda from Cheam Church,' Surrey Archæol. Coll., vol. iii., p. 325.

he says in his 'Life of Lord Keeper Williams,' folio, 1693, p. 11, "have been rector of Cheam now above 30 years." He repaid his debt to his patron by becoming his biographer.

A new *Church* (St. Philip), E.E. in style, was erected on Cheam Common, 1873-74, from the designs of Mr. H. H. Carpenter. At *Cheam School*, once in high repute, the Rev. Wm. Gilpin, author of 'Forest Scenery,' was for some time master, and Glover, the author of 'Leonidas,' was educated. In its later days Cheam School was converted into a Pestalozzian Academy. A new Cheam School (Rev. Robert Tabor) was erected in 1867 from the designs of Messrs. Slater and Carpenter. *Nonsuch Palace* stood a little W. of Cheam. (*See* NONSUCH.)

CHELSFIELD, KENT, a pretty country vill., lying 1½ m. on the E. of the Sevenoaks road, 2 m. beyond Orpington, and a Stat. on the S.E. Rly. (Tunbridge direct line), 15 m. from London: pop. of the par. 903.

The *Church* (St. Margaret), somewhat rude, but venerable and picturesque, will repay a visit. It stands just outside the vill., on the W., the way to it being by a field-path lined with large lime trees. It is of flint and stone, the W. end overgrown with ivy, and consists of nave and chancel, with aisles, and on the N., between the nave and chancel, a massive E.E. tower, capped with a shingled spire, and containing 5 bells. The interior is less venerable in aspect than the exterior, having been restored and refitted, but it is spacious, and has considerable character. The nave is Dec.; the chancel, E.E. At the E. end are three lancet windows, separated by detached banded shafts, and filled with painted glass. On the N. side, by the priest's door, is a hagioscope, partly blocked up. N. of the chancel, within an arched recess, is a coped tomb, of Purbeck marble, to Robert de Bruñ (d. 1417), which has had small brasses of the Crucifixion, with the Virgin on one side and St. John on the other; but only the body of St. John is left. A corresponding tomb of black marble, but without brasses, to George Smyth (rector 1668), occupies the opposite recess. On the chancel floor are undersized brasses of Wm. Robroke (rector 1420); Alice, wife

of Thos. Bray, and 4 sons (1510); another without name or date, but of the end of the 15th cent., to a man and wife (the former gone), 6 sons (of whom 2 are priests), and 5 daughters. *Monts.*— Peter Collet, alderman (d. 1607), with kneeling effigies of alabaster, coloured, of Collet and his wife, with 2 daughters kneeling behind her, and 2 younger deceased children, recumbent below. Alongside is a small effigy of a grandchild of Ald. Collet. *Mural*, of a civic celebrity of the last century, Ald. Brass Crosby, who, as Lord Mayor, not only set at liberty Miller, the printer arrested in the City under the Speaker's warrant for printing the Wilkes debates, but ordered the officers of the House of Commons to give bail to answer a charge of assault. For this Crosby was committed to the Tower (March 18, 1771), where he remained till the Parliament was prorogued, six months later—he, during that interval, almost rivalling Wilkes in popularity. He died a few months after his release from the Tower. *Obs.* the handsome new font.

The chief seat is *Woodlands* (W. Waring, Esq., lord of the manor). The vill. stands on high ground, and there are extensive views from the fields and lanes close by: the finest, perhaps, being that from *Well Hill*, a short distance E. There are also pleasant walks *across the fields* N.W. to ORPINGTON, and S. to HALSTEAD, both places worth visiting (*see* those headings).

CHELSHAM, SURREY (Dom. *Celesham*, perhaps from *Ceosel*, gravel, and *ham*, referring to the remarkable gravel beds noticed below), 2½ m. E. by N. from Warlingham Stat. of the S.E. Rly. (Caterham branch): pop. 399. From *Warlingham Common* continue nearly E. by Bull Green, Holt Wood, and The Ledgers, to Chelsham ch.

Chelsham is a charming place for a holiday ramble. The scenery is unusually varied, and there is much to employ the geologist, the botanist, the antiquary, and the sketcher. There is no vill.: the ch. stands on high ground (Chelsham is one of "the four places on the hills," *see* CATERHAM), and from the ch.-yd. there is a fine view N., the Crystal Palace forming a conspicuous landmark.

The *Church* (St. Leonard) is small;

rough-cast; has a nave with Perp. windows, chancel with Dec. E. window, S. porch, and a heavy sq. W. tower. In the head of a window, N. of the nave, are two or three fragments of old painted glass; in the chancel is a piscina; the font is E.E., of Purbeck marble. The ch. was restored in 1871, when a new E. window and 2 lancets were inserted in the chancel, and 3 new windows in the nave; new and higher roofs have been substituted for the old ones, and new seats for the old pews, and the old rood screen repaired, altered, and refixed, whilst outside the old brick buttresses of the tower have been replaced by stone ones. The building is undoubtedly improved by these changes, but the visitor must remember that all that looks characteristic is *new* work, not old. The tower formerly contained two bells, but in 1834 some thieves entered the ch. one night and stole one of them; neither thief nor bell was ever discovered. The three yews in the ch.-yd. were planted by Wm. Phillips, a schoolmaster of Chelsham, in 1746.

The stately modern Jacobean mansion W. of the ch., is *Ledgers* (Baron Sir A. Cleasby). *Chelsham Court*, now a farmhouse, is ½ m. S.

A short ½ m. farther, S.W., is *Worms Heath*—glorious with fern and furze and " never bloomless heather "—affording splendid prospects, and where are several pits, traditionally said to have been hiding-places during the ravages of the Danes (but *see* BLACKHEATH and CHADWELL). These pits are, however, very different from the Chadwell Danes' Holes. They are mere hollows dug in the gravel, and vary in size from 20 yards to less than 10 in diameter, and in depth from 6 to 10 or more feet. They are basin-shaped, the sides sloping evenly at about the angle at which gravel would rest after the edges of a hole with steep or vertical sides had been acted upon by rain and frost. It is not easy to guess for what purpose these pits were dug. The large recent gravel-pit of the ordinary kind, close at hand, points out a more obvious and easier way of excavating for the material, and yet that is perhaps the most probable purpose that can be suggested. There is a peculiarity in the gravel that is worth noticing. The pebbles are water-worn, and for the most part cemented together by a rich red-rusty clay, which has in some cases become so hardened as to convert the gravel into a conglomerate. The cement is then of such hardness, and adheres so firmly to the pebbles, that they may be broken rather than detached from the mass. Examples are very common, the blocks being locally known as *plum-pudding stones*. This part of Worms Heath is called *The Camp*, but there are now no traces of an entrenchment. On *Botley*, or *Bottle* [i.e. *Battle*] *Hill*, 1¼ m. S.E. of Worms Heath, are vestiges of an ancient camp, "oblong and single-ditched." On *Nore Hill*, nearer Worms Heath, used to stand one of the Government semaphores: from it there is a wide prospect. On the W. side of Worms Heath is *Slines Oaks* (Rev. E. F. Beynon), a good house in a beautiful park.

CHERTSEY, SURREY (A.-S. *Cero-tæsai, Cerotesege,—i.e.* Cerota's ey, or island; Dom. *Certesyg*), a mkt. town pleasantly situated on the l. bank of the Thames, 19 m. from London by rd., and a Stat., 22½ m., on the Chertsey and Virginia Water branch of the L. and S.W. Rly.; pop. of the town 3146. Inns: the *Swan*, Windsor Street; *Crown*, London Street.

Chertsey was celebrated in former times for its Abbey, and is still distinguished as the last retreat of the poet Cowley, and by the vicinity of St. Anne's Hill, the favourite residence of the statesman Fox. The town grew up under the wing of the great monastery, which seems to have been originally founded under Egbert, King of Kent, in 666, by the famous A.-S. saint Erkenwald, the founder of Barking Abbey. But the oldest charter is one of Frithwald, subregulus of Surrey, printed by Kemble,[*] who assigns the date " before 675." It sets forth the boundaries of the abbey lands with much minuteness and precision; and most of the landmarks have been identified by Mr. Corner in a paper full of interest, not only to the local antiquary, but to every student of our early history.[†] Frithwald says in his charter, "I give grant and transfer for the

* Codex Dip. Ævi Saxonici, vol. v., p. 14.
† Trans. of the Surrey Archæological Soc., vol. i., p. 77, etc.

augmentation of the monastery, which was first established under King Egbert and called Cirotesege, the land of 200 inhabitants, and five dwellings in Thorp. And not only do I give the land, but I also confirm and surrender myself and my only son, in obedience to Erkenwald the Abbot." The charter is signed by Frithwald and Erkenwald, and for confirmation by Wulfhere, King of the Mercians.

Chertsey was the first religious house established in Surrey, and Erkenwald ruled over it till he was elected Bishop of London in 675, but it does not appear to have become as celebrated for the miracles performed in it as the sister foundation. (See BARKING.) Its site was a grassy island formed by the Thames and the little stream now known as the Abbey River or Bourne. The grants to the monastery were confirmed by Offa, King of the Mercians, in 787, by Ethelwulf, King of Wessex, in 827, and by King Alfred about 890; but somewhat later the Danes burned the ch. and conventual buildings, and slaughtered Beoçca, the abbot, and the monks, 90 in number. It was re-established as a Benedictine convent by Edgar in 964; its possessions were augmented by Edward the Confessor, and on several subsequent occasions it received royal favours. Its most flourishing period was, perhaps, during the reigns of Edward II. and Edward III., when its abbot was John de Rutherwyke, who, according to the Chertsey Ledger Book, preserved among the Exchequer Records, "might be termed the convent's second founder." The superior of the monastery, a mitred abbot, and a baron by tenure, lived in great dignity and splendour. At the Dissolution the net revenue was £659. On the surrender of the monastery, July 6, 1537, the abbot and monks were removed to the dissolved priory of Bisham in Berkshire, which Henry had refounded for a mitred abbot and 13 Benedictine monks; but a few months later the abbot was compelled to surrender the new monastery, and the monks were finally dispersed.

In the great ch. of Chertsey Abbey many distinguished personages were interred; but it is chiefly remarkable as having been the resting-place for a short period of the remains of Henry VI. It was when on her way "toward Chertsey, with her holy load," that the Lady Anne encountered Richard of Gloucester.* The body was in fact conveyed from Blackfriars to Chertsey by water, and was interred there with much solemnity. It was removed to Windsor by Richard III. in the second year of his reign. Chertsey appears to have been in some favour with King Henry, for he had granted to the abbot the right of holding a fair on St. Anne's Hill, on the 26th of July (St. Anne's Day). This fair is now represented by the so-called "Black Cherry Fair," which is held in the town on the 6th of August. Another great fair, for horses, cattle, and poultry, is held on September 25th. This is commonly known as the "Goose and Onion Fair," a fair for geese and onions being held at the same time, though distinct from the cattle fair: the tolls of these fairs are still taken by the owner of the Abbey House.

Of the once stately buildings, which occupied an area of four acres, few vestiges remain. A lane beyond the parish ch. leads direct to the abbey bridge, crossing the little Abbey river, where will be found the fragment of an arch, which, with the wall in which it stands and portions of a large barn opposite, serve to mark the locality of Erkenwald's foundation. The precise date of the demolition of the buildings is not known. Aubrey writes in 1673, "Of this great abbey scarce anything of the buildings remains except the out-walls about it. . . . The town lies very low; and the streets are all raised by the ruins of the abbey." † Stukeley, writing to Dr. Ducarel, Oct. 1752, declares that the ancient buildings had then all but disappeared. "So total a dissolution I scarcely every saw. . . . Of that noble and splendid pile, which took up four acres of ground and looked like a town, nothing remains. . . . Human bones of the abbots, monks, and great personages, who were buried in great numbers in the church, were spread thick all over the garden, which takes up the whole church and cloisters; so that we may pick up handfuls of bits of bone at a time everywhere among the garden

---

* King Richard III., act i., sc. 2.
† Antiq. of Surrey, vol. iii., p. 174.

stuff. Foundations of the religious buildings have been dug up, carved stones, slender pillars of Sussex marble, monumental stones, effigies, crosses, inscriptions, everywhere, even beyond the terraces of the pleasure-garden." *

The site of the abbey is now occupied by a market-garden. The ground had been several times examined, and various relics exhumed, but in 1853, and subsequently, systematic excavations were made all over the site, under the direction of Mr. S. Angell, an architect resident within the precincts of the monastery, and have yielded very valuable results. The ground plan of the ch., which appears to have been 275 ft. long by 63 ft. wide, with three apses, was laid open in 1861, as well as that of an adjoining building of considerable extent, supposed to have been the chapter-house. The stone seats running round this apartment, and supporting a series of bases of columns of Purbeck marble, were found in an undisturbed state. A coffin of Purbeck marble, containing the body of a priest wrapped in lead; richly sculptured capitals of Purbeck marble, and many other architectural fragments; a metal chalice and paten, and a large number of encaustic pavement tiles, of a character peculiar to Chertsey, were discovered. Specimens of the tiles, which are very remarkable, have been deposited in the Architectural Museum, and copied in colours by Mr. H. Shaw in his 'Specimens of Tile Pavements.' Some may still be seen *in situ*, and some are in the Museum of the Surrey · Archæological Society at the Town Hall. Mr. Shaw says that the Chertsey pavement, "in its original state, must have been one of the most gorgeous in point of design, as it is one of most beautiful in point of execution, of any example of the 13th cent. yet discovered." It is remarkable that some fine pavement tiles exhumed on the site of Hales Owen Priory, Worcestershire, in the autumn of 1870, were identical in design—the subjects being from the story of Tristram—with some of those from Chertsey Abbey, and must, indeed, have been moulded with the same stamp. The ch. and chapter-house, with their architectural vestiges, were suffered to remain

undisturbed, but subsequent neglect and exposure to rain and frost have reduced them to a miserable condition. In the garden may still be traced the conventual stews or fish-ponds, running parallel to each other like the bars of a gridiron.

The site and buildings of the abbey were granted by James I. to his physician, Dr. Hammond, to whose son, the eminent divine who attended Charles I. at Carisbrooke, and is said to have been born in the abbey here in 1605, they descended. Sir Nicholas Carew, of Beddington, the next owner, " built a fair house out of the ruins," which was pulled down in 1810. The site of the abbey ch. passed through various hands, till in 1861 it was purchased by Mr. T. R. Bartrop, of the Abbey Mills.

The *Town* consists mainly of two long streets, crossing each other in the centre, and named, from the direction in which they run, London Street, Windsor Street, and Guildford Street. The ch. stands near the centre of the town, and near it is the Town Hall, a neat red-brick building erected in 1851. The market is held in and about the market-house on Wednesday. Chertsey has a considerable agricultural trade; there is a brewery; and the Abbey Mills still flourish on the ancient site.

The par. *Church* (All Saints), rebuilt in 1806-8, all but the chancel and tower (and that was repaired and heightened with brick), is large, but of the merest builder's design. In 1869 the interior was 'restored,' partially remodelled, the tall pews cut down, the chancel altered, and oak stalls introduced, a reredos of Caen stone with shafts of Devonshire marble erected, and the E. window filled with painted glass by Clayton and Bell, as a memorial to the late Rev. J. C. Clark, of Cowley House, a great benefactor to the town.

A few *monts.* are worth looking at. In the chancel one to Eliza Mawbey (d. 1819, æt. 20), which has a fine bas-relief, by Flaxman, of Christ raising the Daughter of Jairus. A black marble tablet with a long insc. to Laurence Tomson (d. 1608), a great traveller, wit, and scholar, " distinguished by his acquaintance with 12 languages, with theology, with civil and municipal law, and with the whole circle

---

* Gent. Mag., March 1797.

of polite literature and science," celebrated as Professor of Hebrew at Geneva, much employed by Walsingham, and author of an English translation of the New Testament, which was twice reprinted, in the reign of Elizabeth. In the S. aisle is a marble tablet to CHARLES JAMES FOX, erected by his widow "to the best of husbands and the most excellent of men." Fox was buried in Westminster Abbey : his widow, who survived him till 1842, lies in a vault at the N.E. end of Chertsey ch.-yd. In the tower is a peal of 6 bells : one, said to have been brought from the abbey, has inscribed on it, in A.-S. capitals :

ORA : MENTE : PIA : PRO : NOBIS : VIRGO : MARIA.

During the winter months the curfew bell is still tolled every evening at 8, with the curious addition that at the close, after a brief pause, the day of the month is tolled.

Cowley House (C. J. Worthington, Esq.), the house in which Cowley spent his last days—

"Courtly, though retired ;
Though stretched at ease in Chertsey's silent bowers,
Not unemployed, and finding rich amends
For a lost world in solitude and verse," *

is on the W. side of Guildford Street, near the rly. stat. Disappointed in his hopes of the Court, Cowley resolved to husband his small fortune, and indulge a desire he had long cherished, "by withdrawing himself from the tumult and business of the world, and consecrating the little rest of his time to those studies to which Nature had so motherly inclined him, and from which Fortune, like a step-mother, had so long detained him." He first took a house at Barn Elms, but was there "afflicted with a dangerous and lingering fever," and as soon as his health permitted (April 1665) removed to Chertsey, having obtained, says his friend and biographer Bp. Sprat, "by the interest of the Earl of St. Alban's and the Duke of Buckingham, such a lease of the Queen's lands there as afforded him an ample income." In his Essay ' Of Greatness,' he has described the sort of retreat he longed to possess : "A little convenient estate, a little cheerful house, a little company, and a very little feast." The house itself he would

* Cowper, Task, Book V.

have " a convenient brick house, with decent wainscot, and pretty forest-work hangings :" the grounds, " herb and flower and fruit gardens." And this was pretty much what he obtained. It was a little house, with ample gardens and pleasant meadows attached. Not of brick indeed, but half timber, with a fine old oak staircase and balusters, and one or two wainscoted chambers—which yet remain much as when Cowley dwelt here, as do also the poet's study, a small closet with a view meadow-ward to St. Anne's Hill, and the room, overlooking the road, in which he died.

"I thought when I went first to dwell in the country, that without doubt I should have met there with the simplicity of the old poetical Golden Age. I thought to have found no inhabitants there, but such as the shepherds of Sir Philip Sidney in Arcadia, or of Mons. d'Urfé upon the banks of Lignon ; and began to consider with myself, which way I might recommend no less to posterity the happiness and innocence of the men of Chertsey : but, to confess the truth, I perceived quickly by infallible demonstrations, that I was still in Old England, and not in Arcadia or La Forrest." *

Cowley lived here little more than two years in all. He was driven from Barn-Elms by illness, and he tells his friend Sprat, in a letter dated Chertsey, May 21, 1665,—which Johnson † maliciously "recommends to the consideration of all that may hereafter pant for solitude "—

"The first night that I came hither I caught so great a cold, with a deflexion of rheum, as made me keep my chamber ten days. And, two after, had such a bruise on my ribs with a fall, that I am yet unable to turn myself in my bed. This is my personal fortune here to begin with. And, besides, I can get no money from my tenants, and have my meadows eaten up every night by cattle put in by my neighbours. What this signifies, or may come to in time, God knows ; if it be ominous, it can end in nothing less than hanging."

What it came to Sprat tells us :—

"Having languished under this for some months, he seemed to be pretty well cured of its ill symptoms. But in the heat of the last summer, by staying too long amongst his labourers in the meadows, he was taken with a violent defluxion, and stoppage in his breast and throat. This he at first neglected as an ordinary cold, and refused to send for his usual physicians, till it was past all remedies ; and so in the end, after a fortnight's sickness, it proved mortal to him."‡

Cowley died July 28, 1667. His body

* Cowley, Essays,—Dangers of an Honest Man in Much Company.
† Life of Cowley.
‡ An Account of the Life of Mr. Abraham Cowley, prefixed to his Works, ed. 1688.

was conveyed with great pomp by water to London, and buried in Westminster Abbey: hence the allusion in Pope's 'Windsor Forest'—

"Here his first lays majestic Denham sung;
  There the last numbers flow'd from Cowley's
    tongue.
  Oh early lost ! What tears the River shed,
  When the sad pomp along his banks was led !"

Cowley's House is still sometimes called by its old name, the *Porch House*, from a porch with chamber above, which projected 10 ft. into the highway, but which was pulled down in 1786, by Alderman Clark, "for the safety and accommodation of the public." In the garden is a fine group of trees, including a horse-chesnut of great size and beauty, "beneath whose shadow the poet frequently sat." Formerly the stranger had little difficulty in obtaining admittance, but it is now a family residence, and neither house nor grounds can be seen without special leave.

Chertsey Bridge, more substantial and pict. than convenient, is nearly ½ m. E. of the town. It is of stone, has 7 arches, and was constructed in 1780-85, from the designs of Mr. James Payne, at a cost of £13,000. By it are broad green meadows, and the river affords some good trout, perch, and jack fishing. *Chertsey Deep* extends from the weir to 80 yards E. of the bridge; in 1870 a trout of 14 lb. 9 oz. weight was caught off the weir. The *Cricketers*, Bridge Road, is the anglers' inn.

From Chertsey there are pleasant walks in all directions, and on every side stately domains and handsome villas. S.E. by *Woburn Park* (W. J. Alt, Esq.), once famous as *Woburn Farm*, is *Addlestone*. 1 m. N.W. of Chertsey is *St. Anne's Hill* (Rt. Hon. Lady Holland), a spot interesting in itself, and as the favourite residence of Charles James Fox. *Fan Grove* (R. J. Noad, Esq.), 1 m. S. of St. Anne's Hill, is a well-placed mansion, erected in 1820 by Gen. Sir Herbert Taylor. *Ottershaw*, 2 m. S. from Chertsey, is an eccl. dist., with a handsome ch. and parsonage, erected by G. G. Scott, R.A., at the cost of Sir T. E. Colebrooke, Bart., M.P., whose fine seat, *Ottershaw Park*, lies a little farther S. The house is a modern Italian structure, standing in grounds of great extent and

beauty. W. of Ottershaw is *Potter's Park* (A. Savory, Esq.), and nearer Chertsey *Botleys* (Mrs. Gosling), a spacious mansion, with attached Ionic columns and pediment, erected in 1765 by Sir Joseph Mawbey (and figured in the 'Vitruvius Britannicus,' vol. ii.) Some way W. of Botleys is a noble modern Elizabethan manor-house, erected from the designs of Mr. G. Basevi. By it is *Silverlands* (F. A. Hankey, Esq.), formerly the seat of Adm. Hotham. *Anningsley* (the Hon. Mrs. James Norton), S.E. of Ottershaw Park, was the residence of Thomas Day, author of 'Sandford and Merton.' (*See* ADDLESTONE.)

Lyne, 1 m. W. of St. Anne's Hill, is a dist. chapelry of Chertsey. Here is *Lyne Grove* (Hon. Mrs. Cavendish). The little cruciform ch. of the Holy Trinity was erected in 1849, from the designs of Mr. F. Francis. *Long Cross* is another chapelry, with a small ch. built in 1848, on the edge of a wild heath which stretches away to Bagshot.

CHESHUNT (Dom. *Cestrehunt;*

A.-S. *Ceaster*, a castle, *hunt*, a chase: later *Cheston*), occupies the S.E. angle of Herts; and is 13 m. from London by rd., and 16 m. by the Grt. E. Rly. (Hertford line): pop. of par. 7518 (*i.e.*, Cheshunt vill., etc., 3602; eccl. dist. of Waltham Holy Cross, 3104; St. James Goff's Oak, 812). Inns: *Green Dragon*, Church Gate; *Woolpack*, Cheshunt Street; *Four Swans*, Waltham Cross.

Cheshunt village stretches N. from Waltham Cross for 3 m., on both sides of the Cambridge road. The Lea river, which divides Herts from Essex, bounds it on the E., and between the Lea and the Cambridge rd., the Lea and Stort Navigation and the Grt. E. Rly. run almost parallel, whilst the W. side of the par. is traversed by the New River; and here the New River Comp. have vast reservoirs which store up 75 million gallons of water. Cheshunt proper, or *Church Gate* (*i.e.* Church *Street*),—comprising the ch., Cheshunt College, a gathering of genteel residences, and a few dependent shops and cottages,—is above ½ m. from the main rd., W. of Turner's Hill. The business section lies along the highroad, and is known as *Cheshunt Street*. Goff's Oak, 1½ m. W. of the ch., and Waltham Cross, on the S., are hamlets of Cheshunt: the last has a separate notice.

By some antiquaries Cheshunt has been identified with the Roman *Durolitum*. Dorolitum is now relegated to the neighbourhood of Romford, but there is little doubt that Cheshunt was a Roman station or military post. This is indeed almost implied in the old name, *Cestre*, or *Ceaster*. Coins, from Hadrian to Constantine, have been found here; and built into the front of the Roman Urn Inn, at the corner of Crossbrook Street, on the highroad, is an urn which was dug up close by. The name of the height W. of the inn, *Aldbury*, also points to an ancient station.

The manor of Cheshunt was given by the Conqueror to his nephew, Alan Earl of Brittany, along with the earldom of Richmond, and it was held as an appendage to the earldom by, among others, John of Gaunt, and Ralph Nevil Earl of Westmoreland. Having reverted to the Crown, Cheshunt was given, with the title of Duke of Richmond, by Henry VIII., to his "base son," Henry Fitzroy. He dying without heir, Edward VI. granted the manor to Sir John Gates, and it has since passed through a succession of private hands. Nothing is left of the manorhouse. Of the subordinate manors, two have some interest from their associations. *Moteland*, or *St. Andrews-le-Mote*, which was given by Henry VIII. to Cardinal Wolsey, and in the next century belonged to the Dennys and Dacres, whose monts. are conspicuous in the ch.; and *Theobalds* (originally Cullynges, afterwards Tongs, Thebaudes, and Tibbolds), which belonged to Burleigh, who often entertained his imperious mistress here, and which his son transferred to James I. in exchange for Hatfield. Theobalds was given by Charles II. to George Monk, Duke of Albemarle, and on its reversion to the Crown, on the death of Christopher, 2nd Duke, without heirs male, the manor was granted to Ralph, Duke of Montagu, who married Albemarle's widow, but William III. gave the palace and park to his favourite Bentinck, Duke of Portland. Montague sold the manor to a Mrs. Thornhill, from whom it passed by marriage to the family of the Cromwells. Of Theobald's palace the memory alone is preserved in *Theobald's Park*, the pro-

perty of Sir Henry Meux, Bart., but now occupied by Ald. J. Cotton.

Of the manor-house of *St. Andrews-le-Mote*, a portion remains. It is a plain red-brick fabric, standing in a naked meadow (part of a park of about 40 acres) on the rt. of *Goff's Lane*, ¼ m. N. of the ch., and is known as *Cheshunt House*, or the *Great House*. The building is a portion of that said to have been erected by the O'er-great Cardinal, though there is no evidence that he resided here. But if of the time of Wolsey, it has been greatly altered. In 1750 it was "modernized and cased with brick" by the then lord of the manor, John Shaw, Esq., but the last and most material change was made in 1801, by the Rev. Chas. Mayo, who pulled down the larger part of the building in order to obtain materials for repairing the remainder. It has long been abandoned as a residence, but is kept in indifferent repair, and a portion of it is occupied by a labouring family, who show it to visitors. The principal feature is the *Great Hall*, 37 ft. by 21, and 36 ft. high. It has an open timber roof, panelled wainscot walls, and marble floor; and contains several portraits of doubtful authenticity, a couple of busts of Roman emperors, old weapons, banners, suits of armour, fragments of tapestry, an early harpsichord (which has been a fine instrument, and is a better specimen than any in the South Kensington Museum), and various other objects. Among the portraits are Cardinal Wolsey (the usual profile); Charles I., and Charles II., attributed to Vandyck; King William III., and Queen Mary; Abps. Laud and Juxon; Lord Falkland, Sir J. Shaw, and various members of the Mayo family. With few exceptions, the pictures are of little value, and the portraits of doubtful ascription: but it is sad to see the place and its contents so entirely neglected. The children of the people who have charge of the house, and other country children, a rude and rough lot, use the Great Hall as a play-place, and do as they please with its contents. The damage done in the rooms during the last few years is palpable. Vaults beneath the principal apartments are termed a chapel and a prison, and you are shown a common chopping block, which you are told was used "in Cromwell's time" in beheading the prisoners. The moat, marking the site of an earlier manor-house, is still traceable in the park on the opposite side of the lane.

A peculiarity of the Cheshunt manors is, that an irregular line, known as the *Banks line*, runs N. and S. through the parish, and that E. of it, or *below bank*—by far the larger and more valuable portion—the land and tenements are subject to Borough-English, *i.e.* descend to the youngest son, whilst W. of the line, or *above bank*, the eldest son succeeds.

The *Church* (St. Mary), a Perp. edifice, was erected by Nicholas Dixon (d. 1448), who was rector of Cheshunt for 30 years, " also Clerk of the Pipe Office in the Exchequer, Under Treasurer, and at last Baron of the Exchequer."* It consists of nave, aisles, chancel, and tower at the W., which has an angle turret, and contains a peal of 6 bells : the whole embattled. Having become much dilapidated, the church was restored and enlarged in 1873, and a new chancel, with a south aisle, erected under the superintendence of Mr. Joseph Clarke. The body of the church and tower remain rough-cast as of old ; the new chancel is faced with whole flints in irregular courses : in style it agrees with the rest of the building. The W. window, which had been bricked-up for many generations, was restored, the galleries were removed, the plaster ceiling cleared away, and the open timber roof once more revealed. The E. window is of course new, and longer than the old one.

In the chancel are showy marble *monts.* to Robert Dacres, privy-councillor to Henry VIII., and his wife, erected 1543 ; to Margaret, daughter of Sir Thomas Dacres, jun. ; and to Henry Atkins, d. 1635, " physician in ordinary for the space of 32 years to King James and King Charles." On the floor is an inscribed stone to Nicholas Dixon, the founder of the ch. At the end of the N. aisle, a marble statue of Daniel Dodson, d. 1761. *Brasses:* Damoselle Johanne Clay, d. 1400 ; John Roger, d. 1413 ; and Constancia Vere, d. 1502. In the ch.-yard lies the Hon. John Scott, d. Dec. 24, 1805, the only son of Lord Chancellor Eldon. He had the previous summer rented a house at Wood Green, and expressed a " particular wish

* Chauncy, Hist. Ant. of Hertfordshire, vol. i., p. 588.

to be deposited in Cheshunt churchyard, and a blue box with me." The inscription on the mont. was written by Lord Stowell.*

At *Cheshunt Common*, the N. end of the par., and near Goff's Oak, is a small cruciform ch. (St. James), erected in 1861. A small Benedictine nunnery, originally belonging to the Canons of Cathele, but granted by Henry III., in 1240, to the prioress and nuns of Cheshunt, existed here till the Dissolution. The site and some vestiges of the buildings are preserved in the *Nunnery Farm*, on the rt. of the highroad by the 14 m. stone, and between the railway and the Lea.

Cheshunt had a weekly market granted it by Edward III. in 1344, but it probably fell into abeyance at an early period. Church Gate is now a quiet, genteel place. Nearly opposite the ch. is *Cheshunt College*, founded at Trevecca, S. Wales, in 1768, by Selina Countess of Huntingdon, for the training of young men for the ministry of the Connexion ; and after her death removed to Cheshunt, 1792. Besides class and living rooms, it has a chapel and library, master's house ; built in 1863, and good grounds. The very conspicuous new semi-Gothic brick and stone building, with entrance tower 100 ft. high, erected in 1870-71, from the designs of Messrs. Lander and Bedells, contains spacious lecture and students' rooms, but is only a portion of a more extensive structure, which will include a hall, library, and chapel, on a larger scale than those at present in use. The college has theological, classical, Hebrew, and philosophical tutors, and provision for 30 students. Not far from the college is a lane still known as *Dr. Watts's Lane*, from a questionable tradition that it was the favourite stroll of the great nonconformist divine during his visits to Richard Cromwell.

Pengelly House (Benj. Attwood, Esq.), near the ch., occupies the site of the residence of Richard Cromwell, the deposed Protector. He lived here, from his return to England in 1680, an easy Epicurean sort of life, under the assumed name of Clarke, and died here in his 83rd year, July 12, 1712. He was buried at Hursley in Hampshire. The Cromwells settled in

* H. Twiss, Life of Lord Eldon, chap. xxii.

Cheshunt, and it is not a little remarkable that the royal manor which Charles II. gave to Monk for restoring the monarchy should, by marriage, have eventually vested in the last male descendant of Oliver Cromwell, himself an Oliver, who died here May 30, 1821, aged 71. Sir Rbt. Heron relates in his 'Notes' (1851) that the last Oliver was very desirous of leaving his name to his son-in-law, Mr. Thomas Artemidorus Russell, of Cheshunt Park (who married Oliveria Cromwell), and applied several times for the royal licence that Mr. Russell should assume it; but the old king, George III., positively refused, always saying " No, no; no more Oliver Cromwells." George IV. is said to have met a like application, made to him when Prince Regent, with an equally decided refusal. The last Oliver was a worthy man, of mild manners, resembling in character his immediate ancestor Henry, Lieutenant of Ireland. Mr. Russell's son, Cromwell Russell, married Averella, daughter of the Rev. W. A. Armstrong, of Pengelly House, Richard Cromwell's residence; and their daughter, Olivera, married the Rev. Paul Bush, rector of Dulse, near Liskeard, and carried with her to Ireland a large number of Oliver Cromwell's letters (printed in Carlyle's ' Cromwell '), the great seal of Richard Cromwell, and other Cromwell relics, made heirlooms by her grandfather.

At Cheshunt also lived in learned retirement, after dismission from high office, another of the men whose names figure in English history, Lord Somers. Among other notable inhabitants of Cheshunt, may be mentioned Wm. Herbert, the editor of ' Ames's Typographical Antiquities,' who d. here in 1795, and was buried in the ch.-yard; and James Ward, R.A., the well-known animal painter, who died at Roundcroft Cottage, Nov. 1859, in his 90th year.

Though not so lordly a neighbourhood as of old, Cheshunt has still a great many excellent mansions. Among these may be mentioned *Cheshunt Park* (F. G. Debenham, Esq.), 1 m. N. of the ch., long the seat of the Cromwells, and their heirs the Russells; *Aldbury House*, ½ m. S. of the ch.; *Claremont* (H. T. Jenkins, Esq.), ¾ m. N.E. of the ch.; *Wood Green Park* (James Bentley, Esq.), 1½ m. W. of the

ch.; and *The Cedars*, Theobalds (Lady Prescott).

When at *Cheshunt Street*, the stranger should visit the *Old Nurseries*, of Messrs. Paul, which furnish the annual displays of roses that win such general admiration at the Horticultural and Botanical Gardens. The collection of roses is unrivalled in this part of England, but apart from the roses the nursery will repay a visit.

Goff's Oak, a hamlet 1½ m. W.N.W. of Cheshunt ch., is so named from a famous oak which stands at the S. edge of Cheshunt Common, and in front of a little country inn named after it. It has been a majestic tree, but the head is gone, and the trunk, a mere shell, bound together by iron ties, and supported by props; it still however shows some verdure (Aug. 1873). It is 22 ft. in girth at 4 ft. from the ground. To reach Goff's Oak take the first lane (Goff's Lane) on the l. past (N. of) the ch., and continue along it for about 1½ m.

CHESSINGTON, SURREY (the mark of the *Ceassingas*, Kemble; Dom. *Cisedune*), a retired agricultural par. on the S.W. of Malden, to which it is ecclesiastically attached, and 2 m. N.W. of the Ewell Stat. of the L. and S.W. Rly. (Epsom br.): pop. 280. The land is clay, mostly enclosed, but there are some patches of heathy common. The manor was associated with that of Malden as a foundation gift to Merton College, Oxford (*see* MALDEN), to which it still belongs.

Chessington *Church* is partly E.E., but was restored in 1854, and enlarged in 1870, and, while greatly improved in ecclesiastical character and convenience, has lost its air of unpretending antique rusticity. A marble slab to Samuel Crisp, Esq., d. 1783, has a poetic inscription by Dr. Charles Burney. Crisp was the friend and correspondent of Fanny Burney; a good critic, but not a good writer. After the failure of his tragedy of ' Virginia,' he retired, says Macaulay,[*] "to a solitary and long-deserted mansion, built on a common in one of the wildest parts of Surrey. No road, or even a sheepwalk, connected his lonely dwelling with the abodes of men. The place of his retreat was strictly concealed

---

[*] Essays.

from his old associates." Burney was, however, an exception. He was a frequent visitor at the solitary mansion, *Chessington Hall* (G. Chancellor, Esq.) Crisp lived here 30 years, going to London occasionally in the spring. Chessington is hardly so solitary a place now as in those days, but it has still a lonely look. By the brook, S. of the ch., is an artificial mound, now covered with wood, known as *Castle Hill:* Roman coins have been found near it.

CHEVENING, KENT, $1\frac{1}{2}$ m. W. from the Dunton Green Stat. of the S.E. Rly. (Tunbridge line), and $3\frac{1}{2}$ m. N.W. of Sevenoaks. The vill. is charmingly situated on the E. side of Chevening Park and S. slope of the chalk hills, at the bottom of which flows the little river Dart, or Darent. The par., nearly 6 m. long, but narrow, has an area of 3773 acres, includes the hamlets of Bessell's Green and Chipstead, and part of the eccl. district of Ide's Hill, and contained 954 inhab. in 1871. Inn, the *Stanhope Arms*, by the park gates.

The manor of Chevening belonged to the see of Canterbury from 1281 to 1537, when it was surrendered to the Crown by Abp. Cranmer. A subordinate manor is of more historical interest. It was held by Adam de Chevening, *temp.* Henry III.; passed to the De la Poles, *t.* Henry VI.; and to the Lennards, *t.* Henry VIII. The last of the direct male line of the Lennards, Thomas Lord Dacre, was created Earl of Sussex by Charles II. His daughters and coheirs sold Chevening in 1717 to Gen. James Stanhope (grandson of Philip, 1st Earl of Chesterfield), commander of the British army in Spain in 1710, Secretary of State 1714, and First Lord of the Treasury 1717; created Visct. 1717, and Earl Stanhope 1718; d. 1721, and buried at Chevening, but commemorated by a mont., by Rysbrack, in Westminster Abbey. Chevening has since remained in his descendants, the present possessor being the distinguished historian.

The house was built by Richd. Lennard, Lord Dacre (d. 1630), "on a plan of Inigo Jones." It is large and stately, having a centre with attached Ionic columns, and wings, but has been so often altered as to retain little of its original architectural character. In it are several fine historical portraits; among the more noteworthy are Ann Hyde, Duchess of York, by *Lely;* Lady Eliz. Butler, Countess of Chesterfield, one of the beauties of the court of Charles II., by *Lely;* the great Earl Stanhope, by *Kneller;* Charles, 3rd Earl, the inventor of the Stanhope printing-press, and a very prominent politician of the days of the first French Revolution, a good portrait, by *Gainsborough;* Philip, 4th Earl of Chesterfield (author of the 'Letters'), by *Gainsborough*—thinly painted, but a capital picture; the great Earl of Chatham, by *Brompton*, a $\frac{3}{4}$-length, feebly painted, but has the traditional reputation of being a good likeness, which is the more likely since it was, as is stated, a present from himself; and Mary Lepell, the "beautiful Molly Lepell" of Swift and Chesterfield's ballad, Gay's "Youth's youngest daughter, sweet Lepell," afterwards Lady Hervey.

Besides the pictures, the house contains a library of 16,000 volumes, as also many objects of artistic and antiquarian interest; and a brief quotation from Mrs. Grote's 'Personal Life of George Grote'* will indicate the wealth of literary and social associations with which the historian of the reign of Anne has enriched Chevening :—

" A visit on our part at Chevening (1860) must not go unrecorded. . . . On one evening we, that is to say, Lord Stanhope, Dr. William Smith, Lady Stanhope, and myself, sat down to whist. After a while, Dr. Smith said across the table, 'Mrs. G., just turn your head round and see what is going on yonder.' I did so, and beheld the Dean of St. Paul's [Milman], the Historian of Greece, and the erudite scholar, George C. Lewis, all intently occupied in the same way as ourselves! It was indeed a very amusing spectacle to us. Mrs. Reeve was the fourth player at this unique whist-table."

The house is not shown, but the gardens and grounds, which are very beautiful, are open to the public on Wednesday afternoon. The lake, lawns, and terraces are much admired; a pile of Roman altars and monumental stones, brought from Tarragona by the first Lord Stanhope, will interest the antiquary; and the road, which winds up the combe at the back of the house—formed under the superintendence of the great Lord Chatham—leads to a view of exceeding beauty. The park is broad, open, and undulating;

---

* Chapter xxix., p. 247.

well wooded, with beeches and yews spotting the hill sides and summits; lovely green dips and wide and splendid prospects. The walk or drive through the park to Knockholt, 1½ m., is extremely fine. The old British trackway, known as the Pilgrim's Road, was formerly a public way through Chevening, but was closed by an Act of Parliament obtained by Lord Stanhope in 1780; it may still be traced across the park N. of the house, by the rising bank.

The *Church* (St. Botolph), on the rt. of the road opposite the park, has some E.E. features, but is chiefly Perp. It is of Kentish rag, and consists of nave, aisles, and chancel, with S. aisle or Stanhope chapel, and at the W. end an embattled tower with angle stair turret. The int., well restored in 1855, has a good open timber roof, and contains many interesting monuments. In the *Stanhope Chapel* are recumbent effigies, on mattresses of unusual design, of John Lennard, d. 1585, and w. Eliz.: the knight in full armour, and both good examples of the monumental sculpture of the period. A tall and showy mont. in coloured marbles of Sampson Lennard, d. 1615, and his w. Margaret Fiennes, Baroness Dacre, d. 1612, with their recumbent effigies in alabaster, under a semicircular panelled canopy, crowned with coats of arms; on one side 3 sons kneeling, on the other 5 daughters. Tablet erected by his great-grandson to the great Earl Stanhope, whose crested helmet, coronet, and sword are here. A mont. with recumbent statue of Lady Frederica Louisa Stanhope, daughter of the Earl of Mansfield. She d. in childbirth, 1823, æt. 23; the statue of the mother with the child resting on her bosom is one of Chantrey's most simple, graceful, and pathetic designs, and is well chiselled. The chapel contains many tablets to members of the Stanhope family, and the painted glass in both the windows was designed and executed by Emily, Countess Stanhope, d. 1873. N. of the chancel is a mural mont. of Lady Ann Herrys of Chipstead, d. 1613; it has a kneeling effigy, with figures of 2 daughters, supporting angels, etc. On the S. another, with kneeling effigies of Robt. Cranmer, Esq., of Chipstead, d. 1619, his wife, and daughter. *Brass*, on S., of an ecclesiastic (in long robes), d. 1596, wife, 7

sons, and 2 daughters; the name is gone, but above is a coat of arms with 12 quarterings: these, together with the entry of death in the parish register, enable the mont. to be identified as that of the Rev. Griffin Floyd, Rector of Chevening, with his family. The chancel window is a memorial to F. Perkins, Esq., of Chipstead Place. On S. of nave are 2 Easter sepulchres, and 2 ambreys, or credences, with piscinas under. The village is picturesque. The cottages are singularly neat and well kept, and their gardens abound in bright flowers.

A mile S.E. of Chevening ch. is the village of *Chipstead*, very prettily situated on the little river Darenth, on which is a mill. *Chipstead Place*, the stately seat of Mrs. Candy, late in the occupation of Sir Morton Peto, Bart., is at the E. end of the village. It contains a library of rare books, and some choice pictures. The grounds, which are very fine, stretch S. to *Bessell's Green*, another hamlet of Chevening, lying on the Westerham road, midway between Brastead and Sevenoaks. Here is *Park Point*, the seat of Sir S. Hancock. *Morant's Court*, about a mile E. of Chevening ch., on the way to Dunton's Green, Otford, "lies in Chevening likewise" as Philipott wrote,[*] "and contributed both seat and surname to a knightly family who were proprietors of it. King Edward II., in the 14th year of his reign, granted charter warren to Jurdan and William de Morant, in all their lands in Chevening, Shoram, Otford, Brastead, Sundridge, and Chidinston. William de Morant was sheriff of Kent the 12th and 13th year of Edward III., and had issue Sir Thomas Morant, whose heir general brought this seat to Peckham, in which family the title lay couched till our father's memory, and then it was demised to Blackswell, who, some few years since, hath by deed and other conveyance, settled his right in it on Mr. Watson of the county of Oxford." And so it passed on to its present owner, J. W. Tonge, Esq., who, with Earl Stanhope and Earl Amherst, is chief lord of the lands in Chevening. From Morant's Court Hill, N. of the house, on the rd. to Knockholt, a wide prospect is obtained over a remarkably interesting country.

---

[*] Villare Cantianum, folio, 1659, p. 113.

CHIGWELL, Essex (A.-S. *Cingwella*, Dom. *Cinguehella*), a vill. on the Ongar road, 10½ m. from Whitechapel ch., and 1½ m. E.N.E. from the Buckhurst Hill Stat. of the Epping and Ongar Rly. [by the fields on rt. of rly.: cross the Roding by the *Moat*, and the lane on rt. leads direct to the ch.] The par. had 4463 inhab. in 1871 (an increase of 2000 since 1861), but this includes the hamlets of Chigwell Row, Buckhurst Hill, etc. The vill. is small, quiet, and country-like, with at one end the ch., on one side of the rd., and opposite it a long low plaster-fronted half-timber inn, with projecting upper storeys terminating in gables—seemingly earlier than the time of Charles I., whose effigy serves for its sign of the *King's Head*. It was at this inn that the Verderers' or Forest Courts were held, till their desuetude in 1855.

Chigwell *Church* looks more pict. from the rd. than close at hand. An avenue of clipped yews leads to the principal entrance, and farther E. is a second avenue. The ch. is in part ancient, but defaced with plaster. On the S., under a wooden porch, is a Norm. doorway, with plain zigzag moulding; the windows are chiefly Perp., and poor. The chancel is modern. Inside are one or two *monts*. of interest, *Obs.* that of Thos. Coleshill (d. 1595), servant to Edward VI., Q. Mary, and Q. Elizabeth, with kneeling effigies of himself and wife. Also the very large and good *brass*, to Sam. Harsnett (d. 1631), sometime vicar of Chigwell, afterwards Bp. of Norwich, and Abp. of York. He is in cope (one of three instances known) and mitre, and holds the pastoral crook in his l. hand. This brass is of exceptional interest to ritualists and ecclesiastical antiquaries, in that it gives the latest examples known of the stole, albe, dalmatic, and cope in the English Church. The other brasses mentioned in the books have been stolen.

Abp. Harsnett founded a Grammar and an English school here. The Grammar school, having fallen into some neglect, a new scheme for its management was sanctioned by the Court of Chancery in 1867. Abp. Harsnett directed that the master should be "neither papist nor puritan," "no tippler, haunter of ale-houses or puffer of tobacco;" but "apt to teach and severe in government." For phrase and style he must use only Tully and Terence; for poets read only the ancient Greek and Latin; and he is to be careful to introduce "no novelties, nor conceited modern writers." Under the new scheme the master will enjoy a little more license, at least as to conceited modern writers and puffing of tobacco. William Penn was educated in Chigwell School, and there it was that, "about the 12th year of his age, anno 1656," he first had those divine visitations, with "an inward comfort, and, as he thought, an external glory in the room," described by himself in his 'Travels,' and by Antony Wood in the 'Athenæ Oxoniensis.'

Chigwell contains several good seats, some standing in spacious and well-wooded grounds: among them are *Belmont*, by the ch.; *Rolls Park* (J. H. Crossman, Esq.), ½ m. N.; *Woollaston* (Miss Bodle), farther on the road to Abridge; and *Hill House* (C. Dames, Esq.) At the W. end of the lane by the ch. are vestiges of an old moated mansion. Lying between Epping and Hainault forests, and extending into both, Chigwell used to be an exceedingly attractive place. But since 1858 Hainault has been disafforested, and the portion of Epping lying within the par. has been enclosed, and Chigwell is now denuded of nearly all that was characteristic, and much that was beautiful, in it. It is still green and pleasant, but is becoming daily duller, more genteel, and more commonplace.

CHIGWELL ROW, Essex, extends along the N.W. edge of Hainault Forest, 1 m. E. of Chigwell, to which par. it belongs. It has been supposed that the name Chigwell (A.-S. *Cingwella* = Kingswell) is derived from a spring at Chigwell Row. The water was once in repute for its cathartic qualities, and was strongly recommended by Dr. Frewen, a popular physician of the last century, who was a native of Chigwell, but there is no evidence that it was known in early times.

Chigwell Row consists chiefly of a line of good suburban residences on the N. side of the road, with one or two mansions, as *Forest House* (B. Cotton, Esq.); some cottages, and a couple of inns, the *Maypole* (commemorated in 'Barnaby Rudge,' though this is not the house there described), and the *Bald Hind*, much frequented by Londoners in the summer season, though far less than before Hainault was disafforested and enclosed (1858). A belt of green lawn stretches by the roadside, but in losing its forest Chigwell Row has lost its great charm. The most perfect fragment of the forest remaining is a bit of *Crabtree Wood*, on the rt. of Forest Gate, ½ m. beyond the Maypole. About Chigwell Row, and especially from Grange Hill, by the Bald Hind, are extensive views across the Thames, to Knockholt and the Kentish hills, and more W. by the Crystal Palace to the Surrey Downs; but the forest foreground, which gave so much richness to the picture, is wanting. The new *Church*, opposite the Maypole, was built in 1867, from the designs of Mr. J. Seddon, on part of the enclosed forest.

CHILDERDITCH, ESSEX (Dom.

Ciltendis), 2¼ m. S.E. from Brentwood Stat. of the Grt. E. Rly. (turn rt. from the stat. and go by Warley Common and the barracks), an agric. par. of 267 inhab.; there is no village.

A mile S. of *Childerditch Common*—the merest collection of cottages—the *Church* (All Saints and St. Faith) stands alone on high ground, in a secluded and pleasant position. Around the ch.-yard are fine old elms; S. is a broad view over the lowlands; S.E. are the Laindon Hills. The little church was an old, dilapidated pile of flint and stone, repaired with brick, and propped on the N. by wooden shores: rude but picturesque. At the W. end was a tower, brick below, wood above, with a short wooden spire. The int. was plastered, had tall pews, some curious woodwork, but no monts. This quaint old structure was pulled down in the spring of 1869, and a new ch. of Kentish rag, with Bathstone dressings, designed by Messrs. Nichols, erected on its site. The new ch., which is late E.E. in character, consists of nave and chancel, with bell gable. The font—*t.* Henry III.—is the only relic of the old ch. *Childerditch Hall* (J. F. Butler, Esq.) is ¼ m. N. from the church.

Little Warley ch. is ¾ m. from Childerditch: go directly S.W. from the ch.-yd. across the fields. Eastward there is a pleasant way—but rather hard to find—

across the fields, and by the S. end of *Thorndon Park* (Lord Petre's), to *East Horndon* ch. 1½ m.

CHILD'S HILL (see HAMPSTEAD).

CHINGFORD, ESSEX (Dom.

Cinghefoet, or *Cingeford*, i.e. King's Ford: the meadows below the old ch. are still called the King's Mead), an agricultural par. and vill., pop. 1268, of much interest from the character of the scenery, and a pleasant place for a summer stroll, lies on the road to Waltham Abbey, 9 m. from Shoreditch ch.: a Stat. was opened on the Forest br. of the Grt. E. Rly., near Chingford new ch. in 1874.

Chingford is mostly on the high ground E. of the Lea, running on the one hand down to the meadows by that river, on the other E. and N. into Epping Forest. The houses are widely scattered, the largest number being collected about *Chingford Green*, the others at *Chingford Hatch*, *Forest Side*, etc. It includes two manors. Chingford St. Paul belonged to St. Paul's Cathedral from the time of the Confessor to its forced surrender to Henry VIII. in 1544. It has since been in private hands. The old manor-house, *Chingford Hall*, by the Lea, close to Chingford Mill, is now a farmhouse. The other manor, Chingford Comitis, or Chingford Earl's, was held at the Domesday Survey by Orgar the Thane. Each included meadow and forest land (with pannage for 1000 hogs), and rights on the Lea: the former had 5 manses or farms, 2 fisheries, 8 villans, 6 bordarii, and 4 slaves; the latter a mill, 4 fisheries, 7 villans, 6 bordarii, and 2 slaves. Lysons thinks the manor-house of Chingford Earl's was that now known as *Queen Elizabeth's Lodge*, in which the manor and forest courts were held. For a long period, however, the seat of the lord of the manor being *Friday Hill* (R. B. Heathcote, Esq.), about 1 m. E. of the ch.; that of the present lord of Chingford St. Paul's (R. Hodgson, Esq.) is *Hawkwood House*, 1 m. N. Morant[*] describes a remarkable tenure by which an estate in this par. called *Brindwoods* was formerly held under the rectory:—

"Upon every alienation the owner of the estate,

---

[*] History of Essex, vol. i., p. 57.

with his wife, man-servant, and maid-servant, each single upon a horse, come to the parsonage, where the owner does his homage and pays his relief, in the following manner. He blows three blasts with his horn, and carries a hawk on his fist, his servant has a greyhound in a slip, both for the use of the rector that day. He receives a chicken for his hawk, a peck of oats for his horse, and a loaf of bread for his greyhound. They all dine; after which, the master blows three blasts with his horn, and they depart."

By the end of the last century the memory of the custom was lost alike by the rector, tenants, and parishioners.[*]

Old Chingford Church (St. Peter and St. Paul) stands on the brow of the hill overlooking the broad valley of the Lea. Disused, semi-ruinous, and overgrown with ivy, in the midst of an old well-filled ch.-yd., among mouldering grave-stones, and surrounded by venerable elms, it would be hard to find its fellow for sombre picturesqueness within a much greater distance of London. The building appears to be mostly of Perp. date, but when inside you see that the main fabric is older, the windows being insertions. It consists of nave and S. aisle, chancel, and baptistery, with a low massive tower at the W. end. Fortunately, when the dilapidated condition of the ch. rendered a new one advisable, it was decided to erect it on a more convenient site; and the picturesque character of the old pile saved it from destruction. But as the body of the ch. was dismantled, only the chancel (for funeral services) being locked, rough usage and neglect brought it into a semi-ruinous state, and at length the roof of the nave fell in. This compelled attention, and in the summer of 1873 the roof was restored, and the main fabric repaired, happily without injury to its picturesqueness. Some of the old monts. are still within the chancel; but they are very much dilapidated. The brasses once there have been stolen.

The *new Church* stands on the centre of Chingford Green, ¾ m. N.E. of the old ch. It was built in 1844, and is a commonplace sample of the Gothic of that date; of white brick, with squares of black flints; wide in proportion to its length, with a tower and stone spire in the centre of the W. end. In it is the E.E. font from the old ch.

Whether *Queen Elizabeth's Lodge* was

the manor-house, as Lysons thinks, or, as tradition holds, a hunting lodge of the Maiden Queen when she drove the hart in this part of the forest, it is a building that even in its decay will repay a visit, or if the house does not, the surrounding scenery will. To reach it, go past the new ch., N.E. across the Green, to where the lane runs into a scrubby common by 2 or 3 mean cottages, and turn short to the rt. The lodge will then be seen before you between two magnificent elms. It is a tall, irregular, half-timber building (unhappily defaced by a uniform coating of yellow wash), with gable ends and high-pitched roofs; a long barn on one side, seats round the old elm in front, and a large horse-block before the door: altogether a very picturesque building, looking upon a broad open space, spotted over with crooked oaks, and affording a fine view across Epping Forest to High Beech and Buckhurst Hill. The inside of the lodge may be seen on application. The basement is chiefly occupied by the kitchen, with its old-fashioned fireplace, dogs, and projecting chimney. The first floor has 2 or 3 rooms which, though very low, we see by the wide arched fireplace and tapestried walls were intended for persons of some honour. But the great room is on the second floor; it is about 40 ft. by 20, extending the whole length of the house. The walls are plastered, but timber uprights support the beams of the oak roof. When the manor courts were held in it, the walls were hung with tapestry. The staircase, built out from the house, is of large proportions, with massive timbers; the stairs, of solid oak, about 6 ft. wide, are in fours, there being to the 24 steps 6 broad landings. The topmost landing was of old known as the *horse block*, the tradition being that when Elizabeth visited the lodge she always *rode* upstairs to the great chamber—a tradition so firmly held that to prove its feasibility, an enthusiastic forester, about fifty years ago, repeated the feat on an untrained pony.

The open space in front of the lodge has always been a favourite resort of the East-end holiday folk, for whom 'tea and refreshments' are provided at the lodge. On a fine summer's day, on Monday especially, numerous picnic and 'van' parties may be seen, with swings improvised

---

[*] Lysons, Environs, vol. i., p. 657.

between the oaks, and gipsies with their donkeys in attendance.

The ground, sloping gently from the lodge on all sides, used to be everywhere unenclosed, the tract beyond being open forest, with some famous unlopped trees, but chiefly, as in other parts of Epping Forest, of pollard oak. About 1845 the whole of the manor land, some 300 acres, was appropriated. On the Chingford side roads have been laid out and villas built. On the N. the fine wild forest tract has been enclosed, the trees grubbed up, and the forest ways stopped. There is, however, a strip of open forest land left, N. of the lodge, towards *High Beech*, along which there is a forest road. This part of the forest is famous for beeches, many-coloured fungi, spleen-worts, and mosses. The great pond in the hollow—just below Queen Elizabeth's Lodge—is a noted hunting-ground for microscopists and entomologists ; and the wild birds and aquatic plants whose haunt it is will afford pleasure to naturalists who look down upon *entromostaca* and *coleoptera*. The lover of scenery will be no less delighted with the wild undressed picturesqueness of the pond, fringed with forest trees, and overgrown with bulrushes and bur-reeds, about which water-hens hide and gambol.

The *Obelisk* on the height nearly $\frac{1}{2}$ m. N. by W. of Chingford new ch. (it will be seen on the l. in going to Q. Elizabeth's Lodge) was erected by the Ordnance Survey, and is maintained at the desire of the Astronomer Royal. It stands precisely N. of the Transit-room of Greenwich Observatory, is used for occasional observation and verification, and may be regarded as a visible representation of a portion of the " Meridian of Greenwich."

CHIPPING BARNET, Herts (*see* Barnet).

CHIPPING ONGAR, Essex (*see* Ongar).

CHIPSTEAD, Kent (*see* Chevening).

CHIPSTEAD, Surrey (Dom. *Tepestede*, probably a clerical error for *Cepestede*), on the chalk downs, W. of the Brighton road, 17 m. from London, 2 m.

N. from the Merstham Stat. of the L., B., and S. C. Rly.; pop. 628. There is no vill., and nothing but the church to visit ; but there are good views from the hills, and W., and towards *Shabden Park* (John Cattley, Esq.) some wild woodland lanes, overhung by oak and beech, with fenny ponds abounding in bulrushes and sedges, and enlivened by the moorhen.

Chipstead *Church* (St. Margaret) stands on the hill away from the houses, in a remarkably picturesque spot, with fine views on either side, but especially N. It is cruciform, and has still a venerable look, though it has been restored (nave 1827, chancel and transepts partly rebuilt 1858). The W. and N. doors and columns of S. aisle are Norm.; the chancel is E.E., with 4 long lancets, and an unusual exterior hood moulding, and there are some E.E. windows on N. of the nave. The low thick central tower has Perp. windows, and the date 1631 on the top moulding. There is a good S. porch. A stone seat is carried along the S. wall of the chancel, and above is a piscina. Some fragments of old painted glass are in both the E. and W. windows.

Obs. on N. wall of nave, a *mont.* (with bust) of Sir Edward Banks (d. 1835), builder of " the three noblest bridges in the world "—those of Waterloo, Southwark, and London, and " the founder of his own fortune." Banks worked as a ' navvy ' in the construction of the Merstham iron tramroad along here, took a fancy to the place, and when he died, 40 years later, requested that he might be buried in the quiet ch.-yd. Alice Hooker (d. 1649), eldest daughter of the author of the ' Ecclesiastical Polity,' was interred within the altar rails. The battered helmet hanging in the chancel belonged to a Stephens of Epsom, of whose family there are several memorials. In the ch.-yd. are several tombs, more conspicuous in themselves than in their tenants. N. of the ch. is an immense yew —the trunk 24 ft. in circ. at 4 ft. from the ground—and all around are noble elms.

CHISELHURST, or CHISLE-HURST, Kent, is delightfully situated on an elevated common, in the midst of a thickly wooded tract, 3 m. E. of Bromley, and $\frac{1}{2}$ m. E. of the Chiselhurst Stat. of the S.E. Rly. (Tunbridge line): inn, the *Tiger's*

Head, by the church; pop., including the ecc. dists. of Sidcup and All Saints, Foot's Cray, 3313; without them, 2253. The name is derived from the A.-S. *Ceosil*, a pebble, and *hurst*, a wood: and very noticeable beds of water-worn pebbles may be seen by the rly. and elsewhere, whilst there are still left woods of some extent on all sides of the village.

The manor of Chiselhurst was originally an appendage to Dartford. It was given by King John to Hugh Earl of St. Paul, a Norman nobleman, but on the seizure of Normandy by the French King, escheated to the Crown, and was granted to John de Burgh, "till the King should think fit to restore it to the Earl of St. Paul or his heirs." It was afterwards assigned, on like conditions, to the Earl of Albemarle, on whose death it was restored, in 1263, to Guy Earl of St. Paul. On the death of Guy it again reverted to the Crown, and in 1322 was assigned to Edward Earl of Kent. After passing through various hands, it was forfeited to the Crown on the death of the Earl of Warwick, the King Maker, at the battle of Barnet. It was then held by George Duke of Clarence, till his attainder in 1477. Elizabeth granted, in 1584, a lease of Dartford and Chiselhurst for 21 years to Edmund Walsingham, whose son, Sir Thomas Walsingham, purchased the fee of the manors in 1611. Dartford was disposed of in two or three years, but Chiselhurst remained with the Walsinghams till 1660, when it was sold to Sir R. Betenson, from whom it has descended by marriage to its present owner, the Earl Sydney. The *Manor House* stands near the church, a large and stately Elizabethan brick mansion, with quaint porch, and a turret which affords extensive views. The hall entrance and some of the principal rooms are characteristic and handsome; but the whole has suffered restoration. In the grounds are terraced lawns, alleys of yews and box, trained yew trees, and some fine firs and cedars. Elizabeth's famous minister, Sir Francis Walsingham, was born at Chiselhurst in 1536, and is said to have made this house his residence; but Chiselhurst manor belonged during Sir Francis Walsingham's manhood to Sir Thomas and Sir Edmund Walsingham, and we know that Sir Francis Walsingham purchased Barn-Elms about 1568, and there spent his

later years. The subordinate manor of Scadbury belonged to Sir Francis Walsingham's branch of the family.

Chiselhurst *Church* is picturesque itself, and stands in a pict. situation—at one end of a common glowing with the golden blossoms of the gorse, and amidst splendid trees. The entrance to the ch.-yard is by a lich-gate, recent or elaborately restored, with coffin-rest, inscriptions, etc. Around the ch.-yard are noble trees, and *obs.* on S. of the ch. the fine yew with a comfortable seat under it. The ch. was Perp. (it was rebuilt 1422-60), but showed traces of its E.E. predecessor. It was, however, restored, but virtually rebuilt, under the direction of Mr. B. Ferrey, F.S.A., in 1849, and can hardly be regarded as other than a modern church. It consists of nave and aisles, chancel, chapel on the N., and a tower on the N.W., with a shingle spire 110 ft. high, erected in 1858, the old spire having been burned the previous year. The clock and bells were destroyed at the same time, but a new clock by Dent, and a new peal of 8 bells by Warner, have taken their place, and, as a brass plate on the wall records, on Nov. 22, 1864, a complete peal of grandsire triples, consisting of 5040 changes, was rung on them, "being the first rung by a Chiselhurst band."

The interior of the ch. is light and pleasing in appearance, and has a good timber and plaster roof. The elaborate mediæval decorations of the chancel were executed in 1866. The reredos is of carved stone, coloured and gilt; on either side of the E. window are large figures of the evangelists on gold grounds; above are angels with censers; and the walls and roof are brightly coloured, gilt and diapered, and powdered over with emblems. The windows are filled with painted glass, mostly memorial. The font, late Norm., has a central stem of Purbeck marble, and four smaller columns at the angles. *Brass*, half-effigy on wall of chancel, Alan Porter, rector, 1482. Of the *monts.* obs. that in the N. chapel of Sir Edmund Walsingham, d. 1549, and Sir Thomas, d. 1630, by whom it was erected, 1581—an altar tomb, with a canopy supported by Corinthian columns and decorated with gilt foliage; Thomas, 1st Visct. Sydney, d. 1800, and other members of the Sydney family; the Betensons, etc. On the l. wall are a helmet and sword. In the S. aisle, Sir Philip

Warwick, d. 1683, "an acceptable servant to king Charles I. in all his extremities, and a faithful one to king Charles II." Warwick retired in 1667 from public life to Chiselhurst, and here wrote his well-known 'Memoirs of Charles I.' Like his 'Discourse of Government,' it was a posthumous publication. In the N. aisle are memorials of the ducal family of Ancaster. Of recent monts., *obs.* that of William Selwyn, Esq., d. 1817, with alto-rilievo by Chantrey; also tablet to Prince Hoare, the writer on art, d. 1834. Besides those whose names occur in the ch., the name must be recorded, among Chiselhurst worthies, of Sir Nicholas Bacon, father of the great Lord Bacon, who was born here in 1510.

N. of the Rly. Stat., and W. of Camden Park, is *Christ Church*, consecrated July 1872. It is an Early Dec. building of Kentish rag, with Bath-stone dressings, designed by Mr. Habershon, and consists of nave with clerestorey, apsidal chancel, and entrance tower with tall spire at the W., and occupying an elevated site it forms a landmark for a wide district.

Besides the Manor House, already noticed, the mansions in and around Chiselhurst are very numerous. *Camden Place* owes its early fame as well as its name to the Father of English Antiquaries, and conferred its name on one of our most distinguished lawyers, but has acquired more than European celebrity as the place where Napoleon III. spent the last months of his strangely chequered life, and as the present residence of his widow and son. William Camden purchased the estate in 1609, removing to it Aug. 15th of that year, and, as we learn from his Diary, thenceforth spent his summers here, and his winters at his house in Westminster. He wrote his 'Annals of the Reign of Queen Elizabeth' (fol., 1615) at Camden Place, and there died, Nov. 9th, 1623 : he was buried with great pomp and ceremony in Westminster Abbey. The next noted owner of the house was Charles Pratt, Lord Chief Justice, who in 1765 was created Baron Camden, and in 1786 Earl Camden, "of Camden Place, Chiselhurst, Kent." The estate was sold by his son, the 2nd Earl.

Camden Place has some painful associations. In speaking of her early married life, Mrs. Somerville writes :—

"We became acquainted with the family of Mr. Thomas [Thomson] Bonar, a rich Russian merchant, who lived in great luxury at a beautiful villa at Chiselhurst, in the neighbourhood of London, which has since become the refuge of the ex-Emperor Napoleon the Third and the Empress Eugénie. The family consisted of Mr. and Mrs. Bonar—kind, excellent, people—with two sons and a daughter, all grown up. We were invited from time to time to spend ten days or a fortnight with them, which I enjoyed exceedingly. . . . . I spent many pleasant days with these dear good people ; and no words can express the horror I felt when we heard that they had been barbarously murdered in their bedroom. The eldest son and daughter had been at a ball somewhere near, and on coming home they found that one of the men-servants had dashed out the brains of both their parents with a poker. The motive remains a mystery to this day, for it was not robbery." [*]

The story is so remarkable as to be worth telling somewhat more accurately. On the evening of Sunday, May 30, 1813, Mr. Thomson Bonar, an old man of 70, went to bed at his usual hour ; but Mrs. Bonar did not follow him till 2 in the morning, when she ordered her maid to call her at 7. At that hour the servant went into the bedroom, and found her master dead on the floor, her mistress in her bed, fearfully wounded and insensible, in which state she continued till 10 o'clock, when she expired. No noise had been heard by any one during the night ; the window of the drawing-room was found open, but there were no signs of its having been forced from the outside, and nothing had been stolen. Suspicion soon fastened on the footman, Philip Nicholson, who was said to have been drinking for some days, and appeared moody and sullen. He was a man of 29, of Irish birth, who had served in the 12th Light Dragoons, but was discharged on account of having broken his wrist, and had only been in Mr. Bonar's service three weeks. When arrested, he obtained leave to go to his room, and there cut his throat, but not so as to cause death, and the wound was quickly attended to. A few days later he made a full confession. He was lying half asleep on a settle in the kitchen till his mistress and fellow-servants went to bed. About 3 o'clock, when the house was still, he went up to the bedroom, armed with a poker, with which he struck his mistress twice across the head, and

[*] Personal Recollections, from Early Life to Old Age, of Mary Somerville—by her daughter, Martha Somerville, 1873, pp. 76, 77.

left her insensible. He then struck his master, who was still asleep, but the blow fell on his face, and the old man sprang up, but before he could get out of bed the assassin repeated the blow. The old man, however, succeeded in grappling with him, but was soon overpowered, and the deed was finished. The murderer then went downstairs, stripped, and thoroughly washed himself; eat his supper; opened the drawing-room window, that it might be supposed the murderer came in that way, and went out to hide his clothes, which had become saturated with blood during the death struggle, under a furze-bush on the common; then returned to his room and went to bed—but "could not sleep." He had, he asserted, no enmity to Mr. or Mrs. Bonar; his motive was neither revenge nor a desire of plunder; he acted solely upon an irresistible impulse. He was tried, condemned, and on Aug. 23, 1813, just 3 months after the murder, hanged on Penenden Heath.*

Camden Place became in 1871 the residence of Napoleon III., shortly after the termination of his German captivity, and here he died, January 9th, 1873. The Empress Eugénie and the Prince Imperial now live here in strict retirement.

Camden Place is on the W. side of the Common. The front of the house faces the Common, from which it is only separated by a carriage-drive and a grove of elms. It is a tolerably spacious and comfortable-looking Elizabethan mansion of light and dark red brick. The principal front, of two storeys, has an attic balustrade, and a slightly advanced centre, with, on the second storey, a clock, supported by a large figure of Time and other allegorical devices, under an arched pediment. On each side of the principal front is a low projecting wing. Over the entrance is a balcony. On either side are fine cedars. The garden front has the pleasantest outlook. The window with a balcony, on the first floor, next to the projecting semicircular wing, is that of the room in which the Emperor died. The rooms specially associated with the Emperor—his study and the room in which he died—are preserved as when he used them, but it is hardly necessary to add that they

are not open to visitors. A glimpse of the garden side of the house and grounds may be obtained without intrusion from the footpath in the park : the entrance is by a gate in the park fence, opposite the first little cluster of houses on the way to the rly. station.

Before leaving Chiselhurst, a visit will probably be made to the Roman Catholic *Chapel of St. Mary*, where rest the remains of the late Emperor. To reach it take the lane directly opposite the church, by the side of the Tiger's Head; the chapel is about 300 yds. down at the corner of a lane on the rt. It is a small, plain, unassuming structure, which has evidently had greatness thrust upon it, standing in a humble little graveyard in a secluded, out-of-the-way nook, overshadowed and half hidden by tall elms. The building comprises merely a nave and small chancel, with entrance porch, and over the chancel arch a bell-cote for the Sanctus bell; Dec. in style, but with no attempt at external ornamentation. The interior is also unornamented, except about the altar. For the reception of the Emperor's remains, which were temporarily deposited in the sacristy, the Empress has built an elegant mortuary chapel (designed by Mr. H. Clutton) on the S. side of the chancel (the chancel is directed S.W.), and reached from the chapel by two steps through a double bay, divided by jasper columns. It is a very carefully finished little building, the outer walls of Bath stone, the interior of Caen stone; late French Decorated in style, the walls terminating externally in a pierced parapet; and has 3 windows at the side and a rose window at the end. The interior has a groined roof, and the capitals and tracery show much delicate work. At the end is an altar; in the centre, on a tessellated pavement, stands the sarcophagus, of polished Peterhead granite, the gift of Queen Victoria, with the inscription,

NAPOLEON III.

R.I.P.

In this the coffin containing the remains of the late Emperor was placed, with great religious solemnity, on the 9th of January, 1874, in the presence of the Empress, the Prince Imperial, and an august assemblage.

In the little burial-ground will be noticed

---

* Gentleman's Mag., lxxxiii., p. 582, etc. ; Journals of the time.

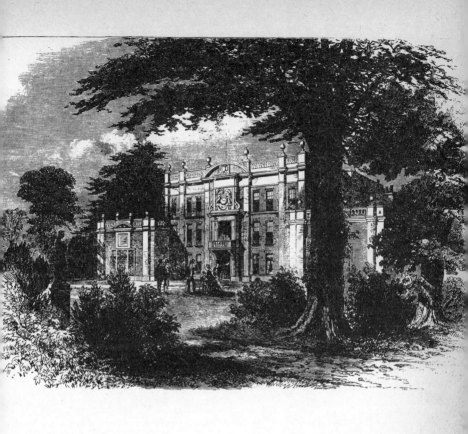

Camden Place, Chiselhurst

Croydon, from the south-east (see p.125)

already a sprinkling of crosses marking the graves of members of the household and followers of the Emperor, the latest memorial, and nearest to the mortuary chapel, being one to " Joseph Michel Xavier Français, Prince Poniatowski, Senateur de l'Empire Français," b. at Rome, Feb. 24, 1813, d. in London, July 3, 1873; and widely known as a diplomatist and amateur musician.

The chapel is open for the usual Sunday services, but on other days visitors are only admitted to the chapel " between 3 and 5 p.m. by orders, which can be obtained by applying, *through the post only*, to the Rev. J. Goddard, Chiselhurst."

Frognal (or Frogpool), the residence of Sir Philip Warwick, now the seat of the Earl Sydney, is a plain, comfortable house, very pleasantly situated, 1½ m. N.E. of Chiselhurst. *Kemnal* (A. F. Slade, Esq.), 1¼ m. N., occupies the site of an old manor-house. *Coopers* is the seat of Lord Richard Cavendish.

The walks on every side are full of beauty. In this neighbourhood occur several of the caverns in the chalk, described under CHADWELL. There they are called Danes' Holes; here they are known as *Draw-pits*. In Camden Park (the footpath mentioned above will lead near the spot) is a connected series of these pits, which extend for some distance under the park. After having been long closed by the falling in of the sides, they were carefully examined in 1857. At the bottom were found great quantities of bones of the horse, ox, pig, dog, wolf, and deer. All were of existing species, with the possible exception of a skull of the *Bos longifrons;* but the presence of undoubted jaw-bones of wolves, and the fact of several fragments of Romano-British pottery being found among them, were incontestible proofs of the antiquity of the cavern. Locally this pit is known as the *Swallow*, and Mr. Latter, in a paper read before the Kent Archæol. Soc., thinks he has identified it as the *Swelgende*, or swallow, a boundary mark used in a charter of Athelbert, King of Wessex, in 862. Another pit was cut through in constructing the rly. a little to the l. of Chiselhurst Station.

CHISWICK, MIDDX., (*Cheswich,*

1210; *Chesnyke*, 1470,) a vill. on the Thames, 5 m. W. of Hyde Park Corner, immediately beyond Hammersmith : ¾ m. W. of the ch., in Burlington Lane, is a Stat. of the S.W. Rly. (Loop-line, 8½ m. from Waterloo Stat.), but connected also with the L. C. and D., and the N. London lines. Pop. of the par., including the hamlets of *Turnham Green* and *Strand-on-the-Green*, 8508.

The Thames, making a great curve here, washes three sides of the parish. The surface is· flat, the soil good, and a considerable part is laid out as market-gardens. There are in the vill. two large ale breweries (Messrs. Fuller and Messrs. Sich), maltings, etc. But to the visitor Chiswick is chiefly remarkable for the Palladian villa of the Duke of Devonshire, the Gardens of the Horticultural Society, and Hogarth's House and Tomb. The *Mall*, along the Thames towards Hammersmith, is still a pleasing walk; but the quaint old Red Lion, with the old whetstone chained to the lintel of the door, and the well-known Chiswick House or Hall, have disappeared. *Chiswick Hall*, formerly *College House*, was a country residence of the Masters of Westminster in the time of Busby, and a retreat for scholars in visitations of plague or sickness. Later, it was widely known as the *Chiswick Press*, from which the Messrs. Whittingham sent forth so many excellent specimens of English typography. The house was pulled down early in 1874, when it was found that, concealed under stucco and modern carpentry, the lower walls were of very early date, built of rubble, of great thickness, and decidedly ecclesiastical character : but no sufficient note seems to have been made of them. When we saw them they were razed nearly to the foundations. Obs. *Chiswick Ait*, or *Eyot*, the first on the Thames above London, used as an osier-bed, and on which, at the proper season, may generally be seen a swan's nest.

The manors of Chiswick (the Dean's and the Prebendal—known originally as Suttune or Sutton) belonged to the Dean and Chapter of St. Paul's as early as the reign of William I., though not mentioned in Domesday. Both have long been held on lease by private persons, the prebendal manor by the Dukes of Devonshire.

Lands within the prebendal manor descend to the youngest son.[*]

Eminent Inhabitants : Sir Henry Sidney (d. 1586), Lord President of Ireland, and father of Sir Philip Sidney, had a house at Chiswick, from which his wife, Lady Mary Sidney, dates her letters in 1547 and 1578.[†] Sir Thomas Chaloner, who discovered at Guisborough in Yorkshire the first alum mines worked in England, wrote a treatise on the virtues of nitre, and whom Puttenham compares, "for eglogue and pastorall poesie to Sir P. Sidney, and the gentleman [Spenser] who wrote the Shepherd's Calendar," d. 1615, at his house at Chiswick, and was buried in the chancel of Chiswick ch. His sons Thomas and James, disgusted at the seizure of the alum mines by Charles I., took an active part against him, were both judges at his trial, and Thomas signed the warrant for his execution. Sir Wm. Russell (afterwards Lord Russell of Thornhaugh), famous for his military prowess, lived at the house afterwards known as Corney House. Here Elizabeth visited him in 1602: "I send you," writes Sir William Brown to Sir Henry Sidney, "all the Queen's entertainment at Chiswick."[‡] The house descended to his only son, Francis, 1st Earl of Bedford (d. 1641), of whose connexion with Chiswick the memory is preserved by a stone let into the outer wall of the ch.-yard, setting forth that

"This wall was made at ye charges of ye Right Hon. & Truelie pious Lorde Francis Russel Earle of Bedford, out of true Zeale and care for ye keeping of this Church Yard and ye Wardrobe of God's Saints whose Bodies lay therin buried, from violating by Swine and other prophanation, so witnesseth William Walker, V. A. D. 1623."

Robert Carr, Earl of Somerset, the unworthy favourite of James I., in a house engraved by Kip, sold 1682 to the 1st Earl of Burlington, and pulled down 1788. Carr mortgaged his house at Chiswick to make up the dower of £12,000 of his only child, Ann Carr, married to Lord Russell, afterwards 1st Duke of Bedford, by whom she was the mother of Lord William Russell.[§] Gervase Holles says,

"The first time I saw the Earl of Somerset at his house at Chiswick [after the Earl of Clare's de-

cease], he stood a pretty while sad and mute. Then he began thus : 'You and I, Mr. Holles, have lost a good friend.' And then throwing up his eyes, he thus proceeded : 'Next the loss of myself, the loss of my Lord of Clare was the greatest calamity that ever befel me. I was once upon the top and able to confer favours . . . but in my calamity, and when I was under foot, whether I look upon your nation, or my own countrymen, that I had deserved well of, I found not one faithful friend but my Lord of Clare." [*]

The wretched Countess of Somerset d. here, 1632, in disgrace and poverty :—

"I will add the testimony of the minister of Chiswick, who was with the lady in her last sickness, when she was past hope of life, and speaking with her of this business, she did then protest upon her soul and salvation that the Earl of Essex was never her husband." [†]

Mary Cromwell, Countess of Fauconberg, third daughter of Oliver Cromwell (d. 1713); Frances, youngest daughter of Oliver Cromwell, married first to Rich, then to Russell (d. 1709) : both the sisters are buried in Chiswick ch. without a monument. Barbara Palmer, Countess of Castlemaine and Duchess of Cleveland (d. 1709) : she is buried in Chiswick ch., without a mont. Margaret Cecil, Countess of Ranelagh (d. 1728) : the Kneller, or Hampton Court Beauty, Fielding likens with Sophia Western. She also lies in Chiswick ch., without a mont. Sir John Chardin, the celebrated traveller (d. 1712). Sir Stephen Fox (d. 1716), father of Henry Fox, 1st Earl of Holland, and grandfather of Charles James Fox.

"1682. *Oct.* 30.—I went with my Lady Fox to survey her building, and give some directions for the garden at Chiswick ; the architect is Mr. May ; somewhat heavy and thick, and not so well understood ; the garden much too narrow, the place without water, near a highway, and near the great house of my Lord Burlington, little land about it, so that I wonder at the expense ; but women will have their will.

"1683. *June* 16.—At Chiswick, at Sir Stephen Fox's, where I found Sir Robert Howard, (that universal pretender) and Signior Verrio, who brought his draught and designs for the painting of the staircase of Sir Stephen's new house." [‡]

Alexander Pope, his father and mother, in Mawson's Buildings, a group of five red brick houses, still standing on the road from the river to the Kew and London road. They lived here before Pope's retirement to Twickenham, and portions of his translation of the Iliad in the British

* Lysons, Environs, vol. ii., p. 123.
† Sidney Papers, vol. i.
‡ Sidney Papers, vol. ii., p. 231.
§ Strafford Papers, vol. ii., p. 58.

* Collins's Hist. Collections, p. 97.
+ Bishop Goodman, Court of King James, vol. i., p. 222.
‡ Evelyn, Diary.

Museum are, after his "paper-sparing" fashion, written on the backs of letters addressed "To Mr. Pope, at his house in ye New Buildings, Chiswick," and the like. Pope's father died at Chiswick in 1717, and was buried in the church.

Richard Boyle, the architect Earl of Burlington (d. 1753) : ("Who plants like Bathurst, and who builds like Boyle ? " *) He built Chiswick House (*see* below). William Kent, painter, gardener, architect (d. 1748). He is buried in Lord Burlington's vault. James Ralph (d. 1762), and buried in the ch.-yard ; made immortal in the Dunciad :—

" Silence, ye wolves ! while Ralph to Cynthia howls,
    And makes night hideous—Answer him, ye owls !"

William Hogarth (d. 1764), and buried in the ch.-yard ; and in the same house, the Rev. H. F. Cary, translator of Dante (*see* below). Rousseau when in England boarded at a small grocer's shop at Chiswick. " He sits in the shop," says a writer of the time, "and learns English words, which brings many customers to the shop." † Charles Holland, the comedian (d. 1769). He was the son of a baker in Chiswick, and was buried in the ch. Foote attended his funeral : " Yes," he said, "we have just shoved the little baker into his oven." ‡ Rose, the translator of Sallust (d. 1786), kept a school at Chiswick : Dr. Charles Burney was one of his tutors, and married his daughter. Griffiths, the bookseller, whose name is so intimately connected with the chequered career of Goldsmith, died at Chiswick in 1803, and is here buried. George, Earl Macartney, ('Account of the Russian Empire,' and 'Journal of the Embassy to Spain,') died here in 1806, and was buried in the ch.-yard. Ugo Foscolo died here in 1827 (*see* below).

The *Church* (St. Nicholas) stands near the river. The tower, of flint and stone, Perp., was erected at the cost of Wm. Bordall, vicar of Chiswick, who d. 1435. Portions of the old nave and chancel remain, but brick aisles were carried out on either side in the last half of the last and early in the present century, of the usual churchwarden character. Recently

* Pope.
† Caldwell Papers, vol. ii., p. 71.
‡ Cradock, vol. i., p. 33.

some improvements and partial restorations have been made in the interior ; the pews have given place to low open seats ; the W. window has been opened ; an organ chamber erected, and a new organ provided ; the chancel rebuilt, decorated, and a new memorial E. window inserted.

The *monts.* are numerous. *Obs.* the large Jacobean structure against S. wall of chancel, with effigies of Sir Thomas Challoner (d. 1615), and his wife kneeling under a pavilion, the curtains of which are supported by 2 armed soldiers. N. wall, Charles Holland, the actor (d. 1769), with bust, and an insc. by Garrick. E. wall, mont. to Thomas Bentley (d. 1780), Wedgwood's partner and most intelligent artistic adviser. Mural mont. to Charles Whittingham the printer (d. 1841).

In the *Churchyard*, obs. S. of the ch. a large altar-tomb covering the remains of WILLIAM HOGARTH, d. Oct. 26, 1764, his sister (d. 1771), his widow (d. 1789), the daughter, and his mother-in-law (d. 1757), the widow of Sir James Thornhill. Besides the usual names and dates, it has a mask, laurel wreath, pencil, palette with the painter's famous Line, a book inscribed ' Analysis of Beauty,' and the verses—

" Farewell, great painter of mankind,
    Who reach'd the noblest point of art ;
    Whose pictured morals charm the mind,
    And through the eye correct the heart !
    If genius fire thee, reader, stay ;
    If nature move thee, drop a tear ;
    If neither touch thee, turn away,
    For Hogarth's honour'd dust lies here.
        D. GARRICK."

A small granite slab at the foot records that it was " restored by Wm. Hogarth of Aberdeen in 1856."

Not far off is a tall mont. to *Philip James Loutherbourg*, R.A.,— Stanfield's predecessor in landscape and scene painting,—d. at Hammersmith Terrace, March 11, 1812. Close to this is an upright headstone, to *Wm. Sharp*, the famous historical line engraver, d. July 25, 1824 ; and near this again (on the N. wall of the engine-house) a slab to James Fittler, A.R.A., d. Dec. 2, 1835, well known by his engravings after West and Loutherbourg. S. of these is a coffer-shaped tomb of polished grey granite, with a bronze wreath of laurel on the top, designed by Baron Marochetti 1861, placed over the remains of Ugo Foscolo, the Italian poet. The recently added inscription will best tell the tale of his interment, removal, and present resting-place. On the E. end of tomb—

UGO FOSCOLO,
Died Sept. 10, 1827, aged 50.

On S. side—

From the sacred guardianship of Chiswick,
To the honours of Santa Croce, in Florence,
The Government and People of Italy have transported
The Remains of the wearied Citizen Poet,
7th June, 1871.

On N. side—

This Spot where for 44 years
The Relics of
UGO FOSCOLO
Reposed in honoured Custody,
Will be for ever held in grateful Remembrance
By the Italian Nation.

Other monts. include those of Lord Macartney, and of Dr. Rose, with a long poetical insc. by Murphy.

Hogarth's House.—The house in which for many years the great painter spent his summers, and in which he died, stands on the S. side of *Hogarth Lane*, not far from the ch. It is an old-fashioned red-brick building, said to have been previously the residence of his father-in-law, Sir James Thornhill. In Hogarth's day, standing in the open country, and surrounded by tall elms, it must have been a pleasant summer abode, but it has of late been a good deal blocked up by mean houses, and is itself dirty, dreary, dilapidated, and semi-ruinous,—the porch broken down, and portions of the ornamented brickwork with it. The house is now let in tenements; the lower rooms unsavoury, and denuded of everything Hogarthian; and the little windows filled with a wretched display of withered apples, nuts, and sweets. The chief room on the first floor is now a lodger's bedroom, as poor and dismantled as the rest. The outbuilding known as 'Hogarth's Painting-room,' is a mere wreck. In an alcove at the end of the garden were the thoroughly characteristic stones he set up over his dog and bullfinch. Over the bird was "Alas, poor Yorick." Over the dog, "Life to the Last enjoyed, here Pompey lies,"—a parody, of course, on Churchill's epitaph. On a recent visit (April 1874), we were told that though the garden was uprooted, these remained,

"it being in the agreement when the house was let that they should not be disturbed." Seeing only a row of pigstyes along that end of the garden, we led the way there and asked for an explanation. "The stones *are* there : under that bed of concrete. We were not to take them away, and so we laid the concrete over them, and now any one has the satisfaction of knowing that they are safe"—under a bed of concrete with a pigstye over them !

Mrs. Hogarth lived here for a quarter of a century after her husband's death; of late in very straitened circumstances, but tenaciously maintaining as much as she was able of her old state, and keeping up the little customs he had established. Sir Richard Phillips relates with what pomp and form he used, when a school-boy at this "simple and primitive village," to see

"The widow Hogarth, and her maiden relative Richardson, walking up the aisle [of Chiswick ch. on a Sunday] dressed in their silken sacks, their raised head-dresses, their black hoods, their lace ruffles, and their high-crooked canes, preceded by their aged man-servant Samuel: who, after he had wheeled his mistress to church in the Bath chair, carried the prayer-books up the aisle, and opened and shut the pew." [*]

"In the garden [of Hogarth's house] there was a large mulberry tree. I was told by an old person who remembered Mrs. Hogarth, that she regularly invited the children of the village every summer to eat the mulberries; a custom established by her husband, and probably not discontinued by Mr. Cary." [†]

The mulberry tree remains, mutilated like everything else, but not irreparably injured.

Cary, the translator of Dante, shortly after his appointment to the curacy of Chiswick in 1814, purchased Hogarth's house, and, with a short interval, lived in it till he removed to an official residence at the British Museum in 1826.

Chiswick House.—The Jacobean mansion of the Earl of Somerset was purchased towards the end of the 17th cent. by the Earl of Burlington. From him it descended to the last, or architect-earl, the friend of Pope and Gay, who, having decided to pull down the old house, built a new one near it (1730-36). The wits dealt somewhat severely with its littleness

---

[*] Morning's Walk to Kew.
[†] Leslie, Life of Reynolds, vol. i., p. 234.

and its inconvenience, but the men of taste were in raptures with its elegance :—

"His lordship's house at Chiswick, the idea of which is borrowed from a well-known villa of Palladio [that of the Marquis Capra at Vicenza], is a model of taste, though not without faults, some of which are occasioned by too strict adherence to rules and symmetry. . . . . Yet these blemishes, and Lord Hervey's wit, who said *the house was too small to inhabit, and too large to hang to one's watch*, cannot depreciate the taste that reigns in the whole. The larger court, dignified by picturesque cedars, and the classic scenery of the small court that unites the old and new house, are more worth seeing than many fragments of ancient grandeur which our travellers visit under all the dangers attendant on long voyages." *

Lord Hervey, not content with the *bon-mot* quoted by Walpole, extemporized an Epigram from Martial on Chiswick House :—

"Possess'd of one great Hall for state,
Without one room to sleep or eat :
How well you build let flattery tell,
And all mankind how ill you dwell." +

The edge of this reproach was somewhat blunted by the addition, in 1788, of two wings, designed by James Wyatt for the 5th Duke of Devonshire. Since then there have been no material additions to the house, but some improvements have been made in the arrangements, and under the late Duke everything was done that could be thought of to embellish the interior. But Chiswick House was from the first regarded as a summer villa, and the garden and grounds were treated as part of the design, and lavishly decorated with urns, obelisks, sculpture, and buildings. Walpole wrote, "The garden is in the Italian taste, but divested of conceits, and far preferable to every style that reigned till our late improvements. The buildings are heavy and not equal to the purity of the house. The lavish quantity of urns and sculpture behind the garden front should be retrenched." Thomson in his 'Liberty' cites Chiswick as one of those

"Sylvan scenes, where Art alone pretends
To dress her mistress, and disclose her charms."

From Gay's 'Epistle to the Earl of Burlington' we learn that the Earl was wont to enjoy the society of his poetic friends in his "Chiswick bowers," and that here

"Pope unloads the boughs within his reach,
The purple vine, blue plum, and blushing peach."

Many of the statues in the grounds and buildings are true antiques, having been selected from the best of those which had been buried under the rubbish in the gardens of Arundel House. The lions and other animals are by Scheemakers. The rusticated gate was originally erected in 1625, by Inigo Jones, for Lord Treasurer Middlesex, at Beaufort House, Chelsea. When Beaufort House was pulled down in 1738, Sir Hans Sloane gave the gate to the Earl of Burlington, who removed it here. The grounds were greatly extended by the late Duke of Devonshire, and the gardens brought, under Sir Joseph Paxton's direction, to the highest point of floricultural excellence. The new approach from Turnham Green, a broad road lined with lime trees—now in full vigour—and known as the Duke's New Road, was also made by him.

"*June* 1, 1813.—Drove with the Duke of Devonshire, in his curricle, to Chiswick, where he showed me all the alterations that he was about to make, in adding the gardens of Lady M. Coke's house to his. The house is down, and in the gardens he has constructed a magnificent hothouse, with a conservatory for flowers, the middle under a cupola. Altogether it is 300 ft. long. The communication between the two gardens is through what was the old greenhouse, of which they have made a double arcade, making the prettiest effect possible." *

In these grounds the late Duke used to give open-air entertainments that were among the chief attractions of the season. Not only did he receive his own sovereign here, but the Emperor of Russia, the King of Prussia, and other high and mighty potentates, with, of course, the leading members of the nobility, the leaders of society, and the lions of the day.

"*May* 17, 1828.—I went to the Duke of Wellington, who gave me some hints, or rather details. Afterwards I drove out to Chiswick, where I had never been before. A numerous and gay party were assembled to walk and enjoy the beauties of that Palladian dome. The place and highly ornamented gardens belonging to it resemble a picture of Watteau. There is some affectation in the picture, but in the *ensemble* the original looked very well. The Duke of Devonshire received every one with the best possible manners. The scene was dignified by the presence of an immense elephant, who, under the charge of a groom, wandered up

---

* Walpole, Anecdotes of Painting, vol. iv., pp. 232, 233.
+ Lord Hervey's Memoirs, vol. ii., p. 145.

---

* Miss Berry's Journal, vol. ii., pp. 535, 536.

and down, giving an air of Asiatic pageantry to the entertainment." *

Charles James Fox was in his last illness removed to Chiswick House, Aug. 29, 1806, and he d. there a fortnight later, Sept. 13. His bedchamber was that which opens into the Italian Saloon, and a mountain ash which grew near his window, with its clustering berries, was an object of great interest to him. " Every morning he returned to look at it. . . . His last look on that mountain ash was his last look on nature." † George Canning was in like manner brought here in the month preceding his decease. He died Aug. 8, 1827, in the room in which Fox breathed his last.

"It is a small low chamber, over a kind of nursery, and opening into a wing of the building, which gives it the appearance of looking into a courtyard. Nothing can be more simple than its furniture or its decorations. . . . On one side of the fireplace are a few bookshelves; opposite the foot of the bed is the low chimneypiece, and on it a small bronze clock, to which we may fancy the weary and impatient sufferer often turning his eyes during those bitter moments in which he was passing from the world which he had filled with his name and was governing with his projects. What a place for repeating those simple and touching lines of Dyer :

'A little rule, a little sway,
A sunbeam on a winter's day,
Is all the proud and mighty have
Between the cradle and the grave.'" ‡

Chiswick House is now rented by H.R.H. the Prince of Wales, and occupied chiefly by the royal children, but during the summer the Prince and Princess usually spend some time here, and give occasional garden parties in the grounds, now no less classic than the house.

Corney, the residence of Lord Russell and of the Earl of Macartney, passed, like most of the property in immediate contiguity with Chiswick House, into the hands of the Duke of Devonshire. The mansion was pulled down, and the grounds added to those of C. House. Some noble specimens of the tulip tree are on the lawn which fronts the site of Corney House. The Grove, between Chiswick House and the river, also the property of the Duke of Devonshire, is famous for its

* Sir Walter Scott's Diary, Lockhart's Life of Scott, chap. lxxvi.
† Earl Russell's Life of Fox; Trotter's Memoir of Fox, p. 451.
‡ Sir H. Bulwer's (Lord Dalling) Historical Characters (Canning), vol. ii., p. 402.

magnificent Spanish chesnuts, the largest of which is above 26 ft. in girth. Grove House, in the last century the seat of Earl Cowper, is now in the occupation of R. Prowett, Esq., but that portion of the park by the rly. stat. has been laid out in streets, and built over. The fantastic red-brick structure, with tall capped towers, beyond the Grove, towards Strand-on-the-Green, is Grove End (J. Pullman, Esq.), erected in 1861.

The Gardens of the Horticultural Society lie between Chiswick House and Turnham Green. Though of less popular interest since the formation of the Society's gardens and conservatory at South Kensington, the Chiswick gardens are well worth a visit, and are full of interest to the student. They are now used as nursery and fruit gardens, for the culture of the seeds and rare plants collected by the Society from all parts of the world; as a school of horticulture; and for raising plants and flowers for the show gardens at S. Kensington, and for distribution among the Fellows of the Society. It was here that the Duke of Devonshire found the future Sir Joseph Paxton, then young and untried, training creepers at 12s. a week.

At what is called Chiswick New Town is a chapel of ease, erected in 1848. The hamlet of TURNHAM GREEN, and its dependant STRAND-ON-THE-GREEN are noticed under those headings.

CLAPHAM, SURREY, is within the 4 m. circle, but though daily becoming more a part of London, it yet retains so much of its old extra-urban character as to claim a brief notice here. It lies between Brixton and Battersea, and may be reached by the Crystal Palace (High Level) and the South London Rlys. The Clapham Junction of the L. and S.W. Rly. is more than a mile on the Battersea side of Clapham.

The name Clapham, i.e., Clapa's ham, is supposed to be derived from its owner, Osgod Clapa, at whose daughter's marriage feast at Lambeth, the king, Hardacnut, died, according to the Saxon Chron., June 8th, 1042. But to this there is the objection pointed out by Mr. Brayley that in the Chertsey Register the place is named Clappenham in the reign of Alfred; in the Dom. Survey it stands as Clopeham.

It is of course possible that there was an earlier Clapa than Osgod.

Clapham has increased so largely of late years in houses and pop. (in 1871 it numbered 27,347 inhab.) that it has become a town in size and appearance, if not in rank. But now, as of old, it is chiefly remarkable for its *Common*, of 220 acres, redeemed from a morass, and planted in 1722 by the exertions of Christopher Baldwin, Esq. The Common, in parts still overgrown with heath and furze, and with its fine groups of trees and great ponds, is in appearance something between a park and a common; well kept, and in excellent condition. It is now (1874), by recent Parliamentary action and purchase of manorial rights, secured in permanence for public use, and placed under the management of the Metropolitan Board of Works. The pleasure fairs held on the Common on Good Friday, Easter and Whit Mondays, and the Derby Day, were abolished in 1873.

Skirting the Common are several of the roomy old red-brick mansions, with great elms before them, the abode of wealthy citizens, which once nearly surrounded it, but they are giving place to brick and compo Gothic and Italian villas.

In a large house on the upper side of the Common, at the corner of what is now the Cavendish Road, since refronted and altered, lived (and d. 1810) Henry Cavendish, "the Newton of Chemistry," distinguished as the founder of pneumatic chemistry, and by his successful researches on the composition of water, and his famous experiment, made here, for the determination of the earth's density. " The man who weighed the world," wrote his cousin, the late Duke of Devonshire, in his ' Hand Book for Chatsworth,' " buried his science and his wealth in solitude and insignificance at Clapham." To such an extent did he carry his solitary habits that he would never even see, or allow himself to be seen by, a female servant; and, as Lord Brougham relates, " he used to order his dinner daily by a note, which he left at a certain hour on the hall table, whence the housekeeper was to take it." His shyness was, not unnaturally, mistaken by strangers for pride :—

"While travelling in England in 1790, with George Forster, Humboldt obtained permission to make use of the library of the eminent chemist and philosopher Henry Cavendish, second son of the Duke of Devonshire ; on condition, however, that he was on no account to presume so far as to speak to, or even greet, the proud and aristocratic owner should he happen to encounter him. Humboldt states this in a letter to Bunsen, adding sarcastically, ' Cavendish little suspected at that time that it was I who in 1810 was to be his successor at the Academy of Sciences.'" *

At Clapham Common, in the house of his servant and friend Will Hewer, died (1703) Samuel Pepys, author of the incomparable ' Diary.' Hewer's house, a large mansion, with a spacious gallery occupying the whole length of the house, was built by Sir Dennis Gauden for his brother, Dr. John Gauden, Bp. of Exeter, the presumed author of the ' Eikon Basilike,' and after his death (1662) became the residence of Sir Dennis himself, who collected a fine library and gallery of works of art, and died here in 1688. Hewer afterwards purchased the house and estate, and died here in 1715. The house was pulled down about 1760.

"23 *Sept.* 1700.—I went to visit Mr. Pepys at Clapham, where he has a very noble and wonderfully well-furnished house, especially with Indian and Chinese curiosities. The offices and gardens well accommodated for pleasure and retirement." †

Clapham Common and its immediate vicinity was, in the early years of the century, the seat of the knot of zealous men who, labouring together for what they believed to be the interests of pure religion, the reformation of manners, and the suppression of slavery, came to be known as the *Clapham Sect.* ‡ One of the most distinguished of them, William Wilberforce, lived at the house known as *Broomfield*, on the S.W. side of Clapham Common, and there his no less distinguished son, the late Bp. of Winchester, was born, Sept. 7th, 1805. " Conterminous with his fair demesne " was that of Henry Thornton, the author and prime mover of the conclave, whose meetings were held, for the most part, in the oval saloon which William Pitt, "dismissing for a moment his budgets and his subsidies, planned to be added to Henry Thornton's newly purchased residence. . . . It arose at his bidding, and yet remains, perhaps a solitary monument of the architectural skill

* Bruhn's Life of Alex. von Humboldt, Eng. trans., 1873, vol. ii., p. 68.

† Evelyn, Diary ; "your Paradisian Clapham,' Evelyn terms it in writing to Pepys, Jan. 20, 1703.

‡ For their names and deeds see Sir James Stephen's Essays in Eccl. Biog., vol. ii., pp. 289—385.

of that imperial mind. Lofty and symmetrical, it was curiously wainscoted with books on every side, except where it opened on a far extended lawn, reposing beneath the giant arms of aged elms and massive tulip-trees." * In this saloon, and on the far extended lawn, after their long years of effort, assembled "in joy and thanksgiving and mutual gratulation over the abolition of the African slave trade," Wilberforce, Clarkson, Granville Sharp, Stephen, Zachary Macaulay, and their younger associates and disciples.

But "the villa-cinctured common" was also the birthplace or cradle of another and hardly less remarkable and far-reaching religious movement, or institution. Just as it was "the dwelling-place or the haunt of every one of the more eminent supporters" of the anti-slavery movement, so was it the home or haunt of the founders of the Bible Society, its earliest ministers or secretaries, and, "above all, the first and greatest of its Presidents— John Lord Teignmouth."

A tract of some 250 acres of bare upland immediately to the E. of Clapham Common, known as Bleak Hill, was in 1824 taken by Mr. Thos. Cubitt, the creator of Belgravia, laid out with broad roads and open spaces, planted, and built over with capacious detached villas, and named *Clapham Park*. This is now the Belgravia of Clapham, though it has an attractive rival in a newer builder's park, the *Cedars*, which stretches from the opposite side of the common towards Battersea Rise, and is spotted over with large and costly residences of the latest model.

The old parish church stood on high ground between Larkhall Lane and Wandsworth Road, about ¼ m. N. of the present parish ch., on the site now occupied by St. Paul's ch. It was small and plain, and, becoming unsafe, was taken down in 1775. In a chapel built especially for their reception were "some very sumptuous monts." to Sir Richard Atkins, Bart. (d. 1689), and his wife Rebecca, with recumbent marble effigies; and others with kneeling figures to their son and daughters. When the ch. was pulled down, these and other monts. were destroyed, and the statues consigned to one

of the vaults. The only mont. preserved was that of Will Hewer.

The new par. *Church* (Holy Trinity), erected 1774-76, at a cost of over £10,000, at the extreme N. end of the Common, is a very ugly brick building, without aisles, and having an odd dome-crowned tower at the W. end. It contains a mont. to John Thornton by Sir Richard Westmacott; a mural mont. with medallion portrait of John Jebb (d. 1833), "the Learned, the Wise, the Good Bishop of Limerick [whose remains] are deposited in the tomb of the Thorntons, by permission of a family to which he was united by a bond of no common friendship;" and a mural tablet to the verbose Dr. John Gillies (d. 1836), the author of a forgotten 'History of Greece,' and translator of Aristotle's Ethics.

St. Paul's is a plain chapel-like brick building, erected in 1814 from Mr. C. Edmond's designs, on the site of the old par. ch. On the S. exterior wall is the mont., with bust, of Will Hewer, which was saved at the demolition of the old ch. Inside is a mont. by Chantrey, to J. B. Wilson, Esq. (d. 1835).

St. James's, Park Hill, an early Gothic building of brick and stone, erected from the designs of Mr. C. Vulliamy in 1829; *All Saints'*, Clapham Park, built in 1858; *Christ Ch.*, Union Grove, built in 1862; and *St. Stephen's*, Grove Road, are Gothic structures calling for no particular remark.

St. John's, in the Clapham Road, erected in 1842, is a Greek temple, with a hexastyle Ionic portico and no steeple, but instead a cross on the apex of the pediment. Here for many years preached to large congregations the Rev. Robert Bickersteth, the present Bp. of Ripon. *St. Saviour's*, Cedars Road, is a handsome cruciform building, Dec. in style, with a central tower in three stages, with pinnacles, 120 ft. high, erected from the designs of Mr. J. Knowles in 1864, at the cost of the Rev. W. Bowyer and Mrs. Bowyer. A recumbent statue of Mrs. Bowyer, on an altar tomb, was placed under the tower, immediately in front of the altar rails, with the feet towards the altar; but the bishop of the diocese objected to this as unseemly, and the ch. remained in consequence unconsecrated till 1873, when the mont. was removed to

* Stephen, Essays, vol. ii., p. 290.

the N. transept. The windows are filled with painted glass by Clayton and Bell.

Two of the most ecclesiastical looking buildings by the Common, with their lofty spires quite dwarfing the parish ch., do not belong to the Establishment. One is the Roman Catholic ch. and college of St. Mary, built in 1851; the other the Congregational ch., Grafton Square, built in 1852. There is also a large and showy classical Presbyterian ch.

CLAREMONT, SURREY (*see* ESHER).

CLAYGATE, SURREY (pop. 576),

a manor and ecc. district in Thames Ditton par., 2 m. S.E. from the Esher Stat. of the L. and S.W. Rly. The district is chiefly agricultural, but the neighbourhood is pleasant, and buildings are increasing. The chief seat is *Ruxley Lodge* (Lady Foley), noted for its fine views, and marked by the noble pair of cedars on the lawn. The *Church* (Holy Trinity), built in 1840 from the designs of Mr. H. E. Kendal, was enlarged and much altered in 1866.

CLAY HILL, KENT (*see* BECKENHAM).

COBHAM, SURREY (Dom. *Coven-ham*),

17 m. from London, and 4½ m. S.W. from the Esher, and 4 m. S. from the Weybridge Stat. of the L. and S.W. Rly. ; pop. of par., 2133.

The village consists of two parts, *Church Cobham*, built around the ch., on the rt. bank of the Mole, and *Cobham Street* (or *Street Cobham*) ½ m. N.W. on the main Portsmouth road. The soil and surface are very varied : along the Mole, which winds in a curious way through the par., it is alluvial (brick earth and gravel); S. clay; whilst N., on both sides of the valley, is Lower Bagshot sand. Of old this part was wild common, like so much still left farther W., but the greater portion was enclosed under Acts obtained in 1770 and 1793, these being among the earliest Acts for the enclosure of commons and waste lands in this county. The occupations are mainly agricultural.

Church Cobham is a good-sized collection of shops and dwellings, several of which are large, and some old. The ch., the bridge, and the mill, with the river

winding round, and almost encircling a broad meadow opposite the village, impart character and picturesqueness to it. The *Church* (St. Andrew) is large; chiefly Late Dec., except the tower, which is of Norman date. It consists of nave, aisles, chancel, and massive W. tower, crowned with a tall shingle spire. It has suffered many repairs and improvements, and in 1866 was restored and enlarged. The *monts.* are numerous, but of persons more distinguished by wealth than attainments. *Obs.* bas-relief by Mr. R. Westmacott, jun.—"the Pilgrim at rest"—on the mont. of W. H. Cooper, Esq., also two *brasses* by the pulpit steps. N. of the ch. notice the ostentatious mausoleum of Ald. Harvey C. Combe (d. 1818) the great brewer, M.P. for London, and friend of C. J. Fox. S.W. of the ch. is a large yew.

Just beyond the ch., on the Ockham road, the Mole is crossed by a brick bridge of 9 arches, and near it is a large water mill. S. is *Cobham Park*, the extensive demesne of C. Combe, Esq., and formerly the residence of Gen. Lord Ligonier. The house was erected in 1750. A lane on rt. of the park leads by Pointers Green to Ockham. *Cobham Lodge* (Miss Molesworth) is at Downside (where is another and more pict. water-mill). S. of C. Park, and W. of this, is *Pointers* (W. Deacon, Esq.), and *Hatchford*, the handsome seat of Capt. the Hon. Francis Egerton, R.N.

Cobham Street, as noticed, lies N.W. of Church Cobham on the Portsmouth road. It contains many substantial houses, and though the glory of the posting trade has departed from it, and its great inn, the *White Lion*, is but a ghost of its former self, it has a thriving look. The bridge here was, it is said, originally built by the good Queen Maud, wife of Henry I., as an act of charity for the repose of the soul of one of her maidens, who was drowned in crossing the ford ; but a precisely similar story is told of her in relation to the construction of the bridge at Stratford-le-Bow. The present structure was erected in 1782. Immediately beyond the bridge is the principal entrance to *Pain's Hill* (Chas. J. Leaf, Esq.), in the last century regarded as one of the greatest triumphs of landscape gardening in England. The larger part of the estate is in Walton par., but as it belongs to Cobham by its position, this appears the most convenient place for a brief notice of it. The house, which stands on an elevation sloping down to the Mole, is a large square building, with a lofty projecting tetrastyle Corinthian portico, erected about 1790, by B. B. Hopkins, Esq.; but altered, especially internally, and the conservatory added, for Mr. Cooper by Decimus Burton about 1832. The grounds were laid out by a former proprietor, the Hon. Charles Hamilton, in the reign of George II. The surface is considerably varied, but the views belong rather to the grounds than extend from them. They include hillside and dell, hanging woods, an artificial lake of 30 acres, fed by the Mole, numerous imitation ruins, grottoes, and towers, a temple of Bacchus, a group of Roman altars and sepulchral inscriptions arranged in a mausoleum near the head of the lake, and in the most broken part of the property a thicket. This part especially delighted Horace Walpole. He says,

"I mean that kind of Alpine scene, composed almost wholly of pines and firs, a few birch, and such trees as assimilate with savage and mountainous country. Mr. Charles Hamilton, at Pain's-hill, in my opinion has given a perfect example of this mode in the utmost boundary of his garden. All is great and foreign and rude; the walks seem not designed, but cut through the wood of pines; and the style of the whole is so grand, and conducted with so serious an air of wild and uncultivated extent, that when you look down on this seeming forest, you are amazed to find it contain a very few acres." *

"In your next expedition you will see Claremont and Lord Portman's which joins my Lord Lincoln's, and above all Mr. Hamilton's at Cobham, in Surrey, which all the world talks of, and I have seen seven years ago." †

Whateley‡ is even more eulogistic. Mr. Hamilton was as careful in the situation and grouping of his trees as in the arrangement of his temples and ruins. Many of the views were formed from the pictures of Gaspar Poussin and Claude Lorraine. It is needless to remark that so elaborately artificial a construction of natural scenery was a mistake in taste. The object seems to have been to combine the greatest possible variety of scenes and periods within the comparatively limited space—for Hamilton possessed less than

* On Modern Gardening, p. 30.
† Gray (the poet) to Dr. Wharton, Aug. 13, 1754.
‡ Observations on Modern Gardening.

100 acres, whilst the present demesne exceeds 450. Not only had he Greek and Roman temples and ruins, but a Gothic chapel, mediæval keep, grottoes, waterfalls, and Italian and Alpine landscapes, and besides all else a hermitage, for which it is said he advertised for a live hermit, offering £700 to any one who would lead a true hermit's life, sleeping on a mat, never suffering scissors to touch his beard or nails, and never speaking a syllable to the servant who brought his food. A man was found to undertake the enterprise, but he tired before three weeks. Much of Hamilton's work has been removed or altered, but his grounds are still the most attractive portion of the park. Many noble trees remain. The cedars are numerous and very fine : *obs.* those on the lawn ; also the superb tulip tree, cork trees, Scotch firs, and several remarkable oaks. There is a fine view of the W. side of the island by Woollett. Cobham is a favourite resort for anglers, the Mole here affording some good chub, trout, and jack fishing.

COLNBROOK, Bucks (17 m.), on the Colne and borders of Middx., 2 m. N. from Wraysbury Stat. of the L. and S.W. Rly. (Windsor br.), through Horton ; pop. 1153. Inns, the *White Hart*, at the entrance of the town from Horton, a good house, with bowling-green and grounds, much in favour for trade dinners and pleasure parties ; the *George*, near the ch., at which Elizabeth is said to have stayed a night when carried as a prisoner from Woodstock to Hampton Court.

The town no doubt took its name from the Colne, but the old rhyme of Thomas of Reading makes the river as well as the town derive its name from Thomas Cole, the Reading clothier, who was treacherously murdered by the landlord of the Ostrich inn. Camden and Gale make Colnbrook to have been *Ad Pontes* of the *Ant. Itin.*, but later antiquaries prefer Staines. From its position on the great W. road, Colnbrook was of old a place of some note. Edward the Black Prince, with his prisoner John, King of France, was met here by Edward III. Charles I. received here a deputation from the Houses of Parliament. Colnbrook was incorporated in 1544 ; had a bailiff and 12 burgesses, a market-house in the main street, and a market on Tuesdays; all which have long passed away. During the coaching days it retained something of its ancient noise and stir; it is now a dull, sleepy, country roadside village of a long main street and 2 or 3 shabby offshoots, the many inns alone testifying to its old character. Of these inns, the decayed hostelry the *Ostrich*, near the middle of the High-street, a large rambling half-timber building, very much out of repair, and defaced by yellow-wash, is the oldest, and is worth notice. Several other of the houses are old, and too often semi-ruinous.

Colnbrook forms "a consolidated chapelry;" the houses are in 2 counties and 4 parishes; the larger portion (the town proper), W. of the Colne, is in Bucks, the N. side of the street being in Langley and Iver parishes, the S. in Horton; whilst the part E. of the river is in Middx. county and Stanwell par. The *Church*, erected in 1849, stands by the avenue that leads to Richings. It is of flint and stone, Early Dec. in style, has a bell-cote on the W. gable, and a porch on the S. side.

The Colne divides here into 4 channels, and is crossed by as many bridges. By the town it works 2 large mills; below, it flows as of old "through meadows trim with daisies pied," a rushy stream betwixt willowy banks. Horton is but a mile away S., and all around are Milton's "daily walks and ancient neighbour-hood;" whilst on the other side (¾ m. N.) is Richings, the paradise of Prior, Pope, and Gay, and in the next generation of Shenstone and Moses Browne. (*See* HORTON; RICHINGS.)

COLNEY HATCH, MIDDX. (anc. *Colne Hatch*), a hamlet of Friern Barnet, and a stat. of the Grt. N. Rly., 6½ m. from King's Cross. A vill. of smart villas with shops, a Railway Hotel, and church, chapels, and schools on one side of the rly., and of cottages on the other, has grown up since the opening of the stat. and the construction of the asylum, and is steadily enlarging its boundaries.

The eccl. dist. is called *New Southgate*, —a name that is intended to supersede that of Colney Hatch. The *Church* (St. Paul's), a neat Gothic building (late E.E. in character), was consecrated July 1873.

The building opposite to it is a Baptist chapel; and the long low brick structure, with a square campanile chimney shaft next the chapel, a pumping station of the New River Waterworks.

On the opposite side of the rly. is the *Middlesex County Lunatic Asylum*. This immense structure covers an area of 25 acres, affords accommodation for over 2000 patients; and includes bakery, brewery, laundry, and every other adjunct required for so large an establishment, on the most complete scale, and worked by the patients. The first stone was laid by the Prince Consort in 1849; it was opened July 17th, 1851, but has since been much extended. The architect was Mr. S. W. Daukes. Throughout it is of brick; the stone dressings and architectural orna-ment being confined to the principal front, which is 1881 ft. long, and plain Italian in style. It stands on an elevated and healthy site, in grounds of about 100 acres, with a farm adjoining of 140 acres. The patients average 800 males and 1200 females; and, under the superintendence of Dr. E. Shephard, are kept without shackle or even strait-waistcoat. The officers and attendants number nearly 300. The asylum cost about half a million; the annual expenditure is some what under £60,000.

Just outside Colney Hatch, at the corner of the lane to Southgate, are the *Clock and Watch Makers' Almshouses*, a comfortable and picturesque looking building of red and black brick, Dom. Gothic, with chapel in the centre, erected in 1857. By it is an entrance to the *Great Northern Cemetery*.

COLNEY HEATH, HERTS, a rambling hamlet, 4 m. E.S.E. of St. Albans, on the road to North Mimms. St. Mark's, Colney Heath, was constituted an eccl. dist. out of the parishes of St. Peter and St. Stephen, St. Albans, and Ridge; pop. 818. A little Perp. ch. was built in 1844. The country is wild, open, and out-of-the-way; and there are pleasant walks to *N. Mimms Park* (Visct. Greville), and W. by *Tittenhanger Park* (Countess of Caledon) to *London Colney*, 2 m.

Colney Street is a pretty hamlet on the St. Albans road, 2 m. farther. All these places derive their name from the little river Colne.

COMBE WOOD, SURREY, a wild little forest-like tract, W. of Wimbledon Common, towards Kingston, to which par. it belongs. The surface is broken into hill and dell, and, with some good trees, is rich in copse and underwood, tangled bramble and knee-deep fern and prickly gorse. On the highest part used to stand an Admiralty semaphore; lower, and farther S., are the springs which supply Hampton Court with water; and Yarrel mentions it as one of the few places in this part of the country in which the white-tailed eagle has been shot. Until trespassers were warned off under threat of prosecution, the wood was a favourite haunt of the ornithologist, botanist, and sketcher. Sketchers, indeed, still go there, for there are open paths, though rambling is forbidden; but in former days it was the frequent goal of a London artist's holiday. Leslie tells a story of Combe Wood that curiously illustrates the simple frugal manners of even the more eminent painters of 50 years ago :—

"I was amused with an account Constable gave me of a walk he took with him [Stothard] in 1824, from London to Combe Wood, where they dined by the side of a spring. They set out early in the day, provided with some sandwiches for their dinner. Before they reached the wood, Stothard, seeing Constable eating a sandwich, called him 'a young traveller,' for breaking in on their store so early. When they got to the spring, they found the water low and difficult to reach; but Constable took from his pocket a tin cup, which he had bought at Putney unnoticed by Stothard. The day was hot, and the water intensely cold; and Stothard said, 'Hold it in your mouth, sir, some time before you swallow it. A little brandy or rum now would be invaluable.' 'And you shall have some, sir, if you will retract what you said of my being *a young traveller*; I have brought a bottle of rum from town, a thing you never thought of:' for though Constable carried their fare, Stothard was the caterer. As they lay on the grass, enjoying their meal under the trees that screened them from a midsummer's sun, Stothard, looking up to the splendid colour of the foliage over their heads, said, 'That's all glazing, sir.'" *

All the stories of Combe Wood are not quite so Arcadian. Wm. Gibson was executed at Kennington Common, Aug. 29, 1755, for robbing a gentleman and lady at Combe Wood. Gibson had "a private cave" in Combe Wood, in which he concealed himself in the daytime, and turned out at night to rob. His cave was discovered, and he captured, by some gentleman shooting in the wood. Before

he took to the road he had been a master maltster at Leeds. Later, the wood was a usual lurking-place of Jerry Abershawe, the highwayman, whose favourite ride was Wimbledon Common, and his hostel, the *Bald-faced Stag*, close by. For one of his exploits about here Jerry was hung on Kennington Common, Aug. 3, 1795, and then suspended from a gibbet on Wimbledon Common.

At the Domesday Survey there were 2 manors of *Cumbe*, one held by Humphrey the Chamberlain of the Queen ("a woman who held this land having put herself with it under the protection of the Queen"); the other by Ansgot, the King's interpreter. The manors were united in the hands of William de Neville, *t.* Edw. III., and thenceforward called Combe-Neville. Having been made over to the prior and canons of Merton, it reverted to the Crown at the Dissolution, and subsequently passed through various hands, till it was purchased for Lord Spencer in 1753. The manor-house was pulled down about 1750. Its successor, the present *Combe House* (Lord Dunraven), occupies a commanding site by Combe Lane, at the S. edge of the wood, about $1\frac{1}{4}$ m. E. of Kingston. It was occupied for several years by the Earl of Liverpool (the Prime Minister of the Regency), who entertained the Prince Regent and the allied sovereigns in 1814, and d. here Dec. 4, 1828. It is now the property of the Duke of Cambridge.

COOPER'S HILL, SURREY, the Mount Parnassus of Sir John Denham, is about $\frac{1}{2}$ m. N.W. of Egham. The way to it is by a long winding lane which leaves the main street on the rt. a little way beyond Egham rly. stat.: the wicket-gate leading to the top of the hill will be seen on the rt. just before reaching *Kingswood Lodge*.

Apart from its associations, Cooper's Hill well deserves a visit. The view from it is one of the loveliest in the neighbourhood of London. It commands the Thames, Runnimede, Windsor Castle, and St. Paul's Cathedral.

"My eye descending from the Hill, surveys
Where Thames among the wanton valleys strays.

*   *   *   *   *

O could I flow like thee, and make thy stream
My great example, as it is my theme!

---

* Autobiography, vol. i., p. 134.

Though deep, yet clear; though gentle, yet not dull;
Strong without rage, without o'erflowing full."

'Cooper's Hill,' written in 1640, and first published in 1642, was the earliest local poem in the English language. Dryden pronounced it "the exact standard of good writing;" and Pope, in his 'Windsor Forest,' declares that

"On Cooper's Hill eternal wreaths shall grow
While lasts the mountain, or while Thames shall flow."

Somerville's clarion sounds a feebler note :—

"Tread with respectful awe
Windsor's green glades; where Denham, tuneful bard,
Charm'd once the list'ning Dryads with his song,
Sublimely sweet." *

Denham's father had a house (now the vicarage) at Egham, and the poet, therefore, was familiar with the locality. (*See* EGHAM.) The view from Cooper's Hill embraces nearly every point noticed in that from *St. Anne's Hill;* but here the towers of Windsor standing out from a rich woody environing confer an additional grandeur. The Thames, too, is a more important feature; and at the base of the hill is the meadow

"Where was that Charter seal'd, wherein the Crown
All marks of arbitrary power lays down." †

But in one respect St. Anne's Hill is the happier. Every part of it is open, and seats are conveniently placed for the best points of view. Here the visitor is confined to a narrow, uneven field-path, and warned that he will be prosecuted if he trespasses from it. The spot from which Denham made his poetical survey is traditionally said to be now included in the grounds of *Kingswood Lodge* (W. B. Eastwood, Esq.), on the S.E. side of the hill: a seat marks the site.

On the W. side of the hill, on an estate formerly called *Ankerwyke Purnish,* and given to the nuns of Ankerwyke, on the opposite side of the Thames, by Abbot Hugh of Chertsey, *temp.* Stephen, stands the INDIAN CIVIL ENGINEERING COLLEGE, founded by Government in 1871,

* The Chase.
† Denham.

for the scientific training of young men as Civil Engineers for service in India. The original portion of the very striking range of buildings was erected some few years ago as a first-class Elizabethan mansion, but almost before it was finished it was thrown upon the market, and was purchased by the Government, then seeking a convenient site for the proposed college. The house was greatly added to, and the whole remodelled, by Sir Digby Wyatt, and made the splendid pile the visitor now sees. In it provision is made for 150 students, besides a president, resident professors, and a large staff of teachers and officials; with the extensive appliances required by the very comprehensive scheme of education. A grander site was never found for a great educational establishment.

COULSDON, SURREY (Domesday *Colesdone*), 1½ m. S.W. of the Kenley Stat. of the Caterham Rly. (S.E. line); pop. 1591, (of whom 79 were in Caterham Valley eccl. dist., and 282 in the Reedham Orphan Asylum); a retired vill. on the chalk hills.

Coulsdon *Church* (St. John the Evangelist) is chiefly Dec., but the arches which separate the nave and aisles are E.E. It is of rough-cast, and battlemented, has a rather long chancel, a heavy W. tower (in which are 5 bells) with short shingled spire and massive buttresses, and a Perp. porch. The chancel has a 3-light Dec. window, filled with modern painted glass; on the S. side are 3 E.E. sedilia and a piscina. *Obs.* the curious *mont.,* on S. wall, of Grace Rowed, d. 1635. By the ch.-yard are some noble elms. The *Grange* (J. Douglas, Esq.) has pretty grounds extending from the ch. to the trim village green. *Coulsdon Court* (E. Byron, Esq.) is a large modern mansion on the hill farther N. *Purley Lodge* and *Reedham* (*see* CATERHAM JUNCTION) are in Coulsdon par. From Coulsdon there is a charming walk by Coulsdon Common (leaving the windmills on the l.), through the Rookery, to *Chaldon;* or, leaving the windmills on the rt., across Caterham Common to *Caterham;* or E., across Kenley Common to *Warlingham.*

On Farthing Down, in this par., ½ m. W. of the ch., and overlooking Smitham

Bottom and the main line of the S.E. Rly., occur several small *barrows*. Manning and Bray* mention the opening of one, about 40 years previously, when a perfect skeleton was found. In the autumn of 1871, eight or ten more were opened by the Hon. G. Leveson Gower, F.S.A., Mr. J. Wickham Flower, and Mr. E. V. Austin, when in those not previously opened perfect skeletons were found, in every instance laid in the solid chalk at an almost uniform depth of 3 ft. 6 in., extended at full length, with the arms close to the sides, the head to the W., the feet to the E. In most cases every tooth was in its place both in the upper and lower jaws. In one barrow there were 2 skeletons lying side by side, and about 3 in. apart; apparently a male and female, one being much smaller than the other. In others the skeletons were probably of males. Only in one, which contained a skeleton only 5 ft. 3 in. long, was any ornament or weapon found; and in this, lying close to the skull, were two bronze pins and an iron knife. Near the barrows are traces of an earthwork, which appears to have been more perfect when Manning wrote, as he describes it as consisting of a vallum and double ditch, extending for about a quarter of a mile. The British and Roman road, *Stane Street*, passed through Coulsdon.

COWEY STAKES, near Walton-

on-Thames, the supposed site of the ford by which Cæsar crossed the Thames in his second invasion of Britain. The exact spot is about a furlong W. of Walton bridge, the ford extending from the Surrey meadow towards Halliford on the Middlesex side of the river, "not transversely straight across the stream, but forming a curve, nearly in a semicircle," according to the statement of a Mr. Crawter, "who was well acquainted with the river there," made to Mr. Bray in 1806, when making inquiries on the spot for Manning's 'History of Surrey,' and before the bed of the river was deepened for the purposes of navigation.

Cæsar tells us that, Cassivellaunus, having been elected to the command of all the British forces, he determined to carry the war into his territories. These were divided from the maritime states by the Thames, about 80 miles from the sea. . . .

* History of Surrey, 1804-7, vol. ii., p. 448.

"The river could only be crossed on foot at one place, and there with difficulty. When Cæsar came there he found a large force drawn up on the opposite bank. The bank also had been defended by sharp stakes fixed in front, whilst similar stakes fixed under water were concealed by the stream. Cæsar having learnt these things from prisoners and deserters, sent forward his cavalry, and ordered the legions to follow immediately. But the soldiers went so swiftly and with such an impetus, though only their heads were above the water, that the enemy, unable to withstand their impetuosity, fell back from the bank, and took to flight." *

Bede, writing early in the 8th cent., says that the remains of the stakes are there to this very day: and on examining them, they are seen to be as thick as a man's thigh, encompassed with lead (*circumfusæ plumbo*), and fixed immovably at the bottom of the river.† Bede does not, however, name the place where these stakes were found. This was first done, as he himself points out, by Camden.‡ "It is impossible," he says, "that I should be mistaken in the place, because here the river is scarce six feet deep; and the place at this day, from these stakes, is called Cowey Stakes." And he adds that the ford is about 80 miles from "that sea which washes the E. part of Kent where Cæsar landed," and consequently the distance which he named.§

A century and a half later (1734) Gale visited the place, and found many of the stakes still in the river. "The wood proves its own antiquity, being by its long duration under the water so consolidated as to resemble ebony, and it will admit of a polish, and is not the least rotted." ‖ He goes on to say that the stakes "exactly answer the thickness of a man's thigh, as described by Bede," but he could not learn whether the ends fixed in the river were covered with lead. Gale fully adopted Camden's view, and supported it by argument and citation of authorities, as well by the result of his personal investigation. Other corroborative features have since been pointed out. As late as 1807 there was a ford here, the line of which had been traced by persons wading through the current when the waters were low.¶

* De Bell. Gall., v., 11, 18.
+ Ecc. Hist., i., cap. 2.
‡ Britannia, ed. 1586.
§ Gibson's Camden, vol. i., p. 236.
‖ Archæol., vol. i., p. 183.
¶ Bray.

On St. George's Hill, a little over 2 m. S., are the remains of " an ancient British stronghold which commands the whole valley " (*see* ST. GEORGE'S HILL) ; whilst " a boundary dyke runs from the rampart towards Walton."* And further, the name of the opposite village, Halliford, indicates that " at the time the name was given there was a ford in the neighbourhood." Now it is, as Dr. Guest observes, a remarkable fact that

"From Hurlyford (by Marlow) to the sea, a distance of nearly 100 miles, taking into account the windings of the river, there is but one place on the banks of the Thames which bears a name ending in the word *ford*. This single solitary place is Halliford, at the Cowey Stakes.+ Cæsar says there was but one ford on the Thames—meaning of course the lower Thames, with which alone he was acquainted ; and we give the name of *ford* to only one place on its banks. Our topography is in perfect agreement with his statement ; and, to my mind, this coincidence is almost decisive of the question."‡

But it must not be concealed that several of the antiquaries who examined the spot while the stakes existed arrived at a different conclusion from Camden and Gale. Some, like Daines Barrington and Lysons, thought the stakes had originally been part of a fishing weir ; others, like Bray, that they had formed the foundations of a bridge. Unfortunately, none remain to be examined now. The attention called to them caused pieces to be sought after by the collectors of ' curiosities.' An old Earl of Sandwich, who came here to fish, gave the boatmen half a guinea apiece for them. The fishermen were glad to get them out of the way of their boats and nets, and the bargemen found them interfere with the navigation. Barrington was told by the fisherman that the stakes were ranged *across* the river, and consequently not so as to oppose any impediment to Cæsar's passage. But the most specific account of their appearance and arrangement is that of Mr. Bray, who, in 1806,

"Was informed by one Simmons, a fisherman, who had lived here, and known the river all his life, that at the place called Cowey Stakes, he had weighed up several stakes of the size of his thigh, about 6 ft. long, shod with iron, the wood very black, and so hard as to turn an axe. . . . One

remained in the river which they were not able to weigh : it was visible when the water was clear : his net had been caught and torn by it. His tradition is that they formed part of a bridge built by Julius Cæsar, and he described them to have stood *in two rows*, as if going *across the river*, about 9 ft. asunder as the water runs, and about 4 ft. asunder as crossing it." *

The objection raised by Barrington from the stakes crossing the river, and a later one that they were " of too permanent a character to have formed any part of the British defences, which must have been prepared somewhat hastily," were for the first time fairly met by Dr. Guest in the paper already cited. He thinks the stakes were not fixed in the bed of the river merely to prevent Cæsar's passage :—

"I believe them to have been fixed there for a very different purpose, years before Cæsar came into the island. I think the stakes formed part of what may be called a fortified ford, and were distributed so as to stop all transit over the river, save along a narrow passage, which would bring the passenger directly under the command of the watch stationed on the northern bank to guard the ford and receive the toll. The shallow at Cowey was probably of considerable extent, and through its whole length must have extended the line of stakes which Cæsar observed on the N. bank. But there must also have been two other lines of stakes across the river, to mark out and define the passage. The remaining portion of the shallow was, no doubt, covered with the short stakes that were concealed by the river."

Of the ingenuity of this theory there can be no question, any more than that, with Dr. Guest's other arguments, it goes far to remove the difficulties remaining in the way of accepting the Cowey Stakes as the true locality of Cæsar's passage. But if the statements made to Mr. Bray by the fishermen were correct, that the line of the ford "formed a curve, nearly in a semicircle," and that the two rows of stakes were only "four feet asunder as crossing the river," it would not be easy to see how even Roman soldiers, up to their chins in the water, could have made good their way along such a passage in the face of a strong opposing force, even though, as Dr. Guest suggests, "the enemy's position was carried by what, in modern military language, is called *a rush*." The curve formed by the stakes in crossing the river is accounted for by the shallow, which would naturally take that direction ; its making "nearly a semicircle" is probably the exaggeration of an

* Guest.

+ Deptford, Brentford, and the like are only seeming exceptions. The fords from which they were named were over the tributaries by the confluence of which with the Thames they stand.

‡ Address at Archæol. Inst., July 19, 1866.

* History of Surrey, vol. ii., p. 759.

inaccurate observer, but the ends may have opened outwards so as to facilitate the entrance of horses and cattle, and thus have apparently increased the curvature.

It is of course extremely difficult to arrive at anything like certainty on a question of this sort : but it appears to be admitted that Cowey Stakes is the place referred to by Bede, and which in his day, and before tradition had become confused by admixture of published assertions, was believed to be the scene of the passage ; it is about the distance from the sea mentioned by Cæsar ; there was a ford here ; and stakes of unknown antiquity existed till the present century in great numbers, no similar stakes having been found in any other locality suggested for the passage. On the whole it is beyond question that this accords with the requirements of the case much better than Kingston or any other place yet named on the Thames. (*See* SURBITON ; TEDDINGTON.) The topographical objections raised in vol. ii. of the Emperor Napoleon's History of Julius Cæsar, are based on inaccurate information as to the locality, and the very serious mistake of supposing the condition of the Thames in Cæsar's time, when it ran uninterruptedly to the sea, to be the same as now, when, as Dr. Guest remarks, "from Teddington westward it is a canal, crossed every 2 or 3 miles by weirs and locks."

COWLEY, MIDDX., a vill. of 491

inhab. (of whom 200 are within the eccl. dist. of St. Andrew Hillingdon); on the road from West Drayton to Uxbridge, 1 m. S. of the latter, 1½ m. N. of the former (both stats. of the Grt. W. Rly.)

Lysons derives the name from the A.-S. *Col leag*, the cold meadow, but the more probable derivation is *Cow ley*, the cow's meadow. In Dom. it is *Covelei :* at this time half the land was meadow, and there was "pasture for the cattle of the manor," besides pannage for 40 hogs, and a mill of 5*s.* rent. The manor belonged to Westminster Abbey. By the 14th cent. it was in the hands of the Pecche family : hence the present name, Cowley Peachey.

There are strolls of quiet beauty about the lanes and meadows, but little of general interest at Cowley. The vill. is in three parts : the largest, *Cowley Street*, on the road to Uxbridge ; a farm and a small cluster of clean cottages about the ch., ¼ m. to the E.; and another cluster called *Cowley Peachey*, where the ways meet by the canal farther S. The occupations are agricultural. The chief trade is due to three large corn mills. At the crossing of the ways in Cowley Street is the trunk of an elm, which must have been a magnificent tree before it lost its head.

The *Church* (St. Lawrence) is small, partly E.E., partly Dec., but plain, and coated with plaster. The chancel window is a triple lancet, under a string-course ; the S. windows are Dec. From the W. end of the tall tiled roof rises a low wooden tower and short spire, built in 1780. On the S. is a new flint and stone porch, and outside steps give access to the squire's pew on S. of the chancel. Inside are several *monts.*, but none of much account. In the chancel is a small *brass* of Walter Pope, yeoman (d. 1502), and wife.

In the ch.-yard (without a stone) lies the unhappy Dr. Dodd, executed for forgery, June 27, 1777. Barton Booth, the actor, was buried here, 1733 ; also, 1773, his second wife, as Hester Santelow a favourite actress and dancer : it was she who erected the mont. to Barton Booth in Westminster Abbey. Booth had property in Cowley, afterwards held by John Rich, the original harlequin.* The Rev. John Lightfoot, author of 'Flora Scotica,' d. 1788.

The brook that flows E. of the ch. is the *Blackwater*, or Cowley Brook. Among the seats are—*Cowley House* (Major W. E. Hilliard) ; *Cowley Hall* (G. A. Mosse, Esq.) ; *The Grove* (W. May, Esq.)

CRANFORD, MIDDX., a pleasant

village, of 557 inhab., on the little river Crane, 2 m. S. by W. from the Southall Stat. of the Grt. Western Rly.

Cranford Bridge, which occupies the site of the old *ford* over the *Crane* (whence the name), is on the Maidenhead road, 2 m. beyond Hounslow ; the village proper lies along the lane extending northwards from it, and the church stands in the Earl of Berkeley's park beyond the village. The parish is large and level ; the land for the most part arable ; there are broad wheat-fields, large orchards, abundant timber trees—altogether a fruit-

---

* T. Davies, Life of Garrick, vol. ii., p. 357.

ful, well cultivated, and pleasant land, rather than one remarkable for scenery. Inns, *Berkeley Arms*, Cranford Bridge, a good old house, small, but comfortable, and *White Hart*, once famous as a posting-house, and a resort for London parties.

Till their proscription the manor belonged to the Knights Templars ; in 1363 it passed to the Knights Hospitallers ; on the suppression of monasteries it was transferred to private hands, and in 1604 became the property of Sir Thomas Aston. On Aston's death, James I. was anxious that the Countess of Essex should buy or rent the house ; but house and manor were purchased for £7000, in 1618, by Elizabeth, daughter and heir of Lord Hunsdon, and wife of Sir Thos. Berkeley, and Cranford has been a residence of the Berkeleys ever since.

Cranford House, a plain, comfortable-looking modern mansion, consists of the additions made to Aston's house by Vice-Admiral James, Earl of Berkeley, towards the middle of the last century, the old house having been since pulled down. Somehow the reputation of being haunted has always clung to it ; and Grantley Berkeley, in his 'Life and Recollections' (p. 209), has a full account of the ghost of a female, " dressed as a maid-servant, with a sort of poke-bonnet on, and a dark shawl drawn or pinned lightly across her breast," which he and his elder brother (the present Earl) saw in the kitchen at Cranford ; and of another, of a man, which his father (the late Earl) saw on the wine-cellar steps, and which disappeared in the wine-cellar. In the house are portraits of Henry Carey, 1st Lord Hunsdon, Sir Francis Drake, William Harvey, Sir William Temple, and Dean Swift, besides members of the Berkeley family.

Cranford *Church* stands in the park, close to the mansion. It is partly of Perp. date, much patched, somewhat decayed, and of little architectural value, the tower and chancel alone being old, but it contains some interesting monuments. To inspect them, however, the visitor must choose a proper (though hardly orthodox) season, the lord of the domain being seemingly of like mind respecting Cranford Church to Izaak Walton respecting the cowslip meadows of his silver Lea, that " it is too pleasant to be looked on but only on *holy* days." A

large board at the park gate conveys a peremptory intimation that no one is allowed to enter except " to go to the parish church at the time of Divine service." Application at the lodge is unavailing : admission can only be obtained by special permission.

First among the monts. is that of Sir Roger Aston (d. 1612), gentleman of the bedchamber to James I., a post he esteemed so highly that he had his letters of appointment enclosed in his tomb. The mont. is " of alabaster, tutch, rance, and white and black marble," according to the terms of an agreement for its execution made by Sir Roger a few months before his death, with " William Cure Esq. the King's Master Mason," who undertook to " hew, cut, work, carve, make up and finish," the same with " the seven pictures of Sir Roger, his two wives and 4 daughters kneeling " thereon, according to the best of his art, for the sum of £180. The tomb is large, showy, and well executed ; the knight and his two wives kneel in the central compartment, the daughters two in each wing of the triptych ; Corinthian columns form the divisions ; arms, pyramids, and scrolls are above. On the S. wall of the chancel is an effigy of Lady Elizabeth Berkeley, Lord Hunsford's daughter, habited in a shroud. Tombs and tablets of later Berkeleys are numerous, but the visitor will turn with greater interest to the slab, on N. wall of the chancel, that records that there was interred the witty *Thomas Fuller*, author of ' The Worthies,' who was rector of Cranford from 1658 till his death in 1661. His residence, the *Moat House*, from which he dates the Dedication to his ' Appeal of Injured Innocence,' was pulled down in 1780 : it stood by the lane N.E. of the ch. His successor in the rectory was the hardly less famous John Wilkins, but he has no memorial here. He lived to become Bishop of Chester, and, dying in Chancery Lane, was interred in St. Lawrence Jewry.

For some years the observatory attached to the residence of Warren De la Rue, Esq., F.R.S., made Cranford a place of interest to the world of science, on account of the valuable observations and experiments, especially in photo-astronomy, carried on there. But the observatory is now dismantled ; and the great reflecting telescope and other valuable apparatus have been presented to Oxford University, where suitable buildings are now (1874) being constructed for their reception.

CRANHAM, Essex (Dom. *Wocheduna*), 4½ m. E.S.E. from Romford Stat. of the Grt. E. Rly. (through Hornchurch and Upminster) ; an agricultural par. of 437 inhab. : there is no village.

The *Church* (All Saints) stands nearly ½ m. from the road, on an upland affording a broad prospect towards the Laindon Hills. It is of flint and stone, irregularly laid ; in part very old, and, despite whitewash, picturesque. On each side of the chancel are three lancets ; the E. window is later. At the W. end is an odd-looking tower, consisting of a low, very wide, semioctagonal, red brick base, running up by a tiled roof to a small square wooden belfry, which is crowned with a slated roof.

Cranham Hall, by the ch., was of old the manor-house, the manor being named "Cranham Hall, otherwise Bishop's Ockenden." In it lived for 40 years, and died (July 1, 1785), General Oglethorpe, the first of our legislators who sought to ameliorate the miserable condition of imprisoned debtors ; the founder of the colony of Georgia as "a place of refuge for the distressed people of Britain, and the persecuted Protestants of Europe," and the leader of the first band of colonists, and founder of the city of Savannah (Feb. 1732) ; celebrated in verse by Pope ; the friend of Johnson, Burke, and Goldsmith, and familiar by name to every reader of Boswell. Oglethorpe invited Goldsmith to visit him here, "if a farm and a mere country scene will be a little refreshment from the smoke of London." * The present hall (R. W. Bunter, Esq.) is later than Oglethorpe's day, but the stately old-fashioned garden, with its large wrought-iron gate, remains almost unaltered. Oglethorpe was buried in Cranham ch., where is a tablet with a long insc. to his memory, written by Capel Lofft and Moses Brown, but it neither gives the year of his birth nor his age at death— though he lived to be very nearly 90. Near the hall are *Cranham Lodge* (W. Holmes, Esq.), N. of the ch., and *C. Place* (S. R. G. Francis, Esq.)

* Prior's Goldsmith, vol. ii., p. 422.

CRAYFORD, Kent (A.-S. *Creccanford*), so named from the ford by which the old Watling Street here crossed the Cray (*Crecca*), is situated on the Dover road, 13 m. from London, and 15 m. by the North Kent Rly. Inn, the *Bear*, a good house ; pop. 3887.

Crayford is one of the first places mentioned in the Saxon Chronicle : "An. 457. This year Hengest and Æsc his son fought against the Britons at the place which is called *Crecganford ;* and there slew 4000 men." The Britons, it is added, "then forsook Kent-land, and fled in great dismay to London."

In the Domesday Survey the manor (held by the Abp. of Canterbury) is entered as *Erhede*, alias *Crayford*, and it is so described in all deeds down to Henry VIII.* The sub-manors of Newbury and Marshal Court were purchased by Admiral Sir Cloudesley Shovel about 1694. The seat of Sir Cloudesley, known as the *Mansion House*, which had been used for a linen manufactory, was, when Hasted wrote (1786), part pulled down, part converted into the workshops of "an eminent calico printer and whitster." At that time Crayford consisted of "a narrow, ill-built street of nearly half a mile." It has since widened its boundaries, and several large mills have been constructed, but the old part remains ill built and narrow. The calico printing works continue in full operation, though calico is almost exclusively a northern manufacture ; but the printing is confined to high-class goods. There are also large silk, wool, muslin, and shawl printing works (at one of which 150,000 shawls have been printed in a year,) and an establishment for printing felt carpets. The river is navigable to within a mile of the vill., just above which point the Cray in the olden times turned an iron mill used for making "armour plates "—a manufacture revived on a larger scale and for a very different article in our own day. Crayford forms now a rather curious combination of an agricultural and factory village.

The *Church* (St. Paulinus) is Perp., (with modern 4-light Dec. window inserted in the chancel), of flint and rubble, with tooled dressings ; large, and comprises nave and N. aisle, chancel, and massive

* Hasted.

embattled W. tower, of stone, with stair turret at N.W. angle, carried half way up, and a peal of 5 good bells inside. The interior of the ch. was carefully restored in 1861 by Mr. Clarke, who removed the plaster ceiling, and restored the open timber roof. Obs. *mont.* at E. end of N. aisle, with recumbent alabaster effigy of Wm. Draper (d. 1650), and above, his wife Mary (d. 1652) ; both the figures are on their rt. sides, the elbow leaning on a cushion. At the head is a small kneeling figure of a son, at the foot a girl, and below an infant. At the top of the mont. is a coat of arms with the original embla-zoning. On the N. wall of the chancel a small mural mont., with kneeling effigy of Mrs. Blanche Marler, *t.* James I. (n.d.) There is also a mont. of the widow of Sir Cloudesley Shovel, who d. 1732, at May Place. The altar-piece was the gift of Sir Cloudesley Shovel. The painted glass in the E. window is a memorial of the late F. C. Jackson, Esq. *Obs.* piscina, S. of the altar.

The *Manor House*, a little way N. of the ch., is the seat of Sir F. Currie, Bart. *May Place* (E. Horner, Esq.) is a short distance farther, N.W. In the neighbour-hood of Crayford are many of the deep excavations in the chalk, known in some places as Danes-holes, and noticed under CHADWELL (which *see*), Chiselhurst, Black-heath, and Tilbury. The most consider-able, though not the nearest, is a group in *Joyden's Wood*, 2 m. N. of Crayford, a place worth visiting on its own account. At Slade's Green pit, on the road to Erith, Mr. Boyd Dawkins, F.R.S., found, April 1872, the skull and horns of a musk sheep : the specimen is now in the museum of the Geological Society. Bones of the mam-moth, elephant (*E. antiquus*), cave lion, bear, and other animals, and some flint implements, have also been found here. (*See* ERITH.)

CRAYS, THE, KENT. The four contiguous parishes situated on the little river Cray, above Bexley, which form the subject of the following articles, are lo-cally known as THE CRAYS. Their order in descending the river is—*St. Mary Cray*, *St. Paul's Cray*, *Foot's Cray*, and *North Cray*. We have for convenience brought them together in their alpha-betical order. Crayford, which lies on

the Cray immediately below Bexley, is sometimes spoken of as one of the Crays, but it is separated from them by Bexley, and usually ranks apart. The scenery of the Crays is varied and pleasing : there are woods to explore ; hop gardens, fruit farms, paper mills, to visit ; churches and antiquities to examine : altogether a day may be very well spent in wandering over them.

FOOT'S CRAY (so named from its owner under Edward the Confessor, Godwin Fot, but in charters written *Votes*, and *Foet's Cray*) is situated on the Cray, where it is crossed by the Maidstone road, 14 m. from London, 1½ m. S.E. of the Sidcup Stat. of the S.E. Rly. (loop line); pop. 390 (but 295 are within the eccl. district of St. John's, Sidcup). Inn, the *Tiger's Head.*

The vill., which is partly in Chiselhurst par., consists mainly of small houses, col-lected on both sides of the road, W. of the river, with a large paper mill on the stream. The *Church* (All Saints) stands among trees by the river, a short distance N. of the vill. It is a small plain flint and stone building, partly E.E., with Perp. windows inserted. Rising from the roof is a small wooden tower with low shingle spire. It was very picturesque, but suf-fered somewhat in that respect when restored, 1864-5, at which time some new windows were inserted, and the old tracery rechiselled. Several of the windows have been filled with painted glass. The font is plain, sq., late Norm. In a recess in the N. wall, under a low obtuse arch, are the mutilated recumbent effigies of Sir Simon Vaughan, lord of the manor, and his wife (*temp.* Edward III.) Lady Fan-shawe's " second daughter, Elizabeth, that I had left with my sister Boteler at Frog Pool, to see if the air would recover her ; but she died of a hectic fever, July 1656, and lies buried in the church of Foot's Cray." [*]

In the ch.-yard, against the S. wall of the ch., is a cast-iron slab (with crossed bones at top) to the memory of Martin Manning, yeoman (d. 1665), and his wife (d. 1681) ; a relic of the days when the iron trade was a staple of Kent ; the in-scription is still (1873) legible and in good condition. E. of the ch. is the tomb of

* Memoirs, p. 124.

Sir Richard Madox Bromley, K.C.B., of The Elms (d. 1865).

Foot's Cray Place, N. of the ch. (E. Elias Hope, Esq.), was built in 1752 by Bourchier Cleve, a pewterer of Cheapside, "from a design by Palladio." The chief feature is the octagonal hall, which is the whole height of the building ; there is an engraving of the house by Woollett. It was the residence of Nicholas Vansittart, Lord Bexley, Chancellor of the Exchequer in Lord Liverpool's ministry, 1812—23, and in his later years known as president of the Bible Society, and an active supporter of other religious associations, who died here, Feb. 8, 1851. He bequeathed Foot's Cray Place to his nephew, Arthur Vansittart.

NORTH CRAY, so called from being the most northerly of the Crays, is about ½ m. from Foot's Cray ch., across the fields ; pop., with Ruxley, 562.

The occupations are agricultural ; the peculiarity, the many large fruit farms. The ch. stands on high ground E. of the river. The little vill. is ¼ m. N. on the road to Bexley. The *Church*, erected in 1851, is of hammered rag with Bath stone dressings ; Dec. of a French type. The chancel was added in 1871 as a memorial to Mr. and Mrs. Western Wood, by their children. It is richly finished and fitted : architect of both church and chancel, Mr. E. Nash. At the N.W. is a stone tower with shingled spire ; on the N. a porch. The interior is well finished, has an open timber roof, good wood carvings in the chancel, and a mont. to Mrs. Gosling, with alto-rilievo by Chantrey, and painted glass in several of the windows. W. of the ch. is the tomb of Western Wood, Esq., of North Cray Place, M.P. for London (d. 1863).

North Cray Place, a pleasantly situated mansion, by the ch., was the residence of the Marq. of Londonderry, best known as Lord Castlereagh, who d. here by his own hand, Aug. 12, 1822. He was interred in Westminster Abbey. The house is a long, rather low, but comfortable looking building with a verandah extending along the entire front. *Mount Mascal* (R. H. Alexander, Esq.) is nearer Bexley. There are several other good seats. E. of the ch. is the still extensive *Joyden's Wood*.

Ruxley, or *Rokesley*, which gives name to the hundred, was formerly an independent parish, but was united to North Cray in 1557, on the petition of the patron, Sir Martin Bowes, setting forth the poverty of the living, and the decayed and ruinous condition of the ch. Indeed, he says, there was "no one, such was the scarcity of clergy in these parts, who could be conveniently found to serve it, insomuch that a priest could not be provided for scarce a fourth part of the year." The materials of Ruxley ch. were directed to be employed for the repair and maintenance of North Cray ch. When Hasted wrote (1777), "the ancient structure had been used for many years as a barn for the use of Ruxley Farm,"* and nearly a century later it is still so used. It is of course entirely dismantled, and greatly mutilated, but tolerably sound, though the walls are merely of chalk, partly faced with flints. The windows are blocked up, and the tracery destroyed : but the ch. is evidently Late Dec. The sedilia still remain. The desecrated ch. stands by *Ruxley Farm* (Mr. R. Allen), on the top of a gentle slope, 1 m. S. of North Cray ch., but nearer Foot's Cray, on the road to Farningham. *Obs.* the large elm N. of the ch., and the cedar in the farm garden. Its spreading arms show its magnificent proportions, but its head broke off under the weight of the snow in the storm of Jan. 11, 1866.

ST. MARY CRAY (Dom. *Sud Crai*, as being the most S. of the Crays, but known as St. Mary Cray as early as *temp.* Edward I.), pop. 1681, is a stat. on the L. C. and D. Rly.

The extensive and complex looking range of buildings by the stat. is the paper mill of Messrs. Joynson, one of the largest and most complete in the kingdom, and worth seeing if permission can be obtained. Close by the mill is the *Church*, a large cruciform building, with a tower and shingled spire at the W. end. It is of stone and flint ; in style Late Dec. and Perp., and was restored in 1862. S. of the chancel is a hagioscope. *Brasses*, N. of chancel, Richard Abery (d. 1508), and wives Joan, Agnes, and Elynor, four small figures. S. of altar, Richard Manning (d. 1604), effigy in long robe, and wife Rachel. Richard Greenwood, of this par., merchant (d. 6th Dec. 1773, æt. 81),

* History of Kent, vol. i., p. 156.

and beside it another to his wife Philadelphia (d. Sept. 24, 1747), but apparently engraved at the same time as the preceding. These brasses are remarkable (the former especially) as the latest known. Mr. Greenwood is represented in the ordinary suit of a century back—wide sleeved coat, long embroidered waistcoat, knee breeches, and wig; and he is pointing to a ship, of which the stem is seen on one side, the stern on the other.

St. Mary Cray is a long, busy-looking, but not very attractive village. Till 1703, when the market-house was blown down in a storm, a market used to be held here. In the neighbourhood are hop gardens, nurseries, and fruit farms. The principal seats are *Kevington* (R. B. Berens, Esq.), and the *Rookery* (W. Joynson, Esq.)

St. Paul's Cray, ½ m. N. of St. Mary Cray, pop. 625, is beautifully situated where the stream runs in a narrow valley between the hills. The scattered cottages hardly form a village; the ch. stands apart on the hillside, and the most conspicuous object by the river is the large but not picturesque water mill of Mr. W. Nash.

The manor house was one of those given by the Conqueror to Odo, Bp. of Bayeux. Later "it gave surname," as Philipott quaintly expresses it, "to Sir Simon de Crey, who was lord warden of the Cinque Ports in the 3rd and 4th years of Edward I.;" it then passed to the Champneys, and in the reign of Richard II. it belonged to Henry le Scrope, " governor and supervisor of all the king's castles"; in the reign of Henry VII. it passed to Sir Gilbert Talbot; in that of Elizabeth, by marriage to the Danbys; and since then through various hands. Besides the paper mills, there are large brick and tile works; but the main occupation is agriculture: hops, peas, and fruit are extensively cultivated.

The *Church* (St. Paul or Paulinus) will repay a visit. The ch.-yard, which is entered by a modern lich-gate, affords pleasant views along the river. The body of the ch. is rough-cast, the chancel of flint and stone, with Roman tiles worked in at the angles. It consists of nave and S. aisle, a lower chancel and N. chapel, and a tower with short, thick shingled spire. The N. aisle has been removed, and Perp. windows inserted under two of the nave arches: the chapel was originally

a continuation of this aisle. The S. aisle was pulled down in 1839, and rebuilt on a wider scale. In the nave and tower are narrow lancets; the E. window is Perp. of 3 lights. The W. window has dogtooth moulding, but this, like the rest of the carving, was re-chiselled when the ch. was restored in 1864. The interior is chaste and simple; the stained wooden waggon roof is new; the chancel has been rather elaborately decorated. All the windows are filled with painted glass, two of them being memorials of the late R. Paterson, Esq., of Leesons. *Obs.* the lock to the old oak door of the tower, inscribed,

"John Mock
Made this lock, 1637."

The principal seats are *St. Paul's Cray Hill*, E. of the ch. (J. Chapman, Esq.); *Leesons* (Miss Paterson), and *Craylands* (W. May, Esq.)

CRICKLEWOOD, Middx. (*see* Willesden).

CROCKERN HILL, Kent (*see* Eynesford).

CROCKHAM HILL, Kent (*see* Westerham).

CROSSNESS, Kent (*see* Erith).

CROUCH END, Middx. (*see* Hornsey.

CROYDON, Surrey (Dom. *Croindene*, the signification of which is uncertain, though it may be derived from *croie*, chalk, and *dene*, a valley, Old Croydon, lying in a hollow at the edge of the London clay basin at its junction with the chalk; and it is noteworthy that the old pronunciation was Craydon), a market town on the Brighton rd., 10 m. from London: pop. of the par., which is 36 m. in circuit, and includes the hamlets of Croham, Combe, Addiscombe, Shirley, Woodside, Waddon, Haling, and part of Norwood, 55,652. Inns, the *Greyhound* (chief), *Crown, King's Arms.*

Railway Stats.—Croydon has 8 rly. stats. For the Epsom br. of the L. Br. and S. C. Rly. there are the *West Croydon*

Stat., at the entrance to the town in the London Road, which serves alo for the Wimbledon, Croydon, and Epsom br. of the L. and S.W. Rly., and is the principal stat. for the passenger traffic with London; *Waddon*, the extreme W., is on the same line. *Thornton Heath*, in Colliers-Water Lane, at the extreme N., and *Selhurst*, are stats. on the Streatham br. *East Croydon* stat., Addiscombe Rd., is for the main Brighton and S.E. lines. *New Croydon* stat., alongside the E. Croydon, and really one stat. with it, and *South Croydon* stat., at the extreme S. of the town, are for the Brighton and S.E. short traffic. *Addiscombe Stat.*, Clyde Road, Upper Addiscombe Rd., about ½ m. E. of the E. Croydon stat., is for the Beckenham and Mid-Kent line of the S.E. Rly. By one or other of these stats. ready access is given to any part of the town and its immediate vicinity, and from them all over 300 trains are despatched daily. There is a Central Croydon stat., in Katharine Street, but it is not now used.

Croydon is a place of great antiquity. It was at one time considered to be the Roman station *Noviomagus*, but that is now placed at Holwood Hill (*see* KESTON): Roman coins have, however, been found here. The manor was given by the Conqueror to Archbishop Lanfranc, and has belonged ever since to the Abps. of Canterbury, who had a palace here—to be noticed presently.

At the time of the Domesday Survey, Croydon had a ch. and a mill; land for 20 ploughs; in demesne 4 ploughs, and 48 villans and 25 bordarii (cottagers) with 34 ploughs; and wood for 200 swine. In the Confessor's time it was assessed for 80 hides; now for 16 hides and one virgate.

The statement of the Survey points to a very different condition of things from what will now be found in Croydon. But the Croydon of that day possessed not only a ch., but a mill. The site of the ancient mill was probably at Waddon, but until lately there was another mill near the ch., though now there is no indication of either mill or mill-stream. The ch. now stands on a dry though low site; quite recently it stood on an island, being completely surrounded by water. Some of the head-streams of the Wandle rose at Scarbrook, and in the grounds of

the archiepiscopal palace immediately N.E. of the ch., united in 'My Lord's Pond' (or according to some *Laud's* Pond), then in divergent streams ran on either side of the ch.-yard to join another brook which came from the S., and was traceable for a longer or shorter distance according to the season, and which—a shallow stream some 10 or 12 ft. wide—crossed the road by the ch.-yard. Here, W. of the ch., the water was pent back to form a large mill-dam, at the W. end of which was the mill—of late a calico printing work. Mr. Anderson [*] writes, " Mr. Harris informs me he can distinctly remember, 60 years ago (*i.e.*, about 1810-12), catching trout in this stream opposite our old church." We have seen the stream opposite the old ch. so swollen as to render the streets impassable on foot for some distance on either side. This state of things was brought to an end about 1850, when a complete system of drainage was adopted in Croydon. The stream in this lower part of the town was carried off by a great culvert, and the upper waters diverted by drain-pipes; and now not only is no surface water visible, but it requires some local experience and a trained eye to discover any traces of the old ponds and water-courses.

The main part of the old town lay to the W. of the present town, extending from the ch. and palace, Lower Croydon, a considerable distance towards Beddington; it has long passed away, but some ruins of it existed when Ducarel wrote in 1783.

The inundations here were usually connected with a phenomenon, easily explained now, but which in earlier times was regarded with superstitious awe, known as the "Rising of the Bourne Water." In his description of Caterham Aubrey says,—

"Between this place and Caulsdon, in the bottom commonly called Stoneham-lane, issues out sometimes (as against any change in our English Government) a bourne, which overflows, and runs down in Smitham Bottom to Croydon. This is held by the inhabitants and neighbourhood to be ominous, and prognosticating something remarkable approaching, as it did before the happy restoration of King Charles the Second, of ever glorious memory, in 1660; also before the Plague of London

[*] Croydon Church, Past and Present, p. 15.

in 1665 ; and in 1688, the eve of another change in the Constitution."

The Bourne Water broke forth in the winter of 1872-73, and continued during January 1873 to increase in volume, but disappeared before reaching Croydon, being carried into the Wandle by the drains just noticed.

Henry VIII. had a distaste for Croydon on account of its low site and dampness; as he told Cranmer with some sharpness :

"I was by when Otford and Knol were given him. My lord [Cranmer], minded to have retained Knol unto himself, said that it was too small a house for his Majesty. 'Marry,' said the King, 'I had rather have it than this house (meaning Otford) for it standeth on a better soil. This house standeth low and is rheumatick, *like unto Croydon*, where I could never be without sickness.'" *

The King referred to the Archbishop's palace, but from a notice of Croydon written in the reign of Elizabeth, and quoted by Steinman,† the town generally would not appear to have been a very desirable abode : "The streets are deep hollow ways and very dirty, the houses generally with wooden steps into them, and the inhabitants in general smiths and colliers." Nor would it appear to have improved much in the following century :—

" In midst of these stands Croydon, cloth'd in blacke,
In a low bottom sinke of all these hills ;
And is receipt of all the durty wracke,
Which from their tops still in abundance trills,
The unpav'd lanes with muddy mire it fills
If one shower falls ; or if that blessing stay,
You well may smell, but never see your way.

* * * * *

And those who there inhabit, suting well
With such a place, doe either Nigros seeme
Or harbingers for Pluto, prince of Hell.

* * * * *

To all proud dames I wish no greater hell
Who doe disdaine of chastly profered love,
Than to that place confin'd there ever dwell." ‡

The colliers, or charcoal burners, of Croydon, and their sooty looks, long furnished a topic for merriment to poets and playwrights. Thus Crowley, in his ' Satirical Epigrams' (1551), has one on ' The Collier of Croydon,'—

---

* Ducarel, Some Account, etc., in Bib. Top. Brit., vol. ii., No. 12.
† History of Croydon, p. 5.
‡ P. Hannay, Nightingale and Other Poems, 1622.

"It is said that in Croydon there did sometime dwell
A collyer that did al other colyers excel.

* * * * *

. . . The colliar that at Croydon doth dwell
Men think he is cosin to the collyar of hell."

And Greene, in his ' Quip for an Upstart Courtier ' (1592), " Marry, quoth he, that lookt like Lucifer, though I am black, I am not the Divell, but indeed a Collyer of Croydon." ' Grim, the Collier of Croydon, or the Devil and his Dame,' is the title of a comedy written about 1662, but the same Grim had figured a century earlier in the comedy of ' Damon and Pythias' (1566), in the ' History of the Collier,' played before Queen Elizabeth in 1577, and in ' Like will to Like, quod the Devil to the Collier' (1568), in which Tom Collier, Nichol Newfangle, and the Devil dance together to the tune of ' Tom Collier of Croydon hath solde his cole.' * But the colliers were not so black as they looked, nor did they all dance with the Devil. If they had their Toms and Grims, they had also their Bunyans, if we may read literally a passage in the ' Egloges' of Alexander Barclay (author of the ' Ship of Fooles,' himself long a resident in Croydon, and buried in the ch., June 10, 1552), who says, " While I in youth in Croidon town did dwell . . . I hearde the collier preache."

The colliers' trade decayed as the use of Newcastle coal became general, but it was long in dying out. Ducarel writes in 1783,† " the town is surrounded with hills well covered with wood, whereof great store of charcoal is made." This is probably about the last mention of its once famous staple : in the 2nd ed. of the ' Ambulator,' 1782, it is said " the adjacent hills being covered with wood, great quantities of charcoal are made and sent to that city " (*i.e.*, London); but in subsequent editions the passage is omitted.

Very different in appearance from the damp and grimy old town is its comparatively modern, clean, and well-built successor, the site of which, according to Ducarel, was a common field, with the present High Street, a mere bridle-way through it, when the old town flourished. This street extends now for nearly 1½ m. N. and S.,—others, short

---

* Steinman.
† Some Account of Croydon.

and steep, branching off towards the ch. westward, with one or two on the E. The older part still derives a certain old-fashioned air from its gables, its hospital, almshouses, the relics of the old palace, and its swinging inn-signs, which here and there, as in the days of the Stuarts, are suspended quite across the streets. These vestiges of antiquity are, however, year by year diminishing. Lecture-rooms, shops with showy plate-glass windows, and joint-stock banks in the latest architectural mode are occupying all the available sites in the leading thoroughfares. Monotonous streets and lines of villas are fast encircling the town, the neighbourhood of which being pleasant and picturesque, and within easy reach of the city, is a favourite residence for men of business, who may be seen flocking to the morning trains in surprising numbers.

Croydon is the place of election for the eastern division of the county, and an assize town—the summer assizes being held alternately here and at Guildford. The Town Hall, in which the assizes are held, is a substantial semi-classical edifice, built in 1809, by S. P. Cockerell (father of the late distinguished R.A.) A spacious Public Hall, for lectures, concerts, and assemblies, was erected in the Wellesley Road in 1860, and greatly enlarged in 1873. There are also a theatre, a market-house in the High Street, a butter market, barracks in the Mitcham Road, prison at the back of the corn market, etc., which, however, are not likely to attract the visitor.

Abp. Kirwaldy procured a grant of a weekly market for Croydon in 1273. The corn market, an important one, is held in the market-house every Thursday and Saturday. A market for cattle is held on Thursdays in Selsdon Road, close by the South Croydon Rly. Station. There is a wool fair in July, and one for sheep and lambs in August ; but the great fair is on October 2nd and 3rd, for horses, cattle, and sheep. It is also a pleasure fair, resorted to not only by holiday-makers of the surrounding district, but by country people from a considerable distance, and by great numbers of Londoners. Walnuts are brought for sale in large quantities, it being, at least hereabouts, an article of the popular faith that " walnuts come in

at Croydon fair : " in the booths, roast geese and pigs are provided for the especial delectation of the country folks. Five newspapers are published in the town weekly, and 2 twice a week.

Old Croydon *Church* (St. John the Baptist), in the low part of the town, W. of the High Street, was one of the largest and finest churches in the county. It was of flint and stone, with a tall and massive tower at the W. end ; Perp. in style, the greater part having been built (or modified from an earlier ch.) by Abp. Courtenay, 1382—96, and completed, 1414—43, by Abp. Chicheley, founder of All Souls' College, Oxford, but restored or rebuilt by Abp. Warham, 1504—33. But though the oldest visible architectural features of the ch., and those few, were of the Dec. period, carved capitals, voussoirs, heads, mouldings, and other fragmentary details of an earlier ch., of Norm. and E.E. date, were found after the fire to have been worked up in the old ch., or buried within the walls, and the walls themselves were ascertained to have been pierced for windows at three several times—presumably after the original erection at the rebuildings of Abps. Chicheley and Warham.

The *interior* of the ch., very impressive in appearance, had been carefully restored by Sir G. G. Scott, 1857—59. Besides some ancient monts. with effigies, and a few brasses, there were monts. with effigies of Abp. *Grindal*, d. 1583—the mont. with Corinthian columns, supporting an entablature with obelisks of coloured marble ; the effigy recumbent and coloured : Abp. *Whitgift*, d. 1604, of alabaster, similar, but inferior, to Grindal's ; and Abp. *Sheldon*, d. 1677, amazing in design, but magnificent in materials, and admirably executed by Joseph Latham and Bonne — whom Walpole designates as "two obscure statuaries" of the reign of Charles II. This mont. excited great contemporary admiration. In the ' Present State of England,' 1683, it is described as entirely finished by English workmen ; and Evelyn admired it far more than its neighbours :—

" The tombs in the church at Croydon of Abps. Grindal, Whitgift, and other Abps. are fine and venerable, but none comparable to that of the late Abp. Sheldon, which being all of white marble, and of a stately ordnance and carvings, far surpass'd the rest, and I judge could not cost lesse than 7 or £800." *

A mural mont. with the indents of brasses was usually ascribed to Abp. Warham, but was really that of his uncle, Thomas Warham, d. at Haling, 1478. Abps. buried here, but without important monts., were—Wake, d. 1737 ; Potter, d. 1747 ; and Herring, d. 1757. The coffins of the Abps. were all enclosed in stone tombs *above* the floor of the ch., except that of Sheldon, which was 2 ft. below it. The organ was famous as the masterpiece of Avery (1794), and was enlarged and the hydraulic apparatus added by Hill in 1859. A fine peal of bells used to ring forth a psalm tune 4 times a day.

Unhappily, on the night of Saturday, Jan. 5th, 1867, the roof of the ch. ignited by the overheating of a flue-pipe which had been incautiously placed too near the timbers, and in the midst of a snow-storm of unusual severity the ch. was in an hour or two entirely destroyed, with the exception of the tower, the walls of which were left standing. A subscription was at once opened for rebuilding the ch., and Mr. (now Sir G. G.) Scott was commissioned to prepare the designs with all convenient speed. The venerable character and associations could not be replaced, but the lines of the old fabric were taken as the basis of the new ; the old walls were as far as practicable preserved ; the old tower was retained, and the style and general character of the ancient edifice carefully followed, without being servilely copied, in the new design.

The new ch. was consecrated on Jan. 5th, 1870, the third anniversary of the fire. It comprises a nave, with clerestorey, of six bays, 91 ft. 6 in. in length, 32 ft. 6 in. in width, and 53 ft. 6 in. in height to the ridge, with aisles 21 ft. 6 in. wide ; chancel 56 ft. long, and 27 ft. wide, with aisles 25 ft. wide ; tower, and N. and S. porches. The tower at the W. and the porch at the S. are the old tower and porch restored. The tower is 28 ft. square ; 100 ft. high to the paparet, and 121 ft. to the top of the crocketed angle pinnacles. The entire length of the ch. is 176 ft., or 18 ft. longer than the old ch., the additional length being given to the chancel. The entire width is 76 ft. The

* Diary, June 13, 1700.

interior of the new ch. is admirable in effect, yet chaste and simple, rich in material, and carefully finished. The nave and chancel roofs are of oak, those of the aisles of pine. The large E. window, of 7 lights, and of excellent design, is filled with painted glass : subject, the leading events in the life of Christ. The W. window and several of those in the body of the ch. are also filled with painted glass. Under the E. window is an elaborate reredos of coloured marbles and alabaster, with representations, in high relief, of the Crucifixion in the centre, the Nativity and Ascension on the sides, and figures of angels and evangelists above.

Avery's fine organ was destroyed in the fire, but a new one of equal power was erected in its place by Hill. The seats in the body of the ch., for 1500 persons, are of oak ; the choir stalls exhibit some good carving. A peal of 8 musical bells, with improved machinery for playing the chimes, and a finger-board for playing by hand, more than supplies the loss of the old peal. Some of the monts. which were not irretrievably ruined, including that of Abp. Sheldon, have been re-erected in their old places, but they are melancholy wrecks. Grindal's mont. was irreparably injured. The mutilated fragments lie in a vault beneath the organ. Along with them are the remains of Whitgift's tomb : his effigy perished in the fire. Sheldon's mont. has been re-erected, but not restored : the face of the effigy is entirely demolished. Flaxman's exquisite rilievo of the ascending spirit on the mont. of Mrs. Bowling was hopelessly shattered. The almost forgotten slab which records the burial here, in 1816, of John Singleton Copley, R.A., father of Lord Lyndhurst, escaped destruction. The lectern, a brass eagle with outspread wings, noticed in all accounts of the ch., was saved.*

There are 7 or 8 other churches in the

* Fortunately, full and careful notes and drawings of the architectural features and monts. of the old ch. had been made before the fire by a competent resident artist, Mr. J. Corbet Anderson, transcripts of which appeared as a series of coloured lithographic 'Views of the Monuments in Croydon Church,' fol., 1855 ; 4to, 1856 ; and 'Antiquities of Croydon Church,' with woodcut illustrations, imp. 8vo, 1867 ; these were remodelled, and a full account of the new ch. added, in a final work— 'Croydon Church, Past and Present,' sm. folio, 1871.

parish (5 in the town), all recent and Gothic, but scarcely calling for visit or comment; the most pleasing architecturally are St. Peter's, South Croydon, and St. Andrew's, Southbridge Lane, designed by Mr. B. Ferrey; also about 20 chapels, few of which make any architectural pretension: the best are the new Baptist and Presbyterian chapels.

The remains of the *Palace* of the Archbishops of Canterbury are behind the ch. "Croydon House is no wholesome House," wrote Abp. Grindall in 1575; and when Abp. Abbot cut down the timber which environed it, Lord Bacon is reported to have said, " By my troth he has done very judiciously, for before, methought it was a very obscure and darke place, but now he has expounded and cleared it wonderfully well." Notwithstanding this "expounding," however, and in spite of large sums expended here, after the Restoration, by Abps. Juxon and Herring, the palace continued "unwholesome" and "incommodious." It ceased to be used as even an occasional residence from the election of Abp. Secker in 1758, and lay quite deserted till sold by auction, under the provisions of an Act of Parliament, in October 1780. Addington Park, 3½ m. from Croydon, the present archiepiscopal residence, was purchased in 1807. (*See* ADDINGTON.)

During its days of prosperity Croydon Palace was honoured by a visit from Queen Elizabeth, who was entertained here by Abp. Parker in April 1567, and again in July 1573. On one of these occasions the marriage-hating queen took leave of the archbishop's wife with the well-known speech, "Madam I may not call you; mistress I am ashamed to call you; and so I know not what to call you; but, however, I thank you." Grindal, Abp. Parker's successor, was not so honoured; but Whitgift, who succeeded him, received Elizabeth here in August 1600. The latest archbishops who resided for any length of time at Croydon were Potter and Herring.

In its original state, the palace with its offices formed an irregular quadrangle, about 156 ft. from E. to W., and 126 ft. from N. to S. Of the existing remains, the Guard Chamber was built by Abp. Arundel (1396—1413); the Hall by Abp. Stafford (1443—52); the Chapel by Abps. Laud and Juxon (1633—63). These remains are worth seeing. The *Hall*, through which Elizabeth's brocade once rustled, and in which Sir Christopher Hatton received the seals as Lord High Chancellor, but which is now attached to a great washing and bleaching establishment (Mr. Oswald), and steams with soapsuds, is of Perp. character, and has its timber roof tolerably perfect. The hall has been partitioned across, and divided into floors of rafters from which to suspend blankets, etc., for drying in wet weather. The walls are thickly covered with whitewash, and all the carvings defaced except on the corbels which support the principal timbers of the roof. These consist of shields of the arms of the Cardinal Abp. Stafford and his successors. The bearings retain their original blazoning, and may be easily examined, the upper floor being on a level with them. The exterior of the hall is as much defaced as the interior; but observe a Perp. entrance porch, with low groined roof in good preservation. The *Guard Chamber* or *Gallery*, 50 ft. by 22, having near the centre on one side a large bay window, and on the other a lofty fireplace, has been a fine room, but is now divided for laundry purposes, and the mouldings, stonework of windows, etc., have all been irretrievably damaged. Other portions of the palace have been preserved in the adjoining dwelling-house, but are not of such interest as to justify a stranger in intruding on the privacy of the occupant. A little N. is the *Chapel*, now used as a school. The interior woodwork, placed here by Abps. Laud and Juxon, has been thickly covered with a dirty yellow paint, and boarding has been carried up from the screen to the roof, so as to cut off the W. end of the room, and what is known as "Queen Elizabeth's Pew." This is a recent piece of vandalism. The gateway of the porter's lodge still serves as the entrance to the premises, but the house which was over it is entirely gone.

Whitgift's Hospital, the third point of interest for the tourist, stands in the higher part of the town, where a crossroad leads from the High Street towards Addiscombe. The building, a somewhat plain specimen of Elizabethan architecture, cost the archbishop above £2700; and it is endowed with lands which produce a large and increasing annual rental.

It supports a warden, schoolmaster, and 22 poor brothers, who, besides lodging, receive each £40 per annum, and 16 sisters, who receive each £30. The school was intended to receive 10 poor boys and as many girls. It is now a sort of national school, and affords education to a large number of children. Oldham, the poet, was usher here for three years ; here wrote his satires on the Jesuits, and was found here by the Earls of Rochester and Dorset, and Sir Charles Sedley, by whom he was introduced to the Earl of Kingston, in whose house he died in 1683. By a new scheme, sanctioned by the Charity Commissioners, the increased revenue has been also made to provide, what was greatly wanted in the town, a Middle Class Grammar School, for which a handsome Elizabethan building, with a central entrance tower, has been erected at a cost of £15,000, from the designs of Mr. A. Blomfield, at North End (a little N. of Whitgift Hospital), of sufficient capacity to accommodate 300 boys.

The Hospital, of dark red brick with stone quoins, and displaying the founder's initials in the gables, forms a quadrangle, the area of which is laid out in grassplots. The building was restored in 1860. Over the entrance are the arms of the see of Canterbury, with the inscription, " Qui dat pauperi non indigebit." In the chapel, at the S.E. angle, which retains all its ancient fittings, is a portrait of Abp. Whitgift ; also the portrait of a lady, supposed to be one of the archbishop's daughters ; and a curious outline drawing of Death the Skeleton digging a grave. The ancient wooden goblets—one of which bore the inscription,

"What, sirrah ! hold thy pease,
Thirst satisfied, cease"—

formerly preserved in the hall, are no longer to be seen. But a black-letter Bible (Baker's ed. 1595) said to have been presented to the hospital by Queen Elizabeth, is carefully cherished. Above the hall and inner gatehouse are some panelled rooms reserved by the founder for his own use, in which he frequently entertained his " entire and honourable friends " on their visits to Croydon : they are now occupied by the warden, who very readily and courteously shows them to the curious visitor.

Besides Whitgift's, there are three other almshouses at Croydon. Two are in Church Street : *Ely Davy's*, founded in 1447 for 7 poor men and women ; and the *Little Almshouses*, founded about 1528, for 24 poor parishioners. The *Royal Masonic Benevolent Institution*, for aged and decayed Freemasons, a handsome Tudor building of red brick and stone, is by the railway, close to the E. Croydon station.

Croydon, the first place to apply for powers under the Health of Towns Act, has carried out a complete system of connected water supply and pipe drainage, and done something towards solving the difficult question of the economical appliance of sewage. The Board of Health have 400 acres of loamy land at Beddington, which they let on lease, the tenant being bound to distribute the whole of the sewage over the land. The sewage is received in furrows about 16 yards apart, and thence gradually poured over the intervening land. Here it is said to part with its noxious as well as its fertilizing qualities, and to pass away an inodorous and limpid stream, purer than the Wandle into which it flows. About 250 acres are laid down in grass (the strong Italian rye-grass chiefly), and the yield has been four and in some parts five heavy crops in the year. But what is most important, whilst these arrangements, with the ample supply of pure spring water obtained by the Board of Health from artesian wells sunk into the upper chalk, have added much to the comfort of the inhabitants, they have effected a marked improvement in the general health.

Croydon includes several manors, or reputed manors, and old estates. Of these *Addiscombe* and *Shirley* have separate notices. (*See* those titles.) *Benchesham*, called from its owner Walter Whithorse, shield-bearer to Edward III., *Whitehorse*, extends into Norwood (including the once noted Beulah Spa), and gives their name to *Bensham Lane* and *Whitehorse Road*.

Haling, at the S. of Croydon, belonged at his d., 1478, to Thomas Warham, citizen of London, uncle of Abp. Warham. By the Abp. it was transferred in 1536 to Henry VIII. Queen Mary granted it to Sir John Gage, on the attainder of whose son, John, for complicity in the Babington conspiracy, it reverted to the Crown. It was then leased to Charles Earl of Nottingham, the celebrated Lord Admiral and Lord Steward, who died here in 1624. After awhile Haling was restored to the Gages ; was sold in 1707 to E. Stringer, Esq., whose widow married (1712) Wm. Parker, from whom it has descended to the present owner, W. Parker-Hamond, Esq. The house (occupied by J. Watney, Esq.) is finely situated. The grounds are well wooded and pleasant. The grove at the back of the house, and its evergreens, are celebrated in some dull verses by the laureate Whitehead, entitled, 'An Epistle from a Grove in Derbyshire to a Grove in Surrey : and the Answer.' In this grove is one of the oldest cedars in the country. Part of Haling Park has been laid out for building villas on.

Waddon manor was granted by Henry I. to the monks of Bermondsey, who exchanged it for the advowson of Croydon, with the Abp. of Canterbury, by whose successors it has ever since been held. Waddon lies on the Wandle, 1 m. W. of Croydon ch. It is a pretty spot, and the walk by the Wandle, past Waddon Mill to Beddington, is extremely pleasant. The river here used to afford some good fishing. At Waddon is an inn, the *Hare and Hounds*, in some favour with holiday-makers. *Waddon Court* (Mrs. Lanfear) stands on rising ground a little S. of Waddon Mill.

Croham manor extends over *Croham Hill* and *C. Hurst*, about 1 m. S.E. of the town : it forms part of the endowment of Whitgift Hospital. It is a charming walk (but threatened by the builder),—abounding in ferns and wild flowers, and through groves famed for nightingales—by Croham to Sanderstead. Close to Sanderstead, but in Croydon par., is *Selsdon* (G. R. Smith, Esq.), a large and stately castellated mansion, finely situated, and commanding wide views.

The archbishops of Croydon, as we have seen, had their palace in the low grounds, by Croydon ch., and there they had ample gardens, orchards, and fish-ponds. But they also had a deer park on the eastern heights (now known as Park Hill, a little S. of E. Croydon Rly. Station). William Walworth, the Lord mayor who slew Wat Tyler, was keeper of *Croydon Park*, having

received the appointment of Abp. Courtenay. With the exception of a brief alienation to Henry VIII., Croydon Park has always belonged to the see of Canterbury : it is now much built over. *Duppa's Hill*, W. of the town, affords extensive views. A portion of it has been set apart as a public recreation ground ; the rest is built upon. From it there is a pleasant stroll over Banstead Downs.

CRYSTAL PALACE (*see* SYDENHAM).

CUDDINGTON, SURREY (*see* NONSUCH).

CUDHAM, KENT (pronounced *Coodham*) ; pop. 1068 ; lies to the W. of the Sevenoaks road, about 3 m. S.W. of the Chelsfield Stat. of the S.E. Rly. (Tunbridge line), and about 17 m. from London.

The par. is large ; the houses are widely scattered, and the place has an unusually secluded air ; but visitors must not now look for the "wild and solitary" aspect ascribed to it when the *Cudham Woods* stretched intact for over two miles through the heart of the parish. Some insulated patches remain, but cornfields, and fields of strawberries and raspberries (largely grown here and at Farnborough for the London market), have taken the place of woodlands, and the pedestrian will have to keep to narrow and ill-sheltered lanes instead of wandering at will among shadowy forest paths.

Cudham *Church* (St. Peter and St. Paul) stands on high ground midway between the churches of Down and Knockholt, and its shingle spire is a conspicuous landmark. It is of flint and stone, but patched with brick, rough-cast; and old windows have been stopped up and new windows inserted. The oldest parts are E.E., but at the Perp. period there were added on the S. side a porch near the W. end, farther E. a tower and spire, and beyond that a short aisle. Altogether it has an irregular, unpretending, but picturesque appearance, very much in keeping with its situation. S. of it are two remarkable yew trees. The easternmost is 29 ft. in girth, but hollow; the other 28½ ft., and sound.

Two m. W. by N. on the road to Keston is the hamlet of *Leaves Green :* a few cottages, fruit farms and orchards, and a clean inn, the *King's Head.* A like distance S.W., through Cudham Wood, is *Aperfield Court Lodge*, the seat of John Christy, Esq., and not far from it the little hamlet of *Aperfield*.

DAGENHAM, ESSEX (12 m.), 2½ m. N.W. from the Rainham Stat. of the Grt. E. Rly. (Southend line); pop., including *Becontree Heath*, 2879.

Dagenham is a long straggling vill., chiefly of cottages, some pretty good, some decent, but too many poor, low, and dirty thatched mud huts. The *Church*, near the E. end of the vill., has a modern brick nave, an old chancel with a triple lancet E. window, and Dec. windows on the S.; but all altered: the others are modern. The tower is in part old, but cased with brick, and has a tall slated spire. An insc., "Wm. Mason, archt., 1800," records the date and perpetrator of the alterations. The int. has tall pews and galleries. *Brass*, Sir Thos. Urswyk, Recorder of London, and Chief Baron of the Exchequer (d. 1470), in judicial costume, wife, 4 sons and 9 daughters. Langhorne the poet was for some time curate here.

Becontree Heath, which gives its name to the hundred, is 2 m. N. of Dagenham. The heath is enclosed, and is a collection of mean houses, with a beer-shop and Wesleyan chapel. *Dagenham Common*, the last of the open heathland, fell under the Enclosure Act of 1862. The occupations are chiefly agricultural, a considerable portion of the land being marsh.

Dagenham Breach, or, as it is now called, *Dagenham Lake*, is an inlet of the Thames, above 1½ m. in length, with an area of nearly 60 acres, formed, as its name implies, by a breach in the Thames wall. As early as 1376 a terrible inundation broke down the banks of the Thames at Dagenham, and laid the lands belonging to the Abbey of Barking under water; which calamity the convent set forth in a petition of the following year as a plea for exemption from contributing an aid to the king, on

account of the expenses they had been at in endeavouring to repair the injury.* Similar occurrences are recorded subsequently; but the present breach was made in a storm, Dec. 17, 1707, "by the blowing up of a small sluice or trunk made for the drain of land-waters, and might, if proper and immediate help had been applied, have been easily stopped with a small charge." † Immediate help not being applied, a breach was made 400 ft. long, and above 1000 acres of land inundated. After several unsuccessful attempts to close the breach, the task was undertaken by Capt. Perry, who had already distinguished himself by somewhat similar works in Russia. After five years of persevering labour in the face of the most trying difficulties, including the failure of more than one contractor, he restored the embankment, and drained the land, except the portion now known as Dagenham Breach, or D. Lake. The total expenditure was returned by the trustees under the Act of Parliament at £40,472. An interesting account of the operations (the work above cited) was published by Capt. Perry, whose exertions seem to have been very inadequately rewarded.

The unreclaimed portion remained a large sheet of reedy water, with clear open reaches, known to London anglers as ' The Dagenham Lake Subscription Water,' and well stocked with pike, carp, roach, and eels. But in 1864-5 a company was formed, and an Act obtained for purchasing Dagenham Lake, and converting it into a dock. Sir John Rennie and Mr. J. Murray were appointed engineers, and some progress was made with the works; but they were stopped by the monetary difficulties of 1866, and have not been resumed. According to the prospectus,

* Lysons, vol. ii., p. 610.
† An Account of stopping Dagenham Breach, by Captain John Perry, London, 1721.

Dagenham Dock "will be one of the largest in the port of London, and be capable of receiving the largest ships afloat. The average width will be 600 ft., and the length about one mile. . . . The tidal basin will be 450 ft. long and 250 ft. wide, the gates to which will be 70 ft. wide, with 27 ft. water on the sill at ordinary high tide."

It is to Dagenham Breach, oddly enough, that the once famous *Ministerial White-bait Dinner* owed its existence. So important was the maintenance of the embankment considered to be that a commission was appointed to make a periodical inspection. This inspection in course of time became little more than an excuse for an annual holiday. The Commissioners, mostly City magnates, with Sir Robert Preston, M.P., as President, went down in state, together with some representatives of the Admiralty, and after their official inspection, dined together at the Breach House. At first it was merely a holiday dinner of fish fresh caught in the lake, and the delicious whitebait caught in the river off the Breach. Pitt when in the height of his *City* popularity was invited by one of the Commissioners to join them at their fish dinner. The dinner was successful, and next year Mr. Pitt was again invited, and with him several of his colleagues and political friends. This was continued, the dinner becoming every year more sumptuous, and assuming the character of a Ministerial festival, till the inspection was given up, and the Breach House applied to another purpose, when the dinner was transferred to one of the Greenwich taverns, where it flourished, whether Whig or Tory were lord of the feast, down to 1870. The dinner appears to have been held at Dagenham, and the invitations issued by Sir Robert Preston, till that gentleman's death in 1834, after which the dinner became strictly Ministerial.* Mrs. Elizabeth Fry used for some years (1826 onwards) to spend her summers in a cottage by Dagenham Lake, " surrounded by trees, mostly willows, on an open space of lawn, with beds of reeds behind them, and on either side covering the river bank."†

* Letter of Mr. Croker, in Notes and Queries, Sept. 1, 1855, p. 168.
† Memoirs of Elizabeth Fry.

DAGNAM PARK (*see* ROMFORD).

DARENTH, KENT, on the rt. bank of the river of the same name, 1½ m. N. from the Farningham Road Stat. of the L. C. and D. Rly., 2 m. S. from Dartford. The little vill. contains but a small proportion of the 670 inhab. of Darenth par. More are collected in the hamlets of *South Darenth*, 1 m. higher up the river, and *Green Street Green*, 1½ m. W.; the remainder are in scattered farms and cottages.

On the Darenth is the paper mill of Mr. T. H. Saunders, but the bulk of the inhab. are occupied in the fields, orchards, and market gardens. Darenth is charmingly situated on a hillside overlooking the river, which, dividing at South Darenth, and uniting just below Darenth, encloses a long narrow willowy island, and makes the foreground of many pretty little landscapes, to which the chalk hills of Horton Kirby and Farningham form a suitable distance. The lane up the hill, by the ch., leads past a plain country ' public,' the *Fox and Hounds* (which has a capacious old chimney corner), to *Darenth Wood* (½ m.), a rare place for a spring or summer stroll, and singularly rich in birds, butterflies, and insects, endless wild flowers and ferns, hazel and underwood. In this wood may be traced an earthwork ; on the neighbouring hills are vestiges of barrows ; at Horton Kirby Saxon graves have been found.

The antiquary will, however, be more interested in the *Church* (St. Margaret). Its erection has been attributed to Bp. Gundulph, the architect of the White Tower (of London), which would carry it back to the Conqueror, but Mr. Parker thinks that it is not earlier than Henry I. From 940 to 1195 Darenth belonged to Christ Ch., Canterbury, and it may therefore be presumed that the ch. was built by that priory, but the work is ruder than what remains of the period at Eynesford, St. Nicholas at Wade, and other Kentish churches which belonged to the same house. (*See* EYNESFORD.) It stands on the hillside, and is approached by an avenue of horse-chesnuts. It consists of a nave and N. aisle, a long narrow chancel, or rather chancel and sanctuary, and a tower at the W., of white flints, with square pyramidal shingled spire. The rough-cast of the exterior partly conceals the Roman tiles which are worked up in the W. walls, and the character of the masonry : *obs.* on l. of the tower an original square tile flue. The oldest part is the chancel, which is Early Norm., and displays very rude work ; the nave is Late Norm. ; the aisle has Dec. windows. The chancel proper is very low, and covered with a curious plain quadripartite stone groining, over which is a small chamber, built probably when the ch. was altered in the 14th cent., in order to raise the gable, and place the chancel roof more nearly on a level with that of the nave. At the E. end are 3 narrow lancet-like windows, but with round arches, cut out of a single block of stone, and having a rude zigzag moulding. Above these, on the exterior, are what appear to have been 2 large windows, filled up, and a sort of cross in the angle of the gable ; but they are merely reveals ; there has never been any external opening into the room over the chancel, and these blind windows have been made to fill what the builders fancied would be an awkward blank in the gable.

The chancel was restored a few years back ; the nave, as far as means allowed, with exceeding care, by Mr. Burges, in 1867. The rude coloured ornamentation is faithfully copied from that found everywhere under the whitewash. Masons' marks have been noticed in several places; those over the N. doorway are rough indications of proposed carvings. The *font,* circular, and sufficiently large for baptising infants by immersion, has round it a series of rude but elaborate sculptures, in 8 compartments, formed by semicircular arches. They have been erroneously described as representing events in the history of St. Dunstan. One subject is the rite of Baptism (by immersion) ; another David playing on the Harp ; 4 are symbolical animals.

A mile S.E. of the ch. stood the chapel of St. Margaret Hilles, a separate precinct till 1557, when it was united to Darenth, and the chapel dismantled and allowed to go to ruin. The hamlet of *Green Street Green,* spoken of above, must not be confounded with Green Street Green by Farnborough. (*See* FARNBOROUGH.) Like that, however, it is a good-sized roadside vill., and has an old inn.

DARTFORD, KENT (A.-S. *Darentford ;* Dom. *Tarenteford,* the name being derived from its situation at a ford over the Darenth, Darent, or Dart ; the root being the Celtic *Dwr,* water), is a market town on the Dover road, and a stat. on the N. Kent Rly., 17 m. from London Bridge ; pop. 8298. The Darenth, famous of old for its salmon, widens below the town into a navigable creek (Dartford Creek), receives the Cray on the l., and falls into the Thames about 3 m. below Dartford. The broad open level tract between the town and the Thames is known as *Dartford Marshes,* and is locally divided into the *Dartford Salt Marsh* and the *Dartford Fresh Marsh.*

The town consists of a long street lying in a hollow, on a stratum of drift gravel several feet thick, between 2 rather steep chalk hills, named respectively East and West Hill, with a few short streets running out on either side. The ch. stands by the river near the E. end of the High-street, partly blocking the approach to the bridge. The tower is said to have been built originally by Bp. Gundulph, in order to defend the ferry. The first bridge was erected towards the close of the reign of Henry VI. Little advantage has been taken of the broken surface to render the town picturesque. The houses in the main street are for the most part commonplace, and the outskirts poor and dirty. There are however several old houses remaining, though disguised by modern fronts or other alterations—such is that at the corner of Bullis Lane, by the entrance to the ch., the overhanging upper storeys of which may be seen in Bullis Lane.

Though a thoroughly country-looking town, Dartford has some large manufacturing establishments, including extensive engineering works; the factory for Bank of England notes and paper moulds ; on the Darenth large paper mills both above and below the town ; corn mills, bandana and silk printing mills, and the well-known gunpowder mills of Messrs. Pigou and Wilks ; at West Hill lime and whiting works, besides breweries, tanneries, and the like. A corn market is held weekly, and a cattle market monthly, at the Bull Hotel ; and altogether Dartford is a place of considerable trade and local importance.

From its low site the town is very liable to be flooded. The last great flood was in Jan. 1866, when, after heavy snow, the Darenth overflowed its banks, and the streets were for 4 or 5 days under water ; on Jan. 18th there was a depth of 3 ft. of water in the High-street, and 2 ft. in the ch.—as recorded by a line cut in the N. wall of the nave.

Dartford has witnessed some historic events, the outbreak of the great popular insurrection under Wat the Tyler being the chief. According to tradition, Wat Tyler's house was on the N. side of the High-street. Isabel, sister of Henry III., was married here by proxy to the Emperor Frederic II., in 1235 ; the marriage in person was celebrated with much pomp at Worms, July 20th of the same year. Edward III., on his return from France in 1331, held a tournament here, and in 1355 founded, on West Hill, a priory of 24 Augustinian nuns, in remembrance of his victory at Crecy. A daughter of Edward IV. was prioress, and usually a lady of noble county family was at the head of the priory, which long continued to be a favourite retreat for the ladies of Kent. Bridget, 3rd daughter of Edward IV., entered as a nun in 1490, and d. here in 1517, æt. 37. At the Dissolution, the priory had a net yearly revenue of £380. Of the buildings Henry VIII. " made a fit dwelling place for himself and his successors, which remains to this day, however somewhat ruinous."* Henry granted the house to Anne of Cleves ; Elizabeth is said to have resided for a few days in it ; by James I. it was conveyed, with other royal property, to Robert Cecil, in exchange for Theobalds. The lower portion of a brick gate-house and part of the garden wall remain, but nothing earlier than temp. Henry VII.

On the opposite side, or E., of the town, was a chantry dedicated to St. Edmund the Martyr, given to the priory by Edward III. It was near this chantry that Christopher Maid was burned for heresy, July 17th, 1555, as narrated by Foxe. A monumental cross has been erected to the Protestant martyr in the Upper Burial-ground. A hermitage, with a small chapel dedicated to St. Katharine, was founded about 1235 close to the ferry ; the last hermit recorded was in 1518.

* Weever, Anc. Fun. Mon ; 1631, p. 135.

Dartford was the first stage from London of the pilgrims to Becket's shrine at Canterbury, hence the number of hostelries in the town. An altar dedicated to St. Thomas was set up for their use in the ch. ; and here it was that they laid in their stock of pilgrims' tokens.

The *Church* is large, and has many points of interest. It comprises nave with aisles of unequal width (N. 18 ft. 6 in., S. 13 ft.), clerestorey, and chancel with aisles, originally used as chapels. The interior was restored and considerably altered (chiefly for congregational convenience) in 1866, under the direction of Mr. A. W. Blomfield. The exterior is poor and very much shut in. In 1792 the W. corner of the N. aisle was rounded off, and a piece taken from the ch.-yard in order to widen the roadway and get rid of a dangerous turn. The lower part of the W. tower is a portion of the Norman structure erected by Bp. Gundulph, and is a rude work of chalk and Kentish rag; the W. porch, restored 1869, and the upper storey of the tower, are later additions : notice the unusual position of the clock face, on one side of the belfry light. The great W. window is of good and unusual flowing tracery (Late Dec.) ; the E. window, Dec., was substituted for a smaller one when the chancel was restored, and at the same time the chancel arch was considerably raised. *Obs.*, on either side of the chancel arch, the entrance and stairs leading to the rood loft, brought to light on clearing away the plaster in restoring the ch. Also at the E. end of the S. aisle a large fresco of St. George and the Dragon, discovered in 1833. It is 19 ft. by 12, occupying the whole available wall space, and appears to be late 15th cent. work, but it is much injured, and from its position, behind the organ, it is seen with difficulty : a very inexact engraving of it appeared in the *Gent. Mag.* for Aug. 1836, p. 134, and is repeated (but absurdly coloured) in Dunkin's 'History of Dartford,' p. 57. In the chancel, S. of the altar, is a piscina, on the N. an ambrey.

The *Brasses*, which formerly paved the chancel, have all been removed to the walls. Those of value remaining are— Richard Martin and wife, 1402, a large and well-executed work, with a marginal inscription. Martin is represented in the robe of a civic dignitary : engraved in Haines. Richard Burlton and wife, 1496, with a curious inscription. Wm. Death "once prinsipall of Staple Inne," and wives, Elizabeth, æt. 40, had 10 sons—1 in her arms, she having died in giving birth to him—and 6 daughters ; and Anne. Capt. Arthur Bostock, 1612. Of the *Monts.*, the most interesting is that, in a chapel N. of the chancel, to Sir John Spilman, "a high German," d. 1626, and first wife, d. 1607. Spilman was jeweller to Q. Elizabeth, and built the first paper mill here, and one of the first in England.* The mont. has kneeling effigies of Sir John and his wife, under life-size and coloured : it was removed to its present situation and restored at the cost of the Fraternity of Paper Makers. Spilman's descendants retained the mill till about the middle of the 17th cent., when they fell into poverty, and from 1689 to 1700 some of their names constantly appear in the parish books as receiving relief, and the children as apprenticed by the parish. The mill was converted into a gunpowder mill in 1732—that now worked by Messrs. Pigou and Wilks. Richard Trevithick, the inventor of the locomotive steam-engine, died in comparative poverty at the Bull Inn, April 22nd, 1833, and was buried 4 days later in the Upper Burial-ground, but no mont. marks his grave.

The other buildings of a public character, such as the Town Hall behind the High-street, the Grammar School, West

* It is usually said to be the first, but the paper for the work of Bartholomeus, *De Proprietatibus Rerum*, printed by Wynkin de Worde in 1495, was made, as some verses at the end of the book state, "by John Tate the younger . . . . in Englond." Tate's mill was on the river Bean, on the Stevenage side of Hertford, and was 'rewarded' by Henry VII. in 1498 and again in 1499, and visited by that monarch in 1507 (Dr. Rimbault in *N. and Q.*, Series I., vol. ii., p. 473 ; and see vol. v., p. 83). Spilman's mill, which seems to have been on a large scale, is celebrated by Thomas Churchyard, in his Description and Plain Discourse of Paper, who says that

"Tho' his name be *Spill-man*, by degree,
Yet *Help-man* now he shall be calde by mee,
Six hundred men are set at work by him,
That else might starve, or seeke abroad their
   bread ;
Who now live well, and go full brave and trim,
And who may boast they are with paper fed."

But though Dartford cannot claim the honour of the first paper mill, the first mill for rolling and slitting iron was erected here by a Brabant named Godfrey Box in 1590.

Hill, and the County Court, Spital Street, are recent, and not of a kind to call for further notice.

Dartford Heath, though encroached on by enclosures, is still a broad tract stretching away for nearly 2 m. S.W. of the town, overgrown with heath and furze, and rewarding the botanical collector with orchids, and the bird-fancier with the Dartford warbler, though the latter is by no means peculiar to, or indeed common on, the heath from which it derives its name. Here also the archæologist may find matter for speculation in the hollows or shallow pits which he may find by hundreds about the heath, sometimes 2 or 3 together, sometimes as many as 30 or 40, and which some believe to be the sites of ancient British dwellings :— one enthusiastic local antiquary indeed fancies he has found in these and the deeper pits in the neighbouring woods evident traces of the ancient "city of Cassivellaunus." These hollows have mostly, as Johnson said of the huts in the Hebrides, "a tendency to circularity," but some are oval, others oblong, the longest diameter never perhaps exceeding 20 ft. The long lines of shallow excavations on the Crayford side of the heath are merely relics of the great camp held on the heath towards the end of the last century. Neither of these must be confounded with the pits sunk by means of a deep shaft into the chalk, and noticed under CRAYFORD, CHADWELL, and elsewhere. Of this latter kind, one or two occur about Dartford Heath, but they are numerous in *Joyden's Wood*, 1 m. S.W. of it. The most accessible specimens, however, will be found in the adjacent *Stankey's Wood*, where they mostly consist of a double chamber, reached by a shaft from 60 to 80 ft. deep. Extensive earthworks are also traceable here. Roman remains, comprising coffins, urns, fragments, and numerous coins of the emperors, have been found on East Hill.

DATCHET, Bucks (Dom. *Daceta*), on the Thames, opposite Windsor, from which it is 1¼ m. E. ; and 24 m. from London by the Windsor br. of the L. and S.W. Rly. ; pop. 990.

The village is a quiet genteel place of abode, and dull and uncharacteristic in appearance, as such places usually are ; but the neighbourhood is beautiful and interesting. The *Church*, St. Mary, the chief building, completed in 1860, stands on the site of the old ch., a small building, partly E.E., but for the most part of the Dec. period, which was pulled down in 1857. The present building is Dec. in style; has nave, with aisles of unequal width, and chancel; on the N. a transept, and a tower, sq. at the base, octagonal above, and crowned by a spire; and on the S. a porch. The painted windows, by O'Connor, are in memory of the Prince Consort. The archt. was Mr. David Brandon. The parsonage and schools were built about the same time. The old half-timber brick and plaster fronted house of 5 gables, opp. the ch., was originally the mansion of Lord Howick: in recent times a workhouse; subsequently the par. school, but of late repaired and let out in tenements.

Above Datchet the banks of the Thames are very picturesque, the towers and trees of Windsor forming at every turn a new combination with the river. " The muddy ditch at *Datchet Mead*, close by the Thames side," into which Falstaff was thrown "glowing hot, like a horse-shoe, hissing hot," was not, however, as the name would seem to indicate, here, but on the other side of the river, near the end of Datchet Lane. The river above Datchet has always been in high esteem with anglers. Here Izaak Walton was wont to fish for "a little trout called a samlet or skegger-trout, that would bite as fast and freely as minnows, and catch 20 or 40 of them at a standing." [*] Here with him sometimes fished, and sometimes made verses, "that undervaluer of money, the late provost of Eton College, Sir Henry Wotton." Wotton built a fishing-house by the Thames side, about half-way between Datchet and Eton; Verrio the painter afterwards built himself a summer lodge on the site. No vestige of either is left, but the site is marked by a well-known fishing-cottage, *Black Pots*. Datchet was the resort of another mighty angler, Charles II.—

"His sceptre dwindled to a fishing-rod!
* * * * * *
But see he now does up from Datchet come,
Laden with spoils of slaughter'd gudgeons home."
Rochester.

[*] Complete Angler, chap. iv.

The communication between Datchet and Windsor was of old by a ferry, till Queen Anne built a wooden bridge. This fell down in 1797, and it was not till 1812 that another was built, a rude wooden structure that lasted till 1851, when it was removed, and two iron bridges substituted, each of a single span; one, Victoria Bridge, some little distance higher up the river, uniting Datchet with Windsor; the other, Albert Bridge, lower down the river, running toward Old Windsor.

By the Thames side, about 1 m. below Datchet, is an old mansion, now a farmhouse, called *Place Farm*, but perhaps better known as *King John's Hunting Lodge*—a picturesque old structure, with quaint gables and a rude porch, overshadowed by 2 magnificent walnut trees. The "huge oak timbers, low roofs, and grotesque carvings" of the interior bear equal testimony with the outside to a very respectable antiquity, but the oldest part is centuries later than the reign of John. Mr. Jesse [*] says that a subterraneous passage has been "traced for some distance from the house, leading directly towards Windsor." It is hardly necessary to add that it never reached there: it is probably nothing more than a drain.

DAWLEY FARM, par. of HAR-LINGTON, MIDDX., ½ m. E. of the Hayes Stat. of the Grt. W. Rly., was for ten years, 1726—35, the rural retreat of the celebrated Lord Bolingbroke.

"I am burying myself here that I may get a day or two for Dawley, where I hope you will find me established at your return. There I propose to finish my days in ease, without sloth; and I believe I shall seldom visit London, unless it be to divert myself now and then with annoying fools and knaves for a month or two." [†]

"I am in my Farm[‡] and here I shoot strong and tenacious roots; I have caught hold of the earth (to use a gardener's phrase) and neither my enemies nor my friends will find it an easy matter to transplant me again." [§]

Lord Bolingbroke bought Dawley of Charles Earl of Tankerville, and rebuilt the house. There is a view of the earlier house in Kip, but none of Bolingbroke's Farm. The Pope Correspondence abounds

[*] Favourite Haunts.
[†] Bolingbroke to Swift, Feb. 17, 1727.
[‡] "And what he built a Palace, calls a Farm." (Dawley Farm, a poem, 1731.)
[§] Bolingbroke to Swift, Feb. 1728.

in references to Dawley. Pope himself was often here, Dawley being within an easy distance of Twickenham. Here, as he writes to Mallet, he came to try the regimen of asses' milk ; and it was on his return from hence, in Bolingbroke's carriage and six, that he was upset in crossing a bridge, and nearly drowned.* Voltaire visited Bolingbroke in 1726, and was a frequent guest at Dawley during the two years he remained in England.

"I now hold the pen for my Lord Bolingbroke, who is reading your letter between two hay-cocks ; but his attention is somewhat diverted, by casting his eyes on the clouds, not in the admiration of what you say, but for fear of a shower. He is pleased with your placing him in the triumvirate between yourself and me ; though he says he doubts he shall fare like Lepidus, while one of us runs away with all the power, like Augustus, and another with all the pleasures, like Antony. It is upon a foresight of this, that he has fitted up his farm, and you will agree that his scheme of retreat is not founded upon weak appearances. . . . . . As to the return of his health and vigour, were you here, you might inquire of his hay-makers ; but as to his temperance, I can answer that (for one whole day) we have had nothing for dinner but mutton-broth, beans and bacon, and a barndoor fowl. Now his lordship is run after his cart, I have a moment left to myself to tell you, that I overheard him yesterday agree with a painter for two hundred pounds, to paint his country hall with trophies of rakes, spades, prongs, etc., and other ornaments, merely to countenance his calling this place a Farm." ✛

Goldsmith in quoting this letter ‡ observes :—

"What Pope here says of his engagements with a painter, was shortly after executed : the hall was painted accordingly in black crayons only, so that at first view it brought to mind the figures often seen scratched with charcoal, or the smoke of a candle, upon the kitchen walls of farm-houses. The whole, however, produced a most striking effect ; and over the door at the entrance into it was this motto : *Satis beatus ruris honoribus.*"

Black crayons seem an odd material to paint a large hall in, and Goldsmith is an unsafe authority on a technical question. But Lysons, evidently unacquainted with this passage in Goldsmith, has seemingly corroborated it by an independent witness. After citing Pope's letter, he adds : "The Editor of the Biographia Britannica observes, from his own knowledge, that it *was* so painted in black crayons ;" but on comparing the two passages it is clear that the writer in the 'Biographia' is simply following Goldsmith. Lady Lux-

borough's account of the decorations is, however, sufficiently explicit to show that the work was of a kind much in vogue at that time for wall-painting, and known as *chiaroscuro*,—the walls of the Upper Painted Hall, Greenwich Hospital, are so painted :—

"When my brother Bolingbroke built Dawley, which he chose to call a farm, he had his hall painted in stone-colours, with all the implements of husbandry placed in the manner one sees or might see arms and trophies in some general's hall ; and it had an effect that pleased everybody. I believe Pope mentions it in one of his letters to Swift." *

The contemporary poem entitled ' Dawley Farm,' though fully describing the paintings, merely says of the style,

"No gaudy colours stain the rural hall ;
Blank light and shade discriminate the wall."

Of the house and its master it is intensely eulogistic :—

"See emblem of himself his villa stand
Politely finish'd, regularly grand,
* * * * * *
Conversing with the mighty names of old,
Names like his own in Time's bright lists enroll'd,
Here splendidly obscure, delighted lives,
And only for his wretched country grieves." †

As is well known, Bolingbroke soon tired of this splendid obscurity. In 1735 he withdrew to France ; and two or three more brief extracts will suffice to show the close of his connection with the Farm.

"Let me depend on you and Bathurst for enabling me to live like a cosmopolite the rest of my days.—For this purpose you must dispose of *Dawley* for me. Were my father likely to die this measure would be prudent, and since he is likely to live it is necessary. To what purpose should I keep an expensive retreat where in all probability I shall never return ?" ‡

"Lord Bolingbroke has been here a few days, and is come to sell Dawley to pay his debts ; and he will return to France." §

"Lord Bolingbroke executed his deeds for the sale of Dawley on Friday, and set sail the next day for France from Greenwich." ‖

In a subsequent letter (May 1, 1739) Pope tells Swift that Dawley is sold for £26,000. The house, except one wing, was pulled down. The site was bought by the Earl of Uxbridge, and, after passing through one or two other hands, became

* See Bolingbroke's Letter to Swift, Sept. 22, 1726.
✛ Pope to Swift, Dawley, June 28, 1728.
‡ Life of Bolingbroke, 1771, p. 65.

* Lady Luxborough's Letters, p. 22.
† Dawley Farm, Gent. Mag., vol. i. (1731), p. 262.
‡ Bolingbroke to Sir W. Wyndham, Chantelon, Jan. 5, 1737.
§ Alderman Barber to Swift, July 2, 1738.
‖ Pope to Ralph Allen (Dec. 1738), quoted in Ruffhead's Life of Pope, p. 530.

in 1797 the property of Mr. Peter De Salis, in whose descendant it remains. About 1799 the Grand Junction Canal was carried along its northern border, and 40 years later the Great Western Railway cut through the southern side of the grounds. The present *Dawley* or *Doyley Court* is in Hillingdon parish.

DEEPDENE (*see* DORKING).

DENHAM, BUCKS (Dom. *Daneham*), lies a little to the N. of the road to Wycombe, and E. of the river Colne, about 2 m. N.W. from Uxbridge Rly. Stat. ; pop. of the par. 1234.

The little vill. is very prettily situated on a feeder of the Colne, with the park of Denham Court on one side and that of Denham Place on the other. The vill. itself looks old and decayed, but none the less picturesque. In it are a few half-timber dwellings, and by the entrance to the ch.-yard is an old brick house with 3 stepped gables, now used as the workhouse.

The *Church*, St. Mary, of flint and stone, consists of a nave and aisles with clerestorey, chancel, and large low sq. embattled tower ; is partly Dec., S. aisle and 3-light E. windows, partly Perp., but was restored, altered, and enlarged in 1861, under the direction of Mr. G. E. Street, R.A. In the chancel is a *mont.* with recumbent effigies of Sir Edm. Peckham, d. 1564, and his wife Anne. By the S. door is a mont. to their son, Sir Robert Peckham, Privy Councillor to Q. Mary, who d. and was interred at Rome, 1569, but whose heart was brought for burial here. Another mont. with a bust is to Sir Roger Hill, founder of Denham Place, 1670 ; and there are several others to members of the Bowyer and Way families. Here also is one of the very rare *brasses* of abbesses—Agnes Jordan, last abbess of Syon, 1545.

From the ch. an avenue of fine lime trees, ½ m. long, runs E. to *Denham Court* (Col. Lambert), formerly the seat of the Bowyers, but enlarged and modernized by its present owner. Dryden was a frequent visitor to Sir Wm. Bowyer ; here " the version of the First Georgic, and a great part of the last Æneid was made,"[*] and he wrote of the place, " Nature has conspired with art to make the garden one of the most delicious spots in Eng-

land. It contains not above 5 acres, just the compass of Alcinous' garden, but Virgil says, *Laudato ingentia rura exiguum colito.*" Charles II. is said to have been concealed for awhile at D. Court, and 4 curious paintings on panel are preserved in the house as a memorial of the devices resorted to by Lady Bowyer to mislead his pursuers. In the 1st, Charles is represented in the kitchen as a scullion ; in the 2nd, hiding among the rushes in the moat ; the 3rd shows the turkey bleeding at the head which Lady Bowyer hung over the panel behind which Charles was concealed, to keep off the bloodhound that was tracking him ; the 4th is a portrait of Lady Bowyer.

Denham Place (B. H. W. Way, Esq.), a large red-brick mansion, standing in the midst of a pleasant little park immediately W. of the vill., was built by Sir Roger Hill, about 1670, on the site of the old manor-h. of the Peckhams. Denham Place was in 1836 the residence of Lucien and Joseph Bonaparte ; Capt. James Cook was a frequent visitor ; and it was the favourite rural retreat of Sir Humphry Davy, who has in his *Salmonia* celebrated his angling exploits in the neighbouring Colne, and described the charm of the scenery. *Denham Fishery* is a very pretty house and grounds by the Colne, here spreading out into a broad clear stream. The trout fishing for which this part of the river was once so famous has deteriorated, but Col. Goodlake has (1874) placed in the water a stock of American brook trout, " a fine sporting fish " (*Buckland*), with every promise of success. The *Tile House* (Lady Drummond), is a good house, surrounded by spacious grounds, 2½ m. N. of the village. Other seats are *Denham Mount* (W. James, Esq.), and *The Cedars* (E. Mounsey, Esq.)

DEPTFORD, KENT, of old famous for its naval ship-building and victualling yards, lies on the Thames, immediately W. of Greenwich, 4 m. from London by road, and by the L. and Greenwich Rly. It consists of two parts, Deptford St. Nicholas, or Lower Deptford, by the Thames (pop. 6474), and Deptford St. Paul, or Deptford Upper Town (pop. 53,714), which extends inland to Lewisham, and is bounded E. by Greenwich, and W. by Rotherhithe and Peckham.

---

* Malone, Life of Dryden.

The name, spelled *Depeford* in ancient charters, *Depford* by Chaucer—

" Sey forth thi tale, and tarye nat the tyme ;
  So heer is *Depford*, and it is passed prime : " *

—is supposed to be derived from A.-S. *deóp* and *ford*, the *deep ford*, now crossed by the bridge over the Ravensbourne, just before it widens into Deptford Creek ; but it may possibly come from the Danish *Dyb*, deep, and *fiord*, an inlet, bay, or station for ships, the Northern fleet having lain long at anchor here (1013—16) whilst the army was encamped at Greenwich— the name of which is by many derived from the Danish. The rise of the tide in the Thames at Deptford is at spring-tides 19 ft. 2 in., at neap tides 15 ft. 3 in.

" This town," writes Lambarde, 1570,† " being a frontier betweene Kent and Surrey, was of none estimation at all, untill that King Henrie the eight, advised (for the better preservation of the Royall Fleete) to erect a Storehouse, and to create certaine officers there : these he incorporated by the name of the Maister and Wardeins of the Holie Trinitie, for the building, keeping, and conducting, of the Navie Royall."

The loss by fire of their early records renders it difficult to ascertain precisely the duties at this time imposed on the Corporation of the Trinity ; but there can be little doubt that Lambarde was misinformed as to their having the direction of the building, keeping, and management of the Royal Navy, though Camden, Stow, and others adopt his statement. No mention of any such service is made in the Charter of Incorporation, or of any voice being allowed the Brethren in the construction of the ships or conduct of the Navy. A guild of seamen was probably in existence before, and the charter of Henry gave it a legal standing and increased authority. The " Bretheren of the Guild or Fraternity " may make laws for their own governance, and " for the relief, increase, and augmentation of the shipping of this our realm of England," but nothing is said about our navy. What they did in connection with it was probably in the way of advice, when counsel was asked of them as the most experienced " shipmen or mariners of this our realm of England." The establishment of the Corporation here is a proof that Deptford was already a rendezvous for shipping and the resort of seamen ; but there can be no doubt that it was the foundation of the naval yard that gave importance to the place.

The Dockyard was founded in the early part of the reign of Henry VIII.; the great storehouse on the N. side of the great quadrangle was erected in 1513 : out of these, under the successive sovereigns, grew up by slow steps the vast double establishment of the Royal Dock and Victualling Yard. " A Note how many ships the King's Majesty (Henry VIII.) hath in harbour, on the 18th day of September, in the 13th year of his reign ; what portage they be of ; what estate they be in the same day ; also where they ride and be bestowed," the first authentic statement extant of its kind, enables us to see what use was made of Deptford as a naval station in 1521 :—

" The *Mary Rose*, being of the portage of 600 tons, lying in the pond at Deptford, besides the storehouse there, &c.—The *John Baptist*, and *Barbara*, every of them being of the portage 400 tons, do ryde together in a creke [the Ravensbourne] of Deptford Parish, &c.—The *Great Nicholas*, being of portage 400 tons, lyeth in the east end of Deptford Strand, &c. . . . The Great Barke, being of portage 250 tons, lyeth in the pond at Deptford, &c.—The Less Bark, being of the portage of 180 tons, lyeth in the same pond, &c.—The twayne Row Barges, every of them being of portage 60 tons, lye in the said pond, &c.—The Great Galley, being of portage 800 tons, lyeth in the said pond, &c."*

Eventually the Dockyard came to be one of the most complete in the kingdom in its arrangements for the construction of wooden ships, and many of the largest and finest of our old men-of-war were launched from it. When iron began to supersede wood, and a heavier class of vessels was required, the shallow water in the river opposite the slips, and other inconveniences of the site, caused the yard to be pretty much restricted to the building of gunboats, and it was finally decided to abandon the dockyard and transfer the workmen to other establishments. The last ship launched from Deptford Dockyard was the screw corvette *Druid*, on the 13th of March, 1869, in the presence of the Princess Louise and Prince Arthur ; the Princess acting as sponsor to the vessel, and cutting the cord which released it from the shore. The Dockyard was finally closed on March 31st, 1869.

---

* Cant. Tales : Prologue of the Reeve, 51.
† Perambulation of Kent, reprint, p. 386.

* Charnock, Hist. of Marine Architecture, vol. ii., p. 105.

Immediately W. of the old Dockyard is the Victualling Yard, or, to use the full official title, the *Royal Victoria Victualling Yard*,—the whole of the land having been procured from time to time from Sir John and Sir Frederick Evelyn, and, in 1869, from W. J. Evelyn, Esq. It comprises extensive ranges of stores, workshops, and sheds, with river-side wharf, and all necessary machinery and appliances. It is the largest of the three great naval victualling yards (the others are at Gosport and Devonport), and is in effect the depôt from which the other yards are furnished. From it the navy is supplied with clothing, bedding, provisions, medicines and medical comforts, and that elastic class of necessaries termed 'sundries.' At the proper season cattle are received and slaughtered ; beef and pork salted and packed in barrels ; meat boiled and preserved in tin canisters ; wheat ground ; biscuits made ; and the barrels in which all are stored manufactured in a large steam cooperage. The articles prepared and in store necessarily fluctuate in quantity, but in a single year 5,000,000 lb. of beef and 3,000,000 lb. of pork ; 7,000,000 lb. of wheat, 1,200,000 lb. of cocoa, 1,000,000 lb. of peas, 800,000 lb. of salt, and 1,600,000 lb. of sugar, have been received, besides a proportionately large quantity of vegetables. The average quantity of meat salted annually exceeds 1,500,000 lb. ; preserved in tins, 1,000,000 lb. A stock of medicine sufficient for 5000 men for 6 months is kept constantly in store, but the demand for it is so great and regular that supplies arrive and leave almost daily. The general direction of the Yard is in a resident Captain Superintendent, who has as his immediate assistants a Storekeeper and Master Attendant. In all about 500 persons are employed in the yard.

The Dock and Victualling Yards have, of course, received many distinguished visitors. Edward VI. was one, and he has left a record of his visit, and the provision made for his entertainment :—

"*June* 19*th*, 1549.—I went to Deptford, being bedden to supper by the L. Clinton, where before souper i saw certaine [men] stand upon a bote without hold of anything, and rane one at another til one was cast into the water. At supper Mons. Vieedam and Henadey supped with me. After supper was ober a fort made upon a great lighter on the temps [Thames] which had three walles and

a Watch Towre, in the meddes of wich Mr. Winter was Captain with forty or fifty other Soldiours in yelow and blake. To the fort also apperteined a galery of yelow color, with men and municion in it for defence of the castel ; wherfor ther cam 4 pinesses with other men in wight ansomely dressed, wich entending to give assault to the castil, first droue away the yelow piness and aftir with clods, scuibs, canes of fire, darts made for the nonce, and bombardes assaunted the castill beating them of the castel into the second ward, who after issued out and droue away the pinesses sinking one of them, out of wich al the men in it being more than twenty leaped out and swamme in the temps. Then came th' Admiral of the nauy with three other pinesses, and wanne the castel by assault, and burst the tope of it doune, and toke the captain and under captain. Then the Admiral went forth to take the yelow ship, and at length clasped with her toke her, and assaulted also her toppe and wane it by compulcion, and so returned home."[*]

"On the 4th of April 1581, Queen Elizabeth visited Captain Drake's ship called the Golden Hind. Her Majesty dined on board ; and after dinner, conferred the honour of knighthood on the Captain. A prodigious concourse of people assembled on the occasion ; and a wooden bridge, on which were a hundred persons, broke down, but no lives were lost. Sir Francis Drake's ship, when it became unfit for service, was laid up in this yard, where it remained many years ; the cabin being, as it seems, turned into a banquetting-house : 'We'll have our supper (says Sir Petronel Flash, in a comedy called Eastward-hoe, written by Ben Jonson and others) on board Sir Francis Drake's ship that hath compassed the world.' It was at length broken up, and a chair made out of it for John Davis, Esq., who presented it to the University of Oxford." [†]

A very different personage may give his own account of his visit as "one of the principal officers of the navy" (clerk of the acts) on occasion of a reported "rising of Fanatiques":—

"*January* 12*th*, 1661.—With Colonel Slingsby and a friend of his, Major Waters, (a deafe and most amorous melancholy gentleman, who is under a despayr in love, as the Colonel told me, which makes him bad company, though a good natured man) by water to Redriffe, and so on foot to Deptford. We fell to choosing four captains to command the guards, and choosing the place where to keep them, and other things in order thereunto. Never till now did I see the great authority of my place, all the captains of the fleete coming cap in hand to us. I went home with Mr. Davis, storekeeper, (whose wife is ill, and so I could not see her) and was there most princelike lodged, with so much respect and honour, that I was at a loss how to behave myself.

"13*th*.—To the Globe to dinner, and then with Commissioner Pett to his lodgings there, (which he hath for the present, while he is in building the King's yacht, which will be a very pretty thing, and much beyond the Duchman's,) and from thence

---

[*] Cott. MSS., British Museum, Nero C. X., f. 19, quoted in Cruden's Hist. of Gravesend, p. 141.

[†] Lysons, Environs, vol. i., p. 466.

The Royal Dockyard, Deptford

Dorking (see p.150)

by coach to Greenwich church, where a good sermon, a fine church, and a great company of handsome women. And so I to Mr. Davis's to bed again. But no sooner in bed, but we had an alarme, and so we rose: and the Comptroller comes into the yard to us; and seamen of all the ships present repair to us, and there we armed, with every one a handspike, with which they were as fierce as could be. At last we hear that it was five or six men that did ride through the guard in the towne, without stopping to the guard that was there; and, some say, shot at them. But all being quiet there, we caused the seamen to go on board again.

"14th.—The arms being come this morning from the Tower, we caused them to be distributed. I spent much time with Lieutenant Lambert, walking up and down the yards, and he dined with us. After dinner Mrs. Pett lent us her coach, and carried us to Woolwich, where we did also dispose of the arms there, and settle the guards.

"15th.—Up and down the yard all the morning, and seeing the seamen exercise, which they do already very handsomely. Then to dinner at Mr. Ackworth's, where there also dined with us one Captain Bethell, a friend of the Comptroller's. A good dinner and very handsome. After that, and taking of our leave of the officers of the yard, we walked to the waterside, and in our way walked into the rope-yard, where I do look into the tar-houses and other places, and took great notice of all the several works belonging to the making of a cable. . . . . The King [Charles II.] hath been this afternoon at Deptford, to see the yacht that Commissioner Pett is building, which will be very pretty."*

Peter the Great visited the dockyard in 1698 for the purpose of studying naval architecture, residing during his stay in Evelyn's house, Sayes Court. In the dockyard he did the work of an ordinary shipwright, but he also paid close attention to the principles of ship designing. His evenings were spent in a public-house with his attendants and one or two chosen companions, smoking and drinking beer, with an occasional fillip of brandy.

Shortly after the final closing of the dockyard it became necessary, under the provisions of the Contagious Diseases (Animals) Act, 1869, to provide a place for the sale and slaughter of foreign animals brought into the port of London, and the Corporation of the city of London having undertaken the duty, purchased the major part of the dockyard for about £95,000, for the site of the new market. They then expended upon the works requisite for converting it into a cattle market about £140,000, and on the 28th December, 1871, it was opened under the title of the *Foreign Cattle Market*. The market occupies an area of over 22 acres,

and provides covered pens, each pen having its water trough and food rack for 4000 cattle and 12,000 sheep, with an open space for some thousands more. The ship-building slips of the old dockyard, with their immense roofs, at least 400 ft. long, familiar objects of old from the Thames, were adapted as pen-sheds, and connected by ranges of substantial and well-ventilated buildings. The old workshops were converted into slaughter-houses for oxen, the boat-houses for sheep, and fitted with travelling pulleys, cranes, and various mechanical appliances for saving labour and minimizing the sufferings of the animals; and in them 700 cattle and 1600 sheep have been killed and dressed in a day. The market has nearly 1100 ft. of river frontage; and three jetties, with a connected low-water platform, provide ample means for landing animals at all states of the tide. Only the animals were wanting to its complete success. But these—owing to some new Orders in Council—ceased to come, and since June 1873 the market has been virtually closed.

William the Conqueror gave the manor of Deptford, or West Greenwich, to Gilbert Magminot, in whose male descendants it remained till 1191, when it passed to a heiress, Alice, the wife of Geoffrey de Say, who gave it to the Knights Templars. It was, however, recovered to the family by his son Geoffrey giving in exchange for it the manor of Saddlescombe, in Sussex. With his other estates it was seized by King John, but restored by Henry III. in 1223, and remained in the possession of the Says till the end of the 14th cent. It then passed through various hands till it finally reverted to the Crown in the early part of the 16th cent. Since the Restoration it has been vested in the Crown, the stewardship being held with that of Greenwich.*

Saye's Court, the site of the manor-house of the Sayes, was with a portion of the demesne lands leased by the Crown to the family of the Brownes; and in 1613 Sir Richard Browne purchased the greater portion of the manor. A "representative of that ancient house," Sir Richard Browne, a follower of the Earl of Leicester, was a privy councillor and clerk of the Green

---

* Pepys, Diary.

* Philipott; Hasted; Lysons.

Cloth, under Elizabeth and James I., and d. at Saye's Court in 1604. He it must have been, and not an Evelyn, as Sir Walter Scott wrote, by a not unnatural slip of the pen, who, taking " a deep interest in the Earl of Sussex, willingly accommodated both him and his numerous retinue in his hospitable mansion," the "ancient house called Saye's Court, near Deptford;" and which hospitable service led to the events recorded in chaps. xiii.—xv. of 'Kenilworth,' among others the luckless visit which Queen Elizabeth paid her sick servant at Saye's Court—" having brought confusion thither along with her, and leaving doubt and apprehension behind." The last Sir Richard Browne, d. 1683, was Clerk of the Council to Charles I., and his ambassador to the Court of France from 1641. John Evelyn, that " perfect model of an English gentleman," as Southey terms him, " whose *Sylva*," as Scott writes, " is still the manual of British planters, and whose life, manners, and principles, as illustrated in his Memoirs, ought equally to be the manual of English gentlemen," married, June 27th, 1647, Mary, the only daughter and heir of Sir Richard Browne; and Sir Richard, being resident in Paris, gave up Saye's Court to his son-in-law. The estate had been seized by the Parliamentary Commissioners, but Evelyn succeeded in buying out, towards the close of 1652, those who had purchased it of the Trustees of Forfeited Estates. Thenceforth he made it his residence, at once setting about the works that did so much to render Saye's Court classic ground:—

"*Jany.* 17, 1653.—I began to set out the ovall garden at Sayes Court, which was before a rude orchard, and all the rest one intire field of 100 acres, without any hedge, except the hither holly hedge joyning to the bank of the mount walk. This was the beginning of all the succeeding gardens, walks, groves, enclosures, and plantations there.

"*Feby.* 19.—I planted the orchard at Sayes Court, new moone, wind W." *

Evelyn lived chiefly at Saye's Court for the next 40 years, and carried out there, as far as the site allowed, the views he set forth in his *Sylva*, to the great admiration of his contemporaries. Roger North, in his Life of the Lord Keeper Guildford, describes the grounds as " most boscar-

esque, being, as it were, an examplar of his book on Forest Trees;" and Pepys, in his homely way, well illustrates its character and that of its owner:—

"*May 5th*, 1665.—After dinner, to Mr. Evelyn's; he being abroad, we walked in his garden, and a lovely noble ground he hath indeed. And, among other rarities, a hive of bees, so as, being hived in glass, you may see the bees making their honey and combs mighty pleasantly." . . . .

"*Nov. 5th* (Lord's Day), 1665.—. . . . By water to Deptford, and there made a visit to Mr. Evelyn, who, among other things, showed me most excellent painting in little; in distemper, in Indian incke, water colours: graveing; and, above all, the whole secret of mezzo-tinto, and the manner of it, which is very pretty, and good things done with it. He read to me very much also of his discourse, he hath been many years and now is about, about Gardenage; which will be a most noble and pleasant piece. He read me part of a play or two of his making, very good, but not as he conceits them, I think, to be. He showed me his 'Hortus Hyemalis;' leaves laid up in a book of several plants kept dry, which preserve colour, however, and look very finely, better than an Herball. In fine a most excellent person he is, and must be allowed a little for a little conceitedness; but he may well be so, being a man so much above others." *

Among the MSS. at Wotton (quoted in Appendix to his *Memoirs*), Evelyn has left a pretty full account of what he did at Saye's Court:—

"The hithermost Grove I planted about 1656; the other beyond it, 1660; the lower Grove, 1662; the holly hedge, even with the Mount hedge below, 1670.—I planted every hedge and tree not onely in the garden, groves, etc., but about all the fields and house since 1653, except those large, old and hollow Elms in the Stable Court and next the Sewer; for it was before, all one pasture field to the very garden of the house, which was but small; from which time also I repaired the ruined house, and built the whole end of the kitchen, the chapel, buttry, my study, above and below, cellars and all the outhouses and walls, still house, Orangerie, and made the gardens, etc. to my great cost, and better I had don to have pulled all down at first, but it was don at several times."

Evelyn's pride in his house and grounds, and the perfect order into which he had brought them, received an unexpected blow. In June 1696, having succeeded to Wotton, he let Saye's Court " for three years to Vice-Admiral Benbow, with condition to keep up the garden." The condition was ill kept, and he writes a few months later that he has "the mortification of seeing every day much of my former labours and expense there impairing for want of a more polite tenant."†

* Evelyn, Diary.

* Pepys, Diary.
† Letter to Dr. Bohm, Jan. 18th, 1697.

But a still less polite tenant was soon forced upon him—Peter the Great.

"*Jany.* 30th, 1698.—The Czar of Muscovy being come to England, and having a mind to see the building of ships, hir'd my house at Sayes Court, and made it his Court and Palace, new furnished for him by the King."

How the Czar conducted himself in the house we learn from a letter Evelyn received from his servant :—

"There is a house full of people, and right nasty. The Czar lies next your Library, and dines in the parlour next your study. He dines at 10 o'clock and 6 at night, is very seldom at home a whole day, very often in the King's Yard, or by water, dressed in several dresses. The King is expected there this day, the best parlour is pretty clean for him to be entertained in. The King pays for all he has."

Evelyn records his leaving, April 21st, after a stay of about three months, and soon after adds—

"*June* 9th.— I went to Deptford to see how miserably the Czar had left my house after 3 months making it his Court. I got Sir Christopher Wren the King's surveyor, and Mr. London his gardener, to go and estimate the repairs, for which they allowed £150 in their report to the Lords of the Treasury." *

They allowed, in fact, something more than £150, as is shown by the Treasury Minute (not printed in the *Memoirs*) :—

"John Evelyn Esq. in recompence for the damage done to his House, goods, and gardens at Deptford by his Csarizes Mätie and his retinue while they resided there, according to the estimation of Sir Christopher Wren, Knt., and George London, Esq. Allowed by Virtue of a Warrant from the late Lords Commissioners of the Treasury held the 21st day of June 1698—£162 .. 7 .. 0."

At the same time Evelyn's tenant, Vice-Admiral Benbow, received, " for like damage done to his goods according to the estimation of Joseph Sewell - - - £133 .. 2 .. 6."

It was the Czar's chief delight to be trundled in a wheelbarrow over Evelyn's lawns and flower-beds and through the hedges, reserving for a special stimulant, when ordinary privet failed, a thick and lofty holly hedge that Evelyn particularly prized, and to which its owner's great joy resisted the utmost efforts of the imperial hedge-breaker :—

"Is there under the heaven a more glorious and refreshing object of the kind, than an impregnable hedge of about four hundred feet in length, nine feet high, and five in diameter; which I can shew

in my now ruined garden at Sayes Court, (thanks to the Czar of Muscovy,) at any time of the year, glittering with its armed and varnished leaves ; the taller standards at orderly distances, blushing with their natural coral ? It mocks the rudest assaults of the weather, beasts, or hedge-breakers— *Et illum nemo impune lacessit.*"*

It may be noted in confirmation of the stories of Peter's rough play in the garden, that Sir Christopher Wren, in his report on the damage done to Evelyn's house and grounds (May 9, 1698), under the heading " what can be repaired again and what cannot," enters :—

"1°. All the grass work is out of order and broke into holes by their leaping and showing tricks upon it.—2°. The bowling green is in the same condition. . . . 6°. The great walks are all broke into holes and out of order." Finally, "George London his Maj. Master Gardener, certifies that to put the gardens and plantations into as good repair as they were before his Zarrish Majesty resided there will require the sum of £55." Admiral Benbow was allowed "for wheelbarrows broke and lost " by the Czar, £1.

Evelyn did not return to Saye's Court after Peter's residence there, except for an occasional visit. After Evelyn's death Saye's Court was neglected, and at the end of the 18th cent. Lysons writes, "There is not the least trace now, either of the house or gardens at Sayes Court ; a part of the garden walls only, with some brick piers, are remaining. The house was pulled down in 1728 or 1729, and the workhouse built on its site." Part of the grounds was taken into the Naval Dockyard, on another part rows of mean cottages were built ; the only portion unappropriated was that left for the workhouse garden : and thus it remained a miserable squalid spot till quite recently. When the Dockyard was closed, and about to be converted into the Foreign Cattle Market, the present representative of the Evelyns (W. J. Evelyn, Esq., of Wotton) determined, 1869, to purchase back from the Government as much of the site of Saye's Court as was available, and restore it to some semblance of its old condition. The neighbourhood is very poor, and has become poorer since the closing of the Dockyard. Mr. Evelyn is landlord of the greater part of the parish, and now proposes to make Saye's Court a *Recreation Ground* for the inhabitants. In all there are about 14 acres of open ground, but a portion

* Sylva, ed. 1704, vol. i., p. 265.

will be attached to the house which stands on the site of Evelyn's mansion. The public garden and playground will be about 10 acres in extent. The garden is laid out and partly planted with trees, shrubs, flowers, and wall fruit—all brought from Wotton, as was also the sod which forms the lawns and borders the walks. There are broad walks, one of which will have at the end a statue of the Queen ; another, one of Peter the Great ; while a statue of John Evelyn, we may hope, will face the entrance. A spacious house, formerly a model-house belonging to the Dockyard, is being converted into a Museum, and made more ornamental in character. When finished, it is proposed to place in it geological and natural history collections, and a library, and to fit up a part of it as a reading-room. In the centre of the garden is a covered stage for a band. The works are being carried out with great care and thoroughness, and we hope the new Saye's Court will have as honourable and lasting a reputation as the old one.*

The entrance to Saye's Court is in Princes Street, Evelyn Street. *Obs.* by the new plant-house a rude stone marking the spot where Peter the Great planted a mulberry tree ; the tree having been cut down by an Admiralty official in 1857. The workhouse mentioned above as erected on the site of Evelyn's house is still standing (though no longer a workhouse), and looks more like an adaptation of a part of the old house than a building of the year 1729.

Apart from the Naval Yard and Saye's Court, the town has little to attract or interest a visitor. In the lower town, towards the river, the streets are narrow, irregular, and dirty, and lined with a sordid array of small, mean, and for the most part wretchedly poor dwelling-houses, and small dingy shops. The district contains however, besides the Government yard, many large and important engineering establishments, factories requiring river-side premises, soap-works and the like. Away from the river the streets are wider, the shops smarter, the dwellings wholesomer in aspect, and there are still broad open market-gardens, with an outer belt of villa and cottage residences, and a sprinkling of old-fashioned red brick mansions.

St. Nicholas Church, the oldest in Deptford, stands by what is called the Stowage, Deptford Green, a little W. of the Dockyard, on the site of an older ch. pulled down in 1697, as being inadequate to the wants of the increased population. Evelyn * notes that "At Deptford they had been building a pretty new church ;" but whatever may have been its beauty, it was so badly built that it had to undergo a thorough restoration 17 years later. It is a plain dull red brick structure, consisting of nave and aisles, chancel, and a tower of flint and stone at the W. end, of Perp. date, but somewhat patched, the only relic of the old ch. The interior contains numerous *Monts.* of former Deptford celebrities, among others the Browne family, including the 2 Sir Richards, buried " in the ch.-yard under the S.E. window of the chancel. ;"† Capt. George Shelvocke, d. 1742, who "in the years of our Lord 1719, 20, 21, and 22 performed a voyage round the globe of the world, which he most wonderfully, and to the great loss of the Spaniards, compleated, though in the midst of it he had the misfortune to suffer shipwreck upon the Island of Juan Fernandez, on the coast of the kingdom of Chili ;" also his son Geo. Shelvocke, F.R.S., and secretary to the Post Office, d. 1760, who in early life accompanied his father in his long voyage, and afterwards wrote an account of it; Peter Pett, d. 1652, and other members of that famous family of naval shipbuilders. In the register of the old ch. are entries of the burial of " Christopher Marlow, slaine by ffrancis Archer, the 1 of June 1693;" and "Capt. Thomas Pearse and Lt. Logan, shot to death for losing the Sapphire cowardly : buried Aug. 26, 1670."

St. Paul's Church, on the W. side of the High Street, near the Rly. Stat., was built in 1730, on the division of the par., and is a good example of the classic style of the reign of George II. It is a solid-looking stone building, with a lofty

---

* We are indebted to the courtesy of John Evelyn Liardet, Esq., the resident manager of the Evelyn estate, who takes a warm interest in the project, for guidance over the grounds and buildings, and inspection of the working plans and drawings.

---

* Diary, August 1699.
† Evelyn.

flight of steps and a circular portico of the Corinthian order, over which is a taper spire, and has nave, aisles, and a shallow chancel. The interior is singularly sombre, with heavy galleries and tall pews, carved pulpit, and chancel fittings of dark Dutch oak, of substance and workmanship worthy the vicinity of the Royal Dockyard. The *Monts.* include one by Nollekens to Admiral Sayer, d. 1760, who "first planted the British flag in the Island of Tobago." In the ch.-yard is a mont. to Thomas Hawtree, d. 1759, and his wife Margaret, d. 1734 :

" She was an indulgent Mother, and the best of Wives,
   She brought into this world more than three thousand lives."

The explanation of this is that she " was an eminent midwife ; " and she evinced the interest she took in her calling by giving a silver basin for christenings to this par., and another to the par. of St. Nicholas.* The Rev. Charles Burney, D.D., the Greek scholar and critic (son of the author of ' History of Music '), whose fine classical library was purchased after his death, 1817, for the British Museum for £13,500, was rector of St. Paul's. The Parsonage is one of Vanbrugh's eccentric red-brick structures.

Recent churches, for newly formed ecclesiastical districts, are *St. Peter's*, Wickham Road ; *St. John's*, Upper Lewisham Road ; *St. James's*, Hatcham, consecrated in 1850, but only recently completed ; and *St. Luke's*, Evelyn Street, a well-built and handsome Gothic ch., erected in 1872, mainly at the cost of W. J. Evelyn, Esq. Chapels of all grades are numerous, and one or two are of some architectural pretensions.

As has been noticed, the Trinity House was founded at Deptford, and the corporation held their meetings here till about 1817, when on the completion of the new Trinity House on Tower Hill, London, their old hall at Deptford was pulled down. Their connection with Deptford is, however, marked by their 2 hospitals for decayed master-mariners and pilots, and their widows : one by St. Paul's ch. ; the other, known as the Trinity House, Deptford, founded in 1670, by Sir Richard Browne, John Evelyn's

* Lysons.

father-in-law, who gave the ground, and Capt. Maples, who gave £1300 towards the building. This is a large and noteworthy old red brick pile in Church Street, behind St. Nicholas ch. In the great room at the back of this building, which serves for hall and chapel, the Master and Elder Brethren of the Trinity House used, till within the last few years, to assemble on Trinity Monday, and, after the transaction of formal business, proceed to St. Nicholas ch., where there was a special service and sermon. That ended, they returned to London by water—the shipping and wharves on the Thames being gaily decked with bunting—and closed the day by a grand banquet at the Trinity House. The meeting and banquet are now held at the Trinity House, Tower Hill, the sermon at St. Olave's, Hart Street (Pepys's ch.)

Hatcham is an outlying manor of Deptford ; and *New Cross*, where are important stations and works of the L. Br. and S. Coast and S.E. Rlys., is in Deptford parish ; but both may be considered as belonging to the outer circle of the metropolis, and do not call for special notice here. At New Cross (Counter Hill, Upper Lewisham Road) is the *Royal Naval School*, a good building of the Wren type, erected in 1850, but since enlarged. The school, which was founded in 1833, has an average of 200 pupils, mostly the sons of naval and military officers, gives an excellent general education, but with special reference to the naval service, and has sent out many pupils who have distinguished themselves in the several branches of that service.

DERHAM, or DYRHAM PARK, MIDDX. (*see* MIMMS, SOUTH).

DITTON, LONG, SURREY (Dom. *Ditone*), an extensive agric. par. of 1836 inhab. The vill. comprises a few scattered houses and farms, about 1½ m. S.W. of the Surbiton Stat. of the L. and S.W. Rly.

The *Church* stands in a charming situation, on high ground at the end of a long narrow lane half hidden among the trees. It is intensely ugly, but its ugliness is partially veiled by ivy. Architecturally it is somewhat curious. It was built about 1776, from the designs of Sir Robt. Taylor, Soane's predecessor at the Bank of England. It is of brick ; in form a Greek cross (63 ft. by 46), with a low cupola at the intersection, and dimly lighted by a single window at the end of each arm of the cross. The manor of Ditton belonged to the priory of St. Mary, Without, Bishopsgate, till the Suppression ; afterwards to the Evelyns, by whom it was sold to Lord Chancellor King, in whose descendant, the Earl of Lovelace, it remains. Another manor, Taleorde at the Dom. Survey, now *Talworth* or *Tolworth*, was for a time in the possession of Hugh le Despenser, Earl of Gloucester ; later in that of Edmund of Woodstock, Earl of Kent, uncle of Edward III. ; and now belongs to the Earl of Egmont. The manor-house, *Tolworth Court House*, on the l. of the road from Kingston to Ewell, where it crosses the Hog's Mill-stream, is now a farm-house with slender indications of its former state. *Tolworth* hamlet lies along the Ewell road, at the foot of Surbiton Hill, about ½ m. on the Kingston side of Tolworth Court House.

DITTON, or THAMES DITTON,

Surrey (Dom. *Ditune*), so called to distinguish it from Long Ditton, which adjoins it on the S.E., is a vill. and stat. on the L. and S.W. Rly., 14 m. from Waterloo : pop. of par., 2545. Inn, the *Swan*, on the Thames, opposite Hampton Court Park, well known to anglers and boating parties, and famed alike for good dinners and for the beautiful views up and down the river :—

> " Here lawyers free from legal toils,
> And peers released from duty,
> Enjoy at once kind Nature's smiles,
> And eke the smiles of beauty.
>
> *   *   *   *
>
> The 'Swan,' snug inn, good fare affords
> As table e'er was put on,
> And worthier quite of loftier boards
> Its poultry, fish, and mutton.
> And while sound wine mine host supplies,
> With beer of Meux or Tritton,
> Mine hostess, with her bright blue eyes,
> Invites to stay at Ditton."*

There are two deeps at Ditton under the care of the Thames Angling Preservation Society : one opposite Boyle Farm of 512 yards ; the other of 250 yards from Keene's Wharf, northward.

The vill. lies a little way back from the Thames, with the church just out of the main street, the houses straggling away on the one hand to Weston Green, on the other to Gigg's Hill. Thames Ditton *Church* (St. Nicholas) was originally a chapel-of-ease to Kingston, but was made parochial by Act of Parliament in 1769. Having become dilapidated, it was rebuilt in 1864, and a new nave, aisle, chancel, and porch added on the S. : archt., Mr. B. Ferrey. The body of the ch. is of flint and rubble, Dec. in character, the base of the tower being older ; the belfry is of wood. Several painted glass windows have been inserted. In the interior are 2 or 3 interesting *brasses*, taken up when the ch. was rebuilt and carefully replaced. *Obs.* a showy but well-engraved plate of Erasmus Fforde, treasurer to Edward IV., d. 1553, and wife Julyan, d. 1559. In the centre is a shield of arms with helmet, crest, and motto : on one side Fforde with 6 sons kneeling, on the other his wife with 11 daughters. Other brasses are of Wm. Notte (d. 1576) with 14 sons, and his wife (d. 1587) with 5 daughters. Cuthbert Blakeden, sergeant of confectionery to Henry VIII. (d. 1540), John Boothe (d. 1548) and Julyan, "wife of the said Cuthbert and John." The recent monts. are several of the families of Taylor and Sullivan of Imber Court ; one, with bust, of Col. Sidney Godolphin, governor of Scilly, and father of the House of Commons (d. 1732) ; and one of Admiral Lambert (d. 1836). The font is noteworthy for the rude carvings on the side of the bowl ; the support is recent.

About Thames Ditton are several good seats. *Boyle Farm*, the residence of Lord St. Leonards, lies between the ch. and the Thames. The house is large ; the river front, with its gables and battlements—a sort of Strawberry Hill Gothic —rather picturesque.

> "Mrs. Walsingham is making her house at Ditton (now baptized Boyle Farm) very orthodox. Her daughter, Miss Boyle, who has real genius, has carved three tablets in marble with boys, designed by herself. Those sculptures are for a chimney-piece ; and she is painting panels in grotesque for the library, with pilasters in black and gold." *

Mr. Croker observes in a note to this passage † that "Boyle Farm was cele-

---

* Theodore Hook, Lines composed in a Punt off the Swan at Thames Ditton, in Hall's Book of the Thames, p. 317.

* Horace Walpole to Earl of Strafford, July 28, 1787.

† Walpole's Works, vol. ix., p. 102.

brated in 1827 for a very gorgeous fête given by five young men of fashion, one of whom was Miss Boyle's son." Miss Boyle married first Lord de Roos, and afterwards Lord Henry Fitzgerald, and resided at Boyle Farm. The expenses of the fête were met "by a subscription of £500 each from Lords Alvanley, Castlereagh, Chesterfield, Robert Grosvenor, and Henry de Roos. . . . Pavilions on the banks of the river; a large dinner tent on the lawn capable of holding 450 ; and a select table for 50 laid in the conservatory. Gondolas floated on the water, containing the best singers of the Italian Opera ; and in a boat Vestris and Fanny Ayton, the one singing Italian, the other English. There were illuminations throughout the ornamental grounds, and character quadrilles were danced by the beauties of the season. This was long remembered as the Dandies' Fête." *

Tom Moore writes in the dedication of his 'Summer Fête,' to the Hon. Mrs. Norton (Nov. 1831), "For the groundwork of the following poem I am indebted to a memorable fête given some years since at Boyle Farm, the seat of the late Lord Henry Fitzgerald, where you, Madam, were one of the most distinguished ornaments." The fête he describes as one

"Of some few hundred beauties, wits,
Blues, dandies, swains, and exquisites."

Lord Francis Egerton (afterwards Earl of Ellesmere) also wrote what Moore terms "a playful and happy *jeu-d'esprit*" on the subject.

Ditton House (W. W. F. Dick, Esq., M.P.), adjoining Boyle Farm, was formerly a residence of the Earl of Darnley. *Imber* or *Ember Court*, by the Mole, which flows through the grounds, about a mile E. of the vill., is a large plain mansion, the old brick front having been covered with stucco, and wings added in the last century. The manor of Imber was empaled as part of the Chase of Hampton Court by Henry VIII., "in the latter days of the king, when he waxed heavy with sickness, age, and corpulency, and might not travel so readily abroad, but was constrained to seek his game and pleasure ready at hand." Shortly after the death of the

king the inhabitants of Thames Ditton and adjoining parishes petitioned the Council of State for relief, and, an inquisition having been made, the enclosed lands were ordered to be dechased and the deer removed to Windsor and elsewhere. Charles I. granted the manor of Imber to Sir Dudley Carleton, Viscount Dorchester. After several transfers it became the property of the Bridges, and was carried by the marriage of Ann Bridges in 1720 to Arthur Onslow, afterwards celebrated as Speaker of the House of Commons, who made Imber Court his principal residence. His son, Lord Cranley, sold the manor in 1784 to George Porter, Esq. Imber Court was for awhile the residence of Sir Francis Burdett. It is now the seat of C. J. Corbet, Esq.

Gigg's Hill, on the Portsmouth road, a little S. of Thames Ditton, noted for its common and its inn, the *Angel*, both favourite resorts of cricketers ; *Weston Green*, on the S.W. ; and *Ditton Marsh*, by Esher Rly. Stat., are hamlets of Ditton.

A long iron spear - head and some bronze weapons, in good preservation, were found in the Thames at Ditton in 1862, and presented to the British Museum by Lord Lovelace: they are figured in the Archæol. Journal, vol. xix., p. 364. A small bronze spear, also in the British Museum, had been found near the same spot some years earlier.

DODDINGHURST, ESSEX (*Dodding's-hurst*, the forest home of the Dodings, a family traceable over a large part of England; Dom. *Doddenhenc*) ; pop. of par. 426 ; lies about midway, 4 m., between Brentwood and Ongar. There is no village : the place consists of a few farms, and a very few cottages, scattered among pleasant but lonely green lanes and broad meadows, abounding in corn and wood.

The *Church* (All Saints) stands alone on the N. side of the Kelvedon road. It is small, covered with plaster, and has red tiled roofs ; consists of a nave and chancel, a wooden tower rising from the W. roof, and thin shingled spire. The ch., originally E.E., has been greatly altered. The doorway under the porch retains the sharp dog-tooth moulding, and

* Life of Thomas Slingsby Duncombe, vol. i., p. 169.

W. of it is a lancet window, blocked up ; but the other windows are mostly Perp. The E. window is of flowing tracery. A single lancet in the chancel is the only window on the N. side of the ch. At the S.W. is a deep old oak porch (16 ft. by 11 ft.) of good character and in good preservation. The interior is plain, and contains no monts. It was partially restored and the tall pews removed in 1853. The neat school-house by the ch. was built in 1857, The large gabled brick house in the grounds close to the ch. is *Doddinghurst Hall*, the old manor-house, now a farm-house. By the roadside at *Kelvedon Common*, in Doddinghurst parish, still stands a substantial pair of stocks—not often, we may hope, called into requisition.

DORKING, Surrey (locally *Darking*, and commonly so written, 1500—1800 ; Dom. *Dorchinges ;* probably the mark or settlement of the Deorcingas), a mkt.-town on the Pip brook, a tributary of the Mole, which flows a little to the E. at the foot of Box Hill. Dorking is at the junction of the road to Horsham with that from Reigate to Guildford, and has stats. on the L., B., and S. C. Rly. (Leatherhead and Horsham line), 26 m. from London Bridge, and on the S.E. Rly. 29 m. Pop. of the town 5419, of the par. 8567.

The *Town* is well built, clean, has good shops, lies in a sheltered valley, and used to have a certain air of old-fashioned picturesque rusticity, but every year something more of this is worn off, and the town itself becomes less and less interesting to a stranger. It lies, however, in the midst of the most charming scenery of Surrey, is a good centre for its exploration, and possesses two excellent inns—the *Red Lion*, originally the "Cardinal's Cap," and the *White Horse*, anciently the " Cross House," it being rented from the Knights of St. John of Jerusalem at Clerkenwell, and bearing their cross as its sign. Once Dorking had several of these old hostelries, the largest being the Queen's Arms, which reached from the corner of West Street to the present Bell Inn ; and the Chequers, changed at the Restoration to the Old King's Head, which occupied the site of the present Post Office. The old buildings have almost all disappeared. The quaint old Market House was pulled down in

1813, to make way for a smart new one, but the new one was never built. Yet though without a market-house, Dorking has a weekly mkt. for corn (on Thursdays), and a monthly one for fat stock. Its specialties, however, are lime and Dorking fowls ; the former burnt in large chalk-pits N. of the town (which the geologist should not fail to visit), and in great request with builders for its property of hardening under water ; the latter distinguished by their colour, form, and an additional claw, the pride of every poultry-wife, and a leading feature at every poultry show. A large trade is done in corn and flour.

Dorking *Church* (St. Martin's) was rebuilt in wretched taste in 1835-7, except the chancel, which was retained for baptisms. The old and the new chancels were alike swept away in 1868, and a larger one erected from the designs of Mr. H. Woodyer. The new chancel rendered the inconvenience and artistic incongruity of the nave more apparent, and in 1872 Mr. Woodyer was commissioned to erect a new nave and transepts, and in 1873 a tower and spire 200 ft. high. The new ch., of black flint with Bath-stone dressings and tracery, is an excellent specimen of current Gothic architecture. In the ch. are tablets to Abraham Tucker, author of 'The Light of Nature,' and Jeremiah Markland, the learned editor of Euripides. In the ch.-yard lies John Hoole, the translator of Tasso and Ariosto.

St. Paul's Church, at the W. end of the town, was erected in 1857, from the designs of Mr. Benj. Ferrey, at the cost of J. Labouchere, Esq., of Broom Hall, but enlarged in 1864 by the addition of a N. aisle, and in 1869 of a S. aisle. The fine E. window was erected by Mrs. Hope as a memorial of her husband, H. T. Hope, Esq. The neat semi-Gothic building near the ch. is a well-fitted Cottage Hospital. The Independent Chapel in West Street is noteworthy for the long time it has been established, and as numbering among its ministers Mason Good, author of the once popular ' Treatise on Self-Knowledge,' and Dr. Andrew Kippis, editor of the ' Biographia Britannica.'

Of the objects and places of interest around Dorking, precedence must be given to *The Deepdene* (Mrs. Hope), close to the town on the S., long the well-known residence of H. T. Hope, Esq. The Deepdene was for some centuries the property of the Howards, into whose hands it passed (with the manor of Dorking) through the Fitzalans and the Warrens. It was sold in 1791 to Sir Wm. Burrell, from whose successor it was purchased by Thomas Hope, Esq., the author of ' Anastasius.' He built the greater part of the present house. The S.E. or principal front (Italian, and unusually good) was added by his son, A. J. Hope. The house is always shown during the absence of the family ; and no stranger should pass through Dorking without making an effort to see it.

The chief glory of the *house* at the Deepdene is the sculpture, the greater part of which was collected by the author of ' Anastasius' and the 'Essay on Architecture.' In the *Vestibule* is *Banti's* statue of Napoleon holding the globe in his outstretched hand. The *Entrance-hall*, beyond, is very striking. It is of stately proportions, has an arcade round three of its sides, and on the fourth the grand double staircase of stone. The floor is of polished marble, with occasional mosaics, some of which are ancient. Around, and in the upper and lower galleries, is arranged the principal collection of sculpture. Of the antique, observe especially a so-called *Hyacinthus*, of which the left hand holds a bronze flower ; a portrait statue of the *Emperor Hadrian ;* and behind in the gallery some figures of the early Greek period. Of the modern, the finest are two of *Thorwaldsen's* best works — the 'Jason with the Golden Fleece,' and the ' Shepherd Boy from the Campagna.' The ' Jason,' a grand and heroic figure, has an especial interest as the turning-point of the artist's life and reputation. Thorwaldsen, disheartened, was on the point of leaving Rome, when Mr. Hope paid an almost accidental visit to his studio. Here he saw the design for the Jason, immediately ordered it in marble, and the sculptor at once became famous. In the gallery behind is an alto-rilievo presented by Thorwaldsen to Mr. Hope, and representing Genius pouring oil into a lamp, whilst History below is recording the triumphs of Art. At the other end is a bas-relief by *Flaxman*. The group

of ' Cephalus and Aurora,' by the same sculptor, in the hall, should not pass unnoticed. Observe also a ' Girl Bathing,' by *R. J. Wyatt*. In the centre of the hall is a fine copy of the ' Florentine Boar,' in white marble, by *Bartolini*.

In the *Sculpture Gallery*, opening into the *Conservatory*, among other admirable things, observe the antique *Minerva*, a grand figure, 7 ft. high, found in 1797 at the mouth of the Tiber ; and a marble vase of unusual size. Here is also a late and amended replica of *Canova's* ' Venus coming from the Bath.' With it may be compared a copy in the hall, by *Bartolini*, of the first version of the statue, from which it will be evident that Canova's alterations were really improvements. Both in the sculpture gallery and in the hall will be noticed several copies in marble of famous ancient and modern statues.

In the *Etruscan* or *Music room* is an interesting collection of early Greek and Etruscan vases and antique bronzes. The seats here, as well as much of the furniture in the principal apartments, are from the designs of Mr. Thomas Hope himself, whose book on ' Household Furniture' was published in 1807.

In the *Billiard-room* are several pictures from the ' Iliad ' by *Westall ;* some views in India by *Daniel ;* two curious ' Scenes on the Boulevards ' and ' at the Tuileries,' by *Chalon ;* and a few ancient paintings. The *Large Drawing-room* is lined with panels of painted satin, and contains some fine Sèvres and Dresden china. In the *Small Drawing-room* observe two fine enamels by *Bone*, ' Mr. Hope as Anastasius,' and ' Lady Beresford ;' also *Canova's* ' Psyche with the Casket,' which stands at the end of the room, and various rich antique cinquecento bronzes and ornaments.

In the *Dining-room* are two allegorical pictures, with figures the size of life, by *P. Veronese*, representing, one ' Strength led by Wisdom,' and the other the artist himself turning away from Vice to Virtue ; ' St. Michael overcoming Satan,' by *Raphael ;* and a Magdalene by *Correggio*. In the *Small Dining-room* are — a portrait of Lady Decies by *Sir Joshua Reynolds ;* one of *Haydon's* earliest pictures, a ' Repose in Egypt ;' *Martin's* well-known ' Fall of Babylon,' one of the best of his gigantic subjects ; 'Edward III. and Queen Eleanor,' by *Hilton ;* and, by *J. W. Glass*, a Scottish artist, ' The Night March '—troopers in bright armour crossing a ford by moon-light, the effect of which is well given.

In the *Boudoir* is a large collection of enamels, chiefly by *Bone ;* a fine portrait of Mrs. Hope ; a pleasing collection of miniatures ; and a number of Dutch paintings, brought from the town-house, chiefly views of streets and buildings in Holland, by *G. Berkheiden.* Flaxman's original drawings for his Dante and Æschylus are preserved in the library.

The art-treasures in the house at the Deepdene are at least equalled in beauty by the scene without. The *Dene* itself, a long steep glade, carpeted with turf, and closed in by a woody amphitheatre, opens close to the house. The lower part forms a flower-garden ; and the whole scene, with its occasional cypresses and sunny patches of greensward, is of almost un-equalled beauty. A walk leads to the upper part, through a beech-wood, in which much of the undergrowth consists of self-sown rhododendrons. At the head, and looking down over the Dene, is a small Doric temple, with the inscription ' Fratri Optimo H. T. H.'

The view here, although very striking, is hardly so fine as that from below. The ' Dene ' is no doubt the " amphitheatre, garden, or solitarie recess," seen and com-mended by Evelyn on the occasion of his visit to Mr. Chas. Howard in 1655. A more recent visitor to the Deepdene, Mr. Disraeli, wrote here the greater part of his romance of ' Coningsby.'

Behind the temple, on the top of the hill, is a terrace with a fine beech avenue, commanding noble views over the tree-covered Wealds of Surrey and Sussex. Brockham spire, close below, the range of the chalk towards Reigate, and East Grinstead tower on its distant high ground, make good landmarks. This ter-race formerly belonged to *Chart Park,* the house of which stood below. It has long been destroyed, and the park added to that of the Deepdene. In that part which lies below the terrace are some groups of very large oriental planes, some of which measure upwards of 10 ft. in circumfer-ence at 1 ft. from the ground. There are also some large Scotch pines, of which the vary-

ing growth and character may be well studied here ; and some grand old cedars of Lebanon, ranging in colour from the black green of the yew to the silvery grey of the deodara. Other trees of un-usual size,—hawthorns, Sophora japonica, Salisburia, and Liquidambar, are scattered through the park. The best views from the terrace are commanded from a summer-house at the S. end, looking on one side into Chart Park, and on the other over the wood called " The Glory." From the opposite end are views (but not so good) toward Boxhill and Norbury Park.

The whole of the ground about the Deepdene is varied and beautiful. A large tulip-tree on the lawn fronting the house should not pass unremarked. It measures 10 ft. in circumference. A walk, open to the public, leads through the Deepdene park into that of Betch-worth, which, like Chart, now forms part of one domain. (*See* BETCHWORTH PARK.)

The walk through the Deepdene woods, to the clump of Scotch firs called " The Glory," is open to the public. It lies at the back of Dorking. Spaces have been cut through the woods for the sake of the distant views, which are good, and seats are placed at intervals. Beyond the clump a path leads to one of the most pic-turesque of Surrey lanes, hedged in by lofty banks, and rich in wild flowers.

Facing the grounds of Deepdene, about ¾ m. S.W. from Dorking, is *Bury Hill* (Robert Barclay, Esq.), a fine mansion with richly wooded grounds, command-ing splendid views, gardens, a Pinetum, and a well-provided observatory. The park is open to the public, and on a height, called the *Nower,* a summer-house has been erected for the accommodation of visitors. Nearly opposite Bury Hill, on the N., is *Milton Court,* a red brick Elizabethan mansion, where Jeremiah Markland lived and laboured for many years, and where he died in 1776. On Milton Heath, adjoining the road, is a tumulus, marked by a clump of fir-trees. About 1½ m. farther (beyond *Westcot* or Westgate, where is a pretty little ch., erected in 1852 from the designs of G. G. Scott, R.A.) is *The Rookery,* the birth-place (1766) of Malthus, the political economist.

Fronting Deepdene and The Glory, but

on the N. side of the rly., is *Denbies* (George Cubitt, Esq., M.P.), the stately residence built by the late T. Cubitt, Esq., C.E. It is understood to have been designed as a hunting-lodge for the Prince of Wales, and was frequently visited by the late Prince Consort, who planted an oak in the grounds. The house contains some fine oak carving and some good pictures. On a clear day St. Paul's and the towers of Westminster are distinctly visible from the terrace and the heights above, to which a bridle-path open to the public leads, passing close by the house. The ride or walk may be continued across *Ranmore Common*, by White Down and Hawkhurst Downs, towards Guildford, returning to Dorking by Gomshall and Wotton. Wide and magnificent views are commanded the whole way. Or, if the visitor pleases, he may cross Ranmore Common towards Polesdon, descending upon Westhamble. The finest views of Box Hill are obtained from this route. There is also a pleasant walk, through very picturesque and varied scenery, along the E. side of Ranmore Common, and over Fetcham Downs to Leatherhead.

At *Ranmore*, the handsome new *Church* of St. Barnabas, erected by Sir G. G. Scott, R.A., at the cost of the late Mr. Cubitt, should be visited. It is cruciform, with a large octagonal tower containing 8 bells, and a spire 150 ft. high; E.E. in style, very richly ornamented both outside and in, and exquisitely finished.

A more distant, but not the least beautiful, excursion to be made from Dorking, is that to the summit of *Leith Hill* (993 ft., the highest ground in this part of England). Leith Hill is about 5 m. S. by W. from Dorking, and far beyond our limits, but the stranger in Dorking should not fail to ascend it if practicable : the views from it are the most extensive and finest in this region of fine views, and the scenery around the base is singularly varied and charming. "Twelve or thirteen counties can be seen from it," says Evelyn. Aubrey reckons as visible parts of Sussex, Surrey, Hants, Berks, Oxfordshire, Buckinghamshire, Hertfordshire, Middlesex, Kent, Essex, "and, by the help of a telescope, Wiltshire." On July 15, 1844, the air being remarkably clear, a party of the Ordnance Surveyors then encamped on the hill, saw with the naked eye an observatory, only 9 ft. square, near Ashford, in Kent ; and with a small telescope, a staff only 4 in. in diameter, on Dunstable Downs. "The spires of 41 churches in London were also visible, as well as the scaffolding around the new Houses of Parliament."[*] The smoke-cloud of London, with the heights of Highgate, may readily be made out on a clear day, when the roofs of the Sydenham Palace glitter in the sun like a spark of diamond. From one point the high grounds about Nettlebed in Oxfordshire are sometimes visible, and the sea opens southward through Shoreham Gap. Westward, the sandhills bordering the chalk lift themselves, fold behind fold, toward the Hog's Back, like so many bastions stretching forward into the oak-covered Wealden. The area included in the view from the highest point of the hill is about 200 m. in circumference.

Box Hill, on the N.E. of Dorking ; the lovely vale of *Mickleham*, which extends from the foot of Box Hill to Leatherhead ; *Betchworth Park*, now united with the grounds of Deepdene ; *Betchworth* village ; its neighbour *Brockham*, and other places of interest in the vicinity of Dorking, are described under their respective titles.

Dorking and the neighbourhood afford much to interest the geologist. The town is on the Folkstone Sands, the Deepdene and S. of it are on the Hythe Sands, whilst a little farther S. you enter upon the great Wealden district. Immediately N. of Dorking is a narrow strip of gault ; beyond that, by Box Hill, clay with flints ; and farther N. chalk ; whilst at Betchworth, on the E., is a great line of fault extending from S.E. to N.W., through the entire series, and another still larger extending E. and W. from S. of Deepdene to Hawkhurst Down. Mantell has described the geological features of the district in detail in vols. i. and v. of Brayley's 'Surrey.' The district is also a favourite collecting-ground for the botanist and entomologist, it being very rich in ferns and orchids, and some unparalleled takes having been made of the rarer and most prized beetles.

DOWN, KENT, a pleasant retired

---

[*] Brayley, History of Surrey, vol. v., p. 51.

vill. of 523 inh., 3½ m. S.W. from the Orpington Stat. of the S.E. Rly. (Tunbridge direct line), but it may be reached by a lane, about a mile long, from Keston ch., or by field-path and lanes (running S. by E. with the ch. spire before you), 2 m. from Farnborough.

The village is built around the intersection of four lanes, the ch. occupying the centre. The cottages have well-kept gardens ; among them are some houses of a better class,—one, *Trodmore Lodge*, immediately S. of the ch., being a restored red brick Jacobean mansion with a prospect tower taller than the ch. spire ; the grounds abound in fruit and timber trees, and altogether the place has a more than commonly agreeable country aspect. The occupations are agricultural ; the farms are chiefly arable, but fruit is largely grown for the London market.

The *Church* is small, Perp., but covered with plaster, and consists of a nave and chancel, and a tower at the W. end, with a shingle spire, and brick buttresses. The *interior* is plain, fitted with high pews, and has no monts. of interest. Around the ch.-yard are tall elms, and on the S. opposite the porch is a venerable yew tree with a trunk 23 ft. in girth. Just beyond the ch. is the vill. pump, having a modern mediæval roof-covering and inscription.

High Elms, the seat of Sir John Lubbock, Bart., M.P., lies 1½ m. from Down ch., on the way to Farnborough. Charles R. Darwin, Esq., the author of ' Natural Selection,' also resides at Down. Other seats are *Down Court*, ¼ m. S. of the vill., and *Orange Court* (C. Harris, Esq.), ¾ m. N.

DRAYTON, or WEST DRAYTON

(A.-S. *Draegtun ;* Dom. *Draitone*), a vill. 3½ m. S. from Uxbridge, and a stat. on the Grt. W. Rly., 13¼ m. from Paddington ; pop. 984. The collection of houses, with the *De Burgh* and *Railway* Inns, by the rly. stat., is *Yiewsley*, a hamlet of Hillingdon ; West Drayton proper is nearly ½ m. S. of the stat.

West Drayton lies low, and has the Colne running along its W. side, the Grand Junction Canal and Grt. W. Rly. on the N. The country is level, but there are shady lanes and broad green meadows, though sulphurous and manury smells from brickfields, canal, and wharves somewhat interfere with the sense of enjoyment. By the Colne are extensive flour-mills ; also the largest mill-board mills (Messrs. Mercers') in existence, where large heaps of ship-rope may be seen soaking in clay, and stacks of old book-covers imbibing air and moisture preparatory to reissue. The vill. is commonplace, the redeeming feature being the large village green.

The *Church* lies away from the vill. on the S., enclosed within private grounds. In 1550 Sir Wm. Paget procured an Act of Parliament empowering him to enclose the ch.-yard within his garden-wall, "free ingress and egress to and from the parish church being reserved to the vicar and inhabitants."[*] As a consequence, the tall outer gates are kept strictly locked except during divine service. This, however, is of little consequence, the ch. having lost by restoration most of its interest. It is of flint and stone, chiefly Perp. in style, and consists of nave with clerestorey and aisles, a rather deep chancel, and a square W. tower partly covered with ivy. Within are several monts., helmets, and banners of the Paget and De Burgh families ; a *brass* without insc., and another to Jas. Goode, M.D., d. 1581, and wife, with 6 sons and 5 daughters. The font, an elaborately carved one of Perp. date, is engraved in Lysons. The E. and some of the nave windows are filled with painted glass. The disused ch.-yard is prettily laid out in flower-garden style.

The mansion of the Pagets, adjoining the ch.-yd., was pulled down by the Earl of Uxbridge in 1750, and the estate shortly afterwards sold. The new ch. by the Green is Roman Catholic : the first stone was laid by Abp. Manning, Oct. 26, 1868 : architects, Messrs. Wilson and Nicholl. The principal seats are *Drayton Hall* (Hubert De Burgh, Esq., Lord of the Manor), and *Drayton House* (E. H. Rickards, Esq.)

About ¾ m. S. of the rly. stat. is *Thorney Broad*, a favourite fishery, where some trout are taken, and where is good bottom fishing. West Drayton races are among the most frequented of the lower-class suburban gatherings.

DULWICH, Surrey (anc. *Dil-*

---

* Lysons.

wisshe and *Dylawys*), is a hamlet and manor in Camberwell parish: pop. 4041. Inns, the *Greyhound*, a good house, near the College; the *Crown*, nearly opposite. The L. C. and D. Rly. has a stat. ½ m. S.W. of the College, the L. B. and S.C. Rly. one the same distance N.

Though we can no longer speak of

"The sylvan wilds
Of Dulwich yet by barbarous arts unspoiled,"

the greater part of the Wood having succumbed before the builder, and new houses having sprung up wherever land was obtainable, the *village* is still rural, well timbered, and very pleasant. The great attraction at Dulwich, however, is the *College of God's Gift*, founded by Edward Alleyne the player, a contemporary of Shakspeare, which contains an important collection of pictures bequeathed by Sir Francis Bourgeois in 1811. To this gallery the public are admitted, without charge and *without tickets*, every weekday—during the summer months from 10 till 5, in the winter from 10 till 4.

The College stands at the S. end of Dulwich, among green meadows and fine old trees; but although it is not without a grave air of dignity and seclusion, it retains little of the original architecture, nearly the whole having been rebuilt at differert periods. The college forms 3 sides of a quadrangle; the entrance and gates, on which are the founder's arms and motto, "God's Gift," closing in the fourth side. The chapel, dining-room, library, and apartments for the master are in front. In the wings are apartments for 24 brethren and 6 sisters, who each receive 20*s.* a week.

In the *Dining* and *Audit Rooms* are some interesting portraits, many of which belonged to the founder, whilst some others were bequeathed to the College by William Cartwright, the actor, in 1686. Among them remark Edward Alleyne, the founder—a full-length in a black gown; Joan Woodward, his first wife; the actors Richard Burbage, painted by himself, Nathaniel Field, one of Shakspeare's fellow-players, William Sly, Richard Perkins, Thomas Bond, and William Cartwright (this last is by *Greenhill*, by whom also are the portraits of Charles II. and Henrietta Maria, as well as that of the artist himself); Col. Lovelace the poet, in armour, with long

black hair—" an extraordinary handsome man, but proud," *Aubrey*; Henry Prince of Wales; the poet Drayton, a fine thoughtful manly head; Sir Martin Frobisher, the naval hero; and Elizabeth Queen of Bohemia. In the Audit Room is a curious emblematical painting, the history of which is unknown. It represents a merchant and his wife, with a tomb between them, crowned with a human skull, on which rest their hands. Below the tomb lies a corpse.

The *Library* contains about 5000 vols., some of which formed part of Cartwright's legacy. Here are also the Spanish and Italian books of John Allen, the friend of Lord Holland, master from 1820 to 1843. The chimneypiece in this room was made of the "upper part of the queen's barge," bought by Alleyne the founder in 1618. To these rooms visitors are only admitted by special order.

The *College Chapel* serves also as the parish ch. of Dulwich. The altarpiece is a copy of Raphael's Transfiguration. The font, of variegated marble, given to the College in 1729, has a covering of gilt copper, on which are the Greek words (to be read either backward or forward)— Νιψον ανομημα μη μοναν οψιν—placed by Gregory Nazianzen above the holy water stoup in S. Sophia. In the chancel is a marble slab marking the tomb of Edward Alleyne the founder, d. 1626.

Alleyne, the Garrick of his time—"Ævi sui Roscius," says the inscription over the porch—whose fortune was acquired partly by marriage, and partly by his own exertions, expended in the purchase of land and on the building of this College £100,000. "I like well," wrote Lord Bacon, "that Alleyne performeth the last act of his life so well." He retired from the stage, and commenced his work here, in 1612; and finally established the "College of God's Gift" for the inmates already mentioned, together with 30 out-members. The master and warden were always to be of the blood, or at least of the surname, of the founder, whose seal-ring was to be worn by each master in succession. The manor of Dulwich, consisting of about 1400 acres, is attached to the College, besides much house property in London. Owing to the extension of building and the greater value of land, the wealth of the College had enormously increased, and an Act was passed in 1857 by which the existing corporation was abolished, and a new scheme, proposed by the Charity Commissioners, adopted. By it, after awarding during their lives annual incomes to the master, warden, fellows, and brethren, the net income of the College is divided into four parts ; three to be devoted to the purposes of education, and the remaining one to the support of aged men and women. The educational establishment is to consist of an Upper and a Lower School, with an adequate staff of masters. In the upper school instruction is to be given in the principles of the Christian religion, English literature and composition, Greek, Latin, and modern languages, mathematics, the natural sciences, chemistry, the principles of civil engineering, and all the usual branches of a liberal education. In the lower school the subjects taught are nearly the same as in the upper school, with the exception of Greek. Boys are admissible between 8 and 15, preference being given to those whose parents reside in the parishes to which the founder confined the benefits of his bounty—St. Saviour, Southwark ; St. Luke, Middlesex ; St. Botolph, Bishopsgate ; and St. Giles, Camberwell, in which the college is situated. There are to be 24 foundation scholars, of whom not less than one-third must be chosen from the lower school. A new school has since been built, which will be noticed presently.

The entrance to the *Picture Gallery* is from the road on the N. side of the College. The collection, originally made by Mr. Desenfans for King Stanislaus of Poland, was retained by the collector in his own hands on the fall of that country; and at his death in 1807 was bequeathed to his friend Sir Francis Bourgeois. Sir Francis left it, 1811, to this College; and with the assistance of Mrs. Desenfans a gallery for its reception was built, 1814, from the designs of Sir John Soane, having a mausoleum attached, in which are interred Sir F. Bourgeois and Mr. and Mrs. Desenfans.

The great charm of the Dulwich Gallery is its perfect quiet. Even now that the railway has been brought almost to the door, the pictures may at any time be inspected with ease and comfort. There are five rooms. Beginning with that at the entrance, the following pictures should especially be noticed. (The numbers correspond with those on the frames.)

First Room.— 1. Portraits of Mrs. Sheridan and Mrs. Tickle, *Gainsborough ;* one of his best pictures. 9. Landscape with cattle and figures, *Cuyp*, a charming picture. 30, 36, and 205. Landscapes with cattle and figures, (30 bright sunny effect, 36 clear evening, 205 quite Cuyplike,) *Both.* 45. Skirmish of Cavalry, *Snayers.* 63 and 64. Landscapes, *Wouvermans.* 102. Flowers in a Vase, *Daniel Seghers.* 104. An old building, with figures (careful and choice), *C. Dusart*, scholar of Ostade. 107, Interior of a Cottage, is a clever work by *Ostade.* 85 and 106 are assigned, perhaps correctly, to *Gerard Dow.*

Second Room.—113. A Calm, *Vandevelde* (injured by cleaning). 121, 140. Flowers, *Vanhuysum*, (121, beautiful in colour and delicacy of touch ; 140, an earlier work, extremely minute and elaborate). 125 is a pretty good specimen of *Wouverman's* manner. 131. Landscape, with a watermill, (well and vigorously painted, but much blackened,) *Hobbema.* 133. Portrait of a young man, here assigned to an unknown artist of the Florentine school, but considered by Dr. Waagen a good work of Da Vinci's scholar *Boltraffio.* 139, etc., half a dozen small and slight but characteristic works by *D. Teniers.* 141. Landscape with figures (a sweet sunny effect), *Cuyp.* 143. A Mother and Sick Child, *Sir Joshua Reynolds :* Death and the Angel in this picture are failures. 144. A Halt of Travellers, *Wouvermans*, much better and less artificial than 136 and 137. 147. Landscape with cattle and figures, *J. B. Weeninx.* Waterfall, *Ruysdael.* 159. Landscape, *S. Rosa.* 163. Landscape with cattle and figures, *Cuyp.* 166. A Brisk Gale, *Vandevelve.* 168. Samson and Delilah, much repainted, if really by *Rubens.* 169. Landscape with cattle and figures, *Cuyp ;* very beautiful sunset. 173. Landscape with figures, *Wouvermans.* 175. Landscape, *Rubens.* 179. Jacob's Dream, a celebrated picture, here assigned to *Rembrandt*, but probably not by his own hand. 182. A Sketch, *Rubens.* 185. The Chaff-cutter, *Teniers.* 190.

Boors merrymaking, a capitally painted *Ostade*.

Centre Room. — 191. Judgment of Paris, *Vanderwerf*, much admired, but thoroughly conventional. 194. Portrait of the Duke of Asturias, afterwards Philip IV., *Velasquez*. 197. Fête Champêtre ; 210. The Bal Champêtre, *Watteau :* the latter most characteristic of his quaint, artificial French grace, but sadly cracked ; the former a less pleasing picture, but in better preservation. 206. Rembrandt's Servant Maid, is a well-painted picture, if not truly assigned to *Rembrandt*. 200. Landscape with cattle and figures (a gem, but the sky injured by cleaning), *Berghem*. 209. Landscape with cattle at a fountain, *Berghem*. 214. Portrait of the Earl of Pembroke, *Vandyck*. 215. Villa of Mæcenas (a replica of the famous picture engraved by Rooker), *R. Wilson*. 217. St. Veronica, *C. Dolce*. 218. Portrait of the Archduke Albert, here assigned to the school of *Rubens*, but Waagen thinks it is by the master himself. 228. Landscape with cattle and figures, *Wouvermans*. 239. Landscape with cattle, *Cuyp*. 241. Mill, *Ruysdael*.

Fourth Room. — 248. Spanish Flower Girl, *Murillo ;* fine from the contrast and harmony of colour. 252. Massacre of the Innocents, intensely artificial and untrue, but worth looking at as a fair sample of *Le Brun's* manner. 254. Death of Cardinal Beaufort, *Reynolds ;* a crude sketch, not a picture. 257. Landscape, *G. Poussin ;* very fine in its way. 260. Landscape, *N. Poussin*, much darkened. 271. Soldiers gaming, *S. Rosa*. 276. Landscape, *G. Poussin*. 283. Spanish Beggar Boys, *Murillo ;* a picture of which there are many duplicates : this is no doubt an original. 284. Rape of Proserpine, *F. Mola*. 285. Samuel (not the popular kneeling Samuel), *Sir J. Reynolds*. 286. Spanish Peasant Boys, *Murillo :* this picture, like No. 283, has been often repeated : " Happy in intention, the execution in parts hard and feeble," says *Waagen ;* but the hardness and feebleness disappear almost magically when the picture is seen by the softened light of an afternoon sun. 299. A Locksmith, *Caravaggio*. 305. The Triumph of David, *N. Poussin*. 309. Philip IV. of Spain, *Velasquez*. 319. Cocles defending the

Bridge, *Lebrun*. 337. Mater Dolorosa, *C. Dolce*.

Fifth Room. — 306 and 307. Saints, formerly attributed to Perugino, now to Raphael, but probably by one of Raphael's scholars (*Waagen*). 329. Christ bearing his Cross ; unknown, perhaps *Morales* or *Murillo*. 333. A Cardinal blessing a Priest, *P. Veronese*. 336. Assumption of the Virgin, *N. Poussin :* a noble picture. 339. Martyrdom of S. Sebastian, a celebrated but much overrated picture, *Guido*. 340. Mrs. Siddons as the Tragic Muse, *Reynolds :* one of his most famous works. A similar picture, perhaps the earlier of the two, is in the collection of the Marquis of Westminster ; in each the painter's name is inscribed on the hem of the robe, almost the only instance of Sir Joshua having put his name on a picture. 345. Adoration of the Magi, on stone, *Alessandro Turchi*. 347. Assumption of the Virgin, *Murillo ;* very beautiful in colour. 348. The Woman taken in Adultery, *Guercino*. 352. Children, *N. Poussin*. 353. Portrait of an Old Man, *Holbein*. 355. The Mother of Rubens ; a life-size portrait, finely painted, but whether rightly ascribed to *Rubens* may be doubted.

Many of the other pictures are interesting, but the visitor who is pressed for time will do well to give his attention to those here noticed.

The new *Schools* are at *Dulwich Common*, about ¼ m. S. of the College (take the road on l. of the College from the village). The available resources of the College having been increased by a sum of about £80,000, received as compensation from the railways, it was decided in 1865 to proceed with the erection of new schools in which might be carried out the scheme of instruction noticed above. The designs of Mr. Charles Barry, the College architect, being approved, the first stone of the new building was laid June 26, 1866 ; on July 5, 1869, the Upper School was transferred to the completed wing ; and on June 21, 1870, the building was formally opened by H.R.H. the Prince of Wales.

The schools comprise three distinct blocks : a centre building, containing the public and official rooms ; the great hall (a noble room), the lecture theatre, library, etc. ; and two wings connected with the centre building by corridors or cloisters—the south wing being appropriated to the upper school and residence of the second master, the north wing to the lower school and master's residence. In style, the building is Northern Italian of the 13th cent. The walls are of red brick, more richly embellished with terra-cotta ornament than any building of recent erection. The front of the centre building is most ornamented, but the decoration is carried entirely round the building. For the most part, the ornament is architectural, but a distinctive and appropriate feature is a series of heads, in very high relief from concave shields, of the principal poets, historians, orators, and philosophers of Greece, Rome, Italy, Germany, and England, from Homer, Herodotus, and Plato, down to Shakspeare, Milton, and Macaulay—the name of each being legibly but unobtrusively inscribed in the hollow of the shield. As a whole, the building has an air of stateliness and propriety, whilst the details are throughout pleasing and often beautiful. It cost about £100,000. When fully completed, the building will provide accommodation for between 600 and 700 boys, in two schools of equal size. The ground has an area of 45 acres, of which 30 acres have been appropriated to the schools and play-fields.

Two new *Churches* merit notice. St. Stephen's, Penge Road, *South Dulwich*, a short distance from the new school, is an elegant and. well-finished E.E. building, erected in 1869 from the designs of Mr. C. Barry. St. John's, *East Dulwich*, erected in 1865, if less artistic in finish than St. Stephen's, is still a favourable example of contemporary Gothic : both are placed in the midst of rapidly growing districts.

E ALING, MIDDX., on the Uxbridge road, 6½ m. from Hyde Park Corner : the Ealing Stat. of the G.W. Rly. (5½ m.) is a little N. of the vill. Ealing par. is extensive, including that part of Brentford town called Old Brentford, Ealing ch. being the mother ch. to Brentford. The entire parish contained 18,189 inhab. in 1871 ; Ealing proper, the Local Board District, 9959.

The older part of the village consists of the street which runs from the Uxbridge road, southwards, to the old ch., lined with houses old and new, patches of greensward, gardens, shops, inns, and chapels, very irregular, in parts very picturesque. *Ealing Common* lies E. of the main street, and has about it many good old-fashioned mansions, among others the Manor House, and the residence of the Rt. Hon. Spencer H. Walpole, M.P., and on every side are modern villas and cottages of the semi-detached class. The chief manor has from time immemorial belonged to the see of London. Lands within the manor descend to the youngest son, but in default of male issue are divided among daughters equally.*

Ealing *Church* (St. Mary), the old ch.

as it is commonly called, was a plain red brick barn of the early 18th cent. meeting-house style (it was built in 1739) ; but was entirely remodelled in 1867 under the direction of Mr. S. S. Teulon, and in the words of the Abp. of Canterbury, "transformed from a Georgian monstrosity into a Constantinopolitan basilica." This was effected by filling the heads of the old round arched windows of the nave with tracery, carrying out buttresses, adding an apsidal chancel with aisles, and an ambulatory, baptistery, and S. porch, and varying the surface by the introduction of coloured bricks in the arches and elsewhere. The western porch and lofty spire, which form an important feature in the design, were added in 1873. The interior has been in like manner recast by the removal of the old galleries, the substitution of low seats for the high pews, and a new roof in place of the original flat ceiling, the general effect being increased by surface decoration and the insertion of painted glass in the 5 windows of the apse, and 10 in the body of the ch., all by Heaton and Butler, and the erection of an elaborate reredos. On the walls are some tablets, among them one to Robert Orme, the historian of India, d. 1801. In the ch.-yard is an altar tomb to John Horne Tooke, d. 1812,

---

* Lysons, Environs, vol. ii., p. 147.

author of the 'Diversions of Purley.' Sir F. Morton Eden, author of 'State of the Poor,' was buried in Ealing ch. 1809.

The *New Church* (Christ Church), near the rly. stat., was erected at the cost of Miss Lewis, daughter of Gentleman Lewis (left the stage 1809, d. 1813), who lived at Ealing, was much attached to the place, and in whose memory part of the fortune he left was thus appropriated. The ch. was designed by Messrs. Scott and Moffatt, and consecrated June 30, 1852. It is of stone, Early Dec. in style, and consists of nave, aisles, chancel with large 5-light window, porch on the N.W., and at the W. a tower and lofty spire. The hand of Sir Gilbert Scott will be traced in the design, and the student of contemporary Gothic will be interested in comparing it with his works of a quarter of a century later. The Independent chapel, 1859, and the Wesleyan chapel, 1865, are both showy buildings.

Among the eminent inhabitants of Ealing may be named—the learned Bp. Beveridge, who was vicar of Ealing 13 years, 1661—1673; Dr. John Owen, the Puritan divine, who d. here Aug. 24, 1683; Serjeant Maynard, the famous lawyer of the Commonwealth and Restoration periods, d. at Gunnersbury House, Oct. 1690; John Oldmixon, the historian, who died at his town residence, Great Pulteney Street, and was buried in Ealing ch. July 12, 1742; Henry Fielding, the novelist, who resided at Fordhook House (on the main road near Acton) till his departure for Lisbon, June 26, 1754; Dr. King, the author of a pleasant volume of 'Anecdotes,' d. 1763; and Thomas Edwards, the opponent of Warburton, and author of 'Canons of Criticism,' a work famous in its day, and not out of date yet, who resided for some years at Pitshanger.

Of the many fine seats in Ealing par., one or two have attained more than local celebrity. *Castle-bear Hill* (now written *Castle-bar*, T. E. Harrison, Esq.) was the seat of Lord Heathfield, the heroic defender of Gibraltar, when General Eliott. A villa on Castlebar Hill was for some time the residence of Mrs. Fitzherbert, and afterwards of the Duke of Kent (father of the Queen), who in 1819 introduced a Bill into the House of Commons, through Ald. Wood and Mr. Hume, to enable him to dispose of it by lottery, but being op-

posed by the Government it was withdrawn.

Gunnersbury Park (Baron Lionel de Rothschild), a subordinate manor, anc. written *Gunyldsbury*, ("it is not improbable," says Lysons, "that it was the residence of Gunyld, niece of King Canute") after a long succession of distinguished owners, including Sir John Maynard, who, as already noticed, d. here in 1690, was purchased in 1761 for Princess Amelia, daughter of George II. The princess's parties acquired great celebrity. What they were like is well told by Horace Walpole, a frequent guest:—

"Ever since the late king's death, I have made Princess Amelia's parties once or twice a week." *

"I was sent for again to dine at Gunnersbury, on Friday, and was forced to send to town for a dress coat and a sword. There were the Prince of Wales, the Prince of Mecklenburg, the Duke of Portland, Lord Clanbrassil, Lord and Lady Clermont, Lord and Lady Southampton, Lord Pelham and Mrs. Howe. The Prince of Mecklenburg went back to Windsor after coffee, and the Prince and Lord and Lady Clermont to town after tea, to hear some new French players at Lady William Gordon's. The Princess, Lady Barrymore, and the rest of us, played three pools at Commerce till ten. I am afraid I was tired and gaped. While we were at the Dairy, the Princess insisted on my making some verses on Gunnersbury. I pleaded being superannuated. She would not excuse me. I promised she should have an Ode on her next Birthday, which diverted the Prince; but all would not do." †

The verses are printed in Walpole's Letters (vol. ix., p. 55), but have nothing distinctive. It was here the attempt was made to bring about a meeting of George III. with his dismissed Minister, Lord Bute, by a piece of feminine strategy very distasteful to the monarch:—

"His aunt, the Princess Amelia, had some plan of again bringing the two parties together, and on a day when George III. was to pay her a visit at her villa of Gunnersbury, near Brentford, she invited Lord Bute, whom she probably had never informed of her foolish intentions. He was walking in the garden when she took her nephew down stairs to view it, saying there was no one there but an old friend of his, whom he had not seen for some years. He had not time to ask who it might be, when, on entering the garden, he saw his former minister walking up an alley. The King instantly turned back to avoid him, reproved the silly old woman sharply, and declared that, if she ever repeated such experiments, she had seen him for the last time in her house." ‡

* Walpole to Sir Horace Mann, May 29, 1786.
† Walpole to the Hon. H. S. Conway, June 18, 1786.
‡ Lord Brougham's Hist. Sketches of Statesmen, vol. i. (Lord North).

Gunnersbury House (said to have been built by Inigo Jones, but according to Lysons by his pupil Webb) was sold, on the death of the Princess, and in 1801 pulled down, the materials sold by auction, and the grounds, 83 acres, divided into lots, and sold at the same time. The purchaser of the chief part of the grounds (76 acres), Alexander Copland, Esq., built himself a new house, the basis of the present mansion. Great additions have been made to it by its present owner, Baron Lionel Rothschild, and it is now one of the most sumptuous dwellings in the vicinity of London. In it are many noble paintings, including Murillo's 'Good Shepherd,' and other famous works by the old masters, as well as many modern pictures, statues, a fine collection of majolica, and other articles of *vertû*. The grounds and gardens are also of great richness and beauty ; and the parties and garden fêtes of the present owner are at least as distinguished as those of the Princess Amelia.

Elm Grove, previously Hickes-upon-the-Heath, a short distance E. of the ch., was successively the residence of Pope's friend Sir Wm. Turnbull, Secretary of State; Dr. John Egerton, Bp. of Norwich ; and the Rt. Hon. Spencer Perceval, Prime Minister, shot by Bellingham in the lobby of the House of Commons, May 11, 1812. *Ealing Grove* was successively the residence of Joseph Gulston, Esq., the celebrated collector of engravings, the Duke of Marlborough, and the Duke of Argyll. The *Manor House*, Ealing Green, is now the residence of Miss Perceval ; *Hanger Hill House*, N. of the Grt. W. Rly., is the finely situated seat of Sir Joshua Walmesley.

Ealing School, or Ealing Great School, long enjoyed the reputation of being one of the first private boarding-schools in the country. In its best days it had about 300 scholars, among them being many who have attained distinction in different walks of life—as Thackeray, Sir Henry Rawlinson, Lord Lawrence, Bp. Selwyn, and Charles Knight.* An effort has been made of late to revive the school. At Ealing is the *Home for Little Girls*, where over 100 destitute girls are educated and trained for service.

* Passages of a Working Life, vol. i., p. 54.

Little Ealing is a hamlet about midway between Ealing and Brentford. Zachary Pearce, Bp. of Rochester, who was educated at a private school in Ealing, occasionally resided in the house that had been his father's, at Little Ealing, and there died Jan. 29, 1774. *Little Ealing Park* (J. S. Budgett, Esq.), S. of Little Ealing, was the property of Sir Francis Dashwood, and afterwards of Earl Brooke and Lord Robert Manners.

EAST BARNET (*see* BARNET, EAST).

EAST BEDFONT (*see* BEDFONT).

EASTBURY HOUSE (*see* BARKING).

EAST HAM, ESSEX (Dom. *Hamme*,

which includes both East Ham and West Ham), 1 m. W. of Barking, 5½ m. from London by road, and 4¾ m. by the Southend Rly.; pop. of the entire par. 4334, but this includes portions of the eccl. districts of Forest Gate, 779, and Victoria Docks, 1322 : East Ham proper contains 2233 inhabitants.

The village straggles for above a mile along the lane which runs from Little Ilford to the Thames opposite Woolwich, the chief part being S. of the Barking road. The rly. stat. is at the extreme N. of the vill., the ch. at the extreme S., 1½ m. from the stat. There is little noteworthy in its history or appearance. The manor belonged, in the time of the Confessor, to the Abbey of Westminster ; was alienated before 1226, and afterwards belonged to the Montfichets. In 1319 it was divided, and a moiety since known as East Ham Hall granted in reversion to the abbot and convent of Stratford, by whom it was held till the Suppression ; the manor-house, near the ch., is now a farmhouse. The occupations are mostly agricultural. A large proportion of the land is laid out as market-gardens, East Ham being noted for the growth of onions, and especially pickling onions, which are pulled by the rood and sold by the gallon. A ton of seed is sown yearly by one farmer. Potatoes are also largely grown. Between the vill. and the Thames is the broad tract of marsh land known as East Ham Level, famous for grazing.

The *Church* (St. Mary Magdalene), stands S. of the vill., at the edge of the marsh. It is of flint and stone, partly of Norman date, much patched and somewhat dilapidated; has nave, chancel, and apse, and a low massive W. tower (the upper part modern), with double buttresses at the angles. An avenue of limes runs from the W. door to the road; S. of the ch. is a good-sized yew tree—the trunk 7 ft. in girth: altogether, though lonely looking and somewhat neglected, it is, with its surroundings, a more than commonly picturesque vill. ch., and the architecture is worth examining. The nave windows are mostly modern and poor, but traces will be observed of some small E.E. windows built up. The apse has been added on to the chancel, is narrower, and has a lower roof. It is lighted by 3 narrow lancets, and has a low priest's door on the S. The decorations—patterns in red and green, with some figures—on the walls of the apse, were brought to light on removing the whitewash in 1850. On the S. of the chancel will be observed some Norman arches with zigzag mouldings; on the S. of the apse a double piscina. *Obs.* behind the altar the *Mont.* of Edmund Nevil, with kneeling effigies of himself and wife (d. 1647). The insc. styles him "Lord Latimer and Earl of Westmoreland," but he had no legal right to such a distinction, the title ceasing with the attainder in 1570 of Charles the 6th earl, and Edmund Nevil's claim having been expressly disallowed by the Lords Commissioners in 1605. *Brasses.*—Hester, "the virtuous loving and obedient wife of Francis Neve," citizen and merchant-taylor of London, d. 1610. æt. 58; and Elizabeth, wife of Richard Heigham, Esq., d. 1622. The learned but too credulous antiquary, Dr. Stukeley, author of the 'Itinerarium Curiosum,' was buried in the ch.-yard, March 9, 1765, "in a spot which he had long before fixed on, when on a visit to Mr. Sims the vicar," without any mont., the turf, by his own request, being laid smoothly over his grave.

Beyond the ch., the East Ham Level extends to the Thames, 1½ m., and across it the Metropolitan Northern High Level Sewer is carried towards Barking in a turf-covered embankment about 20 ft. high. The sewer is admirably constructed of brick, and consists of 3 channels, each 9 ft. in diameter. In excavating, Dec. 1863, for ballast to form this embankment, at the base of the old river bank on which the ch. stands, and about 900 yards W. of it, the workmen came upon what appears to have been a rather extensive Roman Cemetery. A stone coffin with a coped lid, containing 2 skeletons; 3 leaden coffins placed N. and S.; skeletons believed to have been interred in wooden coffins; cinerary urns, fragments of Samian ware, etc., were exhumed, the whole affording evidence of a considerable Roman colony having been placed here on the margin of the river. About a mile to the W., nearly opposite Woolwich, are vestiges of a Roman Camp,* while at Uphill Farm, 1 m. E., is the encampment noticed under BARKING. East Ham Level was a portion of the æstuary of the Thames until the construction of the river wall, in all probability a Roman work.

The works seen covering a large slice of the East Ham Level, by the river, belong to the Chartered Gas Company, are named *Beckton,* and are among the most extensive yet constructed. They were laid out in 1869; occupy an area of 150 acres; comprise 4 retort-houses, each 300 ft. by 90, containing 1080 retorts, each 20 ft. long; 4 gas-holders of a diameter of 180 ft., and capable of containing in the aggregate 4 million cubic feet of gas. Along the Thames is a substantial river wall of brick and stone, 1000 ft. long, from which extends a massive iron pier, 400 ft. long, with a head of nearly twice that extent for landing coals from the lighters by machinery. A double line of railway runs from the pier to the retort-houses; and a private road above 3 m. long from the works to the Barking road. Alongside the rly. are sheds for holding 80,000 tons of coal under cover. Besides the gas-works, there are workmen's and officers' houses, and a capacious canteen. The lately dreary marsh has thus been converted into a busy if not altogether lovely colony. The cost of the Beckton works was over £700,000. The gas passes to the City and the West-end of London through 8 m. of iron tubes of 8 ft., and 3 m. of 3 ft. diameter. When in full operation the works can make 10 million cubic

* Archæol. Journal, vol. xxi., p. 93.

feet of gas a day, and they are so planned as to be capable of enlargement to any extent, without deranging the regular operations. The public road from the ch. across the Marsh goes to North Woolwich, where is a steam ferry to Woolwich.

A new *Church* (Emmanuel) was erected in 1863, close to the Barking road, for the inhabitants of the upper part of the vill. It is of Kentish rag, in irregular courses, Early Dec. in style; cruciform, with a square central tower and low roof-spire, borne on 4 massive columns. The archt. was Mr. A. W. Blomfield. In East Ham parish are the *Industrial School*, for the Union of St. George-in-the-East, which at the census of 1871 had 188 boys and 153 girls; the *St. Nicholas Roman Catholic School*, at the Manor House, with 259 boys and the same number of girls; and *St. Edward's Reformatory*, Boleyn Castle, Greenstreet, with 158 male and the same number of female inmates.

Greenstreet and *Plashet* are hamlets of East Ham. *Greenstreet House*, now called Boleyn Castle (a little way up Green Street, the turning in the Barking road, midway between Ilford Lane and Plaistow, on the rt.), is a red brick mansion, believed to occupy the site of the seat of the Nevils. The most rem. feature is a lofty tower, locally known as *Anne Boleyn's Tower*, from a tradition that she was confined in it. A late owner believed he had "somewhere seen a letter of Henry VIII., dated from Greenstreet,"* but we know of no more definite evidence of the royal ownership or tenancy. From the summit there is a wide view over the East Ham and Plaistow Levels.

Plashet is a quiet out-of-the-way place, ½ m. N. of Greenstreet. *Plashet House* (T. Mathews, Esq.,) was, from 1808, for many years the residence of Mrs. Fry, who here received the visits of the King of Prussia and many other royal and notable persons. Maria Edgeworth wrote after a visit, April 24, 1822, "Mrs. Fry's place at Plashet is beautiful, and she is as delightful at home as at Newgate."

EAST HORNDON, ESSEX (*see* HORNDON, EAST).

* Gent. Mag., 1824, p. 219.

EAST MOLESEY, SURREY (*see* MOLESEY, EAST).

EAST SHEEN, SURREY (*see* SHEEN, EAST).

EAST TILBURY, ESSEX (*see* TILBURY, EAST).

EASTWICK, HERTS (Dom. *Estewicke*), on the N. bank of the Stort, 1 m. N.W. from Burnt Mill Stat. on the Grt. E. Rly. (Cambridge line), 4½ m. S.W. from Sawbridgeworth, is a very thinly populated place, the entire parish containing only 104 inhabitants. The vill. is a collection of about half a dozen cottages, a blacksmith's shop, a neat semi-Gothic inn, the *Pyrgo Arms*, the school-house, and church,—the vicarage standing on one side in a pleasant little park. But though now hardly a village, of old it had a weekly market on Tuesday, and an annual fair of 3 days, granted by Henry III., and confirmed *temp.* Edward I.

The *Church* (St. Botolph), the only object of interest, is a small cruciform building of flint and stone, rough-cast, except the lower part; with a tower and thin shingle spire at the W., and an old porch at the N.W. It is throughout E.E., except the E. window, which is Perp. The interior is whitewashed, has high pews, and a heavy gallery at the W. *Obs.* the chancel arch, which is E.E., of unusually good form and moulding, borne on detached shafts of Purbeck marble (whitewashed). S. of the chancel is a square recess with piscina and credence, and within the altar rails are some encaustic tiles of good pattern, *in situ*, uncovered in July 1869. *Obs.* in centre of chancel a *brass* to

"Robert Lee, Esquire, his Body is buried here,
Who served with King Edward, first, a Sewer many Year,
And after to King Philip and Mary Queen of late,
And lastly with Queen Elizabeth, our Noble Prince in State,
And of the ancient Bagley House in Cheshire born was he,
And in this Tomb with Jane his Wife here buried both they be."

Lee died in 1564; his effigy is lost, but that of his wife, d. 1595, remains. In the N. transept is a recumbent statue of a cross-legged knight in chain armour without name or insc. It is of Purbeck marble (Chauncy mistook it for "brass," *i. e.*, bronze) and remarkably perfect. The country about Eastwick is pleasant : the surface is undulating ; there are shady lanes, finely timbered parks, and a succession of pretty willowy meads bordering the Stort.

EAST WICKHAM, KENT (*see* WICKHAM, EAST).

EDGWARE, MIDDX. (anc. and down to the reign of Henry VII., *Eggeswere*), a small town on the road to St. Albans, and on the anc. Watling Street, extending from Kingsbury on the S. to Elstree on the N., and bounded E. and W. by Hendon and Little Stanmore ; 8 m. from Hyde Park Corner, and the terminus of the Highgate and Edgware branch of the Grt. N. Rly., 11¼ m. from King's Cross. Inns, the *Chandos Arms ;* the *Boot.* The par. of Edgware contained only 655 inhab. in 1871, but the W. (or left) side of the main street is in Little Stanmore par.

The town stretches for more than a mile along the highroad, which widens considerably opposite the ch. It consists of a very irregular mixture of houses— shops, mostly small, cottages, and private dwellings—the best at the N. end ; with two or three old inns, now curtailed in extent and style, but evidently of some consequence in the old coaching days ; and one, the Chandos Arms, reminding the visitor of the splendour of the neighbouring palace (*see* CANONS). The blacksmith's shop, a relic of a sort of middlerow on the l. of the road, is that in which, according to tradition, worked the musical blacksmith, whose performance on the anvil whilst Handel took shelter from a shower, suggested to the great musician the well-known melody named after him. Edgware had a weekly market, on Thursday, but it had been "for some time discontinued" when Lysons wrote. In 1867, however, the Privy Council licensed the holding of a cattle market at the Crane Inn yard on the last Thursday in every month.

Towards the close of the 12th cent. the manor of Edgware belonged to Ela, Countess of Salisbury, the wife of William Longspée. In the 14th cent. it passed by marriage to the Le Stranges ; was alien-

ated in 1427, and in 1443 was sold to the newly founded College of All Souls, Oxford, whose property it still is. The manor of Boys (*Bois*), or Edgware Boys, was held by the Priory of St. John of Jerusalem, from whom, by sale or exchange, it passed to the Dean of Westminster, who, in 1483, surrendered it to the king. Henry VIII. granted it in 1544 to Sir John Williams and Anthony Stringer, who the same year sold it to Henry Page, Esq. From him it passed to the Coventry family, in whom it remained till sold by the Earl of Coventry in 1762 to the son of Lord Chief Justice Lee, whose representative still holds it.

Edgware *Church* (St. John of Jerusalem) is curiously uninteresting. The tower, of flint and stone, square, with an octagonal angle turret, and modern battlements, is old but poor ; the body of the ch., which was rebuilt in 1765, and renewed about 1845, is of brick whitened over ; cruciform, the windows modern Perp., the E. window, of 3 lights, being filled with painted glass. Neither exterior nor interior will long detain the visitor : both are alike uninteresting. The only *Mont.* of mark inside is one to Randulph Nicoll, a native of the place, d. 1658, who, if the inscription may be trusted, was a prodigy of learning and ability. *Obs.* mural *brass* of a child in swaddling-clothes, Anthony, son of John Childe, goldsmith, d. 1599, æt. 3 weeks. The ch.-yard is small, ill-kept, and has no monts. claiming notice. Francis Coventry, author of ' The Life of Pompey the Little,' and Prof. Thomas Martyn, the botanist, held the living. Near the ch. was a cell or station belonging to the abbey of St. Albans, which served as a hostelry for the monks in their journeys to and from London.

On the road, about 1 m. beyond the town, is *Brockley Hill,* by Camden and most subsequent authorities supposed to be the site of the Roman station *Sulloniacæ.* Roman remains have been found here, at Pennywell, a little N., and one or two other places in the vicinity, and the great Roman road (on the line of the older Watling Street) ran through it to St. Albans. The supposed site lies on the rt. of the road by the 10th milestone—the gate leading into the enclosure is opposite the lane to Stanmore. The surface is much and irregularly broken, and overgrown with wild roses, brambles, and thistles, with a few elms, chesnuts, and scrubby firs. About the summit are several hollows, and on the N. the remains of a large artificial pond, from which you may yet occasionally startle a moor-hen. The hill slopes away on the N.E. and E., affording fine views over a wide stretch of country. The S. slope is under crops.

EDMONTON, MIDDX. (Dom.

Adelmeton, later *Edelmeton*), a village which straggles for nearly 2 m. along the road to Ware from Tottenham to Enfield, the Tottenham part being called Upper Edmonton, the Enfield end Lower Edmonton; Stats. on the Grt. E. Rly., Angel Road and Church Street, on the Hertford or Low Level, and at Silver Street and Church Street on the High Level branches, serve both districts. Edmonton parish comprises 7480 acres, and in 1871 contained 13,860 inhab., but this includes the eccl. districts of Upper Edmonton, Southgate, and Winchmore Hill: Edmonton alone had 4097 inhab.

The village is built along a slightly raised crest, having the Lea River on one side and the New River on the other : the higher ground on the W. arable, the lower, by the Lea, marsh land. Of old, Edmonton was noted for its market gardens, and they are still extensive, potatoes being very largely grown. There are also nurseries and farms, as well as several factories; but with the development of railway facilities Edmonton is assuming more and more the aspect of a suburban village. The history of the place is little more than a history of the several manors, to relate which would be alike tedious and unprofitable : an ample account of them will be found in Lysons's, 'Environs of London,' vol. ii., pt. 1, p. 162, etc., ed. 1811, and in Robinson's 'Hist. and Antiquities of the Parish of Edmonton,' 1817. The inhabitants of Edmonton had right of common upon Enfield Chase, and when the Chase was divided, in 1777, a tract of 1231 acres was allotted to the parish. Upon part of the Chase a fair, known as Bush Fair, was held twice a year. James I. threw this part of the Chase into his park of Theobalds, but granted a patent for holding the fairs elsewhere, and, under the name

of Beggar's Bush Fair, they continued to be held until they gradually fell into abeyance only a few years since.

The *Church* (All Saints) is situated in Church Street, Lower Edmonton, a turning on the l. of the London road by the 7 m. stone, and the High and Low Level Rly. stats., leading to Winchmore Hill. It is a large building, chiefly of the Perp. period, but was cased with brick and altered throughout, with the exception of the tower, in 1772. In 1866, however, the interior was carefully restored, new Perp. windows inserted in the chancel, and a S. aisle added to it. The tower is of flint and stone ; Perp., square, with an angle turret at the S.E., and battlemented, and has in it a peal of 8 bells. The *Monts.* are of no account. There are small *brasses* of John Asplin, Godfrey Askew, and Elizabeth " the wyfe of them both," about 1500 ; Edward Nowell, Esq., d. 1616, and wife Mary, d. 1600. The others have disappeared.

In the ch.-yard, W. of the ch., is an upright stone, not mentioned in the present Isaac Taylor's ' Family Pen ' : " Isaac Taylor, Gent., formerly an eminent engraver in London, who died Oct. 17, 1807, aged 77 years." But the most interesting mont. is that of CHARLES LAMB, a tall upright stone, with a long poetical inscription by Cary, the translator of Dante : it will be found on the rt. of the path, S.W. of the ch., half-hidden behind the more showy tombs of Wm. Bridger, of Bishopsgate, and Wm. Cobbett, not of the ' Register.' Lamb lodged for the last year or two of his life in Church Street, at the house of a retired haberdasher, Mr. T. Walden, and there he died, from erysipelas following an accidental fall, Dec. 27, 1834. His sister, Mary, died in Alpha Road, St. John's Wood, May 20, 1847, and the brother and sister now lie in the same grave.* The house in which Lamb lived and died, *Bay Cottage*, is on the left going from the ch. towards the highroad, a small white house, lying back from the street, next door to ' the Lion House,' which will be at once recognized by the lions supporting shields upon the gate piers, and nearly opposite the Girls' Charity School. Church Street has

* Proctor's Life of Charles Lamb, p. 320.

another literary memory. John Keats served his apprenticeship here, 1810—16, to Mr. Hammond, a surgeon, and whilst here wrote his 'Juvenile Poems,' published in 1817.

Edmonton was not, however, without earlier literary associations. Weever writes, under Edmonton Church,—"Here lieth interred under a seemelie Tome, without inscription, the Body of Peter Fabell (as the report goes) upon whom this Fable * was fathered, that he by his wittie devises beguiled the Devill: belike he was some ingenious conceited gentleman, who did use some sleighty trickes for his owne disports. He lived and died in the raigne of Henry the Seventh, saith the booke of his merry pranks."† This book is the famous 'Merry Deuill of Edmonton: As it hath been sundry times acted by his Maiesties Servants, at the Globe on the Bankeside,' in which was set forth not only "the Lyfe and Death of the Merry Devill," but also "the pleasant pranks of Smugge the Smyth, Sir John, and mine Hoste of the George, about their stealing of venison, By T. B."; and which, despite the initials, it was long the fashion to attribute to Shakspeare, as it still is to Michael Drayton. The Prologue to the play says that the merry devil was "Peter Fabel, a renowned scholar;" and adds:

"If any here make doubt of such a name
In Edmonton, yet fresh unto this day,
Fix'd in the wall of that old ancient church,
His monument remaineth to be seen."

But the monument, with or without the name, has long been lost. Besides its fiend, Edmonton had also its witch:

"The town of Edmonton hath lent the stage,
A Devil and a Witch, both in an age." ‡

Ford's play was founded on a true tragedy, the nature of which is sufficiently indicated in the title-page of a contemporary pamphlet quoted by Lysons: 'The Wonderfull Discoverie of Elizabeth Sawyer, a Witch, late of Edmonton; her conviction, her condemnation, and death; together with the relation of the Divel's accesse to her, and their conference together. Written by Henry Goodcole,

Minister of the Word of God, and her continual visitor in the Gaole of Newgate.' 4to, 1621.

The George inn, the pleasant pranks of whose host are related in the 'Merrie Devil of Edmonton,' was not situated here, but at Waltham. Edmonton has, however, one inn of fame, The Bell, at which John Gilpin did not dine. The Bell is on the London side of Edmonton, on the left of the road from town, a house of Cowper's time, but altered, and the balcony removed—a sad desecration. Outside, answering the purpose of a sign, is a painting of Gilpin's ride from Ware, and the landlord designates his house 'The Bell and Johnny Gilpin's Ride.' The Bell is still a favourite resort of London holiday-makers, has capacious rooms, large garden and grounds, and in the summer a superb display of flowers. Charles Lamb, naturally regarding the house with a sort of affection, used to accompany the friends who visited him at Edmonton as far on their way home as 'Gilpin's Bell,' and there take with them a parting cup—generally of porter.

Another inn, named in our literature the "honest ale house, where we shall find a cleanly room, lavender in the windows, and 20 ballads stuck about the wall," with a "hostess both cleanly and handsome and civil," to which Piscator led his Scholar on the Third Day, has been identified by Sir Harris Nicolas * with Bleak Hall, at Cook's Ferry, on the Lea, Edmonton. But this is a mistake, as Isaak Walton's inn was above Waltham, whereas Cook's Ferry is some miles below it. Now, however, the little fisherman's inn known as Bleak Hall has disappeared, and Cook's Ferry has given place to a bridge.

Tillotson resided at Edmonton parsonage for several years whilst Dean of St. Paul's, and occasionally after he became Abp. of Canterbury. He here spent the day before his consecration in fasting and prayer.* Brook Taylor, the author of the standard work on Perspective, was born at Edmonton; Barclay, of Dictionary fame, was for awhile curate; and Nahum Tate, the unmelodious successor of Sternhold and Hopkins, held the living.

---

* Weever does not often perpetrate a pun, and this was appropriated by Fuller (see The Worthies: Middlesex).
† Funeral Monuments, p. 534, ed. 1631.
‡ Prologue to Ford and Dekker's tragi-comedy of the Witch of Edmonton.

---

* Notes to Chapter ii. of the Complete Angle.
† Works, folio, vol. iii., p. 635.

Wyre Hall, a fine old Jacobean mansion, often mentioned in books, was demolished in 1818. *Bury Hall*, Bury Street, once the residence of Bradshaw, who presided at the trial of Charles I.; *Hyde House ; Bush Hill Park ; Arnold's* or *Arno's Grove*, and other good mansions, are in the parish, but mostly away from the village, and noticed under SOUTHGATE and WINCHMORE HILL.

Besides the old church, there are three others in the parish, but only one, St. James, Upper Edmonton, belongs to Edmonton proper ; the others, Southgate and Winchmore Hill, are each 2 m. distant, and virtually distinct parishes. The showy Gothic church-like structure in the main street is the Congregational chapel, successor, we believe, of the old Presbyterian chapel in which Dr. Richard Price, the author of ' Observations on Civil Liberty,' which called forth Burke's ' Reflections on the French Revolution,' and the friend of Franklin, Howard, and Priestley, commenced his ministry.

EGHAM, SURREY (Dom. *Egeham*), on the old Western road, 1 m. W. of Staines, with which it is connected by a bridge over the Thames ; 18 m. from London by road, and 21 m. by the L. and S.W. Rly. (Reading line) : pop. of the par., which is very extensive, 5895. Inns : *King's Head, Catherine Wheel, Crown*.

In the old coaching days, Egham was a busy place ; now it is little more than a village of sober, old-fashioned, red brick dwellings, many of them well built and of a well-to-do aspect ; inns, larger and more numerous than the inhabitants seem to require ; and a dull semi-classical church at the London end. The manor of Egham was part of the vast property bestowed by Frithwald, sub-regulus of Surrey, on the newly founded Abbey of Chertsey. (*See* CHERTSEY.) In 1538 it was surrendered to Henry VIII., by whom it was granted to Lord Windsor, but resumed, in exchange for other estates, in 1542. By Charles I. it was made part of the jointure of Henrietta Maria, and though dispossessed of it by the Parliament, she regained possession at the Restoration. On her death it was settled on Catherine of Braganza, but the reversion was shortly after alienated from the Crown, and it has since remained in private hands. The sub-manor

of Milton was purchased in the reign of Henry VIII. by Fox, Bishop of Winchester, and made part of the endowment of his foundation of Corpus Christi College, Oxford.

The *Church* was built in 1817-20, on the site of an interesting but dilapidated edifice, partly of Norman date. It is a brick cube, having at the W. end Ionic pilasters and a pediment, over which is a square tower with miniature pediments and a cupola. Unattractive as it is exterior, the interior is of interest for various memorials rescued from the old ch. A slab inserted in the E. wall of the S. aisle has an inscription in early English letters (similar to one in the chancel of Great Bookham ch., Surrey), recording the erection of the chancel by John de Rutherwyke, Abbot of Chertsey (d. 1437). Above this stone is a *brass* of Anthony Bond, citizen and writer of the ' Court Lette of London,' d. 1576, and his two wives. On S. staircase, an alabaster mont. of Sir John Denham, Chief Baron of the Exchequer, and father of the poet, d. 1638, in the most elaborately absurd taste of the time. Sir John is represented in his winding-sheet rising from the tomb, amidst a wild confusion of skeletons, cerecloths, and Latin inscriptions, and within a framework of Corinthian columns. In a corresponding place on the opposite staircase are the half-length effigies of the baron's two wives, the second holding in her arms a naked infant, " of whom she died in childbed," whilst on an outer ledge is a small kneeling figure of her son, the poet, in scarlet jacket, cloak, and ruff. The first wife's first husband, Richard Kellefet, Queen Elizabeth's " chief Groome in her removinge gardrobe of beddes, and Yeoman also of her standing gardrobe of Richmont," is commemorated in a tablet under the N. gallery. Here also is a tablet, with military decorations, to Sir Felton E. B. Harvey, Bart., d. 1819, who as Col. of the 14th Light Dragoons served with Wellington during the Peninsular campaign, and lost his right arm at the passage of the Douro. Sir Felton Harvey is the officer of whom it is related that leading a charge of the 14th after he had lost his arm, a French officer who was about to strike, seeing he was defenceless, laid his sword on his shoulder, and rode on—the men of the 14th, who witnessed the act, opening out to let him pass free. The officers of the 14th sought in vain, by means of a flag of truce, to ascertain the name of the gallant Frenchman, who it was supposed must have fallen in the fight. On the E. wall of the nave, among other records, is a bust of Robert Foster, d. 1663, Chief Justice of the Court of King's Bench. The verses on the oval tablet to the Rev. Thos. Beighton (d. 1771) were written by Garrick. Within the altar railings, on the N., is a mural mont. to Geo. Gostling, Esq., d. 1820, with an alto-rilievo, by Flaxman, of Religion holding a tablet on which is a bust of the deceased; and on the S. are others to members of the Gostling family, by E. H. Baily, R.A. The altar-piece, ' Elijah raising the Widow's Son,' is by Richard Westall, R.A.

On the N. side of the High Street are *Strode's Schools and Almshouses*, founded and endowed in 1703 by Mr. Henry Strode, for the free education of the children of Egham, and the maintenance and clothing of 12 poor persons. The charity is under the direction of the Coopers' Company, by whom the present buildings were erected in 1828-37. *Denham's Almshouse*, a plain brick building on West Hill, was built and endowed by Baron Denham for 5 poor widows; over the doorway is the inscription, ' *Domum Dei et Deo*, 1624.'

One or two of the old mansions deserve notice. *The Vicarage*, ¼ m. E. of the ch., of old called *The Place*, was the seat of the elder Denham, and built by him; "a house," writes Aubrey, " very convenient, not great, but pretty, and healthily situated; in which his son Sir John (though he had better seats) took most delight." It is a comfortable looking red-brick house, the older part with mullioned windows and something of a Jacobean fantasy about it, but the rest evidently later than the time when the poet was compelled by gambling debts and the civil law to sell this and his other property, and so sever his hereditary connection with Egham. *Great Fosters* (Baroness Halkett), 1½ m. S. of Egham, is a good-sized and very complete Elizabethan mansion, with the royal arms and the date, 1578, over the porch. The drawing-room ceiling bears the date 1602, and, like the ceilings of the dining and some other rooms, is enriched with numerous heraldic and

other devices—the silver boar ducally gorged, the armillary sphere, etc.—which antiquaries have as yet failed to appropriate. A local tradition makes the house to have been a hunting seat of Queen Elizabeth; another, her prison in the days of Queen Mary: the earliest facts known in its history are that it was the residence of Judge Dodderidge, d. 1628; and afterwards of Chief Justice Sir Robert Foster, whose mont. is in the ch. From the latter it has been supposed to have derived its name: but it is described as "my house of fforsters" in Sir John Dodderidge's will. It, as has been suggested, was probably the official residence of the keeper of the forest here (*forester, forster*): Creswell, the keeper of the forest in Norden's time, was buried at Egham in 1623.[*]

The country around Egham is full of interest. Less than ½ m. S. of it is *Runnimede*, on which the notorious Egham Races are run; a little farther is *Cooper's Hill*, (see those headings); *Englefield Green* is about 1 m. to the W.; Windsor Great Park, in its finest part, *Bishopsgate*, is under 2 m.; and the Wheatsheaf entrance to *Virginia Water* is but little more, S.W. About the Thames, near Egham, are several eyots (whence perhaps the name *Egeham*, A.-S. *Ege*, an island), pretty to look at and profitable as osier plantations; the river affords good fishing.

ELSTREE, Herts, 10 m. from

London by the Midland Rly., 3 m. N. of Edgware, on the road to St. Albans: pop. 525. Inns: *Red Lion*, and *Plough*. The Rly. Stat. is about ¾ m. N.E. of the vill. by the hamlet of Boreham Wood. Elstree vill. stands in 4 parishes and 2 counties: the N.E. portion, with the ch., is in Elstree, the N.W. in Aldenham par., both belonging to Herts; while the S.E. is in Edgware, and the S.W. in Little Stanmore par., which belong to Middlesex. Norden, writing in the reign of Elizabeth, derives the name from Eaglestree,—that is, he says, " *Nemus aquilinum*, a place where it may be thought that eagles bred in times past,"[†] and Chauncy approves the derivation:

---

[*] Notes and Queries, 4th Series, vol. i., p. 505, and vol. ii., p. 463.
[†] An Historicall and Chorographicall Description of Hertfordshire, p. 16.

"Offa, the great and noble Founder of the Church of St. Albans, gave among other things to God and St. Alban, by the Name of *Eaglestree, Nemus Aquilinum*, a Grove, where 'tis thought Eagles usually bred in times past; for though it is now hilly and heathy, yet formerly this place did greatly abound with stately Trees, where such Fowls delighted to resort and harbour : And at the time of the Conquest, it was a waste Piece of Ground overgrown with Wood, which is the Reason no mention is made of it in Domesdei Book."*

Lysons more reasonably suggests that the name is rather a corruption of *Eald Street*, the old road, *i.e.* the ancient Watling Street, upon which it is situated. By several of our earlier antiquaries Elstree was supposed to occupy the site of the Roman station, Sulloniacæ, but that is now with better reason placed at Brockley Hill, somewhat more S. (*See* EDGWARE.)

Till the Dissolution the manor belonged to the abbey of St. Albans, then passed to the Dennys, then to the Briscoes of Aldenham, and finally became the property of the Byngs of Wrotham Park, now represented by the Earl of Strafford. Elstree stands very high, and extensive and beautiful views are obtained from the open ground on all sides of it. From the garden of the Plough Inn, St. Albans with the abbey ch. and the tower of St. Peters, is seen framed like a picture by the trees in the adjoining meadow. The vill. is quiet, clean, and cheerful, and has an air of old-fashioned rural comfort. As you ascend the height on which it stands from the Edgware Road, a large old red brick mansion on the rt., and a broad open meadow on the l. bordered with tall shady elms, and the Elstree reservoir partially revealing its lake-like proportions below, produce an uncommonly picturesque appearance, which is little diminished as you enter the village itself, one of the first objects noticed being the gable end of a cottage on the l., which in summer is literally covered with roses.

The old *Church*, St. Nicholas, was popularly supposed to have been built of stones brought from the ancient Sulloniacæ; the present is a modern Gothic structure, of average character, built of black flints. It consists of nave, aisles, and chancel (in which is a large 5-light E. window filled with painted glass, a memorial to the late Rev. John Morris, D.D., erected by his

pupils), and a tower at the S.W. with shingle spire. The monts. are unimportant ; but in the ch.-yard are buried (without monts.) two persons, Martha Reay, or Ray, and William Weare, whose murders, among the most notorious in the annals of crime, have been celebrated in the most ludicrous verses of the kind extant. Miss Reay, the mistress of the Earl of Sandwich, and mother of Basil Montagu, the editor of Bacon, was killed in the Piazza Covent Garden, as she was leaving the theatre, April 7th, 1779, by the Rev. Mr. Hackman :—

> " A Clergyman, O wicked one !
> In Covent Garden shot her ;
> No time to cry upon her God,
> It's hoped He's not forgot her !"

Hackman was hanged at Tyburn 12 days after the murder. Miss Reay was the daughter of a labourer at Elstree, which accounts for her burial here. Weare, a betting man, was murdered in 1823, by his associates Thurtell and Probert, near Probert's cottage, Gills Hill, about 2½ m. beyond Elstree, on the road to St. Albans. (*See* RADLETT.)

> " They cut his throat from ear to ear
> His brains they battered in
> His name was Mr. William Weare,
> He dwelt in Lyons Inn."

Elstree Reservoir, the large sheet of water in the valley W. of the vill.—nearly ¾ m. long, and ¼ m. across where widest—almost rivals that at Kingsbury in the number and variety of waders and wild fowl which frequent it (*see* KINGSBURY) ; and though less striking in itself, is more picturesque in its surroundings. When the water is drawn off for the supply of the Grand Junction Canal, "and when it has been much reduced by evaporation and want of rain, the herons are here in all their glory. They are then enabled to wade out to some distance, and regale themselves among the roach and eels with which the reservoir abounds."* Elstree Reservoir is a favourite resort of London anglers : it is especially noted for pike, roach, and perch. The water is preserved: day tickets for pike fishing, 2s. 6d., for bottom fishing, 1s. Boats and punts may be hired.

ELTHAM, KENT (A.-S. *Ealdham*,

---

* Chauncy, Hist. Antiq. of Hertfordshire, vol. ii., p. 372.

* Harting, Birds of Middlesex, p. 162.

the old town or dwelling ; Dom., *Alteham*), a suburban vill., interesting as containing the banqueting hall of a royal palace, and for the associations connected with it, on the road to Maidstone, 8 m. from London. The Eltham Stat. of the S.E. Rly., North Kent line, is at *Mottingham*, ¾ m. S. of the vill. Inns : *Greyhound* ; *Chequers*, old-fashioned, with gardens. Pop. of the parish, 4064, but this includes the eccl. districts of St. Peter, 1366, and Holy Trinity, 1271 : that of Eltham proper (the mother ch.) is 1885.

Though now and long a mere village, Eltham had a market (granted to John de Vesci in 1284, and held, on Tuesdays, as late as 1602,) and two annual fairs. The manor belonged to Edward the Confessor, and was given by the Conqueror to his half-brother, Bishop Odo, on the confiscation of whose estates it was divided, and a moiety, granted to the Mandeville family, was called Eltham-Mandeville. The reunited manor passed to John de Vesci, and after his death, 1289, was held by Anthony Bec, Bishop of Durham, but on his decease reverted to Sir Gilbert de Aton, created Lord Vesci, who assigned it to Geoffrey le Scrope of Masham. By him it was transferred to Queen Isabel, and thenceforth was vested in the Crown. Leases have, however, been granted at different times, as by Henry VIII. to Sir Henry Guildford for 40 years; by Edward VI. (1550) to Sir John Gates ; by Elizabeth to Lord Cobham in 1592, etc. In 1628 it was leased to the Earl of St. Albans and others in trust for Queen Henrietta. After the death of Charles I. it was seized, with the other Crown estates, by the Parliament, surveyed, and sold to Nathaniel Rich. Upon the Restoration, Sir John Shaw purchased the subsisting term, and in 1665 obtained a fresh lease, which has since been renewed from time to time to his descendants.[*]

Henry III. kept the Christmas of 1270 at Eltham, and this appears to be the first reference to a royal dwelling here. Leland speaks of Bishop Bec as the very author or first beautifier of the palace, but Hasted attributes its origin to John de Vesci. Bec, the proudest prelate of his time, died at his house at Eltham in 1311.

[*] Hasted ; Lysons ; Dugdale, Baronage ; Philipott, Villare Cantianum, etc.

Soon it became a royal abode, and references to it are frequent. Edward II. was often here ; and here, in 1316, his queen, Isabella, gave birth to a son, known as John of Eltham. Edward III. in 1329, while yet under the tutelage of his mother, held a Parliament here, and another when his strength was decaying, in 1375. In 1363, when at the summit of his glory, he gave a sumptuous entertainment to John, the captive king of France. His feeble successor, Richard II., " resided much at Eltham, and took great delight in the pleasantness of the place ;" here kept his Christmas in 1384 and two following years ; entertained Leo, the fugitive king of Armenia ; held the secret council recorded by Froissart, who was at the time a visitor in the palace ; and here received (1386), somewhat gruffly, the petition of the Commons requesting him to amend the extravagance of his household expenditure. Henry IV. kept here the Christmas of 1401, when 12 aldermen and their sons repaired thither to entertain the Court with a masque, which so delighted the king that he " gave them thanks for their admirable performance." The Christmases of 1405, 1409, and 1412 were also held here, and here he was seized with his last illness. Christmas was kept here by Henry V. in 1414, and by Henry VI. in 1429, with, as we are told, much splendour. But Eltham was probably at its greatest splendour in the days of Edward IV., who expended large sums on the repairs of the palace, and is by some considered as the builder of the magnificent Banqueting Hall. At his Christmas festivities in 1482, 2000 persons are said to have been entertained daily. Eltham was the favourite residence of Henry VII., who, according to Hasted, " built a handsome front to the palace towards the moat," and " most commonly dined in the great hall, and all his officers kept their tables in it." Under his son its fortunes began to wane. He was here at the Christmas of 1515 :—

" After the Parliament was ended, the king kept a solempne Christmas at his manor of Eltham ; and on the xii night in the hall was made a goodly castel, wonderously set out, and in it certeyn ladyes and knyghtes, and when the king and queen were set, in came other knightes and assailed the castel wher many a good strype was gieuen, and at the last, the assaylantes were beaten awaye. And then issued out knightes and ladies out of the castel which ladyes were ryche and straungely disguysed, for all theyr apparel was in braydes of gold, fret with mouing spangels, sylver and gilt, set on Crymosyn satten lose and not fastened : the mens apparell of the same suyte made lyke lulys of Hungary, and the ladys heddes and bodyes were after the fassion of Amsterdam. And when the daunsing was done, the banquet was served in of ii.c. dyshes, with great plenty to every body." *

Ten years later Henry again kept Christmas at Eltham, but this time, the plague being in London, " with a small number, for no manne might come thether, but suche as wer appoynted by name : this Christmas in the kinges house was called the still Christmas," though, as Hall continues, the Cardinal kept open household at Richmond " to lords, ladies and all that would come, with plays and disguisings in most royal manner." In the January following Wolsey came to Eltham, and stayed a fortnight, during which time he " made many ordinances concerning the king's house, which be at this day called the Statutes of Eltham, the which some said were more profitable than honorable." † These statutes are the basis of the regulations for the royal household still in use. A little later Henry completed his palace at Greenwich, and Eltham ceased to be a royal abode. Elizabeth, however, visited it once or twice ; as did James I. in 1612, which appears to have been the last time it was so honoured. But though the Court had removed from Eltham, the town continued for some time to be a place of much resort, and here was held a very popular Motion, puppet-show, or marionnette exhibition. " The divine Motion of Eltham," as Peacham termed it, is referred to more than once by Ben Jonson :—

" See you yon Motion ? not the old fa-ding,
　Nor Captain Pod, nor yet the Eltham thing." ‡

" My very house turns round with the tumult. I dwell in a windmill ! The Perpetual Motion is here and not at Eltham." §

During Elizabeth's reign Sir Christopher, the dancing Lord Chancellor, was keeper of the palace, an appointment in which he was succeeded by Lord Cobham in 1592. In the early years of the Commonwealth the palace was the residence of the Earl of Essex, who died here Sept. 13, 1646.

In 1649 a survey of the manor of Eltham

was made by order of Parliament. The mansion, called Eltham House, was found to be built of brick, wood, and stone, and to consist below-stairs of one fair chapel, one great hall, 36 rooms and offices, with two large cellars ; and above-stairs 17 lodging rooms on the King's, 12 on the Queen's side, and 9 on the Prince's side,— in all 38, with various small rooms and closets ; and 35 bays of building round the courtyard, which contained 78 rooms, and occupied an acre of ground. The chapel and the great hall were the only rooms, furnished. Being much out of repair the whole was sold, and the materials valued at £2753. Attached to the house were three parks,—the Great Park, the Little or Middle Park, and Horne or Lee Park,—comprising in all 1314 acres, and containing about 7700 trees, of which about 4000 were old and decayed, and the remainder fit for the use of the navy.

The parks had already (1648) been disparked, and the deer destroyed, and now, as already mentioned, Nathanael Rich purchased the house and great part of the demesne lands. Evelyn describes its condition a few years later : " Went to see his Majesty's House at Eltham, both palace and chapel in miserable ruins, the noble wood and park destroyed by Rich the rebel."* " Scarcely a tree being left to make a gibbet," according to ' The Mysteries of the Good Old Cause,' 1660.

The site of the palace is about ¼ m. S. of the main street of Eltham, midway between the village and the rly. stat. Its general form was that of a large irregular quadrangle with 4 inner courts ; the buildings, the growth of centuries, differing considerably in style, and constructed, as already noticed, of stone, brick, and timber. A strong external wall surrounded them, and beyond this was a moat 60 feet wide, except at the N. entrance, where it was 115 feet. The number of the rooms has been already given from the Parliamentary survey. The chapel, the banqueting hall, and the other state apartments were on the W., the kitchen and domestic offices towards the E. Of this vast pile only the *Banqueting Hall* remains, except as scattered fragments, and the hall probably only escaped from its obvious use as a barn. The hall is in suf-

---

* Hall's Chronicle, The vii. yere of Kyng Henry the VIII.
† *Ibid.*　　　　　　‡ Epigrams.
§ Epicene, Act v., Scene 3.

---

* Diary, April 22, 1656.

ficient preservation to afford a good notion of the magnificence of the entire structure. But it has had some narrow escapes. Long used as a barn, it had been sorely mutilated, and was greatly dilapidated, when, during the alterations at Windsor Castle, it was suggested by Sir Jeffrey Wyatville that the magnificent timber roof would make an excellent roof for St. George's Hall. On examination, however, it was considered to be too much decayed for removal, and in 1828, at the intercession it is said of the Princess Sophia, then residing in the Ranger's House, Greenwich, the hall was repaired, and the roof rendered secure. Since then little has been done to it : no longer a barn, the hall is now only used occasionally for drill by the Eltham Volunteers.

The hall is of brick, but has been partially faced with stone. The exterior is sadly decayed, but observe before entering the tracery of the five double windows, between buttresses, on each side, and those of the bays at the N. end. The interior, 100 feet long, 36 wide, and 55 high, will by its magnificent roof recall to the memory Westminster Hall, though it differs from that and other great banqueting halls by having been lighted from both sides : now the windows are for the most part blocked up, and the roof only held together by wooden shores and scaffolding. The roof is an open hammerbeam one of the Westminster Hall type, but its pendants and decorative carvings are gone. The remarkably fine bays at the end of the hall, and the remains of the screen, should be examined.

The ivy-clad bridge by which the hall is reached is of coeval date, and has noteworthy groined arches and buttresses. The moat which it crosses is for the greater part drained and planted, but a portion by the bridge is filled with water, and is the haunt of some choice aquatic birds. The *Court House* (R. Bloxham, Esq.), by the moat, the buttery of the palace, retains its old barge-board gables and quaint attics, but it has been much altered, and a new wing was added to it in 1859. Before leaving, notice the gate opposite the palace gardens, which was the entrance to the tilt-yard, and the fragments of wall by the moat. Other vestiges are still traceable, as are also several vaults and subterranean passages, which popular

opinion avers extended to Blackheath, but which were no doubt drains, though one or more may have served as sally-ports. Ample details concerning the building will be found in J. C. Buckler's ' Eltham,' and Dunnage and Laver's ' Elevations, Details, and Views of the Great Hall of the Royal Palace of Eltham,' 4to, 1828.

As we have seen, sad havoc was made by the Parliament with the trees in the three parks, but *Middle Park*, which remains, shows that there was certainly not so entire a clearance made as was asserted. In our own day Middle Park has gained a certain notoriety as the home of the famous racehorse stud of Mr. Wm. Blenkiron. Here used to be gathered at the annual sale of yearlings perhaps the largest and most fashionable assemblage of " patrons of the turf " ever seen on such occasions, and here were obtained the probably unrivalled prices of 2500 guineas (1867) and 2000 guineas (1868) for a yearling. After Mr. Blenkiron's death the stud was sold by auction, July 1872, for £107,100 ; the celebrated horse Gladiateur, for which Mr. Blenkiron gave £6090 at Count Lagrange's sale, was bought by Mr. Ray for £7350 ; whilst Blair Athol brought £13,125, the largest sum known to have ever been given for a horse : the purchasers were the Stud Company, who have since Mr. Blenkiron's death continued the Middle Park business at Cobham in Surrey. The memory of the Middle Park establishment is perpetuated in the " Middle Park Plate," founded in 1866, and which is one of the chief races at the Newmarket Second October Meeting.

The village, which lies a short distance N. of the palace, wears an air of old-fashioned respectability, and some of the houses are worth looking it. The *Church*, St. John the Baptist, is for the most part plain modern brick, but the wooden tower and shingle spire at the W. are old, and the N. aisle, of stone, has, on a label over the doorway, the date 1667. The interior is without interest. In the ch.-yd. is the mont., marked by an urn, of George Horne, Bp. of Norwich (d. 1792), author of the once popular ' Commentary on the Book of Psalms.' Thomas Dogget, the comedian, now best known as the founder of " Dogget's coat and silver badge," rowed for on the Thames by London watermen's apprentices on the 1st of August, the "anniversary of the accession of George I.," was buried here Sept. 25th, 1721. Here also lies Thomas Cadell, the well-known publisher (buried January 3rd, 1803), and Sir William James (d. 1783), the captor of Severndroog, on the western coast of India, 1755; as a memorial of whom, and in celebration of the great event in his career, his widow erected the tower called Severndroog, on Shooter's Hill, in this parish.

Well Hall (E. Langley, Esq.), a long, low, red-brick, farm-like, Elizabethan house, on the rt. of the road to Woolwich, and just opposite the field-path to Kidbrooke, was the residence of Sir Thomas More's favourite daughter, Margaret Roper; and here Holbein's famous picture of 'More and his family' was kept till 1731, when it was carried to his seat in Yorkshire by Sir Rowland Winn, to whom it had come by marriage, and whose descendant, Mr. Charles Winn, now owns it.

Among other notables who have dwelt in Eltham was Vandyck, the painter, who lived here in the summer, tempted, it may be, by the residence in the Park Lodge of his friend Sir Theodore de Mayerne, the king's physician, who was chief ranger of the park before it was seized by the Parliament. According to Walpole,[*] " in an old house at Eltham, said to have been Vandyck's, Vertue saw several sketches of stories from Ovid in two colours, ascribed to him "—but if they were his, all trace has long been lost of them, and of the house also. The quarrelsome Commonwealth Major, John Lilburne, " Freeborn John," Cromwell's opponent in the army and in the House of Commons, here spent his last years "in perfect tranquillity." Having joined the Quakers, "he preached among that sect in and about Eltham, till his death " there, August 29th, 1657. Here Dr. James Sherard formed his famous botanic garden, of which he published an account, the 'Hortus Elthamensis,' in the preparation of which he was assisted by Dillenius, who came to England in 1721 specially to superintend Dr. Sherard's garden, an event which Dr. Lindley says "forms an im-

portant point in the history of botany in this country." Lysons speaks of Dr. James Sherard as the founder of the botanical professorship at Oxford, and in this he is followed by most subsequent writers on Eltham. The founder of the professorship was William Sherard, the Oriental traveller, the brother of James, who, however, was a zealous promoter of the science and patron of botanists.

ENFIELD, MIDDX. (Dom. *Enefelde*, probably from A.-S. *æn* or *én*, and *feld*, a forest clearing), about 9 m. from London by road. The Grt. E. Rly. has a branch line to Enfield, with a terminus, by the town (Nag's Head Lane, S.E. of the ch.); and the Grt. N. Rly. has also a short line with the terminus $\frac{1}{2}$ m. W. of the ch.; and there are stats. on the Hertford line of the Grt. E. Rly., by the Royal Small Arms Factory and at Ponders End. Enfield par. is very large, containing 12,653 acres, and being $8\frac{1}{2}$ m. long, from E. to W., and from 3 to 6 m. wide, from N. to S. The river Lea is its E. boundary, East Barnet and Hadley its W., Edmonton the S., and Cheshunt, South Mimms, and Northaw the N. The pop. in 1871 was 16,054, but this includes the eccl. districts of Clay Hill, Enfield Highway, Jesuschurch, and Trent Christchurch: the town district contained 5087 inhabitants. Enfield par. is divided into 4 quarters: *Town Quarter*, comprising the central portion of the par. and the E. side of Chase Side; *Chase Quarter*, the whole of Enfield Chase, Windmill Hill, and the W. side of Chase Side; *Bull's Cross Quarter*, Enfield Wash, Forty Hill, and the N.E. section of the par.; and *Green Street Quarter*, Green Street, Ponders End, and Enfield Highway. Enfield gave the title of Baron to the Earls of Rochford; the first Earl, who married Joan, daughter of Sir Henry Wroth of Durants, Enfield, was in 1695 created Baron of Enfield by William III. It now confers the title of Viscount on the Earl of Strafford as his 2nd title; and according to the courtesy of the peerage it is borne by his eldest son, Baron Strafford of Harmondsworth.

As will be inferred from what has been said, the houses are very widely spread. One important section, a good-sized vill. in itself, stretches for nearly 2 m. along the highroad to Hertford,—the S. portion, ad-

* Anecdotes of Painting in England, vol. ii., p. 166.

Eltham Palace

Lamb's House at Enfield (see p.186)

joining Edmonton, being known as Ponders End, the central as Enfield Highway, the N. as Enfield Wash, beyond which houses extend in a thin line to Waltham Cross; whilst on the E. by the Lea, at *Enfield Lock*, about a mile from Enfield Wash, is the Royal Small Arms Factory, with about it a cluster of small houses, inns, and shops, such as meet the requirements of the artisans, schools, a literary institute, and a chapel-of-ease. Enfield Town is on the crossroad to Barnet, about a mile W. of Enfield Highway; Baker Street, Clay Hill, and Forty Hill extending northwards from it towards Cheshunt, lined the whole way with good old red-brick mansions, standing for the most part in well-timbered grounds. Through this central portion of Enfield the New River winds from N. to S. for many a devious mile, adding variety and charm to the umbrageous scenery. Enfield Chase, the W. half of the par.,—high, breezy, and gently undulating, nearly all enclosed, yet little built upon,—contains some good seats with noble parks, and still retains traces of its old forest-like character, whilst the upper parts afford wide and beautiful views.

Enfield has eight manors, two of which, Enfield and Worcester, were formerly royal manors, each having its palace and park, and with these the historical interest of Enfield is chiefly associated. In the time of the Confessor the manor of Enfield was held by Osgar, master of the horse to King Edward. At the Domesday Survey it belonged to Geoffrey de Mandeville, a powerful Norman baron who accompanied William to the Conquest of England. The account of Enfield in the Domesday Book supports the above derivation of the name, and gives an unusually bright picture of an English village in the early years of the Conquest. Evidently it was a large village within a cleared portion of the forest. The manor is assessed at 30 hides. There is land for 34 ploughs. The lord has 4 ploughs, the villans have 16. One villan holds a hide, and 3 villans half a hide each; a priest and 17 villans one virgate each; 36 villans half a virgate each; 20 bordarii one hide and one virgate; 7 cottars 23 acres, and 5 cottars 7 acres. There are also 18 cottars holding no land, and 6 serfs or bondmen. A mill produced 10 shillings; the fishponds 8 shillings. The meadow land is sufficient for 24 ploughs; there is pasture for the cattle of the village, and pannage for 2000 hogs. The meadows produce a rental of 25*s.*; wood and pasture 43*s.*; and there is a park. The whole value was £50 in King Edward's time, and it is reckoned at the same amount now.

Unlike so many of the places enumerated in the Survey, Enfield had suffered little from Norman rapacity. It was, as we see, a village of over 100 householders, with large and small holdings, arable and pasture land, ploughs, cattle, and a large number of swine, for which the neighbouring forest afforded an unlimited supply of acorns and beech-mast (pannage); had a mill, and fishponds; a park, in which no doubt was the mansion of the lord; a priest, and, we may assume, a church; and if we find that 6 of the inhabitants were bondmen, we learn, on the other hand, that there were 5 sokemen who held 6 hides of land at their own free disposal: "they may give or sell it without the leave of their lord."

Early in the 13th cent. the manor passed, by a female heir, to Henry De Bohun, Constable of England and Earl of Hereford. In 1347 Humphrey de Bohun obtained the royal licence to fortify and embattle 10 of his manor-houses, of which Enfield was one. Alianore, or Eleanor, daughter of Humphrey last Earl of Hereford, married Thomas of Woodstock, the son of Edward III., who was murdered at Calais by direction of his nephew, Richard II. On the death of Alianore (the Duchess of Gloucester of Shakspeare's Richard II.) in 1399, the manor of Enfield was inherited by her sister Mary, wife of Henry of Lancaster (Bolingbroke), and thus became vested in the Crown, and annexed to the Duchy of Lancaster. Richard III. granted the manor to the Duke of Buckingham in 1483, but it reverted to the Crown on the Duke's attainder in the following year, and though the manor-house and demesne lands have long since been alienated, the manor remains parcel of the Duchy of Lancaster. Early in the 16th century the manor was leased to Lady Winkfield, but it reverted to the Crown in the latter part of the reign of Henry VIII. The children of Henry were brought up at Enfield, not, however, in the ancient manor-house of the Bohuns, which had before this time fallen into decay, but at Elsynge Hall, otherwise known as Enfield House; and on New Year's Day, 1543, the Scottish nobles who had been made prisoners at Solway Moss were taken, on their way back to Scotland, to visit the Prince Edward at Enfield, " and dined there that day, greatly rejoicing, as by their words and countenance it seemed, to behold so proper and towardly an Ympe." * The Princess Elizabeth was residing at Enfield at her father's death ; and Prince Edward, who was then staying at Hertford Castle, was at once brought by his uncle, the Earl of Hertford, and Sir Anthony Brown to Elsynge Hall, and there, in the presence of his sister, first informed of the death of his father and his own accession to the throne. He remained at Enfield over Sunday, so as to allow his uncle, who had determined to assume the protectorate, time to make his arrangements and secure the assent of those immediately about the king's person to his regency.† In 1552 Edward settled the manor on the Lady Elizabeth for her life, and probably on that occasion rebuilt the manor-house. His early death allowed Elizabeth brief space for the enjoyment of her new abode ; but in April 1557, whilst she was in captivity at Hatfield House, she was brought to Enfield Chase by her kindly keeper, Sir Thomas Pope, with "a retinue of 12 ladies in white satin, on ambling palfries, and 20 yeomen in green on horseback, that her grace might hunt the hart. On entering the Chase she was met by 50 archers in scarlet boots and yellow caps, armed with gilded bows, one of whom presented her with a silver headed arrow, winged with peacocks feathers." ‡

After her accession to the throne, Elizabeth was several times at Enfield with her court,—Sept. 8—22, 1561 ; July 25—30, 1564 ; July 25, 1568, and again in 1596 : of this last visit there is a note by Cary, Earl of Monmouth : "The Queen came from Theobalds to Enfield House to dinner, and she had toils set up in the park to shoot at the buck after dinner." It is uncertain whether the earlier of

these visits was to the manor-house or to Elsynge Hall ; but, apart from the statement of Lord Monmouth, there could be no doubt that the last visit was to Elsynge Hall, as she had leased the manor-house to Henry Middlemore, Esq., in 1582, for a term of 51 years, and it did not therefore revert to the Crown during her lifetime. The reversion of the house and demesne lands was granted by Charles I. in 1629, in fee to trustees for the City of London, by whom they were conveyed to Sir Nicholas Raynton, and they have since remained in private hands.

The site of the original castellated manor-house of the De Bohuns is uncertain. Camden mentions that in his time there were "almost in the middle of the Chase the ruins and rubbish of an ancient house which the common people from tradition affirm to have belonged to the Mandevilles, Earls of Sussex." *Camlet Moat*, as it is called, is now within the bounds of Trent Park, and is a large oblong quadrangle, the longest side about 150 ft., overgrown with trees and bushes, and surrounded by a wide moat. Lysons thought there were "very strong reasons for supposing the tradition illfounded. . . . Camlet Moat may have been formerly the site of the principal lodge, and the residence of the chief forester." * Robinson mentions other traditions that in his day attached to Camlet Moat. One was that it was "the lurking-place of the notorious highwayman robber *Turpin*, whose grandfather, one Nott, kept the Rose and Crown by the Brook (BullBeggar's-hole), Clay Hill." † The Rose and Crown is barely 2 m. E. of Camlet Moat, whilst Finchley, a chief theatre of his exploits, is 3 or 4 m. in the opposite direction. Another story is connected with "a deep well at the N.E. corner of the area, paved at the bottom, in which it has been pretended that an iron chest, full of treasure, is concealed, which cannot be drawn up to above a certain height ; and that the last or one of its owners, to whom the whole Chase belonged, being attainted of treason, or some high crime, hid himself in a hollow tree, and, sinking into this well, perished miserably." The house, according to the same veracious chronicler,

* Holinshed, Chronicles of England, fol. 1589.
† See Wightman's Letter to Cecil in the Introduction to Literary Remains of King Edward VI. (Roxburgh Club), p. ccxlvii.
‡ Norden ; Nichols, Progresses of Queen Elizabeth, vol. i., p. 17.

* Environs, vol. ii., p. 183.
† Hist. and Antiq. of Enfield, vol. i., 58 n.

" had brazen gates, which could be heard to shut as far as Winchmore Hill, which is at least two miles distant."

The more probable site of the original manor-house is that pointed out by Lysons in a meadow called Oldbury, near Nags Head Lane, about ¼ m. S.E. from the ch. (laid down and named *Moat* in the Ordnance Map, a little on the rt. of the lane from the ch. to Enfield Highway). It is "an oblong area of 3·35 acres [4·07 acres according to the following dimensions], surrounded by a deep and wide moat with high embankments. The south side is 132 yards long, with a vallum 12 yards high, and the north side 160 yards long, with the vallum 15 yards high, and 16 yards wide at the base. The east and west sides are 135 yards long, the vallum on the west side showing an entrance in the middle, corresponding with another in the inner vallum, which is 40 yards long at the east and west, and 96 yards at the north and south. The moat is from 10 to 12 yards wide, except on the north, where it is 32 yards wide. At the northwest corner is a mount, indicating a small keep, and opposite to it on the other side of the moat is a deep well." *

Enfield Palace, as the house which Edward VI. rebuilt for the Princess Elizabeth has long been named, is situated on the S. side of Enfield High Street, nearly opposite the ch. Originally a large, but never a very stately building, the principal front, facing the W., consisted of a centre with boldly projecting wings, bay windows, and tall gables. The present palace is only a part of Edward's building, the larger portion having been pulled down in 1792, and several small houses built with the materials. What remains is not very palatial in aspect, and is much shut in by mean shops and dwelling-houses. It comprises a portion of the centre and S. wing; is of red brick, much altered and added to. The ornamental features of the exterior have nearly all disappeared.

" A part of one of the large rooms on the ground floor," however, "still remains nearly in its original state, with its fine fretted panels of oak and its ornamental ceiling with pendents of four spreading leaves, and enrichments of the crown, the rose, and the fleur-de-lis. The chimney piece is of stone, beautifully cut and supported by Ionic and Corinthian columns, decorated with foliage and birds, and the rose and portcullis crowned ; with the arms of England and France quarterly in a garter, and the royal supporters, a lion and a dragon. Below is the motto, *Sola salus servire Deo sunt cætera fraudes.*. The letters E. R. are on this chimney piece, and were formerly on each side of the wings of the principal building. The monogram is clearly that of Edward VI., as the same room contains part of another chimney piece which was removed from one of the upper apartments, with nearly the same ornaments, and the motto, *Vt ros super herbam est benevolentia Regis,* alluding no doubt to the royal grant. Several of the ceilings in the upper rooms are decorated in a similar manner to those below." *

The palace was let by Sir Nicholas Raynton in 1635 to Sir Thomas Trevor, Baron of the Exchequer, who held it till his death in 1656. About 1660 it was let to Robt. Uvedale, LL.D., master of the Grammar School; who established an academy in it which soon acquired a great reputation, his pupils in the plague year, 1665, including the Earl of Huntingdon, Viscount Kilmorey, Lord Coleraine, Sir Jeremy Sambrooke, Bart., and sons of Sir Baldwin Wyke, Bart., and other persons of distinction.[†] Dr. Uvedale was much attached to the study of botany, corresponded with the leading contemporary botanists, and formed an almost unequalled *hortus siccus*, which was purchased for a large sum by Sir Robert Walpole, and is now in the British Museum. His garden at the palace is the subject of a very eulogistic notice in a view of the gardens around London in 1691, by J. Gibson.[‡]

" Dr. Uvedale, of Enfield, is a great lover of plants, and, having an extraordinary art in managing them, is become master of the greatest and choicest collection of exotic greens that is perhaps anywhere in this land. His greens take up six or seven houses or roomsteads.[§] His orange trees and largest myrtles fill up his biggest house, and another house is filled with myrtles of a less size, and those more nice and curious plants that need closer keeping are in warmer rooms, and some of them stand where he thinks fit. His flowers are choice, his stock numerous, and his culture of them very methodical and curious ; but to speak of the garden, in the whole, it does not lie fine to please the eye, his delight and care lying more in the ordering particular plants, than in the pleasing view and form of his garden."

His connection with the palace is, how-

---

* Ford's Enfield, p. 23 ; Lysons, Environs, vol. ii., p. 183 ; Robinson's Hist. of Enfield, vol. i., p. 61.

* Ford's Enfield, p. 25.
+ Robinson's Hist. of Enfield, vol i., p. 48.
‡ Archæologia, vol. xii., p. 188.
§ We here see the origin of the term "greenhouse."

ever, now best preserved by the great *cedar* immediately behind the house, which forms a conspicuous object from many parts of the town, and is justly prized by the inhabitants. It is believed to be the first cedar planted in this country, and "tradition hands down to us that the plant was brought immediately from Mount Libanus in a portmanteau, probably by one of his scholars."[*] Planted between 1662 and 1670, in 1779 it had attained a height of 45 ft. 9 in., though 8 ft. of the top was broken off by a high wind in 1703. In Nov. 1794 "a strong gale from the N.W. deprived it of the whole of the upper part, which fell with a tremendous crash, and in its fall several of the lower branches were much injured." In 1793 it measured 13 ft. 6 in. in girth, and in 1873, 16 ft. 2 in., at 3 ft. from the ground.[+] A seedling from this tree, planted by Mr. Ford at Old Park in 1846, measured in 1873, 5 ft. 7 in. in circumference; and another planted there in 1851 had in 1873 attained a height of 33 ft.[‡]

Old Park was the Home Park of Enfield Manor House, and was known as the Frith, or *Parcus Intrinsecus*, to distinguish it from the Chase, which was the Outer Park, *Parcus Extrinsecus*, or as it was commonly called the Great Park. Old Park, with the hop-garden and the warren, was given by Charles II. in 1660 to George Monk, first Duke of Albemarle. By the death of the second duchess it escheated to the Crown, and was granted by William III., in 1689, to the Earl of Rutland; it afterwards passed through various hands, and is now the property and residence of Edw. Ford, Esq., author of the History of Enfield. The house appears to have been originally a ranger's lodge of the time of James I.; parts have been pulled down, and the remainder transformed into a comparatively modern residence: but there "still remain in the library the original open chimney and hearth with fire-dogs, and a curious old reredos, with figures of the time of

James I."[*] Camden mentions as existing in his time, on the lawn in front of the house, "a Roman Oppidum, surrounded on three sides by a circular entrenchment from which various interesting relics have, at different times, been obtained." The park and grounds contain some remarkably fine oaks; an ilex which "rests its branches on the ground in every direction, and has a spread of upwards of 70 feet in diameter;" and a Portugal laurel 30 ft. high, and 105 ft. in diameter, the largest probably in England. *Chase Side House*, the pleasant residence of Philip Twells, Esq., M.P.; and *Chase Park*, the seat of Mrs. Adams, were, with their fine grounds, formerly parts of Old Park.

The *Parcus Extrinsecus*, ENFIELD CHASE, will be noticed under that heading.

Worcesters, for awhile another royal manor, belonged in the reign of Edward II. to Sir Bartholomew de Enefield; in 1374 was purchased by John Wroth, from whose daughter and heir two-thirds of the manor passed to her cousin, Sir John Tiptoft, and on his death to his son, the Earl of Worcester, Lord High Treasurer to Henry VI., who was executed in 1471: "then did the axe at one blow cut off more learning in England than was left in the heads of all the surviving nobility."[+] His estates were forfeited, but restored by Edward IV. to his son, upon whose death, without succession, the manor became the property of Thomas Lord Roos, who had married Philippa, sister of the first Earl of Worcester. From Lord Roos it passed to Sir Thomas Lovell, K.G., Treasurer of the Household, and one of the executors of Henry VII. Lovell lived here many years, and probably rebuilt the house: Lincoln's Inn gateway, Chancery Lane, was built by him. He was in 1516 honoured with a visit, at his house at Enfield, by Margaret, Dowager Queen of Scots, and sister of Henry VIII. Lovell died at his manor-house 1524, and Lysons gives a long account of the ceremonies at his funeral (one of extraordinary pomp), and the procession to Holywell Priory, Shoreditch, where he was interred, copied from the original in the Heralds' College. From Lovell the manor descended to

---

* Robinson.
+ Dr. Robinson (Hist. of Enfield, vol. i., p. 116) gives a diagram of the tree, with admeasurements made in 1821, showing the girth at 12 different places: its perpendicular height was then 64 ft. 8 in.
‡ Ford's Enfield, p. 171.

* Ford.
† Fuller, Worthies (Cambridgeshire).

Thomas Earl of Rutland, grandson of Eleanor, another of the coheirs of Lord Roos. In 1540, the manor with the manor-house, Elsynge Hall, was given by the Earl of Rutland to Henry VIII. As we have seen, Henry employed it as a nursery for his children. Edward VI. settled the manor, along with that of Enfield, on his sister Elizabeth for her life; and Elizabeth, after her accession to the throne, on several occasions, kept her court at Elsynge Hall, or Enfield House, as it was now commonly called. By Elizabeth, or James, the manor was granted to Cecil, 1st Earl of Salisbury, but a special reservation was made of the manor-house. In 1616, the 2nd Earl of Salisbury alienated the manor to Nicholas Raynton, who was already in possession of the "very ancient house called Enfield House (otherwise Elsynge Hall)." It afterwards passed successively to the Wolstenholmes and Armstrongs, and in 1799 was purchased by James Meyer, whose great-nephew is the present owner.

Elsynge Hall has long been pulled down, and the place where it stood forgotten. Lysons, writing at the end of the 18th cent.,* says, "its site is not now known." He thought it probable, however, that it stood about a quarter of a mile from Forty Hall, near the stream of water which runs to Enfield Wash, where the inequalities of the ground and the remains of fish-ponds show there has been a building, and where tradition says that Queen Mary had a palace. Dr. Robinson, 20 years later, repeats Lysons' statement. According to Mr. Ford, however, the site was more to the W., " and is still discernible towards the bottom of the avenue at Forty Hall, between the house and the Maiden-bridge-brook. Here, in dry seasons, the outlines of an extensive fabric may be traced on the ground by the withering of the grass;—the remains of foundations have frequently been dug up, and about the year 1830, under a lime tree in the avenue, an unfortunate bullock fell through the decayed brickwork into a vault below." †

The present manor-house of Worcesters is *Forty Hall* (Jas. Meyer, Esq.), at Forty Hill, about 1½ m. N.E. from the ch., on the

l. of the road to Cheshunt. The house, a large and stately brick mansion, was built, 1629-32, by Inigo Jones for Sir Nicholas Raynton. The principal rooms are large, well-proportioned, and have panelled ceilings, with good scrollwork. The house contains some good pictures : among others, ' Uriah conveying the letter from David,' purchased at the Lansdowne sale 1800, as by *Raphael*, "from the Orleans collection," but we find no such picture in the catalogue of that collection; the 'Three Marys,' by *Annibale Carracci*; a 'Holy Family,' by *Rubens*; 'The Miraculous Draught of Fishes,' by *D. Teniers*; 'The Toilet,' by *G. Metzu*; The Carnival, St. Mark's, *Canaletto*; two landscapes by *Both*, from the Lansdowne collection, and a·fine portrait of Sir N. Raynton by *Dobson*. The quaint but picturesque gateway leading to the stables was erected by Inigo Jones. The house stands in a richly timbered park of some 280 acres. *Obs.* the fine cedars on the lawn : one has a clean trunk for a height of 60 ft. ; another is 15 ft. in girth at 4 ft. from the ground ; a third 13 ft. 8 in. at 4 ft., with a spread of branches 92 ft. in diameter. The splendid double avenue of limes was planted by Sir N. Raynton in the reign of Charles I. The horse-chesnut near the lodge entrance of Forty Hall is that selected by Loudon, in his 'Arboretum,' as a grand specimen of the tree in its prime : it is 80 ft. high, and has a girth of 11 ft. at 4 ft. from the ground. In the wood is a magnificent Spanish chesnut above 99 ft. high, with a clear stem for upwards of 70 ft., and a nobly spreading head : the trunk is 15 ft. 7 in. at 5 ft. from the ground.*

Forty Hill has been long famous for its trees. The elms (well known by Lewis's engraving, 1818), though still fine, are greatly reduced in number and grandeur. One noble tree was cut down to form the keel of the British Queen, "the largest vessel that had then been built, being 35 ft. longer than any ship in the British navy; " and since then several more of the trees have been sacrificed for a like purpose. The largest of the remaining trees lost its head in a great storm in 1863. "This tree measured at the ground 26 ft. ; and at 4 ft., 18 ft.

---

* Environs, 1st ed., 1791 ; 2nd, 1810.
† History of Enfield, p. 75.

* Ford.

12

6 in." * From several parts of Forty Hill the wooded character of the neighbourhood is well seen; and extensive distant views are obtained. On its N. side is *Myddleton House* (H. C. B. Bowles, Esq.), the beautiful grounds of which adjoin those of Forty Hall. It was built on the site of an old house called Bowling Green, in 1818, by H. C. Bowles, Esq., and was named in honour of Sir Hugh Myddleton, to whose patriotism and energy London is indebted for the New River. Mr. Bowles was the fortunate possessor of shares in the N. R. Company; the river runs through and is a great ornament to the grounds, and Sir Hugh lived in the vicinity whilst this portion of the works was being constructed. The house has been enlarged by its present owner, and, though not of much architectural value, is a spacious and comfortable looking mansion. Included in the estate is the site of the old *White Webbs House*, given by Queen Elizabeth to her physician, Dr. Huicks; but which fell under suspicion at the time of the Gunpowder Plot, in consequence of its having been ascertained that Guido Vaux had been in the habit of visiting it prior to his apprehension, that "Mrs. Vaux had spent a month there, when mass was said by a priest," indeed, as Guido afterwards admitted, had "taken the house and furnished it at her own expense," and that Garnet (the Jesuit) had been there under assumed names. The house was searched, but the Report to the Council says "the search ended in the discovery of Popish books and relics, but no papers or munitions, and the house was found to be full of trapdoors and passages." The old house, which was of considerable extent, was pulled down in 1790. Its site was near White Webbs Lane, formerly known as Rome Lane—probably from some tradition connecting it with the Plot. "The remains of the fish-ponds and orchards are still discernible, and the ale house known as the King and Tinker probably still retains some portions of the old outbuildings. With this little beershop is popularly identified the ballad of King James and the Tinker, the incident of which is supposed to have occurred during the residence of James I. at Theobalds." † The tradition, though Mr. Ford

favours it, will hardly hold water. The ballad of 'King James and the Tinkler' is eminently a border ballad, and is popular throughout the northern counties; *tinkler* is the northern term for a tinker, but was never used, so far as we know, in the south: and in the received version of the ballad (though not in that printed by Mr. Ford), the tinkler says, "The king's on the *Border* a chasing the deer." * The ballad must therefore, we fear, be dissociated from Enfield, notwithstanding the beerhouse sign. The present *White Webbs Park* dates from 1787, when the estate was purchased by Dr. Wilkinson, who increased the domain and built the house in 1791. House and park have been enlarged by the present owner, H. Wilkinson, Esq. The park now comprises 250 acres, 100 of which are woodland, and covered with oak and underwood, a relic of the old Chase; the remainder of the park is also rich in timber, whilst on the hill-top is a thick plantation of Scotch firs, which form a conspicuous object from the surrounding country. The house contains a collection of paintings (including portraits of the Dukes of Monti Leoni, fulllength, by *Velasquez*, from the Auldjo collection; John Locke, by *Kneller;* portraits of his daughters, and a landscape, by *Gainsborough;* Charity, by *Sir J. Reynolds;* portrait of himself, by *Wilson;* Lady Jersey, and a son of Col. Hill, by *Sir Thomas Lawrence;* and others attributed to *Tintoretto, Rosalba, Zucchero, Greuze,* etc.); terra-cottas by *Donatelli, Flaxman,* etc.; miniatures (among others, one of Alfieri with the autograph of Byron); Limoges enamels, and enamels by *Bone* and *Petitot;* Della Robbia, Capo di Monte, and Sèvres wares; carved ivories; bronzes; buhl, tortoiseshell, and other fancy cabinets, and old furniture; vases, busts, and an illuminated missal from Newstead Abbey.

Enfield Town, as we have said, stands nearly midway between the Chase and Enfield Highway, and occupies a tolerably central position in the wide parish. Edward I., in 1303, granted by charter a licence to Humphrey de Bohun and his heirs to hold a market at Enfield weekly

---

* Ford.   † Ford's Enfield, p. 79.

* Mr. Ford's version reads, "the King is a hunting the fair fallow deer"—which has hardly the old ballad ring.

on Mondays. James I. renewed the grant (altering the day, however, to Saturday), and at the same time established a Court of Pie Powder. The market has long been abandoned, and the Pie Powder forgotten, but the market-place in the centre of the town remains unbuilt on, and imparts to it an open characteristic aspect. Formerly it must have been eminently picturesque. The main street passes through the market-place. On one side was the palace, its great cedar rising above it, and none of the mean shops about it which now nearly conceal it from the view. On the other side was the broad open market-place, flanked on one hand by a large quaintly gabled inn, with its swinging sign suspended from an elaborate handwrought iron standard, and on the other an ancient wooden tenement. The farther or N. side of the square was bordered by a smaller hostelry (the King's Head, still standing), and the tower and S. side of the old ch. In the centre of the place, and in front of the ch., stood the market-house, an octagonal wooden building, consisting merely of a tall roof supported on a central and 8 outer columns. Near the market-house stood the stocks and whipping-post, and there was a portable pillory—only to be brought into the square, however, on special occasions. Even as late as 1827, if we may trust a charming etching of that date by George Cooke from a drawing by Stanfield, the market-place retained much of its old character. The large inn, with its double gable of Jacobean type and swinging sign, was still there (it is now converted into a very sober-looking office of the Local Board), as well as the rude old half-plaster houses beside it; but the stocks were gone, and the market-house had just given place to the present Market Cross—built in 1826,—a poor attempt at a Gothic cross in brick, covered with cement: restored 1866. The stocks may be found by the police-station; but the whipping-post and pillory have disappeared altogether.

The *Church* (St. Andrew) stands, as has been said, on the N. side of the market-place, and within a spacious but over-crowded ch.-yard. It is of flint and stone, but covered externally with cement, Perpendicular in style, and consists of nave, with clerestorey, chancel, and aisles, W. tower (in which is a peal of 8 bells), and

S. porch. The long side of the ch., lying parallel to the market-place, plaster-covered, and having continuous lines of ugly (and comparatively modern) battlements alike on tower, nave, aisles, and chancel, can hardly be called picturesque, and certainly is not impressive. Of old the monotony was broken by a quaint muniment-house with a round stair turret, built upon, and projecting over the S. porch, but this was removed when the ch. was enlarged in 1824. The *interior* is of more interest. It has a larger and loftier look than you anticipate as you *descend* to it—the floor being some feet below the ch.-yard, which has risen by the slow accumulation of ages. The nave is separated from the chancel by a lofty arch; the aisles run the whole length of both nave and chancel, making the interior a parallelogram 100 ft. long and 63 ft. wide. There are galleries, but they are set well back, and by no means injure the appearance of the building. The ch. has been several times altered, repaired, and 're-stored;' the last and most thorough restoration of the interior being made in 1866, when, in addition to substantial and decorative repairs, new roofs were placed on the nave, aisles, and chancel. From the portions of old walls, windows, etc., then brought to light, it is clear that though seemingly of the Perp. period, the ch. has grown into its present form by extension and reconstruction. The modified lancet window with the hagioscope under it in the S. wall of the chancel, opened in the restoration of 1866, shows that portion of the ch. to be of late E.E. date: this was of course the outer wall of the chancel; the aisle was a much later addition. The mouldings of the nave and chancel arches show the body of the ch. to be of the 14th cent.; the clerestorey is late 15th; the N. aisle was rebuilt, or extended, in the 16th cent. The S. aisle was built, or rebuilt, as late as 1824. The stencil decoration of the chancel, the encaustic tiles and garish glass in the E. window, all date from 1866. The sedilia and piscina occupy the place of those uncovered in 1852, but are themselves modern. *Obs.* the recess in piers of chancel arch for staircases to the rood-loft.

Monts.—The oldest mont. is one of great interest; it is an altar-tomb to the Lady

Jocosa (or Joyce), daughter and coheiress of Charlton, Lord Powes, and wife of John Baron Tiptoft, d. 1446, and stands within the E. arch on the N. side of the chancel; the canopy over it is of later date. The tomb has on each side 4 panels with shields of arms, and on the top a slab of grey Purbeck marble, on which is inlaid a remarkably fine and well-preserved *brass*, with a full-length effigy of Lady Tiptoft, her hands raised and joined as in prayer, under a triple cusped and crocketed conopy. From the shafts which support the canopy hang 6 shields bearing the arms of Powes, Tiptoft, and Holland. At the angles were emblems of the Evangelists, of which, however, only that of St. Matthew remains, though in the engraving of the brass in Robinson (1823) 3 are figured. Round the margin is the insc. setting forth the lady's connections and date of decease, and ending with the usual invocation. The brass will interest the student of costume. The lady wears a flowing dress deeply edged with ermine, which covers the feet, and over it an ermine surcoat, and sleeveless jacket with a narrow border of ermine. Over all is a long heraldic cloak embroidered with the lions of Powes and Holland, fastened by a richly jewelled cord, the long ends of which terminate in tassels. The head-dress is the large and elaborate horned coiffure of the time, bordered with jewels, and surmounted with a coronet. Her hair is concealed by a cover-chef. A rich necklace with a pendent jewel, narrow bracelets on her wrists, and a ring on the third finger of her right hand, complete the costume. It may be compared with the somewhat earlier, but very similar, brass of Eleanor de Bohun, Duchess of Gloucester, in Westminster Abbey. The canopy above the tomb was erected in the 16th cent., by an Earl of Rutland, in memory of one of his ancestors, but, as there are on it only armorial bearings without an inscription, it is uncertain to which : it has lately been restored at the expense of the Duke of Rutland. Gough, the antiquary, Dr. Sherwen, and Mr. Schnebbelie, the draughtsman to the Soc. of Antiquaries, explored the vault beneath the tomb, Oct. 23rd, 1788, but found only fragments of a wooden coffin, and a few mouldering bones. By the vestry door in the N. chancel aisle is a lofty and very

elaborate marble monument to Sir Nicholas Raynton, of Forty Hall (d. 1646), and his wife Rebecca (d. 1640). In the principal storey, under a canopy borne on 2 Corinthian columns of black marble, is the recumbent effigy of Sir Nicholas, in full armour, partly covered with the robe of Lord Mayor. He has a massive collar of SS., roses and portcullis ; his head raised, and leaning on his right hand, the elbow resting on a cushion. In the stage below is a like recumbent effigy of his wife, habited as Lady Mayoress with ruff and chain, her l. arm resting on a cushion, and holding a book in her right hand. Beneath are smaller effigies of Sir Nicholas and Lady Raynton kneeling on opposite sides of a desk, with books open before them, 2 sons kneeling behind the knight, and 3 daughters behind the lady, while at the foot of the desk is an infant in a cradle. At the summit, rising from a broken pediment, are the shield and crest of Raynton, and above it a smaller shield of Moulton, and on the sides Raynton, and Raynton impaling Moulton. In the S. aisle is a mural mont. of coloured marble with small effigies of a man and woman kneeling at a desk (the man's head gone), to Dorothie, wife of Robert Middlemore (d. 1646). Over it a larger mont. to Francis Evington, d. 1614, with small kneeling effigy. In S. chancel aisle, an elaborate marble mont., with good bust, under tent drapery, of Thomas Stringer, Esq., M.P., of Durants, d. 1706. N. aisle, a kneeling effigy of Robert Deicrowe, d. 1586. Around the walls are various mural monts. to local magnates and parochial benefactors, but the only one of any general interest is that to John Abernethy, the surgeon, who died at Enfield, 1831. On the floor of the N. aisle are *brasses* of William Smith, d. 1592, "who in his life served king Henry VIII., king Edward VI., Queen Marie, and now Queen Elizabeth," and Jane his wife. On the same slab are indents for children, but the brasses are gone. Among the tombs in the ch.-yard are those of Lord and Lady Napier of Murchiston, and various local celebrities.

The plain old red-brick building, with 3 gables, on the W. side of the ch.-yard is the *Grammar School*, founded towards the end of the 16th cent. : long ill-managed, it was in 1873 closed, preparatory to being reopened under a new scheme drawn up by the Endowed Schools Commissioners.

A chapel of ease to the mother ch. (St. Michael and All Angels) was built in 1873, chiefly at the cost of G. Batters, Esq., of Brigadier Hill, N. of the town. It is a good E.E. edifice, designed by Messrs. Slater and Carpenter, and will consist of nave, aisles, apsidal chancel, and tower ; but the tower and western portion of the nave are left for erection hereafter. At *Enfield Highway* is the district ch. of St. James, erected in 1831, and to which a new chancel, with painted glass windows, was added in 1863 by the Rev. J. Harman, as a memorial to his wife. Jesus Church, *Forty Hill,* was erected and endowed in 1835 by C. P. Meyer, Esq., of Forty Hall. St. John the Baptist, *Clay Hill,* is a graceful little E.E. ch. of brick and stone, with a bell-cote at the W., built, with the parsonage, in 1857, from the designs of Mr. P. St. Aubyn : the *int.* is admirably fitted, and all the windows are filled with painted glass. Christ Church, *Cock Fosters,* or Trent Christ Church, as the eccl. dist. of 730 inhabitants is called, is a plain ivy-covered building erected in 1837, at the cost of R. C. L. Bevan, Esq., of Trent Park.

Though Enfield Town is the centre of the parish, contains the mother ch., some good shops, the market cross, and is the seat of the petty sessions and the local and parochial boards, a much larger portion of the population is settled in *Enfield Highway,* which stretches along the Hertford road from Ponders End on the S. to beyond Enfield Wash on the N., with a good many streets running off on the rt. towards the Lea, along which are several large factories. The eccl. dist. of Enfield Highway had in 1871 a population of 8027, including that of the colony which has grown up in connection with the Royal Small Arms Factory.

Ponders End is now a busy hamlet, having its rly. stat. (Grt. E., Cambridge line) in South Street, Rly. Tavern, and several good inns, gas and water works, and large factories. It still contrives, however, though with difficulty, to sustain somewhat of its old character of rural gentility. Here was of old the manor-house of

Durants, Durance, or *Durrant's Har-*

bour. In the reign of Edward I. the manor belonged to Richard de Plessitis, from whom it passed, 1336, by marriage to Thomas Durant, whose only daughter, Maud, marrying John Wroth, carried it to the Wroth family, in whose possession it remained till 1673, when the executors of Sir Henry Wroth (d. 1671) sold the manor to Sir Thomas Stringer, who married a daughter of the notorious Judge Jeffreys (a sometime resident at Enfield, and a frequent visitor at Durants). It has since changed hands frequently, and is now the property of Woodham Connop, Esq. The Manor House, a moated house with bridge, gate-house, posterns, etc., stood N. of Ponders End, a little E. of the highroad. It was accidentally burned towards the end of the 18th cent., from too many logs being heaped on the hall fire, at a meeting of tenants. Sir Thomas Wroth, "of the Bedchamber and a favorite to King Edward VI." is celebrated by Fuller as a sufferer and exile for conscience' sake under the Marian persecution.[*] Sir Robert Wroth (d. 1614) was the friend of Ben Jonson, who has addressed to him one of the happiest of his epistles :—

> " How blessèd art thou, canst love the country, Wroth,
> Whether by choice, or fate, or both !
> And though so near the City, and the Court,
> Art ta'en with neither's vice nor sport.
>
> * * * *
>
> But canst at home, in thy securer rest,
> Live with unbought provision blest ;
> Free from proud porches, or the gilded roofs,
> 'Mongst lowing herds, and solid hoofs ;
> Along the curlèd woods, and painted meads,
> Through which a serpent river leads
> To some cool courteous shade, which he calls his,
> And makes sleep softer than it is.
> Or if thou list the night in watch to break,
> A-bed canst hear the loud stag speak,
> In spring, oft rousèd for thy Master's sport,
> Who for it makes thy House his Court." [†]

The last line is of course an allusion to James I., who was a frequent visitor at Durants when hunting the deer at Enfield Chase. "To the noble Lady, the Lady Mary Wroth," wife of Sir Robert, and daughter of Robert Sidney, Earl of Leicester, Jonson not only dedicated his 'Alchemist,' but inscribed a Sonnet, in

[*] Church Hist. of Britain (Dedication of B. v., Sect. iii., to the Right Worshipful Sir Henry Wroth, Knt.) ; Worthies of England (Middlesex).

[†] Ben Jonson, The Forest, iii.

which he declares that since he has read her verses he has become

" A better lover, and much better Poët,
Nor is my Muse, or I, asham'd to owe it." *

Lincoln House (J. F. Bunting, Esq.), on the W. side of the road at Ponders End, is an old mansion, said to have been the residence of William Wickham, Bp. of Lincoln, a native of Enfield, 1594, and afterwards of the 2nd and 3rd Earls of Lincoln, 1600—1612. It appears to have been originally an irregular but picturesque brick building, with buttress-like pilasters, but a large portion of the house was burned down some years since, and has been altered in rebuilding. Before the alterations, the hall and principal rooms had elaborately ornamented ceilings, panelled wainscoting on the walls, and heraldic glass in the windows.

Enfield Wash, at the N. end of Enfield Highway, is a busy populous place with a rly. stat. (Ordnance Factory ½ m. E. of the highroad), many shops, inns, and good private residences. It owes its name to the little stream which, rising in the Chase, here crossed the road, and spreading out made the *wash*, through which horses and carriages had to flounder, but which is now carried under it, and turning to the S.E., falls into the Lea a little below the Ordnance Factory. A hut on the E. side of the road at Enfield Wash, at the corner of the lane leading to the marsh, was the asserted theatre of the strange case of Elizabeth Canning, which in the middle of the last century created an amount of excitement in the country comparable in a small way to that of the Claimant in our own time. Canning was a servant who, having had a holiday on New Year's Day, 1753, was returning home at night when, as she affirmed, on passing the gate of Bethleham Hospital she was attacked by two men, robbed, maltreated, and dragged away in a half-insensible condition to a cottage, which she afterwards found was that kept by Mother Wells, a gipsey at Enfield Wash. There, besides Wells, were another gipsey named Mary Squires (who assisted in further robbing her, and cut off her stays), and a young woman named Hall. In this den she was kept, with only an occasional crust of

* Underwoods, p. 196, ed. 1640.

bread and water, for a month, when she managed to escape by pulling down a board nailed in front of a window, and dropping into the lane. On gaining the road, she inquired the way to London, and reached her home at night in a wretched condition. Her statement naturally excited great commiseration. Search was made, she identified the house and room in which she had been kept, and (though the room differed in many respects from her description) no doubt at this time seems to have been entertained as to the truth of her story. The three women were taken into custody, and Wells and Squires committed for trial. Hall was discharged, but, being again apprehended on a warrant, she made a confession confirming in the main the statements of Canning. At the trial Canning and Hall repeated their respective stories : the two gipseys were convicted; Wells was sentenced to be burnt in the hand and imprisoned, and Squires to be hanged. But now came a strong reaction. The contradictions in the evidence of Canning led to private inquiries, and the Lord Mayor (Gascoigne) laid the result before the King, who referred the memorial to the Attorney and Solicitor General, on whose recommendation the two women were pardoned, and Canning prosecuted for perjury. Subscriptions were raised for conducting her defence; but after a patient trial of seven days she was found guilty, and sentenced to a month's imprisonment, and transportation for seven years. The town was in an uproar. Every one was either a *Canningite* or an *Egyptian*. The mob, who were of the former, attacked the Lord Mayor, broke the windows of his coach, and committed other excesses. The wealthier of her supporters published pamphlets,* and got up subscriptions. Orator Henley preached in her favour, and one zealot found an

* Lysons, Environs, vol. ii., pp. 212-13, gives a list of 36 pamphlets on the Canning case, published at prices varying from 6*d.* to 6*s.*, and 14 prints, including views and ground-plans of the house, and portraits of the several personages. Borrow, 'Romano Lavo-Lil,' p. 217, has a very inaccurate account of the affair. Among other things he says—"Two gipsy women were burnt in the hand in the most cruel and frightful manner, ... and two gipsy men, their relations, sentenced to be hanged, for running away with" the "horrible wench."

indisputable proof of her innocence and veracity in certain conjunctions of the heavenly bodies. What follows reads like a leaf out of one of De Foe's novels. Several hundred pounds being subscribed for her benefit, she was "allowed to transport herself," *i.e.*, choose her ship and pay for her passage, to America. There, practically a free woman, the little fortune with which her supporters had provided her, enabled her to make what is termed "a very advantageous marriage" with a planter, and she had a prosperous career till her death in 1773.

East of Enfield Wash is

THE ROYAL SMALL ARMS FACTORY, situated at Enfield Lock, between the river Lea and the Lea and Stour Navigation, about 1¼ m. from the main road at Enfield Wash. It is, however, best reached from the *Ordnance Factory Stat.* of the Grt. E. Rly. (Cambridge line): cross the line and continue along Armoury Lane, ½ m., to the Lea Navigation, where turn to the rt., and at the end of the lane cross the bridge, and the gate is on the l. The factory covers a large area; the buildings, which occupy three sides of a quadrangle, are neat and substantial in appearance, but quite devoid of ornament; the interior a series of large workrooms, filled with machinery of the highest class, and much of it of exceeding beauty and refinement. The first room you enter, called the *Action Shop*, from everything relating to the action (or breechloading and lock apparatus) being finished in it, is 200 ft. by 219 ft., and contains some 800 machines.

A small factory was founded by the Government at Enfield early in the century, but the present establishment is of much more recent date. Machinery for the manufacture of rifles was introduced from America, and the Enfield Factory set to work in January 1857. At first the machinery was placed under the supervision of Mr. Perkins, who brought it over from America, and remained at the factory about 3 years; since then it has been managed entirely by the factory officials, the first Superintendent of the Factory being Colonel Manley Dixon, R.A., who retained that post till 1872, when he was succeeded by Colonel Fraser, the present Superintendent. The rifle originally produced was that known as the *Enfield;* the

machinery was afterwards modified to produce the Snider, and to convert the Enfield into that arm. Since 1872 it has been entirely remodelled to manufacture the Martini-Henry, the most perfect military arm yet produced. The remodelling and development of the machinery has been going on with wonderful rapidity during the past two years, with a continuous extension of the automatic principle, and with the constant aim of improving the quality and lessening the cost of manufacture. The Enfield machinery is probably the most perfect in any gun-making establishment, whether private or governmental, extant.

A general idea of the works may perhaps be most readily given by stating briefly what is shown to visitors. The butt and stock, of walnut, are obtained, roughly blocked out, from Italy. The butt is here passed in succession through a series of ingenious turning machines, which, without any hand-labour, shape, smooth, and polish it, the cutting apparatus, with a curious movement, following the varying curves of a steel guide the exact size and shape of the finished butt, the last machine leaving it perfect in form and finish, and ready to be transferred to a new set which cut out the parts required for the reception of the action, true to the 500th of an inch. The fore-end, from its simple character, is shaped and finished with still greater celerity and equal accuracy, a barrel taken at hazard at once fitting exactly into the groove of any finished stock without the slightest alteration or adjustment of either.

The *barrel* in the rough, merely a steel rod pierced through, has hitherto been obtained from private firms (mostly Sheffield houses), but rolling mills are being erected, so that shortly the whole process of manufacture will be conducted at Enfield. The grinding of the barrel, the most unhealthy of manufacturing processes—it is said a grinder scarcely ever lives to be more than 40—has hitherto been carried on by hand-labour, it being the only important exception to the automatic character of the manufacture. Now, however, after numberless experiments, a simple and beautiful machine has been perfected at the factory (all attempts to produce such a machine at Birmingham, Liège, and elsewhere having failed),* and before this volume is in the hands of the reader, grinding will have been replaced by turning, and the process be as innocuous as any other branch of the manufacture. The boring, rifling, and finishing are effected with extraordinary rapidity by automatic machines of great seeming simplicity. These, but especially the rifling processes, are among the most beautiful and interesting in the factory. The barrel has 7 grooves, which make 1 turn in 22 inches. They are formed by passing a cutting tool 7 times through each groove in the barrel, and so exquisitely accurate is the work that the barrel with its grooves bears to be tested to the 1000th of an inch. The size of the barrel and depth of the grooves are tested by hardened steel gauges, the straightness and finish of the bore having previously been tested by 'shading.' A mechanical test for ascertaining the straightness of the tube before rifling has been lately introduced, which effects the same object as the shading with greater rapidity, and therefore economy. The polishing and browning of the barrels, fixing studs, adjusting sights, etc., are executed in an adjoining room. Every barrel, we should have stated, is proved by fixed charges of gunpowder at the principal stages of the manufacture, and again, when finished, at the long range.

Just as the stock and barrel, so may the *action* be followed step by step, from commencement to completion. In the *Smithery*, in which there are 180 dome furnaces, the action frame, breech block, or body, which is a frame about 5 in. long, 1½ wide and 3 deep, with thin sides and thick ends, and open at top and bottom, is forged from a solid steel bar, heated red-hot, and, with the aid of dies and punches, brought into shape by four blows of a steam hammer. Here also the lever, trigger, tumbler, striker, guard, and other parts of the breech action are forged and prepared for the finishing-room. The finishing of these several parts, the making and testing of the spring, and the fitting of the firing mechanism generally, cannot fail to interest the visitor, who will be hardly less struck

by the curious adaptive pliability of several of the tools, than by the precision of the results. All, or nearly all, the higher class tools, machinery, and gauges are made in the factory, and the tool-room is to a mechanician one of the most interesting rooms in the establishment.

The great aim in these works has been not merely to produce the best and most effective weapon ever put into the hands of a private soldier, and to produce it at the lowest possible cost by means of automatic machinery, but to make all the separate parts of the instrument interchangeable, so that the several parts being kept in store, if any part of a rifle be damaged or rendered unserviceable, the regimental armourer has merely to remove the injured portion, take the corresponding piece from his repository, and, such is the unerring precision with which it is made, at once fit it into its place without trouble or loss of time. The immense value of such a system in actual service, and its convenience and economy at all times, are self-evident. The firing mechanism is much simpler than that of any other breech-loader; the Snider breech, for example, being composed of 39 pieces, and the Enfield of 50, while the Martini-Henry has only 27.

Ordinarily, from 1600 to 1800 finished rifles are turned out at the factory every week; but under pressure (as in April 1873), 3300 per week have been made. The recent improvements in the machinery will, with the alterations in progress, it is believed, before long, enable the Factory to produce 6000 rifles a week if required. But whilst the manufacture of new rifles is the chief business of the Factory, swords and bayonets are also made. At present about 1500 artizans are employed in the Factory, the larger part of whom are engaged in attending on the automatic machines, and paid by piecework; the rest are skilled workmen employed as overlookers, and in testing the work in its various stages.*

The Royal Small Arms Factory is open to visitors (without previous application)

---

* The only successful machine for grinding gun-barrels was too complex and costly for ordinary military arms.

* We have to acknowledge our obligation to Colonel Fraser, the Superintendent of the Factory, for the ready courtesy with which he afforded us access to all parts of the establishment; and to Lt.-Colonel Dyer, R.A., the Assist. Superintendent, for his kindly guidance and information.

every Monday and Thursday, from 9 till 12 a.m., and from 2 till 4 p.m. The proof-house, immediately S. of the Factory, and the Long Range a little higher up the Lea, are of course not open to visitors.

Clay Hill, N.W. of Forty Hill, is a pretty secluded hamlet lying to the left of Baker Street, containing many comfortable old houses nestling among contemporary trees, a neat inn (the *Fallow Buck*), and the dainty little ch. noticed above. Among the seats in the neighbourhood is *Claysmore* (J. W. Bosanquet, Esq.), a stately mansion, celebrated in the days of its late owner, Mr. Harman, for its artistic contents: the grounds are extensive, varied, and informal, and command wide views over the Chase. *Bull's Cross* (Inn, the *Pied Bull*), immediately beyond Forty Hill, is another quiet little hamlet, believed to have derived its name from a cross which of old stood here: in a deed of 1483 it is named Bedell's Cross. From it there is a most pleasant private road (the gates are closed every night at 9) to Theobalds Park. Here is *Capel House* (James Warren, Esq.), a long low mansion which occupies the place of the old manor-house of Pentriches, sold by Queen Elizabeth in 1562. In the grounds are some fine cedars and other forest trees, and three of the largest copper-beeches in the country.

Baker Street, N. of Enfield Town, of old the genteelest of the Enfield suburbs, still contains several of those good old red-brick houses which contribute so much to the character of the place. One of the most noteworthy, now known as *Gough's Park* (Miss Child), was for 33 years the residence of Richard Gough, the antiquary (editor of Camden's 'Britannia'), who d. here 1809.* It stands at the upper end of Baker Street, and will be recognized by the iron screen and gates in front of it. These gates should be noticed by the visitor; they are among the best specimens of ironwork to be now seen round London: there are other good examples in Enfield, but none equal to this. Gough's antiquarian and other collections were for the most part dispersed: but he bequeathed his unrivalled collection

of books on British Topography to the Bodleian Library, where they hold an honoured place. The house now occupied by Alderman Challis was the residence of John Abernethy, who lies in Enfield ch. The most important house in Baker Street is, however, *Enfield Court*, the seat of Col. A. Plantagenet Somerset. It dates from the 17th cent., but has been greatly enlarged, and has attached to it a circular riding-house, 63 ft. in diameter, often lent by the owner to his townsfellows, for recreative purposes. The grounds are a quaint mixture of old and new, and very pleasant. At the end of the broad terrace, 400 ft. long, and once bordered with hedges of clipped yew, by a rectangular 'canal,' is an old brick and stone two-storey summerhouse, the 'gazebo' of our ancestors.

Cock Fosters is a little secluded hamlet on the S.W. side of Enfield Chase, and 4 m. from Enfield Town. Inn (with good garden), the *Cock*. The ch. has been noticed above. The name has caused some speculation. There can be little doubt that Forsters is a corruption of *foresters* (in either the English or French form). The derivation of Cock is not so palpable. It has been suggested that it comes from *bicoque*, a small house, hut, a collection of huts; Cotgrave renders it "*Bicoque*, a little paltry town," and if the huts of the Chase foresters and woodmen were collected here, the place may have been called *Bicoque Forestière;* but a more obvious explanation is, that here may have been the house of the chief forester, *Coq de Forestiers.*

Besides the eminent persons already noticed as resident at Enfield, two or three more may be mentioned. A cottage at Chase Side, between the workhouse and the Gordon estate, once a house of more pretension, but still containing some woodwork and panelling of the 16th cent., has, according to local tradition, the distinction of having been the abode of *Sir Walter Raleigh*, who certainly attended the Court of Elizabeth at Enfield. A very different politician, *Major Cartwright*, whose statue frowns down on the enclosure in front of Burton Crescent, lived at Enfield for many years, and died here in September 1824, at the ripe age of 85. Isaac Disraeli, author of the 'Curiosities of Literature,' and father of

---

* Gough completed his British Topography here: the Advertisement to his 2nd ed. is dated "Enfield, St. George's Day, 1780."

the distinguished Conservative chief, was born at Enfield in 1766, and resided here till his marriage in 1804—by which removal Enfield just lost the honour of being the birthplace of the more famous son. Mr. Disraeli, in the Memoir of his father prefixed to his edition of the 'Curiosities of Literature' (1858), after speaking of his grandfather's settlement in England, says, "He made his fortune in the midway of life, and settled near Enfield, where he formed an Italian garden, entertained his friends, played whist with Sir Horace Mann, who was his great acquaintance, and who had known his brother at Venice as a banker." It is somewhat singular that the house should have passed out of memory. Mr. Ford, however, who has collected and collated the local traditions, believes that "the probabilities are in favour of that used as the Great Eastern Railway Station, which, with its beautiful façade and tracery-work of carved brick (probably unrivalled in England), is doomed to destruction by the march of mechanics."[*] It has since been destroyed, and on its site stands the terminus of the Grt. E. Rly., but the central part of the façade was purchased for the South Kensington Museum, where it has been erected as a screen in the architectural section.

Charles Lamb came in 1825 to lodge at "a Mrs. Leishman's, Chase, Enfield. Her husband," as he wrote, "is a tailor, but that, you know, does not make her one": it is now known as the Manse, but has been much enlarged since Lamb lodged in it. The following year he took what, in a notelet to Talfourd, he calls an "odd-looking gambogish-coloured house" at Chase Side, but which he described more favourably to his old friend Crabb Robinson.[†] "I am settled for life, I hope, at Enfield. I have taken the prettiest, compactest house I ever saw, near to Andrew Robinson's." It was also near to his friend Serjeant Wilde's (afterwards Lord Truro) ; but the cares of housekeeping proved too oppressive, and after a short trial he and his sister removed to lodgings "twenty-four inches farther from town," where they stayed till their removal to Edmonton, a year or two before his death. The

"gamboge-coloured house" at Chase Side has been transformed past recognition. Lamb's favourite walks here were to the top of Forty Hill on the one hand, and along the Green Lanes on the other. Charles Babbage, the mathematician, and inventor of the calculating machine, Capt. Marryat, the novelist, and Concha, the Spanish general, shot at the head of his army at Estella, July 1874, were schoolfellows at Enfield,—"Babbage, diligent and conscientious, Marryat very much the reverse ;" indeed, as his daughter writes, "he appears to have considered 'running away' to be his mission, and most conscientiously endeavoured to fulfil his destiny by doing so whenever he could find an opportunity."

"Whilst at a school at Ponders End, kept by a Mr. Freeman, that gentleman was surprised one day to detect him, with a book in his hand, in the 'dignified but graceful' position of standing on his head (like Mrs. Vincent Crummles), which, from the circumstance alluded to, naturally (or unnaturally) formed his centre of gravity. But Mr. Freeman must have been still more surprised when, on asking his pupil why he chose so peculiar a mode in which to study his lesson, he received the answer, 'Well ! I've been trying for three hours to learn it on my feet, but I couldn't, so I thought I would try whether it would be easier to learn it on my head." [*]

Mrs. Church, as will be seen, says that the school was at Ponders End ; but Mr. Ford, no doubt more accurately, says, that "the Rev. Stephen Freeman's school was at the red-brick house at the upper end of Baker Street, in Enfield." Marryat was taken from school when 14, having "run away again, and been captured in the horsepond at Edmonton, by a party of the boys and old Bunn the usher."

ENFIELD CHASE was of old a royal hunting-ground apportioned off from the great Forest of Middlesex, which stretched across the county in a S.W. direction from Waltham, where it joined the Forest of Essex, to the forests of Bucks and Berks. Enfield Chase formed part of the manor of Enfield, granted to Geoffrey de Mandeville by the Conqueror, from whose family it passed to the Bohuns, and from them, as already stated under ENFIELD, to Henry IV., since whose time it has remained annexed to the Duchy of Lancaster. The term Chase is applied

---

to it in a document of 19 Edward II.: its more general designation was *Parcus Extrinsecus*, the Outer Park. The ancient Chase extended from Enfield westwards to Hadley and Barnet, S. to Edmonton, Winchmore Hill, and Southgate, and N. to Potter's Bar, South Mimms, and Northaw. Its form is very irregular in the old maps and surveys, but probably the numerous angles and indents were due to encroachments. Its greatest length from Potter's Bar to Winchmore Wood was about 6 m., its width 5 m.

From the time Enfield reverted to the Crown, Enfield Chase was probably an ordinary hunting-ground of the Court. Elizabeth we know came here many times to hunt the hart, and kept her court in her adjacent palace. At this time it was doubtless as Drayton wrote—

"A Forrest for her pride, though titled but a Chace." *

James I. took so much delight in Enfield Chase, that, in order to enjoy it the more thoroughly, he constrained his Minister, Sir Robert Cecil, to exchange his favourite mansion, Theobalds, for the palace at Hatfield. But having obtained possession of Theobalds, James took in 500 acres of the Chase, to add to his park, which he then "surrounded with a brick wall 10 m. in circumference." He frequently stayed at the house, and at last died there.† (*See* THEOBALDS.) By a survey of the Chase, made by order of Parliament in 1650, with a view to its enclosure and sale, the Chase was estimated to contain 7900 acres, and valued at £4742 8s.; oak-timber (exclusive of 2500 trees marked for the navy) £2100; hornbeam and other wood £12,100; deer £150. A memorial of the inhabitants of Enfield asserted, however, that this survey estimated the Chase at 3000 acres less than a prior survey: the difference, as they imply, arising from unchecked encroachments. The work of sale and enclosure was proceeded with, and appropriations made chiefly to officers of the army, but the inhabitants claiming rights of common, created such disturbances that it was found necessary to send down soldiers to maintain

order; these in their turn were charged with excesses, and the House of Commons was compelled to appoint a committee to report on the whole proceedings. Matters seem, however, to have been left to take their own course, as a survey made in 1686 * states that "at the death of King James, the Chase was abundantly stocked with deer, but the army of the Parliament during the Civil War destroyed the game, cut down the trees, and let the ground out in small farms." At the Restoration it was again seized for the Crown, stocked with deer, and planted with young trees. Macaulay's striking description of it shortly after will be remembered: "At Enfield, hardly out of sight of the smoke of the capital, was a region of five-and-twenty miles in circumference, which contained only three houses, and scarcely any enclosed fields. Deer, as free as in an American forest, wandered there by thousands."† This is, however, a little too strongly coloured. The authority cited is Evelyn, who says:—

"2 *June*, 1676.—I went with my Lord Chamberlaine to see a garden at Enfield towne; thence to Mr. Sec. Coventry's lodge in the Chase. It is a very pretty place, the house commodious, the gardens handsome, and our entertainment very free, there being none but my Lord and myselfe. That which I most wondered at was, that in the compass of 25 miles, yet within 14 of London, there is not a house, barne, church, or building, besides three lodges. To this lodge are three great ponds and some few inclosures, the rest a solitarie desert, yet stor'd with not less than 3000 deere. These are pretty retreats for gentlemen, especially for those who are studious and lovers of privacy."

Evelyn is plainly thinking only of houses of the better class—pretty retreats for gentlemen; there must have been cottages for foresters, woodmen, labourers, and the like.

In a survey of 1700 it was estimated that the Chase then contained 3947 acres of wood, consisting of oak, beech, and some ash, which in the whole might amount to 631,520 trees, whereof most part were 30 feet high. At length came the end. In 1777 an Act was passed for disafforesting and dividing the Chase, and allotting it to the parishes and individuals who claimed right of common. For the purposes of the Act a new survey was made

---

* Polyolbion, 16th Song.
† Clutterbuck, Hertfordshire; Chauncy, Hist. Antiq. of Hertfordshire.

* Quoted by Robinson, vol. i., p. 197.
† Macaulay, History of England, ch. iii. (vol. i., p. 323, ed. 1858).

under the direction of Mr. F. Russell, Surveyor-General, when the Chase was found to contain, "including roads, lodges, and encroachments, 8349 acres, 1 rood, and 30 perches, or thereabouts," of which 3218 acres were allotted to the king; 313 acres to the lodges; about 700 acres to individuals; 1732 acres to the parish of Enfield; 1231 acres to that of Edmonton; 1026 acres to South Mimms; and 240 acres to Hadley. The deer, which were very numerous, were taken to Lord Bute's Park, Luton Hoo, Bedfordshire. The enclosure proceeded slowly. The greater part of the Enfield allotment remained as waste land until 1801. "Within living memory it was possible to travel from Hadley Church through Enfield Chase, Epping and Hainault Forests, to Wanstead, without ever leaving the green turf, or losing sight of forest land." [*]

The Chase is now nearly all enclosed, and, with the exception of the parks and lodges, under tillage. Two or three unbroken vestiges of the Chase however remain to indicate the character of the whole—Hadley Common, the portion allotted to Hadley parish, which the parish had the wisdom to leave untouched (*see* HADLEY); Winchmore Hill Wood, the extreme S. point of the Chase, somewhat disturbed by the railway, but still wild woodland, and what is called the Rough Lot in Trent Park; to which may perhaps be added the woodland portion of White Webb's Park.

The old forest-like character of the chase has of course passed away, but the parks and lodge grounds contain many noble trees, and preserve to it still something of a sylvan character. Along the Ridge Road, and from the higher parts generally, alike from the open ways and from Trent Park, there are very wide prospects over Epping Forest to the Kent hills, and across Hertfordshire and Middlesex to Bucks and Berks. The roads too are good, and altogether it is a pleasant country to explore; in the early days of the enclosure this could hardly have been the case: "Such, however, was the state of these roads within the last fifty years, that the late Lady Elizabeth Palk, who resided at the Rectory, was accustomed, when she intended to call on Mrs.

Elphinstone, at East Lodge, to send out men two or three days in advance to fill the ruts with faggots to enable her carriage to pass." [*]

The boundaries and entrances to the Chase are still indicated by the names of hamlets and other outlying places, as Potter's Bar, Northaw, Cattle Gate, Stock Gate, Bohunt or Bohun's Gate, and Southgate. For the head-keepers of Enfield Chase there were three lodges, named respectively the East, West, and South Baileys. *East Lodge* was a brick and tile building, occasionally used by Charles I. as a hunting lodge. After the division of the Chase it was occupied by Alexr. Wedderburn, afterwards Lord Loughborough, Lord Chancellor, and Earl of Rosslyn. The old house was pulled down and a new one erected by the present occupant, G. J. Graham, Esq.

West Lodge (J. W. Cater, Esq.) is a neat, unpretending building erected in 1832, the foundations of the old house having given way. The grounds are small, but very pleasant. It stands on the rt. of the road from Cock Fosters, immediately N. of Trent Park. It was Evelyn's account of his visit to West Lodge, it will be remembered, that formed the basis of Macaulay's, and probably of Sir Walter Scott's, notice of Enfield Chase.

South Lodge (G. R. Burnet, Esq.) is about 1½ m. W. of Enfield, on the road to East Barnet. In the last century it was for several years the residence of the great Earl of Chatham, to whom it had been bequeathed with a sum of £10,000. Chatham spent a good deal of time and money on the improvement of the grounds, about 50 acres in extent,[†] but after a time grew tired of the place and left it. There are several other 'lodges' about Enfield Chase, but they are merely modern titles.

When the Chase was divided, two estates were set apart from the royal allotment, and formed into parks. *Trent Park* consisted of 200 acres, granted on lease by George III. to his favourite physician, Dr. Jebb. The king afterwards made Sir Richard Jebb a baronet, and named his

---

[*] Robinson, vol. i., p. 210; Ford, pp. 43, 100.

[*] Ford, p. 100.
[†] Walpole, Anecdotes, (on Modern Gardening,) iv., p. 267, praises the taste in gardening shown by "the great Lord Chatham in his villas in Enfield Chase and Hayes."

estate Trent Park. The estate has since been greatly extended, and now comprises over 1000 acres. The house, the seat of R. C. L. Bevan, Esq., is spacious, and, the newer portion especially, stately. But the glory of the place is the park, which is in some respects the finest in this part of the country. It is greatly varied in surface, has fine drives, splendid views, and noble trees—beech and oaks of great height and magnitude, extraordinarily large hornbeams and hawthorns, patriarchs of the ancient Chase ; and not least to be prized are untouched fragments of the forest itself, the Rough Lot already mentioned. Here too is *Camlet Moat*, before noticed as a supposed site of the manor-house of the Mandevilles and Bohuns, a supposition to which Sir Walter Scott, who makes Camlet Moat the scene of the murder of Lord Dalgarno, has given countenance :—

"The sun was high upon the glades of Enfield Chase, and the deer, with which it then abounded, were seen sporting in picturesque groups, among the ancient oaks of the forest, when a cavalier and a lady on foot, although in riding apparel, sauntered slowly up one of the long alleys which were cut through the park for the convenience of the hunters. Their only attendant was a page. . . . . The place at which he stopped was at that time little more than a mound, partly surrounded by a ditch from which it derived the name of Camlet Moat. A few hewn stones there were, which had escaped the fate of many others that had been used in building different lodges in the forest for the royal keepers. These vestiges, just sufficient to show that here in former times the hand of man had been, marked the ruins of the abode of a once illustrious but long-forgotten family, the Mandevilles, Earls of Essex, to whom Enfield Chase, and the extensive domains adjacent, had belonged in elder days. A wild woodland prospect led the eye at various points through broad and apparently interminable alleys, meeting at this point as from a common centre." *

The traditions attached to Camlet Moat have been noticed under ENFIELD. The old way through Trent Park is now closed to strangers.

Beech Hill Park, an estate of 270 acres, was granted to F. Russell, Esq., Surveyor-General and Secretary to the Duchy of Lancaster, who drew up the scheme for dividing the Chase : since his death the estate has passed through several hands, and is now the property of Chas. Jack, Esq. The house is large and good ; the park open and charmingly

* Fortunes of Nigel, chap. xxxvi.

situated ; but far too many of the old trees have been converted into timber.

ENGLEFIELD GREEN,

SURREY, 1 m. W. from Egham, to which parish it belongs, a large open tract of elevated country, delightfully situated S. of Cooper's Hill, and in the immediate vicinity of Windsor Park and Forest, Virginia Water, Runnimede, and the Thames. On both the E. and W. sides of the Green, and in the immediate vicinity, are many excellent seats, the healthiness and beauty of the neighbourhood, and the contiguity of Windsor Castle, having attracted to it many noble and wealthy families. Englefield Cottage, on the Green, was for some years the residence of Mrs. Robinson (Perdita), who died here in Dec. 1800. Benedetto Pistrucci, the medallist and engraver to the Mint, spent his last years at Flora Lodge, Englefield Green, where he died September 16th, 1855. Among the many seats in the neighbourhood may be noticed—*Round Oak*, on the N.W., the fine house and grounds of the Marquis of Carmarthen ; *Portnal Park* (long the seat of the late Col. H. Salwey) ; *Purnish*, Englefield Green (Mrs. Brigstock) ; *Kingswood Lodge* (W. B. Eastwood, Esq.) ; *Millicents* (R. Sutherland, Esq.) ; *Lime Lodge* (Major Spence) ; *Castle Hill* (J. Shepherd, Esq.) The neat little Gothic church, St. Jude's, Englefield Green, built in 1859, is a chapel-of-ease to the mother church of Egham. A fair is held annually on Englefield Green on the 29th of May.

EPPING, or EPPING STREET,

ESSEX (*Eoppa ing*), a market town 16½ m. from Whitechapel by road, and about the same distance by the Epping and Ongar branch of the Grt. E. Rly.; the Stat. is a little E. of the town : pop. of the par. 2275.

The manor of Epping belonged to Harold. It was given by the Conqueror to Waltham Abbey, and at the Dissolution passed to the Crown : it is now held by the Duchy of Lancaster.

The town stands on hilly ground, 380 ft. above the Ordnance datum, and consists of a single wide irregular street, stretching for more than a mile along the Newmarket road. It has the look of a quiet, easy-going country town, a little livelier than usual on Fridays, when the market, noted for calves and poultry, is held by the shambles near the centre of the street. In the last century Epping butter and Epping sausages used to command the highest prices in the London market, but though both are still made, the supremacy is hardly maintained. The trade of the town is mainly agricultural. There are some substantial-looking private houses in the street, and one or two good shops, but small shops and cottages prevail. The smart Town Hall, erected in 1865, provides the townsfolk with a concert and lecture room, and the Epping Harmonic Society and a Literary Institute furnish singers and lecturers. The large number of 'publics' (some now closed) tells of former prosperity. Epping inns, however, had the reputation of serving as harbours for the highwaymen who infested this part of the Newmarket road,— of Gregory in the early part of the 18th cent., and the more famous Dick Turpin, among others. Pepys stayed at Epping (Feb. 27 and 28, 1660) ; he does not say at what inn, but he "had some red-herrings to breakfast, while my boot-heel was a-mending, by the same token the boy left the hole as big as it was before." The *Old Lion*, a great rambling house that has seen better days, is a good illustration of the olden times. The front is of timber-framing and plaster pargetting, worked, for the most part, in the zigzag pattern common in old cottages hereabouts, but in part tooled in a sort of star pattern ; evidently it was a place of business in coaching and posting times. The *Cock* is now the chief inn and posting house.

The *Church* of Epping Street (St. John the Baptist), near the London end of the town, a chapel-of-ease to the mother ch. of Epping Upland, is a modern pseudo-Gothic chapel-like building, with galleries ; of no beauty or interest inside or out. It occupies the site of a chapel built by the monks of Waltham, who held the curacy : after the Dissolution it was settled in trust for the use of the town. Dr. Mason Good, M.D., was a native of Epping ; his father was minister of the Independent Chapel, one of the oldest in the county. The present building, however, only dates from 1774, and it has been of late enlarged and modernized. The *parish Church*, St. Mary, is at

Epping Upland, or *Old Epping*, a lonely little vill. 2 m. away to the N.W. (take the lane on l. near the W. end of Epping Street, and go across Forty Green and by Epping Bury,—a very pleasant walk, especially if the field-paths be followed, for which the ch. tower forms a good landmark). The ch.—very prettily situated on high ground, with a little inn (where nothing can be got) and half a dozen houses about it—consists of a long, low, rough-cast nave and chancel, with a tall, weather-worn brick tower, which has stout angle buttresses and some good mouldings (and inside a peal of 5 bells). The nave windows are Perp., but they appear to be insertions; there is an altered lancet in the chancel, and an E. window of pretty good Perp. tracery. The *interior* is plain, with a plaster ceiling, and contains nothing worth notice, unless it be the unusual position of the communion table, it being placed at a distance from the E. wall, with a railing round it.

Copped Hall, the fine seat of George Wythes, Esq., is about a mile S.W. of the town. It was built of white pressed bricks, for John Conyers, Esq., in 1753, but was enlarged and improved by James Wyatt. It is a spacious building, a centre with pediment and two wings, and standing on an elevation is conspicuous for miles round. The old Copped Hall, a large quadrangular red-brick mansion, built by Thorpe for Sir Thomas Heneage in the reign of Elizabeth, with a great gallery 56 yds. long (blown down in Nov. 1639), stood more to the S., on lower ground, and within the parish of Waltham : the present building is at the southern extremity of Epping parish. Charles Sackville, the witty Earl of Dorset, and the patron of wits and poets, lived at Copped Hall, and here Shadwell wrote part of his 'Squire of Alsatia.' Charles II. dined with the Earl of Middlesex at Old Copped Hall in June 1660 ; and William III., when on his way to Newmarket, dined and stayed the night here, April 4, 1698. The painted glass formerly in the chapel of Old Copped Hall is now in the ch. of St. Margaret, Westminster.

Epping Green is a little solitary-looking hamlet, about ¾ m. N.W. from Epping

Upland, and comprises three or four farmhouses, a few tumble-down cottages, a smithy, butcher's and general shop, a 'public' (the *Cock and Magpie*), and small school and chapel. A little way l. of the road, a short mile on the London side of Epping Street, and fairly within the borders of Epping Forest, is the ancient earthwork *Ambresbury*, or *Ambers Banks*. (*See* AMBRESBURY, p. 11.)

EPPING FOREST, that portion of the ancient Forest of Essex which lies N. and W. of the Roding between the town of Epping and Forest Gate, near Stratford. In its original untouched condition, the Forest of Essex appears to have stretched across the county from the Forest of Middlesex at Waltham (*see* ENFIELD CHASE) to Colchester and the sea. The first important inroad on this great waste was probably made under a charter of King John (March 25th, 1204,) disafforesting all that part of the forest lying to the N. of the Highway from Stortford to Colchester. A perambulation made in pursuance of the 'Charta de Foresta,' 29th Edward I. (1301), farther reduced the boundaries ; but probably the disafforesting was carried out slowly and partially, as a new charter was issued in the 8th year of Edward IV. (1468-9) reciting and confirming that of John issued 2 centuries earlier.* By grants, enclosures, and encroachments, the forest was gradually diminished in extent as, with the growth of the population, the land grew in value, until it was limited to the S.W. portion, which then, no longer the Forest of Essex, came to be known as the Forest of Waltham. Of this forest "the bounds and metes" were "set out and finally settled" by an Inquisition and Perambulation made, Sept. 8th, 1640, by virtue of a Commission under the Great Seal, in pursuance of the Act of 16 Charles I., for Settling the Bounds of the Forests. The boundaries of Waltham Forest, as thus defined, comprised 12 parishes wholly within the forest, and 9 partly within it ; and included what have since been known as Epping and Hainault Forests. The

* Printed in the Appendix (p. 83) of the Report of the Committee of the House of Commons on Royal Forests (Essex) 1863, where will be found most of the documents referred to in this notice.

area of the Forest, according to a computation made from their survey by a Commission in 1793, was in all about " 60,000 statute acres, of which about 48,000 acres are the estimated contents of enclosed private property, and the remaining 12,000 acres, the amount of the unenclosed woods and wastes." Of this unenclosed land 9000 acres belonged to Epping Forest, 3000 to Hainault.

From this time encroachments, authorized and unauthorized, went on until Mr. Howard, one of the Commissioners of Woods and Forests, to whose charge the Royal Forest of Waltham was confided, stated before a Committee of the House of Commons, in 1863, that of the 9000 acres of which Epping Forest consisted in 1793, they could not then " make out more than 7000 acres in round numbers," and that 2000 acres had " been lost by enclosures, but at what time we cannot ascertain." But this was very far from being the entire loss the forest had sustained. As a royal forest, the Crown originally possessed the ownership of the soil ; this in course of time it had entirely parted with, but still retained the right of vert and venison, *i.e.*, the right to keep an unlimited number of deer with " their herbage, vert and browse," which is held to include " a right over all the beasts of the forest, the trees and underwood and whatever grows within it ; and the power of granting licenses to hunt and shoot within its boundaries." There are also Commoners' Rights, by which every householder within the bounds of the forest paying a yearly rental of £2 has the right of pasturage for cattle, except during Fence Month (the 15 days before and after Old Midsummer Day), and within certain limits the lopping of trees for fuel.

So long as the Crown rights were enforced the forest must of necessity remain open. No enclosure could be made, no fence set up, no tree be cut down. There were wardens, foresters, verderers and a verderer's court—all the proper machinery, in short, for preventing or punishing encroachments and other forest offences. But the Commissioners of Woods and Forests refused to enforce the law. They held that the business of their department was to manage the Crown lands for purposes of revenue, and as the forest was in this respect comparatively unproductive they considered that the best thing to do was to sell the Crown rights to the lords of the several manors, and have done with them. With this feeling, about the time that Hainault was disafforested, authority was obtained from the Treasury, and the Crown rights over about 4000 acres were sold for the magnificent sum of £15,795.

The entire destruction of Hainault, and the curtailment of Epping Forest to less than half its recent dimensions, with the threatened loss of the remainder—for now the landowners began on all sides to enclose without troubling themselves about the rights of Crown or Commoners, having learnt that the former would not interfere, whilst the latter could not on account of the expense—aroused a strong and bitter feeling in the population of the East-end of London. They regarded 'the Forest' as their especial recreation-ground. The extent to which they resorted to it had indeed been little known except to themselves, or it may be doubted whether so grave an inroad on their enjoyment would have been sanctioned. When an inquiry was instituted by the House of Commons in 1863, a witness, well acquainted with the district, assured the Committee that on Sundays and Mondays, supposing the weather to be reasonably fine, the average number of "working people from the thickly populated districts" of the East who resort to the forest was at least 50,000. On Easter Monday, the great East-end holiday, the number would be "not less than 200,000." On other and quieter days it was resorted to by family and picnic parties, and especially by parties of school children, who were taken there in vans as well as by railway. One van-owner told the Committee that he had been engaged in taking these parties to the forest for 25 years : " 30 and 40 vans in a day—different schools ; " and once he had sent 60 vans, each van carrying from 35 to 40 children. But, further, the forest was the chief collecting-ground of the East-end naturalists, a humble but numerous class—bird-fanciers, and collectors of rare ferns, mosses, butterflies, and insects. It was hardly surprising, therefore, that the imminent danger of losing their chief source of outdoor enjoyment should have aroused much angry feeling ; and as the popular sentiment was supported by the voice of the

magistrates, clergymen, and sanitary authorities, who all agreed as to the injury likely to ensue from cutting off so important a means of promoting the health, comfort, and innocent enjoyment of the enormous, rapidly increasing, and terribly overcrowded population of the East-end, it soon came to be felt that the question was one of more than local concern. After several ineffectual efforts, the House of Commons by a series of enactments (1869) prohibited any further enclosures, and referred all questions of compensation, interference with rights, etc., to a Royal Commission, who were to ascertain the extent and limits of the rights of the Crown, lords of manors, and commoners ; to institute inquiries into sales of Crown rights, acts of enclosure, etc., which have occurred during the last 20 years, and to report thereon with a view to such further legislation as the House may deem fit.* The work of the Commission proved to be more onerous than was anticipated, and a new Act was passed in 1873 granting the Commissioners two years longer in which to complete their inquiries and draw up their final report. Meantime the forest has happily been secured from further encroachment, and its management transferred from the Office of Woods and Forests to the Board of Works ; whilst the Corporation of London has undertaken to watch over and protect the public interest in its preservation, and by prompt and vigorous measures has succeeded in checking the smaller enclosures of land, the raising of fences, cutting down or lopping trees, and other waste and injury which were being perpetrated in defiance of the House and its Commissioners.

The result of all these proceedings, now extended over a quarter of a century, is that Epping Forest, though reduced to considerably less than half its former size, is still an open woodland of nearly 3000 acres area. The great extent and *continuity* of the forest—its distinctive feature—is gone. From Wanstead, Walthamstow, and Snaresbrook, and indeed the whole lower end, the forest character has disappeared ; Chingford-Fairmead and Loughton are spoiled, though about both these places many

* 34 and 35 Vict., cap. 93, etc.

pretty bits are left; but High Beech and its neighbourhood, always the finest part of Epping Forest, is still wild and still lovely.   From High Beech to Epping (including Ambresbury), and again towards Theydon on the one hand and Nazing on the other, there are also many outlying fragments of the old forest that, if not much in themselves, serve as pleasant breaks in the surrounding scenery.

The major part of the forest was oak and hornbeam, with a considerable number of beech and an abundance of hawthorns, sloes, and rough underwood.   But within the last 20 years more than a million forest trees have been cut down.   Of the part left, the most striking feature is the beech wood at High Beech; but there are many good oaks there and at Chingford: hornbeams still predominate in other parts of the forest.   In point of scenery, High Beech is by far the most attractive portion of the forest left. (*See* HIGH BEECH.) Though of course greatly injured by the enclosures and the extensive destruction of trees, Epping Forest is still a very interesting place, alike to the lover of scenery, and to the student of natural history.   A larger number and variety of birds may be found there than in any other place within the same distance of London.   By day the singing birds are numberless, and by night owls and night-jars alternate with the nightingale—which some believe is heard here earlier and later than elsewhere.*   For the rarer plants the forest is still the best collecting-ground on this side of London, though it must yield precedence to Darenth Wood, and perhaps one or two others of the Kentish woodlands.   Ferns flourish wonderfully, but the Osmunda, the Lady Fern, and some other of the more highly prized and rarer varieties, have been extirpated.   Chingford-Fairmead and the neighbourhood produces an unrivalled variety of fungi, and the club mosses and orchids are also numerous and beautiful. For the entomologist Epping is at least as productive a hunting-ground as for any of his brother naturalists.†

The deer which once gave so much animation to Epping Forest are now nearly extinct.   From the Report of the Commission of 1793 we learn that the forest was then well stocked with both red and fallow deer; and Sir Jas. Tylney Long, Bart., at that time warden of the forest, although he was " not able to ascertain what number of bucks and does are kept or abide in the forest in general," reported that " About five brace of bucks, and three brace of does, have been, one year with another, killed in the forest, by warrants of authority from His Majesty; and about fourteen brace of bucks and seven brace of does for individuals who claim a right to have venison in the forest. My claim," he adds, " to red or fallow deer in the said forest is without stint." We can ourselves remember when it was no rare thing to meet with a goodly drive of deer in Epping Forest.   But in 1863 Mr. Howard told the Committee of the House of Commons that " there are no longer any deer in Epping Forest: practically they do not exist . . . . there may be a dozen perhaps."   Col. Palmer stated that " one of the under keepers told him the other day he saw 9 deer altogether."   In the autumn of 1873 a woodman whose life is spent in the forest told us he knew of three, but he would not tell where they lurked.   Col. Palmer, the Verderer of the Forest, believes that " the destruction of the deer has been mainly owing to the forest not being kept up" by the proper enforcement of the Crown rights.

The *Epping Hunt* on Easter Monday has long been so familiarly associated with Epping Forest that it seems requisite to add a brief note respecting it.   The popular notion was that the Easter Hunt was a privilege held by the City of London, and embodied in its charters, and that, at least in the good old days, the Lord Mayor and Aldermen took part in the sport.   Some such notion seems indeed to have found its way into the House of Commons, and some little surprise was expressed in the Committee of 1863, where it was termed " the hunt of the citizens," that Mr. Alderman Copeland, M.P., who appeared as the unofficial representative of the Corporation, did not assert the privilege.   " Then the City of London does not claim the privilege of hunting on

---

* Ample information on the birds of Epping Forest will be found in Mr. Gibson's Birds of Essex, 1862; and see a note by Mr. English, of Epping, in Mr. Walker's useful little Saturday Half Holiday Guide, p. 29.

† Messrs. Doubleday, Entomologist, vol. i., etc.

Easter Monday?" remarked a member, and the Alderman answered, "Not that I am aware of." But the City has always claimed the right of hunting in Epping Forest, though not on a particular day; grounding its title on the Charter of Henry I., which, however, only states that "the Citizens shall have their grounds for hunting, as well and as fully as their ancestors had : namely in Chiltre [the Chilterns], Middlesex and Surrey" *—Essex not being named. But the confirmation of the right by subsequent sovereigns is understood to include Essex in the hunting grounds, and it is noted that Edward IV. invited the Mayor (Sir William Heriot) and the citizens of London to a grand hunt in Waltham Forest, and that "the mayor and his brethren" attended : and this hunt, according to civic authority, was on Easter Monday. The City greatly prized its hunting privileges, and at an early date had its huntsman, with the title of Common Hunt, an office of dignity and emolument, which was retained till 1807, when, on the decease of the then Common Hunt, the office was abolished.

But whatever may be the real or supposed corporate connection with the Easter Hunt, the City has always been associated with it in the popular mind ; and the citizens' doings on that occasion have been keenly quizzed by satirists, from Tom D'Urfey to Tom Hood. Thus, D'Urfey :—

" Next once a year into Essex a hunting they go ;
To see 'em pass along, O, 'tis a pretty show
Through Cheapside and Fenchurch street, and so to Aldgate Pump,
Each man with spurs in horse's sides, and his back-sword 'cross his rump.
My Lord Mayor takes a staff in hand to beat the bushes o'er,
I must confess it was a work he ne'er had done before.
A creature bounceth from the bush, which made them all to laugh,
My Lord he cried, ' A hare ! a hare !' but it proved an Essex calf." †

And Hood tells how, at the hunt,

" Some lost their stirrups, some their whips,
Some had no caps to show ;
But few, like Charles at Charing Cross,
Rode on in *Statue quo*." ‡

The Easter Hunt was "a noted hunt" during the first quarter of the present century. "I went to the hunt," said Alderman Copeland, "in 1810, and have continued, I believe, till within these last ten years to do so. I recollect perfectly well when I was young, the neighbouring gentry and nobility coming in their carriages, and *I have seen certainly* 200 *men in pink* attend that hunt. . . . . It is a widely different thing now." Lieut.-Col. G. Palmer, hereditary verderer of Waltham Forest, who "always understood" that by their charters "the Lord Mayor and Aldermen have the privilege of hunting and killing a stag once a year," told the committee that he had seen "as great a show there in former times as there used to be at Epsom races."

The meet was on the ridge above Fairmead, the house of assembly being the Roebuck at Buckhurst Hill. A good forest buck was selected, its broad antlers dressed with ribbons, and as it was uncarted about midday, it was seldom that a good run was not ensured, whatever might be the fortunes of the motley crowd that followed. Lord William Lennox has published his recollection of an Easter Hunt of this period, "which for fun, life, and absurdity," he says, "could not be excelled."

" From 9 till 11 o'clock the road to Woodford was lined with carriages of every form and description, from the barouche and four down to the taxed cart; and an incredible number of horsemen appeared, among whom were many Cockney Nimrods in smart red coats, white corduroy breeches, top boots, &c. . . . . About 12 the deer, which had travelled in his own carriage from the Bush at Wanstead, was uncarted, his branching antlers being decorated with gaudy coloured ribbons. After a few minutes law, the hounds were laid on. Away went sportsmen, horsemen, footmen, deer and hounds, towards Buckhurst Wood, from thence to Deadman's Wood, returned to Fairmead Bottom, and on to Loughton Wood, from thence to Robinson's Range, Golden Hill, and Queen Elizabeth's Lodge ; here the noble animal, being hardly pressed, plunged into Burleigh's Pond, from which he was taken alive, and reserved for another year's sport." *

The good time hardly outlasted the first quarter of the century. The newspapers of 1825-26 † refer to the declining state of the hunt. The forest authorities ceased to supply the buck. The publicans clubbed together and bought or hired a tame deer, which, prior to the

---

* Liber Albus, p. 116.
† Pills to Purge Melancholy, vol. iv., p. 42, ed. 1719.
‡ The Epping Hunt, with cuts by George Cruikshank, 1826—where Cruikshank's cuts give a far livelier notion of the hunt than his colleague's verses.

* Drafts on my Memory, vol. i., p. 23.
† See also Hone's Every-Day Book, vol. ii., p. 460.

Epping Hunt

Claremont House, Esher (see p.205)

start, was carried round to all the public-houses in the district and exhibited at 2d. or 3d. a head, the start being consequently deferred till the afternoon. The enclosure in 1853 of that part of the forest in which the meet was held brought the hunt to a sudden stop, and in its old form it has not been renewed. A sorry parody of it is, however, still rehearsed. The landlord of the King's Oak at High Beech provides a deer, and advertises "the real original Easter Hunt." In 1873 there was on Easter Monday a larger and rougher assemblage of holiday folk there than usual, and a great number of the stalls and betting games commonly seen in the purlieus of a racecourse; but the only persons even decently mounted were the police inspectors on duty, who rode about as vigorously as aides-de-camp at a review, and the only representative of the "200 men in pink" was the sad and serious-looking huntsman, who appeared overcome with the responsibilities of his position—or the strength of the King's Oak alc. The miserable deer was kept outside the tavern door till late in the afternoon before it was uncarted. A duller travestie was never witnessed. A rival Easter Hunt was provided by a neighbouring publican, but was a still more ludicrous failure. The "hunt" on Easter Monday, 1874, was even worse than that of 1873. The real Epping Hunt is a thing of the past, and it is time the parody was suppressed.

Another noteworthy feature in Epping Forest should not pass unnoticed—*the Gipseys*. There are far fewer than there used to be, but you may still see their tents about Wanstead Flats, or wherever they are permitted to pitch them ; and the women and children are sure to muster strongly at all holiday gatherings.

"Epping Forest . . . . the loveliest forest in the world ! Not equal to what it was, but still the loveliest forest in the world, and the pleasantest, especially in summer; for then it is thronged with grand company, and nightingales, and cuckoos, and Romany *chals* and *chies* [gipsey lads and lasses]. As for Romany-chals there is not such a place for them in the whole world as the Forest. Them that wants to see Romany-chals should go to the Forest, especially to the Bald-faced Hind on the hill above Fairlop, on the day of Fairlop Fair. It is their trysting-place, as you would say, and there they muster from all parts of England, and there they whoops, dances, and plays." *

---

* Borrow, Romano Lavo-Lil, p. 324.

EPSOM, SURREY (*Ebba's Ham*, the Home of Ebba ; Dom. *Ebesham*), famous for its horse races and medicinal salts; a mkt. town seated in a depression of the great chalk Downs of Surrey, immediately S. of Ewell, 15 m. from London by road, and 18½ by the L. Br. and S. C. J'y. (Croydon branch, S.E. of the town), and L. and S.W. Rly. (Wimbledon br., near the centre of the town): pop. 6276. Hotels and Inns : *King's Head ; Albion; Spread Eagle ; Railway:* large and good. The *King's Head* was Pepys' inn, and occasionally that of more questionable company : "To the King's Head, and hear that my Lord Buckhurst and Nelly are lodged at the next house, and Sir Charles with them : and keep a merry house." * The *Spread Eagle* is, at racing time, the head-quarters of the sporting fraternity, of whom a notable assemblage may be seen outside it on a Derby morning. The *Albion* is more of a family hotel.

At the Domesday Survey *Ebesham* belonged to Chertsey Abbey. It contained two churches and four mills ; there were in it 34 villans, 4 bordarii, and 6 bondsmen ; and the wood supplied pannage for 20 swine. The manor was surrendered to Henry VIII. in 1538, and granted the same year to Sir Nicholas Carew, of Beddington, on whose attainder and execution shortly after it reverted to the Crown. In 1589 it was granted by Elizabeth to Edward D'Arcy, her Groom of the Chamber, who quickly disposed of it to George Mynn, of Lincoln's Inn. Mynn's widow bequeathed it to her daughter Elizabeth, wife of Richard Evelyn, younger brother of the author of the Diary. It then passed through several hands, till, in 1819, it devolved by marriage on J. Ivat Briscoe, Esq., in whose descendant it remains. The old manor-house, Epsom Court, is now a farm-house.

The town is a large, rambling, and, except in the Derby week, rather dull place. It has many good and not a few poor houses, spacious and well-filled shops, court-house, market-house, clock-house, water and gas works, banks, a Board of Health, and a weekly newspaper. The noticeable building of coloured bricks with red bands, in the midst of the High

---

* Diary, July 14, 1667.

Street, serves a double purpose : the main building is for the fire-engine, the tall tower serves as a clock-house, and exhibits two illuminated dials at night. The market, chiefly for corn, long discontinued, was revived in 1833, and is held on Wednesdays. A pleasure fair is held on Clay Hill, July 25th. Brewing and malting are carried on in the town, and there are large brick-fields and nurseries in the vicinity, but the main dependence of the place is on the resident gentry, and the races and racing establishments.

The *Church* (St. Martin) at the upper end of Church Street, on the E. side of the town, was built in 1825, when the old ch. (of flint and stone) was taken down, with the exception of the tower. The present building, designed by Mr. Hatchard, is of brick, faced with black flints, with bands of brick, and Bath-stone dressings : by no means to be commended as a work of art, and not likely to tempt the sketcher by its beauty or picturesqueness; but a neat and convenient building inside. The old tower stands at the N.W. corner of the ch., to which its open arches serve as an entrance porch, and it contains a peal of 8 bells. The E. window, poor in colour and worse in design, is by Wailes of Newcastle. *Monts.*—In the chancel are 3 mural monts. with rilievi by Flaxman : on N. wall, to John Henry Warre, d. 1801, a small whole-length female figure with votive urn; on S. wall, one to John Braithwaite, d. 1800, with figure in altorilievo; and another to John Parkhurst, author of the well-known Greek and Hebrew Lexicons, d. 1797, with small symbolical figures—Hope, Faith, etc. Another tablet, on S. of chancel, to Mrs. Susan Warre, has a female figure kneeling with an infant in her arms, by Chantrey. At the E. end of the nave is another tablet, with emblematic figures by Flaxman, to Eleanor Belfield, d. 1802. On the S. wall is the mont., preserved from the old ch., of Richard Evelyn, of Woodcote, d. 1669.

There is another ch. (Christ Church) at *Clay Hill,* a small red-brick building, erected in 1845, but it is of no better design than the mother ch. The Independent chapel in Church Street, known as the *Old Chapel,* is noted as one of the oldest Nonconformist chapels in the county. Isaac Watts, whilst a visitor to Sir J. Hartop, whose seat was close by,

used often to preach here ; and here for many years ministered the Rev. John Harris, author of the once enormously popular 'Mammon.'

The *Almshouses*, in East Street, founded in 1703 by John Livingstone for 12 poor widows, were rebuilt in 1871 in a better style, and now form comfortable dwellings. The rather picturesque red-brick and stone building, a spacious structure in the Tudor Collegiate style, immediately N. of the town, is the *Royal Medical Benevolent College*, "established in order to provide an asylum and pensions for aged medical men, and the widows of medical men in reduced circumstances, and a school, partly gratuitous, for the sons of medical men." The college was opened in 1855. In June 1874, there were 24 medical men, or their widows, in the asylum, who each received annuities of £21, with furnished rooms and an annual allowance of $3\frac{1}{2}$ tons of coal ; and an equal number of outdoor annuitants who received £21 a year each. In the school there were 50 foundation scholars, "the necessitous orphans and sons of medical men," who "receive an education of the highest class, and are boarded, clothed, and maintained at the expense of the college ; " besides 150 resident scholars. The buildings comprise the school, asylum, masters' houses, and a neat chapel, and stand in about 18 acres of ground.

Epsom Wells.—In the last half of the 17th and early part of the 18th centuries, Epsom was a place of great fashionable and even royal resort, on account of its medicinal waters, for a while rivalling Tunbridge Wells in the number and quality of the visitors. The character of the Epsom water was, it is said, discovered by accident in the latter part of the reign of Elizabeth, and began to be celebrated in the reign of James I. Fuller, however, who wrote when the wells were in the height of their fame, puts their actual discovery late in the reign of the latter monarch. The medicinal waters of Ebesham, he says,

"Were found on this occasion some two and forty years since (which falleth out to be 1618). One Henry Wicker, in a dry summer and great want of water for cattle, discovered, in the concave of a horse or neat's footing, some water standing. His suspicion that it was the stale of some beast was quickly confuted by the clearness thereof. With his pad-staff he did dig a square hole about it, and so departed. Returning the next day, with some difficulty he recovered the same place (as not sufficiently particularized to his memory in so wide a common); and found the hole he had made, filled and running over with most clear water. Yet cattle (though tempted with thirst) would not drink thereof, as having a mineral taste therein."*

The water was "at first only used outwardly for the healing of sores. Indeed simple wounds have been soundly and suddenly cured, which is imputed to the abstersiveness of this water, keeping a wound clean, till the balsam of nature doth recover it. Since it hath been inwardly taken, and (if the inhabitants may be believed) diseases have here met with their cure, though they came from contrary causes." But no doubt, as he shrewdly remarks, "Their convenient distance from London addeth to the reputation of these waters; and no wonder if citizens coming thither, from the worst of smokes into the best of airs, find in themselves a perfective alteration."† The well was enclosed in 1621, and a shed erected for the convenience of visitors. Dudley, 3rd Lord North, in his 'Forest of Varieties,' folio, 1645, loudly asserted the virtues of the springs of Tunbridge and Epsom, which he claims to have first made known "to the citizens of London and the king's people." But it was not till after the Restoration that Epsom Wells became fashionable. Charles II. with his Court frequently repaired hither to drink the waters, and brought their dissipated habits with them. Where King and Court went commoners soon followed—Pepys among the number :—

"*July 26th,* 1663 (Lord's day).—Up and to the Wells, where a great store of citizens, which was the greatest part of the company, though there were some others of better quality. . . . . Then rode through Epsom, the whole town over, seeing the various companies that were there walking; which was very pleasant to see how they are there, without knowing what to do, but only in the morning to drink waters. But, Lord! to see how many I met there of citizens, that I could not have thought to have seen there; that they had ever had it in their heads or purses to go down thither."‡

He was there on another "Lord's day" (July 14th, 1667), being "up, and my wife, a little before four," to make ready, when his wife "vexed" him "that she

was so long about it, keeping us till past 5 o'clock, before she was ready." However they got off, provided with "some bottles of wine, and beer, and some cold fowle," in a "coach and four horses," and so "talking all the way to Epsom, by 8 of the clock, to the Well; where much company, and I did drink the water : they did not, but I did drink 4 pints," a pretty liberal allowance. After spending the day in sightseeing, "By and by we took coach and to take the ayre. . . . I carried them to the Well, and there filled some bottles of water to carry home with me; and there I talked with the two women that farm the well, at £12 per annum, of the lord of the manor." * The well continued to prosper. Shadwell wrote his comedy of 'Epsom Wells' (1673), which had a run at the Duke's Theatre ;† the *London Gazette* (June 19, 1684) announced that "the post will go every day to and fro betwixt London and Epsom, during the season for drinking the waters;" ‡ and the Lord of the Manor now (1690) laid out walks through the town, with branching avenues, planted avenues of trees, and built, besides other apartments, a ball-room 70 ft. long. A rival establishment was set up in the town itself, but for a while both continued to flourish. During the reign of Anne it was at the height of prosperity. George, Prince of Denmark, leaving the cares of state to the Queen, was a very regular visitor at the Epsom Spa. In 1711, John Toland, the sceptical author of 'Christianity not Mysterious,' then resident at Epsom, wrote an inflated rambling 'Description of Epsom, with the Humours and Politics of the Place,' which might well have suggested Macaulay's striking description of Tunbridge Wells.§ He pictures the town and company that filled it ; the luxury, and dissipation ; the country people bringing "to every house the choicest fruits, herbs, roots, and flowers, with all sorts of tame and wild fowl, with the rarest fish and venison, and with every kind of butcher's meat, among which Banstead Down mutton is the most relishing

---

* Fuller, Worthies (Surrey), vol. iii., p. 203, ed. 1840.
† Ibid.
‡ Diary, vol. ii., p. 198.

* Diary, vol. iv., p. 118.
† And continued to be popular long afterwards (Tatler, No. 7, April, 1709); though it may have been revived on account of the renewed celebrity of the Wells at this time.
‡ Quoted in Brayley's Surrey, vol. iv., p. 354.
§ History of England (ch. iii.), ed. 1858, vol. i., p. 359.

dainty ; " the " court and city ladies, who, like queens in a tragedy, display all their finery on benches before their doors ; " the behaviour of the damsels, admiring, envying, and cozening one another ; the public breakfasts, music and dancing every morning at the Wells ; midday races, and outdoor sports ; card parties, gambling-rooms, and the like. Toland says that he had often counted 70 coaches in the ring (the present racecourse on the Downs) of a Sunday evening. Among the sports most in favour, he mentions wrestling, running, trying to catch a pig by the tail, and the like ; and the Tatler tells us that an announcement which drew together all the beaux and fair ladies in their coaches was " that on the 9th instant, several Damsels, swift of foot, will run a race for a Sute of Head Clothes at the Old Wells." *

Epsom grew from a little country village to a gay and brilliant town. New buildings of all descriptions were laid out, lodging-houses and hotels of the most luxurious description were opened, and one, the New Inn, was said to be the largest in England. The milliners' and jewellers' shops rivalled in their displays those of London, Bath, and Tunbridge Wells; and hackney coaches and sedan chairs were numbered and ranged as in the metropolis.

The quarrels of the rival well-houses, the excesses of the disorderly class who resorted to the wells for the purpose of preying on the unwary, and the changes of fashion, at length brought about a decline. Efforts were made to revive the interest. Pamphlets were published setting forth the virtues of the waters; new attractions were announced ; but the fame once lost could not be recalled, and before the close of the century the wells were utterly neglected.

"The hall, galleries, and other public apartments, are now run to decay ; and there remains only one house on the spot (the Old Well), which is inhabited by a countryman and his wife, who carry the waters in bottles to the adjacent places." †

In 1804, the mansion and what was left of the buildings at the Old Wells were pulled down, and a small dwelling-house erected on the site ; and in 1810 we find it

recorded that " the Well is now deserted and almost forgotten," while of Epsom itself it is said, " Except during the time of the races few places can be more dull or uninteresting. The assembly-room, now disused, is partly shut up or let out in small tenements ; and several costly buildings are uninhabited." *

The well still remains, and may be tested. It will be found on Epsom Common, a short $\frac{1}{2}$ m. from the town, on the rt. of the road to Ashtead. The water is strongly impregnated with sulphate of magnesia, the Epsom salts of the druggist, with very small portions of the muriates of lime and magnesia, and has been pronounced to have a considerable affinity to the true Seidlitz water. When first extracted from the Epsom water, the sulphate of magnesia, under the since familiar name of Epsom salts, was sold, it is said, at 5s. an ounce. As is known, it is now manufactured on a large scale and at a very low price, but none is made at Epsom.

Epsom Common, without the attraction of the wells, is worth visiting. It is a broad open heath of about 400 acres, covered thickly with furze, somewhat moist perhaps in wet seasons, but a very pleasant, breezy place, with roads in all directions.

Epsom Races are the present glory of Epsom. When racing commenced here is not known, but the tradition that when James I. resided at Nonsuch Palace horse-races were run for his entertainment on the Downs is not improbable. References to meetings for horse-racing on Banstead Downs (the name by which these downs were then and long after generally known, *see* BANSTEAD) occur earlier, but it is not till after the Restoration that they become frequent, and then the race meetings seem to have been only occasional. They commenced to be run annually about 1730. For a time there were spring and autumn meetings, but they have long been timed as at present. There is a Spring Meeting in April, but it lasts only 2 days, and is attended by few besides betting men. The May Meeting lasts 4 days, from Tuesday to Friday, before Whitsuntide (unless Easter occurs in March, when it takes place *after* the Whitsun week), Wed-

---

* Letters from Epsome, Tatler, June 30, 1709.
† Ambulator, 1782, p. 83.

* Hunter's History of London and Environs, vol. ii., p. 154.

nesday being the Derby, Friday the Oaks Day. The *Derby* was established by Edward, 12th Earl of Derby, in 1780 ; the *Oaks* by the same nobleman, in 1779, and named after his seat, "The Oaks" (*see* WOODMANSTERNE), as the Derby was named after himself.

The Derby Day is the prime festival of England. For it even Legislation is adjourned. It is computed that since the railway facilities have been completed by the extension of the line to the foot of the race-hill, not less than 200,000 persons have assembled on the Downs on the Derby Day. Whatever be the number, there can be no doubt that the spectators make the sight. The vast crowd, the major part men, in a state of wild excitement,—the great shout, so startling to those who hear it for the first time, "They're off,"—the strain as the horses rush down the slope at Tattenham Corner, and the cry of one and another name as either of the leaders seems to be clearing his opponent, and then the turbulent excitement at the winning-post,—make up a scene such as is unmatched in England, and probably elsewhere. The *Derby* is a 1½ m. race for 3-year-old colts and fillies, and is usually run in from 2 m. 43 s. (Kettledrum, 1861), or 2 m. 43½ s. (Blue Gown, 1868), to 2 m. 52½ s. (Pretender, 1869). The value of the stakes during the last few years has varied from £4850 (1872), to £7350 (1866).

The *Oaks* is, like the Derby, run over a mile and a half course, but is for 3-year-old fillies only ; and the winning time is on the average a few seconds longer. The stakes range from £4100 (1871) to £5225 (1865). The Oaks, traditionally the Ladies' Day, is on the Friday after the Derby. The crowd is less, but the appearance of the course much more brilliant.

The grand stand, the best and most substantial in the kingdom, affords magnificent views, marked on one side by Windsor Castle, on the other by St. Paul's Cathedral, but stretching far beyond both ; and views hardly less extensive are obtainable from many parts of the Downs. The Downs, at other than racing times, afford delightful walks. Especially so are those across Walton Heath to Walton-on-the-Hill, to Hedley, Betchworth, or Reigate, or in the other direction by Langley Bottom to Leather-

head or Mickleham, or, again, the shorter strolls to Banstead and Sutton.

Some of the seats in Epsom and the vicinity are interesting. *Pitt Place*, near the ch., so called, as is said, from having been built by a disused chalk quarry (though it should be noted that Lady Chatham was Lyttelton's 1st cousin), is notorious as the scene of the death of Thomas, 2nd ("the bad") Lord Lyttleton (Nov. 27, 1779), with which the oft-told ghost story is connected. *Woodcote Park* (Robert Brooks, Esq.), whose magnificent woods are so noticeable on the right nearly the whole way from the town to the race-hill, was for some generations the seat of the Lord Baltimores. The present mansion was erected by Charles, 6th Lord Baltimore (1715—51), but it has been much altered since. It is a very stately structure, consisting of a tall centre and wings connected by curved arcades, and stands in a noble park of 350 acres. The state rooms have ceilings painted by Verrio. *Woodcote House*, by Woodcote Green, is a good old-fashioned mansion built by Sir Edward Northey, Attorney-General to William III., Queen Anne, and George I., now the residence of E. J. Northey, Esq. *Durdans*, in Chalk Lane, long the residence of Sir Gilbert Heathcote, occupies the site of a 'palace' built by George, 1st Earl of Berkeley, with the materials of Nonsuch Palace, which he had purchased of the profligate Duchess of Cleveland, to whom it had been given by Charles II. It was unpleasantly associated with the intrigue between Lord Grey of Warke and his wife's sister, the youngest daughter of the then Earl of Berkeley, which caused so much scandal. It was afterwards the residence of the Earl of Guildford, and then of Frederick Prince of Wales (father of George III.) when drinking the Epsom waters and pursuing his favourite pastime of hawking on the Downs. It was pulled down shortly after the prince quitted it, and the present more modest structure erected.

ERITH, KENT (usually derived from A.-S. *Ær*, or *Ærra*, and *hythe*, the old, or former haven ; the suggestions of Dr. Morris,* *E-rith*, water channel ; and

* Etymology of Local Names, p. 35.

Mr. Taylor,* *ora*, a shore, and *hythe*, seem scarcely applicable to this place). Erith is a small town, the next on the right bank of the Thames below Woolwich, 14 m. from London by road, and 15¾ m. by the N. Kent line of the S.E. Rly.: pop. 5421; of the entire par., which includes Belvedere and Abbey Wood, 8289. Inns, *Pier Hotel, Prince of Wales, Yacht.*

Lambarde (1570) sets forth 'briefly,'

"The narrative of a thing done at this place, by Dunstane the Archbishop of Canterburie, almost a hundreth yeeres before the coming of King William the Conqueror. A rich man (saith the text of Rochester) being owner of Cray, Eareth, Ainesford, and Woldham; and having none issue of his body, devised the same lands (by his last will, made in the presence of Dunstane, and others) to a kinswoman of his owne, for life, the Remainder of the one halfe thereof, after her death, to Christes Church at Canterbury, and of the other halfe to Saint Androwes of Rochester, for ever: he died, and his wife tooke one Leoffun to husband, who (overliving her) reteined the lande as his owne. . . . Hereupon complaint came to one Wulsie, for that time the Shyreman, or Judge of the Countie (as the same booke interpreteth it) before whome, both Dunstane the Archbishop, the parties themselves, sundrie other Bishops, and a great multitude of the Lay people, appeered, all by appointment at Eareth: and there in the presence of the whole assembly, Dunstane (taking a crosse in his hand) made a corporall oath upon the booke of the Ecclesiasticall lawes, unto the Shyreman (which then tooke it to the King's use, because Leoffun himselfe refused to receave it) and affirmed, that, the right of these landes, was to Christes Church, and to Saint Androwes. For ratification and credite of which his oath, a thousand other persons (chosen out of East, and West Kent, Eastsex, Middlesex, and Sussex) tooke their oathes also, upon the crosse after him. And thus, by this manner of iudgement, Christes Church and Saint Androwes were brought into possession and Leoffun utterly ejected for ever." †

If held by the Church, it must have been seized by the Crown, as it was one of the manors given by the Conqueror to his half-brother Odo, Bp. of Bayeux. In the 13th cent. it belonged to the Badlesmeres of Leeds Castle, but escheated to the Crown on the execution of Ralph, "the rich Lord Badlesmere," in the 15th of Edward II. The attainder of Ralph was, however, reversed by Edward III., and Erith restored to his son. It passed by marriage to Roger Mortimer, Earl of March; and afterwards in like manner to the house of Lancaster; and thus, in the person of Edward IV., reverted to the Crown, in whose possession it continued till Henry

VIII., in 1544, granted it to Elizabeth Countess of Shrewsbury, whose tomb is in the ch. By her daughter it passed to Sir Henry Compton, in whose family it remained till towards the end of the 17th cent., when it was sold to a Mr. Lodowick. It now belongs to Colonel Wheatley.

"The towne of Eareth," according to Lambarde, "is an ancient corporation either by reputation or chartre." In 1312-13, Bartholomew Lord Badlesmere obtained for Erith the grant of a weekly market to be held on Thursday, and two annual fairs of 3 days each. Market and corporation have long disappeared, but a fair is still held on Whit Monday. Erith stands, by the river-side, on the E. termination of the line of low hills, described under BELVEDERE and ABBEY WOOD, which stretch westwards to New Cross, and mark a fault in the strata through which the Thames flows, arising either from elevation of the upland tract or subsidence on the N. The point of upland on which Erith is built has on the W. the Erith and Plumstead Marshes, and on the E. those of Dartford and Stone. The town consists for the most part of a long narrow street of small houses. Of old it had a considerable maritime business, at first as being a naval station, and later from the East India Company's fine ships anchoring off here to discharge a portion of their cargo. The navy used to assemble here as late as the end of the 17th cent. Pepys records several official visits to the fleet off Erith;* and James II., when providing for the escape of the royal family to France, issued his warrant (Nov. 30, 1668), "Order the Isabella and Ann yachts to fall down to Erith to morrow." Charnock says that the great Henry-grace-à-Dieu was built for Henry VIII. at Erith, and he supposes by contract at a private yard.† Official documents at the Record Office ‡ show, however, that the Great Harry and 3 galleys were building at Woolwich at the same time (Dec. 1512); but there are contemporary entries for the payment of the "wages of divers and sondre personns, as shipwrightts, calkers and laborers that wrought

---

* Words and Places, 2nd edit., p. 354.
† Perambulation of Kent, reprint, p. 398.

* June 13th, 1661; Nov. 16th, 1665, etc.
† History of Marine Architecture, vol. ii., p. 42.
‡ Quoted in Cruden's History of Gravesend, p. 143.

and labored in carting and making of a new *docke at Erythe*, for the bringing in of our soveryn lord the king's reall shipp, named the Soverin, in the sayed dock, as for amendyng, reparyng and calkyng of the sayed ship, as of heving forthe afflote out of the same docke, by the time and space of viij. weks," * (Dec. 9, 1512—Feb. 4, 1513). There was also a wharf at Erith used for naval purposes. The present pier was built in 1834, when it was sought to make Erith a steamboat station, and the pleasant public gardens by the pier were laid out in the hope of attracting summer visitors. If in this Erith has not been successful, it has found compensation in the establishment of iron and other factories, which have caused a large increase of population and extension of business. Outside the town are extensive clay-pits and brick-fields, and a great sand-pit, where sand is largely dug for ship ballast and iron castings. Parts of the little town are not unpicturesque, especially where glimpses are caught of the river, whilst W. the wooded heights of Belvedere form a fine background.

The *Church* (St. John the Baptist) is by the rly. stat., at the edge of the marsh, ½ m. W. of the town. It used to be a favourite object with steamboat and other travellers on the Thames, standing, half buried in ivy, by the river-side, at the edge of the long dreary marsh; but in recent restorations the ivy has been pretty nearly cleared off, and the once venerable ch. stands out clean, spruce, and new as the rly. stat. beside it. But however it may look, it is old, and it is worth visiting. It is of flint and stone; small, but has nave, aisles, and chancel, and a thick short W. tower, with stout brick buttresses, and an octagonal slated spire. In it is a peal of 6 bells, rung from the ground floor. The interior has been very thoroughly restored. The chancel, E.E. in style, has 3 lancets, filled with painted glass, as are also the windows of the N. aisle. The Dec. E. window is recent. The windows of the nave are Late Dec., but the nave piers are earlier. The roof is plastered, but portions of the old timber framing are seen over the nave and aisles. *Obs.* ambrey on l. of altar, and on rt. a small piscina with Dec. head. In the

* *Ibid.*, p. 149.

wall of S. aisle is a hagioscope directed towards the altar. Above the chancel arch is a figure of the Saviour with extended arms, within the oval of a vesica. *Monts.*—At the E. end of the S. aisle a large and costly altar tomb, with alabaster effigy of Elizabeth Countess of Shrewsbury, d. 1568, lying on a mat which is rolled at the end to form a pillow. The figure is well carved, but much mutilated. Near it is a tall Gothic tabernacle tomb to Wm. Wheatley, lord of the manor, d. 1807. The mural mont., with mourning female, to Lord Eardley, d. 1824, is by Chantrey. On S. wall of chancel is a mural mont. to Marie Countess de Gersdorff, daughter of Lord Saye and Sele, d. 1826. There are several brasses, but some are partially or entirely covered by the seats. The most valuable are—one of Roger Sincler, " serviens Abbatis et Cōventus de Lesens " (1425) ; the other of John Aylmer, d. 1435, and wife. On leaving the ch., notice on the S. wall of the chancel a small sundial " given by S. Stone, May, 1643. *Redibo tu nunquam.*"

Immediately S. of the town is the great *Sand Pit*, or *Ballast Pit*, as it is more commonly called, from the sand being excavated for ship ballast, a place of much interest to the geologist for its fine sections of the Thanet Sands, here represented by a loamy sand 60 ft. thick, resting on a clayey basement bed about 2 ft. thick, in which are embedded large unrolled green-coated flints, locally known as bull-head flints, whence the deposit is known as the Bull-Head bed. The sand is excavated down to this bed, which immediately overlies the chalk. Above the Thanet beds, on the hill-side a little S., may be seen a good exposure of the Woolwich and Reading series, and of the Oldhaven beds (here rolled pebbles).

About ½ m. farther S., on the rt. of the Crayford road, is another great excavation, the *Erith Brick Pit*, or White's Pit, which should be visited, as it is even more interesting in a geological point of view than the Ballast Pit. It lies in the ancient bed of the Thames, and exposes a portion of the steep bank. Here the Thanet beds, which, as we have seen, are 60 ft. thick at the Ballast Pit, are only 15 ft. thick. They overlie the chalk, which here rises to a height of 45 ft. above the Ordnance datum line, both chalk and sand having been sharply cut, and the latter partially denuded, by fluviatile action. A good section is here shown of the chalk and sand, the ancient bank of the Thames, with the gravel not merely resting conformably on the top of the sand, but following the denuded surface of the chalk, and filling up the hollows. In this gravel will be noticed many detached masses of unarranged Thanet Sand, and bull-head flints. The brick-earth beds over the gravel contain bones of fossil elephants, tigers, wolves, oxen, and horses: *Elephas antiquus* and *primigenius*, *Bos longifrons* and *primigenius*, *Equus fossilis*, *Canis lupus*, and *Felis spelæa* (the great cave tiger); but the brick-pit about a mile farther, on the l. of the Crayford road, is far richer in these remains, Mr. Dawkins enumerating no fewer than 16 species of mammalia found there.[*] The Cyrena (*Corbicula flumentalis*) abounds in these pits.

The Erith Marshes stretch W. from Erith to Plumstead, and as they are below the high-water level, the Thames is only kept from flooding them by the great river wall which along the whole of its lower course borders the Thames and the creeks running into it. These marshes, like those on the opposite shore, have a superficial stratum of alluvial clay (marsh clay) from 4 to 10 ft. thick, beneath which is a peat bed, seldom more than 2 ft. thick, in which occur trunks and roots of yew, oak, alder, and hazel; nuts, leaves, and seed-vessels; wing-cases of beetles; bones of the horse, ox, deer, etc. Remains of this submerged forest, as it has been somewhat ambitiously designated, may be very well seen outside the river wall at low water. The marshes form rich grazing land; mineral oil, glue, manure, and other unsavoury factories have been built on them; and at Crossness, the point of land N.W. of Erith ch., are large gunpowder magazines. A terrible disaster occurred here Oct. 1st, 1864, when two of these magazines, containing upwards of 50 tons of gunpowder, exploded. The buildings were of course entirely destroyed,

and all the persons (10 in number) in them killed. A breach 100 yards long was made in the river wall, and Plumstead and Erith marshes would have been flooded but that the explosion occurred nearly at low water, and by the promptness, skill, and energy of the engineers, sappers and miners, and workmen, from Woolwich Arsenal, the breach was sufficiently stopped to keep out the rising waters. Much damage was done to the houses of Erith and Belvedere; indeed, for miles around the houses were sensibly shaken, and the explosion was felt at places 50 m. distant.

At Crossness is the *Southern Outfall of the Metropolitan Main Drainage.* The works, which were formally opened by the Prince of Wales, April 4, 1865, occupy an ornamental group of brick buildings relieved by coloured bands, and comprise, besides the great engine and boiler houses, pretty villas for the enginemen and chief officers, and about 20 neat cottages for the workmen, with a large and handsome school, which serves also for a chapel and lecture-room. A lofty minaret-like chimney serves as the central feature of the group of buildings, and is a conspicuous landmark from the river, as well as across the marsh. The residences stand on a terrace-like embankment, beneath which is the great reservoir, $6\frac{1}{2}$ acres in area. The sewage of the whole S. of London is brought into this reservoir, through nearly 10 m. of main drains and tunnels, and is lifted from it into the Thames, during the two hours following high water. The lifting apparatus consists of two immense compound pumps, each having four plungers, which are worked by four beam engines, each of 125 horse power. These engines lift about 10,000 cubic ft. a minute, but are capable of working to twice that amount in case of a sudden storm or heavy rainfall. The interior of the engine-house displays more ornament than is usual in such places; the machinery is of surprising magnitude and beauty of finish, and the whole is kept scrupulously clean, so that instead of its being the offensive place that might be expected, it may be examined with pleasure, and will be found very interesting. Great care has been taken to provide for the health and comfort of the little colony who are settled in this lonely and far from cheer-

---

[*] Boyd Dawkins, 'On the Age of the Lower Brick Earths of the Thames Valley,' Quarterly Journal of Geol. Soc., vol. xxii., p. 91; Whitaker 'On the Lower Tertiaries of Kent,' *Ibid.*, vol. xxii., p. 404; Tylor, 'On Quaternary Gravels,' *Ibid.*, vol. iv., p. 450; Proc. of Geol. Association, vol. iii., p. 83.

ful marsh. But one thing is wanting. They have no drinkable water. All that they now use is brought in tanks, by barges, from Barking. An attempt was made to obtain pure water by boring, but after reaching a depth of 950 ft. the work was temporarily abandoned, the cost of boring at that depth being £14 a foot. It has, however, been decided to resume operations, and a contract was taken (Feb. 1874) to complete the well and bore-hole for the sum of £5252. It is anticipated that the well will supply sufficient water for the engines, which require 500,000 gallons daily, as well as for the houses. F. E. Houghton, Esq., the resident engineer, has a detailed section of the bore on an ample scale, which will be found of interest by the geologist.

Erith Reach, the reach of the Thames off Erith, extends from Rainham Creek to Coldharbour Point, and is 1¼ m. long.

ESHER, SURREY (Dom. *Aissele ;* 1 John, 1199, *Ashal*), a very pretty vill. between Kingston and Cobham, on the old Portsmouth road, 15 m. from London by road, and by the L. and S.W. Rly. : pop. 1815. Inn, *The Bear*, a noted house. The Esher and Claremont Stat. is at Ditton Marsh, ¾ m. from the village of Esher. On leaving the stat., turn to the rt., and the wooded heights of Claremont will serve as a guide to the little village that lies under their shadow. *Sandon Farm*, by the stat., occupies the site of *Sandon Hospital*, founded early in the reign of Henry II., by Robert de Wateville, and enriched by many subsequent benefactions, one of which, by William de Perci, provided for the maintenance of 6 chaplains, and the keeping a lamp and candle of 2 lb. weight continually burning before the altar of the Virgin Mary, in the chapel where was buried the heart of the donor and the body of his wife.* The pestilence of 1348-9 swept off the master and all the brethren of the hospital. In 1436, on the plea of its reduced condition, it was united to the Hospital of St. Thomas, Southwark, and at the Dissolution it shared the fate of the other religious houses. The chapel was left standing long after the other buildings

were destroyed ; but no vestige of it remains.

At the Domesday Survey the manor of Esher appears to have belonged to the Abbey of Leutfrid's Cross, though Bp. Odo of Bayeux owned some of the land. In the reign of Henry III. the abbot sold this manor to Peter de Rupibus, Bp. of Winchester, and it remained in the possession of the see, Esher Place being the residence of the bishops, till 1537, when Stephen Gardiner, Bp. of Winchester, conveyed house and manor to Henry VIII.,* who had just constituted Hampton Court a manor, and was converting the country round it into a chase. Queen Mary, however, almost immediately on her accession to the throne, was induced by Bp. Gardiner to reconvey the manor and estate to the see of Winchester. Elizabeth, holding this conveyance good, purchased the manor of the bishop in 1583, and granted it a month later in fee to the Earl of Effingham, by whom it was sold to Francis Drake. After this it shifted rather quickly from hand to hand till, early in the 18th cent., it was purchased by Holles Pelham, Duke of Newcastle. After his death, in 1768, it was sold to Lord Clive, and then in succession to Viscount Galway, the Earl of Tyrconnell, and Charles Rose Ellis, by whom it was sold to the Crown in 1816.

The river Mole winds very deviously along the meadows W. of Esher, on its way to the Thames at East Molesey, 2 or 3 m. lower. Along the Mole, and by Ditton Marsh and the Rly. Stat., are river drifts and alluvium ; bordering this, along the lower part of Esher, and on its S.E. side, is the London clay, whilst the higher grounds of Claremont, Fairmile, and Esher Common, are the Lower Bagshot sand, thus affording considerable variety of soil and some difference of vegetation. The meadows bordering the Mole are beautifully green and pleasant, but too apt to be flooded in wet seasons. Hampton Court shows well across them from the higher grounds.

The village itself is pleasant, and still rural ; has a good old-fashioned inn, and a few good houses. The rude erection of flint and stone at the N. entrance of the village, with the Pelham arms, and

* Dugdale, Monasticon, vol. vi., part ii., p. 675 ; Brayley, History of Surrey, vol. ii., p. 433.

* State Papers, vol. viii., part v., p. 2.

the initials H. P. over the centre arch, affords a comfortable seat within an arched recess, and beside it is a well. It stands by Esher Place, is evidently a Traveller's Rest, and, in all probability, was the gift of Mr. Pelham to the village; but it has somehow acquired the name of Wolsey's Well, and is so designated by Mr. Howitt (for some years a resident at Esher) in his 'Visits to Remarkable Places.' In Esher lived the novelists Jane and Anna Maria Porter; the picture of the Saviour, over the communion table in the old ch., was painted by their brother, Sir R. Ker Porter, and presented by him to the parish; and their mother lies in the ch.-yard. The Rev. Philip Francis, the father of the more famous Sir Philip Francis, opened in 1751 an academy at Esher, and here published his well-known translation of Horace; and through him the village was very near having the honour of contributing to the education of the historian of the ' Decline and Fall ':—

" My unexpected recovery again encouraged the hope of my education; and I was placed at Esher, in Surrey, in the house of the Rev. Mr. Philip Francis, in a pleasant spot, which promised to unite the various benefits of air, exercise, and study (January 1752). The translator of Horace might have taught me to relish the Latin poets, had not my friends discovered in a few weeks that he preferred the pleasures of London to the instruction of his pupils."*

The *Old Church* (St. George), E. of the main street, behind the Bear Inn, is still standing, though disused except for burial services. The ch., small and mean, comprises a nave and chancel, with an ungainly excrescence on the S., built by the Duke of Newcastle as a chamber pew for the lords of Claremont and Esher Place. In the little belfry are 3 bells, one of which, says tradition, was brought from over the sea by Sir Francis Drake, and given by him to the parish. The donor of the bell, if a Drake, was more probably the Francis Drake, lord of the manor in the reign of James I. *Monts.*—Richard Drake, d. 1603, equerry to Queen Elizabeth, a small kneeling effigy in armour. The Hon. Mrs. E. C. C. Ellis, of Claremont, d. 1803, an elegant tablet by *Flaxman*. In the ch.-yard is the tomb of " Jane Porter, a Christian Widow," d. 1831, the mother of

* Gibbon, 'Memoirs of My Life and Writings,' in Lord Sheffield's Life of Gibbon, p. 48.

Sir R. Ker Porter, and of his sisters Jane and Anna Maria.

The new ch. (Christ Church) on the Green, on the opposite side of the road, was erected in 1853, from the designs of Mr. Benj. Ferrey, F.S.A. It is large, well built, E.E. in style, cruciform,—the S. transept forming a 'royal closet' or private pew for Claremont. At the W. end is a tower and tall spire. Leopold, King of the Belgians, contributed largely to its erection. The tower has a peal of 6 bells; the chancel windows are filled with painted glass. *Obs.* the large and roomy schools, built in 1859.

The grounds of *Esher Place* extend from the village to the Mole. The history of the manor and estate has been told. The original house, built by Bp. Waynflete about the middle of the 15th cent., as a residence for the Bps. of Winchester, stood on the low marshy meadow close by the Mole, " a moist and corrupt air," as Wolsey complained when a prisoner here, " continuing in which I cannot live." Waynflete's house was a large and stately brick structure, with spreading wings; gate-houses bearing on escutcheons his own arms and those of his see; capacious dining hall, chapel, and whatever else was requisite for the dignity and hospitality of the lordly Bishop of Winchester. Wolsey, on his appointment to the see of Winchester, 1528, purposed remodelling and extending Esher Place, as a compensation for the loss of Hampton Court, which he had found it prudent to present to the king; and it was perhaps on account of the alterations he was making in it that, when commanded (Oct. 19, 1529) to repair immediately to his house at Esher, he found the house desolate, and had to remain with his retinue " for the space of 3 or 4 weeks without either beds, sheets, tablecloths, dishes to eat their meat in, or wherewithall to buy any," and he sick almost to death in body and mind. Cavendish gives a strangely graphic and pathetic account of the events and personages at Esher during those dreary weeks. It was whilst a prisoner at Esher that Henry forced from him a formal cession of York House, the town mansion of the Archbishops of York. At length, at his repeated entreaties, he was allowed to leave Esher, and " be removed to some other dryer air and place," the King's Lodge at Richmond being allotted him as a temporary abode till he should be able to continue his journey into Yorkshire.

When the estate was purchased by Henry Pelham, brother of the Duke of Newcastle, in 1729, little was left of Waynflete's mansion but the gate-house known as Wolsey's Tower. Mr. Pelham added wings and offices to the gate-house, and converted it into a comfortable dwelling. The additions were meant to harmonize with the older building, but Walpole refers to them as a proof how little Kent, by whom they were designed, "conceived either the principles or the graces of that architecture."* In the grounds, however, Kent showed to greater advantage: "Kent is Kentissime there," said Walpole. "Esher I have seen again twice, and prefer it to all villas, even Southcotes."† Pope in like manner celebrates—

"Esher's peaceful grove,
Where Kent and Nature vie for Pelham's love."

Thomson's lines on Esher's groves are too well known, and Moore's and Dodsley's too feeble, to quote. A less familiar passage from Colley Cibber may serve as an illustration of what some of Pelham's friends thought, or at least wrote, of his famous villa:—

"Let me therefore only talk to you, as at Tusculum (for so I will call that sweet Retreat, which your own hands have rais'd) where like the fam'd Orator of old, when publick cares permit, you pass so many rational, unbending hours: There! and at such Times, to have been admitted, still plays in my Memory, more like a fictitious, than a real Enjoyment! How many golden Evenings, in that theatrical Paradise of water'd Lawns, and hanging Groves, have I walk'd, and prated down the Sun, in social Happiness! Whether the Retreat of Cicero, in Cost, Magnificence, or curious Luxury of Antiquities, might not outblaze the simplex Munditiis, the modest Ornaments of your Villa, is not within my reading to determine: But that the united Power of Nature, Art, or Elegance of Taste, could have thrown so many varied Objects, into a more delightful Harmony, is beyond my Conception."‡

A plan of the grounds and views of the buildings, engraved by J. Rocque, were published in 1739; and a large line engraving by Luke Sullivan (March 1, 1759) gives a capital idea of Pelham's house,

then occupied by Miss Frances Pelham, and of the gay parties that assembled in the garden. After Mr. Pelham's death, the estate passed from hand to hand till, in 1805, it was purchased by Mr. John Spicer, who pulled down Pelham's house, and built a new one on higher ground. The present *Esher Place* is a good-sized, semi-classic structure, faced with cement, with an Ionic portico to each front, and contains several large and handsome rooms: it is now the seat of Money Wigram, Esq. The principal rooms command fine views. The old gate-house, known as *Wolsey's Tower*, but which is no doubt a part of Waynflete's original building, is still standing. The park is not open to strangers, but a good view of the tower, with Esher Place and the woods beyond, is obtained across the bridge of Wayland's Farm. The tower, an excellent example of old brickwork, is three storeys high, and consists of a centre and two octagonal turrets, with battlements and machicolations. In one of the turrets is a good brick newel staircase. The rooms are small and dilapidated. It is partly overgrown with ivy, and is a picturesque object. The park has an area of over 160 acres, contains many noble trees, and from the higher parts affords views of great extent and beauty, including within their range Hampton Court and the valley of the Thames, with St. Anne's Hill, Cooper's Hill, Windsor Castle, and the churches of Bray and Maidenhead; southward, Leith Hill and Hindhead are seen on a clear day.

Claremont, on the opposite side of Esher, is still richer in associations than Esher Place, though they are of a more recent date. In the reign of Anne, Vanbrugh purchased a piece of land here, and built himself a brick house of moderate dimensions, but in his usual fanciful style, and laid out the grounds with more than ordinary skill, if we may trust Garth's verses on 'Claremont'—

"Where Nature borrows dress from Vanbrugh's art."

This estate was afterwards bought by Thomas Pelham Holles, Earl of Clare (created Duke of Newcastle in 1715), who enlarged the grounds into a park, which Kent laid out, added a new wing to the house, and called the place after his then

* Anecdotes, vol. iv., p. 241.
† Walpole to Montagu, Aug. 1784.
‡ Dedication to An Apology for the Life of Mr. Colley Cibber, Comedian, p. xi., ed. 1740.

title, *Clare-mont.* The Duke died in Nov. 1768, and the following year Claremont was sold to Lord Clive, to whose genius England owes her Indian empire. Lord Clive pulled down the old mansion, and commissioned Capability Brown to erect a new and more magnificent one on the hill, instead of the low site on which Vanbrugh's house stood. This is said to be the only house Brown built, though he altered a great many. He also remodelled the park and grounds, making short work with Kent's improvements. It is said that Lord Clive gave him unrestricted freedom as to outlay, and that the expenditure amounted to £100,000.* By the time Lord Clive could inhabit his mansion, his health had hopelessly given way ; the attacks on his administration of India in Parliament, and the inquiry into his conduct by a Select Committee of the House of Commons, crushed his spirit and soured his temper ; the stories that were spread of his cruelties, coupled with the rumours of his secluded habits and moroseness of temper, seem to have led the peasantry of the neighbourhood to "look with mysterious horror on the stately house," and it was whispered among them that " the great wicked lord had ordered the walls to be made so thick in order to keep out the devil, who would one day carry him away bodily."† Clive, as we know, died by his own hand, Nov. 22, 1774, but at his town house (Berkeley Square), and not here, as sometimes said.

After Clive's death, the estate, on which money had been so unsparingly lavished, was sold for a comparatively small sum to Viscount Galway ; from him it passed to the Earl of Tyrconnel, who, in 1807, sold it for £53,000 to Charles Rose Ellis, Esq. Mr. Ellis made it his residence, and retained possession of it till 1816, when, in prospect of the marriage of the Princess Charlotte with Prince Leopold, it was purchased by the Commissioners of Woods and Forests for the sum of £69,000.

From their marriage (May 2, 1816) Claremont was the residence of Prince Leopold and the Princess Charlotte till the death of the Princess, Nov. 6, 1817,—

"that melancholy November, when the death of the Princess Charlotte diffused throughout Great Britain a more general sorrow than had ever before been known in these kingdoms."* Prince Leopold continued to reside at Claremont, affectionately cherishing every memorial of the Princess, till his election in 1831 as King of the Belgians, and he retained his interest in the place till his death. For some years Claremont was a favourite retreat of Her Majesty and Prince Albert, the rooms usually occupied by them being on the first floor, the ground floor being reserved for more formal receptions.†

When Louis Philippe took refuge in England after the French Revolution of 1848, the Queen assigned him Claremont as a residence, and he retained it till his death, Aug. 26, 1850. Louis Philippe occupied the ground floor ; the gallery he converted into a private chapel ; the Princess Charlotte's bedroom, at the S.W. angle, was his cabinet ; and the Princess's dressing-room the bedroom in which he died. He was buried at Weybridge. (*See* WEYBRIDGE.)

By an Act passed in 1866 (the 29 and 30 Vict., cap. 62) it was provided that

"It shall be lawful for Her Majesty to retain and have the use and enjoyment during her life and pleasure of the mansion, near Esher, called Claremont, and its fixtures and furniture, with the park, pleasure grounds, and gardens thereto belonging (containing by estimation 332 acres or thereabouts), and certain plantations and lands (containing by estimation 132 acres or thereabouts), with a spring of water rising therein, from which the said mansion is supplied with water, and the waste lands parcel of the manors of Esher and Melbourne or Waterville Esher."

Claremont is now the occasional residence of the Queen and members of the Royal Family. It was for some time after their marriage the residence of the Marquis of Lorne and H.R.H. the Princess Louise, Marchioness of Lorne.

The house is one of those large, regular buildings which a century ago were regarded as the perfection of architectural purity and classical taste. It is an oblong, 135 ft. by 102, of brick with stone dressings, and has for its principal feature a

---

* Manning and Bray, History and Antiquities of Surrey, vol. ii., p. 742 ; Brayley, History of Surrey, vol. ii., p. 442.

† Macaulay, Essays (Lord Clive).

* Southey, Colloquies, vol. i., p. 1.

† Many interesting particulars of the residence of Princess Charlotte and Prince Leopold at Claremont will be found in Lady Weigall's Brief Memoir of Princess Charlotte, 1874 ; see also the Memoir of Baron Stockmar, vol. i., 1873.

tetrastyle Corinthian portico, the entire height of the house, reached by a lofty flight of steps, and containing in the tympanum of the pediment the arms of Lord Clive. The hall is an oval, 33 ft. by 25, and 18 ft. high, opening to a splendid suite of rooms on the ground floor, and leading to the upper rooms by a grand staircase, the columns and pilasters of which are of Siena marble. The house still retains many memorials of the Princess Charlotte : portraits of the Princess by *Lawrence*, and of the Princess and Prince Leopold by *Dawe;* Dr. Fisher, Bp. of Salisbury, and Dr. Short, who shared in her instruction ; in the Queen's room, several small portraits of the Princess's favourite horses and dogs ; in the hall, a cast in iron of the Warwick Vase, a present to her from the King of Prussia, and a variety of other objects. In the grounds, about ½ m. N.W. from the house, is a Gothic building which was intended as a sort of summer-house for the Princess, but, being left unfinished at her death, was completed as a memorial of her by Prince Leopold, and is known as the *Mausoleum of the Princess Charlotte.* The grounds about the house are rich in choice exotic trees, shrubs, and flowers, and the park contains much fine timber, a lake of 5 acres, and from the higher parts affords wide and varied prospects.

Beyond Claremont, on the Portsmouth road, is *Fairmile*, a very pleasant spot, now beginning to be dotted over with villas, generally in the old English style. Just off the road on the left is a large sheet of water surrounded with firs, which, always picturesque, at sunset on fine evenings and by moonlight presents some very striking effects. E. and S. of this is the broad, breezy, heath-clad *Esher Common. Stoke Wood*, near the Common, abounds in all kinds of birds—the note of the cuckoo by day and the nightingale by night is almost unending. *West End*, W. of Claremont, is a level marshy tract of about 130 acres, stretching down to the Mole. Among the seats in Esher and its immediate neighbourhood are *Esher Lodge* (J. F. Eastwood, Esq.); *Esher House* (Mrs. General Cookson) ; *The Manor House* (P. D. Hickman, Esq.); *Sandown House* (J. P. Currie, Esq.); and *West End Lodge* (Abel Jenkins, Esq.)

ESSENDON, HERTS, about 3 m. (by field-paths) E. of the Hatfield Stat. of the Grt. N. Rly., is an agric. vill. and par. (pop. 645), pleasantly situated on high ground overlooking the valley of the Lea, in the midst of a richly wooded and fertile country. The vill. is small, and has nothing in it calling for remark.

The *Church* (St. Mary the Virgin) stands on the W. of the road, with a broad open field behind, where the natives play cricket, and a little inn on one side of it. Except the tower, which is of the Dec. period, but rough-cast, the ch. is modern, with round-headed windows of ordinary carpenter's type. The tower is tall, battlemented, has a short wooden spire, and contains a ring of 5 bells. The interior is plain and pewed. In the chancel is an alabaster mont. to Wm. Priestly, d. 1664 ; also a brass, with kneeling effigies of Wm. Tooke, "Auditor of the Courte of Wardes and Liveries," d. 1558, Ales his wife, and their 9 sons and 3 daughters. There are also slabs to various owners of Bedwell Park. Notice the fine cedar in the ch.-yard.

Bedwell Park (Mrs. Hanbury) stands in a large and beautiful park. The house is old, but was considerably modified by the late owner, R. C. Hanbury, Esq., M.P. In it are some good paintings, and among them an Assumption of the Virgin by Murillo, one of the finest of his many repetitions of the theme. *Essendon Place* (Baron Dimsdale), and *Camfield* (E. Potter, Esq.), 1 m. S. by W. from the vill., are other fine seats. There is a charming walk of about a mile through Bedwell Park to Little Berkhamstead.

ETON, BUCKS (Dom. *Ettone*), on the l. bank of the Thames, which separates it from Windsor ; 22 m. W. by S. from London by road, 26 m. by the Windsor branch of the L. and S.W. Ryl. : the Stat. is near the foot of the bridge on the Windsor side of the river. The pop. of the vill. (Local Board District) was 2806 in 1871, but this includes the staff and students of Eton College. Inn, the *Christopher*, a house of fame.

The vill. consists of a single long narrow street, in effect a continuation of the main street of Windsor, with which it is united by an iron bridge, built by Mr. Hollis in 1824. The houses, especially at the

Windsor end, are for the most part old-fashioned and small, but there are several good shops, and towards the college end houses of a better class: the unwonted number of prim-looking private dwellings is explained by their being the licensed lodging-houses for students who reside outside the college. The street broadens out into an open green lined with fine old elms in front of the college, to which they make a stately and suitable approach ; and here are the masters' houses of more than average architectural character, and sufficiently spacious to accommodate a given number of boys as boarders.

Apart from the college, Eton has no history worth telling. The manor was made over to the college in the reign of Edward VI., and the grant of a market originally made in 1204 to Roger de Cauz, who then held the manor by the serjeanty of falconry, was renewed to the college, but it has long been disused. The college chapel was originally parochial as well as collegiate, and the parishioners used consequently to attend its services, till a mean brick chapel-of-ease was built for their use in the town. On the site of this, the present handsome parish *Church* (St. John the Evangelist) was erected from the designs of Mr. Benj. Ferrey, F.S.A. The first stone was laid by the Prince Consort in Sept. 1852, and it was consecrated in June 1854. It is a spacious and lofty structure, Early Dec. in style, and comprises nave with aisles and clerestorey, chancel, and at the W. end of the N. aisle a tower and spire 160 feet high. The E. window, of 6 lights, is filled with painted glass by O'Connor, as a memorial of the Prince Consort. A neat little district ch. for a congregation of 200 was built at *Eton Wick* in 1867 : archt., Mr. A. W. Blomfield. It consists of nave, chancel, and small S. transept, and has an open timber roof.

ETON COLLEGE, the "College of the Blessed Marie of Eton beside Wynde-sore," was founded by Henry VI., in connection with, and as a nursery for, King's College, founded by him at Cambridge. The foundation charter, dated Windsor, Sept. 12, 1440, is still in good preservation among the college muniments. An Act of Parliament was passed the following May confirming the charter, and the buildings

were formally commenced by the king laying the first stone of the chapel on the 3rd of July, 1441. Henry had set his heart on making his college at Eton the best grammar-school in the land. He provided most liberally for its erection and endowment from his own property, and appropriated to it the estates of such of the alien priories as were available for the purpose. Ample and very definite directions in his own handwriting exist for the construction of the college buildings. Laying aside " all superfluity of too curious work of entayle and busy mouldings," he willed that the structure "be edified of the most substantial and best abiding stuff, of stone, lead, glass and iron, that may goodly be had and provided thereto ; and that the walls of the said College of Eton, of the outer court, and of the walls of the garden about the precinct be made of hard stone of Kent." For the chapel he has no such fear of too curious work. He desired that it should be in all respects superior to the New College Chapel, Oxford,—the college which stood in the same relation to Winchester as he desired King's College, Cambridge, to bear to Eton. Henry lays down the plan and specifies the dimensions of his chapel with such precision that an architect would have little difficulty in transferring them to paper in the form of a ground plan, as indeed Prof. Willis has done. So eagerly did the king at this time press forward his work, that in little more than two years from laying the foundation-stone the buildings were so far advanced that on the Feast of St. Thomas (Dec. 21), 1443, the Royal Commissioners gave formal possession of them to the provost, clerks, and scholars. The buildings were, however, far from finished, and the misfortunes of the remaining years of Henry's reign impeded the progress of the parts which had been commenced, and caused the parts which were only projected to be abandoned. Thus the present chapel, noble structure as it appears, is only the choir of the chapel which Henry designed to erect. However, Henry saw the buildings so far completed as to admit of the commencement of his earnestly desired collegiate operations, and he induced William de Waynflete (afterwards Bp. of Winchester and Chancellor of England), the munificent founder of Magdalen College, Oxford, to exchange the head-mastership of Winchester School for that of Eton, and to bring with him 5 fellows and 35 scholars from Winchester.

The completion of Henry's designs was prevented by Edward IV., who regarded his predecessor's foundation with dislike, despoiled it of "moveables of great value," appropriated to himself a portion of its revenues, and obtained a bull from Pope Pius II. empowering him to dissolve the College of Eton, and unite it with that of Windsor. The courage and prudence of Westbury, who had succeeded Waynflete as Provost of Eton, happily averted the danger, and Edward so far forgave the resistance offered to his behests that he subsequently appears as a benefactor in the college rolls. At the suppression of religious houses the revenues of Eton College were returned at £1100; but in the Act for the Dissolution of Colleges and Charities, in the reign of Edward VI., Eton was specially exempted. It also escaped almost unscathed through the only other period of danger which has threatened its existence. When the Puritans obtained supremacy in the Commonwealth, Francis Rous (Speaker in the Barebones Parliament, and afterwards a member of Cromwell's Upper House) was appointed Provost of Eton, and he loyally asserted and maintained its rights. Cromwell himself seems to have regarded Eton with anything but ill-will, and it is noteworthy that he was the last to contribute the royal gifts of wine and venison, which had previously been annual. From the Restoration the course of Eton College has been one of almost unvarying prosperity and continuous progress.

The original foundation was for a provost, 10 sad priests, 4 lay clerks, 6 choristers, 25 poor grammar scholars, with a master to teach them, and 25 bedesmen, who were to offer up their prayers for the king. There are now on the foundation a provost, 7 fellows, one of whom is vice-provost, head-master, under-master, and 3 conducts, 7 clerks, 10 lay-clerks, 70 king's scholars, and 10 choristers. Besides these, there are over 700 scholars (*Oppidans*) not on the foundation. The good things of the college include the scholarships at King's College, Cambridge, of which four are given annually, two postmasterships at Merton College, Oxford, and 40 livings,—besides exhibitions and prizes within the college.

The Old Buildings, fittingly approached by the well-known Elm Walk, consist of two quadrangles, and comprise the chapel, hall, schools, provosts' and masters' houses, election hall and audit chamber, lodgings of the fellows, and various offices. The New Buildings are attached to the N. side of the Old Buildings. Henry, as we have seen, willed that his college should be built of stone, but almost the only part so built is the chapel. The Old Buildings are throughout of good dark red brick with stone dressings, and massive clustered chimney shafts, in that appropriate Tudor Collegiate style which our universities have rendered so familiar. The entrance to the first quadrangle, or *School Yard*, as it is termed (in Henry's original 'Avise' of the buildings it is always termed the *Quadrant*, and is laid down on a much larger scale than the actual quad.), is by a sombre central gateway, and immediately opposite you is the Clock Tower, a tall gate-house with a great clock-face, of the type of those at Hampton Court and St. James's. The school buildings occupy three sides of the quadrangle, the chapel the fourth—your right as you enter; in the centre is a bronze statue of the founder by Bird. On the N. side of the quad. is the *Lower School*, above which is the old dormitory, the well-remembered *Long Chamber* of old Etonians, now divided into separate compartments, and only retaining as an honoured relic one of the old well-hacked chest-like bedsteads with which it used to be lined. The more modern-looking building on an arcade on the W. side of the quad. is the Upper School, erected by Dr. Allistree when head-master, from the designs of Sir Christopher Wren. As a building, however convenient, it does little credit to the genius of the architect (in extenuation of whose shortcomings, however, it should be remembered that he was restricted to an outlay of £1500); but the goodly array of busts of famous Etonians—beginning with Gray, Fox, and Wellesley—does much, and as it increases will do more, to brighten the interior.

The *Chapel*, which occupies the S. side of the churchyard, is the chief architectural feature of the college. In form and general character it resembles King's College Chapel, Cambridge, but is much smaller and less ornate. It is, however, a part only of what its founder intended his chapel to be. In his will (dated May 1448, the 8th year of the works) he gives the dimensions of the choir, which correspond pretty closely with the present chapel, but directs a nave to be added on the W. of such a size as would have carried it into the street of Eton, which must have been turned to make room for it. This nave was, however, never even begun. The length of the actual building, including the ante-chapel, is 175 feet. It has suffered in its architectural character from the irregular and uncertain manner in which, owing to the failure of funds, its construction was carried on, and the haste with which it was eventually finished; still it is an impressive edifice, and its appearance has been greatly improved by the very elaborate restoration carried out under the direction of Mr. H. Woodyer during 1848-60, when all the classic additions made by Wren were swept away, the mean forms replaced by dark oak stalls and seats, and the flat plaster ceiling by a good open-timber roof. All the windows have been filled with painted glass—that in the great E. window by Willement, the others chiefly by O'Connor and Wailes. In the course of this restoration there was exposed a double row of very remarkable mural paintings in oil beneath the windows on each side of the chapel. They represented the Miracles of the Virgin, and no doubt formed part of the original decorations of the chapel. Their refined style and execution pointed to an Italian origin (and we know that Italian artists were employed in England about that time), but unhappily the subjects and mode of treatment made their retention inadmissible in a Protestant church. The upper row was therefore erased; the lower row covered with canvas, and hidden under the new wainscoting: careful drawings were, however, first made of the whole series; one set in outline, by Essex, is in the possession of the provost.

Several *monts.* in the chapel deserve notice. Besides the long line of provosts and head-masters, many eminent persons have been buried here—Grey, Earl of Wilton, Henchman to Henry VIII., and Longland, Bp. of Lincoln, his confessor; Francis Rous, the Puritan provost; Dr. Allistree, who built the Upper School; Nathaniel Ingelo, author of 'Bentevoglio and Urania'; Sir H. Wotton; and among more recent worthies, the late Marquis Wellesley. At the N. end of the chapel is a fine monument with a coloured effigy of Dr. Murray, 13th provost, which was carefully restored in 1859 by the Highland clan of Murray. On the floor are a few brasses, but none of much interest.

The little *Chantry Chapel* on the N. was erected in the reign of Henry VII., by Provost Lupton, whose rebus, a tun with the word *Lup* above it, is carved over the door. Within the chapel, besides the tomb of the founder, is a statue of Henry VI. by Bacon.

In the graveyard is the tomb of Hales, the "Ever Memorable"; and here may be traced some vestiges of the old parish ch., partially destroyed to make way for the college chapel.

The gateway of the Clock Tower leads to the second or Inner Quadrangle, locally known as the *Green Yard*, smaller than the outer quad., and differing from it in being surrounded by a cloister. Here is the entrance to the *Hall*, the dining-room for the Fellows on the foundation, with a daïs at the farther end for the dignitaries; a spacious room, resembling in its general character the college halls of Oxford and Cambridge, but smaller: it has been thoroughly restored. The panelling is decorated with the arms of provosts and benefactors. The E. window is filled with painted glass by Hardman, representing scenes in the life of Henry VI. On the walls are portraits of Etonians, among others a good one of Sir R. Walpole.

S. of the Hall is the *Library*, a fine suite of rooms, containing a noble collection of MSS. and printed books. In Oriental MSS. it is especially rich. Among the more curious European MSS., is an Heraldic History of the World, full of whole-page (folio) illuminations, portraits of famous personages from Adam and Noah, down to Alexander and Cæsar; representations of the Siege of Troy, the Destruction of Babel, and other momentous events; views of Jerusalem, Jericho, and other cities of antiquity, and a vast variety, besides, of German 15th cent.

work. An exquisitely illuminated Service Book, duodecimo size, on vellum, which belonged to Queen Mary, and bears her autograph, will interest the visitor. Among the printed books, several are remarkable for their rarity and beauty. Such are—a fine copy of the Mazarene Bible; the Nibelungenlied, folio, printed on vellum and richly bound, presented to the college by the late King of Prussia, one of 3 copies so executed; Granger's 'Biographical History of England,' bound in many folio volumes, one of the most amply illustrated copies known. The library is rich in choice copies of the Greek and Roman authors, and there is a fairly good collection of our own early printed books.

"The Provostship of Eton," wrote Thomas Fuller, " is accounted one of the genteelest and entirest preferments in England "; yet, when Bacon asked James I. to bestow it upon him, the king expressed surprise at his desiring " so mean a thing." The Provost's Lodgings contain many interesting portraits, including most of the provosts and many of the old scholars whose deeds have rendered Eton illustrious. Among the provosts are—Sir Thomas Smith, the famous scholar and statesman of the reign of Edward VI. and Elizabeth, a copy by *P. Fischer* from the original by Holbein. Sir Henry Savile, eminent alike as a mathematician and scholar, editor of the works of St. Chrysostom, founder of the Savilian professorships of astronomy and geometry at Oxford, and for more than a quarter of a century Provost of Eton: a full-length, in black robe and lace ruffs, painted at the age of 72. Sir Henry Wotton, ambassador from James I. to Venice and the Netherlands : immortalized by Izaak Walton; half-length, seated, resting his head on his left hand; inscribed " Philosophemur." Sir Francis Rous, the Puritan provost, a fast friend to Eton; half-length, seated, in official robes as Speaker of the House of Commons, with the mace before him. In the other rooms are portraits of the founder, Henry VI; bust to hands; in dark robe and cap trimmed with minever, and collar of SS. ; also his father, Henry V., in a furred robe with crimson sleeves and collar. A curious portrait of a lady whose only costume is a necklace, respecting which it has long been the college tradition that when Edward IV. was despoiling and trying to suppress Eton College, Jane Shore was induced by her confessor, Bost (afterwards Provost of Eton), to intercede with the king, which she did so effectually that he not only abandoned his purpose, but became a friend to the college, and that Bost, in gratitude, begged her portrait, that he might place it in the college in commemoration of her benevolence. Unfortunately for the tradition, the portrait was sent to the First National Portrait Exhibition, when it was pointed out (we believe first by Mr. G. Scharf) that the necklace bore the device of another lady, and one even more famous in her way, Diana of Poitiers; and on comparing the face with that of the acknowledged portraits of Diana, no room was left for doubt that the college portrait was really a portrait of that lady, and Bost's memory was thus relieved from the odium of asking for a picture of his fair penitent in such an unsaintly lack of costume. Queen Elizabeth, with certainly no deficiency of dress, is a good and expressive portrait.

The portraits of eminent Etonians, taken many of them when young, are extremely interesting : among them are such men as Bp. Pearson, Sir Robert Walpole, Gray, Fox, Canning, Hallam, Wellington, the Marquis Wellesley, Lord Metcalfe, etc. Some of these are valuable only as likenesses, but others are more or less excellent examples of the pencils of Reynolds, Romney, Lawrence, Phillips, and other distinguished portrait painters. Of the landscapes, the most curious is a large birdseye view of Venice, painted for Sir Henry Wotton, when ambassador there.

The *New Buildings*, on the N. of the older structure, erected about 1847, from the designs of Mr. H. Woodyer, form with their tall angle tower and varied chimney shafts a picturesque group. They are of red brick with stone dressings, and agree in style as well as material with the Old Buildings, but the rooms are loftier, and the whole has an air of greater freedom, cheerfulness, and amplitude. In them are the dormitories for the elder foundation scholars, the Boys' Library, of several thousand volumes, and a Museum.

A postern gate leads from the college to the *Playing Fields* (locally the *Shooting Fields*), delightful in themselves and in their associations, and made universally familiar by Gray's famous verses. Broad emerald meads, adorned everywhere with grand old elms, in groves or groups, or standing apart in solitary state,—meads

"Whose turf, whose shade, whose flowers among
    Wanders the hoary Thames along
        His silver winding way—"

with the "distant spires, the antique towers that crown the watery glade," and the majestic mass of Windsor Castle, changing in aspect at every step, but from every point crowning and ennobling the landscape,—scenery and associations combined, make the Eton Playing Fields a place in its way without rival in England, or perhaps elsewhere.

We must not leave Eton College without a few words on its gala days. Of these the most famous was the *Montem*. From the early times of the college this ceremonial was celebrated every third year. At first it was held on the first Tuesday in Hilary Term, which then commenced on the 23rd or 24th of January; but about a century ago, in the head-mastership of Dr. Bernard, the day was changed to Whit Tuesday, and the procession assumed the semi-military character it retained till its abolition. The scholars, in fancy dresses, marched from the college in military array, under the orders of a Marshal as commander-in-chief, a colonel, captains, and an ensign bearing a large flag, to a barrow known as *Salt Hill*, about half a mile beyond Slough, on the Bath road. Ascending the barrow, the ensign thrice waved the flag with much mock solemnity. Great crowds of spectators, including large numbers of old Etonians and gaily dressed ladies, lined the road, and assembled at Salt Hill; and the special feature of the festival was the 'salting' or levying contributions on the spectators by two 'salt bearers,' assisted by a numerous band of 'scouts' or 'servitors.' Originally the bearers carried salt, a pinch of which was offered in return for the donation, but later a card was given upon receipt of the 'salt-money,' on which was printed some such motto as "Mos pro Lege," or, as on the last occasion (1844), "Pro More et Monte." For many years the salt-money averaged £1000, and on the last Montem was nearly £1400. After deducting expenses, the surplus was given

to the Captain of the school, as an outfit on his proceeding to King's College. In the olden times the gathering was a brilliant one, and the festival as harmless as it was pleasant; but the railway came to Slough, and brought with it crowds of undesirable visitors. At each returning Montem the evil increased, until at length the authorities, however reluctant, felt that it must be brought to an end: it was accordingly abolished in 1846.

The boys' festivals now held are the 4th of June, or *Speech Day*, when the memory of George III., whose birthday it was, is celebrated, and *Election Saturday* (the last Saturday in July), when the candidates for Cambridge are elected: on both days there is a procession of the college 8-oar boats—Eton boys, as all know, are proficients in rowing—from the Brocas (the broad meadow above Windsor Bridge) to Surley, 3 m. up the river; a banquet or supper at Surley Hall; and a return procession to Windsor,—the evening being wound up by a display of fireworks from the Windsor Eyot.

Founder's Day is commemorated by a grand banquet, given in the Hall by the heads of the college, on the 6th of December, the anniversary of the foundation of the college by Henry VI.: but in this the boys have no share.

EWELL, SURREY (Dom. *Etwelle, Ætwelle* = At well, the vill. standing at the head of the Hogs-Mill, or Ewell River, which falls into the Thames at Kingston), pop. 2214, is situated about a mile N.E. of Epsom, and 14 m. from London: the Ewell Stat. of the Epsom line (L. Br. and S. C. Rly.) is ½ m. S. of the village, that of the L. and S.W. Rly. about the same distance N. Inn, *The Spring*, an excellent house.

At the Domesday Survey, Etwelle belonged to the king, and it continued in the possession of the Crown till Henry II., in 1156, gave all his lands in Ewell to the Prior and Canons of Merton. At the suppression of Merton Priory, in 1538, the manor reverted to the Crown, but was alienated by Letters Patent of Elizabeth, 1563, to Henry Fitz-Alan, Earl of Arundel, and has since been in private hands. As late as the 17th cent. Ewell had a weekly market, and a small market-house at the N. entrance to the village by the junction of the London and Kingston roads; but the market has long been disused, and the market-house pulled down. It is near the site of the old market-house that the spring mentioned above rises, and from it the Spring Hotel takes its sign. Two annual fairs are still held at Ewell, one of which, on the 29th of October, for sheep and cattle, and known as *Ewell Great Sheep Fair*, is one of the most important autumn fairs in the county. Ewell is now perhaps mainly dependent on the wealthy inhabitants, but there are extensive coarse pottery and brick works, maltings, farms, and along the Hogs-Mill large flour-mills, and the gunpowder works of Messrs. Sharpe and Co., which spread over a wide plot of ground in detached buildings: these works were established here in 1720, and have on the whole been creditably free from accidents, but an explosion which occurred in September, 1865, did great mischief, and is said to have been felt through a circuit of 20 miles.

The *Church* (St. Mary), built in 1848, is a commonplace Early Dec. building, with a tall square embattled tower at the W. end, in which is a peal of 6 bells, brought from the old ch. tower. In the chancel are some brasses, brought from the old ch., of which the most interesting is one with a small kneeling effigy in a heraldic mantle of the Lady Jane, wife of Sir John Iwarby of Ewell, d. 1515. Also from the old ch. a tomb with recumbent effigy, in flowing wig and the robes of Lord Mayor, of Ald. Sir William Lewen, d. 1721. There are also numerous tablets and one or two memorial windows to various members of the Glyn family. The ivy-covered tower of the old ch. has been retained for use as a chapel on occasion of burials in the old ch.-yard.

Near the ch. is *Ewell Castle* (A. W. Gadesden, Esq.)—a modern antique, built in 1814. The adjoining grounds are those of *Ewell Grove*; farther N. is *Ewell House* (H. J. Tritton, Esq.). Nonsuch House has a separate notice (*see* NONSUCH). Richard Corbet, the jovial poet-Bishop of Norwich, was born at Ewell, in 1582. He was the son of Vincent Corbet, a wealthy gardener at Ewell, whose many excellent qualities have been celebrated in a graceful poetical Elegy by his son, and in a long and highly laudatory 'Epitaph on Master Vincent Corbet,' by Ben Jonson.*

EYNESFORD, or EYNSFORD,

KENT (Dom. *Elesford*), on the rt. bank of the Darenth, in a lovely valley bordered by chalk hills, and in the midst of hop gardens and cherry orchards, 1¼ m. S.W. of Farningham, and 20 m. from London: Stat. ¼ m. S. of the vill., on the Sevenoaks branch of the L. C. and D. Rly. Pop. 1433, but this includes the eccl. dist. of Crocken Hill, which has 628 inhab. Inns: *Plough; Five Bells*.

One Ælfege gave the manor of Eynesford to Christ Church, Canterbury, about 950. After the Conquest, it was held of the archbishops by the De Eynesfords, who built a castle here, and died out *temp.* Edward I., when manor and castle passed to the great Kentish family of the Criols, and since through many hands to Sir Percival Hart Dyke, Bart. The *Castle*, the outer walls of which enclosed nearly an acre, stood by the Darenth, beyond the village on l. of the road to Farningham. All that remain of it are some shapeless fragments of flint walls, with many Roman bricks intermixed, by means of which the date (Norman) is determined, and the outline and outer bounds may still in part be traced. The moat is converted into an orchard. What could be learnt from a careful examination of the ruins when they were in a more perfect condition than they are now, may be seen in Mr. Cresy's paper in the Archæologia, vol. xxvii., App. A little lower down the Darenth are Mr. F. Fowler's large mills.

Flour and paper mills and fruit orchards —and this is a great fruit district—furnish the chief employment, and help to give the village that mingled manufacturing and agricultural aspect which is seldom altogether comely to look upon. With the river flowing along one side of the main street, and across the other, and with a number of old rickety half-timber houses about it, and the old church towering over it, the vill. has, however, in many parts a picturesque appearance, and the church, though ill-kept, is well worth visiting.

* 'Poems written by the Right Rev. Dr. Richard Corbet, late Bishop of Norwich,' 1672, p. 31; Ben Jonson, Underwoods, 1640, p. 177

The *Church* (St. Martin) stands high, by the crossing of the ancient Watling Street and the street to Maidstone; is large, cruciform, originally Norman, with an E.E. apse, a large W. tower (in which are 6 bells), short shingled spire, and a wooden porch projecting westward. Under this porch is the entrance doorway, which has a Norman arch of excellent work. The body of the church is of flint, the nave windows Perp., but those of the transepts as well as of the apse are E.E. The interior has a plain nave, fitted with high pews, but the chancel has been restored, and received a new roof. S. of the altar is a double piscina, and there is another in the S. transept. The brasses are all gone.

The stone coffin now in the chancel was dug up some years back in the ch.-yard. When the chancel was restored, the stucco was cleaned from the external walls, and some windows that had been long blocked up were opened.

Crocken Hill (pronounced *Croking Hill*), a chapelry in Eynesford par., and an eccl. dist. formed in 1852 out of the parishes of Eynesford, St. Mary Cray, and Sutton-at-Hone, pop. 793, lies about midway between Eynesford and St. Mary Cray, and 1 m. S. of the Swanley Junction Stat. of the L. C. and D. Rly., in a thriving but little-visited hop and fruit district. A neat E.E. church, All Souls, was built here in 1851, and has lately been improved.

F**AIRLOP,** ESSEX (*see* BARKING SIDE).

FARLEY, SURREY, (A.-S. *Fearlege,* Dom. *Ferlega,*) 2½ m. N.E. from Warlingham Stat. of the Caterham Rly. (S.E. line), through Warlingham and Farley Wood: pop. 127. Farley stands high on the chalk, in the midst of a picturesque, well-wooded, and singularly quiet, secluded country. There is no village; not even a 'general shop' or 'public.' The *Church* (St. Mary) is small, of flint and stone; consists of a nave and chancel, with a bell-turret in the roof; is E.E. in style, and has 2 narrow lancets at the E. It has been carefully restored, but has lost as well as gained something in the process. In the chancel is a *brass*, with effigies of John Brock, d. 1495, his wife, and 5 children. *Obs.* the grand old yew W. of the ch.; and, close by, *Farley Court,* of old the moated manor-house, now a most comfortable-looking and picturesque farmhouse, surrounded by goodly trees. The manor belongs to Merton College, Oxford, in whose gift is the living.

FARNBOROUGH, KENT, on the Bromley and Sevenoaks road, 14 m. from London, 3½ m. from the Bromley Stat. of the S.E. and L. C. and D. Rlys., and 2 m. S.W. from the Orpington Stat. of the S.E. Rly. (Sevenoaks and Tunbridge line), by a very pretty road: pop. of par. 1086 (including 212 in the Bromley Union Workhouse, which stands in this parish). Inn, *George and Dragon.*

An ordinary roadside village, Farnborough has little in itself or its history to interest a tourist, but from it there are charming walks towards Down and Keston. Farnborough is a chapelry annexed to Chelsfield—the united living, a very valuable one, being in the gift of All Souls College, Oxford. The *Church* (St. Giles) dates from the 13th cent., but was rebuilt in 1639, having been partially destroyed in a great storm. The chancel is the only part that retains the original lancet windows, and it is propped up with modern brick buttresses. The low square tower, of flint and brick, was rebuilt in 1838, and its crocketed cement finials are worthy of the period. The interior is plastered and ceiled. The churchyard affords views S. and S.W. over a richly wooded country. In the parish are extensive fruit farms: above 300 acres of strawberries are grown here for the London market.

Greenstreet Green, 1 m. S.E. (where is the large ale brewery of Messrs. Fox), and *Lock's Bottom,* 1 m. N.W. (where are the Bromley Union House, and a good inn with large garden, the *White Lion*), are hamlets of Farnborough.

FARNINGHAM, KENT (Dom.

Ferningeham), pop. 854, a small town, 17 m. from London by road, and 1½ m. S.W. of the Farningham Rd. Stat. of the L. C. and D. Rly.

The town is on the highroad to Maidstone, and on the river Darenth, which is here crossed by two bridges. It was formerly a place of some importance, had a weekly market, and an annual fair which lasted 4 days. It has still a considerable trade, but the market, chiefly for cattle, is only held on the 3rd Wednesday in each month, and the fair of one day (Oct. 15th) is mostly for colts. The town, little more than a village, of one long street, straggles down to the river: the shops are few; the private houses numerous, but not crowded. By the bridge, below the ch., is a mill, the successor of one that stood here in the reign of Stephen, and close to it the *Lion*, a good house with pretty gardens, much resorted to as a family hotel; by anglers, the river affording some fair trout fishing; and by Londoners for trade dinners. There is also a good farmers' inn, the *Bull*.

South of the river is the *Church* (St. Peter and St. Paul); E.E.; has a large nave, without aisles, a chancel much lower and narrower than the nave, with 3 lancets under a string-course at the E. end; large Perp. square tower (containing 5 bells) with angle stair-turret, and a modern brick porch on the N. The interior is plain, ceiled, but showing portions of the timber roof; has an early W. gallery, and high pews. The windows of the chancel and nave have painted glass. The font is octagonal, Perp., with elaborate carvings on the sides, but mutilated, and the subjects difficult to make out; and an old wooden cover. On S. wall of chancel is a piscina, trefoiled under a square head, and beside it the large arch of an E.E. tomb. N. of chancel is a *Mont.* (*n. d.*, temp. James I.) to Antony Roper and wife, with portions of the original colour remaining on the kneeling effigies. *Brasses:* in chancel, Wm. Gysborne, vicar, 1451, half effigy; nave, Alais Taillor, 1514, small; Wm. Petham, 1517, and wife Alice, effigy lost; Thomas Sibill, 1519, and wife Agnes. On the N. side of the ch.-yard are two small but healthy yews. In the neighbourhood are several hop-gardens.

From Farningham is a pleasant walk of 2½ m. S. by (or, if the lower road be taken, through) Eynesford (where are the ruins of a castle, and extensive cherry orchards,) to *Lullingstone Castle*.

FAWKHAM, or FALKHAM (pron. *Fakcham*), KENT, 3 m. E.S.E. from Farningham Rd. Stat. of the L. C. and D. Rly.: go by rd. E. by S. from South Darenth to *Deane Bottom*, thence a little more S. by field and ch. path: pop. 262.

Fawkham *Church* (St. Mary) is very small; the windows Dec. in style, but insertions in older walls; has nave without aisles, chancel, small octagonal wooden bell-cote, short shingled spire rising from the W. end of the nave roof, and wooden porch on S. It was restored in 1870. The interior is plain. In the chancel is a double piscina with central shaft. In N. wall is the arch of an Early altar tomb—name unknown; and on its upper slab stands a rude old iron-bound chest. The ch.-yard is treeless. The ch. stands in a hollow, and by it are two or three cottages. There is no village proper; but at *Fawkham Green*, nearly 2 m. S. (you may go to it by the road or through Parkfield Wood) are the village shops and a decent inn, the *Rising Sun*. The chief seats are the *Manor House* (H. Booth Hohler, Esq.) and *Pennis House* (D. F. Cooke, Esq.).

FELTHAM, MIDDX. (Dom. *Felteham*), a village 3 m. S.W. of Hounslow, 13 m. from London, and a Stat. (14¾ m.) on the Windsor br. of the L. and S.W. Rly.: pop. of par. 2748, but this includes 921 persons in the Middlesex Industrial School.

The manor of Feltham belonged to the Hospital of St. Giles-without-the-Bars till the Dissolution, when it was forfeited to the Crown. In 1631 it was granted in fee to trustees for Lord Cottington, and three years later a large part of the village was burned.* The manor, with the advowson, was sold to Sir Thomas Chamber in 1670, and has since changed hands many times.

The vill. is a long, straggling collection of small houses, with a few old-fashioned cottages and shops. There are also some

* Garrard to Lord Strafford, April 1st, 1634, in Strafford Papers, vol. i., p. 227.

newly built villas, and N. and W. of the vill. and at *Feltham Hill*, 1 m. S., are some good seats. The country around is flat, and mostly laid out as market-gardens and orchards.

The *Church* (St. Dunstan) is a plain brick edifice, erected in 1802 and enlarged in 1856: it has a tower and wooden spire. Inside are one or two monts. from the older ch. In the church-yard was interred Wm. Wynne Ryland, engraver to the king (George III.), eminent as a line engraver and etcher, and the first to practise the chalk or dotted style, who was executed Aug. 29, 1793, for forgery on the East India Company.

The large red-brick building seen in the fields N., is the *Middlesex Industrial School*, or Reformatory for boys convicted of crime. In its general character the building appears to have been modelled on the type of Wren's Chelsea Hospital, and, like that, is of red brick and stone, except the chapel, which is wholly of stone, and Dec. in style. It will accommodate about 1000 boys, who must be between 7 and 14 years of age, and may be sentenced to detention here from 1 to 3 years. It was opened January 1st, 1859, but has since been greatly enlarged.

FETCHAM, SURREY (Dom. *Feceham*),

1 m. W. of Leatherhead. To reach the little secluded vill. take the first turning on the rt. after crossing Leatherhead Bridge, by the Rising Sun, a little inn occupying the site of an old chapel; then the lane opposite the mill-pond—a fine sheet of water 7 acres in area which works a large mill,—and ½ m. farther is Fetcham Church, within the borders of *Fetcham Park*. The vill. stretches to the rt., or northward.

Fetcham *Church* has an ivy-covered tower and long sloping roofs, but was thoroughly renovated and despoiled of much of its picturesqueness in 1857. It is of flint and chalk, cruciform, and has some portions of Norman date. The tower contains 3 bells. In the chancel is one of those elaborate parti-coloured monuments with which the 17th cent. delighted to disfigure quiet country churches:

> "Knowe that this is sett
> But to upbrayde the World, if it forgett
> To speake the Virtues"

of Henry Vincent, Esq., d. 1631, whose effigy is given above, and his arms—both properly blazoned—underneath.

Fetcham Park (G. B. Hankey, Esq.) is a large, formal, stucco-fronted mansion standing in a well-timbered park. Other seats are *Elmer House* (W. J. Thompson, Esq.), and Fetcham Lodge (Roger Cunliffe, Esq.) From Fetcham there is a pleasant walk onwards by Eastwick Park to Great Bookham (1 m.), or across the fields, 2 m., to Stoke D'Abernon.

FINCHLEY, MIDDX. (anc. *Fyncheslee*),

a pleasant rural village, 8 m. N. of London, lying between the Barnet road and Hendon. The parish, which is very large, extending northwards about 3 m. from East End to Whetstone (the greater part of which is in Finchley par.), had 7146 inhab. in 1871: the district of the mother-church, excluding the outlying hamlets, had, however, only 2213 inhab. The Finchley Stat. of the Highgate and Edgware br. of the Grt. N. Rly. is by the village, and there is another stat. at East End. The High Barnet br. has stats. at East End, Torrington Park, and Whetstone.

Finchley is not mentioned in the Domesday Survey; but from time immemorial the manor has belonged to the see of London; and King John in the 1st year of his reign granted to the bishop and his Finchley tenants freedom from toll, a grant that was confirmed by Charles II. A manor, called Finchley manor, was held by the Marches and Leyndons in the 15th cent., and by the Comptons in the 16th; Anne Countess of Pembroke having in 1577 the use of it for her life, with remainder to Thomas, second son of Lord Compton and his heirs. Midway between the ch. and East End is the *Manor House* (Geo. Plucknett, Esq., J.P.), a large old mansion, much altered, but retaining the old oak-panelled hall, in which justice is still duly administered to local misdemeanants. The moat, enclosing a spacious oblong area, is still extant, but divided by the public road.

The vill. (called *Church End*) is long, rambling, still rural, and not unpicturesque, the country lanes and road changing imperceptibly into the village street; everywhere trees mingling with the houses, and the village culminating in a striking group of buildings,—the ch. the centre, the old part of Finchley College on one side, the new building with its tall tower—both noteworthy red-brick structures—on the other. But the builder is steadily gaining ground here as elsewhere. Streets, terraces, villas, and cottages are rising all around, and the outlying hamlets threaten soon to become good-sized villages. There is a little inn with a quaint garden, *The King of Prussia*, at Church End ; but the larger house, a great favourite with holiday-makers, the King's Head, is gone. Along the Barnet road the inns are of course numerous.

Finchley *Church* (St. Mary) is of stone, Perp. in style, and was thoroughly restored in 1872, when the plaster which previously covered it was removed, a new S. aisle added, the interior renewed and reseated, and the general appearance of the ch., both inside and out, much improved. It now consists of nave with aisles, chancel, and at the W. end a low battlemented tower, with, at the S.E. angle, a good stair-turret, carried only to the 2nd storey, and terminating in a conical stone roof; this, however, is recent work : before the restoration of the ch., the turret had a very rude termination. The interior of the ch. is very neat. At the W. end is a gallery. The roofs of the aisles and chancel are open timber, that of the nave flat, with ornamental plaster panels in wooden framework. The window tracery is all new. The only *mont.* worth noting is that of Wm. Seward, F.R.S. and F.S.A., d. 1799, the author of the well-known, and to the literary workman very serviceable, ' Anecdotes of Distinguished Persons,' 5 vols., 1795. In *brasses* the ch. is somewhat richer. The oldest is an effigy of Richard Prate, d. 1487. In the chancel is one of Simon Skudemore, gent., d. 1609, and wife ; and on the same slab, a small plate of Nicholas Luke, gent., and wife Elizabeth (daughter of S. Skudemore) with their 3 sons and 3 daughters (imperfect). In the N. aisle is a quadrangular mural plate of Thomas White, citizen and grocer of London, d. 1610, with his 3 wives, Mary (with 5 children), Mary (4 children), and Honnor (4 children).*

The obelisk in the ch.-yard marks the burial-place of Major Cartwright, the once popular political reformer, the associate of Horne Tooke, Hardy, and Thelwall, and brother of the inventor of the power-loom, d. Sept. 23, 1824. Thomas Payne, " Honest Tom Payne," the bookseller of the Mews Gate, where for 40 years his little shop was the daily haunt of scholars and book-collectors, was buried here, Feb. 9, 1799.

Two of the rectors of Finchley have exchanged the living for a mitre : Wm. Coton, promoted to the bishopric of Exeter, 1598 ; and John Bancroft, Bp. of Oxford, 1608. Bp. Bancroft was succeeded in the rectory by John Barkham, D.D., by whose labours others acquired celebrity. A sound scholar, a good antiquary, and a judicious collector, especially of coins and medals, he was most remarkable for the application he made of both. His coins he gave to Abp. Laud, and Laud afterwards presented them to Oxford University, where they are cherished as the Abp.'s gift. He assisted Speed in the composition of his ' English History,' and wrote for it the life and reign of King John, and the larger part of that of Henry II. ; and he is the real author of the ' Display of Heraldry,' fol., 1610, which John Gúillim published under his own name.

Christ College was established by the present rector of Finchley, the Rev. Thos. Reader White, warden of the college, with a view to providing a first-class education at a moderate cost. The mansion adjoining the ch.-yard serves as the Lower School, but it also contains the Dining Hall of both schools. The New Buildings opposite are appropriated to the Upper School. In all, the college has now about 200 scholars.

Finchley, writes Dr. Hunter in 1810, " is chiefly known by being annexed to the extensive *Common*, a place formidable to travellers from the highway robberies of which it has been the scene." The common, he adds, is " estimated to contain 2010 acres, the waste and uncultivated state of which so near the metropolis, is disgraceful to the economy of the country."* Monk, on his march to London, prior to the restoration of Charles II., drew up

* Haines, Manual of Brasses.

* History of London and its Environs, 4to, 1811, vol. ii., p. 86.

his army on Finchley Common, Feb. 3, 1660. But as long as it remained unenclosed Finchley Common was the usual rendezvous for troops on this side of London. Thus when the Pretender was at Derby in 1745, a camp was formed here of veteran soldiers and London volunteers—whose 'March to Finchley' gave occasion to one of Hogarth's most celebrated pictures. Again on Finchley Common were encamped the troops hastily collected on account of the Gordon riots in the summer of 1780.

As late as 1790 Finchley Common was dangerous to traverse at night. In that year Sir Gilbert Elliot (by no means a timid man), writes to his wife when within a few stages of London, that instead of pushing on that night, as he easily could, he shall defer his arrival till the morning, for " I shall not trust my throat on Finchley Common in the dark." * All this is changed now. The Common, the favourite haunt of Dick Turpin and Jack Sheppard, is enclosed, and either cultivated or built over. A traveller by the Great North Road would traverse the whole length of it without suspecting he had been near a common, much less one of such sinister celebrity. Jack Sheppard was captured at Finchley (1724) disguised in a butcher's blue frock and woollen apron; two watches were found concealed upon him, one under each armpit. At the London end of what was Finchley Common, nearly opposite the Green Man Inn at Brown's Wells on the Barnet road, is 'Turpin's Oak,' a fine old tree, still vigorous and green, though it has lost its head. Behind this, the tradition is that Turpin used to take his position. Pistol balls, supposed to have been discharged at the trunk to deter highwaymen, have been frequently extracted from the bark.

On Finchley Common has grown up the hamlet of *North End*, where are some good shops, inns, and many private houses, with a *Church* (Christ Church), erected in 1870, from the designs of Mr. J. Norton, but of which only the nave has been built. The rather showy Dec. Gothic church, with a slated spire nearly 100 feet high, on the W., is a Congregational church, erected in 1865, from the designs of Messrs. Searle.

* Life and Letters of Sir Gilbert Elliot, first Earl of Minto, vol. i., p. 372.

A mile farther along the road is the hamlet of WHETSTONE (*see* that heading). The hamlet of *East End* lies S.E. of Finchley (Church End), and extends to the Barnet road. A church (Holy Trinity) was built here in 1846, but the aisles were added recently. At East End is the cemetery for Marylebone parish, a well-arranged ground of 33 acres, with neat chapel and offices. The cemetery for Islington and St. Pancras parishes, of 88 acres, taken out of Finchley Common, is also in Finchley parish, but farther S., on the E. side of the Barnet road : here was interred, in 1855, Sir Henry Bishop, the musical composer ; his grave is marked by a granite mont. with a bronze medallion.

Of late Finchley has obtained much attention from geologists, it having been discovered that Finchley occupies an insulated glacial bed of an irregular triangular shape, the base extending from near Hendon to Muswell Hill, the apex being a little S. of Barnet. The vill. (Church End) and the central portion of the par. are on the boulder clay, while the outer parts are on the underlying glacial gravel, which crops out as a narrow fringe all round the clay, where that has been removed by denudation. The two deposits vary in thickness; together they average 30 to 35 ft. The gravel abounds in sub-angular iron-stained chalk flints and flint pebbles, with pink, grey, and whitish quartzite pebbles, and some of white quartz. A few shells, chiefly *Gryphæa*, are also found in it. The boulder clay, here for the most part brown and sandy, is full of small fragments of chalk, whence it is named by Mr. Searles Wood the chalky clay. It also includes in a confused mass blocks of sandstone, limestone, good-sized boulders of granite, and fragments of slate, coal, clay, etc., mostly from the north of England. Fossils are very abundant, especially belemnites and gryphæa (*incurva* and *dilatata*), fishes' teeth, bones of saurians, etc. Good sections of the clay may be seen at the brickfields by the ch., and in the Islington and Marylebone cemeteries.*

* Searles V. Wood, jr., on the 'Pebble Beds of Middlesex, Essex, and Herts,' in Quarterly Jour. of Geol. Soc., vol. xxiv., p. 464. 'The Relation of the Boulder Clay without Chalk of the N. of England to the Great Chalky Boulder Clay of the S.,' in Quarterly Jour. of Geol. Soc., vol. xxvi.,

FOOT'S CRAY, Kent (*see* Cray, Foot's).

FOREST GATE, Essex (*see* West Ham).

FOREST HILL, Kent (*see* Sydenham).

FORTIS GREEN, Middx. (*see* Hornsey).

FORTY HILL, Middx. (*see* Enfield).

FRIERN BARNET, Middx. (*see* Barnet, Friern).

FROGNAL, Kent (*see* Chiselhurst).

FROGNAL, Middx. (*see* Hampstead).

FULHAM, Middx. (A.-S. Chron. *Fullan-hamme*; Dom. *Fulcham*), on the Thames, opposite Putney, with which it is united by a wooden bridge; 4 m. S.W. from Hyde Park Corner. Pop. of the parish 23,350, but this includes the eccl. districts of Moore Park, 6803; North End, 5250; and Walham Green, 6174; the district of the mother-church had 5123 inhab. in 1871. Hammersmith was a hamlet of Fulham till it was constituted a separate parish in 1834.

There has been some speculation on the derivation of Fulham. "*Fullonham*," says Norden, "as Master Camden taketh it, signifieth *volucrum domus*, the habitacle of birds, or the place of fowles." But the authors of our A.-S. Dictionaries have adopted a very different derivation, more conformable to the earliest form of the word, though far from satisfactory: thus, Somner has "Fullanham, or Fulham, quasi Foul-ham, from the dirtiness of the place"; and Lye, "Fullanham, *cænosa*

habitatio"; whilst Bosworth gives "Fúllanhámes—*fúle*, foul, muddy; *hám*, home, dwelling—Fulham, Middlesex." *

From long before the Conquest, with the brief interval of the Commonwealth period, the manor of Fulham has belonged to the see of London. It is said to have been given to Erkenwald, Bp. of London, by Tyrhtilus, Bp. of Hereford, with the consent of Sigehard, King of the East Saxons, and Coenred, King of the Mercians. In 879 "a body of pirates (Danes) drew together and sat down at Fullanhamme, by the Thames;" stayed there during the winter, and in the summer of 880 "went over sea to Ghent in France, and stayed there one year." †

After the so-called Battle of Brentford, 1642, the army of Charles I., having established its head-quarters at Kingston, the Parliament called out the trained bands of London to join the force under Essex, which encamped at Turnham Green and Fulham, 24,000 strong; and Essex, to be prepared against all exigencies, "caused a bridge to be built upon barges and lighters over the river Thames, between Fulham and Putney, to convey his army and artillery over into Surrey, to follow the King's forces; and he hath ordered that forts shall be erected at each end thereof to guard it; but, for the present, the seamen with long boats and shallops, full of ordnance and musketeers, lie there upon the river to secure it." ‡ The bridge was built a short distance below the present wooden bridge, and when Faulkner wrote, 1813, the "*tête du pont*" on the Putney side of the river was "still plainly discernible." In 1647, Charles I. being at Hampton Court, the Parliamentary army marched through London and encamped between the city and Hampton; "and the Council of Officers and Agitators, sate constantly and formally at Fulham and Putney, to provide that no other settlement should be made for the government

---

p. 90, and subsequent papers: Mr. Whitaker's Memoir 'On the Geology of the London Basin,' in vol. iv. of the Geol. Survey; and H. Walker, F.G.S., Proc. of Geol. Assoc., vol. ii., p. 289; but especially Mr. Walker's pamphlet, 'The Glacial Drifts of Muswell Hill and Finchley, 1874, which is a handy guide to the geology of the district.

* Camden, Britannia; Norden, Spec. Brit.; Middlesex, 1593, p. 20; Dictionaries, *in loc.*

† Anglo-Saxon Chron. 879-880; Asser, De Rebus Gestis Ælfredi, and the later chroniclers, Ethelward, Florence of Worcester, Simon of Durham, and Henry of Huntingdon, follow the A.-S. Chron. almost verbally.

‡ Memorable Accidents, Tuesday, 15 November, 1642, quoted in Faulkner's Historical Account of Fulham, p. 257.

of the kingdom than what they should well approve." *

The line of houses is now virtually unbroken from London, and Fulham has become a portion of the outer fringe of the great city. But the *village* proper, Old Fulham, retains something of its ancient local and independent aspect. As you approach it by the Fulham Road, there are stately old mansions on either hand, half hidden or overtopped by elms, limes, and cedars, of very respectable antiquity and aristocratic bearing, but many verging on decrepitude and superannuation. The High Street has much the appearance of a dull little country town; shops and private dwellings are intermixed; many of the houses are small, old, low, of red brick with tall tiled roofs; the larger ones are mostly appropriated to meaner uses than of yore. Short streets open on either hand, more or less resembling in character the main street. Where the High Street bends round to Bridge Street, a glimpse may be caught on the rt., looking up Church Row, of the old church, with the tall trees of the Palace grounds beyond, whilst in front are the bridge and quaint bridge-house with the roof crossing the roadway, the Thames, and beyond it the tower of Putney Church. Much has been done during the last few years, and with marked success, to denude Fulham of its distinctive and picturesque features, but it still preserves more of its special character than any other of the river-side villages within the metropolitan circle.

The *Church* (All Saints) stands at the end of Church Lane, near the river, the ch.-yard extending to the E. end of the Palace grounds. It consists of nave, aisles, and chancel, with a tower at the W. end. It is of stone, but covered with plaster throughout, except the tower, the best feature of the exterior, which has been skilfully repaired, is 95 feet high, in 5 stages, with an angle turret rising well above the battlements. The body of the ch. is Perp. in style; the tower has a large W. window of (modern) flowing tracery. In the tower is a fine peal of 10 bells, cast (or recast) by Ruddle, a noted hand, between 1729 and 1766. The interior of the ch. is plain, in good re-

pair, but nearly devoid of ornament; has a pointed ceiling, covered with plaster, coloured of a bluish-grey; the large E. window, of 5 lights, has been restored and filled with painted glass; the other windows are mostly modern, round arched, and without tracery: one or two of the windows have armorial bearings. A gallery is carried round three sides of the ch., and there are tall pews. On the S. side of the chancel is a sedilia, with a cusped arch and canopy: perhaps the original seat of the bp. when attending service in the parish ch.; the bp.'s pew is now at the S.W. end of the nave. The organ, a very good one by Jordan, 1700, is in a handsome carved oak case.

Monts.—On entering the ch. by the tower, a showy mont. will be observed on the rt. to John Viscount Mordaunt of Avalon, father of the great Lord Peterborough, d. 1675. The ornamental portion was executed by John Bushnell, the sculptor of the statues of Charles I. and II. in the old Royal Exchange, and of the kings on Temple Bar, a noted hand at designing sumptuous monts.; the statue by Francis Bird, who carved the Conversion of St. Paul on the W. pediment of St. Paul's Cathedral, and the statue of Queen Anne in front of it. Lord Mordaunt is represented in classic costume, holding a baton in his rt. hand, as Constable of Windsor Castle. The statue, which is of marble, somewhat larger than life, stands on a large black marble slab; pedestals of black marble on either side support his coronet and gauntlets, and oval tablets above them bear a long eulogistic inscription and an ample pedigree. Bird received £250 for the statue, while the entire mont. cost £400, a large sum in those days. On the wall opposite is a plain brass plate within a Gothic frame to Bp. Blomfield, d. 1857, who was buried in the new portion of the burial-ground, opposite the vicarage. Here also is placed a remarkable lozenge-shaped brass, found buried in the ch. in digging for the foundation of a column in 1770, to Margaret Svanders, d. 1529, a native of Ghent, wife of Gerard Hornebolt, painter of Ghent, and mother of Dame Susan, wife of John Parcker, bowyer to King Henry VIII. The plate is of good Flemish work, and gives a half-length effigy, evidently a portrait, in a shroud, with an angel on either side supporting the inscription ; below is a shield of arms.* In the chancel is an elaborate mural mont. to Lady Margaret Legh, d. 1603, wife of Sir Peter Legh, of Lyme, Cheshire. She is represented seated under a semicircular arch, in a ruff, veil, and farthingale, her hair in very small curls, an infant in swaddling-clothes on her rt. arm, and another on a pedestal on her l. ; above her a shield of arms, hour-glasses, and various ornaments. Near this is an altar tomb under an arch ; the brass of a knight in armour (engraved in Faulkner), arms and inscription gone. On the S. side is a plain altar-tomb to Sir William Butts, chief physician to Henry VIII., and founder of the College of Physicians, 1545 : the brass on which he was represented as a knight is gone, but his features are well known by Holbein's portrait of him. Above this is a plain slab to Sir Thos. Smith, d. 1609, Clerk of the Council and Master of Requests to James I. In the aisles are monts. to Bp. Gibson, d. 1748 (of coloured marble), and Bp. Porteus, d. 1809, a plain marble tablet. A superb marble mont., about 14 ft. high, to Dorothy Clarke, d. 1695, daughter and coheiress of Thos. Hyliard of Hampshire, and wife first to Sir Wm. Clarke, Secretary at War to Charles II., and afterwards of Samuel Barrow, d. 1682, physician in ordinary to that king (and author of the Latin verses prefixed to Milton's 'Paradise Lost'). The mont. has a shield of arms supported by angels, above an urn from which depend wreaths of flowers, and is in its way an admirable piece of work : it was carved by Grinling Gibbons, and cost £300. With it may be compared the earlier mural mont. of Catherine Hart, 1605, with her effigy in ruff, stomacher, and hat, kneeling, 2 sons kneeling in front of her, her rt. hand resting on the head of one who holds in his hand a skull (emblem of his decease), behind her 2 daughters kneeling. Others are to Thomas Carlos, 1665, son of the Col.

Careless who concealed Charles II. in the oak, and was allowed to change his name to Carlos as a recompense ; William Rumbold, 1667, Clerk Comptroller of the Great Wardrobe, and Surveyor-General of the Customs ; Hester Nourse, 1705, mother of the maids of honour to Queen Catherine ; Jeffrey Ekins, Dean of Carlisle, d. 1791 ; Catherine Elizabeth, Viscountess Ranelagh, 1805 ; Martha Ogle, Baroness de Stark of the Holy Roman Empire, 1805, and several others. The inscription to Bp. Henchman, 1675, mentioned by Bowack, has disappeared.

In the ch.-yard, E. of the ch., are the altar tombs, mostly with no other ornament than the arms of the diocese of London, of Bps. Compton, d. 1713 ; Robinson, 1723 ; Gibson, 1745 ; Sherlock, 1761 ; Hayter, 1762 ; Terrick, 1777 ; and Lowth. 1787. In the vault of Lowth is interred his friend Christopher Wilson, Bp. of Bristol, d. 1792. Close to the tombs of the bishops are others ornamented with the civic mace, cap, and sword, of Ald. Sir Francis Child, 1713 ; Ald. Sir William Withers, 1768, Lord Mayor of London, etc. Here too is the tomb of Joseph Johnson, bookseller of St. Paul's, the friend of Fuseli, the publisher of Cowper, Darwin, and the Olney Hymns, of the scientific writings of Priestley, and the political ones of Gilbert Wakefield, for selling the last of which he had to suffer 9 months' imprisonment in the King's Bench. Directly opposite the chancel window is a plain stone inscribed " Theodore Edward Hook, d. 24th August 1841, in the 53rd year of his age." Several other notable personages lie in Fulham ch.-yard, and among them (Dec. 5, 1747) Vincent Bourne, in accordance with the desire expressed by him in his will " to be interred with privacy in some neighbouring country church." The gates of the ch.-yard are kept locked on week-days, but the key may be obtained close by.

Along the N.W. side of the ch.-yard are Sir William Powell's Almshouses, founded 1680, for 12 poor widows : they were rebuilt in 1869, of light brick and stone, in a style of rather fanciful Gothic.

A pleasant stroll of about ¼ m. along the raised pathway. *Bishop's Walk*, which runs from the W. end of the ch.-yard, leads to the entrance to Fulham Palace. It has the Thames on one hand, the bishop's

* In an office book of Henry VIII., there is an entry, Feb. 1538, to "Gerard Luke Horneband, painter, 56s. 9d. per month." He is noticed in Descamps, the Dictionaries of Painters, and elsewhere, as Gerard Lucas *Horrebout* or *Horebout;* is said to have imitated Holbein, and d. in London in 1558 : it is not improbable from the style that he designed the brass.

grounds on the other, and, the palace and grounds being private, affords the best view obtainable of both. The low situation of the palace is here very noticeable. In fact at the unusually high tide of March 20, 1874, the water flowed over the walk, making breaches in several parts of it, and carrying away the timber staging by which it is supported, and flooded a large part of the palace grounds. Some days later there might still be seen a good-sized pond in a hollow of the lawn S. of the palace, whilst the long meadow at the end of the walk, looking towards Craven Cottage, appeared as a handsome lake, with the peculiarity of having several fine trees rising from its midst.

Fulham Manor House—*Fulham Palace* as it is now usually designated—has been for three centuries the summer residence of the Bishops of London. The building, a somewhat heterogeneous brick structure, has no great antiquity or striking architectural merit. The house and grounds, about 37 acres in all, are surrounded by a moat, which is crossed by two bridges.* The older portion of the palace consists of two courts. The entrance is by an arched gateway which leads into the Great Quadrangle. This part was built in the reign of Henry VII., by Bp. Fitzjames, whose arms are on the wall and over the gateway. The principal room in the quad. is the Hall, completed by Bp. Fletcher, father of the dramatist, in 1595 ; repaired by Bp. Sherlock, 1748-61 ; converted into a chapel by Mr. Cockerell, for Bp. Howley, about 1825 ; and restored to its original purpose by Mr. Butterfield, for Bp. Tait, in 1868. It is a good room, 50 ft. by 27, and contains the arms of the bishops in the windows. The Library, as altered by Bp. Howley, is a handsome room, has a good outlook over the grounds and river, contains an excellent collection of books, and portraits of the bishops—all more or less interesting on account of the men, and some valuable as pictures. Among them are Bp. Tunstall, a copy after Holbein : Edwin Sandys (afterwards Abp. of York), in episcopal robes, hands resting on a cushion, a book in rt. hand ; Ridley, the martyr, in epis-

copal habit, book in l. hand, a good and characteristic head ; Grindall and Laud, copies after Vandyck, said to be by Old Stone ; Abbot, afterwards Abp. of Canterbury, attributed to Cornelius Jansen, to whom, also, is ascribed the portrait of Bp. Bancroft ; Compton, a copy after Kneller ; Juxon ; Sheldon ; Henchman ; Robinson, noteworthy as having been painted in Sweden when he was ambassador there ; Beilby Porteus, a half-length seated, by Hoppner, R.A. ; Gibson ; Terrick ; Lowth ; etc. The Great Dining Room was built by Bp. Terrick, 1764-77, but altered by Bp. Howley.

In 1715 Bp. Robinson presented a petition to the Abp. of Canterbury stating that "the manor-house or palace of Fulham was grown very old and ruinous ; that it was much too large for the revenues of the bishopric ; and that a great part of the building was become useless." * In consequence of this petition, Commissioners, among whom were Sir Christopher Wren and Sir John Vanbrugh, were appointed to examine and report upon the building. They recommended that the offices adjoining the kitchen, and all the buildings N. of the great dining-room, should be taken down, when there would remain between 50 and 60 rooms, which would be sufficient for the bishop and his successors ; and this advice was followed. Little seems, however, to have been done to the portion left standing, and Bp. Terrick, on his appointment to the see, in 1764, found the palace so dilapidated that he rebuilt the river front, fitted up a chapel, and repaired the remainder. This new portion is a long plain brick structure, the only pretence to ornament being the battlements on the summit, but it contains some good and convenient apartments. Bp. Tait (the present Abp. of Canterbury) made some additions to the offices, and substantial and ornamental repairs to the building, but his chief work was the erection of a new *Chapel*, which was consecrated May 6, 1867. It is attached to the S.W. portion of the older building, and is a small, well-finished, brick edifice, designed by Mr. W. Butterfield, of little pretension outside, but richly and elegantly fitted internally. The most striking of

---

* The moat is nearly a mile in circuit, and there is said to be a (very unlikely) tradition that it was originally the trench around the Danish camp, 879-80.

* Lysons, vol. ii. p. 227.

the ornamental features is an elaborate mosaic on the E. wall, by Salviati, from a design by Mr. Butterfield, representing the Adoration of the Shepherds at Bethlehem.

Fulham Palace has received several royal visitors. Norden says that Henry III. often lay there. Bp. Fletcher, the father of the poet, who is said to have "bestowed great sums of money in reparation of his episcopal houses," was "at an extraordinary charge" on that at Fulham, in the hope that "one day, after the end and purification of her displeasure," Queen Elizabeth would honour him with a visit.* His hope was vain, but she visited his successor, Bancroft, on two occasions, in 1600 and 1602. Bancroft also received a visit from James I. before his coronation. In 1627, Charles I. and his Queen dined here with Bp. Mountaigne. In 1647, Fulham Palace having been sold by the Parliament to Col. Edmund Harvey, Oliver Cromwell was entertained here in right royal fashion.

The grounds of Fulham Palace have from the time of Bp. Grindall been famous for their beauty and good gardening; and though many of the rare trees and choice shrubs and evergreens mentioned by Lysons have been lost, the grounds of Fulham Palace, alike for their verdure, flowers, and trees, and the views from the lawns and walks, are among the most charming in the vicinity of London.

A short distance N.W. of the palace is *Craven Cottage*, one of the best-known seats on Thames side. It was built by Lady Craven, afterwards Margravine of Anspach, and was regarded as "the prettiest cottage extant." The style was not a little fanciful. The entrance hall was Egyptian, "an exact copy of one of the plates in Denon's Travels in Egypt." The cornice and ceiling of the chief or central saloon was supported by large palm trees, the decorations and furniture conformable, the whole being intended to convey the idea of a Persian chieftain's principal room. Then there was a Gothic chapel, later called the Gothic dining-room, which purported to be an imitation of Henry VII.'s chapel at Westminster Abbey. The library was semicircular in form, luxuriously fitted up, and well

supplied with books. A spacious rustic balcony afforded an excellent view of the river. Along the Thames side was constructed a raised terrace. The grounds were laid out with great taste, and have always been much admired. After the Margravine, Craven Cottage was for some years occupied by Dennis O'Brien. It was then purchased by Walsh Porter, who spent a large sum in altering and embellishing it, and resided in it till his death in 1809. About 1842 it was the residence of Sir E. Lytton Bulwer (Lord Lytton),* who is said to have written more than one of his novels in the library.

Returning by Bishop's Walk, and leaving on our l. the fine lime avenue, a stucco-fronted Gothic house by the riverside, nearly opposite the church, at the corner of Church Lane, the narrow passage leading to the bridge, will be sure to catch the eye. Originally called *Vine Cottage*, it was purchased, made a storey higher, and fitted up at a great cost, and in a very fantastic fashion, with a 'robber's cave,' 'lions' den,' and the like, by Walsh Porter, who is said to have here entertained George IV. on many occasions, while Prince of Wales. It was afterwards occupied by Lady Hawarden, and by Wm. Holmes, Esq., M.P., who in 1834 sold it to Thomas Baylis, F.S.A., and T. Letchmere Whitmore, F.S.A. These gentlemen made it their residence, entirely remodelled it, imparted to it its present Gothic form, filled the interior with an extraordinary collection of art and antiquarian knick-knackeries, and gave to it the name of *Pryor's Bank*. The contents have long since been dispersed by the auctioneer's hammer (1841—1854); but of them, of the gatherings of literary and other celebrities, the masques and revels performed within the walls of Pryor's Bank, and the prose and verse to which it gave rise, an ample account will be found in Crofton Croker's 'Walk from London to Fulham.' Next door to Pryor's Bank is *Ashton Lodge* (Thos. Baylis, Esq.), and next to that stood *Egmont Lodge*, the residence of Theodore Hook, who died there 1841. Egmont Lodge was pulled down when the aqueduct of the Chelsea Water Works Com-

---

* Birch's Queen Elizabeth., vol. ii., p. 113.

* Life and Labours of Albany Fonblanque, p. 55.

pany was erected across the Thames in 1855. On the opposite side of the lane stood the residence of Granville Sharpe, who died there in 1813. The house was pulled down, and St. John's Place, a row of mean tenements, erected on its site, in 1844.

On the right on entering the town is *Holcroft's* (Mrs. Baker), built at the beginning of the 18th century by the wealthy Robert Limpany: it was the residence successively of Sir Martin Wright, Justice of the King's Bench, and the Earl of Ross. Afterwards, as *Holcroft's Hall*, it was occupied by Sir John Burgoyne, who gave here a series of dramatic entertainments, under the management of the Hon. Mr. Wrottesley, which were much talked of at the time, and which led to the marriage of Mr. Wrottesley with Miss Burgoyne, the daughter of Sir John, who had gained great applause by her acting. Later the house was rented by Mr. Charles Mathews and Mdme. Vestris, who changed its name to *Gore Lodge*, and in it Mdme. Vestris died in 1856. Directly opposite to it stood *Claybrooke House*, a good Elizabethan mansion, so called from a wealthy family of that name who owned it in the 17th cent. It afterwards belonged to the Limpanys and Frewens; it was pulled down some 30 years ago, and *Holcroft's Priory* (Capt. L. Curtis, R.N.) built on its site.

A little farther from the town, on the N. side of the road, is *Munster* (formerly *Mustow*) *House*, in the 17th cent. the seat of the Powells (of whom Sir Wm. Powell founded the almshouses): it afterwards passed to Sir John Williams of Pengelly ; was for awhile used as a school; was then occupied by Mr. Sampeyo, a Portuguese merchant; was then inhabited for some years by John Wilson Croker, Esq., M.P., Secretary to the Admiralty, prominent as a politician, and the editor of Boswell's Johnson; and after him by the Rev. S. R. Cattley, editor of Fox's 'Acts and Monuments,' or Book of Martyrs. It is now a private lunatic asylum.

By the river, E. of the bridge, are several once lordly mansions, but now wearing a deserted aspect. *Stourton House*, at the bridge foot, unoccupied and dismal, was a seat of the Lord Stourtons in the 14th and 15th centuries. *Ranelagh House* (J. Johnstone, Esq.), a little lower down the river, belonged in the last century to Sir Philip Stephens, Bart., one of the Lords of the Admiralty, and afterwards to Lord Ranelagh. Beyond this is *Mulgrave House*, a seat of the Earl of Mulgrave, and afterwards of Viscount Ranelagh. Still farther were seats of the Earl of Egremont, Sir Evan Nepean, the Countess Dowager of Lonsdale, and other distinguished persons; but though one or two of the houses remain, fashion has evidently deserted this part of Fulham. One of the houses still standing, *Broom House* (Miss Sulivan), is said to have been the residence of Bernard Lintott, Pope's publisher, but was more probably that of his son. *Hurlingham House* is now best known by the grounds, dear to pigeon-shooters and polo players.

On the E. side of the Fulham Road, not far from Walham Green, and concealed by a high brick wall, is *Ravensworth House*, the seat of the Earl of Ravensworth. The house looks but of moderate proportions, but is more capacious than it looks. Lord Ravensworth entertained the Queen and Prince Consort here, June 26, 1840. The grounds of Ravensworth House owe their charm to a former possessor, J. Ord, Esq., Master in Chancery, who about the middle of the 18th century planted them with so much skill that in a few years they took rank among the best around London: Lysons gives a full account of them,[*] but many of the rarer trees and plants described by him have since perished. Not far from Ravensworth House, on the opposite side of the road, is a large house formerly known as *Bolingbroke Lodge*, which tradition affirms was the residence of Lord Bolingbroke, and of course a resort of Pope, Swift, Gay, and others of that brotherhood. The house has long been divided, and now bears the names of *Albany Lodge* and *Dungannon House*. The latter used to be called *Acacia Cottage*, from a tree in the garden, and while so called was the residence, till his decease, of Johnson, the bookseller of St. Paul's Churchyard. Later it was occupied by Mr. C. Hullmandel, who first successfully introduced the practice of lithography into England. On the same side of the road is *Arundel House* (J. W. May, Esq.),

---

* Environs of London, vol. ii. p. 229.

an old mansion, refronted, which about 1819 was the residence of Henry Hallam, the historian of the Middle Ages. *Chesterfield House*, in the King's Road, was the residence of Dr. Burchell, the African traveller.

At *Purser's Green*, where the Fulham and Parson's Green roads separate, a stone will be observed let into the wall by the carriage entrance of Park House, with the inscription "Purser's Cross, 7th August 1738." It commemorates the death of a highwayman under rather singular circumstances. Recognized while refreshing himself at a public-house in Burlington Gardens as having committed a robbery on Finchley Common, he had barely time to remount and ride off. He was closely pursued, and his pursuers increased in numbers as he rode through Hyde Park, the cry being taken up by gentlemen and their servants riding there. On reaching Fulham Fields, and finding himself closely beset, he flung the contents of his purse among the men working there, put his pistol to his ear, and fell dead before any one could arrest him. His name was unknown; no one came forward to acknowledge him; and, as the result of a coroner's inquest, he was buried in the cross-road here with a stake driven through his body,—and this stone is his *hic jacet*. *Park House* occupies the site of an older mansion belonging to Sir Michael Wharton, and was at one time known as *Quibus Hall*. The new house was first called *High Elms*. A house opposite, now known as *Audley Cottage*, was for some years the residence of Thomas Crofton Croker, F.S.A., who wrote an ample account of the house and its contents, which is reprinted in his amusing 'Walk from London to Fulham.' Mr. Croker called his house *Rosamond's Bower*, this having formed part of a sub-manor called Rosamond's, which before 1481 belonged to Sir Henry Wharton, and in 1725 was divided between the coheirs of Sir Michael Wharton, and shortly after sold. There is a tradition that a palace of Fair Rosamond stood on the site of the manor-house.

Parson's Green, a little to the E. of Purser's Cross, so called from the parsonage which stood of yore on the W. side of the Green, was a century ago a very

favourite place of abode.* Though fallen from its high estate, it still preserves something of the old bearing. Several of the best houses have indeed been pulled down or altered, and others are empty and half-ruinous, but some remain, the Green is still verdant, and the elms vigorous. S.W. of the Green is *Peterborough House*, (W. Terry, Esq.), a good mansion which occupies the site of one of some celebrity. The older house, then called *Brightwells*, was the residence of John Tamworth, Privy Councillor to Queen Elizabeth, who d. there in 1599. It was afterwards purchased by Sir Thomas Knolles, who sold it in 1603 to Thomas Smith (afterwards Sir Thomas), Clerk of the Council and Master of Requests to James I. His widow married Thomas Earl of Essex, who made it his residence. By the marriage of Sir Thomas Smith's daughter and heiress it was conveyed to Thomas Carey, second son of Robert Earl of Monmouth, who rebuilt the house, and named it *Villa Carey*. Francis Cleyne then in great repute for painting ceilings, etc., in grotesques, was employed on the decorations.† Carey's daughter married John Mordaunt, a younger son of the 1st Earl of Peterborough, who was created Viscount Mordaunt by Charles II. for services rendered during the Commonwealth and at the Restoration, and whose mont. is in Fulham ch. His son Charles (the great) Earl of Peterborough resided much at Parson's Green, and frequently received Locke, Pope, Swift, and other eminent men as his guests. Lord Peterborough's second wife, the celebrated Anastasia Robinson, lived with her mother in a house close by, Lord Peterborough never publicly acknowledging the marriage till a few months before his death Whilst Lord Peterborough loved to gather literary and political celebrities about him, his wife used at her house to hold musical assemblies, at which Bonancini, Martini, and other leading musicians used to assist, and which were attended by all the fashionable world.‡ The grounds of Lord Peterborough's house were very

---

* "In Parson's Green are very good houses for gentry; where the Right Hon. the Earl of Peterborough hath a large house with stately gardens."—Stow's Survey of the Cities of London and Westminster, by Strype, 1720, vol. i., p. 44.
† Walpole, Anecdotes of Painting, vol. ii., p. 227.
‡ Hawkins, History of Music, vol. v., p. 305.

famous : Swift says in one of his Letters that Lord Peterborough's gardens are the finest he has seen about London. After Lord Peterborough's death the house was sold to a Mr. Heavyside, "lately an eminent timber merchant," from whom it was purchased in 1794 by John Meyrick, Esq., the father of Sir Samuel Meyrick, the antiquary and writer on armour. Mr. Meyrick pulled down the old house, and erected on its site the present house, in which he died in 1801. The red-brick gateway of old Peterborough House is still standing a few yards beyond the present mansion.

Not far from Peterborough House, on the same side of the Green, stood a cheerful-looking old-fashioned house which was the residence of Sir Edward Saunders, Lord Chief Justice of the King's Bench in 1682. This was the house to which Samuel Richardson removed from North End in 1755, and here he is said, both by Lysons[*] and Faulkner,[†] to have written 'Clarissa Harlowe' and 'Sir Charles Grandison': but the first 4 vols. of 'Clarissa Harlowe' were published in 1747-8, and 'Sir Charles Grandison' in 1754 : to North End therefore, and not to Parson's Green, belongs the honour of these works. (*See* NORTH END.) Noticing his removal to Parson's Green, his biographer observes, " he now allowed himself some relaxation from business, and spent the greater part of his time at his country residence, where he was seldom without visitors."[‡] He died in his Parson's Green house, July 4, 1761. His widow resided there till her death in 1773. Thomas Edwards, the author of 'Canons of Criticism,' died whilst on a visit to Richardson at Parson's Green, January 3, 1757.

East End House, a plain white house on the E. side of the Green, was built by Sir Francis Child, Lord Mayor of London 1699 (whose tomb is in Fulham ch.-yard), and, after remaining long in the possession of his family, became the residence of Admiral Sir Charles Wager. Early in the present century it was the residence of Mrs. Fitzherbert, when George IV., then Prince of Wales, was a frequent visitor. The porch, by which it will be

recognized, was built by Mrs. Fitzherbert. It is now unoccupied, and seems going to decay. The adjoining house, a noteworthy old brick edifice, which looks as though it ought to have a history, is in like condition. Sir Thomas Bodley, the founder of the Bodleian Library, Oxford, resided at Parson's Green 1605-9 ; as at the same time did Rowland White, Sir Robert Sydney's correspondent. When Lord Bacon fell into disgrace, he procured a licence (Sept. 13, 1621) to retire for 6 weeks to the house of his friend Lord Chief Justice Vaughan, at Parson's Green; but when the time expired, the king refused to renew the licence.[*]

Among many eminent persons who have been residents in or closely connected with Fulham, are John Norden, who dates the preface to his Speculum Britanniæ, 1598, "from my poore house, neere Fulham." John Florio, whose translation of Montaigne's Essays was we know familiar to Shakspeare, had a house in the High Street. for which he was rated (Oct. 12, 1625) 6s. for the relief of the poor. Henry Condell, the Shakspeare player, also had his 'country house' here ; whilst Burbage's was at North End. Somewhat later, George Cartwright, the actor, lived and wrote here his long-forgotten tragedy 'Heroic Love, or the Infanta of Spain,' 1661. Still later, towards the end of the century, it was for a time the abode of the odd, rambling, and scribbling bookseller, the author of 'The Life and Errors of John Dunton,' 1705, "a faithful and painful collection," as Swift and Dunton concurred in calling it. Dunton does not mention Fulham in his 'Life and Errors,' but there may be a reference to it at the end of his 'Idea of a New Life.' "I now live in a *Cell*, and study the art of living *incognito*."[†]

Fulham looks its best from the Thames. The shabbiness of too many of the houses is thence little apparent. Those by the river are for the most part of the better class. and stand on sunny lawns, screened by tall and shadowy trees. The quaint old wooden bridge is too well known to need description. With the sister churches, Putney at one end and Fulham at the other, their lofty towers each peering out

---

* Environs, vol. ii., p. 238.
† History of Fulham, p. 308.
‡ Mrs. Barbauld's Life of Richardson, prefixed to his Correspondence.

* Lysons, vol. ii., p. 239.
† Life and Errors, vol. i., p. 332.

from a cluster of irregular roofs and gables, it was only a few years ago the most noticeable bridge between London and Windsor; but a good deal has been done to destroy the quaint aspect of the bridge, though as much to lessen its inconvenience for navigable purposes, by throwing two or three of the central arches into one; whilst the effect of the whole as a picture has been irretrievably marred by the construction of the Aqueduct of the Chelsea Waterworks Company across the river immediately above the bridge. The Act for the construction of a wooden bridge from Putney to Fulham was passed in 1726, and the bridge was completed in 1729. The 'plan' of the bridge was drawn by Cheselden, the great surgeon,* to whose ingenuity it certainly does more credit than to his sense of beauty; the builder was Mr. Phillips, carpenter to George II.; the cost £23,075. It is 789 ft. long, and 24 ft. wide. It is from the Aqueduct just above Fulham Bridge that the Oxford and Cambridge boats start for their annual race.

Somewhat over half a mile below Fulham Bridge, a new bridge was opened in 1873, which connects the King's Road, Fulham, with York Road, Wandsworth. It was designed by Mr. J. H. Tolmé; is of iron, a lattice girder bridge, of five spans, borne on coupled wrought-iron cylinders, 7 ft. 6 in. in diameter. The three stream spans are each 133 ft., the shore spans 113 ft.; the width between the main girders 30 ft.

Fulham has always been famed for its nurseries and market-gardens, and though both have been abridged, and are continuously lessening by the progress of the builder, they are still extensive, and kept in the highest style of culture. The market-gardens are chiefly in the level and once marshy tracts by the Thames,— the Town Meadows E. of the town, and the Fulham Common Fields stretching towards Hammersmith.

The manufactures are not important, though there is a Pottery, the history of which is of some interest. It was established here in 1671, by John Dwight, M.A., of Christ Church, Oxford, who had been registrar to Brian Walton, Ferne, and

Hall, successively Bps. of Cheshire, and who after numerous experiments took out a patent (April 23, 1671,) which was renewed for a further 14 years, June 12, 1684, for the making of "earthenwares, known by the name of white gorges (pitchers), marbled porcelain vessels, statues and figures, and fine stone gorges never before made in England or elsewhere." Mr. Chaffers,* who has carefully investigated the history of the Fulham ware, says that Dwight was certainly the "inventor of porcelain in England," as well as the first to make the Hessian and other German wares. But it is curious that though the works have continued in operation to the present day, not a single example of the fine porcelain goods is known to exist. On the other hand, the imitation *grès de Cologne* is not uncommon, though usually passed off as of German manufacture.

About 1753 was also established at Fulham a manufactory of Gobelin tapestry, by one Peter Parisot, who brought over workmen from Chaillot. The project was patronized by the royal family, and the fabrics were greatly admired, but they were too costly for ordinary purchasers, and the manufacture soon declined.

There is reason to assign a counterfeit manufacture of some notoriety to Fulham. False or loaded dice were, in the reigns of Elizabeth and James I., called *Fullams*, and "not improbably," as Gifford suggests, "from their being chiefly manufactured there." There were *high fullams* and *low fullams*, according as they were loaded for the high or low number. Hence Ben Jonson—"Who! He serve? S'blood, he keeps high men and low men, he! He has a fair living at Fullam." †

The eccl. districts of *North End* and *Walham Green* have separate notices. *St. James, Moore Park*, is a new eccl. district formed in 1868: pop. 6803. It occupies the S.E. side of the par. between the Fulham Road and the river, and includes the extensive works of the Imperial Gas Company. It is a poor district of recent growth, without any object of general interest. A house by the river-

---

* Faulkner, History of Fulham, p. 6.

* Marks and Monograms on Pottery, 3rd. edit., 1870, p. 653; Art Journal, Oct. 1862.
† Every Man out of His Humour, Act iii. sc. 2, and Gifford's note, B. J. Works, vol. ii. p. 111.

side, called *Sandford Manor*, now included within the Gas Company's premises, was, according to tradition, a residence of Nell Gwynne. The *Church* is a large cruciformlate E.E. brick building, erected in 1867, except the chancel, which was added in 1873, from the designs of Mr. Darbishire.

GATTON, SURREY (A.-S. *Gatctune*, Dom. *Gatone*, so named probably from its situation on the old road, which is carried through a narrow valley (*gate*) at the edge of the chalk); 1 m. N.W. from Merstham Stat., and 2 m. N.E. from Reigate Stat. of the S.E. Rly. Gatton House and Church are on clay overlying the Upper Greensand. Upper Gatton is on the chalk, and there are quarries of 'firestone' similar to that of Merstham. There is no vill., and in all only 36 houses, with 207 inhabitants, in the parish.

Roman remains have been found at Gatton, and there is a tradition that a body of Danish soldiers were defeated and slaughtered by the women of the district at a spot still known as Battle Bridge, the neighbouring farm being called Battle Farm : Manning suggests that it may have been a party of fugitives from the Danish army defeated at Ockley by the West Saxon King Ethelwulf, 851, that the Gatton women encountered. Gatton was one of the many manors conferred on Bishop Odo by the Conqueror, and was forfeited with the rest of his estates in the next reign. It was then held by Herefrid, and his descendants the De Gatons, till the 14th cent. In the middle of the 15th cent. it belonged to John Tymperley, who received, 1449, a grant of free warren, and a licence to impark and enclose with pales and ditches 580 acres of his manor of Gatton, and 250 acres at Merstham. In 1451 Gatton was empowered to return 2 members to Parliament. Except during a short period in which it was held by the Crown, and included among the estates granted by Henry VIII. to his divorced wife Anne of Cleves (who parted with it the same year to Sir R. Copley) the fortune of the manor seems to have been thenceforth chiefly influenced by its possession of the parliamentary franchise. As early as the reign of Henry VIII. it is recorded that Sir Roger Copley, Knt., " being the burgess and only inhabitant " of the borough and town of Gatton,"

elected the two honourable members ; and as late as that of George III., the then lord of the manor, Mark Wood, Esq., returned the two members by his single vote. On very rare occasions the number of voters reached 20, but the election was always in the hands of the lord of the manor. The trustees of Lord Monson purchased the manor in 1830 for £100.000 —a main element in the valuation being of course the elective power. Two years after came the Reform Act, and Gatton was disfranchised.

Gatton House, the property of Lord Monson, but now in the occupation of R. MacCalmont, Esq., a large and stately Italian structure, owes its present form to Frederick John, 5th Lord Monson, who remodelled and greatly extended the former plain mansion. The *Hall*, the chief feature of the house, was constructed by Lord Monson on the model of the Corsini Chapel, Rome. It has a pavement of rich coloured marbles, purchased by Lord Monson at Rome for £10,000 ; the walls are also lined to some height with various coloured marbles, above which are 4 fresco paintings by *Severn*—Prudence, typified by Queen Esther ; Resolution, by Eleanor, queen of Edward I. ; Meekness, by Ruth ; Patience, by Penelope. A copy of the Warwick vase in white marble, statues, and candelabra add to the splendour of the hall. Among the pictures at Gatton, the most interesting perhaps is a Holy Family by *Leonardo da Vinci*, one of the best of the master's earlier works, and well known by the fine engraving by Forster. A portrait of Lorenzo de' Medici, in a robe trimmed with ermine, by *Sebastian del Piombo*, though much darkened, is a fine picture. *Raphael*, by himself, is of less certain authenticity. The same perhaps may be said of an Entombment, attributed to *Titian*. A Virgin and Child, a Saint with the Infant Christ, and a David with the head of Goliah, are in their several ways good examples of the pencil of *Guido*. Other pictures worthy of note are—The Cardplayers, attributed to *N. Maes*; Women with Fruit, by *Rubens*; two large views of Venice by *Canaletto*; portraits of Sir John Monson and of his wife (temp. Charles I.), by *Cornelius Jansen*; portrait of the Countess of Mexborough, by *Reynolds*; but some of these are in private rooms, and can only be seen by special leave. Visitors are permitted to see the hall, corridors, etc., on any week-day.

Gatton *Church*, stands close to the house. It is mainly of Perp. date; but was entirely remodelled by Lord Monson in 1834, and has been altered since. It comprises nave, chancel, and short transept; tower at the W. with slender spire, and a porch on the N. with room over. The interior is interesting as containing 2 rows of richly carved stalls with misereres, brought by Lord Monson from a monastery at Ghent; a pulpit and altar from Nürnberg, the designs for which are said to have been made by Albert Dürer, and altar rails from Belgium; while the wainscoting of the nave, the canopies, and the painted glass were brought from the cathedral of Aürschot in Louvain, and the carved door from Rouen. The large octagonal mausoleum on the N. of the ch. was erected by the local freestone, by the Lord Monson who rebuilt the house and remodelled the ch., and who was interred in it in 1841.

The house commands a fine view over the great lake and across the park, rich in beech and elm, and picturesquely broken in surface. A pleasant walk by the lake leads towards Reigate. You leave the park by a lodge close to a suspension bridge which crosses the old London road. A good view is obtained from this bridge, but a far finer from the beech wood on the down above: to reach it, take a path a little way up the lane to the W.

Upper Gatton Park, the seat of Charles K. Freshfield, Esq., M.P., about ¾ m. N.W. of Gatton Park, is a handsome mansion, standing on high ground, and embracing an extensive prospect. *Nutwood Lodge* (H. E. Gurney, Esq.) is also pleasantly situated.

GEORGE'S HILL, ST., Surrey,

an oblong mass of Bagshot Sand rising to an elevation of 500 feet, and famous for its views, is situated about a mile S. from the Weybridge Stat., and 2 m. S.W. from the Walton Stat. of the L. and S.W. Rly. The hill is a part of the estate of the Dowager Countess of Ellesmere, and is enclosed, but the gates are open, and convenient paths are cut on all sides, and to the summit. The hill-top is a cap of the middle Bagshot, or Bracklesham beds, overlying the Lower Bagshot beds which form the base of the hill. The sides of the hill are greatly broken, but the ascent to the summit is quite easy by the paths from either of the gates. The area enclosed is about 1170 acres, but a good deal of this consists of fir plantations, which, however, are being thinned out with great advantage to the prospects.

On the summit of the hill, towards the S.E., is a large entrenchment, which since the publication of Gough's ed. of Camden's 'Britannia' has been known as *Cæsar's Camp*, but for which designation there is certainly no early authority. (*See* COWEY STAKES.) The entrenchment is irregular in form, ¼ m. long from N. to S., and about half that width; the circuit, including the angles, is ¾ m., the area enclosed about 14 acres. The general form is very fairly laid down in the Ordnance Map, but the W. side, where there is a double fosse and vallum, is more rounded (convex), the E. more irregular, and the angles less sharp, than there indicated. On the S. a well-defined angular bastion is carried out with a sharp glacis-like scarp on three sides. From the E. of the rampart an embankment (or, as Dr. Guest considers it, a boundary dyke) extends N. towards Walton. The opinion that this was a Roman camp, and probably that formed by Cæsar,[*] is not supported by Cæsar's narrative, or by the extremely irregular nature of the work. That, taken in connection with the dyke above referred to, and other vestiges of earthworks in the vicinity, leaves little doubt that this was a British work, and one of considerable importance as overlooking and commanding a wide extent of country. It is of course possible, and from its value as a military station highly probable, that it was held by the Romans during their occupation of the country, when the S. bastion and one or two other

---

[*] Gale, Archæologia, vol. i., p. 188.

portions, which look like Roman work, may have been constructed.

But apart from the camp, St. George's Hill will abundantly repay a visit. The air is delicious ; the scenery, from whichever side the ascent be made, rich and various ; oak, elms, and pines supply a welcome shade ; in the early summer the hawthorns add beauty and fragrance ; ferns, heath, and broom grow luxuriantly ; rabbits abound, and birds on every hand pour out their melody ; whilst from the summit the eye may on a clear day range over portions at least of Surrey, Berks, Buckinghamshire, Middlesex, Hertfordshire, Essex, and Kent, the prospect being enlivened or bounded by such landmarks as the Wycombe beeches, Windsor Castle, Cooper's Hill, Moor Park, Bushey Heath, Hampton Court, Richmond Hill, which shuts out London, the hills of Harrow, Highgate, and Hampstead, Knockholt beeches, and the Surrey Hills to the Hog's Back and Hindhead.*

GERARD'S, GERRARD'S, and of old JARRET'S CROSS, Bucks, about 3 m. N.W. from the Uxbridge Stat. of the Grt. W. Rly., and midway between Uxbridge and Beaconsfield, is a broad open common of nearly 1000 acres, covered with furze and heather. A little vill. has grown up where the road from Chalfont to Windsor crosses the main road from London to Oxford ; and on the Common some distance S. of the vill. a fine church was erected in 1859, at a cost of £10,000, by the Misses Reid, as a memorial to their brother, Major-Gen. Reid, late M.P. for Windsor. In 1860 the eccl. dist. of St. James, Gerard's Cross, was formed out of portions of the parishes of Chalfont St. Peter, Fulmer, Iver, Langley Marsh, and Upton ; in 1871 it contained 117 houses and 607 inhabitants.

The *Church* is noteworthy as the first built in England in the Lombardo-Byzantine style. In form it is a Latin cross, having an octagonal cupola 67 feet high,

rising from the intersection of the arms of the cross, with four square turrets at the inner angles. and a campanile 80 ft. high at the N. W. corner. The nave is 100 feet long, the transepts 60 feet, the width of both about 21 feet. The architect was Sir W. Tite, F.S.A. The surrounding scenery is open, varied, and pleasant ; and many good villa residences have been erected during the last few years.

W. of the Common is *Bulstrode*, the seat of the Duke of Somerset. Bulstrode belonged to a family of that name who, according to a silly story told at length in Sir B. Burke's 'Vicissitudes of Families,' received their name from the then head of the family, one Shobbington, having at the head of his servants, tenants, and neighbours, mounted on bulls, instead of horses, attacked and defeated an army of the Conqueror. William was so struck with his prowess that he invited him to his camp in order to come to terms. He accordingly went, still astride his bull, accompanied by his 7 sons, and after a conference the king granted him his land and favour. Shobbington, in commemoration of the event, assumed a bull for his crest, and the cognomen of Bulstrode. The Bulstrodes held the manor till the 17th cent., when it was purchased by Sir Roger Hill, by whom it was sold to Judge Jeffreys, who in his patent of baronetcy is styled Sir George Jeffreys of Bulstrode. In 1686 Jeffreys, then Lord Chief Justice, built a stately mansion, in part out of the materials of the old house, and in it is said to have often received James II. His son-in-law, Charles Dee, Esq., sold Bulstrode to William III.'s favourite, William Bentinck, 1st Earl of Portland, who was very fond of the place, and of the gardens, and who died there Nov. 30, 1709. Bulstrode was a place of note in the time of the 2nd Duke of Portland— who by the way was robbed by a highwayman (Dick Turpin as was said) within his own park. Walpole describes Bulstrode, at this time.*

---

* Skrine (who resided near the foot of the hill), has given a full and faithful account of the view in his *Rivers of Note in Great Britain* (1801), pp. 355— 359, but it is right to add that the growth of the trees on the upper part of the hill has rendered it now difficult to make out many of the objects mentioned, and impossible to see them all from any single point.

" Bulstrode is a melancholy monument of Dutch magnificence ; however there is a brave gallery of old pictures, and a chapel with two fine windows of modern painted glass. The ceiling was formerly decorated with the assumption, or rather *presumption* of Chancellor Jeffreys, to whom it belonged ;

---

* Letter to Bentley, June 5, 1755.

but a very judicious fire hurried him somewhere else."

The pictures and works of art were largely increased by Margaret, widow of the 2nd Duke, whose residence here is celebrated in the 'Letters' of Mrs. Montagu, and the 'Autobiography' of Mrs. Delany. George III. often visited the Duchess Dowager at Bulstrode, calling with some of his family in a very homely way. It was on one of these visits that Mrs. Delany was first introduced to the royal family, with whom she afterwards became so great a favourite. She writes to Mrs. Port, of Ilam, that on the 12th of August, 1778, being the birthday of the Prince of Wales, the King, Queen, and several of the royal family came over from Windsor to breakfast with the Duchess at Bulstrode. Mrs. Delany was in her own room, but

" Down came Lady Weymouth with her pretty eyes sparkling, with the Queen's commands that I should attend her. . . . I kept my distance till the Queen called me to answer some question about a flower, when I came, and the King brought a chair, and set it at the table opposite to the Queen, and graciously took me by the hand and seated me in it,—an honour I could not receive without some confusion and hesitation. 'Sit down! sit down!' said her Majesty; 'it is not everybody has a chair brought them by a King.' It would take a quire of paper to tell you all that passed at Bulstrode that morning."

Jeffreys' house was pulled down by the 3rd Duke, and a new castellated mansion begun from the designs of James Wyatt, but it was left unfinished. The manor was sold by the 4th Duke of Portland, and the deer all killed and buried in the park. The Duke of Somerset purchased Bulstrode in 1810, and contemplated the erection of a new and more magnificent residence than either of its completed or unfinished predecessors. But though Sir Jeffrey Wyatville was commissioned to make the designs, the work proceeded no farther, and Bulstrode lay neglected till 1860, when the present Duke of Somerset directed the ruins of Wyatt's buildings to be removed, and commissioned Mr. Benj. Ferrey, F.S.A., to design an entirely new structure, to stand upon a more elevated site a little to the E. of the former residence. This is a spacious but not lofty edifice, in what Mr. Ferrey designates "the old English manorial character, with brick walls, relieved in parts by facial

ornaments of vitrified brick devices, Bath stone dressings, and ornaments." * The *Park*, of nearly 800 acres, is undulating in surface, richly timbered, and affords many beautiful near and distant prospects. At its E. extremity, by Gerard's Cross, is a circular earthwork enclosing an area of 21 acres. There is a public way through the park.

By the park gates, at the Beaconsfield end of Gerard's Cross Common, is the *Bull Inn*, a posting-house, famous in the days of Oxford stage-coaches, and now a pleasant, quiet family hotel, and a comfortable halting-place for the tourist.

GIDEA HALL, Essex (*see* Romford).

GILL'S HILL, Herts (*see* Radlett).

GODSTONE, Surrey, on the road from Reigate to Westerham, 1½ m. E. of Bletchingley : the *Godstone Road* Stat. of the S.E. Rly. is 2½ m. S. of the vill. : pop. of the parish 2254, exclusive of the eccl. dists. of Blindley Heath and Felbridge, 1491. Inns, *Clayton Arms; Railway Hotel*, by the rly. stat.

It has been suggested that the name was given with a reference to the god Woden ; and Mr. Taylor gives support to this view in the remark that "like Godmundham it was a pagan site consecrated to Christian worship,"† though elsewhere he conjectures that "Godstone may possibly be referred to the root" *gate*, a pass through a hill or cliff.‡ This last, however, is scarcely applicable to the site of the village, neither is it supported by the earliest known forms of the name. *Wachelstede* in the Domesday Survey, and *Wolcnestede* in the 'Testa de Nevill.' The old form was probably a patronymic ; the present one may have been derived from a cross (at the crossways N. of the ch.), or other stone to which some reverential feeling was attached.

Godstone stands partly on the Lower Greensand (Folkstone beds), and partly

* Builder, Dec. 14, 1861, in which are plans, elevation and description of the new building by the architect.
† Words and Places, 2nd ed. p. 337.
‡ *Ibid.*, p. 252.

on the Gault. Tilburstow Hill is a mass of Greensand, and here occurs a considerable fault or dislocation of the strata. At the foot of the hill the Surrey *firestone* is largely quarried by the Godstone Stone Co. The *Paludina limestone*, or Sussex marble, is also obtained. At the S. foot of the hill is a mineral spring, once in great repute for its medicinal qualities. The view from the summit of Tilburstow Hill is very fine.

The village, or, as it is locally designated, town, is built about the N. part of a large Green, on the S. of which is a great sheet of water, the ' Town Pond,' which works a mill. The open Green, the irregular arrangement of the houses, the fine horse-chestnuts, and the large pond, make from various points some very pretty pictures ; and happily the general aspect is that of cleanliness and comfort. The ch. is some way E. of the vill. All around are good residences, in well-wooded and well-kept grounds ; and the walks on all sides are delightful.

Godstone *Church* was old, some portions being of E.E. date, but much defaced, and rough-cast. The chancel was renovated in 1864, but the whole ch. underwent restoration, enlargement, and partial rebuilding in 1870-71, under the direction of Sir G. G. Scott, R.A. The old S. transept was removed, and a new S. aisle added ; the nave roof opened ; new W. window, and W. and S. doorways of Norman character inserted ; the tower restored, and spire heightened ; a new S. porch added ; the interior refitted ; a costly reredos erected ; and memorial painted glass placed in several of the windows. The old *monts.* were carefully preserved. Of these the most interesting are those of the Evelyns in the chapel or dormitory on the N. of the chancel.

" *Oct.* 14.—I went to Church at Godstone, and to see old Sir John Evelyn's *dormitory*, joining to the church, pav'd with marble, where he and his lady lie on a very stately monument at length ; he in armour, of white marble. The inscription is only an account of his particular branch of the family on black marble." *

The mont. is a costly and well-executed one. The knight is represented in armour ; " Dame Thomasin his wife, . . . whom he espoused ye 24th of Nov., 1618," has a loose

robe. As Evelyn's note intimates, the mont. was erected during their lives, and the date of death has not been added. Adjoining the Evelyn dormitory is that of the Boone family, with their various memorials. Notice before leaving the fine views from the ch.-yard.

Besides the Town Pond, on the Green, several others, as Rose's Pond, Turner's Pond, etc., will be observed in the neighbourhood. They abound in carp, tench, perch, and pike, and are described as " good fishing lakes."

Relics from former times are not wanting. On *Castle Hill*, by Leigh Place, S.E. of the ch., are remains of an ancient earth-work. On the Bletchingley side of the Green are two small barrows ; two others are N. of the Green ; whilst others occur on the line of the Pilgrims' Road, traceable towards Oxtead. Traces of a still earlier road may be seen about Tilburstow, and perhaps such names as Stanstreet and Stretton Borough are survivals of its course.

Marden Park, now in the occupation of J. H. Puleston, Esq., M.P., on the chalk hills, 1½ m. N. of Godstone, was the seat of Sir John Evelyn (whose mont. we have seen in the ch.), from whom it passed to Sir Robt Clayton, a " prodigious rich scrivener," with whose descendant, Sir William Clayton, Bart., it remains.

" 12 *Oct.*, 1677.—With Sir Robert Clayton to Marden, an estate he had bought lately of my kinsman Sir John Evelyn of Godstone in Surrey, which from a despicable farme house Sir Robert had erected into a seate with extraordinary expence. 'Tis in such a solitude among hills, as being not above 16 miles from London, seems almost incredible, the ways up to it so winding and intricate. The gardens are large, and well wall'd, and the husbandry part made very convenient and perfectly understood. The barnes, the stacks of corne, the stalls for cattle, pigeon houses, etc., of most laudible example. Innumerable are the plantations of trees, especially wall-nuts. The orangerie and gardens are very curious. In the house are large and noble rooms. . . . This place is exceeding sharp in the winter by reason of the serpenting of the hills ; and it wants running water ; but the solitude much pleas'd me. All the ground is so full of wild thyme, marjoram, and other sweete plants, that it cannot be over-stock'd with bees ; I think he had neere 40 hives of that industrious insect." *

The park, especially the lower part, called the *Deer Park*, is still as wild and picturesque, and as fragrant with thyme

---

* Evelyn, Diary, 1677.

* Evelyn, Diary.

and marjoram, and all other sweet plants, as when Evelyn visited it, and the trees are far more nobly developed. The walk to it from Godstone, and through it to Woldingham, is very fine. At the Godstone end of the park is a somewhat dilapidated tower, called the Castle, which commands views over a wide stretch of country. In the garden is a marble pillar erected by Sir Robert Clayton in commemoration of Thomas Firmin, the philanthropist (d. 1697). *Leigh Place* (Mrs. C. H. Turner), once a seat of the Evelyns ; *Godstone Court* (Mrs. Stenning), and several other good residences, are in the neighbourhood.

Blindley Heath, a hamlet of Godstone, 2½ m. S. of Godstone Road Stat., was formed into an eccl. dist. in 1843. It is a pretty little place on the edge of the Weald, and had 862 inhabitants in 1871. The *Church* (St. John the Evangelist), erected in 1842, from the designs of Mr. Whichcord, is E.E. in style, and consists of nave and chancel, with W. tower and octagonal spire.

Felbridge, another hamlet, 8 m. S. of Godstone, and an eccl. dist. (of 316 inhab.), formed in 1864 out of the parishes of Godstone and Tandridge, Surrey, and East Grinstead in Sussex, has a neat E.E. ch. (St. John the Divine), erected in 1865.

GOFF'S OAK, HERTS (*see* CHESHUNT).

GOLDER'S GREEN, a hamlet

of Hendon, MIDDX., a little outlying cluster of cottages, with an inn, the *White Swan*, whose garden is in great favour with London holiday-makers. It lies along the main road, midway between Hampstead and Hendon, the little Brent brook forming its N. boundary. Of the remaining Green, by Littlewood, the larger portion was enclosed in 1873-4. From the village there are pleasant walks by lanes and field-paths on one side to Hendon, or the Edgware Road by Gutterhedge or Clitterhouse farms ; on the other to Hampstead Heath or Finchley. Along the road to North End, Hampstead, are several good residences. The farthest house, on the top of *Golder's Hill*, close to North End, was the residence of Jeremiah Dyson, Clerk to the House of Commons, the warm friend of Akenside the poet—whom he allowed £300 a year " till he should be able to live like a gentleman by his practice as a physician." Akenside was a frequent guest, and not unfrequent resident, at his friend's house, returning to it whenever out of health or spirits.

> " Thy verdant scenes, O Goulder's Hill,
>   Once more I seek a languid guest :
> With throbbing temples and with burden'd breast
> Once more I climb thy steep aerial way.
> O faithful cure of oft-returning ill,
>   Now call thy sprightly breezes round,
>   Dissolve this rigid cough profound,
> And bid the springs of life with gentler movement play." *

Dyson survived the poet, and published in 1772 a handsome 4to ed. of his Complete Works : he died at his house on Golder's Hill, Sept. 16, 1776. Another poet has noted the feelings with which he regarded the house.

> " I am not unfrequently a visitor on Hampstead Heath, and seldom pass by the entrance of Mr. Dyson's Villa, on Golder's hill, close by, without thinking of the pleasures which Akenside often had there." †

GORHAMBURY, HERTS, the seat

of the Earl of Verulam, stands in the midst of a fine park of 600 acres, about 1½ m. W.N.W. of St. Albans. The road to it from St. Michael's Church was until 1828 the highroad to Holyhead : it is now the private road from St. Albans to Gorhambury.

The manor was one of the early possessions of the Abbey of St. Albans. It is usually said to have derived its name from Geoffrey de Gorham, Abbot of St. Albans 1119—45 (or a later abbot, Robert de Gorham, 1151—66), but it is more likely that the abbot derived his name from the place. Be that as it may, it remained the property of the monastery till the suppression of religious houses. It was then granted by Henry VIII., May 20, 1540, to Ralph Rowley ; and by the marriage of Rowley's daughter passed to John Maynard, who in 1550 sold it to Nicholas (afterwards Sir Nicholas) Bacon, Keeper of the Privy Seal to Queen Elizabeth, and father of the great Chancellor. On his

---

* Akenside, Ode on Recovery from a fit of Sickness in the Country, 1758.
† Wordsworth to Dyce, Life of William Wordsworth, vol. ii., p. 350.

death it passed to Anthony, his eldest son by his 2nd wife, who dying unmarried, devised it to his brother Francis Lord Bacon (created Lord Verulam 1618, and Visct. St. Albans 1620), whose seat it remained till his death, 1626, when it descended to his cousin and heir, Sir Thomas Meautys, who erected the statue of Lord Bacon in St. Michael's ch. Meautys' widow married Sir Harbottle Grimston, Bart., whose son purchased the reversion of the estate, which has since continued in his descendants, created successively Viscount Grimston, and, 1815, Earl of Verulam.

Norden, writing in 1593, says that the house at Gorhambury "was raised from the foundation by Sir Nicholas Bacon ; " but there was probably an earlier one. Bacon's house must have been of moderate dimensions, for Elizabeth, on one of her visits to the Lord Keeper, remarked, " My Lord, your house is too little for you ; " to which he replied, "No, Madam, 'tis your Highness hath made me too great for my house." Lord Bacon enlarged and completed the house (Aubrey says he built a new one), and made it his chief country residence. The house was suffered to become dilapidated, and being condemned as past repair, was pulled down, with the exception of a fragment to be mentioned presently, upon the erection of the present house—much to the regret of Horace Walpole, who describes it as " in a very crazy state but deserved to be propped." Walpole adds, " the situation is by no means delightful," * but in this opinion few will agree with him. The fullest and best account we know of the building as it was shortly before its demolition is contained in a letter from Bp. Hurd to Bp. Warburton, June 14th, 1769 :—

"In my way hither, I digressed a little to take a view of Gorhambury. . . . This antient seat, built by Sir Nicholas Bacon, and embellished by Lord Bacon, Mr. Meautys, and Sir Harbottle Grimston, successively masters of it, stands very pleasantly on high ground in the midst of a fine park, well wooded. There is a gentle descent from it to a pleasant vale, which again rises gradually into hills at a distance, and those well cultivated, or finely planted. The house itself is of the antique structure, with turrets, but low, and covered with a white stucco, not unlike the old part of your Lordship's palace at Gloucester. It is built round a court, nearly square, the front to the S., with a little turn, I think, to the E. The rooms are numerous, but small, except the hall, which is of moderate size, but too narrow for the height : the chapel neat, and well proportioned, but damp and fusty, being (as is usual with chapels belonging to the Lay Lords) seldom or never used. On the west side of the house runs a gallery, about the length of that at Prior Park ; the windows, especially the end window at the west, finely painted ; the sides covered with pictures of the great men of the time, I mean the time of the Stuarts ; and the ceiling, which is coved, ornamented with the great men of antiquity, painted in compartments. At the end of the gallery is a return, which serves for a billiard-room. Underneath the gallery and billiard-room, is a portico for walking, and that too painted. I should have observed that the chamber floor of the front is a Library, furnished, as it seemed to me on a slight glance, with the books of the time, as the gallery is with the persons. The furniture altogether unique, and suitable to the rest. It· is impossible that any fine man or woman of these times should endure to live at this place : but the whole has an air of silence, repose, and recollection, very suitable to the idea one has of those

'Shades, that to Bacon could retreat afford ;'
and to me is one of the most delicious seats I ever saw." *

What remains of Bacon's house will be found a short distance W. of the present mansion. The ruins comprise the wall of the hall, some traces of the tower which stood at the farther end of the building, and the boldly projecting entrance porch, a characteristic Elizabethan fragment, with medallions of the Roman emperors in the spandrels of the arches, and the royal arms under the crowning pediment. Within an arched recess, away from the house, is a headless, life-sized statue, said to be Henry VIII.

The present mansion was erected by Lord Grimston between 1778 and 1785, and was the last private work of Sir Robert Taylor (d. 1788), the architect to the Bank of England, who began life with 18 pence, and died worth £80,000. It is a large semi-classic edifice, consisting of a centre of stone, with a grand portico supported on Corinthian columns, and two wings of brick, covered with stucco. The hall, library, and reception-rooms are spacious, well-proportioned, and contain a good collection of pictures, chiefly portraits. These, if permission can be obtained, are exceedingly well worth seeing. *Obs.* especially—*Sir Nicholas Bacon*, in furred robe and deep ruff, black cap on head, and staff in hand—a huge, burly person, as we know he was: Queen Eliza-

* Letter to Countess Ossory, Sept. 6th, 1787.

* Letters from a late eminent Prelate to one of his Friends, p..429.

beth is reported to have said of him that "his soul was well lodged in fat." *Lord Chancellor Bacon*, by Vansomer, full-length, in Chancellor's robes and tall black hat, the seal on a table by him—the famous portrait engraved by Lodge. This and the statue in St. Michael's ch. are the two best likenesses of him. It is a very characteristic though somewhat coarse head, with a bright intellectual look that reminds one of Aubrey's remark, "He had a delicate lively hazel eye: Dr. Harvey told me it looked like the eye of a viper." *Sir Nathaniel Bacon*, half-brother of Francis Bacon, by *Himself.* This is a remarkable portrait. Nathaniel Bacon was a man of rare accomplishments: a scholar; proficient in science as it was then understood; a musician; he studied painting in Italy and Holland, and this portrait is probably one of the best ever painted in England by an amateur. He has here represented himself seated at a table in his study; writing materials, books, and an open volume of maps are before him; his palette is suspended on his easel; music and musical instruments lie about, and a large dog is watching him from under the table. The picture is well and carefully painted, and with all the multifarious details there is nothing slurred or amateurish about it. Alone it would suffice to show that he had a full share of the genius and intelligence of the Bacon family. One could wish that Nathaniel, who was singularly qualified to appreciate his mental character, had left us a portrait of his brother, the great Chancellor, but none is extant. We have, however, two other examples here of Nathaniel Bacon's skill as a painter: a portrait of his wife —a bright, intelligent-looking woman, daughter of Sir Thomas Gresham, the Royal Merchant, in a wonderful costume; and what is entitled 'the Cook Maid,' a large painting of a woman with a turkey in her lap, sitting before a table covered with dead birds, large and small, and several that would hardly find admission into the cuisine now: a picture bearing testimony to a careful study of the Dutch painters of 'still life,' yet quite free from servile imitation.

Turning from the Bacon portraits, we have portraits of Queens *Mary* and *Elizabeth*—the latter ¾-size, in black dress, open ruff, je t l stomacher and farthingale,

painted by Hilliard, and presented to the Lord Keeper by the Queen herself. *James I.*, painted for Sir Thos. Meautys, a good full-length, engraved for the Granger Society. *Countess of Suffolk*, wife of the Lord Treasurer, and mother of the infamous Countess of Essex and Somerset. *Robert Devereux*, 2nd *Earl of Essex*, ¾-size, of a grave, earnest countenance, and very well painted. The Lord Treasurer, *Weston, Earl of Portland*, by Vandyck, ¾-size, in official costume, blue ribbon on breast, treasurer's staff in right hand: one of Vandyck's serious, thoughtful, and thoroughly English heads. *Philip Earl of Pembroke and Montgomery. Algernon Percy, Earl of Northumberland*, and *Anne Cecil* his wife, a replica of the Kimbolton portrait. *Abbot, Abp. of Canterbury*, half-length, in full episcopal habit. *Catherine of Braganza*, Queen of Charles II., as St. Catherine. *Cecil*, 2nd *Lord Baltimore*, son of the founder of the colony of Maryland, ¾-size, by Mytens: the Portland portrait appears to have been painted as a companion to this. *Heneage Finch*, 1st *Earl of Nottingham*, half-length, by Sir Peter Lely, in his robes as Lord Chancellor. *Henry Rich*, 1st *Earl of Holland*, captured by the Parliamentarians at Kingston, and beheaded, March 1649. *Sir Harbottle Grimston*, half-length, by Sir P. Lely, seated, in official robes as Speaker of the House of Commons. This, a very good portrait, may be compared with a really wonderful one of his ancestor, *Edward Grimston*, ambassador from Henry VI. to the Duchess of Burgundy, a small ¾-length, on panel, in rich dress, painted whilst he was at Burgundy, by Peter Christus, in 1446, and still in perfect preservation and apparently untouched: of its kind almost unique. And with these two should be compared or contrasted their descendants, *James*, 2nd *Visct. Grimston*, his Brother and Sisters, in one of Sir Joshua Reynolds' charming family pictures, in which the young visct., as a sportsman, is handing a partridge to one of his sisters. There are other portraits of members of the Grimston family worth looking at as examples of the art of Kneller; by whom also is a good portrait of *George I.* Among many more are *Congreve* the dramatist; *William Pitt*, by Hoppner; and a portrait, not to be overlooked, of *William Chiffinch*, the "Backstairs Chiffinch," and dissolute favourite of Charles II., engraved in Harding.

GRAVESEND, KENT, a municipal and parliamentary borough and market town, on the rt. bank of the Thames, 26½ m. below London Bridge by the river, 22 m. by road, and 23¼ m. by the S.E. Rly., N. Kent line. The town and municipal borough comprises the parishes of Gravesend and Milton, and contained 21,265 inhabitants in 1871 ; the parliamentary borough includes also a portion of Northfleet parish, and contained 27,493 inhabitants.

The name, *Gravesham* in Dom., is probably A.-S. *geréfas ham,* the home or seat of the reeve, bailiff or steward, and it may have been so named as has been suggested from its being "the dwelling-place within the united manors (of Milton, Gravesend, and Parrock) of the reeve or representative of the superior lord." There is, however, no reference in the Domesday Book to any such officer, and the place appears to have been at that time of little consequence. It had a church and a hythe, or landing-place, and Milton had a church, a mill, and a hythe, to which last three serving-men, probably boatmen, were attached, the hythe at Milton being then, as it still is, the chief landing-place, or Town Quay. But Gravesend, as occupying the first convenient site for a landing and trading place in ascending the river, and being in proximity to the ancient Watling Street, would no doubt be early chosen for a settlement. Within the parish, and especially by the Watling Street, celts, Roman coins, and other remains, and a large number of Saxon coins, have been found, testifying to the abode here of three races prior to the Norman Conquest. By the close of the 13th cent. Gravesend (the *ham* had now given way to *end*) had become a place of some trade, with a weekly market, and a regular traffic by boat with London : and it is noticeable that already (1293) the Gravesend boatmen had become notorious for their extortionate conduct ; * a habit

which amidst the vicissitudes of six centuries they have never deviated from. In the 14th cent. (1370), we find Gravesend able to furnish two ships of 20 tons each for the conveyance of men for the army in France. Ten years later the French galleys sailed up the Thames and burnt a great part of the town. In the following years Gravesend shared in the commotions excited in these parts by Wat Tyler's resistance to the harsh efforts made to enforce the poll-tax.

Soon after this (1401), and partly as a compensation for the losses sustained from the French attack, Henry IV. renewed to the men of Gravesend the right of the Long Ferry, or the sole privilege of conveying passengers by boat to and from London, at certain fixed rates, which had, according to the patent, been their privilege " from the time whereof the memory of man is not to the contrary," but which the men of London had of late disputed, and in part dispossessed them of. This grant was confirmed by Henry V., Henry VI., and Edward IV. Its value will be understood when it is remembered that for centuries the route for travellers from London to the Continent was by water to Gravesend, and thence by post-horses to Dover, the place of embarkation for Calais, and the converse. Thus as late as 1506, when Wolsey was sent by Henry VIII. on an embassy to the Emperor Maximilian,

"Having his depeach, he took his leave of the King at Richmond about noone, and so came to London aboute foure of the clocke, where the barge of Gravesend was ready to launch forth, both with a prosperous tyde and with winde ; without any abode hee entered the barge, and so passed forth with such happy speede, that he arrived at Gravesend within little more than three houres, where he tarried no longer than his post horses were providing, and then travelled so speedily, that he came to Dover the next morning, whereas the passengers were ready under sayle-to Calais, into the which passenger without tarrying he entered, and sailed forth with them, that long before noone he arrived at Calais." *

Elizabeth, by proclamation, commanded the Lord Mayor, Aldermen, Companies, etc., of London, on occasion of the arrival in this country of royal personages, ambassadors, etc., to proceed in their robes

---

* The jury of assizes assembled at Canterbury this year presented that the boatmen of Gravesend "did take from passengers unjust fares against

their will : that is, where they had formerly taken a halfpenny from a person for his passage to London they then took a penny."—Cruden, History of the Town of Gravesend, p. 56.

* Stow, Annals, p. 498, ed. 1631.

and liveries to Blackheath, if they came by land, but if they came by water to attend them in their barges at Gravesend.

One of the earliest of these royal receptions recorded is that of Arthur Count de la Roche, the Bastard of Burgundy, who arrived here May 29, 1467,

"accompanyde with many noble lordes, knyghtes, squyers, and oother, aboute the noombre of 400, with 4 kervelles of forstage [caravels or light vessels with forecastles] richely apparailde and enforcid with alle maner abilements of were, penons, banners, gytons, stremers; his gubon [cabin] also hangid with arasse within, and without richly beseen." He had come in response to the challenge of Anthony Woodville, Lord Scales, afterwards Lord Rivers (brother of Elizabeth Queen of Edward IV.) to joust with him at a grand tournament to be held in Smithfield. The Count was received at Gravesend by Garter King at Arms, who with the king's barges and a great retinue, had been some time waiting for him, and conveyed in great state up the river. At Greenwich he was met by the "Earl of Worcester, Constable of England, accompanied with many other lordis, knyghtes, squyers, and many aldermen and rich comeners of the Citee of London, ordeyned in 7 barges and a gally, and richly beseen and araide in coveryng with clothis of gold and arasse." *

In May 1522, the Emperor Charles V., accompanied by Henry VIII. and Cardinal Wolsey, who had met him at Dover, passed, with their respective cavalcades, through the town, and embarked at the landing-place, where 30 barges were waiting to receive them. Twenty years later, 1544, Henry VIII. landed at Gravesend on his way to join the army then about to invade France. In 1606, Christian IV. of Denmark, with his Queen and Court, came here in 7 ships of war, and were received with great ceremony by James I., Prince Henry, and a large attendance of courtiers, who had come from Greenwich Palace in 35 barges, the King's own barge being "built in the fashion of a little castle, enclosed with carved and gilt windows and casements, the roof having battlements, pinnacles, pyramids, and fine imagery." The royal festivities here and at Rochester lasted over three weeks, and it was at these banquets, where the two monarchs pledged each other in endless health-drinkings and embracings, each toast being accompanied by "sound of drums and trumpet and artillery," that the practice of excessive drinking at the dinner-table was said to have been first introduced into England by the Danish King. But if so, it was speedily adopted: "I think," says Sir John Harrington in describing the proceedings, "the Dane hath strangely wrought on our good English nobles; for those whom I could never get to take good liquor, now follow the fashion, and wallow in beastly delights." * In October 1612, Frederick, the Elector Palatine, landed here on his arrival in England to espouse the Princess Elizabeth. In August 1614, James I. and Prince Henry dined with the King of Denmark at the Ship Inn, the house where Pepys often dined half a century later. James left when the dinner was ended, but the Prince stayed with his uncle till he sailed with his fleet for Denmark ten days after.

The next royal visit was of a different kind. Prince Charles (afterwards Charles I.), in starting on his wild incognito visit to the Court of Spain, crossed with his companion, the Marquis of Buckingham, by the ferry from Tilbury to Gravesend, when finding they had no silver, they gave the ferryman a gold piece of the value of 22s., mounted their horses, and rode hastily away. Suspecting that they were not the plain merchants they affected to be, the boatman hurried to the mayor and stated his suspicions. Officers were sent in pursuit, but it was not till they had reached Canterbury that the fugitives were overtaken, arrested, and carried before the mayor of that city. The mayor, mistrusting their explanation, expressed his determination to detain them in custody, when Buckingham took off his false beard, gave his real name, and having stated that his purpose was to view the Channel fleet privately, they were allowed to proceed. The next time Charles, now King, visited Gravesend, June 16, 1625, was with his young bride, Henrietta, whom he had met at Dover three days before, and was escorting by easy stages to London.

Count Koningsmark after the murder of Mr. Thynne, Feb. 1682, made his way to Gravesend in the hope of escaping out of the country, but was arrested as soon as he stepped ashore. In 1688, Queen Mary, wife of James II., was with her infant son

---

* Excerpta Historica, p. 172.

* Letter to Mr. Secretary Barlow, in Nugæ Antiquæ, vol. i., p. 348.

a fugitive at Gravesend, where she embarked in a yacht bound for France. The following day, Dec. 11th, the King himself arrived at Gravesend by water. His purpose was to leave the country, but being stopped by the mob at Faversham. he returned by land to Whitehall. Five days later, however, Evelyn writes, " I saw the king take barge to Gravesend—a sad sight ! " * It was the end : he passed into France, and saw England no more. George I. on his accession to the throne was welcomed at Gravesend by the mayor and corporation with a loyal address. George II. made Gravesend his usual place for embarking or landing on his frequent journeys to Germany, but his visits do not appear to have excited much enthusiasm among the townspeople.

The latest of the royal landings, and those on which the inhabitants most delight to dwell, were those of the Prince of Wales with his young bride, the Princess Alexandra, on the 7th of March, 1863 ; and on the same day, 11 years later, the Duke and Duchess of Edinburgh, on both of which occasions the decoration of the pier and the enthusiasm in the town excited the liveliest interest in the young princesses thus happily welcomed to their new country. Yet another splendid reception remains to be noticed, that of the Shah of Persia, June 18, 1873 ; and also the departure of the Emperor of Russia, May 21, 1874.

The Gravesend barges seem to have been heavy, slow, and far from comfortable vessels, and the lighter and faster tilt-boats that were introduced at the close of the 16th cent. were regarded as a great improvement, though the old barges continued for many years to share in the traffic.† How far from luxurious was the accommodation on board tilt-boats, even

when they were the only public conveyances between London and Gravesend, and how uncertain was the journey, we know from many sources. We may, however, cite two incidental illustrations. In May 1730, John Sherwin. an old, disabled, and discharged soldier, who earned a living by exhibiting conjuring tricks at fairs and public-houses, was, with his wife, apprehended at Gravesend on a charge of highway robbery, for which another man was already in custody. At the trial it became evident that the charge again Sherwin was made with a view to avert suspicion from the real culprit, and Sherwin and his wife were acquitted, whilst the other man was convicted. Sherwin now published and hawked about a pamphlet containing an account of his "remarkable case " under the odd title of ' The Gotham Swan,' in which is a description of the tilt-boat accommodation of ' which we have spoken. On the morning of the robbery he and his wife started early from London in order to go to Maidstone fair.

" I got to Billingsgate by seven, took water at eight for Gravesend, but fell short a mile and a half : the watermen landed their passengers at three o'clock, except myself, wife, and son ; for John Bull advised me to sit in the boat because I was lame, for he would strive to run to town. We did so, and I and my son laid down on the straw, covering ourselves with the tilt, and I fell asleep. In half an hour after he came and helped me out of the boat, over a lime-hoy, and had much ado to get me ashore ; telling us at the same time he could not get to Gravesend till three hours after, the tide ran so strong against them. I got on shore, and being cold and chilly went to an alehouse to clean and brush our clothes from the straw."

Curiously enough we have an equally minute contemporary account of a voyage to Gravesend and back in a tilt-boat, but this time by a person well known to fame, William Hogarth, who had for companions his brother-in-law, Mr. John Thornhill (son of Sir James Thornhill), and three friends Messrs. Forrest, Scott, and Tothall ; but they, it will be seen, fared little better than the old soldier, and like him had to wash themselves and clean their clothes after their journey. They had started from Covent Garden at 1 in the morning and embarked at Billingsgate, the usual starting-place of the Gravesend boats, but had to remain till 1 in the afternoon for the tide, the Gravesend boats leaving Billingsgate at high water, and Gravesend at low water.

---

* Diary, Dec. 18, 1688.

† Sir Thomas Heneage writing to Sir Christopher Hatton, May 2, 1585, says " Her Highness [Queen Elizabeth] thinketh your house will shortly be like a Gravesend barge, never without a knave, a priest, or a thief." (Sir H. Nicolas, Life of Sir C. Hatton, p. 426.) Where Elizabeth got her knowledge of the Gravesend barge it would be hard to say. But the commonness of the barge and its passengers seems to have been a subject of frequent allusion. Thus Sir Henry Wotton writes to Milton going to Italy, " Thence by sea to Genoa, where the passage into Tuscany is *as diurnal as a Gravesend barge*." (Reliquiæ Wottonianæ, p. 343.)

"Then set sail in a Gravesend boat we had hired for ourselves. Straw was our bed, and a tilt our covering. The wind blew hard at S.E. and by E. We had much rain and no sleep for about three hours. At Cuckold's Point we sung St. John, at Deptford Pishoken; and in Blackwall Reach eat hung beef and biscuit, and drank right Hollands." At Purfleet they took on board a pilot, and there Hogarth fell asleep and slept the rest of the way. . . . . "We soon arrived at Gravesend, and found some difficulty in getting ashore, occasioned by an unlucky boy's having placed his boat between us and the landing-place, and refusing us passage over his vessel; but, as virtue surmounts all obstacles, we happily accomplished this adventure, and arrived at Mr. Bramble's at six There we washed our faces and hands, and had our wigs powdered, then drank coffee, eat toast and butter, paid our reckoning, and set out at eight." They journeyed on foot to Rochester, and thence to the Isle of Sheppey. returning to Gravesend on the evening of the 29th. The next morning,—"Wednesday, at eight, we arose, breakfasted and walked about the town. At ten went into a boat we had hired, with a truss of clean straw, a bottle of good wine, pipes, tobacco, and a match. . . . We came merrily up the river, and quitting our boat at Billingsgate, got into a wherry that carried us through bridge, and landed at Somerset water-gate, whence we walked all together, and arrived about two, at the Bedford Arms, Covent Garden." *

An Act of Parliament was passed in 1737 for regulating the Gravesend boats, and gradually larger and better vessels were employed. When steam-packets were first introduced, 1815-16, there were 26 sailing boats, of from 22 to 45 tons each, engaged in the Long Ferry. The last tilt-boat was withdrawn in 1834.† The steam-boats, by bringing an extraordinary influx of holiday and pleasure visitors, commenced an era of unlooked-for prosperity to the town. The opening of the railway greatly increased the number of visitors, and the trade of the town, but was little less injurious to the steam-packets than they were to the tilt-boats.

The traffic of the Short Ferry to Tilbury, 1 m., is now carried on by the steam-boats which ply between Gravesend and the Tilbury Stat. of the London and Southend Rly. In 1799 an Act of Parliament was obtained for making a *tunnel* between Gravesend and Tilbury. The projector and engineer was Mr. Ralph Dodd, who estimated the cost at £15,995. As the first step towards its formation, a shaft 10 ft. in diameter was sunk to a depth of 85 ft. ; when, as the water which flowed

into it could not be kept under, and the funds of the company were exhausted, the works were of necessity abandoned. The expenditure on the shaft had exceeded the estimate for the tunnel—which was not even begun.

Gravesend had grant of free-warren and a market as early as 1268, but it received its first Charter of Incorporation from Queen Elizabeth, July 22, 1562. According to the preamble, it was granted on account of the ruin and distress caused by "the diminution or discontinuance of the common passage between the Town of Dover and the City of London, of old time much frequented and used." This diminution is attributed to the loss of Calais four years before. The charter constituted the inhabitants a body corporate to be governed by 2 portreeves and 10 jurats, and to have a corporate seal, a boat with one mast and sail, 6 rowers hooded in the forepart, and at the helm a hedgehog steering. The hedgehog was the crest of Sir Henry Sydney, steward of the royal honour of Otford, through whose influence the charter was obtained. The charter was amended by a second granted in 1568, which created courts of record, portreeve, and piepowder, and confirmed the grant of a fair and market, and the privileges of the Long Ferry. A new charter was granted by Charles I. in 1632. This, however, was seized, like other municipal charters, by Charles II. in 1684. A new charter was given by James II. in 1687 ; its validity was on more than one occasion questioned, but the matter was finally set at rest by the Municipal Corporations Act of 1835. The corporation now consists of a mayor, 12 jurats, and 24 common-councilmen. The parliamentary franchise was conferred on Gravesend by the Act of 1867. and it now sends one member to the House of Commons.

As a trading town Gravesend was for centuries mainly dependent on the shipping which anchored off it on their way to or from London. As early as the first half of the 14th cent. a searcher was stationed here, whose duty it was to board and examine every outward-bound ship, and satisfy himself that the Port and Customs regulations had been complied with. Officers of the same name and nearly similar duties continued to be

---

* Forrest, An account of the five days peregrination of Hogarth and others, begun May 27, 1732. London, 1772.

† Cruden, History of Gravesend, p. 521.

stationed here till 1825, when the office was abolished. As the outer boundary of the port of London, all outward-bound vessels receive here their final clearances. Formerly, ships lay here some time, and this was the customary place for taking in their sea stores, while the seamen, being paid an advance on their wages, bought clothes and other requisites for the voyage. But the construction of docks up the river, and alterations in the Customs arrangements, cut off that source of trade, and Gravesend is, as we said, now mainly dependent on the summer visitors. Still there is some shipping trade, and the river and river-side are as much alive as ever with ships and sailors. The emigrant ships anchor here to take their passengers on board, and undergo inspection by the emigration officers, and all outward-bound vessels here receive their bills of lading. Inward-bound ships are boarded here by the revenue officers, and take on board their river pilots. But they make only a brief stay unless they be colliers, which anchor at Gravesend till directed to proceed by the harbour-master, —the number of colliers admitted to the Upper Pool, London, being strictly limited. At times a large fleet of colliers lies off here, and on occasions of a contrary wind the river is here as crowded with ships as at London ; and at night, when all the vessels have their lights up, presents a striking appearance. The town imports coal and timber, but the fishery furnishes the chief employment of the seafaring population. The larger smacks are chiefly employed in the North Sea fishery ; * the smaller (of 15 tons and under) in shrimp fishing in the river. Shrimps are taken by the Gravesend fishermen in prodigious quantities. They are very largely consumed at Gravesend by the summer visitors—there are whole streets of 'tea and shrimp houses '—but the main dependence of the fishermen is on the London market.

Gravesend is the head-quarters of the Royal Thames Yacht Club, and yachting adds much to the profit of the town, and to the pleasure of the visitors. The Club

* Sir Walter Scott writes in the Diary of his Voyage in the Lighthouse Yacht, 1814, " August 11. There were two Gravesend smacks fishing off the isle [of Orkney]. Lord what a long draught London makes."—Lockhart, Life of Scott, chap. xxviii.

House, on the Marine Parade, is a spacious and attractive building. Gravesend is a great pilot station, and has a large number of watermen who find ample occupation in conveying passengers to and from the vessels anchored off here. The Custom House staff numbers about 300 men, including those on board the guard-ship. By the river, and within the town limits, are barge and boat building yards, iron foundries, rope walks, breweries, steam flour mills, soap and other factories. Beyond are extensive market gardens, renowned for asparagus and rhubarb ; cherry and apple orchards ; and some hop gardens. Gravesend now supports three weekly newspapers, yet there was not a printing press in the town till 1786, when Mr. Pocock set up that with which he printed his 'History of Gravesend.' A corn market is held on Wednesday, a general market on Saturday, and a cattle market monthly.

The old town was crowded within a contracted space by the river-side, from which the narrow High Street rose steeply southwards. Parallel streets, with a labyrinth of narrow and crooked cross-lanes and passages, grew up slowly as the town increased in population. Of old, Gravesend could have been but thinly peopled. Since 1800 the population has multiplied five-fold, and the growth of the town has more than kept pace with the increase of the population. New and wider streets have been opened in the old town, a new town has sprung up of broad streets lined with shops, dwellings, and lodging-houses, varying in style according to the locality, and beyond that an outer belt of villas, some of which are of considerable size and pretension. Indeed, though the High Street, still the main thoroughfare, is even now inconveniently narrow, and far from attractive, and the streets leading east and west from it are narrow, mean, and dirty, it would be difficult from the present appearance of the town to conceive the confined and squalid aspect it must have presented a century ago. In 1773 an Act was obtained for paving and cleansing the town, and from it the general improvement of the place must be dated. The state of the High Street at that time is thus described by a contemporary. " Before the passing of the Act, the town was most irregularly paved; the kennel then went down (uncovered) near the middle of the High Street; almost every tradesman had a sign, and in the night when the wind blew strong, a concert of squeaking music filled your ears with sounds not the most pleasant."* Along this narrow, ill-paved street, nowhere 30 ft. wide, and only 16 ft. at the river end, with an open kennel running along its centre, emperors, kings, queens, cardinals, and the splendid cavalcades we have described, had in those good old times to make their way. The houses, too, were mostly of wood, with projecting porches, penthouses, bay windows, and overhanging eaves, and sign-boards hung out from every door. A painter like Baron Leys might have brought out the quaintly picturesque phase of such a street with a procession like one of those noticed passing along it, but the reality must have presented many inconveniences alike to natives and visitors.

The great danger in such a town was from fire. And Gravesend has suffered severely from fires. The worst was that still remembered as the Great Fire of August 1727, which consumed the ch., several streets, including a large part of the High Street, with all the inns in the lower part of it, shops, wharves: in all it was said above 250 houses, or the greater part of the town. Serious fires occurred also in 1731, 1748, and on other occasions, the last being as late as August 1850, when above 40 houses, and among them the London and County Bank, were destroyed. But, as out of all evil some good comes, these fires were more than anything else the means of bringing about the widening of old streets, the opening of new ones, the erection of less combustible houses, and the general improvement of the town.

The churches and public buildings of Gravesend have few attractions for a visitor. The parish church, St. George, was built in 1732, on the site of that burned in the great fire of 1727. It was built by a Parliamentary grant of £5000, and a subscription, which the king and queen headed with the handsome donation of 1500 guineas. It is generally stated that the new ch. was dedicated to

* Pocock, History of Gravesend, p. 243.

St. George "in compliment to the king," but this could hardly have been the case, as the older ch. was also dedicated to St. George. It is a spacious but commonplace brick and stone building, and consists of nave with aisles, chancel, and W. tower and spire, 132 ft. high, in which is a good peal of 8 bells. The district ch. of St. James, in the London road, is a Gothic building, erected in 1851.

Milton parish church (St. Peter and St. Paul) is a handsome old building, half hidden behind a screen of tall trees, on the l. of the road to Rochester, in what must have been the country when the ch. was built. It is for the most part Perp. in style, and is supposed to date from near the end of the 14th cent., but portions of it appear older. It had been greatly altered and patched at various times in true churchwarden fashion, but has within the last few years been thoroughly restored — first the chancel, and since the body of the ch. It now presents a handsome, but somewhat trim, exterior, whilst the interior is in harmony with the latest ecclesiological notions. The E. window, with its painted glass, is new; so is the roof; but the corbels, on which the principals rest, are the original ones recarved. On the S. of the chancel are a piscina and 3 sedilia, with well-moulded arches. In the tower is a peal of 6 bells. Milton has two ecclesiastical district churches: Holy Trinity, in Milton Place, a cruciform Dec. building erected in 1845; and Christ Church, in Porrock Street, a neat Gothic edifice erected in 1853. There are besides a spacious Roman Catholic Church (St. John the Evangelist). several Dissenting chapels, and a Jewish synagogue.

The *Town Hall*, on the l., and near the centre of the High Street, was erected from the designs of Mr. A. H. Wilds, in 1836, on a site where had stood two or three town-halls in succession since the first was built there in 1573. The present edifice has a Grecian Doric elevation of Bathstone, the principal feature being a tetrastyle portico, in the pediment of which, besides the town arms, are colossal statues of Minerva, Justice, and Truth. The Great Hall, on the principal floor, is a large and handsome room; beneath it is the market; at the sides are corporation and police offices, cells, etc. The

Assembly Rooms in Harmer Street, built in 1842 for a Literary Institute, is another semi-classical (Ionic) building, with a concert-room for 1000 persons, billiard-rooms, etc. The *Grammar School* is a good Gothic building, but as a school is of a lower grade than its name would imply. A more recent and better example of Collegiate Gothic is the *College for Daughters of Congregational Ministers,* Milton Mount, erected 1872-73, from the designs of Mr. E. C. Robins. The building has a frontage of 200 ft., and is 3 storeys high, with a dining-hall at right angles to it, the centre and the ends being slightly advanced. The dormitories (each child having a separate chamber) are on the upper floor, the schools, class-rooms, and library on the ground floor. The institution is a useful and well-managed one. Other schools and benevolent institutions abound. There are also a theatre, library, etc., but none are architectually noteworthy.

The townspeople pride themselves most, perhaps, on the piers. The *Town Pier*, completed in 1832, from the designs of Mr. W. T. Clerk, C.E., was greatly admired at the time of its construction. It is built on cast-iron arches of 40 ft. span, and extends 127 ft. into the river, but has a total length from the quay of 157 ft., with a uniform width of 40 ft. At the extremity is an extended platform, or T head, 76 ft. long and 39 ft. wide, supported on strong iron columns. On it is a cast-iron column 35 ft. high, with gas lantern and reflectors. This is the chief landing-place for the London steamers, and on it is a ticket-office or station in connection with the London, Tilbury, and Southend Rly., for the convenience of whose passenger traffic the pier was covered in and otherwise altered in 1854. The *Terrace Pier* was constructed, from the designs of J. B. Redman, C.E., in 1843-45, when the steamboat traffic was at its height. It is a light but solid-looking structure, having an extreme length of 240 ft., its river length being 190 ft.; a width of 30 ft., and a T head 90 ft. by 30, on which is a tall, light turret. The platform is laid on iron girders, supported on 20 thick Doric iron columns based on brick piers. The pier is covered throughout, and has sliding shutters or *jalousies* at the sides, thus forming an agreeable promenade in almost any weather. Before the opening of the railway, from a million to a million and a quarter of passengers landed annually from the steamboats at these two piers, and above a quarter of a million in the month of June. Now the Terrace Pier is a pleasure or promenade pier, and connected with it are the Terrace Gardens, formed about the same time as the pier on the site of the old Blockhouse Fort. The gardens and pier afford an excellent view of the river, and make an agreeable lounging-place In the summer a band plays during the day, and occasionally the pier is used for balls.

The favourite hotels, as the Clarendon, the Roebuck, etc., are mostly at the riverside, and near the piers. There is a varied and interesting, though not very clean or fragrant, walk by the shore westwards to Rosherville hotel, gardens, and pier, 1 m.; and eastwards to the Fort, and the basin of the old Thames and Medway canal. Here, too, are bathing machines and bathing establishments, Clifton Baths on the W., and the Albion Baths at Milton on the E. The *Fort* has been lately reconstructed, and mounted with heavy ordnance,—one 25-ton gun and 20 of 12 tons each. A small garrison is maintained in the fort, and there is a volunteer artillery corps trained to work the guns. It is intended to act in combination with Tilbury Fort on the opposite bank, and with Shorne Fort and East Tilbury Fort lower down the river : together, as is believed, rendering the Thames secure from the passage of an enemy's ship. Barracks were erected in Wellington Street in 1862, which cover a large area, and are somewhat better-looking than the average of such buildings.

Windmill Hill, of old the chief attraction of the London holiday visitors, has sadly deteriorated. Sixty years ago a learned topographer, after spending much labour in describing what he called the " bewitching views " over which the eye might range from the summit, concluded with the assertion that "few spots in the island, or in Europe, can vie with this." * However that may have been, it was a spot which the townspeople should have secured in perpetuity as

* H. Hunter, D.D., History of London and its Environs, 4to, 1811, vol. ii., p. 421.

Gravesend

Greenwich (see p.248)

a recreation ground. Instead of which, they first suffered it to be given up to taverns and low refreshment hovels, and then to be seized hold of by speculative builders. Now there is merely a small dirty, disreputable bit of open ground, from which, between the hideous villas and squalid tenements that surround it, some fragments only of the old views can be obtained. The mill, or a wooden erection on its site, very much out of repair, and not very clean, contains a camera, and admits the curious at a few pence a head.

From Gravesend there are easy walks or rides to *Springhead*, now perhaps the most popular resort of summer visitors, noted for watercresses, fruit, and light refreshments ; *Cobham*, 5 m. S. by E., with *Cobham Hall*, the splendid seat of the Earl of Darnley, renowned for its pictures, and the beauty of the park, and *Cobham Church*, with its almost unrivalled brasses and monuments ; *Gad's Hill*, 4 m. S.E., the scene of Falstaff's adventure, and now for ever associated with the last days of Charles Dickens ; *Shorne Church*, 3 m. E.S.E., which may be visited along with Gad's Hill, and which is worth visiting for its architecture, monts., and brasses; and *Chalk Churh.* 2 m. E., which has a remarkable W. porch, with curious grotesque figures of a morris-dancer, and an attendant, between whom is a statue of the Virgin, to whom the ch. is dedicated.

GRAYS, or GRAY'S THUR-ROCK, Essex, a small town and port, on a little creek of the Thames, between Fiddler'sReach and Northfleet Hope; 21 m. from London by road, 20½ m. by the Southend line of the Grt. E. Rly. : pop. 2806. Inns : *King's Arms*, a good house ; *Railway Hotel.* The original name is said to have been Thurrock simply, the prefix, Gray's, being given to it, from the noble family who were for three centuries its owners, in order to distinguish it from the adjacent parishes of West Thurrock and Little Thurrock.

The manor was granted to Henry de Gray by Richard I., and confirmed by John. It passed by female heirs, in the 16th cent., to the Zouch family ; and now belongs to Jas. Theobald, Esq. A charter for a market, to be held weekly on Friday,

was obtained by Richard de Gray in the reign of Henry III. The market day was afterwards altered to Thursday, but it has long been given up. The town consists mostly of a main street running from the rly. stat. to the wharves by the river, and narrowing greatly after passing the market-place. Nothing is to be said for the beauty, and not much for the picturesqueness of the town. It is old, irregular, and, like all these small Thames ports, lazy-looking and dirty ; but new houses are rising outside it, and it is said to be prosperous.

The only building of any interest is the *Church* (St. Peter and St. Paul), a cruciform structure of flint and stone, with, on the N.W., a thick low square tower, crowned by a slated spire. It is mostly E.E. in date, with later windows inserted, but has a Norman door N. of the nave. It was partially restored, and lengthened, westward, in 1866. The encaustic tiles which pave the vestry were discovered outside the ch.-yard.

The port is frequented by hoys, barges, and small-craft ; a shoal 'The Black Shelf,' W. of the Creek impedes the navigation for vessels of heavier burden. The shoal is said to have resulted from the bursting of the river wall near Purfleet, in 1690, and consequent inundation of the long stretch of marsh-land between Grays and Purfleet. Much of the trade of Grays is due to the great *Chalk-pits* N. of the town. The pits are very large, united by a tunnel, and communicate with a wharf on the Thames by a tramway, along which a cumbrous locomotive is puffing all day long. In the E. pit, lime is largely burnt, and in the W. is a whiting factory. The chalk, which is of great thickness, is overlaid with green-coated flints and Thanet Sands, abounds with characteristic fossils, and shows on the S.E. side some good examples of sand-pipes. In the course of the works, caverns or pits, like those described under CHADWELL, have been from time to time come upon, and in them urns and broken pottery (Romano-British), and bones of animals, have been found. The shafts appear to have been intentionally filled with earth, but at what time is unknown. From these chalk-pits flows regularly an almost unlimited supply of excellent water. E. of the pits, towards Chadwell, occurs the newer deposit, about 15 ft. of blue clay, know as *Grays Brickearth.*

The geology of Grays and its neighbourhood is of unusual interest and importance, and has been carefully and well worked out by several distinguished geologists. Prof. J. Morris, F.G.S., who has made the district his own, has kindly favoured us with the following note on its leading features.

The physical features and varying character of the neighbourhood of Grays depend on the geological structure modified by subsequent fluviatile and atmospheric denudation. The strata belong to four periods, which in descending order are—

1. Alluvial marsh land = Recent.
2. Brick-earth and mammalian beds = Newer Pliocene.
3. Thanet sands = Lower Eocene.
4. White chalk = Mesozoic.

The Thames at Grays flows over a bed of chalk which is seen to rise above the level of the river on each side. This chalk, which is here extensively quarried, belongs to the upper, or chalk with flints. It is stratified, or bedded, and traversed by lateral or main joints which assist the working of it, the flints occurring in more or less regular nodular layers. This chalk is a continuation of that which on the Essex side commences at Purfleet, and there crosses the river into Kent. It is worked for the manufacture of whiting, and for burning for lime, the flints being partly exported for use in pottery and porcelain works. It contains the usual characteristic fossils of the formation: some sponges, *Echinoderms,* as Cidaris, Galerites, Ananchytes; *Brachiopods,* as Terebratula, Rhynchonella; *Bivalve Mollusca,* as Pecten, Spondylus, Inoceramus; *Fishes,* as Ptychodus, Galeus, etc., and occasionally drifted wood perforated by the Teredo.

The next overlying formation is that of the Thanet sands, which is seen in the large pit at the N. side reposing on a somewhat undulating or eroded surface of the chalk, having at its base a layer of green-coated flints, known as the Bull's-head bed. These sands are here comparatively thin and unfossiliferous, but in the Isle of Thanet (whence their name)

they are much thicker, and contain fossils. These sands occur in a similar position at Purfleet, and on the opposite side of the Thames, where they are worked for ballast at Erith and Woolwich, and extend under London, and are partly the source of the artesian well supply to the metropolis.

Geologically speaking, a great hiatus occurs between these sands and the next formation or Brick-earth beds exposed near Grays, for the rest of the lower, middle, and upper Eocene beds are wanting, as well as the Miocene, and older Pliocene strata; great physical changes have occurred, and a long period of time has elapsed, so that a large portion of the present land of Europe has been formed, and even the Alps and Pyrenees elevated, during the intermediate period. The brick-earth beds are generally considered to have been formed in the intermediate or after the Glacial period which occurred in northern Europe. They are valley deposits formed by a river wider and deeper than the present Thames, for they occur on each side of the river of great thickness and at a greater elevation than its present level. The brick clay reposes on a bed of gravel overlying the chalk, and is covered by a considerable thickness of ferruginous sands, presenting a false-bedded or wavy structure due to the change in the direction of the currents during their deposition. It is from these beds that a rich mammalian fauna has been obtained, comprising species of elephant, hippopotamus, rhinoceros, horse, ox, deer, and bear, associated with numerous species of land and fresh-water shells, mostly identical with those now living in the vicinity, together with three others *not now* known as British—two belonging to Europe, and the third a species of Cyrena (C. fluminalis), at present only living in the Nile; there are also remains of leaves and parts of trees, indicative of an exogenous vegetation. The alluvial land is due to the silt deposited by the present river, and varies in thickness in different parts of its course, sometimes consisting of a great depth of peat, the result of the decay of a former marsh vegetation.

In the large chalk pit, the bed of ferruginous gravel may be seen overlying the Thanet Sands, and then the chalk on the slope of the hill, the latter being perforated by deep sand-pipes or pot-holes, into which the gravel and sand were slowly let down as the chalk was gradually excavated. It is through this higher gravel and associated beds, and the underlying Thanet sands down to the chalk, that the valley has been partly excavated in which the brick-earth and mammalian remains previously noticed have been deposited.

Belmont Castle (— Smith, Esq.), standing on very high ground, above and N.W. of the great pit, commands extensive prospects, and forms a conspicuous object from the river. From Grays, a pleasant walk of about 2 m., across the fields, due N., leads to *Stifford;* and another of 3 m. N.W. by Baker Street to *Orsett;* whilst *West Thurrock.* 1½ m., on the W., and *Little Thurrock*, ¾ m. E., are worth visiting. (*See* those places.)

Off Grays is moored the Goliath Training Ship, an old man-of-war, one of the last of the three-deckers, but never put in commission. It was fitted by the Government and lent for use as a training ship for pauper boys from Forest Gate School District. There are now nearly 400 boys on board, who are carefully trained under the superintendence of Capt. Bourchier, R.N., for service in the Royal and Mercantile Marine. The ship is kept by the boys in first-rate order ; the boys are healthy, active, and full of life ; have a good band (27 of them were enrolled in the army as musicians in 1873) ; and are so well drilled that they won the first prize for school drill at South Kensington in 1872. Attached to the ship as a tender is a smart sailing brigantine, which the boys, under the command of an officer, regularly navigate to Sheerness for water and to Blackwall for stores, and in suitable weather make occasional trips with to sea. Over 200 of the boys are annually drafted into the army, navy, or mercantile service.

GREAT ILFORD, Essex (*see* ILFORD, GREAT).

GREENFORD, MIDDX., in legal

documents usually written *Greenford Magna,* or *Great Greenford,* to distinguish it from Greenford Parva, or Perivale

(A.-S., and Dom., *Greneforde,* the greenford, so named from the ford over the Brent river immediately E. of the village) ; pop. 578 ; is situated N.W. of the Brent, about 1¾ m. N. of the Hanwell Stat. of the Grt. W. Rly., and 3 m. S. of Harrow. Inn, the *Red Lion.*

The manor of Greenford was given by King Ethelred to Westminster Abbey, and it remained the property of the Abbey till the Dissolution, when it was appropriated to the bishopric of Westminster. Bp. Thirlby, the only Bp. of Westminster, surrendered the manor to the Crown in 1550, when it was transferred to the Bp. of London, in whose successors it has continued.

The land is a fertile clay, but good water is not readily obtainable, and the place has continued therefore to be left pretty much to the agriculturist. The scenery around, if not very striking, is quiet and pleasing : broad meads, through which the Brent meanders deviously, alternate with gentle uplands and leafy lanes ; while a few cottages and farmhouses, and at rare intervals houses of a better class, are dispersed irregularly along the roads and byways. The village consists of a dozen or two cottages and village shops, and a couple of small inns, with, at the upper end, the parsonage, two or three other comfortable-looking residences, and on the l. of the road the village church.

The *Church* (Holy Cross) is small : it comprises nave and narrow chancel of flint and stone, but rough-cast, tall red-tiled roofs, in which are plain dormer windows, at the W. end, a wooden tower with octagonal spire, in which are 3 bells, and a rude S. porch. In the main it is Perp. in character, but some of the windows are mere carpenter's work. The interior is plain, has a high open timber roof, a W. gallery (unused), and tall pews. The chancel arch, a rude E.E. one, was taken down, and a new and larger one substituted, in 1871. In the windows of the chancel is some old painted glass, chiefly heraldic, saved from destruction, and placed where it now is, by a late rector, the Rev. Edward Betham. At the S.E. end of the nave is a mural *mont.*, with an effigy of Bridget, wife of Simon Caston (d. 1637), kneeling before a desk on which is an open book ; before her kneel her 5 daughters; under an arch above is her husband in mourning attitude and habit. *Obs.* on the N. wall of chancel a half-length *brass* of Thomas Symon, rector of the parish 1518. Behind the organ is another imperfect brass. John de Feckenham, last Abbot of Westminster, held the rectory of Greenford, 1554-56. Edward Betham, rector towards the close of the 18th century, deserves remembrance as having at his own cost built the school-house, provided by an endowment for the salary of the master and mistress, and for gifts to certain poor aged parishioners. He also largely helped forward the progress of the Botanic Garden of Cambridge by a gift of £2000; and left a sum of £600 for the erection of a statue of Henry VI. (by Bacon) in Eton College chapel. From Greenford ch.-yard a footpath leads direct to *Northolt ch.*, 1 m. N.W.

The hamlet of *Greenford Green*, about 1 m. N. of Greenford, and 1½ m. S. of Harrow, has little of the rural quiet of the parent village. Here are the chemical works of Messrs. Perkin and Sons, at which was achieved that remarkable industrial triumph of chemical science the production of aniline dyes, which has effected a complete revolution in the dyeing branches of the great cotton, woollen, and silk trades. The works, now of great extent, will be recognized for miles around by their lofty chimney stacks.

GREENFORD PARVA, Middx. (*see* Perivale).

GREENHILL, Middx. (*see* Harrow).

GREENHITHE, Kent, on the rt.

bank of the Thames, 4 m. W. of Gravesend, and 20 m. from London by road, 19¾ by the S.E. Rly. (N. Kent line). Pop. 1452. Inns: *Pier Hotel* (a favourite house for yachtsmen); *Railway Hotel.* The pier, at which the Gravesend packets call at stated times, was erected in 1842.

Greenhithe lies in the hollow of the great bend of the river at the junction of Long Reach with Fidd'er's Reach, whence perhaps its name, from A.-S. *gréne* and *hith*, a haven = the green haven; the Thames here looking still its best and greenest. The village stretches along the river in a single street of about ½ m., at the foot of a chalk hill, with a marsh on either side—Stone Marsh on the W., Swanscomb Marsh on the E. In itself it has little to boast of, but there is the river in front always alive with every kind of craft; on the higher grounds are good houses, and beyond a pleasant country to stroll over. It is not surprising therefore that Greenhithe is in favour, not only as a residence, but as a quiet retreat for a short summer holiday. Yachting, boating, and other river-side matters give some employment, but the chief occupation is afforded by the chalk, lime, and Roman cement works, and fruit and market gardens. The chalk pits have been worked from a very early period, and some of the disused ones, of great extent, are curious and picturesque. The railway runs through the centre of one; in another are several cottages, as odd-looking as they are oddly placed; whilst the bottoms are either cultivated or covered with good-sized trees and shrubs. Wild flowers too (including some rare species) abound in them, and they are among the favourite hunting-grounds of entomologists.

Greenhithe is a hamlet of Swanscombe par., but was, with the help of a small slice from Stone par., created an ecclesiastical district in 1856. The *Church* (St. Mary the Virgin) is a neat Dec. Gothic building, erected in 1855, and consists of nave and aisles, chancel, bell-cote, and N. porch. *Ingress Abbey* (S. C. Umfreville, Esq.), on a gentle slope E. of the village and overlooking the Thames, is a semi-Gothic mansion erected by the late Ald. Harmer with the stone from old London Bridge. It occupies the site of a cell or grange belonging to Dartford Priory. The estate (called by Philipott *Ince Grice*) was owned by the father and grandfather of Sir Henry Havelock, the hero of the Indian mutiny,—who, however, was not born here, as has been stated. *Cliff House* (the Rev. J. Fuller Russell) contains a celebrated collection of works of Early Christian art.

It was from Greenhithe that Sir John Franklin and Captain Crozier, in the 'Erebus' and 'Terror,' sailed, June 19, 1845, on their ill-fated voyage to the Polar Seas.

Off Greenhithe lies the *Worcester Training Ship*, for imparting to "youths destined for the sea a sound mathematical and nautical education," with a view to fitting them to become efficient officers in our mercantile marine. The Worcester school was founded in 1862. There are now about 150 youths on board. A gold medal is given by the Queen annually to the youth who exhibits in the most marked degree "the qualities which will make the finest sailor;" and a sextant by the Elder Brethren of the Trinity House. Near to it is moored the *Chichester Training Ship*, for educating homeless and friendless boys from the London streets as sailors for the Royal Navy and merchant service. The ship was stationed here in 1867, and already some 1400 boys have been rescued from the streets, trained, and sent to sea. About 200 boys are on board the ship,—all it can properly accommodate. The training appears to be excellent, and the condition of the boys speaks well for the care that is taken of them. The Admiralty, in testimony of their approval of the system pursued, have granted (July 1874) a second ship, the frigate 'Arethusa,' which will hold 300 boys, and the Baroness Burdett Coutts has given £5000 towards fitting it up. The institution is a branch of the National Refuges for Homeless and Destitute Children: offices, 8, Great Queen Street, Holborn.

A pleasant walk of ½ m. across the fields, W., leads to the interesting ch. of Stone; 2 m. farther W. is Dartford; 1½ m. S.E., by way of Knockholt, brings you to the pretty village and curious ch. of Swanscombe.

GREENSTED, or GREEN-
STED-JUXTA-ONGAR, Essex (from A.-S. *gréne* and *stede*, a place or station = the green place; Dom. *Gernesteda*), ¾ m. W. of Ongar Rly. Stat. (Gt. E. line), by the Avenue (the entrance is opposite the Cock inn) and field path,—a charming walk. Pop. 121.

Greensted is as pretty and secluded a spot as can be found within the like distance of London. There are in all only 26 houses in the parish, and most of these are gathered about Greensted Green, 1 m. W. of the ch. Besides these, there are a couple of mansions, *Greensted Hall* (Capt. J. P. Budworth), and *Greensted Green* (Mrs. Smith), the Rectory, three good farm-houses, and half a dozen cottages,

but neither inn, public-house, or beer-shop. Abundant trees, shady lanes, and open field paths make this still as ever a green and pleasant place. But the great point of interest is the *Church* (St. Andrew), believed to be a genuine A.-S. wooden building of the year 1013.

In 1010 the remains of St. Edmund were brought to London to prevent them falling into the hands of the Danes, then ravaging Suffolk. Three years later they were restored to their former resting-place, St. Edmund's Bury. On its way back the body of the martyr king "was lodged (hospitabatur) at Aungre (Ongar), where a wooden chapel remains as a memorial to this day."[*] The nave of Greensted ch. has been from an early period believed to be this wooden memorial chapel. The appearance of the building vouches for its antiquity. The inhabitants of Greensted have always had a tradition that the corpse of a king rested in it; and the ancient road to Suffolk ran through Greensted. It is to be considered, on the other hand, that the ch. is dedicated to St. Andrew, instead of St. Edmund, but the date and circumstances of the dedication are unknown, and too much weight must not be attached to what may have been merely accidental.

The little church consists of the wooden nave, 29 ft. 9 in. long, 14 ft. wide, and 5 ft. 6 in. high to the plate into which the upright timbers are inserted, and on which the roof rests; a brick chancel of later date (both nave and chancel having tall tiled roofs); a wooden porch on the S., and square wooden tower and shingle spire at the W., both recent. The nave is formed of split trunks of oaks, about 18 in. in diameter, the bottoms let into the sill with a tenon, the tops sloped off to an edge, which is let into a groove in the roof-plate, and secured with narrow wooden pins. The sides were brought as closely as possible together, grooved, and fastened by tongues of oak inserted between them. The interior was covered with plaster; the exterior left as roughly adzed into shape. On the S. side there are 22 of these upright trunks and 2 door-posts, with an opening for the entrance; on the N. 25.

---

[*] Dugdale, Monasticon, 1655, citing as his authority a MS. *Registrum cœnobii S. Edmundi*: Letheuillier Vetusta Monumenta, vol. ii., pl. 7.

The ends were nearly similar, but the E. end was removed to make way for the chancel: part of the W. end remains.

In 1848 it was observed that the sill had decayed, that the bottoms were wormeaten and unsound, and that the building was becoming unsafe. Mr. T. H. Wyatt, who was entrusted with the restoration, found it necessary to take down the oaken trunks; but after sawing off the decayed ends, they were carefully replaced, the chancel was underpinned, the tower and spire were renewed, and the whole thoroughly repaired ; and now the little church appears to be as sound as when first built. Nothing could exceed the care and taste with which the work was effected, or the watchfulness that has since been bestowed upon it. The principal new work was an open timber roof of 3 bays, and an E. window of moulded brick, similar to the priest's door on the S. of the chancel. The old pews were removed and open seats substituted, and the porch and pathway leading to it paved with encaustic tiles. During the restoration a piscina was uncovered at the S.E. angle of the chancel, and some early surface decoration on the chancel arch. *Obs.* the crowned head of old painted glass, now placed in the centre of the quatrefoil window, between the nave and tower : it is believed to have been brought from Hardwicke House, Bury St. Edmunds. Mural *Mont.* to Jone, sister to Sir Thomas Smith, d. 1585, with kneeling effigy, coloured. The ch. books, Bible, Prayer, and Altar books, presented by Capel Cure, Esq., deserve notice. The covers were made " with much care and cost from spare sections of the ancient timbers upon the restoration of the church."* The ch.-yard, like the ch., is kept in admirable order, and with the fine trees which surround it, the flowers, shrubs, and simple graves, is quite a model country ch.-yard.

On the lawn of Greensted Farm, opposite the ch., is what looks much like a font, and some have suspected that it was obtained from the ch. It was really brought about 20 years ago by the tenant, from a farm previously held by him near Bury St. Edmunds. There it had for some time been used to receive water from a

pump. But there was a spring on the farm carefully banked round, shallow but ever-flowing, known as the Lord's Well (a well on an adjoining estate was called Our Lady's Well), and believed to have been a holy well, and it is supposed that this basin may have belonged to that. It is a large square stone basin, with well-moulded, arched, and cusped panels on the sides, and crocketed flying buttresses : it is evidently ecclesiastical, though not a font, and may well have served as the basin of a holy well.

GREEN STREET GREEN, Kent (*see* DARENTH ; FARNBOROUGH).

GREENWICH, Kent, a market-town and parly. borough on the rt. bank of the Thames, immediately E. of Deptford, from which it is divided by the river Ravensbourne. Greenwich is 4 m. from London by road, or by the Greenwich Rly., and 5 m. by river from London Bridge. The parish of Greenwich contained 40,412 inhabitants in 1871 ; the parliamentary borough, which includes also Deptford, Woolwich, and Plumstead, and part of Charlton, 169,361. *Inns :* the river-side houses, *Ship,* W. of the Hospital; *Trafalgar, Yacht, Crown and Sceptre,* E. of it : all celebrated for whitebait dinners.

The name, *Grénawic* (A.-S. Chron.), *Grenviz* (Dom. Surv.), *Grenewic* (Flor. Wig.), *Greenwic* (Henry of Huntingdon), is " literally the green village,"* as explained by those who are content with an A.-S. derivation. At present a Scandinavian parentage is more popular, according to which Greenwich is " the green reach," the name being given to it when the Danish fleet lay off here " for many months together."† But to this etymology there is the obvious objection that *Grénawic* is the name of the place in the A.-S. Chron., which is a contemporary record,‡ and the A.-S. writers would assuredly use the old and popular rather than a recent and alien name, if newly imposed, would be.

---

* Lysons, vol. i., p. 496 ; Bosworth, A.-S. Dict., *in loc.*

† Taylor, Words and Places, p. 164 ; Worsaae, Danes and Norwegians in England, etc.

‡ The Danish fleet was not here before 1009-10, and the chronicle was certainly commenced earlier.

---

* Rev. P. W. Ray, History of Greensted Church.

The Danish army was encamped between 1011—14 at Greenwich, about the high but sheltered ground, E. of the town and park, known as East and West Combe. (*See* BLACKHEATH, p. 50.) Part of the fleet lay off Greenwich, the remainder had its winter quarters at the Ravensbourne Creek at Deptford. It was to Greenwich that, after their raid upon Canterbury,1011, the Danes brought Abp. Ælfeg (Alphege) as prisoner. He was kept in the camp for 8 months, when, on Saturday, April 19th, 1012, the army being greatly excited by his continued refusal to pay ransom, "they led him to their husting . . . . and there they shamefully slaughtered him: they cast upon him bones and the heads of oxen, and then one of them struck him on the head with an iron axe, so that with the blow he sank down."* Ælfeg was in due season canonized, and the par. church, erected on the traditional site of his martyrdom, was dedicated to him.

The manor of Greenwich was originally an appendage to that of Lewisham, and is said to have been given with it to the Abbey of St. Peter at Ghent, by Elthruda, niece of King Alfred. On the suppression of the alien houses, 1414, it was transferred to the Carthusian priory at Shene. It passed to the Crown in 1530. A sub-manor was at the Dom. Survey held by the Bp. of Lisieux or Bp. Odo, on whose fall it reverted to the Crown. Greenwich appears to have been a royal residence as early as 1300, when the King (Edward I.) "made an offering of 7s. at each of the holy crosses in the chapel of the Virgin Mary at Greenwich, and the Prince made an offering of half that sum."† Henry IV. dated his will, Jan. 22, 1408, from his manor of Greenwich. His successor granted the manor to Thomas Beaufort, Duke of Exeter, for his life. On Beaufort's death, in 1417, it was transferred to Humphrey Duke of Gloucester, who in 1433 obtained a parliamentary grant to enclose and empale a park of 200 acres, and erect therein "towers of stone and lime after the form and tenure of a schedule to this present bill annexed." Four years later a similar licence was granted to the Duke and Eleanor his wife to build with stone and embattle their manor of Greenwich. The Duke enclosed his park, erected within it a tower on the hill where the Observatory now stands, and rebuilt the palace on the site now occupied by the W. wing of Greenwich Hospital. The tower was known as Greenwich Castle; the palace he named *Placentia*, or the Manor of Pleasaunce. On his death in 1447 manor and palace reverted to the Crown.

"Afterwards King Edward IV. bestowed some cost, to enlarge this work. Henry VII. followed, and beautified the house, with the addition of the brick front to the water side. But Henry VIII., as he exceeded all his progenitors in setting up sumptuous houses, so he spared no cost in garnishing Greenwich." *

Henry VIII. was born at Greenwich, June 28, 1491, and baptized in the parish church by Fox, Bp. of Exeter, Lord Privy Seal; his godfathers being the Earl of Oxford, and Courtney, Bp. of Winchester. When he came to the throne he made Greenwich his chief residence, sparing no cost in making it, as Lambarde writes, "a pleasant, perfect, and princely palace."† The palace at Greenwich was the scene of the chief of those sumptuous festivities for which his court was celebrated.‡ It was at Greenwich that he married, June 3, 1509, his first wife Katharine of Aragon. On May day 1511, " his grace being young and willing not to be idell rose in the morning very early to fetch May, or green bows, himself fresh and rychely appareyled, and clothed all his knyghtes, squyers and gentlemen in whyte satyn and all his garde and yomen of the croune in white sarcinet; and so went euery man with his bowe and arrowes shotyng to the wood." The same week Henry held here the first of several tournaments, at which the king with two companions "chalenged all commers to fighte with them at the barriers with targot and casting ye spere of 8 fote long, and that done his grace with the sayde two aydes to fight euery of them 12 strokes with two-handed swordes." § Similar joustings, of which Hall gives

---

* Ang.-Sax. Chron., An. 1012 (Mon. Hist. Brit., p. 418).
† Lysons, vol. i., p. 496; Ordonances for Govt. of Royal Households, p. 30.

* Philipott, Vill. Cant., p. 162.
† Perambulation of Kent, p. 390 (reprint).
‡ Lysons, vol. i., p. 499.
§ Hall, Union of the two Noble and Illustre Famelies of Lancastre and York, 1548 (p. 515, reprint).

ample particulars, were held in succeeding years. Here too he kept the feast of Christmas in 1511, and several following years, introducing on the first occasion a masked dance, till then unknown in England.

"On the daie of the Epiphanie at night, the kyng with 11 other were disguised, after the maner of Italie, called a maske, a thyng not seen afore in Englande, thei were appareled in garmentes long and brode, wrought all with gold, with visers and cappes of gold and after the banket doen, these Maskers came in, with sixe gentlemen disguised in silke bearyng staffe torches, and desired the ladies to daunce, some were content, and some that knewe the fashion of it refused, because it was not a thyng commonly seen. And after thei daunced and commoned together, as the fashion of the Maske is, thei tooke their leaue and departed, and so did the Quene, and all the ladies." *

On the 18th of February, 1516, the Princess, afterwards Queen, Mary, was born at Greenwich. In May following the marriage of Henry's sister, Mary, Queen Dowager of France, with Charles Brandon, Duke of Suffolk, was publicly solemnized in the parish church; and the same year three queens, Katharine of Aragon, Margaret of Scotland, and Mary, Dowager of Scotland, graced the Christmas festivities with their presence. Of the many splendid receptions and sumptuous entertainments of foreign princes and ministers, that of the French ambassador, on Sunday, May 5th, 1527, may serve as an example. First there was a grand mass at which Cardinal Wolsey, the Abp. of Canterbury, and "10 prelates mitred" assisted. The French ambassadors, "in the name of the king their master sware to observe the peace and league concluded between them for the term of the two princes lives;" and desired the hand of the Princess Mary for the Duke of Orleans, the second son of the King of France—but this demand was deferred because of her tender age. Then there were solemn jousts, at which the best knights of England displayed their skill and gallantry. A banqueting-house had been erected on one side of the tilt-yard, and fitted up so richly that according to the old chronicler "it was a marvel to behold." When the feast was ended, shows and masques were played, and Latin orations delivered, the King and Queen sitting under their cloths of estate with the ambassadors on the right side of

the chamber. After this, from an artificial mount and fortress came down 8 lords in rich dresses of cloth of silver and gold, who took ladies and danced with them. Then from out of a cave issued the Princess Mary with her 7 ladies, and danced with 8 lords, and as they danced suddenly appeared 6 personages apparelled in cloth of silver and black tinsel, and hoods on their heads, with tippets of cloth of gold, their garments being long, "after the fashion of Ireland," who danced with as many ladies. But a greater surprise was in store. For now 8 other lords, in gorgeous robes of gold and purple satin, "great, long, and large, after the Venetian fashion," and wearing beards and visors, approached with minstrelsy and danced with the ladies, till the Queen drew near and plucked off the mask of their leader, who was seen to be the King; and other ladies unmasking his followers, the rest of the lords were known. Then the King and all sat down to a banquet "of so many and marvellous dishes that it was wonder to see . . . and there was joy, mirth, and melody, . . . till the night was spent and the day even at the breaking."*

Here, Sept. 7, 1533, the Princess Elizabeth was born; and, after a jousting on May-day, 1536, her mother was arrested. In January 1540 was the magnificent reception and marriage of Anne of Cleves. (See BLACKHEATH.)

Edward VI. kept Christmas, 1552, in Greenwich Palace, George Ferrers of Lincoln's Inn being "the Lord of Merrie Disporte;" and on the 6th of July following the young King died there. Elizabeth spent most of her summers at Greenwich. It was her birthplace; she liked the house and the scenery, enjoyed the river, and almost to the last was fond of walking in the park.† In her early years she presided at jousts, masques, and banquets; later at courts and councils, and the reception of princes and ambassadors. Hentzner the German traveller, who was here in 1598, has given us the most graphic account of Greenwich Palace in the later days of the Maiden Queen. He was admitted to the Presence Chamber, which was hung with rich tapestry, and "the floor, after the English fashion strewed

---

* Hall, p. 526.

* Hall, p. 724.
† Rowland White to Sir R. Sidney, June 11, 1600: Sidney Papers, vol. ii., p. 201.

with hay " (rushes). At the door stood a gentleman dressed in velvet, with a gold chain, ready to introduce to the Queen any person of distinction who came to wait upon her. It was a Sunday, when the attendance was greatest, and there were waiting in the hall the Abp. of Canterbury. the Bp. of London, a great number of councillors of state, officers of the court, foreign ministers, noblemen, gentlemen, and ladies. The Queen passed through on her way to prayers, preceded in regular order by gentlemen, barons, earls, knights of the Garter, all richly dressed and bareheaded. Immediately before the Queen came the Chancellor, with the seals in a red silk purse, between two officers bearing the royal sceptre and the sword of state. The Queen wore a dress of white silk bordered with pearls of the size of beans, her train borne by a marchioness. As she turned on either side, all fell on their knees. She "spoke graciously first to one, then to another, whether foreign ministers, or those who attended for different reasons, in English, French, and Italian." The ladies of the court, very handsome and well shaped, and for the most part dressed in white, followed next to her, and 50 gentlemen pensioners, with gilt battleaxes, formed her guard. In the ante-chapel, next the hall, she received petitions most graciously, and to the acclamation " Long live Queen Elizabeth !" she answered, " I thank you, my good people." In the chapel there was good music ; the service lasted only half an hour. After it she returned, in the same state she had entered. The table had been set " with great solemnity " in the banqueting-room, but the Queen dined in her inner and private chamber. " The Queen dines and sups alone with very few attendants ; and it is very seldom that any body, foreign or native, is admitted at that time, and then only at the intercession of somebody in power." *

James I. settled the palace and park on his wife, Anne of Denmark, for life, 1605; and she rebuilt in brick the garden front, and laid the foundation of " the House of Delight," which now forms the central building of the Royal Naval Schools. Charles I. resided at Greenwich till the

commencement of the Civil War ; and Henrietta Maria " so finished and furnished " the house which Anne of Denmark had begun that, as a contemporary wrote, " it far surpasseth all other of that kind in England." * Henrietta employed Inigo Jones to superintend the building, which was completed in 1635. The Queen was anxious to form a cabinet of pictures at Greenwich, and to have the walls and ceilings of her oratory and other rooms painted by Jordaens or Rubens, and negotiations were entered into with those painters for the purpose, but pecuniary and political difficulties intervened.† Rubens on various occasions attended the court of Charles at Greenwich. The ceilings in the palace were painted for Charles I. by Gentileschi.

On the night of the 3rd of November, 1642, the Parliament sent three companies of foot and a troop of horse to search the palace and town for arms. Nothing of consequence was found, but the palace passed out of the royal keeping. When the Crown lands were sold, Greenwich was reserved, and eventually it was appropriated as a residence for the Protector. On the Restoration it reverted to the Crown. The palace had, however, fallen into such disrepair, that it was decided to pull it down and erect a new one. Denham the poet was at this time the royal surveyor (or official architect), but as he knew nothing of building he called in Webb, who is said to have used the designs of his master and relative, Inigo Jones.

" *Oct.* 19, 1661. — I went to London to visit my Lord of Bristoll, having first ben with Sir John Denham (his Majesties surveyor) to consult with him about the placing of his palace at Greenwich, which I would have had built between the river and the Queenes house, so as a large square cutt should have let in the Thames like a bay ; but Sir John was for setting it on piles at the very brink of the water, which I did not assent to, and so came away, knowing Sir John to be a better poet than architect, tho' he had Mr. Webb (Inigo Jones's man) to assist him."

" *Jany.* 24, 1662. — His Majesty entertain'd me with his intentions of building his Palace of Greenwich, and quite demolishing the old one ; on which I declar'd my thoughts."‡

" *March* 4, 1664. — At Greenwich I observed the

---

* Hentzer, Itinerarium, etc. ; A Journey into England (Walpole's Version).

* Philipott, Vill. Cant., p. 162.
† Sainsbury, Original Papers relating to Sir P. P. Rubens, pp. 211—234.
‡ Evelyn, Diary.

foundation laying of a very great house for the King, which will cost a great deal of money."

"*July* 26, 1665.—To Greenwich, where I heard the King and Duke are come by water this morn from Hampton Court. They asked me several questions. The King mightily pleased with his new buildings there."

"*March* 16, 1669.—To Woolwich. . . . Thence to Greenwich by water, and there landed at the king's house, which goes on slow, but is very pretty."*

The King showed at first great eagerness for the construction of the palace and the improvement of the grounds, but he soon cooled, and the progress was slow. Eventually one wing—the W. wing of the present Hospital—was finished, at a cost of £36,000, and nothing further was done to the building either by him or his successor.

William III. divided his time between Kensington and Hampton Court. Greenwich was no longer thought of as a royal residence; but Queen Mary conceived an even nobler use for it. Charles II. had in 1682 laid the first stone of a Hospital for Disabled Soldiers. Chelsea Hospital was however only finished, under the auspices of William and Mary, in 1690. Mary thought there should be a similar hospital for disabled seamen. Amidst the rejoicings called forth by the great victory of La Hogue, May 1692, the feelings of the Queen were harrowed by the large number of maimed and wounded sailors landed at our naval ports. William was in Holland, and Mary as his vicegerent, after making every possible provision for the wounded, " now publicly declared in her husband's name that the building commenced by Charles should be completed, and should be a retreat for seamen disabled in the service of their country."†

The next step appears to have been the issue of a patent, in 1694, by the King and Queen, granting the unfinished Palace of Greenwich, with lands adjoining, to the Lord Keeper Somers, the Duke of Leeds, and others, in trust, to be converted into a hospital "for the relief and support of seamen of the Royal Navy . . . who by reason of age, wounds, or other disabilities shall be incapable of further service at

sea, and be unable to maintain themselves ; and also for the sustenance of the widows, and maintenance and education of the children of seamen happening to be slain or disabled in such sea service." Before any practical steps were taken to carry out the project, the Queen died, Dec. 28, 1694 ; and William, reproaching himself for having so coldly seconded his wife's efforts, at once determined that the hospital should be completed as a memorial of her public and private virtues.

In the new commission, Evelyn, who had served on that for completing Chelsea Hospital, was appointed treasurer, Feb. 1695 ; and Wren, the architect of that hospital, was named to the same office in this, with, on Evelyn's nomination, Vanbrugh for secretary.

An appeal was made to the public for subscriptions. The King promised £2000 a year, and the scheme was launched. Wren soon had his designs ready, and on their being formally approved, the works were commenced.

"*June* 30, 1696.—I went with a select Committee of the Commissioners for Greenwich Hospital, and with Sir Christopher Wren, where with him I laid the first stone of the intended foundation, precisely at 5 o'clock in the evening, after we had dined together. Mr. Flamsteed, the K.'s astronomical Professor, observing the punctual time by instruments." *

Evelyn notes the laying of the foundation-stone of the hall and chapel, June 9, 1698, the establishment of a lottery in the beginning of 1699, to help the lagging funds, all other lotteries being prohibited, and so on, down to the opening of the hospital, January 1705, which he happily lived to see.

"1705.—I went to Greenwich Hospital where they now began to take in wounded and worn-out seamen, who are exceeding well provided for. The buildings now going on are very magnificent." *

Evelyn resigned the treasurership, on account of age, in Aug. 1703, up to which time " there had been expended in building £89,364." Wren acted as architect gratuitously—it was his contribution to the hospital fund. The building was, however, still far from complete, and the works were continued with more or less regularity to the reign of George II. ; the pavilions at the extremities of the terrace

---

* Pepys, Diary.
† Macaulay, History of England, chap. xviii., (vol. vi., p. 251, ed. 1858,) who quotes as his authority Baden to the States-General, June, $\frac{7}{17}$, 1692.

* Evelyn, Diary.

and the Infirmary being added in the reign of George III.

Greenwich Hospital, in its completed form, comprises four distinct blocks of buildings, on a raised terrace 865 feet long. The two blocks nearest the river, known respectively as King Charles's and Queen Anne's Buildings, stand on either side of the Great Square, 270 feet wide; the two blocks S. of them, King William's and Queen Mary's Buildings, are brought nearer to each other by the width of the colonnades; and the cupolas at the inner angles, which at once attract the eye when the building is viewed from the river, form a fine central feature, and impart unity to the composition as a whole.

King Charles's Building, the W. block facing the river, is in part the palace erected by Webb for Charles II., from Inigo Jones's designs. It is built about an inner quadrangle, is of Portland stone, and has four nearly corresponding fronts, the E. and W. having each a central hexastyle Corinthian portico with entablature, and pediment with allegorical sculpture in the tympanum; and at each angle an advanced pavilion with Corinthian pilasters.

Queen Anne's Building, the corresponding block facing the river, resembles it, except that the pediments are without sculpture: it was begun from Wren's designs in 1698, and completed in 1728.

King William's Building, the S.W. block, comprises the great or painted hall, the dining hall of the original institution, vestibule, and cupola. This part was completed sufficiently for use at the opening in 1705, but the decoration of the walls was not commenced till some years later, and the W. front, a parsimonious brick fabric, the work of Vanbrugh, was only finished in 1726.

Queen Mary's Building, at the S.E., like the corresponding block, has massive Doric columns, and is finished in a much plainer manner than originally intended. The N. end has the lofty cupola, answering to that of King William's Building, the base of which serves as the vestibule to the Chapel, which was originally designed to correspond to the Great Hall. The Chapel was, however, destroyed by fire January 2, 1779, and the present structure erected in its place, from the designs of James Stuart (Athenian Stuart), and opened for service in 1789. The Chapel is 111 feet long and 52 wide, with side galleries for the officers. The interior is richly decorated with coloured marbles, scagliola, and fancy woods, sculpture, carving, and painting. The entrance portal is an elaborately sculptured marble screen, with a frieze, by Bacon, 12 ft. high. Within is a hexastyle Ionic portico with fluted marble columns 15 ft. high, supporting a gallery in which is a fine organ by Green. At each end of the chapel are four marble columns of the Corinthian order, 28 ft. high, on scagliola bases. Over the windows are representations in chiaroscuro of the principal events in the life of Christ. In recesses above the gallery doors, etc., are figures by Benjamin West, P.R.A., of prophets, evangelists, etc.; and over the altar is a large painting (25 ft. high and 14 wide) by West of St. Paul at Melita. On either side of this are marble statues by Bacon of Angels bearing the emblems of the Passion. As an example of imitative Greek art, the chapel cannot be considered very successful, nor is the effect ecclesiastical; but it is probably one of the most ornate Greek interiors produced during the prevalence of the classical mania, and it has an air of richness, elegance, and stateliness not often seen. It used to be open on week-days, and was visited by most who went to the Painted Hall, but it is now closed except during divine service.

The Colonnades to King William's and Queen Mary's Buildings are each 347 ft. long, with returns of 70 ft. Each contains 300 coupled Doric columns, 20 ft. high. They are excellent illustrations of Wren's eye for scenic effect.

The Pavilions at the extremities of the Terrace were erected in 1778. *Obs.* the good ironwork of the E. entrance gate, and the Celestial and Terrestrial globes at the W. entrance. The globes are of stone, 6 ft. in diameter. On the celestial globe meridians and circles, and on the terrestrial the parallels of latitude and longitude were laid down, and the globes adjusted with great accuracy, by the authorities of the Observatory. These globes used to form the theme for many an old pensioner's disquisition to an appreciative circle of holiday-makers. The statue in the centre of the Great Square is of George II., by

Rysbrach. The granite obelisk on the River Terrace, in front of the hospital gates, is a memorial of the gallant young Frenchman, Joseph René Bellot, who perished in the search for Sir John Franklin, Aug. 1853.

Greenwich Hospital covers a larger area than any of the royal palaces except Windsor, and with that exception is by far the noblest and most impressive. The site by the river, thronged with the shipping of the world, the size of the buildings, their solidity, grandeur of scale, and uniformity of character with variety of detail, the harmonious grouping of the detached masses, and essential unity secured by the lofty, well-formed, and happily-placed cupolas and long vista-like colonnades, the breadth and play of constantly varying light and shadow,—all combine to produce on the spectator the feeling that he is in the presence of one of the master works of architecture. The seamen for whom this great work was erected have departed, and in losing them Greenwich Hospital has lost its distinctive and most glorious association ; but it seems to be the opinion of all who know the old pensioners, and the present race of sailors, that the new arrangement, by which they receive their pensions in money, and live as they please, with their relatives or friends, is better for them mentally as well as physically, and is better liked by them.

In the old times the Hospital wards, dining and mess rooms, hall, and chapel, were open to inspection, but now the only part that can be seen is the Hall, or, as it is more generally called,
The Painted Hall, originally intended for the hospital refectory, and which it was proposed to restore to its original purpose, though for naval students instead of old seamen ; but this intention has not been carried out, and the Hall is now only used as a Gallery of Naval Pictures. The Hall is a magnificent and admirably proportioned room, 106 ft. long, 56 wide, and 50 high, sufficiently and well lighted for a dining-hall, but very inadequately for a picture gallery. It is approached by a noble vestibule, open to one of the lofty cupolas, from which it receives a sombre shadowy light. Beyond the great hall is a raised apartment, the Upper Hall. The walls and ceilings of all were painted by Sir James Thornhill. The painting of the

hall was commenced in 1708, and finished in 1727, the artist being paid (after a contest) at the rate of £3 a square yard for the ceiling, and £1 a yard for the sides. On the walls are fluted Corinthian pilasters, trophies, etc., the deceptive accuracy of which, and of the open portholes of the ships on the ends of the hall, was a never-ending source of admiration to the pensioners, and the visitors to whom they acted as guides. The ceiling is covered with an amazing number and variety of allegorical personages and figures, the meaning or purpose of which is hard to find out. The grand feature of the design, however, is the great oval frame in the centre of the ceiling, upheld by 8 gigantic slaves, and surrounded by an interminable variety of maritime trophies and commercial emblems and objects, while in the centre, under a purple canopy, are William and Mary enthroned, and attended by the Cardinal Virtues. Apollo, Hercules, and other of the old gods and heroes; Truth and Liberty, Wisdom, Fame, Tyranny, Envy, Calumny, Covetousness, and other attributes, good and evil ; Neptune and Amphitrite, and the river deities Thames, Humber, Severn, and subject streams; Dryads and Hamadryads; Time, and the Astronomers from Tycho Brahe and Copernicus to Newton and Flamsteed ; the Four Elements, the Hours, the Signs of the Zodiac, and a multitude of other beings and symbols, find their place in this marvellous composition, which, from the time Sir Richard Steele first sounded its praises, never ceased to find confiding admirers down to our own more captious age, when even its undoubted merits of honest purpose and careful workmanship, and adaptation to the character of the architecture, fail of recognition.

The hall, as was said, was built for the common refectory of the institution, the lower part being appropriated to the pensioners, the upper to the officers. But when the number of pensioners outgrew the capacity of the great hall, dining-rooms were provided in the basements of the several buildings, and the hall ceased to be used. The idea of employing it as a National Gallery of Marine Paintings originated with Lieut.-Genl. Locker, in 1795, but his suggestion was not carried out till 1823, when his son, Mr. Commissioner Locker, submitted the scheme to

George IV., who gave it his "cordial approval," and, as the nucleus of the gallery, transferred to Greenwich Hospital the series of portraits of British admirals in the royal collections at Windsor Castle and Hampton Court. William IV. added some naval pictures, and the royal example found liberal imitators. All the pictures it should be borne in mind, have been presented to the Gallery. The Commissioners have no funds applicable for the purchase of paintings. The collection is extensive and valuable. As works of art, some of the pictures are of small account, but few are without interest for the person or subject represented. Beginning with Willoughby, Hawkins, and Drake, and with a representation of the 'Defeat of the Spanish Armada,' we have representations of a large proportion of our bravest admirals, and many of our most famous sea-fights.

We will first glance over the *Portraits:* the numbers are those on the frames. 1. Sir Walter Raleigh, as admiral, a copy of the picture by Zucchero at Longleat. 4. Admiral Jennings, who fought so bravely at Gibraltar : as a picture noteworthy as by old *Jonathan Richardson*. 5. Charles Howard, Earl of Nottingham, Lord High Admiral in command at the defeat of the Spanish Armada, wholelength, *Zucchero*, from Hampton Court. 10. Hawkins, Drake, and Cavendish, halflengths, on one canvas, from the originals by Mytens at Newbattle Abbey.

6. Sir Christopher Myngs ; 7. Sir Thos. Tyddiman ; 8. Sir John Harman ; 14. Edward Montague, 1st Earl of Sandwich ; 41. Sir Joseph Jordan ; 42. Sir William Berkeley ; 44. Sir Thomas Allen ; 90. George Monk, Duke of Albemarle, General of the Fleet ; 94. Sir Jeremy Smith ; 96. Sir William Penn ; 97. Sir John Lawson ; 98. Sir George Ascue, or Askew : these 12 pictures form the series of half-length portraits of the admirals in command under the Duke of York in the engagement with the Dutch fleet, June 1, 1666, painted by Sir Peter Lely for the Duke ; and for the faithfulness of which we have Pepys's voucher : "*April 18th*, 1666.—To Mr. Lilly's, the painter's ; and there saw the heads, some finished, and all begun, of the Flaggmen in the late great fight with the Duke of York against the Dutch. The Duke of York hath them

done to hang in his chamber, and very finely they are done indeed."* The wholelength of Prince Rupert, painted by Lely as one of the series of admirals, was retained at Windsor Castle, but a copy was made for the Painted Hall, (No. 99).

12. Robert Blake, General of the Fleet, *H. P. Briggs, R.A.* 16. Sir Cloudesley Shovel, half-length, *Michael Dahl.* 17. Admiral George Churchill, half-length, *Sir Godfrey Kneller.* 18. Field-Marshal the Hon. Edw. Boscawen, Admiral and Commander-in-Chief of the Marine Forces, whole-length, after Reynolds. 19. Adm. Sir Charles Saunders, *Brompton.* 20. Adm. Sir R. Stopford, *Say.* 22. Visct. Keith, ¾-length, *W. Owen, R.A.* 24. Earl St. Vincent, wholelength, after Hoppner. 26. Visct. Hood, whole-length, after Gainsborough. 30. Adm. Rodney, after Reynolds. 31. Adm. Benbow, half-length, *Kneller.* 32. Alexander Hood, 1st Visct. Bridport, halflength, *Reynolds.* 33. Adm. Sir Wm. Whetstone, half-length, *Dahl.* 35. Edw. Russell, Earl of Oxford, half-length, *Bockman.* 36. Adm. Sir George Rooke, half-length, *Dahl.* 37. Adm. Sir Charles Hardy, *Romney.* 38. Adm. Sir Edw. Hughes, whole-length, *Reynolds.* 43. Prince George of Denmark, whole-length, *Kneller.* 46. Capt. James Cook, the great circumnavigator, half-length, *N. Dance, R.A.*, a portrait familiar from the engravings : very characteristic head. 48. James II. as Lord High Admiral, whole-length, after Lely. 50. Adm. Sir Francis Beaufort, *S. Pearce.* 51. William IV., whole-length, *Morton.* 53. Vice-Adm. Sir Hyde Parker. 55. Adm. Sir John Munden, *M. Dahl.* 57. Rear-Adm. Kempenfeldt, of the Royal George, *Tilly Kettle.* 58. Rear-Adm. Sir Thos. Dilkes, *Kneller.* 59. Adm. Lord Anson, half-length, after Reynolds. 69. Adm. Sir Charles Napier, whole-length. 71. Adm. Sir Thos. Hardy, Nelson's friend, half-length, *Evans.* 73. Adm. Sir J. R. Warren, *J. Opie, R.A.* 75. Nelson, copy of, wholelength, by Hoppner, presented by George IV. 77. Lord Collingwood, whole-length, *H. Howard, R.A.* 84. Rear-Adm. Sir Edward Berry, *J. S. Copley, R.A.* 87. Rear-Adm. Sir A. J. Ball (the Sir A. Ball of Coleridge's 'Friend'), *H. W. Pickersgill, R.A.* 89. Adm. Lord Hawke, *Francis Cotes, R.A.* 91. Algernon Percy, 10th

---

* Pepys, Diary.

Earl of Northumberland, Capt.-Genl. and Governor of the Fleet, half-length, by *Old Stone*, after Vandyck. 93. Adm. Gell; a manly, well-painted head, *Sir J. Reynolds*. 95. Adm. George Byng, 1st Visct. Torrington, whole-length, *Davidson*. 100. Rich, Earl of Warwick and Holland, whole-length, after Vandyck. 101. Adm. SirJames Wishart, half-length, *Dahl*, from Hampton Court.

Among the other paintings, obs.: 11. Defeat of the Spanish Armada, 1588, a large and well-painted but somewhat melodramatic picture, and a good example of *Loutherbourg's* marine style. 15. Battle off Cape Barfleur, 1692, *R. Paton*. 23. George III. presenting a sword to Earl Howe, on board the Queen Charlotte, at Spithead, June 1794, *H. P. Briggs, R.A.*, very poor, and terribly cracked; it was purchased by the Directors of the British Institution for 500 guineas, and presented to Greenwich Hospital in 1829. 25. "The Glorious 1st of June," 1794: the Queen Charlotte, bearing Lord Howe's flag, commencing the action; a fine showy scenic work (12 ft. by 8½ ft.), *P. J. de Loutherbourg*, presented by George IV. 28. Adm. Duncan receiving the sword of the Dutch Admiral de Winter, on the quarter-deck of the Venerable, Oct. 11, 1797, *S. Drummond, A.R.A.* This picture (8 ft. 10 in. by 6 ft. 7 in.), was commissioned in 1825 by the British Institution for 500 guineas. When finished, in 1827, the artist was awarded a premium of £50 "in approbation of his work," and the picture was presented to Greenwich Hospital. 34. The French Fleet under De Grasse repulsed at St. Kitt's, by Sir Saml. Hood's Fleet, Jany. 1782, *N. Pocock*. 40. Destruction of a division of the French Fleet in the harbour of La Hogue, May 23, 1692; a good copy by *George Chambers* of West's picture in the Grosvenor Gallery. 47. Death of Capt. Cook, *Zoffany*. 61. Defeat of the Spanish Fleet off Sicily, by Adm. Sir George Byng, Aug. 1718, *R. Paton*. 66. Bombardment of Algiers by the combined English and Dutch Squadrons under Visct. Exmouth and Vice-Adm. Baron Van de Capellen, Aug. 27, 1816, *G. Chambers*. 67 and 85; six small pictures in two frames, the Burning of the Luxembourg Galley, 1727, and escape of part of her crew. 72. Death of Nelson (8 ft. 7 in. by 6 ft. 4 in.), *A. W. Devis, R.A.*; an

old-fashioned realistic picture, very much in favour with the old salts. 76. Battle of Trafalgar (12 ft. by 8 ft. 6 in.), *J. M. W. Turner*. This is one of Turner's largest pictures, and is a work of great power. As a representation of a sea-fight, however, it altogether transcends probability. As long as the pensioners were the habitual frequenters of the hall, this picture, though they regarded it with a sort of awe, was a never-failing puzzle to them: tactics, ships, rigging, weapons, and water were alike incomprehensible. Unhappily it is much dilapidated, and has suffered severely from the restorer. 81. Nelson's Victory over the French Fleet in Aboukir Bay, Aug. 1, 1798, *G. Arnold, A.R.A.* This picture, a very different one to the last, was a commission, the result of a competition offered by the British Institution: Mr. Arnold received £200 as the prize, £500 for his picture, and £50 in approval of the manner in which he completed the commission: the directors presented the picture to the Hospital in 1829. 86. Nelson boarding the San Josef, in the action off Cape St. Vincent, Feb. 14, 1797, *G. Jones, R.A.* This was another of the naval pieces commissioned by the directors of the British Institution for presentation to Greenwich Hospital. 92. Nelson boarding the San Nicolas at the Battle of St. Vincent, *Sir Wm. Allen*. Obs. the marble statues, at the angles of the Hall, of Admiral Exmouth, by *M'Dowell;* Sir Sydney Smith, by *Kirk;* Adm. De Saumarez, by *Steele;* and Capt. Sir Wm. Peel, by *Theed*.

In the *Vestibule* are some more sea-fights and other marine pictures, and a few *portraits*. 105. Vasco de Gama, from the original at Lisbon. 106. Columbus, from the original in the Royal Gallery at Naples. 121. Andrea Doria, from the original by Sebastian del Piombo; 122. Adm. John Forbes, *Romney;* 116. John 4th Earl of Sandwich, whole-length, *Gainsborough;* 118. Adm. the Hon. Sam Barrington, *Reynolds;* Adm. Sir James Clark Ross, purchased by subscription, 1871.

The *Upper Hall* is painted in a style corresponding to the Painted Hall, but here walls as well as ceiling are covered. On the walls are represented the landing of the Prince of Orange at Torbay, and of George I. at Greenwich. Other paintings allegorize, in a great many heterogeneous figures and attributes, the Public Weal and Public Safety, whilst on the ceiling sit, enthroned sublime, Queen Anne and the Prince of Denmark, attended by a crowd of emblematic beings, and supported by the four quarters of the globe. In a glass case in this room are preserved the coat and waistcoat, and also the watch, worn by Nelson at Trafalgar, and a letter written by him; and in another case the coat he wore at the Battle of the Nile, in 1798 : the former presented by the Prince Consort, the latter by William IV. Bronze bust of William IV. by Chantrey, presented to the hospital by Queen Adelaide. The models of old men-of-war, Franklin relics, and other objects formerly exhibited here, have been removed to the new Naval Museum.

The *Nelson Room* contains the portrait of Nelson by *Abbot*, the most faithful and characteristic likeness extant; Apotheosis of Nelson, by Benj. West, an extraordinary jumble of realism and allegory; and some half-dozen pictures of events in the great admiral's career, by Richard Westall. Here too are several portraits of admirals, and an interesting view of Greenwich Palace in 1690, by *Vosterman*, but unfortunately placed where it is impossible to be properly seen.

The hospital was opened as an asylum in 1705, when 42 disabled seamen were admitted; five years later it had 300 inmates; by 1770 the number—increased no doubt greatly by the events of the Seven Years' War—amounted to 2000. The Revolutionary War brought the number up to 2700, the largest number the buildings could accommodate. This for many years continued to be the nominal standard; but after a time the number of in-pensioners began to diminish, whilst the out-pensioners steadily increased. The revenue of the hospital had necessarily expanded at least in proportion to the number of pensioners maintained by it. The £2000 a year granted by William III. had been from time to time augmented by parliamentary votes; there had been large private gifts and bequests; a 'duty' of 6d. a month imposed on seamen; the tolls of Greenwich market; various lands and leases, the most important of all being the princely domains in Northumberland and Cumberland of the Earl of Derwentwater, forfeited on account of

the Earl's share in the rebellion of 1715. From all these sources the annual income of Greenwich Hospital amounted to nearly £170,000. Complaints of want of economy in the employment of this large revenue, the evidently increasing disinclination of seamen to enter the hospital as in-pensioners, and a doubt whether the institution was adapted to the existing social condition of the class it was intended to benefit, led to a Commission of Inquiry, and in 1865 to an Act of Parliament by which improved arrangements were made as to out-pensions, and advantageous terms were offered to such inmates of the hospital as were willing to retire from it, with a view to closing it as an almshouse. Out of 1400 in-pensioners then in the hospital, 987 at once elected to leave. A second Act, 1869, effected a final clearance, and in 1870 Greenwich Hospital ceased to be an asylum for seamen, though the Act of 1869 provides that in case of war the buildings shall be at all times available for their original purposes.

When the Pensioners left their old home, it became of course a grave question what to do with the buildings. They were among the most magnificent and the most extensive of our public buildings, and there was a general feeling that an edifice constructed for so noble a use must not be appropriated to any mean or alien purpose. Eventually it was decided to make it the seat of the *Royal Naval College*, ultimately perhaps to become a great maritime university. The interior of King Charles's Building was remodelled, and converted into class-rooms for the naval students. The rooms in Queen Mary's Building were renovated and fitted up as general and mess rooms for the Engineer officers and students, and dormitories for the naval students. The hospital chapel in this block became the College Chapel. The Painted Hall, in King William's Building, was proposed to be the College Dining Hall, and some day may be so used. The rest of the building has been remodelled so as to provide a lecture theatre and comfortable mess-rooms. The other block, Queen Anne's Building, has been fitted up as a *Naval Museum*, primarily for the use of the college, but which will, when completely arranged, be opened to the public. It contains the models of ancient and modern

17

ships formerly exhibited at South Kensington, and a great variety of other objects of maritime interest brought from that institution, from the Painted Hall, Woolwich, Portsmouth, and different naval stations both at home and abroad. It occupies 17 rooms, and is by far the finest and most comprehensive collection of the kind ever seen in this country.

The *Royal Naval College* was formally opened Oct. 1, 1873 (partially in the preceding February), and receives as students officers of all grades, from captains and commanders to sub-lieutenants, of the Navy, Royal Marine Artillery, Royal Marine Light Infantry, Naval Engineers, and a limited number of apprentices selected annually by competitive examination from the Royal Dockyards. By special permission, officers of the mercantile marine, and private students of naval architecture and marine engineering, are admitted to the college classes, but must reside outside the precincts of the Hospital. At its head is a flag officer as President, who is assisted by a naval captain in matters affecting discipline ; and by a Director of Studies, who is charged with the organization and superintendence of the whole system of instruction and the various courses of study. For the carrying out of a complete system of scientific and practical instruction, there is a large staff of professors, lecturers, and teachers.

Seamen's Hospital.—When the buildings described were appropriated as a Naval College, there remained the *Infirmary*, immediately W. of the Hospital, a substantial brick building, forming a closed square of 2 storeys, erected in 1763. This the Government assigned to that excellent institution the Seamen's Hospital Society, whose hospital ship, the Dreadnought, moored off Greenwich, was for years so familiar to all passengers on the Thames. The Infirmary was opened in 1870, as a *Free Hospital for Seamen of All Nations.* The building, which appears to be well adapted to its purpose, can provide space for 300 beds, besides all necessary surgical and medical rooms, officers' apartments, a chapel, library, and museum. From 2000 to 3000 patients pass through the hospital every year.

The Queen's House, in the Park, behind Greenwich Hospital, begun by Anne of Denmark and finished by Henrietta Maria,

after being long used as the Ranger's Lodge, was in 1807 appropriated to the use of the Royal Naval Asylum for the maintenance and education of seamen's children. The Queen's House forms the centre of the *Royal Naval School*, as the institution is now called, and is the building seen beyond the central avenue of the Hospital. It is a semi-classic structure of the Inigo Jones type, with the date 1635 on the front, but has been altered since then. The wings, Roman-Doric in style, and each 315 ft. by 51, are united to the central building by a colonnade 180 ft. long. The handsome stone building on the W., with the Admiralty arms in front, is a capacious *Gymnasium*, erected in 1872-3 from the designs of Col. Clarke, and unusually complete in its arrangements : the Gymnasium proper is a fine room, 180 ft. long and 76 wide, covered by an elliptical roof of 8 wrought-iron ribs. There is also a spacious swimming-bath, all the boys being taught to swim. The model ship on the lawn in front of the school is a corvette, the Fame, built especially for its present service by Messrs. Green of Millwall, in 1873. It is fully rigged, with masts, spars, sails, etc.

The school educates, maintains, and clothes 800 boys—now being raised to 1000—the sons of seamen of the Royal Navy. The boys receive up to the age of 14 a good general education, with a special training for sea-service ; whilst there is an upper school, in which those boys who show aptitude are retained for two or three years longer, and taught mathematics, with navigation or engineering.

GREENWICH PARK was enclosed by Humphrey Duke of Gloucester in 1433 : the wall round it was built by James I. In its present form it is the work of Charles II., who very shortly after his restoration commissioned Le Notre to lay out Greenwich Park, the king himself watching with great eagerness the progress of the works. Pepys notes that already, in the spring of 1662, "the king hath planted trees and made steps in the hill up to the castle, which is very magnificent."[*] The castle occupied the site of the Observatory, and traces of Le Notre's terraces may still be observed in the hillside leading to it. Evelyn records that

---

[*] Pepys, Diary, April 11th, 1662.

" the elms were planted by his majesty in Greenwich Park" in the spring of 1664.* The straight avenues and regular lines of trees still testify to the genius of Le Notre, but the brave neglect of two centuries has allowed nature to reassert her rights. The avenues are chiefly of elms and chesnuts, but about the slopes of the Observatory Hill are several rugged and picturesque old Scotch firs. The elms are most numerous, and many are noble trees. The chesnuts in Blackheath Avenue have passed maturity, and every year is telling upon their strength. Many have magnificent trunks, but all have lost their tops. A few exceed 18 ft. in girth. Chesnuts of large size are also dispersed in solitary state. The oaks are comparatively few, but among them are some of the largest trees in the park. In the upper part of the park are thorns of ripe antiquity and rare picturesqueness.

The park is only 190 acres in area, but it is greatly varied in surface, and hence its great charm. Everywhere the scenery is different, and everywhere beautiful; while from the high and broken ground by the Observatory and One Tree Hill the distant views of London and the Thames, with its shipping, are of matchless beauty and interest. The park is the most popular of our open-air places of resort, and on a fine holiday is really a remarkable spectacle. It says something for the conduct of the crowds who resort here, that the deer, of which there is a large number in the park, are so tame and fearless that they will not only feed from visitors' hands, but even steal cakes from unwary children.

The *Ranger's Lodge*, on the Blackheath side of the park, and *Montague House*, which formerly stood close by it, as well as Vanbrugh Castle and its companion, are noticed under BLACKHEATH, p. 49, where also will be found an account of the barrows, opened in 1784, by Croom's Hill Gate. The manors of *East* and *West Combe* are noticed in the same article.

Samuel Johnson lodged at Greenwich, " next door to the Golden Heart, Church Street," soon after he came to London, in the early summer of 1737. He came here to complete his tragedy of 'Irene,' and, as he told Boswell, he " used to compose

while in the Park; but did not stay long enough at that place to finish it."* The first time he took his faithful follower " to make a day of it," he brought him to Greenwich, July 30, 1763. " I was much pleased," writes Boswell, " to find myself with Johnson at Greenwich, which he celebrates in his 'London' as a favourite scene. I had the poem in my pocket, and read the lines aloud with enthusiasm:

' On Thames's bank in silent thought we stood,
  Where Greenwich smiles upon the silver flood:
  Pleased with the seat which gave ELIZA birth,
  We kneel and kiss the consecrated earth.'" †

But his enthusiasm for the place was less fervid than for the poem, and the experience of a quarter of a century had abated the zeal of the philosopher:

" We walked in the evening in Greenwich Park. He asked me, I suppose by way of trying my disposition, ' Is not this very fine?' Having no exquisite relish of the beauties of nature, and being more delighted with the busy hum of men, I answered, ' Yes, sir; but not equal to Fleet Street.' JOHNSON, ' You are right, Sir.'" ‡

The *Royal Observatory*, whence is reckoned the first meridian of longitude, occupies the site of a tower built by Humphrey Duke of Gloucester, as a stronghold, and used sometimes as a residence, sometimes as a prison. In the reign of Elizabeth it was called *Mirefleur*, and was, according to Hentzner, believed to be the Tower of Miraflores referred to in ' Amadis de Gaul.' When Charles II. decided to found a Royal Observatory, adopting the advice of Sir Christopher Wren, he ordered the tower to be pulled down, and the Observatory to be built on its site. The foundation-stone was laid Aug. 10, 1675; in Aug. 1676, Flamsteed, the first Astronomer Royal, received possession of the new buildings, and in September made his first observations. Flamsteed remained for 43 years at the head of the Observatory, having lived long enough to see it take rank with the best of the older observatories of Europe. His observations were published under the title of · Historia Cœlestis Britannica,' in three vols., folio, the third vol. containing his Catalogue of 2935 Stars, reduced to the

---

* Boswell, Life of Johnson, vol. i., p. 116.
+ So Boswell: Johnson wrote the line
  " Struck with the seat that gave Eliza birth."
‡ *Ibid.*, vol. ii., pp. 240—249, ed. 1844.

year 1689, a work which holds a high place in the history of astronomy. Flamsteed was succeeded by Halley, and there has since been at its head an unbroken succession of eminent and laborious men down to the present distinguished Astronomer Royal, Sir G. B. Airy, who succeeded Mr. Pond in 1835.

Greenwich Observatory has little to recommend it as a building. It was erected in haste from the materials of the old tower, and some spare bricks that lay available at Tilbury Fort, the King giving £500 for its construction. Yet the quaint old pile, with its familiar turrets and domes, has served its purpose well, and is now so ennobled by the associations of two centuries, that its removal for any new building, though of greater scientific and architectural propriety, would be regarded with general regret. Greenwich is, however, most admirable for the excellence of its instruments and the number and methodical arrangement of its observations and computations. It is, in fact, a place of various, systematic, and unceasing observation, record and reduction of astronomical, magnetic, and meteorological phenomena : not of unusual phenomena merely, or mainly, but of those which are of regular and continuous occurrence. As a place of this kind of work it is of necessity closed to the public. •

Not being generally accessible, it will be sufficient to mention the principal instruments in the Observatory. Chief is the *Great Transit Instrument*, erected in 1851, by which all observations, alike of right ascension and polar distance, are now made. It is a magnificent instrument by Simms, the mounting and engineering work being by Ransomes and May. The telescope is 12 ft. in length and 8 in. aperture, the axis 6 ft. between the pivots. Two horizontal telescopes, of about 5 ft. focal length, and 4 in. aperture, serve for obtaining the error of collimation; and a chronographic apparatus registers the transits of galvanic contact. The *Transit Clock* is a beautiful instrument, with dead beat escapement. The *Mural Circle* of Greenwich is an instrument of historical fame, as introducing in the observatories of this country an exactitude of working previously unknown in practical astronomy. It is 6 ft. in diameter, and was made by Troughton in 1812. The *Alt-*

azimuth, which is placed in the new South Dome, one of the most important of the improved instruments introduced by the present Astronomer Royal, is a massive and complex structure in which the combined talents of the optician, instrument maker, and engineer had to be called into requisition. This is now the chief instrument employed in the lunar observations which are so distinctive a feature in the work of this observatory : its special purpose is the making observations of the moon out of the meridian. The *Equatorial*, in the N.E. Dome, was made by Ramsden, and presented to the Observatory by the executors of Sir George Schuckburgh. The *Great Equatorial*, a much more powerful instrument, was made by Mr. Simms, 1859, and mounted by Messrs. Ransome. The object glass by Merz of Munich is 16 ft. 6 in. focal length, with a clear aperture of $12\frac{1}{2}$ in. The *Reflex Zenith Tube*, erected in 1852, is used for determining the value of aberration, by means of observations made near the zenith.

A part of the actual work of the Observatory, besides that already referred to, is the *constant* observation of the larger planets on the meridian—a work carried on with undeviating assiduity and punctuality—and fortnightly observations of the small planets made alternately with the Observatory of Paris. Special observations of stars are made with reference to all important astronomical phenomena, and what may be called experimental observations for determining particular points of inquiry. An account of what has been done, as well as of what is in progress, is given in the annual Report of the Astronomer Royal, and the results are issued at intervals in a more substantial form in the shape of such works (to mention only the latest) as the Astronomer Royal's 'Corrections of the Elements of the Lunar Theory,' 1859 ; the 'Greenwich Catalogue of 2022 Stars,' 1864 ; and 'Catalogue of 2760 Stars,' 1870. An important practical branch of the work of the Observatory is the "distribution of time" and the rating of ship's chronometers. All Government chronometers, and 40 from the chronometer makers, for competitive trial, are sent here and rigidly tested by exposure to sudden and extreme changes of temperature, — passing, for example, in the winter months from an oven to a shed open to the N. The time-ball on the E. turret is intended to give captains of vessels about to leave the river the means of rating their chronometers. The ball is raised half-mast high at 5 m. before 1 p.m., at 2 m. before 1 is raised to the top, and falls at 1 precisely. Time is also, at stated hours, sent by electricity to public offices, postal telegraph, railway, and various other stations.

The *Magnetic Observatory* stands within the enclosure some little way S. of the Royal Observatory building. Here by means of the dipping needle, declination, balance, and bifilar magnetometers, and of various other instruments of extreme refinement and delicacy, in connection with electric and photographic apparatus, the various observations, researches, and computations relating to this important branch of science are regularly carried on.

The self-registering anemometers in the W. turret, and on the roof, the pluviometers, barometers, thermometers, and other more or less familiar instruments, often employed in a very unfamiliar manner, that may be observed in or upon various parts of the buildings, belong to the *Meteorological Observatory*—the third great branch of this right royal workshop. The most recent addition to the regular work of the Observatory is that of systematic spectroscopic observation of the sun, and the practice of photo-heliography. Besides all this regular work, there is always a great deal that, though only occasional and in a measure supplementary, is in its way hardly less important or laborious : thus in 1873-4 there have been the preparations for observing the Transit of Venus of Dec. 1874, including the selection of stations, the outfit of the several expeditions, and the training of the observers. The preparation of the Nautical Almanac is also carried on here. On the outside wall by the entrance gate are fixed an electro-magnetic clock ; barometer ; thermometer, showing highest and lowest temperature during the past 24 hours ; *standard* yard, foot, and inch measures, marked by large metal knobs; and (1874) a balance by which, during office hours, any pound weight may be tested, the number of grains it is in error being shown on a scale.

The *town* of Greenwich has not much in it to interest the visitor. Originally and for centuries a small fishing town, it has grown into a place of great local importance, has a large population, considerable trade, and extensive manufactures, including engineering establishments, steel and iron works, iron steamboat yards, artificial stone and cement works, rope yards, a flax mill, an extensive family brewery, and maltings. Having thus grown up gradually, or rather intermittently, to its present size, the streets are very irregular in plan and diversified in character, but neither imposing nor picturesque, and the public buildings are hardly worthy of the vicinity of the royal hospital and park. Among them are a market, theatre, literary institute and lecture hall, public baths, banks, etc.

The par. *Church* (St. Alphege) is one of the "50 new churches" provided for by the Act of the 9th of Queen Anne, and was built on the site of the old church, the roof of which fell in and seriously damaged the rest of the fabric, Nov. 29, 1710. The new ch. was designed by John James (James of Greenwich), and consecrated by Bp. Atterbury, Sept. 10, 1718. A thoroughly solid-looking structure of Portland stone, cruciform in plan, with a tower of 3 stages, in character Roman Doric of the period, the church is far removed from the ecclesiastical taste of the present day, but was regarded with favour in its own. The interior is spacious, has a broad nave with aisles, shallow transepts, and a coved recess for chancel. It was remodelled in 1870, when the tall square pews were converted into open sittings, and various alterations made. The galleries, pulpit, and fittings generally are of dark oak. The columns, etc., of the Corinthian order. The decorations of the altar recess are ascribed to Sir James Thornhill. *Obs.* picture on the S. wall of Charles I. at his devotions—probably preserved from the old ch. ; on the E. wall, portraits of Queen Anne and George I., and on the N. wall a representation of the tomb of Queen Elizabeth. Among the monts. is one to Julius J. Angerstein, Esq., whose fine collection of pictures formed the nucleus of the National Gallery. Thomas Tallis, d. 1585, the great composer of church music, and musician in the royal chapel in the reigns of Henry VIII., Edward VI., Queens Mary and Elizabeth ;

Robert Adams, architect. d. 1595 ; William Lambarde, the antiquary, and author of the ' Perambulation of Kent,' d. 1601 ; Ralph Dallans, the organ builder, d. 1672 ; Thomas Philipott, writer of the ' Villare Cantianum,' d. 1682 ; Adm. Lord Aylmer, Governor of Greenwich Hospital and Ranger of the Park, d. 1720 ; General Wolfe, the victor of Quebec, d. 1759 ; Lavinia Duchess of Bolton (Polly Peachum), d. 1760, and other notable personages were interred here, but the earlier monts. perished with the old church, with the exception of that of William Lambarde, which was rescued from the wreck and removed to Sevenoaks ch.

Other churches are—the *New Church* (St. Mary), by the principal entrance to the park, designed by Geo. Basevi ; first stone laid June 17, 1823 ; consecrated July 25, 1825 : a well-built semi-classic edifice of Suffolk brick and Bath stone ; the chief feature of the exterior being a tower of 2 stages at the W. end of the ch., with, in front of it, a tetrastyle Ionic portico. The interior has galleries. Over the altar is a picture of Christ giving Sight to the Blind, by *H. Richter*, which was purchased from their exhibition, 1816, by the Directors of the British Institution, for 500 guineas, and presented by them to St. Mary's ch. *Trinity Church*, Blackheath Hill, an early modern Gothic ch., with two spires, is noticed under BLACKHEATH. *St. Paul's*, Devonshire Road, *Christ Church*, Trafalgar Road, and *St. Peter's*, Bridge Street, are of more recent erection, but neither of them calls for special notice. The Roman Catholic church on Croom's Hill is a costly structure ; and there are Congregational, Baptist, Wesleyan, and Scotch Presbyterian chapels of more or less architectural pretension.

One or two of the almshouses are noteworthy. *Queen Elizabeth's College*, in the Greenwich Road, nearly opposite the Rly. Stat., was founded by William Lambarde, author of the ' Perambulation of Kent,' and is said to have been the first founded after the Reformation. Lambarde, in 1574, obtained letters patent from the Queen empowering him to build and endow an almshouse for 20 poor men and their wives, to be called " The College of the Poor of Queen Elizabeth ; " it was completed and the poor admitted to it in Oct. 1576. The endowment, greatly aug-

mented in value, is under the control of the Drapers' Company, who have of late built additional houses and made other improvements. Each of the inmates has a separate tenement and garden, and an annuity of £20 a year. *Norfolk College*, or *Trinity Hospital*, a brick quadrangle, with a tower, by the river-side E. of Greenwich Hospital, was founded, 1613, by Henry Howard, Earl of Northampton, for the maintenance of a warden and 20 pensioners, 12 of them to be chosen from the poor of Greenwich, and 8 from Shottesham, Norfolk, the founder's birthplace. The institution is under the management of the Mercers' Company. Besides lodging, the pensioners receive 10*s.* a week each. In the chapel is a large and elaborate mont. of the Earl (d. 1614), with a kneeling effigy in full armour under a canopy, and statues of the cardinal virtues at the angles. The mont. was removed, with the body of the earl, from the chapel of Dover Castle, where he was originally interred. *Obs.* on stone let into the wall of the College Wharf by the river, opposite the entrance to the College, the line cut to mark the " remarkable high-tide, March 20, 1874 ": the line is 2 ft. 4 in. above the pavement. The *Jubilee Almshouses*, Greenwich Road, were founded by subscription of the townspeople, in 1809, in commemoration of the 50th anniversary of the accession to the throne of George III. Additional houses have since been built on various public occasions, and there are now 20 in all: each of the occupants receives an annuity of £10. There are besides Hatcliffe's and Smith's Almshouses ; Roan's School, the Greycoat School, the Greencoat School, the Girls' School (all for clothing as well as educating the children), and numerous benevolent institutions. Roan's School is now being remodelled under a scheme, approved by the Endowed Schools Commission, which gives power to build schools for 300 boys and as many girls, who are to pay a small fee for tuition.

GROVE PARK, near Watford, HERTS, the seat of the Earl of Clarendon, 1½ m. N.W. from the Watford Stat. of the L. and N.W. Rly. The entrance is on the l. of the road to Abbot's Langley, directly after passing the grounds of Cassiobury. The Grove was at the beginning of the

15th century the property and seat of the Heydons, the founders of the Morison chapel on the S. side of the chancel of Watford church. From them it passed to the Hampdens, of Bucks; then to the Ashtons, to whom it belonged till the early part of the 17th century. It afterwards belonged to the Grevilles; was in 1736 the seat of Lord Doneraile; and was bought in 1753 by the Hon. Thomas Villiers (2nd and youngest son of Wm., 2nd Earl of Jersey), the 1st Earl of Clarendon of the new creation (d. 1786).

The house is of red and grey brick, semi-classic in style, with pilasters, a balustrade, and round ends to the principal front; of three floors, with a few dormers in the roof. Of moderate dimensions and comparatively plain exterior, the interior has some noble rooms, and is handsomely fitted; but its main interest lies in the collection of portraits formed by the first Earl of Clarendon, the famous Lord Chancellor. The grounds of Grove Park join those of Cassiobury on the S., and Langley Bury on the N. The Park is flat, but well-timbered, and affords some good walks. From the Park there is a pleasant walk through "the Black Avenue" to Chandler's Cross.

The *Clarendon Portraits*, about 100 in number, are scarcely a moiety of the famous collection formed, as Evelyn, who advised the Chancellor in the selection, states, " with a purpose to furnish all the rooms of state and other apartments [of Clarendon House] with the pictures of the most Illustrious of our Nation, especially of his lordship's time and acquaintance, and of divers before it."* The avidity with which Lord Clarendon sought these pictures gave rise to some scandal. Some were, no doubt, gifts made in hope of securing the favour of the Minister, then in the plenitude of his power, or peace-offerings from those who had incurred his displeasure; but the great bulk of them were direct commissions to the painters, or purchases fairly made. On the sale of Clarendon House the portraits were removed to Cornbury House, Oxfordshire, where, whilst in possession of Lord Clarendon's son, Lord Cornbury, they were seriously thinned by executions and forced

sales, and the collection was only saved from utter dispersion by the house and contents having been purchased of his elder brother by Lord Rochester. Henry, 4th Earl, bequeathed his pictures, plate, and books as heirlooms to the possessors of the estate; but on his death, in 1752, the bequest was contested by his surviving sister, Catherine, Duchess of Queensbury, and set aside so far as related to the pictures. These were ordered to be divided, —one half being assigned to Lord Clarendon's eldest daughter, Lady Essex, the other to the Duchess of Queensbury. The pictures selected by the Duchess were taken first to her country seat, Amesbury, Wilts; afterwards removed to Ham; and on the d. of the Duke of Queensbury, 1810, passed to Archibald, 1st Lord Douglas, who removed them to Bothwell Castle, Lanarkshire, where they still are. The other half has since remained at Grove Park—a heirloom of the Villiers, Earls of Clarendon.

Many of the portraits are copies, but even these, as portraits of the most distinguished contemporaries of Clarendon, collected by himself, and therefore to be regarded as likenesses of the leading actors in the great events of the time, are valuable and interesting. But the larger number are by Vandyck, Jansen, Sir Peter Lely, and other eminent painters, and of very considerable artistic merit. The house is not shown, and the collection can only be seen by special permission: here, therefore, it will be enough to cite only the more noteworthy portraits.* 6. Queen Elizabeth, $\frac{3}{4}$-length, nearly life-size, in black gown with large buttons, and high standing ruff, a row of pearls round neck, *Zucchero*. 8. Lord Burleigh, $\frac{3}{4}$-length, in crimson velvet gown; wand of lord treasurer in rt. hand, *Mark Garrard*. 15. James I., bust, repeated from the picture at Hampton Court, *Vansomer*. 17. George Villiers, Duke of Buckingham, full-length, standing: from the collection of Charles I.,

---

* Letter to Pepys, August 12, 1689, (Evelyn's Correspondence).

* The history of the collection, as well as biographies of the principal persons represented, is given in Lady Theresa Lewis's ' Lives of the Friends and Contemporaries of Lord Chancellor Clarendon; Illustrative of Portraits in his Gallery;' 3 vols., 8vo, 1852. A list of the original collection as given by Evelyn, and a full ' Descriptive Catalogue of the Pictures now at Grove Park,' will be found in vol. iii., pp. 250—435.

C. Jansen. 20. William Herbert, 3rd Earl of Pembroke, full-length, in black silk dress, a replica of the portrait at Wilton, *Vandyck* (or *Vansomer?*). 21. The Earl of Portland, full-length, standing; in black with white lace ruffles; blue ribbon and George; a repetition, but only ¾-length, is at Gorhambury, *Vandyck.* 22. John Fletcher, the poet, Beaumont's associate: the only portrait of him known; engraved in his Works (1647), where it is said that " his inimitable soul did shine through his countenance in such air and spirit that the painter confessed it was not easy to express him: as much as could be you have here, and the graver [Marshall] hath done his part"; small ¾ size; a grave face, sandy brown hair; close black vest and falling ruff; pen, inkhorn, and paper, with verses on table on rt. 24. Henry Comte de Berghe, in steel armour, good, *Vandyck.* 25. Charles I. on horseback; a study for the celebrated picture at Blenheim, *Vandyck.* 26. Queen Henrietta Maria, full-length, in white satin; very fine, and in excellent condition; throughout by Vandyck's own hand: the Windsor portrait is a repetition; engraved in Lodge. 27. Princess of Wales, Duke of York, and Princess Mary, children of Charles I., full-length, cabinet size, good, *Vandyck,* signed and dated 1635. 28. Algernon Percy, Earl of Northumberland, full-length, standing; replicas at Cassiobury and Woburn, *Vandyck.* 29. William Villiers, Visct. Grandison: full-length, standing; in red dress: the Duke of Grafton has a duplicate—which is the original is uncertain, *Vandyck.* 30. Sir John Minnes, Lord Admiral, Governor of Dover Castle, and author of the verses on Suckling's defeat: attributed to *Vandyck,* but doubtful; engraved by Charles Warren. 31. George Hay, Earl of Kinnoul; whole-length, in steel armour, truncheon in rt. hand; a true *Vandyck.* 32. Philip Herbert, Earl of Pembroke and Montgomery, full-length, standing; original at Wilton, *Vandyck.* 33. Lady Aubigny; ½-length, *Vandyck.* 34. William Cavendish, Earl, Marquis, and Duke of Newcastle, whole-length, standing, in black dress; head and hands very fine: repetitions at Althorpe and Burleigh, *Vandyck.* 35. Arthur, 1st Lord Capel, ½-length; steel gorget over a buff jerkin; good, *Vandyck.* 36. Lady Capel,

Vandyck. 37. James Stuart, Duke of Richmond and Lenox; whole-length, standing; in black dress, with star, ribbon, and George; very fine: the Duke of Buccleuch's picture with a dog slightly altered from this; Lord Darnley's is a copy, *Vandyck.* 38. Thomas Howard, Earl of Arundel, full-length, in armour, ascribed to *Vandyck.* 39. Lucius Cary, Lord Falkland, ¾-length, standing; a very fine head. At the Manchester Exhibition, 1857, this picture was absurdly catalogued as by Holbein; it is now ascribed to *Vandyck,* but is more probably by *Jansen.* It has been several times engraved. 40. Diana Lady Newport, ¾-length, seated. *Sir P. Lely.* 41. Marquis of Hertford, ascribed to *Vandyck.* 42. Earl and Countess of Derby and Child, full-length: the Earl, in black, with a black cloak, is pointing with his l. hand to the Isle of Man in the distance; the Countess in white satin: remarkably fine, *Vandyck.* 43. Elizabeth, Queen of Bohemia, full-length, standing, *G. Honthorst.* 44. Lord Keeper Coventry, ¾-length, in baron's robes; very fine, *C. Jansen.* 46. Lord Goring, ½-length, in armour, *Vandyck.* 50. Waller, the poet, ¾-length, seated in an arm-chair, good, *Lely.* 54. Lord Chancellor Clarendon, ¾-length, seated, in his Chancellor's robes: a fine portrait, *Lely.* 60. Charles II. when a boy, full-length, in red dress, stick in hand: a clever copy from Vandyck by *Lemput.* 61. Catherine of Braganza, wife of Charles II., bust, in the dress she wore when she arrived in England, *P. Stoop.*

" May 30, 1662.—The Queene ariv'd with a traine of Portuguese ladies in their monstrous fardingals or guard-infantas. . . . Her Majesty in the same habit, her foretop long and turn'd aside very strangely. She was yet of the handsomest countenance of all the rest, and tho' low of stature pretily shaped, languishing and excellent eyes, her teeth wronging her mouth by sticking a little too far out; for the rest lovely enough." *

62. Mary Princess of Orange, daughter of Charles I. and Henrietta Maria, *Hanneman.* 63. James II., ¾-length, standing, in complete armour, and full-bottomed wig, *Wissing.* 64. Anne Hyde, Duchess of York, bust, oval; a good picture, *Lely.* 65. Duke of Monmouth, whole-length, in armour; by his side a coarse-looking man in brown dress, in a stooping posture, is pointing to a globe, his finger directed

---

* Evelyn, Diary.

to England—perhaps intended for Robert Ferguson, the prime instigator of Monmouth's expedition, though in the ordinary accounts described as an astrologer. The picture is probably that referred to by Walpole: C. Jansen's "son drew the Duke of Monmouth's picture, as he was on the point of sailing for his unfortunate expedition to England."* 67. Lord and Lady Cornbury, ¾-length, sitting in garden: good, *Lely.* 68, 69. Laurence Earl of Rochester: the first a good picture, *Wissing*; the second unfinished, *Lely.* 70. Countess of Rochester, *Lely.* 72. Anne Hyde, Countess of Ossory, *Wissing.* 77. Bp. Henchman, ¾-length, in episcopal robes: a well-painted head, *Lely.* 79. Mary Duchess of Beaufort, ¾-length, standing, *Lely.* 78. Henry Lord Capel, a good head, *Lely.* 81. Sir Geoffrey Palmer, in robes as Attorney-General: a well-painted head, *Lely.* 82. Judge Keeling, *Lely.* 86. William III. when Prince of Orange; small full-length, in armour, standing, *Wissing* 87. Queen Mary, ¾-length, sitting: a replica of the Hampton Court and Woburn pictures, *Wissing.* 89. Edward Villiers, 1st Earl of Jersey, *Kneller.* 90. Princess, afterwards Queen,

Anne, ¾-length, seated, *Wissing.* 91. Queen Anne, full-length. standing; in royal robes, with ribbon and George, *Kneller.* 92. Sarah Duchess of Marlborough, oval, like the Windsor portrait, *Kneller.* 94. Henry. 4th Earl of Clarendon, when a boy, *Kneller.* 96, 97. Two portraits of Jane, the beautiful Countess of Rochester, by *Dahl.* 101. Catherine Hyde, Duchess of Queensbury—a feeble portrait of the lovely, witty, and eccentric Duchess, Prior's "Kitty, ever young." 109. Thos. Villiers, 1st Earl of Clarendon (of the second creation). 113. William Murray, Earl of Mansfield, probably by *Hudson*: a very different portrait from that by Reynolds at Caen Wood. 114. Dr. George Clark, *Hogarth.* 116. Lady Lansdowne, *Kneller.* 118. William, 3rd Earl of Jersey, ½-length, *Gainsborough.*

Besides these, there are in the Hall three large paintings of incidents in the life of St. Buenaventura, by *Herrera;* and in the corridor and elsewhere other Spanish and Flemish pictures, and a series by Stubbs, the Landseer of the last century.

GUNNERSBURY (*see* EALING).

HADLEY, or MONKEN HADLEY, MIDDX., adjoins the town of Barnet on the N.; 1 m. N. of the High Barnet Stat. of the Edgware and High Barnet line, and a like distance W. by N. of the Barnet Stat. of the main line, of the Grt. N. Rly.: pop. of the par., which includes part of Barnet High Street, 978. According to Lysons and others it owes its name to "its elevated situation, *Headleagh* signifying in the Saxon a high place." It lies between the great N. road and the W. margin of the forest tract known as Enfield Chase, and the *ley* in its designation probably points to it as a clearing in the high forest land.

The manor belonged to the Mandevilles till the middle of the 12th cent., when it was alienated by Geoffrey de Mandeville to the Abbey of Walden—whence the designation *Monken* (or Monk's) *Hadley.* After

the suppression of religious houses, Hadley manor was given, 1540, to Thomas Lord Audley, but was in 1544 again surrendered to the king. In 1557 Queen Mary granted it to Sir Thomas Pope; in 1574 it was alienated to William Kympton. It was sold by him in 1582, and remained for a century in the hands of the Hayes family. It has since many times changed owners, and is now held by H. Hyde, Esq.

The village lies along Hadley Green on the E. of the highroad, but many of the larger and better houses skirt the S. side of the Common, the broad open space which stretches away E. of the ch. *Hadley Common* is a very attractive spot, the only unenclosed relic of the ancient Enfield Chase. When the Chase was disafforested and enclosed in 1777, about 240 acres of it were allotted to Hadley parish, and the whole of this, with the exception of the rector's glebe, of 50 acres, has been suffered to remain open. It is a wild

---

* Anecdotes of Painting, vol. ii., p. 10.

undulating tract, high and level on the W. and N., but falling rapidly away to the E. The upper part is kept as common land, and the inhabitants pasture their cattle on it. The lower part, very generally known as *Hadley Wood*, is a rough bit of native forest—green glades and hollow dells, abundant trees, not remarkably large, but evidently indigenous, with luxurious underwood—running away eastward of the rly. in a narrow slip to the hamlet of Cock Fosters. The upper part of the Common, sometimes called *Gladmore Heath*, but better known as *Monkey* (*i.e.*, Monken) *Mead*, is very generally regarded as the site of the Battle of Barnet. (*See* BARNET, p. 30.) In the survey of Enfield Chase made in 1658 it is called *Great Monkey Mead*, and is set down as containing 101 acres, while *Little Monkey Mead*, a narrow strip stretching N. from it to Ganwick Corner, is reckoned at 34 acres. The Common affords wide and varied views, reaching across Essex to the Kentish hills. From some points it is said that on a clear day ships may be seen sailing along the Thames. The wood is a favourite resort for picnic and school parties.

At the S.W. extremity of the Common, nearly opposite the ch., is the bare and barkless shell of a mighty oak, the "gaunt and leafless tree" on which Lord Lytton, in the closing scene of the Battle of Barnet, makes the wizard Friar Bungay hang his hated rival, the luckless mechanician, mathematician. and philosopher, Adam Warner, whilst at its foot lay the corpse of his daughter Sibyll, and the shattered fragments of the mechanical 'eureka' on which he had spent the labour of his life.* The huge trunk measures 30 ft. at the ground, 17 ft. at 4 ft. from it, expanding again to 20 ft. a foot higher. A few yards farther, on the rt. of the road to Cock Fosters, is an elm of even more majestic proportions, known as the *Latimer Elm*, from a tradition that Latimer preached under its spreading branches. It has lost its head, but it is still vigorous, and in the summer of 1874 was full of leaves. It measures 36 ft. at the base, and over 20 ft. at 4 ft. from the ground. Still farther E., and some distance apart, are two more

* Last of the Barons, Book xii., chap. iv.—vii.

giant elms: the largest, (opposite the great gates within which the old workhouse formerly stood,) is also the most perfect, it having its head entire, though the trunk is a shell. It measures (Aug. 1874) 30 ft. at 1 ft. 6 in. from the ground, and 22 ft. 8 in. at 4 ft.

Hadley *Church*, St. Mary, at the entrance of Hadley Common, is a large cruciform building, Perp. in style. It is a good example of the style; but the ch. was restored, and to a considerable extent rebuilt, in 1848—50, under the direction of Mr. G. E. Street, when several new windows were inserted, the mouldings and tracery renewed, and the walls refaced. It is of black flint and Bath stone, except the tower, in which the red ironstone is largely used, the quoins being of Bath stone. It comprises nave with aisles, chancel, transepts, W. tower, and S. porch, added in 1852 as a memorial to the late rector. The tower has the date of its erection, 1494, over the W. door; but the great W. window and those in the belfry are recent insertions. At the S.W. angle is a newell turret carried well above the parapet. From it projects the ancient iron *beacon*, one of the last of its kind left: it was erected by the monks to guide wayfarers crossing Enfield Chase by night, and travellers to or from St. Albans, or the north. Both the tower and chancel are partially covered with luxuriant ivy, the stems of which are of great thickness.

The *interior* of the ch. is handsome, but in the main new. The chancel and transept arches are of good form and proportions; the nave, of four bays, opening into the tower, has depressed arches resting upon octagonal piers, and an elaborate hammer-beam roof. Large hagioscopes enable the altar to be seen from the transepts. The windows are filled with painted glass: that of the E. window by Warrington, the others by Wailes of Newcastle. The chancel has carved oak stalls; the seats in the body of the ch. are of oak with carved standards. The handsome carved pulpit and font are recent. In the chancel is a piscina, and there is one in each transept. *Mont.* in chancel of Sir Roger Wilbraham, d. 1616, Solicitor-General in Ireland in the reign of Elizabeth, Master of Requests to James I., founder of the Hadley almshouses; of coloured marbles, semi-classic in style, with busts of Sir Roger and wife, by Nicholas Stone, and for which, as we learn by his Pocket-book, he was paid £80. The other monts. are unimportant. Laid in the new pavement of the nave are *brasses* to Walter Fermor, merchant, wife and children, 1609 ; Wm. Gale, M.A., 1614 ; a lady with horned head-dress of the 15th cent. ; and two or three others, also without inscriptions, but of later date.

In the ch.-yard are the tombs of Joseph Visct. Micklethwaite, d. 1734 ; Mrs. Hester Chapone, the once popular authoress, who ended her days at Hadley, Dec. 1801 ; John Monro, M.D., celebrated as a physician, and writer on Insanity, d. 1791 ; and several of persons of local note.

Near the ch. are two ranges of almshouses : one founded by Sir Roger Wilbraham, in 1616, for 6 decayed housekeepers, for each of whom there is an endowment of £18 a year ; the other founded by Sir J. P. Paget for 3 poor men and as many women, and rebuilt in 1832.

At the upper end of Hadley Green, locally known as *High-stone*, at the parting of the roads to Hatfield and St. Albans, stands the *Obelisk* (mentioned under BARNET) erected in 1740, and which records that "Here was fought the famous battle between Edward IV. and the Earl of Warwick, April 14th, 1471, in which the Earl was defeated and slain." The fighting probably extended, as already stated, from near this spot, along Gladmore Heath, or Monkey Mead. The Obelisk was originally erected about 200 yards farther S. Just beyond the Obelisk, but in South Mimms par., is Wrotham Park, the seat of the Earl of Strafford.

Among the many good residences in Hadley are the *Manor House* (Henry Hyde, Esq.), on the Green ; *Hadley House* (L. C. Tennyson D'Eyncourt, Esq.), on the Green ; the *Priory* (R. A. Glover, Esq.), near the ch. ; *Gledsmuir House* (Capt. C. Hemery) ; and *Mount House* (Mrs. Green). This last is of some interest to the admirers of Coleridge. In 1836, two years after Coleridge's death, his friend and disciple, Prof. J. H. Green, relinquished his practice as a surgeon, resigned his professorship at King's College, and gave up his other employments, and

retired to Mount House in order to devote himself to the task of systematizing and publishing the philosophical doctrines he had received from Coleridge. Here, on this self-imposed labour, he spent nearly 28 years—living to complete the book, but not to carry it through the press. He died Dec. 1863 : the book was published in 1866.*

HAILEYBURY, HERTS (*see* AN-WELL).

HAINAULT FOREST, ESSEX, that portion of the Forest of Waltham lying S. and E. of the river Roding. (*See* EPPING FOREST.) The name, formerly *Hen holt*, has been derived from the A.-S. *hean*, poor, of little value (having reference to the character of the land, as in Hendon, Henley, etc.), and *holt*, a wood. Dr. Morris has suggested that it may come from *hayn*, a cleared and enclosed space, and *holt*.† It is not unlikely, however, looking at the character of the district, that it was originally *héan holt* = the high wood.

Hainault Forest extended N. and S. from Aldborough Hatch to Forest Gate, beyond Chigwell Row, about 4 m., and E. and W. from Woodford nearly to Havering, about 3½ m., and was divided into East and West Hainault Walks. The greater part was in the manors of Barking and Dagenham, but it extended into the parishes of Woodford, Chigwell, Lambourne, and Navestock. The entire area, according to the perambulation of the Commissioners of Land Revenue, 1793, and the estimate of the Commissioners of Woods and Forests, was about 17,000 acres, but of this only 4000 acres remained unenclosed in 1851, of which the King's Woods, or royal forest, comprised 2900 acres. The Commissioners of 1793 reported that though no timber had been cut from the King's Wood for the use of the navy for above 50 years, it was particularly well fitted for the growth of oak for the navy. In our time Hainault

---

* Spiritual Philosophy ; founded on the Teachings of the late Samuel Taylor Coleridge. By the late Joseph Henry Green, F.R.S. Edited, with a Memoir of the Author's Life, by John Simon, F.R.S.

† Etymology of Local Names, p. 55.

Forest was a wild forest tract, of rough uplands and moist dells, for the most part covered with pollard oak and hornbeam, and dense underwood, but with broad, wild, common-like spaces overgrown with furze, broom, and heather, while in some parts oak, ash, and beech grew unpruned, and of great size.

Hainault Forest, or so much of it as was within the manors of Barking and Dagenham, belonged from a very early period to the Abbey of Barking. On the suppression of religious houses it passed to the Crown. In the reign of Charles I. the manor of Barking was alienated, and from time to time other portions of the property were sold, but generally the soil of the King's Woods and the timber growing on it were reserved, as well as the rights of vert and venison. Hainault thus remained a royal forest, however diminished in extent, down to 1851, when it was resolved to disafforest and enclose it. An Act was accordingly obtained (14 and 15 Vict., cap. 43,) empowering the Government, after ascertaining and compensating the claims of the lords of manors, freeholders, and commoners in respect of their several forestal and common rights, to destroy or remove the deer, cut down the timber, enclose and appropriate the land, make roads, etc. The Crown obtained by allotment and purchase 2040 acres of land and the whole of the timber; the remainder was appropriated to the several parishes and lords of manors. In 1853 the work of reclamation commenced. The trees, over 100,000 in number, were all felled, and produced nearly £21,000, which sufficed to pay the preliminary expenses. The Crown lands were thoroughly drained and fenced, and at a cost of about £42,000 were converted into a compact property of about 3½ sq. m. The land was divided by rectangular roads, and laid out in farms, which are sufficiently described under ALDBOROUGH HATCH.

It was on a portion of Hainault Forest, now occupied by the Crown Farm, that the noted *Fairlop Fair* was formerly held. (*See* BARKING SIDE, p. 24.) The unenclosed fragments of the Forest, Crabtree Wood, etc., are noticed under CHIGWELL ROW, p. 99.

HALING, SURREY (*see* CROYDON).

HALLIFORD, MIDDX., (A.-S. *Haleghford,* later *Hallowford* and *Halford,*) consists of Lower Halliford, a hamlet of Shepperton, by the Thames-side, midway between Walton Bridge and Shepperton; and Upper Halliford, a hamlet of Sunbury, ¾ m. N.E. of Lower Halliford, and the same distance W. by S. of Sunbury.

Lower Halliford is a little collection of dwellings nestling about a sharp curve of the Thames—solid old-fashioned houses, with gardens sloping down to the water, some smarter residences of the modern villa class, a shop or two, and a couple of inns. Along and across the river there are charming views—Oatlands lying directly opposite, Walton and Ashley Park on one side, Weybridge on the other. The *Red Lion* is a favourite house of call for anglers, boatmen, and holiday parties, the narrow creek affording convenient shelter for punt or wherry, and the river off here excellent barbel fishing. By some, Halliford is conceived to owe its name to the ford a little to the E., by which probably Cæsar crossed the Thames (*see* COWEY STAKES); and if so it would be, as Dr. Guest has remarked, the first place from the river's mouth named after a ford over the Thames. But it should in fairness be noticed that the stream from Littleton flows to the Thames *between* Upper and Lower Halliford, and though now of little consequence, it may of old have formed a sort of creek, fordable near the present Hoo Bridge, and Halliford would then belong to the same class of river-side names as Deptford and Brentford. Roman remains have at different times been found in the vicinity, but apparently no British. In March 1868, some labourers digging in a field between Halliford and Littleton exhumed skeletons, pottery, and various small and generally imperfect bronze ornaments: but they appear from the descriptions to have been Saxon.

Upper Halliford is a moderate-sized agricultural hamlet. The manor belonged to Westminster Abbey, with a brief interval, from the time of King Edgar to the Dissolution.

HALSTEAD, KENT, a little E. of the Sevenoaks road, about 1 m. S.

from the Chelsfield Stat. of the S.E. Rly. (Direct Tunbridge line), and 18 m. from London: pop. 365.

The *vill.* consists of a few scattered cottages; the church, nearly half a mile distant, stands within the grounds of Halstead Place. It is an agricultural vill., but much of the land is cultivated as fruit farms, and a good deal is still woodland. The surface is much broken; the lanes are pleasant, and the uplands afford extensive prospects. Halstead *Church* (St. Margaret) consists of a nave, chancel, N. chapel, and W. tower and spire. The tower is old, and some traces of old work (including a piscina) may be found in the chancel; but the body of the church, though old, has been modernized (brick and stucco, with plain round-headed windows), and is of no value or beauty; whilst the interior is filled with high pews and a gallery, and has only commonplace monts. *Brasses:* Wm. Burys, in armour, 1444; Wm. Petley, d. 1528, and wife Alys.

Halstead Place (T. F. Burnaby-Atkins, Esq.) is a large plain red-brick mansion standing in a spacious and well-wooded park. Observe the noble elms about the house and the ch. path. *Broke House* is close to the hamlet of *Bo-Peep*, 1 m. N. From the ch. there is a very pretty walk through the park southward towards Knockholt, and one across the fields N. towards Chelsfield.

HAM, SURREY, a hamlet and eccl. district of Kingston-upon-Thames (pop. 1347), lying between the Kingston road and the Thames, next to Petersham and nearly midway between Kingston and Richmond.

Ham is not mentioned in the Dom. Survey; but lands at Ham were granted by Athelstane in 931 to his minister Wulfgar. Henry II. granted the manor to Maurice de Creoun. About 1271 it passed to Sir Robert Burnel; afterwards by marriage to the Lovels. It was forfeited to the Crown on the attainder of Francis Visct. Lovel ("Lovel our Dog") after the battle of Bosworth. Ham was one of the manors bestowed by Henry VIII. on his divorced wife, Anne of Cleves. By James I. it was given to his eldest son Prince Henry, on whose decease it was transferred to his brother Prince Charles.

In 1671 the manor of Ham was granted, with the lordship of Petersham, in fee to John Earl of Lauderdale and his wife Elizabeth Countess of Dysart, and to her heirs by her first husband; and it has since remained the property of the Tollemache family. (*See* HAM HOUSE.)

The village is very irregularly built, and comprises a street of commonplace houses, a number of houses of a better class, with some good old red-brick mansions, several cottages about the borders of a large common, and others of recent erection on ground newly laid out between the Common and the Thames. The meadows, with the avenues known as Ham Walks by the Thames, belong to Petersham. With these meadows are associated Gay and his great protectress the "old Duchess of Queensbury," once "Kitty beautiful and young," celebrated by Prior, Pope, and Swift, as well as Gay. She lived for many years in the house afterwards occupied by Lady Douglas, and brought here her moiety of the Clarendon Portraits. (*See* GROVE PARK.)

" Ham's embowering walks,
Beneath whose shade in spotless peace retired,
With her the pleasing partner of his heart
The worthy Queensbury yet laments his Gay." *

Gay is still to a certain extent the presiding genius of the Ham meadows, as Thomson is of the neighbouring Richmond Hill; and a summer-house by the riverside between Ham Walks and Richmond is (or used to be) commonly pointed out by Thames boatmen to Cockney visitors as the place in which "Gay wrote Thomson's Seasons."

Ham Common is a broad rough tract of about 20 acres of barren sand, bounded on the E. by the richly wooded uplands of Richmond Park, into which at Ham Gate there is an entrance by a ladder stile, whilst reaching half-way across the Common on the N. is a wide avenue of elms, which extends for nearly a mile —and free to all—to the famous closed gateway of Ham House.

On the S. side of the open common is *Ham Church* (St. Andrew), a chapel-like Dec. Gothic building (Gothic of forty years since) of white brick and stone, erected in 1832, when Ham, which till then had been a hamlet and chapelry of

* Thomson, Seasons (Summer).

Kingston parish, was made an eccl. district.

Ham House belongs to Ham by position, and is the manor-house, but is locally in Petersham par.: it is noticed in a separate article. Other seats are *Morgan House*, long the residence of the Duc de Chartres; the *Manor House* (S. Gilbert G. Scott, R.A.); *Latchmere House*, (Joshua Field, Esq.); *The Elms* (T. James, Esq.), etc.

Hatch (the place in official documents is called Ham-with-Hatch) adjoins Ham Common, and is in fact a part of it. Here is the *National Orphan Home*, founded in 1848 for the education of girls for domestic service. The Home was rebuilt in 1861, and enlarged and completed in 1871. It is now capable of maintaining 200 children, were the funds sufficent: in December 1874 there were 134 orphan girls in the Home: Office, 58, Pall Mall.

HAM, EAST, Essex (*see* East Ham).

HAM HOUSE, Petersham, Surrey, the seat of the Earl of Dysart, a Jacobean brick mansion of good character, the scene of the Cabal, and the place set apart for the retreat of James II., stands on the rt. bank of the Thames, 1 m. above Richmond Bridge, and opposite Twickenham.

It was built in 1610 (the date and the words *Vivat Rex* are over the principal entrance door) for Sir Thomas Vavasor, knight marshal of the Household to James I., and (1611) colleague of Bacon as Judge of the Marshal's Court. From him it passed to John Ramsay, Visct. of Haddington in Scotland, Baron Kingston-upon-Thames, and Earl of Holdernesse in the English peerage, d. 1625, by whose executors it was sold to William Murray, Lord Huntingtower, and afterwards Earl of Dysart. On his decease the estate passed to his daughter Elizabeth, who became Countess of Dysart, and married first Sir Lionel Tollemache, by whom she had 5 daughters, and secondly (1672) John Maitland, Earl and afterwards Duke of Lauderdale, created, 1674, an English peer by the titles of Baron of Petersham and Earl of Guildford. Lauderdale was one of the members of the notorious Cabal ministry—and according to Macaulay the most rapacious and dishonest of the five—who are traditionally said to have held their private councils at Ham House. Lauderdale greatly altered and wholly refurnished the house "with more than Italian luxury." [*]

"27 *August*, 1678.—To Ham, to see the house and garden of the Duke of Lauderdale, which is indeede inferior to few of the best villas in Italy itselfe; the house furnish'd like a greate Prince's; the parterres, flower gardens, orangeries, groves, avenues, courts, statues, perspectives, fountaines, aviaries, and all this at the banks of the sweetest river in the world, must needes be admirable." [†]

The great Duke of Argyll—

" Argyle, the State's whole thunder born to wield, And shake alike the senate and the field " [‡]—

grandson of the Duchess of Lauderdale, was born in Ham House, Oct. 10th, 1678, and d. at Sudbroke, Petersham, close by, in 1743.

Lauderdale d. without issue in 1682, and the house has since continued the property and the residence of the Tollemache family. In December 1688, while James II., still king, but powerless, was at Whitehall, and William, as yet only Prince of Orange, but virtually sovereign, was about to enter London, and take up his abode at St. James's, the peers assembled in council at Windsor agreed that it was inconvenient, and might be dangerous, for the two princes to have their hostile garrisons within a few hundred yards of each other.

" The assembled Lords, therefore, thought it advisable that James should be sent out of London. Ham, which had been built [§] and decorated by Lauderdale, on the banks of the Thames, out of the plunder of Scotland and the bribes of France, and which was regarded as the most luxurious of villas, was proposed as a convenient retreat."

A deputation of the lords was sent to James at Whitehall to announce their decision.

" The King was awakened from his first slumber; and they were ushered into his bedchamber. They delivered into his hand the letter with which they had been entrusted, and informed him that the Prince would be at Westminster in a few hours, and that His Majesty would do well to set out for Ham before ten in the morning. James made some diffi-

---

[*] Macaulay, History of England, chap. iii.
[†] Evelyn, Diary.
[‡] Pope.
[§] This, as we have seen, is incorrect; Lauderdale only altered and refurnished the house, built by Vavasor 60 years before.

Ham House

Branch Hill, Hampstead (see p.288)

culties. He did not like Ham. It was a pleasant place in the summer, but cold and comfortless at Christmas, and was moreover unfurnished. Halifax answered that furniture should be instantly sent in. The three messengers retired, but were speedily followed by Middleton, who told them that the King would greatly prefer Rochester to Ham." *

Notwithstanding Lauderdale's alterations, and the many subsequent mutations in architectural taste, Ham House retains its Vavasor and Jacobean character unimpaired—the best specimen of its time and style in the vicinity of the metropolis. The garden walls and great gate are equally good and untouched examples of the Lauderdale and Charles II. epoch. The house is of brick, with a tall slated roof. The principal front, which faces the river, presents a long façade, with many windows, an ornamented central entrance, and advanced wings terminating in semi-hexagonal bays. Above the ground-floor windows is a range of busts (of lead, but painted stone colour) within oval niches; like ranges of busts being carried along the walls, which, bounding the lawn, extend from the house to the terrace and sunk-wall that separate the gardens from the meadows. On the lawn fronting the house is a colossal statue of the Thames. Altogether a quaint but uncommonly pleasing combination. The back is equally quaint, and equally picturesque; but it is even more weird-looking, desolate, and decaying. The walks are grass-grown; the grand old gnarled pines "a forest Laocoon" seem writhing in a death-struggle. The lofty ornamental iron gates, flanked with piers and urns, and carrying the arms of Tollemache and Murray, which Walpole a century ago complained were never opened, have remained closed ever since, unpainted and rusting away. They have only, it is said, been opened once since they closed on Charles II., and it may be that another sovereign must come before they again turn on their hinges. But the aspect of utter neglect which this back of the house presents is well calculated to foster superstitious fancies. It was this house, with its contorted firs and dreamy avenues, that inspired the vision of the haunted house in Hood's impressive poem ' The Elm Tree.'

The avenues and the meadows, the Ham Walks so often referred to by the writers of Queen Anne's time, have always been celebrated, and are in their way unrivalled. (*See* HAM WALKS.) The great avenue by the Thames side is over half a mile long; the Petersham Avenue is little less; while from the back of the house to Ham Common the " dappled path of mingled light and shade " extends for nearly a mile. Within the gates, house and gardens seem alike unchanged : terraces, parterres, bowling-green, fountains, flowers,—all are as of old.

Inside the house, the antique character has been maintained almost unmodified—at first from neglect, of late from choice and feeling. The " old Countess of Dysart," who d. in the house in 1840, at the age of 95, preserved scrupulously the ancestral furniture and state. Walpole, visiting it when his niece, Charlotte Walpole, had become Countess of Dysart, and mistress of Ham House, wrote thus of it a century since :—

" I went yesterday to see my niece in her new principality of Ham. It delighted me and made me peevish. Close to the Thames, in the centre of all rich and verdant beauty, it is so blocked up and barricaded with walls, vast trees, and gates, that you think yourself an hundred miles off, and an hundred years back. The old furniture is so magnificently ancient, dreary and decayed, that at every step one's spirits sink, and all my passion for antiquity could not keep them up. Every minute I expected to see ghosts sweeping by; ghosts I would not give sixpence to see, Lauderdales, Tollemaches, and Maitlands. There is one old brown gallery full of Vandyck's and Lely's, charming miniatures, delightful Wouvermans and Poelemburghs, china, japan, bronzes, ivory cabinets, and silver dogs, pokers, bellows, etc., without end. One pair of bellows is of filigree. In this state of pomp and tatters my nephew intends it shall remain, and is so religious an observer of the venerable rites of his house, that because they were never opened by his father but once, for the late Lord Granville [whose daughter he had married] you are locked out and locked in, and after journeying all round the house, as you do round an old French fortified town, you are at last admitted through the stable-yard to creep along a dark passage by the housekeeper's-room, and so by a back door into the great hall. He seems as much afra d of water as a cat, for though you might enjoy the Thames from every window of three sides of the house, you may tumble into it before you guess it is there. . . . . . Think of such a palace commanding all the reach of Richmond and Twickenham, with a domain from the foot of Richmond Hill to Kingston Bridge, and then imagine its being as dismal and prospectless as if it stood ' on Stanmore's wintry wild ' ! I don't see why a man should not be divorced from his prospect as well as from his wife for not being able to enjoy it." *

---

* Macaulay, History of England, chap. x.

* Horace Walpole to Montagu, June 11, 1770.

Forty years later, Queen Charlotte, in a letter to one of her own family, (Sept. 7, 1809,) described in her imperfect English a visit she made to Ham House, and the impression it made on her :—

"The Rain having ceased Ldy. Caroline wished to show me from Ham walks the View of the River and likewise that of Lord Dysart's Place and as She has been favoured with a Key She offered to carry us there, we walked and most delightfull it was there, and saw not only the House, but all the Beautifull Old China which a Civil Housekeeper offered to show us. It is so fine a Collection that to know and admire it as one ought to do would require many Hours, but when all the Fine Paintings, Cabinets of Excellent Workmanship, both in Ivory and Amber also attrack Yr. Notice Days are required to see it with Advantage to one-self. The House is much altered since I saw it by repairing and tho' the old Furniture still remains it is kept so clean, that even under the Tattered State of Hangings and Chairs One must admire the good Taste of Our forefathers and their Magnificence. The Parqueté Floors have been taken up with great Care, Cleaned and relaid and in order to preserve them the Present Lord has put Carpets over them, but of Course not Nailed down. I saw this time also the Chapel which is so dark and Dismal that I could not go into it. Upon the whole the Place remaining in its old Stile is Beautifull and Magnificent both within and without, but truly Melancholy. My Lord is very little there since the Death of His Lady for whom he had the greatest regard and attention." *

The chief apartments are the *Central Hall*, a large and stately room, paved with black and white marble, and surrounded by an open gallery. From it ascends a grand staircase of six flights, with massive balustrades of solid walnut, ornamented with military trophies. The state reception room, called the Queen's Audience Chamber, but also known as the Cabal Chamber, a rather dark room at the back of the house, has the initials I. L. E., (John, Elizabeth, Lauderdale,) beneath a coronet. It is hung with old tapestry, as are also some of the smaller rooms. In the Queen's Closet is a chimneypiece of good work. The Blue and Silver Room is ornamented with the Tudor-shaped crown. A suite of rooms known as the Duchess of Lauderdale's, is remarkable as having been preserved—furniture, fittings, and all else—just as they were left by the imperious beauty. In a sort of boudoir or dressing-room, opening from her bedroom, are her arm-chair and writing-desk, her tall walking-cane, a shorter cane, and

* Extracts of the Journal and Correspondence of Miss Berry, vol. ii., p. 423.

other articles of personal use. Here, too, are various drawings and other memorials of her presence. The North Drawing-room is, however, perhaps the most perfect example of the Lauderdale time and state. All the rich old furniture, including the great cabinet of ivory and cedar, remains ; there is an elaborate marble chimneypiece, with its sculptured allegories, and bronze andirons on the hearth. The Library looks the perfect retreat for learned leisure, and is full of rare books in choice old bindings : it contains, or at one time contained, as many as 14 Caxtons, and some of the rarest Wynkyn de Wordes. Here are also preserved many papers of great historical interest. Much of the panelling throughout the house is of the Charles II. period, and some of the recesses are filled with sea-fights painted by the elder Vandevelde expressly for the places they occupy. Some of the ceilings are by Verrio. The Gallery on the W. side of the house, over 80 ft. long, is hung, as Walpole mentions, with portraits said to be by Vandyck and Lely ; the light is bad, and they are seen with difficulty, but the ascription of some at least of the Vandycks is questionable. The Tapestry Room has four subjects copied from Raphael's Cartoons—Paul Preaching at Athens, Elymas struck with Blindness, the Death of Ananias, and Peter and John at the Beautiful Gate. It is believed they were some of those wrought at Mortlake. The Chapel mentioned above, by the Hall, has been recently very richly fitted by Lady Huntingtower for the Roman Catholic service.

Among the few really important pictures, the following deserve notice. A Portrait of James I. when old : there is a small copy of it at Hampton Court. Duke and Duchess of Lauderdale, half-lengths on one canvas, *Lely*. Charles II., a good portrait, *Lely*. Sir Henry Vane, the elder ; ¾-l., his hand on a stick ; a well-painted portrait in Vandyck's manner. Wm. Murray, Earl of Dysart, in armour. The Countess of Bedford, daughter of Carr, Earl of Somerset, and the divorced wife of the Earl of Essex. mother of William Lord Russell. Vandyck, holding a sunflower, a copy of a picture often copied. The miniatures are rather numerous. and unusually good and interesting ; and the china, jewellery, and various other items antique articles of an ornamental character. are curious and attractive. The house can only be seen by special permission.

HAM WALKS, called by Thomson, in his ' Seasons,' " Ham's umbrageous walks,"* occupy the meadows facing Ham House—" where silver Thames first rural grows,"—and extend from the house as far as Twickenham Ferry. The walks are " all overarched with lofty elms," in groves and avenues of magnificent trees. Time is. however, telling upon them, and the storms of the last winters have laid many a giant low.

Ham Walks were a favourite lounge of Swift, Pope, and Gay : of Swift whilst at Sheen, of Pope whilst Gay lived in the house of the old Duchess of Queensbury ; † and they are often referred to in Walpole's letters. The ' Daily Post' of Friday, June 4. 1728, contained the following advertisement :—

" Whereas there has been a scandalous paper cried about the streets under the title of ' A Pop upon Pope,' ‡ intimating that I was whipt in Ham Walks on Thursday last : this is to give notice that I did not stir out of my house at Twickenham on that day, and the same is a malicious and illgrounded report. A. P."[OPE]

Dennis asserted that for long after the publication of 'The Dunciad,' in 1728, Pope " never dared to appear without a tall Irishman to attend him."§

HAMMERSMITH, MIDDX., a town and member of the parliamentary borough of Chelsea ; pop. 42.691. Virtually a suburb of the metropolis, Hammersmith extends from Kensington along the Western Road to Turnham Green, and by the Thames to Chiswick. It is 3½ m. from Hyde Park Corner ; the L. and S.W.. the Metropolitan Extension. and the N. London Rlys. have stats.: the Metropolitan in the Broadway, the L. and S.W. in the Grove, a short distance W., and the N. London in the Brentford Road, at the extreme W. of the

town. Till 1834 Hammersmith was a *side* (or division) of Fulham par. ; it is now the parent parish of 4 separate eccl. districts.

Of old, besides the business that accrued from its position on a great line of road, Hammersmith was noted for extensive market-grounds, orchards, and dairy farms ; possessed various good mansions, and, as its local historian reported, was " inhabited by gentry and persons of quality, and a summer retreat for nobility and wealthy citizens." Now the builder has very nearly supplanted the gardener and farmer ; the mansions are for the most part pulled down, occupied as schools or institutions, been subdivided, or given place to factories, and nobility and wealthy citizens seek more distant and romantic regions for their summer or autumn retreats. But as the fields have been built over, Hammersmith has grown in population and importance. There are now large engineering establishments, distilleries, lead mills, oil mills, a coach factory, boat-builders' yards, and brick fields, besides the extensive pumping works of the West Middlesex Water Company.

The main street of Hammersmith (the Western Road, here called *King Street.*) about 1½ m. long, and towards its E. end widening into the *Broadway*, is lined throughout with shops of the usual suburban character : the quaint old inns and posting-houses have been transformed, and the whole wears a modern aspect. At the Broadway the main street is crossed by a road from Brook Green and the Uxbridge Road, which is continued S. over the Suspension Bridge into Surrey. Facing the river from the Suspension Bridge to Chiswick stretches the *Mall*, once the fashionable part of Hammersmith, and affording a pleasant promenade, shaded by the tall old elms which here line the Thames. It is divided into the Upper and Lower Mall by the Creek, a dirty inlet of the Thames, which is crossed by a wooden foot-bridge, built originally by Bishop Sherlock in 1751, and known as the High Bridge ; the region of squalid tenements bordering the Creek having acquired the cognomen of *Little Wapping*, probably from its confined and dirty character. Just over the bridge, at the entrance to the Upper

---

* So Armstrong, Art of Preserving Health, 4to, 1744, invokes
          " the friendly gloom that hides
    Umbrageous Ham."
† Swift to Gay, Nov. 10, 1730.
‡ Reprinted in Gulliveriana and Alexanderiana, 8vo, 1728, p. 321; it was generally attributed to Lady Mary Wortley Montagu.
§ Dennis on the Dunciad, p. 12.

Mall, is a little inn, the *Doves*, known in the days when coffee was less of a home beverage than now, as the *Dove Coffee House*, and "wits and citizens resorted to it in the season to sip their coffee, enjoy the sweet prospect of the river, and talk over the literature and politics of the day." In a room overlooking the river, Thomson is said to have written part of his 'Winter,' "when the Thames was frozen, and the surrounding country covered with snow."* Thomson's room is on the first floor, a bright, pleasant apartment, affording an excellent view of the long reach of the Thames across Chiswick. The humble tea garden, reaching from the house to the river, is quite hidden from this room by the limes which shade it. The adjoining cottage, now called The Seasons, then an appendage to the Doves, was a favourite smoking retreat of the late Duke of Sussex, who is said to have kept here a choice assortment of meerschaums. Along the Upper Mall are still a few of the good old-fashioned brick houses that once lined its whole extent. But oil mills and factories have driven away the "noble and fashionable" occupants, and the houses left are mostly altered, mildewed, or mouldering. Between the Mall and King Street is a populous district of mean houses; N. of King Street, a flat, uninteresting region, are the better built districts of Ravenscourt, Brook Green, and Shepherd's Bush,—all within Hammersmith parish.

The Parish *Church*, St. Paul, was built originally as a chapel-of-ease to Fulham, and was consecrated by Bishop Laud, June 7, 1631. It has been often repaired, and was enlarged and restored in 1864. It is of brick, but covered throughout with stucco ; is of the corrupt style of the time, and is of little architectural or other interest. It consists of nave, aisles, short transepts, and W. tower, in which are 8 bells, with a bell turret instead of spire. The interior is roomy, has an ornamental ceiling, a large altar-piece of carved oak, and some contemporary

painted glass, scriptural figures and emblems, and the arms of Sir N. Crispe and other benefactors of the church. *Monts.*— On S. of chancel, one of black and white marble of Edmund Lord Sheffield, Earl of Mulgrave, commander of a squadron against the Spanish Armada, for his service on which occasion he was made a Knight of the Garter by Queen Elizabeth, and President of the North under James I., d. 1646. N. of chancel, tomb with bust of Ald. James Smith, d. 1667, founder of Bookham Almshouses, and father of 20 children. Sir Edward Nevill, d. 1705, Justice of the Common Pleas. But the most remarkable mont. is that of Sir Nicholas Crispe, d. 1666 : "a man of loyalty, that deserves perpetual remembrance." * Against the N. wall of the nave is a bronze bust of Charles I., with the inscription beneath it, "This effigies was Erected by the Special Appointment of Sir Nicholas Crispe Knight and Baronet, As a grateful commemoration of the Glorious Martyr King Charles the First of blessed Memory." Beneath this, on a pedestal of black marble, is an urn with an inscription setting forth that "Within this urn is entombed the Heart of Sir Nicholas Crispe, Knt. and Baronet, a loyal sharer in the sufferings of his late and present Majesty." Crispe lost his fortune and became an exile in the royal cause ; but after the return of Charles II. was restored to his office, and created a baronet. On wall of S. aisle, a tablet to "Thomas Worlidge, Painter," d. 1766. This is the celebrated engraver : he was originally a painter, but abandoned the pencil for the etching needle, and thus made himself famous. He lived and worked in a thatched cottage in Lee's Nursery, which had been constructed with large vaults for a wine store, when the nursery was a vineyard, and a British Burgundy was made from the grapes grown there.† A tablet commemorates Arthur Murphy, d. 1805, the dramatic writer, essayist, and translator of Tacitus. Another is the memorial of Sir Elijah Impey, the Indian judge, d. Oct. 12. 1809.

Near the church are the Latymer Schools, founded by Edward Latymer, who in 1624 bequeathed the rental of 35

---

* In the garden is one of the old ale-house boards, now rarely seen, for playing a rustic substitute for bagatelle. Here they call it "bumble-puppy," but it differs materially from the bumble-puppy described in Strutt's Sports and Pastimes (B. iii., chap. vii., § 13), being merely a bridge with numbered arches, through which large marbles are bowled.

* Johnson, Life of Waller.
† Faulkner's Fulham, p. 21.

acres of land for clothing 6 poor men, and clothing and educating 8 boys. The property has greatly increased in value, and now maintains 30 men, and clothes and educates 100 boys and 50 girls.

St. Peter's district ch., at the W. end of the town, is a substantial semi-classical building, erected in 1829. *St. Mary's*, in the Hammersmith Road, belongs to *North End*, and is noticed under that heading. *St. John the Evangelist*, Dartmouth Road, N. of King Street, is a noticeable brick ch., erected in 1861 from the designs of Mr. Butterfield. It consists of nave with clerestorey, aisles, and chancel, but has at present no tower. A somewhat severe specimen of E.E., the exterior is not particularly attractive, but the interior is striking from its altitude, breadth, and boldness of character.

Close by St. John's Church is the *Godolphin School*, founded in the 16th cent., under the will of William Godolphin, but remodelled as a Grammar School according to a scheme approved by the Court of Chancery in 1861. The buildings, which comprise a school-room for 200 boys, class-rooms, a dining-hall, dormitories, and a master's residence, are of white brick and stone, Early Collegiate Gothic in style, agreeing in general character with the neighbouring ch. They were completed in 1862, from the designs of Mr. C. H. Cooke.

Hammersmith contains an unusual number of Roman Catholic establishments. The parent institution appears to have been a School for Ladies, founded in 1669, in the Broadway, on the site, as has been said, of an ancient Benedictine convent, and which was generally known as the Nunnery. Towards the end of the 18th cent. it became a refuge for nuns driven from France by the Revolution, and shortly after was placed under the English Benedictine Dames. It is now a theological institute. The large brick buildings (designed by Pugin) in the Fulham Road, a little S. of the parish ch., are the *Convent of the Good Shepherd*, and an *Asylum for Penitent Women*. In King Street East is the *Convent of the Little Daughters of Nazareth*, where the sisterhood have a home for aged, destitute, and infirm poor persons, and a hospital for epileptic children. At Brook Green is a cluster of Roman Catholic

institutions. The *Ch. of the Holy Trinity* is a spacious stone building of considerable architectural pretension; Early Dec. in style, with a tower and lofty stone spire at the N.E. : the interior is very rich. By it is a large range of almshouses of stone, Late Collegiate Gothic in style; and on the opposite side of the road a large gloomy pile—St. Mary's Normal College. Close by are a Roman Catholic Reformatory for boys and another for girls. Industrial Schools, Day Schools, etc., are in other parts of the parish.

The town has also its full share of Dissenters' chapels ; and of public buildings, but of neither class any of architectural or historical interest. The public buildings include a Town Hall, in King Street, 2 Lecture Halls, Baths and Washhouses, a Police Court, Office of the Board of Works, and the West London Hospital, King Street East, which appears to be growing into an important institution. The town supports two weekly newspapers.

The *Suspension Bridge* which here crosses the Thames was erected 1824—27, from the designs of Mr. Tierney Clark. It was the first suspension bridge constructed near London, and in outline and simplicity of style, remains the best-looking bridge of its kind on the Thames. It has a water-way of 688 ft., and a central span of 422 ft. The suspension towers are 48 ft. above the level of the roadway, which is 16 ft. above high water. The platform is carried by 8 chains, arranged in 4 double lines.

The most celebrated of the Hammersmith mansions was *Brandenburg House*, which stood by the river-side, about $\frac{1}{4}$ m. below the Suspension Bridge. It was built by Sir Nicholas Crispe, in the early part of the reign of Charles I., at a cost of nearly £23,000, and even in that age of costly dwellings was celebrated for its splendour. When the army of the Parliament was stationed here in Aug. 1647, Fairfax made Crispe's house his headquarters. Crispe had fled to France, but after the death of the king returned to England, and having submitted to a composition, obtained possession of his house. Crispe d. in 1666, and in 1683 his nephew sold the house to Prince Rupert, who gave it to his mistress. Margaret Hughes the actress—" the pretty woman newly come, called Pegg, that was Sir Charles Sedley's mistress," whom Pepys "did kiss" at the king's house, "a mighty pretty woman, and seems, but is not, modest." * She lived in her fine house at Hammersmith for ten years, when she sold it to one Timothy Lannoy, "a scarlet dyer." His son's widow married James Murray, Duke of Athole, and they lived in the house till 1748, when it was purchased by George Bubb Dodington, afterwards Lord Melcombe. Dodington altered and modernized the house at a great expense, and added a sculpture gallery which he filled with antiquities. Having furnished it with ostentatious luxury, he named it La Trappe, calling himself and associates the Monks of the Convent.† He died here in 1762, when the estate passed to his nephew, Thomas Wyndham. It was afterwards let to Mrs. Sturt, whose gay parties made the house more famous than it was in Mr. Dodington's day.

"Last night we were all at a masquerade at Hammersmith, given by Mrs. Sturt . . . . It is the house that was Lord Melcombe's, and is an excellent one for such occasions. I went with Lady Palmerston and Mrs. Crewe, Windham and Tom Pelham. We did not get home till almost 6 this morning. The Princes [the Prince of Wales, afterwards George IV., and his brothers] were all three at Mrs. Sturt's in Highland dresses, and looked very well. Their knees were bare, and I saw the Prince of Wales make a lady feel his bare knee." ‡

In 1792 it was purchased by the Margrave of Brandenburg-Anspach, who, shortly after his marriage, in 1791, with the widow of Lord Craven, transferred his states to the King of Prussia for an annuity of 400,000 rix-dollars during the lives of himself and the Margravine, and settled in England. He died in 1806. The Margravine made many alterations in the house, now named Brandenburg House, and added a small theatre, in which dramatic performances were enacted by various distinguished amateurs, the Margravine herself "sometimes gratifying her friends by exerting her talents

* Diary, May 6th, 1668.
† In vol. iv. of the Vitruvius Britannicus are 3 plates of Brandenburg House, as altered by Dodington—the elevation towards the Thames, ground plan, and section of gallery.
‡ Sir Gilbert Elliot to Lady Elliot, June 13, 1789. Life and Letters of Sir Gilbert Elliot, first Earl of Minto, vol. i., p. 325.

both as a writer and performer." She was a prominent personage in her day, and while here. according to her relative Mr. Grantley Berkeley, was "in the habit of driving a curricle and four white ponies, her most frequent companions being the celebrated Duchess of Gordon, who, with her three famous beauties, were often guests at Brandenburg House ; as well as the Countess of Cork."* She died in 1828, leaving the bulk of her property to the Hon. Keppel Craven, one of her sons by her first husband, the Earl of Craven. Mr. Keppel Craven was a member of the household of Queen Caroline, wife of George IV., and it was probably in consequence of this connection that she was led to rent Brandenburg House, May 1820, pending her trial in the House of Lords. During the trial she resided at Brandenburg House, and all the while the popular enthusiasm kept the neighbourhood of the mansion in constant turmoil :—

> "All kinds of addresses,
> From collars of SS
> To vendors of cresses,
>   Came up like a fair ;
> And all through September,
> October, November,
> And down to December
> They hunted this hare,"—

as Theodore Hook wrote, with much more in the same strain, in the 'John Bull.'

The unhappy Queen died here, Aug. 7, 1821 ; and in May, 1822, the materials of Brandenburg House were sold by auction, and the house pulled down. In the grounds, but not on the site of the original mansion, there is now a house called Brandenburg House, occupied as a private lunatic asylum. Close by, and partly in the grounds of Brandenburg House, stands the huge workhouse of the Fulham Union. Opposite Brandenburg House, Mrs. Billington, the most famous of British singers, had a villa, which she fitted up with great elegance, and in which she resided till she left England, in 1817, to join her worthless husband, Felissent, in Italy, where she died the

* My Life and Recollections, vol. iv., p. 224. Many particulars of the latter days of the Margravine will be found in the Diary of the Duke of Buckingham and Chandos. For a more ample account her own Memoirs will of course be consulted.

following year, as was said, from his ill-treatment. It was afterwards occupied, in succession, by Sir James Sibbald, Bart., Vice-Admiral Ross-Donnerly, and Capt. Marryat, the novelist.

In Queen Street, opposite the ch., is a large brick mansion with a central pediment and classic portico, which was the residence of Edmund Sheffield, Earl of Mulgrave and Baron Butterwick, who died here in 1646. The house, then known as *Butterwick Manor House*, was afterwards modernized and divided, and the newer moiety, called *Bradmore House*, was in 1736 purchased by Elijah Impey, father of the Indian judge, whose family long resided in it. The other half, Butterwick House, was pulled down some years ago, and the site built over.

The ancient manor-house of *Pallenswick*, subsequently *Ravenscroft*, at the N.W. extremity of Hammersmith, "was probably the country seat of Alice Perrers," the fair favourite of Edward III.* The manor was purchased for her in 1373. The house was surrounded by a moat, and stood in a park which extended from King Street to the New Road. A lodge or inn at the New Road end is supposed to have been the house hired by Miles Sindercombe for his proposed attempt to assassinate Cromwell, Jan. 1657, as he rode to Hampton Court.

The *Lower Mall*, now pretty well abandoned to inns, rowing-club houses, boat yards, oil mills, and shabby dwellings, was once a fashionable locality, and contained several good mansions. In a house near the High Bridge, the remarkable mechanical genius, and friend of Charles II., Sir Samuel Morland, spent his last years :—

"25 *Oct.*, 1696.—The Abp. and myself went to Hammersmith, to visite Sir Sam. Morland, who was entirely blind ; a very mortifying sight. He shew'd us his invention of writing, which was very ingenius ; also his wooden kalender, which instructed him all by feeling ; and other pretty and useful inventions of mills, pumps, etc., and the pump he had erected that serves water to his garden, and to passengers, with an inscription, and brings from a filthy part of the Thames neere it a most perfect and pure water. He had newly buried £200 worth of music books 6 feet under ground, being, as he said, love songs and vanity. He plays himself Psalms and religious hymns on the Theorbo."†

Morland's house, since known as Walborough House, was purchased for a residence, in 1703, by Sir Edward Nevill, one of the Justices of the Common Pleas. Morland's pump and inscription have long disappeared.

In the *Upper Mall* dwelt for some years Queen Catherine, widow of Charles II. After she quitted it, 1692, to return to Portugal, the house descended through various hands, serving as an academy, before it was pulled down, about 1800. In the Queen's time the garden was celebrated for its abundant flowers—but mostly of the common kind, "the Queen not being for curious plants or flowers." In the reign of Anne, her physician, the celebrated Dr. Radcliffe, had one of the chief houses on the Upper Mall. He intended to convert it into a public hospital, but did not live to carry out his purpose. Lloyd, the nonjuring Bishop of Norwich, was Radcliffe's neighbour at the Upper Mall, where they lived in great intimacy and amity. *Sussex House* was purchased of the Duke of Sussex, by Capt. Marryat, the novelist, who furnished it luxuriously, and lived in extravagant style, giving parties and "conjuring soirées," in which Theodore Hook used to assist.

Beyond the Mall is *Hammersmith Terrace*, so named from the pleasant walk by the river at the back of the houses, and common to all. In the last house, Arthur Murphy, the dramatist, lived, and made his translation of Tacitus.* Two or three doors off (No. 13, the last house with a portico) lived for many years Philip James de Loutherbourg, R.A., the precursor of Stanfield as a painter alike of panoramas, stage scenery, and sea-pieces. Loutherbourg was a simple-hearted, benevolent creature, but he bewildered himself with mesmerism, became a disciple of Brothers the Prophet, and himself took to prophesying, and curing the sick and the lame.

"Loutherbourg, the painter, is turned an inspired physician, and has 3000 patients. His sovereign panacea is barley-water. I believe it is as efficacious as mesmerism."†

---

* The Dedication, to Burke, is dated "Hammersmith Terrace, 6th May, 1793."

† Horace Walpole to Countess of Ossory, July 1, 1789.

---

* Lysons, Environs, vol. ii., p. 232.

† Evelyn, Diary.

In 1789 was published 'A List of a Few of the Cures performed by Mr. and Mrs. Loutherbourg, of Hammersmith Terrace, without Medicine. By a Lover of the Lamb of God.' In this it is stated that "Mr. De Loutherbourg has received a most glorious power from the Lord Jehovah, *viz.* the gift of healing all manner of diseases incident to the human body, such as blindness, deafness, lameness, cancer," and so forth. He also cast out evil spirits; while such trifles as "fever and gout he cured instantly." The writer says, "Mr. De Loutherbourg told me he had cured, by the blessing of God, 2000 persons since Christmas." He gives the particulars of a great many of the cures in order "to convince the unbelieving that miracles have not ceased." For a failure of one of his predictions a mob assembled and broke his windows, and Loutherbourg ceased to practise and to prophesy. He died here March 11th, 1812, and was buried in Chiswick ch.-yard. Sir Christopher Wintringham, Bart., physician to George III., lived for some time at No. 15.

Other eminent inhabitants of Hammersmith include—Sir Leoline Jenkins, Secretary of State to Charles I., who died here 1685. William Sheridan, Bishop of Kilmore, but deprived for refusing to take the oath of allegiance to William III., d. at Hammersmith 1711. Sir Philip Meadows, ambassador from Cromwell to the King of Denmark; knighted by Charles II.; and Commissioner of Trade and Plantations, and Knight Marshal, under William and Mary, and Anne; died at Hammersmith 1718, aged 94. The Rev. Mikepher Alphery, a member of the imperial family of Russia, who left that country on account of political risks, became a clergyman of the English Church, was ejected from his living (Wooley, in Huntingdonshire) by the Puritans, and lived on his 'fifths' at Hammersmith, till the return of Charles II. restored him to his benefice, which, however, as years drew on, he resigned, to return to Hammersmith, that he might spend his last days there with his eldest son. At Fair Lawn House, Charles Burney, the great Greek scholar, kept school from 1786, till he obtained the living of Deptford in 1793. Samuel Taylor Coleridge was living at No. 7,

Portland Place, in 1811. In Portland Place also lived William Belsham, the essayest and historian; here he wrote the larger part of his voluminous 'History of Great Britain to the Peace of Amiens,' and here died, Nov. 27th, 1827.

The Hamlet of *Brook Green*, already noticed for the Roman Catholic colony established there, lies between the Broadway and Shepherd's Bush. Like the northern side of Hammersmith generally, it has suffered from the encroachment of the builder, but there is still a long slip of open green—in all 6½ acres—with elms and chesnuts bordering it, though green and trees are alike in somewhat shabby condition.

Shepherd's Bush, which lies N. of Brook Green, by the Uxbridge Road, also a hamlet of Hammersmith, has a separate notice.

HAMPSTEAD, Middx., famous

for its Heath, pure air, and fine scenery, lies N. by W. of London on the outer edge of the metropolitan boundary; the 4 m. circle cuts the S. slope of the hill on which the vill. is built, and the 4½ m.-stone is at the commencement of the Heath, N. of the town. The N. London and Hampstead Junction Rly. has stats. at the Lower Heath, and in the Finchley Road; the Midland Rly. at Finchley Road, West End, and Child's Hill. The Heath being a great pleasure resort, Hampstead abounds in inns: those about the Heath are the *Castle* (best known as *Jack Straw's Castle*) on the summit, an excellent house; the *Vale of Health Hotel*, in the hollow to the E.; the *Spaniards*, by the lane leading to Highgate; and the *Bull and Bush*, North End. Till about 1598, Hampstead was a chapelry of Hendon par. It is now, not merely a separate par. of 32,281 inhab., but the mother ch. of 8 eccl. districts, which have been wholly or in part formed out of it. The district of the mother church, Hampstead proper, had 5935 inhabitants in 1871.

Hampstead stands on one of the highest hills round London. The town occupies its southern slopes, the Heath its summit, which is 443 ft. above the sea-level. The upper part of the hill is of sand, mostly coarse, yellow, ferruginous, and unfossiliferous, but occasionally fine and light coloured, and in places inter-stratified with thin seams of light-coloured sandy clay or loam : a capping, in fact, of the Bagshot Sand series, about 80 ft. thick, which overlies a stratum of dark sandy clay, 50 ft. thick, and in the lower part rich in fossils, that may be seen between the Lower Heath and Parliament Hill, where it is worked for brick-making. Beneath this, and crop-ping out on all sides towards the base of the hill, is the London Clay, here 400 ft. thick. The London Clay being impervious to water, the sand resting upon it forms a water-bearing stratum, and hence from the sides of the hill, at nearly the same level, issue the copious springs for which Hampstead has long been noted. In the long course of ages the effluent water has cut for its passage the series of diverging chines or narrow valleys which add so much to the charm and variety of the scenery.*

Some of these springs are chalybeate, the most celebrated of this class being that known as The Wells, to be noticed presently. The Conduit in the Shepherd's or Conduit Fields, W. of Belsize, formerly supplied a large part of Hampstead with water of singular purity for domestic pur-poses, and continued to be much used till the supply was spoiled by the falling in of the Midland Rly. tunnel. The springs on the E. are the sources of the Hampstead Ponds and of the Fleet River ; that on the W., near the ch., is the source of the Bayswater Stream ; one farther N. below the flagstaff, forms the Leg of Mutton Pond ; and others still farther round to the N. are among the head-waters of the Brent. As early as 1543-4 it was proposed to collect the Hampstead waters for the service of the City of London, the water from the Conduit being reserved for the inhabitants of Hampstead. In 1590 a scheme was put forward for drawing "divers springs about Hampstead Heath into one head and course," for the supply and scouring of the Fleet river. In 1672 the ponds and works were leased to the Hampstead Water Company, who collected the water from the springs and wells—adding later

two artesian wells sunk on the Mansfield estate—into the Hampstead and High-gate Ponds as reservoirs, and thence sup-plied Kentish Town, Camden Town, and part of Tottenham Court Road, as well as Hampstead. The works were some years ago transferred to the New River Company, and the Hampstead Company was dissolved.

Both Camden and Norden make Wat-ling Street to have crossed Hampstead Heath, but the ancient way could not have come nearer to the present Heath than Kilburn. Hampstead had, however, its early inhabitants. Stone and bronze implements have been found on the N. side of the Heath ; and Roman urns, containing burnt bones, vases, lamps, etc., by the Wells.

The manor of Hampstead (*Heamstede, Hamstede*, in charters *temp*. Ethelred, 986, of doubtful authenticity, Edward the Confessor, 1066 ;† from *heam*, a home, and *stede*, a place,) was given by Ethelred to the Abbey of Westminster, and re-mained its property till surrendered, with the rest of the abbey estates, to Henry VIII., Jan. 16, 1539. It formed part of the endowment of the new bishopric of Westminster, Dec. 1540 ; but when Dr. Thirlby, the first and only Bp. of West-minster, was promoted to Norwich, and Westminster was reduced to a deanery, Hampstead was resumed by the Crown. Edward VI. granted it, 1551, to Sir Thomas Wroth, in whose family it con-tinued till 1620, when it was sold by John Wroth to Sir Baptist Hickes, afterwards Lord Campden. By the marriage of his daughter to Sir Edward Noel, afterwards Lord Noel and Visct. Campden, it passed to the Gainsborough family ; and was sold in 1707 by Baptist, 3rd Earl of Gainsborough, to Sir Wm. Langhorne, Bart., a wealthy East India merchant, who bequeathed it, with his other manor of Charlton, Kent, to his nephew, Wm. Langhorne Games, on whose decease it passed by entail to a distant relative, Mrs. Margaret Wilson. Eventually, through female heirs, it passed to Sir Thomas Spencer Wilson, Bart., in whose family, who have assumed the name of Maryon-Wilson, it continues, the present

---

* See an excellent paper by Caleb Evans, F.G.S., On the Geology of Hampstead, Proc. of Geol. Assoc., vol. iii., 1873.

† Kemble, Cod. Dip. Ævi Saxonici, vol. iv., p. 177.

owner being Sir John Maryon-Wilson, Bart.

The manor of Shuttop, or Shot-up Hill, belonged to the Knights Templars till the suppression of the order, when it was transferred to the Priory of St. John of Jerusalem, and at the Dissolution was surrendered to the Crown. Henry VIII. granted it in 1547 to Sir Roger Cholmeley, and it has since passed through various hands. The other manor, Belsize, originally Belses, was given by Sir Roger le Brabazon, in 1317, to the Abbey of Westminster, and is still the property of the Dean and Chapter. The manor-house became by lease the residence of Sir Armigal Waad, Clerk of the Council to Henry VIII. and Edward VI., who attained some notoriety by a voyage to Newfoundland in 1536. Sir Armigal died in 1568, at Belsize House, which then became the residence of his son, Sir Wm. Waad, Clerk of the Council to Queen Elizabeth, who sent him on embassies to Germany, Portugal, and Spain. Under James I. he was Privy Councillor and Lieutenant of the Tower. In 1660 Belsize was leased to Daniel O'Neale, Gentleman of the Bedchamber to Charles II., who nearly rebuilt the house. He had married Catherine, daughter and coheir of Thomas Lord Wotton, to whose son by a former marriage, Charles Henry, created Baron Wotton, the lease of Belsize House passed. On Lord Wotton's decease, 1683, the lease was renewed to his half-brother, Philip, 2nd Earl of Chesterfield, in whose family it continued for nearly a century, but the house was thenceforth occupied by under-tenants. Early in the 18th cent. Belsize became, as we shall see presently, notorious as a place of public entertainment, but being restored to its old use, was for several years (1798—1807) the residence of the Rt. Hon. Spencer Perceval. The house, originally a large but plain Elizabethan mansion, with central tower and slightly projecting wings, remodelled in the reign of Charles II., and subsequently much altered, was pulled down in 1852. The site of the house and grounds, about a mile in circuit, is now covered by a little town of villas, Belsize Park, etc., to which the old avenue serves as the entrance from Haverstock Hill. Pepys and Evelyn visited the house whilst Lord Wotton occupied it,

and their notes will give some notion of its character :—

"17th Aug., 1668.—To Hampstead to speak with the Attorney General [Sir Geoffry Palmer, Bart., who died at his house at Hampstead May 1670], whom we met in the fields. by his old route and house ; and after a little talk about our business of Ackeworth, went and saw the Lord Wotton's house and garden, which is wonderfully fine : too good for the house, the gardens are, being indeed the most noble that ever I saw, and brave orange and lemon trees."

Evelyn's account of it is hardly so favourable :—

"2 June, 1677.—We return'd in the evening by Hamsted, to see Lord Wotton's house and garden, Belsize, built with vast expense by Mr. O'Neale, an Irish gentleman who married Lord Wotton's mother, Lady Stanhope. The furniture is very particular for Indian cabinets, porcelain, and other solid and noble moveables. The gallery very fine, the gardens very large, but ill kept, yet woody and chargeable. The soil a cold weeping clay, not answering the expense."

Hampstead springs became noted for their medicinal qualities towards the close of the 17th cent. At the beginning of the 18th, they leapt into sudden popularity. A resident physician, Dr. Gibbons, the Mirmillo of Garth's ' Dispensary,' pronounced them " not inferior to any of our chalybeate springs, and coming very near to Pyrmont in the quality of the waters; " and published a list of cures in proof of their efficacy. It was a time when chalybeates were the universal specific. Crowds flocked to Hampstead ; and for those who were unable to come to the waters, the owners of the rival springs sent the water every morning to London. One advertised that the true waters are to be had in London at the Sugar Loaf, Charing Cross ; Nando's Coffee-house, Temple Bar ; Sam's Coffee-house, near Ludgate ; the Salmon, in Stock's Market ; and various other inns and coffee-houses ; whilst another, still more accommodating, offered to forward it every morning to the water-drinkers' own houses.

"The Chalybeate Waters at Hampstead, being of the same nature and equal in virtue with Tunbridge Wells, Sold by Mr. Richard Philps, Apothecary, at the Eagle and Child in Fleet Street, every morning at 3 pence per flask ; and conveyed to persons at their own houses for one penny per flask more. The flask to be returned daily."*

Like Tunbridge and Epsom, and the other so-called ' watering-places ' of that

* Advt. in the Postman, April 20, 1706 ; quoted in Park's Hampstead, p. 52.

time, Hampstead became "the resort of the wealthy, the idle, and the sickly." "Houses of entertainment and dissipation started up on all sides." Taverns had their long-rooms, assembly-rooms, card and concert-rooms, and even chapels; out of doors were gardens, bowling-greens, races on the Heath, a fair by the Lower Flask. The comedy of 'Hampstead Heath,' played with some success at Drury Lane in 1706, and which John Kemble lent Mr. Park for his Hampstead history, opens after this fashion :—

"*Smart.* HAMPSTEAD for awhile assumes the day : the lovely season of the year, the shining crowd assembled at this time, and the noble situation of the place, gives us the nearest show of Paradise.

"*Bloom.* London now indeed has but a melancholy aspect, and a sweet rural spot seems an adjournment o' the nation, where business is laid fast asleep, variety of diversions feast our fickle fancies, and every man wears a face of pleasure. The cards fly, the bowl runs, the dice rattle, . . .

"*Smart.* Assemblies so near the town give us a sample of each degree. We have court ladies that are all air and no dress ; city ladies that are over-dressed and no air ; and country dames with brown faces like a Stepney bun ; besides an endless number of Fleet Street sempstresses, that . . .

"*Arabella.* Well, this Hampstead's a charming place—to dance all night at the Wells, and be treated at Mother Huff's—to have presents made one at the Raffling-shops, and then take a walk in Cane Wood with a man of wit that's not over rude." *

"Consorts of vocal and instrumental Musick by the Best Masters," continued to be advertised in the London papers for many years as being given at "the Great Room at the Wells," usually at "11 in the forenoon,"—tickets, "by reason the room is very large, at one shilling each ; and there will be dancing in the afternoon as usual." Some of the advertisements add that, besides stables and coach-houses, there is the "further accommodation of a stage coach, and a chariot from the Wells at any time in the evening or morning." But the most remarkable 'accommodation' at the Wells was that announced in the following advertisement :—

"Sion Chapel, at Hampstead, being a private and pleasure place, many persons of the best fashion have lately been married there. Now as a

minister is obliged constantly to attend, this is to give Notice, that all persons upon bringing a Licence, and who shall have their Wedding Dinner in the Gardens, may be married in that said Chapel *without giving any fee or reward whatsoever:* and such as do not keep their Wedding Dinner at the Gardens, only Five Shillings will be demanded of them for all fees." *

The earliest of these Sion Chapel advertisements known is of April 1710, so that the practice of these irregular, or, as they were commonly called, Fleet Marriages, must have gone on for several years. The Wells was the chief establishment ; but arrangements for supplying the matrimonial demand appear to have been made by the landlords of other houses. Marriages in these unlicensed places were put an end to by Lord Hardwicke's Act, 1754 ; but they had ceased long before that date at Hampstead.

The Wells, the oldest, and long the chief of the Hampstead houses of entertainment, stood on the hill-side E. of the village, at the corner of the Well Walk, which leads from Flask Walk to the East Heath. The property somehow got into the Court of Chancery, and a decree of the Court informs us that in 1719 the Wells comprised a "tavern. coffee-room, dancing-room, raffling-shops. bowling-green," etc. The site is marked by the present Wells Tavern, a very modern structure, which, like its predecessor, has its grounds or tea-gardens. but of greatly curtailed dimensions. The 'dancing-room,' or 'long-room' as it was usually called, was converted into a chapel about 1732, when the popularity of the Wells had greatly abated, and the local gentry had transferred their patronage to the long-room of the Flask. It continued to be used as a proprietary chapel for over a century ; but was never. we believe, consecrated. It is now the head-quarters of the Hampstead (3rd Middlesex) Volunteers.

The spring still flows, though the supply has been diminished through the formation of deep drains and railway tunnels. The water runs slowly from a neat stone fountain recently erected a short distance beyond the Wells Tavern, on the opposite side of Well Walk. The fountain bears on its face the words "The Chalybeate

---

* Park's Hampstead, pp. 242—245. There is a notice of the Hampstead Raffling-shop in the Tatler, No. 59, where it is said to have been set up by a Practitioner in the Law as an "easier way of conveyancing and alienating estates from one family to another."

* Read's Weekly Journal, Sept. 8, 1716 ; quoted by Park, p. 256.

Spring," and any one may satisfy himself of its medicinal properties. Whilst here observe the grove of elms on the l. side of Well Walk. The seat at the end of the grove was the favourite resting-place of John Keats, when here in almost the last stage of consumption :—

"Winding southwardly from the heath, there is a charming little grove in Well Walk, with a bench at the end ; whereon I last saw poor Keats, the poet of the 'Pot of Basil,' sitting and sobbing his dying breath into a handkerchief— glancing parting looks towards the quiet landscape he had delighted in—musing as in his Ode to a Nightingale." *

The extreme popularity of the Hampstead springs does not appear to have been of long continuance. An attempt was made to revive the interest in them by the publication, in 1734, of a treatise by a resident physician, John Soame, M.D., entitled, 'Hampstead Wells : or Directions for the drinking of those Waters ; shewing, 1. Their Nature and Virtues. 2. The Diseases in which they are most beneficial. 3. The Time, Manner, and Order of drinking. 4. The Preparation of the Body required. 5. The Diet proper to be used by all Mineral Water Drinkers. With an Appendix relating to the Original of Springs in general ; with some Experiments of the Hampstead Waters, and Histories of Cures.' Fresh analyses of the waters were published later ; but fashion had turned elsewhere, and the Hampstead Wells were forsaken. The gentry of Hampstead, however, continued till the end of the century to meet in the Long Room for tea, evening, and card parties, concerts, and dances. The 'Assembly' was held from Whitsuntide till October, a guinea subscription admitting a gentleman and 2 ladies to the ball-room every other Monday. When Akenside the poet attempted, about 1746, to establish himself as a physician at Hampstead, his friend Jeremiah Dyson used to take him to the Long Room assemblies, etc., to introduce him to the leading families,— with, however, very little success. Hampstead folk thought him disputatious and proud :—

"Hampstead could not be suited to a man like Akenside. The inhabitants were respectable and rich ; but many of them were not only respectable and rich, but purse-proud, and, therefore, supercilious. They required to be sought ; their wives and daughters expected to be escorted and flattered ; and their sons to be treated with an air of obligation. . . . After residing two years and a half at Hampstead, therefore, Akenside returned to London, and took up his abode in Bloomsbury-square, where he continued to live during the remainder of his life." *

The *Upper Flask*, on the higher ground at the edge of the Heath, like the Wells, had its Long Room, card-rooms, and bowling-green,—the last seemingly under distinct management.

"The Upper Flask Bowling Green at Hampstead Heath is to be let with the Tap or Without. Inquire there or at the Sun Tavern in Holborn, London." †

It became early noted as the summer resort of the Kit-Cat Club.

"Or when, Apollo-like, thou'rt pleas'd to lead
Thy sons to feast on Hampstead's airy head,
Hampstead, that towering in superior sky
Now with Parnassus does in honour vie." ‡

Richardson makes Clarissa Harlowe escape for awhile from the pursuit of Lovelace to the Upper Flask :—

"The Hampstead Coach, when the dear fugitive came to it, had but two passengers in it. . . The two passengers directing the coachman to set them down at the Upper Flask she bid them set her down there also. They took leave of her very respectfully no doubt, and she went into the house, and asked if she could not have a dish of tea and a room to herself for half an hour. They showed her up into the very room where I now am,"§ etc.
Mrs. Barbauld, long a resident at Hampstead, says she "well remembers a Frenchman who paid a visit to Hampstead for the sole purpose of finding out the house where Clarissa lodged, and was surprised at the ignorance or indifference of the inhabitants on that subject. The Flask-Walk was to him as much classic ground as the rocks of Mallerie to the admirers of Rousseau." ‖

Richardson's example was followed by other novelists. Henry Brooke laid the scene of his popular 'Fool of Quality' (1766) at Hampstead ; and Fanny Burney takes Evelina (1778) to the Hampstead tea-gardens.

---

* Bucke, Life of Akenside, p. 70.
† Advt. in the Tatler, No. 131, Feb. 7, 1710.
‡ Sir Richard Blackmore. The Kit-Cats, a Poem, 1708. When Steele was living at Haverstock Hill, it is said that "Here Pope and other members of the Kit-Cat Club . . . used to call on him, and take him in their carriages to the place of rendezvous." The anecdote is perhaps doubtful ; if true, it would prove that the Kit-Cat summer meetings were held at the Upper Flask as late as 1712.
§ The first four vols. of Clarissa Harlowe were published in 1748.
‖ Life of Richardson.

---

* Hone, Table Book, 1827, col. 810.

Two years after Richardson wrote, the Upper Flask became the property of Lady Charlotte Rich, and was probably soon after converted into a private residence. In 1771 it was purchased by George Steevens, the editor of Shakspeare, who spent £2000 in improving the house and grounds, and converted it into a very comfortable abode. Here he lived a solitary life for nearly 30 years, and here died, Jan. 22, 1800.

"Whilst his last edition of Shakspeare was going through the press, he quitted his house at Hampstead, every morning at one o'clock, and walked to the chambers of his friend, the late Isaac Reed, Esq., of Staples Inn, of which he had a key for the purpose of admitting himself ; here he devoted some hours of each night [? morning] to the purpose of correcting the proofs, and by these extraordinary efforts of activity and perseverance he accomplished the laborious task of getting the whole work, consisting of 15 vols. in 4to, through the press within 20 months."[*]

Another account[†] makes him start, regardless of the weather, "with the patrole every morning between 4 and 5 o'clock " —a much more reasonable hour. It is said that he always took with him a nosegay, tied to the top of his cane, for his friend Sir Joseph Banks. The house, which has had a new plain brick front since Steevens inhabited it, is the last on the rt. of Heath Mount (the main street to the Heath), at the corner of the East Heath Road, directly opposite the reservoir of the New River Company and the flower-bed of the Met. Board of Works. The Long Room was formed into a separate dwelling. The grounds, of about 2 acres, are bordered by noble old elms.

Belsize House, nearer town, was opened as a place of entertainment in 1720.

" Whereas that the ancient and noble house near Hampstead, commonly called *Bellasis House,* is now taken and fitted up for the entertainment of gentlemen and ladies during the whole Summer season the same will be opened on Easter Monday next, with an uncommon solemnity of music and dancing. This undertaking will exceed all of the kind that has hitherto been known near London, commencing every day at 6 in the morning, and continuing till 8 at night, all persons being privileged to admittance without necessity of expence."[‡]

In 1729 " Galloway Races " were advertised to be run at Belsize House for a £10 plate : gentlemen were to pay 1*s.* entrance, ladies nothing.—" P.S. There is a very good ordinary at 2 o'clock, two cooks which dress everything to perfection, and a good set of musick every day during the season."

A handbill of somewhat later date gives a representation of the house, the only one known ; and in announcing the opening of "the park, wilderness, and gardens," adds the assurance that there had been engaged "twelve stout fellows, compleatly armed, to patrole between Belsize and London." The proprietor, one Howell, nicknamed ' the Welch Ambassador,' gave prizes to be run for, had carp fishing in the pond, stag hunts in the grounds, and gambling tables in the house. Tea, chocolate, and ratafia, with an ample variety of wines, were the viands ; fish of many kinds and venison pasties were among the dishes. There was provision fit for princes ; but those who could not afford silver might spend their pence there. Belsize became popular with all classes, and the 12 stout fellows required for the protection of the visitors had to be increased to 30.

" Last Saturday their Royal Highnesses the Prince and Princess of Wales dined at Belsize House, near Hampstead, attended by several persons of quality, where they were entertained with the diversion of hunting, and such other as the place afforded, with which they seemed well pleased, and at their departure were very liberal to the servants." [*]

" On Monday the appearance of nobility and gentry at Bellsize was so great that they reckoned between three and four hundred coaches, at which time a wild deer was hunted down and killed in the park before the company, which gave near three hours' diversion."[†]

The place appears to have soon acquired notoriety as a scene of riot and dissipation. The Middlesex magistrates, at the quarter sessions of June 1722, issued a precept for the prevention of "unlawful gaming, riots, etc., at Belsize House ; " and in the same year it was spoken of in very strong terms in ' Belsize House, a Satire exposing, etc., etc. By a Serious Person of Quality.'

" This house, which is a nuisance to the land,
Doth near a park and handsome garden stand,

---

* Lysons, Environs, vol. ii., p. 352.
† Park, Topography of Hampstead, p. 353. The statement is in the main transcribed from Mathias's Pursuits of Literature, note to l. 116 of Part ii.
‡ Mist's Journal, April 16, 1720 (quoted by Lysons).

* Read's Journal, July 15, 1721 (Lysons).
† St. James's Journal, June 7, 1722 : quoted by Park.

Fronting the road, betwixt a range of trees,
Which is perfumed with a Hampstead breeze;
And on each side the gate's a grenad.er,
Howe'er they cannot speak, think, see, nor
  hear." *

Belsize House continued to be a place of entertainment for more than 30 years longer. Foot races were advertised to be run in the grounds as late as the summer of 1745. We have already told its later history.

The *Spaniards*, at the N.E. edge of the Heath, and just outside Hampstead par., occupies the site of a lodge built for the keeper of Park-gate—the toll-gate at the Hampstead entrance to the Bp. of London's lands.† When Hampstead became a popular resort, the lodge was taken " by a Spaniard, and converted into a house of entertainment." Later, a Mr. Staples added gardens, in which, " out of a wild and thorny wood, full of hills vallies and sand pits, he hath now made pleasant grass and gravel walks, with a mount, from the elevation whereof the beholder hath a prospect " reaching to Hanslope steeple, near Stony Stratford, Langdon Hills in Essex, Banstead Downs in Surrey, Windsor Castle, Berks, and various other distant objects and places.‡ " A South View of the Spaniards," by Roberts, after Chatalain (1750), shows the arbours in the garden, but barely indicates the " many curious figures depicted with pebble-stones of various colours "—among them being a rainbow and star, the sun in its glory, Adam and Eve, Salisbury spire, an eclipse —which are catalogued at length by the authority just cited. The Spaniards still has its garden and bowling-green, but the curious figures are gone, and so has the mound, and with it the larger part of the prospect—partly, perhaps, owing to the growth of the neighbouring trees, and the erection of two or three large houses between it and the Heath.

---

* Mr. Howitt, Northern Heights, p. 22, supposes they were living soldiers, posted there on account of the insecurity of the roads : " Two sentinels, moreover, were regularly posted at the door of the house." But grenadiers of this kind—flat boards cut into shape and painted—used till quite recently to be the common guardians of the entrances of suburban tea-gardens. A pair might be seen so posted at the neighbouring Load of Hay, Haverstock Hill, till the house was rebuilt some six or eight years ago.

† Park, pp. 15, 252.

‡ MS. Description of Middlesex, quoted by Park, p. 252.

Another noted place of entertainment, *New Georgia*, was in Turner's Wood, now enclosed within Lord Mansfield's grounds. The rooms were low and irregular, but contained many " humorous contrivances to divert the beholder," and " the grounds and wilderness were laid out in a delightful romantic taste." One of the most admired of the " humorous contrivances " was a chair which sank into the ground on a person sitting in it.

Of the present houses, *Jack Straw's Castle*, on the summit of the Heath, is most in repute. It is noted for its dinners, wines, and lodgings ; has long been a favourite trysting-place for artists and men of science and letters; and will be remembered as the usual goal of Charles Dickens in his rides to Hampstead, by the repeated allusions to it in his letters and Forster's Life. It was on the slope behind the Castle that the corpse of the unhappy John Sadleir, M.P. for Sligo, was found on the morning of Sunday, Feb. 17, 1856, and beside it a phial of essential oil of almonds, and the silver cream-jug into which he had poured the fatal draught. Hampstead is an awkward place for a suicide to select. The lord of the manor possesses very extensive rights, among them being that of deodand, and is therefore, in the case of a person who commits suicide within the manor, entitled as heir to " the whole of the goods and chattels of the deceased, of every kind, with the exception of his estate of inheritance, in the event of a jury returning a verdict of *felo de se*." Sadleir's goods and chattels were already lost or forfeit; but the cream-jug was claimed and received by the lord as an acknowledgment of his right, and then returned.

One of the few remaining examples of the old Hampstead tavern-garden is that of the *Bull and Bush* at North End. Its central feature is a room within a belt of yew trees, and a platform over it, to which the verdure forms a canopy ; and there are tall holly hedges, clipped and trained in arches, etc., bright flowers, and a bowling-green. The assembly and card-rooms of the *Holly Bush Tavern*, Holly Bush Hill, W. of the High Street, have another kind of interest. They were the studio and picture-gallery of the " strange new dwelling " which Reynolds's rival, George Romney, built for himself, when, tired of the dirt and narrowness of Cavendish Square, he resolved to withdraw to the pure air and retirement of Hampstead to paint the vast "historical conceptions for which all this travail had been undergone, and imagined that a new hour of glory was come,"* but which proved instead a brief hour of mental gloom and physical depression, to be followed by a speedy flight and early death.

The *Town* straggles up the slopes of the hill, towards the Heath on the top, in an odd, sideling, tortuous, irregular, and unconnected fashion. There are the fairly broad winding High Street, and other good streets and lanes, lined with large old brick houses within high-walled enclosures, over which lean ancient trees, and alongside them houses small and large, without a scrap of garden, and only a very little dingy yard; narrow and dirty byways, courts, and passages, with steep flights of steps, and mean and crowded tenements ; fragments of open green spaces, and again streets and lanes bordered with shady elms and limes. On the whole, however, the pleasanter and sylvan character prevails, especially W. of the main street. The trees along the streets and lanes are the most characteristic and redeeming feature of the village. Hampstead was long ago termed "the place of groves," and it retains its early distinction. It is the most sylvan of suburban villages. The groves and avenues are still flourishing ; especially delightful are those about Frognal, Montague Grove, the Grove, and most of all that now best known as Judges' Walk, with its grand prospect over Hendon and Herts, Harrow (hill and spire), and from the extreme end Windsor Castle and Cooper's Hill. Judges' Walk, or Judges' Avenue, according to a tradition (seemingly a very modern one), was so named from the judges having held their sessions there during the great plague of London. But Judges' Walk is probably only one of those fanciful names in which "watering-places" delight (as all will remember who have been at Tunbridge Wells or Matlock), and of which Hampstead affords other examples in Mount

Vernon, Vale of Health, Pilgrims' Lane, Squire's Mount, and the like. The name by which it occurs in old books and maps is *Prospect Walk* or *Terrace*. Thus Mrs. Barbauld writes to her brother, shortly after settling at Hampstead, 1787 : "Hampstead is certainly the pleasantest village about London. The mall of the place, a kind of terrace, which they call Prospect Walk, commands a most extensive view over Middlesex and Berkshire,"* etc.

The *Church*, St. John, is little more than a century old. The former ch., rambling, mean, and ruinous, was pulled down in 1745, and the present building erected in its stead, from the designs of Mr. H. Flitcroft, but has been somewhat altered since. It was consecrated by Bp. Gilbert (of Llandaff) Oct. 8, 1747. The ch. is a plain brick building of ordinary 18th-cent. style, but has the peculiarity of having the tower at the E. end, no chancel, and short transept-like projections at the W., so that it looks like a ch. turned round. The tower has a quaint, picturesque character ; though it is less elaborate than that originally designed, and the spire (of copper) is much lower. However it may be architecturally, the tower is a pleasing feature in the landscape, and from the elevated site it is conspicuous over a wide area. The interior of the ch. is of no interest, and the monts. on the walls are not to persons of much account. It has lately (1874) been proposed to remove the tower, and erect a chancel at the E. end. But this, as a matter of taste, would be a great mistake. Hampstead is essentially of 18th-cent. creation. Its houses are 18th-cent. brick houses ; its historical or social associations are all of the 18th cent. Church Row, at the end of which the ch. stands, is a rare old street of red-brick dwellings, contemporary with the ch., which crowns the group; and it would be a rude shock at once to the picturesque and historical character of the place to supplant the familiar old ivy-clad tower by a newfangled modern Gothic apse.

The ch.-yard contains the tombs of several eminent persons. Under the yewtree, S.E. of the ch., is that of Sir James Mackintosh (d. May 30, 1832), his wife,

* Allan Cunningham, Lives of British Painters, vol. v., p. 126.

* Le Breton, Memoirs of Mrs. Barbauld, p. 62.

children, and grandchildren: a plain altar-tomb without rails.

" Poor Mackintosh . . . He lies in the church-yard which I see from my windows." *

Beyond this is a taller tomb, within railings, where lie Joanna Baillie, the author of 'Plays of the Passions,' (d. Feb. 26, 1851), her elder sister, Agnes (d. April 1861, aged 100 years and 7 months), and their mother, Mrs. Dorothea Baillie, widow of the Rev. James Baillie, Prof. of Divinity at Glasgow. The Miss Baillies lived for half a century at Hampstead, chiefly at Bolton House, Windmill Hill, where they were visited by many of the most eminent of their contemporaries. At the E. end of Joanna Baillie's tomb, fronting the path, is an upright granite slab to the memory of Lucy Aikin, who lived in all more than 30 years at Hampstead, and d. there Jan. 29, 1864. Follow this path a little farther, and you will reach the mont. (a tall altar-tomb within railings, close to the wall at the S.E. corner of the ch.-yard) of that original and thoroughly English land-scape painter, John Constable, R.A., "for many years a resident in this parish," d. March 31, 1837. His wife and some of his children lie in the same grave. Near the entrance to the ch.-yard is the humble gravestone of Henry Cort (d. 1800), whose grand improvements in the manufacture of iron enriched many with unimagined wealth, but left him destitute. Other more or less distinguished persons interred here, often without monumental record, include—George Sewell, M.D., author of 'Sir Walter Raleigh, a Tra-gedy,' a translation of Ovid's Metamor-phoses, and miscellaneous poems and essays, who practised for some years with success as a physician at Hamp-stead, but died here in poverty in 1726. James MacArdell, the eminent mezzo-tint engraver, d. 1765 (his tombstone is lost), and his fellow-pupil, Charles Spooner, d. 1767, who was buried beside MacArdell by his own request. Nathaniel Booth, last Lord Delamere (d. 1770), and several members of his family. Anthony Askew, M.D., a distinguished physician and classical scholar (d. 1774). Another well-known mezzotint engraver, and author of the 'History of Worcester, Valentine Green, lived for many years

at Hampstead, and his wife has a mont. in the ch.-yard, but he lies elsewhere. John Harrison (d. 1776), the eminent chronometer maker, inventor of the grid-iron pendulum, and "of the time-keeper for ascertaining the longitude at sea," which received the government reward. James Pettit Andrew, F.S.A. (d. 1797), author of an "anecdotal and chrono-logical" 'History of Great Britain' from Cæsar's invasion to the Death of Henry VIII., 2 vols. 4to, 1794. The Rev. George Travis, D.D., Archdeacon and Prebendary of Chester (d. 1797), author, among other controversial works, of "some angry letters" against Gibbon's criticism on the text of the 'Three Heavenly Wit-nesses,' of which Gibbon wrote: "The brutal insolence of Mr. Travis's challenge can only be excused by the absence of learning, judgment, and humanity; and to that excuse he has the fairest or foulest pretension" *—so mildly wrote controversialists one of another in those days! Travis was answered by Porson, in his "merciless" 'Letters to Archdeacon Travis,' which Gibbon considered "the most acute and accurate piece of criti-cism since the days of Bentley." John Carter, F.S.A. (d. 1817), whose faithful and spirited etchings of our cathedrals and other ecclesiastical buildings did much to revive and purify the taste for Gothic architecture.

It will be enough to give the names and sites of the district churches—several of which belong rather to London than the environs. Christ Church, Hampstead Square, a roomy Perp. edifice with a lofty spire, a landmark for miles around, was erected in 1852. St. Saviour's, Eton Road, near the foot of Haverstock Hill, a rather pleasing Dec. building, with a very deep chancel, dates from 1856, but the tower and spire are of more recent erection. St. Paul's, Avenue Road, a somewhat peculiar brick building, 1860. St. Peter's, Belsize Park, a neat Dec. cruciform ch. erected in 1860. St. Ste-phen's, Hampstead Green, 1870, is more pretentious and more picturesque, of early semi-French character, very ir-regular outline, and unusually rich in external ornament: archt., Mr. S. S. Teulon. St. John's, Episcopal chapel,

---

* Lucy Aikin to Dr. Channing, July 15, 1832.

* Memoirs of My Life and Writings. p. 101.

Downshire Hill, is a plain brick 18th-cent. barn.

The Dissenters' chapels are of some interest. The old Presbyterian church is believed to have been founded in the reign of Charles II. Like many of the early Presbyterian churches, it became Unitarian; and had for some years (1785—99) the Rev. Rochemont Barbauld for minister. The present Unitarian chapel is an elegant little Gothic building in Pilgrims' Lane. An orthodox Presbyterian church, Trinity Church, has been built on the E. side of the High Street. The Independent chapel is said to owe its origin to the anti-Unitarian preaching of Whitefield on Hampstead Heath. The showy Gothic building on Green Hill is a Wesleyan chapel; and that with the two towers on the rt. of Heath Street, Baptist. The Roman Catholic church of St. Mary, Holly Place, will be recognized by the statue, in a niche over the entrance, of the Virgin with the Infant Jesus in her arms.

In the town are—a Literary Society, a Public Library and Reading Room, and an Art Club which has its meetings and periodical exhibitions at the Holly Bush Assembly Room. The new Fire Brigade Station, at the parting of the roads by Heath Street, is a noticeable building of coloured bricks, with a lofty watch tower, commanding a wide stretch of country: the archt. was Mr. G. Vulliamy. Another noteworthy building is the spacious Militia Barracks, nearly opposite the Wells Tavern, erected in 1863, from the designs of Mr. H. Pownall. The centre is the old mansion known as Burgh House.

The principal benevolent institutions are —The Soldiers' Daughters' Home, Rosslyn Hill, founded in 1855, in connection with the Central Association for the Relief of the Wives and Children of Soldiers on Service in the Crimea. The buildings, which are spacious, substantial, and carefully adapted to their purpose, were erected in 1858, from the designs of Mr. Munt, but since enlarged. They stand in charming grounds, a part of those of Rosslyn House, in which the children were at first lodged. In August 1874 there were 163 children in the home, but there is ample room for 200, if the income were sufficient for their maintenance. A kindred institution, The Sailors' Daughters' Home, originally established in Frognal House, now occupies a large and handsome building, erected for it in the Greenhill Road, near the parish church, by Mr. Ellis, in 1869: it has about 100 children. Both are admirable institutions, and the children look healthy and cheerful. The Orphan Working School, Haverstock Hill, is another valuable institution, the oldest and one of the best of its kind. Founded in 1758, to receive, maintain, and educate orphan children from all parts of the kingdom, it has gone on extending its arrangements and modifying its plans to meet the requirements of the times, and at the end of 1874 had 400 children under its care, who are well housed and taught, and as far as may be fitted for practical life. The Hampstead Reformatory for Girls, occupies a good-sized private house in Church Row. The very useful North London Hospital for Consumption, established in 1860, a roomy old mansion on Mount Vernon.

Several houses are noteworthy on account of their age or occupants. The memory, and little more, remains of a few houses of Elizabethan or Jacobean date. One of these, a low brick building, oddly called the Chicken House, stood in the High Street, near the entrance of the town, and some fragments are still traceable behind the modern shops. In a window was a small portrait of James I., and another of George Villiers, Duke of Buckingham; and an inscription in French under the former stated that the king slept in this room Aug. 25, 1619. Samuel Gale the antiquary "died of a fever at his lodgings The Chicken House," Jan. 10, 1754. In it, too, before his purchase of Caen Wood, lodged Lord Mansfield. Probably at this time, but certainly later, it had been converted into an inn: some years later it was a notorious resort of thieves; afterwards it was divided into tenements, and suffered to go to ruin.

Lower down the hill, on the l., was a large square building of 3 floors, in which lived Sir Henry Vane ("The Lord preserve me from Sir Henry Vane!") and which he is supposed to have built. He was here when arrested by order of Charles II. The house was afterwards the property, and for many years the residence, of Joseph Butler, Bishop of Durham, author of 'The Analogy,' who filled the windows with painted glass, chiefly of scriptural subjects. The house was pulled down to make way for the Soldiers' Daughters' Home.

Somewhat lower, and a little to the W. of the road, is *Rosslyn House* (C. H. L. Woodd, Esq.), a large rambling building which owes its present form to Alexander Wedderburn, Lord Loughborough and Earl of Rosslyn. When purchased by Lord Loughborough, it was an old mansion, which had been for many years the residence of the Carey family, and was known as Shelford Lodge. Lord Loughborough added the great oval rooms at the end, and otherwise altered the building and greatly improved the grounds. It was afterwards the residence of Robert Milligan, the founder of the West India Docks; and then of Sir Francis Freeling, the Secretary to the Post Office; and later of Admiral Sir Moore Disney, and the Earl of Galloway. Eventually it passed into the hands of the speculative builder; the house was let to the Soldiers' Daughters' Home; a large part of the grounds was sold and built over. Shortly after the house, with the remaining portion of the grounds, was purchased and carefully restored by Mr. Woodd.

Branch Hill Lodge (S. Basil Woodd, Esq.), the large red-brick house on the rt. in going from Holly Bush Hill towards the Heath, was rebuilt about 1745 by Sir Thos. Clark, Master of the Rolls. He bequeathed it to his old patron Lord Chancellor Macclesfield, who lived in it for some time, when it was occupied successively by Thos. Walker, Master in Chancery, Lord Loughborough, Col. Parker, and Thos. Neave, Esq., the last of whom formed here a noted collection of painted glass.

Frognal Hall (J. T. Airey, Esq.) was about the middle of the 18th cent. the residence of Isaac Ware the architect; it was afterwards the seat of the Guyon family; then of Richard Pepper Arden, Lord Alvanley, Master of the Rolls, and afterwards Chief Justice of the Common Pleas, who d. here March 29, 1804. Other good residences are *Frognal House* (J. Rowe, Esq.); *Frognal Lodge* (Mrs. P. A. Taylor); and *Upper Frognal Lodge* (J. G. Weir, Esq.) *Frognal Priory*, as it is called, is a much-visited lath-and-plaster ruin standing in spacious but desolate grounds at the S. end of Frognal. The house was built by a dealer in Wardour Street antiquities, known as Memory-Corner-Thompson, so as to have a sort of Jacobean aspect, real old carved woodwork being wrought into the window frames, and the summit finished with stepped gables. The interior was filled with real and supposititious antiquities, —Queen Elizabeth's bedstead and bedroom furniture, cabinets, china, and the like,—and became a noted show-place. After Thompson's death, 1836, it passed to less reputable hands, and eventually into the law-courts. Now, as we have said, the house is a ruin, and not an unpicturesque one, especially when the morning sun, shining through the screen of trees, dapples the front with mingled light and shade, though it has of late lost something by the fall of the portico.

Erskine House, the plain white house with a long portico adjoining the Spaniards Tavern, was the residence of Thomas Lord Erskine, the famous advocate. When Erskine purchased the house it was a very small place, but had good grounds, and commanded extensive prospects, and he at once set about its improvement. During his residence here of a quarter of a century he spent a large sum of money upon it, and "having surrounded it with evergreens of different descriptions has lately given it the name of Evergreen Hill." * A great deal of his time was spent on his garden, which was on the opposite side of the road, and connected with the house by a subterranean passage: the garden has long been taken into Lord Mansfield's grounds; the house has been little altered. The splendid holly hedge on the l. of the road going to the Heath from the house, is said to be of Lord Erskine's planting. Erskine was fond of assembling here many of the prominent politicians and wits of the day; and here occurred his last meeting with Burke. They had differed over the French Revolution, and it was long since they had met.

"He [Burke] came to see me not long before he died. I then lived on Hampstead Hill. 'Come Erskine,' said he, holding out his hand, 'let us forget all! I shall soon quit this stage and wish to die in peace with everybody, especially you!' I reciprocated the sentiment and we took a turn round the grounds. Suddenly he stopped. An

* Park, Topography of Hampstead, 1818, p. 319.

extensive prospect over Caen Wood broke upon him. He stood wrapped in thought, gazing upon the sky as the sun was setting. 'Ah, Erskine!' he said, pointing towards it, 'this is just the place for a reformer; all the beauties are beyond your reach —you cannot destroy them.'"

Whilst living here, Lord Erskine lost his first wife: a graceful mural monument to her, "the most faithful and the most affectionate of women," the work of the younger Bacon, is in Hampstead church.

The large square white house adjoining Lord Erskine's on the Upper Heath, *Heath House* (H. Stedall, Esq.), was occupied by Edward Coxe, Esq., author of Miscellaneous Poetry, 1805, in which he has celebrated the wanderings of Murray " and Pope on Hampstead Hill," and afterwards by Sir Edward Parry. The house next it, *The Firs* (Mrs. C. C. Luch), "was built by Mr. Turner, a tobacconist in Fleet-street," * who deserves to be remembered for having planted the avenue of Scotch firs in front of the house which now forms so picturesque a feature of the Upper Heath.

From The Firs a short walk (along a road made by Mr. Turner) leads to *North End*, a pleasant hamlet where have lived several of our literary contemporaries. The large house on the l., by the avenue, now called *Wildwood House* (Wm. Haynes, Esq.), but then known as *North End House*, is that in which for a while lived the great Lord Chatham. He was here in 1766, and again during the period when he remained "inaccessible and invisible," and " afflicted "—to use the words of Earl Stanhope,—" by a strange and mysterious malady . . . able at intervals to take the air upon the heath, but still at all times inaccessible to all his friends."† This time he came to North End shattered in health, March 1767; but deriving no benefit, returned to Burton Pynsent in September. Whilst here, though Prime Minister, he "would see no one on business, except once the Duke of Grafton, at the king's urgent entreaty."‡ The house has been raised a storey, and transformed in aspect, within the last few years, but Chatham's room is still retained.

* Park, p. 15, n.
† Hist. of England, 3rd ed., vol. v., p. 178. See also Grenville Papers, iii., 320; iv., 159; Fitz-maurice, Life of Lord Shelburne, vol. i., p. 409.
‡ Walpole's George III., vol. iii., p. 51, n. Chatham's Letter to the Duke of Grafton on this occasion, dated North End, May 30, 1767, is printed by Lord Stanhope, Hist. of Eng., vol. v., p. xix., App.

Mr. Howitt relates some curious particulars relative to the place, and Chatham's residence in it, but does not give his authority for them :—

"The small room, or rather closet, in which Chatham shut himself up during his singular affliction—on the third storey—still remains in the same condition. Its position from the outside may be known by an oriel window looking towards Finchley. The opening in the wall from the staircase to the room still remains, through which the unhappy man received his meals or anything else conveyed to him. It is an opening of perhaps 18 inches square, having a door on each side of the wall. The door within had a padlock, which still hangs upon it. When anything was conveyed to him, a knock was made on the outer door, and the articles placed in the recess. When he heard the outer door again closed, the invalid opened the inner door, took what was there, again closed and locked it. When the dishes or other articles were returned, the same process was observed, so that no one could possibly catch a glimpse of him, nor need there be any exchange of words."*

At the other end of the avenue is another house, *The Hill* (Mrs. Gurney Hoare), which has acquired fame from an occasional resident. Whilst the seat of Mr. Samuel Hoare, the banker, The Hill was "the head-quarters" of the poet Crabbe in his annual visits to London; and here Coleridge. Wordsworth, Rogers, Campbell, Joanna Baillie, who lived close by, and other of his eminent friends and admirers, used frequently to be invited to meet him.

"During his first and second visits to London, my father spent a good deal of his time beneath the hospitable roof of the late Samuel Hoare, Esq., on Hampstead Heath. He owed his introduction to this respectable family to his friend Mr. Bowles, and the author of the delightful 'Excursions in the West,' Mr. Warner; and though Mr. Hoare was an invalid, and little disposed to form new connections, he was so much gratified with Mr. Crabbe's manners and conversation, that their acquaintance grew into an affectionate and lasting intimacy. Mr. Crabbe in subsequent years made Hampstead his head-quarters on his spring visits, and only repaired thence occasionally to the brilliant circles of the metropolis."†

Crabbe himself wrote, "My time passes here I cannot tell how pleasantly. To-day I read one of my long stories to my friends and Mrs. Joanna Baillie and her sister. I rhyme at Hampstead with a great deal of facility, for nothing interrupts me but kind calls, or something pleasant."

* Howitt, Northern Heights, p. 90.
† Life of the Rev. George Crabbe, by his Son.

"Our haughty life is crowned with darkness,
   Like London with its own black wreath,
On which with thee, O Crabbe! forth-looking,
   I gazed from Hampstead's breezy Heath."*

Steele 'retired' for a while to a small house on Haverstock Hill—it may be, as Nichols somewhat unkindly suggests, that "there were too many pecuniary reasons for this temporary solitude."

"I am at a solitude, an house between Hampstead and London, wherein Sir Charles Sedley died. This circumstance set me a thinking and ruminating upon the employments in which men of wit exercise themselves. . . Sir Charles breathed his last in this room."†

In Sir Richard Phillips's time it had been "converted into two small ornamental cottages for citizens sleeping boxes. . . . Opposite to it the famous Mother or Moll King built three substantial houses; and in a small villa behind them resided her favourite pupil Nancy Dawson. . . . An apartment in the cottage was called the Philosopher's Room, probably the same in which Steele used to write. In Hogarth's March to Finchley this cottage and Mother King's house are seen in the distance. . . . Coeval with the Spectator and Tatler this cottage must have been a delightful retreat, as, at that time, there were not a score buildings between it and Oxford-street and Montague and Bloomsbury Houses. Now continuous rows or streets extend from London even to this spot;"‡ and we may add, Montague and Bloomsbury Houses have long ceased to exist.

In old engravings of Steele's Cottage (two of which are now before us) St. Paul's Cathedral is shown in the distance. The cottage, which stood on a slight elevation on the W. side of Haverstock Hill, nearly opposite the Load of Hay, hardly answered in its later days to Sir Richard Phillips's description, it being a plain low whitened cottage, and the only ornament a scroll over the central window. It was pulled down in May 1867. The site is marked by a row of houses called Steele's Terrace, and the Sir Richard Steele Tavern.

Besides those whose houses or monts. we have named, there have been several other persons of sufficient eminence resident at Hampstead to call for mention. Philip Lord Wharton, "an old Roundhead, who had commanded a regiment against Charles the First at Edgehill," § and who lived to take an active part against James II., died at Hampstead,

where he had lived many years. Sir Geoffry Palmer, Manager of the Evidence against the Earl of Strafford, Attorney-General to Charles II., Chief Justice of Chester, and author or editor of several vols. of highly prized Reports, d. here in 1670. Sir Wm. Jones, another of Charles II.'s Attorney-Generals, and M.P. for Plymouth, and many other distinguished lawyers, have lived for a longer or shorter time at Hampstead.

Gay was carried to Hampstead in 1722, when it was thought he could hardly live a day, and under the care of Arbuthnot he here recovered.* Two years later Arbuthnot himself came here for a like purpose, but with only temporary success. His regimen was peculiar :—

"I saw Dr. Arbuthnot who was very cheerful. I passed a whole day with him at Hampstead. He is in the Long Room half the morning, and has card parties every night. Mrs. Lepell and Mrs. Saggioni and her sons and his two daughters are all with him."†

Dr. John Armstrong, the author of the once popular didactic poem 'The Art of Preserving Health,' visited and recommended "Hampstead, courted by the western wind." His brother, Dr. George Armstrong, was settled as a physician here, but the poet was never more than an occasional resident. Maynwaring, the author of 'The Medley,' and Thos. Javon, Wilkes, Cibber, Bullock, and a whole bevy of playwrights and actors, lived here for a time.

Here, in 1748, Samuel Johnson wrote 'The Vanity of Human Wishes.'

"Mrs. Johnson, for the sake of country air, had lodgings at Hampstead, to which he resorted occasionally, and there the greatest part, if not the whole, of this Imitation [of the Tenth Satire of Juvenal] was written. The fervid rapidity with which it was produced is scarcely credible. I have heard him say, that he composed seventy lines of it in one day, without putting one of them upon paper till they were finished."‡

The poem has no touch of local colour, unless indeed his strolls on the Heath may have suggested the lines—

"The needy traveller, serene and gay,
Walks the wild heath, and sings his toils away."

"For the gratification of posterity let it be recorded, that the house so dignified was the last

---

* Wordsworth, Extempore Effusion upon the Death of James Hogg, 1833; Works, vol. v., p. 336.
† Steele to Pope, June 1, 1712.
‡ Sir Richard Phillips, Monthly Mag.
§ Macaulay, Hist. of England, ch. x.

* Roscoe's Pope, vol. viii., p. 170.
† Pope to Martha Blount, 1734.
‡ Boswell, Life of Johnson, ed. 1836, vol. i., p. 221.

at Frognal (southward) now occupied by B. C. Stephenson, Esq., F.S.A."*

Thomas Day, the author of 'Sandford and Merton,' after his marriage, took a small lodging at Hampstead, and stayed here through the winter, "being in no haste to purchase a house; as he thought that by living in inconvenient lodgings, where he was not known, and consequently not visited by anybody except his chosen few, he should accustom his bride to those modes of life which he conceived to be essential to her happiness:"† and the lady, a rich heiress, whom he had long hesitated to marry on account of her wealth, performed her part in this novel matrimonial experiment with abundant cheerfulness.

Leigh Hunt lived at Hampstead, 1816 and following years; and in more than one of his smaller poems he has celebrated its beauties. His cottage, in the Vale of Health, "the first one that fronts the valley," was pulled down to make way for the ugly large hotel that now defaces this part of the Heath. Shelley and Keats were Hunt's guests, and Hazlitt, Haydon, and Procter frequent visitors.‡ Keats, indeed, took so great a liking to Hampstead from his stay at Hunt's, that he became a resident here from 1817 till he left England for Italy in 1820. Here he wrote his 'Ode to a Nightingale,' 'St. Agnes,' 'Isabella,' 'Hyperion,' and began the 'Endymion,' which he finished at Burford Bridge. The house in which he lodged for the greater part of the time, then called Wentworth Place, is now named Lawn Bank, and is the end house but one on the rt. side of John Street, next Wentworth House. His walks were in his later months limited to the Lower or the Middle Heath Road, the seat at the top of Well Walk being his goal and resting-place. Hunt as well as Hone has recorded Keats's melancholy musings here: "It was on the same day, sitting on the bench in Well Walk (the one against the wall) that he told me, with unaccustomed tears in his eyes, that his heart was breaking."§

Hampstead has always been a favourite haunt of painters, and many of them have lived here. Blake lodged at the farmhouse at the N. end of the Heath, by the field-path to Finchley,—part of the time, we believe, as the guest of John Linnell, who had hired the house for the summer, as other landscape painters have done since. Collins lived first in a small house at North End, and afterwards in a larger one on the Heath. Constable, whose tomb it will be remembered records his having been "many years an inhabitant of this parish," lived and died at No. 5, now No. 24, Well Walk, a few doors from the Wells Tavern. Sir Wm. Beechey lived in the Upper Terrace. Wilkie came here by the advice of Dr. Baillie, with great benefit to his health. Stanfield resided many years at Greenhill. His house, on the rt. in going down the hill towards London, is now named *Stanfield House.*

The large house next but one below Stanfield's was for many years the residence of the eminent publisher Thomas Longman, who died there Feb. 5, 1797. Mr. Longman's house was afterwards occupied by Lord Ashburton. On its site now stands the large new Wesleyan chapel. The grounds are covered with villas.

Hampstead Heath is a broad, elevated, sandy tract occupying the summit and northern slopes of Hampstead Hill. It has no historical associations, like Blackheath, though "High on bleak Hampstead's swarthy moor they started for the North;"* but, like most of the heaths in the vicinity of London, it has its recollections of highwaymen, their doings, and their executions:—

"As often upon Hampstead Heath,
Have seen a felon, long since put to death,
Hang, crackling in the sun his parchment skin
Which to his ear had shrivell'd up his chin."†

Perhaps the only relic of those emblems of Hampstead civilization is the mantle-tree over the fireplace in the kitchen of Jack Straw's Castle, which is said to have been made from the gibbet-post on which was suspended the corpse of Jackson, a notorious highwayman, executed on Hampstead Heath for the murder of

---

* Park, Hampstead, p. 334. It is, we believe, the house on the l. opposite West-End Lane.
† R. L. Edgeworth, Memoirs.
‡ Leigh Hunt, Lord Byron and his Contemporaries, vol. i.; Autobiography.
§ Leigh Hunt, Byron and his Contemporaries, vol. i., p. 440.

---

* Macaulay, The Armada.
† The Triennial Mayor, or The New Raparees, 1691.

Henry Miller, March 1673. * 'Jackson's Recantation . . . . wherein is truly discovered the whole mystery of that wicked and fatal profession of Padding on the Road,' was published in 1674.

Until 1700 the Middlesex elections were held on Hampstead Heath : the first election held at Brentford was in 1701. The Heath is now the most frequented of the open spaces round London. It is estimated that a fine Whit-Monday brings at least 50,000 people, and every fine Sunday or holiday a proportionate number.

Originally about 500 acres in extent, the Heath has been reduced, by the extension of the village, and occasional enclosures, to about 240 acres. Partly, no doubt, owing to these encroachments, it is of very irregular shape. The surface is much broken, and many of the deeper valleys have ponds,—some, like Leg of Mutton pond on the N.W., and those by the Vale of Health and the Lower Heath, of considerable size. From the higher parts views of great extent, ranging from the Surrey Downs and Hampshire Hills, by Windsor Castle and Harrow, and extending N., it is asserted,† to Hanslope spire, within 8 m. of Northamptonshire, and the Langdon Hills of Essex on the E. The W. view, with Harrow in the background, is perhaps the most picturesque, especially from those points whence the Kingsbury Lake is seen like a gleam of silver in the mid-distance, and a group of elms or firs gives strength and character to the foreground.

The fate of Hampstead Heath as an open space was long uncertain. The late Lord of the Manor was debarred from granting more than a 21 years' lease for building. For nearly 40 years he continued his efforts to obtain from Parliament powers to grant leases for 99 years to build on the Heath, on enclosures abutting on it, and on adjoining lands. He failed, and it is probable that if he had succeeded he would have preserved at least a part of the Heath as ornamental ground in connection with the houses he

proposed to erect; though he threatened, if thwarted, to " make an Agar Town of it." The Metropolitan Commons Act, 1866, secured the Heath from enclosure, and in 1870, the manor having passed to a new lord, the Metropolitan Board of Works were able to purchase the manorial rights for the sum of £45,000, and secure the Heath in perpetuity for public use. For several years prior to 1870, the Heath sands, in great request for brickmaking, had been dug in prodigious quantities, with the result of levelling many of the lesser elevations, scooping out deep pits, undermining trees, and extirpating large tracts of furze, broom, and heather. The Board of Works have happily done little in the way of improvement, and nothing towards rendering the Heath prim or park-like. Under their 5 years of judicious neglect, Nature has begun to reassert her rights. The bare sands are becoming clothed with verdure ; the banks, especially on the N., are purple with heather, the harebell is once more becoming common, the furze and broom have spread vigorously and bloomed abundantly, and the brake is everywhere fresh and flourishing. Hampstead Heath, in fact, looked better in the summer and autumn of 1875, than it had looked for the previous thirty years, and promises to look still better in the years that are to come.

Kilburn, 1½ m. S.W. of Hampstead, and of old a hamlet of Hampstead par., is now a populous suburb of London, with long rows of terraces, streets, and villas, rly. stats., 3 or 4 churches, chapels of all orders, schools, etc. At a very early date there was established at Kilburn a cell or priory for nuns, which was in 1376 under the order of St. Augustine; and which continued till suppressed in 1536. Some fragmentary vestiges of the buildings remained till the last few years. Near the site of the Priory was a mineral spring, which about the middle of the last cent. had its Long Room for the " reception of company . . . . and fit either for music, dancing, or entertainments," and set up as a rival to Hampstead Wells, which it at least equalled in dissipation. As late as 1818 it remained " a tea-drinking house well known as Kilburn Wells to the holiday folk of London." A part of the modern Kilburn bears the name of Kilburn Priory; while another is called Goldsmith's Place,

---

* Park, Hampstead, p. 305.
† The original authority for this assertion is an anonymous "MS. Description of Middlesex," quoted in Park's Hampstead, p. 252 ; it is repeated in all subsequent accounts of Hampstead ; but we have never met with any one keen-eyed enough to discern the spire.

from a fondly cherished tradition that in a house which stood where now this place stands Goldsmith wrote his 'Deserted Village,' and 'She Stoops to Conquer.'

West End is an outlying member of Hampstead, about ½ m. W. of the mother ch. ; the hamlet for the most part built a round a triangular green, now let on building leases. *North End* and *South End* are, as the names imply, situated some distance N. and S. from the village : near South End is the site of the Fever Hospital, the proposed erection of which is so warmly resented by the inhabitants. *Frognal* is the western side of Hampstead village.

HAMPTON, Middx. (Dom. *Hamntone*),

on the Thames, 13 m. W. of London, 14¾ m. by the Thames Valley branch of the L. and S.W. Rly. The par. extends from Hampton Wick, opposite Kingston-upon-Thames to Sunbury, and includes Hampton Court and Bushey Park within its boundaries. Pop., exclusive of the eccl. district of Hampton Wick, 3915. Inns : the *Red Lion*, in the centre of the vill, a good house; *Bell*, by the ch., much in favour with anglers ; *Railway Hotel*, by the stat.

The manor and honour of Hampton are noticed under HAMPTON COURT. Hampton village lies along the outer curve of a reach of the Thames, about a mile above Hampton Court. It consists for the most part of small houses ; but outside it there are many of a better description. The site is low, but the soil is gravel, and the scenery pleasant. Though somewhat impaired by the extensive works of the London water companies, this long reach of the Thames is still fresh, verdant, and picturesque. Along the bed of the river stretches a line of six or eight of the eyots, which, where untouched, always give so much character to the Thames. On either hand are broad meadows; the elms of Bushey Park, and beyond them the towers and trees of Hampton Court, and in the distance the massive tower and crowded roofs of Kingston are seen in one direction, Apps Court and the wooded hills of Surrey in the other.

The *Church*, St. Mary, at the entrance to the vill., is a neat, commonplace, white brick Perp. building, erected about 1830. It has nave and aisles, and at the W. end a square tower with pinnacles. Within are some *monts.* from the old ch. Under a canopy supported by Corinthian columns,

the tomb, with effigy, arms, long rhyming and punning epitaph of Mrs. Sebel Penn, d. 1562, nurse to King Edward VI.

" No plant of servile stock, a Hampden by descent, Unto whose race 300 years hath friendly fortune lent."

Edmund Pigeon, Esq., Yeoman of the Jewel-house to Henry VIII., Edward VI., Queen Mary, and Queen Elizabeth ; by the last of whom he was made Clerk of the Robes and Wardrobes (no date) ; also his son Nicholas Pigeon, who succeeded his father in those offices, and d. 1619. Theophilus Dillingham, Esq. (son of Archdeacon Dillingham) d. 1769, *æt.* 93 : mural slab, marble, with medallion. Elizabeth Mostyn, d. 1785, daughter of Sir Roger Mostyn and Lady Essex Finch. Richard Tickell, 1793, author of ' Anticipation,' a noted pamphlet, verses, and an opera; and grandson of the more eminent poet : " threw himself from one of the uppermost windows of the palace at Hampton Court, an immense height." [*] Richard Cumberland, d. 1794, son of the dramatist. John Beard, d. 1791, the famous vocalist. He quitted the stage on his marriage, 1739, with Lady Henrietta Herbert, daughter of James Earl of Waldegrave, and widow of Lord Edward Herbert ; but returned to it after some years' absence, and acquired great popularity both as actor and singer. He married for his second wife (1759) a daughter of John Rich, the patentee of Covent Garden Theatre, of which he became manager on the death of his father-in-law. The mont. is lost of Edward Progers, Page of Honour to Charles I., and Groom of the Bedchamber to Charles II., d. 1714, according to Le Neve " at the age of 96; of the anguish of cutting teeth, he having cut four new teeth, and had several ready to cut, which so inflamed his gums that he died."

In the ch.-yard lies " Huntington Shaw of Nottingham, an artist in his own way," d. 1710. This is he who wrought those admirable iron gates of Hampton Court, among the finest examples of English wrought iron extant, some of which have been removed for preservation from the weather to the interior of the palace, and others to the South Kensington Museum. Thomas Rosoman, d. 1782, for many years proprietor of Sadler's Wells Theatre, and

---

[*] Walpole to Miss Berry, Nov. 7, 1793.

who has bequeathed his name to Rosoman's Row and other places in its vicinity.
Thomas Ripley (d. 1758), the architect of
the Admiralty, and of Wolterton, and
thrice snarled at in Pope's verses. A
heavy granite cross by the S. door to the
Rev. G. F. W. Mortimer, D.D., Canon of
St. Paul's, and for 25 years head master
of the City of London School, d. 1871.

Garrick Villa, as it is now called, but
which, whilst the great actor occupied it,
was known as *Hampton House*, stands a
little E. of the ch. Garrick became tenant
in January 1754, purchased the estate in
the following July, and made it his country
seat till his death in January 1779. He
altered and enlarged the house, and gave
it in 1755 an entirely new front, designed
by Adam, of which the chief feature is a
tetrastyle Corinthian portico, reaching,
with its pediment, above the attic. The
grounds, which are separated from the
house by the road, extend to the river in
a wide lawn. Garrick added considerably
to the grounds, and had them and the
neighbouring eyot, which forms a part of
the property, laid out and planted under
his own direction. On the lawn he erected
an octagonal "Grecian Temple," with an
Ionic portico, to receive Roubiliac's statue
of Shakspeare. For this statue Garrick
stood as model, and gave the sculptor a
vast deal of trouble during its execution.
Roubiliac finished it in 1758, and received
300 guineas for his labour.

"John and I are just going to Garrick's, with a
grove of cypresses in our hands, like the Kentish
men at the Conquest. He has built a temple to
his master Shakspeare, and I am going to adorn the
outside, since his modesty would not let me decorate it within as I proposed," with certain mottoes.*

The grounds are over 11 acres; the eyot
4½. As seen from the river, the lawn,
with its trees, shrubs, and temple, and
the portico of the house rising high beyond,
has always been one of the attractions
of this part of the Thames.

Garrick furnished his house handsomely,
and hung on the walls many good pictures,
though ill-natured censors said that representations of himself, or of the scenes in
which he acted, were disproportionately
numerous. Among these were some of
Zoffany's clever pieces ; † while his general

pictures included Hogarth's Election
series. Garrick's dinners and garden
parties were very attractive ; night fêtes
are described in which his grounds were
lit by thousands of coloured lamps; and
Horace Walpole met at his Hampton
table "the Duke of Grafton, Lord and
Lady Rochford, Lady Holderness, the
crooked Mostyn, and Dabreu the Spanish
minister ; two regents, of which one is
lord chamberlain, the other groom of the
stole ; and the wife of a secretary of state.
This is being *sur un assez bon ton* for a
player."* Once a year the player had a
different festivity. On the 1st of May he
threw open his grounds to the village
children, and regaled them with cakes
and wine. On Johnson's first visit to
Hampton House, Garrick asked him how
he liked it. "Ah, David!" replied the
moralist, "it is the leaving of such places
that makes a death-bed terrible."

Hampton House continued to be the
residence of Mrs. Garrick for 43 years after
her husband's death, and during that
time it remained, with its contents, intact.
She would have nothing touched that was
his. On her death, in 1822, the contents
were sold by auction, and dispersed. The
statue of Shakspeare, which Garrick bequeathed to the British Museum after
his wife's decease, is now in the Entrance
Hall of that building. In June 1864,
the house and grounds were sold by
auction for £10,500, to Mr. Edward Grove,
the clothier of New Cut, Lambeth. The
house has since been enlarged, but remains substantially unchanged in appearance. Only the attic and top of the
portico are visible from the road, the
house being shut off by a tall brick wall :
the temple may be seen from the road,
on the opposite side to the house.

The large white-brick buildings, with
the half-dozen tall campanile smoke and
ventilating shafts, just beyond the vill.,
are the pumping works, and beyond these
are the filtering beds, of the Grand Junction, the West Middlesex, and the Southwark and Vauxhall Water Works Companies, for supplying London with water.
These companies, with the Chelsea and
Lambeth Works at Kingston, have parliamentary powers to take from the

* Horace Walpole to George Montagu, Oct. 14,
1756.
† At Petworth is a painting by Hodges and
Zoffany of Garrick at his villa.

* Walpole to Bentley, Aug. 4, 1755 ; Letters,
vol. ii., p. 457.

Thames 100,000,000 gallons of water a day. But even all these works have proved insufficient to satisfy the monster maw of London ; and now a large red-brick building will be noticed nearly completed a little higher up and on the opposite side of the river, with immense filtering beds beyond, for the Lambeth Company ; and a little inland, between Sunbury and Hanworth, a great pumping station has been constructed, with lofty sq. shaft, and extensive reservoirs, for furnishing an extra supply to the East London Water Works at the opposite extremity of London.

Hampton may be considered the head-quarters of the Thames Angling Preservation Society, and here and a little higher up on the Surrey side are the ponds and streamlets made by the Thames Conservancy, and maintained by the society for hatching and rearing fish ova—chiefly salmon, grayling, and trout. The young fish are kept in the streams for eight or nine months, when, being considered able to take care of themselves, they are turned into the river. About 50,000 fish are annually sent into the Thames from these ponds, and anglers acknowledge a decided improvement in the fishing. The river here is strictly preserved along what is known as *Hampton Deep*, which extends from the lawn of Garrick Villa to Tumbling Bay, 960 yds. From 20 to 30 lb. of roach or perch are accounted a good day's fishing.

Hampton Races, one of the most popular of the "suburban gatherings," are held in June, on *Molesey Hurst*, exactly opposite Hampton Ch., on the Surrey side of the Thames. There is a ferry from Hampton to Molesey Hurst, and a bridge from Hampton Court to East Molesey. The first bridge at Hampton Court was a wooden one, erected in 1708 : the present iron girder bridge of five spans was built in 1865.

New Hampton, on the N. extremity of the par., by Hampton Hill and the Hanworth road, has grown within the last few years into a considerable village. It was made a chapelry in 1864; has a neat E.E. red-brick church, St. James, built in 1873 ; and in 1871 had 1322 inhabitants.

HAMPTON COURT, MIDDX., the
palace of Wolsey and of Henry VIII.,

then of all our sovereigns in succession from Edward VI. to George II.; and now, by royal goodwill, a palace free to the enjoyment of every one, stands on the l. bank of the Thames, midway between Hampton village and Hampton Wick, and 12 m. W. from Hyde Park. The L. and S.W. Rly. Stat. for Hampton Court is at East Molesey, on the opposite side of the Thames, but within sight of the palace. On crossing the bridge from the station, the West Gate of Hampton Court, the best approach to the buildings, is on the rt., close to the foot of the bridge.

The State Apartments and Grounds are open free to the public *every week-day*, except Friday, from 10 a.m. to 6 p.m., from the 1st of April to the 30th of September, and from 10 till 4 from the 1st of October to the 31st of March : on *Sundays*, the State Apartments are not open till 2 p.m. A summer's day may be pleasantly spent in examining the palace and its contents, and wandering about the grounds, Bushey Park, and the Thames. Hotels : the *Mitre*, by the bridge ; *King's Arms*, by the Lion Gate ; and, opposite it, the *Greyhound*, by the entrance to Bushey Park.

The manor of Hampton (*Hamntone*), belonged in the reign of Edward the Confessor to Earl Algar, and was worth £40 per annum. At the Domesday Survey it was held by Walter de St. Waleric, and produced £20. At the beginning of the 13th cent. it was the property of Joan, relict of Sir Robert Gray. Lady Gray, who died in 1211, gave the manor to the Knights Hospitallers of St. John of Jerusalem, by whom it was held till the suppression of the order ; but the prior and brethren granted a lease of the manor, Jan. 11, 1515, for 99 years to Thomas Wolsey, Archbishop of York, for a yearly rental of £50, out of which there was to be "allowance . . . in the payments of the rent" of £21, "towards and for the exhibition of a preste for to mynister divine servi e within the Chapell of the said manor," so that Wolsey would seem to have had a good bargain.

When he purchased Hampton, Wolsey was in the plenitude of his power. He was created Cardinal in September of the same year, and it may have been in anticipation of his increase of dignity that he bought

Hampton in order to convert the manor-house into a palace. Without delay, and at a vast cost, Wolsey raised so large and stately a palace that, as Stow says, " it excited much envy," which the magnificence of his style of living in it was not calculated to lessen. Skelton, though his bitter enemy and satirist, probably only gave utterance to what many felt:

" Why come ye not to court?—
  To whyche court?
  To the Kynge's courte,
  Or to Hampton Court?—
  Nay, to the Kynge's court:
  The Kynges courte
  Shulde haue the excellence;
  But Hampton Court
  Hath the preemynence,
  And Yorkes Place,
  With my lordes grace,
  To whose magnifycence
  Is all the conflewence,
  Sutys and supplycacyons,
  Embassades of all nacyons." *

Cavendish, Wolsey's gentleman-usher, has celebrated both in verse and prose the magnificence of his master's favourite palace, and the splendour of his court. His account of the grand banquet given by the Cardinal to Montmorenci, the French ambassador, and his suite. in 1527, will be found in all the descriptions of Hampton Court, but an extract or two may have place here.

"Then was there made great preparation of all things for this great assembly at Hampton Court. The Cardinal called before him his principal officers, as steward, treasurer, comptroller, and clerk of his kitchen, to whom he declared his mind touching the entertainment of the Frenchmen at Hampton Court, commanding them neither to spare for any cost, expense, or travail, to make them such a triumphant banquet as they might not only wonder at it here, but also make a glorious report of it in their country, to the great honour of the King and his realm. To accomplish his commandment they sent out caters, purveyors, and divers other persons, my Lord's friends, to make preparation; also they sent for all the expert cooks and cunning persons in the art of cookery which were within London or elsewhere, that might be gotten to beautify this noble feast. . . . Then my Lord Cardinal sent me, being his gentleman usher, with two other of my fellows, thither to foresee all things touching our rooms to be nobly garnished. . . . . . . The day was come to the Frenchmen assigned, and they ready assembled . . . . . and every of them was conveyed to their several chambers, having in them great fires and wine to their comfort and relief, remaining there until their supper was ready. The chambers where they supped were ordered in this sort: first the great waiting chamber was hanged with rich arras, as all others were, and furnished with tall yeomen

to serve. There were set tables round about the chamber, banquetwise, covered with fine cloths of diaper; a cupboard was there garnished with white plate, having also in the same chamber to give the more light, four great plates of silver set with great light, and a great fire of wood and coals. The next chamber, being the chamber of presence, was hanged with very rich arras, and a sumptuous cloth of estate furnished with many goodly gentlemen ready to serve the tables. The boards were set in manner as the other boards were in the other chamber before, save that the high table was set and removed beneath the cloth of estate toward the middest of the chamber, covered with fine linen cloths of damask work sweetly perfumed. There was a cupboard, made for the time, in length of the breadth of the nether end of the same chamber, six desks of height, garnished with gilded plate, very sumptuous and of the newest fashions, and the nethermost desk was garnished all with plate of clean gold, having two great candlesticks of silver and gilt, most curiously wrought, the workmanship whereof with the silver cost 300 marks, and lights of wax as big as torches, burning upon the same. This cupboard was barred all round about that no man came nigh it; for there was none of the same plate occupied or stirred during this feast, for there was sufficient besides. The plates that did hang on the walls to give light in the chamber were of silver and gilt, with great pearchers of wax burning in them, a great fire burning in the chimney, and all other things necessary for the furniture of so noble a feast. Now was all things in a readiness, and supper time at hand. My Lord's officers caused the trumpets to blow to warn to supper, and the said officers went right discreetly in due order, and conducted these noble personages from their chambers unto the chamber of presence where they should sup. And, they being there, caused them to sit down; their service was brought up in such order and abundance, both costly and full of subtleties, with such a pleasant noise of divers instruments of music, that the Frenchmen (as it seemed) were rapt into a heavenly paradise." The Cardinal was not yet there, but "before the second course, My Lord Cardinal came in among them, booted and spurred, all suddenly, and bade them *proface* . . . . and straightways, being not shifted of his riding apparel, called for a chair, and sat himself down in the midst of the high paradise, laughing and being as merry as ever I saw him in all my life. Anon came up the second course, with so many dishes, subtleties, and curious devices, which were above a hundred in number, of so goodly proportion and costly, that I suppose the Frenchmen never saw the like: the wonder was no less than it was worthy indeed. . . . . Then my Lord took a bowl of gold, which was esteemed of the value of 500 marks, filled with hippocras,* whereof there was

---

* Skelton's Poetical Works, Dyce's ed., vol. ii., p. 39, 'Why Come ye Nat to Courte?' lines 398—412.

* A drink made of wine mixed with spices and sugar. Skelton charges the Cardinal with too great fondness for this and other dainties—

" To drynke and for to eate
  Swete ypocras and swete meate
  To kepe his flesh chast,
  In Lent for a repast
  He eateth capons stewed
  Fesaunt and partriche mewed,
  Hennes, checkynges, and pygges."
      (Why Come ye Nat to Courte?
          l. 214, etc.)

plenty, and putting off his cap, said ' I drink to the King, my sovereign lord and master, and next unto the King your master,' and therewith did drink a good draught. And when he had done, he desired the Grand Master to pledge him, cup and all, the which cup he gave him ; and so caused all the other lords and gentlemen in other cups to pledge these two royal princes. Then went cups merrily about, that many of the Frenchmen were fain to be led to their beds." Various pastimes followed, the Cardinal treating his guests "so nobly and with so familiar countenance and entertainment, that they could not commend him too much. And whilst they were in communication and other pastimes, all their liveries were served to their chambers. Every chamber had a basin and an ewer of silver, a great livery pot of silver, some gilt, and some parcel gilt ; yea and some chambers had two great pots of silver in like manner, and one pot at the least with wine and beer, a bowl, or goblet, and a silver pot to drink beer in ; a silver candlestick or two, with both white lights and yellow lights, of three sizes of wax, and a staff torch, a fine manchet, and a cheat loaf of bread. Thus was every chamber furnished throughout the house, and yet the two cupboards in the two banqueting chambers were not once touched. Then being past midnight, as time served, they were conveyed to their lodgings to take their rest for that night." *

Du Bellay, Bishop of Bayonne, who was in the suite of Montmorenci, bears testimony to the admiration with which his countrymen regarded the entertainment, particularly noting the chambers that Cavendish has described so fully. " The very chambers had hangings of wonderful value, and every place did glitter with innumerable vessels of gold and silver. There were two hundred and fourscore beds, the furniture to most of them being silk, and all for the entertainment of strangers only." This was the last entertainment the Cardinal gave in his gorgeous palace, and probably the last occasion on which he presided as host within its walls. It had, in fact, already ceased to belong to him. The envy which it excited among the courtiers had extended higher. The king asked Wolsey why he had built so costly a house. " To show how noble a palace a subject may offer to his sovereign," replied the adroit courtier. The king accepted the gift (1526), and " in recompense thereof licensed the Cardinal to lie in his manor of Richmond at his pleasure." †

Thenceforth Henry made Hampton Court a frequent residence. Its fame reached the ear of Henry's great rival in

splendour Francis I. Wallop the English Ambassador having mentioned that Henry was at Windsor, Francis asked him where that was, and how it stood ; and being told that it stood upon a hill by a goodly river,—

" ' Je vous prie, Monsr. Ambassadour,' quod He, ' que ryver est cella ?' I saied it was the Themys. ' Et Hampton Court,' quod He, ' est il sur la mesmes ryver aussy ?' I saied, ' Ye, that theye bothe stode uppon the same ryver with dyvers other goodly howses, namyng Richemount for one, declaring to hym at lenght the magnificence of them all three, and specially of Hampton Court ; of which He was very desierous to here, and toke grete pleasure to commun with me thereon, shewing me He hard saye that Your Majestie did use much gilding in your said howses, and specially in the rowffes, and that He in his buildyng used litle or none, but made the rowffes of tymbre fyndly wrought with dyvers cullers of woode naturall." *

Henry was at Hampton Court when he received news of the death of Wolsey. Cavendish, after watching his master through his last illness, and seeing his remains laid reverently in his grave in Leicester Abbey, rode with all haste to Hampton Court to apprise the king of the particulars.

"Repairing to the King, I found him shooting at the rounds in the park, on the backside of the garden. And perceiving him occupied in shooting, thought it not my duty to trouble him : but leaned to a tree, intending to stand there, and to attend his gracious pleasure. Being in a great study, at the last, the King came suddenly behind me, where I stood, and clapped his hand upon my shoulder ; and when I perceived him I fell upon my knee. To whom he said, calling me by name, ' I will,' quod he, ' make an end of my game, and then I will talk with you,' and so departed to his mark, whereat the game was ended. Then the King delivered his bow unto the yeoman of the bows, and went his way inward to the palace, whom I followed ; howbeit he called for Sir John Gage, with whom he talked, until he came at the garden postern gate, and there entered ; the gate being shut after him, which caused me to go my ways. And being gone but a little distance the gate was opened again, and there Sir Harry Norris called me again, commanding me to come in to the King, who stood behind the door in a night-gown of russet velvet, furred with sables : before whom I kneeled down, being with him there all alone the space of an hour and more, during which time he examined me of divers weighty matters concerning my Lord, wishing that liever than £20,000 that he had lived. Then he asked me for the £1500 which Master Kingston moved to my Lord before his death. ' Sir,' said I, ' I think that I can tell your grace partly where it is.' ' Yea, can you ?' quod the King, ' then I pray you tell me, and you shall do us much pleasure, nor it shall not be unrewarded.'" Having satisfied his Majesty in whose hands the

* Cavendish, Life of Wolsey, Singer's edition, p. 195, etc.

† Cavendish, Life of Wolsey.

* Wallop to Henry VIII., in Calendar of State Papers.

money was, "'Well then,' quod the King, 'let me alone, and keep this gear secret between yourself and me, and let no man be privy thereof, for if I hear any more of it, then I know by whom it is come to knowledge.' 'Three may,' quod he, 'keep counsel, if two be away; and if I thought my cap knew my counsel, I would cast it into the fire and burn it. And for your truth and honesty ye shall be one of our servants, and in that same room with us, that ye were with your old master.'" *

Henry spent a good deal of his time at Hampton Court, being in these early days much given to hunting, hawking, fishing, shooting at the rounds, bowls, and other outdoor diversions in fair weather, and tennis, backgammon, and similar games—at which he staked heavily and lost much—in wet weather, and on long evenings. † In 1533 Anne Boleyn presided as Queen at superb banquetings, with masques, interludes, and sports. On the 12th of October, 1537, Edward VI. was born at Hampton Court, and twelve days after his mother, Jane Seymour, died there. In the summer of 1540, Anne of Cleves was here awaiting her decree of divorce. That announced "she removed to Richmond; and Catherine Howard, was openly showed as Queen at Hampton Court." Here on the 12th of July, 1543, Catherine Parr was married and proclaimed Queen, and here a few months later her brother was created Earl of Essex, and her uncle ennobled. Henry kept the Christmas of 1543 at Hampton Court in great state, his chief guest being Francis Gonzaga, viceroy of Sicily. ‡ At the Christmas of 1544, Henry held here a Chapter of the Garter, at which the Earl of Surrey was present; and on this or an earlier occasion Surrey became enamoured of his Geraldine :—

" Bright is her hue, and Geraldine she hight.
Hampton me taught to wish her first for mine;
And Windsor, alas! doth chase me from her sight " §

Henry added largely to the buildings and grounds of Hampton Court, "so as to make it a goodly sumptuous and beautiful manor, decent and convenient for a King, and did ornate the same with parks, gardens, and orchards, and other things of great commodity and pleasure thereto adjoining, meet and pertinent to his Royal

Majesty.". These are the terms of the preamble of the Act for creating the *Honour of Hampton*, 1538; but the Order of the Privy Council issued in the next reign for dechasing the honour, explains that at this time " His Highness waxed heavy with sickness, age, and corpulency of body, and might not travel so readily abroad, but was constrained to seek to have his game and pleasure ready and at hand." This royal hunting-ground comprised not merely the manor of Hampton Court as "the chief and capital place and part of the said Honour," with the adjacent manors on the Middlesex side of the Thames, but also the parishes and manors of Walton-upon-Thames, Oatlands, Weybridge, Byfleet, Cobham, Esher, Thames Ditton, and East and West Molesey, in Surrey, the whole being surrounded by a wooden paling, and stored with deer. Only two other honours had been thus created,* and this was the last.

No wonder that, as soon as a new king came to the throne, there should be " divers supplications exhibited unto the King's most Excellent Majestie of many poor men of these parishes," setting forth that " forasmuch as their commons, meadows and pastures be taken in, and that all the said parishes are overlaid with the deer now increasing daily upon them, very many households of the same parishes be let fall down, the families decayed and the King's liege people much diminished, the country thereabout in manner made desolate," and praying to be relieved. Or that the King, the Lord Protector, and the Council, taking into consideration that " over and besides " what was thus set forth, ": the King's Majesty loseth yearly, diminished of his yearly revenues and rents to a great sum," should order the honour to be " dechased . . . so much of the deer within the said chase shall be spent or put into the Forest of Windsor," or other of the royal parks ; and " at Michaelmas next the pale shall be taken down and transported to the help of other of the Kings Maties Parks and Chases, and the land therein enclosed and emparked restored to the old tenants, to pay again the former rents." This was done and the country laid open, but the

---

* Cavendish, Life of Wolsey, p. 398.
† Sir H. Nicolas, Privy Purse Expenses.
‡ Lysons; Stow; Holinshed.
§ Surrey, Description and Praise of his Love, Geraldine.

---

* Lysons, Environs, vol. iii., p. 53; Madox, Baronia Anglica, p. 9.

district thus enclosed has ever since been considered a Royal Chase, and the office of " Lieutenant and Keeper of Her Majesty's Chase of Hampton Court " has continued to be held along with that of Chief Steward of the Honour, and Ranger of the Parks.*

Edward VI. was at Hampton Court in the autumn of 1549, with his uncle, the Protector Somerset, Cranmer, Cecil, Paget, and other members of the Council, when Somerset received intelligence of the confederation against him of the members of the Council assembled in London and the Earl of Warwick. who had just returned after suppressing the Norfolk insurrection. Somerset in the utmost alarm issued a strange proclamation, summoning all loyal subjects to come armed to the help of the king, and followed it up by measures equally the result of panic, so that Hampton Court was for some days in a state of extraordinary excitement.

" The King's Majesty straitly chargeth and commandeth all his loving subjects with all haste to repair to His Highness at his Majesty's Manor of Hampton Court, in most defensible array, with harness and weapons to defend his most royal person and his most intirely beloved uncle, the Lord Protector, against whom certain hath attempted a most dangerous conspiracy. And this to do in all possible haste. Given at Hampton Court, the first day of Oct, in the third year of his most noble reign." †

The lords seized the Tower of London, displaced the lieutenant, and substituted an officer of theirs. How Somerset sought to meet the danger is told by the king and the council :—

" The next morning, being the 6th of October and Saturday, he [Somerset] commanded the armour to be brought down out of the armoury of Hampton Court, about 500 harnesses, to arm both his and my men ; with all the gates of the house to be rampiered—people to be raised." ‡

Somerset did raise the people about Hampton Court, " writing and crying out that certain Lords had determined to repair to the Court and to destroy the King." " And when he had thus gathered the people and commons together at Hampton Court, then he brought his Majesty into the base court there, and so after to the gate to

them that were without ; and after he caused his Highness Good Prince to say—' I pray you be good to us and our Uncle." *

Such measures were of little avail. That same 6th of October, " at nine or ten o'clock of the night," Somerset hurried the king to Windsor. A few days later the proud Protector was a prisoner, and saw Hampton Court no more. In 1551 Edward VI., at Hampton Court, created Somerset's deadly enemy, the Earl of Warwick, Duke of Northumberland, and the Marquis of Dorset, Duke of Suffolk.

Immediately after their solemn entry into London following their marriage, Queen Mary and King Philip withdrew to Hampton Court, where they lived in great retirement, and winning little popularity : " The hall-door within the Court was continually shut, so that no man might enter unless his errand were first known; which seemed strange to Englishmen that had not been used thereto."† Hither the Princess Elizabeth was summoned from Woodstock, and hard pressed to abjure Protestantism by Gardner and others of the queen's confessors and councillors ; and seems to have owed her safety to the interposition of Philip. According to Holinshed, she was on one occasion conducted by torch-light to the queen's bed-chamber, when kneeling down she declared herself a true and faithful subject. During the interview Philip was concealed behind the tapestry, ready, as is conjectured, to have interposed if the violence of the queen's temper had proceeded to extremities. A week later she was released from her strict surveillance ; and the following Christmas (1554),‡ which was kept at Hampton Court with a splendour that had no return in the unhappy queen's reign, the

* Lysons.
† Tytler, England under the Reigns of Edward VI. and Mary, Original Letters, etc., vol. i., p. 205 ; another proclamation was issued dated H. Court, Oct. 6 : comp. Froude, Hist. of England, vol. v., p. 232 n., and Calendar of State Papers, Domestic Series, vol. ix. (Lemon), p. 23.
‡ Journal of Edward VI.

* Letter of the Council 'To my Lady Marie's Grace and my Lady Elizabeth's Grace,' Oct. 9, 1549, Tytler, vol. i., p. 249.
† Holinshed, Chronicle, vol. iv., p. 64.
‡ Lysons (vol. iii., p. 63) says' that " Philip and Mary kept their Christmas at Hampton Court in 1558," while Nichols places it in 1557 ; but Mary died in November 1558, and the only Christmas Philip spent in England was that of 1554, which must therefore have been the Christmas described by the Chronicler. Froude, Hist. of England, vol. vi., pp. 358, 359, places the meeting in which Philip is said to have been concealed behind the tapestry in July 1555 ; but it was in 1554 she was sent for from Woodstock.

Princess Elizabeth was the principal guest:

"On Christmas-eve the great hall of the palace was illuminated with 1000 lamps, curiously disposed. The princess [Elizabeth] supped at the same table with the King and Queen, next the cloth of state; and after supper was served with a perfumed napkin and plates of confects by the Lord Paget. But she retired to her Ladies before the revels, maskings, and disguisings began. On St. Stephen's day she heard mattins in the Queen's closet adjoining to the chapel, where she was attired in a robe of white satin, strung all over with large pearls. On the 29th day of December she sate with their Majesties and the nobility at a grand spectacle of jousting, when 200 spears were broken. Half of the combatants were accoutred in the Almaine, and half in the Spanish fashion." *

It was to Hampton Court that Mary retired, April 1555, for perfect quiet when daily expecting to become a mother; and the proclamation announcing her "happy deliverance of a prince" is subscribed "from our house of Hampton Court," though occasion was never found to fill the blank left for the date.†

Elizabeth occasionally resided at Hampton Court, but preferred Greenwich. She was there in 1559, August 10—17; 1568, 1570, 1572 (in September of which year she "fell sick of the smallpox at Hampton Court"), 1579, and 1582; and kept Christmas there in 1568, 1572,‡ 1575, and again in 1593, when, on New Year's Day, Thomas Churchyard presented Her Majesty with "A Pleasant Conceite, Penned in Verse."

Whilst Mary Queen of Scots was at Bolton Castle, Elizabeth summoned a great council of the lords at Hampton Court, October 30, 1568, to consider the allegations against Mary respecting the murder of Darnley. A conference was appointed to be held at Westminster, and this was adjourned to Hampton Court, where Elizabeth still was. Here it assembled December 3rd. and on the following day the Regent Murray produced the casket containing the letters and verses which proved so fatal to Mary.§

Hentzner, the German traveller, visited Hampton Court in 1598, and has given an ample but not very exact account of it: he seems to have been most interested in the furniture and decorations; "all the walls of the palace," he writes, "shine with gold and silver." *

James I., shortly after his arrival in England, took up his abode at Hampton Court, and here was held (Jan. 14—17, 1604) the famous conference between the representatives of the Established Church and the Presbyterians; the former consisting of the Abp. of Canterbury, the Bp. of London, 7 other bishops, 5 deans, and 2 doctors; the latter, of 4 of their leading ministers, Dr. Reynolds being their spokesman. The conference lasted three days, but the Presbyterians were only admitted on the second and third, when Reynolds was browbeaten by the bishops, and "soundly peppered" by the pedant king, who announced his resolve to "have one doctrine, one discipline, one religion in substance and in ceremony." James's oratory so delighted the bishops that the Bp. of London fell upon his knees and protested his "heart melted with joy that Almighty God, of his singular mercy, hath given us such a king as, since Christ's time, the like hath not been," and the Abp. exclaimed, "Undoubtedly your Majesty speaks by the special assistance of God's spirit."† "I wist not what they meant," wrote an auditor;‡ "but the spirit was rather foul-mouthed." The conference, as Fuller notes, "produced some alterations in the Liturgy;" but its best result was the resolution for a new translation of the Bible: its evil fruit, the intensifying the differences between churchmen and nonconformists, and thus preparing the way for the disastrous events of the next reign.

Charles I. was often at Hampton Court, sometimes, as in 1625, because the plague raged in London (when all communication between that city and Hampton Court was forbidden by proclamation), and sometimes for pleasure; and he and his queen enriched it with many works of art. In July 1625 the king gave formal receptions at Hampton Court to the ambassadors of France and Denmark, and one from Bethlem Gabor, Prince of Transyl-

---

* Brit. Mus. Cott. MSS., Vitell. F., quoted in Nichols' Progresses of Queen Elizabeth, vol. i., p. 18.

† Froude, vol. vi., p. 346.

‡ "Here, we play at tables, dance, and keep Christmas,"—Letter of Sir Thomas Smith, Hampton Court, 1572; Life, p. 239. Nichols, Progresses, i., 75; i., 263; ii., 392; and iii., 232.

§ Froude, vol. ix., p. 335.

* Sir Paul Hentzner, A Journey into England in the Year 1598.

† Fuller, Church Hist., Book X., s. 20.

‡ Harrington, Nugæ Antiquæ, p. 162.

vania, the French ambassador being, at the earnest request of the queen, contrary to all court etiquette, lodged within the palace. Charles was here with his court in Oct. 1627, Oct. 1628, again in 1632—1636, and again in the autumn of 1638, when on the 2nd of Oct. he knighted Balthazar Gerbier, the painter and projector, who had been negotiating for him at Brussels and the Hague a settlement of the Spanish difficulty, and the purchase of works of art.*

On the 10th of Jan. 1642, Charles sought refuge here with his queen from the tumultuous assemblies in London. It was the last time he was here as master : his next visit, August 24, 1647, was as a prisoner. He remained here three months under a very mild restraint ; his children who were at the Duke of Northumberland's, Syon House, had free access to him, and his old servants were about him.

"The King lived at Hampton Court rather in the condition of a guarded and attended prince, than as a conquered and purchased captive ; all his old servants had free recourse to him ; all sorts of people were admitted to come to kiss his hands and to do obeisance as to a sovereign. Ashburnham and Berkeley, by the Parliament voted delinquents, came to him from beyond the seas, and others by permission of the army." †

"Hampton Court was prepared and put into as good order for his reception, as could have been done in the best time. . . . . The King enjoyed himself at Hampton Court much more to his content than he had of late ; the respects of the chief officers of the army seeming much greater than they had been ; Cromwell himself came oftener to him, and had longer conferences with him ; talked with more openness than he had done, and appeared more cheerful. Persons of all conditions repaired to his Majesty of those who had served him ; with whom he conferred without reservation ; and the citizens flocked thither as they had used to do at the end of a progress, when the King had been some months absent from London : but that which pleased his Majesty most, was that his children were permitted to come, in whom he took great delight." ‡

The manor of Hampton Court was sold by the Parliament, in 1651, to John Phelps and others ; and in the court rolls of 1654 Phelps's name occurs as lord of the

manor.* But in Sept. 1653 it was "Ordered, That the house called Hampton Court, with the outhouses and gardens thereunto belonging, and the little park wherein it stands," which had been valued at £10,765, "be stayed from sale, until the Parliament take further order."

"For the house of Hampton Court having been ordered to be sold that day, which place I thought very convenient for the retirement of those that were employed in Public affairs, when they should be indisposed, in the summer season, I resolved to endeavour to prevent the sale of it, and accordingly procured a Motion to be made at the sitting down of the House to that end, which took effect as I desired. For this I was very much blamed by my good friend, Sir Henry Vane, as a thing which was contrary to the interest of a Commonwealth. He said that such places might justly be accounted amongst those things that prove Temptations to Ambitious Men, and exceedingly tend to sharpen their Appetite to ascend the Throne." †

A year or two later both house and manor had passed into the possession of Oliver Cromwell, who thenceforth made the palace one of his principal residences. In it his daughter Elizabeth was married to Lord Falconbridge, Nov. 18, 1657, and his favourite daughter, Lady Claypole, died August 6, 1658. A fortnight later Cromwell was himself stricken with fever, and removed to Whitehall, where he died Sept. 3rd. For the amusement of his leisure hours the Protector is said to have had the organ removed from Magdalen College, Oxford, and erected in the great gallery of Hampton Court. ‡

Soon after his marriage Charles II. brought his queen to Hampton : he in a measure refurnished the house and remodelled the gardens.

"*May* 25, 1662.—I went this evening to Hampton Court to see the new Queene.

"*May* 31.—I saw the Queene at dinner ; the Judges came to compliment her arrival, and after them the Duke of Ormond brought me to kiss her hand.

"*June* 8.—I saw her Majesty at supper privately in her bed-chamber.

"Hampton Court is as noble and uniforme a pile, and as capacious as any Gotiq architecture can have made it. There is incomparable furniture in it, especially hangings designed by Raphael, very rich with gold ; also many rare pictures, especially the 'Cæsarian Triumphs' of Andr. Mantegna, formerly the Duke of Mantua's ; of the tapestrys I believe the world can show nothing nobler of the kind than the storys of Abraham and Tobit. The gallery of hornes is very particular for the vast

---

* Sainsbury, Original Papers relating to Rubens, p. 211 ; Walpole, Anecdotes of Painters, vol. ii., p. 95 : Walpole says, perhaps by an error of the copyist, that Gerbier "was knighted at Hampton Court in 1628."

† Lady Hutchinson, Memoirs of Colonel Hutchinson, ed. 1846, p. 305. See also Lady Fanshawe's Memoirs.

‡ Clarendon, Hist. of the Rebellion, B. x., vol. iii., pt. 1, p. 67, ed. 1720.

* Lysons, vol. iii., p. 52.

† Ludlow, Memoirs, vol. ii, p. 678.

‡ Hawkins, Hist. of Music, vol. iv., p. 45.

beames of staggs, elks, antelopes, etc. The Queene's bed was an embroidery of silver on crimson velvet, and cost £8000, being a present made by the States of Holland when his Majesty returned, and had formerly ben given by them to our King's sister, the Princesse of Orange, and being bought of her againe was now presented to the King. The greate looking-glasse and toilet of beaten and massive gold was given by the Queene Mother. The Queene brought over with her from Portugal such Indian cabinets as had never before ben seene here. The great hall is a most magnificent roome. The chapell-roof excellently fretted and gilt. I was also curious to visite the wardrobes and tents and other furniture of state. The park, formerly a flat naked piece of ground, now planted with sweete rows of lime trees ; and the canall for water now neere perfected ; also the hare park. In the garden is a rich and noble fountaine, with syrens, statues, etc., cast in copper by Fanelli, but no plenty of water. The cradle-walk of horne-beame in the garden is, for the perplexed twining of the trees, very observable. There is a parterre which they call Paradise, in which is a pretty banquet-ting-house set over a cave or cellar. All these gardens might be exceedingly improved, as being too narrow for such a palace." *

William III. liked the situation of Hampton Court, its proximity to the Thames, its distance from London ; pulled down two courts of Wolsey's palace, and commissioned Wren to erect on their site a suite of state apartments that might rival those of Versailles ; extended the grounds and remodelled King Charles's French gardens in the Dutch taste ; and, in fine, spent so much time, money, and thought upon Hampton that the Londoners grew angry, and his Ministers expostulated with him on his neglect of the capital. Obliged to select an abode nearer London, William chose Kensington, partly because he could at any time ride across to his " country house," see the progress of his alterations there, or enjoy a gallop in the park. It was to Hampton Court he drove straight, without entering London, on returning, broken down in health from his last visit to Holland, Nov. 4, 1701. Three months later (Feb. 20, 1702), whilst ambling through the park on his favourite horse Sorrel, the horse struck his foot against a molehill, stumbled, and threw the king. His collar-bone was found to be broken, and he was carried to Kensington, where he lived little more than a fortnight.

His successor lived much at Hampton Court. Pope has told all that need be said about the dull routine of her residence :

" Close by those meads, for ever crown'd with
    flowers,
Where Thames with pride surveys his rising
    towers,
There stands a structure of majestic frame,
Which from the neighb'ring Hampton takes its
    name.
Here British statesmen oft the fall foredoom
Of foreign tyrants, and of nymphs at home ;
Here thou great Anna ! whom three realms obey,
Doth sometimes counsel take,—and sometimes
    tea." *

George I. and George II. spent a good deal of time at Hampton Court, but the Court life was as dull in their reigns as in that of their predecessor, and hardly so respectable. George I. tried to relieve the tedium by having some plays acted, but the stolidity of the Court seems to have infected the players, who were dismayed at finding that " at Court, where the Prince gives the treat and honours the table with his own presence, the audience is under the restraint of a circle, where laughter, or applause raised higher than a whisper, would be stared at. . . . This coldness or decency of attention, at Court, I observed had but a melancholy effect upon the impatient vanity of some of our actors, who seemed inconsolable when their flashy endeavours to please had passed unheeded. Their not considering where they were quite disconcerted them." † However, they seem to have pleased.

" I shall proceed to speak of the theatre which was ordered by his late Majesty (George I.) to be erected in the great old hall at Hampton Court ; where plays were intended to have been acted during the summer-season. But before the theatre could be finished, above half the month of September being elapsed, there were but seven plays acted before the Court returned to London. This throwing open a theatre in a royal palace, seemed to be reviving the old English hospitable grandeur." After noting that the King appeared most pleased with Shakspeare's Henry the Eighth, Cibber adds, " This calls to my memory an extravagant pleasantry of Sir Richard Steele, who being asked by a grave nobleman, after the play had been presented at Hampton Court, how the King liked it, replied, ' So terribly well, my Lord, that I was afraid I should have lost all my actors ! For I was not sure the King would not keep them to fill the posts at Court, that he saw them so fit for in the play.' . . . . Since that time, there has been but one play at Hampton Court, which was for the entertainment of the Duke of Lorraine (Oct. 2, 1731) ; and for which his present Majesty (George II.) was pleased to order us a hundred pounds." ‡

* Rape of the Lock, opening of Canto iii.
† Cibber's Apology, p. 451.
‡ Apology for the Life of Mr. Colley Cibber, Comedian, pp. 446—457.

Of Court life in George II.'s time there is a cabinet picture. perfect in its way, by his Majesty's Vice-Chamberlain and Lord Privy Seal.*

" I will not trouble you with any account of our occupations at Hampton Court. No mill-horse ever went in a more constant track, or a more unchanging circle ; so that by the assistance of an almanack for the day of the week, and a watch for the hour of the day, you may inform yourself fully, without any other intelligence but your memory, of every transaction within the verge of the Court. Walking, chaises, levees, and audiences fill the morning ; at night, the King plays at commerce or backgammon, and the Queen at quadrille, where poor Lady Charlotte runs her usual nightly gauntlet—the Queen pulling her hood, Mr. Schutz sputtering in her face, and the Princess Royal rapping her knuckles all at a time. . . . . The Duke of Grafton takes his nightly opiate of lottery, and sleeps as usual between the Princesses Amelia and Carolina ; Lord Grantham strolls from room to room (as Dryden says, 'like some discontented ghost that oft appears, and is forbid to speak,') and stirs himself about as people stir a fire, not with any design, but to make it burn brisker ; which his lordship constantly does to no purpose, and yet tries as constantly as if it had ever once succeeded. At last the King comes up, the pool finishes, and every one has their dismission." †

George II. was the last monarch who resided at Hampton Court, though it enjoyed a glimmer of royalty at the end of the century, when the Prince of Orange, driven from the Netherlands by the revolution, occupied for several years (1795—1813) the vacated palace of the English king. Since the palace ceased to be one of the royal residences. the private apartments have been appropriated as dwellings at the pleasure of the sovereign, chiefly for members of noble families, but sometimes for persons otherwise distinguished : thus Faraday, the eminent chemist, was granted a residence in 1858, which he occupied till his death in 1867. Dr. Johnson applied, April 11, 1776, to the Lord Chamberlain for a grant of apartments, thinking that " to a man who had had the honour of vindicating his Majesty's Government, a retreat in one of his houses

* Lord Hervey has treated the subject on a large canvas and with a fuller pencil in his ' Memoirs of the Reign of George the Second,' edited by Mr. Croker, 1848. Life at Hampton Court in the reigns of Anne and the first two Georges is abundantly illustrated in the Pope Correspondence, and in the Memoirs and Letters of Lord Hervey, Lady Sundon, Lady Suffolk, Horace Walpole, etc.

† Lord Hervey to Mrs. Clayton, July 31, 1733 ; Memoirs of Lady Sundon, vol. ii.. p. 231.

may not be improperly or unworthily allowed." This application seems to have been unknown to Boswell or to Croker—as why it was unsuccessful is to us.

For a long series of years the State Apartments and grounds were neglected and forlorn. Visitors were comparatively few, for even in summer few cared to pay the entrance fee in order to be hurried through the rooms by an ignorant guide. In November 1838, the State Apartments and the grounds were thrown open to the public without fee and without restriction ; and now every possible facility is afforded for seeing them, and studying their contents at leisure and in comfort. The largest number of visitors to Hampton Court since it was opened to the public was in the Exhibition years,—350,848 in 1851 ; 369,162 in 1862. In 1873 there were 217,589 visitors, and this is about the average. Nearly 30.000 persons passed through it on Whit Monday 1872.

Wolsey's palace consisted of 5 great courts surrounded by public and private rooms, and all the adjuncts of archi-episcopal dignity and enjoyment. For his palace Wolsey brought water of great purity from springs in Combe Wood, midway between Kingston and Wimbledon, Surrey, by leaden pipes under the Thames ; also from a branch of the Colne near Longford, by a canal over 11 miles long, still called the Cardinal's or the King's river. The buildings were probably incomplete when they passed into the king's hands ; and Henry spent large sums upon them, added considerably to their extent, and erected the present great hall and chapel. Little further alteration, probably, was made in the buildings till 1690, when William III., intending to make the palace his chief residence, commissioned Sir Christopher Wren to erect a new suite of State Apartments more in accordance with the taste of the day than the sombre rooms of the Tudor king. Wren demolished two of Wolsey's courts, and remodelled a third, and erected the long uniform southern and eastern fronts, towards the Thames and the gardens, in a semi-classic style, having no affinity to the older structure. Wren's building is. however, a good one of its kind. The elevations are imposing from their extent, and have much simple dignity of character. The garden front is about 330 ft. long, the river front somewhat less. The rooms, through which we shall pass, are stately and well-proportioned, though they have the inconvenience of being all rooms of passage. The Tudor palace is built throughout of a mellow red brick; Wren's additions are also of red brick, but of a lighter colour, with a larger use of stone in columns and dressings.

The best entrance to the palace is by the large gates at the foot of Hampton Bridge. You thus come to the oldest part of the building first; and having familiarized yourself with that, and with Henry's great hall, pass through the state rooms and study the pictures at your ease, and then enter the gardens from the centre of Wren's eastern façade.

Leaving the low line of cavalry barracks on the l., you obtain from the *Green*—the Outer Court of the original building—an excellent view of the W. front of Wolsey's palace, perhaps the finest and most striking example of Tudor palatial architecture left. Between the outer court and the west front was the Moat, crossed here by a bridge which led to the central gate-house. Moat and bridge have long disappeared, but the gate-house is still the approach to

The *Western* (or Entrance) *Court*, a fine quadrangle, 167 ft. by 161 ft., at once recalling the familiar quads. of Eton, Oxford, and Cambridge, but richer in treatment. Observe here and throughout the old buildings the fine chimney-shafts. Directly in front is the tall western gate-house, with its handsome oriel, turrets decorated with terra-cotta busts of the emperors Trajan and Hadrian, and over the gateway the arms and motto of Wolsey. Around the court are ranges of private apartments. The gateway leads to the *Middle* or *Clock Court*, so called from the curious old clock in the highest storey of the tower. On the N. side of this court is the great hall: on the S., where is now Wren's Ionic colonnade, were Wolsey's state rooms. The rooms on the E. are those occupied in 1795 by the Stadtholder. The terra-cotta busts of the Roman emperors around this and the Western court were presented to Cardinal Wolsey by Leo X., and have been attributed, we

know not on what authority, to Della Robbia. When these courts were restored a few years back, the busts were restored also, so that it would be useless to look to them now for evidences of Robbia's skill. Under the colonnade is the entrance to King William's State Apartments; but before visiting them it will be well to look at the hall, the entrance to which is by the stairs on the l. under the arch of the clock-tower.

The *Great Hall* was erected by Henry VIII., on the site of Wolsey's hall, which was demolished to make room for it. The building was commenced in 1531, and finished, except perhaps some ornamental details, in 1536. It is of noble proportions, being 106 ft. long, 40 ft. wide, and 60 ft. high. It was probably built on the lines of Wolsey's hall, and it is noteworthy that it is of nearly the same dimensions as his great hall at Oxford, though a still finer room.* Entering the hall from under the dark Minstrel's Gallery, the effect is very striking. High up along both sides of the noble room range wide Tudor windows filled with gaudy heraldic emblazonings; on the walls beneath them hang tapestries, faded indeed, but telling of antique splendour; at the far end is the broad dais, with on one side a tall oriel; horns, arms, and armour decorate the walls, and over all bends the grand old open hammer-beam roof, with its long rows of arches, mullions, bossed pendants, and carved corbels, rich in gilding and colour. Still finer, however, is the effect looking towards the gallery from the dais. The hall was restored when opened to the public some years back, and it may be thought has been somewhat over-decorated, but it will be remembered that Henry was, as his French visitors noted, fond of gilding richly the walls and roofs of his palaces, and traces of gilding and colour are said to have been found here sufficient to justify the artists in their endeavour to bring the hall back to its pristine condition. The glass in the several windows was painted by Mr. Willement. The great W. window of 7 lights, over the gallery, has in the centre a portrait of Henry, and in the several compartments his arms and devices, and

---

* The hall of Christ Church, Oxford, is 8 ft. longer, but of the same width, and 10 ft. lower.

those of his queens, and below those of his children, all fully emblazoned. The corresponding window at the E. gives the genealogy of the king, with the arms, badges, and devices of the houses of York and Lancaster. The fine oriel on the rt. of the dais is dedicated to Wolsey, whose arms and those of his several dioceses are duly represented. The windows at the sides of the hall (12 in number) contain alternately the badges and devices of the king, and the pedigrees of his wives. Altogether the windows furnish a tolerably complete heraldic study of the history of the Tudor king. The tapestry on the walls beneath the windows represents in 8 compartments the principal events in the life of Abraham. It is of arras, and pronounced of good workmanship, by those skilled in such matters. The designs, which have been assigned to B. Van Orley, are quaint, the drawing dry ; what the colour may have been the silk is too faded to tell. At the entrance of the hall is some more tapestry, of still earlier date, and even more faded ; whilst on the screen are the arms of Wolsey in three compartments, in tapestry, and on each side those of Henry VIII. It was in this hall that George I. had the theatric performances already spoken of—the first play, Hamlet, being acted on the 23rd of September, 1718.

Beyond the hall is the *Withdrawing Room*, or *Presence Chamber*, also a handsome, well-proportioned, and well-lighted room, about 62 ft. by 29½, and 29 ft. high, with, near its S. end, a semicircular oriel, filled with painted glass, the entire height of the room. The ceiling is flat, ribbed, and decorated with pendants, with the Tudor badges of the rose, portcullis, fleur-de-lis, etc. ; the royal arms impaled with those of Seymour in the centre, and the initials H. J. with the true lovers' knot, serving to indicate the date of the building. The carved oak mantelpiece is of later date than the room, and was brought here some years ago from Hampton Wick : the portrait of Wolsey in the centre is a modern copy. The walls are hung with faded tapestries : those on the N. end, Wolsey's own, represent "the three fatall ladies of Destenye," the others various mythological and allegorical subjects. Above them is a series of 7 cartoons in monochrome by *Carlo Cignani*.

The *Chapel*, of about the date of the Presence Chamber, as is shown by the arms of Henry impaled with those of Seymour, and the initials H. J. over the door, is not open to visitors, except at the Sunday morning service, but may be seen on application. It is small, but characteristic, and has a good groined roof, coloured and gilt on the restoration of the chapel a few years back, and made as splendid as when Hentzner visited it in Queen Elizabeth's day. Wren altered and repewed the chapel, and added an organ by Father Schmidt, with richly carved case by Grinling Gibbons.

The entrance to the *State Apartments* is under the colonnade at the S.E. corner of the Clock Court. They are all in the building erected by Wren for William III., and form two suites of rooms extending nearly the whole length of the river and garden fronts, and on two sides of the Fountain Court. The rooms vary greatly in size, according to the purposes for which they were designed, but generally they are good and characteristic specimens of the palatial architecture of the time, and will repay more close attention than is usually bestowed upon them : it is greatly to be regretted that in order to exhibit the pictures several of the larger rooms have been divided for about three-fourths of their height by screens, thereby entirely spoiling their well-planned proportions. The carvings generally were executed by Grinling Gibbons, or under his direction. Most of the rooms contain furniture or upholstery of the time of William III., Anne, or George I. ; but their chief attraction is the collection of pictures, about 1000 in number, contained in them. Of so large a collection it would be impossible even to name more than a few, were all excellent. But many of them have been removed from the other royal collections, whilst some of the best of those formerly here have been sent to Windsor Castle or Buckingham Palace, or, like the portraits of admirals, to Greenwich Hospital ; and the paintings now here form a very heterogeneous assemblage. Many are of great value ; but many are misnamed, or, in the case of the historical portraits, misappropriated. Considering the number of persons who visit these rooms annually, it would be a public service to distinguish in an official catalogue the pictures which possess an ascertained history, or are of undoubted authenticity. The collection, and especially the historical portraits, in which it is so remarkably rich, would then, if judiciously arranged, be of essential educational value.

Before ascending the *King's Staircase*, by which you reach the State Apartments, it will be well to halt at the foot of the stairs to let the eye, when accustomed to the light, rest for a moment on this prodigious illustration of the mural decoration of the close of the 17th cent. The staircase is one of the best examples left in this country of the "grand staircase" which was so important a feature in the palaces of the Louis XIV. era, with which this was intended to compete. The paintings by Verrio are an amazing confusion of mythology and chronology. Heathen gods and goddesses, Æneas and the 12 Cæsars, Julian the Apostate with Mercury as his secretary, William and Mary, and an endless array of Virtues and Attributes sprawl over the walls and ceilings, amid clouds, thrones, and rainbows, in inconceivable attitudes and wonderful attire. Walpole says that Verrio, from attachment to the fallen king, refused at first to paint for William, and when he condescended to serve him, painted his "great staircase as ill as if he had spoiled it out of principle." * But as far as we can judge (for it has been *restored*) this staircase is as well painted as any of his elsewhere, contains as many gods and goddesses, and has had quite as much labour, ultramarine, and gilding bestowed upon it.†

Guard Chamber, the first of the state rooms, is a noble hall, 67 ft. long, 37 wide, and 30 high. The upper part is decorated with trophies of arms, halberds, swords, muskets, etc., sufficient to arm 1000 men : below are portraits of English admirals, chiefly by *Bockman*, and scenes by *Rugendas* from Marlborough's campaigns in the Netherlands. No. 9, the Exterior of the Colosseum, wrongly attributed to *A. Canaletto*. 20. Queen Elizabeth's Porter, —a huge fellow 9 ft. 3 in. high, with a hand 17 in. long, cleverly painted though ill drawn,—*Zucchero*, is worth noting. *Obs.* the two iron gates removed for pre-

servation from the park about ten years ago. They were executed, under Wren's direction, by Huntington Shaw, of Nottingham, (who, as we have seen, lies in Hampton ch.-yard), and are among the choicest specimens of English wrought-iron work extant : some of his other gates were removed to the South Kensington Museum.

First Presence Chamber.—Observe the carvings, in this, as in succeeding rooms, by Grinling Gibbons ; the vista extending the whole length of this S. front of the building ; and the charming views from the window seats : and bear in mind that you cannot return the way you came, but must go through the whole suite. In this room are the HAMPTON COURT BEAUTIES, the famous series of portraits of the ladies of the court of William and Mary, painted for the queen by Sir Godfrey Kneller, in imitation of, or rivalry with, the Beauties of the Court of Charles II. by Sir Peter Lely. King Charles's Beauties were deposited in Windsor Castle, and thence known as the Windsor Beauties ; but they are now at Hampton Court. The Hampton Court Beauties have been engraved by Faber. Eight of them are in this room, whole-lengths, nicely painted, though not with so light a hand as Lely's. They include the Duchesses of St. Albans and Grafton, the Countesses of Essex, Peterborough, Dorset, and Ranelagh, Lady Middleton, and the charming Miss Pitt : but as beauties are meant to be seen, when the pictures are re-arranged, these should be brought nearer the eye.

"As you talk of our beauties, I shall tell you a new story of the Gunnings. They went the other day to see Hampton Court ; as they were going into the Beauty-room, another company arrived ; the housekeeper said, 'This way, ladies ; here are the Beauties.' The Gunnings flew into a passion, and asked her what she meant ; that they came to see the palace, not to be showed as a sight themselves." *

"Reader, perhaps thou hast seen the statue of Venus de' Medici ; perhaps too thou hast seen the Gallery of Beauties at Hampton Court. Yet it is possible thou may'st have seen all these without being able to form an exact idea of Sophia Western ; for she did not exactly resemble any of them : she was most like the picture of Lady Ranelagh." (No. 37.) †

---

* Anecdotes, vol. iii., p. 67.
† Verrio died at Hampton Court in 1707, a pensioner on the bounty of Queen Anne.

* H. Walpole to Sir Horace Mann, Aug. 31, 1751 ; Letters, vol ii., p. 265.
† Fielding, Tom Jones, B. iv., ch. 2.

William III. is here in a large allegorical picture (No. 29) by *Kneller ;* and in two historically curious representations —Embarking from Holland (38), and Landing at Brixham (51). With these last compare an equally curious picture of Charles II. taking leave of the Dutch Court at his Restoration (62)—bought with the two preceding pictures by the Commissioners of Woods and Forests in 1840. The pictures attributed to Leonardo da Vinci, Giorgione, Caravaggio, and other great Italian masters, may be passed by, but the fine portrait of James, 1st Marquis of Hamilton, by *Mytens* (44), in the Grinling Gibbons frame over the fireplace, should by no means be overlooked; nor should the loosely-draped Margaret Lemon by *Vandyck* (47); the whole-length in armour of Peter the Great (57) by *Kneller*, painted in 1698, the year of his visit to England : the background is by W. Vandevelde; or the badly lighted but fine whole-length, by *Kneller* (65), of Mary of Modena.

Second Presence Chamber.—In this room are several good pictures, but they have been cleaned, over-varnished, and are seen with difficulty. Queen Esther before Ahasuerus, *Tintoretto*, good and vigorously painted. 70. An Italian Lady, in a green robe, good, but not by *Sebastian del Piombo*. 72. A Sculptor, *Bassano*, an admirable portrait. 73. Diana and Actæon, certainly not by *Giorgione;* if Venetian at all, it is by a much later painter. 85. Charles I. on horseback, *Vandyck :* the well-known portrait of Charles in armour under an arch, his white horse led by his equerry, the Duc D'Epernon, of which there are several repetitions, the best being that at Windsor Castle: this is probably a copy by Vandyck's assistants for presentation. 82 and 90. Philip IV. of Spain, nad his Queen, the sister of Henrietta Maria, *Velasquez ;* unusually bright in colour, but no doubt genuine. 91. A Knight of Malta, *Tintoretto ;* a capital head, the rest blackened ; cross on breast and l. arm. 97. Holy Family, *Dosso Dossi ;* of no great value, but noteworthy as a fair example of the artist. 98. Christian IV. of Denmark, *Vansomer ;* one of several replicas. 102. An Italian Knight, *Pordenone ;* vigorous and well-coloured. 104. Family of Pordenone, the painter, his

fat wife and 8 children : a characteristic group.

Audience Chamber.—106. Triptych, newly mounted and placed on a stand in centre of the room : central compartment, the Crucifixion ; on l. wing, Christ bearing the Cross ; on rt., the Resurrection ; back of l. wing, the Ecce Homo ; of rt., the Virgin and St. John. A work of strongly marked early German character ; powerful in colour, fine in effect, and elaborately finished, but whether rightly attributed to *Lucas Van Leyden* is open to question. Two or three portraits ascribed to *Titian* deserve notice as manly well-painted heads,—113, the best, is, however, not Ignatius Loyola ; 116, called Titian's, is a remarkably fine head. 115. Holy Family, with St. Roch, *Jacopo Palma*, genuine, and excellent in its conventional way. The same may be said of 118, Virgin and Child, with Donors, *Paris Bordone*, though a weaker picture. 110, Mary Magdalen Anointing the Saviour's Feet ; 121, Christ Healing the Sick ; and 131, The Woman taken in Adultery, are large decorative works in the manner of P. Veronese, worthy of attention as unusually good examples of the pencil of *Sebastian Ricci*. 128. The Queen of Bohemia, daughter of James I., *Honthorst*, hangs over the fireplace, an excellent picture : *obs.* the frame, carved, but not gilt, and the finely carved wreaths on the sides and above the frame. 136. *G. Bassano*, a capital portrait. 148. Andrea Ordini, *Lorenzo Lotto*, another good portrait of a sculptor. 149. Alessandro de' Medici, *Titian—not* de' Medici, it has been engraved as Boccaccio. The scriptural subjects in this room, attributed to Titian, are certainly not by him.

King's Drawing-room.—151. David with the Head of Goliath, *D. Feti*, only noteworthy as a good example of a master whose works are not common in our galleries. 154. The Expulsion of Heresy, a soundly painted picture, but wrongly ascribed to *P. Veronese*. 155. Duke of Richmond and Lenox, *Vansomer*, wh.-l., in red dress, with garter, and holding the white staff of Lord Steward of the Household : *obs.* the carved wreaths (by Gibbons) round the frame. In this room are 7 paintings ascribed, and probably correctly, to *Giacomo Bassano ;* the most characteristic is 157 the Apotheosis of a Saint, a bright and well-coloured though otherwise uninteresting work. 164. Venus, *Titian*, a replica, or very early copy, of the well-known painting with a servant taking clothes from a trunk in the background. Other Titians and Giorgiones are in this room of more than doubtful authenticity, and a Tintoretto (171) and P. Veronese (165, 178), which may have proceeded from the schools, but certainly not from the pencils, of those masters. *Obs.* before leaving this room the fine views of the grounds from the windows, and the pretty effect of the terrace, lawns, and flower-beds.

King William III.'s Bedroom.—A handsome room, with some of Gibbons' charming carvings over the fireplace; one of Verrio's very best ceilings; and some quaint old furniture, needlework, clock, and crockery; and, on the walls, the famous BEAUTIES OF THE COURT OF CHARLES II., painted by Sir Peter Lely, and brought hither from Windsor.

"There was in London a celebrated portrait painter, called Lely, who had greatly improved himself by studying the famous Vandyck's pictures. . . . The Duchess of York being desirous of having the portraits of the handsomest persons at Court, Lely painted them, and employed all his skill in the performance; nor could he ever exert himself upon more beautiful subjects. Each picture appeared a master-piece, and that of Miss Hamilton [afterwards Countess de Grammont, No. 207] appeared the highest finished : Lely himself acknowledged that he had drawn it with a peculiar pleasure. The Duke of York took a delight in looking at it, and began again to ogle the original." *

Grammont's Memoirs are the best commentaries on these sleepy-eyed voluptuous nymphs, their " bed-gowns fastened with a single-pin," and nothing loath to discover their charms. But they might be better displayed. Here they are at least half hidden ; perhaps out of pity to the less frail, and it must be confessed less lovely, Beauties of Hampton Court. Kneller was no match for Lely in this line.

King's Dressing-room.—Notice Verrio's Mars and Venus on the ceiling. 211. The Continence of Scipio, *S. Ricci*, one of his large, showy, clever, conventional furniture pictures, worth looking at as marking the fashion of a day gone by. 212. Robbers in a Cave, *S. Rosa*.

King's Writing Closet.—227, a Sybil,

* Count de Grammont, Memoirs of the Court of Charles the Second, chap. ix.

and 229, Joseph and Potiphar's Wife, by *Orazio Gentileschi*, and 226, *Artemisia Gentileschi*, portrait of Herself, deserve notice as the work of a painter and his daughter much patronized by Charles I., his queen. and nobility, and whose names often occur in the letters and memoirs of the time. Charles invited Gentileschi to England; allowed him £500 for outfit and expenses of his journey ; furnished him a house "from top to toe" at a cost of over £4000, and gave him a pension of £100 a year : altogether an extraordinary amount in those days.* The Potiphar's Wife was one of the pictures he painted for the King. He was to have decorated Greenwich Palace, but political troubles intervened. Artemisia Gentileschi attained popularity here as a portrait painter, and probably many portraits in great English houses attributed to more eminent names are from her pencil. 237. Moses Striking the Rock, *Salvator Rosa*, deserves a better light. The Landscape, 239, attributed to him, has been terribly scrubbed. So palpable a misappropriation as 241, Daughter of Herodias with the Head of John the Baptist, to L. da Vinci, ought not to be persisted in.

Queen Mary's Closet.—251. A Holy Family, is a favourable example of *Giulio Romano's* ordinary manner. A Madonna (249) by *Bronzino*, and one (262) by *P. F. Mola*, claim a passing glance.

Queen's Gallery, a fine room. 80 ft. long and 25 wide, overlooking the Home Park, and affording quite a different view from the rooms we have passed, has been hung with the series of 7 copies in tapestry from Le Brun's Life of Alexander which were brought to light from their temporary concealment in 1865. They are sadly faded, but interesting to amateurs of needlework.

Queen's Bedroom.—Fitted with Queen Anne's state bed and furniture ; the ceiling painted by *Sir James Thornhill*. Over the doors are full-length portraits of James I. and his Queen by *Vansomer*. James I. (308) in a black dress, by a table, on which are the crown and sceptre ; Anne of Denmark, 273, in a hunting dress, with hat and red feather, leading two dogs ; interesting as illustrating the cos-

* Sainsbury, Original Papers relating to Rubens.

tume of the day. 275. St. Francis with the Infant Saviour, *Guido*. Of the Nursing of Jupiter, 291, Jupiter and Juno, 302, and half a dozen others in this room, ascribed to Giulio Romano, it may safely be said with Waagen,[*] "they belong to him only by invention:" they are however of about his time, and probably proceeded from his school. 301. Judith with the Head of Holofernes, *Guido*. 306. Portrait of a Lady, *Parmegiano;* notice the curious and elaborate dress and turban. 307. The Baptism of our Lord, *Francia*, a large and no doubt genuine picture; the Saviour, nearly life-size, stands in a shallow stream, the figure very carefully studied, and altogether a valuable example of the master.

Queen's Drawing-room.—The central room of the garden front: *obs.* the ceiling, painted by *Verrio*, and the fine view from the central window of the grounds, and three spreading fan-like avenues. This room contains pictures painted by *Benjamin West* for George III., 17 in all, and some of large size. They include portraits of George III. and his family, and subjects from the Scriptures, and classical and modern history. Those best worth examining are (311) the Death of Bayard, and (320) the Death of General Wolfe, a duplicate of the picture in the Grosvenor Gallery, familiar to all by the engravings.

Queen's Audience Chamber.—In this room are several contemporary historical representations, absurdly attributed to Holbein, of little artistic value, but extremely interesting to the student of English history and antiquities. 331. The Meeting of Henry VIII. and the Emperor Maximilian, very curious for the costumes; 337, Henry VIII. Embarking at Dover, still more curious for the shipping; 342, Henry VIII. and Francis I. at the Field of the Cloth of Gold, in which the splendid array of the two kings is set forth with wonderful detail; and, 339. The Battle of the Spurs. 340. Henry VIII. and Family, *Holbein*, a very important work. The king is seated on his throne, under a rich canopy; on his l. the queen, on his rt. Prince Edward; beyond these are the Princesses Mary and Elizabeth. Will Somers, the king's jester, with a

monkey on his shoulder, is on the extreme rt.; Somers' wife at an open door on the extreme l. The king and queen are in golden robes; the background is an elaborate Renaissance colonnade, also richly gilt. The queen is described on the frame and in the catalogue as Jane Seymour, but Jane Seymour died 12 days after the birth of her son, who is represented as a boy 6 or 8 years old; there can be no doubt it is Catherine Parr who is represented, as Mr. Scharf pointed out long ago. Among the portraits, *obs.* 345, Henry Howard, Earl of Surrey, *Holbein*, full-length, in red dress, legs apart; a duplicate of the celebrated portrait. 346. Anne of Denmark, full-length, in hunting costume, with 5 dogs, black servant holding horse, Theobalds in background: signed and dated 1617, *Vansomer*. 349. Queen Elizabeth in fanciful straight-down dress, with scroll of more fanciful verses, supposed to be her own inditing, at her feet, *Lucas de Heere*.

Public Dining-room, contains some good modern portraits. By *Gainsborough* are,—352, Fisher, the composer, leaning on a piano; and 353, Col. St. Leger: two very characteristic examples; 367, Bp. Hurd, and one or two more. 363. Gentz, the German statesman and writer, *Sir Thos. Lawrence*. Also two earlier portraits, which should not be overlooked. 365, *Robert Walker*, by himself; and, 376, The Painter and his Wife, *Dobson*.

Prince of Wales's Presence Chamber, contains (377) Count Gondomar, *Mytens*, and some other interesting portraits and subject pieces: but the chief picture is (385) Adam and Eve, *Van Grossaert*, called *Mabuse*, painted after his return from Italy, and very carefully finished. It belonged to Charles I., and the gallery in which it hung at Whitehall was called from it the Adam and Eve Gallery.

Prince of Wales's Drawing-room, also contains several good portraits. *Obs.* (413) Louis XVI. of France, *Greuze*, in original presentation frame; and, by the same artist, (429) Madame Pompadour, at tambour work, half-length, in an oval frame.

The next rooms, the *Prince of Wales's Bedroom*, the so-called *Queen's Private Chapel, Private Dining Room, Queen's Chamber, King's Dressing Room, George the Second's Chamber, Dressing Room,*

---

[*] Art Treasures in Great Britain, vol. ii., p. 358.

and *Private Chamber*, and two or three closets, all contain pictures, among which are some bearing great names, a few historical portraits, and some good fruit and flower pieces, but the visitor will not care to linger over them.

The *South Gallery*, running along the S. side of the Fountain Court, is a handsome room, 117 ft. long and 23½ ft. wide, built by Wren for the reception of Raphael's Cartoons, now removed to South Kensington, but which will probably find their ultimate destination in the enlarged National Gallery. The panels constructed for the cartoons are now filled with large paintings, and the room, greatly to the injury of its proportions, has been divided by tall screens, on which are hung the smaller pictures. The gallery contains in all 214 pictures, a large number being historical portraits, and many of great value and interest. We can note but a few, by way of sample. 559. Margaret Douglas, Countess of Lennox, in a black furred robe ; engraved by the Grainger Society : this picture is attributed to *Holbein*, but it is dated 1572, and Holbein died in 1543 ; it could not, therefore, be painted by him. 560. Mary Queen of Scots, *Zucchero*, full-l., in a black dress, holding a rosary : doubtful. 563. Henry VIII. at the age of 35, half-length, in rich slashed doublet and jewelled shirt ; *not* by Holbein, but by *Fr. Clouet (Janet)*, and so described in Catalogue of Charles I.'s pictures. 573. Sir George Carew, to waist, l. hand in vest, gloves in rt. hand ; a good and genuine portrait, but not by Holbein, as it is dated 1565. 591. Lady Vaux, *Holbein*, holding a clove-pink in rt. hand ; delicately painted, and probably authentic. 594, Erasmus reading ; 597, Erasmus with hands on book, engraved in Nat. Portrait Gallery ; both ascribed to *Holbein*, but probably early and very good copies. 595. "Children of Henry VII.," *Mabuse*, should be, as Mr. Scharf has shown, children of the King of Denmark. 598. Francis I., *Holbein*. 601. Henry VIII. and Jane Seymour, Henry VII. and his Queen in the background ; a small but very precious copy by *Remée van Leemput*, made in 1667 for Charles II., from the fresco painted by Holbein in 1537, on the side of a room in Whitehall, which was destroyed with that building by fire in 1697. 616. Queen Elizabeth,

bust, *Zucchero*. 619. Queen Elizabeth, half-length, holding George in rt. hand. 635. Queen Elizabeth, *Lucas de Heere ;* the noted allegorical portrait in which Juno, Minerva, and Venus are retiring in utter amazement and confusion at sight of the wit, wisdom, and beauty of "the comeliest queen that ever was," as Gascoigne calls her in his Woodstock verses. 636. The Princess Mary, *Holbein*. 631. Mary Queen of Scots, *Fr. Clouet ;* small, in close white cap, as widow, the Reine blanche, of Francis II. ; by no means handsome, but the pallor is due to the fading of the carnations. 632. Francis II., small, *Fr. . Clouet.* 639. The Earl of Darnley and his brother Charles Stuart, *Lucas de Heere ;* Darnley aged 17, his brother 6 ; inscribed and dated 1563. 645. The King and Queen of Bohemia dining in public, *Van Bassen :* a curious contemporary illustration of a custom often referred to by D'Ewes, Evelyn, and other memoir writers. 707. Villiers Duke of Buckingham, *C. Jansen ;* half-length of the duke assassinated by Felton. 710. *Raphael :* a genuine portrait, but not of Raphael. 711. Sir Theodore Mayerne, *Rubens :* genuine, but much repaired. 742. Small equestrian portrait of Louis XIV., *Van der Meulin.* 759. James Stuart, the Old Pretender, *B. Luti.* 763, 764. James I. and his Queen, *Vansomer.* 765. Elizabeth, Queen of Bohemia, daughter of James I., *Derick.*

Passing through the Anteroom, we reach the long gallery on the W. side of the Fountain Court, of old known as the Admiral's Gallery, now called the *Mantegna Gallery*, from its containing the drawings of the Triumph of Julius Cæsar by *Andrea Mantegna*. These are a series of nine grand designs, each 9 ft. square, executed in tempera on twilled linen, for Ludovico Gonzaga, Duke of Mantua, for a frieze in the palace of St. Sebastian, and purchased of a later Duke by Charles I.[*] After the death of Charles I. they were sold for £1000 ; but on the Restoration were repurchased by Charles II., and de-

---

[*] The Mantegna drawings were not purchased as part of the Mantua collection, as usually stated, but formed a supplementary purchase, with the marbles, for £10,500 : the agent declaring the Triumph to be "a thing rare and unique, and its value beyond estimation." Daniel Nys to Secretary Lord Dorchester, Feb. 2, 1629, in Sainsbury's Rubens Papers, p. 328.

posited in Hampton Court. They occupy nearly the whole length of the gallery : are much dilapidated, have been badly repainted, and are ill seen from hanging opposite the windows, and being covered with glass. However, they are worth all the pains required to study them. They are wonderfully designed, full of invention, fertility of resource, and artistic power. The figures are nobly conceived, and admirably drawn ; and the whole has more of the antique feeling and spirit than perhaps any similar work of even that brilliant period of the Renaissance when Mantegna painted. The colouring has been too much tampered with to judge of its original effect ; but no doubt it was light as now in key, but brighter and truer. In this room is a curious portrait (798) of Sir Jeffry Hudson, the famous dwarf, painted, as we know from King Charles I.'s catalogue, "by Dan Mytens, and the landskip by Cornelius Johnson" (C. Jansen), who received £40 for their labours.

Queen's Guard Chamber, a handsome room about 60 ft. by 30, but now, unhappily, broken up and disfigured by partitions. It contains portraits of Locke (824) and Newton (846) by *Kneller;* 830. The Duke of Gloucester, *Kneller;* 839. Pope Benedict XIV., *Batoni;* 843, Robert Boyle, *Kersboom :* 845, George Prince of Denmark, *Dahl;* 852, *Sir P. Lely*, by himself; and several landscapes and figure-pieces of little account.

The Anteroom and the *Queen's Presence Chamber*, the latter a fine room, disfigured by two tall partitions, contain many naval pieces, British victories, by Vandevelde and Paton ; naval reviews by Serres ; storms, naval dockyards, etc. ; also some interesting views of Greenwich Hospital, St. James's Park, etc., painted in the last century, and a few miscellaneous pieces.

But by this time the visitor will be glad to escape from pictures and refresh his wearied senses in the ever-verdant grounds. These charming gardens owe their general form to Charles II., whose gardener, Rose, laid them out under the king's inspection. The fine yews and laurels are of this date. They were extended and remodelled by William III., under whose personal direction his gardeners, London and Wise, dug the canals, planted the lime avenues, arranged the topiary work, and formed

the terraces and broad gravel walks. Queen Mary took no less interest in the place than her husband, lived in a garden-house whilst Wren was altering the palace, and formed her choice flower-gardens and greenhouses for rare exotics, under the supervision of Dr. Leonard Plunked, a noted botanist whom she engaged as her superintendant.[*]

The Grounds have been altered, and the trees allowed to take their natural shapes, of late years ; but much of the original formal trimness is retained, with great benefit to the character and charm of the place. The canal with its bordering avenues of limes. three-quarters of a mile long, is one of William's devices. Another is the oval basin with its fountain and gold fish. The two fronts of Wren's state apartments are seen to great advantage from the oval basin, and so too, in the opposite direction, are the three branching avenues of which Hampton Court is so proud. The river terrace is another fine feature. The Private Garden, a dainty old-fashioned flower garden of the rarest beauty, and admirably kept, may be seen on application to the gardener, who expects a small fee. The *Vine* is also to be seen for a trifling payment. It is in a lean-to house at the S. end of the palace, 90 ft. long. The vine, a black Hamburgh, was planted in 1769, has a stem 38 in. in circumference, the leading branch is 110 ft. long, and it bears on an average 1500 bunches : in 1874 there were 1750. The *Royal Tennis Court*, N. of the garden front, is reputed one of the best in the country, but it is not open to the public. A doorway a little beyond it leads to the *Wilderness*, a pleasant shady retreat of about 11 acres, with winding walks amidst groves of good-sized trees. Nearer the Lion Gate is the *Maze*, the most popular spot in the grounds with holiday visitors and children. The Lion Gate, the northern entrance to the palace grounds, is directly

---

[*] P. Rigaud's large plate, 1756, 'The Royal Palace of Hampton Court,' bound up in vol. v., No. 33, of the Illustrated Clarendon in the Print Room, British Museum, and a 'Perspective View of the Royal Palace and Gardens at H. Court,' of about the same date (No. 31 of the Illustrated Clarendon), show the gardens in all their prim formality—beds perfectly straight, shrubs cut into obelisks, etc.

opposite to the gates of Bushey Park, and the famous chesnut avenues.

Hampton Court Park comprises 576 acres, and contains many fine oaks and elms ; cork-trees flourish there, and there are some large Lombardy poplars. Bushey Park contains about 994 acres. The two form in effect a single domain, divided only by the public road.

Whilst Hampton Court was a royal abode, there was a courtly village adjacent to the palace. Wren, among a crowd of courtiers, had a dwelling in it, and several of the stately old houses may yet be seen about the Green.

"In the Survey of 1653 mention is made of a piece of pasture ground near the river, called *The Toying Place*, the site, probably, of a well-known inn, near the bridge, now called the Toy." * This inn had attained sufficient consequence in the last half of the 17th century to issue its trade tokens ; and it continued to be a popular resort for Londoners to the close of its existence. It was taken down in 1857 to make way for private houses.

HAMPTON WICK, MIDDX., on the
Thames, opposite Kingston-upon-Thames, with which it is united by a bridge ; 12 m. from London by road, and 14¼ m. by the Loop line of the L. and S.W. Rly.; and 2½ m. E. of Hampton. Pop. 2207. Inns : *White Hart ; Old King's Head.*

The vill. is pleasantly situated, lying close to the Thames, and Hampton Court and Bushey Parks ; and there are about it many good villas. *Bushey House* was the seat of the Duc de Nemours. Hampton Wick was created an eccl. dist. in 1831. The *Church*, St. John the Baptist, Church Grove was erected in 1829-30, from the designs of Mr. Lapidge, the architect of Kingston bridge. It is of Suffolk brick and Bath stone ; Dec., of bald character ; has nave, narrow aisles, and short spire. The E. window is filled with painted glass. Timothy Bennet, who secured the public way through Bushey Park, was an inhabitant of Hampton Wick. (*See* BUSHEY.) Steele dates the dedication (to Charles Lord Halifax) of the 4th vol. of the Tatler, "From the Hovel at Hampton Wick, April 7, 1711;" and in it says, "I could not but indulge a certain vanity in dating

from this little covert, where I have frequently had the honour of your Lordship's company, and received from you many obligations. The elegant solitude of this place, and the greatest pleasures of it, I owe to its being so near those beautiful manors wherein you sometimes reside." The Earl of Halifax was Chief Steward of the Honour and Manor of Hampton Court, and built the Lodge, Bushey Park, for his residence.

HANWELL, MIDDX. (Dom. *Hanewelle*), on the little river Brent, and the Uxbridge Road, 8 m. W. from Hyde Park Corner, 7½ m. from Paddington by the Gt. W. Rly., which has a stat. here : pop. 3766, of whom 1319 were in the Central London District School. Inns : *King's Arms ; Duke's Head ; Old Hat*, on road to Ealing,—garden and bowling-green.

Hanwell manor was given to Westminster Abbey by King Edgar, and confirmed by the Confessor.* It now belongs to the see of London. The neighbourhood is green and pleasant, gently undulating, mostly pasture land, with the Brent, a thin stream, winding through it. By the ch. the Brent has scooped out a deep broad hollow, across which the Gt. W. Rly. is carried by the Wharncliffe Viaduct, a much-admired brick structure of 8 principal arches, nearly 700 ft. long and 70 ft. high: a similar viaduct is in course of construction alongside it.

The *Church*, St. Mary, stands on high ground N. of the Uxbridge Road, with lawn-like fields sloping down to the Brent, here thick with rushes and water-lilies. It occupies the place of a mean brick ch. built in 1782, and is a handsome building of black flints and brick with stone dressings, erected from the designs of Messrs. Scott and Moffat, in 1841 ; it is E.E. in style, and consists of nave with aisles and clerestorey, chancel, and tower and spire at the W. end. Jonas Hanway, the founder of the Marine Society and the Magdalen Hospital, and one of the earliest promoters of Sunday-schools, was buried in the ch.-yard, September 13, 1786.

On the l. of the Uxbridge Road, nearly opposite the ch., but in Norwood par., is the *County Lunatic Asylum*, generally

---

* Lysons, Environs, vol. iii., p. 75.

* Kemble, Cod. Dip. Ævi Saxonici, No. 824, vol. iv., p. 177.

known as Hanwell Asylum, an immense structure, built in 1831, but since much altered and enlarged. The average number of inmates is about 1750, of whom nearly 1100 are females. Under the management of Dr. Conolly the asylum acquired great celebrity, on account of his having introduced and successfully carried out for a long series of years the system of entire " freedom from restraint on the part of the patients, ample occupation, amusement, and absence of seclusion ; with constant kindness of manner and sleepless vigilance on the part of the attendants, and unceasing watchfulness by the superiors:"* a system now happily established in all our larger asylums. In extent, appliances, and general character the Hanwell Asylum is very similar to that described under COLNEY HATCH, p. 115.

In Cuckoo Lane, N. of the ch. (take the turning rt. of the ch., skirting Hanwell Park), is Cuckoo Farm, the *Central London District Schools*, an extensive range of brick buildings erected in 1858, where about 1250 children from the City of London Union and St. Saviour's Union are trained : the boys cultivate the farm and learn common trades ; the girls are prepared for service. In the Uxbridge Road is the *Roman Catholic Convalescent Home*, erected in 1869 by the Baroness Weld, from the designs of Mr. F. Welby Pugin. By it is the R. C. ch. of Our Lady and St. Joseph. Here too is the Kensington Cemetery.

There are several good seats in Hanwell. The principal are—*Hanwell Park*, (B. Sharpe, Esq.), a charmingly situated and well-wooded property on the high ground E. of the ch. ; *The Grove* (Mrs. Buchan) ; and *The Spring* (The Rt. Hon. Sir A. Young Spearman, Bart.)

HANWORTH, MIDDX. (Dom.
Hanexorde), an agric. vill., and the site of a royal hunting seat, 3 m. S.W. from Hounslow, 1¼ m. N.E. from the Sunbury Stat. on the Thames Valley line, and 1½ m. S. of the Feltham Stat. on the Windsor line of the L. and S.W. Rly.; pop. 867. Inn, the *Swan*, a good country house.

The manor belonged in the 13th cent. to the Hamdens ; passed, 1294, to Henry Dayrell, in whose family it remained till 1377, when it was conveyed to Thomas Chamberlayne, by him the following year to Thomas Godlak ; afterwards passed successively to the Rothwells and Crosbys, and in 1519 had become the property of the Crown. Henry VIII. had a "place and park," apparently a hunting seat, here, in which he took great pleasure ; and to it Montmorenci, the French ambassador, and his suite were sent by the king's desire, " there to hunt and spend the day until night,"* whilst the great banquet, described under HAMPTON COURT, was preparing. Later, Henry settled Hanworth upon Catherine Parr, who after the King's death resided here with her second husband, the Lord Admiral, Sir Thos. Seymour. In 1548 the Princess (afterwards Queen) Elizabeth stayed some time at Hanworth, and here, according to the "confession" of Catherine Ashley, her waiting woman, occurred some of the horse-play which was made one of the articles of accusation in the impeachment of the Lord Admiral. "At Hanworth, in the garden, he [Seymour] wrated with her, and cut her gown into an hundred pieces, being black clothes." On another occasion, " This examinate lay with her Grace ; and there they tytled my Lady Elizabeth in the bed, the Queen and my Lord Admiral."† Elizabeth was at this time in her 15th year.

In 1558 the manor was granted for her life to Anne Duchess of Somerset, the widow of the Protector, and mother of the Earl of Hertford. In 1578 the Duchess entertained Elizabeth at Hanworth, when the Queen, at the request of the Countess of Hertford, sat to Cornelius Ketel for her portrait.‡ In 1594 Hanworth was leased for 80 years to William Killigrew. In Sept. 1600, Elizabeth again visited Hanworth, dined there, and hunted in the park. § William Killigrew, the friend and servant of Charles I. and II., and author of some dramatic pieces, wa

---

* English Cyc. : Biography, art. Conolly ; Sir James Clark, Bart., A Memoir of John Conolly, M.D., 1869.

---

* Cavendish, Life of Wolsey.
† Nichols, Progresses of Queen Elizabeth, vol. iii., p. 514.
‡ Walpole, Anecdotes, vol. i., p. 235.
§ Nichols ; Lysons.

born at Hanworth Park in 1605. His more celebrated, though less respectable, brother, Thomas Killigrew, was also, according to the biographies, born at Hanworth; but, as Lysons noted long ago, his baptism is not recorded in the register, and in a copy of Diodati's Bible, sold in Dean Wellesley's library, 1866, among several entries on the back of the title-page in Thomas Killigrew's handwriting, is one stating that he was "born at Lothbury, London, on February the 7th, 1611." In 1627 Hanworth became the property of Sir Francis Cottington, who in the following year was created Baron Cottington of Hanworth. Lord Cottington made many alterations in the place, much to his own satisfaction.

"There is a certain large room made under the new building with a fountain in it, and other rare devices, and the open gallery is all painted by the hand of a second Titian. Dainty walks are made abroad, insomuch that the old porter with the long beard is like to have a good revenue by admitting strangers that will come to see these rarities. . . . My wife is the principal contriver of all this machine, who with her clothes tucked up, and a staff in her hand, marches from place to place like an Amazon commanding an army."*

In August 1635 Lord Cottington entertained the Queen, Henrietta Maria, and her court at Hanworth. Lord Cottington was greatly trusted by Charles I., on whose fall Hanworth was confiscated, and given to President Bradshaw. On the Restoration, Lord Cottington's cousin and heir recovered Hanworth, but sold it in 1670 to Sir Thomas Chamber, whose granddaughter, Mary, carried it by marriage to Lord Vere Beauclerk, who was created (1750) Baron Vere of Hanworth, and left the manor to his son Aubrey, who in 1786 became Duke of St. Albans.

"The Duke of St. Albans has cut down all the brave old trees at Hanworth, and consequently reduced his park to what it issued from—Hounslow Heath: nay he has hired a meadow next to mine, for the benefit of embarkation; and there lie all the good old corpses of oaks, ashes, and chesnuts directly before your windows, and blocking up one of my views of the river!"†

Hanworth House was destroyed by fire March 26, 1797. It had been so much altered that little of interest remained. Its contents were equally unimportant.

* Lord Cottington to Earl of Strafford, 1629: Strafford Papers, vol. i., p. 51.
† Horace Walpole to the Miss Berrys, June 8, 1791; Letters, ix., p. 324.

The moat and a few vestiges of the house may be seen immediately W. of Hanworth ch. [Turn off from the village on l. through the park gate at the end of the short lane by the school-house, take the lower path across a little foot-bridge, and you will see the ch. before you.] The grounds, now called Queen Elizabeth's Gardens, retain much of their old-world character, contain old yews, pines, and cedars, ponds, waterfall, etc., but the property was (June 1875) announced for sale, and may become the prey of the builder. The present *Hanworth House* stands on somewhat higher ground than the old house, and nearly ½ m. N.E. of it. It is a well-built commonplace mansion, with colonnade, and tall clock-tower, from which a wide prospect is obtained, with Windsor Castle and the Grand Stand, Epsom, as landmarks. The park (of 108 acres) still contains much fine timber, chiefly oak and elm, and is intersected by the King's River, cut by Wolsey for the supply of Hampton Court.

Hanworth *Church*, St. George, as we have said, stands in the park, immediately E. of the old mansion. It was built in 1865, from the designs of Mr. S. S. Teulon, on the site of the former par. ch.; is of stone in irregular courses, early Dec. in style, and comprises nave, semicircular apsidal chancel, with pinnacled buttresses, a square tower with tall octagonal stone spire on the N.W., and stone porch on S.W. *Obs.* large hollow yew S.W. of ch.

A portion of the extensive gunpowder works of Messrs. Curtis are situated at Hanworth on the Isleworth river. A terrible explosion occurred at the Hanworth Mills in June 1869.

HAREFIELD, MIDDX., on the Colne, about 4 m. N. of Uxbridge, and 21 m. from London; pop. 1579. Inns: *Breakspear Arms*; *Vernon Arms*. Harefield occupies the N.W. angle of Middx., and is bounded N. by Rickmansworth, Herts, W. by Denham, Bucks, from which it is separated by the River Colne, which, with the Grand Junction Canal nearly parallel to it, runs along the W. side of the parish.

Harefield is a place rich in associations, and has about it much quiet sylvan beauty. It lies in a valley, with on the one hand uplands abounding in elms and oaks and lordly houses, on the other the little river flowing gently amid broad willow-fringed meadows. The village stretches for some way along the road; has many poor and some good cottages, and the usual shops; lime and brick works; by the river a paper mill; by the canal coal and timber wharfs. The ch. stands on one side of the vill., in the grounds of Harefield Place; in the street are a rather showy Wesleyan Chapel and a Working Men's Club and Reading Room, both Gothic, and both built at the cost of Mr. R. Barnes of Manchester. Altogether a flourishing and comfortable looking country village.

The manor (Dom. *Herefelle*) belonged to the Countess Goda in Edward the Confessor's time; at the Domesday Survey it was held by Richard, son of Gilbert Earl of Briou. At this time there were two mills, meadow for a plough, pasture for the vill. cattle, pannage for 1200 hogs, and 4 fish-ponds furnished 1000 eels. The inhabitants were a priest, 8 bordarii, 3 cottagers, 10 villans, and 3 bondsmen. The total annual value was £12; in King Edward's time £14. In the 13th cent. the manor was the property of the Bacheworths. Sir Richard de Bacheworth assigned the manor in 1315 to Simon de Swanland, who married the daughter and coheir of his brother Roger; Sir Richard soon after joining the order of the Knights Hospitallers, whilst his wife took the veil. Later in the 14th cent. the manor passed, by his marriage with the granddaughter of Sir Simon de Swanland, to John Newdegate, afterwards knighted for his services in France under Edward III. In 1585, John Newdegate, the 8th in lineal descent from Sir John, exchanged Harefield with Lord Chief Justice Sir Edmund Anderson for the manor of Arbury in Warwickshire. Sir Edmund sold Harefield in 1601 to Sir Thomas Egerton, Lord Keeper of the Great Seal, and his wife Alice, Countess Dowager of Derby. The Lord Keeper died in 1617, the Countess in 1637, when the manor descended to Anne Stanley, her eldest daughter by her first marriage, who married, 1st, Grey Lord Chandos, and 2nd, Mervin Earl of Castlehaven. On the death of the Countess of Castlehaven, the manor passed to her eldest son by her first husband, George Lord Chandos, who died in 1655, leaving Harefield to his widow. Lady Chandos shortly after married Sir William Sedley, who died in 1656, and in 1657 she took a third husband, George Pitt, Esq., of Strathfieldsaye. Having vested her estates in Mr. Pitt, he, in February 1675 sold the manors of Harefield and Moor Hall to Sir Richard Newdigate, grandson of the John Newdegate why had alienated them to Chief Justice Anderson. The estates thus restored have ever since continued in the Newdegate family (who have resumed the old spelling of their name as well as the old estates), and are now the property of C. Newdigate Newdegate, Esq., M.P.

"It is remarkable that this manor (with the exception of a temporary alienation,) has descended by intermarriages, and a regular succession (in the families of Bacheworth, Swanland, and Newdegate,) from the year 1284, when by the verdict of a jury, it appeared that Roger de Bacheworth and his ancestors had then held it from time immemorial. It is the only instance in which I have traced such remote possession in the county of Middlesex." [*]

Harefield Place, the ancient manor-house and seat of the Newdegates, stood close by the church, in a park just outside the village, and approached "under the shady roof of branching elm star-proof."[†] Norden describes it as "a fair house, standing on the edge of the hill; the river Colne passing near the same, through the pleasant meadows and sweet pastures, yielding both delight and profit." Whilst in the occupation of the Lord Keeper Egerton and the Countess of Derby, the old house received illustrious guests. In 1602 Queen Elizabeth visited Harefield, where she was entertained with all possible pomp, and remained three days. She arrived July 31, and was met as she entered the grounds "near the Dairy-house" by a bailiff and a dairy-maid, who recited a long eulogistic dialogue, while "Her Majesty, being on horseback, stayed under a tree (because it rained) to listen to it." Then another Dialogue of Welcome between Place and Time—Place being arrayed "in a parti-coloured robe, *like the brick house*," Time, "in a green robe, with a hour-glass, stopped not running." [‡] In the morning she was addressed as

"Beautie's rose and Virtue's book
Angel's mind and Angel's look."

---

[*] Lysons, Environs, vol iii., p. 107.
[†] Milton, Arcades.
[‡] Newdegate MS., printed in Nichols, Progresses of Queen Elizabeth, vol. iii., pp. 586—593.

It has been said that the Lord Chamberlain's company was brought down to Harefield to play Othello before her, Shakspeare himself being probably present to direct the performance of his new play.* The statement is, however, not free from suspicion—and the play is not alluded to in the Newdegate MS. The Queen depàrted on the 2nd of August, when Place, instead of her parti-coloured robe, came " attired in black mourning," as a poor widow mourning before her Grace, " amazed to see so great happiness so soon bereft me." The abundant indoor entertainment was a happy provision, for the Queen seems to have been " close imprisoned ever since her coming," by the rain—

" Only poor St. Swithin now
   Doth hear you blame his cloudy brow."

The Countess of Derby in her second widowhood resided much at Harefield Place ; and Milton during his residence at Horton is believed to have been a frequent visitor. At any rate he wrote his exquisite Arcades as the poetic " part of an entertainment presented [1635] to the Countess Dowager of Derby, at Harefield, by some noble persons of her family [her grandchildren] in pastoral habit."

The house thus ennobled was burnt down in 1660, the fire being occasioned, according to a tradition preserved by Lysons, by the carelessness of the witty Sir Charles Sedley, whilst reading in bed. A new house was built a little distance from the old site, but that was pulled down at the end of the last century, and not a vestige remains of either, or of the star-proof avenue under which Elizabeth listened to her Welcome, and which Milton celebrated. The present Harefield Place, a little more to the S. of the ch., the seat of C. N. Newdegate, Esq., M.P., is a comfortable, commonplace, modern mansion.

The *Church* (St. Mary) is of the late Dec. period, but was restored a few years ago by Mr. Newdegate, and new windows inserted, the E. and W. having flamboyant tracery. Except on the S., which is of flint and stone in alternate squares, the exterior has been covered with plaster. It consists of nave, aisles, and chancel, a low square embattled tower

* Collier, New Particulars regarding the Works of Shakspeare, 1836 ; Egerton Papers, printed by the Camden Society.

at the N.W., in which are three bells, and a stone porch on the N., of recent erection. The *int.*, much altered when restored, though not venerable in itself, wears an air of antiquity and dignity from the number of stately monuments it contains. The seats of oak, open, with poppy-head terminals, are recent. The fine carved oak about the altar, chancel rails, etc., was brought from a religious house in Belgium. The stalls, six on each side of the chancel, with their carved reversible seats, are original. The E. end of the N. aisle is shut off by a parclose, and forms the Breakspear Chantry. The corresponding portion of the S. aisle was no doubt applied to a like purpose, as there is at the end a good original piscina ; it was the burial-place of the Newdegates, and is known as the Brakenburye Chapel.

Brasses and Monuments.—In S. aisle, tablet with brass of Edetha, widow of William Newdegate (wearing a horned head-dress), d. 1444. At N.E. corner of S. aisle, a low altar tomb, with brasses, of John Newdegate, Serjeant-at-law, d. 1528, and wife Amphelicia, d. 1544. Sir John Newdigate, d. 1618, and wife, with their effigies in alabaster, coloured. Several monts. to other members of the Newdegate family are in this aisle. On S. wall of chancel, an altar tomb, under a tall groined canopy, to John Newdegate, d. 1545, with brasses of himself, wife, 8 sons, and 5 daughters, kneeling before faldstools. Mural mont. of Sir Richard Newdigate, d. 1710, and wife Mary, d. 1692 : the mont. a very handsome one of its kind, the work, it is said, of Grinling Gibbons, was erected in memory of Lady Newdigate, of whom there is a well-executed recumbent effigy. Sir Richard Newdigate, d. 1727, with bust; and several more. But the most magnificent mont. in the chancel is that of Alice Spencer, Dowager Countess of Derby, and widow of the Lord Keeper Egerton, d. 1637. The mont. is of coloured marbles, in two stages ; on the upper is a highly coloured recumbent alabaster statue of the Countess, under a curtained canopy, which is crowned with the arms of Stanley with all their quarterings, impaling the arms and quarterings of Spencer of Althorp ; in the lower stage, under arches, are kneeling effigies of her three daughters, that on the l, being the Lady Chandos, in the centre the Countess of Bridgwater, on the rt. the Countess of Huntingdon. In the Breakspear Chapel are an altar tomb without inscription ; brass with inscription to George Assheby, d. 1474 ; and brasses with effigies of George Ashby, clerk of the signet to Henry VII., and clerk and counsellor to Henry VIII., d. 1514, and wife Rose ; and William Ashby, d. 1537, and wife Jane. On N. wall, mural mont., with effigies under a canopy borne on Corinthian columns of black marble, of Sir Robert Ashby (in armour, kneeling), d. 1617, and son, Sir Francis, d. 1623. Several other monuments of Ashbys are on the walls. On the wall passing from the chapel is a mont. of John Pritchett, Bp. of Gloucester, d. 1680. The others are of little consequence. All the principal monts. were restored and recoloured when the ch. was restored. *Obs.* helmet (early 15th cent.) and armour in chancel.

The manor of *Moor Hall* was given by Alice, daughter of Baldwin de Clare, to the Priory of Knights Hospitallers at Harefield.* This was no doubt, as Lysons supposes, a cell of the Priory of St. John, Clerkenwell. It stood on the road to Denham. The site is now a farm ; the little 13th century chapel, still remaining, and externally tolerably perfect, is used as a barn. The manor, since its forfeiture to the Crown, has followed the fortunes of Harefield. *Brakenburyes*, the seat of the Swanlands, midway to Uxbridge, is likewise now a farmhouse. *Breakspears*, or Breakspear House, ½ m. S.E. of the village, is an old mansion, occupying the site of one which, according to Camden, took its name from the family from which Nicholas Breakspear (Adrian IV.) was descended. More modern accounts say, without any authority, and in contradiction to the known events of his life, that Nicholas himself resided here. It is now the seat of W. W. Drake, Esq. *Harefield Park* (W. F. Vernon, Esq.), N. of the vill. ; *Harefield Grove* (J. Boord, Esq.), on the Rickmansworth road ; and *Harefield House* (Rt. Hon. Sir J. Byles), are the other principal seats.

HARLESDEN, MIDDX. (*see* WILLESDEN).

HARLINGTON, MIDDX., a long

straggling village, stretches from Harlington Corner, by the 13th milestone on the Bath road, northwards for a mile along a cross road to Uxbridge ; the ch. is 1 m. S. by W. from the Hayes Stat. of the Gt. W. Rly. : pop. 1296. Inns : *White Hart*, looks rural and comfortable ; *Lion* ; *Crown.*

Harlington (Dom. *Herdintone*), was called *Hardington* till near the end of the 16th cent. The manor belonged to the Harpeden family during the first half of the 14th cent. ; it then passed in succession to the Mirymanths, 1363 ; Lovells, 1474 ; Roper, 1559 ; Bird, 1584 ; Langworth, 1589 ; and Coppinger, 1590. In 1607 Francis Coppinger sold the reversion to Sir John Bennet, to whose son, Sir Henry, the notorious Cabal minister the manor gave, 1664, the title of Baron, and afterwards, 1672, Earl. (*See* ARLINGTON.) The manor remained in the Bennet family till 1724, when it was sold by Charles Earl of Tankerville to the celebrated Lord Bolingbroke. From him it passed by sale, 1738, to a Mr. Stephenson ; was bought by the Earl of Uxbridge in 1757, and sold by him in 1772 to Fred. Augustus Earl of Berkeley, the owner of the sub-manor of Harlington-cum-Shepiston, in whose family the reunited manors remain. The manor of *Dawley* (Dom. *Dallega*) was, with brief intervals, united with that of Harlington till 1772, when Dawley was alienated to Peter de Salis, Esq. It is now the property of Count de Salis. (*See* DAWLEY COURT.)

Harlington, a quiet rural village, with no very marked feature, has a cheerful well-to-do look. The cottages have plenty of bright flowers in the front gardens, and apples and plums in the back. The country is level, lying at the N.W. end of Hounslow Heath, some 250 acres of which belong to Harlington par. Much of the ground is devoted to market gardens and orchards, the cherry prevailing. The lanes are shady, and the country green and pleasant.

The *Church* (St. Peter and St. Paul), near the N. end of the vill., is small but interesting. It comprises nave with buttresses, chancel, W. tower, and S. porch, the upper part oak. The body of the church is covered with plaster. The tower of flint and stone, Perp., restored, has buttresses, a newel angle turret, pinnacles, and battlements. The S. doorway, under the porch, is Norman, and of its class unusually good : a chevron, above it an elaborate cable, then beaked heads, and above them embattled and medallion mouldings rising from grotesque capitals. The nave windows are Dec., those of the chancel a sort of flamboyant. The *int.* is plain ; the roof ceiled, but the tie-beams exposed ; a W. gallery, and some good old open oak seats. *Brasses* and *Monts.*—On floor in centre of chancel, small brass without date, but early 15th cent., with half-length effigy of John Monmouthe, rector, a priest in chasuble, the inscrip., pray for the soul, carefully effaced. N. wall of chancel, a canopied altar tomb with effigies in brass of George Lovell, Lord of the Manor, d. 1544, and wife. On the same wall a tablet, with a poetic inscription, to Joseph Trapp, D.D., d. 1747, rector 1733—47 (presented to the living by Lord Bolingbroke), Professor of Poetry at Oxford, and author of 'Prelectiones Poeticæ,' a translation of Virgil which gained him little credit, a tragedy, and some volumes of sermons. S. of the altar, an altar tomb, with recumbent marble statue, by Lucas, of Gerome Fane de Salis, Count of the German Empire, of Dawley Court, d. 1836, and on the N. side a corresponding tomb, with statue by Theed, of the Countess de Salis, d. 1856. On the S. wall a mont. to Sir John Bennet, K.B., Lord Ossulston, d. 1695, with marble busts of Lord Ossulston and his two wives. On the floor, Charles, Earl of Tankerville, d. 1767. The font, of Sussex marble, large, late Norm., has a thick central shaft and four smaller, and round-arched panelling on the sides. The tower contains 6 bells, and the leads afford a fine view, with Windsor Castle and the Crystal Palace as conspicuous landmarks : *obs.* the magnificent cedar in neighbouring garden. The ch.-yard is bordered by a row of tall Lombardy poplars. Opposite the porch is a grand old yew, still sound and full of verdure. Lysons, writing towards the close of the last century, describes it as " cut in topiary work ; " and in 1729 was published a large copper-plate engraving of the tree, with verses by " Poet John Saxy," the parish-clerk of Harlington. The print, in some request among collectors of curious engravings, shows a seat round the trunk, and the tree cut into a circular disk about 10 ft. from the ground, as Poet Saxy writes,—

" So thick, so fine, so full, so wide,
A troop of guards might under it ride."

About an equal height above this is a similar but much smaller disk, and some 15 ft. higher a globe, on which, as the crowning ornament, is perched a cock, the centre of the tree, which serves as a pedestal, being a truncated cone.* The tree, according to its poet,

" Yields to Arlington a fame,
Much louder than its Earldom's name."

For the last half century the tree has been allowed to grow at its own will, and all traces of topiary work have disappeared. When Lysons wrote, the trunk measured 15 ft. 7 in. at 6 ft. from the ground ; it now, 1875, measures 17 ft. 10 in. at 4 ft. from the ground. N. of the ch. is another good but much smaller yew.

The principal seats are *Harlington Lodge* (John D. Allcroft, Esq.), *The Cedars* (Daniel Sharp, Esq.), *The Grove* (R. Capper, Esq.)

HARMONDSWORTH, MIDDX.,

(Dom. *Hermodesworthe*, from the patronymic *Hermode* or *Harmond*, and A.-S. *worth*, a farm or enclosure,) adjoins Harlington on the W. ; is ½ m. N. of the Bath road, 5 m. W. of Hounslow, and 1½ m. S. of the W. Drayton Stat. of the G. W. Rly. ; pop. 1548.

The country is flat, the soil fertile, and the occupations almost exclusively agricultural. Large corn and green crops are raised, but vegetables for the London market engage at least an equal share of attention, and fruit is much grown. Of the 3480 acres of which the parish consists, 1176 belonged to Hounslow Heath, but these are now all enclosed and cultivated, not an acre having been spared as open ground. The scenery is tame, but trees are abundant, and often of large size ; the old Powder Mill River winds through the par., and the Colne along its

* In a S.E. view of the ch. now before us, " J. Hampner, del. Jan. 3, 1803," the body of the tree is much thicker than in Saxy's eng., and there is a third disk instead of a globe at top, the crowning ornament being still a cock, though grown somewhat out of shape. The N. yew is also a curious piece of topiary work.

W, border, dividing it from Buckingham-shire.

The village of Harmondsworth is small and not remarkable ; but there are some good houses on its E. side ; in the main street one or two half-timber (but yellow-washed) tenements, with projecting upper storeys and overhanging thatch eaves, and a fine elm on what should be a green by the church. The *Church* (of the Virgin Mary) is large and interesting. In its present form it is mainly of the Perp. period, but it was then clearly re-built from a much earlier church, parts of which were retained. It consists of nave with aisles, chancel, and N. aisle, a good (modern) wooden S. porch, and a battlemented tower at the S.W. The body of the ch. is built of black flints, but the squared stones of the earlier build-ing are largely worked up in the walls, especially those of the chancel, and upon some of them vestiges of carving may be traced. Especially curious is the doorway under the porch. It is of very fair Norman work, and evidently, from the junction of the stones and its unusual place, cutting the E. wall of the tower, has been taken down from the original church and re-erected on a somewhat narrower scale. The arch is semicircular, the innermost fascia being flat, and orna-mented with square panels, in which are circles with crosses and flowers of 4 and 5 leaves, and which are not merely carried round the arch, but down to the ground on both sides. On either side of this is a thin shaft much worn, but on which the carving that originally covered them can still be made out. From the caps. springs a good and freely executed semicircular beaks-head moulding, and above this is a quadruple chevron mould-ing carried down to the ground, but only half the width, on the left side. *Obs.* too the door, of oak of great thickness, studded over with broad-headed nails, and having the original massive hinges. The lower part of the tower is of early date, the upper part is of brick and modern, but the whole is covered with plaster. In it is a peal of 5 musical bells, (of the 17th century), and there is a clock-bell in the open turret on the roof of the tower.

The church was carefully restored in 1863-4 ; the interior was much improved, but for the old and small windows new ones were substituted in the chancel and partially in the nave. The nave is divided from the aisles by cylin-drical pillars and pointed arches of early date ; *obs.* the discontinuance of the re-moulding on the middle of the arch of the eastern bay, and the brackets to which the rood screen was attached. The open roofs are old, but repaired when the plaster ceiling was removed : note the hammer-beam roof to chancel aisle. *Obs.* also the original Perp. open oak seats, of good design, in aisles and lower end of nave, to which the new ones have been made to correspond. On S. of the chancel are three sedilia, and a piscina with credence over it. On the walls are several mural monts., but none of general interest. The brasses which were on the floor, being detached and placed in a chest in the tower, were all stolen by the workmen at the restoration of the church. At the S.W. end of the nave is an excel-lent plain late Norman *font* of Sussex marble. It is octagonal, of sufficient size for baptism by immersion, and has a very thick central shaft, with 8 thin ones around it. If the day be clear, it will be well before leaving the church to obtain permission to ascend the tower. The view over the level country resembles generally that of Harlington, but is more open to the horizon : Windsor Castle on one hand, and the Crystal Palace on the other, are the landmarks.

Immediately N.W. of the church is a very remarkable old *Barn*, probably mo-nastic. At the Dom. Survey the manor of Harmondsworth belonged to the Abbey of the Holy Trinity at Rouen. Later, the Abbey is said to have had a cell or branch estab.lishment (Benedictine) here, of which this was the barn. It is of extra-ordinary size, being 191 feet long and 38 feet wide, and is divided into 3 floors. The walls are of conglomerate (pudding-stone), found in these parts. The open roof, of massive oak, is an excellent ex-ample of old timber-work. The body of the barn is divided into a nave and aisles by two rows of oak pillars of immense thickness, which rest on square blocks of sandstone. But unusual as are the di-mensions of the barn, it was a century back much larger. It then had a pro-jecting wing at the N. end so as to form an ∟. This wing was taken down about the same time as the Manor House by which it stood, and rebuilt at *Heath Row*, 1½ m. S.E. of Harmondsworth church. This, which is known as Tithe Barn, exactly resembles the Manor Barn in structure, except that the walls are of brick, and of course modern—the oak columns and roof are the originals. It is 128 feet long and 38 wide, and is divided into 2 floors. The Manor House which stood by the church and great barn, was a rich and quaint pile; its many gables had ornamented barge boards, and there was a good deal of decorative work in other parts; but it had got much out of repair, and was pulled down in 1774. The manor passed from the abbey to William of Wykeham, who settled it upon his newly founded college at Winchester. It was surrendered to the Crown in 1544, and granted by Edward VI. in 1547 to Sir William Paget, Secretary of State, by whose descendant, the Earl of Uxbridge, it was sold in 1855. It is now the property of Mr. Wools. Subordinate manors, in which were included the hamlets of Longford, Sibson, etc., and some manor farms, also belonged to the Pagets, but have been sold at different times, and are now the property of the Earl of Strafford and others.

Longford, the largest collection of houses in the par., including three roadside inns, is about ½ m. S. of Harmondsworth, where the Bath road is carried over the Colne by King's Bridge, which occupies the place of the *long ford*, to which the hamlet owes its name. The fishery here is in good repute among anglers; as is also the *King's Head* Inn.

Heath Row, so called from its position by Hounslow Heath, where is the Tithe Barn, is also on the Bath road, but at the opposite (E.) extremity of the parish. A short distance E. of the vill., on what was Hounslow Heath, are remains of a Roman camp, about 300 feet square, which Stukeley as usual believed to have been one of Cæsar's stations after he passed the Thames in pursuit of Cassivellaunus. Half a mile N. of The Magpies, Heath Row, and a mile E. of Harmondsworth, is a third hamlet, *Sibson* or *Sipson* (anc. *Sibbeston*), where are some good old farms and cottages.

HARROW ON THE HILL,

MIDDX., famous for its church, its hill, and the prospects from it, and above all for its school, is situated 10 m. N.W. from Hyde Park Corner by road; the Harrow Stat. of the L. and N.W. Rly. (11½ m.) is 1¼ m. N. of the town. Pop. of the town (Local Board Dist.), 4997; of the entire par., including the eccl. dists. of Harrow Weald, Roxeth, and Wembly, 8537. Inns: *King's Head Hotel*, High Street; *Railway Hotel*, by the Stat. The Mitre, on the S. slope of the hill, belongs locally to Sudbury.

Harrow Hill rises, abrupt and isolated, some 200 ft. from the plain, a mass of London clay capped with sand, an "outlier" of the Bagshot beds. With the spire of the church which crowns its summit — King James's "only visible church"—Harrow Hill is a conspicuous, and, from its form, a pleasing feature in the landscape for many miles on every side, but especially S. and W.: "lofty Harrow," it will be remembered, is prominent in Thomson's "boundless landscape," seen from Richmond Hill. Of the view *from* Harrow Hill we shall speak presently. The town—it had a market, granted in 1262, but long abandoned—occupies the crest and follows the slopes of the hill. The School dominates and colours it, and has seized upon the best positions. As a rule the shops are small, but those which provide for the school, and the many affluent families the school has led to settle around it, are of course exceptions. Besides the school buildings, there are many masters' houses sufficiently spacious to receive boarders, and many good private residences, the former invariably and the latter mostly, modern Domestic Gothic, of a kind to harmonize with the school buildings, together giving to the town a thoroughly distinctive character—a character that every visitor feels is at once unique and appropriate. Of late years the town has been much improved in its sanitary and social arrangements. It has its Local Board of Health; Gas and Water Works; a Literary Institute, Young Men's Society, Workmen's Hall, a Public Hall and Assembly Room, built in 1874, and a Cottage Hospital, for which a neat building was erected opposite the cricket-field in the Roxeth Road in 1872. Harrow has also its fortnightly Gazette.

In the Domesday Survey the name is written *Herges;* an early Latin form is *Herga super Montem;* in 1398 it appears as *Harewe at Hill.* Lysons supposes the name to be derived from the A.-S. *hearge*, "which is sometimes translated a troop of soldiers, and sometimes a church;" and he adds, "I am inclined to adopt the latter derivation, and to suppose that *the church upon the hill* might have been before the Norman Conquest a prominent feature of this part of the country." But *herige* was a legion or division of an army; and, as from its commanding position Harrow would certainly be made a military station by the Romans, it is probable that the name was given to it as the camp or station of a legion.

The manor belonged to the Abps. of Canterbury long prior to the Conquest. It was exchanged for other lands by Cranmer, in 1543, with Henry VIII., who in 1546 granted it (with the subordinate manors) to Sir Edward (afterwards Lord) North. It continued in the North family till 1630, when it was sold to Edmund Philips, and George and William Pytts. By the marriage of Alice daughter of Edmund Pytts, it passed to James Rushout, created a baronet in 1661. His grandson, Sir James Rushout, Bart., was created Baron Northwick in 1797; and the manor is now held by George, 3rd Lord Northwick.

The manor-house was occupied as an occasional residence by the Abps. of Canterbury; and it is related that in 1170 Thomas à Becket spent some days here, having been stopped on his way to Woodstock, where he was about to visit Prince Henry, then newly associated with his father, Henry II., in the government, and ordered to return to his diocese. Nizel de Sackville, the rector of Harrow, and Robert de Broc, the vicar, treated the archbishop with so much disrespect that he excommunicated them from the altar of Canterbury Cathedral, on the Christmas Day before his murder. The site of the manor-house is unknown: the archbishops appear to have removed their residence to Heggeston (now Headstone), near Pinner.

Harrow *Church*, St. Mary, stands on the brow of the hill. It was founded by Abp. Lanfranc, *t.* William I., but the only portion of his building remaining is the lower part of the tower, the W. entrance of which has the round Norman arch with chevron mouldings. The present ch. is of flint and stone; cruciform; with at the W. end a tower and tall wooden spire covered with lead, a stone porch on the S., with a priest's chamber, or parvise, over it, and a 15th cent. wooden porch on the N. The nave piers are E.E.; the aisles, clerestorey, transepts, and stone porch Perp.; the chancel Dec. The ch. was thoroughly restored a few years back under the direction of Sir Gilbert Scott, when the chancel was lengthened, and a N. aisle added to it; the fine open timber Perp. roof, with upright figures of angels playing on musicial instruments, on the corbels, was exposed and repaired; open oak seats were substituted for pews; the E. window was filled with painted glass, by Wailes, as a memorial of the Rev. J. W. Cunningham, d. 1861, many years vicar of Harrow, and other memorial windows inserted. Much of the carving and tracery was rechiselled, or replaced by new. The font, a circular basin rudely carved, on a thick cable pedestal, probably the original font of Lanfranc's ch., after being for half a century in the vicarage garden, has been restored to the ch., and now stands near the S. door.

In the ch. are some noteworthy *brasses.* Sir John Flambard, d. near the end of the 14th cent.; effigy life-size, in full armour, with dog at feet: under it are the following curious hexameters, the exact meaning of which has hitherto evaded the many attempts which have been made to decipher them: the general purport is of course clear enough:

" Jon me do marmore Numinis ordine Flam tum lat'
Bard q° 3 verbere stigis E fun'e hic tueatur."*

---

* Perhaps the late Mr. Husenbeth's version is the most satisfactory. His reading is interesting as indicating "how the jingle of rhymes is kept up" in some of these mediæval inscriptions. The *jingle* is plainly the parent of verses like those of Skelton:

" Jon me
do marmore
Numinis ordine
Flam tumulatu
Bard quoque
vulnere
Stigis e funere
hic tueatur."

" (I) John resign myself | in marble, by God's decree is buried Flam and Bard | may he (God) preserve (him) from the punishment and burial of hell." (Notes and Queries, 2nd series, vol. ix.)

John Byrked, rector of Harrow, d. 1418 ; effigy of priest under a canopy, head gone. Simon Marchford, priest, 1442, head lost. William Wightman, d. 1579, wife and 5 children. Small brasses of a priest, half-length, no date ; one in transept of a man, 3 wives, 5 sons, and 6 daughters ; and one or two more. *Obs.* particularly the mural brass on N. side of nave of John Lyon, "late of Preston in this parish yeoman." d. Oct. 11, 1592, the *Founder of Harrow School*,—" to have continuance for ever ; and for maintenance thereof, and for releyffe of the poore, and of some poore schollers in the universityes, repairinge of highwayes, and other good and charitable uses, hath made conveyance of lands of good value to a corporation granted for that purpose." Among the *monts.* are one or two with kneeling effigies in alabaster coloured, but of little value ; one to Dr. Summer, d. 1771, Master of Harrow School, with an insc. by Dr. Parr ; Thomas Ryves, F.R.S., d. 1788 ; Sir Samuel Garth, d. Jan. 18, 1719, (in chancel—the vault selected and prepared by himself,) physician and author of ' The Dispensary.' The tower contains a peal of 8 musical bells.

The ch.-yard has few if any tombs of interest on account of the persons interred within them, but it contains one that for another reason has as many visitors as any in an English ch.-yard.

"There is a spot in the churchyard, near the footpath, on the brow of the hill, looking towards Windsor, and a tomb under a large tree, (bearing the name of Peachie, or Peachey,) where I used to sit for hours and hours when a boy. This was my favourite spot." *

Byron's Tomb had come to be so called from the tradition of the school long before its confirmation by the above passage, or the poet's verses ' On a Distant View of the Village and School of Harrow on the Hill ' :—

' Again I behold where for hours I have ponder'd,
  As reclining, at eve, on yon tombstone I lay ;
Or round the steep brow of the churchyard I wander'd,
  To catch the last gleam of the sun's setting ray."

Byron's Tomb is an ordinary altar tomb, now enclosed by railings, by the

* Byron to Mr. Murray, May 26, 1822 ; Works, v. 334, ed. 1832.

footpath S.W. of the ch., and the "large tree," an elm, now known as Byron's Elm, still overshadows it. But the large slab of blue limestone on which the poet used to recline, is split across, a portion of it lost, and the surface so worn that the name on it can no longer be read.

The prospect as seen from the tomb— more readily from the terrace outside the ch.-yard,—is really very fine, especially on a clear summer's evening. It reaches W. and S.W. across Roxeth Common, and a broad expanse of level, but richly wooded and cultivated scenery, the distance stretching round from the Surrey hills to Bucks and Berks. On this side Windsor Castle is the chief distant object. From other parts of the hill, the Crystal Palace, the tower on Leith Hill, the obelisk in Ashridge Park, the Langdon Hills in Essex, the Kentish Downs and Knockholt Beeches may be made out by keen eyes—or a telescope. The coign of vantage for a panoramic view is the roof of the ch. tower.

Harrow School was founded in 1571, by John Lyon, yeoman, of Preston, a hamlet of Harrow, whose mont. we have seen in the ch. Lyon carefully guided its infant steps, and for 20 years watched its growth, when, in 1590, two years before his death, he put forth his matured scheme for its future governance. The school statutes are laid down by him with great plainness of speech and precision of detail. He not only declares who are eligible as scholars, and what they are to be taught, but settles the number of forms, what books shall be used, the hours of attendance, the number of holidays, and the modes of discipline, and forbids any other games than "driving a top, tossing a hand-ball, running and shooting," the last being especially insisted on. For "a large and convenient school-house, with a chimney in it," and "meete and convenient rooms for the school-master and usher to inhabit and dwell in"—for honest John Lyon contemplated no such array of head, under, and assistant masters as now graces Harrow—he appropriated the sum of £300. To the master he allotted a salary of £26 13s. 4d., and £3 6s. 8d. to be paid him on the 1st of May "for provision of fuel ;" to the usher £13 6s. 8d., and the same sum as the master for fuel. A sum of £20 was to be paid annually for two exhibitions to Caius College, Cambridge, and two to any college in Oxford. The management he entrusted to six "governors," with the Abp. of Canterbury as visitor for the decision of controversies. Harrow School has long outgrown Lyon's stipulations, and taken a foremost rank among the "Eight Great Schools" of England. It has fluctuated like most great schools, but its course has generally been an onward one, and it has never been more flourishing than now. Its masters have almost always been men of mark, and among its scholars are some of our chief men. Sir William Jones, Parr, Sheridan, Perceval, Byron, Peel, Palmerston, are among the scholars, poets, and statesmen who once were "Harrow Boys."

The *School Buildings* are immediately S. of the ch. The School House, erected in pursuance of Lyon's instructions in 1595, is a good old red-brick and stone Elizabethan structure, without much external ornament, unless it be the lion which typifies the founder, but meet and convenient, as he desired it to be, for the purpose for which it was built. It is wholly appropriated to school purposes, masters and boys alike dwelling in the town. The school-room, dear to all Harrovians, is a good old room, some 50 ft. by 21, with the walls well scored with old boys' names, not a few of which are dearly prized. This was of old the room in which the annual gatherings of scholars and friends were held, and speeches and essays recited, but in Dr. Butler's mastership, in the early days of the present century, it was deemed necessary to have a new and larger Speech Room built. Now, however, Harrow has outgrown that—it never had much architectural merit,—and under the mastership of another Dr. Butler, on Speech Day, July 2, 1874 (Speech Day is always the first Thursday in July), the first stone of a new Speech Room was laid by the Duke of Abercorn.

The new Speech Room will be erected out of the Lyon Memorial Fund, raised by old Harrovians in 1871, the tercentenary of the foundation of the school. It will stand nearly opposite the College Chapel, on the other side of the road, and is intended to harmonize with it in style. It is to have two towers, with tall spires, —not so tall, we may hope, as to overtop the church spire, or to materially interfere with the familiar contour of Harrow Hill. The archt. is Mr. W. Burges.

Till 1839 the boys attended Harrow Church ; but in that year—Dr. Wordsworth being head-master — a *College Chapel* was built at the N. end of the High-street, from the designs of Mr. C. R. Cockerell, R.A. It was a neat red-brick building, designed to harmonize in character with the school buildings. It was admired at first, but with the advance of Gothic taste fell into disfavour, and in 1854 was taken down, and a new chapel erected on its foundations— but with a greater extension eastward— from the designs of Sir G. G. Scott, R.A. The present College Chapel, which was consecrated by the Bp. of London (Dr. Tait, now Abp. of Canterbury), Nov. 1, 1857, is an elegant and admirably finished stone building, of 13th cent., French type, evidently modelled on the Ste. Chapelle, Paris, and, like that, has a lofty apsidal chancel, with a crypt beneath. The tall, slender flèche was added by subscription in 1863, as a memorial to a much-esteemed under-master, the Rev. Wm. Oxenham. All the windows are filled with painted glass—those on the S., with the whole S. aisle, forming a memorial of the officers educated at Harrow (21 in number) who fell in the war in the Crimea.

By the Chapel is the *Library*, or, as it is otherwise named, the *Vaughan Library*, it having been erected in commemoration of the head-mastership of Dr. Vaughan, under whom Harrow School attained an unexampled state of prosperity. The first stone was laid by Lord Palmerston, on Speech-day 1861, and it was opened in 1863. The archt. was Sir Gilbert Scott. The Library is a Gothic building, like the Chapel, with which it is intended to harmonize, rather than with the other school buildings. It is of coloured bricks, a little fanciful in parts, but very pretty. The interior is a noble room, and well fitted and furnished. Besides the books, it contains portraits of Byron, Palmerston, and other illustrious Harrovians. A fitting adornment of the new Speech Room would be a like series of marble busts.

Among other additions made to the school buildings under Dr. Butler's head-mastership, the following claim notice as valuable in themselves. and possessing some architectural character. The *Sanatorium*, an admirably planned and fitted building, erected at a little distance from the school, in 1864 ; a large and commodious *Gymnasium*, built at the bottom of the steps which lead from the playground, and opened in 1874 ; and Laboratories and Natural Science Schools, erected in 1874-5, near the new Speech Room. These last were all designed by Mr. C. F. Hayward, F.S.A., and may be said to be rather intended to accord with the Vaughan Library than the Lyon School-house,— coloured bricks being freely employed, and the turrets and windows being rather French and Gothic than English and Elizabethan. The Gymnasium and Laboratories, as well as the Speech Room, have been built out of the Lyon Memorial Fund of 1871.

Roxeth, which extends away S.W. from the new Gymnasium, may fairly be reckoned a part of Harrow, being joined to it by the many new buildings; but it was formerly an outlying hamlet, and is now an eccl. district. It has a Gothic ch. (Christ Church) of flint, stone, and brick, built in 1862, and some good modern residences. Note the picturesque effect of the hill, with the ch. and group of school buildings on its brow, from the hill foot and the open part of Roxeth Common.

Greenhill, another eccl. dist., lies between Harrow town and rly. stat. It has the look of a suburban railway growth, and is not attractive. The ch., St. John the Baptist, a little cruciform fabric of parti-coloured bricks, with a prodigious roof, was erected in 1866 from the designs of Mr. Bassett Keeling.

Sudbury adjoins Harrow on the S.E. ; at its eastern end is a stat. on the L. and N.W. Rly. Sudbury was a hamlet of Harrow, but was united with Wembly in 1848, and made an eccl. dist., for which a neat E. E. ch., St. John's, was erected. The manor of Sudbury goes with that of Harrow. Of old there was a broad heath-like tract, Sudbury Common, where now runs the rly. ; but it was enclosed in 1803, and is now all cultivated or built over. By the rly. stat., and towards Harrow,

many villas and cottages have been built, and the place is becoming populous. Here is the *Girls' Home*, a branch refuge for homeless girls of the National Refuges Institution, whose training ship for homeless boys we noticed under GREENHITHE (p. 247). In the comfortable new house, Sudbury Hall, over 100 destitute girls are trained for domestic service. *From* Sudbury there are pleasant walks—on the one hand to Wembly, on the other to Perivale and Greenford.

Harrow Weald is the broad level tract N. of Harrow, extending from Harrow Stat. to Stanmore. Of old, as its name implies, a wild woodland, it has long been enclosed and cultivated ; but it still has a good deal of timber ; and the walk across it to Stanmore Common is very pleasant. The hamlet of Harrow Weald, about ¾ m. N. of Harrow Stat., was constituted an eccl. district in 1845, when a neat E.E. ch.. All Saints, was built. The pop. was 1465 in 1871. The village has little to attract or interest the stranger, but there are some good farm-houses and private residenees. *Weald Park* (Alex. Sim, Esq.) is a spacious castellated mansion, standing in well-wooded grounds. The better-known domain, *Bentley Priory* (Sir John Kelk, Bart.), belongs to Harrow Weald, but is so much a part of STANMORE that it will be more conveniently noticed under that heading.

WEMBLY and KENTON have separate notices.

HARTLEY, KENT, 2 m. S.E.
from the Fawkham Stat. of the L. C. and D. Rly. ; pop. 252. Inn, *King's Arms.*

Hartley (in Dom. *Erclei*) belonged to Bp. Odo; reverted to the Crown; in the reign of Henry III. was the property of the Lords of Montchesney; was conveyed by marriage to William de Valence, Earl of Pembroke, and on the death of Aymer de Valence passed to the Hastings, and from them to the Grays, and so on to the Penhales, Cressels, Sedleys ; for, as Philipott moralizes in treating of this manor, " no eminence of birth or dignity can chain the possession of a place to a family, when the title leans upon the wheel of an inconstant and ebbing estate." *

---

* Vill. Cant., p. 181.

Harrow on the Hill

Hatfield House (see p.327)

Col. G. Palmer Evelyn is now lord of the manor.

Hartley can hardly boast of a village—certainly not of a village shop. It is a quiet, out-of-the-way place, with hop-gardens on every hand, three or four comfortable-looking farm-houses, a smith's forge, and a very few scattered cottages. The *church*, All Saints, is the only object of interest. Restored in 1862, and standing in a treeless ch.-yard, it is not now very picturesque, but it is worth examining. It is small, of black flint and stone, the W. end propped by brick buttresses, and has a wooden bell-cote with shingled spire. The nave walls and N. windows are of late Norman date, but the other windows are insertions of the Dec. period; the E. window was renewed in 1862. The *int.* is plain; has open seats; no monts. The roof is ceiled, but the principals are shown. The font, good Dec., is octagonal, with quatrefoils on the sides, and 8 thin shafts of Weald marble.

HATFIELD, or BISHOP'S HAT-FIELD, HERTS,

an old market town, and the site of the stately mansion of the Marquis of Salisbury, is situated on the North Road, 20 m. from London, 7 m. W. of Hertford, and 5 m. E. of St. Albans. Pop. of the par. (which is the largest in the county,—has an area of 12,312 acres, and includes the eccl. dist. of Lemsford, and the hamlet of Newgate Street) 3998. The Hatfield Stat. of the Grt. N. Rly. (17½ m. from King's Cross) is on the W. of the town. Inns: *Salisbury Arms*, Fore Street; *Red Lion*, North Road.

The *Town*, a quiet, old-fashioned place, in appearance a large country village rather than a town, lies along a hill-side, overshadowed by the towers and oaks of Hatfield House; a town of narrow streets, old houses, shops curiously low, with little in it to interest any one, but everywhere clean, cheerful, and, as you pass upwards towards the church and park, pleasant and picturesque to look upon. There is a modern, but not attractive, suburb, known as the New Town, ½ m. N. of the old one. Away by the Lea are some large mills. HATFIELD HOUSE forms a separate article. The church is the only other object of interest.

The *Church*, St. Etheldreda, is, after St. Albans Abbey Church, the largest in the county. It dates from Norman times; but the only fragment left of the original building, so far as we know, is a late Norm. arch in the S. transept. The building in the main is of the Dec. period; but it was restored, and much of it rebuilt, in 1872, under the direction of Mr. D. Brandon, F.S.A. It is of flint and stone; cruciform; and comprises a nave, 102 ft. by 20, with aisles; chancel, 41 ft. by 20, with chapels on both the N. and S. sides; transepts with aisles; embattled tower and spire at the W.; and porches on the N. and S. The windows throughout were renewed when the ch. was restored; but the old work (the tracery which remained was terribly decayed) was carefully followed. The spire and the porches are entirely new; the latter, open oak, were made from the timber of the old roof. The flint facing on the external walls is also new. In the tower is a peal of 5 good bells. The interior is effective and handsome, and has been restored with great care. New and rather richly decorated roofs have replaced the old, which were hopelessly decayed. For the old high pews substantial open oak seats, of uniform pattern throughout, have been substituted. A new chancel arch, with shafts of red Mansfield stone, has been erected, and the chancel has received a new roof. An elaborate reredos has been added of Caen stone and marble, with representations of the Marys at the Cross in the centre, and on the sides St. Etheldreda and St. Alban, carved by Mr. Earp, and mosaics by Salviati—the gift of Dr. Drage and the Rev. J. Robinson. The new E. window has been filled with painted glass as a memorial of members of the Salisbury family. Memorial windows have also been placed in the transepts and elsewhere. The fine piscina on the S. wall of the chancel was brought to light during the recent restoration, when was also discovered another at the E. end of the nave. The pulpit, of Caen stone and marble, carved by Earp, was the gift of Mr. Wynn Ellis; the font, of Tisbury stone, with clustered shafts of coloured marble, was given by the Marchioness of Salisbury.

The *Salisbury Chapel*, on the N. of the chancel, was erected by Robert Cecil, Earl of Salisbury (d. 1612), the builder of Hatfield House, whose mont. is at its E. end. The tradition that this is of Italian execution is confirmed by its appearance. It is well executed, and a good example of the costly work of the time. On a slab of black marble, supported by white marble statues of the virtues—Fortitude, Justice, Prudence, and Temperance—is the recumbent effigy of the Earl in his robes, and holding his treasurer's staff in his hand ; beneath is the recumbent marble figure of a skeleton on a mat. The chapel on the S. of the chancel, known as the *Brocket Chapel*, has been restored at the cost of Mr. Wynn Ellis, whose property it is. In it are several monts. (some with effigies) of the Brockets and Reads of Brocket Hall. The most noteworthy are a mont. to Dame Eliz. Brocket (d. 1612), wife of Sir John Brocket ; and one to Sir James Read (d. 1760), with two busts by Rysbrack. The mural tablets have been removed from the aisles, and brought together in the ground-floor of the tower.

Lemsford Mills, on the Lea, close to Brocket Hall, and 2½ m. N. of Hatfield town, is an eccl. dist. of 451 inhab., formed in 1858. It is a pretty rural hamlet, with corn mills on the Lea ; a country inn, the *Roebuck;* and, opposite the entrance gates of Brocket Hall, a neat little E.E. church, St. Mark, erected in 1858 by the Countess Cowper as a memorial of the late Earl.

Wood Hill, 2½ m. S.E. of the town, is a curiously out-of-the-way, wild-looking little hamlet, lying on the S.E. edge of Hatfield Park, for whose use a good-sized chapel-of-ease was built a few years back.

Newgate Street, 6 m. S.E. from Hatfield, on the Middlesex border, is a larger hamlet, and, notwithstanding its name, as quiet, secluded, and rural a spot as could easily be found so near to London. It has a *ch.,* St. Mary, of more than usual excellence, built and endowed a few years back by Thos. Mills, Esq. It is of stone, E.E. in style, cruciform, with square tower and spire, and has all the windows filled with painted glass.

Brocket Hall is, as old Chauncy wrote, "situated upon a dry hill in a fair park, well wooded and greatly timbered." It stands on the Lea, just beyond Lemsford Mills. The name comes from the Brockets, its early owners. It passed by marriage, early in the 17th cent., to the Reads, from them to the Loves, and in the next century by purchase to the Lambs. The present mansion was begun by Sir Matthew Lamb, and completed by his son, Sir Peniston Lamb, Bart., created (1776) Baron, and (1780) Viscount Melbourne. It is a large and stately, though somewhat formal, structure of 4 storeys, with the offices below. In front of it the Lea spreads out so as to form a broad sheet of water, crossed a little higher by a stone bridge of 3 arches, which serves as the approach to the hall. Both house and bridge were designed by James Paine, the architect of Chertsey Bridge. The grand staircase and drawing-room have been much praised for their fine proportions. The park is varied in surface, affords some good views, and contains some fine trees : a large oak near the hall is called Queen Elizabeth's, from a tradition that when under the charge of Sir Thomas Pope, at Hatfield, she was permitted to come here for occasional change, and used to sit under this oak. Brocket Hall has the distinction of having been successively the residence of two Prime Ministers—Lord Melbourne, who d. here, Nov. 24, 1848, and Lord Palmerston.

Ponsbourne Park, by Newgate Street, was in the reign of Henry VI. the manor-house of the Fortescues. In the reign of Elizabeth it belonged to the Crown, and was conveyed with other manors to Sir Henry Cock. It has since passed through many hands, and is now the property and seat of J. W. Carlile, Esq.

Pope's, 2 m. to the W. of Hatfield, was another sub-manor. It was to Pope's, then the residence of David Mitchell, Esq., that Gray's friend West, when failing in health, went, March 1742 ; but the change wrought no improvement, and he died there the following June. Gray addressed his friend several letters here,[*] and here West wrote the beautiful little ode ("if it deserves the name") beginning—

> "Dear Gray, that always in my heart
> Possessest far the better part ; "

in return for which Gray composed and sent his Ode to the Spring, but before it arrived West was dead. He lies in Hatfield ch.-yard. Pope's is now a farm.

---

[*] "It is from this place [Pope's], and from the former date [March 1742], that this third series of letters commences."—Mason, Memoirs of Gray, prefixed to his Works, vol. i., p. 312, ed. 1807.

HATFIELD HOUSE, the magnificent Jacobean mansion of the Marquis of Salisbury, stands in a fine park immediately E. of Hatfield town. The manor (*Hetfelle* in Dom.) is said to have been given to the Abbey of Ely by King Edgar. It remained the property of the Abbey till 1108, when Ely was raised to a bishopric by Henry I., and Hatfield passed with the other conventual possessions into the hands of the bishop. The Bishops of Ely made Hatfield a residence, and built themselves a sumptuous palace there, whence the place came to be designated *Bishop's Hatfield*, to distinguish it from Hatfield Regis, Hatfield Broad Oak, Hatfield Peveril, and other places of a like name. It has been supposed that there was also a royal palace here, and that William of Hatfield, 2nd son of Edward III., was so called from having been born in it ; but there can be no doubt that his birthplace was Hatfield in the West Riding of Yorkshire, his mother Philippa having given a thank-offering to the neighbouring Abbey of St. Roch on the occasion.*

The manor was conveyed to Henry VIII., Nov. 24, 1538, by Thos. Goodrich, Bp. of Ely, in exchange for lands in Cambridge, Essex, and Norfolk, and the palace became a royal abode. During Henry's later years it was Prince Edward's occasional residence. Shortly after coming to the throne Edward VI. granted Hatfield to his sister, the Princess Elizabeth, who made it her usual abode.† In the reign of Mary, Elizabeth, after her harsher confinement, at Ashridge, the Tower, Richmond, Woodstock, and elsewhere, was removed in 1555 to Hatfield Palace, and placed under the charge of Sir Thomas Pope, by whom she was treated with kindness and respect. She was allowed to visit Enfield Chase, and shoot at the hart ; on three or four occasions was summoned to Court ; and on the Shrovetide of 1556 " Sir Thomas Pope made for

the Ladie Elizabeth, all at his own costes, a greate and rich maskinge in the greate halle at Hatfelde ; where the pageauntes were marvellously furnished. . . . . And the next day the play of Holofernes." But this was too much for the sour Queen, who wrote sharply to Sir Thomas that she " mysliked these folliries," and " so their disguisings were ceased." * The three years Elizabeth remained here were spent chiefly in solitude and retirement ; " she prudently declined interfering in any sort of business, and abandoned herself entirely to books and amusement . . . principally employing herself in playing on the lute or virginals, embroidering with gold and silver, reading Greek and translating Latin."† At length came her release. On the 17th of Nov., 1558, Mary died, and Elizabeth was Queen. She was soon surrounded by the leading men in the country, and, with the astute William Cecil as her principal Secretary, held at Hatfield her first Privy Council, on Sunday, Nov. 20, and, with increased numbers, another on the following day.‡ On Wednesday, the 23rd, she set out for London, attended by an escort of 1000 gentlemen. Only once again, July 30, 1568, when on a progress in Essex and Herts, does she seem to have visited Hatfield, and of that visit no particulars are recorded.

James I. was entertained at Theobalds by the Lord Treasurer, Sir Robert Cecil, younger son of the great Lord Burghley, from the 4th to the 7th of May, 1603 ; when the King became so enamoured of the place, and the facilities it afforded for his favourite diversion of hunting, that he prevailed on his host, whom he created Lord Cecil, to exchange Theobalds with him for his manor and palace of Hatfield, the King undertaking to build Cecil a new house at Hatfield.§ Accordingly, the larger part of the old palace was pulled down, and a new mansion erected in the utmost magnificence of the time, on a more elevated site, and somewhat farther to the E. At the same time, mindful of his own and perhaps thinking also

---

* Drake, Eboracum, p. 490 : Clutterbuck, Hist. of Herts, vol. ii., p. 334. Equally mistaken seems to be the attempt made by Chauncy, and since commonly repeated, to identify Hatfield as "the place which the Saxons call *Hæthfelde*" (Bede, Hist. Ecc., lib. iv., cap. 17.), where was held, 680, the synod presided over by Abp. Theodorus : that Hæthfelth was probably Hatfield Chase.

† Nichols, Progresses of Queen Elizabeth, vol. i., p. 3.

* MS. letter in Trin. Col., Oxford, printed by Nichols, vol. i., p. 16.

† *Ibid.*, vol. i., p. 28.

‡ *Ibid.*: comp. Froude, Hist. of Eng., vol. vii., p. 15.

§ Grant of the Manor of Hatfield, Brit. Mus., Addit. MS. 6693, p. 105.

of his master's pleasures, Cecil, now Earl of Salisbury, enclosed two large parks, one for red the other for fallow deer. The house was completed in 1611 ; but Lord Salisbury was already in ill-health, and died in May of the following year. Since his death Hatfield House has continued to be the chief seat of his descendants : the title of Earl being in 1789 exchanged for that of Marquis of Salisbury. In the time of the 5th Earl, Hatfield House had been suffered to get very much out of order, but his successor spent large sums in " restoring it to its pristine magnificence," the architect employed being a Mr. Donowell. Walpole, who saw the house shortly after, was " not much edified " by the *improvements* effected —but these, whatever they were, have since been pretty well swept away. By an unfortunate fire (Nov. 27, 1835,) in which Mary Amelia, widow of James 1st Marquis of Salisbury, was burnt to death at the age of 85, the W. wing of Hatfield House was almost totally destroyed, but it was shortly after restored with scrupulous care to its original state.

James I. paid an early visit to Hatfield House, and his state bedroom is religiously preserved with its sumptuous original furniture intact. Charles I. was here, but as a captive, and not of his free will. In 1800 George III. and Queen Charlotte were royally entertained at Hatfield House, and on the 13th of June the King held a grand review in Hatfield Park. In 1846 Queen Victoria and the Prince Consort stayed some days here, when among other festivities a state ball was given in the Long Gallery ; and on July 12, 1874, the Marquis of Salisbury gave a magnificent entertainment to the Prince and Princess of Wales, the Crown Prince and Princess of Germany, the Duke of Connaught, Duke of Teck and Princess Mary, and some 900 noble and distinguished personages.

What the Earl of Salisbury left of the old palace has since been carefully maintained. The central gateway, opposite the E. end of Hatfield ch., now serves as the strangers' entrance to Hatfield House and Park. Passing through it, you enter an oblong court, bounded by the west wing of the bishop's palace. It is wholly of deep red brick, earlier and plainer in style than the older parts of Hampton Court, and

probably a portion of the edifice erected by John Morton, Bp. of Ely, 1478—86, who " bestowed great care upon his house at Hatfield," and in effect rebuilt the greater part of it. Elizabeth probably dwelt on the side of the palace demolished by the Earl of Salisbury, though Mr. Robinson thinks she may have occupied the rooms which remain.* These are now used as offices. The largest, which is believed to have been the great hall of the old palace, is now a stable for 30 horses. It is large and lofty, and has a timber roof springing from stone corbels.

The adjacent *West* or *Privy Garden*, an almost unique and happily unimpaired example of the Jacobean pleasure garden, was laid out by James I., who planted the four mulberry trees still growing in its four corners. It is only about 150 ft. square, and is, as Bacon would have a princely garden to be, " encompassed on all the four sides with a stately arched hedge," though the arches are not set, as he orders, " upon pillars of carpenter's work." † On the S., E., and N. sides are avenues of limes. In the centre is a basin of rock-work, now the home of gold fish. At the angles are ' plots,' with a mulberry tree in the midst of each.

Cecil's Hatfield House is perhaps the most majestic of the Jacobean mansions which have come down to us virtually unaltered. The design is commonly assigned to John Thorpe, the originator of the Elizabethan style, and the greatest architect of his time : but it is not in the list of his buildings in his book of plans (now in the Soane Museum), and it is doubtful whether he was living at the date of its erection (1610-11), as the last of his dated buildings was Holland House, 1607, the earliest being Kirby's, 1570. If not by Thorpe, Mr. Robinson thinks it may have been by John of Padua, from the decidedly Florentine character of the arcade in the principal front ; ‡ but this is certainly a mistake, as John of Padua flourished in the reign of Henry VIII., who in 1544 allowed him, as royal architect, a fee of 2s. a day ; and though the grant was renewed to him in the reign of Edward VI., it is not likely he would

* Vitruvius Britannicus : Hist. of Hatfield House, fol. 1833, p. 9.
† Essays : of Gardens.
‡ Hist. of Hatfield House, p. 14.

erect palaces in the reign of James I. Whoever was the architect, it is quite in the Thorpe style, and a highly effective example of it. Looking at the size and splendour of his house, it appears to have been built at a very moderate outlay—even if we assume that the old palace furnished the bricks. From the accounts, still preserved, it appears that the whole cost of the building was only £7631 11s. 3d.* Some of the particulars are very curious : one entry may be quoted as illustrating the rate of payment to skilful carvers in the early years of the 17th cent.

" Item, for cuttinge of 48 stone Lyons which stande in the open worke of masonrye about the house, for 11 tafferils more, for the carving of the pew heads in the chappell, the stone pedestalls in the open worke before the house, the chimney-peece in the upper Chappell, and the Corinthian heads which stand on the top of the stayre cases one the Northe side of the house, all which comes to . . . . £130 14 2 "

Hatfield House is in plan a parallelogram, 280 ft. long and 70 ft. wide, with, on the S., or principal front, two wings. each projecting 100 ft., and 80 ft. wide ; and forming, with the centre, three sides of a court, 140 ft. long. This S. front is very noble. The wings are connected by a centre, Italian Renaissance in character, of 2 orders, the lower Doric, the upper Ionic, with a highly enriched Elizabethan central gate-tower and stepped gables. The basement is an arcade extending the whole distance between the wings, the 8 arches being carried on fluted Doric pilasters, with arabesque ornaments. Above the principal floor, at 50 ft. from the ground, is a pierced parapet, and over this rise the gables. The central tower, in which is the elaborate entrance porch, projects boldly, is 70 ft. high, and is divided into 3 storeys, the 3rd exhibiting the full armorial bearings of the Earl of Salisbury ; in the parapet is the date of the completion of the building, 1611, and above the Earl's crest and coronet. A clock turret with cupola crowns the whole. The wings have projecting angle turrets, 50 ft. high, with cupola roofs 20 ft. high,

enriched central porches, and handsome oriels. The materials are brick, with stone pilasters, parapets, and dressings, and, being happily free from any incrustation of London smoke, have, with the weathering of two centuries and a half, toned down into delightful harmony. The ornamental gates in front of the house were erected on the occasion of the visit of Her Majesty in 1846.

The N. front, though less ornate, is large in style and very effective : the principal feature is the central compartment, with the enriched entrance of bold design. The ends are also good in their way : the E. end especially, as seen in combination with the garden and terrace, has a charming air of quaint antiquity.

The State Rooms are stately and superb ; as a whole, perhaps the finest remaining examples of their class and time. The *Hall*, or, as it is sometimes called, the Marble Hall, is a spacious and lofty room, 50 ft. by 30, with a coved ceiling, divided into panels, containing the heads of the Cæsars, and amply lighted by a great oriel at the upper end, and 3 on the S. side. At the lower end is a massive carved screen, overlaid with heraldic bearings ; the walls are wainscoted with oak, and hung with tapestry.

The *Grand Staircase*, 35 ft. by 20 ft. 9 in., of 5 landings, has massive carved balusters with naked figures playing on bagpipes and other uncouth musical instruments, and lions holding heraldic shields. On the walls are portraits of the Cecils by Zucchero, Vandyck, Lely, Kneller, Reynolds, and Beechey. *Obs.* the open-work wicket-gate on the first landing, put there, as is supposed, to prevent the dogs from intruding into the state apartments above.

The *Long Gallery* is striking from its unusual proportions, 163 ft. by 20, and 16 ft. high. It has a floor of dark oak, grotesque panelling on the walls, a flat " fret sealinge " of complex pattern, now picked out with gold, two massive fireplaces with dogs, is lit by a long line of side windows, and fitted with coats of mail and rare old furniture— among other things being some choice antique Japan cabinets, Queen Elizabeth's cradle, and many curious old pictures.

King James's Room, originally " The Great Chamber," at the E. end of the

* Robinson, p. 16.

gallery, is a superb room, 59 ft. by 27 ft. 6 in., and 21 ft. high, gorgeous in carving, gold, and colour, and lighted by 3 tall oriels. The great feature of the room is the grand chimneypiece, 12 ft. wide, of coloured marbles, the supports being Doric columns of black marble. Above, in a niche of dark stone is a life-size bronze statue of James I., crowned and holding a sceptre in his rt. hand. Silver fire-dogs, silver gilt candelabra, chairs and sofas with gilt frames and crimson velvet cushions, form the furniture; and on the walls are the family portraits, and other important works.

Under the Long Gallery, and of the same size, is the *Armoury*, where among other interesting suits of armour are many Spanish pieces, relics of the Great Armada, which were thrown ashore when the ships were wrecked, and sent to Burghley as trophies.

At the W. end of the gallery is the *Library*, a room corresponding in size and place to King James's Room, at the E. end. The room is a noble one, and well fitted, but its great attraction is the fine collection of printed books, MSS. (many with choice illuminations), and state papers. The latter include Lord Burghley's Diary, a mass of documents relating to the chief events in the reign of James I., and upwards of 13,000 letters of the first Cecils, extending from Henry VIII. to James I., all carefully arranged, classified, and catalogued. It also contains a fine portrait, by *Zucchero*, of Robert Earl of Salisbury, the founder of the house, 1608, *æt.* 48, in his robes as Knight of the Garter, and other pictures and objects of interest and curiosity.

Other state rooms are the *Summer Dining Room*, under King James's Room ; the *Winter Dining Room*, a handsome room, 31 ft. by 29, containing many curious and interesting portraits, as Peter the Great of Russia, and Charles XII. of Sweden, by *Kneller*, Henry IV. of France, James I. and Charles I. by *Van Somer*, and the Duke of Wellington by *Wilkie ;* and the *Drawing Room* connected with it. The *Chapel* contains King James's organ in a very rich case, and has an unusually fine painted window of Flemish work, representing in compartments various Scriptural subjects. The whole

of the ground floor of the E. wing is occupied by private apartments.*

Most of the principal rooms contain portraits of members of the Salisbury family. Besides these, and others already mentioned incidentally, there are many of personages of historic fame. Of Queen Elizabeth there are no fewer than 5 portraits, including the remarkable half-length by *Zucchero*, in which she is represented in an extraordinary jewelled head-dress, with huge transparent wings, and a still more extraordinary yellow gown embroidered with mouths, eyes, and ears, a serpent on her sleeve, and a rainbow in her hand, and which is inscribed, " Non sine sole Iris." Another is by Hilliard. Of Mary Queen of Scots there are two portraits : one in an oval frame, attributed to *Zucchero ;* another by *N. Hilliard*, dated 1578, *æt.* 36, and painted when she was a prisoner at Sheffield. Of James I., the best is one by *Mytens*. Henry Grey, Duke of Suffolk, father of Lady Jane Grey, a worldly Jewish countenance, half-length, *Mark Garrard*. Henry Herbert, 2nd Earl of Pembroke, ¾-l., *Vansomer*. Robert Dudley, Earl of Leicester, ½-l., in white doublet richly embroidered in gold, and furred cloak, *Mark Garrard*. William III., *Kneller*. A repetition of the Hampton Court Beauty, Lady Ranelagh, by *Kneller*. Algernon, 10th Earl of Northumberland, Countess, and child, ½-l., *Vandyck*.

Amomg the Salisbury portraits may be noticed—Thomas Cecil, Earl of Exeter, and his half-brother Robert, Earl of Salisbury, ancestors of the two great Cecil families, *Zucchero*. Mildred Coke, Lady Burleigh, 2nd wife of the great Lord Burghley, and mother of Robert Earl of Salisbury, *Zucchero*. James Cecil, 1st Marquis of Salisbury, *Beechey*. Mary, 1st Marchioness of Salisbury, whose sad death we have mentioned, a charming wholelength, walking in a garden, *Reynolds*.

Near the house are a riding-school and a tennis-court, both large buildings.

The gardens and grounds about the house are laid out with great taste, and kept in perfect order. When Evelyn

---

* The architectural features of Hatfield House are shown with great clearness in the plates drawn and engraved by Mr. H. Shaw for Robinson's Hist. of Hatfield House.

" went to see my Lord of Salisbury's palace," March 11, 1643, he thought " the most considerable rarity besides the house (inferior to few then in England for its architecture) was the garden and vineyard rarely well watered and planted ; " and Pepys, who was here many times (and on one occasion as he walked through the house " would fain have stolen a pretty dog that followed me, but could not, which troubled me "), was also delighted " above all with the gardens, such as I never saw in all my life ; nor so good flowers, nor so great gooseberries, as big as nutmegs " *—and now, after more, than two centuries have passed away, the gardens retain all their pre-eminence.

The park, the finest in the county, is of great extent, undulating, with the Lea flowing through it on the N., and abounding in noble trees. Some of the trees are famous. The Lion Oak, near the house, is over 30 ft. in girth, of most venerable antiquity, and though dilapidated from age, still verdant. More famous, however, is Queen Elizabeth's Oak, by the avenue—Hatfield Park is celebrated for its avenues—leading towards the kitchen garden, vineyard, and river Lea. According to a constant tradition, Elizabeth was sitting reading under this oak when the news was brought her of the death of Queen Mary : in a cabinet in the library is kept the broad-brimmed hat she wore when she received the message. The oak is now little more than a hollow trunk, the upper part being all gone, but it still throws out leaves from a few thin branches, is railed round, and carefully preserved. When Queen Victoria visited Hatfield, she carried away an acorn from the tree as a relique ; and very curiously this acorn was the last the tree ever bore. The avenue leads by the Gardener's Lodge to the *Vineyard* mentioned above. It is very carefully kept, and curious as almost the last of its age remaining. Beyond it are equally curious yew hedges, and a delightful terrace by the Lea, here crossed by a Gothic bridge of recent erection.

HAVERING-ATTE-BOWER,

Essex, a little rural village, and the site

of a royal palace, 3 m. N. of Romford : pop. 369. Inn, the *Orange Tree.* Havering gives its name to the liberty and peculiar of Havering-atte-Bower, which comprises 16,000 acres, and includes the parishes of Havering, Romford, and Hornchurch. To reach the vill., turn to the l. (N.) on leaving the Romford Rly. Stat. (Grt. E. Rly.), cross the High Street, Romford, to North Street, directly before you, by the Golden Lion Inn. This soon becomes a pleasant country road, and you follow it to Havering. The grounds, with overhanging trees, on rt. of the road after leaving Romford, belong to *Marshalls* (E. O. Coe, Esq.) At the parting of the roads, take the rt. ; the large white house, with battlemented turrets, among the trees in front, is *Bedfords* (J. Stone, Esq.) At the cross-roads, take that in front, and leaving Bower House on the rt. (*obs.* the broad prospects both rt. and l., and backward over the Thames), you pass the inn, and reach the village green, with the ch. on its farther side.

The name, *Haveringæ* in Dom., is no doubt the A.-S. patronymic *Hæfering*, though Morant derives it from A.-S. *hæfer*, a goat, and *ing*, pasture,* and tradition from the Confessor's famous gift of his ring to the pilgrim—" Have ye ring." According to the legend, King Edward being present at the dedication of a church in Essex, to St. John the Evangelist, an aged pilgrim drew near to the king and asked an alms in the name of St. John. The king had no money, so he gave his ring to the pilgrim, who took it and departed. Some time after, according to one version,—that very day, according to another,—two English pilgrims in the Holy Land, being benighted, were guided on their way by a venerable man, who found them a lodging, inquired their country, and asked much of the life and well-doing of their king. When they were about to take leave in the morning, their host told them that he was St. John, and having given them a ring bade them return straightway, deliver it to their king, and say, " I greet thee well : and by the token that ye gave me this ring at the hallowing of my church, within six months ye shall be

---

* Evelyn, Diary, March 11, 1643 ; Pepys, Diary, July 22, 1661 Aug. 7, etc.

* Hist. of Essex, vol. i., p. 58.

with me in paradise." All which, of course, duly happened.

Some early versions of the legend name the church *Clavering* in Essex, others merely say that it was a church of St. John. The weight of literary authority is decidedly in favour of Clavering, but local probability is as decidedly the other way. Edward had a house at Havering which he valued, and often visited, for the same reason that King James I. long after liked and visited it—its proximity to Waltham Forest, and its consequent convenience for hunting, of which he was passionately fond. Clavering is at the other end of the county, far away from the forest, and in no other connexion associated with the Confessor. What is still more to the point, Havering ch. is dedicated to St. John the Evangelist ; Clavering ch. to St. Mary and St. Clement. Lastly, the neighbouring ch. of Romford, the capital of the liberty of Havering-atte-Bower, and to which the royal chapel at Havering was considered a chapel of ease, is dedicated to St. Edward the Confessor, and the most prominent decoration of the old church (now rebuilt) was the legend of the ring.*

Edward loved Havering as much for its solitude, and as affording opportunities for devotional retirement, as for the pleasures of the chase : but, as happened to holy men of old in other country retreats, the singing of the nightingales disturbed his meditations, and he prayed that they might be banished ; after which nightingales were never heard within the park at Havering †—till our own degenerate times.

* The story is related by the writer of the De Inventione S. Crucis apud Waltham, by Ethelred, in the Life and Miracles of the Confessor, in Brompton's and Roger de Hoveden's Chronicles, the French metrical Life of the Confessor, and in Caxton's Golden Legends ; and comp. Professor Stubbs, notes, pp. 22 and 24, to his ed. of the De Inventione, Freeman, Norman Conquest, vol. ii., p. 512, and Waterton, in Archæol. Journal, vol. xxi., p. 105. By the 13th cent. the legend had become extremely popular. Statues of Edward, St. John, and the two pilgrims, with other references to the legend, were carved on the shrine in the chapel of the Confessor in Westminster Abbey, embroidered on the hangings of the choir, and painted in a window of the S. aisle ; whilst statues of the Confessor and St. John as a pilgrim were erected over the entrance gate in Dean's Yard and in Westminster Hall. Dart, Antiq. of Westminster ; and Stanley, Westminster Abbey.
† Camden, Remains, p. 483.

The manor continued after the Conquest to be held by the Crown, and a royal hunting-lodge, which appears to have been called The Bower, was built "of stone and leaded." To it, at the beginning of 1377, Edward II., after he had invested the prince (afterwards Richard II.) with the succession to the throne, withdrew, and he only left Havering to die at Sheen. It was after dining at his house at Havering that Richard II. went to Plashy to sup with his uncle, the Duke of Gloucester, before arresting and condemning him to death. Edward IV. was here hunting in the summer of 1482, when " lowlinesse and genlenesse had so far furth in hym encreased that " . . .

" Beeynge at Haverynge at the bower, he sente for the maire and aldermen of London thether onely to hunte and make pastyme, where he made them not so hertye but so familiare and frendly chere, and sent also to their wiues such plenty of venison, that no one thyng in many daies before gatte him either more hartes or more hertie fauour emongest the comon people, which oftentymes more esteme and take for greate kindnesse a little courtesie then a greate profite or benefite."*

Edward VI. was here for some time in his childhood. Queen Elizabeth frequently spent a few days at Havering in the summer season. She was here in July 1561, 1568, 1572, 1576, 1578, and 1588, on which last visit she confirmed to the inhabitants of Havering their privilege of freedom from purveyors. James I. used to close the hunting season by a visit to Havering.

" That Prince Henry died not without vehement suspicion of poison, this I can say of my own knowledge. The King's [James I.] custom was to make an end of his hunting at his house at Havering in Essex, either at the beginning or in the middle of September. Prince Henry did then accompany him. I was beneficed in the next parish, at Stapleford Abbot's. Many of our brethren, the neighbour ministers, came to hear the sermon before the King, and some of us did then say, looking upon Prince Henry, that certainly he had some great distemper in his body." †

James appears to have been the last royal resident in the Bower. From the survey of it drawn up in 1596 by the keeper of the house, Samuel Fox (son of the Martyrologist), it was then a good deal out of repair, and little probably was done to restore it in the succeeding years. It was, however, in existence after

* Hall, Chronicle, reprint, p. 346.
† Bishop Godfrey Goodman, Court of King James I., vol. i., p. 247.

the Commonwealth. Later, it is spoken of as ruinous and uninhabitable. In the middle of the 18th century parts of the walls were standing, "but not enough to show its original form or extent." * In 1827 "not a vestige" remained.† Some low mounds, and the irregular surface of the ground in the park near the green, suffice, however, to mark the site it occupied. Havering Park was divided and leased, but the manor remains in the Crown.

The successor of the royal bower is *Bower House* (C. P. Matthews, Esq.), erected, some way S. of the Palace, in 1729, by Sir J. Smith Burges, from the designs of Henry Flitcroft, the architect of the church of St. Giles in the Fields. It is a good and comfortable house, with views over a wide stretch of country, embracing some 7 or 8 miles of the Thames, with the Kentish Hills beyond, and W. much of Essex and Herts, with the queenly dome of St. Paul's rising above the smoke-cloud of London ; but on this side the view has been sadly injured by the destruction of Hainault Forest. In the hall of Bower House is a stone of the royal bower with the arms of the Confessor cut on it, and an inscription recording the erection of the present building. *Havering Park* (D. Macintosh, Esq.) is a modern Italian villa, occupying, with the pleasant grounds, a portion of the royal park.

There was a second royal residence, not so ancient as Havering, but of very early date, at *Pyrgo*, (variously Pergo, Pirgo, and Purgo), about a mile N.E. of the Bower. Pyrgo seems to have appertained to the Queens, and to have been reserved as their residence in widowhood. Eleanor, queen of Edward I., was one of its earliest occupants, and Joan, widow of Henry IV., died in it, July 1437. Q. Elizabeth granted house and park, in 1559, to Sir John Grey, 2nd son of the Marquis of Dorset. Grey more than once entertained the Queen here ; and here the Lady Katherine Grey (sister of Lady Jane Grey), after her committal to the Tower for marrying the Earl of Hertford, was permitted to retire on account of her failing health. From the Greys, Pyrgo passed by purchase to

Sir Thomas Cheke, grandson of the famous Sir John ; and since through many hands. The house, described as " a venerable structure," was in 1770 sold for the materials to a bricklayer in Ilford, who pulled down the wings and chapel. The rest was retained for several years. The present house (Major-Gen. Fytche) was built in 1852 ; and altered and enlarged by Mr. Barry in 1862.

Havering *Church*, St. John, stands on the W. side of the vill. green. It is a commonplace modern brick building, with Perp. windows, an ivy-covered chancel, wooden belfry, and short spire. The int. is plain, with high pews, and no monts. of interest. The font is the only vestige of the royal chapel. At the opposite corner of the green, facing the lane to Noakes Hill, is an immense elm, hollow, the top dead, and several of the upper branches gone : a magnificent ruin. Beneath it, *obs.* that venerable symbol of civilization, the stocks and whipping-post.

HAYES, KENT (anc. *Hese*), 12 m.

S.E. from London, 2 m. S. from the Bromley Stat. of the S.E. and L. C. and D. Rlys. ; pop. 621. Inn : the *George*, by the ch., a good house. The sign is said to have been painted by Millais, but is now too much blackened to be made out. To reach Hayes, turn l. on leaving Bromley Stat., and take the lane on rt. before reaching Leaves Green—a pleasant lane overhung with elms, with hop gardens and wheat fields on either side.

The vill., quiet and respectable, and chiefly dependent on the wealthy residents, consists of a few ordinary houses and shops. The *Church*, St. Mary, was a small and rather rude-looking edifice of hammered flint and stone, and comprised only a nave and chancel, with a small chapel on the S. ; but it was restored in 1861-2, under the direction of Sir Gilbert Scott, the chancel lengthened, and a large 3-light window, with circular head, inserted, an aisle added on the N., and a new and taller octagonal shingled spire placed on the embattled W. tower. The ch. is late E.E.; but the windows in the chancel and N. aisle are of course new. The int. has now a very neat, but very new, aspect. The nave, of 4 bays, has a good plain timber roof ; the windows

---

* Morant, Hist. of Essex, vol. i., p. 59.
† Nichols, vol. iii., p. 70.

in the chancel and N. aisle are filled with painted glass; the floor throughout is paved with encaustic tiles. The S. chapel, now used as a vestry, contains a piscina. *Brasses:* half-lengths of John Osteler, Sir John Andrew, and Sir John Heygge (1523), rectors of the parish. *Mont.:* a large mural marble tablet to Sir Vicary Gibbs (d. Feb. 8, 1820), Chief Baron of the Exchequer and Lord Chief Justice of the Common Pleas. Sir Vicary had a villa on Hayes Common. William Pitt was baptized in Hayes Church, and Bruce, the African traveller, married there. S. of the ch. is a large but hollow yew.

Close by the ch. is *Hayes Place,* the residence, and scene of the closing days, of the great Lord Chatham, and the birthplace of his illustrious son, William Pitt. When purchased by Lord Chatham, then the Rt. Hon. William Pitt, in 1757, Hayes Place was an old mansion, formerly the seat of the Scotts, and afterwards of the Harrisons, with a very few acres of ground attached. Chatham pulled down the house, and built a new one, and extended the grounds by purchase to about 100 acres. He took great delight in the place and his improvements—himself directing " with the prophetic eye of taste " the laying out of his grounds, so as to extort the warm praise of Horace Walpole.* Here his famous son, the younger William Pitt, was born, May 28, 1759. Here, during the disturbed ministerial crisis of May 1765, Pitt lay suffering from a severe attack of gout ; or, as Burke wrote, " on his back at Hayes talking fustian." On coming into possession of Burton-Pynsent, he sold Hayes Place (1766) to the Hon. Thos. Walpole ; but he soon repented ; and when the following year he was utterly prostrate, he became possessed with a morbid belief that only the air and scenery of Hayes " would save him." At length, on the renewed assurance that this was Lord Chatham's firm impression, Mr. Walpole consented, Oct. 1767, to reconvey the property to him.† Lord Chat-

* Essay on Modern Gardening, Anecdotes, vol. iv., p. 267 ; and see Grenville Correspondence, vol. i., p. 408.
† See the curious particulars in H. Walpole's Memoirs of the First Twelve Years of the Reign of George III., vol. iii., p. 42 ; Chatham Correspondence, vol. iii., p. 289 ; and Lord Albemarle's Memoirs of the Marquis of Rockingham, vol. i., p. 185, etc.

ham's last years were on the whole pleasantly spent at Hayes,—much of his time being given to the improvement of his estate, and the training of his favourite son. After his fatal fit on his last appearance in the House of Lords, he was removed as soon as practicable to Hayes Place, and there expired May 11, 1779.

Hayes Place was sold in 1785 to Mr. (afterwards Sir) James Bond, and by him, in 1789, to George Viscount Lewisham, afterwards Earl of Dartmouth. It has since passed through several hands, and is now the seat of Edw. Wilson, Esq.

"The house and grounds of Hayes, which had been purchased by Lord Chatham, were disposed of by his eldest son some years after his decease. So far as can be judged at present, the house has been little altered since his time. The best bedroom is still pointed out as the apartment in which William Pitt was born; it was probably also the apartment in which his father died." *

Immediately S. of Hayes is *Hayes Common,* of 220 acres, secured to public use, and placed under the charge of a board of conservators, 1869. Opening on to Keston Common it forms a broad expanse, high and breezy, bordered by goodly elms and beech, covered thick with gorse, several varieties of bright-coloured heaths, wild thyme, harebells, and ferns ; on all sides are wide prospects over Bromley, Beckley, and Chislehurst, and far away into Kent, with the Crystal Palace, a conspicuous landmark, and a mill and groups of red-tiled cottages for the sketch-book. On the high-ground in front, and a little to the l., is *Holwood,* the favourite residence of Chatham's famous son, William Pitt. (*See* KESTON.) Other seats are *Hayes Court* (H. A. Smith, Esq.), *Boston House* (Capt. A. Torrens), *Pickhurst* (S. H. De Zoete, Esq.)

HAYES, MIDDX. (Dom. *Hesa*), a

pleasant wayside village, lies a little to the l. of the Uxbridge Road, 12 m. W. from Hyde Park Corner, and about 3 m. S.E. from Uxbridge. The Hayes and Harlington Stat. of the Grt. W. Rly. is a full mile S. of Hayes. Pop. 2654.

The manor of Hayes, like that of Harrow (*see* HARROW-ON-THE-HILL),

* Earl Stanhope, Life of William Pitt, vol. i., p. 1.

was held by the Abps. of Canterbury till surrendered in 1543 by Cranmer to Henry VIII., by whom it was given in 1546 to Sir Edward North. In 1613 Lord North sold it to John and Richard Page. It has since been many times transferred, and now belongs to Sir Charles Henry Mills, Bart. The archbishops used the manor-house as an occasional residence. Anselm was in 1095 directed by William II. to repair to his manor at Hayes, and abide the king's commands. Here he was waited on by the body of the bishops, who attempted in vain to induce him to submit to the king. The local tradition says that Cranmer occupied the manor-house, and that "Queen Elizabeth used sometimes to stay at Pinkwell, and with her unrivalled train of courtiers and statesmen worshipped God in our parish church." * The old house remains, though a good deal modernized; it is now the residence of the rector. Part of the moat is also left; and there is of course the old story of the subterranean passage, which in this case is asserted to lead to the church. Ghosts, too, haunt the house and grounds, or used to do so,†—as they do or did most of the old houses in this district. (*See* CRANFORD.)

The country hereabouts is flat ; the soil clay, loam, and gravel ; the occupations are mainly agricultural, but brickmaking is also largely carried on. The Paddington Canal skirts the eastern side of the par. ; the Grand Junction Canal and the Grt. W. Rly. the southern. The district is considered healthy, and the lanes are green and pleasant. There are many farms ; few good residences ; fewer resident gentry ; "the farmers have been and are the greatest autocrats the parish possesses." The inh. have the reputation of being rough and rustic in manner, " of great combative tendencies," and behind the age in views and customs. Mummers and hand-bell ringers still make their rounds at Christmas ; as late as 1754, cock-throwing was practised in the churchyard on Shrove Tuesday ; within living memory a vicar used to come every week

from the King's Bench prison, and preach, with the sheriff's officer behind him in the pulpit ; and another vicar gave two boys who quarrelled after the confirmation service half-a-crown to "fight it out." But times are changing even at Hayes. The Grt. W. Rly. has opened a station at Botwell ; the ch. has been restored, and is well filled ; and our local authority admits that "a better state of things has now dawned upon us." *

The village, or, as the inh. name it, Hayes Town, is an irregular, commonplace collection of houses ; but a large proportion of the pop. is collected in the outlying hamlets of Hayes End, Yeading, West End, and Botwell.

The only building of any interest in Hayes town is the *Church*, St. Mary, a large and good fabric of flint and stone, carefully restored by Sir Gilbert Scott in 1873-4. It comprises nave with aisles and clerestorey, a very deep chancel, embattled tower of 3 storeys at the W. end, and an open timber porch on the S., in which is a bracket for a portable stoup. The larger part of the ch. is of the Perp. period ; but there are two lancets in the chancel, and a late Dec. window in the S. aisle. The int. has been greatly improved in appearance by the restoration, though it has lost the air of antiquity. Most of the windows have been renewed. The roof of the nave is coved and panelled, with bosses at the intersections of the ribs, carved with the instruments and emblems of the Passion, and the arms of England and Aragon. The aisles have low open timber roofs. In restoring the ch. some paintings were uncovered in the N. aisle ; but they were difficult to make out, and have probably not been preserved. The oil painting of the Adoration of the Shepherds has been removed. In the chancel are a piscina and sedilia, with canopies borne on Sussex marble shafts. The font, of Norman date, has a circular bowl for baptism by immersion, with rudely carved foliage round it, and supported on a thick central and 8 thin shafts. The pews have been cleared away, and chairs provided. *Monts.*—In chancel : mural mont., Sir Edward Fenner, of Hayes (d. 1611), Judge of the King's Bench ; and his son Edward (d. 1614),

---

* Eliz. Hunt, Hayes Past and Present, 1861, p. 5.

† "Who shall recount the awful tales which in my childish days were told of the beings that used to flit about its walks and gardens."—*Ibid.*, p. 15.

* Hunt, Hayes Past and Present, pp. 4, 15.

with half-length effigy, in armour and ruff, truncheon in rt. hand. S. aisle: altar-tomb of Thomas Higate (d. 1576), having brass with effigies of Higate, his wife, 5 sons, and 4 daughters. At E. end of N. aisle: altar-tomb of Walter Grene, about middle of the 15th cent.; on the top effigy in armour, at the angles shields of arms, three perfect, the fourth lost. The entrance to the ch.-yard is by an old and good *lich-gate*, resembling that at Heston. In the ch.-yard are two yews, on the N. and E. of the ch.

Hayes Park is a sub-manor. The house, a very good one, in a finely timbered park, is now a first-class lunatic asylum for ladies. There is a second female lunatic asylum at Wood End.

Hayes End is a good-sized hamlet, 1 m. N.W. from Hayes Town, on the Uxbridge Road.

Yeading (formerly *Yelding*) is a hamlet on the Yeading Brook and Paddington Canal, 1 m. N.E. of Hayes Town. The inhabitants are much employed in brickmaking, and have not the highest reputation. The native annalist writes*: "Sure I am that at Yeading dirt, ignorance, and darkness reign supreme;" but we know many worse places, and have always found Yeading folk civil.

Botwell, the hamlet in which ,is the Hayes Stat. of the Grt. W. Rly., is "a place but little more civilized than Yeading," † and need not detain us therefore.

The principal seats are *Hayes Court* (M. Newman, Esq.), *Botwell Lodge* (E. H. Shackle, Esq.), *Park House* (T. Shackle, Esq.)

HEADLEY, Surrey (Dom. *Hallega*),

a straggling village on the Downs, 2½ m. N. by W. of Betchworth Stat. on the S.E. Rly., and 3 m. S.E. from Leatherhead Stat. of the L. and S.W. Rly.: pop. 337. The country is charming, the air good, and there are several excellent seats, including *Headley Grove* (J. Bridge, Esq.), and *Headley House* (G. Lyall, Esq.) The neat little church, erected in 1855, is of flint and stone, E.E. in style, with a square tower and tall shingled spire at the W. end, added in 1859. *Obs.* the fine view from the ch.-yard. The odd sort of grotto

here, surmounted with a cross, is intended as a memorial of the old church, from fragments of which it was constructed: inside it will be noticed the old font, creed, and commandments. The walks across the Downs, over Juniper Hill to Mickelham, or more to the right over Mickelham Downs to Leatherhead, are greatly to be commended.

HENDON, Middx., lies to the rt.

of the ~~Uxbridge~~ Road, 7 m. N.W. from London, 3 m. N.W. from Hampstead: pop. 6972; but this includes the eccl. districts of All Saints, Child's Hill, 2138, and St. Paul, Mill Hill, 1335. Hendon proper had 3499 inh. in 1871. Inn, the *Greyhound*, by the ch., a good house. Hendon Stat., on the Midland Rly., is 1 m. N. by E. of the vill. On leaving the stat. turn l. and keep along the lane and through Burrows, leaving the pond on the rt.

The name, *Handone* in Dom., is derived by Norden, who "lived at Hendon during the greater part of King James's reign," from *Highendune*, "which signifieth Highwood, of the plenty of wood there growing on the hills." To this Lysons objects on the ground that *Heandune* "will be found to mean rather, the high down or hill." Mr. Taylor, the latest writer on the subject, asserts that Hendon is "from the A.-S. *hean*, poor."* But the soil is fertile rather than sterile, and it is to *heán*, high, rather than *hean*, poor, that we may look for the probable derivation.

Hendon par. is 7 m. long from N. to S., and from 2 to 4 m. wide. At its S. end the little river Brent, which has most of its head-streams in this par., forms a large lake. (*See* Kingsbury.) Northwards the ground rises into moderate elevations, by Hendon vill., Mill Hill, and Highwood Hill. The country is exceedingly pleasant, green, abundantly wooded, the trees large and various; undulating, the hills affording very pleasant views, the valleys many pretty field paths and quiet shady lanes, with hedges full of hawthorns, wild roses, honeysuckles, and brambles, and bluebells and arums everywhere by the waysides. The vill. is of some extent, and used to be rural and

---

* Eliz. Hunt, Hayes, p. 4.
† *Ibid.*

* Norden, Middlesex, p. 21; Lysons, Environs, vol. ii., p. 393; Taylor, Words and Places, p. 470.

Hendon

The Gate-house, Highgate (see p.344)

somewhat picturesque, but it has been so much improved of late years that it now hardly differs from any other suburban or railway vill. Recently a great many villa and cottage residences have been built at Hendon, and the number seems likely to be largely increased.

At the Dom. Survey, and for an uncertain time before, the manor belonged to the Abbey of Westminster. Alienated in the reign of Stephen, it was restored to the abbey in 1312, and continued to be held by it till the Dissolution, when it was transferred to the newly created see of Westminster. Bp. Thirlby surrendered it in 1550 to Edward VI., who the same year "bestowed it upon Sir Edward Herbert, Knt., as a favour at the time of his baptism, whereof King Edward was a witness." * It was held by his descendants till 1757, when it was sold by Henry Arthur Earl of Powis to the celebrated David Garrick. On his death, in 1790, it was sold to Mr. J. Bond, and has since passed through several hands.

The manor-house was an occasional residence of the Abbots of Westminster. Wolsey, after his fall, rested in the Abbot's house the first night on his way to York. The Abbot's house was succeeded by an Elizabethan mansion, which was successively the seat of Sir Edward Herbert, Sir John Fortescue, the Nicolls and Snows. This house gave place to a new one towards the end of the 18th cent., which had, among other occupants, the Earl of Northampton, Mr. Aislabie, and Lord Chief Justice Tenterden.

Hendon *Church* occupies a commanding site on the summit of the hill immediately N. of the vill. It is however a poor building, and not in the best condition. It consists of nave with aisles and clerestorey, chancel with aisles, and a tower at the W. end. The body of the ch. is covered with plaster; the tower, small and poor, is of stone, uncovered, except by ivy, but much weather-worn, and the battlements patched with red brick. The ch. is Perp., the windows mostly modern and poor, and those of the N. clerestorey have carpenters' frames. The interior is encumbered with deep galleries. The nave arches are borne on octagonal piers, probably of an earlier ch. The chancel

* Norden, Spec. Brit. ; Middlesex.

has been restored and decorated, and the E. window filled with painted glass. The font is Norm., large and square, with an arcade of intersecting arches on each of the four sides. *Monts.*—On N. of chancel, of Sir Wm. Rawlinson, one of the Commissioners of the Great Seal under William and Mary, d. 1703 ; life-size marble statue, semi-recumbent, the face turned to the spectator, with chancellor's robe, purse, and flowing wig; sometimes ascribed to Rysbrack, but which from the date could not have been executed by him. Edward Fowler, Bp. of Gloucester, d. 1714. Marble tablet, by Flaxman, to Charles Colmore, Esq., d. 1795. In the nave is a large and elaborate incised cross, but the brass is unfortunately lost. In N. aisle, tablet to Charles Johnson, the dramatist, d. 1748. The tower contains a peal of six bells.

The *Churchyard* is of exceptional beauty, carefully planted, and well kept. The view from the N. side of the old ch.-yard is very fine, embracing Harrow, Edgware, Stanmore, and the Buckingham hills, Elstree, and distant Hertford heights, Highwood and Mill Hill. Something was lost of the beauty of the views, though the panoramic range was extended, when the grove of trees which skirted the brow of the hill was cut down to form the new burial-ground. The best point of view now is from the large ash tree. In the ch.-yard are many large tombs, marking the family vaults of the Earls of Mansfield, and many local magnates. Among others buried here are James Parsons, M.D., d. 1770, eminent as a physician, man of science, and antiquary ; Sir John Ayloffe, Bart., keeper of the state papers, and distinguished as an antiquary, d. 1781 ; Nathaniel Hone, R.A., d. 1784, who acquired an unenviable notoriety by his picture of The Conjuror; Abraham Raimbach, d. 1843, so well known by his fine engravings after Wilkie. On the E., S.E., and N. of the ch. are moderate sized yews; farther E. are deodars and other handsome evergreens. Note the avenue of clipped limes from the entrance gate to S. door of ch. From the E. end of the ch.-yard is a very pretty footpath to Mill Hill.

In the vill. are almshouses for six men and four women, founded by Robert Daniel in 1681—a noticeable red brick building, repaired in 1853. The Metropolitan Convalescent Institution has a branch establishment at Burrows for 40 little girls—an admirably managed home. In the fields is a Gothic Roman Catholic ch., with the chancel unbuilt.

Brent Street is a genteel hamlet on the Finchley Road. Here are some good houses—one was the seat of the Whichcotes and of Sir Wm. Rawlinson—and a spacious Gothic Congregational chapel. The Knights Hospitallers had lands, some say a house, at Hendon; and the monastery of St. Bartholomew held the manor of *Renters.* Another sub-manor was *Clitheroes,* 2 m. S.E. of Hendon, where is now a picturesque old farm-house known as Clutterhouse Farm. The hamlets of GOLDER'S GREEN and MILL HILL have separate articles. *Child's Hill* is noticed under HAMPSTEAD ; *Highwood Hill* under MILL HILL ; the *Welsh Harp* and *Kingsbury Lake* under KINGSBURY.

HERTFORD, the county town of

HERTFORDSHIRE, and a parliamentary borough, lies in the valley of the Lea, where that river receives its tributaries the Beane, just above, and the Maran, below the town ; 2 m. S.W. from Ware, 21 m. N. from London by road, 26 m. by the Gt. E. Rly., and 28 m. by the Gt. N. Rly. Pop. of the municipal borough, 7169 ; of the parliamentary borough, which includes also part of Bengeo, 7894. Hertford formerly returned two members to Parliament, since 1867 only one. Inns: *Salisbury Arms,* Fore Street; *Dimsdale Arms,* Fore Street ; *White Hart,* Market Place ; *Green Dragon,* Maidenhead Street ; *Railway* taverns by the Rly. Stats.

"In this year," 913, says the Saxon Chronicle, "King Edward [the Elder] commanded the northern burh to be built at Heortford, between the Memera, the Benefica, and the Lȳgean [Lea]." This has been read as though Edward built the town of Hertford ; * but it was no doubt a castle or fortress he constructed, " not of great extent but handsome," as Henry of Huntingdon adds," † as a pro-

tection against the ravages of the Danes, who had in the previous reign taken and burnt the town, and were again threatening the country. There was probably a town here as early as 673, when Theodorus, Abp. of Canterbury, assembled a synod of bishops at *Herutford,* to consider the celebration of Easter, the intrusion of bishops, clerical discipline, marriage, and other important matters.*

Whence the name *Hertford* was derived has been disputed. Chauncy is angry with Norden for adopting the obvious etymology of the hart's ford, and would prefer to believe with Camden that it came from a British word meaning the *red ford,* so called " from the red gravel at the ford." † Mr. Taylor, however, assures us that " Hert-ford gives us the Celtic *rhyd,*" a ford, and that the *ford* is merely " the superimposition " of the Saxon synonyme. But later, when he comes to treat of names of places derived from wild animals, forgetting his Celtic *rhyd,* he instances the stag as giving the name to Hertford.‡ Whatever may have been the origin of the name, there can be no doubt that the A.-S. *Heortforda* means the hart's ford. And this has ever since been the accepted derivation of the inhabitants. Thus when Elizabeth granted arms to the borough in 1561, they were blazoned " Argent, a Hart couchant in a Ford, both proper:"§ though as now borne the hart is not couchant, but statant.

Hertford Castle was regarded as a place of importance in early times. William I. gave the custody of it to Peter de Valoines, or Valence, a powerful Norman baron, and thenceforth for centuries it had a succession of noble governors. In 1216 Hertford Castle surrendered, after a siege of some continuance, to Prince Louis of France, but was given up when his cause became hopeless. At a tournament held here June 27, 1241, Gilbert Earl Marshal was killed, as was also Robert Say, one of his knights, while many esquires were wounded. In 1345 Edward III. granted

* Chauncy, Hist. Antiq. of Hertfordshire, vol. i., p. 458 ; Kemble, Saxons in England, vol. ii., p. 321.

† " Edwardus rex . . . construxit Herefordiam, castrum non immensum sed pulcherrimum," Hist. Angl., lib. v.

* Bede, Hist. Eccl., lib. iv., cap. 5.

† Chauncy, vol. i., p. 452 ; and comp. Norden, Spec. Brit., Herts, p. 17, and Camden, Britannia, p. 413.

‡ Taylor, Words and Places, 2nd ed., 1865, pp. 213, 466.

§ Chauncy, vol. i., p. 484.

to his son, John of Gaunt, Earl of Richmond, who had married Blanche, youngest daughter of Henry Duke of Lancaster, the castle, town, and honour of Hertford, that he might there, "according to his estate, keep house, and decently make his abode;" and in 1362, on occasion of creating him Duke of Lancaster, entailed the honour of Hertford upon him and his heirs male. Gaunt had for a time John King of France and David King of Scotland as prisoners within his castle. Isabella, widow of Edward II., spent the last year of her weary captivity at Hertford Castle, and not at Castle Risings, as generally stated. After her death, Aug. 22, 1358, her body lay in the chapel of the castle, watched day and night by 14 poor persons (who each received 2*d*. a day and his food), till Nov. 23, when it was removed for interment to the church of the Grey Friars.* In 1399, while Richard II. was a captive in the Tower, Gaunt's son, Henry of Lancaster, stayed in his castle at Hertford, whence, accompanied by a goodly array of nobles and prelates, he rode into London to receive the enforced abdication of the unhappy Richard, and himself assume the crown. Henry IV. settled his castle of Hertford upon his wife Joan; it was forfeited by her attainder in the next reign, when Henry V. conveyed it to his wife, Katherine of France. In like manner, Henry VI. granted Hertford Castle, on his marriage, to Margaret of Anjou, in whose name courts continued to be held at Hertford as long as Henry retained a semblance of authority. Henry VIII. is supposed to have intended to make Hertford Castle a residence, and for that purpose caused a survey to be made of it; but it is more likely he thought of it for some of his children.

"This castle adjoineth to the King's town of Hertford, was parcel of his duchy, hath competent lodgings for his Grace, if it shall be his pleasure to lie there for a season. There is a fair river that runneth along by the north side thereof, the water serveth all the offices; there is very little garden ground, but a large court-yard, almost built round with fair lodgings; a small park, little more in compass than a mile, distant from the castle not a quarter, having a convenient lodge built with

timber. 'Tis well stored with timber trees: fuel, wood, and coal in these parts: £6 or £7, or a less sum, would yearly keep the castle and the houses about it staunch and dry. When the King shall please to lodge there, £40 or £50 must be bestowed upon the hostry, pastry, and such other offices, to make it convenient for his Grace; because they are now ruinous and decayed; wherefore the last year, William Byrd, the King's Receiver, by his warrant allowed £71 ,, 17 ,, 5 towards the repair thereof." *

Prince Edward was residing at Hertford Castle, when his father, Henry VIII., died. The king's death was kept secret till arrangements could be made for the new reign. Edward was not informed of it till the next day, Jan. 29, 1547, when he was taken by his uncle, the Earl of Hertford, and Sir Anthony Brown, to Enfield, and there the intelligence was formally communicated to him and his sister, the Princess Elizabeth. In 1561 Q. Elizabeth visited Hertford, and granted arms and a charter to the borough. James I. is also said to have been here. Charles I., May 3, 1630, alienated the castle and manor of Hertford to William Earl of Salisbury, by whose descendants they have since been held. Hertford Castle was taken possession of by the Parliament, and it was at Hertford that Cromwell by his prompt sharp measures put an effectual stop to the agitation of the Levellers in the Commonwealth army. In 1841, and again in 1846, Hertford was visited by the Queen and the Prince Consort; and by the Prince and Princess of Wales, on occasion of a visit to Panshanger, Nov. 28, 1874.

Of the old castle little is left but an embattled wall, some fragments of towers, and a mound. A mansion was built on its site about the time of James I.; but it has been so often and so much restored, modernized, altered, and added to, as to retain little of its original character. Before the completion of the college at Haileybury, Hertford Castle was occupied by the East India Company as a training school for their civil service. It is now the residence of Philip Longmore, Esq., part of it being fitted as the Judges' lodgings, and occupied by them at the Assizes.

Hertford sent two members to Parliament from the reign of Edward I. (1298) to that of Henry V., when the bailiff and

* E. A. Bond, Notices of the Last Days of Isabella, Q. of Edward II., drawn from an Account of the Expenses of her Household; Archæologia, vol. xxxv., p. 456.

* Report, 1552-3, Chauncy, vol. i., p. 480.

burgesses petitioned the king that they might be eased of the charge, "for that they were reduced to that poverty, that they were not able to pay their ways," and their prayer being granted the borough remained for 200 years without members. In 1624 the borough, in a petition to the House of Commons, set forth their ancient right to return two burgesses to Parliament, and asked that it might be restored to them. The claim was examined in committee, and led to "a great debate," when it was resolved that "to send and maintain burgesses in parliament is no franchise but a service, and that the service could not be lost by the discontinuance;" whereupon writs were issued, and Hertford continued to return its two members till 1867, when the number was reduced to one.

Around the market-place are several timber-framed houses with pargetting (ornamented plaster-work between the timbers), and two or three have the timber in the first floors very fairly carved; else there is little of antiquity in the town. The Shire Hall, a spacious but not handsome building, erected in 1780, contains the law courts, grand jury room, council chamber, a large assembly room for public meetings and county balls, and the usual municipal offices. The Corn Exchange has a semi-classical façade of Bath stone, surmounted by a statue of Ceres. The Market Hall is large, and covered with a glass roof. In the building is a Free Library, with a good reading room, maintained by the borough rates. There are besides literary and other institutes; and three newspapers are published weekly. The market, held on Saturday, is the largest corn market in the county. Corn and malt are the staple trade : there are no manufactures. On the Lea are large flour and oil mills. The Lea is navigable for barges, and there is a good carrying trade, chiefly in corn and malt.

Of 5 churches formerly in the town, All Saints is the only old one left, and that was *restored*, enlarged, and modernized in 1872-3. It is a large cruciform building, with a square tower and short spire at the W. end, in which is a peal of 10 bells; is of various dates, from E.E. to Perp., and of little architectural value. The window tracery is all new. Rising from amidst trees in a large ch.-yard; the ch. with its double chesnut avenue, has, however, something of a picturesque dignity. The int. has a broad open effect, and one or two of the *monts.* are noteworthy. *Obs.* in chancel, marble mont. of Sir John Harrison, M.P., of Balls Park, Farmer of the Customs to Charles I. and Charles II., and father of Lady Fanshawe, d. 1669. Marble tablet to the officers and privates of the 49th (Hertfordshire) regiment, who fell in the Crimean campaign, 1854. St. Andrews, at the W. end of the town, occupies the site of a small ch. of Perp. date, pulled down in 1870. The present church is a small cruciform building with an apsidal chancel; Early Dec. in character, with rose windows and plate tracery, designed by Mr. J. Johnson. The tower and spire were added by Lord Cowper in 1875. Christ Church, Port Vale, is a pretty little E. E. ch., built and endowed 1868, by J. Abel Smith, Esq., M.P.

A priory was founded, in the reign of William I., on the left bank of the Lea, behind the present Bluecoat School, by Ralph de Limesi. It was afterwards transferred to St. Albans Abbey, and made a cell to that house for 6 brethren. It received additional endowments, including the church of Amwell, and remained vested in the Abbey till the Dissolution, when it was granted by Henry VIII. to Sir Henry Denny. A Roman Catholic ch., St. Mary, was built on the site of the old priory in 1859. Congregational and other dissenting churches have in the last few years added somewhat to the previously scanty ecclesiastical architecture of the town.

There are many schools, but the one that gives character to the place is *Christ's Hospital School*, the preparatory school for Christ's Hospital (the Bluecoat) School, London. The school is a large, comfortable-looking, old-fashioned, red-brick building, forming 3 sides of a quadrangle, with a large hall erected in 1800, and ample playgrounds, at the E. end of the town, on the l. of the road to Ware. In it are about 420 boys and 20 girls; and there is an infirmary for 100 boys. The boys are drafted to the London school at the age of 12. Hertford has also a Grammar School (Hales), the Green Coat School, the Cowper Testimonial School for boys, the Abel Smith Memorial School for girls, and the Brown Industrial School for girls. In the North Road is the Hertford General Infirmary. The County Prison is in the Ware road.

Balls Park, S.E. of the town, on the rt. of the road to Hoddesdon, the seat of the Marquis Townshend, is a stately brick structure, erected by Sir John Harrison in the reign of Charles I.* The house stands on high ground, in a small but pleasant park, and has 4 uniform fronts, built about a central court. It continued to be the seat of the Harrisons till the middle of the 18th cent., when it passed by marriage to Charles, 3rd Visct. Townshend, Secretary of State to George II.

Brickendon is a liberty in All Saints par. 1½ m. S. of Hertford. The manor belonged to the monks of Waltham at the Dom. Survey, and was held by them till the Dissolution. Edward VI. granted it to John Aleyne, and it has since passed through many hands. Brickendon is a secluded little hamlet, with a good old farm-house; *Brickendonbury*, the fine seat of Mrs. Ellice, approached from Hertford by a noble avenue over a mile long; and farther S. what remains of the Brickendon Woods.

Little Amwell, another liberty in All Saints par., is noticed, with *Haileybury*, under AMWELL.

HERTINGFORDBURY, HERTS,

beautifully situated on the Maran, 1 m. W. of Hertford; and a stat. on the Gt. N. Rly. (Hertford and Welwyn br.) Pop. 828. Inn, the *White Hart*, a convenient country inn, by the river, mill, and Panshanger Park.

Panshanger, the main attraction of Hertingfordbury, is noticed under that heading. Hertingfordbury is hardly a village; there are a few houses gathered about the ch., a few more at *Cole Green*, 1¾ m. W., where also is a rly. stat., and others in the hamlets of *Roxford*, on the Lea, 1½ m. S.W. of Hertingfordbury ch., *Eason Green*, and *Lilly Green*, between Roxford and Cole Green.

Hertingfordbury *Church*, St. Mary, stands on high ground E. of the vill. It is an old rough-cast village ch., not

materially altered by recent restorations. It consists of a nave with an aisle and the Cowper chapel on the N., chancel, and, at the W. end, a tower with slate roof and short slender spire. The body of the ch. is Dec., with some Perp. windows inserted on the S.; the chancel E.E.; the Cowper chapel brick and modern. The int. is plain, partially restored, and has open seats, a carved reading desk, and Dec. font —all recent. *Monts.*—On S. of chancel, Sir Wm. Harrington, with recumbent effigies in alabaster of the knight and his wife, arms, and a long rhyming inscription. George Mynne, of Hertingfordbury, d. 1581, kneeling effigies of himself and wife, Elizabeth, daughter of Sir Thomas Wroth, of Durance, who took to her 2nd husband Nicholas Boteler, Esq., and d. 1613. N. side an elaborate mont. with recumbent effigy of Lady Calvert, d. 1622. There are also many tablets in the nave and aisle to the Keightleys and other old families, and one (on S. wall) to Sir Gore Ouseley, Ambassador Extraordinary to Persia, d. Nov. 1844. The Cowper chapel is devoted to monts. of the Cowper family. The most important is that by Roubiliac to Spencer Cowper, one of the Justices of the Common Pleas, d. 1727. Besides Panshanger, the principal seats are *Woolmers* (W. H. Wodehouse, Esq.), near Lilly Green; *Cole Green House* (J. C. Allen, Esq.); and *Moat House* (Capt. J. W. J. Gifford).

HESTON, MIDDX. (anc. *Hestune*),

about 10½ m. W. of Hyde Park Corner, by road; 1¾ m. N. from the Hounslow Stat. of the L. and S.W. Rly., and a like distance S. from the Southall Stat. of the Gt. W. Rly.; pop. 2840. The entire parish, which includes Hounslow and the chief part of Spring Grove, the cavalry barracks, and the large Roman Catholic orphanage at North Hyde, had 8432 inhab. in 1871.

Heston was of old famous for its fertility. Long before his time, writes Camden, it furnished bread to the royal table; and Norden described it as

"A most fertile place of wheate, yet not so much to be commended for the quantitie, as for qualitie; for the wheate is most pure, accompted the purest in many shires; and therefore Queen Elizabeth hath the most part of her provision from that place for manchet for her Highness's own diet, as is reported."

* "15 *April* 1643.—Near the town of Hertford, I went to see Sir J. Harrison his house new built." —Evelyn, Diary.

Heston maintains its reputation for fine wheat, and large crops are grown, but vegetables and fruit for the London market now obtain a large and increasing share of attention. The bulk of the population is dependent on the farms and market gardens, but brickmaking employs many. The village consists of three or four irregular streets converging upon a dirty little triangular Green, in the centre of which is a shabby brick pound, and just off it the ch. About the vill. are a few old timber-framed houses. There are several good old brick residences—the vicarage by the ch. is a comfortable-looking example—one or two stately mansions, and many cottages, both good and bad. The vill. and the lanes are rich in large elm and walnut trees, and the level meadows look green and flourishing.

The *Church*, St. Leonard, lies a little to the E. of the Green. The entrance to the ch.-yard is by a large picturesque old oak *lich-gate*, with one wide door turning on a central pivot, and self-closing by means of a rude pulley-wheel in the roof, and a stone weight enclosed in an iron frame—a primitive but effective piece of machinery. Heston ch. was one of the most interesting in this part of Middlesex. In the main Perp., having been plainly rebuilt on the lines of an older ch., it contained some features of each distinct period of ecclesiastical architecture. The S. arcade of the nave and S. aisle were E.E., the aisle opening by a Norm. arch into a Perp. chapel, or chancel aisle; the N. aisle, much wider than the S., was Dec. The chancel, with its chapels, the tower, and porches were Perp. Roofs, vestiges of the rood staircase, and other interesting details, remained in fair preservation. In 1865 the ch., with the exception of the tower, was levelled to the ground, in spite of earnest protests by architects and archæologists, and a new ch. erected from the designs of Mr. J. Bellamy, partly on the old foundations, but larger, affording 650 instead of 500 sittings. It is of Kentish rag, with Bath-stone dressings; Early Dec. in style; and comprises nave and chancel, with double aisles of equal height to each; W. tower, and N. and S. porches. Some parts of the old ch. have been copied, and some of the shafts and other parts rechiselled and worked up in the new

building,—but divested of all archæological value. The tower is, however, the old one, and good of its kind; Perp. of 3 storeys, with large W. window, and an angle turret carried well above the battlements. The large wooden W. porch is a copy of the old one. *Obs.* the nearly perfect stoup by the W. door. The *int.* is spacious, lofty, and light. Some of the windows are filled with painted glass. In the chancel is a curious *brass* to Mordecai Bownell, vicar, and wife Constance (d. 1581). The figure of the man with six children kneeling before him is lost. The woman is lying in bed covered with a worked counterpane, on which is laid an infant in swaddling-clothes; by her head is an angel; above her the demi-figure of the Saviour, with the rt. hand raised in benediction.* Two or three inscribed brasses are of no particular interest. There are also some *monts.* of the Childs family, of Osterley. The *font*, large and octagonal, is worth looking at: the carved oak cover is later.

From the back of the ch.-yard there is a pleasant walk of about a mile, eastward, by tall elms, and across a wheat-field, to OSTERLEY HOUSE, of which a notice will be found under that heading.

Anthony Collins, the celebrated free-thinking writer and controversialist, and correspondent of John Locke, is said to have been born at Heston, June 21, 1676: his father resided many years at Heston, and was buried in the ch., where two of his sisters were baptized, but Anthony himself was baptized in Isleworth ch.

Heston House, a handsome brick mansion at the turn of the road to Cranford, is the seat of Mrs. Rowland Hooper. Other seats are *Heston Hall* (J. R. Hogarth, Esq.), and *Bulstrode House* (Mrs. Robinson).

Sutton, a hamlet, S. of Heston vill., contains some good houses, among others the *Manor House* (Captain A. W. Cole), and *Sutton House* (P. Watson, Esq.)

North Hyde, 1 m. N.W. of Heston, is another hamlet. Here are extensive brickfields, and St. Mary's Roman Catholic Orphanage for Boys, a large establishment under the charge of Brothers of Charity from Malines in

* See eng. and description in Trans. of Lond. and Middx. Archæol. Association, vol. ii., p. 210.

Belgium: at the census of 1871 there were 411 boys in the house.

HIGH BARNET (see BARNET).

HIGH BEECH, EPPING FOREST, a great resort for holiday-makers and excursionists; 2 m. N.W. from the Loughton Stat. of the Gt. E. Rly. (Epping and Ongar line): take the lane opposite Loughton Stat., and keep along it till tempted by a bit of open forest on the l., cross the Epping road, and High Beech Hill and the King's Oak are about ½ m. due N.

High Beech Green is a hamlet and eccl. dist. (pop. 535) of Waltham Abbey, from which it is 3 m. S.E. It is a straggling collection of houses and cottages, with a small brick ch., St. Paul, built in 1836, and of no sort of interest. Near it are *Beech Hill Park* (R. Edwards, Esq.), *Fairmead Lodge* (E. Bartholomew, Esq.), was, 1791—1833, the residence of William Sotheby, author of 'Orestes,' and translator of the 'Iliad,' 'Oberon,' etc., *Wallsgrove House* (T. C. Baring, Esq., M.P.), the *Manor House* (C. W. H. Sotheby, Esq.), and *Alder Grove Lodge* (Prince Lucien Bonaparte). On the Loughton side of Beech Hill, by the Epping road, and serving as a chapel-of-ease to Loughton ch., an elegant little ch., St. Mary, was erected in 1872, from the designs of Mr. A. W. Blomfield. It is of stone, E.E. in style, cruciform, with a semi-circular apse, in which are seven lancet windows, a tower and tall stone spire at the N.W., and a stone porch at the S.W. From many spots amidst the old forest trees the ch. peeps out very prettily, and its spire is a landmark for miles around.

But the great attraction is the forest scenery, High Beech being the finest portion of Epping Forest left unenclosed. The central feature of the district is *High Beech Hill*, an outlier of Bagshot Sand, here attaining an elevation of 759 ft. From its brow is seen a broad sweep of undulating forest; and in the distance, looking across Waltham Abbey, whose tower and town strengthen and vivify the mid-landscape, the eye wanders unobstructed along the valley of the Lea and over the wooded demesnes of Herts to the dim uplands of distant Cambridgeshire, and round to the hills of Surrey and Kent; whilst from the heights southward, by the parsonage and Lappit's Hill, the view extends by way of Middlesex and the Surrey downs, to where.—

"Beyond the lodge, the City lies, beneath its drift of smoke." *

Tennyson was dwelling here—at Beech Hill House, since pulled down—when he wrote his 'Talking Oak,' and grander 'Locksley Hall,' and something of the local colouring was derived from his forest ramblings, "hidden to the knees in fern." High Beech, too, for awhile gave shelter to John Clare, who was brought to Dr. Allen's private lunatic asylum, Fairmead House, July 16, 1837, "a large establishment consisting of half a dozen houses connected together and surrounded by large gardens." † The son of Thomas Campbell, the poet, was at this time an inmate of the asylum, and Clare's constant companion in walks which after a time he was permitted to take about the forest. Clare wrote many little half-crazy poems expressive of his delight in the scenery:—

" I love the Forest and its airy bounds,
  Where friendly Campbell takes his daily rounds.
        *   *   *   *
I love to see the Beech Hill mounting high,
The brook without a bridge, and nearly dry.
There's Buckett's Hill, a place of furze and
  clouds," etc.

But after four years' trial he tired of the place, or of confinement, and started off, July 20, 1841, without a penny in his pocket, to walk to his native Northborough in Northamptonshire, which he reached, worn out with hunger and fatigue, on the evening of the 23rd. He was soon after taken to the County Lunatic Asylum, where he remained till his death, May 20, 1864.

On the E. side of High Beech Hill is the *King's Oak* Inn, the head-quarters of holiday-makers, and in the summer a crowded and noisy place, especially on Saturday, Sunday, and Monday afternoons. The King's Oak is the meet for the counterfeit Easter Hunt. (*See* EPPING FOREST.) Near the King's Oak Inn is an old stump, of late called Harold's Oak, from which the inn perhaps took its sign, The *Robin Hood*, the rival inn, is by the Loughton lane. By the hill-foot is an excavation locally known as Dick Turpin's Cave, from a tradition that it was one of

---

* Tennyson, Talking Oak.
† F. Martin, Life of John Clare, p. 273.

the lurking-places of that notorious high-wayman : this part of the forest had of old an evil reputation in that direction.

Beyond High Beech Hill, to the Wake Arms on the Epping road, about 1½ m., you may explore a charming bit of wild forest, guided by a winding forest road, and keeping the highroad well to your rt. Rough and broken, in parts open, elsewhere thick with pollard oaks and hornbeams, and an ever-varying under-growth of hollies, thorns, and sloes, rose bushes, sweetbriars, and brambles, and not wanting many an unlopped beech, oak, or ash, its sunny glades and gentle undulations reveal as you wander on a thousand peeps of sylvan loveliness. Deep moist dells rich in fungi, or banks of furze, fern, and heaths, foxgloves, and honey-suckles tempt your admiration at every turn, song-birds are on every spray, the call of the cuckoo is heard the summer through, and not unfrequently you may catch a glimpse of a nimble woodpecker, blue-tit, or wryneck. A mile beyond the Wake Arms is the earthwork known as *Ambresbury Banks*. (*See* that heading.)

Beech Wood is on the other (S.) side of High Beech Hill. Of no great extent, you might fancy it a fragment stolen from Minstead or Lyndhurst by some good fairy before the New Forest was despoiled. Certainly it is the finest piece of wild beech wood for many miles round London. The beeches are not of such venerable an-tiquity, and have no such gnarled and rugged boles, or wild fantastic roots, as those of Burnham ; but then, unlike the Burnham beeches, they are all un-lopped, and have sent out their free-grown branches high and wide as nature prompted. Generally they are well-grown, many are large, and some veritable giants.

All this part of the forest is as full of charm to the naturalist as to the lover of forest scenery. Some 15 or 16 varieties of ferns still flourish here, though within the last 10 or 12 years several of the choicer kinds, and among them the Osmunda regalis, lady's fern, and black spleen-wort, have been extirpated. Botanists describe the locality as remarkably rich in flowering plants and fungi ; and butter-fly collectors and entomologists generally find it a productive hunting-ground. Out of 120 kinds of birds which have been observed in Epping Forest, by far the

larger part haunt the purlieus of High Beech. By day the common song-birds— and some that are far from common— abound ; by night the air is vocal with nightingales. Not with nightingales alone, however ; this is a very paradise of owls, who are as noisy as they are numerous. At intervals may be heard the whir of the night-jar ; and bats abound (though they are silent messengers of the night). Mr. Newman names 7 kinds of bats as com-mon here.

HIGHGATE, MIDDX., a suburban village on the Great North Road, 5 m. from the Gen. Post Office by road, 4½ m. from King's Cross by the Gt. N. Rly. (Highgate and Edgware line) : pop. 5339. Inns : *Gate House*, opposite the Grammar School ; *Wrestlers* and *Red Lion*, at N. end of the town ; *Fox and Crown*, West Hill.

Highgate occupies the summit of Hamp-stead's " sister hill," at the junction of the two main northern roads,—from Oxford Street by way of Tottenham Court Road, and Islington through Holloway,—the summit being reached by the steep accli-vities of Highgate Rise and Highgate Hill. The two roads meet in the High Street, where begins the North Town, a broad highway lined with private dwell-ings, shops, and inns, and having at the commencement the Grammar School on one side, the Gatehouse Tavern on the other, and terminating in the slope of North Hill. On the W., by the junction of the roads, are the Grove and Green, where was the large pond referred to below, now filled up and planted. The Green, bordered by groves of ancient elms, seems to have been the centre of the original village, and the place where the villagers met for rural games and holiday diversions. Thus, the Whitsun Morris-dancers, in 'Jack Drum's Entertainment,' 1601, sing,—

" Let us be seene on Hygate Green,
To dance for the honour of Holloway."

Lanes run off rt. and l., from the Gram-mar School to Hornsey, from the Gate-house to Hampstead, main road and lanes being alike lined with good old tree-embowered houses, modern villas with bright gardens, and comfortable cottages ; not without signs of dirt and poverty, but, as a whole, a healthy, prosperous, and pleasant place, as Norden, who evidently knew it well, described it nearly three centuries ago :

"Upon this hill is most pleasant dwelling, yet not so pleasant as healthful ; for the expert inhabitants here report that divers who have been long visited with sickness, not curable by physicke, have in a short time repayred their health by that sweet salutarie aire. At this place — Cornwalleys Esq. hath a very faire house, from which he may with great delight beholde the statelie citie of London, Westminster, Greenwich, the famous river of Thamyse, and the country towards the south verie farre." *

All later writers are agreed as to the beauty of the prospect of the "statelie citie," but the vacant spaces whence the view was obtainable have been so enclosed or built over that it is now hard to find a tolerable stand-point, unless it be on a housetop. A glimpse of London may be caught from the summit of the hill, by Sir Sidney Waterlow's ; a broader view from the archway-bridge in Hornsey Lane. From the upper parts of the cemetery different portions of London may be seen ; but the best view is gained from the terrace behind Highgate church, which is not, however, always accessible. There is a pleasant prospect, though not over London, from "Peacock's Field " (by the birch-tree), where Jackson's Lane runs off from Southwood Lane —but this will soon be lost, as it is "to be let on building leases," under the name of Southwood Lawn. Like Hampstead, Highgate Hill is a mass of London clay with a cap of Bagshot sand, at the highest point 426 ft. above the Ordnance datum.

"Highgate, a hill over which is a passage, and at the top of the same hill is a gate through which all maner passengers have their waie ; the place taketh the name of this high gate on the hill, which gate was erected at the alteration of the way, which was on the E. of Highgate. When the way was turned over the said hill to leade through the parke of the Bishop of London, as now it doth, there was in regard thereof, a toll raised upon such as passed that way with carriage. And for that no passenger should escape without paying toll by reason of the widenes of the way, this gate was raised through which of necessitie all travellers pass. This toll is now farmed of the said Bishop at £40 per annum."†

Lysons thinks the derivation from this high gate, or gate upon the hill, "sufficiently satisfactory, supported as it is by facts, the toll-gate of the Bp. of London having stood from time immemorial on

the summit of the hill." On the other hand, it has been suggested that this is an example of the use of the word *gate* in the sense of road, Highgate meaning the highroad.*

The Gatehouse was a brick building extending across the road from the Gatehouse tavern to the burial-ground by the old chapel. The gateway through which the traffic passed had two floors over it, the access to which was by a staircase on the E. side. Of old, the gateway is said to have been only wide enough to allow a pack-horse with its side-loads to pass through, and though afterwards widened for carriages, the arch was so low that waggons with high loads had to be taken through the yard in the rear of the Gatehouse tavern.† To remedy the inconvenience the gatehouse was taken down and the roadway widened in 1769, and an ordinary turnpike gate substituted. On the front of the gatehouse was a stone inscribed A.D. 1386, but judging from the engravings it had no title to any such antiquity, being probably of about the time of Queen Elizabeth. The road was, however, in existence in the middle of the 14th cent., and the bishops had the right to demand toll on horses and cattle. Our older writers tell a curious story of the formation of the road, which Fuller epitomized in his odd way :—

"A nameless Hermit (dwelling in the hermitage where now the School is) on his own cost, caused gravel to be digged in the top of Highgate Hill, where now is a fair pond of water ; and therewith made a causeway from Highgate to Islington : a two-handed charity, providing water on the hill, where it was wanting, and cleanness in the vale, which before, especially in winter, was passed with much molestation." ‡

In 1363, Edward III. granted to Wm. Phelippe, in consideration of "the pious motive which, for the advantage of our people passing through the highway between Heghgate and Smithfelde, in many places notoriously miry and deep, you unremittingly and continually exert in the emendation and support of that way in wood and sand, and other things of that nature necessary thereto, at your own cost," the privilege of taking customs

---

* Norden, Spec. Brit. : Middlesex, 4to, 1593.
† Norden, *Ibid.*, p. 22.

* Taylor, Words and Places, p. 252.
† Prickett, Hist. of Highgate, p. 13 ; Tomlins, Perambulation of Islington, p. 38.
‡ Fuller, Worthies of England ; Middlesex. Camden and Norden write to the same effect.

of all persons using the road for mer-
chandise ; the said toll to be applied only
to the reparation of the road, and to cease
altogether and not be levied after the end
of the year.* Mr. Tomlins suggests that
this Wm. Phelippe was probably Fuller's
"nameless hermit," and he quotes various
authorities in proof that hermits were
often employed as toll-collectors and engaged in repairing roads.   To the hermitage at Highgate there are several references. The Bp. of London in 1386 collated
" William Litchfield, a poor hermit weighed
down by poverty and age . . . . to the
office of the custody of our Chapel of
Highgate, beside our Park of Hareng, and
of the house to the same chapel annexed,
by other poor hermits hitherto used to be
kept," for the term of his life. The last
hermit mentioned is William Forte, who
received a grant of the hermitage for his
life in 1531.   The Hermitage House was
granted by Queen Elizabeth in 1577 to
John Farnehame, one of her gentlemen
pensioners.†

Till within the memory of the passing
generation a toll of another kind was
levied at the Gatehouse :—

" Some o'er thy Thamis row the ribbon'd fair,
   Others along the safer turnpike fly ;
   Some Richmond Hill ascend, some scud to Ware,
   And many to the steep of Highgate hie.
   Ask ye, Bœotian shades ! the reason why ?
   'Tis to the worship of the solemn Horn,
   Grasp'd in the holy hand of Mystery,
   In whose dread name both men and maids are
      sworn,
And consecrate the oath with draught and dance
      till morn." ‡

Byron wrote these lines in Thebes, and
partly, perhaps, from imperfect recollection, partly from the exigences of rhyme,
somewhat overstated the accompaniments
of the once famous *Highgate Oath.* The
oath was consecrated with libations of
wine, but not often with dance till morn.
Highgate was the halting-place of stage-
coaches to and from the North, and it had
come to be the established custom, when
coaches drew up at the inn doors, to invite
passengers to alight and enter for refreshment. They were led into " the parlour,"
and the subject of the freedom of Highgate introduced. If the person addressed
betrayed ignorance of the oath, he was
told that all who passed through Highgate
must be sworn and admitted to the freedom. The *horns* were brought in by the
landlord, and compliance was generally
extorted from some of the company, the
fine on admission being a bottle of wine,
or " draughts round " in some meaner
liquor : in 1761 the fee was " a shilling
for the oath, to be spent among the company." The horns were a pair of ram's,
stag's, or bullock's horns, mounted on a
pole about 5 ft. high. The person to be
sworn placed his right hand on one of the
horns, when the landlord or his deputy,
after proclaiming " Silence ! " proceeded to
deliver his charge. This was a rude jocular
injunction to the effect that the new freeman must " Take notice what I now say
to you, for *that* is the first word of your
oath,—mind *that !* . . . . You must not
eat brown bread while you can get white,
except you like the brown the best. You
must not drink small beer while you can
get strong, except, etc. You must not
kiss the maid while you can kiss the mistress, except you like the maid the best,
or have the chance to kiss them both ; "
and more to the same effect, concluding
with, " And now, my son, kiss the horns,
or a pretty girl if you see one here, and
so be free of Highgate." The " privileges,"
as they were called, seem to have been a
comparatively late and coarse addition.
In its main features the oath was pretty
much the same in the earliest known
account of it *—a ' Song by the Landlord
of the Horns,' introduced in the panto-
mime of ' Harlequin Teague,' at the Hay-
market Theatre, August 1742—as it was
when dying out a century later.

" An old and respectable inhabitant of the village
says that 60 [now 100] years ago upwards of 80
stages stopped every day at the Red Lion, and that
out of every 5 passengers 3 were sworn. . . . . An
old inhabitant, who formerly kept a licensed
house, says, ' In *my* time nobody came to Highgate
in anything of a carriage, without being called
upon to be sworn-in.   There was so much doing in
this way at one period, that I was obliged to hire a

---

* Patent Rolls, 37 Edw. III., printed by Tomlins, Perambulation of Islington, p. 34.
    † Newcourt, Repertorium, i., p. 654 ; Tomlins,
p. 37.
    ‡ Byron, Childe Harold, Canto i., 70. Washing-
ton Irving describes his Stout Gentleman as one
" who has seen the world, and been sworn in at
Highgate."

---

* In Barnaby's Journal (Itinerarium, 1623, p. 59)
drinking out of the crooked horn (*cornu tortuo-
sum*) at Highgate is mentioned, but nothing is said
of the oath ; it is, however, noticed in the Weekly
Oracle for 1737.

man as a swearer-in. I have sworn-in from 100 to 120 in a day. Bodies of tailors used to come up here from town, bringing 5 or 6 new shopmates to be sworn [St. Monday was usually chosen by this class of novitiates]; and I have repeatedly had parties of ladies and gentlemen in private carriages come up purposely to be made free of Highgate in the same way.'—Officers of the guards and other regiments repeatedly came to the Gate House and called for ' the horns.' Dinner parties were formed there for the purpose of initiating strangers ; and as pre-requisites for admission to sundry convivial societies now no more, the freedom of Highgate was indispensable." *

When Hone wrote (1826) there were " 19 licensed houses in this village, and at each of these houses the horns are kept and the oath administered." In 1842 the oath, though "still occasionally" † administered, was fast falling into disuse— the consequence of the loss of the stage-coach traffic from the opening of the rail-ways. It is now a mere tradition. When the oath was customary, a pair of horns was fixed over the door of every inn ; now only one house (the Green Dragon) has horns outside, and only two (the Gate-house and the Cooper's Arms) possess the original staff and horns inside. Much has been written as to the origin of the custom. The most probable suggestion is that a pair of horns mounted on a staff was the gatekeeper's symbol of authority for taking toll on sheep and cattle passing through the gate, and the possession and exhibition of this symbol led in process of time to the burlesque of taking toll of human travellers, and conferring on them, by virtue of the horns, the freedom of High-gate.

The formation of this road over the hill in the place of the earlier one by Crouch End, Muswell Hill, and Friern Barnet, if it was not the origin of the village, was the main cause of its growth into import-ance. Prior to its construction, Highgate was only known as a portion of Hornsey, and was for the greater part covered with the woods of Hornsey or Haringey Park. The early history of the manor, Hornsey

Park and Lodge Hill, the Bishop of Lon-don's house, at the N.E. angle of what is now known as Bishop's Wood, will be found under HORNSEY. Of the Wood itself the chief portion left is Bishop's Wood, opposite Caen Wood, at the junc-tion of Highgate and Hampstead. (*See* CAEN WOOD.) A smaller fragment, known as *Highgate Wood*, remains on the l. of Southward Lane, near the Wood-man inn (much cut up in forming the Highgate and Edgware Rly.), and a piece, somewhat less injured, at the end of Wood Lane.

Sir Roger Cholmeley, Lord Chief Justice of the King's Bench under Edward VI., having been dismissed from his high office and imprisoned by Queen Mary, for his share in drawing up the late king's will, by which Mary was disinherited, on his liberation withdrew from public life and retired to Hornsey. Here, as his days were drawing to an end, he resolved to devote his property to the foundation of " a Publique and Free Grammar School." For this purpose he obtained, in 1565, charters of Queen Elizabeth, licensing him to found and erect a grammar school at his own charges ; and a grant from Bp. Grindall of the Hermitage chapel, High-gate, and two acres of ground. Later he procured a transfer of Farnham's lease of the Hermitage House. Cholmeley died soon after completing his arrangements, but his trustees carried out his purpose. The first stone of the school and chapel was laid in July 1576, the buildings were completed in Sept. 1578. The chapel was to serve not the school only, but to be a chapel-of-ease to Hornsey par., for the use of the inhabitants of Highgate, the school-master being the minister, who was to teach and read prayers there on all meet and convenient seasons, " saving that on any the first Sunday of every month in the year the said schoolmaster shall not say the morning prayer in the said chapel, because the inhabitants of the said town or hamlet of Highgate," are on that day required to resort to their parish church, "to hear common prayers and sermons, and to receive holy communion there."

The chapel served this double purpose for more than 150 years. In 1833, having become dilapidated, the old chapel was pulled down ; Highgate was, 1834, created an ecclesiastical district, and a new church,

* Hone, Every Day Book, 1826, vol. ii., pp. 81, 86. Hone's is the best and fullest account of the Highgate oath, and that from which all later accounts are taken. He carefully collected all the information then obtainable at Highgate, and en-riched his narrative with a capital cut of Swearing on the Horns, by George Cruikshank, the scene being the parlour of the Fox and Crown, and Hone himself the chief performer.

† Prickett, Highgate.

St. Michael's, erected on a different site. The Old Chapel, always a mean building, had been so often altered as to be altogether without architectural character or picturesqueness. Inside there were a few interesting monts., two or three of which were re-erected in St. Michael's and Hornsey churches; that of Chief Justice Sir Francis Pemberton, d. 1699. was removed to Cambridge, others were lost.*

The Highgate Grammar School underwent various fortunes, but never acquired a high reputation : Nicholas Rowe was, perhaps, the most celebrated of its scholars. In 1824 it was remodelled ; under the mastership of Dr. J. Bradley Dyne, it was greatly raised in character, and at his retirement in 1873 was in a more prosperous state than at any previous period. Of Cholmeley's school-buildings every vestige has long disappeared. A new school-house was built in 1819, but it was an insignificant and inadequate structure, and was taken down, and the present handsome group of buildings erected in 1865—68, from the designs of Mr. F. C. Cockerell. The buildings comprise school, chapel, and library, and are of good red brick, with stone mouldings, pierced parapets, and dressings. The school-house is Collegiate in style, the entrance being marked by a gable in which is a sundial, while over the doorway are three small bas-reliefs. The schoolroom is large, well-proportioned, and has a good open roof. The chapel is early French Gothic, has an apsidal chancel, with 5 memorial lancet windows, and a slender flèche. The chapel was the gift of Mr. G. A. Crawley ; the library was built by old scholars.

The chapel occupies in part the site of the old Highgate chapel, but includes part of the old burial-ground, and covers the vault in which lie the remains of the poet COLERIDGE. To preserve this intact, the chapel was constructed with a crypt, into which is an external entrance from the W. Descending a flight of steps, the visitor sees behind an open grating, a range of small square marble tablets, with initials marking the place of the

coffins : S. T. C. (the poet); S. C. (his wife) ; S. N. C. (his daughter Sara) ; H. N. C. (Henry Nelson Coleridge, the poet's nephew and his daughter's husband); and H. C. (Herbert Coleridge, the poet's grandson, buried here in 1861).

Highgate *Church*, St. Michael, stands some little distance S. of the old chapel and school, facing the entrance to the Grove. It is of white brick and stone, well-built, spacious, and lofty ; comprises nave and aisles with clerestorey, buttresses, crocketed pinnacles, and pierced parapet, chancel with large 5-light E. window, and at the W. end a tower and octagonal stone spire. The style is an impure Perp. (it was consecrated in Nov. 1832). The archt. was Mr. Lewis Vulliamy. Occupying nearly the highest point of Highgate Hill, its tall spire is conspicuous for miles around. The int. of the church is convenient, and well-kept, but in no way remarkable. The only mont. to be noted is a marble tablet with a long insc. to " SAMUEL TAYLOR COLERIDGE, Poet, Philosopher, Theologian," d. July 25, 1834. " This truly great and good man resided for the last 19 years of his life in this hamlet," and " James and Ann Gillman, the friends with whom he lived during the above period," add, with other commendation, that he was "the gentlest and kindest teacher ; the most engaging home-companion."

The house in which Coleridge spent these 19 years, and in which he died, was the third house in the *Grove*, facing the church, a roomy, respectable brick dwelling, with a good garden behind, and a grand outlook Londonwards. In front of the house is a grove of stately elms, beneath which the poet used to pace in meditative mood, discoursing in unending monologue to some earnest listener like Irving or Hare, or an older friend like Wordsworth or Lamb. The house remains almost unaltered ; the elms too are there, but four or five years ago some Vandal deprived them of their heads.

" Coleridge lives in the Grove at Highgate, with a friendly family who have sense and kindness enough to know that they do themselves an honour by looking after the comforts of such a man. His room looks upon a delicious prospect. . . . . Here he cultivates his flowers, and has a set of birds for his pensioners, who come to breakfast with him. He may be seen taking his daily stroll up and down, with his black coat and white locks, and a

* Lysons and Prickett give ample notes of the monts. in the chapel ; and in the Brit. Mus. (Add. MSS. 7943) is a full list of the epitaphs in the Old Chapel burial-ground.

book in his hand ; and is a great acquaintance of the little children." *

" Coleridge sat on the brow of Highgate, in those years, looking down on London and its smoke tumult, like a sage escaped from the inanity of life's battle . . . . . sat there as a kind of *Magus*, girt in mystery and enigma ; his Dodona oak grove (Mr. Gillman's house at Highgate) whispering strange things, uncertain whether oracles or jargon. . . . He would stroll about the pleasant garden with you, sit in the pleasant rooms of the place,— perhaps take you to his own peculiar room, high up, with a rearward view, which was the chief view of all." †

Of the other churches, *St. Ann's*, Brookfield, Highgate Rise, is not in Highgate par., Brookfield being an eccl. dist. of St. Pancras. The ch., a neat Gothic one, with painted glass windows, was erected in 1852, by Miss Burnett, as a memorial of her brother,—Miss (now Baroness) Burdett-Coutts giving the site, and a fine peal of bells. *All Saints*, North Hill, is a pretty little cruciform ch., with a bell-cote, early French Gothic in style, erected in 1865 from the designs of A. W. Blomfield, and enlarged in 1875. The Presbyterian chapel in Southwood Lane is interesting as having been founded as early as 1622. Like many of the old Presbyterian churches it became Unitarian in creed ; and had among its ministers David Williams, "the High-priest of Nature," noteworthy as the founder of the Literary Fund, Rochmont Barbauld (husband of Mrs. Barbauld), and Alex. Crombie, LL.D., a man of some literary celebrity. In 1814 it passed into the hands of the Baptists. The handsome Gothic ch. on the summit of the hill near St. Michael's ch., is a Congregational ch., erected in 1860, and since enlarged. The large brick building, cruciform and Romanesque, opposite the Archway tavern, at the foot of Highgate Hill, is a Wesleyan ch., built in 1873 from the designs of Mr. J. Johnson.

Immediately behind St. Michael's ch., and falling rapidly away to the S., with, from the upper parts a good view over London, is *Highgate Cemetery*, the most beautifully situated of all the suburban cemeteries, and one of the most crowded. Consecrated in 1839, and since greatly extended, it has received a large share of

the men of mark who have passed away in these 36 years. Strolling leisurely about the walks, the visitor cannot but be struck as his eye glances along the forest of monuments, with the many names familiar in art, science, and literature, in the pulpit or on the stage, in public or in social life, from men like Lyndhurst and Faraday, down to Wombwell and Tom Sayers— the latter having by no means the least conspicuous monts.

The ch. and cemetery occupy the site of the *Mansion House*, erected by Sir Wm. Ashurst, Lord Mayor in 1694, and afterwards the seat of Sir Alan Chambre, Justice of the Common Pleas. The house, which appears to have been of good architectural character, is said to have been built from the designs of Inigo Jones— but this is more than doubtful, as Jones died in 1652. When the house was pulled down, the enriched stone doorway, with the arms of Ashurst over it, was re-erected as the entrance to a house on the E. side of the High Street, now occupied by Mr. J. Oakeshott, surgeon.

Nearly opposite the Mansion House, where now stands the Grove (including the house in which Coleridge lived), was another noted mansion, *Dorchester House*, " a capital messuage or mansion-house of Henry, late Lord Marquis of Dorchester." The marquis was "remarkable for having been a bencher of Gray's Inn and a fellow of the College of Physicians." * His daughter, Lady Anne Pierpoint, was married from Dorchester House, July 1658, to John Lord Roos, son of the Earl of Rutland. Eight years after they were divorced by Act of Parliament, whereon ensued the publication of statements by Lord Dorchester and Lord Roos, the particulars of which are given by Walpole in his Royal and Noble Authors. Dorchester House was purchased by a crazy philanthropist, William Blake, " a woolen draper at the sign of the Golden Boy in Maiden Lane, Covent Garden," to use his own words, as " first only a Sumer's recess from London ; " but " which, having that great and noble city, with its numerous Childhood, under view, gave the first thoughts to him of a great Design "—that of establishing in it " a Hospital for 40 poor or fatherless children " of Highgate,

---

* Leigh Hunt, Lord Byron and some of his Contemporaries, 1828, vol. ii., p. 53.
† Carlyle, Life of John Sterling, 1852, p. 68.

* Lysons, Environs, vol. ii., p. 439.

Hornsey, or Hampstead, who were to be "decently cloathed in blew, lined with yellow; constantly fed all alike with good and wholsom diet; taught to read, write, and cast accompts, and so put out to trades, in order to live another day." Blake called his institution the Ladies' Hospital, or Charity-school House of Highgate, hoping to obtain from the ladies of the neighbourhood and of London generally, and through them from their husbands the wealthy citizens, sufficient subscriptions to carry out his benevolent purpose. In furtherance of his design, he printed a strange, incoherent volume entitled 'Silver Drops, or Serious Things,' in which he earnestly appeals to the ladies to come to his assistance, and sets forth the excellence of the undertaking. The book has become a bibliographical curiosity. partly on account of its rarity and the quaint language in which it is written, but also from the circumstance that most of the copies are bound in choice old Morocco (or Turkey, as it was then called), and beautifully tooled at the sides as well as back, whilst several have the name of the lady to whom it was presented on the cover. Blake appears to have had 36 boys in his school in 1667; but subscriptions failed, his affairs became involved, he was compelled to mortgage the house, and after "an essay of the design in the maintenance of children at this school for two years," and having on the building, "and by presents to persons of honesty and piety [probably of his 'Silver Drops'] expended 5000l.," he complains that he "was, for debts contracted only for this hospital and well enough secured, seized, imprisoned above two years, just at the height of his expence, before his receipt of the promised assistances, to have repayed him and enabled his work." This final appeal was issued in the shape of a large print or 'Delineation of the Ladyes Hospital at High-gate,' the margin covered with incoherent statements—from which the above passages are quoted. The school —believed to be the first charity-school founded on the principle of support by voluntary subscriptions—probably came to an end about 1685; but Blake, nothing daunted by his failure, availed himself of the enforced leisure of his prison to draw up a scheme for a great extension of his original design,—which may possibly

have been the germ of the charity-schools which in the next century sprang up in almost every parish. This he published, under the title of 'The State and Case of a Design for the better Education of Thousands of Parish Children successively in the vast Northern Suburbs of London, vindicated.' The house in which Coleridge resided, as well as the two houses before it in the Grove, occupy the site, and were partly built out of the materials of Dorchester House.

On the slope of Highgate Hill, towards Holloway, were several mansions of interest from their owners or associations. *Arundel House*, the seat of the Earls of Arundel in the 17th cent., stood on the l. or E. side of the road, on what is known as the Bank. It is probable that this was the house occupied by Sir Thos. Cornwallis, of which Norden spoke in the passage cited above. In May 1604 Sir Wm. Cornwallis gave a splendid entertainment to James I. and his Queen at his house at Highgate, for which occasion Ben Jonson prepared his dramatic interlude of The 'Penates.' * Sir Thos. Cornwallis died in Dec. 1604, and Sir Wm. is believed to have removed to the family seat in Suffolk: at any rate there is no later mention of the family at Highgate. Whether in the house of Cornwallis or another, Lord Arundel was resident at Highgate in 1617, when the Countess of Arundel, in the absence of the Earl, who was in attendance on the King in Scotland, entertained the Lord Keeper Bacon, the Master of the Rolls, Sir Julius Cæsar, the Lords Justices, and other members of the Council. James I. stayed the evening of Sunday, June 2, 1624, at the Earl of Arundel's house at Highgate, in order that he might hunt a stag in St. John's Wood, early the next morning. The next and most important reference to Arundel House is to the death within it of the great Lord Bacon. The circumstances connected with it are related, in an oft-quoted passage, by Aubrey, on the authority of Thomas Hobbes:—

"The cause of his Lordship's death was trying an experiment, as he was taking the aire in the coach [April 2, 1626] with Dr. Witherborne, a Scotchman, physician to the King. Towards Highgate snow lay on the ground, and it came into my Lord's thoughts why flesh might not be preserved

* Nichols, Prog. of King James I., vol. i., p. 430.

in snow as in salt. They were resolved they would try the experiment presently: they alighted out of the coach and went into a poor woman's house at the bottom of Highgate Hill, and bought a hen and stuffed the body with snow, and my Lord did help to do it himself. The snow so chilled him that he immediately fell so ill, he could not return to his lodgings (I suppose then at Gray's Inn), but went to the Earl of Arundel's house at Highgate, where they put him into a good bed warmed with a panne, but it was a damp bed that had not been laid in for about a yeare before, which gave him such a cold that he died in 2 or 3 days; as I remember, he [Hobbes] told me, he died of suffocation."

Bacon lay here a week, his death occurring on the morning of Easter-day, the 9th of April. The story of stuffing the fowl with snow rests on Aubrey's authority, but it receives some confirmation from a passage in a letter Bacon dictated (being unable to hold a pen), to Lord Arundel, to excuse his taking up his abode at his lordship's house—"but when I came here, I was not able to go back, and therefore was forced to take up my lodging here" —and thanking him for the attention he had received from his servants. He adds, "I was desirous to try an experiment or two touching the conservation and induration of bodies. For the experiment itself it succeeded exceedingly well; but in the journey (between London and Highgate) I was taken with such a fit of casting, as I know not whether it was the stone, or some surfeit or cold, or indeed a touch of them altogether." The subsequent history of Arundel House is without interest. In its later days it was occupied as a school; and it was pulled down in 1825.

In the various accounts of Highgate it is stated that it was from the house of Mr. Coniers at Highgate that the unfortunate Arabella Stuart made her escape, disguised in man's apparel; while some writers suggest that the house was Arundel House.* But the statement is altogether a mistake: the house from which she escaped was Mr. Thos. Conyers', at EAST BARNET.

Cromwell House, at the end of the Bank, just below the site of Arundel House, is so named from a tradition that the Protector once dwelt in it, a tradition abandoned in favour of another that the house was built by Cromwell as a residence for General

Ireton, who had married his daughter. There is no direct evidence of this, but it is not unlikely. Ireton could, however, have lived but little here. He married Bridget Cromwell in 1646; was directly after engaged in active service; on the proclamation of the Commonwealth was sent to Ireland, and died there in Nov. 1651. The story told by Mr. Gibson, that "General Ireton was elected a governor and trustee of the Cholmeley foundation [the Grammar School], but was expelled the trust," * is plainly an invention. Ireton died in the plenitude of his power. The expulsion of Commonwealth men did not commence till after the Restoration. By whomsoever, or for whom, built, Cromwell House is a good example of the carefully finished, artistic, red-brick mansion of the first half of the 17th cent. The rooms are large and of good proportions, and have the ceilings moulded in scroll and floriated patterns. That of the drawing-room has a coat of arms, said to be Ireton's. The staircase, a noble one of oak, has carved balusters, and statuettes on the standards of Commonwealth soldiers in their several uniforms. On the night of Jan. 3, 1865, the house, then occupied as a boarding-school, was partially destroyed by fire. It has been restored, not without material injury to its original character. In place of the old platform on the roof, which afforded a panoramic view of great extent, there has been erected a hideous and unmeaning octagonal turret, covered with cement, and crowned with a dome. Cromwell House is now a *Convalescent Hospital for Children*, a branch of the Hospital for Sick Children, Great Ormond Street. It has accommodation for 56 children, and is an excellent and well-conducted establishment. Adjoining Cromwell House, at the corner of Hornsey Lane, is another large and stately old red-brick mansion, *Winchester Hall* (Mrs. Jeakes). It stands amidst good old trees, and commands from the level roof a wide panoramic view.

Directly opposite Cromwell House is *Lauderdale House*, the seat of the Duke of Lauderdale, the notorious minister of Charles II., and Lord Deputy of Scotland.

---

* Prickett, Hist. of Highgate, p. 121. Howitt, Northern Heights, pp. 370, 374.

* Hist. and Antiq. of Highgate, p. 57.

"*28th July*, 1666.—To the Pope's Head, where my Lord Brouncker and his mistress dined. . . . . Thence with my Lord to his coach-house, and there put six horses into his coach, and he and I alone to Highgate. Being come thither, we went to my Lord Lauderdale's house, to speak with him, and find him and his lady and some Scotch people, at supper: pretty odd company, though my Lord Brouncker tells me, my Lord Lauderdale is a man of mighty good reason and judgment. But at supper there played one of their servants upon the viallin some Scotch tunes only; several, and the best of their country, as they seemed to esteem them, by their praising and admiring them: but, Lord! the strangest ayre that ever I heard in my life, and all of one cast." *

According to a cherished Highgate tradition, Nell Gwynne lived some time at Lauderdale House, and here induced Charles II. to acknowledge her infant, afterwards the Duke of St. Albans, by holding the child out of window, and threatening to let it fall unless he gave it a title. In our own day, Lauderdale House was, 1843, the seat of R. Bethell, Esq., afterwards Lord Westbury and Lord Chancellor; and later for many years the residence of James Yates, Esq., F.R.S., when it was famed for its garden-parties, at which the literary and scientific celebrities were gathered to meet the lions of the season. Since his death, Lauderdale House has been converted into a convalescent branch of St. Bartholomew's Hospital, a lease of it rent-free for 7 years having been granted to the governors of the hospital for that special purpose by its owner, Sir Sidney Waterlow. The Home was formally inaugurated by the Prince and Princess of Wales, July 8, 1872. The house, though altered and modernized, is in the main what it was in Lauderdale's time. It is a long, plain, stucco-fronted house of two stories, with a pediment on each of the two main façades, and a heavy roof. From the garden front, which has a recessed arcade, and is much the more picturesque of the two, there is a good view Londonwards. The terraced garden, with its brilliant flowers and velvet lawns, was in Mr.

Yates's time a charming example of an old-fashioned garden, treated with the best modern skill. A large portion of the grounds has been incorporated with those of Fairseat House.

Next to Lauderdale House stood what was known as *Andrew Marvell's Cottage*, from a constant tradition that it was the residence of the author of the 'Rehearsal Transprosed.' A long, low, modest wood-and-plaster cottage, with a central bay window and porch, set 8 or 10 feet back from the footway, it had a pretty little old-fashioned shrubby garden, with a raised walk, behind. Having fallen out of repair, it was taken down by Sir Sidney Waterlow in 1869. The only vestige of it left is the flight of 3 stone steps which led from the road to the front door.

Just above the site of Marvell's Cottage is *Fairseat House*, a large, irregular, but grandiose, white-brick, Renaissance mansion, of recent erection, the seat of Alderman Sir Sidney H. Waterlow, M.P., who had the honour to receive the Prince and Princess of Wales as his guests, on their visit to Lauderdale House in 1872. The house is spacious, richly fitted, has from the two prospect towers nearly the best views over London which Highgate affords, and the grounds, which include the chief part of those of Lauderdale House and Marvell's Cottage, are extensive and pleasant. Opposite to Fairseat House is Ivy House, for some years the residence of Mr. Charles Knight.

On the Green, by Swain's Lane, may be observed another good but much battered old red-brick mansion, *Church House*, now in the occupation of Mr. Daniel, "cemetery mason," but which a century ago was the residence of Sir John Hawkins, the friend of Johnson and author of a ponderous History of Music, and of his daughter Letitia, the novelist and memoir writer. Sir John was chairman of the Middlesex magistrates, and always rode to the Sessions House, Hicks's Hall, in a stately carriage drawn by four horses. It may not however have been wholly from pride he figured thus: Highgate folk still remember that General Harcourt, a near neighbour of the musical knight, and other residents, "displayed a similar taste in equipage and horses;" * and it

---

* Pepys, Diary, vol. iii., p. 245. Highgate was at this time evidently a place of fashionable resort. Thus the Grand Duke Cosmo "went out again to Highgate, to see a children's ball, which being conducted according to the English custom, afforded great pleasure to his Highness, both from the numbers, the manner, and the gracefulness of the dancers."—Travels of Cosmo the Third, Grand Duke of Tuscany, through England, 1669. 4to, 1821, p. 319.

* Prickett, Hist. of Highgate, p. 117.

must be considered that the bad state of the roads made the steep ascent of Highgate Hill very laborious. From Pepys we have learnt that my Lord Brouncker deemed it necessary to " put 6 horses into his coach " in order to climb Highgate Hill ; and the father of Wilkes of '45 fame, a wealthy distiller of St. John's Street, Clerkenwell, used, a little before Hawkins's time, to ride on Sundays to the Presbyterian chapel in Southwood Lane in his carriage drawn by six horses, his son John and Miss Mead, John's future wife, accompanying him.* Sir John Hawkins's capacious coach-house and stables now serve as the lecture hall and offices of the Highgate Literary Institute.

A house a few yards farther on, the second house past the ch. towards West Hill, was the residence of one who in his day made far more noise than Sir John Hawkins, and nearly as much as John Wilkes, Dr. Henry Sacheverell, who died here June 5, 1724. The house is worth looking at as a genuine untouched moderate-sized gentleman's house of the reign of Queen Anne.

Passing onward by Cutbush's Nursery, noted alike for its flowers and the view from the upper part of the grounds, there will be noticed lying back on the rt. a modest roadside inn, with seats in front, and the royal arms, with a long inscription, over the entrance. This is the *Fox and Crown* (vulg. Fox-on-the-Hill), and the insc. records a remarkable accident which occurred to Her Majesty only a fortnight after her accession to the throne. The Queen was driving over West Hill with the Duchess of Kent, July 6, 1837, when the horses became restive and dashed off at a gallop. West Hill is very steep ; there is an awkward turn of the road just below, and the position was perilous. Turner, the landlord of the Fox and Crown, was watching the coming carriage, saw the danger, and promptly caught a leader's head, and, with ready help, brought the carriage to a stand. Turner received a handsome present, and permission to place the royal arms over his door ; but he died in poverty a few years back. At West Hill Lodge, just below the Fox and Crown, and before

that at the Hermitage, lower down the hill, lived for some years William and Mary Howitt, known by many popular books.

A little lower down the hill on the l. is *Holly Lodge*, the seat of the Baroness Burdett-Coutts. When the residence of the Duchess of St. Albans, Holly Lodge was famous for its fêtes and garden parties ; and those given by the present owner have been at least equally celebrated. One of the most memorable was that given (July 19, 1870) to the Belgian Volunteers, and a party specially invited to meet them, including the Prince of Wales, the Prince and Princess of Teck, the Duke and Duchess of Aosta, and many other distinguished persons. The house has little architectural character externally, having become what it is by frequent additions, but the interior is handsome and commodious, and contains many good pictures and objects of art. The conservatory, in addition to a rich store of exotics, contains a fine collection of minerals, admirably classified and arranged for convenient examination by Professor Tennant. The gardens are kept in the finest condition, and the grounds are varied, well wooded, and in parts, as from the fir hill, afford good views. In Swain's Lane, a short distance from Holly Lodge, is *Holly Village*, a group of 9 detached model houses built by Miss (now the Baroness) Burdett-Coutts in 1865-6, from the designs of Mr. Darbishire. The houses are small, but built of the best materials, and with as much care and finish as though they were mansions. They are early Domestic English in style, all differ in form and details, and have a piquant and attractive aspect. They are ranged around a quadrangle laid out in lawns and flower-beds, and entered by an archway somewhat elaborately decorated with statues and carving.

The long low cottage apposite the principal entrance to Holly Lodge was for many years and until his death, June 1870, the residence of "Judge Payne," the ardent friend and popular advocate of ragged schools and other philanthropic objects. The adjacent mansion was the seat of Sir W. H. Bodkin, Assistant Judge of Middlesex (d. 1874), whose deputy Joseph Payne was.

Nearly opposite the entrance to Holly

---

* Almon, Life and Correspondence of John Wilkes, vol. i., p. 3.

Lodge is Millfield Lane, a few yards down which on the l. is a fantastic looking house of many gables named *Brookfield House* (J. Ford, Esq.), which, when a much less pretentious place, and known as *Ivy Cottage*, was the residence of Charles Mathews (the elder), and contained his noted collection of theatrical portraits : a catalogue of the pictures, and a plan of their arrangement in Ivy Cottage, will be found in C. J. Smith's 'Historical and Literary Curiosities;' the pictures themselves are in the Garrick Club. In Mathews' days, and long after, Millfield Lane was one of the most delightful lanes on this side of London, but within the last few years the hedgerow elms have been ruthlessly cut down, the banks planed away, and high fences erected so as effectually to shut out the views on either hand.

"It was in the beautiful lane running from the road between Hampstead and Highgate to the foot of Highgate Hill, that meeting me one day, he [Keats] first gave me the volume [of his Poems]. If the admirer of Mr. Keats's poetry does not know the lane in question, he ought to become acquainted with it, both on his author's account and its own. It has been also paced by Mr. Lamb and Mr. Hazlitt, and frequented like the rest of the beautiful neighbourhood by Mr. Coleridge, so that instead of Millfield Lane, which is the name it is known by on earth, it has sometimes been called *Poet's Lane*, which is an appellation it richly deserves. It divides the grounds of Lords Mansfield and Southampton, running through trees and sloping meadows, and being rich in the botany for which this part of the neighbourhood of London has always been celebrated." *

Caen Wood, Lord Mansfield's Park (*see* CAEN WOOD), is on the l. of Millfield Lane; on the rt. was Fitzroy House and Park. Fitzroy House, a large square brick building, with capacious and handsome rooms, but of little architectural merit, was built for Lord Southampton in 1780. In 1811 it was the seat of the Earl of Buckinghamshire. In 1828 the house was pulled down, the park parcelled out, and several villas erected on the more convenient sites. In one of these lived Dr. Southwood Smith, the popular physician, author of 'The Philosophy of Health,' and friend and conservator of Jeremy Bentham.

On an eminence originally a portion of Fitzroy Park, was *Dufferin Lodge*, the

* Leigh Hunt, Lord Byron and some of his Contemporaries, vol. i., p. 419.

pleasant rural seat of Lord Dufferin, removed in 1869 to make way for *Caen Wood Towers*, the more pretentious villa of Edw. Brooke, Esq., a costly structure of red brick and stone, with stepped gables, bay-windows, long galleries, and massive towers, completed in 1872, from the designs of Messrs. Salomons and Jones.

In 1746, Marshal Wade, after his removal from his command in the Highlands, bought an old house in Southwood Lane, pulled it down, and built on the site a comfortable roomy brick dwelling in which to spend in quiet his remaining days. After the Marshal's death it was sold by his nephews, to whom he had bequeathed the property. It was for awhile the residence of Mr. Longman the publisher. The house is on the rt. in Southwood Lane, the last but one before reaching Jackson's Lane.

A large square modern brick mansion on the rt. of North Hill, known as *Park House*, was in 1847 rented as an Asylum for Idiots, the first instituted in this country. The asylum having been removed to Earlswood, Park House was purchased in 1863, and converted into the *London Diocesan Penitentiary*. On Highgate Hill, at the corner of Maiden Lane, stood of old a noted roadside inn, the Black Dog. This was afterwards converted into a private dwelling; and this, with the grounds, was purchased some years ago for the use of the Passionist Fathers, a monastery formed, named *St. Joseph's Retreat*, and a large Roman Catholic chapel built. Two or three years back a showy school-house, with tall campanile, was built on the lower part of the estate; and now, Nov. 1875, a large and costly monastery is being erected on the terrace, Italian in style, from the designs of Mr. Tasker.

The immense structure on the rt. in Maiden Lane, just below St. Joseph's Retreat, was erected by St. Pancras parish, in 1870, as an *Infirmary* for paupers. It is a plain brick building, in several blocks connected by corridors, on the pavilion system; has accommodation for nearly 600 patients, and is very complete in arrangements and appliances.

Opposite to it, on the l. in Maiden Lane, but with the chief entrance on Highgate Hill, is the *Smallpox and Vac-*

cination Hospital, erected in 1850—a spacious but unobtrusive brick building, well-placed on the S. side of the hill, and in all respects an admirable institution. Ordinarily about 1000 smallpox patients pass through it annually, but in years when the disease is epidemic more than double that number are received. So excellent are the arrangements, and so careful the supervision, that even in the worst years the nurses and attendants have enjoyed almost entire immunity from the disease.

Near the foot of Highgate Hill, by the kerb opposite the Whittington Stone public-house, at the corner of Salisbury Road, the first turning above the Junction Road from Holloway, is *Whittington Stone*, marking the site of that on which, according to the legend, the runaway apprentice, Richard Whittington, rested, footsore, when he heard Bow bells chime sweetly

" Turn again, Whittington,
   Thrice Lord Mayor of London-town."

In Chatelain's ' Prospect of Highgate from Upper Holloway,' and other old prints, the stone is represented as a truncated shaft on a square base ; and Mr. Tomlin has shown pretty conclusively* that it was a portion of a wayside cross, which probably stood in front of the Lazar-house and Chapel of St. Anthony. This hospital for persons stricken with leprosy was founded in 1473, by William Pole, yeoman of the guard to Edward IV. ; it existed as a spital-house, serving also as a poorhouse, as late as the reign of Charles I., but in 1653 the land was sold, with the buildings on it, and the spital-house was probably removed, as there is no later mention of it ; the field, however, continued—till built over, 1852—to be called the Lazerette or Lazercot Field. Whatever was the original, the stone known as Whittington's remained till removed by one of the parish authorities in 1795. Popular dissatisfaction being loudly expressed at the removal, a new stone, inscribed Whittington's Stone, was soon after set up. This second stone was in 1821 removed by the churchwardens of Islington, in which parish it stands, and a new one erected, bearing the same inscription,

together with the years in which Whittington was Mayor,—1397, 1406, and 1419. This stone was renewed in 1869, a low iron rail placed round it, and a large lamp above, together with a number of small coloured illumination-lamps : Whittington's Stone is, in short, degraded into a public-house signpost.

Sir Richard Whittington, by his will dated Sept. 3, 1421, founded a college of priests and choristers, together with an almshouse for 13 poor men, on the N. side of St. Michael's Church, Paternoster Row. Whittington's College was dissolved in the reign of Edward VI., but the almshouse remained at College Hill, under the direction of the Mercers' Company. At length, in 1822, the Mercers' Company, finding they had a handsome surplus in hand from the Whittington estate, resolved to found new *Whittington's Almshouses*. Led probably by the popular associations, they selected for the site a piece of ground on the rt. of the Archway Road, nearly opposite and within view of the Whittington Stone. The almshouses are a range of modest but comfortable dwellings,with a chapel in the centre, a light, cheerful, Gothic pile, built about a large lawn, on which is a statue of Whittington. The almshouses are for 24 single women over 55 years of age, who receive lodging ' gifts,' medical attendance, and an annual stipend of £30 each. The general supervision is in a tutor (or master), and a matron. Besides there, there are in Highgate the almshouses in Southwood Lane, for 6 poor persons, originally founded by Sir John Wollaston in 1658, and rebuilt, and augmented with an annuity of £5 to each widow, by Edw. Pauncefort, Esq., in 1723,—but the houses are low, close, and gloomy.

The *Archway Road*, more than once referred to, was constructed as a means of avoiding the steep acclivity of Highgate Hill. In 1810 a Company was formed and an Act obtained to carry out the project of Mr. Robert Vazie, for a roadway on the E. of the hill, " from the foot of Highgate Hill, Holloway Road, to rejoin the main road just beyond the 5 m. stone." The new road was to be 1½ m. long, with a tunnel 765 ft. long, 24 ft. wide, and 19 ft. high. The works were commenced, and about 130 yards of the tunnel made ; but in those days the art of tunneling was ill

---

* Perambulation of Islington, p. 141, etc.

understood ; the brick lining was insufficient ; the London clay through which it was carried was treacherous, and suddenly the whole fell in with a noise that startled the neighbourhood. The tunnel was now of necessity abandoned, a wide open cutting substituted, and the present picturesque archway—a lofty single arch below, and 3 smaller arches with a balustrade over it—substituted. The failure of the tunnel was not the only or the chief difficulty in making the road. The subsoil was sand and gravel, and the road being in a deep cutting was exposed to the frequent and sudden influx of water, and all attempts to form a firm roadway failed. The road was formally opened in 1813, but after years of labour, trying numberless experiments, and a great outlay, the works were in 1829 placed temporarily under the management of the Holyhead Road Commissioners. By extensive and judicious drainage, and laying the road-metal in a thick bed of Roman cement, Telford, with his able assistant Macneil, brought the road in a short time into an excellent state. So marked was the success that the Archway Road occupies an important place in the annals of road-making ; whilst the experience gained from the failure of the tunnel is said to have been of material service to Stephenson in constructing his early railway tunnels through the London clay. The cutting of the Archway Road was further of great scientific value ; in that it furnished a large proportion of the fine collection of fossils of the London clay, formed by Mr. N. T. Wetherall, of the Grove, Highgate, which, after yielding a rich harvest to geologists, has now found a permanent home in the British Museum.

The chain of ponds—4 in Lord Mansfield's park, 3 outside, the latter known as the *Highgate Ponds*,—lie to the l. of Millfield Lane, and are described under CAEN WOOD, p. 17. Immediately W. of them is *Parliament Hill*, or as it is sometimes called *Traitors' Hill*, the latter name, as is asserted, being due to a tradition that the conspirators in the Gunpowder Plot were to meet on the hill to witness the effect of the explosion.* The more common tradition is that it was

* Howitt, Northern Heights.

called Parliament Hill from the Parliamentary generals having planted cannon on it for the defence of London. The hill is 307 ft. above the Ordnance datum, and on a clear day commands a wide prospect. London, with the Surrey hills beyond, is well seen from it.

HILL HALL, ESSEX (*see* THEYDON MOUNT).

HILLINGDON, MIDDX. (Dom. *Hillendone*), a vill. on the Oxford road, 14 m. W. of Hyde Park Corner, 1¼ m. S.E. of the Uxbridge Stat., 2 m. N. of the West Drayton Stat. of the Gt. W. Rly. Pop. 8237 ; of the entire parish, which is very large, and includes the greater part of Uxbridge, and the hamlets of Colham and Yiewsley, 11,601. Inn, the *Red Lion*,— a house which entertained Charles I. as an unwilling guest, after his escape from Oxford, with his chaplain, Dr. Hudson, and Ashburnham, his groom of the chamber, when besieged by Fairfax, April 1646.

"After we had passed Uxbridge at one Mr. Teasdale's house a taverne in *Hillingdon*, we alighted and stayed to refresh ourselves, betwixt 10 and 11 of the clocke [Monday morning. April 27] ; and there stayed two or three hours : where the King was much perplexed what course to resolve upon, London, or North-ward ? The considerations of the former vote, and the apparent danger of being discovered at London, moved him to resolve at last to go North-ward and through Norfolke, where he was least knowne. . . . . About 2 of the clocke we tooke a guide towards Barnet, resolving to crosse the roads into Essex."*

Hillingdon stands on the edge of the elevated heathland, which rises northward, by Little Hillingdon, Uxbridge Common, and Harefield ; the river Colne forms its W. boundary, dividing it from Denham and Iver, Bucks ; the Grt. W. Rly. (Uxbridge br.), and the Grand Junction Canal traverse the W. side of the par. Situated where several roads meet, and having about it many good houses, Hillingdon is a pleasant open roadside vill., with the old ch. backed by great elms, and a noticeable yew tree in the ch.-yard, on an eminence facing the main street, and forming a picturesque finish to the scene. The land

* Peck, Desiderata Curiosa, 1735, vol. ii., Lib. IX. No. XXV., fol. 21, 'The Examination of Dr. Michael Hudson before the Committee of Parliament touching the King's Escape from Oxford to the Scots at Southwell.'

is divided into pasture and arable; orchards are numerous, and there are many good seats standing in well-timbered grounds.

Colham, the principal manor, in which that of Hillingdon merged, belonged at the Dom. Survey to the Earl of Arundel; in the reign of Henry I. was forfeited to the Crown; and was in 1246 the property of William de Longespée Earl of Salisbury. It was conveyed by marriage to Eubulo Le Strange, in 1331, and remained the property of the Le Stranges till near the end of the 15th cent., when it passed by marriage to George Lord Stanley, eldest surviving son of Thomas Earl of Derby, who on his marriage was summoned to Parliament as Lord Strange. The manor continued in the Stanley family till 1637, when, by the bequest of Alice Countess Dowager of Derby, it passed to her grandson, George Lord Chandos, whose widow having married, as her second husband, George Pitt, Esq., of Strathfieldsaye, sold the manor in 1669 to Sir Robert Vyner, Bart. It has since passed through many hands. The old manor-house, Colham House, on the Colne at Colham, the occasional residence of the Earls of Derby, was pulled down early in the 18th century.

The *Church*, St. John the Baptist, is built of flint and stone, cruciform, and of large size, but the nave was lengthened, the transepts added, and a new chancel built, when the ch. was *restored*, by Gilbert Scott, in 1848: the old ch. had only nave, aisles, chancel, and tower. The W. tower, square, with double buttresses at the angles, and angle turret of three stages, and embattled, built 1629, repaired 1835, was the only part unaltered at the recent restoration of the ch. The window tracery and the carved stone-work were renewed or rechiselled throughout, and the walls refaced. The interior, as in most of Sir Gilbert Scott's churches, is carefully finished and effective, but, despite the old monts., looks modern. The roofs are all new, and some of the windows have painted glass by Willement. *Obs.* the Perp. font, the carved octagonal bowl being, in heraldic terms, supported by lions sejant and savage men alternately. On the walls are many monts., chiefly of local magnates. The following should be noticed: Sir Edw. Carr, d. 1635, with kneeling effigies

of the knight in armour, his wife and two daughters, under a canopy of coloured marble, supported on Ionic and Corinthian columns. Henry Paget, Earl of Uxbridge, d. 1743, well-carved recumbent marble statue of the Earl in Roman habit. Also various tablets, of Lady Anne Scott, d. 1737, daughter of the Duke of Buccleuch; Thomas Lane, d. 1795, with medallion, etc. *Brasses.*—A good double brass, under canopy, of John Lord Strange, d. 1478, and of his wife, Jane, daughter of Richard Woodville, Earl Rivers, and sister of Elizabeth, queen of Edward IV. Lord Strange is in armour, his lady in long gown and hood. The mont. was erected by their daughter Jane, wife of George Stanley, Lord Strange, in 1509. On floor, a knight in armour with arms and quarterings of Stanley; first half of the 16th cent. Drew Sanders, gentleman and merchant of the staple, d. 1579, and wife. In the ch.-yard, E. of the ch., is the sarcophagus of John Rich, d. 1761, the first and most famous English harlequin, and 40 years manager of the Lincoln's Inn and Covent Garden theatres. There are many tombs in this part of the ch.-yard, but that of Rich will be recognized by the sculptured urn which surmounts it. Rich lived at Cowley Grove.

A new ch., St. Andrews, was erected in 1864-5 by the roadside, at *Hillingdon End*, or *New Hillingdon*, near Uxbridge, where has sprung up a village of genteel houses, which was created an eccl. district in 1865, and had 2673 inhab. in 1871. St. Andrews ch., designed by Sir Gilbert Scott, is a spacious Early Dec. edifice of coloured brick and stone, the chief feature of the exterior being the massive tower and tall spire, at the E. end of the S. aisle, which somewhat dwarfs the body of the building. The interior is wide, lofty, fairly lighted, and effective. The brick walls are left uncovered; the piers which divide the nave and aisles are of brick with stone bands; the roof is of timber; and there is an elaborate reredos of marble, alabaster, and coloured glass, with a rilievo of the Last Supper. Near the ch. is *Hillingdon Cemetery*, consecrated 1867, in which are two chapels by Mr. Benj. Ferrey, F.S.A., of a better order than usual.

Among the seats in and around Hillingdon, the most noteworthy is *Hillingdon*

House, a large plain mansion of two storeys, having a slightly advanced centre with pediment, erected by Meinhardt, last Duke of Schomberg, in 1717. After his death it became, in 1738, the seat of John Visct. Chetwynd. John Chetwynd, Earl Talbot, sold it in 1785 to the Marchioness of Rockingham, and whilst the residence of the Rockingham family, it is often referred to in the Greville and other memoirs. It stands in an undulating, richly wooded park, with a good sheet of water winding through the valley. Other seats are *Hillingdon Court* (Lady Mills); *Cedar House* (J. T. Clarke, Esq.), by the ch., so called from a famous cedar, one of the earliest planted in England, which adorned the grounds till cut down in 1789; *Hillingdon Lodge* (R. C. Walford, Esq.); *Park Field* (D. Rutter, Esq.) *Dawley Court* (W. Fane de Salis, Esq.), in Hillingdon par., but above 2 m. from the ch., is noticed under DAWLEY FARM.

Colham Green, 1 m. S. of Hillingdon, is a hamlet of Hillingdon. The large building that will be noticed here is the Union Workhouse. *Gould's Green*, ½ m. S.E. of Colham, is another hamlet, where is *Moorcroft House*, an upper-class private lunatic asylum. Another hamlet—

Yiewsley, 1½ m. S. by W. from Hillingdon ch., has within the last few years become a somewhat populous place. It adjoins West Drayton, indeed the West Drayton rly. stat. is at Yiewsley, and the two now form a sort of railway town, as little attractive as railway towns usually are. Inns, the *De Burgh Arms; Railway Arms; Trout*. As the sign suggests, there is angling in the neighbourhood. The Colne hardly maintains its old reputation as a trout stream, but there is said to be good bottom fishing. A neat brick ch., E.E. in style, with an apsidal chancel, S. porch, and bell-cote, was erected here in 1869, from the designs of Sir Gilbert Scott. Yiewsley was made an eccl. district in Jan. 1874. Near the ch. is a vicarage, built in 1874; and close by are good schools erected at the same time as the ch. Many houses for city clerks, etc., have been built within a short distance of the station; in the neighbourhood are extensive brick-works; by the Colne and the Grand Junction Canal are flour mills, oil mills, varnish works, etc.

HODDESDON, HERTS (Dom. *Hodesdone*), a small town, partly in Great Amwell par., partly in that of Broxbourne, on the Ware road, 17 m. from London, and 1 m. N. from the Broxbourne Stat. of the Grt. E. Rly.; pop. of the hamlet 2090, of the eccl. dist. 2316. Inns, *Bull; Salisbury Arms*.

Hoddesdon stands on rising ground; the Lea, here tolerably rural and picturesque, is its eastern boundary; and on the W. and N.W. are green lanes, narrow, winding, and overhung with hedgerow elms, running towards the characteristic Hertfordshire slopes of Broxbourne Woods, Bayfordbury, and Amwell. The towns of Hertford and Ware are each 4 m. distant. Hoddesdon is an ordinary roadside town of the West. The houses are ranged for ¾ m. along both sides of the broad highroad, and are of all sizes and kinds, some old, but few unaltered, side by side with showy modern shops with plate-glass fronts. At the entrance to the town, on the rt., is a large mansion, *Rawdon House*, built by Sir Marmaduke Rawdon about 1640, and said, but without sufficient authority, to have been at one time a seat of the Dymocks, the hereditary champions of England. Occupied as a boarding-school by Mrs. Ellis, author of the 'Women of England,' and wife of the Madagascar missionary, and a good deal defaced, it has been thoroughly renovated, and is now the residence of H. Oxenham, Esq. It is a characteristic late Jacobean structure, with an enriched doorway with the Rawdon arms and carved work in the centre, 4 fine bays on the first floor, and a range of curved gables above; but it has been covered with stucco, and has lost much of its primal character. At the back is a low tower with the curved cupola roof so often seen in houses of its time. The int. has some good oak wainscoting and carving. On the rt. of the street, at the farther end of the town, is a large corn mill. Opposite to this are the two chief inns. Matt. Prior wrote in his 'Down Hall'—

" Into an old inn did this equipage roll
    At a town they call Hodsdon, the sign of the Bull,
    Near a nymph with an urn that divides the highway,
    And into a puddle throws mother of tea."

The Bull remains, and, though much altered since Prior wrote, has still the look of an old inn ; but the nymph with the urn (meant for "the effigies of the Samaritan woman ") no longer divides the highway. Its site is occupied by a mean little town-house (police-station and engine-house) with a clock tower. The topographical books, indeed, say that the Conduit, the gift to the town of Sir Marmaduke Rawdon, still remains, but there is not a vestige of it to be seen. The Salisbury Arms, just beyond the Bull, is noteworthy as having its sign suspended across the road from tall supports on either side.

Henry VIII., by a charter dated 1535, granted to Henry Earl of Essex, and Mary his wife, who then owned the manor, the right to hold a market in Hoddesdon every Thursday, and a fair of three days annually. The manor was forfeited to the Crown in the reign of Mary, and granted by Elizabeth to Robert Earl of Salisbury, in whose descendants it has continued. The market appears to have existed when Clutterbuck wrote, 1821, but has long been given up ; the fair is still held, June 29 and 30, as a small pleasure fair. Elizabeth granted a charter, Jan. 4, 1560, for a Grammar School ; it is now kept at Burford House, at the N.E. end of the town.

When Chauncy wrote, about 1700, "the chappel, erected for the ease of the inhabitants thereof, in the middle of this town," had become "through negligence so ruinous, that it was lately pulled down to save charges, so that nothing now remains hereof more than the clock-house, which is kept for the convenience of the inhabitants in this town."* A new church was afterwards built at the N. end of the town, on the l. of the Ware road, a poor little brick barn ; this was transformed in 1865, and made to serve as the nave to a larger structure. The new portion, of red brick, Dec. in style, comprises a wide chancel with two transepts or chapels. A campanile was to have been added, but it has not been built. The former ch. was mean ; the present is ugly. Though an old place, Hoddesdon exhibits few vestiges of antiquity. In 1861

several earthenware vases and other articles of Roman manufacture, were dug up on the N.E. of the town ; and in making a new road from Burford Street to Ware Valley, in August 1874, several vases of red-ware, with well-executed incised patterns, a spear-head, and many coins, were found, and in the immediate vicinity "a large quantity of bones of various animals," marking, as was believed, the site of a Roman cemetery. In the Gentleman's Mag. for April 1830 (p. 305) is engraved the seal, apparently of the middle of the 14th century, of the Hospital of SS. Clement and Loei [Eloy], at Hoddesdon, with effigies of the saints in mitres under canopies ; but nothing is known of the hospital.

Bennett, the editor and publisher of the works of Roger Ascham, the schoolmaster to Queen Elizabeth, kept a school at Hoddesdon, and had for a scholar Hoole, the translator of Tasso. For Bennett's edition, Samuel Johnson, also once a schoolmaster, with David Garrick for his pupil, wrote the life of Ascham. At Hoddesdon lived for some time John Loudon M'Adam, the road-maker. William Ellis, the missionary to the South Sea Islands and Madagascar, lived at *Rose Hill*, up a long narrow lane on the W. of the town, from shortly after his marriage with Sarah Stickney, 1837, till their death within a few days of each other, June 9 and 16, 1872. Mr. Ellis worked as secretary at the office of the London Missionary Society on week days, preached in the little Congregational chapel at Hoddesdon on Sundays, and at odd hours cultivated his roses and orchids at Rose Hill, winning with them, to his great delight, many of the prizes at the London as well as local flower-shows.*

"The *Thatched House* in Hodsden," into which Piscator and his scholar Venator "turned to refresh themselves with a cup of drink and a little rest," after their long morning's walk from Tottenham Cross, and longer talk over the relative merits of hunting, hawking, and fishing, has disappeared ; and the primrose hills and fragrant meadows Izaak Walton so pleasantly describes as he strolls and

---

* Chauncy, Hist. Antiq. of Hertfordshire, vol. i., p. 563.

* A full account of Ellis's life at Rose Hill is given in chapters ix. and x. of his Life, by his son, John Eimo Ellis, 8vo, 1873.

angles along the Lea hereabouts, will, we fear, hardly appear so charming in the reality as they do in the pages of the Complete Angler. *Rye House*, the theatre of the Rye House Plot, and now a popular summer resort and angling station, is on the Lea ¾ m. N.E. of Hoddesdon. (*See* RYE HOUSE.)

There are several good seats in the vicinity. On the W. are *Woodlands*, (Mrs. Warner), a good house, in charming grounds; *High Leigh* (Robert Barclay, Esq.), a spacious mansion, standing in a well-wooded and picturesque park; and *Westfield* (Herbert C. Lloyd, Esq.) The beautiful grounds of Broxbournebury (H. J. Smith-Bosanquet, Esq.) lie to the S.W.

HOLLY LODGE (*see* HIGH-GATE).

HOLWOOD HOUSE (*see* KES-TON).

HOOK, SURREY, a hamlet of Kingston, on the Leatherhead road, 2 m. S. of the Surbiton Stat. of the L. and S.W. Rly.; pop. 364, of the eccl. dist. 522. The hamlet consists of a few cottages by the roadside, with several genteel residences beyond. The manor, called Barwell, belonged to the priors of Merton from a very early period to the Dissolution, when it passed to the Crown. It was granted by Queen Elizabeth to Thos. Vincent, of Stoke D'Abernon; was in 1595 alienated to Edward Carleton, of Stoke; has since been frequently transferred, and is now the property of Lord Foley. The larger part of the old manor-house, *Barwell Court*, about 1 m. S. by E. of the vill., and a little out of the highroad, was long ago pulled down, and the remainder tenanted as a farm; but it has been renovated, and is now the residence of A. B. Cunningham, Esq. The *church*, St. Paul, is a small brick building, in style E.E., of the year 1838, and now, happily, covered with ivy. Hook was made an eccl. dist. in 1839.

HORNCHURCH, ESSEX, about 2 m. E.S.E. of the Romford Rly. Stat. (Grt. E. Rly.), on the road to Upminster: pop. 2476. Inns, *White Hart; Bull.*

The vill., large and busy-looking, ex-tends N. towards Butt's Green, as well as along the road. It has a good-sized brewery (Woodfine's), a well-known steam-engine and agricultural implement factory (Wedlake's), large tile and drain-pipe works, and other establishments; but in the main the business is agricultural, and all around are extensive farms. The par. is bounded E. by the little Rom brook, W. by the Ingerbourn.

The *Church*, St. Andrew, on the rt. of the road at the E. end of the vill., is a large Perp. building of stone, but patched with brick. It comprises nave with clere-storey, aisles (the S. aisle being of brick and modern), chancel, porches, and a battlemented tower at the W. end, of 3 stages, with turrets at the angles, that at the S.W. being the largest and carrying a flagstaff, and a slender spire which rises to a height of 170 ft. On the apex of the E. gable is fixed the carved skull of an ox, with broad-spreading curved horns. The int. is not of much interest. The chancel was restored in 1869: the fine E. window of five lights is filled with painted glass. At the E. bay of each aisle is a good oak parclose. The body of the ch. is filled with tall pews. On the S. of the chancel is a mont. with kneeling effigies. *Obs.* the great horse-chesnut on the N. side of the ch.-yard, and ash on the E.

The horns on the gable of the ch. are commonly supposed to symbolize the name. Its origin is accounted for by a coarse tradition, which is given by Weever.* The received explanation is that the priory founded here by Henry II. as a cell of the Hospice of St. Bernard in Savoy, was called the Monasterium Cornutum, and had the head and horns of an ox for a crest: † but this, of course, does not show how the name originated. On the suppression of the alien priories, William of Wykeham purchased the pro-perty, with the advowson of the living, for his New College, Oxford, to which it still belongs. A curious custom is main-tained here. New College, or the lessee of the tithes, provides once a year a boar's head, garnished with bay leaves and de-corated with ribbons, which is wrestled for in a field adjoining the ch.-yard.

---

* Funeral Monuments, p. 646; Newcourt, Re-pertorium, vol. ii. p. 336.
† Dugdale, Mon. Aug., vol. ii., p. 420.

The Almshouses seen on the l. are Dame Appleton's, founded in 1587 and rebuilt in 1838 ; and two founded by John Pennant in 1587 and restored by Thos. Masheter, Esq., in 1837. The principal seats are the *Hall*, N. of the ch.; *Langtons* (John Wagener, Esq.), W. of the vill. ; *Great Nelmes* (Rev. T. Harding Newman, D.D.), a good house and grounds, 1½ m. N. ; *Ardley Lodge* (Geo. Ralph Price, Esq.); *Fair Kytes* (Joseph Fry, Esq.) ; and *Harrow Lodge* (C. Barber, Esq.)

HORNDON, EAST, Essex (Dom.

Horninduna), about 3½ m. S.E. from the Brentwood Stat. of the Grt. E. Rly., on the road to Tilbury : pop. 470.

East Horndon is rural and secluded, lying out of any great line of traffic, and the inh. wholly engaged in agriculture. The only vill. is at Heron Gate, by Thorndon Park. The *Church*, All Saints, stands some distance out of the road on the l., about 1 m. beyond Heron Gate, on high ground, surrounded by old elms, with a farm, the old manor-house of *Abbot's* or Low Horndon, below it on the S., and no other house near. It is a curious and interesting building, of red brick, of late Perp. date, consisting of nave and S. aisle, short transepts, chancel with chapels, a S. porch and a short thick tower, with heavy buttresses, stepped battlements, and a low, tiled roof-spire. *Obs.* sun-dial, 1728. The int. is plain. with high pews. The chancel roof has bosses at the intersection of the ribs, with shields of arms and roses. On the S. of the chancel is the Tyrell Chapel, in which are several monts. of that family ; on the N. a smaller chapel, with a groined roof, now used as a vestry. The Tyrell monts. include an incised slab on the floor, with curious insc., of Sir John Tyrell, a devoted adherent of Charles I. ; mutilated mont. of Sir J. Tyrell, d. 1422, and wife Alice. In the vestry is a mural brass of a lady of about the middle of the 15th cent. In wall of S. transept, a tomb under a canopy, with indents for brasses, of man, wife, and children, in which, oddly enough, local tradition asserts the head, or, as some say, the heart, of Anne Boleyn was interred. The transepts are remarkable as having an upper chamber, about 12 ft. by 8, approached by a stone staircase in the wall. These doorways having been blocked up, the upper rooms had been lost

sight of till discovered by accident a few years ago. They have been opened to the ch., and now serve as galleries. They were probably intended for the chantry priests serving in the adjacent chapels, though there do not appear to have been any chimneys, or other housekeeping arrangements.

Heron Gate is a hamlet of Horndon, and the only village in the par. It consists of a few cottages by the roadside, near the top of the hill, 1 m. N. of East Horndon ch., and close to Thorndon Park. East Horndon comprised the manors of Heron and Abbots, and Heron's Gate is said to have derived its name from the gate which here served as the boundary of the two manors. The manor-house, Heron Hall, the ancient seat of the Tyrells, a stately brick mansion, with 4 towers at the angles, has long been taken down, but the moat and a few vestiges of the house remain. The last male of the Heron line and his wife are said to have been burnt to death on their wedding night, in a fire which destroyed the ancestral hall. The house stood about ¾ of a mile E. of Heron Gate. The country here is very pleasant ; there are trees by the roadside, good views to the Langdon Hills and across the undulating country S. and S.W., and a charming public path through Thorndon Park by the rookery.

HORNDON-ON-THE-HILL,

Essex, stands on a low hill on the road from Billericay to Tilbury, 2 m. E. by N. from Orsett, and 1½ m. N.W. from the Stanford-le-Hope Stat. of the L. and Southend Rly. ; pop. 611. Inn, the *Bell*.

Once a town with a market every Saturday, Horndon-on-the-Hill is now a quiet, little visited agricultural vill., chiefly interesting to a stranger for the fine views of the lower course of the Thames, the Essex levels, and Kentish hills. The manor-house, *Ardern Hall*, N.E. of the vill., was the seat successively of the Arderns, Fagels, Marneys, Shaas, Poleys, etc. The *Church*. St. Peter, is chiefly Perp., and consists of nave and aisles, chancel, and wooden tower. The neighbourhood lying between the marshes and the uplands affords some characteristic and picturesque scenery, not seldom recalling to the memory the works of one or other of the old Netherlandish landscape painters. Corn is grown largely, and vegetables, and especially peas, are extensively cultivated for the London market. Horndon was once celebrated for the growth of saffron, and there is still a farm here called Saffron Gardens. A Horndon yeoman, Thomas Highbed, was burnt in the market-place for heresy during the Marian persecution : he lived at Horndon House, on the rt. of the Orsett road, ¼ m. W. of the ch., and tilled the adjoining land.

HORNDON, WEST, ESSEX, 2 m.

S.E. from Brentwood ; pop. 81. There is no vill. West Horndon adjoins Ingrave, and the two churches having, early in the 18th cent., fallen to decay, were taken down, the parishes united for eccl. purposes by Act of Parliament under the title of Ingrave-cum-West Horndon, and a new ch. built by James, Lord Petre, in 1734, nearly midway between the two old ones. (*See* INGRAVE.) West Horndon ch. stood on the Brentwood side of Thorndon Hall.

Thorndon Hall, the seat of Lord Petre, has been the property of the Petre family since the manor was purchased of Sir John Mordaunt by Sir Wm. Petre, before 1570. The present mansion was built by James Paine about 1770. It stands in a large and richly timbered park, from which there is an avenue nearly 2 m. long to Brentwood. The house is of white brick, and consists of a centre with a hexastyle Corinthian portico, and wings connected by semicircular corridors. The rt. wing is a Roman Catholic chapel. The reception rooms are much admired. The hall is 40 ft. square, the roof supported on 18 scagliola columns ; the saloon is 60 ft. by 30, the drawing-room is 38 ft. by 26, and richly fitted. The hall and principal rooms have numerous family and other portraits, and a few Italian pictures. Among the portraits are Sir Wm. Petre, by *Holbein*, and the Duke of Norfolk, attributed to the same master; Mrs. Onslow, by *Cosway ;* Lord Derwentwater, with various relics of that unfortunate nobleman; busts of Fox, Lord Petre, and others. The library contains some fine illuminated MSS. George III. and Queen Charlotte stayed at Thorndon Hall on their way to the great review on Warley Common in 1778. This was the first royal visit paid to a Catholic peer since the accession of the House of Hanover, and Lord Petre made magnificent preparations. A state bed was purchased at a cost of £2000, but their majesties brought and used their own bed. The visit caused some comment, and called forth one of Gilray's most powerful and popular caricatures—' Grace before Meat, or a Peep at Lord Petre's '—the king and queen being represented at Lord Petre's dinner-table under a canopy of state, while a priest with a crucifix is invoking the blessing.

HORNSEY, MIDDX., a once rural,

now suburban vill., but still retaining some of its primitive features, 2 m. N.E. of Highgate, 5½ m. from the General Post Office by rd., 4 m. from King's Cross by Grt. N. Rly.: the stat. is about ¼ m. S.E. of Hornsey ch. Pop. of district of the mother ch. 5492 ; of the par. 19,357, but this includes part of Highgate, Muswell Hill, Hornsey Christ Church, and St. Matthias, Stoke Newington. Inns, the *Three Compasses*, by the ch.; *Great Northern Tavern*, opposite the ch.; *Railway Hotel*, by the stat.

In the 13th cent. the name was written *Haringee, Haringhee,* or *Haringey ;* in the reign of Elizabeth, *Harnsey*, but also, when Norden wrote, *Hornsey*. Lysons somewhat fancifully derives the name from "*Har-inge*, the meadow of hares ;" the more likely etymology is the patronymic *Hearing*.

The manor has belonged to the see of London from the earliest date recorded ; the only break in possession being the period of the Commonwealth. The bishops had a seat in Hornsey ; probably, as Lysons conjectures, marked by the mound in Hornsey Great Park spoken of by Norden :—

"A hill or fort in Hornsey Park called *Lodge Hill*, for that thereon, sometime, stood a lodge when the park was replenished with deer ; but it seemeth by the foundation that it was rather a castle than a lodge, for the hill is trenched with two deep ditches, now old and overgrown with bushes ; the rubble thereof, as brick, tile, and Cornish slate, are in heaps yet to be seen, which ruins are of great antiquity, as may appear by the oaks at this day standing, above 100 years' growth, upon the very foundation of the building." *

---

* Spec. Britt. : Middlesex, p. 36.

The site here intended is at the N.E. extremity of *Bishop's Wood* (*see* CAEN WOOD), a mile N.W. of Highgate, and overlooking Finchley Fields. "The form of the moat is still visible, and 70 yds. square; the site of the castle is still uneven, and bears the traces of former foundations; it is somewhat higher than the ground outside the trenches. The portion of the moat which still remains consists of [is formed by] a spring constantly running and is now used as a watering-place for cattle." * Bishop Aylmer's house at Hornsey, "the burning of which put him to 200 marks' expense," must have occupied a different site.†

Hornsey Woods and Great Park were portions of the Forest of Middlesex, and extended over what is now Highgate to Hampstead Heath. They were leased in 1755: Hornsey Woods to Lord Mansfield, the Great Park to Wm. Strode, Esq. Part of Hornsey Wood was incorporated with Lord Mansfield's park; a portion, known as Bishop's Wood, remains as wild woodland, but enclosed and preserved: it lies on the opposite side of Highgate Hill, 2½ m. from Hornsey in a direct line. (*See* CAEN WOOD.) Hornsey Great Park was divided and built over, cultivated, or enclosed as private grounds. Two or three fragments of woods, now known as the Highgate Woods, are still left on the Hornsey side of Highgate, by Southwood Lane, Wood Lane, and towards Muswell Hill. (*See* HIGHGATE.)

In Nov. 1387 the Duke of Gloucester and the Earls of Arundel and Nottingham, united their forces in Hornsey Park, and marched thence on London in order to compel the king, Richard II., to dismiss the Earl of Suffolk from his councils. The Lodge in Hornsey Park, then a residence of the Duke of Gloucester, was in 1440 the reputed theatre of the "necromancy" by which the learned clerk, Roger Bolingbroke, and another priest, Thomas Southwell, sought to compass the death of Henry VI., at the instigation of Eleanor Duchess of Gloucester: and for which Bolingbroke was executed as a traitor at Tyburn, Southwell died in the Tower, and the

Duchess had to do penance in the public streets, — incidents Shakspeare turned to such effective account in the Second Part of King Henry VI. When Edward V., under the escort of his uncle, Richard of Gloucester, made his public entry into London, May 1483, "when the kynge approached nere the cytee, Edmonde Shawe, goldsmythe, then Mayre of the cytie, with the Aldermenne and shreves in skarlet, and five hundreth commoners in murraye, receyved his Grace reverently at Harnesay Parke, and so conveighed him to the cytie, where he entered the fourth day of May, in the fyrst and last yere of his reigne."*

Henry VII. was on one occasion met at the same place by the Lord Mayor and citizens, and conducted in like manner to London.† Jane Porter, in her 'Scottish Chiefs,' relates that the remains of Wallace were secretly removed and deposited temporarily in the chapel of Hornsey Lodge; and that Robert Bruce was concealed at Lodge Hill in the garb of a Carmelite, when Gloucester sent him a pair of spurs as an intimation that he must depart with all speed—but she does not give her authority for these facts, which seem to have escaped the notice of historians.

Lands in the manor of Hornsey descend by the custom of gavelkind. The sub-manor of Brownswood is "the corps of a prebend in St. Paul's Cathedral, and has a court-leet and court-baron." ‡ Other manors are Toppesfield, at Crouch End, Fernfields, and Duckett's, but there is nothing of interest in their descent.

Hornsey *village* is long, irregular, and scattered. By the ch. the street is broad, bordered by elms, and still rural; and the rural character is preserved in the lanes that run off from it, as it is in the extension of the main street towards Muswell Hill. Along the lanes are many good old houses half-hidden behind tall elms, and so-called villas are rising on every side. The New River meanders in devious fashion through the valley.§ The fields,

---

* Prickett, Hist. and Antiq. of Highgate, 1842, p. 20.
† Lysons, Environs, vol. ii., p. 422.

* Hall, Chronicle, p. 351.
† Stow, Annals, p. 792.
‡ Lysons.
§ Hone, Every-Day Book, vol. ii., 1311, gives an engraving of 'The New River at Hornsey': the spot represented was the garden of the Three Compasses inn, but the New River would now be sought

though fast diminishing, are still pleasant, and the heights on either hand afford wide prospects : the new Alexandra Palace is of course conspicuous from all of them.

The *Church*, St. Mary, looks better at a distance than close at hand. The old ivy-covered tower is an attractive object from the neighbouring heights, and picturesque when near ; but the body of the ch. is brick, and Gothic of the year 1833. The old ch., pulled down in 1832, is said by Camden and Norden to have been built with the stones from the bishop's house at Lodge Hill. The tower, the only part left of the old ch., is of reddish sandstone, square, embattled, with a newel turret at the N.W. angle, and has on it the arms of Savage (1497-1500), and Warham (1500-4), successively Bps. of London, thus fixing the date of its erection. In the tower is a peal of 6 bells. The int. of the ch. is kept in excellent order. Several of the windows have painted glass. Among the *monts.* are some worth looking at, saved from the old ch. Mural mont. to George Rey, with kneeling effigies of man, two wives and son, temp. Eliz. and James. Small brass, of about 1520, with good figure of a "chrisom" child (infant in swaddling-clothes). Marble Corinthian column, surmounted with arms, to Lewis Atterbury, LL.D., rector of Hornsey, d. 1731, brother of Bp. Atterbury : the mont. was brought here on the demolition of the old chapel at Highgate, in which Dr. Atterbury was for 36 years the preacher. In chancel, kneeling figure in alto-rilievo, of Francis Masters, a youth of 16, fine in feeling and execution for the period (1680) of its erection. Samuel Buckley, editor of Thuanus, d. 1741. Tablet by Behnes to Samuel Rogers.

Hornsey *Churchyard* is screened by tall elms, wears a secluded and rural air, and has always been a favourite with those who love to meditate among the tombs. *Obs.* at the extreme N.E. corner of the ch.-yd. the last resting-place of the Bard of Memory, a tall altar tomb on a high base, within railings. "In this vault lie the remains of . . . SAMUEL ROGERS,

for there in vain : its course was diverted, and this portion filled up with the vestigia of a London cemetery.

Author of the Pleasures of Memory . . . . Born at Newington Green, 30 July, 1763 ; Died at St. James's Place, Westminster, 18 Dec. 1855." His brother Henry and sister Sarah lie in the same vault. On the same side of the ch.-yd., but S.E. of the ch., is an upright stone to "Anne Jane Barbara Moore. Born Feb. the 4th, 1812 ; died Sept. the 18th, 1817," the youngest daughter of Thomas Moore, who died whilst the poet was residing in what is now called Lalla Rookh Cottage, at the end of the lane running W. from the ch. (*See* MUSWELL HILL.)

Thomas Westfield, Bp. of Bristol, was rector of Hornsey till 1637. Wm. Cole, F.S.A., "the Cambridge antiquary" and correspondent of Horace Walpole, held the rectory, but for little more than a year, 1749-51. John Lightfoot, the learned rabbinical divine, removed to Hornsey soon after his marriage, that he might have access to the books in Sion College library. The preface to his 'Erubhim' is dated "From my study at Hornsey near London, March 5th, 1629."

S. of Hornsey ch., with the New River winding through the grounds, is *Harringay House*, the seat of W. C. Alexander, Esq. Beyond, passing the filtering beds and pumping station of the New River Company, are walks to Tottenham Woods and Wood Green. Westward from the ch. is the pleasant lane to Muswell Hill and Alexandra Park. A footpath from the ch.-yd., S., leads to *Mount Pleasant* (222 ft. high), the E. extremity of what has been styled the Northern Hog's Back ; from which there is a wide view across the valley of the Lea (the massive tower in the mid-distance is that of Tottenham ch.), Epping Forest, and the Essex uplands. In another direction the Alexandra Palace is seen to perfection. A narrow path leads from Mount Pleasant to

Finsbury Park, of about 120 acres, opened in 1869. It occupies the site of a portion of Hornsey Wood, and of the once popular *Hornsey Wood House*. The Wood was at one time notorious as a duelling ground. Hornsey Wood House was at first a little rural inn with a couple of large oaks before it, under which customers sat and took their modest refreshments. In course of time it grew into "a noted tea-house" ; the house was enlarged, large grounds were added and planted, and a lake formed, which grew in favour with cockney anglers. Afterwards, and up to the time of its demolition, 1866, Hornsey Wood House was the aristocratic pigeon-shooting ground. Finsbury Park is laid out in landscape-garden style, affords some pretty views, and would be pleasant if there were a little shade, and walking were not confined to the gravel paths. The name is however a foolish misnomer. The site has always been known as Hornsey Wood; Finsbury lies miles away, with Holloway, Highbury, Islington, and Hoxton intervening ; and it tends to the confusion of local tradition, historical records, and topographical accuracy thus to obliterate, or transfer and confound, local names of well-defined and long-standing usage.

Crouch End, on the S.W. of Hornsey, was a hamlet, and is now an eccl. dist. of 1675 inh., has still some pretty rural lanes, like that to Stroud Green, and good old brick houses ; but all available sites are being fast built over. Christ Church, on high ground at the S. end of the hamlet, near Hornsey Lane, is a good Dec. church, erected in 1863 from the designs of Mr. A. W. Bloomfield, and enlarged, and a tower with tall stone spire added in 1873. Nearly opposite the ch. is a stat. on the Highgate, Edgware, and High Barnet br. of the Grt. N. Rly. Between Crouch End vill. and Priory Lane, Highgate Archway Road, is a pretty field walk over the brow of the hill by the Shepherd's Cot, near which is a fine prospect, in its general features resembling that from Mount Pleasant, but more broken and varied.

Fortis Green is a hamlet of villas and cottages lying between Muswell Hill and the Finchley Road, 1½ m. W. of Hornsey ch. For eccl. purposes it is united with the district of St. James, Muswell Hill.

Hornsey Rise, adjoining Crouch End on the S., belongs to Islington par., and the London district. Here is the *Aged Pilgrims' Friend Society's Asylum*, a cheerful-looking range of cottages for 180 inmates, erected in 1871-75. Opposite to it is the *Alexandra Orphanage for Infants*, 1867-70, which consists of a number of detached Gothic houses varying in character, and built with some attention to picturesque effect : about 150 children are in the Orphanage, but it is desired to raise the number to 400.

HORTON, Bucks (Dom. *Hortone*), 1 m. N. of the Wraysbury Stat. of the Grt. W. Rly., 1¼ m. S.W. from Colnbrook, 18 m. from London : pop. 835. Inn, *The Crown*.

Horton is memorable as the place John Milton, after leaving Cambridge, came to reside at, and where for nearly six years (July 1632 to April 1638), " As ever in his great Task-master's eye," he trained himself for the work he trusted to accomplish. "At my father's country residence, whither he had retired to pass his old age, I, with every advantage of leisure, spent a complete holiday in reading over the Greek and Latin authors." He read not merely the Greek authors "down to the time when they ceased to be Greek," and the chief Latin writers, but employed himself in tracking out the obscure footsteps of the Lombards, Franks, and Germans, till they received their freedom at the hand of King Rodolphus.* But what is now of more importance, it was during his residence at Horton that occurred the grand outburst of poetry which proclaimed the advent of a new poet, and justified the prophecy of his ultimate greatness. Comus, the Arcades, Lycidas, and probably L'Allegro and Il Penseroso, and some of his sweetest sonnets, were written at Horton,—the first two, as we know, for the noble family at Harefield, where, as there is reason to believe, he was a valued guest. (*See* HAREFIELD.) Lawrence, the subject of the sonnet—

" Lawrence, of virtuous father virtuous son,
    Now that the fields are dank, and ways are mire,
    Where shall we sometimes meet, and by the fire
    Help waste a sullen day ? "—

is said to have dwelt in the neighbourhood of Horton. His near relative, William Lawrence—appointed to a judgeship by Cromwell—died at Bedfont, near Staines.† Of Milton's house, the tradition alone remains. It is said to have been pulled down about 1795.‡ The house stood nearly opposite the *ch. ;* the site is now occupied by a modern Elizabethan villa, *Byrken Manor House* (Edw. Tyrrell, Esq.)

* Letter to Carlo Diodati, Sept. 23, 1637 ; Second Defence, etc.
† Warton's Milton, p. 353.
‡ Letter of a late Vicar of Horton, quoted in Todd's Account of Milton's Life and Writings, prefixed to the Works, p. 19, ed. 1809.

In the garden was, till a few years ago, the bole of an old apple tree, under which, as tradition affirmed, Milton was accustomed to sit and meditate; a young apple tree now marks the spot.

Even though it were not so closely associated with the opening manhood of our great poet—"His daily walks and ancient neighbourhood"—Horton would be a pleasant and interesting place to visit. Lying at the S.E. extremity of Bucks, with the Colne, as its eastern boundary, dividing it from Middlesex, and the broader Thames separating it from Windsor, whose

"Towers and battlements it sees
Bosom'd high in tufted trees,"

and the green fields everywhere intersected by willowy watercourses—

"Meadows trim with daisies pied,
Shallow brooks and rivers wide,"—

the scenery about Horton, though level, is very charming in a quiet, sylvan, homely way. The village—hardly a village—is a loosely straggling place, with a great tree at the crossing of the roads. The *Church*, St. Michael, is of various dates, from Norman to late Perp.; and though somewhat patched and defaced by modern mendings, looked, with its heavy, ivy-covered tower, sombre and venerable. It was, however, restored in 1875, and whilst improved in condition, has suffered in appearance. It comprises nave, N. aisle, and short chapel on the S., chancel, and W. tower, with a short turret at the S.E. angle, and two porches. Under the N. porch is a rather rich Norm. doorway, with double chevron moulding. The arcade of the nave and S. aisle is E.E., with cylindrical shafts. The body of the ch. is late Perp., and poor. The font is large plain Norm. On a slab in the ch. are some indents of brasses of a man and wife. In the N. chapel is a costly marble sarcophagus to a member of the Scawen family, as is believed; but there is neither inscription nor heraldic device. The mont. that will most secure attention is a plain blue slab on the floor of the chancel, inscribed, "Heare lyeth the Body of Sara Milton, the Wife of John Milton, who died the 3ᵈ of April, 1637." The poet it will be remembered left Horton for Italy very shortly after his mother's death. Before leaving, *obs.* the two grand old yew-trees in the ch.-yard.

S. of the ch. stood an old mansion, *Place House*, built in the reign of Elizabeth,—the seat of the Brerewoods, afterwards of the Scawens, and then occupied by a succession of tenants. It was taken down in 1785. *Horton House* (W. P. Ainslie, Esq.) is pleasantly situated on a branch of the Colne, some little way S. of the ch. The house is modern, semi-classic, with a portico of four columns, stiff, stately, and commodious.

HORTON KIRBY, KENT (Dom. *Hortune*), on the Darent, 1½ m. N.E. of Farningham, and ½ m. E. of the Farningham Road Stat. of the L., C., and D. Rly.: pop. 1382.

At the Dom. Survey, Horton possessed a church, 2 mills, arable land, meadows, and woods, whence pannage could be had for the swine. Its pop. included 20 bondmen and 16 villans, attached to the soil; but one Godel, who held land, was free to choose his abode, and to have whom he pleased for lord. It does not make a very attractive picture, perhaps, but the place was evidently prosperous, and its value, unlike most places recorded in the Survey, had increased by half since the time of the Confessor. The four Saxon manors had been consolidated into one.

But though the Norman Survey is the earliest written record, Horton has of late unfolded some fragmentary pages of her earlier history. On a woody knoll near the height on the Franks estate, known as the Folly, on the W. side of the Darent, and about ½ a mile from the vill., some labourers, grubbing up trees in the spring of 1866, came upon traces of a building, which, upon careful excavation, proved to be the foundations of a house of moderate size. Admirably constructed with flat bricks and mortar of the best make, it seemed to be a Roman villa of the best period. Nothing beyond the foundations was, we believe, found; but we have heard that some relics have been discovered nearer Farningham. Be that as it may, here is proof that Horton Kirby was not without inhabitants during the Roman occupation. Curiously enough, a year later, June 1867, evidence was unexpectedly found of a later and much larger colonization. In digging for the building of the Boys' Home, near the Rly. Stat., N. of Horton Kirby, on the side of he hill sloping to the river, several graves were opened, close together, and so similar in their contents as to leave no doubt that here was the burial-place of a tribe of rude habits, but who had made some progress in the arts. The graves penetrated but a short way into the chalk—in most cases only a few inches—and were often so short that the bodies had to be much bent to insert them. The bodies appeared to have been placed in coffins, as with them were traces of wood, and a few nails. The bones were much decayed—those of the children had entirely perished—and the crania were all fragmentary. The graves had been dug without any regularity, the heads being directed indifferently to all points of the compass. With them were found many fragments of rude earthenware jugs, dishes, and other household ware, iron rings, knives, and keys, a knife-sheath, a bone spindle-whorl, a whetstone, and several fibulæ—one having a flowing pattern and a small piece of red glass in the centre; the smaller, a cruciform central ornament, with human heads rudely punched out in the interspaces. Unless the last-named article be so regarded, nothing was found to indicate the religious belief of the occupants of the graves; and this circumstance, and the position of the bodies, seemed to suggest that they were heathens. That they were a peaceful people may be inferred from no weapon of any kind having been found. The ornaments on a fibula are of the kind known as late Saxon work; but some of the graves and their contents were of so rude a description as to render it probable that the interments extended over a somewhat long period, and that some may have been British. Later excavations (1872), made on the N. of the rly. embankment, show that the cemetery stretched over a considerable space, reaching far towards South Darenth.*

Horton was one of the many manors given by the Conqueror to Odo, Bp. of Bayeux. On his fall, it appears to have been granted to the bishop's tenant, Anchetil de Ros. It remained in the Ros family—one of whom built Horton Castle

* Notes; Statement by the Rev. R. Coates, Vicar of Darenth, on exhibiting articles found in graves at Horton Kirby, at Archæol. Institute, June, 1867; C. Roache Smith, Gent. Mag. 1866, 1867.

—till about 1292, when it passed by marriage to Roger de Kirby, or Kirkby, of Kirkby Hall, Lancashire, who re-edified the castle, and from whom it derived the addition of Kirby. About the end of the reign of Richard II., it was carried, by the marriage of the heiress of the Kirbys, to Thomas Stonor, of Stonor, Oxfordshire. Horton was forfeited to the Crown, by the complicity of John Stonor in the insurrection headed by Lord Audley in 1496. Henry VIII. granted the manor to Robert Hudston. About the middle of the 17th century it passed by marriage to the Michels; and in 1736 was devised with other lands by John Michel to the Provost and Fellows of Queen's College, Oxford, for the purpose of founding 8 fellowships, 4 scholarships, and 4 exhibitions in that college, the recipients of which are still designated Michel fellows, scholars, and exhibitioners. Horton Kirby Manor remains the property of Queen's College. On the Darent, N. of the ch., are a few unimportant vestiges of the castle.*

The vill. is built about an irregular parallelogram, with the ch. a little N. of it. About it are a few old and some picturesque houses. The neigbourhood is full of beauty. The river is pleasant throughout. The chalk hills on either side vary the aspect of the valley at every turn, and afford wide and diversified prospects. East is the broad open country towards Falkham; S. and W. are the charming valley, park, and woods of Eynesford, Lullingstone, and Farningham; and N. the quaint little Darenth ch., and unspoiled wood beyond. The employments are chiefly agricultural; but the paper mill of Messrs. Spalding, at South Darenth, employs many hands.

South Darenth, on the rt. bank of the river, midway between Horton Kirby and Darenth, has become a busier-looking place than the parent village; but there is nothing in it to call for special notice.

Horton *Church* is a large and interesting cruciform building, venerable in fact and appearance, but on close inspection showing signs of modern renovation. In the main of about the middle of the 13th cent., the chancel and transepts retain their original lancet windows, whilst those

* Hasted, Hist. of Kent, vol. i., p. 293; Philipott, Vill. Cant., p. 192; Oxford Univ. Cal.

of the nave are Perp. insertions. The body of the ch. is of flint, but it is much patched with brick ; and the upper part of the central tower is wholly of brick, and modern. The old S. porch is of flint and stone. *Obs.* on entering, the holy-water stoup on the rt. The *int.*, restored in 1863—not wisely perhaps, but thoroughly —is striking from the great height of the tower-arches and width of the aisles, and the widely separated lancets of the chancel, with the tall, thin, detached, and banded shafts between them. The transepts have wide arcades, with string-course moulding above the windows, and a piscina, marking the place of an altar, at the end of each arcade. The arches at the end of the nave, opening respectively into the N. and S. transept, it will be observed, differ in size and position, while the centre line of the chancel in the nave is nearly 5 feet nearer to the N. wall than to the S. (11 ft. 3 in. and 16 ft.) : the roof is consequently out of line by so much, and the W. window is not directly over the central doorway. The roof is open timber, well restored. The font is E.E., and large. Several of the windows have painted glass. In the chancel are mural *monts.* of the Bathursts of Franks, some partially erased. In the N. transept is a small *brass* of John Browne, Esq. (d. 1599), and wife ; and in the S. transept a larger one of a female, of fair 16th-cent. work, but without an inscription. *Obs.* in the ch.-yard the large hollow yew S.W. of the church.

By the river side, ½ m. S. of the ch., is *Franks* (Fred. Power, Esq.), a stately Elizabethan mansion—a little Hatfield— of red brick and stone, with a rich central doorway, with balcony over, bay windows at each end, many gables, enriched chimney shafts, and spire-capped turret. Before the house a reach of the river expands out lake-like, fringed with ash and alder, and brightened with swans. The interior of the house has some good carved oak, and ornamented plaster-work. Franks, as Philipott notes, "an ancient seat in this par., was the mansion of gentlemen of that sirname, who, about the latter end of Henry III., came out of Yorkshire, and planted themselves at this place ;" but the present mansion was the work of Ald. Lancelot Bathurst, who bought the estate and built the house in the reign of Queen

Elizabeth, as the insc. over the dining-room testifies : " E. R. 1591." Bathurst died in 1594. The house was thoroughly restored in 1862.

The neat group of buildings on the hill-side N. of the ch. is the *Home for Little Boys*, of which the first stone was laid by the Princess of Wales, July 7, 1866, and which was formally opened by the Earl of Shaftesbury in the following year. It now consists of 10 detached houses, each standing in its own large garden, and accommodating 30 boys under the care of a warden and his wife ; a large school-house ; a neat E.E. cruciform chapel ; workshops, infirmary, etc. The buildings, which are of brick, and of a modest, domestic Gothic character, seem comfortable and well adapted to their purposes. The archt. was Mr. T. C. Clarke. The boys must be homeless and under 10 years of age when received ; they are maintained, educated, taught a trade, and leave " prepared for industrial life " at 14.

HOUNSLOW, Middx., a town on

the main western road, partly in the par. of Heston (in which is the chapel), and partly in that of Isleworth ; 9 m. from Hyde Park Corner, and a stat. on the Loop-line of the L. and S.W. Rly. ; pop. 9294 (Heston 4224, Isleworth 5070).

In the Dom. Survey the hundred of *Honeslowe* occurs ; somewhat later the name is written *Hundeslowe*, or *lawe*, whence Lysons suggests as a derivation, " Hounds' law," which may be taken for what it is worth. He adds in explanation, to *lawe* a hound, was an obsolete word for laming him, by cutting out one of the balls of his foot, which was done by the foresters to all dogs kept on the " King's forests," above a certain size ; and " Hounslow-Heath was within the forest of Staines." *

According to a Parliamentary Survey made in 1650, the town of Hounslow contained " 120 houses, most of them inns and alehouses, depending upon travellers." This could hardly be said of it now, though inns and alehouses seem unduly numerous. Hounslow, in fact, was for centuries mainly dependent upon the travellers passing through it. As the first stage from London on the main

* Lysons, Environs, vol. ii., p. 413.

western road, its coaching and posting business was necessarily very great. It is said that in its palmiest days as many as 500 stage-coaches passed through it daily, and that 1500 horses were kept in the town. The opening of the railways destroyed that traffic, and Hounslow was for awhile in a very depressed condition. It has, however, quite recovered. Large numbers of genteel houses have been built in and about it, and the place has now a good local trade. But it is a dull place to visit. The town consists of a long mile of characterless shops, many inns, a commonplace ch., and a town-hall, erected in 1857; and the immediate neighbourhood is flat, monotonous, and uninteresting.

A priory of the Brethren of the Holy Trinity existed at Hounslow in 1296, in which year the prior obtained a charter empowering the brethren to hold a market weekly on Wednesdays, and an annual fair of 8 days' continuance. The priory continued down to the Dissolution, and is often referred to. It had at least one distinguished member, Robert de Hounslow, a native of the town, d. 1430, grand provincial of the order for England, Ireland, and Scotland, and eminent in his day as a writer. The market has long been discontinued.

The chapel of the priory continued to be used as the chapel-of-ease for Hounslow till about 1833, when it gave place to the present ch. of the Holy Trinity. The old chapel was a small building of the Dec. period, but had been so often repaired and altered, and was in so bad a state, that its demolition was not to be regretted. The present ch. is a plain white brick building, Gothic, of the year 1835, and enlarged by the addition of a chancel in 1856. A second church, St. Paul's, Hounslow Heath, a neat E.E. fabric, was completed in 1874, from the designs of Messrs. Habershon and Pike: the eccl. district was formed in 1871.

HOUNSLOW HEATH. The fame of Hounslow is mainly due to its Heath—

"Hounslow, whose Heath sublimer terror fills,
Shall with her gibbets lend her powder mills." *

The Heath stretched from Hounslow town westwards for over 5 miles. By the

* Mason, Heroic Epistle.

Survey of 1546 it contained 4293 acres, but other accounts make the area much greater. On it were vestiges of Roman, and possibly of British camps, and it was the scene of military and other assemblages in more recent times. A tournament was held here in the reign of John. In 1267 the Londoners, with the Duke of Gloucester at their head, took arms against Henry III., and encamped in great strength on Hounslow Heath. Charles I., after an interview with the Parliamentary deputation at Colnbrook, Nov. 1642, marched his army under cover of a fog to Hounslow Heath. Thence Rupert marched on to Brentford, and having compelled his opponents to retreat, returned to head-quarters at Hounslow Heath, where "the King lay that night with the body of his army, and where (if Essex had pleased the next day) there was a large fair heath for the two armies to have tried once again their courage and fortunes." * When Charles was a prisoner at Hampton Court, Fairfax "appointed a general rendezvous for the whole [parliamentary] army upon Hounslow Heath within two days; when and where there appeared 20,000 foot and horse, with a train of artillery, and all other provisions proportionable to such an army." † The meeting was attended by the speakers of the two houses of parliament, with their maces, accompanied by many of the members.

The early summer of 1678 saw Charles II. with his army encamped on the Heath.

"June 29.—Return'd (from Windsor) with my Lord (Chamberlain) by Hounslow Heath, where we saw the new-rais'd army encamp'd, design'd against France, in pretence at least, but which gave umbrage to the parliament. His Majesty and a world of company were in the field, and the whole armie in battalia, a very glorious sight. Now were brought into service a new sort of soldiers called *Granadiers*, who were dextrous in flinging hand granados, every one having a pouch full; they had furred caps with coped crowns like Janizaries, which made them look very fierce, and some had long hoods hanging down behind, as we picture fools. Their clothing being likewise pybald yellow and red." ‡

In June 1686, James II. had an army of 13,000 men, with 26 pieces of artillery,

* Sir Philip Warwick, Memoires of the Reigns of King Charles I., p. 234.
† Clarendon, Hist. of the Rebellion, vol iii., p. 62, ed. 1720.
‡ Evelyn, Diary.

encamped on Hounslow Heath. It was at the time he was pressing forward some of his most obnoxious measures, and, as Evelyn notes, "there were many jealousies and discourses of what was the meaning of this encampment." But whatever was the purpose of the king, it soon became evident that there was no ill-feeling on the part of the soldiers, and the Londoners flocked to the camp in such numbers that the place became, as Macaulay has described it in one of his most brilliant pages, "merely a gay suburb of the capital." *

Again, in the summer of 1687, James had his army on Hounslow Heath, but now the disaffection was hardly concealed. The king was at the camp when the news arrived of the acquittal of the Bishops. He left at once for London, but " he had scarcely quitted the camp when he heard a great shouting behind him. He was surprised, and asked what that uproar meant. 'Nothing,' was the answer, ' the soldiers are glad that the Bishops are acquitted.' ' Do you call that nothing?' said James. And then he repeated, ' So much the worse for them.' " † He might well ask if his courtiers thought that nothing, To him that shouting on Hounslow Heath must have sounded very like the knell of his dynasty. Three years later, on occasion of a French descent on the Devonshire coast, Queen Mary, in the absence of her husband, reviewed the troops assembled on Hounslow Heath, and Marlborough, their commander, warmly complimented the men on their martial bearing. Hounslow Heath saw no more such gatherings till the reign of George III., when the king more than once held grand reviews of regulars and volunteers.

The Heath was however, in the 17th and 18th cents., most celebrated as the haunt of highwaymen. Every great line of road was infested by these " collectors of the highway," as they were termed ; but in the ' Lives of Famous Highwaymen,' Hounslow Heath and Finchley Common figure oftenest. They frequented the Hounslow inns to learn who among the travellers promised the best booty, and the meaner

sort were said to make friends with the grooms and coachmen. "Am I to have the honour of taking the air with you this evening upon the Heath?" asks Matt. of the Mint of Captain Macheath, in the Beggars' Opera ; " I drink a dram now and then with the stage-coachmen in the way of friendship and intelligence ; and I know that about this time there will be passengers upon the Western road, who are worth speaking with."

Noble and vulgar were alike laid under contribution ; and indeed the audacity of the robbers was almost incredible. To be stopped in crossing Hounslow Heath was regarded as almost a matter of course.

"Our roads are so infested by highwaymen, that it is dangerous stirring out almost by day. Lady Hertford was attacked on Hounslow Heath at three in the afternoon. Dr. Eliot was shot at three days ago, without having resisted ; and the day before yesterday we were near losing our Prime Minister, Lord North ; the robbers shot at the postilion, and wounded the latter. In short, all the freebooters that are not in India have taken to the highway. The Ladies of the Bedchamber dare not go to the Queen at Kew in an evening."*

The prime minister escaped more easily than another prime minister's friend. Mr. Northall, Pitt's confidential legal adviser, and secretary of the Treasury under the Rockingham ministry, who had more than once before encountered highwaymen, and one of whom had died by his hand, was stopped on Hounslow Heath, as he was returning from Bath, with his wife and child in the carriage, March 1776, and, on refusing to give up his purse, was shot. He was carried to an inn at Hounslow, where he wrote a description of the robber to send to Sir John Fielding, the Bow Street magistrate, and died as he finished it.† A similar fate befel another well-known personage. Messrs. Mellish, Bosanquet, and Pole, great names in the city, were returning from a stag hunt at Windsor, when on Hounslow Heath the coach was stopped. Purses and watches were quietly surrendered, but one of the robbers fired his pistol into the carriage. The bullet struck Mr. Mellish, who died on reaching the

---

* Evelyn, Diary, June 2, 1686 ; Macaulay, Hist. England, vol. ii., p. 357.
† Macaulay, vol. iii., p. 123.

* Horace Walpole to Sir H. Mann, Oct. 6, 1774 ; Letters, vol. vi., p. 129 ; and comp. his George III., vol. iii., p. 43.
† Jesse, Memoirs of George III., vol. i., p. 354. Lord Stanhope says, Hist. of Eng., chap. xxx. (vol. vii., p. 312) that "he died of the fright" : Northall however, was hardly a man of that temperament.

Magpies. But the assailants were not always so fortunate. Earl Berkeley (the father of Grantley Berkeley, who tells the story,) was wakened out of his slumber as he was being driven over the Heath on his way to Cranford House by the sudden stoppage of the coach, and a head peering in at the window. "Now, my Lord, I have you at last; you said you would never yield to a single robber—deliver!" "Then who is that looking over your shoulder?" said the Earl. Thrown off his guard, the fellow turned round to look, when the Earl shot him dead.* The dramatists and novel writers of course availed themselves freely of Hounslow Heath and its incidents.

"Strap rode up to the coach door, and told us in a great fright, that two men on horseback were crossing the Heath (for by this time we had passed *Hounslow*), and made directly towards us." †

The exploits of the highwaymen, exaggerated by mystery and rumour, attracted no little attention and some admiration. Even in our own day some of the more noted have been rated as heroes. "The Flying Highwayman," wrote the Annual Register for 1761, "engrosses the conversation of most of the towns within 20 miles of London." He rode three different horses—a grey, a sorrel, and a black; he had done rare feats on the Heath, and he "has leapt over Colnbrook turnpike a dozen times within this fortnight." In the last half of the 17th cent. it was no uncommon thing for the gay young cavalier to take to the road as the readiest mode of mending his fortune by lightening the purses of the well-to-do roundhead citizens he held in supreme contempt; but even a century later stories were credited of other than vulgar footpads resorting at times to Hounslow Heath. It is gravely related, for example, that Twysden Bishop of Raphoe, playing the highwayman there in 1752, was shot through the body, and died from the wound at a friend's house; his death being announced as from "inflammation of the bowels." ‡ But though the story may be a tradition of Cranford House,

it was merely one of those good stories which the unscrupulous wits of the time were wont to circulate after dinner or to put forth as hearsay at their clubs.

When caught. short shrift was in those days given to the highwaymen; and the road across Hounslow Heath was made hideous by the gibbets on which their bodies were left to rot. Mr. Crabb Robinson was assured by his coachman—an old man—that "when he was a boy the road beyond Hounslow was literally lined with gibbets, on which were in irons the carcases of malefactors blackening in the sun." * Forty years later some were still there: "In 1804. as I was riding home from school, the man who accompanied me proposed to show me something curious. Between the two roads, near a clump of firs, was a gibbet, on which two bodies hung in chains. The chains rattled; the iron plates scarcely kept the gibbet together; the rags of the highwaymen displayed their horrible skeletons. That was a holiday sight for a schoolboy 60 years ago." † The highwaymen generally went to their doom in their gayest attire. An intelligent Frenchman, travelling in England in 1765, observes that though he heard they were very numerous, he saw no highwaymen except such as were hanging upon gibbets by the roadside: there, he says, "they dangle, dressed from head to foot, and *with wigs upon their heads*." ‡

In 1793 large cavalry barracks were erected on Hounslow Heath, and about the same time the enclosure of the Heath was commenced. For a time enclosure and cultivation went on slowly, but in 20 or 30 years the process was pretty well completed—much to the disgust of a sturdy radical who rode over it (Oct. 1822) :—

"A much more ugly country than that between Egham and Kensington would with great difficulty be found in England. Flat as a pancake, and, until you come to Hammersmith, the soil is a nasty stony dirt upon a bed of gravel. *Hounslow Heath*, which is only a little worse than the general run, is a sample of all that is bad in soil and villainous in look. Yet this is now enclosed, and what they call *cultivated*." §

---

* Gent. Mag., xliv., p. 538; Grantley Berkeley, Life and Recollections, vol. i.; Stanhope, Hist. of Eng., vol. vii., p. 331.
† Smollett, Roderick Random.
‡ Hon. Grantley Berkeley, Life and Recollections, vol. i., p. 213.

* H. C. Robinson, Diary, Sept. 13, 1819, vol. ii., p. 132.
† Charles Knight, Passages of a Working Life, 1864, vol. i., p. 40.
‡ M. Grosley, A Tour to London, vol. i., p. 12.
§ William Cobbett, Rural Rides, p. 61.

The Cavalry Barracks are on the rt. of the road, about ½ m. beyond Hounslow. They contained 544 officers and men, at the census of 1871. Opposite to them, on the l. of the road, is a drill or exercise ground, of about 300 acres, reserved for this purpose at the enclosure of the Heath. The base line, of 27,404 ft., of the first trigonometrical survey executed in England, was laid down by General Roy, on Hounslow Heath, in the summer of 1784; and when the General Survey of the British Isles was undertaken by the Master-General and officers of the Ordnance, in 1791, they commenced their operations by re-measuring General Roy's base line.

Hounslow Powder Mills, which, as we have seen, were with her gibbets supposed to add " sublimer terrors" to the Heath, are situated on the King's and Isleworth rivers, and chiefly in Isleworth parish. Mason's reference was probably to the great explosion which occurred in them on the 6th of Jan., 1772, which caused a prodigious amount of mischief, and was heard, it is said, as far as Gloucester. Walpole gives an amusing account of the damage done to his *castle*, Strawberry Hill. "The N. side of the castle looks as if it had stood a siege. The two saints in the hall have suffered martyrdom! They have their bodies cut off, and nothing remains but their heads."* Many explosions have occurred since; the last serious one was on Nov. 3, 1874, when 5 lives were lost. Every precaution is taken now to prevent such accidents; and by the separation of the buildings, etc., to localize their effects as far as possible if they occur.

HUNSDON, Herts (*Dom. Hones-done*), a vill., and the site of a once royal mansion, is 5 m. E.S.E. from Ware, 2½ E. of the St. Margaret's Stat. of the Grt. E. Rly. (Ware and Hertford line), and about the same distance N.E. of the Roydon Stat. on the Cambridge line: pop. 518. Inn, *Fox and Hounds.*

As early as 1124, Richard, Earl of Hertford, had a park at Hunsdon, from which he covenanted to give a doe yearly to the monks of St. Augustine, at Stoke. At the end of the reign of John it belonged to Sir Walter Montgomery, Earl of Ferrers. In the reign of Edward I. it was held by John Eugaine, and in 1367 passed in default of male heirs to John Golding-ton, whose son sold it to Sir Wm. Oldhall, Kt., and M.P. for the county. Sir Wm. was attainted of high treason, 1460, as an adherent of the House of York; but on the accession of Edward IV. the estates were restored to his son, Sir John Old-hall, who built "a fair house in the mode of a castle." He seems to have shortly after made over the estate in trust; but for what purpose is not clear. However his death at Bosworth Field, and subsequent attainder, carried the manor to the crown, and the king, Henry VII., granted it to his mother, the Countess of Richmond, and her husband, Thomas Earl of Derby, for their joint lives. On their deaths, Henry VIII. granted it, Feb. 1514, to Thomas Duke of Norfolk. He dying, May 1524, the manor reverted to the crown, and Henry built himself a "palace royal here, at great cost and charge, where he was pleased to resort for the preservation of his health."* Hector Ashley in three years received above £1900, on account of buildings at Hunsdon House; but whether as architect is not known.† That he might have "his game and pleasure ready at hand," Henry, after building his palace, in 1531, annexed the manors of Roydon and Stanstead, and made them an honour, with his palace of Hunsdon as the capital place of the honour (*See* HAMPTON COURT.) The house appears, however, to have been most used as a residence of his children.

Edward VI. granted Hunsdon House, May 1548, to his sister, Princess Mary, who made it her residence. Here she heard the news of the death of her brother, and at once took horse for her manor of Kenninghall, that she might be within reach of Framlingham Castle. Mary annexed Hunsdon to the Duchy of Lancaster, and held it during the whole of her reign.

Shortly after her accession to the throne, Elizabeth granted Hunsdon to Henry Carey, son of Sir Wm. Carey and his wife Mary Boleyn, sister of Anne, the Queen's mother, and created him, Jan. 1559, Baron Hunsdon. In Sept. 1571 Elizabeth

---

* Walpole to Hon. H. S. Conway, Jan. 7, 1772, Letters, vol. v., p. 367.

* Chauncy, Hertfordshire, vol. i., p. 387.
† Walpole, Anecdotes, vol. i., p. 200.

visited Lord Hunsdon here, and stayed some days. A painting, well known by the engravings, in which Elizabeth is represented sitting in a state litter, which is borne on the shoulders of 6 noblemen, and attended by a large retinue of lords and ladies, has been understood to represent "Queen Elizabeth carried in state to Hunsdon House," since it was seen by Vertue, in 1737, at Coleshill, in Warwickshire, the seat of the Digby family, and so described by him in his 'Historic Prints,' 1740. The picture was exhibited under that title at the First Special Exhibition of National Portraits, 1866 (No. 256), when it was clearly shown by Mr. G. Scharf, to be *not* the visit to Hunsdon House in 1571, but the procession of Queen Elizabeth in a litter to celebrate the marriage of Anne Russell, daughter of John, Lord Russell, with Lord Herbert, son of Edward, 4th Earl of Worcester, at Blackfriars, June 16, 1600.*

Hunsdon continued in the male branches of the Carey family for over 100 years, when it descended to Anne, daughter of Sir Philip Carey, who married William Lord Willoughby, of Parham, who, on the death of his wife, sold Hunsdon to Matthew Bluck, one of the six clerks in Chancery. In 1702 Elkanah Settle published in a pompous folio, 'Spes Hunsdoniana: a poem on the anniversary birthday of the incomparable youth, Mr. Matthew Bluck, son and heir to the Worshipful Matthew Bluck, Esq., of Hunsdon House, in Hartfordshire.' This incomparable youth, the grandson of the original Matthew, mortgaged Hunsdon House in 1737 to a Mr. Nicolson, who bequeathed it to his nephew, Nicolson Calvert. It is now the seat of James Wyllie, Esq.

When given to Henry Carey, Hunsdon House appears to have been "ruinous and decayed"; but he no doubt speedily put it into a fitting condition to receive the queen as his guest. Norden, in 1593, calls it "an ancient house lately begun to be enlarged with a stately gallery, fair lodgings, and offices," by Lord Hunsdon.†
The house was surrounded by a moat, and approached by two bridges, of three arches; had a stately front, with a handsome central entrance and tall clock tower, and two projecting wings; extensive outhouses, stables, etc.; and tradition still, or but a few years ago, told of a subterranean passage running from it to the Rye House—nearly 3 m. in a direct line. But in process of time Hunsdon House has undergone many alterations. The clock house and the two wings, which are so conspicuous in Chauncy's print, were long ago pulled down, the interior completely modernized, and the stables converted into a farm-house. * A few years since it was entirely restored, and now has the appearance of a handsome Elizabethan mansion of very respectable dimensions. It is of red brick, oblong, with turrets at the angles, gables in the attic, and terra-cotta chimney shafts of good patterns: altogether a noble-looking edifice, backed as it is by the majestic elms in the park.

The *Church* stands close to Hunsdon House. It is small, of flint, stone, and plaster; Perp. in style; cruciform, with a tower and short thin spire at the W. The tower is partly covered with ivy, and contains a peal of 5 bells. On the N.W. is an old wooden porch, and the doorway under it has a bold moulding, the Tudor rose in the spandrils of the arch, and terminal heads to the dripstone. The tracery of some of the windows has been renewed, but altogether it is an interesting ch. of its kind, and the exterior is picturesque, especially as seen in combination with the neighbouring trees and portions of Hunsdon House.

The *interior* is plain, except the chancel, which has modern decorations. The large E. window has a representation of the Crucifixion, and some of the other windows are filled with painted glass. The N. transept is shut off from the body of the ch. by a richly carved screen, and forms the Carey chapel. In it is a large and elaborate mont., blocking up the end window, to Sir John Carey, 3rd Baron Hunsdon, and Lady Mary Hunsdon his wife. On it are recumbent effigies of Lord Hunsdon, in armour, with large trunk breeches, sword by his side, dog at his feet; his wife in long robe and stand-

---

* G. Scharf, F.S.A., Archæol. Journal, vol. xxiii., p. 131.
† Norden, Spec. Brit.: Hertford.

* Nichols, Progresses of Queen Elizabeth, vol. i., p. 288.

ing ruff, with swan at her feet : both richly coloured. The mont. was probably erected by Lord Hunsdon, as the insc. leaves spaces for the dates of decease, which have never been filled. *Obs.* here the good old carving on the pews. On the N. of the chancel is a mont. of Sir Thomas Forster, d. 1612, with recumbent alabaster effigy under a canopy supported on marble columns. Here, also, are several large and showy mural monts. to Blucks, Calverts, Chesters, etc. In the nave is a good mural *brass*, with effigy tolerably perfect, of Margaretta Shelley, d. 1495, wife of Jno. Shelley, citizen and mercer of London.

There is no proper vill. The shops are in *Hunsdon Street*, which lies a mile N. of the ch.; and in the lane that leads to it are a few cottages, and a few more about *Hunsdon Green*, on the N.W. In the neighbourhood are some good seats, the chief being *Hunsdonbury* (J. S. Walker, Esq.), by Hunsdon Green; *Mead Lodge* (Chas. J. Phelps, Esq.), on the S.; *Briggins Park* (Albert Deacon, Esq.), a very pretty estate on the border of Essex, towards Roydon; and *Bonningtons* (Salisbury Baxendale, Esq.)

HYDE, THE, MIDDX., a roadside hamlet commencing at the 6 m.-stone on the Edgware road : Inn, the *King's Arms*. The W. side of the road is in Kingsbury par., the E. in Hendon. Of old it was rural, now it is a mere roadside gathering of small commonplace houses, shops, an inn, a school, and a chapel.

In the summer of 1771 Goldsmith wrote his comedy, ' She Stoops to Conquer,' and in the following years (1772-4) his ' Animated Nature' here—at Mr. Selby's, " a farmer's house near the 6 m.-stone." He took the lodgings, as he said, " that he might have full leisure" for his task; and " carried down his books in two returned post-chaises." The farmer's family were puzzled at his strange ways and fits of abstraction; thought him "an odd character," and always spoke of him as "the gentleman"—partly, perhaps, out of respect to his visitors, among whom were Sir Joshua Reynolds, Sir Wm. Chambers, Johnson, and Boswell.

" Since I had the pleasure of seeing you last, I have been almost wholly in the country at a farmer's house, quite alone, trying to write a comedy. . . . . Every soul is a-visiting about and merry but myself. And that is hard too, as I have been trying these three months to do something to make people laugh. There have I been strolling about the hedges, studying jests with a most tragical countenance. The comedy is now finished." [*]

Boswell brought Mickle (translator of the Lusiad) to visit Goldsmith here :—

" He was not at home ; but having a curiosity to see his apartment, we went in and found various scraps of descriptions of animals scrawled upon the wall with a black-lead pencil." [†]

Mr. Forster, speaking of Goldsmith's " Edgware Road lodging," says that " almost all" of the 'Animated Nature' " was written here *or at Kingsbury*," [‡] not observing that the Edgware Road lodging *was* at Kingsbury. It was whilst here that Goldsmith had the sudden attack of illness, March 1774, which " warned him to seek advice in London," where he died a fortnight later.

ICKENHAM, MIDDX. (Dom. *Ticeham, Ticheham*, later *Tykeham*), 2½ m. N.E. from Uxbridge Stat. (G. W. Rly.), on the road to Ruislip: pop. 386.

Ickenham is an old-fashioned country village, the houses straggling along the lanes, and nestling a little more closely about the village green. There the main roads cross; and there, in the middle of the green, stands the village pump, within a capacious enclosure with seats all round and a tall conical roof overhead—the very place for a little cosy village chat and

scandal on an idle summer afternoon, —and beyond, on the farther side of the green, half hidden behind the tall trees, is the village church : making altogether a very pretty village landscape. Outside the vill., on the Hillingdon road, is the capital 17th cent. mansion of Swakeley, and all around are broad green meadows,

---

* Goldsmith to Bennet Langton, Sept. 7, 1771.
† Boswell, Life of Johnson, vol. iii., p. 220, ed. 1844.
‡ Forster, Life and Times of Oliver Goldsmith, vol. ii., p. 296.

spotted here and there with farm-houses that look the very picture of comfort and prosperity.

The *Church*, St. Giles, is small, the walls partly covered with plaster, the tall roofs tiled, the style early Perp. It consists of nave with N. aisle, brick chancel, wooden belfry and spire rising from the W. end of the nave, and containing 4 bells, wooden porch with tiled roof at the S.W. The interior is poor and without any special feature: the chancel arch was added in a recent restoration. It has some monts. to the Shorditch's, Dixons, Clarkes, and Turners, but none of any general interest; and *brasses* with effigies of Edmund Shorditch and wife, d. 1584; another merchant and wife, seemingly of a somewhat earlier date; and another of a man, of which the inscription is illegible. The octagonal font has been rechiselled.

The manor of *Swakeley* appears to owe its name to Robert Swalclyve, to whom it belonged in the early part of the 14th cent., and from whom it passed to John Charlton in 1350. By the attainder of Sir Richard Charlton in 1486, his property was forfeited, and Swakeley was granted to Sir Thos. Bourchier. Henry Bourchier Marquis of Exeter sold Swakeley in 1552 to Ralph Pexall. The manor was afterwards divided, a portion going to Oliver Becket, another to Bernard Brocas; but after some further changes the whole was reunited in the hands of Sir John Bingley, who in 1629 sold it to Edmund Wright, afterwards Sir Edmund Wright, alderman and (1641) Lord Mayor of London. Ald. Wright built the present mansion in 1638. Sir Edmund's daughter Catherine married Sir James Harrington, Bart., one of the judges of Charles I., who, thus becoming the owner of Swakeley, sold it, in 1665, to Sir Robert Vyner, Bart., noted as Lord Mayor for his entertainment of Charles II. at the Guildhall, and for his facetious manners. We have a picture of Sir Robert in his house shortly after he purchased it.

"*Sept.* 7, 1665.—To Branford. . . . There a coach of Mr. Povy's stood ready for me, and he at his house ready to come in, and so we together merrily to *Swakeley*, to Sir R. Vyner's: a very pleasant place, bought by him of Sir James Harrington's lady. He took us up and down with great respect, and showed us all his house and grounds; and it is a place not very moderne in the garden nor house, but the most uniforme in all that ever I saw; and some things to excess. Pretty to see over the screene of the hall, put up by Sir J. Harrington, a Long-Parliament-man, the King's head, and my Lord of Essex [the parliament general] on one side, and Fairfax on the other; and upon the other side of the screene, the parson of the parish, and the lord of the manor and his sisters. The window-cases, door-cases, and chimnys of all the house are marble. He showed us a black boy that he had, that died of a consumption; and, being dead, he caused him to be dried in an oven, and lies there entire in a box. By and by to dinner, where his lady I find yet handsome, but hath been a very handsome woman: now is old. Hath brought him near £100,000, and now he lives, no man in England in greater plenty, and commands both king and council with his credit he gives them. After dinner Sir Robert led us up to his long gallery, very fine, above stairs, and better, or such, furniture I never did see." *

In 1741 the manor was bought by Benj. Lethieullier, Esq., who, in 1750, sold Swakeley House to Thos. Clarke, Esq. It is now the seat of T. Truesdale Clarke, Esq. The house is a spacious, picturesque, and well-built, red-brick mansion, little altered externally, and in good preservation. The style is wanting in the playful exuberance of the true Elizabethan or Jacobean, but it is stately and effective, and among the majestic elms which surround it, and with the old ch. by its side, Swakeley forms an excellent representative old English manor-house. The principal front has the centre, in which is an enriched doorway, carried up four storeys high, the rest being lower; the projecting wings terminate in large bay windows; along the attic is a great but irregular array of gables, and above are stacks of ornamented chimney shafts. The grounds are very pleasant. Other seats are *Buntings* (W. C. Clarke-Thornhill, Esq.), and *Ickenham Hall* (G. Corderoy, Esq.)

IDE HILL

IDE HILL, KENT, famous for its prospect, a hamlet, and created in 1852 an eccl. dist., of Sundridge par., with the addition of small portions of Chevening and Chiddingstone parishes; pop. 764; 2¼ m. S. from Sundridge, on the road to Chiddingstone, and about 3½ m. S.W. from the Sevenoaks Rly. Stat. by a pleasant walk across Whitley Woods. Inn: the *Cock*, noted for dinners.

A plain brick ch. was erected here by Bp. Porteus in 1807. Failing to satisfy later ecclesiological tastes, it was taken down in 1863, and a new ch. raised to the honour of St. Mary the Virgin. This is a cruciform structure, of Kentish rag with Bath-stone dressings; Dec. in style; and has on the N.E. a tower and shingled spire 90 ft. high, at the junction of the nave and chancel. The int. is rather richly decorated, and several of the windows are filled with painted glass. The archt. was Mr. C. H. Cooke.

But the main interest of Ide Hill is the view. The hill is 700 ft. high, and the summit commands a magnificent stretch of weald country, rich in woods, villages, mansions, farms, not wanting in streams, and having the soft chalk downs to grace the extreme distance. It is one of the finest views of its kind in Kent, and the whole neighbourhood is full of charm.

ILFORD, GREAT, Essex (Dom. *Ilefort*), on the Colchester road, 6½ m. from Whitechapel ch.; 7 m. by G. E. Rly., Colchester line. Inns: *Angel*; *Red Lion*. Ilford is a ward of Barking par., but for ecclesiastical purposes was in 1830 constituted a district par.: pop. 3689.

Ilford, no doubt, owes it name to the ford over the Roding here; but whether it was an "*ill* ford," as Morant supposes, or an "*eald* (old) ford," as Lysons thinks more likely, we will not undertake to determine. It is a respectable roadside town, but looked livelier in the old coaching times, when the *Angel* was a busy posting house, and the other half-dozen inns seldom lacked customers. The Roding has been made navigable for barges to Ilford (2 m. above Barking) where is a wharf. By the river is a large corn mill, and there are extensive lime and brick works.

Ilford *Church* is a neat structure of white brick, E.E. in style; erected in 1831, and extended eastward, and painted windows inserted, in 1866. In the tower is a peal of 6 bells. Better worth looking at is *Ilford Hospital*, on the N. of the main road, originally founded (*temp.* Stephen) by Adeliza, Abbess of Barking, as the Hospital of the Virgin Mary and St. Thomas the Martyr, for 13 "lepers of the king's servants." By the statutes as modified in 1346 by Ralph Stratford, Bp. of London, every leper was obliged on admission to take an oath of chastity, of obedience to the Abbess of Barking, and

not to possess property to his own use. The chief officers were a prior and a master of the lepers elected by themselves. At the Dissolution there were only two poor inmates. Elizabeth granted the site and endowments in 1572 to Thomas Fanshaw, his heirs, etc., on condition that they should keep up the building and maintain therein a master and six poor aged men, with a chaplain to perform divine service in the chapel. The estate has since passed through many hands, and now belongs to the Marquis of Salisbury, who is master of the hospital. The buildings occupy three sides of a quadrangle. The oldest part is the chapel, a long, narrow, rough-cast building; late Perp. in style; but both chapel and houses were in the main rebuilt in 1719.

Will Kemp called at Ilford in his Nine Days' Morris-dance to Norwich, 1599.

"Forward I went with my hey-de-gaies to Ilford, where I again rested, and was by the people of the town and country thereabout very well welcomed, being offered carouses in the great spoon, one whole draught being able at that time to have drawn my little wit dry; but being afraid of the old proverb (He had need of a long spoon that eats with the devil), I soberly gave my boon companions the slip." [*]

Cranbrook House (R. Crook, Esq.), ¾ m. N., was the residence of Sir Charles Montague, d. 1625, whose mont. is conspicuous in Barking Ch. *Valentines* (C. M. Ingleby, Esq., LL.D.), which adjoins it on the N., was erected by Jas. Chadwick, Esq., son-in-law of Abp. Tillotson; and a walk in the grounds is known as Bishop's Walk. In the house is some good carving by Grinling Gibbons. In the field behind Valentines was found, in 1724, a stone coffin, containing a human skeleton, and in 1746 "an urn of coarse earth, filled with human bones." [†] These objects do not appear to have been preserved, or ever described by a competent authority; the former was perhaps, the latter almost certainly, Roman. The Roman road to *Durolitum* passed along here, the great encampment at *Uphall* (*see* BARKING) is in Ilford ward; and various relics of the

---

[*] Kemp, Nine Daies Wonder, ed. A. Dyce (Camden Soc.), p. 5. In the original ed. is a marginal note to the above, "A great spoon in Ilford, holding above a quart." It was probably kept at one of the inns for some drinking mummery, like the horns at Highgate, but we find no other reference to it.

[†] Lysons, Environs. vol. i., p. 626.

Roman occupation have been brought to light in the neighbourhood.

The Ilford brick-fields, by the London road, and at Uphall, towards Barking, are of classic fame in the annals of geological research, on account of the very remarkable remains of the larger mammalia of the pleistocene, or post-pliocene deposits of the Thames Valley found in them. These occur chiefly in the Lower Brick-earth, underlying the Thames Valley gravels, and comprise not only the elephant (*Elephas primigenius*), but 16 other species of mammalia, among them being the rhinoceros (*R. tichorhinus*, *R. leptorhinus*, and *R. megarhinus*), the bear (*Ursus arctus*, and *U. ferox*), tiger (*Felis spelæa*), wolf (*Canis lupus*), bison (*B. priscus*), ox (*Bos primigenius*), great stags (*Megaceros Hibernicus*, and *Cervus elephus*), horse (*Equus fossilis*), and beaver (*Castor fiber*).* The place of these deposits in time, is, probably, as Prof. Phillips remarks, "somewhere between that of the late pre-glacial and early post-glacial ages, when the levels of the country were different from what they are at present." † How different the entire conditions of the country were then from what they are now, the most cursory consideration of even the above imperfect list of the Ilford mammalia will sufficiently indicate. We may add that the magnificent collection of pleistocene mammalia formed by Sir Antonio Brady almost exclusively from the Ilford pits, is now in the British Museum, and an admirable catalogue of it has been drawn up by Mr. W. Davies. As has been pointed out, the occurrence of "the teeth of perhaps 100 elephants in this collection, attests the abundance of these great pachyderms at one time inhabiting the Thames Valley." ‡

ILFORD, LITTLE, Essex, ¾ m. S.W. of Great Ilford, and a stat. on the G. E. Rly. (Colchester Line) : pop. 675, of whom 33 were inmates of the gaol. Inn, the *Three Rabbits*, on the London road.

The ch. and quiet old vill. lie among perfectly flat fields, ¼ m. S. of the highroad,

but the parish stretches some way N. of it, and comprises within its boundaries the *County House of Detention*, better known as *Ilford Gaol*, a large brick structure, erected in 1831, and the *City of London Cemetery*. Little Ilford *Church* (the Virgin Mary), is a mean brick substitute for a venerable ivy-clad building, one of the most picturesque village churches near London, destroyed a few years back. In it are some *monts.* removed from the old ch.—N. of chancel, mural, of William Waldegrave, d. 1610, and wife, d. 1595, alabaster effigies, coloured, with kneeling effigies beneath of their 3 sons and 4 daughters, and at the sides, arms and obelisks : a characteristic example of the monumental art of the time. In the vestry, John Lethieullier, of Aldersbrooke, d. 1724, Smart Lethieullier, "the antiquary of Essex," d. Aug. 27, 1760, and other members of the Lethieullier family, noted in Essex annals. The manor of Aldersbrooke was purchased in 1786 by Sir J. Tylney Long, who pulled down the mansion and built a farm-house on the site. Lysons, writing at the end of the last century, says, "A great mart for cattle, from Wales, Scotland, and the north of England, is held annually, from the latter end of Feb. till the beginning of May, on the flat part of the forest," or Wanstead Flats, and he adds that "a great part of the business between the dealers is transacted at the Rabbits in this parish."* The *mart* has long ceased, and the Three Rabbits is a less important house than of old, but is still frequented by graziers and cattle dealers.

IMBER COURT (*see* DITTON).

INGRAVE, Essex (Dom. *Inga, Ginga ;* anc. *Ginges Radulfi, Ging Raff, Ing Raffe, Ingrafe*),† on the road to Orsett and Tilbury, 2½ m. S. E. from Brentwood ; pop. 633.

Ingrave is pleasantly situated on high ground, with the fine park of Thorndon Hall on the W., and on the E. and S.E. the broad tract known as Ingrave Common, but long since enclosed and cultivated. At the Dom. Survey, the place

---

* Boyd Dawkins, Quart. Journal, Geol. Soc., vol. xxiii., p. 91 ; Proc. of Geol. Soc., 1867 ; Searles V. Wood, Geol. Mag., vol. iii., p. 57.

† Phillips, Geology of the Valley of the Thames, 1871, chap. xviii., p. 472.

‡ Proc. of Geol. Assoc., vol. ii., p. 274.

---

* Lysons, Environs, vol. i., p. 670.

† Chisenhale-Marsh, Domesday Book relating to Essex ; Morant, Hist. of Essex.

belonged to Ranulfus, or Ralph, the brother of Ilger, whence the name *Ging Ralph*, Ralph's ing or meadow. The vill. consists of first a sprinkling of wooden cottages about a small village green and along the road, then of newer and more formal, but very clean, brick tenements, with a few houses of a better class, a triangular green with a small pond and inn. Ingrave was united with West Horndon par. by Act of Parliament, the churches of the two parishes taken down, and a new one built to serve the united par., as an inscription on the tower records, " by Robert James Petre, Baron Writtle," in 1734. (*See* HORNDON, WEST.)

The *Church*, St. Nicholas, stands close to the road, at the N. end of the vill., and is a plain red-brick building with a massive tower at the W., in which is a peal of 5 bells. The int. is as gloomy as the exterior, and only noteworthy as containing 2 brasses of the Fitz Lewis family, the ancient owners of Heron Hall, brought from old Ingrave ch.—Margaret Fitz Lewis, probably wife of Sir Lewis Fitz Lewis, d. 1500, and John Fitz Lewis, d. 1442, and his 4 wives, in heraldic dresses. Nearly opposite to the ch., by the entrance to Thorndon Hall, are the Roman Catholic Schools, built and maintained by Lord Petre—a neat white-brick building, with a statue of the Virgin and Child in a niche in the front.

INGRESS (*see* GREENHITHE).

ISLEWORTH, MIDDX., on the l. bank of the Thames, between Brentford and Twickenham, 8½ m. W.S.W. from Hyde Park Corner, and about ½ m. E. from the Spring Grove Stat. of the L. and S. W. Rly. (Loop-line). The pop. of Isleworth par. in 1871 was 11,498, but this includes 4531 in the eccl. dist. of Hounslow Heath, 1331 in St. Margaret's, and 136 in Spring Grove; the parent district, All Saints', Isleworth, had 4948 inh., and of these 808 were in public institutions.

The name has somewhat puzzled inquirers. In the Dom. Survey it is written *Gistelworde;* later it appears as *Istelworth* and *Istylworth;* and Norden, in 1591, writes " *Thistleworth,* or *Istleworth.*" *Thistleworth* appears to have been the local pronunciation down almost to our

own day. It seems clear, therefore, that the derivation from *isle* is inapplicable, and none quite satisfactory has been suggested. It is probably, a patronymic combined with *worth*, an enclosure.

The history of Isleworth is chiefly connected with Syon. Simon de Montfort and the Barons encamped in Isleworth Park in 1263. The following year a great multitude of the citizens of London, under Sir Hugh le Spencer, Constable of the Tower, and lately created by the Barons Justiciary of England, marched to Isleworth, and "spoiled" the house of Richard, Earl of Cornwall and King of the Romans, who then held the manor, destroyed his water-mills, and did other mischief. The City, for this and other services rendered to the Barons, had shortly after to submit to many indignities. The posts and chains by which the entrance to the City was guarded were removed from the ends of the streets. The Mayor and 40 of the principal citizens, who had gone as a deputation to the king, were seized and thrown into prison, and kept there till a fine was paid which the king at first fixed at 60,000 marks, but at length reduced to 20,000.[*] The site of the Duke of Cornwall's house is uncertain. Lysons thinks it "probable that it was a spot of ground behind the Phœnix yard, called in old writings the Moated Place;" Mr. Aungier places it near Isleworth House; while tradition assigns it a site more to the W.[†] In Aug. 1647 Fairfax had his head-quarters at Isleworth.

In 1415 Henry V. founded a convent of Bridgetines at Twickenham, the first and only house of the order established in England. Sixteen years later, 1431, Henry VI. gave permission to the abbess and convent to remove to a more spacious house which they had erected at Isleworth, settled on them an annuity of 1000 marks, and by Act of Parliament gave them the manor. Syon monastery was dedicated to "St. Saviour and St. Bridget of Syon," and, according to the rules of the order, consisted of the abbess and 59 nuns, 13 priests, 4 deacons, and 8 lay brethren— the number of the apostles and 72 dis-

---

[*] Maitland, Hist. of London, p. 59.
[†] Lysons, ii., p. 453, note; Aungier, Hist. and Antiq. of Syon, p. 231.

ciples of Christ. From various benefactors it received considerable gifts and endowments, and at the Dissolution had a revenue of £1944. The Report of the Commissioners charges the nuns and priests with gross misconduct, but their testimony may fairly be read with some mistrust. Tradition asserts the existence of a tunnel carried beneath the Thames from Syon to the monastery of Sheen, in Surrey, to further the intercourse of the monks and nuns of the two houses. Syon was one of the first of the larger monasteries suppressed. It is said to have been particularly obnoxious to the king, Henry VIII., and to Cromwell, on account of reputed complicity of the inmates with the proceedings of the Maid of Kent. One of the commissioners, Thomas Bedyll, in his Report to Cromwell, has a remark that seems to imply that some such rumour had been circulated. He had, he writes, ordered the confessionals to be walled up, " for that hearing of outward confessions hath been the cause of much evil and of much treason, which hath been sowed abroad in this matter of the King's title, and also in the King's Grace's matter of his succession and marriage." *

Henry retained the monastery of Syon in his own hands till his death. In 1541 it became the prison of Queen Katharine Howard till three days before her execution. The corpse of Henry himself rested here the first night on its way to the vaults at Windsor. Edward VI., in the first year of his reign, gave monastery and manor to the Protector Somerset, who on the site, and from the materials, built himself a stately mansion. On his fall it reverted to the Crown, and in 1553 the King granted it to John, Duke of Northumberland. His was a brief and sorry tenancy. Edward died on the 6th of July 1553, and Northumberland's daughter-in-law, the Lady Jane Grey, was at Syon when the king's death and her own succcession were announced. On the 10th she went by water in state to the Tower, which she was not to leave again alive. Northumberland himself was beheaded on the 10th of August, and Syon again reverted to the Crown. In 1557 Queen Mary restored the monastery, and

recalled the nuns ; but 30 years had passed since their dispersion, most of the elder nuns were dead, and many of the younger, according to Fuller, had married; "however," he adds, "with much ado, joining some new ones with the old, they made up a competent number." * Before two years were over a new Queen was on the throne, and the monastery was again suppressed. Elizabeth in 1560 made Sir Francis Knolles keeper of Syon House for his life, with reversion to his son Robert, but kept the place in her own possession. James I. shortly after his accession granted the house and manor to Henry, Earl of Northumberland. Its subsequent history will be found under SYON HOUSE.

The nuns of Syon, after the final suppression of the monastery, did not at once disperse, like most of the communities. Some, indeed, returned to their families. The abbess, Clementina Thresham, being sick, retired to Rushton, in Northamptonshire, and soon after died there ; Margaret Dely, a nun, was buried, 1561, in Isleworth ch.; but the rest repaired together to the Continent. After seeking in vain an abiding-place in France, Germany, and Flanders, they made their way to Lisbon, where Isabella de Azevedo gave them, 1594, a house and grounds, and they formed a new community of the Sisters of Syon. With many fluctuations of fortune, including the destruction of the convent by the great earthquake of 1755, they held together till 1807, when, on the approach of the French army, the convent was closed, and in 1809 the superior and nine of the nuns removed to England. On the fall of Napoleon, the nuns who had stayed in Portugal returned to their house, and several from England rejoined them. The convent of the Sisters of Syon was re-established ; but after awhile the numbers dwindled, and in 1861 the 12 remaining nuns returned to England, and were received in Spetisbury Convent, Dorsetshire. When the nuns migrated from Isleworth they carried with them the keys of the monastery, as an assertion of their right to their old estate. A late Duke of Northumberland visited the Lisbon convent, and presented the nuns with a silver model of the lost Syon. "We still hold the keys," said the

* Aungier, p. 87.

* Fuller, Church Hist. of Britain, b. vi., sect. 5.

abbess. "I dare say," replied the duke; "but we have altered the locks since then!" *

A chapel was founded at Brentford End, by John Somerseth, Chancellor of the Exchequer to Henry VI., in honour of the nine orders of holy angels—the only chapel, according to the preamble of the charter, which had ever been founded in their honour. On an adjoining piece of land he built a hospital for 9 poor men, who were incorporated as a guild by Henry VI. The guild afterwards received an augmentation of 7 brethren, and funds for a chantry for two priests in the chapel, the estates being made over to Syon monastery. It was suppressed with the other religious houses. Edward VI. gave the estate to the Protector Somerset, and, after many transfers, it now belongs to the Duke of Northumberland. As long ago as 1635 no vestige of the buildings remained, and the site is now uncertain.

Isleworth extends for three miles along the Thames, where the river first becomes sylvan, Kew Gardens and Richmond Lower Park lining the opposite bank. The first mile from Brentford is occupied by the ducal park and palace of Syon. Then comes the ivy-clad ch. and mill, the river-side village, with its good old-fashioned red-brick, middle-class residences, shops, wharves, and boat-houses, and in front of all the long willowy eyot. Farther on and wider apart are fair and stately seats, with velvet lawns sloping to the river, and girt with shadowy trees; and ever and anon, and more frequently as we approach Twickenham, varied with clusters of modern Gothic neo-archaisms, misnamed villas.

From the river the parish stretches back 2½ m. N.W. to Heston; its extreme length, from E. to W., along the Great Western Road, is about 4½ miles. A large part of the ground is laid out in the cultivation of fruit, vegetables, and flowers for the London markets. There are brick-fields, and extensive cement works. A great flour-mill, worked by the Isleworth river and by steam; a large brewery, steam yacht and launch and boat yards, and a fleet of lighters and

barges, give employment to the river-side population. And as a counterpoise to its ducal and dignified side, Isleworth has its rough and grimy region, the trouble of policemen, and terror of quiet-loving villagers, known as the Irish Quarter. In Norden's day there was "a copper and brasse myll wher it is wrought out of the oar, melted, and forged;" and where "workemen make plates both of copper and brasse of all syces little and great, thick and thyn, for all purposes: they make also kyttles." The hammers, "some of wrought and beaten iron, some of cast iron, of 200, 300, some 400 weight," greatly moved the old surveyor's admiration, they being "lifted up by an artificiall engine by the force of the water." This branch of industry has, however, long departed from Isleworth, as has another of later introduction, but of much interest—that of pottery and porcelain. The porcelain works were abandoned towards the end of the last century; but the delft manufacture was continued on a small scale as late as 1811. Specimens of the Isleworth ware are now in request with collectors. The Hounslow Gunpowder Mills are partly in Isleworth par.

The *Church*, All Saints, stands on a raised terrace by the river at the Syon end of the par. Except the tower, which is of stone, and of the Perp. period, the ch. is of brick, and of the years 1705-6. The old ch. being in a bad state, Wren was, in 1701, invited to make designs for a new one. These were pronounced too expensive for adoption, and laid aside; but when the ch. was at last erected, Wren's plans were, it is said, brought out and used—being first altered and improved on economical principles by the churchwardens. Apart from its ivy-covered tower, there could not well have been an uglier ch. than that of Isleworth a few years ago; but it has been transformed, the windows altered, a new roof of higher pitch, and a lofty white-brick Dec. chancel added, greatly to the benefit of the general effect. And the interior is even more improved than the exterior. The body of the ch. is lengthened by the new chancel, and the opening of the tower into the nave; heightened by the loftier roof; and brightened by painted glass windows, the very elegant and novel tinting of the roof, shafts, and decorative

* Aungier, Hist. of Syon Monastery; Lysons, Environs, vol. i.; Fuller, Church Hist. of Britain; Thorne, Rambles by Rivers: the Thames, vol. ii.

features, and the substitution of open seats for high pews. The organ, by Father Schmidt, is of unusual power and sweetness; and the 8 bells in the tower are, according to the Isleworth creed, the most musical by the river-side.

Among the *monts.*, obs. on S. side of the tower, Sir Orlando Gee, d. 1705, steward to Algernon and Joceline, Earls of Northumberland, Registrar of the Admiralty: a marble bust to waist, representing the knight in flowing peruke and long cravat. On the opposite wall, and, like Gee's, brought here from the old chancel, is a mont. with marble bust of Anne Tolson, d. 1750, foundress of the almshouses named after her. E. end of the N. gallery a mural mont. to Catherine, wife of Sir Francis Darcy, d. 1625; with kneeling effigies of Sir Francis in armour, and his wife, under a canopy supported by Corinthian columns. On wall of S. gallery, one to Sir Francis Devaux, F.R.S., physician to Charles II., d. 1694; one with small effigies of 3 children of Sir Thomas, afterwards Visct. Savage, and Earl Rivers; also a mont. by Nollekens to George Keate, d. 1797, known by his Narrative of Capt. Wilson's Voyage to the Pelew Islands. Chiefly in the vestry are some *brasses*, among which should be noticed, a nameless knight in armour, about half life-size, of the latter part of the 15th cent.; two chrisom children, 16th cent.; Wm. Chase, d. 1544, "Serjeant to King Henry VIII., and of his honourable houshold of the hall and woodyerd"; effigy in armour; and, what is not the least interesting, a small effigy of Margaret Dely, "a sister professed yn Syon," at the second suppression of the monastery. She d. Oct. 7, 1561; and this is probably the latest brass of the kind in this country. The brass of Agnes Jordan, abbess of Syon at the first suppression, is in Denham ch. (*See* DENHAM, p. 140.) Margaret Howard, wife of Roger Earl of Orrery, whose marriage to the Earl was the subject of Suckling's beautiful ballad of "A Wedding," was buried at Isleworth. Among the vicars were, John Hall, who, after holding the living for 14 years, was hanged at Tyburn, 1535, for denying the royal supremacy; Nicholas Byfield, 1615-22, author of several theological works, and father of the more famous Adoniram Byfield; Dr. William Cave, author of the

Lives of the Fathers, and other learned books; and William Drake, 1777-1801, distinguished in his day as an antiquary.

The parish register records the baptism, Oct. 5, 1617, of Waller's *Sacharissa*, —Dorothy, daughter of Sir Robert and Lady Dorothy Sidney; the baptism, June 22, 1676, of Anthony Collins, the famous deistical writer (*see* HESTON); and the first marriage, March 1679, to Lord Ogle, of the Lady Elizabeth Percy, afterwards the wife of Thomas Thynne, of Longleat Hall, murdered, Sept. 1682, by Count Koningsmark, and thirdly, May 1683, the wife of the proud Duke of Somerset —thus having in 4 years three husbands, and being yet only 17.

A new district ch., St. John the Baptist, was erected, 1857, at Woodlands, near the rly. stat., on a site given, with a large subscription, by Algernon late Duke of Northumberland. It is a neat E.E. building, and cost about £9000. Near it is a range of almshouses, for 6 poor men and 6 women, built and endowed by the late John Farnell, Esq. Several other almshouses are in the par.: Sir Thos. Ingram's, 1654, for 6 poor women, housekeepers of the par.; Mrs. Anne Tolson's, 1750, and lately rebuilt, for 6 poor men and 6 women; Mrs. Mary Bell's, 1738, for 6 women; and Mrs. Sermon's, for 6 women.

The "Manor-place" of Richard, king of the Romans, has already been spoken of. This was no doubt the palace which Henry IV. is said to have had here. But Isleworth has had other famous mansions. *Worton* was a royal manor till Henry VI. gave it to Syon monastery. It is now the property of the Duke of Northumberland. *Worton Manor House* (F. Walton, Esq.), a good modern mansion, in the Worton Road, midway between Isleworth and Hounslow, was at the close of the last cent. the residence of Col. Fullarton. Wyke manor-house, also given by Henry VI. to the nuns of Syon, stood by Wyke Green. The present *Wyke House* adjoins the entrance to Osterley Park, and is noticed under BRENTFORD (p. 59). A little S.E. of it was *Syon Hill*, built by Robert Earl of Holdernesse, d. 1778: the house has been taken down, but the park remains.

Kendal House, on the rt. of the Twickenham Road, was the residence of Amen-gard de Schulemburg, Duchess of Kendal, mistress of George I.

"In a tender mood he [the King] promised the Duchess of Kendal that if she survived him, and if it were possible for the departed to return to this world, he would make her a visit. The Duchess on his death [1727], so much expected the accomplishment of that engagement, that a large raven, or some black fowl, flying into one of the windows of her villa at Isleworth, she was persuaded it was the soul of her departed monarch so accoutred, and received and treated it with all the respect and tenderness of duty, till the royal bird or she took their last flight." *

Kendal House was sold on the death of the Duchess, and converted into a place of public entertainment, of the kind described under HAMPSTEAD. The style of our ancestors' amusements a century and a quarter ago may be judged from the invitations to Kendal House. There were to be public breakfasts upon Wednesdays and Fridays. The long room for dancing was 60 ft. long, and, like all the other rooms, "elegantly fitted up." "The orchestra on the water is allowed by all that have seen it to be in the genteelest taste, being built an octagon in the Corinthian order, above 50 ft. in diameter, having an upper and lower gallery, where gentlemen and ladies may divert themselves with fishing, the canal being well stored with tench, carp, and all sorts of fish in great plenty." There are "two wildernesses. with delightful rural walks"; a rapid river runs through the grounds; a pleasant grove of trees screens you on hot summer days from the heat of the sun; "there is a man-cook, and a good larder;" and everything is "as cheap, or cheaper, than at any place of the kind." † When the fashion for these places died out, Kendal House was pulled down and the site appropriated.

Close by Kendal House stood another noted mansion, *Gumley House.* It was built towards the end of the 17th cent. by the wealthy John Gumley, whose daughter and sole heiress gave her hand, wealth, and house to Wm. Pulteney, afterwards Earl of Bath, the famous orator and minister of Georges I. and II., and friend and rival of Walpole. Whilst his residence, Gumley House was a place of

* Horace Walpole, Reminiscences of the Courts of George the First and Second; Letters, vol. i., p. ciii.

† Daily Advertiser, April 4, 1750, quoted by Lysons.

mark; after his death it was the residence of Lord Lake; it is now a Roman Catholic convent. Charles Talbot, Duke of Shrewsbury, Secretary of State to William III. and Queen Mary, and whose name is of such frequent occurrence in the history of these reigns, d. at his country seat at Isleworth in 1718. This house, which was much admired in the Duke's time, had a parallel fate to that of Gumley House, terminating as a Roman Catholic school and chapel. It was pulled down in the early part of the present century. Lord Baltimore, Secretary of State to James I., one of Walpole's Noble Authors, and the original grantee and founder of the colony (now State) of Baltimore, had a summer residence at Isleworth,* but where it stood we know not.

Lacy, one of the patentees of Drury Lane Theatre, built himself a large house by the river, which, under the name of *Lacy House,* attained some celebrity; it having been successively the residence of Sir Edward Walpole, his daughter Mrs. Keppell, widow of the Bp. of Exeter, and Richard Brinsley Sheridan. It was taken down several years back. Next to it stood *Seaton House,* the residence of General Bland; afterwards of Lord James Hay, and later of Lord and Lady Frederick Gordon.

Isleworth House (Mrs. M'Andrew) is celebrated for the beauty of the grounds and the charming views of the river and Richmond. The house is a very fine one. The Syon Vista in Kew Gardens was cut by command of William IV.. after a visit to Lady Cooper at Isleworth House, in order to open a view of the Pagoda and Observatory to the front of the house. A house by it had for occupants Lady Charlville, Lord Muncaster, and the Duchess of Manchester. The most noticeable of the recent mansions is *Gordon House,* the fine seat of the Earl of Kilmorey. *Silver Hall,* in the North Road. a good old 17th cent. mansion, so called from an early owner, was pulled down in 1801. A new Silver Hall was built on a somewhat different site, and is now the seat of F. H. N. Glossop, Esq. Besides those incidentally named, Isleworth has numbered among its inhabitants Mrs. Middleton, one of the Beauties of the

* Strafford Correspondence, vol. i., p. 24.

Court of Charles II., who appears to more advantage on Lely's canvas than in the pages of Grammont; Sir Theodore Mayerne, "First Physician to three Kings"—Louis XIII. of France, James I. and Charles I. of England; the Rev. Samuel Clarke, an eminent Nonconformist divine and biographer of the 17th cent.; and Sir Ralph Winwood, ambassador to Holland and Secretary of State to James I.

St. Margaret's, by the river-side towards Twickenham, the seat of the Marquis of Ailsa, was pulled down some years back, and the park broken up and built over, and is now a village of modern villas. A spacious and handsome mansion, built by Lord Kilmorey, but never occupied, was purchased in 1856, and converted into the *Royal Naval Female School*. The institution is for the maintenance and education of the daughters of naval and marine officers. The larger part of the girls are received at an almost nominal charge; a certain portion pay £40 a year each; and some are provided for from the Patriotic Fund. The house is a noble one; there are good grounds, and a pretty little E.E. chapel has been lately added for the children's use. *The Chesnuts* (W. Knox Wigram, Esq.), and *St. Margaret's Lodge* (G. S. Measom, Esq.), are among the larger villas.

IVER, BUCKS (Dom. *Evreham*), 1½ m. N.W. of the West Drayton Stat. of the Grt. W. Rly., 2½ S.W. of Uxbridge, and 17 m. from London: pop. 2239, of whom 680 are in the eccl. dist. of Iver Heath, and 74 in that of Gerard's Cross.

The par. is of great extent, reaching N. and S. from Colnbrook, part of which is in Iver par., to Gerard's Cross. The extreme length is said to be over 10 m. The country is varied, and much of it very pleasing. The upper part is undulating, rising northwards into low hills and open heath, and varied with parks and woodland; the lower, level meadows; the E. side bounded by "the trouty Colne." Iver village is long, rambling, clean, quiet, secluded, and, in parts, picturesque. Of old it had a market and a fair, but the former has long been discontinued, and the latter is only maintained as a little village holiday. Two old inns, the *Bull* and *Swan*, by the ch., mark the former greater size of the place; the Bull is of brick gabled, with a good group of chimney shafts; the Swan, half-timber.

The *Church* (St. Peter) is large, ancient, —ranging in date from Norm. to Perp., but externally showing chiefly its later features,—of flint and stone, mended with brick; and consists of nave with clerestorey, aisles, long chancel, and large and lofty square embattled tower at the W. end, in which are 6 bells. The *int*. is spacious and imposing. The arcade of 5 arches, between the nave and N. aisle, is Norm. On the S. is a gallery. The E. window is a fine one of 5 lights, Dec. S. of the chancel are sedilia and a piscina. The oak stalls have well-carved poppyheads; and there are piscinas at the E. end of the aisles. The Norm. font has a square bowl of Sussex marble, supported on a thick central pedestal and four thin octagonal shafts. *Monts.*—N. of chancel, Lady Mary Salter, d. 1631; recumbent effigy, with boy on each side, between Corinthian columns which support a tall canopy; below, kneeling figures of Dame Salter with 2 daughters behind her, and infant lying with its head on a skull; opposite 2 male figures kneeling. There are other monts. to the Slaters, Bowyers, and other local families; but the most noteworthy, perhaps, is a tablet in the N. aisle to a learned bricklayer:—

Venturus Mandey, d. 1701, of St. Giles in the Fields, London, many years "Bricklayer to the Hon. Soc. of Lincoln's Inn." He was "studious in mathematicks, and wrote and published three Books for the Public good: one entitled Mellificium Monciones, or the Marrow of Measuring; another of Mechanical Powers, or the Mystery of Nature and Art unvayled: the third an Universal Mathematical Synopsis. He also translated into English, Directorium generale Uranometricum, and Trigonometria Plana et Sphærica, Linearis et Logarithmica: Auctore Fr. Bonaventura Cavalerio Mediolanense, and some other tracts which he designed to have printed if Death had not prevented him."

On a large slab in the nave is a *brass*, without name or date, but believed to be of Richard Blount, d. 1508, and wife Elizabeth. It has a figure of a knight in plate armour, with sword on l., dagger on rt. side, spurs, etc.; wife in rich embroidered robe and girdle, pointed head-dress and lappets; 3 sons and 3 daughters. There are also two or three inscribed brasses, without effigies. *Obs.* the great elm W. of the ch.-yard.

St. Margaret, *Iver Heath*, 1¾ m. N. of

Iver vill., is a neat building of flint and stone, late E. E. in character, erected in 1862. It comprises nave, chancel, and low embattled tower. Iver Heath is a secluded little hamlet, in the midst of very pleasing scenery.

Richings, the most celebrated. of the seats in Iver, is noticed under that title. Others are *Huntsmore Park* (Christopher Tower, Esq.), a stately old many-gabled house, standing in fine grounds by the Colne, ½ m. N.E. of the vill. In the Tudor times it was a manor house with a courtyard. *Delaford* (C. Clowes, Esq.), ¾ m. N. of Iver, is a spacious classic edifice, with a semicircular portico, erected by Col. Francis Needham (after-

ward Lord Kilmorey), in 1761, but altered and enlarged in 1802, by Chas. Clowes, Esq., who had purchased the estate in 1790. It stands in a small but pleasant park, through which flows a branch of the Colne. *Iver Grove*, 1 m. W. of the church, was for some years the residence of Admiral Lord Gambier. Queen Elizabeth is said to have stayed at *Rycots*, now a farm-house, surrounded by a moat. Cromwell is claimed as a resident at *Thorney*. Mr. Charles Knight had a small property at Iver, where in early life he spent many summer months.

JUNIPER HILL, SURREY (*see* MICKLEHAM).

KELVEDON HATCH, ESSEX,

(Dom. *Kelvenduna*), 3 m. S. by E. from Ongar Stat., on the road to Brentwood; pop. 401.

Kelvedon Hatch is a secluded and pleasant place; almost exclusively agricultural, but possessing several good seats. There is no vill. proper; the church is in the grounds of Kelvedon Hall, and close by the mansion. The largest gathering of houses is about *Kelvedon Common* and *Kelvedon Mill*, 1½ m. S. of the ch.; but these are partly in Doddinghurst parish. The *Church*, St. Nicholas, is a small and plain red brick 18th century building, with a wooden bell turret and short shingled spire rising from the W. end of the roof, and a wooden porch. On the walls are several old monts., but of no general interest, being chiefly to members of the Dolby, Luther, and Wright families, who have held the manor; and there is a *brass* of a man and his wife, without an inscr., but of about the middle of the 16th cent.

Kelvedon Hall (E. Carrington Wright, Esq.), is a large old red brick mansion, surrounded by fine oaks and lofty elms, which overhang the ch.-yd. The building carried out from the Hall is a Roman Catholic chapel—in curious propinquity, for a country vill., to the par. ch. By the house is a large sheet of water; beyond it are some shady woods. By that E. of the ch. is a pleasant footway (1½ m. N.E.) to Stondon Massey

KEMSING, KENT, 3 m. N.E. from the Sevenoaks Rly. Stat., through *Seal*, and thence by a pleasant walk of a mile along field-paths and hop-gardens; pop. 408.

The village consists of a farmhouse or two with hop-kilns attached; a few cottages of Kentish rag and brick, and one or two of half-timber and plaster; a village smithy, and a couple of 'publics'; in the centre of the village a well (half well, half pond, with steps descending to the spring) dedicated to the Anglo-Saxon saint Edith—who is claimed as a native of Kemsing—and, dominating all, the church, dedicated, like the well, to the local saint. The village is exclusively agricultural; hops being perhaps the staple product. The *Church* is small, and consists of a nave and chancel, a wooden bell turret, with thin shingled spire, rising from the western roof, and a wooden porch on the S.W. The nave windows are late Dec., except a lancet on the S. side, which should be noticed, as it contains a bit of old painted glass worth looking at—a small circular medallion with a representation of the Virgin and Child, on a white diapered ground. The chancel is Perp. The *int.* is plain and fitted with tall pews. There are no monts. of value or interest. In the chancel is a small but quite perfect 14th cent. *brass*, of Thomas Hop, rector of Kemsing, d. 1346.*

---

* Boutell, Mon. Brasses, 95 : it is well engraved in the Reliquary for Jan. 1873.

The ch. was restored and reseated in 1870. S. of the ch. is the shell of a large yew.

Above the ch. rises a ridge of chalk hills, to which a path leads direct from the ch.-yd., through a hop-garden, and across the Pilgrims' Road, making for the yew-tree on the hillside due N. The view from the summit will amply repay the trifling labour necessary to reach it. The *Pilgrims' Road*, here crossed, is the ancient track way traversed by the pilgrims from the W. and S.W. on their way to Canterbury. It may still be traced at intervals along the ridge or slopes of the Downs from Alton in Hampshire, through Surrey (by way of Reigate and Merstham), and across Chevening Park, by Otford to this spot, and thence onwards by Wrotham and Halling, where, crossing the Medway, it again takes to the hills and proceeds towards Canterbury by way of Detling, Hollingbourne, and Charing,—seldom, however, touching the towns or populous villages.

KEN WOOD, MIDDX. (*see* CAEN WOOD).

KENLEY, SURREY, a hamlet of

Coulsdon par., and a stat. on the Caterham branch of the S.E. Rly. Inns, *Kenley Hotel; Rose and Crown*, Caterham Road.

Kenley was until lately only known as a charming but almost houseless district, stretching over hill and dale between Riddlesdown and Coulsdon, and along the Caterham Valley. Now there are a rly. stat., hotel, and water-works; the hillsides are spotted over with villas, smaller houses are creeping along the valley, and shops have been opened to supply the bodily, and a church the spiritual needs of a growing village. Some of the new houses are large and handsome ; the only older one of any size is *Kenley House* (J. Young, Esq.)

The country around Kenley is unusually pleasing. (*See* CATERHAM JUNCTION; COULSDON.) The cuttings of the abandoned Surrey and Sussex Railway afford ready means of observing the geological formation of the district. The cuttings are through beds of chalk banded with flints — the chalk here being some 250 ft. thick. At the mouth of the Kenley tunnel is observable a considerable *fault*,

with the resultant grooves and ridges of the rubbed surfaces. The fossils are chiefly *Micraster cor-anguinam, Ananchytes ovata, Spondylus spinosus,* and *Inoceramus Cuvieri.*[*] The *Church*, All Saints', was erected in 1872 from the designs of Mr. J. Fowler. It is of Kentish rag and stone externally, of brick inside ; is early Dec. in style ; and consists of nave, aisles, and chancel, with a tower and spire on the N.E.

KENTON, MIDDX., a hamlet of

Harrow, from which it is about 2 m. E.— midway between Harrow and the Edgware Road. Though so near to London it remains a secluded rural hamlet of two or three farmhouses, a few cottages, a little inn (the *Plough*), a school-house in which service is held on Sundays, a great house, *Kenton Lodge* (J. D. Smith, Esq.), with a couple of groups of elms before it, and a rookery, and another not far off called *Kenton Grange* (Henry Ricardo, Esq.) The walk to Harrow is pleasant ; still more so is the longer one by Wembly Park to Kingsbury.

KESTON, KENT, on the borders of

Surrey (A.-S. *Cystaninga*, Dom. *Chestan*), famed for its Common, and as the residence of William Pitt, is 3½ m. from Bromley on the road to Westerham : pop. 717. The best way to it from Bromley is through Hayes and over Hayes Common—a very pleasant walk.

Keston is a charming place for a summer ramble. There is no village proper ; a few houses are collected together by the *Red Cross* inn, at Keston Mark, or Keston Cross, on the Hayes side of Holwood, where the Farnborough road crosses the main road from Bromley to Westerham ; a few more by the mill on the Common, where is another country inn, the *Fox ;* and two or three more by the ch., at the S. end of Holwood Park. Keston Common is a prolongation of Hayes Common (*see* HAYES), equally enjoyable and more picturesque, because more broken and varied—though in places somewhat rudely encroached upon.

The name as given above shows its

* Caleb Evans, F.G.S., 'Some Sections of Chalk between Croydon and Oxtead,' Proc. Geol. Assoc., 1870.

antiquity. But it was a Roman and possibly a British settlement before it was Saxon. Holwood House occupies a portion of an extensive encampment, long known as Cæsar's Camp, and which is now generally held to mark the Roman station, *Noviomagus.* From the accounts published when the works were much more perfect than now, it was an oblong earthwork with a double, in parts triple, vallum and deep trenches, the outer vallum being nearly 2 m. in circuit and enclosing an area of over 100 acres. But large portions of the lines have been levelled, laid out as lawns, planted, or converted into arable land ; and what remains untouched is overgrown with trees and shrubs, and would require time and labour to make out. Many Roman remains, foundations of buildings, tiles, broken pottery, and coins of the Middle and Lower Empire, have been found within the lines on Holwood Hill ; and at Blacknest Farm, W. of the ch. The foundations of a circular building, evidently Roman, and, as some believed, a temple, were laid open in 1828 ; and in 1854 at the Lower Warbank extensive remains were discovered, consisting not only of a Roman villa, but vestiges of rude habitations; the site, as was considered, of a British village and the house of its Roman master. These discoveries led to the formation of a sort of club, the Noviomagians, ostensibly to prosecute the investigation of the site, but we have not heard much of the results of their researches beyond some agreeable meetings.

A well just under Warbank, by the roadside and near the entrance to Holwood Park, is known as *Cæsar's Well,* though this appears to be a comparatively modern appellation, and may have been given to it when antiquaries were calling attention to the camp. It is a circular well, has been carefully bricked round, with steps to descend into it, but the brick lining has been allowed to get out of repair, and the steps are lost. The water, fed no doubt by springs in Holwood Park, flows out cool and clear, and running along a short winding channel spreads out into the large sheets of water known as the *Keston Ponds.* These are bordered by trees, and form an agreeable object on the broad common. The well is the reputed source of the *Ravensbourne,*

which flowing by Bromley, Beckenham, and Lewisham falls into the Thames at Deptford Creek. The brick lining and steps were probably of the last quarter of the 18th cent. An account of Holwood and Keston, published in 1792, says that " of this spring an excellent bath was formed, surrounded by pales and trees ; " and another, going more into detail, " *Cæsar's Spring* has long been converted into a most useful public cold bath ; a dressing-house is built on the brink of it ; it is ornamented with beautiful trees, and from its romantic situation forms a most pleasing scene." Further we are told that this part of Keston Common " has long been the promenade of the neighbouring company, and parties of gentry from even so far as Greenwich, have long been accustomed to retire with music and provision to spend in this delightful spot the sultry summer's day, drinking at Cæsar's Fountain," etc.* Dressing-house, pales, and trees have long vanished, but the memory lingered on in the name of the Cold Bath, by which it was spoken of by the country people hereabout within the last 30 or 40 years.

The *Church,* on the rt. of the road at the S. extremity of the Common, in a narrow elm-girt ch.-yard, is a humble country ch., interesting most from its situation and absence of pretension. It is small, consisting only of nave and chancel, with a little wooden bell-cote rising from the W. end of the nave : the strange brick excrescence at the W. end, covering the whole width of the nave, is the vestry. The ch. itself is of whole flints, but patched with brick, with high-pitched, moss-covered, tiled roofs ; late E.E. in style, but most of the windows altered by the village " carpenter and builder." A doorway and one or two lancet windows on the S. have been stopped up, and the E. window altered. The int. is quite plain, fitted with high pews, with a row of hat-pegs on the walls above ; and walls and ceilings are covered thickly with whitewash. Note, however, the late Norman chancel arch. The only *mont.* is a tablet to Geo. Kirkpatrick, of the H. E. I. service. In the ch.-yard, S.E. of the ch., obs. the flat

* Ambulator, 1792; European Mag., Dec. 1792; quoted in Hone's Table Book, 1827, col. 627.

grey granite tomb, with large red granite cross, of a late Lord Chancellor, Robert Monsey Rolfe, Baron Cranworth, d. July 26, 1868.

The park of *Holwood* skirts the E. border of Keston Common. Before Pitt made it famous, Holwood had belonged to a series of undistinguished owners. In 1673 it belonged to Capt. Pearch ; in 1709 to Nathaniel Galton ; from him it passed to the Burrels of Beckenham ; from them in succession to Calcraft, whose parties were celebrated, Ross, Barrow, who transformed the grounds and excavated the lakes, and Randall, "an eminent shipbuilder."

Pitt was born in Hayes, the next village ; and he said to his friend, Lord Bathurst— " When a boy I used to go a-bird-nesting in the wood of Holwood, and it was always my wish to call it my own."* In the autumn of 1785 he purchased it of Mr. Randall, the payments extending from Nov. 1785 to Aug. 1794, and amounting in all to £8950. He entered with ardour upon the possession, and his liking for it never abated.

" He took the greatest delight in his residence at Holwood, which he enlarged and improved (it may truly be said) with his own hands. Often have I seen him working in his woods and gardens with his labourers for whole days together, undergoing considerable bodily fatigue, and with so much eagerness and assiduity that you would suppose the cultivation of his villa to be the principal occupation of his life." †

The cultivation of his grounds was his especial delight. As he wrote, he had a " passion for cutting," and he inspired his friends with a share of his ardour. Thus Wilberforce enters in his Diary : " April 7, 1790. Walked about after breakfast with Pitt and Grenville. We sallied forth armed with bill-hooks, cutting new walks from one large tree to another, through the thickets of the Holwood copses." Within the house his tastes found equally free play. " The apartments," writes George Rose, " were strewed with Greek and Roman classics." The walls of one room he is said to have covered with Gilray's and other political caricatures levelled directly at himself. On the alterations of the house he spent

a good deal of time. When he bought it, it was a small, plain, rectangular brick building, which Mr. Burrows had improved and beautified by covering with plaster. As engraved during Pitt's occupancy, we see a sort of wing carried out at one end, with a semi-octagonal termination ; this Pitt built ; and it reminds one of the saloon he designed for his friend Richard Thornton. (*See* CLAPHAM, p. 111.) The roof of the main building is truncated, terminating in a broad platform enclosed by balusters— an alteration not unlikely to have been Pitt's. " No one," as his friend Lord Bathurst said of him, "had a more exquisite sense of the beauties of the country." He delighted in the prospects from Holwood, ranging as they do over a wide extent of the woods and plains of Kent and Surrey, and embracing almost all the amenities of the scenery of our home counties—water excepted—and this platform must have extended the range to the utmost.

But Pitt's increasing pecuniary embarrassment compelled him to sell Holwood, and Sir George Pocock became its purchaser for £15,000. It again changed hands, and at length was bought by a Mr. John Ward, who, about 1823, pulled Pitt's house down, and erected in its stead the present more pretentious structure—a large semi-classic edifice, with a portico, completed in 1827 from the designs of Mr. Decimus Burton. Mr. Ward uprooted Pitt's plantations as little remorse as he levelled his house; and now there is nothing in or immediately about the house to remind a visitor of its famous owner. The choicest relic lies a little way from it. Through one side of Holwood Park there is a public walk—a very pleasant one, and one not to be overlooked. The entrance to it is by a ladder-style, just beyond the well noticed above. Along the path are one and another quaint antique oak, each larger or wilder than the preceding, till on the rt., close by the path, you come upon one slightly decaying, but of huge girth—a notable tree, for under its shadow Pitt was accustomed to sit and watch the shifting colours of the landscape ; and here he and Wilberforce settled the measures to be adopted for the Abolition of the Slave Trade. Opposite to the tree,

* Earl Stanhope, Life of Pitt, vol. iii., p. 349.
† Diaries and Correspondence of the Right Hon. George Rose, vol. ii., p. 227.

on the l. of the path, is a stone bench, on the back of which is engraven—

"From Mr. Wilberforce's Diary, 1788. 'At length, I well remember, after a conversation with Mr. Pitt, in the open air at the root of an old tree at Holwood, just above the steep descent into the Vale of Keston, I resolved to give notice on a fit occasion in the House of Commons, of my intention to bring forward the ABOLITION OF THE SLAVE TRADE.' Erected by Earl Stanhope, 1862. By permission of Lord Cranworth."

The tree has long been known as *Pitt's Oak*; it is now becoming a fashion to call it the *Emancipation Oak*. Holwood was the seat of Lord Cranworth till his death here in 1868; it is now the residence of Robert Alexander, Esq., C.B.

Other seats at Keston are, *Forest Lodge* (Lady Caroline Legge), and *Ravensbourne* (Mrs. Bonham-Carter).

KEW, SURREY, on the Thames, between Mortlake and Richmond, and opposite Brentford, with which it is united by a stone bridge : pop. 1033. The Kew and Brentford Stat. of the L. and S.W. Rly. is on the Brentford side of the river, and alongside it is a stat. of the North London Rly. The Kew Gardens Stat. of the L. and S.W. Rly. is on the Surrey side, opposite Cumberland Gate, Kew Gardens, and is in connection with the L. and N.W., N. Lond., Grt. W., and L. C. and D. Rlys. By road Kew is 6 m. from Hyde Park Corner. Inns : *King's Arms; Rose and Crown.*

Kew is believed to be first mentioned in "a court roll of the manor of Richmond, in the reign of Henry VII.; it is there written *Kayhough;* in subsequent records its name is varied as *Kayhowe, Kayhoo, Keye, Kayo*, and *Kewe :* its situation, near the water-side, might induce one to seek for its etymology from the word *key*, or quay."* This is scarcely satisfactory. The oldest forms point to an earlier and probably a Celtic etymology. British remains have been found (1860 and following years) in the bed of the river near Kew Bridge, in proximity to portions of ancient piles, in such quantities as to indicate a British settlement, if not, as has been thought, a pile-village like the Swiss *pfahlbauten.* The remains comprised fragments of pottery and household

* Lysons, vol. 1., p. 147. In 1524 it was written *Kai-ho.*

utensils, and bronze spear-heads, swords, and daggers, of the early British and Romano-British periods.

The vill. comprises a few good houses dispersed about the borders of a Green of some 13 acres, near the centre of which is the church, and at the W. corner the principal entrance to Kew Gardens, and a number of smaller houses along the E. side of the Richmond Road, which runs S., by the side of Kew Gardens, from the S.E. corner of Kew Green. Since the opening of the Kew Gardens Rly. Stat., many houses have been built in its vicinity and along the Richmond Road; but there is still a good deal of ground occupied as market gardens.

Kew was a hamlet and chapelry of Kingston-upon-Thames until 1769, when it was constituted a distinct vicarage. The *Church* (St. Anne), a plain brick building with a Doric portico and octagonal clock-turret, was erected in 1714, but has since been enlarged and altered. The int. is chaste, and kept in excellent order ; has an arched ceiling supported on 6 columns, and at the W. end the Royal Gallery built by George III. On the walls are many tablets in memory of persons eminent in their day and now forgotten. The organ is said to have been Handel's ; was long used by George III.; was given to the ch. by George IV.; and is much praised for sweetness of tone. In the vaults the Duke of Cambridge, youngest son of George III., was buried (1850), without Garter King at Arms being present,—the Duke being the first prince of the blood-royal so interred : the coffin has since been removed to the sepulchral chamber abutting on the E. end of the ch., designed by B. Ferrey, F.S.A. In the ch.-yard lie side-by-side, on the S. of the ch., Jeremiah Meyer, R.A. (d. 1789), the eminent miniature and enamel painter of the last cent. (there is a tablet, with bust of him and verses by Hayley, in the ch.) ; Joshua Kirby, F.R.S., architect, and author of the well-known treatise on Perspective ; and Thomas Gainsborough, our great landscape and portrait painter. Gainsborough did not reside at Kew, but was brought here by his own desire, and laid alongside his friend Kirby : his grave is marked by a plain flat blue slab, inscribed with merely his name and dates of birth and death. Here also are the graves of John Zoffany, R.A. (d. 1810); William Aiton, the distinguished botanist, and long head of Kew Gardens (d. 1793); Francis Bauer, F.R.S., the celebrated microscopist and scientific draughtsman (d. 1840); General Douglas and Governor Eyre.

Charles Brandon, Duke of Suffolk, resided at Kew, with his wife Mary, sister of Henry VIII. and widow of Louis XII. of France. Suffolk House was pulled down early in the reign of Elizabeth. Charles Somerset, Earl of Worcester, had a house at *Kai-ho* in 1524. Queen Elizabeth visited Sir John Puckering, Lord Keeper of the Great Seal, at his house at Kew in 1594, and again in 1595. The Lord Keeper's steward had made a careful " Remembrance for Furniture at Kew, and for her Majestie's Entertainment," among the items in which was " What present shall be given by my Lord," and " The like for my lady," which would seem to have been a very needful provision :—

" On Thursday her Majestie dined at Kew, my Lord Keeper's house. . . . Her entertainment for that meal was great and exceedingly costly. At her first lighting she had a fine fanne, with a handle garnisht with diamonds. When she was in the middle way, between the garden gate and the house, there came running towards her one with a nosegay in his hand, delivered yt unto her with a short well-pened speech ; yt had in yt a very rich jewell, with many pendants of unfirl'd diamonds, valewed at £400 at least. After dinner, in her Privy Chamber, he gave her a fair pair of virginals. In her bed-chamber he presented her with a fine gown and juppin, which things were pleasing to her Highnes. And to grace his Lordship the more, she, of herself, tooke from him a salt, a spoone, and a forcke of faire agatte." *

Robert Dudley, Earl of Leicester, about this time had a residence at Kew, which he afterwards sold to Sir Hugh Portman, " the rich gentleman that was knighted by her Majesty at Kew."† Sir Hugh was a Dutch merchant, whence his house came to be popularly known as the *Dutch House.* Opposite to this was a larger mansion, *Kew House*, which in the middle of the 17th cent. belonged to Richard Bennet, whose daughter and heiress married Sir Henry Capel,—created, 1692, Lord Capel of Tewkesbury.

" 27 *Aug.* 1678.—I went to my worthy friend Sir Henry Capel, brother to the Earl of Essex : it is an old timber house, but his garden has the choicest

fruit of any plantation in England, as he is the most industrious and understanding in it." *

Lord Capel was afterwards appointed Lord Lieutenant of Ireland, where he d. in 1696. His widow continued to reside at Kew House, where she died in 1721, and was buried in Kew ch. The property then passed to Samuel Molyneux, Secretary to George II. when Prince of Wales, who had married Lady Elizabeth Capel, daughter of Algernon, Earl of Essex, and grand-niece of Lord Capel. Molyneux was of a scientific turn, and erected in his grounds a large zenith sector, made for him by Graham, with which he and Bradley, then Savilian professor at Oxford and afterwards Astronomer Royal, observed, Dec. 21, 1725, the displacement of the star γ *Draconis*, which led to Bradley's great discovery of aberration—"the first positively direct and unanswerable proof of the earth's motion." A sun-dial on the lawn, facing the present Kew Palace, marks the spot which the sector occupied : the inscription on the pedestal commemorating this fact was placed there by order of William IV. in 1830.

Molyneux died in 1728 ; and in 1730 Frederick, Prince of Wales, took a long lease of Kew House of the Capel family, and employed Kent to decorate the house and lay out the grounds. After his death the Princess Dowager of Wales continued to reside at Kew House, and commenced the formation of the ' Exotic Garden '— the parent of the present Botanic Garden. Sir Wm. Chambers had charge of the works, and he erected various temples and ornamental buildings, of which, in 1765, he published an account in a large folio volume, with 40 fine engravings by Rooker, etc., entitled ' Plans, Elevations, and Perspective Views of the Gardens and Buildings at Kew in Surrey,' and which— " a work to wonder at, perhaps a Kew " —was one of the exciting causes of Mason's famous ' Heroic Epistle.'

After the death of the Princess Dowager in Feb. 1772, George III. occupied Kew House, and subsequently purchased the fee-simple of the estate. He lived here, as Madame D'Arblay writes, in " a very

---

* Rowland Whyte to Sir Robert Sydney, Dec. 15, 1595 : Sydney Papers, vol. i. p. 376.
† *Ibid.*

* Evelyn, Diary. Evelyn records other visits (Oct. 30, 1683 ; March 24, 1688), chiefly noting the improvements in the gardens, the " orangerie and myrtelum most beautifull and perfectly well kept," and the like.

easy, unreserved way, running about from one end of the house to the other without precaution or care. . . . There is no form or ceremony here of any sort. . . . They live as the simplest country gentlefolks. The King has not even an equerry with him ; nor the Queen any lady to attend her when she goes her airings." Addington in 1805, when about to be created Viscount Sidmouth and Lord President of the Council, waited on George III. at Kew, and dined with the King at the homely hour of "rather before one," the dinner "consisting of mutton-chops and pudding."* The King's favourite amusement, whilst here and in health, was improving the grounds and uniting them with those of Richmond Lodge. Here, too, he pursued with zeal his farming operations, having taken for the purpose Keel's Farm in the adjoining parish of Mortlake ; ploughed up and tilled a large part of Richmond New Park, and turned the Old (or Deer) Park, and part of Kew Gardens, into pasture for the large flock of Merino sheep he imported to Kew in 1791,—the progenitors of our present stock. For a while the improvements were entrusted to Capability Brown, whose decided measures and impatience of interference rather tried the King's temper. If Mason may be trusted, when he heard of Brown's death the King went to the under-gardener, and in a tone of great satisfaction said, "Millicent, Brown is dead : now you and I can do what we please here."†

The Dutch House, mentioned above, which was only divided from Kew House by a public carriage road, had been taken on lease by Queen Caroline, when making her alterations in Richmond Old Park ; and, the lease not having then run out, the freehold was, in 1781, purchased by Queen Charlotte, wife of George III., who made it a nursery for her children. Hence the house came to be known as the *Royal Nursery*, and later, from the Prince of Wales, afterwards George IV., receiving his education in it, as the *Prince's House ;* whilst Kew House was known as the *Queen's Lodge*. During his first serious attack of insanity, George III. lived with

the Willises in the Prince's House, the Queen, with the princesses, remaining at the Lodge.* Kew House was partly pulled down in 1802, and subsequently the remainder was demolished. The older house then became the usual suburban residence of the royal family, and obtained the name by which it has since been known of *Kew Palace*. In it Queen Charlotte died, Nov. 17, 1818. After remaining long dismantled and unoccupied, it has been repaired and appropriated as apartments. Kew Palace is a picturesque old red-brick mansion, but hardly justifies its title. It stands in the enclosed ground in front, as you enter the principal gate to Kew Gardens.

Kew House was demolished preparatory to the erection of a new palace at Kew, the King having become much attached to the locality. James Wyatt prepared the designs, and works were commenced by the river-side, opposite the W. end of the eyot and the centre of the town of Brentford. The building was of stone, in form a rectangular castle, with a round tower at each angle, two smaller turrets in each front, and a tall square tower rising from the centre. A low crenellated screen, close to the towing-path, provided a river entrance and servants' apartments and offices. Throughout the walls had battlements, machicoulis, and loopholes ; the windows were but narrow ; the rooms closets. Only the shell was completed. The renewed illness of George III. delayed the works ; his successor, naturally enough, disliked both the site and the building ; and, after standing for years untouched, in 1827 Kew Palace was razed.

Sir Peter Lely had his country seat on the N. side of Kew Green, to which he frequently retired in his later years. It has been long pulled down, but it was occupied by Sir Peter's descendants till the middle of the 18th cent. Stephen Duck, the thresher poet, lived in a house at Kew provided him by his patroness Queen Caroline, and preached at Kew Chapel, where for a time he attracted vast congregations. Among the present residents on Kew Green are H.R.H. the Duchess of Cambridge, at Cambridge Cottage, on the W. side of the Green ;

---

* Madame D'Arblay, Diary, vol. iii.,p. 33 ; Pellew, Life of Lord Sidmouth, vol. ii., p. 342 and n.
† Mason to Walpole, May 19, 1783.

* Rose, Diaries, vol. i., p. 355.

Dr. Joseph Dalton Hooker, the Director-General of Kew Gardens; and till his death, 1875, Sir Arthur Helps. At Cumberland Gate is the residence of Major-General F. P. Nott.

Kew Bridge is a stone structure of 7 arches spanning the Thames and several smaller brick arches on the low Surrey shore. It was designed by James Paine, and built at the cost of Mr. Robert Tunstall; the first stone being laid June 4, 1783, and the bridge opened for public use in Sept. 1789. It was afterwards bought for £22,000 by Mr. G. Robinson, and continued private property till the end of 1872, when it was purchased, under powers of an Act of Parliament, for £57,300, and formally opened free of toll, Feb. 8, 1873. The large and gaily decorated state barge that may be noticed moored on the E. side of Kew Bridge, is the Maria Wood, formerly the City Barge, when the Lord Mayor and Corporation were wont to indulge in swan-upping and other river jaunts, now private property, but much in request for civic entertainments.

KEW GARDENS comprise the Royal Botanic Gardens and the Pleasure Grounds, and are *open every week-day from 1 o'clock till sunset* (Christmas Day alone excepted); *on Sundays from 2 till sunset*. The principal entrance to the Botanic Garden is by the ornamental wrought-iron gates (designed by Mr. Decimus Burton) at the N.W. corner of Kew Green. Another entrance is by Cumberland Gate in the Richmond Road, opposite the Kew Gardens Stat. of the L. and S.W. Rly. The Pleasure Grounds are divided from the Botanic Garden by a wire fence, but visitors can pass freely from one to the other. There are also separate entrances to the Grounds at the *Lion Gate*, Richmond Road, near the Pagoda, for Richmond; *Isleworth Gate*, at the S.W. corner of the grounds, by the Thames for Isleworth; and *Brentford Gate*, at the N.E. angle, for Brentford. The visitor who is not familiar with the Gardens will do well to purchase at the entrance lodge the official 'Route Map' (price 1d.), which not only points out the route by which the plant-houses may be most readily seen, but by a well-arranged "Index to some of the more

Interesting Plants," shows the locality of any particular plant. The official guides to the "Royal Botanic Gardens and Pleasure Grounds" (1s.), and to the Kew Museums (6d.), drawn up by Prof. Oliver, F.R.S., keeper of the Kew Herbarium, furnish full information respecting houses, plants, and contents of the museums.

The foundation of the Exotic Garden at Kew is usually ascribed to the Princess Dowager of Wales. As we have seen in the preceding section, "that great statesman and gardener," Sir Henry Capel, had formed a fine collection of rare plants when Evelyn visited Kew House in 1678. But the Princess, during her long residence at Kew, entirely changed its character. The Gardens were extended, the rarest and choicest plants were collected, houses like the famous orangery, designed by Chambers, were erected, and the whole was placed under the direction of one of the most skilful botanists and gardeners of the time, William Aiton.

"The gardens which the Princess Dowager of Wales has lately laid out at Kew, in the neighbourhood of Richmond, unite all that the English taste has been capable of producing, most magnificent and most variegated. These gardens consist chiefly in thickets of a considerable extent, laid out in such a manner that each forms a whole, from which we pass to another unknown to ourselves, and without so much as suspecting that there was anything farther. In one of these thickets is a Gothic chapel . . . . which forms a saloon as spacious as it is singular. In another, on the summit of a hill made by art, rises a temple in the form of a rotunda, in the most pure taste of Grecian architecture. . . . Amongst the curiosities to be seen at Kew-gardens, we should not forget a considerable collection of foreign plants of all sorts; a quarter is assigned to it in the neighbourhood of the palace, which unites all the conveniences necessary in a botanical garden." *

George III. and Queen Charlotte took a warm interest in the garden, continued Mr. Aiton in its management, erected many new houses, stoves, and pits, employed skilful collectors in various countries, and, with the active assistance of Sir Joseph Banks in securing the co-operation of Capt. Cook and other distinguished navigators, "enriched the Gardens of Kew with the vegetable productions of the southern hemisphere to an extent unparalleled before or since." Mr. Aiton's great

---

* M. Grosley, F.R.S., A Tour to London (in 1765), or New Observations on England, translated by T. Nugent, LL.D., 1772, vol. ii., pp. 117—120.

work the 'Hortus Kewensis,' 3 vols. 8vo, 1789, made the treasures of Kew known throughout Europe, and Darwin's Imperial Kew was seen not to be a mere poetic flourish :

" So sits enthron'd in vegetable pride
  Imperial Kew, by Thames's glittering side ;
  Obedient sails from realms unfurrow'd bring
  For her the unnam'd progeny of Spring," etc.*

From the death of George III. till the accession of Victoria, Kew Gardens were comparatively neglected. In 1838 the Government appointed a Committee to inquire into the management of Kew Gardens, and its Report, drawn up by Dr. Lindley, and presented to the House of Commons in 1840, led to the adoption of Kew Gardens as a national establishment, the appointment of Sir W. Hooker as Director, and the opening of the Gardens to the public. Since then they have been increased in extent from 11 acres to 75, and enriched with plants from every region ; palm and temperate houses of magnificent proportions have been erected; museums formed ; and under the admirable management of Sir W. J. Hooker, and since his decease of his son, Dr. J. D. Hooker, the present Director, Kew Gardens have become the richest, and perhaps the most beautiful and instructive establishment of the kind in Europe.

Referring to the Guides mentioned above for a more particular account of the Gardens and their contents, we here merely draw attention to their beauty and picturesque variety, as deserving admiration equally with their richness and scientific value. The Broad Walk, bordered on each side with clumps of rhododendrons and a line of deodars, is, when the rhododendrons are in bloom, one of the finest walks of its class we possess. The lawns are everywhere diversified with rare and beautiful trees, shrubs, and flowers. In addition to the Pinetum proper, beyond the great Palm House, there is a wonderful variety of the choicest pines, araucarias, cedars, deodars, cypresses, American snowdrop trees and maples, planes, limes, beeches, oaks, and many other hardy trees ; a splendid collection of rhododendrons and other flowering shrubs, and an almost endless variety of flowers. The Herbaceous Beds,

on the E. side of the gardens, in which hardy herbaceous plants are arranged in the Natural Orders to which they belong, have a special interest for the botanical student. The conservatories, palm-houses, stoves, and museums would require many visits to examine thoroughly ; but even the briefest examination will discover unexpected and multifarious objects of interest and beauty.

The large and solid-looking house seen on the rt., after entering by the principal gate, was brought here from the gardens of Buckingham Palace in 1836. Formerly known as the Australian House, it is now called the *Aroideous House*, because chiefly filled with plants of that order. Aroids, as the Guide points out, "chiefly abound in the swamps and humid forests of the tropics, where several species are gigantic climbers : they are represented in Britain by the common Arum (*A. maculatum*)." The larger tropical kinds flourish in this artificial atmosphere. Notice the Dumb Cane (*Dieffenbachia seguina*) of the West Indies, which paralyses the mouth if merely chewed. Besides the aroids and associated species there are fine young palms and other plants here.

For the palms it will, however, be well to go at once to the great *Palm House*, at the end (on the rt.) of the broad walk. The Palm House was completed in 1848, from the designs of Mr. Decimus Burton, and was, with the exception of the great conservatory at Chatsworth, the largest building of the kind that had then been constructed. It is 362 ft. long ; and comprises the centre, 138 ft. long, 100 wide, and 66 high, and two wings each 50 ft. wide and 30 ft. high. It contains about 45,000 sq. ft. of glass.* In its contents the Kew Palm House is quite unrivalled. The collection of palms is magnificent, and there are bamboos, sugar-canes, dragon trees, banyans, India-rubber, figs, numerous flowering climbers, and, indeed, nearly all that is rare and rich in tropical plants for which such a house is a suitable habitat ; and out of a tropical forest probably so superb a display of tropical foliage can nowhere else be seen. The

---

* Darwin, Botanic Garden, Canto IV.

* The Chatsworth Conservatory is 300 ft. long, 145 ft. wide, and 67 feet high to the centre of the coved roof ; it is said to contain about 70,000 sq. ft. of glass.

The Palm House, Kew Gardens

Market Place, Kingston-upon-Thames (see p.399)

staircases and galleries afford the visitor means of looking over and among the trees as well as at them from the floor.

Immediately N. of the Palm House is the *Water Lily House*, in which is a beautiful collection of exotic water-lilies (including the sacred lotus of Egypt), the papyrus, and other choice aquatic plants. The queen of water-lilies, the famous Victoria Regia, has, however, been removed from this house, and is now in the *New Range* (No. 6), N.W. of the mound on which is the Temple of Æolus. This (No. 6) is a large house, and holds a great diversity of plants. The great central compartment is occupied by the Victoria Regia, nepenthes, the mango, and a number of curious pitcher plants. The rt. wing contains a fine collection of orchids and dendrobiums; the left wing is devoted to economic plants, such as the bread-fruit, castor-oil, allspice, nutmeg, gamboge, indigo, orange; whilst the long annexe, beyond the central tank, displays heaths, begonias, pelargoniums, and the like in most tempting varieties. A group of houses a short distance N.W. of the New Range will be found very interesting. The nearest, the *Succulent House*, 200 ft. long and 30 wide, contains an extraordinary collection of cactuses, aloes, euphorbias, opuntias, stapelias, etc.,—some of wondrous beauty, some eminently grotesque. Next is an Ornamental Greenhouse, occupied by a miscellaneous collection of plants, like the Chinese magnolias, gleichenias, mimosas, etc. Beyond this is the *Temperate Fern House*, and on the rt. the larger *Tropical Fern House*, 140 ft. long and 28 wide, filled with the choicest and rarest examples of this beautiful group of plants, and with many remarkable varieties of pitcher plants. There are various other houses, but these will suffice to indicate the range and richness of the living species.

The Museums abundantly illustrate the economic products of the vegetable world. *Museum No.* 1, the handsome Italian building at the head of the Ornamental Water, and directly facing the great Palm House, is devoted to specimens and products of Dicotyledonous plants, or Exogens, the largest and most varied primary class in the vegetable kingdom. The museum has three floors, and the numbering is from the top floor. The arrangement of the objects is according to the orders to which they belong, and is calculated to assist the student, but is hardly so attractive to the non-scientific visitor. Nearly all the articles have descriptive labels attached, but the very useful Official Guide to the Museums (price 6d.) will greatly facilitate the examination. *Museum No.* 2, or the *Old Museum*, at the N.E. corner of the Gardens, is appropriated to specimens and products of Monocotyledonous plants, or Endogens, of which palms and grasses may be cited as typical examples. Here, too, are specimens and products of the Acotyledons, flowerless plants, or Cryptogamia. *Museum No.* 3 is the old *Orangery* on the l. of the broad walk, built by Sir Wm. Chambers in 1761. It is now filled with specimens of timber, including very complete collections of Australian, New Zealand, and Canadian woods, and examples of remarkable trees and miscellaneous objects too large to be exhibited in the cabinets of the other museums. We may add that in addition to the Museums there is a *Herbarium*, "the largest in existence, and constantly increasing by additions from every quarter of the globe." It is not exhibited to the public, but the botanical student can obtain permission to examine it upon application to the Director.

The *Pleasure Grounds*, or *Arboretum*, which adjoin the Botanic Gardens on the S., are open during the same hours as the Gardens, and may be entered from them. The Pleasure Grounds have an area of about 270 acres, and are intersected with broad and picturesque walks, lined with rhododendrons, cypresses, junipers, box-trees, trees and shrubs of the order Rosaceæ, etc., while on the lawns are almost endless varieties of oaks, elms, beeches, maples, hickories, some noble cedars, walnuts, as well as many less familiar kinds; an extensive pinetum, and a collection of rare Antartic plants. In following the walks, the *Syon Vista*, with its borders of deodars, limes, and standard Robinias, and terminated by Syon House and the tower of Isleworth church, should not be overlooked; nor should the still more picturesque walk by the Thames, with the view of the river from the mound at the S. end. Return from it by the *Lake*, 5 acres in extent, and rich in aquatic plants and wooded islands.

The *New Temperate House*, erected from the designs of Mr. D. Burton in 1861-3, stands on a high terrace, and is more solid and ornamental in character than the Palm House. It consists of a centre 212 ft. long, 137 wide, and 66 ft. high, and 2 octagons each 50 ft. in diameter. The original design included 2 wings, each 112 ft. long, to be carried out from the octagons, but these have for the present been abandoned. The house was designed for the reception of trees and shrubs from temperate climates, and especially those of Australia and New Zealand, and already it exhibits a luxuriant mass of foliage. It is especially rich in Australian trees of the genera Eucalyptus, Acacia, Banksia, the characteristic trees of Tasmania and New Zealand, Norfolk Island pines, tree ferns, the Amboyna pitch pine, Himalaya rhododendrons, the pomegranate, the date palm, and trees and shrubs from China and Japan.

A short distance S.E. of the Temperate House is the *Pagoda*, from its height the most conspicuous object in the grounds. It was built by Sir Wm. Chambers in 1761, and is a solid octagonal structure of hard grey bricks, 49 ft. in diameter at the base and 163 ft. high.* It is in 10 storeys, each storey diminishing a foot in diameter and height, and each having a balcony and projecting roof. Originally a Chinese dragon crawled over every angle of each roof, but these have all taken flight. The other Chinese buildings with which Chambers adorned the vicinity of the Pagoda have been demolished, but here, as in the Gardens, some of the classic temples have been allowed to remain.

Obs., before leaving the grounds, the *Flagstaff*, erected in 1861 on a low mound near the Unicorn Gate : it will be seen on the l. on entering the Grounds from the Gardens. It is the trunk of a Douglas Pine (*Abies Douglasii*), a native of British Columbia, and is 159 ft. high—the finest spar, it is believed, in Europe.

Adjoining the Pleasure Grounds on the S. is *Richmond Old Park*, or the *Deer Park*, 357 acres, united to Kew Grounds and Gardens by George III., but again sepa-

* " We begin to perceive the tower of Kew from Montpellier Row ; in a fortnight you will see it in Yorkshire." Horace Walpole to the Earl of Strafford, July 5, 1761.

rated from them. The building near the centre. seen from many parts of the Pleasure Grounds, is the *Kew Observatory* of the British Association, lent to that body by the Queen for magnetic, photo-heliographic, spectroscopic, and meteorological observations.

KIDBROOKE, Kent (*see* Blackheath).

KILBURN, Middx. (*see* Hampstead).

KINGSBURY, Middx. (pop. 622),

on the rt. bank of the Brent, 6 m. N.W. from London, is a thoroughly country vill., and, though lying but 1 m. W. of the 5 m. stone on the Edgware Road, is the richest spot in the county for water-birds and wild-fowl. It may be reached from the Welsh Harp Stat. of the Midland Rly., 1½ m. by Kingsbury Lake, or by a pleasant walk of 2½ m., along bye-lanes and fields, N. from the Willesden Stat. of the N.W., and the North London and Hampstead Junction Rlys., by way of Willesden and Neasdon. *Obs.*, on ascending the hill just before reaching Kingsbury, the picture made by the old-fashioned farm-like cottages on the rt., nestling under the big elms, the avenue in front, and the little church glimmering through the trees—in a homely way, very like one of Creswick's early village scenes.

Kingsbury probably owes its name to the camp mentioned below, and to its belonging to the king—*Cynges-burh* or *byrig*. Lysons conjectured that "some Saxon monarch had a residence here," but the name seems to be the only ground for the conjecture. Edward the Confessor presented it to Westminster Abbey. In the deed of gift it is written *Kyngesbyrig*. In Domesday it appears as *Chingesberie*. At this time it must have been thickly wooded, as it afforded " pannage for 1200 hogs."

The *Church* (St. Andrew) stands away from the houses, on elevated ground, and within what appears to be part of an ancient encampment, which Stukeley very decidedly sets down as a Roman work —" Cæsar's second station after he had crossed the Thames." The ch. is old, weather-beaten, and lonely, and the white owl breeds under the roof-roots. It is very plain, both inside and out, but should be examined by the antiquary. It is said to be built of Roman bricks, and Bloxam found in it vestiges of Saxon architecture, but rough-cast effectually conceals both now. It is small, consisting of nave and chancel of equal height, and a wooden tower and short spire at the W.; the windows have early Perp. tracery; a handsome timber porch of the Dec. period was taken down in 1830. In the chancel are *monts.* to John Bul, d. 1621, Gentleman of the Poultry to Queen Elizabeth and King James; and Thos. Scudamore, d. 1626, servant to Elizabeth and James for 47 years. *Brass,* John Shephard, d. 1520, and wives Anne, with 7 sons and 3 daughters, and Mawde, with 5 sons and 3 daughters. In the ch.-yard, E. of the ch., is the vault of William, 3rd Earl of Mansfield, d. 1840.

The large sheet of water seen E. of the ch. is the *Kingsbury Reservoir,* or, as it is now frequently called, Kingsbury Lake, " a famous resort for water fowl," and a favourite haunt of London anglers; a path from the church style leads to the embankment at the foot of the reservoir, where notice, in the centre, as a fine specimen of massive brick-work and masonry, the great semicircular penstock or weir, by which the surplus water is let off into the Brent. From this embankment the reservoir extends E. for above a mile, and in one part nearly $\frac{1}{4}$ m. wide, crossing the Edgware Road in two branches, at Brent Bridge by the *Old Welsh Harp,* and at Silk Bridge, $\frac{3}{4}$ m. farther. The best view of the whole extent of the lake is obtained from the penstock. The reservoir was formed in 1838, on the Brent, with a N. arm on the Silk stream, in order to supply the locks of the Regent's Canal, and was soon discovered by the waders. A ' List of Water Birds occurring at Kingsbury Reservoir ' was published in the *Zoologist* for 1843; but the most complete account of its winged visitants will be found in Mr. J. V. Harting's admirable little vol., ' The Birds of Middlesex.' From this we learn that no fewer than 46 species of waders and 21 of wild fowl have been observed here at different times. The heron is not uncommon; several varieties of snipe occur; wild duck and teal are numerous in winter; bitterns, curlews, plovers (both

golden and ringed), spoonbills, whimbrels, ruffs are more or less frequent, and even such rare birds as the turnstone, avocet, and bar-tailed godwit are occasionally seen, and, we are sorry to add, almost invariably shot; whilst the smaller birds, as bramblings, larks, greenfinches, goldfinches, lesser redpoles and twites occur in such numbers that Mr. Harting (a resident at Kingsbury) has " frequently seen half-a-dozen London birdcatchers busily employed there with their nets, all day long, in the month of October."

The reservoir is well stored with jack, perch, roach, tench, and carp. The fishing is rented by Mr. W. P. Warner, of the *Old Welsh Harp,* and strictly preserved. Annual subscription, one guinea each rod; day tickets for jack 2*s.* 6*d.*, for roach and general fishing 1*s.* The *Well Springs,* $\frac{1}{2}$ m. N. of the ch., are also " a favourite haunt of the heron" (*Harting*), and here the golden oriole and the tawny owl have been seen; but the establishment of the Hendon races, and the opening of the Welsh Harp Rly. Stat. have done much to destroy the quiet of Kingsbury Lake and to scare away the larger and rarer birds.

A field-path from the N. side of the ch.-yard leads by *Fryern Farm* to *Kingsbury Green,* a larger collection of houses than Kingsbury vill., but having little in it to arrest the visitor. A lane leads from it to *The Hyde* in the Edgware Road, $\frac{1}{2}$ m. W. About half-way up this lane, at the corner of a farmer's drove lane on rt., get over the gate to what looks like an opened barrow, for the splendid view from the summit.

KINGSDOWN, KENT, 21 m. from London by rd., $4\frac{1}{2}$ m. S. by E. from the Farningham Road Stat. of L. C. and D. Rly., through Horton Kirby and Fawkham Green; pop. 421.

Kingsdown is a curiously out-of-the-world place. There is no vill., and the ch. stands in a little clearing in the midst of a nut-wood, with only a small school-house, and one half ruinous and unoccupied dwelling near it. The ch. (St. Edmund the King) has nave (Dec.), chancel (Perp.), with a square tower and spire. It is small, rough-cast, has heavy buttresses on the N., and tall red-tiled roof. The int. is plain, ceiled, filled with high pews, and whitewashed; font old, round,

but covered with plaster and painted. *Obs.* in N. end window of nave a seated figure of Christ, crowned, of untouched painted glass, late 14th cent., and in the next window a standing figure of the Virgin ; also some heraldic fragments.*
In the ch.-yard, S.E. of the ch., is a very large yew, formed of several trunks grown together. On the W. is another less flourishing, but of a single trunk, 22 ft. in girth. The lonely and neglected but picturesque ch., sombre yews, and surrounding wood, form, as the evening is drawing on, a scene to inspire a poet or poetic painter. It is, however, threatened with restoration, when all poetic visions will be swept away.

At *Maplescombe*, 1¼ m. N.W., are some remains of an old church ; but the rd. is not easy to find from Kingsdown ch. (ask for *Mapscombe*), and the ruins are of little account. The country is wooded, hilly, and pleasant, with some good distant views.

KING'S LANGLEY, Herts

(Dom. *Langelei*), 4½ m. N. by W. of Watford, 3½ m. S. of Hemel Hempstead, 19½ m. from London by road, 21 m. by L. and N.W. Rly. (the stat. is ¾ m. S. of the vill.) : pop. 1495. Inn, *Rose and Crown.*

Langelei belonged at the Dom. Survey to Earl Moreton, to whom it had been given by the Conqueror ; but was forfeited by his son, Earl William, for his share in the rising of the Norman barons against Henry I. The manor was retained by the Crown, and Henry III. built here a royal seat, the place henceforth taking the name of *King's Langley* (or Langley Regis), in distinction from the adjoining manor, which, as held by the Abbot of St. Albans, was designated Abbot's Langley (*see* AB-BOT'S LANGLEY). Edmund, 5th son of Edward III., was born at the manor-house, King's Langley, in 1344, whence he was known as Edmund de Langley. His father created him Earl of Cambridge in 1362, and in 1386 Richard II. made him Duke of York. He married Isabel, daughter of Pedro, King of Castile. She was buried, 1394, in the ch. of the Preaching Friars, at King's Langley, and Edmund de Langley was by his desire laid beside her on his death in Aug. 1403.

* They are described by Mr. Winston in the Archæol. Journal, vol. ii., p. 188.

The mont. raised to their memory is now in Langley church.

Richard II., with his Queen and Court, including the Duke of York, many bishops, lords, and ladies, held a royal Christmas at his manor of Langley in 1392. After his death at Pomfret Castle, and the exposure of his body at St. Paul's, March 1400, his corpse was brought to King's Langley, and interred in the ch. of the Preaching Friars. It remained there, however, only till the reign of Henry V., who had it removed and laid beside Richard's first wife, Anne, in Westminster Abbey. At this time and onwards the royal manor seems to have been an appanage of the queens dowager ; it is said that the earliest autograph letter of an English queen is one from Joanna of Navarre, widow of Henry IV., to the Regent, John Duke of Bedford, dated " at our manor of King's Langley." Henry VII. gave Langley manor in 1505 to his consort Katherine for her life. In 1534 Henry VIII. gave it to Anne Boleyn for the like (as it proved very short) term. James I. gave his manor, park, and chase of King's Langley, in 1610, to his eldest son Henry, Prince of Wales, on whose death, in 1612, the lordship was transferred by letters patent to Prince Charles. In 1626 Charles I. granted to Sir Charles Morrison a lease for 99 years of the park, with reversion at the expiration of that term to Sir Baptist Hicks ; and in 1628 alienated the manor to Edward Pitchfield and others, by whom in 1630 it was conveyed to Thomas Houlker. The Parliament, when in arms against Charles I., seems to have regarded this alienation as invalid, as King's Langley is one of the manors contained in the grant to Robert Devereux, Earl of Essex, the Parliamentary general, in 1645, but which his early death rendered void. Houlker's son sold the manor to Henry Smith, Esq., and after one or two more transfers, it passed to the Capels, Earls of Essex, to whom it now belongs.

The royal manor-house stood a little to the W. of the ch. Some shapeless fragments of the outer walls mark the site. About the end of the last century enough of the walls and foundations remained to show that the house was large and nearly square. A mill and farm occupy the grounds.

Roger Helle founded at King's Langley

a priory of Dominican (Black, or Preaching) Friars, which King Edward largely augmented, 1274 and 1280, with gifts of lands and manorial rights. In 1312 the corpse of Piers Gaveston, Earl of Cornwall, the favourite of Edward II., after his execution on Blacklow Hill, was brought to the ch. of the Dominicans for interment ; where, as already mentioned, was deposited in 1400 the corpse of the deposed and murdered monarch, Richard II. The priory received further grants of lands from Edward IV., 1466, and augmentations from private benefactors ; but it appears never to have been wealthy, and at the suppression the revenue was valued at only £127 14s. Philip and Mary, by letters patent of June 25, 1557, restored the priory, and conveyed to it the land and buildings at King's Langley ; but the triumph was brief, as in the first year of Elizabeth, 1559, the establishment was again suppressed, and house and appurtenances resumed by the Crown. Elizabeth gave the living and ch. lands to the Bp. of Ely ; the living is now in the gift of the Abp. of Canterbury. The site of "the late house or priory," 7 acres in extent, was granted by James I., in 1606, to Edward Newport and John Compton, and passed from hand to hand till it fell to William Houlker, who demolished the priory buildings, and so effectually, that now only the memory of them is left.

King's Langley is watered by the little river Gade ; the Grand Junction Canal borders it on the E., and beyond that the L. and N.W. Rly. runs on an embankment at the foot of the hill. The vill. lines the highroad, and consists of small country shops, one or two little inns, private residences, with garden walls and overhanging trees, mills by the river, the ch. on high ground at the London end : altogether a good specimen of a quiet country roadside village. The occupations are in the main agricultural ; but the paper-mills of Messrs. Dickinson, and a brewery, employ many of the men, and straw-plaiting the women and girls. The surrounding country is varied in surface, in parts richly wooded, and there are plenty of green fields, footpaths, and shady lanes.

The *Church* (All Saints) is Perp. ; of flint and stone, the S. side rough-cast ; and consists of nave with aisles, chancel,

square embattled tower at the W., with an angle turret, and a porch of flint and stone. It has been partially restored, a new E. window inserted, and the tracery of the other windows renewed. The *int.* is neat and well kept, but chiefly remarkable for the monts. Of these the most important is that of Edmund of Langley, Duke of York, 5th son of Edward III., and his wife Isabel, which stands on the N. of the chancel, having been removed there from the priory ch. at the Dissolution. It is an altar tomb of white marble about 5 ft. high, with on the top a slab of Purbeck marble. It has no effigy or inscription, but on the front are 4, at the W. end 3 shields, within frames of 8 cusps. When Chauncy wrote, the shields bore the arms of England and France with those of Pedro of Castile, the father of Isabel ; but these have been defaced, and recent restoration has not added to the archæological value of what remained. Another altar tomb of Caen stone has male and female effigies, much worn and injured. There are also *monts.* of the Cheyneys, Dixons, Sir William Glascocke (d. 1688), Master of Bequests and Judge of the Admiralty under Charles II., and others ; and a *brass* of John Carter, of Giffres, d. 1588, and his 2 wives—one with 4 sons and 5 daughters, the other with 5 sons and 4 daughters.

The noticeable red-brick building by the rly.-stat. is the Booksellers' Provident Retreat : it is noticed under ABBOT'S LANGLEY, to which par. it belongs ; as are also the hamlets of *Hunton Bridge* and *Langley Bury*, *Nash Mill*, and *Lavertock Green*.

KINGSTON-UPON-THAMES,

SURREY (Dom. *Chingestun*). a municipal borough and market town on the rt. bank of the Thames, opposite Hampton Wick, with which it is united by a stone bridge, 10 m. from London by road, and 12 m. by the L. and S.W. Rly. ; (Stat. on main line at Surbiton ; on the Twickenham loop line at New Kingston, N. of the town : this stat. serves also for the N. London, and L. C. and D. Rlys.) The pop. of the *borough* was 15.263 in 1871 ; that of the *parish* (exclusive of Ham), 25,159. Inns : *Griffin* ; *Sun* ; *Railway Hotel*, Surbiton Stat.

The name is plainly A.-S., and means

the King's, or royal town. It has been sought to derive it from the stone on which the early English kings sat to be crowned; but the oldest form is *Cyningestun, Cingestune*,[*] king's town, and a charter of King Edred, 946, expressly terms Kingston " the royal town, where kings are hallowed."[†]

Kingston, then, was a place of mark in Saxon times, and it is not improbable there was a Roman settlement here, as in the bed of the Thames and a short distance inland, Roman weapons, pottery, and coins have been at various times exhumed.[‡] Some have supposed from the finding of Roman weapons in the bed of the river that here was the deep ford by which Cæsar crossed the Thames to engage the army of Cassivelaunus ; but that, undoubtedly, was some miles higher. (*See* COWEY STAKES.)

Mention is made in a charter of King Egbert of Wessex, 838, of a great council held at Kingston in that year, at which Golnoth, Abp. of Canterbury, presided, and Egbert, the first king of all England, his son Ethelwulf, and all the bishops and nobles of the land were present.[§] But Egbert's death is placed in the A.-S. Chronicle under 836, and must have occurred in that or the following year ; the council does not appear to be referred to by any contemporary or early authority, and that of the charter is perhaps doubtful.

The authentic chronicles of Kingston commence with the coronation here of Athelstan, son of Edward, in 924 : " And Athelstan was chosen king by the Mercians, and hallowed at Kingston." Subsequently six more of these early kings were crowned at Kingston—Edmund, 940; Edred, 946; Edgar, 959; Edward the Martyr, 975; Ethelred II., 978 ; Edmund

II., 1016. Some add to the list Edward the Elder, 900 ; and Edwig, 955. The last is distinctly stated by Florence of Worcester, who, though not contemporary, is an early authority ; and upon its correctness of course depends whether Kingston was the theatre of the unseemly occurrence related by William of Malmesbury and other monkish historians, when, after the coronation feast, Dunstan followed the king to his wife Elfgiva's chamber, and compelled him to return to the hall. The coronation stone will be noticed presently.

If the Dom. Survey gave a full account, Kingston at the Conquest would appear but a poor specimen of a royal town. It was held by King William as it had been by King Edward, and is now, as then, valued at £30. There was arable land for 32 ploughs, and land for 2 ploughs was held in demesne; 40 acres of meadow, and wood for 6 swine. There were 86 villans, and 14 bordarii with 25 ploughs. Also a church, and 2 ministers; 5 mills of 20s.; 2 fisheries of 10s., and a third fishery, very productive, but free from rent. One or two of the entries are curious. Humphrey the Chamberlain has " one of the villans in charge for spinning (or working-up — *codunandi*) the Queen's wool." Elsewhere it is stated that Walter FitzOther (Warden of the King's Forests) " has a man of the Soke of Kingston, to whom he has given in charge the King's brood mares " (or hunting mares—*equas silvaticas*).

King John visited Kingston on several occasions. In 1200 he gave the townsmen their first charter ; in June 1204 he stayed there 5 days ; in 1205 he paid the town three visits, and he was there in 1207, 1208, 1210, and 1215. Henry III. was there in 1264, having marched from London to seize the castle at Kingston belonging to Gilbert Clare, Earl of Gloucester, one of the insurgent barons—the only mention made of such an edifice. Falconbridge, with an army of 17,000 men, was at Kingston in 1472, in pursuit of Edward IV., but finding the bridge broken down, withdrew to Southwark. Katherine of Aragon stayed a night here on her way from Portsmouth, after her first landing in England, 1501.

Sir Thomas Wyatt, in his insurrection against Queen Mary, finding the gates of

---

[*] A.-S. Chron., A.D. 924; Mon. Hist. Brit., pp. 382, 398.

[†] Kemble, Cod. Dip. Ævi Sax., No. 411, vol. ii., 268 ; so Florence of Worcester, A.D. 924, speaks of Athelstan being crowned at Kingston, "id est, *in regia villa*." (Mon. Hist. Brit. 573 A.)

[‡] Camden ; Aubrey ; Horsley ; Manning and Bray ; Brayley ; Lysons ; Archæologia, vol. xxx. ; Biden. Hist. and Ant. of Kingston-upon-Thames, p. 4.

[§] Brit. Mus. Cotton MSS. Claudius, D. ii. f. 33, etc., quoted by Lysons, vol. i., p. 158 ; Kemble, Cod. Dip. Ævi Sax., No. 240, vol. i., p. 318 ; Wilkins, Concilia i., p. 178 ; and comp. A.-S. Chron. and note b. in Mon. Hist. Brit., p. 344.

London Bridge shut against him, marched after some delay to Kingston—where was then the first bridge across the Thames above London Bridge. He arrived at nightfall of Shrove Tuesday, Feb. 6, 1554, and found the bridge broken down, and 200 soldiers posted on the opposite side to oppose his crossing. These he dispersed with two pieces of ordnance, and seizing some west-country barges and boats, and hastily repairing the bridge with planks and ladders, he carried all his soldiers safely over by 10 at night, and marched on, with a brief halt at Brentford, to Knightsbridge. His defeat, surrender, and execution are familiar to all.

During the contest between Charles I. and the Parliament, Kingston was alternately occupied by the opposed troops. The king was more than once there; and for a time (Aug. 10—27, 1647) it was Fairfax's head-quarters. The last struggle on behalf of Charles I. was made at Kingston by Henry Rich, Earl of Holland, at the head of 600 horse, July 7, 1648. The second Duke of Buckingham of the Villiers family (Dryden's Zimri) and his younger brother, Lord Francis Villiers, were present. The royalists were routed, Lord Holland taken, and Lord Francis slain, while, with his back to a tree, and refusing quarter, he fought against unequal numbers. "On this elm, which was cut down in 1680, was cut an ill-shaped V for Villiers, in memory of him."[*]

"My Lord Francis at the head of his troop having his horse slain under him, got to an oak tree in the highway about two miles from Kingston, where he stood with his back against it, defending himself, scorning to ask quarter, and they barbarously refusing to give it; till with nine wounds in his beautiful face and body, he was slain. The oak tree is his monument, and has the two first letters of his name, F. V., cut in it to this day."[†]

"The Lord Francis, presuming perhaps that his beauty would have charmed the soldiers, as it had done Mrs. Kirke, for whom he had made a splendid entertainment the night before he left the town, and made her a present of plate to the value of a thousand pounds, stayed behind his company, where unseasonably daring the troopers, and refusing to take quarter, he was killed, and after his death there was found upon him some of the hair of Mrs. Kirke sewed in a piece of ribbon that hung next his skin."[‡]

[*] Aubrey, Surrey, vol. i., p. 47.
[†] Brian Fairfax, Memoirs of the Duke of Buckingham, p. 17.
[‡] Ludlow, Memoirs, Vevay ed. 1698, vol. i., p. 256.

Kingston returned members to Parliament in the reigns of Edward II. (1310-13) and Edward III. (1353 and 1374), but not, as would seem, since. The first charter was granted to Kingston, as mentioned above, by King John, 1200, and an amended charter in 1209. Henry VI., in a new charter, 1441, constituted the townsmen a body corporate, and further extended their privileges. New charters confirming, amending, or extending those already given, continued to be granted by successive sovereigns down to James II.; but all these were superseded by the Municipal Corporation Act of 1835, which placed boroughs generally under a uniform system. Kingston is now governed by a mayor, 8 aldermen, and 24 councillors. The market is on Thursday, and is important for corn and cattle. Fairs are still held on the last three days of Whitsun week, on Aug. 2nd and 3rd, and on Nov. 13th and two following days. This last is one of the great horse and cattle fairs of the home counties, and it is customary to have a show of fat (slaughtered) hogs. The pleasure fair, which used to be held in the town, is now held in the cattle fields. The Lent assizes have hitherto been held at Kingston; quarter sessions and a county court are also held there.

The town extends for nearly a mile along the Thames, and for a like distance along the Portsmouth road; there is a spacious market-place, and a considerable mass of houses in cross and bye streets. About the market-place are a few old houses, but their number diminishes yearly, and what are left have undergone frequent renovation. The extension of the town by the L. and S.W. railway station is now known as New Kingston, and another new town appears to be growing up about the station on the loop line. The Hog's Mill, or as it is now called New Mill, river flows through the town, without adding to its beauty or salubrity.

Of the municipal buildings the chief is the *Town Hall*, in the centre of the market-place, an Italian building erected in 1840, from the designs of Mr. C. Henman. It is of white brick and stone, quadrangular, with ornamented turrets at the angles, and in front, above the recessed balcony, a leaden statue of Queen

Anne, removed from the old town-hall, on the front of which it was erected in 1706. In the principal or court-room is a portrait of the same queen by Sir Godfrey Kneller. Beyond the market-place is the *Court House*, erected in 1811, in which the assizes are held, and by it the Judges' Lodgings.

In the open space in front of the Court House is placed the ancient stone on which, according to tradition, the Saxon kings sat when crowned. Of old it stood by the church, afterwards in the market-place by the old town-hall; when that was pulled down, the stone was removed to the yard behind the Court House, and in 1850 it was set up where it now stands. The stone itself, like most of these early sacred stones, a rude, shapeless block, is fixed on a granite base, of so-called Saxon design, on the 7 sides of which are inscribed the names and dates of the kings crowned at Kingston, the two of doubtful authority being omitted. An iron railing of Early English character, with pillars at the angles, surrounds the monument, which as a whole is creditable to the designer, Mr. C. E. Davis. A silver penny of the monarch was inserted in the stone above each king's name.

The parish or old *Church* (All Saints), near the market-place, is one of the largest churches in the county. It is of flint, clunch (or hard chalk), and stone, cruciform, with a massive central tower, in which is a peal of 10 bells. The body of the ch. is of the Perp. period, but the lower part of the tower appears older. In 1445 the tower and spire were greatly damaged by lightning, and, as William of Worcester relates, " one in the church died through fear of a spirit which he saw there." The injury appears not to have been completely repaired till 1505. The spire was again destroyed by lightning in a great storm, Nov. 27, 1703, and the tower so much shattered that it had to be taken down to the springing of the arches of the large windows. The upper part of the tower was rebuilt, as it remains, of brick; but the spire was not restored, and the tower is now terminated, somewhat incongruously, with a large pineapple at each angle, and a tall flagstaff.

The interior is in good preservation, having been thoroughly restored by the

Messrs. Brandon in 1862. The broad nave, its massive columns, lofty arches and aisles, and the two chancels with the great E. window, impart to it an air of size and dignity beyond that of the ordinary parish ch. It is, however, somewhat dark, owing to the heavy painted glass in the windows. Some of the *monts.* are interesting. Under an arch is an altar tomb, with a recumbent effigy in alabaster of Anthony Benn (d. 1618), Recorder of London, and previously Recorder of Kingston, who is represented in his recorder's gown and great ruff. A seated marble statue of Louisa Theodosia, Countess of Liverpool, d. 1821, is a good example of Chantrey's monumental work. A full-length portrait, in high relief, of Henry Davidson, Esq., d. 1827, is from the chisel of Chantrey's pupil, Ternough. Among the *brasses*, notice, on a large slab in the chancel, those of Robert Skern, d. 1437, and his wife Joan, daughter of Alice Perrers, and, as is supposed, of Edward III. The figures are about 3 ft. high, and very well engraved. A small brass has kneeling effigies of John Hertcombe, d. 1488, and his wife Katherine, d. 1477 : he in the habit of a merchant, with scrip and girdle; she in full gown, furred gloves, and square pendent head-dress. Other brasses are to Marke Snellinge, 9 times bailiff of Kingston, d. 1633, and his wife Anne Snellinge, d. 1623; also of the 10 children (" seven sons and daughters three, Job's number right") of " Edmund Staunton, Dr. of D., late minister of Kingston-upon-Thames, now (1653) Presidt. of Corpus Christi Colledge, Oxon," but ejected at the restoration of Charles II., and "silenced for nonconformity" by the Act of 1662. Staunton was not the only, nor the first, unconformable minister of Kingston. " Pious Mr. Udal," for his book, ' A Demonstration of Discipline,' was in 1590 ejected from his living and condemned to death. His sentence was respited from time to time, and he died in the Marshalsea prison in 1592.[*]

Dr. Primrose's parishioners, retaining " the primeval simplicity of manners," among their other simple customs, it may be remembered, " religiously cracked nuts

[*] Lysons, vol. i., p. 181.

on Michaelmas Eve."* In like manner the parishioners of Kingston religiously cracked nuts at Michaelmas, and in the church itself. On the Sunday before Michaelmas Day, *Crack-nut Sunday* as it was called in Kingston, the congregation, old and young alike, attended ch. with their pockets stuffed with nuts, which they cracked during the service, the noise at times becoming so loud that the reading or sermon had to be suspended. The practice was only, and with much difficulty, suppressed about the end of the last century.†

Kingston folk seem always to have loved their diversions. In some valuable extracts Lysons made from the churchwardens and chamberlains' accounts, which reach from the reign of Henry VII., we find repeated entries of charges on account of the "Kynggam," or King-game, no doubt the church-play of the Kings of Cologne, performed in the ch.-yard. It was conducted by the churchwardens, and on the last entry of its performance, 1527, the parish made a clear profit, " all costs deducted," of £9 10s. 6d., a large sum for that time. The costs must have been considerable. At one King-game (23 Henry VII.) there is " Paid for whet and malt and vele and motton and pygges and ger and coks for the Kyngam . . £0 33s. 0d.;" whilst the taberer has 6s. 8d., " the leutare, 2s." At other times, other seasonable plays were performed, but the properties were less extensive and costly. Thus we have one Easter, " For thred for the resurrection, 1d.;" "for 3 yards of dornek [a sort of linen] for a pleyer's cote and the makynge, 15d.; " whilst "a skin of parchment and gunpowder [probably for the thunder] for the play on Easter-day" cost only " £0 0s. 8d.," and the " brede and ale for them that made the stage and other things belonging to the play," no more than 1s. 2d. In 1505 the profit from the Easter play was £1 2s. 1½d. Other plays are named, but the diversions most often referred to are those of the May Day minstrels, morris-dancers, and Robin Hood and Little John, evidently great favourites. " Little John's cote "

cost 8s., whilst " Kendall for Robyn hode's cote " cost only 1s. 3d., " 3 yards of white for the frere's," 3s., and " 4 yards of Kendall for Mayde Marian's huke " [a hooded mantle], 3s. 4d. " Two payre of glovys for Robyn hode and Mayde Marian " cost 3d.; and there was paid " To mayde Marian for her labour for two years," 2s., which was not excessive if she had allowed credit for the first year's labour. A ducking-stool cost the parish £1 3s. 4d. in 1572, but ducking was hardly a pastime, at least to the person ducked.

No reference appears to be made in these old accounts to what was later the most remarkable diversion of the place—the Kingston *Ball-play*. On Shrove Tuesday, at about 11 in the morning, the shops were closed, and foot-balls were paraded round the town with flags and a band of music. At noon the church-bells rang out for the opening of the game, and the mayor started the first ball from the steps of the town-hall. Then till 5 in the evening, when the ch. bells gave the signal for the game to close, the ball was kicked, carried, or hugged, about the streets and to the river, a new ball being supplied when one was cut or lost. The goals for the main game were respectively the Great Bridge and Clattern Bridge (over the Hog's Mill river at the S. end of the town), but other play went on in the byeways. In the olden times it is said to have been a good-humoured though rude game; but of late years it has been a mere " carnival of the roughs." The lamps and windows in and around the market-place had to be boarded over, and the streets were abandoned for the day by all quietly disposed persons. In 1866, the mayor for the first time refused to start the ball; and since then the game, if not wholly suppressed, has been brought more under control. Local tradition accounts for the game by relating that in one of their incursions the Danes were stopped at Kingston by the resistance of the townsmen, till help came from London, when in the battle that ensued the Danes were defeated, and their general being slain, his head was cut off, carried into the town in triumph, and then kicked about the streets. This happened on a Shrove Tuesday, and the ball-play was instituted in comme-

* Vicar of Wakefield, chap. iv. Brand. Pop. Ant. i., 211, Notes to Allhallow Even (3), has curiously changed this to " All Hallow Eve."

† Brayley, vol. iii., p. 41.

moration of the victory. Unluckily for the Kingston tradition, a nearly similar one is repeated in many other towns. At Derby, for example, where football was played in the streets every Shrove Tuesday till within the last few years, it was said to commemorate a victory by the townsmen over a Roman army that was about to assault the town. Football, indeed, so far from being a local game, was played throughout the country on Shrove Tuesday. In London, as we know from Fitzstephen, as early as the 12th cent. it was the custom, on Shrove Tuesday, for the young men of the city to turn out after dinner to play at the famous game of football.

Till 1842 the old ch. was the only ch. in Kingston; now there are six others. *St. Peter's*, Norbiton, erected in 1842 from the designs of Messrs. Scott and Moffat, is a brick ch. of semi-Norman character, with a tower of 3 storeys on the N.W. *St. Mark's*, Surbiton, erected in 1855, is of stone, Perp. in style, and has nave with aisles, chancel, tower, and spire. *St. Andrew's*, consecrated in 1872, a chapel of ease to St. Mark's, is a cruciform Italian building with a campanile. *Christ Church*, Surbiton Hill, is a rather peculiar fabric of parti-coloured bricks, erected in 1863, and since enlarged. *St. John the Evangelist*, Spring Grove, on the outer edge of the town, is a good cruciform ch. of Kentish rag, with Bath-stone dressings, erected in 1873 from the designs of Mr. A. J. Phelps. *St. Matthew's*, 1874, another Gothic ch., in the Ewell Road. The Italian Roman Catholic ch. (St. Raphael) was elaborately restored and decorated in 1874. The Congregational Church, Surbiton, and the Wesleyan Chapel, Kingston Hill, are of more than average architectural pretensions.

The *Free Grammar School*, London Street, was established by Queen Elizabeth on the site of the chapel of St. Mary Magdalene, founded in 1305 by Edward Lovekyn, a native of Kingston, and his brother Richard. In 1355, John Lovekyn, fishmonger, and four times Mayor of London, a kinsman of the founder, rebuilt the chapel and augmented the endowment, so as to provide for a second chaplain; and the eminent citizen and mayor, William Walworth, who it is said had been an apprentice to John Lovekyn,

added funds for the maintenance of a third chaplain. The chapel escheated to the Crown in 1540, and in 1561 Queen Elizabeth, by charter, founded a free grammar school on the site of the chapel, endowed it with lands, tenements, and rents, yielding an income of £19 5s. 11d., and made the bailiffs of Kingston the governors, with the condition that they should pay 20 marks yearly for the support of a master and under master.[*] Lovekyn's chapel still serves as the schoolhouse, but other buildings have been added. The school was in its most flourishing condition towards the middle of the 18th cent., when Dr. Wooddeson was the master, and George Alexander Stevens, the author of the 'Lecture upon Heads,' Lovibond, once known as a poet, and Gibbon the historian were among the scholars.

"In my ninth year (January 1746), in a lucid interval of comparative health, my father adopted the convenient and customary mode of English education; and I was sent to Kingston upon Thames, to a school of about 70 boys, which was kept by Dr. Wooddeson and his assistants. Every time I have since passed over Putney Common, I have always noticed the spot where my mother, as we drove along in the coach, admonished me that I was now going into the world, and must learn to think and act for myself. . . . . My timid reserve was astonished by the crowd and tumult of the school; the want of strength and activity disqualified me for the sports of the play-field; nor have I forgotten how often in the year forty-six I was reviled and buffeted for the sins of my Tory ancestors. By the common methods of discipline, at the expense of many tears and some blood, I purchased the knowledge of the Latin syntax; and not long since I was possessed of the dirty volumes of Phædrus and Cornelius Nepos, which I painfully construed and darkly understood. . . . . My studies were too frequently interrupted by sickness; and after a real or nominal residence at Kingston school of nearly two years, I was finally recalled (December 1747) by my mother's death." [†]

Cleave's Almshouses, Norbiton, were founded under the will of William Cleave, alderman of London, who died 1667, for 6 poor men and as many women "of honest reputation," being single persons and over 60 years of age. The houses are the original range, low and small, with a central common hall, over the doorway of which are the founder's arms and the date of erection, 1668. At Cambridge Road, Norbiton, is the *Cambridge Asylum*

---

[*] Brayley, Surrey, vol. iii., p. 44.
[†] Gibbon, Memoirs of My Life and Writings, prefixed to Miscellaneous Works.

for Soldiers' Widows, founded in 1851, and named in memory of the late Duke of Cambridge. The first stone of the building, a spacious and comfortable looking red-brick edifice, was laid May 1, 1852, by the Prince Consort. A new wing and chapel were added in 1856 : archt., Mr. B. Ferrey, F.S.A. About 50 widows (over 50 years of age at admission) are lodged, provided with light and fuel, and a small weekly stipend. It is a good institution, but suffers from insufficient funds. On Kingston Hill has been erected (1874-5) a *Convalescent Hospital for Children* under 14 years of age, as a branch of the Metropolitan Convalescent Institution, Walton-on-Thames.

The *Bridge* over the Thames, which connects Kingston with Hampton Wick, occupies the site of a wooden bridge, the first erected over the river after London Bridge. The present bridge, of stone, a very handsome structure, was designed by Mr. E. Lapidge. It has five principal arches over the stream, and two smaller ones on each side ; the centre arch being 60 ft. in span, the others 56 ft. and 52 ft. respectively. The entire length is 382 ft.; the width 27 ft. The first stone was laid by the Earl of Liverpool, Nov. 7, 1825, and it was opened by the Duchess of Clarence, afterwards Queen Adelaide, July 17, 1828. The cost was about £27,000. It was opened free of toll by the Lord Mayor and Sheriffs of London, March 12, 1870.

Norbiton and *Surbiton* (North and South Barton), though formerly outlying hamlets, are now merely the northern and southern portions of the town. They have their own churches and chapels, and contain some of the institutions already described, but have no features requiring particular notice. *Canbury* (anc. Canonbury), a manor adjoining Norbury, was so named from having belonged to the canons of Merton priory ; here are still remains of the monastic barn.

The hamlet of *Combe*, 2 m. E. of Kingston, towards Richmond Park and Combe Wood, was, with New Malden, formed into an eccl. dist. in 1867, a neat church (Christ Church), E.E. in style, having been erected the previous year. (*See* COMBE WOOD; MALDEN.) Another collection of dwellings which has grown up by the Robin Hood Gate of Richmond Park, has also been created an eccl. dist. of Kingston par., under 'the title of *Kingston Vale*, but is better known as *Robin Hood*. The ch. (St. John the Baptist), E.E. in style, was consecrated in 1861. The hamlets of HAM and HOOK are described under those headings.

KINGSWOOD, SURREY, 3 m. S.

from the Banstead Stat. of the Epsom Downs br. of the L., B., and S. C. Rly., and about 18 m. from London. Kingswood is a detached liberty of Ewell par., from which it is about 4 m. distant, but being joined with Tadworth, a portion of Banstead par., was in 1838 created an eccl. dist., the pop. of which was 934 in 1871.

Until the Dissolution, Kingswood Manor belonged to Merton Priory ; it then accrued to the Crown, and with the capital manor of Ewell was annexed to the honour of Hampton Court. Elizabeth granted it in 1536 to Wm. Lord Howard of Effingham. In 1651 it was alienated to Sir John Heydon ; from him passed successively to the families of Bludworth, Harris, Hughes, Jolliffe, and Alcock, and now belongs to Sir J. W. C. Hartopp, Bart. Kingswood is hardly a village. The largest collection of houses is at Tadworth. The dwellings are scattered between Banstead Down and Walton Heath, in a delightful though secluded country. The pursuits are mainly agricultural. All around are handsome residences, the chief being *Kingswood Warren* (Sir J. W. C. Hartopp, Bart.), a spacious castellated mansion, rebuilt about 1840 for the late Thos. Alcock, Esq., M.P., from the designs of Mr. T. R. Knowles. The park is well wooded and rich in views. The *Church*, a short distance W. of the Warren, is a handsome cruciform E.E. building, erected at the cost of Mr. Alcock. *Tadworth*, the Banstead half of Kingswood, lies half a mile to the W. The principal seat is *Tadworth Court*, the residence of Lionel Heathcote, Esq., lord of Tadworth manor.

KNOCKHOLT, KENT, 5 m. N.W

from Sevenoaks, 2½ m. S.W. from the Halstead Stat. of the Sevenoaks and Tunbridge br. of the S.E. Rly. : pop. 676.

Knockholt is a scattered agric. village,

and stands on nearly the highest point in the county of the ridge of chalk hills which extends across Kent from Rochester to Westerham, and thence through Surrey by Dorking and Guildford to Farnham. Its lofty site is marked by the *Knockholt Beeches*, a long clump of old but not very large trees standing a little S. by E. of the ch. (a path opposite the ch.-yd. leads directly to them). The beeches are a 'andmark for miles around. They are visible from Leith Hill; are very noticeable from the Crystal Palace; and are plainly seen (without a telescope) as far north as Highgate and Harrow. The views *from* them are correspondingly extensive and varied. From the neighbouring lanes and field paths you also obtain fine views, though the high hedges in fashion hereabouts rather interfere with the distant prospects. The *Church* has been modernized; what is old is hidden under stucco, what is new is of brick. It has a tower of flint and brick. The interior contains no monts. of interest, but has been very neatly restored and fitted with low seats. One of the windows contains some fragments of old painted glass. S. of the ch. is a fine yew (19 ft. 6 in. in girth) with a stout seat round the trunk. Notice the large ash tree at the E. end of the ch.-yd. The principal seat is *Court Lodge* (H. Turner, Esq.) At *Knockholt Pound*, ¾ m. E. of the ch., is a decent country inn, the *Three Horse Shoes*. From Knockholt there are delightful walks by hill-lanes to Brasted or Westerham, or by Chevening Park towards Sevenoaks.

KNOLE, KENT, the noble seat of the Hon. Mortimer Sackville West, stands in a fine park immediately contiguous to the town of Sevenoaks. The park gates are opposite Sevenoaks church.

In the reign of John, Knole belonged to Baldwin de Bethun, Earl of Albemarle. It afterwards passed to the Mareschalls, Earls of Pembroke, and to the Grandisons and the Says, and in the reign of Henry VI. to James Fiennes, or Fynes, created, 1446, Lord Say and Sele, and so barbarously murdered by Jack Cade. His son, Sir William Fiennes, 2nd Lord Say, sold Knole, "with all its appurtenances," for 400 marks, to Thomas Bouchier, Abp. of Canterbury, in 1456. Bouchier enclosed

the park, rebuilt the house, made it his residence, and died in it in 1486. His successor, Cardinal Morton, also d. here, 1500. It continued to be a seat of the Abps. of Canterbury, one of their 16 palaces, till Henry VIII., who had often visited Abp. Warham here and taken a liking to the place, forced Cranmer to an involuntary surrender of it:

"I was by when Otford [another of the archbishop's houses] and Knol were given him [Henry VIII.]. My Lord [Cranmer], minded to have retained Knol unto himself, said, That it was too small a house for His Majesty. 'Marry,' said the King, 'I had rather have it than this house,' meaning Otford; 'for it standeth on a better soil. This house standeth low, and is rheumatic, like unto Croydon, where I could never be without sickness. And as for Knol it standeth on a sound, perfect and wholesome ground: and if I should make abode here, and as I do surely intend to do now and then, I will live at Knol and the rest of my house shall live at Otford.' And so by this means both those houses were delivered up into the King's hands."[*]

The deed of indenture by which Cranmer surrendered Knole to the King is dated Nov. 30, 1537. It remained in the Crown till July 1550, when Edward VI. granted it to John Dudley, Earl of Warwick (created Duke of Northumberland in 1551), who however in 1553 exchanged the lordship and manor with the King for other estates, but reserved to himself the house and appurtenances. These by his attainder the same year reverted to the Crown; and Queen Mary soon after granted the house and manor for her life to Cardinal Pole, whom she had nominated Abp. of Canterbury—the last archbishop who possessed Knole. The cardinal-archbishop died a few hours after Queen Mary, and Knole was at once resumed by the Crown—though the grant to Pole was for his life and a year after, as he should by his will direct. Queen Elizabeth granted Knole in 1561 to Sir Robert Dudley, afterwards Earl of Dudley, but 5 years after he resigned it to the Queen, who granted the reversion of the house and manor (subject to two leases granted by the Duke of Northumberland and the Earl of Leicester) to Thomas Sackville, afterwards Lord Buckhurst and Earl of Dorset. The Earl did not come into possession of Knole till about 1605, when he rebuilt and greatly extended the house, and made

---

[*] Strype, Life of Cranmer, 8vo ed., p. 625, from the MS. of Morrice, Cranmer's secretary.

it his chief residence. The 3rd Earl was compelled by his extravagant expenditure to alienate several of the family estates, and among others the manor of Knole, which he sold, 1612, to Alderman Smith, reserving however a lease of it to himself and heirs, and continuing it as his chief country seat. It was held on this tenure by the Sackvilles till Richard, 5th Earl of Dorset, redeemed the lordship and estate in 1661. The estate and manor continued in the direct male line—the title of Earl having been exchanged for that of Duke in 1720—till the decease of the 4th Duke of Dorset unmarried, when it devolved on his eldest sister, Mary, who married, 1st, the Earl of Plymouth, and, 2nd, Earl Amherst, and died in 1864. By her will and settlements the house and lordship have passed in tail to the Hon. Mortimer Sackville-West, younger son of her sister Elizabeth, Baroness Buckhurst and Countess Delawarr.

The house is of great extent, covering, it is said, an area of 3¼ acres, but externally impressive rather from its dimensions and air of antique dignity than from its architectural merits. The main portion of the structure consists of castellated buildings with embattled gatehouses and square towers ranged about a broad quadrangle, and smaller buildings and offices about inner courts and in the rear.

" Knoll most famous in Kent still appears,
    Were mansions survey'd for a thousand long
        years ;
    In whose dome mighty monarchs might dwell,
    Where five hundred rooms are, as Boswell can
        tell." [*]

The principal front is very long but flat, being unbroken except by the towers of the central gatehouse and the dormers in the wings ; in appearance a college rather than a ducal dwelling. If it were not for the grand open park in which it stands, it would be pronounced gloomy. A tall central gatehouse has square embattled flanking towers. The wings have each five curved and stepped dormer gables. The gatehouse is probably Bourchier's work, 1456-86 ; the rest of the front has been ascribed to Abp. Morton, 1486-1500, but it looks later, and perhaps was rebuilt or altered and the dormers

added by the 1st Earl of Dorset early in the 17th cent. The second gateway, on the S. side of the first court, is no doubt Bourchier's, as are probably the Inner Court, the Hall, Chapel, and probably, as Mr. Loftie suggests, the lower storey of buildings looking out upon the pleasance. Some portions may be assigned to his successors—the Brown Gallery, for example, which is attributed with reason to Abp. Warham ; but most of these earlier portions have been more or less altered. A large part of the building is that erected by the 1st Earl of Dorset, in the reign of James I., but parts are of the time of William III. and later. The way in which it has grown to its present form and character is very observable in going over the different portions of the building, but there is one point where it is strikingly shown :

" The Wood Court is one of the most interesting features of Knole. From it you may see specimens of all the styles of [Domestic] architecture which have prevailed in England for 400 years. Standing with our faces towards the house—that is facing W.—we have on the extreme right the Gothic buildings of the Archbishops. The square towers are very fine. At right angles stand the stables, and the upper storey of this part is of the Tudor period. It still bears the name of the King's Stables. . . . . The portion of the house immediately facing us is composite in character. The lower part is early, the upper part bears more distinct traces of Elizabethan and later work. Farther towards the S., the Stuart period comes in distinctly ; and then we have a window which was probably inserted after 1700. A fire which did some damage here in 1623, will account for other alterations. Another fire about 30 years ago, has left its mark in some modern windows to the right. . . . . The S. end of the Wood Court is occupied by the Laundry, a Stuart building, and its lawn. The S. E. has a small apartment which still retains the name of the *Jail*, and may possibly have been used as a place of punishment for the archbishop's servants. It is of their time." [*]

This mingling of styles and manners, the old with the older, what is merely quaint and old-fashioned with the venerable remains of an age that is fading into poetry, is as remarkable within the house as outside. The old rooms of different periods remain almost untouched ; strange, stately, and uncomfortable ; filled with faded and dreamy old furniture, and endless portraits of the days of Holbein and Mytens, of Jane Seymour and the Earl of

---

[*] Durfey, New Operas, etc., 1721, p. 170, Verses on the Glory of Knoll : Boswell was " groom of the chambers."

[*] Loftie, Knole House, Archæologia Cantiana, vol. ix. ; and comp. Brady, Guide to Knole, pp. 81—90.

Surrey, of Elizabeth and her ruffs, and James I. and his portentous breeches; of Vandyck and Lely, the Clarendons and Grammonts and pretty Stewarts; of Kneller and Dorset, with Dryden and Locke on one side and Sedley and Durfey on the other, and so on down to Sir Joshua Reynolds and Dr. Johnson, Goldsmith and Peg Woffington, and other equally familiar names and faces of the days when George the Third was king.

"Knole—that was a medley of various feelings! . . . . . It wants the cohorts of retainers and the bustling jollity of the old nobility to disperse the gloom. I worship all its faded splendour, and enjoy its preservation; and could wander over it for hours with satisfaction." *

The entrance to the rooms open to the public is by the central gatehouse. This leads to the Green Court, or First Quadrangle, at the opposite side of which is the Second Gateway (*obs.* the fine oriel, and Bourchier's cognizance, the Eagle and Bourchier Knot). Passing through the archway into the Second or Stone Court, we see in front an Ionic portico or colonnade which opens to the hall, with which the tour of the public rooms commences.

The *Hall* is of the Bourchier period, but the ceiling of Lord Buckhurst's adding: a fine room, 74 ft. 10 in. long, 27 ft. wide, and 26 ft. 8 in. high, with a screen and minstrel's gallery at one end, a dais at the other. It is singularly well preserved, and enables a fair notion to be formed of its appearance in the days of the first of the Sackvilles who lived at Knole, when, as we learn from the Household Book, 70 or 80 persons sat daily at dinner in the hall, and my lord had a "constant household of 119 persons, independently of visitors." On screens and walls and windows are bearings of the Sackvilles. One of the Jacobean long-tables stands here, its top marked for the game of shuffleboard. On the hearth are a pair of andirons, or fire-dogs, not originally belonging to Knole, however: they were brought here from Hever Castle, the ancient seat of the Boleyns. One has a crown on the standard, with the royal initials, H. R.; the other Anne Boleyn's badge, the crowned falcon on a stock, and the initials H. A. Among the *pictures*, notice Silenus and

Bacchanals, *Rubens;* Boar Hunt, *De Vos;* George III. and Queen Charlotte, *Ramsay;* Lionel Cranfield, 1st Earl of Middlesex, with Treasurer's stick in left hand; John Lord Somers, *Kneller;* Lord Buckhurst and Lady Mary Sackville, *Kneller;* and a large and curious Procession to Dover Castle, *Wotton.* On the dais is a good life-sized antique marble statue, called Demosthenes, and an inferior recumbent statue of the nymph Egeria.

The *Principal Staircase*—according to Bridgman * there are 80 staircases at Knole—of the time of James I., small, but, as Sir Henry Wotton directs, "of no niggard latitude," leads from the hall to the old state apartments. *Obs.*, on ascending it, the curious monochrome decoration of the walls, the shields of arms in the windows, the leopards sejant on the rail standards, and the quaint carvings beneath. From the staircase you enter the *Brown Gallery*, 88 ft. long, with floor and sides of oak, but low and dark. In the windows are the arms of England in a garter, the Tudor rose, and the Prince of Wales's plume. There is much curious carved walnut furniture, the chair of King James I., inlaid tables, silver sconces of James I. and his queen, and quaint seats and stools with noticeable wrought silk and velvet coverings. Then there are, as Walpole wrote more than a century ago, "sundry portraits of the times; but they seem to have been bespoke by the yard, and drawn all by the same painter."† In the main he was right; the oval portraits may be passed as valueless; but, besides those he goes on to mention, there are several worth looking at. Such are Oliver Cromwell, ascribed to *Walker*, and probably authentic; Thomas Sackville, 1st Earl of Dorset, a so-called "Katherine of Aragon, *Holbein,*" really, what is much better, a charming portrait of excellent Margaret Roper, but whether by the great master is uncertain; Queen Jane Seymour, half-length, *Holbein,* a replica of that in the Belvedere Gallery, Vienna; Queen Elizabeth, in elaborate costume, of little value; William Herbert, 3rd Earl of Pembroke, in furred mantle, with the garter, rt. hand on the treasurer's staff, good; "Milton, when young,"— *not*

---

* H. Walpole to the Countess of Ossery, Sept. 1, 1780: Letters, vii. 434; and comp. his earlier Letter to Bentley, Aug. 5, 1752, vol. ii., p. 296.

* Hist. and Top. Sketch of Knole in Kent, 1817.
† Letter to Bentley, Aug. 5, 1752.

Milton, but probably the Earl of Burlington (Scharf) ; A Masked Ball given by Wolsey to Henry VIII. and Anne Boleyn.

Lady Betty Germaine's Chamber contains a curious old oak bedstead and furniture, heraldic glass, and a piece of tapestry wrought at Mortlake from a picture by Vandyck, representing the painter and Sir Francis Crane, the master of the works. The paintings are of no account. The *Dressing Room* contains portraits of Anne Countess of Dorset, Pembroke, and Montgomery, and her first husband, Richard, 3rd Earl of Dorset, *Jansen ;* Thomas, 1st Earl of Dorset ; Sir Walter Raleigh, in armour ; Villiers, Duke of Buckingham.

The *Spangled Bedroom* contains the furniture presented by James I. to Lionel Cranfield, Earl of Middlesex, and brought here from Copped Hall. *Obs.* the Indian cabinet ; ebony cabinet ; Venetian mirror ; tapestry with Mercury and Argus, and other classical subjects ; and portrait of the Duke of Monmouth. The *Spangled Dressing Room* has several pictures. *Obs.* particularly, James Compton, 5th Earl of Northampton, ascribed to *Vandyck,* but probably by *Dobson ;* some miniatures, and a good Venetian mirror.

Billiard Room.—Sir Kenelm Digby, *Vandyck,* a noble portrait ; Sir Thomas More ; Philip of Spain and his Queen. *Leicester Gallery.*—James I. ; his son Prince Henry ; and Nicolo Molino, the Venetian Ambassador,—all three by *Mytens,* and all in their different ways very characteristic. Henry Howard, Earl of Surrey, ascribed to Holbein, is a replica of the picture formerly in Sir R. Walpole's collection, which Horace Walpole identified as that painted by *Guillim Stretes* for King Edward in 1551 ; * Princess Sophia of Hanover, the ancestress of our royal house, *Honthorst ;* Lionel Cranfield, Earl of Middlesex, and Lady Middlesex—" the citizen who came to be Lord Treasurer, and was very near coming to be hanged ; his countess, a bouncing kind of Lady-Mayoress, who looks pure awkward amongst so much good company." † *Obs.* the elaborate and richly illuminated pedigree of the Sackville, Clifford, and Curzon

families, prepared 1623 by Sir Wm. Segar, and Richard and Henry St. George, Garter, Norroy, and Richmond Heralds, for Edward, 4th Earl of Dorset ; and, before leaving, enjoy the fine views from the windows.

The *Venetian Bedroom,* so called from having been slept in by Nicolo Molino, the Venetian Ambassador, contains the superb furniture, quaintly shaped and carved, and covered with green cut velvet, with which it was originally fitted. The costly state bed was prepared for James II. The toilet-table and mirror are of silver. The portrait of the Empress Catherine II. of Russia, in red military uniform, was given by her to Lord Wentworth. The adjoining *Dressing Room* contains more noteworthy 17th century furniture, and several portraits.

The *Organ Room,* so called from the ancient organ, one of the earliest made in England, and so placed that by opening a window it could assist the choir during service in the chapel below. *Obs.* here, and in the anteroom, the fine early 16th cent. German tapestry, with allegorical and historical subjects.

The *Chapel* is of Bourchier's time, but has been much altered. Under it is a vaulted crypt. The screen is original. The carving in wood of the Crucifixion is said to have been given by Mary Queen of Scots to Robert, 2nd Earl of Dorset, shortly before her execution. In the chapel gallery and chapel room is more tapestry, some of it good.

The *Ball Room* has finely carved panelling on the walls, an elaborate frieze, ornamented ceiling, and rich old marble chimneypiece ; the carved furniture, ebony cabinet carved with the story of Jonah, andirons, and sconces are worth noticing ; and there is an interesting series of family portraits. *Obs.* Robert, 2nd Earl Dorset, and Margaret, 2nd Countess, by *Deheers ;* Edward, 4th Earl, the hero of the murderous duel with Lord Bruce, fought without seconds, under the walls of Antwerp, 1613, and a devoted adherent of Charles I., a fine portrait, in armour and red dress, *Vandyck ;* Charles, 6th Earl,—" Dorset, the grace of courts, the Muses' pride,"—whole-length, in robes and collar of the Garter, white stick in rt. hand, *Kneller ;* John Frederick, 4th Duke of Dorset, *Reynolds,* interesting, though

* Anecdotes of Painting, vol. i., p. 206.
† Walpole to Bentley.

not one of Sir Joshua's finest works; Lord George Sackville, *Gainsborough*, half-length, seated, in court-dress, bright and well painted.

The *Crimson Drawing Room* contains the best and most interesting pictures, apart from the portraits, at Knole. A Sibyl, *Domenichino*, a replica of the Marquis of Hertford's picture. Judith with the head of Holofernes, *Garofalo*, powerfully painted and unpleasant. Cupids at Play, *Parmigiano*, a charming picture. Mary Queen of Scots, *Zucchero*. Henry VIII., *Holbein* (or from his studio), full-faced, ¾-length, on a blue ground. A Morning Party, *Wouvermans*, a fresh, charming work, the inevitable grey horse notwithstanding. Frances, 5th Countess of Dorset, *Vandyck*, a full-length in Vandyck's best style of courtly elegance, and very well painted. Card Players, *Ostade*. By *Teniers* there are two good pictures— A Village Fair, or Kermis, full of life and spirit, and daintily painted ; and A Guard Room with, in the background (and altogether subordinate to the gambling and drinking soldiers, arms and weapons in front) the Angel delivering St. Peter from prison—a curiously Flemish way of regarding a scriptural miracle, worked out with great care and thoroughness. Landscape—Travellers by the Wayside, *N. Berghem*, a bright crisp piece of workmanship, though the landscape is a little too palpably made up. Half a dozen semi-historical and 'fancy' subjects, by *Sir Joshua Reynolds*, help to glorify the room. One is the famous Ugolino and his Children, though grim, not Dantesque, but noteworthy for the free and masterly handling of the brush, every touch doing its appointed task. Samuel, another famous work, though this is only one of several repetitions, as little consonant with Hebrew inspiration as the other with Italian, but interesting as one of the most popular of Sir Joshua's pictures. Robinetta, one of Reynolds's arch little damsels feeding her caged bird, whilst her dog peeps over her shoulder, exquisite in feeling and colour, and painted with the lightest touch. The Fortune Teller, another of the master's best known and most admired works, in fancy the brightest, in colour the best in the room. The portraits of a Chinese Boy, and Madame Schindlerin the singer, will not detain the visitor.

The *Cartoon Gallery*—90 ft. long, 18 ft. wide, and 15 ft. high—is so named from containing early copies in oil, said to be by D. Mytens, of 6 of the celebrated Cartoons by Raphael. The furniture in this room is choice of its kind ; the silver andirons, sconces, chandeliers, and mirror frames are remarkable ; there is a very curious collection of 17th century treasury and travelling chests ; and a piece of tapestry, greatly admired by the lovers of needlework. The pictures to be noted are Lord Albemarle, by *Dobs₃* and George IV., full-length, in regimentals, by *Lawrence*.

The *King's Bedroom*, is so called from having been fitted up for the reception of James I., and only used by him. It contains the original furniture, which is said to have cost £20,000,—the bed alone, a gorgeous but most cumbrous piece, with fittings of gold and silver tissue, having cost £8,000. The tables, sconces, mirror frames, baskets, and vases are of chased silver. The rich silver toilet service which stands on the dressing-table was not a part of the original royal furniture, but bought at the Countess of Northampton's sale in 1743. The cabinets, one of ebony, the other ivory carved, are choice of their kind. In the ivory cabinet are two chamberlain's keys of office.

The *Dining Room* is devoted to portraits of wits and poets. Both the first and sixth earls were poets themselves, and the friends of poets. The poetic brotherhood of Charles II.'s time, from Dryden to Durfey, were often invited to share the earl's social hours at Knole. The portraits of Chaucer, Shakspeare, Sir Philip Sidney, and Sir Walter Raleigh, may be left as of at least questionable authenticity. Ben Jonson, the well-known portrait by *Honthurst*, must not, however, be so passed over ; and the Beaumont and Fletcher are perhaps genuine, as is certainly that of Otway, by *Lely*. Thomas Flatman, at once painter and poet, is by his own hand. Cowley, by *Du Bois*. The *Knellers* are numerous, and some excellent. At their head is the Earl himself. Dryden ranks next. It is of Dryden at Knole, and, as we may suppose, in this room, the story is told, that at one of the after dinner wit combats of the Earl and his friends, it was proposed to try who should write offhand the best impromptu, the poet being judge. Whilst the others were painfully cogitating, the Earl scrawled a few words on his paper, and tossed it to Dryden. "Gentlemen," said the poet, when the other papers were handed in, "you will agree with me that it is hardly necessary to read these, and that the Earl must have the crown, when I read to you his effusion—' I promise to pay Mr. John Dryden on demand the sum of £500. Dorset.'" For glorious John's sake it may be feared the story is too good to be ⁚. The other Knellers include Locke, Newton, Hobbes (doubtful), Sir Charles Sedley, and Betterton the actor —a picture copied by Pope. Congreve, Garth, and Wycherley are copies. A Conversation Piece, *Vandergucht*, is curious as indicating pretty clearly the footing on which some of these guests were received at Knole. The painter has represented himself sketching the likeness of Tom Durfey, as he is talking with Mr. Buck the family chaplain, Lowen the steward, and a Sevenoaks tradesman, "Mother Moss, and Jack Randall." * Durfey was certainly on easy terms with the upper servants, as is shown by his mention of Jourdain the butler, and Boswell, "the groom of the chambers," in his verses on Knole. Vandyck and Sir Francis Crane, *Vandyck*, the picture from which the tapestry portrait was wrought at Mortlake. Addison; Waller; both by *Jervis*. Handel, by *Denner*, hard, but a strong likeness. Gay, *not* by Boll (who died before Gay was born), but by *Aikman*, exhibited as his, and so described by Walpole.† By *Reynolds*, are several of rare interest—His own portrait, holding a paper in rt. hand, clearly and carefully painted, and very characteristic; Johnson, one of the near-sighted, or ' Blinking Sam ' heads, vigorous but a little coarse ; Goldsmith, also a profile, book in rt.

* Brady, Knole, p. 159.
† Anecdotes, vol. iv., p. 40.

hand, engraved ; Edmund Burke, same size, paper in rt. hand, a characteristic head ; Garrick, hands clasped ; Sacchini the composer ; Mrs. Abingdon, whole-length, in a white dress, standing against a pedestal, amid autumn trees, mask of the Comic Muse in rt. hand, arch in expression, brilliant in colour. Sir Walter Scott, *Phillips*, R.A.

Knole Park is of great extent (nearly 1000 acres) and quite exceptional beauty. It stands high, is varied in surface, deep hollows alternating with broad sunny slopes, and running, towards Fawk Common, into rough copse and wild gorse and fern ; well stocked with deer, and richly timbered. "The park is sweet," wrote Walpole, "with much old beech, and an immense sycamore before the great gate that makes me more in love than ever with sycamores." The beeches are even finer than the sycamores. Some on the N. and N.E. of the house are wonderful trees, of vast size and the perfection of beech form, with tall silvery boles, splendid foliage, and wide branches—trees in themselves. The oaks are almost equally fine, and one, now a venerable ruin, its hollow trunk 30 ft. in girth, was known as the Old Oak more than two centuries ago. Public roads and walks traverse the park, and pass by dells and glades of rare picturesqueness, and offer many a charming distant prospect. A broad beech avenue leads to a height at the S. extremity of the park, whence is obtained one of the finest views in the county, looking over Tunbridge Castle, Hever Castle, Penshurst, and Eridge, and the entire Weald of Kent, to Ashdown Forest, and bounded by the Sussex Downs and the hills of Hampshire and Surrey.

[Knole is for the present closed to the public : but in the hope that it may soon be again as accessible as it was till the autumn of 1874, we have described the contents of what were known as the Public Rooms.]

LALEHAM, MIDDX. (Dom. *Leleham*), on the Thames, about midway (2 m.) between Staines and Chertsey, and 20 m. from London : pop. 567. Inn, the *Three Horse Shoes.*

The manor belonged to Westminster Abbey in 1254. The sub-manor of Billets was demised to John Kaye in 1585 for 54 years. Later, Laleham with Billets was annexed to the Honour of Hampton Court, and in 1606 was granted in fee to trustees for Sir Henry Spiller, whose daughter carried it to Sir Thomas Reynell. It was purchased in 1746 by Sir James Lowther, from whom it descended to the Earl of Lonsdale.* It is now the property of the Earl of Lucan.

Laleham is a quiet, commonplace, river-side village, with a few good old-fashioned houses about it, and the church in its midst. The ordinary pursuits are agricultural; but angling attracts many visitors, who make the Horse Shoes their head-quarters. There is good bottom-fishing for chub and barbel along the shallows up-stream, and fly-fishing for trout from Penton Hook to the lock when the water is in suitable condition. The country is flat, and the broad meadows can hardly be deemed picturesque. But the scenery grows in favour with an intelligent resident. Arnold—who lived here for 9 years, from 1819, just before his marriage, till his removal to Rugby in 1828, and for whose sake Laleham will always have a special interest—came to regard the country as "very beautiful. I have always a resource at hand," he wrote, "in the bank of the river up to Staines; which, though it be perfectly flat, has yet a great charm from its entire loneliness, there being not a house anywhere near it; and the river here has none of that stir of boats and barges upon it, which makes it in many places as public as the highroad."† Arnold whilst here took six or eight young men as private pupils in preparation for the universities; and here the sterling manliness of his character was formed, and the preparation made for his future career.

"It was a period on which he used himself to look back, even from the wider usefulness of his later years, almost with a fond regret, as to the happiest time of his life. . . . Without undertaking any directly parochial charge, he was in the habit of rendering constant assistance to Mr. Hearn, the curate of the parish, and in visiting the villagers. . . . Bound as he was to Laleham by all these ties, he long loved to look upon it as his final home. . . . Years after he had left it he still retained his early affection for it, and till he had purchased his house in Westmoreland, he entertained a lingering hope that he might return to it in his old age, when he should have retired from Rugby. Often he would revisit it, and delighted in renewing his acquaintance with all the families of the poor whom he had known during his residence ; in showing to his children his former haunts; in looking once again on his favourite views of the great plain of Middlesex—the lonely walks along the quiet banks of the Thames—the retired garden, with its 'Campus Martius,' and its 'wilderness of trees,' which lay behind his house, and which had been the scenes of so many sportive games and serious conversations—the churchyard of Laleham, then doubly dear to him, as containing the graves of his infant child whom he buried there in 1832, and of his mother, his aunt, and his sister." *

Arnold's is a rather large, solid-looking old red-brick house, with a large garden, on the edge of the village: any villager will point it out.

The *Church* (All Saints) is small, old, and patched. It has a nave and N. aisle, Perp., but mended with modern brick, chancel with aisle, and a short, thick 17th-cent. brick tower at the W. end, upheld by clumsy buttresses. The chief feature of the int. is the E.E. arcade of two bays, with cylindrical shafts, cushion capitals and billet mouldings, and early pointed arches. The only mont. to be noted is that of George Perrott, Baron of the Exchequer, died 1780.

Laleham House, the seat of the Earl of Lucan, is a plain square modern mansion, with a Tuscan portico. The pleasant grounds, of about 40 acres, are noted for the noble elms, shrubberies, and flower gardens. Donna Maria, Queen of Portugal, resided for some time in her minority (1829, etc.) at Laleham House.

At Greenfield, near Laleham, are remains of an extensive earthwork, which Stukeley fancied was the camp formed by Cæsar after he had crossed the Thames, and the spot where he received an embassy from the Londoners.† It seems to have been much more perfect when Stukeley visited it than now.

---

* Lysons, vol. iii., p. 198.
† Letter to J. T. Coleridge, Nov. 29, 1819; Stanleys, Life of Arnold, chap. ii.

* Stanley, Life of Arnold, chap. ii.
† Stukeley, Itinerary, part ii., p. 2 ; Lysons, vol. iii., p. 196.

LAMBOURNE, Essex (Dom. *Lamburna*), lies just off the Ongar road, 2½ m. from the Theydon Stat. of the Grt. E. Rly. (Ongar br.), through Abridge, and 13 m. from Whitechapel by road.   Pop. 939.

Abridge is a hamlet of Lambourne, and contains the shops and inns. (*See* ABRIDGE.) Lambourne *Church* (St. Mary and All Saints) stands on high ground 1 m. S.E. of Abridge and the highroad. It has nave and chancel, with tall tiled roofs. A short wooden tower and spire rises from the W. end of the nave. The N. door is Norm., but the body of the church has been covered with plaster inside and out, and all evidence of antiquity hidden. The windows are modern, and without tracery ; some fragments of old painted glass are apparently Flemish. The interior is cumbered with high pews and a gallery. *Obs. mont.* to Thomas Wynyffe, the deposed Bp. of Lincoln. Lambourne was his first living ; and after his deprivation (1641) he returned to Lambourne to spend his remaining days, and was buried in the ch. 1654. At the foot of the Bp.'s tomb, but without a mont., lies the Rev. Michael Tyson, the antiquary, known by his etchings. Tyson was given the living by his college —Christ Church, Cambridge,—but died shortly after induction (May 4, 1780). *Obs.* alto-rilievo of Hope leaning on an urn, by Wilton, on mont. of John Lockwood (d. 1778). *Brass*, with effigies, of Robert Barefoot, citizen and mercer of London (d. 1646), and Katherine his wife. In the ch.-yard notice the fine views over the forest and away to the Kentish hills ; and the grand old oak on the N.

Close to the ch. is the old manor-house, *Lambourne Hall*, now a farm-house. *Bishop's Hall* (General W. M. Wood), ¼ m. S.W. of the ch., marks the site of a residence of Henry Spenser, the warlike Bishop of Norwich, who in 1381 defeated John Litester and his Norfolk followers. *Patch Park* (E. Eliot Eliot, Esq.) is just beyond the rectory, 1 m. N.E. from the ch. *Knoll Hall*, 1¼ m. S.E. of the ch., a mansion built by the 1st Lord Fortescue, was taken down some years ago, and the site occupied by a farm-house. *Dews Hall*, ½ m. S. of the ch., was the seat of the Lockwoods.

LAMORBEY, Kent (*see* BEXLEY).

LANGLEY BURY, Herts (*see* ABBOT'S LANGLEY).

LANGLEY MARSH, Bucks (anc. *L. Maries* and *Marish*). adjoins Upton, Horton, and Iver. The vill. is 2 m. N.W. of Colnbrook, and a stat. on the Grt. W. Rly., 16¼ m. from Paddington. Pop. 1694, including 474 in the eccl. dist. of St. Thomas, Colnbrook, and 48 in that of Gerard's Cross.

The suffix *Maries* or *Marish* is supposed by Lipscomb to be derived from Christiana de Mariscis, who held the manor after the Montfichets. It escheated to the Crown in the reign of Edward I. ; and was granted by Henry VI. to Eton College in 1447, but resumed, and, in 1492, was assigned by Henry VII. to Elizabeth, Queen Consort. Henry VIII. gave it as dower, in 1510, to his consort Katherine of Aragon. In 1523 he granted a lease of it for life to Henry Norres, Keeper of the King's Woods ; and in 1540 made a further grant to Sir Anthony Denny. Edward VI. granted the reversion to Heneage and Willoughby in 1548 ; and in 1551 assigned the manor to the Princess Elizabeth. Charles I., in 1626, alienated the manor to Sir John Kederminster, whose daughter carried it by marriage to Sir John Parsons. From Parsons it passed to Seymour, then to Masham. In 1738 Lord Masham sold it to the 2nd Duke of Marlborough. Fifty years later it was sold to Sir Robert Bateson Harvey, Bart., in whose family it continues.

The old Manor House—about a mile N. of the church—was pulled down by the Duke of Marlborough about 1758, and the present mansion, *Langley Park*, erected on the site. It is a large square stone building, with a central pediment, in the bald pseudo-classic taste of the time ; but is stately, commodious, and has some noble rooms, in which are many good pictures, and among them Reynolds's masterpiece, Mrs. Siddons as the Tragic Muse. The park is nearly 3 miles long, and has an area of over 300 acres ; is richly wooded, contains 2 lakes, and affords many picturesque views. The *Black Park*, a celebrated feature of Langley Park, N. of the Home Park, acquired its name from the dense fir plantations made by Lord Blandford about a century ago.

Langley Marsh was originally a chapelry of Wraysbury, and though made a separate parish, the living continued annexed to that of Wraysbury till 1856. The population is very much scattered. The vill. is chiefly in a line with the Rly. Stat., nearly ½ m. E. of the church; but there are several outlying hamlets, mostly *Greens*, as *Horsemoor Green*, *Sawyers' Green*, *George Green*, *Middle Green*, *Westmoor Green*, *Imer Green*, and *Langley Broom*.

The *Church* (St. Mary) is exceedingly interesting. It is small: of various dates, and much of it late; very irregular, but withal picturesque. By it, on the S., is an immense yew tree, much split and decayed; the ch.-yard is well kept, and full of rose-trees and flowers; on either side of it is a group of solid-looking old red-brick almshouses—one founded by Sir John Kederminster, the other by a Seymour. The church consists of a nave and N. aisle of the Perp. period, and a somewhat earlier chancel and N. aisle. The chapel or manor pew and library on the S., and the W. tower, of brick, were built by Sir John Kederminster, between 1630-50. The nave is divided from the aisle by wooden columns. There is a plain oak rood screen. In the chancel are 4 sedilia. The elevated chapel on the S., which is separated from the nave by a screen of "Coade's artificial stone," erected in 1792, is now the manor pew. On the front, and around the frames of the latticed door and windows, are admonitory Scripture texts in Latin; on the sides the arms of the Kederminsters, etc.; and above is an eye, with the words "Deus videt" on the pupil. Connected with the pew is the Library, to be noticed presently.

Monts.—A large architectural structure, N. of the chancel, in two divisions: one to John Kederminster (d. 1553), and his wife Elizabeth (d. 1590), with their effigies kneeling before lecterns, on which are open books, and beneath them 2 sons and 3 daughters, the other to Edmund Kederminster, one of the six clerks of Chancery (d. 1607), and wife (d. 1618), kneeling effigies, with 2 sons and 6 daughters. *Brass*—John Bowser, " gent. of Coole Broke in the 64th year of his age . . . . and in the 50 yeare of

the peace of the Gospel in England, 1608, March ye 23;" effigy with long beard, furred gown and ruff.

The *Library*, at the W. end of the manor pew, was founded by Sir John Kederminster. In his will, dated Feb. 22, 1631, he provides for the "library which I have prepared and adjoined to Langley Church," and, "for the benefit as well of ministers of the said town, and such other in the county of Bucks as resort thereunto, I do appoint that those books which I have already prepared, be there duly placed together, with so many more as shall amount to the sum of £20." He expressly forbids any book to be taken out of the library.*

The room is quaint and curious. It is comparatively spacious, panelled, painted white, and has roughly executed but expressive paintings of Prophets, Apostles, and Scriptural Saints; numerous inscriptions; views of Windsor Castle, Theobalds, etc. The Cardinal Virtues support a large coat of arms over the mantelpiece; and here again, as in the pew, is the emblematic eye and "Deus videt." The books are enclosed in 5 presses, with panelled doors. There are about 300 volumes, folios and quartos, some rare and a few illuminated; chiefly the Fathers and early divines; a few medical works, and one of general literature—'Purchas his Pilgrims.' The curious family receipt book, mentioned by Lipscomb, does not appear to be now in the collection. On the wall is a catalogue of the books, written on vellum. Mr. Charles Knight, in a pleasant notice of the library, written after he had been staying a month at Langley, asks whether John Milton may not have availed himself of it during his 7 years' residence at Horton.

"Why not? He who wrote L'Allegro, Il Penseroso, Lycidas, Comus, Arcades, wrote them in his father's house at Horton, within little more than two miles from this spot. From 1632, after Sir John Kederminster founded this library, to 1638, when that broad vellum catalogue was hung upon these walls, John Milton could walk over here through pleasant fields, and pass sweet solitary hours in this room." †

LATTON, ESSEX (Dom. *Latuna*), on the borders of Hertfordshire, 1¼ m.

S.W. from Harlow town (across Mark Hall Park), and 1½ m. from Harlow Rly. Stat. : pop. 225.

Latton consists of a few scattered farms and cottages. and a church standing by a stately mansion (*Mark Hall*, Miss Arkwright), far away from the other dwellings. Standing in the park, on high ground amidst fine trees, the little *Church* (St. John the Baptist) looks picturesque, but is not architecturally remarkable. It is Perp. in style, and consists of a nave and chancel, a chapel on the N. used as the manorial pew, and a large sq. tower on the W., with an angle turret terminating at the belfry floor in a tiled roof ; much mended with brick, and, like the body of the ch., rough-cast. The *int.* has been renovated and reseated, and the E. window filled with painted glass. Of the many *monts.*, the most noteworthy is one on the S. wall of the chancel, with small kneeling effigies of a knight and lady. *Brasses :* Sir Peter Arderne, Chief Baron of the Exchequer, d. 1467, and wife ; John Bohun, d. 1485, and wife ; of about the same period, or a little later, a man and his wife, 3 sons, and a daughter ; a priest with a chalice, and one or two more. In the ch.-yard, E. of the chancel, *obs.* a marble cross to Vice-Chancellor Sir James Wigram, d. July 29, 1866, æt. 72, and wife ; and contiguous to it a massive polished red granite cross to Joseph Cotton Wigram, Bp. of Rochester, d. April 6, 1867, æt. 69.

A small Augustinian priory was founded here before 1270, but it never rose into importance. Part of the priory church, Dec. in style, now serves as a barn. *Latton Priory Farm*, as it is called, is about 3 m. S. of Latton, and ½ m. W. of the Epping road, at Randalls.

LAVER, HIGH, Essex, the burial-place of John Locke, is about 5 m. N. by W. from the Ongar Rly. Stat. of the Grt. E. Rly., through Bobbingworth and Moreton : pop. 497.

High Laver is a quiet country vill. in a secluded part of the county, far from any main road, and about midway between Ongar and Harlow. The occupations are agricultural. There are no resident gentry, but the farms look flourishing, the cottages comfortable, and the country pleasant.

Otes, a manor-house in High Laver par., was in 1690 the seat of Sir Francis Masham, M.P., when Locke, failing in health, and unable to withstand the winters of London, at their invitation, "took up his abode with Sir Francis and Lady Masham at Otes, where he was perfectly at home, and enjoyed the society most agreeable to him." * Lady Masham, daughter of Cudworth, the author of the Intellectual System, and a woman of uncommon intellectual powers, held Locke in great reverence, and devoted herself to solace his last hours. Locke died at Otes, Oct. 28, 1704. The house, a moated Tudor mansion, about a mile N.W. of the ch., continued to be the family seat till the death of the last Lord Masham in 1776. It was pulled down in 1804.

High Laver *Church* (All Saints) stands high on the side of a cross road, by the Hall, of old the manor-house, now a farm. It is of undressed flints and sandstone, and consists of nave and chancel, tower at the W. with short octagonal spire, and a wooden porch at the S.W. The nave is Perp., the chancel has lancet windows, and the W. window is Dec. ; but the church was restored throughout in 1865-6, and lost at once its old rusticity, and all evidences of antiquity : the windows and the tower are in the main new. The *int.*, plain but neat, has been fitted with low seats, and the principals of the roof exposed.

Locke was buried in a vault in the ch.-yard, close to the S. porch. A thick blue slab, on an altar-tomb, bears his name, and the dates of his birth and death (b. Aug. 29, 1632 ; d. Oct. 28, 1704). On the ch. wall above the tomb is a black marble slab, with a long Latin inscription to his memory, written by himself some three or four years before his decease.† Locke's tomb was restored, and enclosed within a Gothic railing, by Christ Church College, Oxford, in 1866. E. of the ch., close to the chancel, are tombs like Locke's of his friends Sir Francis and Lady Masham, Lord Masham, and Lady Abigail Masham —the Mrs. Masham of Swift's correspondence, Queen Anne's bedchamber-woman,

---

* Lord King, Life of Locke, p. 251, Bohn's ed.
† King, Life of Locke, p. 266. Lord King states erroneously that the epitaph was "placed *upon* his tomb ; " the tomb and epitaph are wide apart.

favourite, and mistress, Sarah of Marlborough's foe, and Harley and Bolingbroke's confederate. In all there are 10 or 12 of the Masham tombs, almost exactly alike, clustered about the E. end of High Laver Church.

LAVER, LITTLE, Essex,

contiguous to and on the E. of High Laver—the churches are 1 m. apart—is another thinly peopled agricultural parish (27 houses and 104 inh. in 1871). The village, hardly a village,—half a dozen cottages, shop, farm, and the Leather Bottle—are on the highroad, midway between the churches of the sister parishes. Little Laver *Church* (St. Mary the Virgin), still small, was enlarged as well as elaborately restored in 1872, at the cost of the patron of the living, the Rev. Rd. Palmer, of Purley, Berks, as a memorial of his brother, the Rev. Henry Palmer, the late rector. The *int.* has been handsomely fitted up, and stone pulpit, substantial open oak seats, and carved font erected.

LAVER, MAGDALEN, Essex,

about 1 m. W. of High Laver, a vill. of 175 inh., is so called from the ch., which is dedicated to St. Mary Magdalen, and to distinguish it from High and Little Laver. Magdalen Laver *Church* stands in the open fields, among finely formed and luxuriant trees, and consists of Perp. rough-cast nave and chancel, with tall red-tiled roofs, and old and battered wooden W. tower, painted black, and terminating in a gabled roof. The *int.* is plain, plastered, has high pews, and is kept in excellent condition. A slender oak screen divides the nave and chancel. *Obs.* the helmet with dragon crest suspended against the wall, and the hooks for 3 other helmets. The font is Perp., of fair details. The heads of some of the windows contain fragments of original painted glass.

LAVERSTOCK GREEN, Herts

(*see* ABBOT'S LANGLEY).

LEATHERHEAD, Surrey,

on the river Mole, 3½ m. S.W. from Epsom, 4 m. N. from Dorking, and 18 m. from London by road; a stat. on the Croydon and Dorking br. of the L., B., and S. C.

Rly. (22¾ m.), and the terminus of the Wimbledon and Leatherhead br. of the L. and S.W. Rly. (21 m.) Pop. 2455. Inns, *Swan* hotel; *Bull* commercial inn.

The present form of the name has been reached by slow steps. In the will of Alfred the Great is a bequest to the "custos de *Leodre*"; and it again occurs as *Leodria*. In the Dom-boc it is written *Laret*. In the Testa de Nevill, it occurs (temp. Richard I.) as *Lerred*. In 1203 it is written *Ledred*, and so on with variations as *Leddered* and *Ledrede*, till in the 15th century we have "*Ledered* alias *Leatherhed*," a close approximation to the present form.* The conjectures that have been offered as to the origin of the name seem of little value. Possibly it may be connected with A.-S. *leod*, people, and *red*, counsel = a place of meeting.

At the Domesday Survey, the king held the church of Leret, with 40 acres of land, as an adjunct of Ewell; whilst Odo, Bp. of Bayeux, held the principal manor of Pechevesham, and Richard de Tonbridge that of Tornecrosta (Thorncroft). The subsequent history of these two manors is intricate, and of no general interest; nor does it afford any incidents which require relation. Both manors still exist. Pachensham and Leatherhead, as the first is now called, is in private hands. Thorncroft is held by Merton College, Oxford; Philip Basset and his wife, Ela, Countess Dowager of Warwick, having in 1270 given it, with other lands, to Walter de Merton for the endowment of the college he had founded at Malden, and which was afterwards removed to Oxford.†

The town stands on the rt. bank of the Mole, at the foot of the beautiful Vale of Mickleham, which extends hence to Dorking. The ground rises somewhat steeply from the Mole, many of the houses being built on a series of irregular terraces. The shops are mostly collected about the crossing of the Guildford and Dorking roads, and in the centre stands a steep-roofed clock and engine-house. Several of the houses are old, and some picturesque; but the picturesqueness of the place as a whole, formerly very marked, has been almost improved away of late years. At

---

* Manning and Bray's, and Brayley's Histories of Surrey.

† Brayley, Surrey, vol. iv., p. 430.

one time Leatherhead was of some local consequence. The sheriff's county court was held here, and a market was granted it by Edward III. Long after these had departed, and down to the railway epoch, Leatherhead had a large posting business. Now the town depends on its local trade, and is a very quiet place.

The Guildford road is carried over the Mole by a bridge of 14 arches. On the town side of the bridge is a rude timber-framed house (but much altered) known as the Old Running Horse, which, according to a tradition reaching very far back, was the ale-house of Skelton's Elynour Rummyng, who

> " Dwelt in Sothray,
> In a certain stede,
> Besyde Lederhede . . .
> She breweth noppy ale,
> And maketh thereof port sale." *

The *Church* (St. Mary and St. Nicholas) stands on high ground on the l. of the road to Mickleham. A large rambling cruciform building, with a long chancel, and low massive W. tower, it is chiefly of the 14th century, but the old work was much altered in the recent restoration. The E. window is Dec., the larger window in the S. transept Perp.; both are filled with painted glass: that in the E. window was collected at Rouen by the Rev. Jas. Dallaway. In the latest restoration (1873) open oak seats were substituted for the old pews, the W. gallery was removed, the chancel paved with encaustic tiles, and an elaborate reredos erected. S. of the chancel are three sedilia and a piscina. The *monts.* are not remarkable. They commemorate, among others, Admiral Jas. Wishart, d. 1723; Adm. Rd. Byron, d. 1837; Lieut.-Gen. Langton, d. 1714; Lt.-Gen. H. Gore, d. 1739; Rev. James Dallaway, author of the 'History of Sussex,' of 'Anecdotes of the Arts in England,' and of a work on Heraldry—all of very little value—who died here in 1834, vicar of Leatherhead for 30 years; Richard Duppa, author of the 'Life of Michel Angelo,' d. 1831 ; and Lt.-Col. Drinkwater Bethune, d. 1844, who, when Captain Drinkwater, wrote the 'History of the Siege of Gibraltar,' that stirs the heart like a trumpet. There is also a

brass plate to "fryndly Robartt Gardnar," d. 1571, with a long poetic inscription by Q. Elizabeth's court poet, Thomas Churchyard. The tower contains a good peal of 8 bells ; an excellent view is obtained from the leads.

On the Epsom road is *St. John's Foundation School*, a spacious red-brick Elizabethan building completed in 1873, for the gratuitous instruction of the sons of poor clergymen. The institution was founded in 1850, at St. John's Wood, but having outgrown its original domicile, the present building was erected for the accommodation of 100 boys.

The principal seats are—*Randall Park* (Mrs. Henderson) on the N.W. of the town, the Manor-house of Pachensham, a Tudor mansion erected in 1829, when the old house, which stood on lower ground and nearer the river, was taken down. *Thorncroft* (Mrs. Knight) on the l. bank of the Mole, S.E. of the town, was built in 1772, from a design by Sir Robert Taylor. Its predecessor was the residence of (and is said to have been built by) Robert Gardnar, chief sergeant of the cellar to Q. Elizabeth, whose mont. we saw in Leatherhead ch.; and of Ald. Sir Thos. Bludworth, Knt., and Lord Mayor in 1666, the year of the Great Fire, and who was buried in Leatherhead ch. The present house was long the residence of Col. Drinkwater-Bethune. *The Mansion*, on the rt. bank of the Mole near the ch., occupies the site of one that was the property of Ald. Bludworth, and an occasional residence of Judge Jeffreys, who married Bludworth's sister. There is a tradition that when proscribed at the Revolution of 1688, Jeffreys concealed himself in the vaults of this house. The present house was built about 1710. *The Priory* (Arthur T. Miller, Esq.), very pleasantly situated on a high bank, on the same side of the river, was originally called the *Lynk House*, from its being held by the tenure of providing a link to burn before the altar of St. Nicholas in Leatherhead ch. The house was enlarged, gothicized, and named The Priory at the suggestion of the Rev. Jas. Dallaway, who had concocted a history of a fictitious Cistercian Priory on the site.

Leatherhead Common, a large and pleasant piece of wild heath on the E. of the town, was enclosed in 1862.

* Skelton, The Tunning of Elenour Rummyng, Works, vol. i., p. 98.—Dyce's Ed.

LEAVESDEN, HERTS (*see* WATFORD).

LEE, KENT, lies S. of Blackheath, and between Lewisham and Eltham ; 1½ m. S.E. of Greenwich, and 6 m. from London. Rly. stats., *Burnt Ash Lane*, on the Loopline of the S.E. Rly. ; *Grove Park*, on the L. C. and D. Rly. (Sevenoaks and Tunbridge line). Pop. 10,493 (dist. of mother-ch., 4052 ; Lee Park, 3852 ; Holy Trinity, 1980 ; part of St. Peter, Eltham, 609).

Lee is a large suburban parish, and its convenient distance, the pleasantness of the neighbourhood, and the proximity of Blackheath, have made it a favourite place of residence with City merchants and men of business, for whose accomdation every available piece of ground has been appropriated. Parks (Lee Park, Manor Park, Dacre Park, Belmont Park, Grove Park, etc.), in which the houses are not too closely packed, mingling with the terraces of detached and semi-detached villas and genteel cottages, and a sprinkling of older houses in good-sized grounds, secure the place from the cheerless monotony of some suburban districts, but leave little to interest a visitor. Nor has the place any historical associations. The manor of Lee (it was written in the Domboc as it is written now) was one of those given by the Conqueror to his half-brother Odo, Bp. of Bayeux ; and it has been, with its sub-manors, as frequently transferred as most—but the details are quite devoid of interest.

The old parish *Church* (St. Margaret) having become dilapidated, was, with the exception of a portion of the tower, taken down and a new one built in 1840. This in a few years became too small, or too modest, for the increased congregation, and a larger and more elaborate Dec. ch., with a lofty spire, was built on an adjacent site. The old ch.-yard, well-kept and pleasant to look upon, is the last resting-place of some men of mark. Here was interred, 1742, Edmund Halley, according to the insc. on his tomb " astronomorum sui sæculi facilé princeps ;" and if Newton be omitted this might be said with truth. Nathaniel Bliss, who succeeded Bradley as Astronomer Royal, was also buried here, 1764. Among the tombs are several of the Fludyer, Boone, and Roper families.

Ald. Sir Sam. Fludyer entertained George III. and Q. Charlotte at the Guildhall, with great state, on occasion of his mayoralty, 1761. Trevor Roper, Baron Dacre, d. 1773, and his wife Mary Jane, daughter of Sir Thos. Fludyer, are commemorated in a very long and eulogistic inscription. William Parsons, the comedian, a noted Dogberry, and the original Sir Fretful Plagiary, d. 1795, has a brief epitaph, in verse, that tells

" He science knew, knew manners, knew the age."

Margaret Hughes, probably the handsome actress and mistress of Prince Rupert (see *Brandenburgh House*, HAMMERSMITH), was buried "from Eltham, Oct. 15, 1719." John Charnock, F.S.A. (d. 1807), author of the 'Biographia Navalis,' 6 vols., 8vo, and 'Life of Nelson.' Samuel Purchas is said to have written the greater part of his ' Pilgrims ' at Lee.

Other churches in Lee are—Christ Church, Lee Park, a neat E.E. building erected in 1855; and Holy Trinity, Belgrave Villas, a more pretentious E.E. cruciform structure, of Kentish rag and Bath-stone, completed in 1864 from the designs of Mr. W. S. Barber. St. Peter's, Eltham Road, belongs to Eltham rather than to Lee.

The Merchant Taylors Almshouses, for widows of freemen of the company, at the junction of Brandram Road with the High Road, consists of a range of 30 comfortable-looking houses, within pleasant and well-kept grounds. The Boone Almshouses, near Lee Green, were rebuilt in 1874.

LEITH HILL, SURREY (*see* DORKING).

LEMSFORD MILLS, HERTS (*see* HATFIELD).

LESNESS, KENT (*see* ABBEY WOOD).

LEWISHAM, KENT (Dom. *Levesham*), a large suburban village and parish, 5 m. from London, and 1 m. S. of Greenwich, is situated on the Ravensbourne, the vill. extending for more than 2 m. along the Bromley road. *Stats.* of the S.E. Rly.; *Junction Stat.* for North Kent and Mid-Kent lines, Lewisham bridge; for Mid-Kent, *Catford Bridge; Lady-Well*, near the par. ch.; for the L. C. and D. Rly., *Lewisham Road.* Pop. of par. 36,525, but this includes 8 separated eccl. dists., embracing Blackheath, Brockley, and Sydenham: Lewisham proper had 9387 inhabitants in 1871.

Lying along the valley of the Ravens-bourne, with the country rising gently on either side into low uplands, Lewisham was only a few years ago a pleasant rural district, but it has fallen a prey to the builder, and has become much like any other suburban village. It still, however, retains a few good old houses.

Ælthruda, niece of Alfred, about the year 900, gave the manor of Lewisham to the abbey of St. Peter in Ghent. A cell, known as Lewisham Priory, of the Bene-dictine order, was in consequence esta-blished here. Kilburne says that it was founded, temp. Henry III., by Sir John Merbury; but it is more probable that he added to its endowments, and thus became its second founder. Though sometimes endangered, it lasted till the suppression of alien priories at the be-ginning of the reign of Henry V. It was then transferred, 1414, with the manor, to the priory of Sheen. It reverted to the Crown with the other conventual property in 1538; and was granted for his life to Thomas Lord Seymour in 1547. Edward VI. gave it to John Duke of Northumber-land, on whose execution, in 1553, it reverted to the Crown, but was by Q. Elizabeth granted, 1563, to Northumber-land's brother, Sir Ambrose Dudley, for his life. James I. gave the manor in 1624 to John Earl of Holderness. In 1664 it was sold to Reginald Grahme, who 9 years later conveyed it to Admiral George Legge, afterwards created Baron Dartmouth. His son, William, was in 1711 created Viscount Lewisham and Earl of Dartmouth, and the manor is now the property of his descendant, William Earl of Dartmouth. Billingham, Catford, and Sydenham are manors in Lewisham par.

In the Chamberlain's papers for 1602 is the entry, "On May-day the Queen [Elizabeth] went a-Maying to Sir Richard Buckley's at Lewisham, some three or four miles off Greenwich." Bulkeley's house was probably on the Sydenham side

of Lewisham, where is Oak of Honour Hill, so named, according to the local tradition, from Q. Elizabeth having sat beneath the oak on its summit when she came hither a-maying.

The old parish *Church* (St. Mary) was taken down in 1774, and the present ch. erected on its site. It is a plain oblong structure, of stone, with a shallow semi-circular recess instead of a chancel at the E. end, a portico of 4 Corinthian columns on the S., and a square tower, the lower part of which is ancient, at the W. end. A *brass* to George Hatteclyff, 1514, is the only old memorial of any interest. Two or three of the later *monts.* should be examined. Tablet on E. wall to Mary, daughter of William Lushington, Esq., d. 1797, æt. 16: rilievo by Flax-man of an angel pointing the mourning mother to the text inscribed above. "Blessed are they that mourn," etc., and a poetical epitaph by Hayley. At the W. end (N. of the organ) a tablet to Anne, wife of John Petrie, d. 1787: rilievo of her death-bed, with her husband and children beside it. South of the organ is a companion tablet to Margaret, relict of the Rev. Robert Petrie, d. 1791, with a very fine rilievo by Banks, representing Mrs. Petrie dying in the arms of Religion, and supported by Faith and Hope. Another tablet to a member of the Thackeray family has a bas-relief by Baily. In the ch.-yard is a mont. with some verses from his own 'Fate of Genius,' to the unfortunate young poet, Thomas Dermody, who was buried here July 20, 1802.

Nine more churches are in the parish, but only two of them are in Lewisham proper. *St. Stephen's* was built and en-dowed in 1865 by the Rev. S. Russell Davies. It was designed by Sir G. Gilbert Scott, and is an elegant and carefully fin-ished example of his favourite style of E.E. *St. Mark the Evangelist*, College Park, is a handsome Dec. building, erected in 1870 from the designs of Mr. W. C. Banks. It serves a rapidly growing district of villas, which has already, besides the ch., Con-gregational and Wesleyan chapels of more than average architectural character.

Lewisham Grammar School was founded and endowed by the Rev. Abraham Colfe, vicar of Lewisham, in 1656, for 31 boys; the Leathersellers' Company being constituted trustees for carrying the bequest into effect. The intentions of the founder were extended by a scheme settled by the Court of Chancery in 1857. The foundation includes an upper or Endowed Grammar School on Lewisham Hill, and a lower school, known as the Leathersellers' School, in the village.

Mr. Colfe also left funds for building and endowing 5 *almshouses* for poor godly housekeepers of the parish, above 60 years of age, and able to say the Creed, the Lord's Prayer, and the Ten Commandments. These almshouses still exist, and others have been lately erected in the village, under the will of Mr. John Thackeray, for 6 poor females, who in addition to apartments receive 10*s*. each weekly.

Rushey Green is a hamlet on the Bromley road, now in effect a southern extension of Lewisham village. Here are the *Hatcliffe Almshouses* for 6 poor persons. *Priory Farm*, at the S. end of Rushey Green, occupies the site of the Benedictine priory mentioned above.

Southend, 1½ m. S. of Rushey Green, is the most rural part of Lewisham. Here are several good residences (*The Hall*, Sam. Forster, Esq. ; *Park House*, C. W. Slee, Esq.; *Warren House*, Col. S. Long, etc.); a chapel-of-ease, built and endowed by the late John Forster, Esq.; a large and somewhat picturesque flour-mill on the Ravensbourne, which here runs close to the road ; and a country inn, the Tiger's Head.

Catford and *Catford Bridge*, on the Ravensbourne, ½ m. E. of Rushey Green, and *Hither Green*, ½ m. E. of the village, are other hamlets of Lewisham. *Perry Vale* (or *Perry Slough*, where Dermody died) belongs to Sydenham.

LEYTON, or LOW LEYTON,

ESSEX, on the Epping road, and to the E. of the river Lea, about midway (2 m.) between Stratford and Walthamstow, and 5½ m. from Whitechapel ch. The Leyton Stat. of the Grt. E. Rly. (Epping and Ongar br.) is nearly a mile from the ch. Pop. 5480: the entire par., which is very large, and includes Leytonstone, contained 10,394 inhab. in 1871.

Low Leyton is a long straggling vill., built for the most part on ground slightly

raised above the marshes which border the Lea. It is to its proximity to this river that Leyton is supposed to owe its name. "Layton, or Leyton," writes Norden, " a town upon Ley." This is generally accepted, yet it is hardly borne out by the form of its name in the Dom. Survey, *Leintuna, Leintun.*

Traces of a circular entrenchment 100 ft. in diameter, within a nearly square rampart and outer fosse, at Ruckholt, about 1 m. S. of Leyton ch., indicate the presence of an early British settlement ; and the somewhat extensive lines of walls and foundations of buildings, fragments of pottery, and imperial and consular coins, found at Ruckholt, and near the Manor House, show that there must have been a Roman establishment of some size : though *Durolitum*, with which some antiquaries have sought to identify Leyton, is now placed in the neighbourhood of Romford. The manor of Leyton belonged to the Abbey of Stratford Langthorne from about 1200 to the Dissolution. In 1545 it was granted to Lord Chancellor Wriothesley, who, however, sold it immediately, and it has since been often transferred, and a good deal subdivided.

As elsewhere the fields have been much encroached on; but much land is still under culture as market gardens and nursery grounds, and large quantities of roots and flowers are grown for Covent Garden Market. Potatoes are cultivated extensively, and the marshes afford good grass and pasture. Formerly Low Leyton was the residence of many great City merchants, and other wealthy personages. These have mostly retreated farther from the capital; but several of the solid old mansions are left.

Low Leyton *Church* (St. Mary) is a plain brick and plaster structure, of which no part is older than the last half of the 17th cent., and which was in a great measure rebuilt in 1821—the tower, which was built about 1660, alone being left untouched. But though the ch. is ugly and poor, it contains several interesting *monts*. That indefatigable antiquary John Strype was minister of Low Leyton for 68 years (1669—1737), and till within two or three years of his death continued punctually to perform his ecclesiastical duties, although he had never received institution or induction.* He died at his granddaughter's house at Hackney, Dec. 11, 1737, æt. 94, and was buried in the chancel of Leyton ch. His grave is marked by a plain stone, but this has been covered over by the new floor of the chancel. S. of the chancel is a mont. of Sir Michael Hickes, d. 1612, secretary to Lord Burleigh, and friend of Bacon, Raleigh, and Camden; with life-size alabaster effigies of the knight in armour, and of his widow in mourning habit. On the N. wall an elaborate mont. of Sir Wm. Hickes, Bart., d. 1680; his son, Sir Wm. Hickes, d. 1702; and Marthagnes, wife of Sir Wm. Hickes the younger, d. 1723. On the mont. are marble effigies of the father, recumbent, in a Roman habit, with baton in rt. hand as Lieut. of the Forest of Waltham, and on one side the son in a Roman habit, on the other Lady Marthagnes, both standing. On the S. wall is a brass plate to Lady Mary Kingston, d. 1557, with rhyming inscription—

"If you wyll the truythe have
  Here lyethe in thys grave,
  Dyrectly under thys stone,
  Good Lady Mary Kyngestone,
  Who departed this world, the truth to say,
  In the month of August, the xv day ;
  And, as I do well remember,
  Was buryed honorably 4 day of September,"
  etc.

In the nave are monts. of "the most accomplished cavalier, and right valiant commander, Charles Goring, Baron of Hurst Perpoint and Earl of Norwich," d. 1670 ; of Ald. Sir Richard Hawkins, d. 1735 ; and of many members of the families of Bosanquet, Hawes, Trench, etc. But one that will have more interest is a tablet to William Bowyer (d. 1737), the learned printer, with a long Latin epitaph, by his pupil and partner the elder Nichols, who erected the memorial. *Brass* (small) of Ursula Gaspar, d. 1493. One of Tobias Wood, wife and 12 children, is no longer in its place. The ch.-yard abounds in tombs of local celebrities, among which perhaps the most noticeable is one on the N.E. of the ch. of Sir John Strange, Master of the Rolls, d. 1754, author of two folio volumes of Reports, whose worth is commemorated in an immensely long insc., as well as on a tablet in the ch. Among the tombs is that

of David Lewis, d. 1700, author of 'Philip of Macedon, a Tragedy,' and the friend of Pope. Sir Thomas Roe, or Rowe, the Oriental traveller, sent by Q. Elizabeth, 1614, on an embassy to the Great Mogul, of which, and of his embassy to Constantinople, he published an account, was a native of Leyton. Thomas Lodge, the Shakspearian poet, dates his 'Wit's Miserie,' 1596, "from my house at Low Layton, this 5th of November, 1595."

A second ch., All Saints, was consecrated in Jan. 1865. It is of brick and stone, cruciform, with a long narrow chancel, S. and W. porches, low walls, and high-pitched roofs ; Dec. in style, and the E. window, of 5 lights and rather elaborate tracery, filled with painted glass: archt., Mr. W. Wigginton.

In the Lea Bridge Road are the Almshouses of the Master Bakers' Pension Society. There are also parochial almshouses, a low range of single-roomed tenements by the ch.-yard, founded by John Smith, merchant, in 1656, for 8 poor persons.

Among the old mansions remaining are —*Etloe House*, built by Edward Mores the antiquary, and founder of the Equitable Assurance Society, in 1760, and his residence till his death in 1778. It stands in Church Lane, about ¼ m. N.W. of the ch., by a lane which leads to the Lea, and is a rather peculiar white-fronted building, standing in a good garden, and is now chiefly noteworthy as having been during the last years of his life the residence of Cardinal Wiseman. *Leyton House*, a short distance beyond Etloe House, is the fine seat of W. L. Gurney, Esq., noted for its grounds. *Ruckholt House*, ½ m. S. of the ch., was the stately mansion of the Hickes family. In 1742 and following years it was opened as a place of public entertainment, of the kind noticed under HAMPSTEAD (Belsize House), and ISLEWORTH (Kendal House). Ruckholt House was taken down about 1757. The present Ruckholt House (J. Tyler, Esq.) is a moderate-sized modern house.

At *Knott's Green*, a hamlet of Leyton, 1½ m. N.E. from the ch. on the road to Snaresbrook, is the seat of G. Gurney Barclay, Esq., locally famous for its grounds and gardens, and in the scientific world for its Observatory, in which, under the management of Mr. C. G. Talmage, excellent work has been accomplished. Here also is the seat of Edward Masterman, Esq.

Park House, another fine old mansion, has, by the addition of a new wing and other alterations, been converted into the St. Agnes Roman Catholic Poor Law School.

Lea Bridge, where are a stat. of the Grt. E. Rly., some good nursery grounds, reservoirs of the East London Water Works, a favourite fishing house, and a large number of new villas and cottages, is another hamlet. The mills at *Temple Mills*, on the Lea, 1½ m. S.W. from Leyton ch. by Ruckholt, by some imagined to occupy the site of mills belonging to the Knights Templars, have given place to works of the East London Water Company.

LEYTONSTONE, Essex, a hamlet of Low Leyton, from which it is about 1 m. W., stretches for a considerable distance along the Epping road, and is about 2 m. N. of Stratford. The Leytonstone Stat. of the Grt. E. Rly. (Epping and Ongar line) is close to the ch. Pop. of the eccl. dist. 4914, but this includes 1205 in public institutions.

Leytonstone is pleasantly situated on the edge of Epping Forest, with Wanstead on one side, Snaresbrook on another. In itself it has become a long street of small villas and cottages, with a few older and better houses standing apart in their well-timbered grounds. Here is a very large nursery (Protheroe's), noted for standard roses and other choice flowers, and ornamental trees and evergreens. The public institutions above referred to include the large West Ham Union Workhouse, which had 784 inmates in 1871 ; the Bethnal Green Industrial School, with nearly 400 inmates ; and a Children's Home. Here too is a Roman Catholic Cemetery.

The *Church*, St. John the Baptist, is a white brick and stone building, E.E. of the year 1843 ; poor in details, with a tall W. tower surmounted with pinnacles at the angles. The *int.* is neat and commodious, and the triple lancet in the chancel is filled with painted glass.

LIMPSFIELD, Surrey, a pleasantly situated agric. vill. on the borders of Kent, and on the road from Godstone to Westerham, 4 m. from the former, 3 m. from the latter place : pop. 1292.

At the Dom. Survey, *Limensfeld* was held by the Abbot of Batailge, it being one of the manors with which the Conqueror endowed his newly founded Battle Abbey. Besides the arable land, there were in the manor a mill, a fishery, and a church ; 25 villans, 6 bordarii, and 10 bondsmen. In the woods, pannage for 150 swine ; *3 eyries of hawks*, and 2 stone quarries. The manor was held by the abbey till the Dissolution ; it was then granted to Sir John Gresham, in whose descendants it continued till the death of Sir Marmaduke Gresham in 1742. It was bought by Bourchier Cleeve in 1750, after whose death in 1760 it several times changed owners, till in 1779 it was purchased by Sir John Gresham, the son of Sir Marmaduke. Having thus returned to the Gresham family, it went by the marriage of Sir John's daughter and heiress to Wm. Leveson Gower, Esq., and is now the property of G. W. G. Leveson Gower, Esq.

Aubrey praises the "delicate air" of the neighbourhood, and it is a very pleasant country. The vill. extends N. and E. from Limpsfield Common—large, picturesque, and broken by clumps of firs. A large house in the centre of the village, by the ch., was the property and residence of Mrs. Eugenia Stanhope, widow of Philip Stanhope, natural son of Philip Earl of Chesterfield. She it was who after her husband's death gave to the world Lord Chesterfield's celebrated ' Letters to his Son.'

The *Church* (St. Peter) consists of a nave and S. aisle, a double chancel, and tower, with a short shingled spire at the E. end of the S. aisle. The tower is in part Norm. ; the body of the ch. E.E., with Perp. windows inserted. The whole was thoroughly restored in 1871, chiefly at the expense of Mr. G. W. G. Leveson Gower. In the principal chancel are a piscina and sedilia ; in the tower a holy water stoup. The font is E.E., a square basin on a thick central and 4 smaller angle shafts. In the chancel is a tablet to Eugenia Stanhope, relict of Philip Stanhope, d. 1783. Against the exterior of the W. wall of the ch. is a large mont. to John, 13th Baron Elphinstone, d. 1860.

and his uncle, the Hon. Mountstuart Elphinstone, d. 1859. In the ch.-yard are two good yew trees. The entrance is by a lich-gate.

Hookwood, in richly timbered grounds, near the ch., was of old the seat of the Greshams, but was taken down and the present house built on the site by Vincent Biscoe, Esq., about 1810; it is now the residence of C. N. Wilde, Esq. *Tenchleys* (formerly Tinsley) *Park* (S. Teulon, Esq.) is a short distance from the vill.; *Moor House* (Mrs. Brandreth) is 2 m. E.; *Trevereux* (H. Cox, Esq.) is a large and stately old mansion standing in a fine park at the S.W. extremity of the par.

LITTLE BERKHAMSTEAD, HERTS (*see* BERKHAMSTEAD, LITTLE).

LITTLE ILFORD, ESSEX (*see* ILFORD, LITTLE).

LITTLE STANMORE, MIDDX. (*see* STANMORE PARVA).

LITTLETON, MIDDX., an agric. village, 1 m. N. of Shepperton Rly. Stat. (Thames Valley line), and 16 m. S.W. from Hyde Park Corner; pop. 165. The little village—there are only 28 houses in the par.—lies somewhat over a mile from the Thames, in the midst of a level but pleasant district.

The *Church* (St. Mary Magdalen) stands on the vill. side of Littleton Park. It comprises nave, aisles, and deep chancel, and a square embattled W. tower. The main fabric is E.E., but the clerestorey and some of the windows are Perp. additions. The upper part of the tower is modern. The brick mausoleum on the N. of the chancel was constructed for the Wood family towards the end of the 18th cent. The interior shows the original and added parts better than the exterior. *Obs.* the cylindrical piers in the nave, the obtuse arches on either side, the lancets in the chancel, and the window for lighting the rood-loft. In the chancel is a *brass*, Blanche, wife of Sir Henry Vaughan, d. 1509. The font is E.E., and has an octagonal bowl on a thick round stem. Notice the finely carved cover.

Littleton Park (Thos. Wood, Esq.) has been the seat of the Wood family for two centuries. The mansion is large and stately, and has a noble saloon and other spacious rooms, in which are some good pictures, including Hogarth's Actors Dressing in a Barn (with the artist's receipt for the purchase-money). The late Lieut.-General Wood entertained the Prince of Wales, Prince Hohenlohe, etc., here, March 28th, 1866.

LONDON COLNEY, HERTS, a large village on the river Colne (here a mere brook), from which it derives its name, and on the main northern road; 3 m. S. of St. Albans, and 17½ m. from London. London Colney and the hamlet of Tittenhanger, being portions of the parishes of St. Peter (St. Albans), St. Stephen, Ridge, and Shenley, were in 1826 constituted the eccl. district of St. Peter Colney, and had 843 inhab. in 1871. The ch., a plain square modern building, stands in the centre of the village. The ground is high (238 ft. above the Ordnance datum), the neighbourhood picturesque, and there are pleasant walks to Colney Street, 1¼ m. W., Radlett (the nearest rly. stat. 3 m.), Shenley, and Mimms.

The hamlet of *Tittenhanger*, about 1 m. N.E. of *Tittenhanger Park*, the fine seat and park of the Countess of Caledon, lies to the E. of London Colney. The manor belonged to St. Albans Abbey, and, according to Chauncy, John de la Moote, abbot from 1396 to 1401, "began a fair mansion at Tittenhanger, where he and his successors might retire for their ease and pleasure, and recreate themselves with their friends and relations, but died before he could finish the same."* It was however finished, and on a larger and richer scale, by his successor, John of Whethamsted, and continued to be used by the abbots till all was swept from them at the Dissolution. There is a tradition that Wolsey expended a large sum on it, intending to make it one of his residences. In 1528 Henry VIII. and Q. Katherine stayed at Tittenhanger during the continuance of the sweating-sickness in London. Henry granted the manor to Sir Hugh Paulet, and by marriage it passed to Sir Thos. Pope, who greatly improved the house. His widow bequeathed the manor to her nephew, Thos. Blount. The Blounts became extinct about the middle

---

* Chauncy, vol. ii., p. 387.

of the 18th cent., and the manor went first to the Freemans, and by marriage to Philip Earl of Hardwick. On the decease of the Countess of Hardwick it was inherited by the Countess of Caledon. The house is a large and rather picturesque red-brick Tudor edifice, oblong, with an inner court. The moat which originally surrounded it has long been filled up. The park is small but pleasant, has some fine trees, and the Colne flows along its W. border. Other good seats are—*Colney Park*, Ald. Sir A. Lusk, Bart., M.P. ; *Salisbury Hall*, J. Ball, Esq. ; and *Highfield Hall*.

LONG DITTON, SURREY (*see* DITTON, LONG).

LONGFORD, MIDDX. (*see* HARMONDSWORTH).

L O U G H T O N, ESSEX (Dom. *Lochintuna*), on the eastern edge of Epping Forest, and on the Epping road, 5 m. S. of Epping, and 11¼ m. from London (Whitechapel and Shoreditch churches). The Loughton Stat. of the Grt. E. Rly. (Epping and Ongar line, 12 m.), is the usual stat. for visitors to Epping Forest. Pop. of par. 2438. Inns, *King's Head ; Crown*; *Robin Hood*, by the forest.

Loughton was one of the manors with which Harold endowed his abbey of Waltham, and it remained the property of the abbey till the Dissolution. Edward VI. granted it to Sir Thos. Darcy, but it soon reverted to the Crown, and was annexed by Mary to the Duchy of Lancaster. Early in the reign of Elizabeth it became the property of the Stonard family, and was carried by the marriage of Susan, daughter and heiress of Frances Stonard, to Sir Robert Wroth, of Durants, Enfield. In this family it continued for over a century, when John Wroth dying, 1718, without issue, it passed by his bequest to William Henry Earl of Rochford, who in 1745 sold it for £24,500 to Ald. Wm. Whitaker, merchant, of Lime Street, London, in whose family it has since continued.

Loughton stands on high ground overlooking the valley of the Roding, Lambourne, Chigwell, and what was Hainault Forest, and on the other hand running into Epping Forest at its finest part, High Beech. (*See* EPPING FOREST; HIGH BEECH ; CHIGWELL.) The village is a long straggling place, lively and noisy on holidays, but wearing at other seasons a sober sylvan aspect.

The *Church*, St. John, stands on the rt. of the Epping road, at the N. end of the vill., a more convenient site for the parishioners than that of the old ch., which stood by the Hall, a mile to the E. Loughton ch. is a solid white-brick fabric, Norman, of the year 1846, with a low square tower at the W. end. Most of the windows are filled with painted glass. The churchyard is prettily planted and well kept, and affords some lovely views.

The lane past the ch. leads to the old ch. Of this, the chancel—of flint and stone, Perp., and of no architectural value —alone remains. The lines of the old ch. are, however, traceable by the drains, and the place of the N. porch is marked by the abrupt ending of a fir avenue, which extends from the garden door of the old hall. The ch.-yard is full of tombs of Whittakers and Maitlands and other lords of the soil, and the grave-stones of humbler parishioners, but looks neglected and melancholy.

The ch. stood within the grounds of *Loughton Hall*, the ancient manor-house of the Stonards, Wroths, and Whitakers, but now little more is left of one than the other. Loughton Hall is described as a large and handsome structure, and it boasted of having received many distinguished visitors. Elizabeth visited Loughton Hall in July 1561. James I. was there on more occasions than one. The Princess (afterwards Queen) Anne is said to have retired to Loughton in 1688, but it was most likely only for a night or so when on her way to Nottingham under the escort of Compton, the military Bishop of London. Loughton Hall was destroyed by fire in 1836. The present Loughton Hall, in part constructed from the old hall, is a farm-house. Before leaving, *obs.* the great gates of the old hall, an admirable specimen of hand-wrought iron-work. From the hall there are pleasant walks across the fields to Theydon-Bois, or by lane to Chigwell.

An elegant little ch. (St. Mary the Virgin) was erected in 1871 on the forest side of the parish, as a chapel-of-ease to Loughton. (*See* HIGH BEECH.)

LOW LEYTON, Essex (*see* Leyton).

LULLINGSTONE, Kent (Dom. *Lolingestone*), on the Darent, 1 m. S.W. of Eynesford, and ½ m. W. of the Eynesford Stat. of the L. C. and D. Rly. (Sevenoaks line). At the census of 1871 there were only 5 houses in Lullingstone, including the castle, and 53 inhab.* There is of course, therefore, no village, and, apart from the beauty of the scenery, the interest centres in the castle and the monts. in the church.

In the latter years of William I., Lullingstone was held by Anketul Rosse. It passed by marriage in the reign of John to Wm. Peyforer; and in 1279 was purchased by Gregory Rokesley, Lord Mayor of London. From the Rokesleys it passed by sale in 1359 to Sir John Peche, in whose family it remained till carried by marriage to John Hart, on the death of Sir John Peche in 1522. On the decease of Percival Hart in 1738, it went by marriage to the Dykes of Sussex, and is now the property of Sir William Hart Dyke, Bart., M.P.

Lullingstone Castle lies low, a little to the W. of the Darent, with a splendid park running over the chalk hills behind it. The castle is really a red-brick manor-house of the reign of Elizabeth or early part of that of James, but enlarged, altered, and in good part rebuilt in the latter part of the 18th century. John Thorpe has been said to be the architect, but it is not in his folio Book of Plans. There used to be a household tradition that " Lullingstone Castle is 8 centuries old, and the tower was built before the Conquest—they never built such places since;" but it has probably been silenced by the railway whistle. Originally the house was moated, and portions of the moat remain as ornamental canals. Lullingstone Castle, as you look at it from the lawn, has, with its surroundings, a singularly stately and picturesque appearance. In front is a lake, with immense elms bordering it; behind the house rise splendid cedars; in the garden are lofty firs; on one side is seen the fine old red-brick gate-house (the tower

* When Hasted wrote, just a century ago, there were "but two houses in it besides Lullingstone House."

above referred to), a capital specimen of Elizabethan brick-work, on the other side the church. Notice the shell of an ancient oak, with a vigorous chesnut growing from the centre.

The *Church* (St. Botolph) stands on the lawn close to the castle. It is of the Dec. period, small, and plain externally, but the inside rich and well kept—"it appears more like a nobleman's costly chapel than a common parish church," wrote Hasted of it a century ago, and the same might be as justly said now. The windows have some old painted glass, with saints and their emblems, a martyrdom, arms of the Peches, Harts, etc. The ceiling is a rich example of Jacobean plaster-work. *Obs.* too the excellent old pews, of oak, —all grown, it is said, on the estate. The *monts.* to the Peches, Harts, and Dykes are numerous and costly. S. of the chancel is a graceful mont. to Sir Percival Hart, d. 1580 ; Sir George Hart, d. 1587, and wife, with coloured recumbent effigies. On the N. a freestone effigy. In the chapel is a rich high tomb of Sir John Peche, d. 1522, Capt. of the Body Guard of Henry VIII., and Lord Deputy of Calais, recumbent effigy in full armour, under a lofty canopy. Also several other monts. of later date of both Harts and Dykes, and some helmets and armour that may repay examination. The *brasses* in the chancel include—Sir Wm. Peche, d. 1487, remarkably well engraved, but seemingly of later date. Alice Baldwyn, d. 1533, "late gentlewoman to the Lade Mary, princes of England." Dame Eliz. Cobham, d. 1544, wife of John Hart, by whom she was mother to the Right Worshipful Sir Percival Hart; afterwards wife of George brother to Lord Cobham. *Dole Day* is regularly observed here : on the 1st of January doles of bread and money are distributed from the altar to the few poor of the parish, the church being for the occasion strewed with straw—a survival of the old custom of strewing rushes on church festivals.

The park is large, undulating, richly wooded, and well stocked with deer. There is a public path through it to Park Hill gate; but before taking it ascend the hill E. of the castle, to the great yew tree, for the splendid view over the valley of the Darent.

MALDEN, SURREY (more correctly MALDON—A.-S. *Mældune*, "being compounded of two words, *Mæl*, a cross, and *dune*, a hill;"* Dom. *Meldone*), on the Hog's Mill river, 3 m. S.E. from Kingston, and 10 m. from London. The Worcester Park Stat., on the Epsom and Leatherhead br. of the L. and S.W. Rly., is about ½ m. E. of Malden. Pop. of the par. 416.

In 1240, Walter de Merton, Lord Chancellor of England, and afterwards Bp. of Rochester, purchased the manor of Malden in order to establish a "house of scholars at Malden [domus scholarium apud Meandon], for the support of 20 scholars in the schools of Oxford or elsewhere." The Malden house consisted of a warden and priests, who were transferred, and the estates made over to, Merton College in 1274, when that institution (begun in 1264) was completed. The manor was held undisturbed by Merton College till Henry VIII. began his house at Nonsuch, when he compelled the college to cede him 120 acres for his Great Park—since known as Worcester Park. Elizabeth went still further, for she compelled them to grant her a lease of their manors of Malden and Chessington, with the advowsons of the livings, for the term of 5000 years, at a rental of £40, which she at once ceded to the Earl of Arundel, in exchange for Nonsuch. The college, dissatisfied with this compulsory grant, brought an action of ejectment in 1621, with a view to try its legality, and in 1627 the Chancellor made a decree, by consent, that the lease should be retained for the benefit of the then holder for 80 years, and then revert to the college.

Malden is a vill. of irregularly scattered houses; the occupations chiefly agricultural, the soil clay, the lanes verdant. The *Church* (St. John) was in 1610 rebuilt of brick, except the chancel, which is of flint and stone. It was repaired, altered, and a N. aisle added in 1867. It is small, of no interest, and contains no monts. In the E. window are the arms of Walter de Merton, and of Ravis, Bp. of London in 1609, a native of Malden, and a contributor to the rebuilding of the ch. The carved pulpit is temp. James I.; the

font is large and old, but plain. Rogers Ruding was vicar from 1793 till his death, Feb. 16, 1820, and here wrote his great work, the 'Annals of the Coinage of Great Britain,' 4 vols., 4to, 1817—19.

Worcester Park, ½ m. E. of the ch., was a portion of Nonsuch Great Park. It has been divided, partially built over, and is now a stat. of the Epsom and Leatherhead Rly. *New Malden*, by the S.W. Rly., is a hamlet of Kingston. (*See* KINGSTON-UPON-THAMES.)

MARBLE HILL, MIDDX. (*see* TWICKENHAM).

MARDEN PARK, SURREY (*see* GODSTONE).

MARGARET'S, ST., HERTS (*see* STANSTEAD ST. MARGARET'S).

MARKS, ESSEX (*see* ROMFORD).

MERSTHAM, SURREY (Dom. *Merstan*), a vill. on the Brighton road, 3½ m. N.E. of Reigate, 8½ m. S. by W. of Croydon, and a stat. on the S.E. Rly., 20¾ m. from London Bridge. Pop. 959. Inns: *Feathers Hotel; Jolliffe Arms.* Two centuries ago, Flecknoe found the Merstham inns very unsatisfactory.

"Where I nothing found for supper
But only coarse brown bread and butter,"

a dirty table-cloth, and a "mare mortuum of beer, . . . full of hundred drowned flies." In the bed, besides other discomforts, a "whole warren of starved fleas" grazed on him; and he ends his "littanie" with the pious wish, "the Devil take Mestham for't for me."* But matters have no doubt improved since then.

Merstham (*Mearstam*, the country people call it, and so Cobbett writes it in his 'Rural Rides') is seated in the midst of a hilly district, and the country all around is varied and beautiful. The church and village are on the Upper Greensand; the rly. stat. and lower part of the village are on the Gault; the northern parts are chalk, and on the hill-sides a stiff bluish clay, and clay with flints occur. From the foot of the church hill issues one of the head-

---

* Lysons, vol. i., p. 241.

* Flecknoe, Diarium, 1656. 8th Jornada, p. 41.

springs of the river Mole, and in wet seasons a bourne breaks out from Merstham Hill, and continues flowing for weeks. Merstham stone was formerly much prized for building purposes. It varies greatly in different parts of the parish, and at different depths in the same quarry, the upper beds being coarse, and only available for common work. It is a greyish arenaceous limestone, similar to the *firestone* of Godstone and Reigate—soft when quarried, but hardening by exposure to the atmosphere. So highly was the stone valued at one time, that the Crown took possession of the quarries. Edward III., in 1359, issued a patent authorizing John and Thomas Prophete to dig stone here for the works at Windsor Castle, and commanding the sheriff and others to aid them, and if any men refused to work, to arrest them, and send them in safe custody to Windsor Castle.* Henry VII.'s Chapel at Westminster was built of Merstham stone. The stone is now in request for building furnaces, and for making a fine lime, known in the building trade as Merstham greystone lime. The hillock on which Merstham church stands is a mass of firestone rock. Fitton and Mantell reckon the thickness of the firestone beds at Merstham at 25 ft., the gault 150 ft. A well at the Feathers inn is 210 ft. deep; of which the boring at the bottom, 60 ft., was all in clay and marl.

The manor of Merstham was given by Athelstan, son of King Æthelred II., to the monks of Christchurch, Canterbury. At the Dom. Survey, the Abp. of Canterbury held it "for the clothing of the monks;" and it continued to be held by the Abp. or monks till the Dissolution. Henry VIII. gave Merstham in 1539 to Robert Southwell (afterwards a knight and Master of the Rolls) in exchange for the churches of Warnham, Sussex, and East Peckham, Kent, which the king gave to the newly-constituted dean and chapter of Christchurch. In 1568, Francis Southwell alienated Merstham to Thomas Copley. Afterwards the manor frequently changed hands, till in 1788 it was purchased of the Rev. Jas. Tattersall by Wm. Jolliffe, Esq., M.P. It is now the property of Wm. G. Hylton Jolliffe, Lord Hylton, whose

seat, *Merstham House*, a large irregular mansion, with some fine rooms, and a few good pictures, stands close by the church.

Edward II. is said to have granted the monks of Christchurch the privilege of holding a market in Merstham, but there is no record of its ever having been held. Merstham is now at any rate a mere country vill., not unpicturesque in parts, as by the turn to the Reigate road, where are several old half-timber cottages, and by the entrance gates to Merstham House, where is a quaint old smith's forge. The *Church* (St. Catherine) stands very picturesquely among old trees, on a hillock E. of the vill. It is built of the native stone, has nave and aisles, with a long sloping tiled roof extending over both; chancel and aisles, or sub-chancels, wider than the nave-aisles; a tower at the W. end, with a short octagonal shingled spire; and S. porch. The tower, at least in the lower part, is E.E. (*obs.* the W. door; the mouldings were rechiselled in 1861); the body of the ch. Perp., but some portions are Dec. The columns which divide the nave and aisles are cylindrical on the N., octagonal on the S. The E. window of 5 lights is large and good. *Obs.* double piscina on S. of the main chancel, and a single one in S. sub-chancel. The N. sub-chancel serves as the manor-pew and chapel for the Jolliffe monts. Some of these are good of their kind, but have only family or local interest. A mutilated effigy, with purse hanging on the rt. side, of 14th-cent. date, now in the S. chancel, was found some years since beneath the pavement. *Brasses.*—On an altar-tomb in N. chancel, Sir John Elmebrygge, d. 14— (the date has never been completed), 2 wives, 4 sons, and 5 daughters : only the female effigies remain. Small brass of Peter and Richard Best, d. 1585-7, with effigies of boy in long coats and child in swaddling-clothes. The font is E.E. in date, of Sussex marble, large, square, and rests on a thick central shaft. The int. of the ch. was restored in 1875, the plaster ceiling removed, and the open timber roof exposed.

The first iron railway in the South of England was constructed, 1801-5, from Merstham and Croydon to the Thames at Wandsworth. It was a double line, pro-

* Brayley, History of Surrey, vol. iv., p. 318.

jected to carry lime and stone to London, and bring back coals and manure. It was worked by horses; did not pay; and was at length purchased and taken up by the Brighton Rly. Company. The hills at Merstham are pierced by a tunnel of the Brighton Rly. over a mile long; and it illustrates the different scale on which our actual railways are wrought, that the cost of this Merstham tunnel far exceeded the entire outlay on the old Merstham or "Surrey Iron Rly."

MERTON, SURREY, a long straggling village, 1 m. S. of the Wimbledon Stat. of the L. and S.W. Rly., and 9 m. from London on the Epsom road. *Lower Merton* is on the Wandle, midway (1 m.) between Merton ch and Tooting. There are Rly. Stats. at Merton Abbey and at Lower Merton, available from the Waterlco, Ludgate Hill, and London Bridge Stations; and one called the Morden Stat., but really in Merton, on the Croydon and Wimbledon br. of the L., B., and S. C. Rly. Pop. 2139. Inns, *White Hart ; Grove Tavern.*

The name, A.-S. *Merantune, Meretune,* Dom. *Meretone,* is probably Mere-tun = the town on the Mere, from its position on a mere or lake formed by the waters of the Wandle having flooded the marshes between Phipps' Bridge and Merton Mill. The village consists of two portions, once separated, now connected by a line of dwellings: *Lower Merton,* by the Wandle, where stood the Priory, much occupied by mills and factories; and the ch., village, and neighbourhood, sometimes called *Upper Merton.* S. of the ch. is *Merton Common*—a common no longer.

Merton was the scene of two important events in early English history. In 784, Cynewulf, king of the West Saxons, having come to visit a lady at Merton, was beset by the Ætheling Cyneheard and his followers, and killed, with all his attendants: on the following day the king's thanes and men, having heard the news attacked Cyneheard and slew him, and all his 84 followers save one.* In 871, the English under King Æthelred and his brother Alfred the Ætheling (afterwards our Alfred the Great) fought a terrible battle with the Danes at Merton. During the

greater part of the day the English were victorious, but the Danes held possession of the field of carnage. Bishop Heahmund and many good men were slain there,* and King Æthelred mortally wounded.

The manor of Merton belonged to Harold. At the Dom. Survey it was held by King William, and it remained a possession of the Crown till given by Henry I. to Gilbert the Norman, Sheriff (Vicecomes) of Surrey. Gilbert, born a Norman and bred a soldier, had in 1115 founded an Augustinian priory at Merton, and it was to augment his foundation that he obtained the grant from the king. Merton Priory grew rapidly in reputation, was visited and patronized by Queen Matilda, and soon, at the suggestion of the Prior, was removed to a more convenient site by the Wandle: the original site appears to have been by Merton ch. The original buildings were of wood; the new buildings, of flint and stone, were completed about 1130. There were then 36 brethren in the house.

Merton Priory appears to have risen early into importance. The prior was made a mitred abbot, with a seat in Parliament. From its school proceeded two memorable scholars. One was Thomas à Becket; the other, a native of the village, was Walter de Merton, Bp. of Rochester and Chancellor of England, and the founder of Merton College, Oxford. When Hubert de Burgh, Chief Justiciary of England, incurred the displeasure of Henry III., he fled for sanctuary to Merton Priory. It was at Merton Priory that the Great Council of the Nation was held, 1236, which passed the ordinances known as the Statutes of Merton, and in which the assembled barons answered the attempt of the king and prelates to introduce the canon law by the famous declaration "Nolumus Leges Angliæ mutare." At the surrender of the Priory to the commissioners of Henry VIII., April 16, 1538, its gross revenue was £1039. The Priory was let on lease, but the manor was retained by the Crown. Queen Mary, by letters patent of Nov. 14, 1558, bestowed the priory on the monastery of Sheen;

---

* A.-S. Chronicle, An. 755, 784.

* *Ibid.*, An. 871. Some place the battle at Merton in Oxfordshire, others at Merton, or Marden, in Wilts, but the balance of authority inclines to the Surrey Merton.

but it was resumed by Elizabeth, who granted a lease of it for 21 years to Gregory Lovel, Cofferer to the Household,—buried 1597, in Merton ch., where his mont. is still standing. The manor was sold by James I. in 1610 to Thomas Hunt. Manor and priory have since remained in private hands, and been frequently transferred.*

For awhile the priory estate was held by a Pepys—though not the memorable Samuel—

"*May 21st,* 1668.—To the Office, where meets me Sir Richard Ford, who among other things congratulates me, as one or two did yesterday, on my great purchase ; and he advises me to forbear, if it be not done, as a thing that the world will envy me in : and what is it but my cosen Tom Pepys's buying of Martin Abbey in Surry." †

The priory occupied an area of about 60 acres. In 1648 Merton Priory was one of the "places of strength" in the county of Surrey, ordered by the Derby House Committee to be made defensible. An advertisement for letting it, in 1680, described it as containing several large rooms and a very fine chapel. Fifty years later Vertue described the chapel as entire, and resembling a Saxon building. Lysons, writing in 1792, says that the only vestige of the buildings then left was "the east window of a chapel in crumbling stone." Now only the flint walls of the precinct and a few shapeless fragments of the chapel and mutilated doorway are left.

Within the walls a factory for printing calico was established in 1724, the chapel being utilized as the print-room. A second mill was opened within the walls in 1752, and a third somewhat later. About 1000 persons were employed in them in 1792 ; ten years later the number had fallen to 300.‡ After a time cotton printing was supplanted by silk printing. Merton Priory Mill is now an extensive silk and woollen printing establishment.

* In the British Museum is an excellent impression of the seal of Merton Abbey. It is of the 13th cent., ogival, and has a representation of the Virgin enthroned, under a canopy, with the infant Jesus in her arms, and is one of the finest known. The seal is engraved with much accuracy in the Supp. to the English Cyclopædia, Arts and Sc. Div., col. 1882, and both seal and counter-seal in Brayley's Surrey, vol. iii., p. 460.
† Pepys, Diary. Tom Pepys was Master of the Jewel Office to Charles II. and James II. Merton Priory was for some years his seat.
‡ Lysons, Environs, 1st and 2nd eds. ; Brayley.

Merton *Church* (St. Mary), which stands on somewhat higher ground, ½ m. W. of the priory, is in the main the original ch. built by Gilbert Norman about 1120. It is of flint and stone, covered with plaster, and comprises a nave with S. aisle and very long chancel, N. porch, and short octagonal wooden spire rising from the W. end of the nave roof. Under the porch (which is a rude Dec. work) is a Norman arch with zigzag moulding. One or two lancet windows remain ; the others are Dec. and Perp. insertions. The *int.* is of no interest. In the E. window are the arms of Merton Priory in old painted glass. S. of the chancel is a mural mont. with kneeling effigies, coloured, of George Lovell, Esq., of Merton Priory, cofferer to Q. Elizabeth, d. 1597, his wife, 4 sons, and 4 daughters. In the ch.-yard is the tomb of Mr. Francis Nixon, of Merton Priory, who "first perfected the art of copperplate calico printing," and introduced the process here, to the great profit of the neighbourhood. Another, with long poetic epitaph, is that of the second wife of James Lackington, the once famous bookseller. She was the Dorcas Turton of whom he gives so pretty an account in his Memoirs, and whom he married within two months of the death of that "best of women" his first wife. Lackington had a country house at Merton.

"For four years Upper Holloway was to me an elysium ; then Surrey appeared unquestionably the most beautiful county in England, and Upper Merton the most rural village in Surrey. So now Merton is selected as the seat of occasional philosophical retirement." *

Merton Place was for a few years the residence of NELSON, who delighted in the house and grounds, and used to amuse himself by angling in the Wandle, "having been a good fly-fisher in former days, and learning now to practise with his left hand."† He lived here entirely with Sir William and Lady Hamilton, from Oct. 1801 to May 1803, when he was ordered to sea ; but all the time he afterwards spent on land was spent at Merton. He left it for the last time Sept. 13, 1805, just 5 weeks before Trafalgar. Lady Hamilton made all the

* Memoirs of the Forty-five first Years of the Life of James Lackington, 1794, p. 433.
† Southey, Life of Nelson ; Davy, Salmonia.

arrangements for furnishing and fitting up the house, laid out the grounds, etc., whilst Nelson was at sea; but he gave very precise directions:—

"I would not have you lay out more than is necessary at Merton. The rooms and the new entrance will take a deal of money. The entrance by the corner I would have certainly done; a common white gate will do for the present, and one of the cottages which is in the barn can be put up as a temporary lodge. The road can be made to a temporary bridge, that part of the Nile one day shall be filled up. Downing's canvas awning will do for a passage. . . . The footpath should be turned . . . . and I also beg, as my dear Horatia is to be at Merton, that a strong netting, about 3 ft. high, may be placed round the Nile, that the little thing may not tumble in, and then you may have ducks again in it." *

The Nile was a streamlet which ran through the grounds in artificial windings, so named by Lady Hamilton in honour of her hero. Horatia was of course his daughter. Nelson's manner of life at Merton has been painted with none too favourable a pencil by Lord Minto :—

"I went to Lord Nelson's on Saturday to dinner, and returned to-day in the forenoon. The whole establishment and way of life such as to make me angry as well as melancholy. . . . She [Lady Hamilton] and Sir William and the whole set of them, are living with him at his expense. She is in high looks, but more immense than ever. She goes on cramming Nelson with trowelfulls of flattery, which he goes on taking as quietly as a child does pap. The love she makes him is not only ridiculous but disgusting: not only the rooms, but the whole house, staircase and all, are covered with nothing but pictures of her and of him, of all sizes and sorts, and representations of his naval actions, coats of arms, pieces of plate in his honour, the flagstaff of L'Orient, etc." †

"I went to Merton on Saturday and found Nelson just sitting down to dinner, surrounded by a family party, of his brother the Dean, Mrs. Nelson, their children, and the children of a sister. Lady Hamilton at the head of the table and Mother Cadogan at the bottom. He looks remarkably well and full of spirits. . . . Lady Hamilton has improved and added to the house and the place extremely well, without his knowing she was about it. He found it all ready done. She is a clever being after all." ‡

"Friday night, 13th September [1805].
"At half-past ten, drove from dear, dear Merton, where I left all that I hold dear in this world, to go to serve my king and country. May the great God whom I adore enable me to fulfil the expectations of my country." §

* Nelson to Lady Hamilton.
† Sir Gilbert Elliot to Lady Elliot, March 22, 1802 : Life and Letters of Sir G. Elliot, first Earl of Minto, vol. iii., p. 242.
‡ Elliot to Lady Elliot, Aug. 26, 1805.
§ Nelson's Diary, Nicolas, vol. vii., p. 33.

Lady Hamilton continued to reside at Merton till 1808, when, compelled by pecuniary difficulties, she sold it to Asher Goldsmid. The house has long been pulled down and the ground built over. The names of Nelson Place and Nelson's Arms are now the only memorials of the connection of our greatest naval hero with the village.

MICKLEHAM, Surrey (Dom. *Micleham, Michelham*), in the beautiful Vale of Mickleham, midway (2½ m.) between Leatherhead and Dorking: the nearest rly. stat. is the Box Hill Stat. of the L.,B.,and S. C. Rly., at Burford Bridge, 1½ m. S. of Mickleham ch. Pop. 787. Inns, *Running Horse Hotel*, Mickleham ; *Burford Hotel* (*Fox and Hounds Inn*), Burford Bridge.

The Vale of Mickleham extends for nearly 4 m., from Leatherhead to Burford Bridge, at the foot of Box Hill. Winding, the surface undulating, with for the first mile or more the Mole on your rt. hand, flanked by the lower slopes of Fetcham Downs and the rich woods of Norbury, and on the l. the steep Mickleham Downs, and beyond the dark many-coloured and somewhat fantastic mass of Box Hill, the Vale is beautiful throughout, though by Mickleham vill. high walls too often enclose houses and grounds, and mar the prospect. But the ch. and the school-house perched up on a height are picturesque, and there are tempting-looking byways to the Downs.

The *Church* (St. Michael) looks attractive, but does not gain on close inspection. The massive tower has a Norm. doorway ; the arcades dividing the nave and aisles have semicircular arches ; but the body of the ch. was entirely remodelled, under the pretence of restoration, in 1822-3, and elaborately ornamented—much of the constructive as well as decorative work, however, being mere lath and plaster—and little, if any, of the old work being left unaltered.* The old chancel was removed and a new one substituted in 1872, a reredos of marble and alabaster erected, and the windows filled

* The architect, Mr. P. F. Robinson, published an 'Attempt to ascertain the Age of Mickleham Church in Surrey, with Remarks on the Architecture,' illustrated by 20 plates, thin folio, 1824.

with painted glass. The only mont. to be noticed is an altar-tomb in the Norbury chapel, with *brasses* of "Wm. Widdowsonn, cytizen and mercor of London, and Jone his wyfe," d. 1514. The almshouses by the pretty little school-house, on a high bank near the ch., were built in 1865, in place of a very shabby range destroyed by fire the previous year.

Norbury, so named, as is believed from its position N. of Mickleham, is the pride of the Vale. As early as the Confessor it constituted a distinct lordship then held by the king; at the Dom. Survey by Richard of Tonbridge, and in the reign of Edward II. by Tonbridge's descendant Gilbert de Clare, Earl of Gloucester. For many generations it was held by the Husee family, at first (1315) under the Earls of Gloucester, afterwards in their own right, till in the reign of Henry VI. it went by marriage to Wm. Wymeldon. From the Wymeldons it passed, in default of heirs male, to the Stydolfs, or Stidolphs, an old Kentish family, who made Norbury their residence, and held it through a long course of years.

"*Aug.* 27, 1655.—I went to Box-hill to see those rare natural bowers, cabinets, and shady walkes in the box copses : hence we walk'd to Mickleham, and saw Sir F. Stidolph's seate environ'd with elme-trees and walnuts innumerable, and of which last he told us they receiv'd a considerable revenue. Here are such goodly walkes and hills shaded with yew and box as render the place extreamely agreeable, it seeming from these evergreens to be summer all the winter." *

The Stydolfs died out, and the property passed through various hands, till in 1766 it was bought by one Anthony Chapman, who, true to his name, cut down the "walnut trees innumerable," and converted as much of the other timber as he could venture into cash. When he had exhausted its availabilities, he sold the estate, 1774, to William Lock, a man of very different stamp, the friend of many of the most distinguished men of his time, an excellent scholar and a man of refined taste, who did his best to improve the property. The old house, which stood on low ground by the public road, having become ruinous, Mr. Lock pulled it down, and built a new one on the crest of the opposite hill, the principal rooms thus

commanding one of the richest prospects in a district famous for fine views. The house was in the coldly classic taste of the day, but it contained some good rooms ; one, the Saloon, became celebrated from the novelty of its decoration. It is a room 20 ft. by 23, and was intended to represent a bower enclosed by vine-covered trelliswork. The sides of the room are divided by pilasters which appear to support the trellised roof, through an opening in the centre of which is seen the evening sky. The windows of the south side of the room frame the real scenery of the Vale looking towards Box Hill and over Dorking. On the other sides are landscapes—compositions from the Cumberland lakes—reaching the whole height of the room. The idea was carried out with great care and thoroughness. Intended for a dining-room, the artificial landscapes are all lit by the same early evening sun as in the summer or early autumn the natural landscape would be at the dinner hour. And to assist the effect, the lawns and slopes before the window were planted and arranged to form a pictorial foreground to the natural scene. The landscapes were painted by Barrett (Wilson's more prosperous rival), but Cipriani painted the groups of men in them, and Gilpin the cattle ; while the ceiling, sky, and triallage, with the climbing vines and clustering grapes and honeysuckles, were painted by Pastorini.* Many changes have been made in the house, but happily this saloon, in which Lock often entertained a distinguished circle, has been preserved intact. Lock was himself a man of superior taste and culture, and a warm friend of artists and literary men. The "ingenious critic," whom Johnson cites in his Life of Milton, is, says Boswell, "(as he told Mr. Seward) Mr. Lock of Norbury Park, in Surrey, whose knowledge and taste in the fine arts is universally acknowledged."† And Fuseli's biographer records that "for his taste and critical judgment in the fine arts as well as for the power which he displays in historical painting, . . . Fuseli considered that Mr. W. Lock ranked as high, or higher than any historic painter in England. The society at the house of

---

* Evelyn, Diary.

* William Gilpin, Observations on the Western Part of England ; Brayley, Hist. of Surrey.
† Life of Johnson, vol. viii., p. 11.

Mr. Lock was well chosen and very select; and here he occasionally met Sir Joshua Reynolds and Dr. Moore, the author of Zeluco;"* and Sir Thomas Lawrence, a favourite guest of Norbury—where he made his only effort at modelling on a bust of his host—speaks of Mr. Lock, in his letters, in a like laudatory style. Besides English artists and writers and men of mark, the emigrants who had settled at Mickleham, Talleyrand, Madame de Staël, the Duc de Montmorency, and other notable personages, were welcome guests. It was at Lock's dinner-table in this room that Fanny Burney met and was fascinated by M. D'Arblay; and when her father refused his assent to the marriage, Mr. Lock gave her away at Mickleham ch., provided them a cottage close at hand, and after infinite pains succeeded in soothing the angry father and bringing about a reconciliation. In return, Madame D'Arblay's next book, 'Camilla,' written at Lock's instigation, paints the personages and scenery of Norbury and its neighbourhood—not however with any marked vigour or vraisemblance. After the decease of the younger Mr. Lock, Norbury was sold in 1819 to Mr. F. Robinson, who two years after sold it to Mr. W. Fuller Maitland, and he in 1824 exchanged it with Mr. H. P. Sperling for Park Place, Berkshire. In 1848 the estate was purchased by Mr. Thos. Grissell, the builder, who, with the assistance of Messrs. Banks and Barry as architects, greatly enlarged and improved the house (and abridged the public access to the park), and made it his residence till his death in 1874. It is now in the hands of his trustees. The Park, of about 300 acres, is greatly diversified in surface, richly timbered, and yields many charming prospects. More than a century has passed since the Chapman disposed of its walnut trees, and their place has not been adequately supplied. But there are splendid beeches and very respectable oaks, elms, and chesnuts, whilst on the steep slope of a hill is an almost unrivalled grove of yew trees, of magnificent proportions, unknown antiquity, and most fantastic growth—the chief pride of Norbury, where it is known as the Druids' Grove, the larger or more remarkable trees being distinguished as The

King of the Grove, The Horse and his Rider, and the like.

Juniper Hall (F. Richardson, Esq.), S. of Mickleham, and at the foot of Juniper Hill, was, at the end of the 18th cent. the home of a remarkable cluster of French emigrants. Talleyrand, Greville notes, "has gone to live at Juniper Hill with Madame de Staël."* But there lived also Madame de Broglie, the Comte de Narbonne, the Duc de Montmorency, M. Sicard, Fanny Burney's M. D'Arblay, and several more, for whom the hospitable gates of Norbury were always open.

Fredley Farm was the "cottage-home" of Richard Sharp, the 'Conversation Sharp' of the best society of the early part of the 19th cent.; and here, as he himself has recorded in verse and prose,† and as the memoirs and letters of his contemporaries corroborate, he had as guests Grattan, Mackintosh (who writes with great warmth of 'The Happy Valley,' as he proposes Mickleham shall be named), Romilly, Leonard Horner, Samuel Rogers, the elder Mill, and others of equal celebrity. *Fredley* has, since Sharp's tenancy, been wholly remodelled, and the *farm* sunk. *Mickleham Hall* (G. Wyatt Clarke, Esq.) was built by Sir C. H. Talbot about 1785. It was for a time in the occupation of Lord Albert Conyngham. *Birch Grove*, on Mickleham Down, is the finely placed seat of Winthorp Mackworth Praed, Esq.

Camilla Lacy (J. L. Wylie, Esq.) was built by Mr. William Lock on a pretty spot S. of Norbury Park, for Madame D'Arblay, partly out of the profits of 'Camilla,' whence the name : and here she wrote, "I bury all disquietudes in present enjoyment; an enjoyment more fitted to my secret mind than any I had ever hoped to attain. . . . The serenity of a life like this smoothes the whole internal surface of the mind."‡ Madame D'Arblay, with her husband, quitted Camilla Lacy for France in 1802. The house has since been greatly altered. Other inhabitants of Mickleham of more or less note have been William Guthrie, one of the most popular and one of the most voluminous compilers of the 18th cent., but entirely forgotten in

---

* Knowles, Life and Writings of Henry Fuseli, R.A., vol. i., p. 60.

* Greville, Journal, vol. ii., p. 346.
† Sharp, Letters and Essays in Prose and Verse, p. 248, etc.
‡ Diary and Letters of Madame D'Arblay, vol. ii., p. 322.

the 19th; Samuel Weller Singer, the editor of Spence's Anecdotes and Cavendish's Life of Wolsey, and the author of a History of Playing Cards; Akenside's friend, Jeremiah Dyson, Clerk of the House of Commons, and M.P. for Horsham; Sir Lucas Pepys, the distinguished physician, the Marquis Wellesley, Prof. Daniell, the chemist, James Mill and John Stuart Mill, etc. Close to Burford Bridge is the pretty hamlet of *Westhamble.*

MILL HILL, MIDDX., a hamlet and eccl. dist. of Hendon, from which it is about 2 m. N. The Mill Hill Stat. of the Grt. N. Rly. (Edgware and Highgate line) is ¾ m. S.E. of the vill., that of the Midland Rly. 1¼ m. W. Pop. of the eccl. dist., 1335. Inn: *King's Head.*

The vill. is an irregular, disjointed collection of houses stretching for a mile along the summit of a hill away from any main line of road, and about mid-distance between Edgware and the Barnet road. From every clear spot wide views are obtained, and on all sides is a pleasant open green country. Mill Hill is consequently a favourite place of abode, and many good seats with large and well-stocked grounds occur, and fine large elms line both sides of the way, The *Church,* St. Paul, was begun by Wilberforce, then living at Highwood Hill, in 1829; but some difficulties occurred respecting its consecration, and that ceremony was not performed and the ch. opened till July 1836, a few days after its founder's death. Artistically it is but a sorry specimen of Early Gothic, but is neat and commodious inside, and has supplied a much-felt want.

The long, bald, semi-classic, white brick structure on the opposite side of the way is the *Mill Hill School,* a Congregationalist college on the model of the great public schools of the kingdom, with exhibitions to the universities. The school was founded in 1807, and the present building erected in 1825. The school stands on the site of Ridgeway House, and the once famous Botanic Garden formed by Peter Collinson (d. 1768), one of the ablest botanists of his time. Linnæus visited Collinson here, and planted some trees in his garden. An account of its rarer plants was printed for private circulation at the cost of Mr. Dillwyn, M.P. 'for

Swansea, under the title of ' Hortus Collinsonianus.' After Collinson's death the garden was continued by his brother till the site was purchased for the Congregational school. In the school grounds may still be seen two venerable, though somewhat dilapidated, cedars, which the Duke of Richmond sent to Collinson from Goodwood in 1751.

The large building on the rt. in ascending the hill from the Midland Rly. Stat. is the Roman Catholic Missionary College (' St. Joseph's College of the Sacred Heart for Foreign Missions'). The first stone of the building was laid by Abp. (Cardinal) Manning, in June 1869, and a portion was completed in 1871 : the architect was Mr. G. Goldie. It is a somewhat gloomy looking monastic structure, of stock brick varied with bands and dressings of red and black bricks; is Venetian-Gothic in style, and is built about a cloister court, or quadrangle surrounded by cloisters. The most noteworthy of the several sections is the chapel, which occupies one side of the court, has nave, aisles, side chapels, sanctuary, and semicircular apse, with ambulatory. Between the apse and cloister is a square campanile, 100 ft. high, surmounted by a gilded statue of St. Joseph, which forms a conspicuous object for miles around. The college is intended for 60 students, and has at present about half that number in residence : they are under vows to proceed, on the completion of their educational course, to any station to which they may be sent, and remain among the heathen for life. The grounds are about 40 acres in extent.

Two other Roman Catholic institutions have their homes at Mill Hill : the St. Mary's Franciscan Nunnery, and the St. Margaret's Industrial School, at the N. end of the vill., and not far from the grounds of the Missionary College.

Littleberries (J. F. Pawson, Esq.) is a good old brick mansion, which tradition says was built by Charles II. *Frith Manor House* (M. S. Davidson, Esq.), ½ m. E. of the vill., belonged with the manor to Westminster Abbey; was assigned to the short-lived bishopric of Westminster, and afterwards passed into private hands. The present house is modern. Other seats are, *Bittacy* (H. Eley, Esq.); *Miles Down House* (F. W. Field. Esq.); *Belmont* (J. Macandrew, Esq.), etc.

Highwood Hill adjoins the N. end of Mill Hill, and extends E. to Totteridge, Herts. It is higher, more secluded, and more picturesque than either. At *Highwood House* (Geo. Locket, Esq.), Sir Stamford Raffles, Governor of Java and Bencoolen, founder of the settlement of Singapore, and founder and first president of the Zoological Society, spent the last year or so of his too short life. "A happy retirement," he calls it; a "house small but compact," grounds well laid out and 112 acres in grass, so that he will have abundant occupation; and for society, "Wilberforce takes possession to-morrow" (June 16, 1826,) of the next house, "so that we are to be next-door neighbours and divide the hill between us."* Their neighbourship was brief: Raffles died at Highwood, July 5, 1826. Lady Raffles continued to reside here for many years, and Bunsen makes frequent and admiring mention of his visits. In one of his letters he refers to the mineral spring within the grounds, "enclosed at the expense of Rachel, Lady Russell"; † and gives the tradition of the house respecting it :—

"A visit to Highwood gave an opportunity for commenting upon the dignity, the order, the quiet activity, the calm cheerfulness with which Lady Raffles rules the house, the day, the conversation ; and the place and its neighbourhood were full of those memorials of the honoured dead which served to enhance the natural beauty of the prospect and the interest attaching itself to the residence of Sir Stamford Raffles. The ground of Highwood must have been trodden by the footsteps and hallowed by the life and sorrows of Rachel Lady Russell, even though no family recollection exists to mark the spot which she inhabited. . . . But the beautiful portion of original wood in which Lady Raffles's friends have enjoyed walking with her, contains within its precincts a chalybeate spring, walled round, and marked by an inscription as having been enclosed by Mistress Rachel Russell, at a date when the eldest daughter of Lord and Lady Russell must have been under 12 years old : yet is there nothing unreasonable in the supposition that the mother should have caused the work to be performed as a public benefit (the healing quality of the spring being in repute among the poor), and assign to it the name of her daughter instead of her own. Moreover in that wood there is a spot evidently cleared of trees in a regular circle, from the centre of which it was remembered by the lower class of inhabitants, at the time when Sir Stamford Raffles made the purchase of the ground, that a previous proprietor, about the middle of the last

century, had caused the loose stones to be removed which had formed a 'monument to the memory of the gentleman who was beheaded.' This piece of forest might have been a portion of Lady Russell's own large Southampton inheritance : as an original Russell property it is gone out of remembrance."*

Wilberforce lived in the next house from 1826 to 1831, when, greatly to his regret, he was obliged to leave it. Other houses are *Ivor Hall* (I. E. B. Cox, Esq.), and *Moat Mount* (Serjt. E. W. Cox).

MIMMS, NORTH, HERTS (Dom. *Mimmine*), 3 m. S. of Hatfield, and about the same distance N. by W. from Potter's Bar Stat. of the Grt. N. Rly. ; pop. 1157.

Mimms Street is a pretty hamlet-like village at the S.E. corner of North Mimms Park, in which, ½ m. from the vill., is the ch. ; and there are several little collections of houses or hamlets at *Bell Bar*, by the 17 m.-stone on the Hatfield road ; *Welham Green*, a thoroughly rural hamlet, with a small green and pond, to the left of the Hatfield road ; *Marsh Moor*, a little N. of it ; *Roestock*, to the N.W. ; and *Swanley Bar* and *Little Heath*, on the S.E.

The manor of North Mimms was held by the Bp. of Chester in the reign of the Confessor and at the Dom. Survey, but not in right of his bishopric. It was shortly after alienated to Geoffrey de Magneville, who built the ch. and gave the tithes to the abbey he founded at Walden in Essex. On the failure of male heirs, the manor went to the Says ; and afterwards in the same way to the Fitzpiers. In the reign of Edward III. it belonged to Sir Robert Knolles, a distinguished commander in the French war. In the reign of Henry VIII. it passed by marriage to the Coningsbys ; then by sale to Sir Nicholas Hyde, whose granddaughter conveyed it by marriage to Peregrine Osborne, Baron Osborne, and afterwards Duke of Leeds. It was purchased about 1800 by Henry Brown ; and is now the property and seat of Coningsby Sibthorpe, Esq.

North Mimms Park is large (over 1100 acres), varied in surface, well wooded, and watered by a feeder of the Colne. The house is a spacious and characteristic Jacobean mansion, red brick, with stone

---

* Letters in Lady Raffles' Memoir of the Life of Sir T. S. Raffles, 4to, 1830.

† Lysons, vol. ii., p. 398.

* Baroness Bunsen, A Memoir of Baron Bunsen, vol. i., p. 532.

quoins and dressings, good chimney stacks, and many gables. From the park there is a pleasant way to South Mimms, through Mimms Wood, carpeted in the spring with innumerable blue-bells.

Potterells, the adjacent demesne, is a sub-manor, without any history of interest, but has a pleasant park and good house, the property and seat of W. Cotton Curtis, Esq.

Brookmans is a sub-manor, so named from a family by whom it was held in the reign of Henry IV. It passed in that of Henry VI. to the Fortescues. In 1639 it was purchased by Paul Pindar, Esq., of London; on the death of whose son, Sir Paul Pindar, it went to his daughter, who married Sir Wm. Dudley, and was sold by them in 1666 to Andrew Fountaine, who " built a very fair house upon this manor in the year 1682,"* and in 1701 sold it to John Lord Somers, Baron of Evesham—the great Whig Lord Chancellor and minister. Somers, when disengaged from public affairs, spent much of his time at Brookmans, occupied in literary and antiquarian pursuits, and especially in the formation and arrangement of his choice collections of rare books, historical pamphlets, prints, and medals ; and here he died, April 26, 1716. Somers was never married, and he bequeathed Brookmans to a sister, the wife of Sir Joseph Jekyll, Master of the Rolls, cursorily commemorated by Pope—

"A joke on Jekyll or some odd Old Whig
  Who never changed his principle or wig."†

Jekyll died at Brookmans in 1738, and on the death of his widow, in 1745, the estate descended to her nephew, John Cocks, in whose family it remained till 1784, when it was sold to Alexander Higginson, of London. It was purchased in 1786 (after having passed through the hands of Dr. Humphrey Sibthorpe) by S. R. Gaussen, Esq., and is now the property and seat of his grandson, R. W. Gaussen, Esq.

Brookmans is a large and stately structure, whence, as when old Chauncy wrote, " you have a pleasant prospect from the front thereof towards the east over Essex, and from the back thereof toward the west into Bedfordshire." The park, of 500

* Chauncy, Hertfordshire, vol. ii., p. 441.
† Epilogue to the Satires, Dialogue i.

acres (the estate has 3600, or about three-fourths of the parish), is rich in trees, water, and views. Near the house are extensive private grounds, a pinetum, and gardens, famed for exotic trees, shrubs, and flowers ; and a long avenue leading to the lodge at the London end of the park.

Gobions (locally Gubbins), a sub-manor lying immediately S. of Brookmans, so called from its early owners, was in the reign of Henry VII. " parcel of the ancient revenue " of Sir John More, one of the Justices of the Court of Queen's Bench, and father of Sir Thomas More, who it may be remembered, when Lord Chancellor, never failed, if, in passing through Westminster Hall to his seat in Chancery, he saw his father sitting in court, to fall on his knees and ask his blessing. Sir Thomas, when the estate came to him, lived at Gobions with his house full of his family, including not only children and grandchildren, but his father's widow, relatives, friends, dependants, books, perhaps, too, the " strange birds and beasts " he loved and " kept, an ape, a fox, a weasel, and a ferret," as he did in his house at Chelsea. His ownership of Gobions was but short. After his execution, the king took the manor, and though subsequently Sir Thomas More's son was restored to his honours, he only recovered this estate, of which a lease had been granted for the life of Elizabeth, in reversion. On the death of Elizabeth it was obtained by Cresacre More, and it remained the property of a More till sold by Basil More in the reign of Charles II. to Sir Edw. Desbovery. In 1697 it was sold to one Pitchcraft, packer, of London, who transferred it to Sir Jeremy Sambrooke (who was an active county magistrate, and erected the obelisk in commemoration of the Battle of Barnet, noticed under BARNET and HADLEY). From the Sambrookes it passed in succession to Freeman, Hunter, Holmes, and Kemble, and now belongs to Mr. Gaussen. More's house was pulled down by Mr. Gaussen shortly after he purchased the estate, and the park incorporated with Brookmans. Of the house not a vestige remains, and only a few traces of the once famous gardens.

The *Gateway* (worth seeing) now serves as the S. or London entrance to Brookmans Park. It is of red brick, perhaps as old as the great Chancellor; an arch between square battlemented towers of three stages, a picturesque structure, and remarkable for the very unusual altitude of the arch. By it is a good old brick lodge, and an avenue a mile long leads from it to Brookmans.

Peacham, author of 'The Complete Gentleman,' a well-known work of the early part of the 17th cent., himself a native of North Mimms, tells us that Sir Thomas More wrote his Utopia at Gobions, and Heywood his Epigrams at North Mimms—though More says the Utopia was written in the scraps of time he could steal from his meals and sleep in the midst of many and heavy occupations.*

"Merry John Heywood wrote his Epigrams, as also Sir Thomas More his Utopia, in the parish wherein I was born (North Mims in Hartfordshire near to St. Albans); where either of them dwelt and had fair possessions." †

"To its literary honours I may add that there in all probability Cresacre More composed the account of the life of his great grandfather. North Mimms I am sorry to say has not been careful to preserve the memory of her distingushed inhabitants. On enquiry lately made by a friend residing near that place, it was discovered that there were no memorials of the Mores in the church, and that all the early registers are lost." ‡

The *Church* (St. Mary) stands in North Mimms Park, and near it are 3 magnificent elms. It is of flint and stone, and is said to have been built by Sir Hugh de Magneville, in the reign of Stephen, but the body of the church is much later, and it has been recently restored. It consists of nave, aisles, and chancel, an embattled W. tower, with a thin leaded spire, and a porch of flint and stone at the S.W. In the tower are six bells. The W. door has an E.E. moulding with bell-flower ornaments, and oak leaves on the capitals—weather-worn, but good. The E. and W. windows have flowing Perp. tracery. The *int.* is neat, and has well-proportioned nave arcades. The E. and W. and one or two of the other windows are filled with painted glass. *Monts.*—N. of chancel, figure of Justice holding the scales and a roll of paper, seated on a sarcophagus of black marble, marking the grave of Lord

* Letter to Peter Giles, prefixed to the Utopia.
† Peacham, Compleat Gentleman, ed. 1661, p. 95.
‡ Joseph Hunter, Preface to Cresacre More's Life of Thomas More, p. lvi.

Chancellor Somers, "who lived at Brookmans Park," 1716. The mont. was erected by his sister, Dame Elizabeth Jekyll. On the N. wall of nave a small half-length effigy of George Jarvis, d. 1718. *Brasses.*—In chancel, on an altar tomb, mutilated effigies of Sir Robert Knolles, d. 14—, and wife Elizabeth, d. 1458. Effigy of a knight in armour. Richard Butler and wife, no date. Effigy of Thomas Leucas, d. 1531. Small but unusually fine brass of a priest (no insc., but supposed to represent Wm. de Kesteven, vicar, d. 1361). It is apparently Flemish, and resembles in style that of Abbot de la Mare at St. Albans. He is vested in chasuble and stole, has a chalice on his breast, and over him is a rich canopy, with, on the dexter side, St. Peter, and underneath SS. John the Evangelist and Bartholomew, and in corresponding places on the sinister, SS. Paul, James the Great, and Andrew, with their respective emblems. Above is the Almighty holding the soul of the deceased; at the sides are two angels swinging censers.

MIMMS, SOUTH, MIDDX., so called to distinguish it from North Mimms, Herts, on the St. Albans road, 14½ m. from London, 3½ m. N.N.W. from Barnet, and about 2 m. W. from the Potters Bar Stat. of the Grt. N. Rly. Pop. of the par., 3571, but this runs into Barnet town, and includes the eccl. dists. of Barnet Christ Church, 1598, and Potters Bar, 1198; South Mimms proper had 775 inhab. in 1871. Inns: *White Hart; Black Horse.*

South Mimms is a pretty little vill. standing on high ground (421 ft. above the Ordnance datum) about the junction of several roads. The *Church* (St. Giles) is near the N. end of the vill., close to the White Hart inn. It is an interesting and picturesque building of flint and stone (the S. side covered with stucco), and consists of nave and N. aisle, chancel, W. tower, and porch at the S.W. The tower, tall, massive, with buttresses and good angle turret, and partly covered with ivy, is much above the average of village ch. towers. In it is a peal of 6 bells. The ch. is Early Perp. with flowing tracery, except the N. aisle, which is of brick, rebuilt in 1526. The *int.* is pleasing, but without any marked feature, except that the E. end of the N. aisle is shut off by a carved oak parclose, and forms the Frowyk Chantry (founded and endowed, 1448, by Thomas Frowyk and his wife Elizabeth). The chancel was newly paved and decorated at the restoration of the ch. in 1868. Some of the pews are old and well-carved: obs. those N.E. of the nave. In the windows of the N. aisle are some fragments of painted glass of the date and no doubt part of the original decoration of the rebuilt aisle. *Monts.*—On N. of chancel, an altar tomb with fan-groined canopy, supported on 4 twisted Renaissance columns; without arms or insc. except the initials R. H. In the Frowyk Chantry, a tomb with recumbent effigy of a knight in armour, under a rich open canopy; on shields are the arms of the Frowyks, but no insc. or date. There are two or three brasses, with mutilated effigies or inscriptions of members of the Frowyk family; and on the S. wall of the nave is a tablet with a small figure of a skull within a niche, and the insc.—

"Looke on, why turn awaye thyne eyne
This is no stranger's face, the phesnamy is thyne."

By the ch.-yard, facing the street, is a neat row of almshouses for 6 widows, founded by Jas. Hickson, 1687, at Dancer's Hill, but recently removed here by the Brewers' Company, who are trustees of the charity. There are other almshouses in the parish.

Wrotham Park, the seat of the Earl of Strafford, at the S. end of the par., between the Hatfield and St. Albans roads, immediately beyond the obelisk at Monken Hadley, was built from the designs of Ware, for Admiral Byng, about 1754—only 3 or 4 years before his execution. It has since been the chief seat of the Byng family. The name was given to it from the ancient seat of the family, Wrotham in Kent. The house is a spacious, stately, semi-classic structure of the style which prevailed towards the middle of the last century, and consists of a centre and wings, with recessed tetrastyle portico, and a pediment level with the second storey, in the tympanum of which are the Byng arms, etc. Along the summit is a balustrade. The park, of about 250 acres, is fairly timbered. There is a public foot-path across it from Ganwick Corner.

Dyrham (or *Derham*) *Park* (Captain F. Trotter) ½ m. W. of Wrotham Park, and nearly 2 m. S.W. of South Mimms

ch., derived its name from the Derham family, its owners in the early part of the 14th cent., when by marriage it was transferred to Thomas Frowyk, in whose descendants it continued till the end of the 15th cent. It afterwards belonged to the Laceys and Austens; was then sold to the Earl and Countess of Albemarle; in 1773 was sold to Christopher Bethell, and in 1798 to John Trotter, Esq., the founder of the Soho Bazaar. The mansion is large and good; the park of 170 acres, pleasant and well timbered. The entrance gate by the St. Albans road—a tall central arch between Tuscan columns, with entablature and floral scrolls, surmounted with a large vase, and flanked by small lodges—is the triumphal arch erected in London by General Monk for the entry of Charles II. in 1660.

MITCHAM, Surrey (Dom. *Michelham*), 2 m. S.W. of Tooting, 9 m. from Westminster Bridge, and a Stat. on the L., Br., and S. C. Rly. (Croydon and Wimbledon line); pop. 6498, of whom 453 were in the Holborn Union Industrial Schools.

The par., locally divided by Wykford Lane into Upper and Lower Mitcham, extends from Merton to Beddington, Carshalton, and Croydon. The houses are scattered, but mostly lie along the road from Tooting to Sutton, by the river Wandle, and about Mitcham Common. The soil is rich black mould, and for more than a century Mitcham has been famed for its gardens of sweet-herbs, and flowers. Roses, lavender, and peppermint are grown here in immense quantities for distilling for the perfumer; and liquorice, aniseed, poppies, mint, chamomiles, and other medicinal plants cover hundreds of acres, and perfume the air for a considerable distance. But outside, and fringing these fragrant fields, are many far from fragrant factories, notably snuff, tobacco, and various other mills by the Wandle, japan and varnish manufactories in Lower Mitcham and about Merton Lane, floor-cloth, felt, and telegraph works, tanneries, etc. On the E. of the vill. stretches the broad breezy *Mitcham Common*, of 480 acres, broken northwards towards the Reigate road by low hills and trees, and everywhere pleasant.

Famed of old for "good air and choice company," Mitcham was early a favourite place of residence. Sir Walter Raleigh had a house here, in right of his wife, Elizabeth Throckmorton, assigned her probably as a marriage portion, the Throckmorton-Carews being at that time the owners of the three Mitcham manors, Mitcham (or Canons), Ravensbury, and Bigging and Tamworth. Raleigh sold the property, on his release from the Tower, 1615, to aid in providing funds for his expedition to Guiana. The mansion, which stood at the corner of Wykford Lane, after having long served as a boarding-school, was taken down some years back. Sir Julius Cæsar, Master of the Rolls, owned a house here, through his wife, the widow of a Mr. Dens, and in it, after several disappointments, had the costly honour of entertaining Queen Elizabeth.

"On Tuesday, Sept. 12, 1598, the Queen visited my house at Mitcham, and supped and lodged there, and dined there the next day. I presented her with a gown of cloth of silver richly embroidered ; a black net-work mantle with pure gold ; a taffeta hat, white, with several flowers, and a jewel of gold set therein with rubies and diamonds. Her Majesty removed from my house after dinner the 13th of Sept. to Nonsuch, with exceeding good contentment ; which Entertainment of her Majesty with the charges of five former disappointments, amounted to £700 sterling, besides mine own provisions, and whatever was sent unto me by my friends." *

Donne the poet, before he took orders, lived for two years at Mitcham in poverty and ill-health. One of his letters is dated "from my hospital at Mitcham ;" and in it he says, "there is not one person besides myself in my house well. . . . I flatter myself in this that I am dying too." At Mitcham lived Moses Mendez (d. 1758), a poor poet, but "possessed of an hundred thousand pounds." Mitcham Grove, on the rt. of the road going towards Sutton, was bought by Lord Clive, and given to Alexander Wedderburn (afterwards Lord Chancellor Loughborough) for his defence of his lordship in the House of Commons. Lord Loughborough sold it in 1789 to Henry Hoare, Esq. (the banker of Fleet Street), and he to Sir J. W. Lubbock.† A greater Lord Chancellor,

and worthier man, must have owned a house here (though there is no evidence he lived in it), as Thomas Elrington, Esq., by his will, bearing date 1523, bequeathed to Alice his wife "his chief house at Mitcham, which was given to him by Sir Thomas More." *

The old *Church* (St. Peter and St. Paul), a dilapidated fabric of flint and stone, was taken down in 1820, and a new ch. erected on its site, the base of the old tower being retained. The new ch., consecrated Aug. 1822, is of brick and cement, in the baldest style of the revived Gothic. Inside are some *monts.* from the old ch., but none of interest. One in the N. aisle to Mrs. Eliz. Tait (d. 1821), has a female figure in relief by Westmacott. Outside, under the W. window, is a mont. to Alderman Sir Ambrose Crowley, d. 1713, the Sir Humphrey Greenhat of the Tatler (No. 73), who, in order to check bribery at elections, promised, as an acknowledgment for their favour, a chaldron of good coals gratis to every elector of Queenhithe who engaged to poll for him. In the ch.-yard is the tomb of Mrs. Anne Hallam (d. 1740), an actress famous as Lady Macbeth and Lady Touchwood.

Christ Church, Merton Lane, is a new district ch., with parsonage and mission-house adjoining, Gothic, of brick and stone, erected by Messrs. Francis, in 1874, at the cost of Mr. W. J. Harris, of Corringe Park. Dissenting and Roman Catholic chapels, and national and board schools, are numerous. On Lower Mitcham Green is a neat range of Gothic almshouses, designed by Buckler, and erected and endowed in 1829 by Miss Tate, for 12 poor unmarried women above 55 years of age.

MOLESEY, EAST, Surrey,

at the confluence of the Mole with the Thames, opposite Hampton Court, with which it is united by an iron girder bridge (*see* HAMPTON COURT), 13 m. from London: pop. 2409. The Hampton Court Stat. of the L. and S.W. Rly. is at East Molesey, near the foot of the bridge. Inns : the *Bell*, a good house with garden and bowling-green ; *Prince of Wales Hotel* ; *New Inn* ; *Albion*.

* MS. of Sir Julius Cæsar, in Brit. Mus., quoted by Nichols, Progresses of Q. Elizabeth, vol. iii., pp. 68 and 429 n.
† Lysons, Brayley.

* Lysons, vol. i., p. 258.

In the Dom. Survey, East and West Molesey are both included under *Molesham*, the home or town by the Mole; as Molesey—Mole, and *ey*, an island—seems to indicate that the Mole here formed an island, by dividing, before joining the Thames, as it still does somewhat higher up. The form *Moulsey*, still often used, is a modern and foolish corruption of the old spelling, and ought to be definitely abandoned.

The manor of East Molesey was given by Henry I. towards the endowment of Merton Priory, whence it came to be known as Molesey Prior. In 1536 Henry VIII. obtained East Molesey by exchange from the prior of Merton, in order to incorporate it with his newly formed chase of Hampton Court. A lease of the manor, held by Sir Thomas Heneage, was at the same time renewed; the reversion was in 1571 granted by Q. Elizabeth to Anthony Crane. Subsequently leases were granted to various persons till 1775, from which date the lease has always been granted to the holder of the manor of West Molesey. It is now held by the Rev. H. Hotham.

The vill. extends in a rambling way for some distance about the level meadows on the l. bank of the Mole, a large increase having of late years taken place at the N. end towards the Thames and about the rly. stat., mostly of small houses, and known as *Kent Town*. The whole district is flat, but there are many pretty little bits of Dutch river scenery about the different branches of the Mole, and lanes with the water flowing across the road. At the mouth of the Mole is a large but not picturesque water and steam flour and saw mill.

The *Church* (St. Mary), near the centre of the vill., a mean building, was damaged by fire in 1863, taken down, and a new church, designed by Mr. Talbot Bury, erected on the site, and consecrated Oct. 17, 1865. It is of flint and stone, late E.E. in style, with some plate tracery in the windows, and consists of nave and aisles, with gabled windows and chancel. A tower at the N.W., with slated spire. was added in 1867. The *int.* is neat, carefully finished; has open seats throughout; the chancel windows are filled with painted glass, the E. window having a representation of the Ascension, by Heaton and Butler; the others, the Good Shepherd, St. John, and St. Peter, by Lavers and Barraud; a good new stone pulpit, and an old font restored. A brass from the old ch. to Anthonie Standen, "cupbearer to the King of Scotland, sometime Lord Darley, father to King James, now of England, and also sworne servant to his Majestie," d. 1611. In Kent Town, the new part of the vill., nearer the stat., is a district ch., St. Paul's, erected in 1856. From the bridge-foot and river-side between East Molesey and Molesey Hurst, the best general views are obtained of Hampton Court.

The private ("call it as you please *pilgrim* or *vagabond*") press at which the celebrated Martin Marprelate pamphlets were printed, was first set up at Molesey, whence, on its locality appearing to be suspected, it commenced its wanderings by a removal to Fawsley, Northamptonshire.[*]

MOLESEY, WEST, SURREY, ¾ m. W. of East Molesey, and 1½ m. W. of the Hampton Court Stat. of the L. and S.W. Rly.: pop. 563.

West Molesey is a small straggling village of poor houses, with a few of a better grade, lying along the Walton road some way inland from the Thames. The country is pleasant but flat; and there are two or three mansions with good old elms and oaks in the grounds.

The *Church*, rebuilt, except the tower, in 1843, is of brick, a poor specimen of the Gothic (Perp.) of its time. The N. aisle was added in 1860. The tower at the W. is of flint and stone, partially restored. The windows are filled with painted glass. The font, from the old ch., is Perp., octagonal, with quatrefoils in the panels. In the ch.-yard is the tomb of the Right Hon. J. Wilson Croker, who lived for many years at Molesey Grove.

Among the old tree-embowered mansions and pleasant villas that here stud the Thames or overlook the Mole, are APPS COURT (Mrs. Gill), noticed under that heading; *Molesey Grove*, already mentioned as the residence of Mr. Croker, now the seat of Sir Robert Walpole;

---

[*] Fuller, Church History, book ix., cent. 16; Neale, Hist. of the Puritans, vol. i., chap. viii.

Mole Lodge (Alderman Sir R. W. Carden); *The Grange* (A. J. R. Stewart, Esq.)

The long level meadow by the Thames between East and West Molesey, and opposite Hampton ch. and vill., to which there is a ferry, is *Molesey Hurst*, of old notorious for duels and prize-fights, now devoted to the scarcely more reputable meetings of the Hampton Races.

"Breakfasted at Mr. Maule's very early, and went along with him and the Bailie to see the great fight betwixt Belcher and Cribb at Moseley Hurst near Hampton. The day was very fine, and we had a charming drive out in our coach-and-four, and beat all the coaches and chaises by the way. We had three hard runs with one post-chaise and four very fine horses before we could pass it, and drove buggies, horsemen, and all off the road into lanes and doors of houses &c. this last run. . . . . At length got to the scene of action, which is on the Thames, about 2 or 3 miles above Richmond. Hampton Court is a little way farther down the river. We crossed the Thames to get to the field of battle on the Surrey side. . . . . Moseley Hurst ꞇthe most beautiful meadow I almost ever saw, hard and smooth as velvet, and of a great extent. . . . . We had fully 10,000 I suppose present as it was, and many hundreds of carriages, horses, carts, &c. Among the gentlemen present were the Duke of Kent, Mr. Wyndham, Lord Archibald Hamilton (a famous hand I am told), Lord Kinnaird, Mr. T. Sheridan, &c. &c. and all the fighting men in town of course : the Game Chicken, Woods, Tring, Pitloon &c. Captain Barclay of Urie received us and put us across the river in a boat, and he followed with Cribb, whom he backed at all hands. . . . . The Hon. Barclay [Berkeley] Craven was judge. . . . . Odds at setting-to 5 and 6 to 4 in favour of Belcher." But after a long fight Belcher " was at length obliged to give in. Poor fellow ! " *

MONKEN HADLEY, Middx. (*see* Hadley).

MOOR PARK, Herts (*see* Rickmansworth).

MORDEN, or MORDON, Surrey

(*Dom. Mordone*), 1 m. S.W. from Mitcham, and about the same distance from the Morden Stat. of the L., Br., and S. C. Rly. (Croydon and Wimbledon line), 10 m. from London : pop. 787. Inns : *Crown; George.*

The manor was confirmed by Edward the Confessor to the Abbey of Westminster, and remained its property till the Dissolution. In 1553 it was granted by Edward VI. to Ducket and Whitchurch,

who immediately transferred it to Richd. Garth, Esq., in whose descendants it has continued to ᵗhe present time, those to whom it passed by default of heirs male assuming the name of Garth. The present lord of the manor is Sir Richard Garth, Q.C. The old manor-house, Morden Hall, 1 m. from the ch., is now a farm-house.

The pursuits are chiefly agricultural, and much of the land is in grass. There are brick-fields at Lower Morden, and snuff-mills on the Wandle. The *Church* (St. Lawrence) is a long narrow brick building, the nave and chancel of the same height, erected in 1636. The tower at the W., of flint, low and embattled, belonged to the older ch., as apparently did also the Dec. tracery in the windows. The E. window is filled with painted glass. On the walls are numerous tablets to Garths, Hoares, Meyricks, and other local magnates; also a late brass of a priest, Wm. Booth, rector of this ch.

Morden Park, the seat of Major-Gen. Sir William Erskine Baker, K.C.B., is a spacious mansion seated on an eminence in a pleasant park N.W. of the ch. Other seats are : *Ravensbury Park* (G. P. Bidder, Esq.); *Morden Lane* (Gen. W. C. Hadden); and the *Lodge* (Sir Richard Garth, Q.C.)

MORDEN COLLEGE, Kent (*see* Blackheath).

MORETON, Essex, a small

agric. vill., in a pretty neighbourhood,—quiet, rustic, and abounding in trees,—something over 3 m. N. by W. from Ongar, along a crooked country lane : pop. 484.

The little *Church* (St. Mary the Virgin), which stands by a farm-house beyond the vill., consists of a nave (Perp.), and chancel (E.E.), with a modern red brick tower and shingled spire (in which are 5 bells) at the W., and a wooden porch on the S.W. The *int.*, plain, and without tomb or mont., was restored, the nave in 1865, the chancel in 1868 : architect, Mr. Chancellor, of Chelmsford. The very pretty decoration of the chancel was executed by Mr. Lea, of Lutterworth, from a pattern discovered on scraping the walls. Remains of mural paintings were discovered on removing the whitewash from the walls of the nave, but too much decayed to preserve, or even to make out the subjects. The lancet window, found under the plaster in the chancel gable, was opened, and with the others (two under this at the E., two on the N., and one on the S.) properly displayed. The ch. is worth a visit.

MORTLAKE, Surrey (Dom. *Mortlage*), on the Thames, immediately W. of Barnes, 2 m. E. of Richmond, 8 m. from Westminster Br., and a Stat. on the Richmond branch of the L. and S.W. Rly. : pop. 5119. Inns : *Mortlake Hotel; Ship ; Spur.*

Mortlake, of old a residence of the Abps. of Canterbury, was famous in the reign of Elizabeth as the abode of Dr. Dee ; in the reign of James I. and Charles I. for its tapestry works; in the 18th and early 19th centuries unrivalled for the growth of asparagus ; and now probably best known as the goal of the Universities Boat Race.

The manor belonged to the see of Canterbury before the Conquest, and, except during a brief usurpation by Bp. Odo, it remained its property till it was conveyed, along with Wimbledon, to Henry VIII. by Abp. Cranmer in exchange for other lands. The Manor-house served the Abps. for occasional residence and ceremonies. Anselm celebrated in it the Whitsuntide of 1099. In 1136 Abp. Corboyle lay ill in his house at Mortlake. Abp. Peckham died there in 1292 ; and Abp. Reynolds in 1327. When Abp. Mepham, or Meopham, was excommunicated by Pope John XXI. on account of a dispute with Grandison, Bp. of Exeter, he retired to his house at Mortlake, spent many days there in solitude, and died of grief shortly after, 1333. Nicholas Bubworth, keeper of the privy seal and lord treasurer to Henry IV., was consecrated Bp. of London, 1406, in the chapel of the manor-house. Warham was the last Abp. who resided at Mortlake, the manor being alienated by his successor. The house was afterwards known as the King's. The last notice Lysons found of it was in 1547, but Bray says it was standing in 1663. It was probably taken down shortly after.* The manor is now included in that of Wimbledon.

The vill. consists of a long narrow street of irregular houses, a few of the substantial old red-brick kind, but the greater part mean and flimsy ; the ch. on the l., near the centre of the street ; wharves, boat-houses, malt-kilns, and a large brewery by the river; a green, girt about with modern dwellings, beyond; and a lane lined with tenements, leading to the pretty hamlet of East Sheen.

Works for weaving pictorial tapestry were established here about 1619, by Sir Francis Crane, in imitation of the royal tapestry works of France, then in great repute. The king was interested in the enterprise, and gave Crane £2000 towards the cost of the buildings. At first the designs were obtained from abroad, but in 1623 the services were secured of Francis Cleyn or Klein (he signed his designs indifferently F. C. and F. K.), a native of Rostock, then in the service of the King of Denmark. James I. made him designer to the works at Mortlake, a free denizen of England, and settled on him " a certain annuitie of £100 by the year during his natural life." Cleyn was a ready and skilful designer, and Crane a judicious manager, and the works were remarkably successful. Many large and costly pieces were produced and eagerly purchased for the decoration of patrician halls. The Lord Keeper Williams paid Sir Francis Crane £2500 for the Four Seasons, in tapestry. At Knole are portraits of Crane and Vandyck in silk tapestry, as well as Vandyck's picture from which they were wrought. Charles I. was munificent in his patronage. While at Madrid in 1623 he directed £500 to be paid for a set of Mortlake tapestry, representing the Months, he had ordered to be made for him ; and directly after his accession to the throne he gave an acknowledgment of indebtedness to Sir Francis Crane "for three suits of gold tapestry for our use, £6000;" granted him an annuity of £1000 ; and further, an allowance of " £2000 yearly for the better maintenance of the said works of tapestries for ten years." Somewhat later the king gave to Crane and the Duchess-Dowager of Richmond the exclusive right for 17 years of making copper farthings—no doubt a profitable monopoly. Sir Francis

---

* Manning and Bray, Hist. and Antiq. of Surrey, vol. iii., p. 305 ; Brayley, Hist. of Surrey, vol. iii., p. 464 ; Lysons, Environs, vol. i., p. 266 ; Fuller Church History.

Crane died about 1635 ; his brother sold his interest in the works to the king, and the works were thenceforth known as the King's Works. It was in order to their being copied at Mortlake, that Charles I., at the suggestion of Rubens, purchased the Cartoons of Raphael, long the glory of Hampton Court, and now of Kensington. There is a warrant dated Dec. 3, 1639, to "Sir James Palmer Knt. Gov. of his Ma^{es} workes for making of Hangings at Mortlake," directing him "to sell unto the Earle of Holland 5 peeces of Hangings of the story of the Apostles being of the second sort, for the some of £886. 17. 6, being the price his Ma^{te} allowed for the same." Mortlake copies of the Cartoons are now scarce, but Mortlake tapestry is often met with. From contemporary references it must have been very popular.

"*Timothy.* Why Lady, do you think me
　　Wrought in a loom? Some Dutch piece weav'd
　　at Mortlake?" *

　　" Here some rare piece
Of Rubens or Vandyck presented is :
There a rich suit of *Moreclack*-Tapestry,
A bed of damask, or embroidery." †

During the civil war the Tapestry House was seized as royal property. In the Parliamentary Survey it is described as a building 115 ft. long and 84 ft. deep, having on the second floor one great working room 82 ft. long and 20 wide, wherein are 12 looms for making tapestry work of all sorts, and another room about half as long containing 6 looms, a great room called the limner's room, and on the third floor a long gallery divided into 3 rooms. Charles II. proposed to revive the manufacture, and invited Verrio to England to make the designs; but the king found other use for his money and other employment for the painter, and the tapestry works were left to their fate. Lysons ascertained that the tapestry house occupied the site of Queen's Head Court, and that the house " on the opposite side of the road, built by Charles I. for Francis Cleyn, was pulled down in or about the year 1794." In the Parliamentary Survey this house is called "the limmer's tenement," and valued at £9 per annum. By the ch. register it

* Jasper Mayne, The City Match, fol. 1639.
† Oldham, A Satyr in imitation of the Third of Juvenal, written in May 1682, Works, ed. 1703, p. 443.

appears that Cleyn had 5 children born at Mortlake. Less famous than the tapestry works, but also a manufactory of some note in its day, was that of Delft and earthenware, established here early in the 18th cent., and which finally died out early in the 19th.

The first *Church* at Mortlake was built in 1348, the mother-ch. being at Wimbledon. The present fabric appears from an insc. on the tower to have been erected in 1543 : has been many times altered, enlarged, and improved, the last time in 1860, and is now ugly and uninteresting. The only picturesque feature is the patched, battered, and ivy-clad tower. In it is a ring of 8 bells. Some of the *monts.* are of noticeable people. One is a tablet to Sir Philip Francis, d. 1818, the reputed author of Junius. Another is the white marble sarcophagus of the most commonplace of Prime Ministers, Henry Addington, Viscount Sidmouth, d. at the White Lodge, Richmond Park, in 1814 ; also of Ursula Viscountess Sidmouth, d. 1811, with alto-rilievo of the dying lady and her attendants, and a long prosaic rhyming epitaph. On S.E. wall a costly structure of coloured marbles, with effigies, of the Hon. Francis Coventry, 2nd son of the Lord Keeper Coventry, d. 1699. Alderman Sir John Barnard, d. 1764, Pope's lord-mayor :

" I never (to my sorrow I declare)
　Din'd with the Man of Ross, or my Lord
　　Mayor." *

Dr. Dee, the most famous of English astrologers, was buried in the chancel in 1608. On the N. wall near the chancel is a tablet to the Rev. Richard Byfield, d. 1664, rector of Long Ditton, and one of the Assembly of Divines. The font has Abp. Bourchier's arms on it—a cross engrailed between four water-bougets—and was probably given by him to the ch. The painting of the Entombment by G. Seghers was given to the ch. for an altar-piece by Benj. Vandergucht, the engraver and picture dealer (son of the more eminent Gerard V.), who had a country house at East Sheen : he was drowned by the upsetting of a boat in which he was crossing the Thames at Chiswick, 1794, and buried in Mortlake ch.

In the ch.-yard *obs.* the flat tombstone

* Pope, Epilogue to the Satires, Dial. ii.

with a Latin insc. to John Partridge, the astrologer, and author of the popular almanac named after him. Partridge and his almanac served as a target for the wit of Swift and Steele, the former of whom went so far as to foretell his death in 'Predictions for the year 1708,' in which, under the afterwards famous name of Isaac Bickerstaff, he announced that his first prediction "relates to Partridge the Almanac-maker. . . . I have consulted the star of his nativity by my own rules, and find he will infallibly die upon the 29th of March next, about 11 at night of a raging fever." When the night was passed Swift issued 'An Account of the Death of Mr. Partridge the Almanac-maker, upon the 29th inst.,' with full particulars of the time and manner of his decease. Afterwards Steele described in the Tatler (No. 99) the burial of this professor of physick and astrology "from Cordwainers on Tuesday the 29th instant ; " and Swift wrote an elegy on his death, and wound up with his epitaph :

"Here, five feet deep, lies on his back
A cobbler, star-monger, and quack," etc.

Partridge, taking the announcement seriously, issued an advertisement in which he assured the public that so far from being dead "blessed be God, John Partridge is still living and in health and all are knaves who report otherwise ; " and the others retorted by a 'Demonstration' of his death and burial. His actual burial took place in Mortlake ch.-yard in 1715, seven years after that announced by his persecutors. Tomb of Alderman Barber (d. 1740), who erected the bust in Westminster Abbey of Butler the author of Hudibras, and pilloried by Pope in a couplet intended for the scroll in Shakspeare's hand.

"Then Britain lov'd me and preserv'd my fame
Pure from a Barber's or a Benson's name."

Dr. Dee the astrologer lived in a house near the river-side, no longer standing. Here he was several times visited by Queen Elizabeth, and lived in very expensive style. Being obliged to quit England in 1583, the mob, who regarded him as a magician, broke into his house and, according to his own estimate, damaged his library to the value of £390 ; destroyed his chemical apparatus, which had cost him £200 ; broke a fine quadrant which cost him £20, and took away a magnet

for which he gave £33. Recalled to England by the Queen, he returned to Mortlake, was restored to favour, and received as compensation the promise of various offices, some of which, as the Chancellorship of St. Paul's, he obtained. In 1595 he was appointed Warden of Manchester, but after a long series of disputes with the fellows he returned to Mortlake in 1604. With James I. he was for a time in favour, but shortly fell into discredit, and his last days were passed in poverty, he being obliged to sell his library, as Lilly tells us, piecemeal for his sustenance. He died at Mortlake in 1608, aged 81, and was buried in the chancel of Mortlake ch., where Aubrey was shown an old marble stone as belonging to his tomb.*

"Dr. Dee dwelt in a house neere the water-side, a little westward from the church. The buildings which Sir Fr. Crane erected for working hangings . . . were built upon the ground whereon Dr. Dee's laboratory and other rooms for that use stood. Upon the west is a square court, and the next is the house wherein Dr. Dee dwelt, now [1673] inhabited by a Mr. Selbury, and farther west his garden." †

"1580. Sep. 17.—The Queene's Majestie came from Rychmond in her coach, the higher way to Mortlak felde, and when she came right against the church she turned down toward my house : and when she was against my garden in the felde she stode there a good while, and than cam ynto the street at the great gate of the felde, where she espyed me at my doore making obeysances to her Majestie : she beckoned her hand for me ; I cam to her coach side, she very speedily pulled off her glove and gave me her hand to kiss ; and, to be short, asked me to resort to her court, and to give her to wete when I cam ther." ‡

On another occasion (1575) she came with several of her nobility to see his library, but being told that his wife was lately dead would not enter the house, and Dee had to show her Majesty at the coach-door his glass, or 'black-stone,' about the properties of which she was curious, and which had earned for him the reputation of a magician. This stone was among the curiosities collected by Horace Walpole at Strawberry Hill. It is now in the collection formed by the late Lord Londesborough, and at present deposited in the Alexandra Palace.§

* Aubrey, Antiq. of Surrey, vol. i., p. 8 ; Lysons, vol. i., p. 274 ; Nichols, Progresses of Q. Elizabeth, vol. i., p. 416.
† MS. Ashmole, 1788, fol. 19 ; Diary of Dr. Dee, edited for Camden Soc. by J. O. Halliwell, p. 2.
‡ Dr. Dee's Diary, p. 6.
§ The story of the identification, loss, and reco-

Dee's son, Arthur, subsequently physician to the Emperor of Russia, and to Charles I. of England, was born at Mortlake in 1575, and when a boy acted as his father's *skryer* in discerning spirits, etc., by the black- or show-stone. Anthony Wood relates that when a child he frequently played with quoits of gold, which his father made at Prague by transmutation.

Phillips, the fellow-actor of Shakspeare, describes himself in his will as " Augustine Phillips of Mortlake in the county of Surrey, Gentleman," and directs his body to be " buried in the chancel of the parish church of Mortlake." He died in 1605, and was doubtless buried in the chancel ; but the register between 1603 and 1613 is unfortunately lost. One of his bequests is " a thirty-shilling piece in gold " to his " fellow " William Shakspeare : it is not unlikely that Shakspeare was a visitor to Mortlake in Phillips's day.

According to the local tradition, a house known as Cromwell House was the resi- dence of the great Protector ; it really belonged to his son Henry. It was the residence, in his later years, of Edward Colston, the eminent benefactor of Bristol, who died in it, Oct. 11, 1721. After various vicissitudes, the house was pulled down in 1858, and a new red-brick Tudor mansion, *Cromwell House* (J. Wigan, Esq.), built on the site. John Anstis, Garter-King-at- Arms, author of the ' Register of the Garter,' etc., died, March 1744, at his house at Mortlake.

MOTTINGHAM, KENT, an extra-

parochial hamlet of Eltham, from which it is 1 m. S. by W. ; the Eltham Stat. of the S.E. Rly. (Dartford line) is in Mot- tingham, about ¼ m. from the houses : pop. 475. Mottingham is a little but fast-growing place, with new houses springing up on every side, a temporary ch., and all the signs of suburban progress. The neighbourhood is, however, still open, verdant, and agreeable, and there are good grounds and old houses. *Mottingham House* (F. A. Schrœder, Esq.) marks the

very of "the Black-stone, with which Dr. Dee used to call his spirits" is told at length by H. Walpole in a letter to Sir Horace Mann, March 22, 1771, Letters, vol. v., p. 290. At the Strawberry Hill sale, it was bought by Mr. Smythe Pigott, and at the sale of his collection, Dec. 1853, it was pur- chased for Lord Londesborough.

site, and perhaps retains in part the fabric, of Mottingham Place, a stately mansion built by George Stoddard, Esq., in 1560 ; and *Fairey Hill* (Mrs. Hartley) char- mingly placed a little S. of the hamlet, was in the last cent. the seat of Earl Bathurst, when Lord Chancellor, and afterwards of General Morrison, etc.

" A strange and marvellous accident happened at this place, upon the 4th day of August, 1585, in a field which belongeth to Sir Percival Hart. Be- times in the morning, the ground began to sink, so much, that three great elm trees were suddenly swallowed into the pit, the tops falling downward into the hole : and before 10 of the clock, they were so overwhelmed, that no part of them might be discerned, the cave being suddenly filled with water : the compass of the hole was about 80 yards, and so profound, that a sounding line of 50 fathoms could hardly find or feel any bottom. Ten yards distant from that place there was another piece of ground sunk in like manner, near the highway, and so nigh a dwelling-house, that the inhabitants were greatly terrified therewith." [*]

Little appears to be known of it now : Lysons wrote of it 70 years ago, " The spot where this strange accident is said to have happened, is near the road leading to Fairey Hill ; it presents now only a slight inequality of surface, and is supposed to have been occasioned by the falling-in of what had at some remote period been a chalk-pit." [†]

MOULSEY, EAST, and WEST,
SURREY (*see* MOLESEY).

MUSWELL HILL, MIDDX., on

which stands the Alexandra Palace, about 1 m. W. by N. of Hornsey vill., and 1½ m. N. by E. of Highgate : Muswell Hill Stat., on the Alexandra Palace br. of the G. N. Rly., is 6 m. fr. King's Cross. The hamlet of Muswell Hill, with the addition of a detached portion of Clerkenwell, the priory estate noticed below, forms an eccl. dist. of Hornsey : pop. 1414 (Hornsey par. 1370 ; Clerkenwell, 44). Inns, *Green Man* at the summit, *Victoria* at the foot of the hill.

Muswell Hill is a mass of London clay, similar to the neighbouring hills of High- gate and Hampstead, but somewhat lower, and capped with glacial gravel and boulder clay—the S.E. edge of the North London glacial deposits noticed under

* Philipott, Villare Cantianum, 1659, p. 136.
† Lysons, Environs, vol. i., p. 492.

FINCHLEY. These beds contain fragments of chalk, clay, coal, and slate, and boulders of granite, sandstone and limestone, fossil shells, and other organic remains—"a strange heterogeneous mixture," as Sir Charles Lyell terms it, "of the ruins of adjacent lands, with stones both angular and rounded, which have come from points often very remote." *

The place owes its name to a holy well near the top of the hill. Becoming noted for the cure of diseases, a chapel was erected over the well, in 1112, by the Priory of St. John of Jerusalem, at Clerkenwell, the ground having been given for the purpose by John de Beauvoir, Bp. of London, and lord of the manor of Hornsey. The chapel was known as that of Our Lady of Muswell, and was regarded as an appendage to the priory, whose fortunes it followed. After the suppression of religious houses, the manor of Muswell, with the site of the chapel and farm, was alienated to the Cowpers, and passed through various hands, till purchased by William Roe in 1577, in whose family it continued till the end of the 17th cent., one of the number having built here "a faire house."

"There is on the hill a spring of faire water, which is now within the compasse of Sir Nicholas Roe's cellar in the said house. Here was sometime an Image of Our Lady of Muswell, whereunto was a continuall resort, in the way of pilgrimage, growing (as it goes by tradition from father to the sonne) in regard of a great cure which was performed by th.s water upon a King of Scots, who being strangely diseased, was (by some divine intelligence) advised to take the water of a Well in England ; which, after long scrutation and inquisition, this Well was found, and performed the cure." †

The well still remains on the E. of the Colney Hatch lane, and though covered, the water is accessible by a pump ; but its fame has departed.

Muswell Hill *Church* (St. James), on the crown of the hill, l. of the road to Highgate, is a white-brick E.E. building, with an ivy-covered tower and thin spire at the E. end, erected in 1842, and enlarged, and a good deal altered, in 1874-75. The first incumbent was Dr. Jackson, the present Bp. of London.

On the slope of the hill (l. going towards Crouch End) is the *Grove*, a large white mansion, standing within finely timbered and picturesque grounds and gardens of 16 acres, very famous in their day, laid out by Dr. Johnson's friend, Topham Beauclerk, whose summer residence it was.*

"This morning away to dine at Muswell Hill with the Beauclerks, and florists and natural historians, Banks and Solanders." †

Johnson is said to have frequently visited Topham Beauclerk here, and a walk is still called *Johnson's Walk*. Boswell does not mention these visits, but he records an incident which seems to authenticate them :

"Topham Beauclerk told me, that at his house in the country two large ferocious dogs were fighting. Dr. Johnson looked steadily at them for a little while ; and then, as one would separate two little boys, who are foolishly hurting each other, he ran up to them, and cuffed their heads till he drove them asunder."‡

House and grounds are now incorporated in the Alexandra Park estate, but preserved intact, and the grounds are accessible to visitors to the palace.

At the foot of the hill, lying back on the rt., is a long, low brick cottage, with a verandah in front, and a lawn sloping down to a pond by the roadside, which was the residence of Abraham Newland, cashier of the Bank of England, whose signature to the bank-notes made his name once universally familiar.

"O rare Abraham Newland ! Sham Abraham
    you may,
But you must not sham Abraham Newland."

The poet Moore rented it in 1817, and his eldest daughter, Anne Barbara, died here, and lies in Hornsey ch.-yard. (*See* HORNSEY.)

"*Jan.* 15, 1823.—To the foot of Muswell Hill to look at the Cottage I inhabited there, the only one I do not again see with pleasure." §

From a mistaken tradition that the poem was written in it, the cottage is now named *Lalla Rookh :* the poem was writ-

---

* Lyell, Elements of Geology, chap. xi. ; and see Walker's Glacial Drifts of Muswell Hill and Finchley, 1874.
† Weever, Ancient Funeral Monuments, fol. 1631, p. 499 ; Norden, Spec. Brit.: Middlesex, p. 36.

* Letters from Beauclerk to Lord Charlemont (then in Ireland) from "Muswell Hill, Summer Quarters, July 18, 1774," and on other occasions are printed in Hardy's Life of the Earl of Charlemont.
† Horace Walpole to the Countess of Ossory, June 11, 1773 ; Letters, vol. v., p. 471.
‡ Boswell, Life of Johnson, vol. v., p. 65.
§ T. Moore's Diary.

ten before, but published whilst Moore lived here. The cottage will be easily recognised : it lies next to the Victoria Inn (which nearly faces the entrance to the Alexandra Palace), and has Lalla Rookh painted on the gate-posts.

The *Alexandra Palace* and *Park* occupy the E. portion of the summit, and the S. and E. slopes of Muswell Hill. The estate of 480 acres was purchased in 1859 by a company formed to provide for the north of London an establishment similar to that of the Sydenham Crystal Palace on the south. About 220 acres were appropriated to the palace and public grounds, the rest reserved for villas. After various delays, the palace was completed, and opened May 24, 1873. Sixteen days after it was destroyed by fire. A new building was, however, commenced without delay on the old foundations, but of uniform width throughout, instead of being broken by transepts. It was opened on the 1st of May, 1875.

The new Alexandra Palace is a substantial structure of brick, iron, and glass, unnecessarily ugly externally, from whatever point it be viewed, but of vast extent and capacity, its dimensions being 900 feet by 430, and the area included about 7½ acres. Of the interior, the chief feature is the great Central Hall, 386 ft. long,

184 wide, and 85 ft. to the centre of the semi-cylindrical roof. It has a great organ, and an orchestra for 2000 performers. West of the hall is an enclosed garden, 240 feet by 140. Theatres, concert rooms, picture and sculpture galleries, reading and billiard rooms, corridors, banqueting halls, and a conservatory, occupy their several places, and leave ample room for ethnological models and exhibitions, collections of arms and armour, stalls for objects of ornamental art, and other articles, the particulars of which will be best learnt from the official hand-books.

The grounds are pleasant, in parts well-timbered (with oaks, elms, and chesnuts), and afford fine views across the valley of the Lea, and over more or less of Middlesex, Essex, Kent, Surrey, and Hertfordshire. The best part of the grounds is the Grove, with its delightful old shady walks and avenues, holly hedges, and great oaks, elms, chesnuts, and firs. In one part of the grounds is a Japanese village, in another a lake and pile-dwellings. A racecourse of over a mile, with a grand-stand, has been provided for visitors needing excitement, as well as cricket, croquet, archery, and trotting grounds, a circus, etc. On Whit Monday 1875, no fewer than 94,125 persons visited the palace.

NASING, or NAZEING, Essex (Dom. *Nazinga*), a secluded vill., about 4½ m. N.E. of Waltham Abbey, and a like distance N.W. from Epping ; 17 m. from London : pop. 786. From the Broxbourne Stat. of the Grt. E. Rly. (Cambridge line) a walk of about 3 m. E., past the *Crown* Inn (famous for its flower gardens), across the Nasing Marshes, and along quiet lanes, the last part up a sharp hill—reminding you all the way of the Dutch landscape painters and our own David Cox—will bring you

" To where bleak *Nasing's* lonely tower o'erlooks
  Her verdant fields." *

The *Church* (All Saints), from its position on the crown of the hill, shows well,

and commands fine views over the valley of the Lea. It is of flint and stone, roughcast and weather-beaten, propped by brick buttresses, and much patched. Chiefly Perp., it comprises nave and N. aisle, chancel, and W. tower of brick, embattled, with an octagonal stair turret at the S.E. angle, and short shingled spire. In it are 5 bells. *Obs.* the large Perp. window in the lower part of the tower, and the smaller ones above, of moulded brick. The E. window is filled with painted glass. Notice the curious passage to the rood-loft in pier of chancel arch. The vill. lies along the hill S. of the ch.

Nasing was given by Harold to the Abbey he founded at Waltham, and it remained in the possession of the Abbey till the Dissolution. In 1547 it was granted

---

* Scott of Amwell.

by Edward VI. to Sir Ralph Sadleir, who the same year transferred it to Sir Anthony Denny. Through many hands it descended to the Wake family, and is now the property of Sir Herewald Wake, Bart. The manor-house was at *Nasingbury*, now a farm-house, at the edge of the Lea Marshes, 1½ m. W. of the ch. The Abbot of Waltham had a park at Nasing, which he obtained licence to enclose from Henry III., in 1225. Morant conjectures it was at Fairmead. *Nasing Park* (Robt. Henty, Esq.) is a good house, in a commanding position, immediately S. of the ch. and village.

NASH MILL, Herts (*see* Abbot's Langley).

NAVESTOCK, Essex (Dom. *Nacestoca ; Nasetoca, Nasingstoke, Nastoke*, are early varieties of spelling), 4 m. S. of Ongar by road, 5 m. E. of Brentwood, 19 m. from London : pop. 913.

The par., which extends to South Weald, has a circuit of 25 m. ; the lower parts are a wet and heavy clay, the uplands gravel ; the occupations are chiefly agricultural. The country is secluded, thoroughly rural, undulating, in parts richly wooded, the lanes well lined with trees ; Navestock Park and woods exceedingly picturesque. Altogether, Navestock is a favourable and unspoiled example of Essex scenery.

The manor of Navestock is said to have been given to St. Paul's Cathedral by King Edgar. The authenticity of the grant has been questioned, but Navestock belonged to the Chapter before the Conquest, and it remained its property till the Dissolution. Queen Mary granted the manor in 1553 to Sir Edward Waldegrave, and it has ever since remained in the Waldegrave family, who have at different times bought up and incorporated the sub-manors. The manor-house, *Navestock Hall*, a short distance N. of the ch., was built (or rebuilt) by James, 1st Earl of Waldegrave (created Viscount Chewton and Earl of Waldegrave 1729), and remained the chief residence of the family till taken down, and the materials sold by auction, by John James, 6th Earl, in 1811. The house had been despoiled of some of its treasures before his time.

"The present lord [John, 3rd Earl] bought all

the furniture pictures at Navestock ; the few now to be sold are the very fine ones of the best masters, and likely to go at vast prices, for there are several people determined to have some one thing that belonged to Lord Waldegrave." *

Walpole has sketched it when at its best :—

" I came this morning in all this torrent of heat from Lord Waldegrave's of Navestock. It is a dull place, though it does not want prospect backwards. The garden is small, consisting of two French *allées* of old limes, that are comfortable, two groves that are not so, and a green canal ; there is besides a paddock. The house was built by his father, and ill finished, but an air seigneural in the furniture : French glasses in quantities, handsome commodes, tables, screens, &c., goodish pictures in rich frames, and a deal of noblesse à la St. Germain—James II. Charles II. the Duke of Berwick, her Grace of Buckingham, the Queen Dowager in the dress she visited Madame Maintenon, her daughter the Princess Louisa. . . . . All this is leavened with the late King, the present King, and Queen Caroline." †

The present Navestock Hall is in the occupation of J. Bull, Esq. Navestock Park is of considerable extent, in parts very wild, and contains a long sheet of water, the Lady's Pond. *Dudbrook House*, the seat of Frances Countess Waldegrave, is about ½ m. E. of Navestock Park, towards Kelvedon Hatch.

Navestock *Church* (St. Thomas) stands within Navestock Park. It is small, and rather picturesque ; has nave and S. aisle, small wooden belfry and spire, in which is a peal of 5 bells. The N. door has a good Norm. arch. In the chancel is a mural mont. to " the two first Earls Waldegrave, father and son, both of the names of James, both servants of that excellent Prince George the Second, both by him created Knights of the most noble Order of the Garter." The insc., which runs on to an inordinate length, was written and the monument erected by Walpole's " royal niece," the widow of the 2nd Earl, who afterwards married William Henry Duke of Gloucester. There are several other memorials of the Waldegrave family. The most noticeable, perhaps, is one to Lieut. the Hon. Edw. Waldegrave, drowned at sea 1809, with an elaborate and unsuccessful allegory in marble by Bacon. Another, with a good medallion, is to Lord Radstock, d. 1825.

* Horace Walpole to George Montagu, Nov. 12, 1763 ; Letters, vol. iv., p. 122.
+ Walpole to G. Montagu, Esq., July 26, 1759. Letters, vol. iii., p. 237.

Morant * notices an ancient entrench-ment on Navestock Common, "and near it runs a high bank with a ditch on each side." This is not so readily made out now as it seems to have been a century ago.

Navestock Side, 1½ m. S.E. from Nave-stock ch., is a pretty out-of-the-way ham-let of two or three comfortable farm-houses, cottages, a general shop, a mill, a decent country inn, the Green Man, and *Abbotswick House*, the seat of Ambrose Colson, Esq. *Navestock Heath* is another and smaller hamlet, 1 m. S. of Navestock.

NEASDON, MIDDX., a hamlet and prebendal manor of Willesden, midway (¾ m.) between that vill. and Kingsbury. The Dudding Hill Stat. of the Midland and S.W. Junction Rly. is ¼ m. S. of Neasdon. Inn, the *Spotted Dog*, a sort of suburban tea-garden. The hamlet is a small collection of scattered cottages, with a considerable sprinkling of good houses, some in large grounds. The neighbourhood is green and pleasant.

NETTESWELL, ESSEX (anc. *Netheswelle, Necheswell, Netyswell*), a village on the road from Latton to Parn-don, and 1 m. S. from the Burnt Mill Stat. of the Grt. E. Rly. (Cambridge line): pop. 333.

The vill., *Netteswell Street*, is a rambling collection of detached cottages. The *Church* (St. Andrew) stands apart by a farm-house, and there are broad views over an open flat country from the E. side of the ch.-yard. The ch. is rough-cast, small and plain ; has nave and chancel, wooden belfry rising from the W. end of the roof, with shingled spire, containing 3 bells, and a dilapidated wooden porch on the S.W. At the W. end of the nave are two lancet windows in each side, and 3 in the chancel ; the other windows are Perp., and poor. The *int.* is plain, and has high pews. *Monts.*, to two members of the Marten family, with medallions, and life-size figure of mourning female. Mural tablet to Col. Francis Maule, d. 1829. Notice on the S. wall of nave, W. of the porch, a small but curious terra-cotta heraldic relief—lions supporting a Tudor rose, a hare under the dexter lion, serpent under the sinister.

* Hist. of Essex, 1768, vol. i., p. 181.

NEWGATE STREET, HERTS (*see* HATFIELD).

NONSUCH PALACE, SURREY, a residence of Henry VIII., and Elizabeth, stood a little W. of Cheam, but in the par. of Cuddington (Dom. *Codintone*) : a parish, as they say in the neighbourhood, " without village or shop, church, chapel, school, or public," but which figures in the population returns for 375 inhab. This pop. is, however, chiefly due to the growth of *Worcester Park*, 1½ m. N.W. of Nonsuch, a collection of villas and cottages about a Stat. on the Epsom br. of the L. and S.W. Rly.

Henry VIII. acquired the manor of Cuddington in 1539, in exchange for the rectory of Little Melton in Norfolk, and added it to his Honour of Hampton Court. Henry enclosed nearly 1600 acres of land to form two parks, pulled down the church and manor-house, which stood close together,* and built on the site so magnificent a palace that, as Leland tells in Latin verse, it was called *Nonesuch*, be-cause it was without any equal. It was, however, so far from completed at Henry's death, that Mary thought it "meet rather to be pulled down and sold by piece-meal, than to be perfected at her charges ; " but the Earl of Arundel, "for the love and honour he bare to his old master, desired to buy the same house by the grant of the Queen, for which he gave fair lands unto her Highness ; and having the same, did not leave till he had fully finished it in building, reparations, pavements, and gar-dens, in as ample and perfect sort, as by the first intent and meaning of the said King, his old master, the same should have been performed ; and so it is now evident to be beholden of all strangers and others for the honour of this realme, as a pearle thereof."† Lord Arundel en-tertained Elizabeth several times at Non-such. At her first visit, Aug. 3, 1559, he prepared for her great banquets, especially on Sunday night, together with a masque and all kinds of music till midnight. On the Monday she saw a course from her standing in the outer park ; at night a play was acted by the boys of St. Paul's,

* Losely, MSS., p. 144.
† MS. Life of Henry Earl of Arundel, quoted by Lysons vol. i., p. 112.

under the direction of Sebastian their music-master ; and after that was a costly banquet, with music and drums, the dishes extraordinarily rich gilt, the entertainment lasting till 3 o'clock in the morning. To crown all, the Earl presented the Queen with a cupboard of plate. Her stay lasted a week.* From Lord Arundel, Nonsuch passed to Lord Lumley, who also entertained Elizabeth on several occasions, and who eventually sold the palace, and Little or Home Park, to her Majesty. In her latter years, Elizabeth spent a considerable part of each summer at Nonsuch, "which of all other places she likes best." † It was here that the unfortunate Earl of Essex had that remarkable interview with Elizabeth after his return from Ireland, in Sept. 1599, of which Rowland Whyte gives so quaint an account in a letter to Sir Robert Sydney, dated "Nonsuch, Michaelmas Day at Noone" :—

" Upon Michaelmas Eve, about 10 a clock in the morning, my Lord of Essex 'lighted at Court Gate in post, and made all hast up to the Presence, and so to the Privy Chamber, and stayed not till he came to the Queen's bed-chamber, where he found the Queen all newly up, the hair about her face ; he kneeled unto her, kissed her hands, and had some private speech with her, which seemed to give him great contentment ; for coming from her Majesty to go shift himself in his chamber, he was very pleasant and thanked God, though he had suffered much trouble and storms abroad, he found a sweet calm at home. 'Tis much wondered at here that he went so boldly in to her Majesty's presence, she not being ready, and he so full of dirt and mire that his very face was full of it. About 11 he was ready, and went up again to the Queen, and conferred with her till half an hour after 12. As yet all was well, and her usage very gracious towards him." ‡

Later in the day the Queen's countenance darkened. At night, between 11 and 12, he was commanded "to keep his chamber ; and on the following Monday he was committed to the custody of the Lord Keeper at York House."

James I. settled the palace and parks on his queen, Anne of Denmark ; as did Charles I. on Henrietta Maria. They were of course seized by the Parliament. A lease of the house was granted to Algernon Sydney, the grounds being sold. Later

the Little Park passed to General Lambert, the Great Park to Colonel Pride ; but at the Restoration the grants were resumed by the Crown, and the house restored to the Queen Dowager. In the plague year of 1665, it was fitted up for the offices of the Exchequer. Pepys was down here (Sept. 29, 1665) about his tallies, which, he says, " I found done, but strung for sums not to my purpose. But, Lord ! what ado I had to persuade the dull fellows to it." * In 1670 the palace and park were granted by Charles II. in trust for his mistress, the profligate Duchess of Cleveland, who, as soon as she came into possession, pulled down the palace and sold the materials, and converted the park into farms. Her grandson the Duke of Grafton alienated Nonsuch in 1730. Twenty years later it was bought by Mr. S. Farmer, in whose family it has since remained.

The writers (foreign as well as native) who describe Nonsuch as they saw it in the latter part of the 16th century, seem at a loss for words strong enough to express their sense of its magnificence. Camden calls it " a monument of art," and Paul Hentzner, the German traveller, writes,—

" Nonsuch, a royal retreat built by Henry VIII. with an excess of magnificence and elegance even to ostentation ; one would imagine everything that architecture can perform to have been employed in this one work : there are everywhere so many statues that seem to breathe, so many miracles of consummate art, so many casts that rival even the perfection of Roman antiquity, that it may well claim and justify its name of Nonesuch, being without an equal. . . . The palace itself is so encompassed with parks full of deer, delicious gardens, groves ornamented with trellis work, cabinets of verdure, and walks so embrowned by trees, that it seems to be a place pitched upon by Pleasure herself to dwell in along with Health." †

A more prosaic account, the ' Survey made by order of the Parliament' in 1650, affords, with Hofnagel's print, published in 1582, a more definite idea of what was one of the most curious examples of our palatial architecture. It consists of

" A fair, strong, and large structure, or building of free-stone, of two large storeys high, well wrought and battled with stone . . . . standing round a court of 150 foot long, and 132 foot broad, paved with stone, commonly called the Outward Court : a Gate-House leading into the Outward Court

* Strype, Annals, vol. i., p. 274 ; Nichols, Progresses of Queen Elizabeth, vol. i., p. 74 ; Lysons ; Brayley.
† Rowland White to Sir Robert Sydney, Sept. 8, 1599 ; Sydney Papers, vol. ii., p. 120.
‡ Sydney Papers, vol. ii., p. 127.

* Pepys, Diary, vol. iii., p. 99.
† Hentzner, A Journey into England in the Year 1598, Walpole's translation.

aforesaid, being a building very strong and graceful, 3 storeys high, leaded over head, battled and turretted in every of the 4 corners thereof : also of another very fair and curious structure or building of two storeys, the lower storey whereof is very good and well wrought freestone, and the higher of wood ; richly adorned and set forth and garnished with variety of statues, pictures, and other antick forms, of excellent art and workmanship and of no small cost : all which building, lying almost upon a square, is covered with blue slate, and incloseth one fair and large court 137 ft. broad and 116 ft. long, all paved with freestone, commonly called the Inner Court. Mem., That the Inner Court standeth higher than the Outward Court by an ascent of 8 steps, leading therefrom through a gate-house of free-stone, 3 storeys high, leaded and turretted in the four corners . . . . of most excellent workmanship, and a very special ornament to Nonsuch House. On the E. and W. corners of the inner court building, are placed two large and well-built turrets of 5 storeys, each of them containing 5 rooms, the highest of which rooms, together with the lanthorns of the same, are covered with lead and battled round with frames of wood covered with lead ; these turrets command the prospect and view of both the parks of Nonsuch, and most of the country round about, and are the chief ornaments of Nonsuch House." *

The interior appears from the Survey to have been of correspondent magnificence, but it was the exterior which excited such general admiration, and especially the profusion of " statues, pictures and other antick forms," which, as we see from Hofnagel's print, covered the entire wall space of the principal front. These decorations are said to have been " done with plaster work, made of rye-dough, in imagery, very costly." † Evelyn visited it four years before it fell into the hands of the Duchess of Cleveland :—

" 1665-6, *Jan.* 3.—I supp'd at Nonsuch House, whither the office of the Exchequer was transferr'd during the Plague, ... and took an exact view of ye plaster statues and bass rilievos inserted 'twixt the timbers and punchions of the outside walls of the Court, which must needs have been the work of some celebrated Italian. I much admired how they had lasted so well and entire since the time of Henry VIII., exposed as they are to the air ; and pity it is they are not taken out and preserved in some dry place : a gallery would become them. There are some mezzo-rilievos as big as the life ; the story is of the Heathen Gods, emblems, compartments &c." ‡

Pepys visited Nonsuch about the same time, and was equally delighted with the house, park, and " ruined garden." Evelyn, we have seen, is content to express his opinion that the external decoration

"must needs have been the work of some celebrated Italian," without venturing to name the artist ; but Pepys, with less technical knowledge, and some confusion in artistic chronology, says very decidedly, " All the house on the outside filled with figures of stories, and good painting of Ruben's or Holben's doing." * Mr. J. G. Nichols conjectures, with some probability, that John Hethe, an Englishman in the service of Henry, was " one of those engaged at Nonsuch. . . . By his will dated 1st Aug., 1562, he bequeathed to his second son Laurence ' all my moldes and molded worke that I served the king withall.' " †

The present house, *Nonsuch Park,* (Capt. W. R. G. Farmer) was built, 1802-6, from the designs of Sir Jeffry Wyattville, and is a castellated structure of the order of domestic Gothic rendered familiar by that architect : it has, however, been somewhat altered as well as enlarged during the last few years. It stands in a park of moderate size, reclaimed from the plough since the building of the house. There is a public way through it from Cheam to Ewell, along an old avenue (entering by the projecting lodge on the Epsom road ¼ m. beyond Cheam village—familiar to all who have driven to the Derby). The palace stood at some distance from the present house, but within the park, at the angle formed by the avenue where a footpath branches off towards Ewell : the ground-plan is said to be still traceable. An elm, known as Queen Elizabeth's, stands by the lodge on the Ewell road, and there are some other trees of unusual size in the grounds.

NORBITON, Surrey (*see* Kingston-upon-Thames).

NORBURY PARK, Surrey (*see* Mickleham).

NORTHAW, Herts, lies to the E. of the Great North Road, 15 m. from London, 4 m. N.E. of Barnet, and 2 m. E. of the Potters Bar Stat. of the Grt. N. Rly. Pop. 559.

Northaw (in old books and documents

---

* Archæologia, vol. v.
† Gough, Topography, vol. ii., p. 275 ; Lysons, vol. i., p. 111.
‡ Evelyn, Diary.

* Diary, Sept. 21, 1665.
† Archæol., vol. xxxix.

frequently written *Northall* and *Northalt*) was probably so named from its position, = the north *haw* or *holt*, *i.e.*, wood; Barnet was sometimes called *Southaw*. Northaw stands on high ground outside and N. of the N.W. boundary of Enfield Chase, and Barnet occupies a corresponding site on the S.W. Northaw was probably a waste at the Conquest, as it is not mentioned in the Dom. Survey. Then, or shortly after, the wood or waste of Northaw (*Sylva et Nemus Northagæ*) belonged to St. Albans Abbey, and the Abbot Paul granted a lease of it for his life to Peter de Valoines and his son Roger. The Abbot died in 1093, and Valoines continued in possession by consent; but when, in 1162, the monks wished to resume possession, Robert de Valoines refused to give it up, and appealed to the King, Henry II., then in France. Henry commanded the abbot to give Valoines the wood, but he, taking counsel with his monks, declined. Valoines made complaint to the Earl of Leicester, Lord Chief Justice, and a long irregular litigation ensued. The Pope was appealed to, and issued letters commanding Valoines to make restitution within 30 days under pain of excommunication. But the bishops " feared to publish the excommunication," as being contrary to the King's prohibition, and the Abbot despatched one of his monks with a prayer for inquiry to the King, who directed the Chief Justice to hear and determine the cause. Valoines failed to appear at the third summons, and the Earl " seized the wood which he had forfeited to the King for his contempt ; " and afterwards, Valoines not answering to a forth summons, the Earl " did adjudge the Wood of Northaw to the Abbot by the Judgment of the Court, and thereupon put him into possession by the bough of a tree."* King John confirmed the grant, and thenceforth the Abbots remained in quiet enjoyment till the dissolution of the monastery in 1539.

William Cavendish, Wolsey's gentleman usher, and author of the Life of the Cardinal, of whom we have read under HAMPTON COURT, obtained a grant of Northaw in 1541 from Henry VIII., but alienated it early in the next reign to

Sir Ambrose Dudley, afterwards Earl of Warwick, who "raised here a stately house from the ground, and contrived it in very beautiful order, gracing it with delightful gardens and walks, and sundry other pleasant and necessary devices." * The manor afterwards passed successively, by descent or sale, to Lord Russell of Thornaugh, Sidley, Leman, Strode, and Trenchard. The Earl of Warwick's house was taken down about 1775. The present manor-house is *Nyn Park*, the fine seat of Ashfordby Trenchard, Esq. Other good seats are *The Hook* (N. Brindley Acworth, Esq.), a noble old house in finely wooded grounds S. of the vill.; *Northaw House* (C. W. Faber, Esq.); *The Grove* (F. Lubbock, Esq.); and *Springfield* (Capt. Le Blanc).

The vill. is a scattered collection of good cottages, with several houses of a better class, in the midst of a very pleasant country. The ch. stands on one side of a little green, and opposite to it, under the shadow of a magnificent horsechesnut is the comfortable-looking village inn, the Sun. The *Church* (St. Thomas à Becket—it belonged, it will be remembered, to an Abbey) was built in 1812, on the site of the old ch., by W. Strode, Esq., lord of the manor, and is Gothic of the time; covered with cement, cruciform, and commonplace. The *int.* was remodelled in 1868.

NORTH CRAY, KENT (*see* THE CRAYS).

NORTH END, FULHAM, MIDDX.,

an eccl. dist. of Fulham, extending along the North End road for 1½ m. N.W. from Walham Green to the Hammersmith Road: pop. 5250.

A century ago North End was in the country ; and as late as 1813, if we may trust the map prefixed to Faulkner's Hist. of Fulham, it was still a rural district ; the long lane winding between open fields, mostly market-gardens, with at intervals large houses on either side, but no signs of a village, and no church. Now the houses are nearly continuous, in some places clustered, mostly small and poor, and the mansions nearly all gone. New houses are fast rising, and some

---

* Chauncy, Hertfordshire, vol. ii., p. 384 ; Newcome, Hist. of the Abbey of St. Albans.

* Chauncy, vol. ii., p. 385.

about the Edith Road and Villas are of a better class than at the Walham Green end of the lane.

In 1814 a plain chapel-of-ease was built in the Hammersmith Road ; this is now North End Church (St. Mary), North End having been made an eccl. dist. in 1835.

North End has had some noteworthy inhabitants. A short distance down the North End Road, on the l. from the Hammersmith Road (opposite the Grove), is a large house, now divided, the nearer half stuccoed, the farther red brick, which was for many years the residence of Samuel Richardson, and in which he wrote 'Clarissa Harlowe' and 'Sir Charles Grandison,' and probably part at least of 'Pamela.' "He used to write in a little summer-house or grotto, within his garden, at North End, before the family were up, and when they met at breakfast he communicated the progress of his story, when every turn, and every incident, was eagerly canvassed." * Many are the references to his residence at North End in his voluminous correspondence. Richardson removed in 1755 to Parson's Green, where he died in 1761. (*See* PARSON'S GREEN.) Nearly opposite (where now stand the Grove Cottages) was a large house occupied by W. Wynne Ryland, the celebrated line engraver, who was executed for forgery in 1783. It was afterwards the residence of Dr. Crotch, the eminent musical composer, organist to Westminster Abbey, and principal of the Royal Academy of Music. In the lane opposite the Edith Road lived Cipriani, the popular designer of the middle of the last century ; while Bartalozzi, who engraved many of Cipriani's designs, lived a little way on in the North End Road. Here too, in *Walnut Cottage*, pulled down in 1846, resided for some time Edmund Kean, the great actor. *Normand House*, half hidden by a high wall,—it will be known by its range of 5 wide windows on the first floor, central porch, and date 1664 over the gateway,—is said to have served as a hospital during the plague of 1665. Mr. Crofton Croker says that "Sir E. Lytton-Bulwer resided here," but we find no other authority for

the statement ; it was used as a private lunatic asylum in 1813, and it is so employed now (1876). *Otto House*, which we have just passed, is also a private lunatic asylum. At the *Hermitage*, a spacious house farther S., standing within a high wall, and overshadowed by tall trees, Samuel Foote, the comedian, lived for some years. *Browne's House*, nearer Walham Green, was the seat of Lord Griffin and the Earl Tylney, and in 1718 became the property of Sir John Stanley. In 1736 Mrs. Delaney writes to Dr. Swift, "My employment this summer has been making a grotto at North End for my grandfather Sir John Stanley." It was afterwards purchased by Sir Gilbert Heathcote, and was pulled down on the death of the Dowager Lady Heathcote. *York Cottage* was for many years the residence of J. B. Pyne, the landscape painter. *North End Lodge*, by Walham Green, was the residence of Albert Smith, the popular entertainer, who died there, May 1860. Jacob Tonson lived at North End prior to removing to Barn Elms.

NORTH END, HAMPSTEAD. MIDDX. (*see* HAMPSTEAD).

NORTH MIMMS, MIDDX. (*see* MIMMS, NORTH).

NORTH OCKENDON, ESSEX (*see* OCKENDON, NORTH).

NORTHFLEET, KENT (Dom. *Norfluet*), on the Thames, 1½ m. W. of Gravesend, and a Stat. on the S.E. Rly. (Maidstone line), 21¾ m. from London. Pop. of the par. 6515, but this includes the eccl. districts of Perry Street and Rosherville : Northfleet proper contained 4550 inhab. Inns : *India Arms ; Plough ; Ingress Arms.*

The name appears to be derived from its position on the *fleet*, or streamlet, which, rising in the par. of *Southfleet*, 2 m. inland, flows N., and after passing under Stone Bridge enters the Thames on the W. side of Northfleet. Here the channel is now insignificant, the outfall being regulated, and the ingress of the Thames at high water prevented, by floodgates in

---

* Mrs. Barbauld's Life of Samuel Richardson, prefixed to his Correspondence.

the river wall; but anciently the stream at its mouth formed a large creek or bay—it is still called Northfleet Creek—that in which, according to some authorities, the Danish fleet, or a part of it, lay during the winter of 1013.

Northfleet itself is not inviting to a stranger. Its long mean river-side street stretches along the Thames for 1¼ m. to Rosherville, and the outskirts of Gravesend. The streets inland by the ch., and what was once a green, are little better; but the strange forms into which the chalk cliffs have been excavated—they being carried back to the edge of the highroad—and the way in which the disused pits have become overgrown with scrubby brushwood, and interspersed with scattered cottages, give a singular and occasionally picturesque character to the scenery. One of the larger pits was many years ago converted into a dockyard for shipbuilding, and in it many of the fine old East Indiamen, the pride of our mercantile marine, and also a goodly number of men-of-war, including several of 74 guns, were built, between 1789 and 1825. Afterwards it was employed for building steamers—but the trade has departed from Northfleet. The well-known Rosherville Gardens occupy another of these disused chalk-pits, the sides of which were in parts 150 ft. high. Flints used to be largely wrought here for gun-locks; now at most a few stray flakes and chippings are appropriated by amateur antiquaries. Chalk is still extensively quarried, and there are large lime. whiting, and Portland cement manufactories, sand and ballast yards, and brick-works. The lofty chimney (220 ft. high, and 22 ft. diameter at the base,) that will be observed at one of these cement works, occupies the site and exactly corresponds in dimensions to one that fell at the moment of completion (Oct. 1873), and caused serious loss of life.

The *Church* (St. Botolph) is of Norman foundation, and some portions of the original fabric remain. The nave and aisles are, however, in the main Dec.; the chancel Perp. The nave was restored and reseated in 1846; the chancel in 1863. The general appearance of the *int.* is good. The E. window is a memorial to the Prince Consort. The sedilia were restored at the same time as the chancel.

Obs. the early Dec. rood-screen, with its range of delicately cusped arches borne on slender banded shafts; a work full of excellent detail. The only mont. of note is a tablet with long Latin insc. to Dr. Edward Browne, d. 1710, President of the College of Physicians, physician to Charles II., whom he attended in his last illness, and author of a once much-read 'Account of some Travels in Germany and Hungary,' 1672, 1685, etc., the eminent son of a more eminent father, Sir Thomas Browne, the author of the 'Religio Medici,' and 'Vulgar Errors.' Dr. Edward Browne had a residence at Northfleet, and he bequeathed the house and estate equally between the College of Physicians and St. Bartholomew's Hospital. The *brass* in the chancel floor is of Petrus de Lacy, rector, d. 1375, the builder of the chancel: it is a fine brass, but was unfortunately re-engraved when relaid in the new pavement. Other brasses are, of Wm. Lye, d. 1391; Sir Wm. Rikhill (in armour), and wife; and Thos. Brato, d. 1511, and wife Jone. In the ch. yard *obs.* the pyramidal mausoleum of John Huggins, Esq., of Sittingbourne, with views of Huggins College on two of the sides.

Huggins College, a spacious Gothic building on an elevation near Stone Bridge, comprises 40 comfortable residences and a chapel, with a tall spire, erected and endowed by Mr. John Huggins, in 1847, for persons reduced in circumstances: there are now about 30 residents, who receive £1 a week each.

Northfleet Hythe is a river-side hamlet at the W. end of the par. The districts of PERRY STREET and ROSHERVILLE are noticed under those titles.

Northfleet chronicles are very barren. When, as often happened, Gravesend boats failed to reach that town before the tide turned, passengers were glad to land at Northfleet, which must thus have had many remarkable visitors. Sometimes these unintentional visitants were above the passenger-boat class. On one occasion, Aug. 9, 1609, such a mischance brought to Northfleet two Kings, a Queen and a Prince—James I. of England and his Queen, Christian IV. of Denmark, and Prince Henry.

NORTHOLT, or NORTHALL,

MIDDX. (Dom. *Northala*), 3½ m. N. of the Southall Stat. of the Grt. W. Rly., and about 2 m. S.W. from Harrow : pop. 479.

Northolt is a quiet little country village reached by very crooked lanes. Farming is the chief occupation, the larger part of the land being in grass ; but there are brick-fields in which bricks of superior quality, such as are used for the London sewers, are made, and despatched by the barge-load from a wharf on the Paddington Canal on the E. side of the par. The only object of interest is the *Church* (St. Mary), which stands on a hillock on the E. side of a broad open green, which is crossed by the main road. On the opposite side of the green are half a dozen cottages, and the Crown inn. A pretty little ch. it is, with a few humble gravestones dotting the sward on its S. side, and somewhat more about the yew-tree on the E. The ch. comprises a nave and chancel, with a low wooden belfry and short octagonal spire rising from the W. end of the tall red-tiled roof. The nave is Dec., of flint and rubble, but covered with cement and whitewashed ; the chancel Perp., rebuilt in part of bricks, and a modern Dec. window inserted. The *int.* is plain, the roof unceiled ; the E. window filled with painted glass. Within the chancel rails is the gravestone of Sam. Lisle, Bp. of St. Asaph, d. 1749. *Brasses :* Henry Rowdell, 1452 ; Susan, wife of John Gyfforde, d. 1560 ; Isaiah Bures, vicar of Northall, d. 1610. There is a good octagonal Perp. font. A pleasant field-path leads direct from the ch.-yard to Greenford ch.

NORWOOD, MIDDX., 9 m. W. of

Hyde Park Corner, a precinct and chapelry of Hayes, on the Grand Junction Canal, ¾ m. N. of Heston, and 1¼ m. S. from Southall Stat. of the Grt. W. Rly. : pop. 4889, but in this were included 1908 persons in the Hanwell Lunatic Asylum, and 500 in the Marylebone Union Schools.

Norwood vill. lies a little to the W. of Osterley Park, in a pleasant though flat district. There are neat cottages, many trees, the well-cared-for ch., and close by it a large square mansion, *Norwood Lodge* (W. Unwin, Esq.) Opposite the parsonage, bordered by large elms, is a smooth green, on which on a summer evening a Norwood eleven may be seen vigorously engaged at cricket. Beyond are farms, market-gardens, and orchards ; some hands find employment at brick-making, and there is a wharf on the canal.

The *Church* (dedication unknown) consists of a nave, N. aisle, and chancel, wooden turret and shingled spire, and an old oak porch, restored and glazed. The walls are E.E., with Dec. windows inserted. The fabric was restored and enlarged in 1864, and the external walls refaced with black flints, and a bordering of red, black, and yellow moulded bricks. At the same time the interior was renovated and reseated, the new E. window filled with painted glass, two lancet windows opened in the nave, and two in the chancel. *Obs.* the old glass in the most easterly window of the aisle, with figures of St. John the Baptist and St. Mary ; and other fragments in the W. window removed from the chancel. *Monts.*—On N. of chancel, canopied altar-tomb to Edw. Cheesman, Cofferer to Henry VII., d. 1547. One with life-size semi-recumbent marble statue of John Merick, Esq., of Norcut, d. 1749 ; and tablets to members of the families of Awsiter, Child (of Osterley), Biscoe, Wright, etc. *Brasses.*—S. of chancel, small of Francis Awsiter, in a long robe (d. 1624) ; in nave, to Matthew Huntley (d. 1618), in short cloak, collar and tassels. The font, Dec., is large and good.

Besides the *Lodge*, there are *Norwood House* (W. Rush, Esq.), *The Cedars* (W. E. Berry, Esq.), *Cambridge House* (T. E. Inwoods, Esq.), and other good seats. *North Hyde*, by the Grand Junction Canal, 1 m. W., and *Southall* (with Southall Green), by the Rly. Stat., are hamlets of Norwood. (*See* SOUTHALL.)

NORWOOD, SURREY, of old " a

village scattered round a large wild common," and " a principal haunt of the gipseys," now an extensive region of suburban villas ; and for " Norwood's oak-clad hill," brick-clad may be substituted as the more accurate reading. Norwood is not a parish, but a district of considerably over 30,000 inhab., locally divided into Upper, Lower, and South Norwood, extending from Brixton, Dulwich, and Sydenham to Croydon, and from Anerley to Mitcham, Tooting, and Streatham, and lying partly in Croydon par., and partly in the parishes of Battersea, Lambeth, Streatham, and Camberwell. The Crystal Palace, though always described as in Sydenham, belongs to Norwood.

In the 17th cent. Norwood was really a wood. In his account of Croydon, Aubrey writes (1673-92), " In this parish lies the great wood, called *Norwood*, belonging to the see of Canterbury, wherein was an ancient remarkable tree, called Vicar's Oak, where four parishes meet in a point." * Under this oak the church-wardens, etc., of the several parishes used to dine at their boundary perambulations. Other trees were equally remarkable :

"This wood wholly consists of oaks. There was one oak which had misselto, a timber tree, which was felled about 1678. Some person cut this misselto, for some apothecaries in London, and sold them a quantity for 10s each time, and left only one branch remaining for more to sprout out. One fell lame shortly after ; soon after each of the others lost an eye, and he that felled the tree (though warned of these misfortunes of the other men) would, notwithstanding, adventure to do it, and shortly after broke his leg ; as if the Hamadryades had resolved to take an ample revenge for the injury done to that sacred and venerable oak." +

Norwood was at that time the head-quarters of the gipseys who hovered round London ; and hither the Londoners resorted in fair weather to benefit or otherwise by their palmistry, as they continued to do for more than a century longer.

"*Aug.* 11, 1668.—This afternoon my wife, and Mercer, and Deb., went with Pelling to see the gipsies at Lambeth, and have their fortunes told ; but what they did, I did not enquire." ‡

Long after the Hamadryades had departed, and the last oak and mistletoe had disappeared, the gipseys lingered about Norwood ; but instead of the wood their haunt was the Gipsey Inn, its signpost with the well-known effigy of " Margaret Finch, the Gipsey Queen, aged 109," being the trysting-place for London maid-servants out with their 'followers' for a summer holiday. Now the Norwood gipsey is a tradition—or a pretender.

Norwood is hilly, and for a region of bricks and mortar, non-hypochondriacal : physicians send their patients here, and there are hydropathic and homœopathic establishments, capacious and comfortable hotels, 'family' or otherwise, endless lodging-houses, and the Crystal Palace for a summer and winter garden. Further, Norwood possesses 7 churches, 3 or 4 mission-houses, a full dozen dissenting chapels, Roman Catholic institutions of various kinds, schools beyond count and of every grade and diversity, hospitals and almshouses, Jewish as well as Christian, for foreigners as well as natives, and for the blind as well as those who have their sight. Railway Stats.—Norwood Junction (L., Br., and S. C. Rly. ; Lond., Croydon, and Epsom, and Victoria and Epsom lines), Gipsey Hill, and Lower Norwood of the Crystal Palace and W. End line ; and the Crystal Palace High-level Stat. of the L. C. and D. Rly.,—meet the requirements of the several parts of the district.

The 7 churches are all modern—the oldest Classic, the others Gothic of the fashion of the year of erection. They are : St. Luke's, Lower Norwood; of brick and stone, with a hexastyle Corinthian portico ; completed in 1825 from the designs of Mr. F. Bedford. All Saints, Beulah Hill, South Norwood ; of stone, Perp., with a lofty spire ; erected in 1828 from the designs of Mr. J. Savage. St. Mark's. Victoria Road, South Norwood ; E.E., erected in 1853. St. Paul's, Hamlet Road, Upper Norwood, of coloured bricks and stone ; E.E. (of a French type), erected in 1866 from the designs of Mr. B. Keeling. Christ Church, Gipsey Hill ; late E.E. ; designed by Mr. J. Giles ; completed in 1867. St. John's, Grange Wood Road, Upper Norwood. Holy Trinity, South Norwood ; E.E., of red brick, designed by Messrs. Newman and Billing.

The *North Surrey District School*, Anerley Road, is a very large and very complete establishment, covering an area of 50 acres, and providing accommodation and the means of industrial training for nearly 1000 children from the district unions. Other industrial schools, parochial and denominational, do not call for particular attention. Noticeable for its architectural as well as philanthropic character is the *Jews' Hospital*, Lower Norwood, a good Jacobean structure, erected by Mr. Tillot in 1863 for the maintenance of the aged poor, and the industrial training of friendless children :

* Really five, says Manning—those named above ; Manning and Bray, History of Surrey, vol. ii., p. 536.
† Aubrey, Perambulation of Surrey, vol. ii., p. 33.
‡ Pepys, Diary, vol. iv., p. 496.

there is also a *Jewish Convalescent Home.* An admirable institution is the *Royal Normal College and Academy of Music for the Blind,* Weston Street, Upper Norwood. The schools of the Westmoreland Society for children of parents residing within 75 miles of London are at Lower Norwood. The *Norwood South Metropolitan Cemetery,* founded in 1836, one of the earliest of the great metropolitan cemeteries, occupies 40 acres of the northern slopes of a hill at Lower Norwood, parts of which command good views across Sydenham, Penge, and Beckenham. The grounds are well laid out, but are becoming crowded with monuments. Many men of mark have their last resting-place here.

Among the few houses of note at Norwood, *Knight's Hill* was perhaps the most conspicuous. It was built by Henry Holland, the architect of Carlton House and Drury Lane Theatre (that burned in 1809), for Lord Chancellor Thurlow. The house was much admired; it afforded, we are told, splendid views from the upper storeys, and the grounds were extensive and beautiful. But his lordship would never occupy it, continuing to live in a smaller house, Knight's Hill Farm, close by. Here is the story as told by another Lord Chancellor (Eldon):—

"Lord Thurlow built a house in the neighbourhood of London. Now he was first cheated by his architect, and then he cheated himself; for the house cost more than he expected, so he never would go into it. Very foolish, but so it was. As he was coming out of the Queen's Drawing Room, a lady whom I knew very well stopped him and asked him, When he was going into his new house? 'Madam,' said he 'the Queen has just asked me that impudent question: and as I would not tell her, I will not tell you.'"[*]

The report was that the house and grounds cost £30,000. Both house and grounds have disappeared, having, with his lordship's adjoining manor of Leigham, been appropriated by the speculative builder.

Another once noted place was the *Beulah Spa,* Upper Norwood; founded on a handsome scale, about 1831, for rendering available the medicinal properties of a spring strongly impregnated with sulphate of magnesia. There were grounds of nearly 30 acres, pump and recreation rooms, and an hotel, all designed by Mr. Decimus Burton, and provided with all appliances for well-to-do water-drinkers and valetudinarians; but after a brief day of prosperity, Beulah Spa collapsed, and the site was handed over to the builder. The grounds have, however, been partially preserved, and there is (or was recently) a hydropathic establishment where the curative qualities of the water may be tested.

NUTFIELD, SURREY (Dom. *Notfelle*), a vill. on the road from Reigate to Bletchingley, 2 m. E. of the Redhill Stat. of the S.E., and L. Br. and S. C. Rlys., and 1 m. W. from Bletchingley: pop. 1224, but of these 36 were in the eccl. dist. of St. John Outwood, and 85 in the Gladstone Philanthropic Farm-school and cottages.

Nutfield is a very pretty village, situated on a ridge of the Lower Greensand overlooking the Weald, whence there are charming prospects, and that richness of foliage and colour which is so characteristic of the Lower Greensand formation.

"The little village of Nutfield has long been celebrated for the Fuller's Earth which has for centuries been dug up in its neighbourhood. . . . The beds of fuller's earth are situated near the top of the lowest division of the Shanklin sand, and occupy a line on the N. side of a ridge that extends from the E. of Nutfield nearly to Redstone Hill, on the W. of Copyhold Farm. About 2 m. W. of Nutfield the earth was extracted from a stratum 6 or 7 ft. thick. In some of the pits there are two varieties of fuller's earth, one of an ochreous yellow colour, and the other of a slaty gray. The sulphate of barytes is found in detached nodular masses from a few ounces to 130 or 140 pounds weight . . . . Horizontal and vertical veins of fibrous gypsum, about half an inch in thickness, are disseminated through the fuller's earth."[*]

The district yielding the fuller's earth is about 2 m. long from E. to W., and ½ m. wide. Three pits are worked in Nutfield, and a large quantity is annually sent away. The grey (locally *blue*) earth is used only by the manufacturers of fine cloth, and chiefly sent to Yorkshire; the yellow variety is employed for every fabric of coarse woollen goods, and very widely distributed. The sandstone, both above and below the fuller's earth bed, is employed as a coarse building stone. In the sandstone strata occur various organic

---

[*] Twiss, Life of Lord Chancellor Eldon, vol. i. p. 198.

[*] Mantell, in Brayley's Hist. of Surrey, vol. i., p. 145.

remains. Characteristic fossils are a large ammonite (*A. Nutfieldiensis*), and nautilus (*N. undulatus*). Firestone is also quarried.

The *Church* (St. Peter and St. Paul) stands in a picturesque position N. of the road. It comprises nave with N. aisle and S. chapel, chancel, W. tower, with stair turret, battlements, and short shingled spire. There was a church here at the Dom. Survey, and though no part of the existing fabric is of that period, the nave piers and long chancel are early Dec. The tower, S. chapel, and windows of the nave are Perp.; the porch has a Dec. bargeboard. In the E. wall of the chancel is an ambrey. In the S. wall, under a Dec. canopy, is a slate with a nearly obliterated insc. to the memory of Sire Thomas de Roldham. Another sepulchral arch is in the S. wall of the chapel. There are two small brasses, one of Wm. Grafton, rector, about 1460, the other of a female. In the E. window are some fragments of old painted glass. There are also remains of an oak screen. On leaving,

obs. a tablet on the external wall, by the porch to Thomas Steer, d. 1769, æt. 76:

" He Liv'd alone, He Lyes alone,
To Dust He's gone, Both Flesh and Bone."

Nutfield has the look of a well-cared-for as well as pleasant village. The school-house with its outside staircase and open galleries, and many of the new cottages are unusually picturesque. Some are half timber, others of the native sandstone, and most well adapted to their purpose and position. *Nutfield Priory* is a large and costly mansion, built in 1872 from the designs of Mr. J. Gibson, for Joshua Fielden, Esq., M.P. It is Domestic Gothic in style, with a tall tower somewhat too much like that of a ch. Other seats are: *Nutfield Court* (C. H. Barclay, Esq.); *Tower* (J. Cawley, Esq.); *Hall Lands* (Gurney Fox, Esq.); *Patteson Court* (T. Nickalls, Esq.); *Elstree* (T. Woolloton, Esq.); *Colmongers* (T. Welch, Esq.) An urn containing 900 coins of the lower Empire, and other Roman remains, have been found here.*

O AKS, THE, Surrey (*see* WOODMANSTERNE).

OATLANDS, Surrey (*see* WALTON-UPON-THAMES and WEYBRIDGE).

OCKENDON, NORTH, Essex (Dom. *Wochenduna*), 5 m. N. of Grays Stat. on the Southend Rly., on the road to Brentwood: pop. 324.

" Okendon," as Morant writes, " otherwise in records *Wokynden Septem Fontium*, or *Fontem*, either from some owner of that surname, or from seven fountains or springs formerly famous here."* The latter seems the more likely, but nothing is now known of any such springs here. "A spring of excellent water in the churchyard," used however, as late as 1819, to supply the village. In the reign of the Confessor, North Ockendon belonged to Harold. William I. gave it to the Abbot of Westminster. In the reign of Edward

II. it belonged to John Malegreffe. In 1320 it was owned by Baldwin de Wokyndon, and in the 2nd half of the 14th cent. it passed by marriage to the family of Pointz. By marriage alsoit went to John Maurice, or Morice, of Chipping Ongar, whose eldest son assumed the name of Pointz, and was knighted in 1603. In 1643 a female heir carried the manor to the family of Littleton, descended from the author of the famous work on Tenures. In the same way it passed to a Rede, and afterwards to Littleton Pointz Meynell. It is now the property of Richard Benyon, Esq., late M.P. for Berkshire.

Hardly a village, North Ockendon consists of a slip of green, with about it two or three cottages, a general shop, a smithy, and a little country inn, the Old White Horse. A short distance W. of the vill. are the ch., the pretty parsonage by it, and, screened by a grove of elms, North Ockendon Hall, a large, moated, brick

* Morant, Essex, vol. i., p. 102.

* Brayley, Hist. of Surrey, vol. iv., p. 329; Archæol. Journal, vol. vi., p. 288.

manor-house, the old seat of the Pointz family, now a farm-house. W. of the Hall a portion of the moat remains, and it may be traced round the wall by the ch.-yard.

The *Church* (St. Mary Magdalen) is interesting in itself, and for the Pointz memorials. It is of flint and stone, comprises nave and N. aisle, with the Pointz chapel at the E. end, chancel, a square embattled tower, the W. front covered with ivy, and modern flint and stone porch on the S. The ch. ranges in date from the Norm. to the, Perp. period, but it was thoroughly restored in 1859 at the cost of Mr. Benyon, when much of it was rebuilt, some new windows inserted, and the mouldings and tracery rechiselled. The tower, a good Perp. work, was left intact; in it is a peal of 5 bells. The entrance arch under the S. porch is Norm., with billet and chevron moulding (recut). The nave, aisle, and chapel are Perp., the chancel Dec. (observe the somewhat unusual tracery of the E. window). The int. is of more than average excellence, and has been restored in good taste. There is a good chancel arch, and the original open timber roofs of the nave and aisle have been preserved. Some of the windows have modern painted glass, with which may be compared a figure of the Madonna under a tall canopy, of late 15th or early 16th cent. work, in a window of the Pointz chapel.

In this chapel will be found the most interesting of the *Monts.* The most curious, and well deserving notice, is a series of memorials of successive heads of the Pointz family—in appearance monts., but evidently memorials erected by the same person, and for the most part therefore long after the deaths of the individuals recorded. The series consists of 8 small mural tablets to Pointz Fitz Pointz, son of Nicholas Pointz, who lived in the reign of Edward III.; John Points, *t.* Henry IV.; John Pointz, *t.* Henry VI.; William Pointz, *t.* Henry VII.; John Pointz, *t.* Edward VI.; Thomas Pointz, died 1562; Thomas Pointz, d. 1597 (this for some reason is placed out of its order, on the N. wall); Gabriel Pointz, d. 1606. All the tablets are of the same size, and similar in character and lettering. In each a knight and lady are represented kneeling on the opposite sides of a lectern. All have a close resemblance, and were executed pro-

bably soon after the decease of Gabriel Pointz, the last of the series : definite dates, it will be observed, commence with the fifth in order, Thomas Pointz, 1562, whilst the first was two centuries earlier. Of the John Pointz of the reigns of Henry VIII. and Edward VI.—the 4th in the list, who died in 1558—there is a fine portrait among the Holbein drawings at Windsor Castle, a clean-shaven ¾-face, looking up, not recognizable, if our memory served, in the Ockenden head, which is clearly imaginary. The figures, of alabaster, are in good preservation, but the hands have been mischievously broken off all of them. A costly tomb has life-sized recumbent effigies of Sir Gabriel Pointz (d. 1607), in full armour, and wife in ruff and robes, under a flat canopy, coloured, and diapered with stars, above coats of arms. On the N. wall, large mural mont. with half-sized kneeling effigy of John Maurice Pointz, of Chipping Ongar, d. 1618, 4 sons and 3 daughters. Another, with kneeling effigies of Sir James Pointz and wife. Large marble mont., with bust and weeping cherubs, to Sir Thomas Pointz, Speaker of the House of Commons, d. 1709. *Brasses.*—At W. end of chapel, Wm. Pointz, d. 1502, in full armour, large 2-handed sword at side, feet on dog; wife in long robe; 6 sons and 6 daughters. E. end of chapel, John Pointz, d. 1547. The other monts. in the ch. include one to John Russell of Stubbers (d. 1825), with a good bust by Behnes; and one with medallion of his widow, Eliza Russell (d. 1830). In the rectory is a brass of about 1530, with insc., mutilated, of Thomasyn, wife of Robert Latham, gent., and then of Wm. Ardell, gent.

North Ockendon was the rectory (held by him with the living of Duffield in Derbyshire) of Vicissitude Gifford (the Rev. Richard Gifford, d. 1807), author of some theological tractates and various small poems, from a verse in one of which, that clung to the memory of Johnson, and being quoted by him to Boswell in the 'Hebrides' attained sudden popularity, Gifford acquired his sobriquet :

" Verse sweetens toil, however rude the sound.
    All at her work the village maiden sings,
Nor, while she turns the giddy wheel around,
    Revolves the sad vicissitude of things."

Stubbers, anciently the property of the Coys, a family of Welsh origin, but long the seat of the Russells, and now of C. Bramfell Russell, Esq., stands in the midst of a small but beautiful park, about 1 m. W. of North Ockendon Church.

OCKENDON, SOUTH, Essex, a

roadside vill., 1 m. S. of North Ockendon, and about 4 m. N. of the Grays Stat. of the Southend Rly.: pop. 1243. Inns: *Plough ; Red Lion.*

South Ockendon is much larger than the sister vill., stretches for some distance along the highroad, and has the look of an active and growing place. There is a pleasant and prettily varied walk to it wholly through the fields from Grays by way of Stifford ; but it is easy to lose the path. South Ockendon Church, though its old charm has been destroyed by restoration, is worth visiting. At South Ockendon Hall, now a farm-house, ½ m. N.E. of the ch., at the Mill, S. of it, at Great Mounds, ⅓ m. S. of the Mill, and again at Little Mounds and the Grange, still farther S., are ancient mounds upon which the archæological visitor may exercise his ingenuity.

In the reign of the Confessor, *Wochadune* (as the Norman scribe spells it) belonged to Friebert a Thane, but after the Conquest it was transferred to a Norman noble, Geoffrey de Magnaville, Earl of Essex. In the reign of Stephen it appears to have passed to William D'Ou, probably by marriage. To the D'Ous succeeded the Rokeles, in whom it remained till conveyed by Isola, daughter of Philip de la Rokele, to her husband Sir William de Bruyn, knight of the bedchamber to Edward I., as Isola was lady of the bedchamber to Queen Eleanor. The manor remained in this family till the 16th cent., when it was divided into two manors, Bruyns and Groves, one going to each of the daughters of Sir Henry Bruyn. Elizabeth, the wife of Sir Thomas Tyrell, inherited *Bruyns.* She had for her third husband Sir Wm. Brandon, standard-bearer to Henry VII. at Bosworth, where he fell by the hand of Richard III. Their son, Charles Brandon, Duke of Suffolk, is said to have been born at South Ockendon. The Tyrells held the manor for a long period, when it was alienated to Wm. Petre of Stanford Rivers. To him succeeded Jasper Kingsman of Horndon-on-the-Hill, the Cliffes, and R. Benyon, Esq.,

the present owner. *Groves,* the other moiety, was conveyed by Alice Bruyn to Robert Harleston, her first husband (for like her sister she had three), and the manor remained in the Harleston family till the 16th century, when it went to a Saltonstall, afterwards to Goodere and to Stewart, and is now reunited with Bruyns in the hands of R. Benyon, Esq.

The *Church* (St. Nicholas), which is approached from the Green by an avenue of limes, is in part Norm., and noteworthy. It is one of the seven Essex churches which have round towers, "after the Danish fashion," writes Morant, "and embattled."[*] The ch. was elaborately restored (almost rebuilt) in 1866, when the tower was carried up much higher, and Norm. windows inserted in the upper storey, without improvement to its picturesqueness, proportions, or propriety. Before the alterations, the ch. consisted of a nave, N. aisle, chancel, and large N. chapel, the round tower at the W. end, and a S. porch. A S. aisle and vestry were then added, the tower raised, the chancel rebuilt, the walls uniformly refaced with black flints, and the whole renovated. The N. doorway, under an open wooden porch, though small (8 ft. 2 in. by 4 ft. 2 in.) is a remarkably fine late Norm. work. It has a semicircular arch with 4 richly carved receding reveals, 3 of them with varied chevron mouldings, the uppermost with the billet moulding. The outer shafts have foliated capitals, the next, very slender and banded, have spirals with the dog-tooth ornament, and alternate beads and flowers. This doorway has been carefully repaired, and the decayed parts stopped with a dark cement, but very little, and cautiously, rechiselled. The bands and lower part of the E. shaft are however new.

The int. presents a new aspect, but not more so, perhaps, than was inevitable. The roofs, of plain wood, and ceiled, are in effect new, and the whole has been reseated. The reredos was added in 1874.[†] *Monts.*—In the N. chapel is an elaborate mural mont. of coloured marbles to Sir Richard Saltonstall, Knt., and Lord Mayor,

---

[*] Morant, Hist. of Essex, 1768, vol. i., p. 101.

[†] There is a good architectural description of the ch., of course prior to the restoration, in Buckler's 'Twenty-two of the Churches of Essex,' 1856, p. 32, etc,

d. 1601, with kneeling effigies in recesses, under canopies, of Sir Richard in plate armour, with his scarlet Lord Mayor's robe over it, and his wife in rich coloured dress with falling sleeves. Below are small kneeling effigies of 7 sons (one with a skull below) and 9 daughters. Above are his arms, fully emblazoned. There are other memorials of Saltonstalls, Kingsmans, Drywoods, etc. *Brasses.*—In chapel (removed from the chancel at the restoration of the ch.), a very choice one, with life-sized headless effigy, under a canopy, of Sir Ingelram Bruyn, "Lord of the village and patron of this ch.," d. 1400. He is in full armour with long sword on rt., his feet armed with long spurs resting on a lion sejant : insc. on jupon across the breast. Another is of Margaret, wife of Edward Barker of Chesswycke, in Mydd., d. 1602, noteworthy for the elaborate Elizabethan costume.

ONGAR, or CHIPPING ONGAR,

ESSEX, a small market town on the Dunmow road, 21 m. from London, and the terminus of the Epping and Ongar br. of the Grt. E. Rly.: pop. 946. Inn, *The Lion*, a comfortable house.

In the Dom-boc the name is written *Angra ;* in other old records, *Angre, Angrea, Aungre, Ongre.* The derivation is doubtful. *Chipping* is the old English term for a market, and is prefixed to distinguish this from the neighbouring village of High Ongar. In some documents the name has the addition *ad Castrum*, from the castle which formerly stood here.

The manor was given by the Conqueror to Eustace Earl of Boulogne, whose daughter Maud conveyed it by marriage to Stephen Earl of Blois, and afterwards King of England. Henry II. granted it to Richard de Lucy, Lord of Diss, who built a castle here. From the De Lucys it passed in succession to Richard de Rivers, Sir John Sutton, and, in 1348, to Ralph Lord Stafford, in whose descendants it remained till it escheated to the Crown on the attainder of Edward Earl Stafford in 1521. Henry VIII. gave it in 1541 to George Harper, who sold it in 1543 to Wm. Maurice, or Morice. It next passed by marriage to Sir Fulke Greville, and then to the Whitmores, Goldburghs, Alex-

anders, and Bennetts. The present lord of the manor is Admiral Swinburne.

Ongar is a pretty little town. Its single street runs along a gentle declivity between the Roding and its affluent the Cripsey Brook, which, at the foot of the hill, is crossed by a brick bridge of three arches. Looking up the street from this bridge, gardens and trees everywhere mingling with the houses, shops, and inns, the tall roofs and spire of the ch. crowning the whole, the little town has an unusually bright and pleasant aspect. Ascending the street, it must be admitted the houses look small, and for the most part modern and bald, the market-house ugly, and the streets dull—unless it be on Saturday, when the market is held, or when the "Ongar Volunteers" are parading the town with their band. The trade is that of the centre of an agricultural district.

Ongar *Church* (St. Martin) has nave and chancel, and, rising from the W. end of the roof, a wooden belfry and slender spire. It is small, plain, the walls roughcast ; the chancel, which has 3 lancets, E.E.; the nave Perp. The *int.* is in good order, having been partially restored in 1865. The main beams of the timber-roof are exposed. *Obs.* large piscina on S. of the altar, ambrey on N., and another ambrey in the nave. There are numerous *monts.* to the Alexanders, Bennetts, and other local families ; one to Jane, daughter of the Lord Oliver Cromwell of Finchingbrook, Huntingdonshire, Knt. of the Bath, and wife of Tobias Pallavicine, d. 1637 ; and one to "that truly noble and religious gentleman, Horatio Pallavicine," d. 1648. There is also a brass of a civilian, without insc., of the early part of the 16th cent.

The *Castle* was built by Richard de Lucy, in the reign of Henry II., on an artificial mound which, as Gough pointed out, was probably of Roman construction. Roman remains have been found here, and Roman tiles are worked up in the walls of the ch. (though now concealed by rough-cast), showing the proximity of a Roman station. Ongar Castle, having become dilapidated, was taken down by William Maurice, its owner, in the reign of Elizabeth, and a handsome manorhouse built in its place. This only lasted till 1744, when Mr. Alexander, the then lord of the manor, removed it, and substituted "an embattled summer-house." This in its turn has disappeared, and now no building crowns the hillock, but it is thickly timbered, and is still encompassed by the moat. There is a pleasant view from the top of the mound. The castle stood at the upper end of the town, a little E. of the street. *Castle House*, a picturesque, old-fashioned, many-gabled dwelling in the castle grounds, with the moat close to it, was the first residence in the town of Isaac Taylor, sen., who came to be widely known as Isaac Taylor of Ongar. The Taylors lived three years (1810—13) at the Castle House, and then removed to the Peaked Farm—a mile away in the meadows—a place now utterly transformed, and despoiled of all its picturesque accompaniments. The story of the Taylors of Ongar is told in the 'Family Pen' of the Rev. Isaac Taylor—the third of that name honourably distinguished in our literature. The elder Taylor, his wife, the authoress of many popular books for the young, and their daughter Jane, perhaps better known as a writer than either, were interred in the little burial-ground of the Independent Chapel at Ongar, of which Mr. Taylor was for many years the minister; "but their graves have been enclosed within the enlarged buildings of the chapel: the vestry floor covers them." *

From the N. end of Ongar—the stile is opposite the Cock inn—there is a charming field-path of about a mile (half a mile of it being along an avenue) to the unique little wooden ch. of Greenstead. (*See* GREENSTEAD.) In the opposite direction a pretty field-path of about a mile leads to High Ongar, the subject of the next article.

ONGAR, HIGH, (sometimes called LITTLE or OLD ONGAR,) ESSEX, stands on high ground, about 1½ m. (by road) N.E. of Chipping Ongar: pop. 1157. Inn, *Red Lion.*

The par. is much larger than that of Chipping Ongar: its greatest extent from Weald Bridge to Horton Heath is about 8 m. For an Essex par. it is unusually varied, and affords much pleasant and even picturesque scenery. It is divided

into several manors, but their history is of little interest. *Ongar Park* is a detached portion of the par., cut off from the main part by Greenstead and Bobbingworth.

The *vill.* is small, and not remarkable. The little *Church* (St. Mary the Virgin) is of considerable antiquity, but has been covered with plaster and modernized. Under the S. porch is a Norm. arch of fair details. The chancel has 3 lancet windows. The nave windows are Perp. The tower at the S.W. was erected in 1858, and is of white brick and stone, with lancet windows. The int. has a tall arched roof. There is a brass, without insc., of the beginning of the 17th cent.

Forrest Hill, formerly Folliot's or Folyat's, 1 m. N., a fine mansion in a small but pretty park, is the seat of J. P. Newell, Esq. *Ashe Hall,* or Nash Hall, ¼ m. S.E. of the ch., the ancient seat of the Frenles and Mildmays, is now a farm-house. *Chevers,* 1 m. E. of the ch., a good house on a hillside, was the manor-house of the Chevres, Stalbrokes, Pawnes, etc. *Astelyns,* by Bobbingworth, now a farm-house, was, according to an old tradition, the place where Thomas Duke of Norfolk concealed himself when charged with treason for abetting Mary Queen of Scots. The estate was purchased by Harvey, the discoverer of the circulation of the blood, and bequeathed by him to the College of Physicians. *Marden Ash House,* the seat of Edward Cunliffe, Esq., is in High Ongar par., but situated a little S. of Chipping Ongar. At Marden Ash resides Josiah Gilbert, grandson of Isaac Taylor of Ongar, and himself the author of a well-known work on the Dolomite Region, and of Memorials of his mother, Mrs. Gilbert (Ann Taylor).

ORPINGTON, KENT (Dom. *Orpintun*), 1½ m. S. of St. Mary Cray Stat. of the L., C., and D. Rly., on the road to Westerham: pop. 2371. Inns, *Maxwell Arms; White Hart.*

"Orpington," writes Philipott, "was in the 20th year of William the Conqueror, wrapped up in the ecclesiastical patrimony, and belonged to the monks of Christchurch." * They held it till taken away by Henry VIII. Henry retained it three years, and then granted it to Perci-

---

* Jos. Gilbert, Autob. and Memorials of Mrs. Gilbert (Ann Taylor), vol. ii., p. 320.

* Philipott, Vill. Cant., 1659, p. 258.

vall Hart. Esq., of Lullingstone. Percivall Hart built himself a noble mansion, in which he entertained Queen Elizabeth for three days, July 21—24, 1573.

"*Bark Hart* has obtained a place in the map of Kent, and therefore shall not want one in this discourse. It was built by Percivall Hart, Esq. . . . but it was adorned with this name by Queen Elizabeth, when she was magnificently entertained at this place by the abovesaid gentleman. Upon her reception she received her first caresses by a nymph, which personated the genius of the house ; then the scene was shifted, and from several chambers which, as they were contrived, represented a ship, a sea conflict was offered up to the spectator's view, which so much obliged the eyes of this princess with the charms of delight, that, upon her departure, she left upon this house (to perpetuate the memory both of the author and artificer) the name and appellation of Bark Hart." *

Bark Hart it remains to the present day, and house and manor still belong to a Hart—Sir William Hart Dyke, Bart., of Lullingstone. Bark Hart is the residence of C. A. Dickinson, Esq. The manor of *Little Orpington* belongs to J. G. Stapleton, Esq.

Crofton, a little secluded hamlet, 1½ m. W., was according to tradition a parish in itself, with a goodly village, till destroyed by fire, thus evincing to us, as old Philipott moralizes, "that towns and villages have their stated period of duration, and must at length find a grave like men." *Crofton Court* is the seat of Alfred Aylwood, Esq. Another and certainly baseless tradition is that *Tubbingden*, towards Farnborough, was the birthplace of Thomas à Becket.

Orpington is a good specimen of a Kent village. It stands in the midst of pleasant scenery, the cottages are clean and comfortable, some old half-timber of the true Kent type, with the date 1633, and with them are new ones, good shops, and houses of a more expensive kind, large schools and the like, showing that the place is not merely a relic of the past, but making progress. The N. end of Orpington forms *South Cray*, and derives benefit from the mills, etc., at St. Mary Cray, but Orpington is in the main agricultural. Hops and fruit are the specialty, both of which are largely grown. The river Cray has its source in several springs at Orpington, and forms a respectable stream before it enters St. Mary Cray.

The *Church* (All Saints) is in the main

* Philipott, Vill. Cant., 1659, p. 259.

a building of the early part of the 13th cent. It is of whole flints and stone, and comprises nave, chancel, and N. chapel, and by it a large low square battlemented tower, and a porch of flint and stone on the W. The entrance doorway under this porch has the dog-tooth moulding, and transition Norman details may be seen in the tower—which has, however, been restored. The triple lancets of the chancel are new. The int., restored in 1874, is very handsome. It is well proportioned, has a good open timber roof, neat oak pulpit, lectern, and rood screen ; the floor has low open seats ; the E. windows are divided by slender banded shafts of Purbeck marble, and filled with painted glass ; and a Caen stone reredos. with a representation of the Last Supper, has been erected. S. of the altar are sedilia and piscina ; N. an ambrey. *Obs.* on rt. of the pulpit, the entrance to the rood-loft staircase. The font has a large E.E. octagonal basin : the central stone shaft, and 4 smaller ones of coloured marbles, are new. In the entrance porch is a holy-water stoup. *Obs.* here on l. a damaged altar tomb with canopy. The chapel has a quadripartite vaulting. In the chancel is a *brass* to Thomas Wilkyson, M.A., prebendary of St. Wulfram at Ripon, and rector of Orpington, d. 1504 ; and one in the chapel to another rector, d. 1522.

The ch. and ch.-yard are well kept and picturesque. N. of ch. are two large yews.

OSTERLEY HOUSE, HESTON,

MIDDX., is about 2 m. N.W. from Brentford, and 1 m. E. of Heston ch. The manor of Osterlee belonged in the reign of Edward I. to John de Osterlee. In 1443 it was held by John Somerseth, Chancellor of the Exchequer to Henry VI., who had founded a hospital and chantry for the gild or fraternity of All Holy Angels at Brentford End, of which this manor, or a rent-charge on it, formed part of the endowment. In 1508 Hugh Denys, of Gray's Inn, bequeathed Osterley, with other manors, to the Prior and Convent of Sheen, charged with payments for building additional houses, and the maintenance of 2 priests in the chapel, and 7 poor men in the hospital of All Angels. Twenty years later the manor was conveyed, subject to the same payments, to the Abbess and Convent of Syon at Isleworth. At the Dissolution it was granted by Henry VIII. to Henry Marquis of Exeter, upon whose attainder it reverted to the Crown. Edward VI., in the first year of his reign, gave it to the Protector Somerset, on whose execution, 4 years later, it again reverted to the Crown. In 1557 it was granted to Augustine Thaier, and a few years after became the property of the prince of merchants, Sir Thomas Gresham.

Gresham having enclosed his park, commenced the building of a magnificent mansion, which he completed in 1577, and next year Sir Thomas entertained and lodged Queen Elizabeth at his new house with a degree of splendour that was long remembered.

"Her Majesty found fault with the court of this house as too great; affirming that 'it would appear more handsome, if divided with a wall in the middle.' What doth Sir Thomas, but in the night-time sends for workmen to London (money commands all things), who so speedily and silently apply their business, that the next morning discovered that court double, which the night had left single before. It is questionable whether the Queen next day was more contented with the conformity to her fancy, or more pleased with the surprise and sudden performance thereof; whilst her courtiers disported themselves with their several expressions, some affirming it was no wonder he could so soon *change* a building, who could build a '*Change*;' others (reflecting on some known differences in this knight's family) affirmed that 'any house is easier divided than united.'" *

The splendour of Osterley suffered eclipse on the death of its master. "No sooner was he gone," writes his biographer, "than this fine seat began to fall into decay;" † and Norden, writing whilst Lady Gresham still occupied it, says:

"Osterley, or Oysterley, the house now of the Ladie Gresham's, a faire and stately building of bricke, erected by Sir Thomas Gresham, ... standeth in a parke, by him also impaled, well-wooded, and garnished with manie faire ponds, which afforded not onely fish, and fowle, as swanes and other water-fowle; but also great use for milles, as paper-milles, oyle-milles, and corne-milles, all which are now decaied (a corne-mille excepted). In the same parke was a very faire heronrie, for the increase and preservation whereof

sundrie allurements were devised and set up, fallen all to ruine." *

On Lady Gresham's death the manor passed to Sir Wm. Read, her son by her first husband; but the house became the residence of Sir Edward Coke, then Attorney-General, and afterwards Lord Chief Justice, whose daughter Bridget was baptized in the chapel Jan. 3, 1597. George Earl of Desmond, and his Countess—a great-granddaughter of Sir William Read, and coheiress of his estates—lived many years at Osterley; after Desmond carried her off, sorely against her will, from York House, and the protection of the Duchess of York, "the first ever heard of that ran away with his own wife." † Sir William Waller, the Parliamentary General, purchased Osterley in 1655, and made it his residence till his death in 1668. It then became the property of Sir Wm. Thompson, whose son sold it in 1683 to Nicholas Barbon, M.D., a noted projector. Dr. Barbon soon afterwards mortgaged it to Sir Francis Child, whose son Francis purchased the fee-simple about 1713.

The Childs were citizens of the first rank and opulence, and Osterley was now old and faded. Francis Child, the younger, began to rebuild Gresham's house, and Robert Child about 1770 employed Robert Adam to complete it, and furnish it with all possible magnificence. The wings of the principal front were united by an Ionic portico of 12 columns; walls and ceilings were painted and decorated by Antonio Zucchi; mosaics, marbles, and velvets were imported from Italy; the walls of one room were hung with tapestry made for it at Gobelin; pictures by the Italian and Flemish masters filled the great gallery and drawing-room. A stone bridge was carried over an artificial lake, and a menagerie formed in the grounds.

"On Friday we went to see—oh, the palace of palaces!—and yet a palace *sans crown, sans coronet,* but such expense! such taste! such profusion! and yet half an acre produces all the rents that furnish such magnificence. It is a Jaghire got without a crime. In short, a shop is the estate, and Osterley Park is the spot. The old house I have often seen, which was built by Sir Thomas Gresham; but it is so improved and enriched, that all the Percies and Seymours of Syon must die of envy. There is a

---

* Fuller, Worthies: Middlesex; Mr. Greville, when on a visit to Lord Jersey at Osterley, records, Dec. 29, 1829, what would seem to be a tradition of the house: "It was here that Sir Thomas Gresham feasted Q. Elizabeth, and pulled down a wall in the night which she had found fault with, so that in the morning she found it was gone." Greville, Memoirs, vol. i., p. 261. But the account given in the text is the contemporary story.
Ward, Life of Gresham, p. 17.

* Norden, Spec. Brit. : Middx., p. 37.
† Garrard to Lord Wentworth, Jan. 11, 1635 Strafford Letters, vol. i., p. 357.

double portico that fills the space between the towers of the front, and is as noble as the Propyleum of Athens. There is a hall, library, breakfast-room, eating-room, all *chefs-d'œuvre* of Adam, a gallery one hundred and thirty feet long, and a drawing-room worthy of Eve before the Fall. Mrs. Child's dressing room is full of pictures, gold filigree, china and japan. So is all the house; the chairs are taken from antique lyres, and make charming harmony; there are Salvators, Gaspar Poussins, and to a beautiful staircase, a ceiling by Rubens. Not to mention a kitchen garden that costs £1400 a-year, a menagerie full of birds that come from a thousand islands, which Mr. Banks has not yet discovered; and then, in the drawing room I mentioned, there are door-cases and a crimson and gold frieze, that I believe were borrowed from the Palace of the Sun; and then the Park is —the ugliest spot of ground in the universe—and so I returned comforted to Strawberry. You shall see these wonders the first time you come to Twickenham." [*]

Osterley House is a stately red-brick mansion, nearly square in plan (140 ft. by 127) with turrets at the angles. The raised Ionic portico is approached by a flight of steps, and leads into an open court. The interior is still splendid, and contains some antique statuary and interesting pictures. The great hall, with the fine staircase and ceiling, painted by Rubens with the Apotheosis of William Prince of Orange, assassinated at Delft in 1584, is very striking. In the gallery and drawing-room are portraits of George Villiers, 1st Duke of Buckingham, by *Rubens;* Lord Strafford, in armour, *Vandyck;* and Mr. and Mrs. Robert Child, by *Reynolds;* historical and religious pictures by Guido, Dominichino, and other eminent masters, and some charming landscapes by Claude Lorraine, Nicolas and Gaspar Poussin, Salvator Rosa, Ruysdael, Berghem, etc. The library, decorated by Zucchi, contains some choice illuminated MSS., and Caxton's and other early printed books.[†] A Catalogue of the Library, by Dr. Morell, was printed in 1771. The Park, of about 350 acres, though level, is far from deserving Walpole's reproach, now that another century has imparted a venerable antiquity to the trees. The elms are particularly fine. The lake divides the park, and pleasantly varies the scenery. A public

* Hor. Walpole to the Countess of Ossory, June 21, 1773: Letters, vol. v., p. 474; and see Rev. Wm. Mason, July 16, 1778: Letters, vol. vii., p. 95.

† See Waagen, Galleries and Cabinets of Art in Great Britain, vol. iv., p. 269.

road and path crosses the park from Syon Hill to Norwood.

Osterley is the property of the Earl of Jersey, to whose family it came by the marriage of George, 5th Earl, with Sarah Sophia, eldest daughter of John, 10th Earl of Westmoreland, and granddaughter and heiress of Robert Child, Esq. The house is now the residence of the Dowager Duchess of Cleveland.

OTFORD, Kent (Dom. *Otefort*), 3 m. N. of Sevenoaks, and 2 m. S. of the Shoreham Stat. of the London, Chatham, and Dover Rly. (Sevenoaks br.): pop. 1126. Inn, *The Woodman.*

The vill. lies in a narrow valley cut through the chalk hills by the river Darent, and is pleasant-looking, in parts picturesque, and easily reached from Shoreham by a very agreeable walk past Shoreham Place, and through corn-fields and hop-gardens, leaving road and rly., the whole distance, on the l. Otford was the scene of a great battle in 774, when Offa defeated the Men of Kent; and again in 1016, when Edmund Ironside overtook and defeated the army of Canute. According to Hasted, "The fields here are full of the remains of those slain in the battles; bones are continually discovered in them, particularly when the new turnpike road was made in 1767, many skeletons were found in the chalk banks on each side." Offa gave the manor of Otford to the Abp. of Canterbury in 791, and it was retained by his successors till the reign of Henry VIII., when it was alienated by Cranmer. From a very early period the Archbishops of Canterbury had a *Palace* here, surrounded by a double park and extensive woods; and here one of their number, Abp. Winchelsea, died in 1313. Early in the 16th century, only a few years before it was lost to the see, the palace was rebuilt in a more sumptuous style by Abp. Warham, the wealthiest of English prelates, at a cost of £33,000; and on more than one occasion Warham entertained the King, Henry VIII., in it. Little is visible of its ancient splendour. The ruins stand on one side of a farm-yard W. of the ch., and consist of a roofless tower, and the cloistered side of the outer court. They are of brick, sadly dilapidated, and very dirty. The only picturesque fragment is the tower, which is covered with ivy, and in which remains some of the stone-work of the doors and windows: the cloisters serve as stables and tool-houses.

A little farther (by the watercress beds) is *St. Thomas à Beckett's Well*, a spring which tradition affirms issued forth on à Becket striking his staff into the ground. It is enclosed within a wall, forming a chamber 15 ft. across, and 10 ft. deep, and is said to have been used by the saint as his bath. The water, which is beautifully clear and cool, was once in high repute for its curative qualities, and is still resorted to medicinally. A hospital for lepers existed at Otford in 1228.

The *Church* (St. Bartholomew) is Dec. in style, but was in the main rebuilt, after a fire, in 1637 ; was repaired and altered—thoroughly 'restored'—in 1863 ; and now looks patchy. The body of the ch. is of flint and stone ; the S. aisle and chancel of Kentish rag ; the lower part of the massive tower is rough-cast, the upper brick. The interior has been made more uniform. The large Dec. E. window is a recent insertion. The only *mont.* of interest is one to Chas. Polhill, Esq., on the N. wall of the chancel, which has some local celebrity as being made of 7 different kinds of marble : it has well-carved figures of angels (in white marble) as supporters. S. of the ch. is a yew of good size, and healthy. The neighbourhood is very pretty ; from the heights there are wide prospects over a fertile and undulating country, and along the valley are extensive hop-gardens.

OXTEAD, or OXTED, Surrey

(Dom. *Acstede*), 3¼ m. N.E. from the Godstone Stat. of the S. E. Rly., and 4½ m. S.E. from the Caterham Stat. ; pop. 1164 ; stands in the midst of a beautiful and varied district. The vill., *Oxtead Street*, is a long irregular street, in which are a large brew-house, three or four public-houses (of which the best is the *Bell*) some tolerable shops, and many poor and dirty cottages. Some good residences have been built of late years about the parish, and by the ch. is a fair example of an old one.

The *Church* (of the Virgin Mary), ½ m. N.E. of Oxtead Street, is mostly late Dec.; the tower is E.E.; the large E.

window (French Dec. in style) is recent. *Observe* the sundial by the porch (on S.W.) re-erected in 1815. Inside are several monts. to the Hoskins family, but none of interest except a poor brass to a child, of 1611. Far better is the *brass* to John Ynge, rector, d. 1428. A mural mont. on the N. wall has kneeling effigies of John Aldersley, a prosperous and prolific "haberdasher and merchant-venturor of London," d. 1616, his wife, and their 10 sons and 7 daughters.

Barrow Green, 1 m. W. of the ch., is so called from a large ancient tumulus ; there are others, not so large, in the neighbouring parish of Godstone. Hops are grown about Oxtead and Tandridge.

Barrow Green House is the seat of C. Hoskins Master, Esq., lord of the manor.

"Jeremy Bentham had a country residence called *Barrow Green House*, which he occupied during the summer season, renting it furnished of Mrs. Koe [Roe], widow of Mr. Master, late owner of that place, a life proprietrix. . . . At Barrow Green, James Mill and his children lived (about the years 1812-1813-1814) with Bentham, who kept house for all, as he had done at other country houses, and did likewise afterwards, at Ford Abbey, near Chard. Barrow Green House, some forty-five years afterwards, was rented and inhabited by Mr. Grote, and therein he and Mrs. Grote received more than one visit from John Stuart Mill, who took a lively pleasure in retracing the scenes of his childhood, and in recalling the personal recollections of Jeremy Bentham connected with the spot." [*]

Grote took a short lease of Barrow Green House, Midsummer 1859, and lived there till June 1863.

"A spacious and rural residence, with fifty acres of grass land, offering itself (near Godstone), we entered upon the occupation of 'Barrow Green House' at the end of the London season of 1859, which was passed in Saville Row. We received therein many guests during the months that followed (G. C. Lewis among the number), and found ourselves well satisfied with our new residence, except that the winter of 1859-1860 proved terribly severe, and that the old house was very imperfectly provided with the means of warding off cold. The fire-grates would seem to have been placed there under the 'Commonwealth' or coeval with the chimneys. One of them, in fact, bore the date of 1649, and its capacity of affording warmth corresponded with its age." [†]

Other seats are *Perryfield* (C. M'Niven, Esq.) ; *Shrubhurst* (Colonel C. Sedley Burdett) ; *Stone Hall* (G. Barker, Esq.) ; *Broadhams* (E. Kelsey, Esq.)

---

[*] Mrs. Grote's Personal Life of George Grote, note to p. 24.
[†] *Ibid.*, p. 246.

PAIN'S HILL, SURREY (*see* COBHAM).

PALMER'S GREEN, MIDDX. (*see* SOUTHGATE).

PANSHANGER, HERTS, the seat of Earl Cowper, is in Hertingfordbury par., about 2½ m. W. of Hertford. *Cole Green*, on the St. Albans and Hatfield br. of the Grt. N. Rly., is the nearest rly. stat., about 1½ m. by a charming walk through Panshanger Park; but the distance is very little farther from the *Hertingfordbury* Stat., and the walk is equally beautiful through the other side of the park, by a path nearly parallel to the Maran, here a very pretty stream.

The manor of Blakemere, or, as Chauncy writes it, Blakesware, was bought by the first Lord Cowper—the Lord Chancellor Cowper of the reign of Anne and the early years of George I.—of a merchant of London named Elwes; and in 1720 he added largely to the property by the purchase of an estate at Hertingfordbury of a Mrs. Culling. Blakesmere belonged in the reign of Henry VIII. to the family of the Hangers, whence the name Panshanger appears to be derived. The Chancellor built himself a house at Colne (now Cole) Green, in which he died, Oct. 10, 1723. This continued to be the family seat till 1801, when it was taken down by the 5th Earl Cowper, and the present house erected on higher ground, about 1 m. N., which had been purchased of Lady Hughes.

Panshanger has been altered, enlarged, and modernized, but remains essentially a stucco-fronted, semi-castellated Gothic mansion of the Walpole-Wyatt type, most unsatisfactory when examined closely, but grandiose and picturesque when looked at in connection with its surroundings. The Drawing-room, or Picture Gallery, as it is sometimes called, in which the more important of the paintings are hung, is a noble and richly furnished room, lighted by three lanterns and a large bay window, from which you have a splendid view over the terrace, gardens, and park. Other rooms contain good pictures; but the visitor who obtains permission to view the paintings will do well to devote his attention chiefly to this.

The Italian pictures, which constitute the glory of Panshanger, were chiefly collected by George Nassau, 3rd Earl Cowper, who went to Florence a young man in 1762, married and settled there, was created a Count of the Holy Empire, and there spent most of his remaining years. A collection formed under such circumstances was likely to be exceptionally rich, as this is, in pictures of the Florentine school. The following are some of the more important examples :—

Portrait of a Man, with landscape background, admirably painted, and exquisite in feeling, *Perugino;* Waagen says by Francia ;* but the ascription is probably correct. Madonna and Child, *Raphael;* an early work, much in the manner of Perugino, but very tender and graceful ; and the grave, dreamy expression of the Mother looking out of the picture imparts an elevation of tone sometimes absent in Raphael's later representations of this theme. Finer, however, larger in style, and more mature in thought, is a later Madonna by the great master (it is dated 1508), in which the Mother bends forward in rapt contemplation of the Child, seated on her knee. The face of the Child is not satisfactory, but that of the Virgin gains on you the more it is studied, as indeed does the painting as a whole. By it is a picture that does not suffer even by comparison with Raphael's masterly work, the Holy Family, by *Fra Bartolommeo* (Baccio della Porta). The Virgin is seated in the centre of the picture, under the shade of a palm-tree; by her side is St. Joseph; the infant Saviour on her lap has just given a cross to the young St. John, who is standing by, and who presses it to his breast with a saddened forecasting of the future. This is evidently the key-note of the picture ; and the still, subdued attitude and expressions of the personages, the sombre richness of the colour in sky and landscape, as in the group itself,—all serve to deepen the still, religious pathos of the scene. It is undoubtedly the finest work by Bartolommeo in this country, and among the finest extant. It is about 5 ft. by 4 ft., and in one or two places a little injured by the restorer. Virgin Enthroned,

* Art Treasures in Great Britain, vol. iv., p. 345.

P. Veronese, an altar-piece, with saints and emblems and much ecclesiastical paraphernalia ; very ably painted. A companion piece, the Prodigal's Return, by *Guercino*, is also good in its way. Ecce Homo, *Correggio*, unfinished, but fine in colour and powerful in conception. By Correggio also is a Virgin and Child that may be usefully compared with Raphael's Madonna. Children, *Titian*, of more than doubtful genuineness ; as is also the Pietà, ascribed to *Michael Angelo*, and which Waagen transfers (without much reason perhaps) to Daniel da Volterra. The Nativity, *Carlo Dolce*, full of refinement. Sibyl, *Guido*, freely and well painted. Portrait of himself, *A. del Sarto*. Standing behind a table at which he has been writing, the painter looks with a frank, manly, unembarrassed gaze at his visitor. A capital portrait. So, too, is that of a lady with a music-book in her hand. Two legends of Saints, by *del Sarto*, are obscure to the uninitiated, and not of much artistic value. His other picture, a predella of Joseph making himself known to his brethren, is of a better order. By *Moroni* there is a good and characteristic head of a man. A Mountainous Coast, with fishermen, *Salvator Rosa*, somewhat injured by the cleaner, but a capital work ; the best landscape in the collection. Also by Salvator are another larger and two smaller landscapes, but they are of inferior value.

Of the pictures other than Italian, and chiefly portraits, one of the most remarkable is an equestrian portrait of Marshal Turenne, by *Rembrandt*, on a canvas $9\frac{1}{2}$ ft. by 6 ft., and affording the painter full scope for his vigorous pencil and wondrous combination of light and shade. It appears to be the only life-sized equestrian portrait Rembrandt painted, and the painter can hardly be congratulated on his horsemanship. By *Velasquez*, there is a clever head of a Boy with a Dog. By *N. Poussin*, is a manly, unaffected head of Du Quesnoy (Il Fiammingo) the sculptor, best known by his carvings on ivory of children. Villiers Duke of Buckingham is one of *Jansen's* coarse, unflattering, suggestive full-lengths, which the historical student finds so interesting. Lord Bacon, a half-length by *Van Somer*, is a repetition of a familiar picture. John Duke of Nassau with his

Family, is one of those lordly groups which nobody ever painted like *Vandyck ;* and this is one of his best : it was painted in 1634,—before, therefore, he was rendered careless by the full tide of London prosperity. The portrait by him of Percy Earl of Northumberland is a duplicate of that at Cassiobury. By Sir Peter Lely there are two or three uninteresting portraits. *Sir Godfrey Kneller* has a good half-length of the first Earl, Lord Chancellor Cowper ; of whom, however, there is a more characteristic whole-length, in his Chancellor's robes, with the great seal by his side, a stately work, by the elder *Richardson*,—of whose careful though somewhat dull pencil there are other specimens here.

The Cowper portraits are of course numerous, and to one versed in the family annals would no doubt all be interesting. One group, as an example of the Conversation Pieces that Hogarth often essayed, and Zoffany rendered so popular, and as a representation of the Florentine Earl, the collector of the Panshanger pictures, is worth noting : George Nassau, 3rd Earl Cowper, and his family are represented as a musical party of six the Countess at the harpsichord, my lord playing the violoncello. There are also portraits by Reynolds (one or two very good ones), Hoppner, Northcote, Lawrence, etc.; but these may be left now.

The park is very delightful, and there are several open paths. It is of considerable size, finely timbered, undulating, with the pretty Maran winding through its midst, and below the house expanding into a lake. The ancestral trees of Panshanger are a delight to the eye and the memory. Many are of large size, but more of magnificent form. By the Cole Green gate are several noble old oaks of from 17 to 20 ft. in girth, and most picturesque. But the pride of the park is the famous Panshanger Oak, which stands on a bottom, or broad lawn, a little to the W. of the house, and has been figured in most of the published histories of English trees from Strutt to Loudon. It was known as the Great Oak when Arthur Young wrote his 'View of the Agriculture of Hertfordshire,' and he says it was so known in 1709. It was then estimated to contain 796 cubic feet of timber ; in 1822 Strutt reckoned it to contain

1000 ft. He gave the thickness of the trunk as 19 ft. at 3 ft. from the ground. The trunk now measures 20 ft. 4 in. at 5 ft. from the ground. But it is not so much its size as its perfect form and symmetry that renders it so impressive. It rises from the ground a clear stem without a break for some 12 ft., then its glorious branches spread out equally on all sides, sweeping the ground at their extremities and forming a circle 100 ft. across, the main stem rising upwards without a bend, "tall as the mast of some great ammiral," and sending off at regular distances duly diminishing branches till the whole is a majestic mound of foliage. This magnificent tree is, however, passing or past its prime. Each time we have seen it of late years we have observed more leafless spray at top, and more broken and decaying wood in the great branches below; but it is still a wonderful tree, and worth a long journey to see. Let us add that access to the park, and, upon application, to the grounds, is most liberally accorded; and that permission is very freely granted to see the pictures whenever the rooms are not actually occupied by the family.

PARK STREET, HERTS, a hamlet of St. Stephen's par., St. Albans, from which town it is 2 m. S., and a stat. on the St. Albans br. of the L. and N.W. Rly. Park Street is a little rustic straw-plaiting village on the London road, where it is crossed by the Colne, with trees on all sides, and pleasant lanes leading away to pleasanter Brickett Wood. Within a broad green enclosure at the S. end of the vill., serving alike for Park Street and Colney Street, stands the modest district ch., a recent Norm., white brick, cruciform fabric, with an apsidal chancel, and a bellcote on the W. gable.

PARNDON, GREAT, ESSEX (anc. *Paringdon*), about 2½ m. S.E. from the Roydon Stat. of the Grt. E. Rly. (Cambridge line);—go to the end of Roydon Street, and there inquire the way, by lane and field paths: the road is much longer and less pleasant. Pop. 491.

The village is secluded, stands on high ground, and the scenery is more varied than is common in this part of Essex.

The church (dedication unknown) stands a little W. of the vill., by Hall Farm. It is small, plain, covered with plaster, and has a tall weather-beaten tower of flint and stone on the W.; is Perp. in style, and has been partially restored. The interior is neat, has open seats, and a timber roof, ceiled between the rafters. S. of the altar is a piscina. There are no monts. At *Parndon Cross*, a little S. of the ch., is a decent country inn, the *Cock*, at the parting of the roads, looking very snug and picturesque under the shadow of two immense elms. About the middle of the 12th cent. Roger de Paringdon founded a Premonstratensian monastery here, but it was removed in 1180 to Bileigh, near Maldon.

PARNDON, LITTLE, ESSEX, lies N.E. of Great Parndon (the churches are 1½ m. apart), and ½ m. W. of the Burnt Mill Stat. of the Grt. E. Rly.: pop. 117. The par. is small, and there is no vill. The *Church* (St. James) is an elegant little early Dec. building of French type, erected in 1868, chiefly at the cost of Mr. L. W. Arkwright, in place of a rude and dilapidated Dec. structure. It is of flint and stone, has nave, apsidal chancel, porch on the S.W., and a wooden belfry rising from the W. end of the roof. The interior is prettily finished. The scenery, though flat, is pleasant along the Stoat, which here divides Essex from Herts; and the water-mills (Burnt Mill, Little Parndon, and Hunsdon mills) break the monotony. *Parndon Hall*, the seat of L. W. Arkwright, Esq., lord of the manor, is a spacious modern red-brick and stone mansion. *Gilston Park* (J. Hodgson, Esq.), on the high ground N. of the Stoat, is in Hertfordshire.

PARSON'S GREEN, MIDDX. (*see* FULHAM).

PENGE, SURREY, a detached hamlet of Battersea, but for poor-law and eccl. purposes a separate parish, lies between Norwood and Beckenham, on the N.W. border of Kent, and 7 m. from London. Pop. 13,202 (Penge St. John, 8345; Upper Penge, 4857). *Rly. Stats.* —On main line of L., Br., and S. C. Rly., Penge Stat.; Anerley Stat. Also on London Bridge and Victoria line. On L., C., and D. Rly., at Penge Lane.

Fifty years ago Penge was only spoken of as a common, and the maps show hardly a house upon it. By the Crooked Billet, on the Beckenham road, there were a few dwellings; the Croydon Canal (constructed 1801) with its step-like locks, crossed the Common—then noted for its oaks,—beyond was Penge Wood. Slowly the houses increased in number, till the old canal was bought and converted into a railway in 1839, and Penge Common was fixed on as a convenient stat. for Norwood and Beckenham. Then "the plague of building lighted upon it;" spread more rapidly when Penge Place was taken for the Crystal Palace, Penge Wood was absorbed partly in the palace grounds, and the rest, doubly attractive from its proximity to that popular resort, given over to the builder; and culminated when a Freehold Building Society bought what had been spared of the Common for distribution among its members. Now, Penge is a town in size and population, in appearance a waste of modern tenements, mean, monotonous, and wearisome. It has 3 churches, many chapels, schools, hotels, taverns, inns, 'offices' of all sorts, shops, 4 or 5 rly. stations, and whatever may be looked for in a new suburban rly. town.

The churches are—St. John the Evangelist, Gothic of 1850, originally a chapel, with aisles added in 1861, and transepts in 1866; St. Paul's, Hamlet Road, a commonplace Gothic ch., erected in 1867; and Holy Trinity, South Penge, a somewhat more ambitious parti-coloured brick fabric erected in 1872.

The *Watermen's and Lightermen's Asylum*, opposite St. John's ch., Dulwich Road, a neat structure in good-sized grounds, built and managed by the Watermen's Company, consists of 40 comfortable residences and a lodge, for the reception of decayed watermen and lightermen. Close by it, in Penge Lane, is *King William IV.'s Naval Asylum*, erected from the designs of Philip Hardwick, R.A., at the sole cost of Queen Adelaide, for 12 widows of commanders in the merchant service.

PERIVALE, MIDDX., anc. GREENFORD PARVA, lies to the E. of Greenford (Magna), on the rt. bank of the Brent, 2 m. N. by W. of the Ealing Stat. of the Grt. W. Rly. and about 8 m. from Hyde Park Corner.

Considering its nearness to London, Perivale is a curiously lonely-looking little place. It lies in the valley of the Brent, among broad meadows, the 4 farms being all hay-farms, and no other houses, not even a labourer's cottage, near. In the entire par., of 624 acres, there were in 1871 only 7 houses and 33 inhab. The Church stands at the edge of a field, alongside a low semi-Gothic half-timber parsonage, a farm-house its only other neighbour. The seclusion is delightful; and the green meadows, backed by the hill and spire of Harrow, are pleasant to look upon. The *Church* (dedication unknown) is very small, late Dec. or early Perp., and consists of nave and narrow chancel, rough-cast, wooden tower and short pyramidal spire at the W., and porch on the S.W. The interior is neat, nicely kept, and in good order, having been restored in 1875. In the windows is some late 15th cent. glass—figures of St. John the Baptist, St. Matthew, tolerably perfect, and St. Mary and St. Joseph, much less so. A low 17th cent. screen divides the nave from the chancel; and on the S.W. is a small hagioscope. There are *monts.* to Lanes, Harrisons, Mylletts, and other local families. Before the altar rails, on the chancel floor, is a *brass* to Henry Myllet, d. 1500, his 2 wives and 15 children. Philip Fletcher, Dean of Kildare, brother of Bp. Fletcher, and author of 'Truth at Court,' a poem popular in its day, and forgotten now, was buried here, May 12, 1765.

From the ch. a walk of a short m. due N. leads to *Horsington Hill*, whence there are pleasant views—the best obtainable of Harrow Hill, and a wider one over Harrow Weald and Wembly—and *Horsington Wood*, rich in spring flowers and shady walks, but now enclosed. The City of London District School (Cuckoo Farm) is on the l. of the lane to Greenford.

PERRY STREET, KENT, is a hamlet and eccl. district of Northfleet, from which vill. it is 1 m. S.E.; pop. 1208. Perry Street has grown into favour as a place of residence, and many good moderate-sized houses have been erected. The country is pleasant; the higher grounds afford cheerful and varied prospects. Farming and market gardening are the chief occupations. In 1871 a pretty ritualistic E.E. *church* (All Saints), was erected from the designs of Mr. J. Brooks. It is of Kentish rag, and has a sanctus bell in the bellcote over the chancel arch, which can be rung from the steps of the choir.

PERRY VALE, KENT (*see* SYDENHAM).

PETERSHAM, SURREY, a pleasant village on the Thames between Richmond and Kingston, and about 1½ m. S. of the Richmond Rly. Stat. Pop. 683.

The manor at the Conquest belonged to the Abbey of St. Peter, at Chertsey, whence no doubt the place derived its name (*Patricesham* in Dom.), and the ch. its dedication. At the Dom. Survey there was a ch. at Petersham. On the land were 15 villans and 4 bordarii. A fishery was estimated at 1000 eels and 1000 lampreys—the only instance in the Survey of the home counties in which lampreys are specified. The Abbey retained the manor till 1415, when it was conveyed to the King, Henry V. It was settled by Henry VIII., in 1541, on his divorced wife, Anne of Cleves, who surrendered it, with other estates, to the Crown in 1548. James I. in 1610 granted the manors of Petersham, Ham, and Sheen to his eldest son Henry, Prince of Wales, on whose decease, 1612, they were conveyed to Prince Charles. A lease of Petersham had been granted by James I. to George Cole, whose mont., with effigy, is in Petersham ch. In 1637 a reversionary lease was granted by Charles I. to William Murray, afterwards Earl of Dysart. In 1672 Charles granted the lordship of Ham and Petersham in fee-simple to John Earl of Lauderdale, (whom he created Baron Petersham and Earl of Guildford in England, and Duke of Lauderdale in Scotland) and to his wife, Elizabeth, Countess of Dysart, and to her heirs by her first husband. Petersham thus passed to the Tollemaches, and is now the property of the Earl of Dysart, whose fine seat, Ham House, is in Petersham par. (*See* HAM ; HAM HOUSE.) The barony of Petersham having become extinct by the death, without heirs, of the

Duke of Lauderdale, the title was revived in William Stanhope, who was created, 1742, Viscount Petersham and Earl of Harrington.

Though lying low, Petersham is very pleasantly placed, having Ham Walks and Ham House and grounds on one side, Richmond and Richmond Park on the other, the Thames in front, and Ham Common in the rear. Petersham *Church* (St. Peter) is of red brick, and was built, as an entry in the register records, in 1505. It is small and low, and of unorthodox form, the nave stretching N. and S., while the chancel (a vestige apparently of the earlier edifice, rough-cast, and having an old Dec. window) projects eastward. On the W. is a tower, small and low, with a cupola turret. The int. is not attractive. *Monts.*— N. of chancel, George Cole, Esq., of the Middle Temple, d. 1624, with recumbent effigy in black robe and ruff, parchment roll in rt. hand, under an arch flanked by Corinthian columns ; by him his wife Frances, d. 1633. Tablet to Sir Thomas Jenner, Baron of the Exchequer, and Judge of the Common Pleas, d. 1707. On W. wall, a tablet, erected in 1841 by the Hudson's Bay Company to Capt. George Vancouver, R.N., the distinguished circumnavigator, who died at Petersham in 1798 and was buried in the ch.-yard.

The ch.-yard contains the remains of many persons eminent in place or merit. A large and showy tomb records the interment of Richard Earl of Mount-Edgcumbe, d. 1839. One by the chancel to Vice-Admiral Sir George Scott, d. 1841, has inscribed on another side some much-admired and often-quoted verses on Lady Frances C. Douglas, daughter of the Marquis of Queensbury, who d. 1827, in her 15th year. Other oft-read verses are in commemoration of Patty Bean, who d. 1785, aged 12. Very different is the interest excited by the stone which marks the grave of Horace Walpole's "Elder-Berries," the Mary and Agnes Berry to whom the world is indebted for his Reminiscences, and a large part of his later Correspondence. During the last twenty years of their lives the sisters spent the summer of each year in what they called their "retirement at Petersham." Being at Paris in July 1836, Miss Berry writes in her journal,—

" It is now that I figure Petersham and our quiet

garden there as everything on earth that I most covet, and from which I no longer desire to wander. There in the immediate neighbourhood of a friend [Lady Scott] more my child than any other ever can be—there I feel that I can patiently wait for the last stroke which is to send me to the neighbouring country church-yard, where I have long intended to have my bones deposited." *

She did, however, wander a good deal after this entry, and it was not till nearly 16 years had passed, and she was in her 90th year, that her bones were deposited in the ch.-yard, alongside those of the sister who had been with her through their long life, and in death was not separated. Their grave is marked by a large plain stone, under a lime-tree, by the path N.E. of the ch. The insc. was written by the Earl of Carlisle.

" Mary Berry, born March, 1763, d. Nov. 1852. Agnes Berry, born May, 1764, d. Jan. 1852.

Beneath this stone are laid the remains of these Two Sisters, amidst scenes which in life they had frequented and loved. Followed by the tender regret of those who close the unbroken succession of Friends devoted to them with fond affection during every step of their long career."

Beside their's is another stone, inscribed to one often mentioned in the Journals and Correspondence—Isabella Harrott, died Nov. 1854, aged 90, "For nearly 60 years the faithful and devoted housekeeper to the Misses Berry." On the S. side of the ch.-yard is an unusually elaborate and elegant low tomb, coffer-shaped, with raised centre of red granite, on a base of dull grey granite with polished bosses and pattern, and surmounted with an enriched cross, to Albert Henry Scott, Student of Ch. Ch., Oxford, d. 1865, son of Sir Gilbert G. Scott, R.A., then resident at the Manor House. The celebrated Countess of Dysart and Duchess of Lauderdale was buried (as well as married) in Petersham ch., but the only record of her is in the register. Charles Caleb Colton, the author of 'Lacon,' held the living of Petersham and Kew from 1817 till deprived for misconduct in 1828.

The principal seat, *Ham House*, is described under that title. *Petersham Lodge* was purchased of Gregory Cole by Charles I., at the time he enclosed the New Park, Richmond. In 1682 James II. granted a lease of it to his nephew, Hyde Lord Cornbury, grandson of Lord Chancellor Claren-

don. From him it descended to Henry Hyde, 2nd and last Earl of Rochester, in whose possession it was when, Oct. 1, 1721, it was destroyed by a fire, which destroyed also much rich old furniture, many family pictures, and the Chancellor's priceless library. The *second* Petersham Lodge was built by Richard Boyle, the architect Earl of Burlington, for William Stanhope, 1st Viscount Petersham and Earl of Harrington (d. 1756). William Stanhope, the 3rd Earl, sold it to Thomas Pitt, 1st Lord Camelford (d. 1793), who in 1784 procured an Act of Parliament for the purchase of the fee-simple of the Crown, and in 1790 sold his right to the Duke of Clarence, afterwards William IV. The Duke made it for a time his residence, and then parted with it to William Tollemache, Lord Huntingtower (d. 1833), whose executors sold it for £14,000 to the Commissioners of Woods and Forests, by whom it was pulled down and annexed to Richmond Park. The large cedars on the declivity below Pembroke Lodge by Petersham Lane, mark the situation of the last Petersham Lodge. The grounds were very beautiful and very famous :

" The pendent woods
That nodding hang o'er Harrington's retreat,"

commemorated in 'The Seasons,' are the woods of Petersham Lodge.

Sudbrook is mentioned as a hamlet as early as 1266, but it has for centuries been reduced to a single house. Sudbrook, or Sudbroke, House belonged to John Duke of Argyll, the eminent statesman, who d. there in 1743. From him it passed to his eldest daughter, Lady Catherine Campbell, created Baroness of Greenwich, on whose decease at Sudbrook House, in 1794, it passed to Henry, 3rd Duke of Buccleuch, her son by her first marriage. Later it was the property and residence of Sir Robert Wilmot Horton, Under Secretary for the Colonies, and afterwards Governor of Ceylon, who made extensive alterations in the house and grounds. It was afterwards purchased for the Crown, and the grounds in part annexed to Richmond Park. For several years past *Sudbrook Park*, as it is now called, has been a " hydropathic sanatorium." The house is a large and stately edifice of three storeys, with an elevated tetrastyle portico, approached by a tall double flight of steps.

* Miss Berry's Journal and Correspondence, vol. iii., p. 444.

The grounds, though curtailed, are extensive and beautiful.

Bute House, by the village, was the seat of the Marquis of Bute, and afterwards of Lord Dudley-Coutts Stuart. It is now a "gentleman's boarding-school." The *Manor House*, formerly the residence of Sir Gilbert Scott, R.A., is now the seat of Tanfield G. Headley, Esq. *Douglas House* (C. Home-Drummond-Moray, Esq.), *Montrose House* (R. Fowler, Esq.), and *Petersham House* (S. Walker, Esq.), are among the other seats.

PINNER, MIDDX., nearly 3 m. N.W. of Harrow by road, but nearer by the fields, and about 13 m. from London : the Pinner Stat. of the L. and N.W. Rly. is 1½ m. N.E. of the vill. Pop. 2332, of whom 248 were in the Commercial Travellers' Schools.

Pinner was formerly a hamlet and chapelry of Harrow, and part of the same demesne, but is now a separate parish. Though only a hamlet, it had a market, granted by Edward III. to the Abp. of Canterbury in 1336. The market has long been lost, but of the two annual fairs, granted at the same time, one survives, though shrunken to a small pleasure fair of a single day, Whit-Wednesday. Pinner stands on elevated ground, whence flows one of the feeders of the Colne. The main street is broad, clean, lined, among many modern ones, with several old half-timber houses, with overhanging upper floors and gables. On its N. side is a long, low, old country inn, an excellent specimen of its class, the Queen's Head, bearing on its front the date 1705, and no doubt a genuine relic of Queen Anne's reign. At the upper (E.) end of the street, on the highest ground, soars the weather-beaten church tower, with the bare trunk of a huge elm before it, fitting finish to a scene unusually archaic, rustic, and picturesque for its nearness to London. A charming etching of Pinner, looking towards the church, was made by George Cooke in 1828, when it was even more picturesque than now.

The *Church* (St. John the Baptist) was built in 1321, but it includes parts of an earlier building, and it has been at various times added to, altered and modernized. It is of flint and stone, with patches of rough-cast : cruciform, with an embattled W. tower ; transepts small and low, and tall tiled roofs. Though in the main of the 14th cent., the S. aisle and transepts have lancets. The tower is a good one of the usual Perp. type, with a bold angle turret on the N.W., carried well above the battlements, and a pyramidal tiled roof. The E. window of 5 lights is filled with modern painted glass. In one of the lancets are some fragments of old glass. A mural *mont.* to John Day, minister of Pinner, d. 1622, has his effigy and an insc. commencing—

"This portraiture presents him to thy sight
Who was a burning and a shining light."

Other monts. are to the Clitherow, Page, and Hastings families, and one to Sir Bartholomew Shower, d. 1701, of Pinner Hill, a lawyer famous in his day, and an author of repute, who, the register records, was "buried in sheep's wool only." In the chancel is a mural brass of a chrysom child, 1580.

The Abbot of Westminster was appointed Keeper of *Pinner Park* in 1383. Pinner Park, ½ m. E. of the vill., was included in the grant made by Henry VIII. to Sir Edward North (*see* HARROW) ; was alienated, disparked, and converted into tillage : it is now the property of St. Thomas's Hospital. *Pinner Hill* (W. A. Tooke, Esq.), 2 m. N.W., was the seat of Sir Christopher Clitherow, and afterwards of Sir Bartholomew Shower. It is a good house ; the grounds are very beautiful, and command wide views. A little E. is *Pinner Wood House* (R. H. Silversides, Esq.), where Lord Lytton wrote 'Eugene Aram.' In its vicinity is a fragment of the still pleasant Pinner Wood. *Pinner Place* (Mrs. Garrard) was long the residence of Zephaniah Holwell, Governor of Bengal, and author of a narrative of the sufferings of himself and fellow-prisoners in the Black Hole, Calcutta. The *Manor House* is the seat of H. Morley, Esq.

Pinner Green is a sort of hamlet, ½ m. N. of the vill. Beyond are *Pinner Grove* and *Woodhall. Woodridings*, 1½ m., by the Rly. Stat., is a growing hamlet, with some good residences and a chapel-of-ease. At *Headstone*, 1 m. E. of Pinner, was a residence of the Abps. of Canterbury (*see* HARROW) ; the moat still remains. *Hatch End*, by the rly., 1 m. N.E. of the vill., is a hamlet of small houses, with a landing-place for goods and coals on the rly.

Close to Pinner Rly. Stat., and the rly., are the *Commercial Travellers' Schools* founded in 1845. The building, a pleasing and commodious collegiate Gothic structure, was opened by the Prince Consort in 1855. Wings were added in 1868, rendering it capable of accommodating 300 children; and that number is now fully maintained, in the proportion of about 200 boys and 100 girls. The schools are admirably managed; the boys, who receive a superior education, leave at the age of 15.

PLAISTOW, Essex, a vill. and eccl. dist. of West Ham par., and a Stat. on the L. and Southend Rly., 1 m. E. of West Ham, 4½ m. E. of Whitechapel ch.: pop. 6699 (Plaistow St. Mary, 3448; St. Andrew, 3251). But this is exclusive of the new district in the Plaistow Marshes, Canning Town, and Victoria Docks ("London over the border") which in 1871 had 7874 inhabitants.

The old village of Plaistow, lying loosely along North Street, the Broadway, Balaam Street, and Greengate, with roomy old houses and large gardens, tree-girt and surrounded with green though level fields, secluded, quiet, rural, was in the last and early part of the present century a favourite place of abode with sedate merchants and citizens of credit and renown. Pelleys, Morleys, Gurneys, Frys, Howards, Sturges, Hoares, Martins, Schroders, dwelt within it or on its borders. There was a Friends' Meeting House before there was a ch., and Mrs. Fry, Joseph John, and Samuel Gurney, the Howards, and the Sturges were among the regular worshippers and frequent ministrants. The Independents and other dissenters were strongly represented, and the vill. had altogether a staid and somewhat of a puritanic aspect. Apart from the requirements of the wealthier residents, the occupations of the inhabitants were mainly agricultural and pastoral.

"Upon a fertile spot of land,
Does Plaistow, thriving Plaistow stand,"

wrote an enthusiastic local bard. The raising of potatoes in the fields, and fattening sheep in the marshes, were the chief sources of profit.

"Potatoes now are Plaistow's pride,
Whole markets now are hence supplied;

Nor finer mutton can you spend
Than what our fattening marshes send." *

Entirely changed is the old village now. Unpleasant manufactures, driven from the capital, have settled down in the Marshes. The great Metropolitan Sewer, in the form of a huge grass-covered embankment, has been carried across the level, and through the vill. The construction of the sewer, the opening of the rly., and the proximity of great manufacturing establishments caused a large influx of the labouring classes. The gentry migrated. The handsome old mansions have been pulled down, suffered to go to decay, or diverted to other uses, and the grounds built over. The trees have been felled; the fields, changed into streets which lead nowhere, are left unfinished and fragmentary, and lined with mean little tenements, which, dirty, frail, and gardenless, look as though cast in a mould—and that a bad one—and warped and cracked whilst drying in the sun. The Friends' Meeting House is transformed into a School Board school; the Congregational Chapel into "The Tonic Sol-Fa Press"—with a steam-pipe puffing out all day its unmelodious key-note; and the great house in the Broadway is depressed into a "Destitute Children's Home." One compensation Plaistow has: though Mr. Gurney's stately house has disappeared, his still handsome park has been happily secured as a free public park for ever.

West Ham Park lies just outside Plaistow vill., and Plaistow people have the readiest access to it.

The *Church* of St. Mary, built in 1830, is a small brick edifice of the Gothic then in vogue. St. Andrew's, built in 1870, from the designs of Mr. J. Brooks, is another brick ch., but of an altogether different type. Large, unusually lofty, cruciform, it promises to be an imposing edifice; but left as it is incomplete, it can hardly be considered satisfactory, however much it may be in keeping with its surroundings. The new Congregational Chapel in Balaam Street is a very ecclesiastical looking building.

The old vill. has extended into the Barking Road, and spread out over the marshes, and has been met by straggling

* White, Eastern Counties, vol. ii., p. 299.

streets and houses from Hall Ville, Silver Town, Canning Town, and the Victoria Docks, manufacturing and shipping quarters, built on the marshes between the Lea and the Thames, and reaching back across the Barking Road towards Plaistow proper and West Ham. But these places hardly fall within our province, belonging rather to the outer border of London; and it will be enough to say that they have grown up within the last few years about the great docks, chemical, creosoting, artificial manure, engineering and various other works, without order and without oversight; are dirty, incomplete, unfragrant, unattractive, but in many points of view exceedingly interesting. The Victoria Docks are perhaps the finest on the Thames, and well worth visiting. They have an area of 100 acres, admit ships of the largest size, and are provided with the most perfect hydraulic and other appliances. The entrance lock is 325 ft. long, and 80 ft. wide, and has a depth on the sill of 28 ft. at high water. There are churches at Silvertown; at Nelson Street, Victoria Docks (St. Luke); and in the Barking Road (Holy Trinity); besides chapels, schools, halls, and institutes innumerable.

Aaron Hill, distinguished in his day as a dramatic writer, 'retired' to Plaistow in 1738 to cultivate poetry and his garden, and here wrote several of his pieces, including the adaptation of the tragedy of 'Merope,' the last work he lived to complete. Edmund Burke was also for awhile a resident here.

"About this time [1759] he occasionally resided at Plaistow in Essex. A lady, then about 14 years old and residing in the neighbourhood, informs me that she perfectly remembers him there. His brother Richard, who found employment in the City, was with him frequently; and both were much noticed in the neighbourhood for agreeable and sociable qualities. Among their visitors, calculated to attract notice in the country, were several known as popular authors, and a few as men of rank." *

Luke Howard, F.R.S., lived in a house on the W. side of Balaam Street, opposite the Greyhound. The house is still standing, but has been new-fronted, and the cupola lantern removed from the roof. There he had his chemical laboratory, and there carried out the meteorological observations which resulted in his great

* Prior, Life of Burke, Bohn's ed., p. 63.

work on 'The Climate of London,' and the determination and nomenclature of cloud-forms, universally adopted, and still in use.

PLAISTOW, KENT (*see* BROMLEY).

PLASHET, ESSEX (*see* EAST HAM).

PLUMSTEAD, KENT (Dom. *Plumestede*),

lies immediately E. of Woolwich. The ch., at the eastern extremity of the town, is 1 m. from Woolwich, but the towns run into each other. Rly. stats.: Dartford br. of L. and S.E. Rly., Woolwich Arsenal, for W. end of vill.; Plumstead (by the ch.) for the E. Pop. 28,259; in 1851 only 8373. Inn, *Plume of Feathers*.

Plumstead High Street may be regarded as a part of Woolwich, running into Burrage Town, a new district of workmen's houses, modern cottages, and small villas. Beyond the streets is an agricultural district, a large portion being cultivated as market gardens, and the broad marshes by the Thames kept for grazing. There are chalk and sand pits, brick and tile works, and kilns where drain-pipes, garden pots, and sugar moulds are largely made. Plumstead had once a weekly market, but it belongs to a time beyond memory.

The old *Church* (St. Nicholas), situated at the edge of Plumstead Marsh, by a fine old farm-house, is a somewhat incongruous admixture of styles and periods. It comprises nave and N. aisle, in part Perp. N. transept or chapel, of E.E. date (*obs.* the lancet on the E.); with Perp. window inserted on N. chancel, and tall embattled square brick tower of early 17th century work, with imitation Gothic windows, without cusps. The tower has a peal of 6 bells. The interior is commonplace, and has no monts. of interest. The ch.-yard contains many monts. to military officers, and some whose names will probably be familiar to the visitor. A stone erected, and restored 1870 by subscription, has some lines, often quoted for their oddity, on a boy employed at the Arsenal who was killed whilst in a tree taking cherries, by the owner of the orchard:

"The hammer of Death was given to me
For eating the Cherris off the tree."

But far more strange—a real curiosity of lapidary literature—are some lines on the tomb E. of the ch., of Sir Wm. Green, Bare^t., Chief Royal Engineer, d. 1811 :

"Efficient duty, reminiscent, grave,
  Yet mild philanthropy a reign may save,
If but the mind incline, rare to deny,
  Courteous, humane, to misery a sigh,
To woe and wretchedness a constant friend ;
  Whats this proud course, a rind, an atom, cloud,
Where shines the planet nature's voice is loud,
  Soft sweep the lyre, pity her distress,
Compassions melting mood, his numbers bless,
  On these perhaps our future joys depend."

Originally poet or mason "did not stand upon points," for there was not one from beginning to end of the inscription ; but lately the tomb has been renewed, and the epitaph sprinkled thickly over with points w.th the effect of increasing the obscurity.

St. Margaret's, near the centre of the town, was constituted in 1864 the mother-church, when St. Nicholas was made an eccl. dist. It is a spacious Gothic building, erected in 1853, and comprises nave and aisles, chancel, and tall embattled W. tower. St. James's proprietary chapel is a plain building in the Burrage Road. The Royal Arsenal Chapel is in the High Street.

The manor of Plumstead was given by King Edgar to the abbot and monks of St. Augustine, Canterbury, in 960 ; but taken from them by Earl Godwin and given to his son Tostig. William I. gave it to Odo, Bp. of Bayeux, who, on the intercession of Abp. Lanfranc, restored one moiety to St. Augustine's monastery, and in 1074 added the other. The monks remained in undisturbed ownership till the compulsory surrender of all their possessions to Henry VIII. In 1539 Henry granted the manor to Sir Edward Boughton, whose descendant sold it in 1685 to John Michel of Richmond, Surrey. Michel, in 1736, devised the manor of Plumstead, with other estates, to Queen's College, Oxford, for the foundation of 8 fellowships and 4 scholarships (to which have since been added 4 exhibitions) at that college. The monks of St. Augustine obtained from King John extensive privileges within their Plumstead manor, which were confirmed and extended by succeeding monarchs. These included rights of court-leet and court-baron, free warren, waifs and wrecks of the river, a weekly market, and annual fair. The other manors, Burwash, Bor-stall, and Plumstead Upland, have no features of particular interest.

Plumstead par. includes nearly 1000 acres of marsh. The *Plumstead Marsh* extends from Woolwich Arsenal to Crossness, Erith Marsh being its eastern prolongation. Over this space, bounded inland by the line of low cliffs extending from Woolwich to Erith, 4½ m. long, and 1 m. to 1¼ m. wide, the Thames flowed at every spring tide till kept back by an artificial embankment. As mentioned under ABBEY WOOD, the monks of Lesness Abbey who owned the E. portion of the Marsh, inned the Great Marsh at Plumstead, and a few years later the Lesser Marsh. The monks of St. Augustine, as lords of the Plumstead Marsh, no doubt contributed their share of the cost, though the monks of Lesness, as resident on the spot, would more efficiently conduct the operations. Damage frequently occurred to the river wall, and was as often repaired ; but in 1527 two great breaches were effected, one at Erith and the other at Plumstead, which the engineering skill available was inadequate to remedy, and the whole Marsh, of over 2000 acres, lay under water for 36 years. At length a remarkable man, Jacob Acontius (Giacomo Aconzio), distinguished as a jurist, theologian, (his 'Stratagemata Satanæ,' Basle, 1565, was widely read, and translated into several languages,) and lastly as an engineer, who was an exile in England on account of his having abjured the Romish faith, and a pensioner of Queen Elizabeth, offered on certain conditions to repair the embankments and recover the 'drowned' land. His offer was accepted, and an Act of Parliament passed, 1563, empowering "the said Jacob Acontyus, an Italian and servant to the Queen," at his own "cost and charges, after the 10th of March, 1563, during the term of four years next following, to inne, fence and win the said grounds, or any parcel of them," and in consideration and recompense thereof, he was to have "a moiety of the lands so won for his charges." By Jan. 1565, a commission appointed for the purpose reported that 600 acres had been effectually won and embanked. Acontius did not, however, live to complete his work. In the following year he had farmed his privilege to John Baptista Castilion, perhaps on account of failing health. At any rate his name appears no more, and he is believed to have died the same year, 1566. By 1587, 1000 more acres had been recovered, but 500 acres remained under water till after 1606, when an Act was passed for their recovery. The breach of 1864 and its prompt stoppage are told under ERITH, p. 202, where also will be found an account of the 'submerged forest,' or forest-bed, underlying the Marsh, and the general geological character of the district. The Woolwich Arsenal Butt and Government practice range for testing artillery occupy the W. side of Plumstead Marsh. The Southern Outfall of the Metropolitan Main Drainage is on the E. side of Crossness, and the powder magazines at various points between Crossness and Erith. The river as it rounds the Marsh makes in its downward course the *reaches* of Galleons (1 m. 85 yards); Tripcock, or Barking, (1 m. 1235 yds.); Halfway (2 m. 290 yds.); and Erith (1 m. 770 yds.)

Plumstead Common affords some good views across the river, and formed a pleasant and healthy recreation-ground for the townspeople till the end of 1874, when it was enclosed and appropriated as a riding-school and drill-ground for the mounted troops stationed at Woolwich. The far finer *Borstall Heath* has, however, been secured as an open space for public use and enjoyment. (*See* ERITH ; ABBEY WOOD.)

POLESDEN, SURREY (*see* BOOKHAM, GREAT).

PONDER'S END, MIDDX. (*see* ENFIELD).

POTTERS BAR, MIDDX., a vill.

on the Great Northern Road, 3 m. N. of Barnet, and 14 m. from London : the Potters Bar Stat. of the Gt. N. Rly. is nearly 1 m. W. of the vill. Potters Bar is an eccl. dist. of South Mimms par.: pop. 1198. Inns, *White Horse ; Lion ; Railway Hotel.*

The vill. stretches in a desultory way for ¾ m. along the highroad. The houses are mostly small, but at the N. end are some of good size in large gardens. The *Church,* St. John, on the rt., towards the N. end, is a neat white brick Norm. building,

erected in 1835, chiefly at the cost of George Byng, Esq., for many years M.P. for the county, father of the House of Commons, and lord of the adjacent domain, Wrotham Park. (*See* SOUTH MIMMS.) Several of the windows are filled with memorial painted glass ; and there are *monts.* to the late Earl of Strafford, by Noble, and to Lady Agnes Byng, by Westmacott. In the vicinity are *Oakmere* (H. Kemble, Esq.); *Parkfield* (H. Parker, Esq.) ; *Osborne Park* (G. Gadsden, Esq.), etc. At Potters Bar, Thorpe, the great Elizabethan architect, built a house for T. Taylor, but all traces of it are gone. Potters Bar, with the hamlet of *Ganwick Corner,* lies on the N.W. margin of Enfield Chase ; and when, in accordance with the Act of 1777, the Chase was enclosed, 1097 acres of it were allotted to South Mimms parish.

Bentley Heath, on the N. of Wrotham Park, is a pretty hamlet, with a semi-Norm. ch. (Trinity Chapel), built in 1866 from the designs of Mr. S. S. Teulon, at the cost of the Earl of Strafford.

PURFLEET, ESSEX, the seat of

the Government gunpowder stores, a hamlet of West Thurrock, from which it is nearly 3 m. W., and a Stat. on the Southend Rly. (16½ m.): pop. 163, exclusive of the Garrison and Control Department, 323, and the *Cornwall* Reformatory Ship, 296. Inn, the *Royal Hotel.*

Purfleet stands on the Thames, by the mouth of the Mardyke, a stream which comes down from Bulphan, past Stifford, and forms at its embouchure a small creek or haven, whence the name, anc. *Pourtflete,** from the A.-S. *port,* a harbour, and *fleot,* the mouth of a river, a place where vessels float. The Cockney tradition that the place was so called from Queen Elizabeth's exclamation, " My poor fleet," as she caught sight of her fleet destined to oppose the Armada, when on her way to review the troops before embarkation, is some centuries too modern.

The manor belonged to the priory of St. John of Jerusalem ; after the Dissolution, was held by the Crown till granted by Elizabeth, in 1583, to Sir George

* Morant, Hist. of Essex, vol. i., p. 93.

Hart; afterwards passed to the Lakes, Childs, and others; and is now held by S. C. Whitbread, Esq. Purfleet, like other places along the Thames, has suffered from inundations. The most serious recorded occurred in Dec. 1690,[*] when, from the giving way of the river wall, the marshy tract between Purfleet and Grays was entirely submerged, and an awkward shoal formed off the latter place.

Occupying the first high ground on the Essex shore in descending the Thames, Purfleet, with its fantastic chalk cliffs, military-looking buildings, and sentinels on guard, attracts the notice of most passengers in the passing steamers. From the shore its appearance is not less peculiar. For a long series of years the hills, which here come down to the Thames, were excavated for chalk. Many thousand tons were annually sent away, or converted into lime at the kilns, and deep, irregular, cavernous pits were formed. Walls and cliffs of strange shape were left standing in working the quarry. One of great height, capped by loam, is conspicuous. The quarries themselves have been enclosed. The bottoms are overgrown with wild underwood, shrubs, and verdure, planted with fruit trees, or laid out as gardens, and a few primitive-looking cottages and a chapel built in them. The sandy banks and higher slopes are thickly clad with oak, ash, hazel, and fir; and on the highest point of Beacon Hill is the old wooden lighthouse, or observatory, built many years ago by the Government for watching and signalling, and various experimental purposes, and now maintained chiefly for the extensive view it commands of the lower reaches of the Thames.

There is no village at Purfleet. The inhab. are all in the Government service or connected with the works, and are housed in regulation rows of brick dwellings by the river-side. The Government stores cover a large area, and are jealously walled in. There were powder magazines here in 1759, when they were reported to be in a dangerous condition, unenclosed, out of repair, and propped up by shores. An Act was in consequence passed (31

Geo. II., cap. 11) for purchasing land at Purfleet and erecting thereon a sufficient gunpowder magazine, barracks, guard-house, and other necessary buildings. The old corn-mill on the Mardyke was purchased, the requisite land acquired, and the depôt gradually brought to its present condition. The Powder Magazines, the great reserve store for gunpowder, are now capable of holding 60,000 barrels of gunpowder, and 52,000 barrels (of 100 lb. each) were in store on a recent inspection. The magazines are bomb-proof casemates, disconnected, and under the strictest and most watchful regulation and supervision. Hitherto there has been a happy immunity from accidents. The barracks, guard-house, and officers' quarters are of the usual description. For the use of the Store a fine landing-pier has been constructed, and off it may usually be seen a store-ship or two, a gunboat, or some one or other of the peculiar craft now carrying the R.N. pennant. The old man-of-war moored here is the *Cornwall*, reformatory ship, of the School Ship society. The boys are trained for sea service, and remain, on the average, 2½ years on board.

By the pier is Wingrove's *Royal Hotel*, noted for its dinners and its beds. Here may be had the key of the *Botany Bay Gardens*, formed out of a chalk pit, and much resorted to in the summer. 'The Botany,' as it is called by the natives, is worth a visit, is free from vulgar decorations, and has as its crowning point the Observatory, to which there is an easy ascent by zigzag paths, and which repays the trouble by a splendid view of the Thames—if the day be clear.

From Purfleet there is a pleasant walk to *Aveley* and *Belhus*. (*See* AVELEY.)

PURLEY, SURREY (*see* CATERHAM JUNCTION; COULSDON).

PURSER'S GREEN, MIDDX. (*see* FULHAM).

P U T N E Y, SURREY, on the rt. bank of the Thames, between Barnes and Wandsworth, and directly opposite Fulham, with which it is connected by a wooden bridge (*see* FULHAM); 4½ m. from Hyde Park Corner; and a Stat. on the Windsor br. of the L. and S.W. Rly. Pop. 7492. Inns, *Star and Garter*, by the river ; *Railway Hotel*, by Stat. ; *Fox and Hounds*, Richmond Road ; *Green Man*, on the Heath.

The derivation of the name is uncertain. It occurs as *Putelei* in Dom., and Taylor thinks the *ey* commemorates " an island in the lagoon " on this part of the Thames ; but, as Lysons long before pointed out, the name " in all subsequent records till the 16th century is spelt *Puttenheth* or *Pottenheth*, since which period it has obtained the name of Putney. *Stebonheath* has in the same manner been contracted to Stepney." *

Putney is included in the manor of Wimbledon. In early days the ferry was of importance ; it is mentioned in the Domesday Survey as of the value of 20*s*. per annum, and it continued of importance till the building of the bridge in 1729. Harold held a fishery here, which after the Conquest fell to the Abp. of Canterbury, but " paid no rent." In 1663 the rent was the three best salmon caught during the months of March, April, and May. By a lease which expired in 1780, the rent was raised to £8 per annum. Thirty years later the fishery was still valuable : what would a Putney fisherman think of catching smelts and salmon here now, as they were caught in 1810 ?

> " Smelts are caught here in great abundance in the months of March and April, and are esteemed very fine. The salmon fishery is not very productive, but the fish are of a very good quality, and sell for a high price. Small flounders, shad, roach, dace, barbel, eels, and gudgeons may be reckoned also among the produce of the fisheries here. One or two sturgeons are generally taken in the course of a year ; and sometimes, though rarely, a porpoise. These are claimed by the Lord Mayor, and the fishermen are obliged to deliver them as soon as taken to the water-bailiff. For a porpoise they receive a reward of 13*s*. ; for sturgeons a guinea each." †

Queen Elizabeth made many visits to Putney, to the house of John Lacy, Esq., a wealthy citizen and member of the Clothworkers' Company, who lived in a large house by the river, the ancient seat

of the Waldecks. Nichols says she " honoured Lacy with her company more frequently than any of her subjects." She frequently dined with him, and sometimes stayed two or three nights. Her earliest visits were in 1579, the latest Jan. 21, 1603, when she dined there on her way from Whitehall to Richmond, only two months before her death. At least 12 or 14 visits are recorded in the intermediate years.*

Putney, with Fulham (*see* FULHAM, p. 219), was on various occasions occupied by the Parliamentary forces. In 1647, when Charles I. was at Hampton Court, the Parliamentary generals fixed themselves at Putney. Fairfax had his quarters " at Mr. Wimondsold's, the high sheriff "—the house at which Mr. Lacy had so often received Queen Elizabeth : Cromwell was " at Mr. Bonhunt's," the site of which is not known ; Ireton, at Mr. Campion's, a school when Lysons wrote ; Fleetwood, at Mr. Martin's ; and the other officers in the different mansions, of which, at that time, there seems to have been no deficiency. The generals used to hold their councils—and they had many grave matters to discuss—in the church, seated round the communion table. But they heard sermons there also. On one occasion they received in audience " one Gifthiel, a high German prophet." On another occasion

> " Sept. 18, 1647, after a sermon in Putney church, the General, many great officers, field officers, inferior officers and agitators, met in the church, debated the proposals of the Army, and altered some few things in them, and were full of the sermon, which was preached by Mr. Peters." †

The vill. or town has little in it to attract attention. By the river-side is an irregular collection of houses, some comfortable old brick dwellings, but few of mark, boat-building sheds, boat clubs and boating houses—for this is the headquarters of Thames boating men. It was the starting-place for the Thames regatta in its palmy days ; and it is now, as every one knows, the starting-place in the Oxford and Cambridge boat race. The crews take up their abode at Putney—at the Star and Garter, or at a private house —during their preparatory trials and

* Lysons, Environs, vol. i., p. 296 ; Taylor, Words and Places, pp. 280, 348.

† Lysons, Environs, 2nd ed., 1811, vol. i., p. 312. Two or three years later Faulkner (Hist. of Fulham) complains that the salmon are leaving this part of the Thames. Only one had been caught off Fulham last season (1812).

* Nichols, Progresses of Q. Elizabeth, vol. ii., p. 92 : Lysons, vol. i., p. 299.

† Whitelocke, Memorials, ed. 1732, p. 270.

coaching; and Putney for the previous week, as well as on the day of the race, is, as the old watermen say, "like a fair." The ugly wooden bridge which unites Putney to Fulham, and the still uglier iron aqueduct of the Chelsea Waterworks Comp. immediately above it, from which the University boats start, are noticed under FULHAM. The High Street, the business street of the town, runs up at right angles from the river towards the Heath, a broad clean street with some good, but for the most part commonplace, houses. Beyond the railway is a constantly growing colony of villas.

Putney *Church* (St. Mary) stands at the foot of the bridge. A ch. stood here at an early date, but the present structure was rebuilt, except the tower, in 1836, by Mr. Edw. Lapidge, the architect of Kingston Bridge. The ch. is spacious, well built, of pale stock-brick and stone, and Perp. in style. The massive tower, twin sister to Fulham, is of stone, 4 stages high, with angle turret and battlements : it was repaired and restored when the ch. was rebuilt. In it is a peal of 8 bells. The *int.* is spacious, light, and neatly fitted. The roof is of oak; some of the windows have painted glass. N. of the chancel is a chapel, erected originally in the early years of Henry VIII. by Nicholas West, Bp. of Ely (d. 1533), the son of a baker at Putney. *Bp. West's Chapel* stood originally on the other side of the chancel, but was removed to its present position when the ch. was rebuilt. It can hardly be regarded, therefore, as though it had remained untouched, but it was probably not materially altered, and it is interesting from the late date of its erection. It is small, of good design, and the fan tracery in the vaulting, in which are the Bp.'s arms and initials, show few signs of deterioration.* The painted glass in the E. window was presented by Abp. Longley, when Bp. of Ripon, as a memorial of his mother. There are several monts. from the old ch., but none calling for particular attention. The numerous tombs in the ch.-yard may be passed with a similar remark. John Toland, the celebrated sceptical writer of the 18th cent., spent his last years in penury

in lodgings at a carpenter's in Putney; there wrote his 'Pantheisticon,' and most of his later works; died there, and was "decently buried" in the ch.-yard, March 13, 1722. A few days before he died he composed a Latin epitaph for his tomb, which has often been printed, but we failed to find this or any memorial of him in the ch.-yard.

A new ch., St. John the Evangelist, E.E. in style, was erected in 1859 on Putney Hill, from the designs of Mr. C. Lee, chiefly at the cost of Mr. J. T. Leader, late M.P. for Westminster. All Saints, on the Lower Common, is a picturesque Gothic building designed by Mr. G. E. Street, R.A., and consecrated in 1874.

The *Almshouses* of the Holy Trinity, Wandsworth Lane, were founded and endowed by Sir Abraham Dawes, in the reign of Charles II., for 6 poor unmarried men, and 6 women, but for some time only women have been admitted. A large red-brick building in Wandsworth Lane is the *Watermen's School*, for the maintenance and education of 20 boys, the sons of watermen. It was founded in 1684 by Thomas Martyn, a London merchant, who had been saved from drowning by a Putney watermen. At Melrose House, West Hill, is the *Royal Hospital for Incurables*, founded in 1854 by Dr. Andrew Reed. The building, recently extended by the addition of wings, c in accommodate 200 patients, and contains about 160, whilst upwards of 300 receive pensions at their own homes.

Besides West, the magnificent Bp. of Ely, Putney boasts of two eminent natives, Thomas Cromwell Earl of Essex, the minister of Henry VIII., and Edward Gibbon, the historian. Thomas Cromwell was the son, as is said, of a blacksmith at Putney, and tradition used to point to the site of "an ancient cottage, called the Smith's shop, lying W. of the highway leading from Putney to the Upper Gate, and on the S. side of the highway from Richmond to Wandsworth, being the sign of the Anchor," as his birthplace.

Gibbon was born April 27, 1737, at the house of his paternal grandfather; "a spacious house," he calls it, "with gardens and lands," situate between the roads which lead to Wandsworth and Wimbledon, and in which the celebrated mystical divine and non-juror, William Law, author

---

* Jackson and Andrews, Illustrations of Bp. West's Chapel in the Church of Putney, 4to, 1825.

of the 'Serious Call to the Unconverted' lived and ruled as spiritual director. But a great deal of the sickly child's time was spent with his aunt, Mrs. Catherine Porten, at the house of his maternal grandfather close to Putney Bridge.

"As far back as I can remember the house near Putney bridge and churchyard of my maternal grandfather, appears in the light of my proper and native home. It was there that I was allowed to spend the greatest part of my time, in sickness or in health, during my school vacations and my parents' residence in London, and finally after my mother's death" [1748]. *

Gibbon's house was afterwards the residence of Robert Wood, Esq., M.P., distinguished as a traveller, and the author of the splendid folio 'Ruins of Palmyra, otherwise Tadmor in the Desert,' 1753, and the corresponding volume, 'The Ruins of Baalbec,' fol., 1757. Mr. Wood died at his house, Putney, Sept. 1771, and was interred in the New Cemetery, Upper Richmond Road, where a costly marble sarcophagus was erected, with an inscription, to his memory, written by Horace Walpole. James Macpherson, of Ossian fame, lived in a villa on Putney Heath, afterwards inhabited by Andrew Drummond, Esq. William Pitt, the Minister, d. 1806, at his residence, Bowling-Green House, on the brow of the Heath. The story of his dying alone, deserted by relatives, friends, and servants, is pure fiction. Pitt had taken a dislike to Nollekens, and would never sit to him for his bust; but as soon as the sculptor heard of the Minister's decease, he hurried to Putney, and succeeded in obtaining permission to take a mask of his face.

"On Mr. Nollekens's return from Putney Common, after taking Mr. Pitt's mask, he observed to Mr. Gahagan [his assistant], pointing to it on the opposite side of the coach, 'There, I would not take 50 guineas for that mask, I can tell ye.' He would have done wrong if he had, for from this mask, and Hoppner's picture, which was lent him by Lord Mulgrave, he was enabled to produce the statue erected in the Senate House of Cambridge, for which he received 3000 guineas. . . . He also executed at least 74 busts in marble, for almost every one of which he had 120 guineas ; and there were upwards of 600 casts taken at six guineas each." † A prodigious illustration of Pitt's popularity at the moment of his decease.

Henry Fuseli, R.A., the historical

painter, d. April 16, 1825, at the house on the hill belonging to the Countess of Guildford, where he was on a visit. Douglas Jerrold lived at West Lodge, Lower Common, from 1845 to 1854,—the most prosperous and sunniest period of his life, says his son. It was there he wrote Mrs. Caudle. Leigh Hunt died Aug. 28, 1859, in Putney, at the house of his friend Mr. C. W. Reynell.

Putney Heath, of over 400 acres, is a pleasant breezy tract of sand, heath, and furze,—slightly broken in surface, and affording some good views in the higher parts,—joined on the one hand to the wider Wimbledon Common, and on the other opening upon Richmond Park. Like Wimbledon and neighbouring heaths, Putney was in the olden times a noted haunt of highwaymen. It was also noted for duels, some of which were remarkable. Here, in May 1652, George, 6th Lord Chandos, and Col. Henry Compton fought ; Compton was killed, and 2 years afterwards (May 1654) Lord Chandos and his second, Lord Arundel, were tried and convicted of manslaughter. On a Sunday afternoon in May, 1798, a bloodless encounter took place between the Prime Minister, William Pitt, and Wm. Tierney, M.P. for Southwark. Less happy was the duel fought between two Cabinet Ministers and Secretaries of State 11 years later, near the Telegraph, at 6 o'clock on the morning of the 21st of Sept., 1809, when Lord Castlereagh shot George Canning in the thigh.

Putney Heath has been used for reviews and sham-fights, as well as for real duels. Occasionally, as would seem from an entry of Pepys', it has been used for horse-racing.

"*May 7th*, 1667.—To St. James's ; but there find Sir W. Coventry gone out betimes this morning, on horseback, with the King and Duke of York, to Putny Heath, to run some horses." *

But Putney Heath was perhaps most noted at one time for its Bowling-Green, for more than 60 years (1690—1750) the most famous green in the neighbourhood of London. The house had large rooms for public breakfasts and evening assemblies, and was, while the Bowling Green flourished, a fashionable place of entertainment.

---

* Gibbon, Memoirs of My Life and Writings.
† J. T. Smith, Nollekens and his Times, 1828, vol. ii., pp. 44—48.

* Pepys, Diary.

"This is to give Notice that Ed. Lockett at Charing Cross hath taken the Bowling Green House on Putney Heath, where all gentlemen may be entertained." *

In 1720, Putney was described as a place "graced with large and good buildings, well inhabited by gentry ; and the more for its good air and the diversions its large Heath affords. Where there is a Bowling-green, well resorted unto in the summer season." † That is all that is told about Putney, so that it is plain its Bowling Green was still its chief attraction. And Defoe, in 1722, writes of being insensibly led to "the Bowling Green of Putney, whither the citizens resort twice a week, and where I have seen pretty deep play." ‡

In 1750, Horace Walpole, in giving an account of the apprehension of James M'Lean, "the gentleman highwayman," writes :

"M'Lean had a quarrel at Putney Bowling-green two months ago with an officer whom he challenged for disputing his rank ; but the captain declined till M'Laren should produce a certificate of his nobility, which he has just received." §

M'Lean was executed at Tyburn, Oct. 3, 1750. Whether his connection with the Bowling Green tended to bring it into disrepute does not appear, but it declined, and was shortly after closed. A few years ago some old inhabitants professed to remember it, but probably their recollection was more from hearsay than anything else. The Bowling Green House, a large rambling building, was converted into a private residence, and in it, as

* London Gazette for 1693, No. 2965.
† Stow, Survey of London, by Strype, fol., 1720, vol. i., p. 44.
‡ De Foe, a Journey through England, 8vo, 1722, vol. i., p. 132.
§ Walpole to Sir Horace Mann, Aug. 2, 1750, Letters, vol. ii., p. 219.

already noticed, William Pitt lived for several years, and there died. The next villa, known as Lord Bristol's, was for some time the residence of Mrs. Siddons.

The *Obelisk*, a short distance from Bowling Green House, was erected to commemorate the experiments of Mr. David Hartley (son of Dr. Hartley, author of ' Observations on Man '), who built a house here, 1776, which, by inserting plates of iron and copper between double floors, he professed to make fire-proof. The experiments were many times repeated, and were witnessed by the King and Queen, members of both Houses of Parliament, the Lord Mayor and Corporation, and excited very general interest. On one occasion, several members of the royal family remained in perfect security in an upper room whilst a fierce fire was raging in the room under them : and the same experiment was many times tried by other parties. The trials were pronounced successful. The House of Commons voted Mr. Hartley £2500 to defray his expenses ; he received the freedom of the Goldsmiths' Company, and the City of London erected this Obelisk, the first stone of which, as the insc. on it records, was laid by the Rt. Hon. John Sawbridge, the Lord Mayor, on the anniversary of the Fire of London. Hartley's ' Firehouse ' still stands ; but houses continue to be burnt down. Near the Obelisk was erected, in 1796, the Admiralty Semaphore, or Telegraph, by which Castlereagh and Canning fought their celebrated duel.

The Common was once noted for its tumuli, but they have long since been emptied or levelled.

PYRGO, or PIRGO, ESSEX (*see* HAVERING-ATTE-BOWER).

RADLETT, HERTS, a hamlet and eccl. dist. of Aldenham, 3 m. N. of Elstree, on the road to St. Albans, and a Stat. on the Midland Rly. 15 m. from St. Pancras : pop. 443. Inns : *Red Lion ; Railway*.

The vill. consists of a few plain cottages, an inn, and a convenient rly. stat., very prettily situated in the midst of a farming country, with uplands and park-like grounds, and abundant trees on either hand. The *Church* (Christ Church) was built in 1864 on Cobden Hill, some distance S. of the vill. and stat. It is an early Dec. building of flint and stone, with red-brick bands ; cruciform, with a tower and tall octagonal stone spire at the N.E. angle. Some of the windows have memorial painted glass.

By the stat. is a pretty up-hill lane to Shenley; in the opposite direction is a pleasant walk by lane and field-path to Aldenham (a short 2 m.) The turning by the Red Lion leads, by a crooked lane on the l., to *Gill's Hill*, the scene of the murder of Mr. Wm. Weare, on the night of Friday, Oct. 24, 1823, which excited at the time almost unprecedented interest. Weare was shot by his companion Thurtell, while riding with him in a gig to Probert's house in this lane ; his body was deposited in a pond behind the cottage, while the murderers divided the spoil, and afterwards dragged through a hedge into a field at a short distance from the house. Suspicion having been aroused, the body was searched for and found, and the murderers arrested. Thurtell, a noted betting-man and gambler, son of the Mayor of Norwich, was tried, convicted, and hanged at Hertford. Probert was admitted king's evidence, and set at liberty, but some time after apprehended, tried, and hanged for horse-stealing. The story of the murder was dramatized, and the actual roan horse and yellow gig in which Weare was carried were exhibited on the stage. Carlyle more than once alludes to incidents connected with the murder, and Sir Walter Scott was so fascinated by the story that he describes himself as spending a morning over a variorum edition of the trial ; and more than four years after the murder, when returning from London to the North, he turned out of his way to examine the scene of the tragedy. He writes in his Diary :

"Our elegant researches carried us out of the highroad and through a labyrinth of intricate lanes, which seem made on purpose to afford strangers the full benefit of a dark night and a drunk driver, in order to visit Gill's Hill in Hertfordshire, famous for the murder of Mr. Weare. The place has the strongest title to the description of Wordsworth—

'A merry spot, 'tis said, in days of yore,
But something ails it now—the place is curst.'

The principal part of the house is destroyed, and only the kitchen remains standing. The garden has been dismantled, though a few laurels and flowering shrubs, run wild, continue to mark the spot. The fatal pond is now only a green swamp, but so near the house that one cannot conceive how it was ever chosen as a place of temporary concealment for the murdered body. . . . The dirt of the present habitation equalled its present desolation, and a truculent looking hag, who showed us the place and received half-a-crown, looked not unlike the natural inmate of such a mansion. She

hinted as much herself, saying the landlord had dismantled the place, because no respectable person would live there." *

The house hardly seems to have been so thoroughly dismantled as Scott describes. It is a common rough-cast, one-storey cottage, with a high-pitched tile roof. On the ground floor is a window on each side the door, and three windows are on the floor above. Behind is still the dirty half-drained pond, with a gaunt fir-tree by it, and on this side it might by night make a weird study for a haunted house ; but as the old woman, its sole inhabitant, told Sir Walter, she had seen no ghosts and feared none, so hold its present occupants. The barn, opposite the cottage, which played its part in the story, is now ruinous. A cleft oak up the lane by it marks the place, according to the local tradition, where the body was dragged through the hedge, and near where it was found. Weare was buried in Elstree churchyard. (*See* ELSTREE.)

RAINHAM, ESSEX, on the Ingrebourn, about a mile from its outfall in the Thames at Rainham Ferry ; 5 m. E. of Barking on the road to Grays, 12¼ m. from Whitechapel, and a Stat. on the L. and Southend Rly. : pop. 1122. Inns, *Phœnix*, by the stat., a comfortable house, with outlook over the Thames ; *Angel ; Bell*.

The vill. extends for some distance along the London road, here a crooked street lined with old-fashioned houses and occasional gardens, large coal yards and wharfs by the brook, which forms a creek navigable by lighters to the bridge, and the old church with a large old red-brick house by it, just off the main street. Rainham is the centre and port of an extensive district of market gardens, and a considerable trade is done in carrying potatoes and the like by the lighters to London and bringing back coal and manure. The neighbourhood is pleasing, the cottage gardens abound in flowers, and the walks along the uplands N. and E. afford bright glimpses of the Thames and the Kentish hills.

The *Church* (St. Helen and St. Giles, a unique conjunction) was given by Richard de Lucy, Grand Justiciar of England, 1179, to his Abbey of Lesness, and pro-

* Scott's Diary, May 28, 1828, Lockhart, Memoirs of the Life of Sir Walter Scott, chap. lxxvi.

bably was built, or rebuilt, about that time. The body of the ch. is late Norm., with windows of later insertion. The low massive square tower is E.E., and has heavy buttresses and modern brick battlements. A doorway S. of the chancel has a late Norm. arch, with good chevron moulding and grotesque heads to the small caps. The chancel arch is Norm. with plain mouldings. The pier arcades have square shafts and dentil mouldings to the caps. The only noteworthy memorial is a late 15th cent. brass of a civilian and his wife, without an insc. Charles Churchill, the poet, was curate to his father, who was rector of Rainham, about 1756-58, and is said to have opened a school here, which was not successful.

At Rainham Ferry, at the mouth of Rainham Creek, are wharves and the Three Crowns Inn. Here is the City rifle range, much used by London volunteers.

RANMORE, SURREY (see DORKING).

REDHILL, SURREY, a modern rly. town, and a stat. (20¾ m. from London Bridge) on the L., B., and S. C., and L. and S.E., Rlys., is within the parish, and a member of the municipal borough, of Reigate, from which town it is 1½ m. E. Pop. 9323 (eccl. dist. of St. Matthew 4582, St. John 4741). Inns, *Warwick Hotel; S.-Eastern Hotel*, etc.

When Redhill was made a first-class station of the Brighton and S.-Eastern rlys., its convenience of access, reputed healthiness, and the charm of the scenery drew to it numerous merchants and men of business who prefer living at a moderate distance from the capital. It was of course speedily marked as a quarry by the speculative builder, and on the hill-top has grown up a populous railway town of hideous brick shops and habitations, and around it a belt of ostentatious villas, comfortable looking mansions, and tasteful and ornate dwellings of many varieties, with a superabundance of builders' detached and semi-detached malformations. But the beauty of the neighbourhood has been little impaired. From the hill and heathy common there are fine views, and about the lanes still umbrageous and pleasant walks. John Linnell, our veteran landscape painter, resides here. His studio

has long been the fields of Redhill and Reigate, and the scenery so familiar on his canvas is only a slightly idealized transcript of the natural landscapes of these localities. The views over the Weald, seen from any of the southern heights or slopes on an autumn evening, will at once recall many a familiar composition.

Redhill has a couple of churches, a Roman Catholic chapel, a large Gothic Congregational church, three or four Baptist and various other chapels, schools, institutes; a spacious Market Hall and Assembly Rooms (a respectable Elizabethan building of rough-hewn local stone), a bank, newspaper, and the other appurtenances of advanced civilisation. The corn-market has indeed ceased to be held, but there is a monthly market for cattle. On the Common is an excellent cottage hospital. The older of the churches, St. John the Evangelist, was erected on the slope of the hill in 1843, from the designs of Mr. J. T. Knowles, and is a good and carefully finished Perp. building, with a tower and octagonal spire 120 ft. high. The nave has an open timber roof; the chancel, vaulting with fan-tracery. St. Matthew's was built in 1867, and is a spacious early Dec. building, with a lofty spire.

About ½ m. from Redhill is the *Philanthropic Society's Farm*, a school for the reformation of criminal boys, conducted on the " family organization " so successfully carried out at Mettray. The Redhill Farm was established in 1849. The farm is about 250 acres in extent, and the buildings, designed by Mr. Moffatt, are extensive, complete, and well furnished; not one large building, but five different " houses," with their connected farms, each having its complement of about 50 boys. Besides farming, the boys are taught brickmaking, smith's work, bricklaying, carpentry, shoemaking, and tailoring. The whole work of the farm is done by the boys. When they leave the school, situations are, if possible, obtained for them, if they elect to remain in England; outfit and passage if they choose to go to the colonies. The boys are healthy and look content, and the system is on all hands reported to work well. The Farm can receive 300 boys: at the census of 1871 there were 248.

At *Earlswood*, 1 m. S. of Redhill, is the *Asylum for Idiots*, an admirable institution, founded by the late Dr. Andrew Reed at Highgate in 1847. The Prince Consort laid the first stone of the buildings at Earlswood in 1853, and he formally opened them in 1855. They were much enlarged in 1870, the Prince of Wales having laid the first stone of the additional buildings June 29, 1869. In May 1875 they contained 596 inmates. The grounds, very prettily laid out, are about 80 acres in extent. The Asylum is open to visitors (it will be well to obtain an order at the office, 29, Poultry, E.C.), and any one who desires to see what may be done to ameliorate the apparently hopeless condition of the idiot and the imbecile will do well to visit the Earlswood Asylum.

REIGATE, Surrey, a municipal

borough and market town, 21 m. from London by road, 23 m. by the L. and S.E. Rly.: pop. of the par. and borough, 15,916, but this includes Redhill and outlying parts, and is subdivided into Reigate Borough, 2945, and Reigate Foreign, 12,971. Inns: the *White Hart*, an excellent family hotel ; *Swan, Grapes*, both good commercial houses.

The town is seated on the Folkestone beds of the Lower Greensand formation, near the head of the long and lovely Holmesdale, a valley bounded N. by chalk downs, S. by a steep ridge of greensand. The neighbourhood is exceedingly beautiful. The vegetation along the greensand is proverbially luxuriant; the views from the ridge are rich, varied, and extensive. What they appear to the artist, Mr. Linnell's landscapes—all inspired by this locality—sufficiently attest ; of how much interest the view from the chalk down is to the geologist, Mantell has well told :—

"The view from the summit of the chalk hills, to the N. of Reigate, is as interesting to the geologist as to the lover of the picturesque ; for it presents a magnificent landscape, displaying the physical structure of the Weald, and its varied and beautiful scenery. At the foot of the downs lies the valley in which Reigate is situated ; and immediately beyond the town appears the elevated ridge of Shanklin sand, which stretches towards Leith Hill on the W., and to Tilburstow Hill on the E. The forest ridge of the wealden occupies the middle region, extending westward towards Horsham, and eastward to Crowborough Hill, its greatest altitude, and thence to Hastings, having on each flank the wealds of Kent and Sussex ; while in the remote distance the rounded and undulated summits of the South Downs appear stretched along the verge of the horizon.*

In the Dom. Survey both hundred and town are named *Cherchfelle*, the churchfield, probably from some ch. which stood here, though none is mentioned. The earliest known reference to it as Reygate is in 1279 ; later it is always so called. The form Reigate is probably derived from its position : Reigate = the ridge road, from *rigg*, a ridge or back, and *gate*, a road or passage.

The manor was granted by William Rufus, in the first year of his reign, to William Earl of Warren and Surrey, and it was held with the earldom—though not in the direct line of descent—till 1483 when it lapsed by the death of Richard Plantagenet in the Tower of London. It then reverted to the heirs of Elizabeth Mowbray, Duchess of Norfolk, one moiety going to John Howard, Duke of Norfolk and his son Thomas, 14th Earl of Surrey, the other to Thomas Stanley, afterwards Earl of Derby, and father-in-law of Henry VII. On the attainder of the Duke of Norfolk, his lands escheated to the Crown, and his moiety of Reigate was granted by Edward VI. to William Lord Howard of Effingham. His son, Charles Earl of Nottingham, settled his half-share of Reigate as a jointure on his second wife, Margaret, who, after his decease, married for her second husband William Monson, created Baron Monson, and Viscount Castlemain in Ireland. Having thus acquired one moiety, Lord Monson purchased the other of the 4th Earl of Dorset, and thus reunited the manor. Lord Monson took part with the Parliament against Charles I., and on the Restoration was tried, stripped of his estates, and died a prisoner in the Tower. Reigate was given to James Duke of York, and held by him whilst king. Being forfeited by his abdication, it was granted in 1697, by William III., to the Lord Chancellor Somers. On his death it passed to his sisters, and on the death of the survivor, Lady Jekyll, it descended to her nephew James Cocks, then to his nephew Charles Cocks, created, 1784, Baron Somers of Evesham. From his son, created Viscount Eastnor and Earl

---

* D'. Mantell, Brayley's Surrey, vol. i., p. 147.

Somers in 1821, it came to the present owner, Charles, 3rd Earl Somers.

Reigate was of sufficient consequence to send a representative to the House of Commons in the reign of Edward I., 1297. From the reign of Edward III. it sent two members, till the Reform Act of 1832 deprived it of one. Up to this time it was a nomination borough entirely under the control of the Earl of Hardwick and Earl Somers, a Yorke and a Cocks being invariably returned. Under the new franchise the single member was a Cocks till 1857. The reformed borough had 960 electors in 1866, when a select committee of the House of Commons reported that " bribery and treating had extensively prevailed ... at the elections in the years 1863 and 1865," as well as at previous elections, and Reigate was consequently disfranchised by the Representation Act of 1867. It had, however, been incorporated in 1863, and though no longer a parliamentary, it ranks as a municipal borough, and has a mayor, 6 aldermen, and 17 councillors. A weekly market was granted to Reigate by Edward II. in 1313 : it is still held every Tuesday, and a cattle market on the first Tuesday in each month.

Lying in the main line of the Pilgrims' Way from the West to Canterbury, and at the junction probably of two or three secondary ways, Reigate was an important centre and halting-place for Canterbury Pilgrims. For their special use it had a chapel dedicated to St. Thomas, and hostels no doubt for their lodging and refreshment. After the Reformation the chapel was used as a market hall and assize court, till, becoming dilapidated, it was taken down in 1708, and a new market house and town hall built on its site. The White Hart hotel, which stands opposite to it, may mark the site of the hostel frequented by pilgrims of the higher class, but tradition has fixed on the Red Cross inn at the W. end of the High Street as the representative pilgrim's hostel.

Reigate had its baronial castle and priory, but has figured little in history. In the civil war the town was held alternately by Royalists and Parliamentarians ; royal and noble personages have visited or passed through it; but no stirring incident is recorded. Nor has it been made illustrious by its inhabitants. We have the names of no eminent natives. The philosophical Shaftesbury lived here, but did not, as has been said, write his Characteristics here. He retired to Reigate for a short time, when failing health was about to cause him to quit England for the last time. Two letters to Harley Earl of Oxford and Lord Godolphin are dated Reigate, March 29, and May 27, 1711 ; and he left England in the following July. The house he occupied was afterwards the residence of Mr. R. Barnes, a local celebrity in his day, who so improved the grounds, that Reigate folk designated it " the world in an acre." Another temporary resident in Reigate was Lord Lytton's hero, Eugene Aram, who served for a year as usher in Mr. Alchin's school in Church Street, lodged in a cottage called (for some unexplained and inexplicable reason) Upper Repentance, wore a gold-laced hat and ruffles, and was known as a " gay man."

Reigate Castle was built by one of the Earls of Warren on an elevation N. of the town, and perhaps on the site of an earlier fortress. The date of its erection is not known, but it was seized by the partizans of Prince Louis in the reign of John. When Camden wrote, Reigate Castle was " forlorn, and for age ready to fall ; " and in a survey made in 1623 it was described as decayed. But five-and-twenty years later enough strength remained in it to cause the House of Commons (or Derby House) Committee to direct care to be taken of it, and that it be put " into such a condition that no use may be made of it to the endangering of the peace of the kingdom." The building was in consequence dismantled, but portions of the walls, with low flanking towers, were left at the close of the 18th cent. Nothing remains of the castle now except the strange entrance archway built by Mr. Barnes, in 1787, out of fragments of the old wall. What is called the castle court is the mound on which the keep stood, and is surrounded by a dry ditch. The habitable building stood apart from the keep, and had, besides its mural defences, an outer moat, and the natural steepness of the ground rendered more difficult by artificial means.

In the centre of the court, by a rude recent structure of " rock-work," is the entrance to the *Barons' Cave*, a series of extensive vaults, which local faith, as early as Gough's time, assumed to be the secret conference hall of the barons prior to meeting King John at Runnimede, and that here, in short, Magna Charta was elaborated.[*] This may be dismissed without hesitation as legendary; but the cavern may be visited : the key and candles will be brought for a small gratuity from the cottage close by. A flight of steps and a long sloping tunnel, together 240 ft. long, lead to a chamber 23 ft. long, 13 ft. wide, and 11 ft. high, called, with or without reason, the Dungeon. Left of this is a sort of gallery 150 ft. long, having a semicircular end with a seat round it, and a kind of vaulted roof, 12 ft. high. This is the Barons' Chamber, and here tradition affirms their conferences were held. Nearer to the entrance is a third and larger apartment, with a pointed roof. A closed arch in the Barons' Chamber is pointed out as the entrance to a passage that led to the town, while another passage, tradition asserts, led to the priory. The probability is that these vaults served as cellars for storing provisions, and repositories for articles of value, whilst there was most likely a sally-port from them to the outer moat, which will account for the tradition of tunnels to the town and priory. The passages may be as old as the castle, but the rock is a soft sandstone, and they may have been enlarged or extended at any time : there is nothing in their appearance to determine their date. The rude figures were, we believe, carved, or recarved, by a living local artist. Somewhat similar excavations exist in other parts of the town. The largest and most remarkable of them, to which there was entrance from the cellars of the Red Cross inn, opposite which stood the original market-house, fell-in May 9, 1860.

The Castle Grounds, several acres in extent, were till recently in a wild and neglected state. They have, however, been cleared, planted with shrubs and flowers, and formed into very pretty pleasure-grounds, and a lease of them for 999 years, presented by their owner, Lord Somers, to the town, on condition that they be kept in order and opened free. There are pleasant walks, old elms with seats under them, and from the castle mound splendid views over the town and

priory, and away to Box Hill, Dorking, and the chalk downs.

Reigate *Priory* was founded by William Earl of Warren and Surrey (d. 1240), and his wife Isabel, in honour of the Virgin Mary and the Holy Cross, for a prior and canons of the order of St. Augustine. It seems never to have grown into greatness, and was among the first of the religious houses suppressed, 1535— those, namely, with revenues under £200 per annum—the entire income of Reigate Priory being only £77 14s. 11d. The priory estate was granted (in exchange for the rectory of Tottenham, Middx.) to Lord Effingham, who built himself a mansion on the site. Of the Priory buildings not a vestige is left. Lord Effingham's house, *The Priory*, has been so much altered and modernized as to retain little of its original aspect. The present building is a spacious and comfortable-looking mansion, and contains some fine rooms. The lofty and elaborately carved chimney-piece in the entrance hall (formerly "the great chamber ") is stated alike by Manning and by Brayley to have been brought from Nonsuch Palace; but Evelyn, who saw it at Reigate nearly twenty years before the Duchess of Cleveland dismantled Nonsuch, says that it came from Bletchingly.

" *May* 21, 1665.—I went to Rygate to visit Mrs. Carey at my Lady Peterboro's, in an antient monastery well in repaire, but the park much defac'd ; the house is nobly furnish'd. The chimney piece in the greate chamber, carved in wood, was of Henry 8. and was taken from an house of his in Blechinglee. At Rygate was now the Archbishop of Armagh, the learned James Usher, whom I wente to visite." [*]

The priory estate had been carried by marriage from the Effingham to the Mordaunt family, and was sold by the brilliant and errant Charles Mordaunt, 3rd Earl of Peterborough, about 1680, to a wealthy citizen, Sir John Parsons, who made many costly alterations in the house, converted the great chamber into an entrance hall, and employed Verrio to embellish the chief apartments. The next owner, a Mr. Ireland, pulled down a portion of the house, and altered what was left. Early in the present century the estate was purchased by the Earl of Somers, the house remodelled, brought

---

* Gough's Camden's Britannia, vol. i., p. 252.

* Evelyn, Diary.

into its actual condition, and made the family seat. Lord Somers formed here a small but choice collection of pictures, and a large library of old books. Grote, who resided here from Dec. 1858 to March 1859, found the library a great attraction, " and many a spare hour was passed by him in exploring its treasures, perched upon the steps of the lofty ladder, candle in hand." * It is at present occupied by D. P. Blaine, Esq. The grounds are picturesque, pleasant, and richly wooded.

The town consists of the long High Street stretching for nearly a mile from E. to W., and a second street running from it southward, with various outlying extensions and a genteel northern suburb called Wray Park. Camden's description of it in Elizabethan days, as "carrying a greater show for largenesse than faire buildings," is still applicable. But it is a town whose appearance tells its story pretty clearly. There are old houses, inns, and shops, solid, heavy, and dark ; but they are yearly becoming fewer. Of old a place of local importance, and doing a good trade, in a deliberate, dreamy way, it became in the days of Brighton's coaching glory an active coaching and posting centre, with its White Hart, the Clarendon of the Brighton road. The railway came, and not only drove off the coaches, and avoided the town, but by establishing its great junction station for the Brighton and Dover lines at Redhill, called into existence a new and rival town, which speedily outstripped the elder in size and population, and carried off no small share of its trade. For awhile Reigate was paralyzed, but at length it too got its rly. stat., though only on a subsidiary line. Trade revived ; the beauty of the neighbourhood attracted men of means, and villas sprang up all around, and now the town is putting on a new aspect without altogether casting off the old, and wears a solidity of character that entitles it, as it feels, not merely to hold its head proudly, but to look down patronizingly on its *parvenu* neighbour.

The *Market House* and *Town Hall*, in which also the sessions used to be held, is a small brick building, facing the White Hart, erected in 1798, when it was de-

cided to remove the market from the W. end of the town, where it had been previously held. The Town Hall has been practically superseded by a Gothic *Public Hall*, erected by a company in 1861. It has a large room for public meetings and assemblies, and in it sessions and county courts are held, and a mechanics' institute and museum lodged. The *Grammar School*, founded in 1675, occupies a building on the Redhill road, near the ch. Its reputation was not very high, but it greatly improved under reorganization in 1862, and it was brought under a new scheme, propounded by the Endowed Schools Commission, in 1874. The buildings were extended and improved in 1871.

The par. *Church* (St. Mary Magdalene) stands off the road at the E. end of the town. It is a large and noble-looking building, of squared clunch, and comprises nave and chancel, with aisles to both ; S. porch ; and a fine battlemented tower at the W. end, in which is a peal of 6 bells. The chancel has E.E. windows, but these were inserted when the ch. was 'restored' and transformed in 1845 : the fabric is in the main Perp., though portions of an earlier ch. have been worked up in it. The interior is grave and imposing. The nave aisles are separated by arcades of 5 bays borne on alternate octagonal and cylindrical shafts. The nave has been heightened, received a new roof, and had low open seats substituted for the old pews. The reredos was discovered when the ch. was repaired, and like it underwent restoration. S. of the chancel are 3 sedilia. Several of the windows have painted glass. In the chancel and aisles are some remarkable 17th and 18th century *monts. ;* but the most famous personage interred here, Charles Howard Earl of Effingham, the conqueror of the Armada, has no memorial. In the chancel is a mont., with effigies, of Sir Thos. Bludder of Flanchford, and wife, d. 1618 ; the child that lay at their feet has been removed to an absurd position in a side window. The monts. of the Elyot family were removed from the chancel in 1846—the effigies of Robert Elyot, sen., d. 1609, and of his wife, d. 1612, to the N. aisle ; the kneeling figure of his daughter Katherine, d. 1623, to a niche in the S. aisle. The much-controverted mont. of Edw. Bird, Esq., "who had the misfortune

---

* Mrs. Grote, Personal Life of George Grote, p. 246.

to kill a waiter at a bagnio by Golden Square," and was convicted and hanged for his trouble, July 11, 1714, with his bust in full armour and flowing wig, has been relegated to the belfry. The N. aisle has a prodigious mont. of coloured marbles, with reclining effigy of Richard Ladbroke of Frenches (d. 1730), a zealous member of the Church of England, in full armour and flowing wig, and holding in his left hand a celestial crown. On either side are full-sized figures of Truth and Justice; above are angels with trumpets and palm branches; in the centre a resplendent sun; and over all the armorial bearings of the Ladbroke family. In the ch.-yard is an obelisk to Francis Maseres (d. 1824), Cursitor-Baron of the Exchequer, and author of some tracts on constitutional law and politics. *Obs.* the costly sarcophagus of Mrs. Waterlow, erected in 1874, of granite, Portland stone, marble, and bronze, with figures of angels and bassi-rilievi by Mr. J. Durham, A.R.A.

St. Mark's ch., Wray Park, is a spacious cruciform structure, with a tall tower and spire, early Dec. in style, erected in 1860. A second eccl. dist. ch., St. Luke's, South Park, was built in 1871, of the local stone, with Bath-stone dressings, in the Dec. style; and comprises nave, S. aisle, and chancel; the N. aisle and tower being left for erection at a future day. In Nutley Lane is an endowed Working Men's Ch. and Institute; and there are the usual chapels; but none of historical or architectural value.

A pleasant lane of about ½ m. leads to *Reigate Park*, of old "well-stored with timber trees and replenished with deer," but disparked and denuded of its trees in 1635, by its then owner, Lord Monson. It is now an open space of about 150 acres; short grass and broad terrace at the top, with trees and seats beneath, inviting to contemplate at leisure the prospects, which are among the most extensive in these parts, stretching away over the broad Weald to the distant South Downs, round by Leith Hill and the Gomshall Heights, to the nearer Betchworth Clump and North Downs,—the rough and broken slopes at your feet, rich in ancient thorns and shining hollies, rampant ferns and purple heath, making vigorous foregrounds to the varying landscapes.

Reigate Heath is another picturesque spot,—or was, till defaced and vulgarized by racing encroachments; and there is a charming walk from it to Betchworth, by Wonham Mill, or by Flanchford to Leigh,—but for this choose fair weather. The stranger must remember, as he explores the Weald lanes and field-paths, that he is entering on what has been pronounced (though unfairly) to be in foul weather "the dirtiest country in England." Reigate Hill, and the downs on the other side of the town, afford lovely views, endless pleasant walks, and flowers, ferns, and orchids innumerable.

Flanchford, by the Mole, on the way to Leigh, was the seat of the Bludder, Wyche, and Scawen familes : the mansion was pulled down many years ago. *Frenches*, the seat of the Ladbrokes, stood 1½ m. N.E. of the town. Few old mansions remain ; but modern villas abound. Among them are *Great Doods*, on the London road (A. J. Waterlow, Esq.) ; *Woodhatch*, built from the designs of Mr. J. T. Knowles; *Oakfield* (Sir E. Hornby) ; *Rosenheim* (Sir S. Saunders).

RICHINGS,

RICHINGS, BUCKS, a house and park so called, celebrated for the better part of the 18th cent. in connection with English poets and English landscape gardening, is in Iver par., 2 m. S. of the vill., and 1 m. N. of Colnbrook.

The estate (in early books and documents it is spelled *Rickings* and *Riskings*, while Lord Bathurst almost invariably wrote *Richkings*) was purchased of the Britton family by Sir Peter Apsley, whose granddaughter carried it by marriage to Sir B. Bathurst. On his death, in 1704, Richings became the seat of his son Allan, 1st Lord Bathurst, who improved the house and park, planted the grounds anew, and collected about him the chief wits and poets of the day. Lord Bathurst's gardening became famous :

"Who plants like Bathurst—or who builds like Boyle ? "

" I should be sorry to see my Lady Scudamore's [Holme Lacy in Herefordshire] till it has had the full advantage of Lord Bathurst's improvements ; and then I will expect something like the waters of Riskins and the woods of Oakley [Lord Bathurst's seat by Cirencester] together, which (without flattery) would be at least as good as anything in our world." *

* Pope to Hon. Robt. Digby, Aug. 12 (1724),

Pope was not, however, always so en-comiastic on Lord Bathurst's doings at Richings:—

"In laying out a garden, the first thing to be considered is the genius of the place ; thus at Riskins, for example, Lord Bathurst should have raised two or three mounts ; because his situation is all a plain, and nothing can please without variety."*

"The late Lord Bathurst told me that he was the first person who ventured to deviate from straight lines, in a brook which he had widened at Riskings."

Lord Bathurst himself writes of his grounds—

"Here I am absolute monarch of a circle of above a mile round, at least 100 acres of ground, which (to write in the style of one of your country-men) is very populous in cattle, fish, and fowl. To enjoy this power, which I relish extremely, and regulate this dominion which I prefer to any other, has taken up my time from morning to night. There are Yahoos in the neighbourhood ; but having read in history that the southern part of Britain was long defended against the Picts by a wall, I have fortified my territories all round. . . Now I think of it, as this letter is to be sent to you, it will certainly be opened ; and I shall have some observations made upon it, because I am within three miles of a certain castle " [Windsor Castle].‡

Richings was one of the places that dwelt in Swift's memory when he was hankering to return to England, but could not make up his mind to leave Ireland:—

"I had lately an offer of an English living, which is just too short by £300 a year ; and that must be made up out of the Duchess's pin-money before I consent. I want to be minister of Aims-bury, Dawley, Twickenham, Riskins, and Pre-bendary of Westminster ; else I will not stir a step." §

Swift, Pope, Gay, Arbuthnot, Boling-broke, Prior too, it is said, and Parnell, were frequent visitors at Richings, capped verses there, wrote inscriptions for the gardens, and helped their host with criti-cisms and suggestions in his favourite pur-suit of improving his dominion. But as time wore on Richings became too narrow for Lord Bathurst's ambition, and he turned to Oakley as a wider field for the exercise of that talent for landscape gardening

he here first displayed, and which after-wards made the woods and grounds of Oakley so celebrated. He sold Richings in 1739 to Algernon Lord Hertford, who succeeded to the title of Duke of Somerset in 1747. Lord Hertford changed the name from Richings to *Percy Lodge*, but he, and still more Lady Hertford, strove hard to maintain the poetic character of the place. Her ladyship has left an elaborate study of Richings as it was soon after she entered into possession:—

" We have just now taken a house by Colnbrook. It belonged to my Lord Bathurst, and is what Mr. Pope calls in his 'Letters' his *extravagante bergerie*. The environs perfectly answer that title, and come nearer to my idea of a scene in Arcadia than any place I ever saw. The house is old but convenient, and when you are got within the little paddock it stands in, you would think yourself a hundred miles from London, which I think a great addition to its beauty. . . . I cannot dis-cover who were the first builders of the place. . . . On the spot where the greenhouse now stands, there was formerly a chapel dedicated to St. Leonard, who was certainly esteemed a tutelar saint of Windsor Forest and its purlieus : for the place we left [St. Leonard's Hill] was originally a hermitage founded in honour of him. We have no relics of the Saint, but we have an old carved bench with many remains of the wit of my Lord Bathurst's visitors, who inscribed verses upon it. Here is the writing of Addison, Pope, Prior, Con-greve, Gay, and, what he esteemed no less, several fine ladies. I cannot say that the verses answered my expectations from such authors ; we have, how-ever, all resolved to follow the fashion, and to add some of our own to the collection. . . . There has been only one as yet added by the company. . . . I scarcely know whether it is worth reading or not:

By Bathurst planted, first these shades arose,
Prior and Pope have sung beneath these boughs.
Here Addison his moral theme pursued,
And social Gay has cheered the solitude." *

The paddock she describes as "laid out in the manner of a French park, interspersed with woods and lawns ; " the Abbey Walk, as "composed of pro-digiously high beeches that form an arch through the whole length, exactly resem-bling a cloister ; " and "the canal,"—the "waters of Riskins" that Pope admired so much—" 1200 yards long, and propor-tionately broad." Lady Hertford was of a literary turn, delighted to have literary men about her at Percy Lodge, and was pleased when they praised her gardens, and appreciated her poetry. She was the Cleora of Mrs. Rose, the Eusebia of Dr. Watts. Shenstone eulogized her " rectitude of heart, delicacy of sentiment,

Letters, 4to ed., 1737, p. 196; Works, 1764, vol. v., p. 313.

* Pope : Spence's Anecdotes, ed. by Singer, p. 12 ; and comp. Warton, Essay on Pope, ed. 1782, vol. ii., p. 179.

† Daines Barrington, Archæologia, vol. vii.

‡ Lord Bathurst to Swift, dated Richkings, June 30, 1730.

§ Swift to Gay and the Duchess of Queensbury, August 12, 1732.

* Lady Hertford to Lady Pomfret.

and truly classic ease and elegance of style," and devoted to her an 'Ode on Rural Elegance,' in which, while celebrating her "genius graced with rank," he condemns "the reptile race, that slight her merit, but adore her place,"—that place to which,

"Far happier, if aright I deem,
When from gay throngs, and gilded spires,
To where the lonely halcyons play,
Her philosophic step retires."

And Thomson, in the opening lines of his Spring, addresses her as his Muse :

"O Hartford, fitted or to shine in courts
With unaffected grace, or walk the plain
With innocence and meditation join'd
In soft assemblage, listen to my song,
Which thy own Season paints ; when Nature all
Is blooming and benevolent like thee."

But he did not play the courtier as well in person as in poetry. It was the practice of the Countess, says Johnson, "to invite every summer some poet into the country, to hear her verses, and assist her studies. That honour was one summer conferred on Thomson, who took more delight in carousing with Lord Hertford and his friends than assisting her ladyship's poetical operations, and therefore never received another summons." *

The Duke of Somerset died at Percy Lodge in 1750. His widow lived there almost entirely. She had been used to call it her *Bergerie*, she now termed it her Hermitage. Shd died there July 7, 1754. The estate went to her daughter Elizabeth, Countess of Northumberland, whose husband sold it, when created Duke of Northumberland, 1766, to Sir John Coghill. Coghill's widow, the Countess Dowager of Charleville, alienated it in 1786 to the Rt. Hon. John Sullivan, M.P. Shortly afterwards the house was destroyed by an accidental fire, and Mr. Sullivan built on a more elevated site the present more spacious mansion, a formal but stately building of 3 floors, with central portico, and wings—and resumed the name of Richings. A later Sullivan sold the estate to Mr. Meeking, and *Richings Park* is now the seat of C. Meeking, Esq. The grounds have been greatly altered and extended, retain few traces of Bathurst or Hertford influence, and reach nearly to Colnbrook. The entrance gates to the

* Johnson, Life of Thomson: Lives of the Poets, vol. iii., p. 228, ed. 1821.

private road are at the E. end of that town.

RICHMOND, SURREY, one of the most beautiful and celebrated places in England, lies on the Thames, 8½ m. W. of Hyde Park Corner. It is on the L. and S.W. Rly., but it can also be reached from the Broad Street, Moorgate Street, and Ludgate Hill stats., the N. London, L. and N.W., Midland, and L., C., and D. Rlys. having access to it over a portion of the L. and S.W. line. Pop. 15,113. Inns : the *Star and Garter* on the Hill, and the *Castle* by the river, are among the most famous of English hotels ; the *Queen's*, opposite the Star and Garter, is a first-class family hotel ; the *Roebuck*, by the Terrace, an excellent house for a dinner ; the *Talbot*, High Street, and the *Greyhound*, George Street, may also be commended.

Richmond is not mentioned in Domesday; it was probably then a waste, and included in the manor of Kingston. It first occurs as *Syenes* ; afterwards as *Schenes*, *Schene*, and *Sheen*, by which name it was known till about 1500, when it was called Richmond by command of Henry VII., who before the battle of Bosworth was Earl of Richmond in Yorkshire. The name *Syenes*, *Sheen*, is assumed to be the A.-S. *Scine* (= Germ. *Schön*), splendour, beauty, and to have been applied on account of the charm of the place, or, as Leland and Camden thought, from the magnificence of the royal palace. But the name was in use before any palace existed ; and in the 11th century a waste was little likely to be regarded as pleasant or beautiful.

In the reign of John, Michael Belet held Sheen by the service of being the King's butler, in succession to an ancestor to whom Henry I. had granted the manor and office. Belet left a daughter, who probably died early, as in 1230 the manor was held by her uncle, John Belet. He dying, left two daughters, between whom the manor was divided. One moiety went to John de Valletort, who married Alicia Belet; the other to Jordan Oliver, who married her sister Emma. Oliver's share was alienated to Gilbert Earl of Gloucester, and early in the reign of Edward I. purchased by Robert Burnell, Bp. of Bath and Wells. In 1293, Philip Burnell, the Bp.'s nephew, and John de Valletort, held each a moiety of the manor by the serjeanty of providing two silver cups at the King's coronation. The manor must shortly after have reverted to the Crown, as Edward I. kept house at Sheen in 1300, and the following year received the Scotch Commissioners " at his manor of Sheene upon Thames." * The manor has ever since been held by the Crown, though grants for life have been made to the wife of the sovereign or some member of the royal family ; and occasionally leases of it have been granted to subjects. It is now held by the Queen. The custom of Borough English prevails : lands in the manor descending to the youngest son ; or in default of sons to the youngest daughter.

Edward I., as we have seen, had a house at Sheen. Edward III. is said to have rebuilt the palace; and in it, attended only by a solitary priest, he died, June 21, 1377. Richard II. resided here in the early years of his reign ; and here, in 1394, his first wife, Anne of Bohemia, died ; whereupon, according to Holinshed, he cursed the place where she died, and " caused it to be thrown down and defaced; whereas the former kings of this land, being weary of the city, used customarily thither to resort, as to a place of pleasure, and serving highly to their recreation." It lay neglected till the beginning of the reign of Henry V., who liking the place, rebuilt the palace, and founded "three houses of religion, fast be his place which thei clepe Schene.—on of the monkis of Chartir-hous ; another clepid Celestines : thei kept Seint reule *ad literam*, as thei sey ; thei are constreyned for to be recluses for evyr. The thirde is of the Seynt Bride ordir." Henry's mansion was " of curious and costly workmanship, befitting the character and condition of a king." †

Edward IV. in 1465 granted the manor to his queen, Elizabeth Woodville, for life ; but Henry VII., shortly after his marriage with her daughter Elizabeth, deprived the Queen Dowager of this with her other possessions, and secluded her in the nunnery at Bermondsey, where she died shortly after. Henry was much at Sheen, where he kept great state. In 1492 he held a grand tournament, which lasted throughout May, sometimes within the palace, and " sometime without, upon the Greene without the Gate of the said mannor. In the which space a combat was holden and doone betwyxt Sir James Parkar, knt., and Hugh Vaughan, Gentleman Usher, upon controversie for the arms that Gartar gave to the sayde Hugh Vaughan : but he was there allowed by the King to beare them, and Sir James Parkyr was slain at the first course." *

Whilst Henry was staying in the palace in Dec. 1498, a fire occurred, which destroyed the greater part of the old building, and consumed much costly furniture, plate, and jewellery—the acquisition of jewels being a passion with the otherwise frugal King. The King at once gave orders for rebuilding the palace, and when in 1501 it was sufficiently advanced to be habitable, he directed that it should in future be named *Richmond*, from his former earldom. In January 1507, another fire broke out in the King's chamber, and caused great damage. His new palace nearly proved fatal to the King. In July 1507, a new gallery, in which the King had been walking with the prince his son a few minutes before, suddenly fell down, happily without injury to any one.† Philip I., King of Castile, was with his sister Margaret driven on the English coast in a storm, January 1506, and detained by Henry for three months pending negotiations for his marriage with the lady Margaret. Philip, after having visited Windsor Castle and London, was entertained with great magnificence in Richmond Palace, " where were many notable feates of armes proved both at the tylt and at the tourney and at the barriers."‡ Henry VII. died at Richmond Palace, April 21, 1509.

Henry VIII. was here in Nov. 1510, and commenced the series of splendid entertainments which formed so marked a feature of the early years of his reign.

"His Grace . . . willed to be declared to all

* Ordinances for Govt. of Royal Households : Account of Money paid at the Court at Sheen, 28 Edw. I., pubd. by Society of Antiquaries, p. 71. Matthew of Westminster, etc.

† Capgrave, Chronicle of England ; Book of the Illustrious Henries ; Elmham, Life of Henry V.

* Stow, Annals, Anno 1492.

† Brayley, Hist. of Surrey, vol. iii. p. 62, says that Prince Arthur was walking with his father in the gallery. Prince Arthur died in 1502 : it must of course have been Prince Henry.

‡ Hall, Chronicle, p. 501.

noblemen and gentelmen, that his grace with two aides, that is to wit mayster Charles Brandon and mayster Compton, duryng two dayes would answer all commers, with spere at the tylt one day, and at turney with swordes the other. And to accomplish this enterprice the xiii daye of November, hys grace armed at all peces with his twoo aydes entred the fielde, their bases and trappers were of clothe of golde, sette with redde roses, ingreyled with gold of brouderye. The counter parte came in freshly, appareyled every man after his devise. At these Justes the king brake more staves then any other, and therefore had the pryce. At the Turney in likewyse, the honour was his."*

Henry kept his Christmas at Richmond, and entertained a number of distinguished foreign visitors right royally. On New Year's Day the Queen gave birth to a son, "to the great gladnes of the realme;" but the young prince died at his birthplace on the 22nd of February following. Henry after this does not seem to have made Richmond a frequent residence. The emperor Charles V., on his visit to England in 1522, was lodged for a night in Richmond Palace. In the same year the King granted a lease for 30 years of the manor of Sheen, and the office for life of keeper of Richmond Park and Palace, to Massey Villard and Thomas Brampton. But the royal rights must have been reserved or the grant resumed, as when Wolsey in 1526 presented his newly-erected palace of Hampton Court to the King, Henry "of his gentle nature," as Hall relates, gave the Cardinal permission to reside at Richmond at his pleasure : and so, continues the chronicler, "he laie there at certain tymes. But when the common people, and in especiall such as had been King Henry the seventhes servauntes, sawe the Cardinal kepe house in the manor royall of Richmond, which King Henry VII. so highly esteemed, it was a marvell to here how thei grudged and said, See a Bocher's dogge lye in the Manor of Richemond !" † In July of the same year Wolsey received at Richmond the French Commissioners sent to negotiate a peace with England. The winter following there was plague with "great death" in London, and the King in consequence kept his Christmas at Eltham in such strict retirement that it was called "the still Christmas."

"But the Cardinall in this season, laye at the Manor of Richmond, and there kept open house-

holde, to lordes, ladies, and all other that would come, with plaies and disguisyng in most royall maner : which sore greved the people, and in especial the kynges servauntes, to see hym kepe an open Court, and the kyng a secret Court."*

The manor of Richmond was in 1541 granted by Henry to his divorced wife Anne of Cleves, so long as she should reside in this country ; but was resigned by her to Edward VI. in 1548.

On the 3rd of June, 1550, Edward VI. was present at the marriage, in Richmond Palace, of the Lord Lisle with Anne, daughter of the Protector Somerset, and on the following day at that of Sir Robert Dudley (later Earl of Leicester and favourite of Queen Elizabeth) with Amy, daughter of Sir John Robsart; "after which marriage," as the King records in his diary, "certain gentlemen did strive who should first take away a goose's head, which was hanged alive between two cross posts." Later in the year the King came here on account of the outbreak of the sweating sickness in London :

"*July* 13.—Came this day to Richmond, where I lay with a great band of gentlemen—at least 400, as it was by divers esteemed."

Queen Mary and Philip of Spain stayed here shortly after their marriage, and the Queen was here several times subsequently. The Princess Elizabeth was detained here in the interval between her release from the Tower and her removal to Woodstock. When Queen, she was often at Richmond, leading here, as would seem, a life of less state than in most of her other palaces ; and even in her later years, as one of the gentlemen of the privy chamber at Richmond writes, "I assure you, six or seven gallyards of a mornynge, besydes musycke and syngynge, is her ordinary exercyse." † Here, six years later, Anthony Rudd, Bp. of St. David's, greatly offended the Queen by preaching before her a sermon on the infirmities of age, and in it reminding her that "age had furrowed her face and besprinkled her hair with its meal." Here, according to a local tradition, in a small room, still remaining, over the entrance gateway, the Countess of Nottingham on her death-bed confessed to the Queen

---

* Hall, Chronicle, p. 516.
† *Ibid.*, p. 703.

* Hall, p. 707.
† John Stanhope to Lord Talbot, Dec. 22, 1589, Lodge's Illustrations of History, vol. ii., p. 411.

that she had kept back the ring which the Earl of Essex sent to her after he had been condemned to death. Whether the incident really occurred or not, it is at least certain it did not occur here, as the Countess died at Arundel House, London. It was at Richmond Palace that Elizabeth herself died, March 24, 1602; and another version of the former tradition assigns the room over the gateway as that in which she died: it is hardly necessary to say that the site and a glance at the dimensions of the room are enough to refute the tradition.

James I., in 1610, settled Richmond on his son Prince Henry, who spent large sums in repairing and embellishing the palace, employing Solomon de Caus as his architect.* The prince "kept house" at Richmond in 1612. On his death the grant was transferred to his brother, who as Charles I. settled the manor on his wife, Henrietta Maria, as her dower. Charles made the palace an occasional residence, formed in it a collection of pictures, and is said to have contemplated rebuilding it. In 1636 a masque was performed before the King and Queen by Lord Buckhurst and Edward Sackville. The young prince, afterwards Charles II., was educated at Richmond Palace, under Bp. Duppa. In 1647 the Parliament directed the palace to be made ready for the reception of the King. Charles refused to go there; but he went to Richmond in the August of that year to hunt in the new park, along with the Prince Elector, the Duke of York, and his attendant lords. Two years later a survey was made of Richmond Palace, by order of the House of Commons, when the materials were valued at £10,782. The palace was sold to Thomas Rookesby and others, and was afterwards purchased by Sir Gregory Norton, one of the King's judges, who probably resided in it, as on his death, in May 1652, he was buried at Richmond.

After the return of Charles II., the palace appears to have been dismantled. Several boat-loads of "rich and curious effigies, formerly belonging to Charles I., but since alienated," were taken from Richmond to Whitehall in 1660; and Fuller, writing about the same time of

Richmond Palace, says it is "a building much beholden to Mr. Speed's representing it in his map of this county: otherwise (being now plucked down) the form and fashion thereof had for the future been forgotten."* But though dismantled and perhaps in part plucked down, portions of it were left in a sufficiently perfect state for occupation.

"22d July, 1663.—In discourse of the ladies at Court, Captain Ferrers tells me that my Lady Castlemaine is now as great again as ever she was; and that her going away was only a fit of her own upon some slighting words of the King, so that she called for her coach at a quarter of an hour's warning, and went to Richmond; and the King the next morning, under pretence of going a-hunting, went to see her and make friends, and never was a-hunting at all. After which she came back to Court, and commands the King as much as ever, and hath and doth what she will."†

The Queen Dowager used the palace as an occasional residence till 1665. In 1666 Edward Villiers was appointed keeper of the manor and palace. In the reign of James II. it was held by the Crown, and the house was used for the nursery of the prince, afterwards known as the Pretender. The Princess (afterwards Queen) Anne is said to have applied unsuccessfully to William III. for the use of Richmond Palace, to which she was attached from having lived in it in her childhood. Strype, in 1720, speaks of the palace as "now decayed and parcelled out in tenements." Several houses had in fact been erected on the site under leases from the Crown, little except the offices of the old building being at this time left.

George II. granted Richmond to his consort Queen Caroline, "as he had done," writes Lord Hervey, "several sets of houses, which he used as much as she, that her Majesty, having the nominal property of them, might be at the expense of keeping them."‡

In 1770, the manor, the palace and park excepted, was granted to Charlotte, consort of George III.

Richmond Palace stood just outside the town, N.W. of Hill Street, between the Green and the Thames. A view of the principal or river front engraved in the 'Monumenta Vetusta' of the Society of

---

* The Accounts of the Expenses are printed in vol. xvii. of the Archæologia.

* Exact Account, June 8—15, 1660, quoted by Lysons; Fuller, Worthies of England, Surrey, vol. iii., p. 202.
† Pepys, Diary.
‡ Lord Hervey, Memoirs, vol. ii., p. 39.

Antiquaries, from a picture belonging to Lord Cardigan, shows it to have been a large and magnificent building of three floors, with numerous bays and turrets, rising well above the main structure, and crowned with bulbous cupolas, of which thirteen are shown in the view. The Parliamentary Survey describes it as

"All that capital messuage, palace, or Courthouse, commonly called *Richmond Court*, consisting of one large and fair structure of free-stone of two storeys high, covered with lead . . . and battayled, and hath upon it 14 turrets, all covered with lead, standing a convenient height above the said leads; which turrets very much adorn and set forth the fabric of the whole structure, and are a very graceful ornament unto the whole house, being perspicuous to the country round about." On the first floor was the Great Hall, a "fayr and large room 100 ft. in length and 40 in breadth," with "a screen in the lower end therof, over which is a little gallery, and a fayr foot-pace (dais) in the higher end thereof; the pavement is a square tile, and it is very well lighted and seeled, and adorned with eleven statues in the sides thereof; in the midst a brick hearth for a charcoal fire, having a large lanthorn in the roof of the hall fitted for that purpose, turreted and covered with lead."

At the N. end of the Great Hall was a turret, "which, together with the lanthorn in the middle thereof, are a special ornament unto that building."

The rest of the building is described with equal minuteness. There are the Great Buttery, the Buttery Chamber, the Silver Scullery, the Saucery, and the like on the ground floor. The Privy Lodgings consist of "a very large free-stone building, of curious workmanship, 3 storeys high," with 12 rooms on every storey, including the Robe Rooms, 4 rooms belonging to the Master of the Horse, 3 to the Groom of the Stole; the Lobby, Guard Chamber, Presence Chamber, Privy Closet, Privy Chamber, bed-chambers, pages rooms, and the like. In the midst is a paved court "of 24 ft. broad and 40 ft. long, which renders all the rooms thereof, that lye inwards, to be very light and pleasant." A "round structure of free-stone, called the Canted Tower, 4 storeys high . . . is a chief ornament unto the whole fabrick of Richmond Court." A fair and large structure 3 storeys high, "called the Chapel Building," contains on the third storey a "fayr and large room, 90 ft. long and 30 ft. broad, used for a chapel. This room is very well fitted with all things useful for a chapel; as fair lights, handsome cathedral seats and pewes, a removable pulpit, and a fayr case of carved work for a payr of organs." Other "piles of buildings or structures of stone,"—the Queen's Closet, the Prince's Closet, the Passage Buildings, and "one other structure of stone two storeys high, called the Middle Gate,"—with the Great Hall and Chapel Buildings, surround "a fayr court, paved with free-stone, 67 ft. long and 66 ft. broad, in which court stands one very large fountain of lead."

Beyond these State or Great Hall Buildings was another block, the Wardrobe Offices, of "three fayr ranges of buildings," two storeys high and embattled, lying round a great paved court 198 ft. long and 180 wide, and containing many convenient rooms appropriated to the higher court officials and court offices. Adjoining this, and lying along the N. side of the Privy Garden and facing Richmond Green, was another range of brick buildings, embattled and "adorned with divers pinnacles," and containing the Tennis Court, together with divers choice rooms both below stairs and above. From this again extended the whole S.E. side of the privy garden, a close or privy gallery, 200 yards in length, partly of brick and partly of wood, open below stairs, and closed and floored with plaster of Paris above, "very pleasant and useful to the whole house." Outside the gallery was a building "called the Fryars," no doubt the Priory of Observant Friars founded here by Henry VII.: it was at this time degraded to "a chandler's shop." Beyond were kitchens, flesh, fish, and pastry larders, and all other offices, "part of brick and part of wood tyled," standing "about a little court near adjoining to the riverside." About another small court are the Poultryhouse, Woodyard-lodging, Ale-butteries, an Aumery-room, Scalding-room, etc. Then farther away, and partly by the river and partly on Richmond Green, are the Plummery, Armory, Offices of the Clerk of the Works, and a great many more.

In all, Richmond Palace covered an area of very nearly 10½ acres. It was earlier, it will be remembered, than the oldest part of Hampton Court; but an examination of Wolsey's building would render clear the general plan of Richmond Palace. Little is left of the building now. On the W. side of the Green is the entrance gateway of the Wardrobe Court (now called *Old Palace Yard*), a rude stone building, above the arch of which is an escutcheon with the arms and supporters of Henry VII., defaced, and the red dragon of Cadwallader and white greyhound of the house of York, scarcely decipherable. Within the gateway is a building of red brick and stone dressings, having a turret and battlements, now used as a dwelling. All else has long been razed, and the site for the most part covered with residences, some towards the river, villas of considerable size, and by the Green, the old-fashioned rows known as Maid of Honour Row and Old Palace Terrace.

The *Green* was an important appendage to the palace. On it, as we have seen, the tournaments and royal festivities were held. The Paliamentary Commissioners described it as containing "20 acres more or less . . . well turfed, level, and a special ornament to the place." It had "113 elm trees, 48 whereof stand altogether on the W. side, and include in them a very handsome walk." This was the High Walk of recent times ; the elms have sadly diminished in number, but of late fresh trees have been planted. Richmond Green was a favourite resort in Richmond's fashionable season, a century and a quarter ago.

"To-day, as I passed over Richmond Green, I saw Lord Bath, Lord Lonsdale, and half a dozen more of the White's Club sauntering at the door of a house they have taken there, and come to every Saturday and Sunday to play at whist. You will naturally ask why they cannot play at whist in London on these two days as well as on the other five ; indeed I can't tell you, except that it is so established a fashion to go out of town at the end of the week, that people do go, though it be only into another town. It made me smile to see Lord Bath sitting there, like a citizen that has left off trade ! " *

A park had been attached to the palace from the earliest mention of a royal dwelling at Richmond. This was the present *Old Park*, or *Little Park*, so called to distinguish it from the New or Great Park (*the* Richmond Park of our day) on the opposite side of the town. The Old Park extends northwards from the palace and the Green towards Kew, with the Thames as its western boundary. In the Parliamentary Survey it is described as impaled, and "contayning upon admeasurement, 349 acres, 1 rood, and 10 perches of land." A recent official return makes it 357·2 acres. Wolsey in his fallen state, when broken in health he petitioned to be allowed to remove to a healthier site than Esher, was commanded to repair to the *Lodge* in Richmond Old Park, where he remained from "shortly after Christmas until it was Lent with a privy number of servants, because of the smallness of the house." When Lent came round he removed to a lodging built by Dean Colet in the neighbouring priory of West Sheen, where he spent the season "in godly contemplation." †

A lease of this Lodge was granted by William III. in 1694 to John Latton. In 1704 Queen Anne granted a lease of it for 99 years to James Duke of Ormond, who pulled it down, and built a larger lodge on the site, which he made his residence ; and where, as Lord Stanhope has recorded, after the death of Anne he

collected the Jacobites about him, " held a sort of Opposition Court," and " by the magnificence of his mode of living, and the public levees which he held, seemed to be arrogantly vying with Royalty itself." * A few months later he was impeached by the House of Commons, when he lost heart, gave up all his mighty projects, and escaped as quickly as he could from Richmond Lodge to France, where he spent the remainder of his days. The lease of the Duke's house was sold by auction, June 10, 1719, before the Commissioners of Forfeited Estates, and bought by the Prince of Wales (afterwards George II.) for £6000. The Prince made the lodge his summer residence, and frequently stayed in it after he ascended the throne.

"The late Duke of Ormond in Queen Anne's reign was ranger and keeper of Richmond Park, and his Lodge a perfect Trianon ; but since his forfeiture it hath been sold to the Prince of Wales, who makes his summer residence here. It does not appear with the grandeur of a Royal Palace, but it is very neat and pretty. There is a fine avenue that runs from the front of the house to the town of Richmond at half a mile distance one way, and from the other front to the river side, both enclosed with balustrades of iron." †

Caroline, wife of George II., was greatly attached to Richmond. The Lodge was her favourite abode, and the park and the gardens occupied no small share of her care. She employed Bridgman to lay out the gardens on a larger scale, and to embellish them with more costly buildings than had been previously seen in England. The works excited much admiration, and were duly praised by loyal bards, and mocked by the wits in opposition. Chief among the rarities were the Hermitage, Merlin's Cave, the Grotto, the Dairy, and a Menagerie. Her Hermitage the Queen placed in the midst of a solemn grove, adorned the exterior with a ruined pediment, turret and bell, and the interior with busts of Newton, Locke, Woolaston, and Clerke, with Robert Boyle as the presiding genius, his head encircled with a halo of gilded rays. Merlin's Cave was more elaborate. It was a " Gothic building," roofed with thatch, and placed in a "labyrinth full of intricate mazes." The

---

* Horace Walpole to Sir H. Mann, June 4, 1749 ; Letters, vol. ii., p. 164.

† Cavendish, Life of Wolsey, vol. i., p. 237.

* Earl Stanhope, Hist. of England, chap. iv., vol. i., p. 122.

† De Foe, A Journey through England, 8vo, 1722, vol. i., p. 68 ; King's Anecdotes, p. 7.

interior was circular ; four wooden pillars supported the roof ; in recesses were wax models by Mrs. Salmon, of Fleet Street (the Mdme. Tussaud of that day), of Merlin and his secretary, the Queen of Henry VII., Minerva, Queen Elizabeth and her nurse, the Queen of the Amazons, and other equally veracious effigies. At opposite ends of the room were collections of books, and Stephen Duck, the thresher poet, was constituted keeper and librarian.

" Lord ! how we strut through Merlin's Cave, to see
　No poets there, but, Stephen, you and me." *

" How shall we fill a library with wit,
　When Merlin's Cave is half unfurnished yet."†

　"Lewis the living learned fed,
　And rais'd the scientific head :
　Our frugal Queen to save her meat,
　Exalts the heads that cannot eat." ‡

"Whilst Lord Hervey was going on with a particular detail and encomium on these gates, [to Henry VII.'s Chapel] the Queen asking many questions about them, and seeming extremely pleased with the description—the King stopped the conversation by saying, ' My Lord, you are always putting some of these fine things in the Queen's head, and then I am to be plagued with a thousand plans and workmen.' Then turning to the Queen, he said, ' I suppose I shall see a pair of these gates to *Merlin's Cave* to complete your nonsense there.' The Queen smiled and said Merlin's Cave was complete already ; and Lord Hervey, to remove the King's fears of his expense, said that it was a sort of work that if his Majesty would give all the money in his exchequer he could not have now. ' *Apropos*,' said the Queen, ' I hear the Craftsman has abused Merlin's Cave.' ' I am very glad of it,' interrupted the King, ' you deserve to be abused for such childish silly stuff, and it is the first time I ever knew the scoundrel in the right.'" §

In the early part of his reign George III. lived in Richmond Lodge, and in 1760 settled it on Queen Charlotte in case of her surviving him.　George III. is said to have hated his grandmother, and he certainly showed little sympathy with her favourite works in the Old Park.　By his command Capability Brown swept away all Queen Caroline's buildings, destroyed

* Pope, Imit. of Horace, Book ii., Ep. 2.
† *Ibid.*, Book ii., Ep. 1.
‡ Swift, On Queen Caroline's Hermitage.　Earlier, when George II. became king, Swift had written, in a very different strain, ' A Pastoral Dialogue between Richmond Lodge and Marble Hill,' to be " carried to Court and read to the K. and Q.," though he soon after gave vent to his satirical temper in ' A Scribbling Epigram on Stephen Duck the Thresher and favourite Poet,' in which the Queen and the poet are alike rudely handled.
§ Lord Hervey, Memoirs, vol. ii., p. 49.

the Terrace she had constructed along the river—the finest it was said in Europe,—broke the avenues, and uprooted the trimmed hedges, so that not a trace now remains of any of her doings.

"See untutor'd Brown
Destroys those wonders that were once thy own.
Lo ! from his melon ground the peasant slave
Has rudely rush'd and level'd Merlin's Cave,
Knock'd down the waxen Wizard, seized his wand,
Transform'd to lawns what once was fairy land ;
And marr'd, with impious hand, each sweet design
Of Stephen Duck and good Queen Caroline." *

George III. converted the park into a grazing farm, built a model farm-house at the Green end, destroyed the road which separated the park from the pleasure grounds of Kew, and laid the two together.　(*See* KEW GARDENS.)　About 1760 he pulled down Richmond Lodge, with a view to the erection of a palace on the site ; but though the plans were prepared, and the foundations laid, the building was carried no farther.

Richmond Lodge stood not far from the *Observatory*, erected for George III., in 1768, by Sir Wm. Chambers, and now appropriated to the British Association for carrying on regular Meteorological observations and investigations, as noticed under KEW GARDENS.　A few years after the destruction of Richmond Lodge, the hamlet of *West Sheen*, which stood about ¼ m. N.W. of Richmond Palace, with what remained of West Sheen Priory, was removed, and the ground added to the park.　(*See* SHEEN, WEST.)

Richmond Park.—The *New Park*, as what is now known as Richmond Park was called in order to distinguish it from the already existing park attached to the palace, was formed by Charles I. in the early years of his reign, out of what was for the most part waste and wood land, on the S.E. of the town and hill.　The King, who as Clarendon explains, "was excessively affected to hunting and the sports of the field, had a great desire to make a great park for red as well as fallow deer, between Richmond and Hampton Court, where he had large wastes of his own and great parcels of wood, which made it very fit for the use he designed it to."　Intermingled with these wastes were however many houses

* Mason, Heroic Epistle to Sir William Chambers.

and farms whose owners and tenants "obstinately refused" to part with them, and as the King was bent on obtaining them, and went on building the wall before they had consented to part with the land, "it made a great noise." Laud, then Bp. of London and Lord Treasurer, and Lord Cottington, the Chancellor, endeavoured to divert the King from his purpose, the former because by these measures the King's honour and justice were so much called in question ; the latter "because the purchase of the land and the making a brick-wall about so large a parcel of ground (for it is near ten miles about) would cost a greater sum of money than they could easily provide, or than they thought ought to be sacrificed for such an occasion." * The King had his way ; the wall was completed, and the Earl of Portland appointed first keeper of the New Park in 1637. In 1649 the House of Commons resolved that the New Park at Richmond should be given in perpetuity to the City of London, to be preserved as a park and so remain, as an ornament to the City, and a mark of the favour of Parliament. Later there was a proposal to exchange Richmond for Greenwich Park, but it was not carried out, and at the Restoration of Charles II. the Corporation hastened to return the park to His Majesty, with the assurance that they had always held it for him as trustees. Charles made Sir Daniel Harvey ranger. Anne, on ascending the throne, gave the post to the Earl of Rochester for three lives. After his death, George I. purchased the grant, and appointed Lord Walpole nominally, but actually his father the Minister, to the rangership.

"The Park had run to great decay under the Hydes, nor was there any mansion, better than the common lodges of the keepers. The King ordered a stone lodge, designed by Henry, Earl of Pembroke, to be erected for himself, but merely as a banqueting-house, with a large eating-room, kitchen, and necessary offices, where he might dine after his sport. Sir Robert began another of brick for himself and the under-ranger, which, by degrees, he much enlarged ; usually retiring thither from business, or rather, as he said himself, to do more business than he could in town, on Saturdays and Sundays. On that edifice, on the thatched house, and other improvements, he laid out £14,000 of his own money. In the mean time he hired a

small house for himself on the Hill without the Park ; and in that small tenement the King did him the honour of dining with him more than once after shooting. His Majesty, fond of private joviality, was pleased with punch after dinner and indulged in it freely." *

"During the last years of the late King's life, he took extremely to New Park, and loved to shoot there, and dined with my father and a private party and a good deal of punch. The Duchess of Kendal, who hated Sir Robert and favoured Bolingbroke, and was jealous for herself, grew uneasy at these parties and used to put one or two of the Germans upon the King to prevent his drinking (very odd preventives !)—however they obeyed orders so well, that one day the King flew into a great passion and reprimanded them in his own language with extreme warmth ; and when he went to Hanover ordered my father to have the New Lodge in the park finished against his return." †

On the death of the 2nd Earl of Orford in 1751, the Princess Amelia was appointed ranger, and soon contrived to arouse general dissatisfaction and opposition by arbitrarily closing the park-gates against all but the few to whom she granted tickets. The inhabitants petitioned and remonstrated in vain, when a Mr. John Lewis, a brewer of Richmond, formally claimed admittance, and on refusal appealed to the law. In the first suit as to the passage of carriages, the Princess was successful ; but in a second action, tried before Sir Michael Foster in April 1758, judgment was given fully establishing the right of ingress to the park, and of footway through it ; and in a subsequent session, the Princess having evaded compliance with the judgment, the judge issued peremptory orders for the erection of step-ladders, and directed Mr. Lewis to see that they were "so constructed that not only children and old men, but old women too may get up !" The Princess was so incensed at the decision that according to Walpole "she abandoned the park." Lewis was regarded as the village Hampden, acquired unbounded popularity, and his portrait, with an inscription beneath it, setting forth that by his "steady perseverance . . . the right to a free passage through Richmond Park was recovered and established," was an ordinary ornament in Richmond dwellings, and may still be occasionally seen. Lewis in his last years became

* Clarendon, Hist. of the Great Rebellion, vol. i., p. 100.

* Horace Walpole, Reminiscences, p. xcvi.
† Horace Walpole to Sir Horace Mann, Dec. 1, 1754.

reduced in circumstances, and was maintained by the proceeds of a subscription of the inhabitants of Richmond. Feeling her unpopularity, the Princess willingly accepted the offer of George III. shortly after his accession to purchase the rangership, in order to bestow it, 1761, on the Earl of Bute, who retained the office and resided in the White Lodge till his death in 1792. The King then took the rangership into his own keeping, appointing the Countess of Mansfield deputy ranger.

When Addington, afterwards Viscount Sidmouth, accepted the premiership on the resignation of Pitt, in 1801, the King gave him the White Lodge as a residence. The King lived at this time in the Queen's Lodge at Kew, and he marked the interest he took in Addington by adding 5 acres to the private grounds, and riding over almost daily that he might himself superintend the repairs and alterations, and direct the laying out of the grounds. Mr. Jesse says that the King with his own hands marked out a space of about 60 acres for enclosure, but the more prudent minister begged to have the smaller quantity.* Lord Sidmouth occupied the White Lodge (or *Villa Medici*, as Canning named it in allusion to Addington's cognomen of The Doctor) for 43 years.

Before his marriage, the White Lodge was a residence of H.R.H. the Prince of Wales. It is now occupied by the Duke of Teck and Princess Mary. The White Lodge stands at the end of the Queen's Avenue, which faces you on entering the Park from Richmond Hill, and a short distance E. of the smaller of the two Pen Ponds. The old Lodge, built by Walpole, stood a little way S. of White Lodge: it was taken down in 1841. Two fine old oaks, which stood on the lawn before it, mark the site.

Pembroke Lodge, originally *Hill Lodge* —it derived its present name from having been for many years the residence of the Countess of Pembroke—stands at the end of the New Terrace on the rt. after entering the park from the hill. After the death of the Countess, Pembroke Lodge became the residence of the Earl and Countess of Errol. Since 1847 it has been the summer residence of Earl Russell. The house is plain and unassuming; the site charming; the grounds, though confined, are very beautiful, and command the best views in the park.

"Richmond Park is very large and encompassed with a brick wall. In the middle of this park is a little artificial hill, called *King Henry's Mount;* from whence one hath a full prospect of six counties, with the City of London at nine miles distance, and Windsor Castle at fourteen." *

King Henry's Mount is within the grounds of Pembroke Lodge, far from the middle of the park, and now too much encompassed with trees to allow of anything like the range of view De Foe mentions. The local tradition respecting the origin of the name is that Henry VIII. stood on this mound to watch the ascent of a rocket which was to announce to him the execution of Anne Boleyn! The mound now known as *Oliver's Mount*, from a tradition that the Protector had a camp there, commands a much better view Londonwards than King Henry's Mount. From it St. Paul's, the Houses of Parliament, and the sister hills of Highgate, Hampstead, and Harrow are still visible. Windsor Castle, which used to be seen, is shut out by recent plantations. Some labourers digging gravel by this mound, in Dec. 1834, found the skeletons of three persons laid side by side, about three feet from the surface.†

Thatched Lodge, at the S.W. end of the park, near Kingston Gate, formerly in the occupation of Sir Charles Stuart, K.B., and afterwards of Major-General Sir Edward Bowater, is now the residence of Lady Bowater. At the opposite edge of the park is *Sheen Lodge*, since 1852 the residence of Richard Owen, the eminent anatomist and paleontologist. The garden is noted for possessing some rare foreign trees; the pond in front is well stored with carp. The *Farm House* was for many years the residence of Edward Jesse, when Deputy Surveyor of the Parks, who has given many interesting particulars respecting the natural history of Richmond Park in his pleasant ' Gleanings in Natural History.'

The Park has an area of 2015·5 acres, according to a recent Ordnance Survey

---

* Memoirs of George III., vol. iii., p. 283 ; Pellew, Life of Viscount Sidmouth, vol. i., p. 408.

* De Foe, A Journey through England, 1722, vol. i., p. 68.

† Brayley, Hist of Surrey, vol. iii., p. 73,

estimate, but 2253 according to the old Department return, and is, next to Windsor, the largest round London. It far exceeds in extent the combined areas of Hyde Park, St. James's Park, the Green Park, Kensington Gardens, Regent's Park, Greenwich Park, Battersea Park, Southwark Park, Victoria Park, and Finsbury Park, and is about equal if the new West Ham Park be added to them. Plantations skirt the park on all sides but the E. The substratum of the park is London clay, with deep hollows filled with drift gravel, the flint pebbles in some of these deposits being broken and the edges slightly rounded, in the others whole and smooth. The surface of the park is varied; it is traversed in all directions by footpaths, and wide views are obtained from several places. The old timber is chiefly oak, past its prime, but many of the trees are large, still vigorous, and remarkably picturesque. There are many fine horse-chesnuts, maples (and on both these Mr. Jesse has here seen the mistletoe growing), firs, and by Petersham the cedars once the glory of Petersham Lodge. Hawthorns abound, old, contorted, but exuberant in bloom. The newer plantations, now rapidly maturing, are chiefly of oak, elm, chesnut, beech, poplar, fir, and red and white hawthorns. Along its western side, all the way from the Petersham slopes to Kingston Gate, the park has something of a forest aspect, and there is some fresh, rough forest scenery on the opposite side by Sheen Gate; whilst not less picturesque scenery of another kind is found by the ferny dells and open heathy tracts towards Wimbledon.

In the centre of the park are two large sheets of water, the *Pen Ponds*, nearly 18 acres in area, formed from gravel pits by the Princess Amelia, in the reign of George II. They are a great addition to the scenery, and attract many aquatic birds: at times, as Mr. Jesse tells, some fifty or sixty herons assemble, but they never remain long. Great quantities of eels inhabit the ponds, and have their annual migrations.

"An amazing number of eels are bred in the two large ponds in Richmond Park, which is sufficiently evident from the very great quantity of young ones which migrate from these ponds every year. The late respectable head-keeper of that park assured me that, at nearly the same day in the month of May, vast numbers of young eels,

about two inches in length, contrive to get through the pen-stock of the upper pond, and then through the channel leading into the lower pond; and thence through another pen-stock into a water-course falling into the river Thames. They migrate in one connected shoal, and in such prodigious numbers that no guess can be given as to their probable amount." *

About 1450 fallow and 50 red deer are kept in Richmond Park. The park is well drained, the food and cover abundant, and the venison has the reputation of being the best from any of the royal parks. Sixty bucks are shot annually.

The entrance gates of Richmond Park are on *Richmond Hill*, whence is obtained that "goodly prospect" which, since Thomson described it, now very nearly a century and a half ago,[†] has been the most famous and the most visited in England. Thomson's verses and Turner's painting remain the truest representations of the "glorious view, calmly magnificent," but since Thomson wrote "the boundless landskip" has been limited in range by the erection of houses, and many of the objects and places mentioned by him have been concealed by the growth of trees, or effaced by the hand of time. But the view has rather gained than lost in loveliness. From contemporary, or nearly contemporary prints—Sayer's, Heckel's, Vandergucht's, Farington's, and other engravings, and Sir Joshua's famous view from the window of his house on the hill, are lying before us—it is evident that the plain is now much more thickly wooded, and that the view, with the broad river winding placidly amid the masses of verdure, has in consequence acquired increased richness and grandeur. The view is best studied from the *Terrace*, where it can be contemplated at leisure beneath the shade of the spreading elms, or from the open ground by the Star and Garter.

The view extends, W. and S.W., from the broken declivity of the *Hill*, and the trees at its foot as a foreground, up the wide valley of the Thames,—a thickly wooded tract relieved by open meadows and gentle undulations, the eye resting always on the tranquil surface of the river, with its eyots, skiffs, and swans,—to the beech-clad hills of Buckingham-

* Jesse, Gleanings in Natural History, 1st Series.
† Thomson's Summer, in which the prospect from "Thy Hill, delightful Sheen," is described, was published in 1727.

32

shire, the Surrey heaths and downs, and the Berkshire heights, over which, dimly visible through a veil of purple haze, "majestic Windsor lifts his princely brow." Ham House, with the elm groves and avenues of Ham Walks on one side of the river, and on the other the dark massive forms of Hampton Court and the long chesnut avenues of Bushey Park, are as prominent and effective features in the landscape as when Thomson wrote ; but "the raptur'd eye exulting," looks from the Terrace in vain for "huge Augusta," "the sister hills that skirt her plain," or even "lofty Harrow." though the last may be made out from the garden terrace of the Star and Garter, and all, in clear weather, from some part or other of the park. Jeannie Deans liked "just as weel to look at the craigs of Arthur's seat, and the sea coming in ayont them, as at a' thae muckle trees," * but her historiographer, though he recalls the "more grand and scarce less beautiful domains of Inverary," admits the view from Richmond Hill to be an "inimitable landscape." Canova, too, is said to have sighed for cliffs or crags and classic ruins. In truth, it is a mistaken taste that thinks of mountains, cliffs, and torrents, or the landscapes of Claude Lorraine, when looking at the prospect from Richmond Hill. The view is one of a wide expanse of quiet cultivated scenery. It has a character and charm all its own, and is perfect in its kind. And its charm is not dependent on the hour or the season. It may receive an added grace or assume a nobler beauty at certain seasons or under exceptional atmospheric phenomena, but it is alike exquisite, seen, as we have seen it, in the earliest dawn or broad daylight, when bathed in the crimson glory of a sinking sun, or lit by a full or waning moon ; in the first freshness of the spring, the full leafiness of summer, the "sober gold" of autumn, or the sombre depth of advancing winter.

On the summit of the hill, by the entrance to Richmond Park, is the *Star and Garter Hotel*, renowned for convivial parties, dinners, and wines. Originally a small house of entertainment, erected in 1738 on a piece of Petersham waste, let at £2 a year rental, it gradually extended

till, at the close of the century, it ranked as a first-class hotel. Twenty years later it had come to be recognized as the chief hotel in the vicinity of London. Kings and princes were among its patrons, and returned to it in exile ; Louis Philippe stayed at it for six months after his flight from Paris; Napoleon III. had apartments in it ; and at one time or other it has received almost every distinguished person of the day within its walls. The original Four-in-hand Club used in the season to drive down and dine here every Sunday, and on Sundays it was a favourite resort of foreigners, who escaped thither from the dulness of London. On one Sunday in July 1851, when the hotel was at its highest, under Mr. Ellis's management, as many as 560 dinners were served—the average at that time being about 320. In 1864 the house was transferred to a Limited Liability Company, who built a large and costly extension in the shape of a lofty Italian Renaissance edifice on the park side of the old hotel. A stately dining hall was erected by the architect of the new wing, E. M. Barry, R.A., to connect the two buildings. The comfortable old hotel was destroyed by fire on the morning of Jan. 12, 1870, but a spacious and luxuriously fitted pavilion and banqueting hall was in 1873-4 erected on the site, from the designs of Mr. C. J. Phipps, F.S.A. This building is now appropriated to dinner parties and holiday visitants, the building by the park being reserved for families and residents. From the banqueting hall and private dining rooms there are charming views of the Thames valley, but the best and widest are obtained from the terrace and grounds in the rear of the hotel.

The house next to the Star and Garter from the park, *Wick House* (A. Tod, Esq.), was built by Sir William Chambers for Sir Joshua Reynolds, on the site of a small inn called the Bull's Head, pulled down in 1775. The great painter was in the habit of giving pleasant little dinner parties in the summer at his Richmond villa, when many of the more eminent of his contemporaries gathered around his table.* Mr. Beechey says, "it is remarkable that, though he frequently visited it, he never, it is said, passed a night" at his

---

* Heart of Mid-Lothian, ch. 36.

* Northcote, Life of Reynolds, vol. i., p. 295.

Richmond Hill

Magna Charta Island, Runnimede (see p.516)

Richmond villa; * but this is certainly incorrect. Malone, Reynolds' friend and literary executor, says expressly he "occasionally spent a few days at his villa on Richmond Hill; but he had very little relish for a country life, and was always glad to return to London."† In his later days, however, he seems to have visited it oftener. His niece, Miss Palmer, afterwards Marchioness of Thomond, who at this time kept his house, writes after rather protracted visits in July and Aug., 1789 :—

"A place, to tell you the truth, I hate; for one has all the inconveniences of town and country put together, and not one of the comforts : a house stuck upon the top of a hill, without a bit of garden or ground of any sort near it but what is as public as St. James's Park." ‡

One of the three landscapes painted by Reynolds was the view from the drawing-room window of his Richmond villa. The house has been added to and altered since Sir Joshua's death, but it still bears the impress of Sir Wm. Chambers' genius and Sir Joshua's masculine simplicity of taste.

Ancaster House (Lieut.-Col. F. Burdett), by the park gate, opposite the Star and Garter, was long the residence of Sir Lionel Darell, a great favourite of George III., who frequently visited him here, and observing that the grounds were somewhat confined, not only added to them a portion of the park, but himself directed their arrangement and planting. It is related that riding one day up Richmond Hill to Sir Lionel Darell's, he noticed a handsome new house in course of erection (No. 3 on the Terrace, Capt. G. A. Lloyd), and inquired to whom it belonged. "Blanchard, your Majesty's card-maker," was the reply ; to which the King returned, " Blanchard, hey !—well ! well ! his cards must have turned up trumps."

Mrs. Fitzherbert was resident on Richmond Hill in 1784 when she attracted the notice and won the affections of the Prince of Wales (afterwards George IV.) "According to her kinsman, Lord Stour-

ton, she was the original of the once celebrated ballad, 'The Lass of Richmond Hill,' " * and the lines

" *I'd crowns resign* to call thee mine,
Sweet Lass of Richmond Hill,"

are cited in support of the assertion. But rival claims have been put forward. An early tradition, embodied by the Rev. Thos. Maurice in his ' Richmond Hill, a poem,' and by Dr. Evans, in ' Richmond and its Vicinity,' makes the heroine to be a Miss Cropp, who destroyed herself because her father refused to consent to her marriage with " a young officer of exemplary character—but poor." Leigh Hunt† says the lass of Richmond Hill was understood to be Lady Sarah Lennox, daughter of the Duke of Richmond, of whom George III. was in early life supposed to be enamoured, but her claim is inconsistent with the date of the ballad. Sir Jonah Barrington says the lady was a Mrs. Janson, whose father, a solicitor in Bedford Row, had a country house on Richmond Hill, and the author of the ballad a Mr. Leonard MacNally ; and lastly, to increase the confusion, it has been stated by her grandson that Miss Janson was indeed the " lovely lass," but that she resided at Richmond Hill, Leyburn, Yorkshire, and that Mr. MacNally, the author of the song, afterwards (1787) married her.‡ The song was set to music by James Hook (the father of Theodore), and first sung by Incledon, at Vauxhall, in 1789. It immediately became popular, and, whether the lass was a real, or, as is more probable, only a poetic personage, both song and air have ever since been favourites at Richmond, and regarded as its unquestionable property.

In the richly wooded grounds adjoining the *Terrace*, and commanding views of almost equal extent and beauty, stood *Lansdowne House*, so named from having been for many years the seat of the late Marquis of Lansdowne. Before him it had belonged successively to the Marquis of Anglesey and the Duke of Sutherland. Later (1865, etc.), it was the residence of the Prince de Joinville. The house has

---

* Beechey, Memoir prefixed to the Literary Works of Sir Joshua Reynolds, vol. i., p. 196, note.
† Malone, Some Account of Sir Joshua Reynolds, prefixed to his Works, vol. i., p. lxv.
‡ Leslie and Taylor, Life of Reynolds, vol. ii., p. 542.

* Hon. C. Langdale, Memoirs of Mrs. Fitzherbert, p. 117; Jesse, Memoirs of George III., vol. iii., p. 502.
+ Old Court Suburb, p. 164.
‡ Letter in the Times, March 31, 1856.

since been pulled down, and the ground is for sale on lease for building on.

Cardigan House (J. Willis, Esq.), a little lower down the hill, formerly the residence of the Earl of Cardigan, stands in grounds celebrated for their beauty and prospects : they include the site of the once noted house of entertainment known as Richmond Wells. A spring here was observed to be chalybeate in 1689, soon began to be resorted to, and in 1696 the *Wells House* was built.

"The *New Wells* on Richmond Hill will be compleated for the reception of Company this following May. There is a large and lofty Dining Room, broad walks, open and shady, near 300 foot long, cut out of the descent of the Hill, with a prospect of all the country about," etc.*

"Richmond New Wells are to be disposed of by purchase or lease." †

Assembly, card, and raffling rooms were added, and the place appears to have retained its popularity for many years.

"This is to give notice to all Gentlemen and Ladies, that Richmond Wells are now opened, and continue so daily ; where attendance is given for Gentlemen and Ladies that have a mind either to raffle for Gold Chains, Equipages, or any other Curious Toys and fine old China, and likewise play at quadrille, ombre, wisk, etc. And on Saturdays and Mondays, during the Summer season, there will be Dancing as usual." ‡

Shortly after this the place began to decline ; assemblies were advertised there as late as 1755, but the company became less reputable, and the premises were purchased and annexed to the estate, "in order to get rid of the noise and tumult attending a public resort of this description." The Wells House was pulled down about 1775.§

Downe House (Hon. Mrs. Broadhurst) was for a time the residence of Richard Brinsley Sheridan. The eccentric castellated structure conspicious on the rt. in descending the hill is *Ellerker House* (Rev. J. Askew), for many years the residence of the Hon. Mrs. Ellerker, sister of the Marchioness of Thomond, in whose time the grounds were very celebrated. A large white house nearly opposite was the residence of John Moore, M.D., author

of ' Zeluco,' and father of General Sir John Moore.

Queensbury House, the mansion which acquired so much celebrity during its long tenancy by the Duke of Queensbury (Old Q.), was originally known as Cholmondeley House, having been built by George, 3rd Earl of Cholmondeley, about 1708, on a portion of the ground occupied by the palace. In it was his famous collection of pictures, for the reception of which he erected a spacious gallery. Lord Cholmondeley sold the house to the Earl of Brooke and Warwick ; from whom it passed to Sir Richard Lyttleton, and then to Earl Spencer, who purchased it for his mother, the Countess Cowper. On her death, 1780, it was bought by the Duke of Queensbury, who made it his principal country residence ; brought to it the famous Clarendon (or Cornbury) pictures and tapestry from Amesbury ; and made it famous by his dinners and parties and the distinguished people he collected at them.

"I went yesterday to the Duke of Queensbury's palace at Richmond, under the conduct of George Selwyn the *concierge*. You cannot imagine how noble it looks now all the Cornbury pictures from Amesbury are hung up there. The great hall, the great gallery, the eating room and the corridor are covered with whole and half lengths of royal family, favorites, ministers, peers and judges, of the reign of Charles I.,—not one an original, I think, at least not one fine ; yet altogether they look very respectable ; and the house is so handsome, and the views so rich, and the day was so fine, that I could only have been more pleased if (for half-an-hour) I could have seen the real prince that once stood on that spot, and the persons represented, walking about." *

Walpole recurs to this idea some years later :—

"Richmond, my metropolis, flourishes exceedingly. The Duke of Clarence arrived at his palace there last night, between 11 and 12, as I came from Lady Douglas. His eldest brother and Mrs. Fitzherbert dine there to day, with the Duke of Queensbury, as his grace, who called here [Strawberry Hill] this morning, told me, on the very spot where lived Charles I., and where are the portraits of his principal courtiers from Cornbury. Queensbury has taken to that place at last, and has frequently company and music there in an evening. I intend to go." †

Again he writes :—

"Richmond is still full, and will be so till after

* Advt. in London Gazette, April 20—23, 1696.
† *Ibid.*, April 5—8, 1697.
‡ Craftsman, June 11, 1730 : quoted by Lysons.
§ Brayley, Hist. of Surrey, vol. iii., p. 99 ; Lysons, Environs, vol. i., p. 351 ; Crisp, Richmond and its Inhabitants.

* H. Walpole to Countess of Ossory, Dec. 1, 1786 ; Letters, vol. ix., p. 79.
† Walpole to Miss Berry, Sunday, Nov. 28, 1790.

Christmas. The Duke of Clarence is there, and every night at Mrs. Bouverie's, Lady Di's, at home, or at the Duke of Queensbury's, with suppers that finish at twelve." *

The Duke of Queensbury continued to reside here for many years, but he tired of the country, and even the sight of the river grew wearisome. Wilberforce relates that when a young man he once dined with the Duke of Queensbury at his Richmond villa.

"The party was very small and select, Pitt, Lord and Lady Chatham, the Duchess of Gordon and George Selwyn. . . . The dinner was sumptuous, the views from the villa quite enchanting, and the Thames in all its glory; but the Duke looked on with indifference. 'What is there,' he said, 'to make so much of in the Thames? I am quite weary of it; there it goes, flow, flow, flow, always the same.'" †

At length he found an excuse for leaving it. He began to extend his grounds by enclosing the larger part of the popular Cholmondeley Walk. This the townspeople resented, and as he refused to desist, the parish authorities applied for an injunction, when he left Richmond altogether, and never again visited his mansion. His removal was regretted on account of his magnificent style of living and lavish charity, but personally the Duke was never popular. The house was long left without an occupant. It was then for a time the residence of the Marquis of Hertford. It was demolished in 1830. The present *Queensbury House* (Thos. Cave, Esq., M.P.) was built on a back part of the grounds.‡

Two other mansions built on the river side of the palace have some local celebrity. One, a good old red-brick house with a stately portico facing the Thames, known as the Trumpeting House, from two figures with trumpets which formerly stood in niches on either side of the portico, was built by Richard Hill, Esq., who obtained a lease of the site from Queen Anne in 1708. The house was for some time the residence of Mrs. Way and her sister the Countess-Dowager of Northumberland; afterwards of J. A. Stewart Mackenzie, Lord High Commissioner of the Ionian Islands, and now of the Hon. Mrs. Lee Mainwaring. In the grounds

is an unusually handsome cedar of Lebanon. Next to it is *Asgill House* (J P. Trew, Esq.), a handsome Palladian villa, built by Sir Robt. Taylor for Alderman Asgill, but since enlarged and a good deal altered. Obs. the fine elms, acacias, and Turkey oak on the lawn.

West of the bridge, by Bellevue Terrace, is a large house which was built by George Colman on the site of Queen Elizabeth's Almshouse; it was for some time his residence, and afterwards that of Sir Drummond Smith and of the Countess of Kingston. It has since been much altered.

The large brick house a little higher up the river is that which was occupied by the Duke of Clarence (afterwards King William IV.), and referred to by Horace Walpole. The Gothic house beyond was for a while the residence of Madame de Staël.

Buccleuch House, the stately villa of the Duke of Buccleuch, farther up the river, at the end of the towing-path, is one of the most famous of the river-side residences. The house was built for the Duke of Montagu, and inherited towards the close of the 18th century by the Duke of Buccleuch. The house has an old-fashioned stately aspect, is roomy, and inside sufficiently magnificent. The fine lawns slope down to the Thames, and are connected with the upper grounds by a passage under the Petersham Road.

"I have been this evening to see the late Duke of Montagu's at Richmond, where I had not been for many years. . . . The new garden that clambers up the hill is delightful, and disposed with admirable taste and variety. It is perfectly screened from human eyes, though in the bosom of so populous a village; and you climb till at last, treading the houses under foot, you recover the Thames and all the world at a little distance." *

The river fêtes and garden parties of Buccleuch House are among the most celebrated of their class. One of the most noted was that given to the Queen and Prince Consort June 23, 1842, when there were also present the King and Queen of the Belgians, Adelaide Queen-Dowager, the Duchess of Kent, and various other members of the royal family, and a crowd of foreign princes and British nobles.

Devonshire Cottage, by the Petersham

---

* Walpole to Miss Berry, Dec. 17, 1790.
† Life of William Wilberforce, by his Sons.
‡ Lysons; Brayley; Evans, Richmond and its Vicinity; Crisp, Richmond and its Inhabitants.

* Horace Walpole to Miss Berry, July 29, 1790.

meadows, was the residence of Lady Diana Beauclerk, the Lady Di of Horace Walpole and Dr. Johnson, and in her day was famous for the brilliant little circle that gathered around her. It was afterwards the residence of the more widely noted Georgiana, Duchess of Devonshire, celebrated alike for her wit and beauty, and of no small influence among the Whig politicians of her day. Later it was the residence of the Hon. Mrs. Lamb, widow of George Lamb, brother to Lord Melbourne.

Camborne House, Lower Road, is the residence of the Duchess-Dowager of Northumberland. At *Heron Court*, Hill Street, lived the distinguished diplomatist and author Sir Henry Lytton Bulwer (Lord Dalling and Bulwer). The neighbouring mansion, *Hotham House*, is the seat of Baron J. B. Heath. *Mount Ararat*, near the Vineyard, formerly the seat of Earl Grosvenor, and afterwards of Sir Rose Price, Bart., is now the residence of Admiral R. F. Stopford.

Spring Grove, Marsh Gate, was built early in the 18th cent. by the Marquis of Lothian, and greatly enlarged towards the close of the century by Sir Charles Price. A smaller house at Marsh Gate was for many years the residence of Lord Kenyon, the distinguished successor of Lord Mansfield as Chief Justice of the King's Bench. *Stawell House* (Sir H. Watson Parker), *Egerton House* (Lieut.-Col. Price), and other good seats, are in this vicinity.

Wentworth House, on the N. side of the Green, was the seat of Sir Charles Hedges, Secretary of State to Queen Anne; afterwards of Sir Matthew Decker, who had the honour of entertaining George II. with his Queen in it on the day of his proclamation, and built an additional room for the royal reception. From him it descended to his grandson Viscount Fitzwilliam, who had here the fine collection of pictures, books, and medals which he bequeathed to Cambridge University. After his decease it was successively occupied by the Countess of Pembroke and the Countess of Mulgrave, and is now the seat of R. Laurie, Esq.

Rosedale House, the house in which James Thomson lived and died, is on the rt. in Kew Foot Lane, the lane leading from the Green to the Kew Road. The present house is a large brick house

of three floors,—a centre with a small portico reached by a flight of steps, and two irregular wings. The house Thomson occupied was a mere cottage of two rooms on the ground floor, which now, united by an arch, form a sort of entrance hall, that on the rt. being the poet's sitting-room,— in which he wrote the 'Castle of Indolence,'—that on the l. his bedroom, in which he died, Aug. 22, 1748. After the poet's death the lease of the house was bought by his friend Mr. George Ross, who built the present house, piously enshrining within it the poet's dwelling in the manner just noted. On Mr. Ross's death (1786) it became the residence of the Hon. Mrs. Boscawen (widow of the Admiral), who collected and placed in the Thomson rooms various Thomson relics—his chair, table, etc. After her decease (1805) it was purchased by the Earl of Shaftesbury, and was for more than 40 years the residence of the Countess. It has since suffered many changes, and is now (1876) the Richmond Infirmary. The garden has suffered as much as the house. Thomson was fond of his garden, added largely to it, and spent as much time in improving it as his indolent temperament allowed.

"You must know that I have enlarged my rural domain . . . . the two fields next to me, from the first of which I have walled—no, no, paled—in about as much as my garden consisted of before, so that the walk runs round the hedge, where you may figure me walking any time of the day, and sometimes in the night. You will give me no small pleasure by sending me from time to time some seeds, if it were no more than to amuse me in making the trial. . . . Retirement and Nature are more my passion every day; and now, even now, the charming time comes; Heaven is just on the point, or rather in the very act of giving Earth a green gown. The voice of the nightingale is heard in the lane." *

In Lady Shaftesbury's time the garden was carefully kept and was worth visiting. In it was 'Thomson's Alcove,' a plain summer-house painted green, which local tradition asserted was Thomson's favourite place for poetic composition. On the front was an oval board inscribed,

"Here Thomson sung the Seasons and their change;"

and inside was hung a tablet, on which was the date of the poet's death, and a long florid inscription, commencing,—

* Thomson to Paterson, Kew Lane, April 1748.

"Within this pleasing retirement, allured by the music of the nightingale, which warbled in soft unison to the melody of his soul, in unaffected cheerfulness, and genial though simple elegance, lived James Thomson." Of late the ground has been curtailed, and small houses built on the portion cut off; the summer-house has been removed from its original place, whilst, as we have said, the house itself has been turned into an infirmary: altogether the admirer of Thomson had better leave Rosedale House unvisited, and not dispel any vision he may have formed of the bard's poetic retirement.

Whilst in Kew Foot Lane the visitor may be reminded that in it that diligent antiquary Sir Henry Ellis lived for some years before his appointment as principal librarian at the British Museum.

The *Town* in itself is not particularly interesting. It looks best in a distant view. The main street extends for a mile from N. to S. The extreme breadth of the town is about ¾ of a mile, but the houses are commonplace, and the public buildings unattractive..

The old *Church* (St. Mary Magdalen) is a plain brick building altered and enlarged at different times, with an older tower of flint and stone, in which is a peal of eight bells. The ch. is only interesting for its monts. In the chancel is one to Henry Viscount Brouncker (d. 1688), cofferer to Charles II. On N. wall, Lady Dorothy, wife to Sir George Wright (d. 1631), with small kneeling effigies of the lady and her husband, and beneath three sons and four daughters. Mural brass of Robert Cotton, groom of the privy chamber to Queen Mary, and yeoman of "the removing wardroppe of beds" to Queen Elizabeth, with effigies of Cotton, his wife, and eight children. S. wall, Walter Hickman, of Kew, d. 1617, with small kneeling effigy, and poetic inscription. Lady Margaret Chudleigh, d. 1628, with her effigy, kneeling, and that of her second husband, Sir John Chudleigh. Wm. Rowan, K.C., d. 1767, with bust in flowing peruke. A slab near the altar rails commemorates the once famous tragic actress Mary Ann Yates, d. 1787, and her husband, Richard Yates, also a celebrated actor, d. 1796. On a pier by the pulpit is an elaborate mont. by the younger Bacon to Major George Bean,

R.A., who was killed in the battle of Waterloo.

In the S. aisle is a memorial with a long insc. to Gilbert Wakefield, the well-known classical, biblical, and political writer, d. 1801, and of his brother, Thomas Wakefield, d. 1806, for 30 years minister of this parish: their father, the Rev. George Wakefield, for nine years vicar of Kingston and minister of Richmond, is commemorated by a tablet in the chancel. In this aisle are two monts. by Flaxman, one with a medallion portrait of the Rev. Robert Mark Delafosse, LL.B. (d. 1819), erected by his pupils; the other, erected by the Duchess of Bolton in memory of her sister the Hon. Barbara Lowther (d. 1805), has a medallion portrait, and a figure of a mourning female in high relief: by the pedestal is a lily with three blossoms, one broken off, symbolizing the three sisters—the Duchess of Bolton, the Countess of Darlington, and Mrs. Lowther.

The burial-place of Thomson is indicated by a brass plate inserted in the wall at the W. end of the N. aisle.

"In the earth below this tablet are the remains of JAMES THOMSON, author of the beautiful Poems entitled *The Seasons*, the *Castle of Indolence*, etc., who died at Richmond Aug. 22nd, 1748, O.S. The Earl of Buchan, unwilling that so good a Man, and sweet a Poet, should be without a Memorial, has denoted the place of his interment for the satisfaction of his admirers, in the year of our Lord, 1792."

The Earl of Buchan, who commemorates himself as well as the poet, was the eccentric earl who figures noticeably in Lockhart's Life of Sir Walter Scott, and in the great novelist's diary. It is said that by an enlargement of the ch. subsequent to the poet's interment the present wall is carried directly across his grave, so that his body lies half within, half without the church.

Outside the ch., by the N. door, is a large architectural mont. of Richard Viscount Fitzwilliam, d. 1776; his wife, Catherine, dau. of Sir Matthew Decker; and of their son Richard, 7th Viscount Fitzwilliam, d. 1816, the munificent founder of the Fitzwilliam Museum, Cambridge. Not far off is the mont. of Sir Matthew Decker, d. 1749. On the W. front of the ch., rt. of the tower, is a marble tablet, with medallion portrait, of Edmund Kean, the great tragic actor, who d. at Richmond, May 15, 1833, "erected by his son Charles John Kean," in 1839. Next to it is a tablet to Mrs. Hofland, author of the ' Son of a Genius,' and other popular tales.

Joseph Taylor, the actor, d. 1652, who was instructed in the part of Hamlet by Shakspeare himself, and performed it, as Downes testifies, incomparably well, was buried in Richmond ch.-yard. Here too were interred William Hall, d. 1700, "a superior violin," as Aubrey terms him, gentleman of the king's private band, composer of several airs and author of ' Triplia Concordia;' Edward Gibson, d. 1701, and Richard Gibson, d. 1703. painters, the former the son and the latter the nephew of Gibson the dwarf; James Fearon, a noted actor of Covent Garden Theatre, d. 1787; Joseph Groves, author of a Life of Wolsey and other works; and Heidegger, Master of the Revels to George II. In the new burial-ground lie Lady Diana Beauclerk, d. 1808; Dr. John Moore, d. 1802, author of Zeluco; and Jacques Mallet du Pau, the publicist, and editor of the ' Mercure Britannique,' who d. at the house of his friend Count Lally-Tolendall, at Richmond, May, 1800.

Nicholas Brady lived at Richmond whilst engaged on his metrical version of the Psalms, and by desire of the parishioners served as their curate, 1696, there being then apparently no settled minister at Richmond. Among the entries in the ch. register is one of the baptism of Hester, daughter of Edward Johnson, March 20, 1680-81,—Swift's Stella.

St. Matthias, Mount Ararat Road, a chapel-of-ease to Richmond ch., is a handsome early Dec. ch., erected in 1858, from the designs of Sir Gilbert Scott. It has side chapels, a clerestorey, a good wheel window over the western porch, and a tower and spire 195 ft. high—a conspicuous object from many points of view. St. John's district ch., Kew Road, of a now obsolete type of modern Gothic, was erected in 1831, from the designs of Mr. L. Vulliamy. Holy Trinity district ch. Marsh Gate Road, is a neat cruciform building, erected in 1870.

There are Roman Catholic and dissenting chapels, but of no architectural or historical interest. Of more importance in this point of view is the Wesleyan Theological Institution, for the education of students for the Wesleyan ministry,

erected in 1841-3, from the designs of Mr. A. Trimen, out of the proceeds of the fund raised in 1839 in commemoration of the centenary of the foundation of the Wesleyan societies. It stands near the summit of the hill, is a large and stately structure in the Tudor Collegiate style, 248 ft. long and 65 ft. deep, contains a handsome hall, library, and chapel, and, from the observatory at the top of the central tower, commands a wide and splendid prospect.

Bp. Duppa lived a retired life at Richmond during the civil war and Commonwealth; and when, after the Restoration, he was appointed to the see of Winchester, he occasionally resided there, and there died in 1662. The year before his death he founded an almshouse for ten poor unmarried women over 50 years of age, who from the endowment have each, in addition to their lodging, £1 monthly, "a gown of substantial cloth of bishop's blue" every other year, and a barn-door fowl and a pound of bacon for a Christmas dinner. The original house, a low red-brick building, with an insc. over the entrance, "Votiva Tabula. I will pay my vows which I made to God in my trouble," stood on the hill by Downe House, but was taken down a few years back, and a new one erected in the Vineyard.

To the Vineyard also was removed Queen Elizabeth's Almshouse, which originally stood in the Lower Road. It was founded by Sir George Wright, in 1600, for eight poor women, who each receive £1 monthly, an allowance of bread, cheese, and beer, coals and clothing. Michel's Almshouse, also in the Vineyard, was founded by Humphrey Michel and his nephew John Michel, in 1696, for ten poor men, who receive each £1 10s. monthly, a chaldron of coals yearly, and a great-coat every alternate year. Hickey's Almshouse, founded in 1727, by Wm. Hickey, for six men and ten women, occupies a neat Elizabethan building, erected in 1834, from the designs of Mr. L. Vulliamy, in the Marsh Gate Road. Next to it stands the Church Lands Almshouse, founded by Act of Parliament in 1828: the building was erected in 1843, from the designs of Mr. C. Stow. Houblons' Almshouse, Marsh Gate, was founded in 1758, by two maiden sisters, Rebecca and Susannah Houblons, for nine poor unmarried women. The building, a low brick structure, comprises nine distinct tenements of two rooms each, with a courtyard in front.

Richmond Theatre, a house of fame in the annals of the stage. is at the N.W. corner of the Green. There appears to have been a theatre at Richmond as early as 1715, when " the Duke of Southampton and Cleveland's Servants " performed B. Griffin's tragedy, ' Injured Innocence. or the Virgin Martyr.' In 1719, Penkethman " the droll " opened a theatre for what the Tatler styles " his ingenious company of strollers," in Upper Hill Street (the site now occupied by York Place). and it appears to have been well patronized. Walpole several times refers to it. Theophilus Cibber reopened it in 1756 as "The Cephalic Snuff Warehouse," where, in order to avoid the penalties then in force against unlicensed players, he professed to sell " a most excellent cephalic snuff, which, taken in moderate quantities (in an evening particularly) will not fail to raise the spirits, clear the brain, throw off ill-humours, dissipate the spleen, enliven the imagination, exhilarate the mind, give joy to the heart, and greatly invigorate and improve the understanding." He further announced that " he has also opened at the aforesaid Warehouse (late called the Theatre) on the Hill, an Histrionic Academy," etc. The Cephalic Snuff Warehouse was one of Theo. Cibber's latest speculations : he perished in a vessel in which he embarked for Dublin, October 1768.

The present theatre was built in 1776, for James Dance, who under the name of Love was the most popular Falstaff of his time. Garrick is said to have superintended its construction; it was considered one of the best little theatres in the kingdom, but has since been much altered. It long enjoyed a large share of public favour, was much patronized by George III. and Queen Charlotte, who often visited it, and was noted for the eminent actors who occasionally performed in it, and as a school for those who were seeking a London engagement. Cherry, Beverly, Quick, Munden, Liston, Mrs. Siddons, Mrs. Jordan, and other actors of celebrity have trod the boards, and it was here that Charles Mathews, the elder, made " his first appearance on any stage," Sept. 7, 1793, as Richmond in Richard the Third. Edumnd Kean, in his later years, was lessee of Richmond Theatre, and performed in it so frequently (for awhile on each of the three nights in the week on which it was open) that he came at length to play to " a beggarly account of empty benches "—the receipts on one occasion being £3 13s. 6d.[*] It was in a small room in the house attached to the theatre that the great actor died. The theatre has ceased to attract, is closed, looks dilapidated, and is to let.

The *Bridge* which connects Richmond with Twickenham was commenced in 1774, and completed Dec. 1777, at a cost of £26,000 : the architects were Messrs. Paine and Couse. It has five arches of stone, one serving for the towing-path, and five land arches of brick on the Middlesex shore.

At Richmond Bridge the Thames is about 300 ft. wide. The distance by the river from London Bridge is 16½ m. High water is 75 minutes after the time of high water at London Bridge.

The views from Richmond Bridge are very pleasing, especially up the river, with its eyots, Richmond Hill, Ham Walks, and Twickenham Meadows. A row up the river is still more to be commended. Collins and Wordsworth have thrown a poetic halo over this portion of the river's course.

" Remembrance oft shall haunt the shore
    When Thames in summer wreaths is drest ;
And oft suspend the dashing oar,
    To bid his gentle spirit rest." [†]

"Glide gently, thus for ever glide,
    O Thames ! that other bards may see
As lovely visions by thy side
    As now, fair river ! come to me.
O glide, fair stream ! for ever so,
    Thy quiet soul on all bestowing,
Till all our minds for ever flow
    As thy deep waters now are flowing." [‡]

RICKMANSWORTH, Herts, a

small town on the Chess, near its junction with the Colne, and the terminus of the Watford and Rickmansworth br. of the L. and N.-W. Rly. (20¾ m.); 4 m. W.S.W. from Watford by road, and 18 m.

---

[*] Crisp, Richmond and its Inhabitants, p. 381.
[†] Collins, Ode on the Death of Thomson.
[‡] Wordsworth, Remembrance of Collins, composed upon the Thames near Richmond, 1789.

from London. Pop. 5337. Inns: *Swan*, High Street; *Railway Hotel*, by the Station.

The name—Dom. *Richemaresvorte; anc.* records, *Rickmeresvearth, Rickmeresveard*—is supposed by the county historians to be derived "from its situation in a low flat bottom, or nook of land," at the confluence of the rivers Colne, Gade, and Chess, or Chesham, here a considerable stream : " *Ric* in the Saxon language signifying rich ; *mear* a pool of water; and *wearth*, or *weard*, a piece of land watered by more rivers than one or situated between them."* This is rather too complex to be satisfactory. It more probably signified a town or village (*worth*, an enclosed or protected place) on the Rick mere—the low land at the confluence of the streams being then covered with water. From the Dom. Survey we learn that besides a mill and fishery, there was arable land for 20 ploughs, pasture for cattle, and pannage for 1200 swine, so that the uplands must have been thickly wooded. The inhabitants numbered 45, of whom 5 were serfs, and 22 villans, 5 cattagers, 9 bordarii, and 4 Frenchmen—a sufficiently mixed population.

The chief manor was among the first gifts to the Abbey of St. Albans (A.D. 793), and it remained the property of the Abbey till surrendered to the Crown in 1539. Edward VI. granted it in 1550 to Ridley, Bp. of London, but it was resumed by Elizabeth, and remained in the Crown till granted by Charles I. in discharge of a loan to one Hewet, who sold it to Sir Thos. Fotherley. It has since remained in private hands, and is now the property of J. Swindon Gilliat, Esq. The sub-manors, Moor, Michelfield, and Wood-oaks, are also in private hands ; that of Crossley (or Croxley) belongs to Gonville and Caius College, Cambridge, it having been granted by Queen Elizabeth to Dr. Caius, who gave it to his college.

The *Town* is an irregular straggling place of no architectural character, but country-like, not unpicturesque in parts, and pleasant from its surroundings. It is the centre of a busy paper-making district —there being the extensive paper mills of Messrs. Dickinson at Croxley and Betchworth, M'Murray at Loudwater and Scot's Bridge, and Austin at Solesbridge and Mill End. A large silk mill and an extensive brewery employ many hands ; straw-plaiting and horsehair weaving are among the domestic occupations; and watercresses are largely grown for the London market. From the reign of Henry II. a market was held weekly, till it fell into disuse within the last 20 years. The Grand Junction Canal comes close to the town, and there is a considerable carrying trade.

The *Church* (St. Alban) was rebuilt, except the tower, a few years since. It is a spacious modern Gothic structure, comprising nave, aisles, and chancel. The tower, of the Perp. period, is embattled, and contains a peal of 5 bells. The east window is filled with painted glass, removed from a church at Rouen in the first French revolution, and purchased and presented to Rickmansworth church by a late vicar. *Obs.* mont. from the old church to Robert Cary, Baron of Leppington and 1st Earl of Monmouth, d. 1631, his wife Elizabeth Trevanian, the 2nd Earl, and other members of the Cary family. The first earl was the Robert Carey of the court of Elizabeth, the courtier who carried the news of Elizabeth's death to James, reaching Holyrood House the third day after the event. He is author of the Memoirs which throw so much light on the court and times of Elizabeth. There are also monts. to the Fotherleys, Colts, etc., and a 16th cent. brass. In the ch.-yard are some fine old trees.

The Gothic *Town Hall*, of red brick and Bath stone, was erected in 1870, from the designs of Mr. A. Allom. The chapel, with octagonal tower and spire 75 feet high, is Wesleyan, built in 1867 on the site of a smaller chapel destroyed by fire ; it has a good painted glass east window, representing the Crucifixion, by Messrs. Heaton.

A little S.E. of the town, and divided from it by the river Colne, is *Moor Park*, the stately seat of Lord Ebury. The park was enclosed by licence of Henry VI. in 1426. In the reign of Edward IV. the manor of Moor belonged to Ralph Boteler, was forfeited to the Crown, and granted

---

* Chauncy, Hist. Antiq. of Hertfordshire, vol. ii., p. 342 ; Clutterbuck, Hist. of Hertfordshire, vol i., p. 186 ; Newcome, Hist. of Abbey of St. Albans, p. 516 : this derivation is made up from the vocabulary in Verstegan's 'Restitution of Decayed Intelligence,' ed. 1673, p. 226, etc.

to George Nevil, youngest son of Richard Earl of Warwick, and Abp. of York, who built a house here, in which he lived in great state, and on several occasions entertained the King, Edward IV. On the defection of his brother, the King-maker Earl of Warwick, the Archbishop was commanded to reside at the Moor, but shortly afterwards was arrested on a charge of treason, and sent as a prisoner first to Calais and then to Guisnes. He obtained his liberty in 1476, but " all his plate, money, moveable goods to the value of £20,000, had been seized upon for the king . . . . and with grief and anguish of mind, as was thought," he died shortly after. Henry VII. gave the manor to John Earl of Oxford, as a reward for service rendered him at Bosworth Field ; but before long it reverted to the Crown, and in the next reign formed part of the estate of Cardinal Wolsey.* After Wolsey's fall Moor was retained by the Crown till 1617, when James I. granted a lease of it to Francis, 2nd Earl of Bedford, whose widow sold it to the Earl of Pembroke. The Earl divided the Moor Park estate from the manor, and sold it to Robert Cary Earl of Monmouth, who died at Moor Park in 1639. On the death of Cary's son in 1661, Moor Park was purchased by Sir John Franklyn, from whose son it passed to Thomas Earl of Ossory, son of James Duke of Ormond, created by Charles II. Baron Butler of Moor Park. He sold the seat and park to the Duke of Monmouth, on whose execution it was granted by James II. to his widow.†

The gardens, which were "made by the Countess of Bedford, esteemed among the greatest wits of her time, and celebrated by Dr. Donne, and with very great care, excellent contrivance, and much cost," were at this time very famous. Sir William Temple, who declares Moor Park to be " the sweetest place, I think, that I have seen in my life, at home or abroad," gives in his essay ' On the Gardens of Epicurus,' a full description of the garden at Moor Park, "the perfectest figure of a garden I ever saw, ... for a model to those that meet with such a situation, and are above the regards of common expense." The terrace gravel-walk on to which the best

parlour opens, is about 300 paces long, and broad in proportion, the border set with standard laurels, and two summer-houses at the ends. From this walk are three descents of stone steps into a very great parterre, which is divided by gravel walks and adorned with fountains and statues. At the sides of the parterre are two large cloisters upon arches of stone, and ending with two other summer-houses. Over the cloisters are two terraces, covered with lead and fenced with balusters, the entrance to which is from the summer-houses. Flights of steps lead from the middle of the parterre into the lower garden, "which is all fruit-trees ranged about the several quarters of a wilderness," the walks all green and very shady, with a " grotto embellished with figures of shell rock-work, fountains and waterworks." On the other side of the house is a garden all of evergreens, " very wild, shady, and adorned with rough rock-work and fountains." *

Such was a model garden in the 17th century, and quoting the passage in the 18th century, another courtly essayist on gardening says he will only remark on this description that " any man might design and build as sweet a garden who had been born in and never stirred out of Holborn."†

So tastes change—the garden had been transformed long before. In 1720 it was sold to Benjamin Hoskins Styles, who had enriched himself by successful dealing in South Sea shares, and who spent, as is said, £130,000 of his gains in building and alterations at Moor Park. He employed the then popular architect Giacomo Leoni to enlarge the house (which is said to have been built by the Duke of Monmouth), face it with Portland stone, add wings, and connect them with the main building by a Tuscan colonnade. The mere carriage of the stone for these works is reported to have cost £14,000. The interior was fitted up with corresponding magnificence, Sir James Thornhill being engaged to paint the principal rooms. Further, that he might have a prospect from the house, the hills N. and S. were

---

* Cavendish, Life of Wolsey, p. 245.
† Haywood, On C. J. Fox's James II., . 417.

* Sir Wm. Temple, Miscellanea, the Second Part, ed. 1690, p. 127, etc.
† Walpole, Essay on Modern Gardening : Anecdotes, vol. iv., p. 277.

cut through so as to afford a vista with Watford church as a termination in one direction and Uxbridge in the other—a whim that Pope used to point his satire on modern taste:

> " Or cut wide views through mountains to the plain,
>   You'll wish your hill a sheltered seat again."

This was done, it is added in a note, " in Hertfordshire by a wealthy citizen, at the expense of above £5000, by which means (merely to overlook a dead plain) he let in the north-wind upon his house and parterre, which were before adorned and defended by beautiful woods." * This is overstated, however, for the view from the terrace front towards Watford is very charming, and by no means over a dead level. On the death of Mr. Styles the estate was purchased by the celebrated circumnavigator, Admiral (afterwards Lord) Anson, who spent £80,000 in undoing his predecessor's costly doings, chiefly in the grounds, for the rearrangement of which he called in that famous destructive Capability Brown.

" We went to see *Moor Park*, but I was not much struck with it, after all the miracles I had heard Brown had performed there. He has undulated the horizon in so many artificial mole-hills, that it is full as unnatural as if it was drawn with a rule and compasses. Nothing is done to the house; there are not even chairs in the great apartment. My Lord Anson is more slatternly than the Churchills [of Chalfont], and does not even finish children." †

Lord Anson died suddenly whilst walking in the garden at Moor Park in 1762, and in 1765 his heir sold the estate to Sir Lawrence Dundas,‡ whose son sold it in 1787 to T. Bates Rous, an East India director, who being unsuccessful in commercial speculations, pulled down the wings, erected at so much cost by Mr. Styles, to raise money by selling the materials. It afterwards passed to a Mr. Williams, was purchased by the Marquis of Westminster, and is now the seat of Lord Ebury.

Though denuded of its wings and colonnades, the house is of stately pro-

portions, and looks well beyond the broad terrace. Its chief external feature is a grand tetrastyle Corinthian portico, the columns of which are about 50 feet high. Of the interior, the great hall and the saloon to which it leads are the chief features. The hall is of unusual size and height, with 5 large marble doorways supported by colossal statues, and the walls and ceilings decorated with classical and emblematic compositions painted by Sir James Thornhill ; the saloon has on the ceiling a copy of Guido's Rospigliari Aurora. When these paintings were completed, Mr. Styles refused to pay the stipulated sum, £3500, on the ground that they were not properly executed, and Thornhill sued him for the amount. Richardson, Dahl, and other artists were appointed to examine the work, and their report being favourable, " Mr. Styles was condemned to pay the money, and by their arbitration £500 more for decorations about the house and for Thornhill's acting as surveyor to the building." *

The drawing and dining rooms are handsome apartments, and contain some interesting pictures and objects of taste and curiosity.

The pleasure grounds, of about 25 acres, are laid out near the house in terraces, adorned with vases, sculpture, and fountains, flower-beds in geometric patterns and brilliant with flowers of every hue, and pass away on the one hand into less formal walks backed by evergreens, to kitchen gardens where yet flourish the once famous " Moor Park apricots " and Moor Park lettuces of Lord Anson's introduction, and on the other to the hill and wilderness with its quaint mixture of old trees and tall formal columns—relics of the old demolished colonnades—and broad pond bordered with shrubs and aquatic plants, and alive with song birds and waders.

The Park, of nearly 500 acres, is varied in surface, rich in ancient trees, wild ferny tracts spotted over with deer, and ornamental waters, the favourite haunt of the moor-hen. It is an old tradition that the Duchess of Monmouth, in memory of her husband's execution, pollarded all

---

* Pope, Moral Essays, Epistle iv., line 75.
+ Horace Walpole to George Montagu, July 4, 1760 ; Letters, vol. iii., p. 324.
‡ The house was engraved, during his occupancy, in the Vitruvius Britannicus, vol. v., pl. 20. Plan and Elevation of Moor Park belonging to Sir Lawrence Dundas, Sir J. Thornhill, archt. ; Gandon, delt., White, sc.

---

* Walpole, Anecdotes of Painting in England, vol. iv., p. 42.

the oaks in Moor Park. But this the aspect of the present ancient oaks clearly refutes ; and Sir Joseph Paxton some 30 years ago, after examining them for the purpose, stated decidedly that they could not have been lopped. The trees are among the finest in England, many of them being of vast size, their lowest branches on the ground and their foliage in the fullest luxuriancy.

Other seats are—*Rickmansworth Park* (Joseph Arden, Esq.), a good house standing in grounds which extend northwards from the town to Loudwater, with the Chess on the E. border. *Loudwater House* (J. D'Aguila Samuda, Esq., M.P.) *The Cedars*, Chorley Wood, a handsome modern manor-house, the seat of J. S. Gilbert, Esq.

Hamlets of Rickmansworth are :— *Batchworth*, S. of the town and the Grand Junction Canal. Here are large paper-mills, wharf on the canal, the goods station of the railway, and, at Frogmore Hill, the *Female Orphan Home* for 50 orphans.

Chorley is a pleasant hamlet and eccl. dist. of 955 inh., 2 m. N.W., on the border of Bucks. The ch., Christ Church, erected in 1870, is one of Mr. Street's best country churches, is handsomely decorated, and contains some good painted glass. At Chorley Wood Common is the kennel of the Old Berkeley Hunt.

Croxley Green, 3 m. S.W. from Rickmansworth, on the Colne, which separates it from Middlesex, is an eccl. dist. formed in 1872. The church (All Saints) is a neat E.E. building erected in 1872. The country is very pretty, with Harefield Park on the opposite side of the river. The fishing, for which the district was noted, has been spoiled by the paper-mills.

Mill End, on the Uxbridge Road, and on the Colne, 1 m. S.W. from Rickmansworth, is a busy suburb, with paper-mills, large brewery, tannery, etc. A church, St. Peter, of flint and stone, E.E. in style and cruciform, designed by Mr. Sutton, was consecrated in 1875.

At *Loudwater*, 1 m. N., are Mr. M'Murray's extensive paper-mills ; *Glen Chess*, the seat of W. M'Murray, Esq., and other good houses.

West Hyde, an eccl. dist. (formed in 1846) of 493 inh., is on the Uxbridge

Road, 2½ miles S.W. of the town. The church, St. Thomas, erected in 1845, is of brick and stone, Norman in style and cruciform. Here are chalk pits and a paper-mill—formerly a copper mill. There are besides *Maple Cross*, 2 m. S.W., and several other outlying collections of houses.

RIDDLESDOWN, Surrey (*see* Caterham Junction).

RIDGE, Herts, ¾ m. S.W. of South Mimms, about 3 m. W. from Potter's Bar Stat. of the Grt. N. Rly., by crooked country lanes, and 4 m. N.W. from the High Barnet Stat. (Edgware and Barnet branch) of the Grt. N. Rly. Pop. 448.

The village consists of a dozen country cottages, one or two houses of higher rank, a farm-house, parsonage, the village shop, and the village inn. The ch. stands apart on the rt., venerable in its solitude. It consists of chancel (early Dec.) and nave and tower (Perp.) of flint and stone, with a recent W. window. In it are monts. to the Blounts, who held the manor for several generations. The best known of the name interred here are Sir Henry Pope Blount, d. 1682, who published an account of his 'Voyage into the Levant,' 1636, which passed through several editions, and his sons, Sir Thomas Pope Blount, d. 1697, the author of 'De Re Poetica,' (1694), 'Censura Celebriorum Authorum,' etc. ; and Charles Blount, the deistical writer, but better remembered for his important exertions in emancipating the press from the tyranny of a Licenser. Charles Blount d. by his own hand, Aug. 1693, driven to frenzy by the failure of his efforts to obtain a licence to marry his deceased wife's sister, and her refusal to marry without it. Pope has commemorated him in the line—

"If Blount despatch'd himself, he played the man." *

" The flippant profaneness of the notes " to his translation of Appolonius of Tyana, as Macaulay remarks, " called forth the severe censure of an unbeliever of a very different order, the illustrious Bayle." But Bayle only knew the notes by report (see his *Dict.*, note I. to art. *Apollonius*

---

* Epistle to the Satires, Dialogue I.

de Tyane). Macaulay has devoted several pages of his history (chap. xix.) to Charles Blount. His books were collected and reprinted by Gildon, 1695. The seat of the Blounts was *Tittenhanger*. (*See* LONDON COLNEY.)

RIVERHEAD, KENT, a vill, and eccl. dist. formed in 1874 from Sevenoaks par., is situated at the junction of the Westerham with the London and Maidstone road, 1 m. N.W. from Sevenoaks, and about the same distance from the Sevenoaks (Dunton Green and Tubb's Hill) Stats. of the S.-E. Rly. (Direct Tunbridge line), and L. C. and D. Rly. Pop. 750 ; but the area of the district has been somewhat enlarged since the census of 1871. Inn, the *Amherst Arms*, a good house pleasantly situated by Montreal Park.

Riverhead is a quiet agricultural village, not remarkably picturesque, but attractive from its situation amidst parks, woods, shady lanes, broad open fields, and hop gardens. The *Church* (St. Mary) is a neat, commonplace stone building, Gothic of the year 1831. *Montreal*, the seat of Earl Amherst, is a stately and commodious mansion, standing in the midst of a finely wooded park immediately S. of the village. *Bradbourne Hall* (F. Crawshay, Esq.) is a good house built in 1730 on the site of an older Bradbourne, "a place of account," which belonged to Fulke de Brent in the reign of John, and was forfeited with his other estates in the reign of Henry III. Granted to Baldwin de Beten, Earl of Albemarle, it passed by marriage to William Mareschall, Earl of Pembroke, and then to Roger Bigod, Earl of Norfolk, who in 1283 transferred it to Otho, Lord Grandison. "After this family was worn out," Philipott tells us, it was owned by the Pevenleys or Pemleys, from whom the house "in old deeds is written Pevenley or Pemley Court." From them it passed to the Ashes ; in the beginning of the reign of Elizabeth to Ralph Bosville ; and since, in succession through many hands, to its present owner. Sir Ralph Bosville had the honour of entertaining Queen Elizabeth at Bradbourne, and in the great drawing-room of the present house is a set of tapestry hangings which the Queen is said to have presented to her host. Other seats are *Riverhead House* (C. R. C. Petley, Esq.) ; *Oakhill* (George Lyall, Esq.), etc.

ROEHAMPTON, SURREY, an eccl. dist. of Putney, lies W. of Putney Heath, between it and Richmond Park, about 1 m. S. of the Barnes Common Stat. of the L. and S.-W. Rly. (Richmond line) ; pop. 1497.

The pleasantness of the situation and the proximity of Richmond caused Roehampton at an early period to be in favour as a place of residence. Many of the good old houses remain, but several have been demolished to make way for modern villas, and more seem doomed to be ere long the prey of the builder. The village is small and of little interest. Here was a royal park, originally known as *Putney Park*, but sometimes called Mortlake Park, about 300 acres in extent, its eastern boundary being the lane still called Putney Park Lane. In Mary's reign, Sir Robert Tyrwhit was Keeper of the Park. James I. granted Sir Charles Howard the office for life. Charles I., in the 2nd year of his reign, alienated the park to Sir Richard Weston, a great favourite of the King, who in 1628 appointed him Lord Treasurer, and shortly after created him Lord Weston and Earl of Portland. Weston made Roehampton his chief residence, living here in great state. In May 1632 a chapel in his house was consecrated by Bishop Laud, and a month afterwards Jerome Weston, the Lord Treasurer's son, was married in it to Lady Frances Stuart, daughter of Emme Duke of Lenox,—a splendid wedding, at which Laud officiated, the King gave away the bride, and Ben Jonson wrote the Epithalamium—

" See the procession ! what a holy-day
   (Bearing the promise of some better fate)
Hath filled with cacoches all the way
   From Greenwich hither, to Row-hampton gate.

*   *   *   *   *

See now the chapel opens ; where the King
   And Bishop stay to consummate the rites :
The holy prelate prays, then takes the ring,
   Asks first, Who gives? (I *Charles*) then he plights
     One in the other's hand
      While they both stand
     Hearing their charge ; and then
The solemn quire cries, Joy ; and they return
   Amen." *

---

* Ben Jonson, The Under-Wood, ed. 1640, p. 239.

In 1635 Lord Portland obtained a licence to enclose 450 acres and add them to his park, but he died shortly after, and instead of extending, his son began to alienate the estate. Roehampton Park and mansion he sold for £11,300 to Sir Thos. Dawes, who sold them to Christian Countess of Devonshire — a woman of great ability and influence, who made Roehampton Park a notable place. Hobbes, the metaphysician, lived here as tutor to her son; the leading wits and poets of the day frequently assembled here, and Charles II., with the Queen Dowager and the Royal Family, paid the Countess repeated visits. In 1689 the house was sold to Alderman Sir Jeffery Jefferys, on whose death, in 1707, it was sold to Mr. Bagnall; then passed successively to Mr. Fordyce the banker, Mr. T. Parker, and Joshua Vanneck, afterwards Lord Huntingfield, who pulled down the old mansion, erected a new villa, known as *Roehampton Grove*, from the designs of Wyatt, and altered and modernized the grounds. It subsequently became the property and residence of Mr. Thos. Fitzherbert and of Mr. Wm. Gosling, the banker. It is now the residence of Mrs. Lyne Stephens.

Roehampton Park is now in part occupied by a spacious Gothic edifice, the Roman Catholic *Convent of the Sacred Heart*. The entrance is in Roehampton Lane, N. of the ch. An Orphanage and other buildings were added in 1866, Mr. M. E. Hadfield, archt.

Roehampton House, the seat of the Earl of Leven and Melville, is a red brick house, with wings, erected for Thomas Carey, Esq., in 1712, from the designs of Thos. Archer, the architect of St. John's Church, Milbank, Westminster. The ceiling of the saloon has a Banquet of the Gods on Olympus, painted by Sir James Thornhill. It was for a time the residence of the Earl of Albemarle. The grounds are extensive and beautiful.*

Dover House, the seat originally of Lord Dover, afterwards of Lord Clifden, the Viscountess Clifden, and lately of Mr. Alexander Collie, is a handsome villa in charming grounds, of old famous for its social and literary gatherings.

"*Nov. 12th*, 1829.—At Roehampton at Lord Clifden's from Tuesday the 10th till to-day. Sir James Mackintosh, Moore, Poodle Byng, and the Master of the Rolls. It was uncommonly agreeable." *

Downshire House (D. B. Chapman, Esq.) was so named from having been long the residence of the Marchioness of Downshire.

Mount Clare was built in 1772, by George Clive, Esq., and so named in compliment to his relative Lord Clive, and his Esher mansion, Claremont. In 1780 it was purchased by Sir John Dick, Bart., who employed Signor Columb, an Italian architect, to Italicize the building, and add a Tuscan portico. It was afterwards the residence of Charles Hatchett, Esq., F.R.S., H. Meldrey, Esq., Admiral Sir Charles Ogle, and Robert Hanbury, Esq., M.P.

Besborough House, originally *Parkstead*, was built by Sir William Chambers, for Brabazon Ponsonby, Earl of Besborough, and was celebrated in its day both as a building and on account of the fine collection of works of art and antiquity formed in it by the Earls of Besborough.† After passing through two or three hands, it was purchased and demolished about 1863 by a building society.

Clarence Lodge, Clarence Lane, for awhile the residence of the Duke of Clarence (afterwards William IV.), is now the *Royal School for Daughters of Officers of the Army*.

The Priory, the fine seat of the late Lord Justice Sir J. Knight Bruce, has been converted into a private lunatic asylum. The grounds, of about 40 acres, are varied, well timbered, and very beautiful.

There are several other good seats in this village of villas, but these will suffice to indicate the character of the place. The village proper, never very interesting, has been rendered still less so by recent commonplace dwellings.

The *Church*, Holy Trinity, a rather elegant E.E. building, was erected in 1842 from the designs of Mr. Benj. Ferrey, F.S.A., and altered and enlarged in 1862. The original chapel was that consecrated by Bp. Laud. It was re-

---

* In vol. i. of the Vit. Brit. is an elevation of Roehampton House as originally built by Archer.

* Greville's Memoirs, vol. i., p. 241.
† It is engraved under the name of **Parkstead** in vol. iv. of the Vitruvius Britannicus.

moved, and a larger chapel erected in its stead, in 1727; and this in its turn gave place to the present structure. The large and costly mausoleum just outside the churchyard on the N. (within the grounds of Roehampton Park) was erected from the designs of Mr. W. Burn, to receive the remains of the late Mr. Lyne Stephens, and specially consecrated by the Bp. of London, August 1864.

ROMFORD, ESSEX, a market town on the Colchester road, and a stat. on the Grt. E. Rlwy. 12 m. from London by road or rly. Pop. of the town 6355, of the par. 8239, of whom 373 were inmates of the Union Workhouse. Inns: *White Hart* (a good house), and *Golden Lion*, High Street; *Swan, Dolphin, Lamb*, etc., Market-place.

The name is derived from the ford over the Bourne (called by some writers the Rom), a shallow stream which flows through the middle of the town and falls into the Thames at Dagenham. Letheuillier and others suppose that from its being on the line of the Roman road it was called the *Roman ford*, and by contraction Romford. Others more plausibly suggest that it was the broad ford, from the A.-S. *rum*, broad, the brook here spreading out into a wide and shallow stream. If, however, the *Rom* were the ancient name of the brook. it would simply mean the Ford over the Rom.

Romford had a market as early as 1247. The first mention of the manor is in a record of 1299, when it was held by Henry of Winchester, a Jewish convert. Until about 1780 Romford was a chapelry of Hornchurch. but is now a distinct parish. With Havering-atte-Bower and Hornchurch, originally one parish (*see* HAVERING), it formed the Liberty of Havering-atte-Bower, was governed by its own high steward and justices, and possessed a separate jurisdiction, courts, including a prerogative court for wills, sessions, and commission for trying felons within the liberty.

The town stretches for over a mile along the great Essex road, and is crossed near the centre by another principal street, which leads S. to Hornchurch and Rainham, and N. to Havering. The main street, narrow in the middle, expands towards the ends, the western half form-

ing the High Street, the eastern the Market-place, the cross street being named South Street on one side of the High Street and North Street on the other. Several additional streets have been formed within the last few years, especially S. of the town and about the rly. stat. High Street and Market-place contain some good shops, an unusually large number of inns and public-houses, and a few public buildings. The Market-place extends from W. of the ch. to the extreme E. end of the town, cattle-pens being fixtures in the open street. Formerly there were markets for hogs on Monday, cattle and calves on Tuesday, and corn on Wednesday.; but there is now only one market-day, Wednesday, when Romford presents a busy and noisy but characteristic and not unpicturesque scene. The calves, cattle, and hogs—the specialities of Romford market—are at the E. end of the market-place, westward are farm tools and necessaries, clothes, and miscellaneous goods, fruit and vegetables. The Corn Exchange is on the N. side of the High Street. The market is the largest for corn, calves, and cattle, in the neighbourhood of London. Romford is an agricultural centre, and there are agricultural implement factories, foundries, and the great ale brewery of Messrs. Ind, Coope, and Co. (the entrance to it is on the S. of the High Street, but the works extend to the rly.)

The original chapel of Romford, built about 1323, some distance E. of the town, was taken down in 1407, and a larger one erected on the site of the present ch. Romford Church. dedicated to the Virgin Mary and St. Edward the Confessor (*see* HAVERING-ATTE-BOWER). is a Dec. building, with window tracery inclining to Flamboyant, designed by Mr. J. Johnson, and consecrated Sept. 19, 1850. It is built of hammered Kentish rag with Bath stone dressings, and comprises nave with aisles, chancel with chapels, and on the S. tower a stone spire 160 feet high, and a stone porch. The tower contains a good peal of 8 bells. The interior is spacious, lofty, and effective. In it is the mont. from the old church of Sir Anthony Cooke of Gidea Hall, d. 1576, preceptor to Edward VI., with alabaster effigies of the knight and his wife, kneeling, and long Latin insc., said to have been written by his daughters, celebrated alike for their learning in an age when female learning flourished, and for their fortunate marriages. Mildred married William Lord Burleigh ; Anne married Nicholas Bacon, Keeper of the Great Seal, and was the mother of the great Lord Bacon ; Elizabeth married John Lord Russell, eldest son of Francis Earl of Bedford, and Catherine married Sir Henry Killigrew. Several of the windows have memorial painted glass, by Wailes of Newcastle and others. *Obs.* in the E. window the (restored) figure of Edward the Confessor.

St. Andrew's ch., at the E. end of the town, was erected from the designs of Mr. J. Johnson, in 1863, when the eccl. dist. of St. Andrew was created. The church is a neat late Dec. building of Kentish rag and Bath stone. Not far from it is a Cemetery with a small Norman chapel and lich-gate.

The Town Hall, near the Market-place, is a Corinthian building, tall and narrow. In it is held the Literary Institute. In the Market-place is a Court House ; a County Court has been built near the Rly. Stat., and opposite the Corn Exchange is the London and County branch bank, a showy Italian building with polished granite shafts and much carving.

Gidea (otherwise *Giddy*, *Gedy*, and *Guyddy*), a subordinate manor of Romford, believed to have belonged originally to the Abbey of Westminster, was in the reign of Edward IV. held by Sir Thos. Cooke, Alderman and Lord Mayor of London, who obtained a licence in 1467 to enclose a park and erect a fortified and embattled mansion. Falling however under the royal displeasure for refusing to lend money to the King, he was heavily fined, his goods seized, and he died in 1478, leaving his house unfinished. *Gidea Hall* was only completed in the reign of Elizabeth, by his grandson, Sir Anthony Cooke (whose monument is in Romford church), who had been an exile in the reign of Mary, but returned on the accession of her sister, and had the honour of entertaining the Queen at Gidea in July 1568, as he recorded in an inscription on the front of the honse. Mary de' Medici lodged at Gidea Hall the night before her arrival in London in 1638 ; the King, her son-in-law, who had escorted her from

Chelmsford, staying at his house at Havering-atte-Bower. The estate remained in the Cooke family till 1657, when it was alienated to Richard Emes, by whom it was sold in 1664 to John Burch. After one or more changes, it was purchased by Sir Francis Eyles, Bart., who, about 1720, pulled down the old house and erected in its place the present Gidea Hall, which however owes something of its actual appearance to a subsequent possessor, Richard Benyon, Governor of Fort St. George, and his son, Richard Benyon, Esq., who made great alterations in the grounds, and built the bridge, of 3 elliptical arches, from the designs of Mr. Wyatt. Sir Anthony Cooke's house, of which John Thorpe was the architect, is engraved in La Serres' account of the Queen Mother's Progress in England, and reproduced in Nichols's Progresses of Queen Elizabeth. The present Gidea Hall, on the l. of the road, ½ m. beyond the town, is a bald commonplace rectangular building of brick and stone, but contains some handsome rooms. There is a good engraving of it by Walker from a drawing by Humphrey Repton, 1794. It is now the residence of the Rev. T. Sill Gray, D.D.

Mark's House was a quaint quadrangular half-timber moated manor-house, situated on the margin of Hainault Forest, about 2 m. W. of Romford. The house and manor belonged, 1499, to Thos. Urswyck, Recorder of London ; in 1605 to Sir George Hervey, Lieutenant of the Tower, whose son, Sir Gawen Harvey, bequeathed it to his nephew, Carew Mildmay, from whom it passed to Powlet St. John, who assumed the name of Mildmay in addition to that of St. John, and in whose family it remains. The house, which had been long uninhabited, and was much decayed, was pulled down in 1808.

Dagnams lies at the N.E. extremity of the par., about 4 m. from the town. In 1454 Henry Percy, Earl of Northumberland, died seised of the manors of Dagnams and Cockerells ; as did Sir Wm. Husee in 1495, Peter Christmas in 1517, and Thos. Legatt in 1555. In 1637 it belonged to Lawrence Wright, M.D., whose son Henry was created a baronet by Cromwell in 1658, and by Charles II. in 1660. Sir Henry's daughter, Mrs. Anne Rider, devised the manor to her relative Edward Carteret, Esq., Postmaster-

33

General, during whose occupation Pepys many times visited the house (which he describes as "a most noble and pretty house that ever, for the bigness, I saw") to assist at the courtship and wedding of Mr. Carteret and "my Lady Jem," his patron Lord Sandwich's daughter. The estate was sold in 1749 to Henry Muilman, and again in 1772 to Sir Richard Neave, who pulled down the old house and built the present mansion on a new site. *Dagnams* is now the seat of Sir Arundel Neave, Bart.

Stewards, a town manor, belonged in the first half of the 16th cent. to the Halys family; was alienated iu 1565 to Wm. Cade, and in 1588 to James Quarles, Clerk of the Board of Green Cloth, whose more famous son, Francis Quarles, the author of the 'Book of Emblems,' was born at Stewards in May 1592. The manor passed from the Quarles family in 1708, and has since had many owners.

Hare Hall (R. Pemberton, Esq.), by the hamlet of *Hare Street*, 1 m. beyond Romford, on the main road, is a spacious mansion of Portland stone, comprising a centre with attached columns and pediment, and wings connected by a short colonnade, designed by Paine and erected by Mr. J. A. Wallinger in 1769, on the site of an old family seat. The house contains some noble rooms, commands wide prospects, and stands in good grounds. In a pleasant cottage in Hare Street, now called *Repton Cottage* (A. Graham, Esq.), lived for over 30 years, and died March 24, 1818, Humphry Repton, the celebrated landscape gardener.

At *Noak Hill,* a hamlet 4 m. N.E. from Romford, are the *Priory* (J. Sands, Esq.) and *Home Park* (M. Whittingham, Esq.) Other good seats are—*Marshalls* (O. Coe, Esq.), ½ m. N. of the town on the Havering road; *Priests* (Octavius Mashiter. Esq.), ½ m. farther on the same road; *Eastbury Lodge* (W. H. Clifton, Esq.), London Road, etc.

ROSHERVILLE, KENT, on the

Thames immediately W. of Gravesend, is an eccl. dist. of Northfleet par., founded in 1853, with an area of 170 acres and a population of 757.

The place owes its name to its founder, Jeremiah Rosher, formerly largely engaged in chalk and lime-works here, who created

on the cliffs overlooking the abandoned pits a village of smart villas and "cottages of gentility." The church, St. Mark, built by the Rosher family, and endowed by George Rosher, Esq., of Crete Hall, is a neat modern Gothic structure with several memorial painted glass windows.

Rosherville is, however, most widely known by its gardens, "the place"—as we are told at every rly. stat.—"to spend a happy day," and since Vauxhall the most popular resort on the Thames. Formed out of an abandoned chalk-pit, and originally intended for zoological gardens, *Rosherville Gardens* present in many respects a unique appearance, the cliffs, some of which are 150 feet high, and natural features, having been skilfully taken advantage of, and the floricultural arrangements being profuse and varied. There are, of course, many objects and decorations in more than questionable taste, but if not exactly, as one of the advertisements before us insists,—"sublimely picturesque, truthfully charming, truly rural, veritably salubrious—the Garden of all the Gardens in the world,"—Rosherville Gardens are exceedingly pretty, and will repay a visit. But it should be in the morning: in the afternoon and evening, theatrical and acrobatic performances, ballets and outdoor dancing, fireworks, the company, and the accompaniments, are a trying drawback on the beauty of the gardens.

The Rosherville Hotel is noted for its dinners. A pier, erected in 1840 close to the gardens, serves for passengers by steam-boats and the Tilbury and N. London Rlys.

ROXETH, MIDDX. (*see* HARROW-ON-THE-HILL).

ROYDON, or WOODREDON,

ESSEX, on the borders of Hertfordshire, 22 m. from London by the Grt. E. Rly. (Cambridge line), extends S. from the l. bank of the Stort, 1½ m. before it joins the Lea. Pop. 950.

Roydon was formerly a market town; now there are not more than two or three shops in the wide empty street. There is however still a "commercial inn," *The Temple.* The church (St. Peter's) is between the rly. stat. and the street (from which it is screened by a row of lime trees). It consists of a nave and chancel (Perp.), a north aisle (Dec.) partly covered with ivy, and a sq. embattled tower, of 3 storeys, Dec., with Perp. windows inserted. The int., partially restored in 1854, is low, has open seats, and the chancel is laid with encaustic tiles. In the chancel are three *brasses* to members of the Colte family : one on the N. of Thos. Colte, d. 1471, wife, and son, has the figures very fairly engraved. Of *Nether Hall*, the moated quadrangular castellated mansion of the Colte family, built towards the end of the 15th cent., 1½ m. S.E. from Roydon, only the entrance gate-house remains. It is of brick, with semi-hexagonal flanking turrets, the upper part gone. The mansion was demolished about 1770. The site is occupied by Nether Hall Farm. *Mount Pleasant* (— Webb, Esq.) is ½ m. E. of Roydon.

RUISLIP, Middx. (Dom. *Rislepe;*

anc. *Rueslyppe*, *Ruslip*, *Ryslep*, and *Riselip*), lies between Ickenham and Pinner, about 4 m. N.E. from the Uxbridge Stat. of the Gt. W. Rly., and a like distance S.W. from the Pinner Stat. of the L. and N.-W. Rly., and 17 m. from London. Pop. 1482, of whom 266 are in the eccl. dist. of Northwood.

Ruislip is pleasantly situated in a quiet rural district, between low uplands, watered by the two head branches of the Isleworth River, and backed by Ruislip Park, Wood, and Reservoir. The occupations are agricultural ; much of the land is devoted to pasture, and there is a considerable trade in timber and firewood. In the time of the Confessor, Ruislip Manor belonged to Wlward Wit, the King's thane ; under the Conqueror it was held by Ernulfus de Hesding, who gave it to the Convent of Bec Harlewin, in Normandy. It was transferred in the 13th century to the Priory of Okeburn, and was seized as an alien priory by Henry IV., who granted it for life to his 3rd son, John Duke of Bedford. Reverting to the Crown on Bedford's death in 1436, it was given by Henry VI. for his life to John Somerset, and on his death, 1442, was granted to King's College, Cambridge, in whose possession it remains. A moiety of the sub-manor of Southcote was, at

her attainder in 1378, the property of Alice Ferrers.

The *Church* (St. Martin) stands on high ground, and is a large and interesting building of black flint and stone. It comprises a nave ; aisles, with embattled parapets ; deep chancel, with a fine 5-light E. window ; and, at the W. end of the S. aisle, a tall square embattled tower, with double angle buttresses, stair-turret, and pyramidal roof. The Dec. nave is the oldest part of the ch., the aisles being somewhat later, whilst the chancel and tower are Perp. In the tower is a peal of 6 bells, recast in 1802. *Obs.* on entering the ch. the place of a holy water stoup, on rt. of W. door of N. aisle, and empty niche over the buttress on l. of doorway. The interior is good in character, has a remarkably fine nave of 6 bays, with alternate circular and octagonal piers, a timber roof in square compartments, and retains some of the old open oak seats. The chancel has an open timber roof of 3 bays. S. of the chancel is a chantry chapel. Both inside and out, however, the ch. has undergone restoration ; the body of the church some years back, under the direction of Sir Gilbert Scott ; the chancel in 1869-72, under Mr. R. L. Roumieu, when the present noticeable reredos was erected. The font is late Norm., a square basin of Sussex marble on a thick circular stem. *Obs.* mont. in chancel of Ralph Hawtrey, deputy-lieut. of the county, d. 1638, and wife, Mary, d. 1647, with their busts, "Johannes et Matthias Christmas, Fratres, Fecerunt." Also on S. wall, mont. to Lady Mary Banckes, d. 1661, celebrated for her heroic defence of Corfe Castle against the Parliamentary army. *Obs.* brass with fittings of John Hawtrey, Esq., d. 1593. Other brasses are mentioned by Lysons, but only their indents remain. Here are preserved a curious old iron-bound church chest, with 3 locks, and a quaint carved bread box, dated 1697. On the S.E. of the ch. is a good sized yew-tree.

Ruislip Park, N. of the vill., is a famous fox-hunting meet. *Park House* is the seat of R. Parnells, Esq. On the W. side of Ruislip Park, much frequented by aquatic birds and anglers, is the *Ruislip Reservoir* of the Regent's Canal Comp., a fine sheet of water of 80 acres.

Eastcott, a large and pleasant hamlet,

adjoins Pinner West End. *Eastcott House* (F. H. Deane, Esq.) occupies the site of the ancient seat of the Hawtreys, of whom Ruislip ch. contains so many memorials. *High Grove* (Sir Hugh H. Campbell, Bart.) and *Field End House* (W. Lawrence, Esq.) are other good seats.

Northwood, on the Rickmansworth road, N. of Ruislip Wood, is a long straggling hamlet on the Hertfordshire border, created, with portions of the pars. of Watford and Rickmansworth, an eccl. dist. in 1854. The ch., Holy Trinity, is a neat little Gothic building of flint and stone, consecrated in 1854. Most of the windows are filled with painted glass. Much of the land here is pasture, and many of the inhabitants are employed in hewing and preparing firewood for the London market. The seats are *Northwood House* (R. H. W. Dunlop, Esq.), and *Northwood Hall* (D. Norton, Esq.)

RUNNIMEDE, Egham, Surrey, a long level meadow bordering the Thames, on the N. of Egham, and at the foot of Cooper's Hill:

> " Here was that Charter seal'd wherein the Crown
> All marks of arbitrary power lays down." *

It has indeed been disputed whether Magna Charta was signed and sealed on Runnimede or on the little island at its upper end, now known as Magna Charta Island. Tradition, as far back as Aubrey's day, favoured the island; and in 1834 the then owner, Mr. Simon Harcourt, treating the question as settled, erected a small Gothic building on the island, and in it placed a rough stone, which a bold imagination had assumed to be that on which the Charter was signed, with an inscription to the effect that, " on this island, in June 1215, John King of England, signed the Magna Charta." But Matthew Paris, the contemporary chronicler, and the signature to the charter itself, distinctly state that the charter was signed "in the meadow called Runnimede between Windsor and Staines." A later treaty (Sept. 1217) by which Prince Louis of France agreed to leave the country with his followers, was signed on Magna Charter Island—whence perhaps the confusion.

* Denham's Cooper's Hill.

Runnimede is a triangular slip of meadow, about 160 acres in extent, somewhat over a mile long, and bounded by two other meadows, Longmead on the W., and Yardmead on the S.E. Between it and the Thames is a raised causeway, constructed at the cost of a patriotic merchant, Thomas de Henford, in the reign of Henry III., and since carefully maintained as a barrier against the river floods. The reach of the Thames off Runnimede is picturesque and pleasant, fringed with willows, varied by eyots, and brightened with abundant water-lilies.

According to an early tradition, the armies of the King and the Barons occupied Longmead and Yardmead, leaving Runnimede as a free interspace for negotiations. When Aubrey wrote, the fields had not long been enclosed, and there can be no doubt that when the armies of King John and the confederate Barons were assembled here, the whole tract lay quite open. An Act was obtained in 1814 for the enclosure of the commons and waste lands in the parish of Egham, when such parts of the " Meads called Runney Mead and Long Mead," as had been appropriated as a race-course, were expressly excepted from its operation, and directed to be left unenclosed, and " kept as a Race Course for the Public use, at such times of the year as the races thereon have heretofore been accustomed to be kept." The Egham races are accordingly run on Runnimede in the second week of August, when the famous mead is the great gathering-place of the roughs and pickpockets of London. In the last century there was put forth a proposal to erect on Runnimede a memorial of what is admittedly one of the greatest and most fruitful events in English history, and Akenside wrote some verses to be inscribed on the base of the monument. But the design was never carried out, and the only celebration which Runnimede witnesses of the event which has made its name sacred, is the annual running for the ' Magna Charta,' ' King John,' and ' Runnimede ' Stakes at the Egham races.

Some suppose that horse-racing, far from being of novel introduction at Runnimede, was practised there at so early a period as to have given its name to the meadow: Runnimede or Runney-mede, according to them, being an obvious corruption of 'Running-Mead' (A.-S. *rune*, a race, and *mede*, a meadow). The more reasonable derivation, however, is that suggested by Matthew of Westminster in the 13th, and more distinctly stated by John of Beverley in the 14th century. It was called the 'Field of Council' (from A.-S. *rune*, council), writes Beverley, because here in ancient times the council was wont to assemble.*

RUXLEY, KENT (*see* CRAY, NORTH).

RYE HOUSE, HERTS, the scene of the Rye House Plot, and now a noted fishing-house and place of entertainment, is situated on the l. bank of the Lea, 1 m. N. by E. from Hoddesdon, and close to the Rye House Stat. of the Grt. E. Rly. (Cambridge line), 17 m. from London.

The Rye, a manor of 85 acres, in Stanstead Abbots par., belonged in the reign of Henry VI. to Andrew Ogard, who obtained the royal licence to impark it, "erect a castle there with lime and stone, make battlements and loopholes, and have free warren there." † Towards the end of the reign of Henry VIII., it was purchased by Edward Baesch, "General Surveyor of the Victuals for the Navy-Royal and Marine Affairs," under Henry VIII., Edward VI., Mary, and Elizabeth. His son, Sir Edward Baesch, sold the house and manor to Edmond Field, Esq., in whose descendants it continued almost to our own day.

At the date of the plot, the house was in the occupation of Richard Rumbold, an old officer of Cromwell's, a maltster, a vehement republican, and, according to the royalist witness, the chief in the conspiracy. The purpose of the conspirators, according to the not very trustworthy testimony of the approver Keeling, was to have some 40 or 50 well-armed men concealed in the house and grounds to attack the Guards who were to escort the King from Newmarket, and in the confusion Charles and his brother, the Duke of York, were to be assassinated. The spot was well chosen for the purpose. It was, wrote Bramston, "a place so convenient for such a villany as scarce to be found in England; besides the closeness of the way over a river by a bridge, gates to pass, a strong hedge on one side, brick walls on the other." * Bishop Sprat describes the place as it then was with great clearness and precision, and as we may judge by the existing ground-plans, and the present appearance of the place, with great accuracy.

THE *Rye House* in *Hartfordshire*, about eighteen Miles from *London*, is so called from the *Rye* a Meadow near it. Just under it there is a By-road from *Bishops-Strafford* to *Hoddesden*, which was constantly used by the King when he went to or from *Newmarket*, the great Road winding much about on the Right-hand by *Stansted*. The House is an old strong Building and stands alone, encompass'd with a Mote, and towards the Garden has high Walls, so that Twenty Men might easily defend it for some time against Five hundred. From a high Tower in the House all that go or come may be seen both ways for nearly a Miles distance. As you come from *Newmarket* towards *London*, when you are near the House, you pass the Meadow over a narrow Caus-way, at the end of which is a Toll-gate, which having Entred you go through a Yard, and a little Field, and at the end of that through another Gate, you pass into a narrow Lane, where two Coaches at that time could not go a-breast. This narrow passage had on the left hand a thick Hedge and a Ditch, on the right a long Range of Building used for Corn-Chambers and Stables with several doors and windows looking into the Road, and before it a Pale, which then made the passage so narrow, but is since removed. When you are past this long Building, you go by the Mote and the Garden Wall, that is very strong, and has divers holes in it, through which a great many Men might shoot. Along by the Mote and Wall the Road continues to the *Ware-River* (the Lea) which runs about Twenty or Thirty yards from the Mote, and is to be past by a Bridge. A small distance from thence another Bridge is to be past over the *New-River*. In both which Passes a few Men may oppose great Numbers. In the outer Court-yard, which is behind the long Building, a considerable Body of Horse and Foot might be drawn up unperceived from the Road; whence they might easily issue out at the same time into each end of the narrow Lane, which was also to be stopt up by overturning a Cart." †

The King's return to London at an earlier hour than was expected is said to have disconcerted the conspirators. Whatever was the cause, the King escaped; but the discovery of the alleged plot led to the trial and execution of Russell and Sidney, and years after of

---

* "*Runnimede*, id est, Pratum Consilii . . . eo quod antiquis temporibus ibi de pace regni sæpius consilia tractabant."—Leland's Collectanea, vol. i., p. 281.

† Chauncy, Hertfordshire, vol. i., p. 383.

* Sir John Bramston's Autobiography, p. 182.
† Bp. Sprat, A True Account of the Horrid Conspiracy, etc., fol., 1685, p. 135.

Rumbold and the Earl of Argyll, the exile of a great number of prominent Whigs, and the temporary disruption of the party.

The Rye House was a square brick building, with inner court-yard and great central hall. The larger part of it was pulled down early in the 18th cent., and now only the embattled Gate House is left. If not a portion of Ogard's original building, it cannot be of much later date. It is of red brick, has an entrance gateway with good Tudor arch, in the spandrels of which traces of the Ogard arms may still be discerned, and groined brick vaulting under the archway; bays, carved chimneys, and an angle-turret, from the top of which there is, as Bp. Sprat intimates, a wide view over the meadows in all directions. The interior has lost all vestiges of its original character, except a brick staircase and hand-rail, it having been used for best part of a century, prior to the passing of the Poor Law Amendment Act, as the workhouse for Stanstead Abbots par., and suffered accordingly. For several years past it has been kept as a showhouse attached to the Rye House Inn. The rooms have received fanciful names. One, designated the Dungeon, is shown as the place in which the confederates met to confer on the details of the Plot. Others are filled with rackety old furniture and hangings. In one is the noted Great Bed of Ware, celebrated by Shakspeare, and brought here from its old home, the Saracen's Head at Ware.

Rumbold's malthouse has been converted into a refreshment bar, and a long barn has received a counterfeit open timber roof, some old wood-work from a house at Hoddesdon, been hung with old portraits, tapestry, and testimonials from the managers of trade dinners and children's festivals, designated "The Hall of the Conspirators" and "The Retainer's Hall," and serves as the great dining room for trade and van parties.

A fishing inn has stood by the bridge from time immemorial. Major, in his ed. of the 'Complete Angler,' seeks to identify it with Bleak Hall, Isaak Walton's "honest alehouse, where we shall find a cleanly room, lavender in the windows, and twenty ballads stuck about the wall," and doubtless the original Bleak Hall must have been here or at Broxbourne. But the present inn is of modern erection, and has grown to be a very popular resort for railway and van excursionists, and trade and school festivals, many hundreds and occasionally thousands of visitors assembling here on a summer holiday. The grounds are large, and the gardens pretty, though not equal to those of the Crown Inn at Broxbourne. The fishery extends for about 3 miles, and is strictly preserved. There is good bottom fishing. The fly rods are limited to 25 annual subscribers at 2 guineas each.

ST. ALBANS, HERTS, a market- town and borough (formerly parliamentary), and created in 1875 the seat of a bishopric, stands on rising ground on the l. bank of the little river Ver, or Muse, the main upper branch of the Colne, 21 m. from London by road, 20 m. by the Midland Rly., and 24 m. by the St. Albans br. of the L. and N.-W. Rly., and the Hatfield and St. Albans br. of the Grt. N. Rly. The Midland Stat. is in Victoria Street, ¼ m. E. of the town; the L. and N.-W. at the foot of Holywell Hill, on the S.; the Grt. N. in London Road, ½ m. S.E. Pop. of the borough 8298. Inns, *Peahen; George.*

St. Albans is the most interesting place for its historical associations and anti-quarian remains within the like distance of London. The objects to be visited in and around the town are—the *Abbey Church* and *Gatehouse;* the three parish churches, but especially that of St. Michael, Bacon's church and burial-place; the unique *Clock Tower;* the ruins of *Sopwell Nunnery* (of little account); *Bernard's Heath*, the field of the 2nd Battle of St. Albans; *Gorhambury*, where, besides the present mansion, are the remains of the house built by Lord Bacon's father, and the residence of Bacon himself; the vestiges of the Roman city of *Verulamium;* and the earth-works at Beech Bottom, possibly a relic of the older British *Oppidum.*

History.—The town (*oppidum*) of Cassivellaunus, to which Cæsar pursued that chieftain after defeating him on the banks of the Thames (*see* COWEY STAKES), is believed to have been the precursor of the present St. Albans. Cæsar describes the town as admirably fortified alike by nature and by art. It was surrounded by woods and marshes, and defended by a ditch and rampart. He carried it by assault, but as his soldiers entered it on two sides the defenders escaped by another, leaving, besides great quantities of cattle, many men who were captured, or slain in the fight.* Cæsar's occupation was brief ; and *Verlam* remained till the conquest of Britain by Claudius (A.D. 43), an important British city. It appears to have possessed a mint with the privilege of coining, since a gold coin and many copper coins of Tasciovanus have been found, with the name *Ver.* on the reverse, and several of his successor, Cunobelin, the last King of the East Britons, with V. or Ver. on the reverse, and one at least with the name in full, *Verlamio.*†

When the Romans took possession of the island they founded here a *municipium,* a dignity not conferred on London, though already the commercial emporium of the country.‡ But whether Verulamium occupied the site of the British city, or, as is more likely, a new one, is not certain. It is evident, however, that the Roman name was merely a Latinization of the British Verlam, or Verolam. In the revolt of Boadicea, Verulamium was burned, and the inhabitants put to the sword. It was, however, speedily rebuilt, surrounded by a strong wall, and remained an important station as long as the Romans held the island. The famous conference of Germanus with the teachers of Pelagianism, which led to their conversion and the extirpation of the heresy from Britain, was held, according to the earliest writers who name the place, at St. Albans (429), and this is incidentally confirmed by the statement of Bede (who does not name the place) that after his triumph Germanus and his companions repaired to the tomb of the martyr St. Alban.§

In the 5th century Verulam fell into the hands of the Saxons. The Roman city stood on the low ground to the W. of the present town, with the Ver river for its northern boundary : the church of St. Michael stands nearly in the centre of the ancient city. The Saxons, who seldom occupied the Roman towns,* built a new town on the hill N. of the river.

Fable is abundantly mingled in the monkish narratives of the origin of the Saxon town: we may tell the story briefly. During the Diocletian persecution, Alban, an eminent citizen of Verulam, to be more eminent henceforward as ' the Protomartyr of England,' was condemned to death for having sheltered Amphibalus, a Christian priest, and refused to sacrifice to idols. He was led forth towards the place of execution—a woody height named Holmhurst, on the other side of the Ver ; but when the procession came to the river the narrow bridge was found to be blocked by the multitude flocking to witness the spectacle. Alban, in haste to wear the martyr's crown, prayed that a way might be opened to him, and immediately the waters dried up, and all passed over without hindrance. Arrived at the hill-top, Alban thirsted, and behold a spring gushed forth at his feet. Amazed at these miracles, the executioner refused to perform his office upon so holy a man, and was forthwith condemned to suffer along with him. The day of the martyrdom was the 22nd (or, as was said later, the 17th) of June, the year 304 or 305.† Within twenty years, it is affirmed, a church had been raised on the spot in honour of the first English martyr.‡ A century or so later the place of sepulture was forgotten, though some accounts make the church to have survived, and to have been called after St. Germanus.

Nearly five centuries after the death of St. Alban (793), as Offa, King of the Mercians, was anxiously revolving how he might expiate his share in the murder of Ethelbert, it was revealed to him in a

---

* Cæsar, De Bell. Gall., lib. v., c. 21.
† Mon. Hist. Brit., Plate i. of Coins ; J. Evans, F.S.A., Ancient Coins found at Verulam, 1848, and Coins of the Ancient Britons, Plate vi.
‡ Tacitus, Annales, lib. xiv., c. 33.
§ Bede, Hist. Eccl., lib. i., c. 18.

* Kemble, Saxons in England, vol. ii.
† Bede, Hist. Eccl. Gentes Anglorum, lib. i., c. 7. What little evidence there is for the existence and martyrdom of St. Alban is brought together in ' Councils and Eccl. Documents relating to Great Britain and Ireland,' by Haddon and Stubbs, vol. i. p. 6, etc.
‡ Bede, Hist. Eccl., lib. i., c. 18.

vision that he should seek out the body of St. Alban, and on the spot where he found it erect a monastery. Accordingly the King, with Humbert, Archbishop of Lichfield, and the Bishops of Leicester and Lindsay, followed by a great multitude of priests and people, ascended the hill where the martyr was beheaded. There, guided by a lambent flame which descended on the spot, they found the martyr's relics. On the site Offa built a church, which he dedicated to St. Alban ; and adjoining it erected, in the space of five years, suitable buildings for an abbot and 100 monks of the order of St. Benedict, endowing the abbey with a princely revenue, " that great hospitality might be kept there, because the highway called Watling Street lay near, through which men continually travelled to and from London to the north and back again."

About the abbey, in process of time, grew up a large town, which received the name of the parent monastery. The old city of Verulam was abandoned, and the materials of its houses and walls served for the construction of its successor. So at least say the chroniclers. The truth probably is, that the new town preceded the monastery in point of time, but, overshadowed by the greatness of the religious establishment, its original English name, *Wirlamceaster*, or *Watlingceaster*,* gradually merged in the popular designation of St. Albans town. Some have been disposed to regard Ulsig. or Ulsinus, the 6th abbot, as the true founder of the modern town, he having obtained from King Ethelred, in 950, a confirmation of all former grants to the monastery, and a charter for a market, for which he erected suitable buildings at his own cost, as well as dwellings for strangers whom he induced to settle here, and finally built, at the entrances to the town, a church on each of the three principal roads.

During its early years St. Albans suffered like other towns from the ravages of the Danes, and in the time of Wulnoth, the 4th abbot, there befel the monastery what seemed an irreparable calamity. The Danes not only sacked the abbey, but carried off the bones of the protomartyr, which they deposited in a convent at

* Bede, Hist. Eccl., lib. i., c. 7; Henry of Huntingdon, lib. i.

Owensee. Great was the dismay and distress of the brethren at the loss of their chief treasure, but the one who took it most to heart was Egwin the Sacrist. At length, moved by his tears and prayers, the saint appeared to Egwin in a vision, and having made himself known, bade him take comfort, and told him what course he wished him to pursue, and departed, leaving the room filled with a fragrant odour. Obtaining leave of his abbot, Egwin left the Abbey and travelled to Denmark, and presenting himself at the convent of Owensee, was admitted as a monk. There his piety and diligence were so conspicuous that in course of time he was advanced to the office of sacrist, and thus had access to the feretory in which the relics of his patron saint were kept. Watching his opportunity, he stealthily removed them into a chest which he had prepared, and this he induced an English merchant trading at Owensee to undertake to convey to England, and forward by trusty hands to the Abbot of St. Albans. As soon as he was apprised of its safe arrival, Egwin applied to his superiors, who were of course unaware of the pious theft, for permission to return home. On reaching St. Albans he transmitted to the authorities at Owensee full particulars of what he had done. The Danes denied the truth of the story ; but the miracles wrought by the restored relics testified at once to their authenticity, and to the saint's approval of his servant's conduct.

But even now the relics were not secure. Some 70 years after, in the time of Ælfric II., the 11th abbot, the Danes again ravaged the country, and the abbot, mindful of the former disaster, concealed the martyr's bones in a cavity in the walls of the church. As a further precaution he sent supposititious relics to the monastery of Ely, and entreated the monks to take especial care of the precious charge. When the Danes had left the country, Ælfric reclaimed these bones, but the monks and people of Ely refused to part with them, and when at length they consented to do so, they repeated the trick of the Abbot of St. Albans, and substituted other bones. Again the saint intervened. Appearing to Gilbert, one of the brethren, he told him that the true relics must be brought forth from their hiding-place, and deposited in the shrine in the centre of the church. This was done with great solemnity. But now the monks of Ely publicly proclaimed the artifice they had practised, and declared that the true bones were in their possession. The king, Edward the Confessor, expressed great indignation at the fraud, but the monks held their own, and for a century the "true bones" of St. Alban were exhibited both at St. Albans and Ely. It was only when, on the appeal of Robert de Gorham, the 18th abbot, the Pope sent three bishops to Ely to inquire into and determine the matter, that the monks of Ely acknowledged that they had been outwitted, and that the true relics were at St. Albans.*

By the gifts of successive sovereigns, and the munificence of the pious, the Abbey had greatly increased in wealth, when shortly after the conquest Paul of Caen, a nephew, or as some said son, of Abp. Lanfranc, was appointed abbot. To the Norman, the Saxon buildings seemed all too rude for such an establishment. Paul rebuilt, on a scale of surpassing magnitude, the church, and a large part of the monastery. By a special grant (1154) of Pope Adrian IV. (Nicholas Breakspeare, a native of a neighbouring parish [see ABBOT'S LANGLEY], and a scholar here) the Abbey was made free of episcopal jurisdiction, and only and directly subject to the see of Rome—a privilege which was long a matter of heartburning and contention with the see of Lincoln. The Pope also gave the abbot of St. Albans precedence of all the other English abbots : a precedency which was retained till 1396, when, after an angry contest, the abbot of St. Albans had to give place to his brother of Westminster.

The town shared largely in the prosperity of the Abbey. But it shared also in the risks of conspicuous rank. In the Wars of the Barons, St. Albans was garrisoned for King John ; was threatened by Prince Louis in 1217 ; and a few months later was ransacked by a disorderly band under Fulke de Brent, the abbot having at last to buy him off with a hundred pounds of silver ; for which insult to St. Alban, Sir Fulke not long after met with "guerdon meet," dying a strange death,

as Bishop Pandulph, warned by St. Alban, had foretold. Again, soon after Easter, the town and Abbey were plundered by Prince Louis ; but no such retribution befel the French prince.

A story told by the chroniclers curiously illustrates the condition of a town like St. Albans in the reign of Henry III. The town, they say, was so strongly fortified that throughout the land it gained the name of Little London (*Minor Londonia*): a name by which it was familiarly known for half a century later. In 1265, the year of the struggle between De Montfort and the King, and of the battle of Evesham, the gates were kept shut, and travellers, especially horsemen, were denied a passage. Hearing this, the constable of Hertford, one Gregory de Stokes, boasted that with three of his serving-men he would force an entrance. The gates were opened to him, and with his followers he went up and down the streets, making everywhere some idle speech. At length calling to one of his men, "See where the wind stands," a townsman, thinking he purposed mischief, shouted, "I'll teach thee where the wind stands," and felled him to the ground. Others closed upon the luckless boasters, bound them, and hurried them to the market-place. There they struck off their heads, fixed them upon tall poles, and, after parading them through the principal streets, set them over the town gates. For this piece of rough discipline the town had, however, to pay a fine to the King of 100 marks—equal to about £1500 at the present day.*

The townsmen were at this time in a very excitable condition. There had been another of the outbreaks which were of frequent occurrence in the long struggle of the townsmen against the feudal exactions of the abbots. A coarse cloth was in those days made at St. Albans, and the townsmen claimed the right of fulling it themselves, and of using handmills to grind their corn. But the Abbey mills were an important source of conventual revenue, and the abbots stringently insisted on the townsmen using them alike for fulling and for grinding both malt and corn, and sent their bailiffs to search

---

* The legend is told in full by Matthew Paris, Gesta Abbatum Monast. S. Albani, Rolls ed., pp. 12—18 ; 34—37 ; 175—177.

* Opus Chronicorum, Rolls ed., p. 20 ; Matt. Paris, Gesta Abb. S. Albani, Rolls ed. p. 426, etc. ; Rishanger Chronicle, p. 38.

their houses, and seize and destroy the handmills. The townsmen appealed in vain to the King and his justiciars, and waylaid the Queen on her passage to the Abbey to lay their complaints before her. When the wide-spread popular discontent found vent in the Wat Tyler and Jack Straw risings, the men of St. Albans were only too ready to join in them. In 1381, with one William Grindecobbe as leader, the townsmen rose on the abbot, and forced from him a formal discharge from "all services and customary labours," and the surrender of various muniments and deeds of service. The townsmen put themselves in communication with the rebel priest, John Ball, and Walsingham gives a curious letter which Ball sent to the town. It was directed to John Nameless, John the Miller, and John Carter, and

"Biddeth hem that thei ware of gyle in borugh and stondith togiddir in Goddis name, and biddeth Peres Ploughman go to his werke, and chastise well Hobbe the robber, and taketh with you Johan Treweman and all his felaws, and no mo.

"Johan the Muller hath ygrownde, smal, smal, smal;
The Kingis sone of hevene shalle pay for alle.
Be ware or ye be wo,
Knoweth your frende fro youre foo,
Haveth ynowe, and seythe *Hoo*:
And seketh pees, aud holde therynne.
And so biddeth Johan Trewman and all his felawes."*

The movement was suppressed by the King (Richard II.) in person. John Ball, the priest, was brought to St. Albans, and there hanged and quartered. Fifteen of the townsmen underwent a like punishment. Four of the chief burgesses, and about 80 of less mark, were committed to prison, but eventually pardoned. All concessions made by the abbot were revoked, and on St. Margaret's day "all the commons of the county," over 15 years of age, were made to appear before the king in the great hall of the Abbey, and take an oath of allegiance and fidelity.

Many of the sovereigns of England visited St. Albans, and about 1356 King John of France was a prisoner in the Abbey. It was often visited, too, by foreign as well as English prelates, but for the highest of them the abbot never abated any of his prerogative. Thus

when, in 1280, Peccham, Abp. of Canterbury, asked to be admitted into the Abbey, the abbot only consented on his agreeing not to celebrate mass there. Within the town of St. Albans, and in the towns of Barnet and Watford, only the abbot, his steward, and officers, had right of holding assizes, and deciding pleas in civil and criminal cases, the Barons of Exchequer, and other justices, etc., of the King being expressly forbidden to go within those towns, or intermeddle in any matters concerning them. Indeed, by the grant or charter of 1 Edward IV. it appears, as Newcome remarks, "that a kind of palatine jurisdiction was given to the abbot," such as long after was held by the bishops of Durham and Ely.* The townsmen of St. Albans sent two burgesses to Parliament from the reign of Edward I. (1300) to the 5th of Edward III. (1331), when, at the instance of the abbot, the privilege was intermitted, and only renewed after the Suppression.

In the War of the Roses, St. Albans was the theatre of two important battles. The first was fought on the 23rd of May, 1455. The King, Henry VI., set up his standard on the N. side of the town, at "the place called Boslawes, in St. Peter's-street, which place was called aforetime past Sandeford." The Yorkists, under the Duke of York, and Warwick the Kingmaker, encamped in the Key Fields, E. of the town (immediately S. of the present London Road). The forces met in Holywell Street (as you ascend from the N.-W. Rly. Stat.), the Earl of Warwick having broken into the town "on the gardens side, between the sign of the Key and the Chequer," to the cry of "a Warwick! a Warwick!" The victory was with the Yorkists. The King was wounded in the neck by an arrow, and made prisoner.

The second battle was fought, Feb. 2, 1461, on Bernard's Heath, N. of the town; when the Yorkists, under the Earl of Warwick, were defeated with great slaughter by Queen Margaret at the head of a large force, and Henry fell into the hands of his friends.

Our next note in the history of St. Albans is of a very different kind. From the time of Abbot Paul, if not earlier, the

* Walsingham, Hist. Anglicana, Rolls ed., vol. ii., p. 33.

* Newcome, Hist. of the Abbey of St. Alban, p. 370.

Abbey had its skilful teachers, writers, painters, and illuminators ; * and from the reign of John a school of historians unrivalled by any other religious house, and including such writers as Roger Wendover, Matthew Paris, William Rishanger, Thomas Walsingham, John de Trokelowe, Henry de Blandeforde, and Abbot Whethamstead ; and it was among the first in England to avail itself of the art of printing. Caxton printed his first book in the Abbey of Westminster in 1474. A press was erected in St. Albans Abbey at least as early as 1480, in which year issued from it the ' Rhetorica nova fratris Lauri. de Guili. de Saonâ '; and 'Alberti liber significandi,' 8vo. The more famous ' Boke of St. Albans,' of Dame Juliana Berners, bears the date of 1486.† From this time no more books appear to have been printed in the Abbey, owing as is asserted to Wolsey's distrust of the new art, till about 1534, when John of Hertford printed here some half-dozen books in four years. The suppression of the monastery put a peremptory stop to further operations.

Down to the Suppression the govern-

ment of the town, though the townsmen had struggled long and hard for a share in it, had been exclusively in the hands of the abbot. On the surrender of the Abbey by Abbot Richard Boreman (or De Stevenage), in 1539, all the abbatal rights and privileges reverted to the Crown. Fifteen years later (1554), Edward VI. granted the town a charter of incorporation as a borough, with power to elect a mayor and ten common councilmen. He at the same time restored the privilege of sending two representatives to Parliament—a privilege it retained (despite the Reform Act) till 1852, when the borough was disfranchised for corrupt practices at elections.*

The suppression of monasteries had given the townsmen the management of their own affairs. The Abbey Church was sold to them for a sum of £400, for conversion into a parish church. The Lady Chapel was divided from it and appropriated as a grammar school. The convent grounds and buildings passed into private hands. But for a brief space there were symptoms of reaction. The Protestant King, Edward VI., died, and his Catholic successor was firmly seated on the throne. In 1556, Richard Boreman, the deposed abbot, purchased the site of the late monastery from its then owner, Sir Richard Lee, and transferred it to Queen Mary—the unconcealed purpose being the restoration of the monastery to its old use. But the dream of the Catholic Queen faded quickly away, and the early accession of Elizabeth put an end to all such hopes and fears for ever.

As it had been the site of the first, St. Albans was the scene of almost the latest English martyrdom. On the 26th of August, 1555, George Tankerfield was burned for heresy in a meadow near the west end of the Abbey.

St. Albans was Monk's last stage in his famous march from Edinburgh to London, when Peters preached before him, choosing for his text Psalm cvii. 7 : " He led them forth by the right way, that they might go to the city where they dwelt."

By an Act passed in 1875 Her Majesty may, by an Order in Council, found a new Bishopric of St. Albans, with a diocese

---

* Among their artists were some clever portrait painters. In the British Museum is the very remarkable *Catalogus Benefactorum* of St. Albans Abbey (Nero D. vii., f. 81) of the last half of the 14th century, which was given to Cotton by the Lord Chancellor Bacon. It contains not merely an account of the benefactions to the Abbey, but in many instances gives a portrait of the donor. These portraits are often marked with characteristic expression, and appear to be likenesses. The drawings illustrate also the costumes of abbots, monks, municipal officers, and townsmen, and depict their quaint half-timber dwellings, and have been largely drawn upon by Strutt for his illustrations. Several of the benefactors are merchants, some shopkeepers. Portraits are also given of faithful servants of the Abbey who displayed exceptional courage, or met with rough treatment, in defending its rights and privileges. The painter was Alan Strayner, or Strayler, " who for his pains (however he was well payed) and for that he forgauve three shillings four pence of an old debt owing unto him for colours is thus remembered :

' Nomen Pictoris Alaymus Strayler habetur
Qui sine fine celestibus associetur.' "

Weever, Anc. Funerall Monuments, fol. 1631, p. 577.

† The books known to have been printed here in the interval are : ' Johannis Canonici Questiones super octos libros Phisicorum Aristotelis,' fol. 1481 ; 'Exempla Sacra Scripturæ,' 8vo, 1481 ; 'The St. Albans Chronicle,' fol. 1483. Two or three others are mentioned, but do not appear to have been verified.

* At this time there were 530 electors, of whom half sold their votes : their price was about £2500.

consisting of Herts and Essex, or such parts thereof as may to her seem meet, and may assign as a Cathedral Church the Abbey Church of St. Albans. St. Albans town therefore may any day find itself elevated to the rank of an episcopal city, and the church be a cathedral.

Town.—On quitting the N.-Western Rly. Stat. you cross the Ver, on your rt., and see before you the principal street of St. Albans, running up a pretty steep hill. The houses, wide apart at the base, become more closely packed towards the summit ; but the Abbey, the crowning glory of the town, though it stands on nearly the highest point, is not seen from here,—so closely is it pent in with houses,—nor indeed from any of the main thoroughfares except the north end of St. Peter's Street, whence the massive tower is well seen. About the rly. stat. the houses are modern; but as you ascend the hill, and turn towards the market-place, you pass some quaint old tenements, and find ample evidence that you are in an old town ; yet St. Albans can hardly be said to look venerable, and is certainly not picturesque. Of late it has been passing through a state of transition. It had lapsed into the semicomatose condition of many of our old boroughs, and a few years back wore a dull, decaying, listless aspect, as though, beaten in the struggle for existence, it had been left on one side and forgotten. But a new trade, that of straw-plaiting, was introduced, and took vigorous root; then came the railways; speculative builders followed, and though prosperity has not been unintermitted, the decay has been arrested, some decided progress has been made, and a new impetus will perhaps be imparted by its conversion into an episcopal city.

Straw-plaiting is now the staple industry, while that branch of the trade known as the Brazilian hat manufacture i s peculiar to St. Albans. Some thousands of hands are employed in the straw trade in the town and neighbourhood. On a summer's day almost every house in the back streets may be seen with the street door (opening into the living room) set wide open, and women and girls busy plaiting and talking or singing,—or, often, rocking a cradle with the foot, whilst they ply their nimble fingers without seeming even to look at their work. Plenty of houses

with their inmates so occupied may be seen along Fishpool Street, on the way to St. Michael's. A market for straw-plait is held in St. Peter's Street every Saturday morning at 9 o'clock, and is worth visiting by the stranger who is in the town at that early hour, and may wish to see something of the female peasantry of the neighbourhood and their industry. The Corn-market follows from 12 to 5 ; a market for stock and pigs is held in the broadway facing the Town Hall, and fish, vegetables, and crockery are exposed in the market-place by the Clock Tower. On the Ver is a steam and water-mill (Mr. J. Woollam's)—you pass it in crossing the meadow from the Abbey to Verulam. It occupies the site of the old Abbey Mill; was erected for cutting diamonds, was afterwards a cotton-mill, but has for many years been a silk mill, and now employs some 300 children and adults.

St. Albans is a municipal borough, governed by a mayor, four aldermen, and twelve councillors. The principal corporation building is the *Town Hall*, in St. Peter's Street, a semi-classic edifice erected 1829-30. Here the St. Albans Archæological and Architectural Institute—which has done good service for local antiquities —holds its meetings. The *Corn Exchange*, erected in 1857, close by the Town Hall, and the *Dispensary*, in Holywell Hill, are the only other modern buildings of a public character. The Cross, one of the Eleanor Crosses, and not the worst of them,—like those at Stoney-Stratford, Woburn, and Dunstable, it was the work of John de Bello,[*]—was "pulled down by the authorities " in 1722. Happily, the authorities left one piece of antiquity, though they did nothing for its preservation. This was the *Clock Tower*, "the old town belfry, somewhat equivalent to those in the ancient cities of Belgium,"[†] but unique in this country. It stands in the market-place, on the rt. of the High Street; and over against it, the site marked by a drinking fountain, erected in 1874, stood the Eleanor Cross. It is a lofty tower of flint and stone, of early Perp. character, agreeing very well with the old statement that it was built for a clock-house in the first quarter of the 15th

[*] Hunter, in Archæologia, vol. xxix., p, 182.
[†] Sir G. G. Scott, Report.

cent., but Sir Gilbert Scott is of opinion that its " date is probably about the middle of the 15th century, or a little later." " The lower storey of this curious building," writes Sir Gilbert Scott, " has evidently been built for a shop, having two fronts with stone benches for the display of goods ; the one on the S., the other on the E. One storey over the shop seems to have been in the same occupation with it, and was approached by a separate stair. . . . It is probable, also, that the use of one or more of the upper storeys may have been allowed to the same person, should he have the charge of the bells, though provision is made by a distinct guardrobe for their possible occupation by another party." In the upper storey is a bell of about a ton weight, which within memory was tolled at the curfew hour, and though not, as has been suggested, the " tuneable bell " given by Abbot Roger (temp. Edw. I.) for that special purpose, was no doubt its successor. On it is the legend *De Missi Celis Habes Nomen Gabrielis.* Left long to neglect and ill-usage, the tower had fallen into a deplorable state, full of cracks, mutilated, dirty, when Sir G. G. Scott was in 1864 called in to examine it. His report was favourable, and he was entrusted with its restoration. This he effected thoroughly, and by the summer of 1867 this interesting monument of the past history of the town was restored to its original strength and freshness. A new town-clock was placed in it; the upper storey was made to serve again as a belfry : the ground floor is now (1876) a saddler's shop.

In the Hatfield Road (the turning on the rt. before reaching St. Peter's Ch.), are the *Marlborough Almshouses*, or ' *The Buildings*,' a substantial red-brick structure, consisting of a centre and projecting wings, built and endowed by Sarah Duchess of Marlborough in 1736. It was intended by the famous Duchess for officers' widows, but the benefits of the institution have since been extended. It now provides apartments and an annuity of five shillings a week to thirteen old married couples, and thirteen widows. The building occupies the site of the Manor House, a once noted academy, in which Dr. Doddridge and other distinguished Nonconformists were educated. The great Duke of Marlborough " built for his own

habitation a fair house at the W. end of this borough, near the river, where he has a fair garden, through which passeth a stream in which he keeps trouts and other fish for the convenience of his table." * The house which was at Holywell, was pulled down in 1837.

Besides those already mentioned, St. Albans numbers several eminent natives and residents. Alexander Neckam, 1157—1227, author of ' De Naturis Rerum,' poems, and theological dissertations, the universal scholar of his time, sometimes called Alexander de Sancto Albano, was born at St. Albans, and educated in the monastery, though from some distaste at a slight put upon him by the abbot he migrated to another house. Sir John Mandeville, the famous traveller of the 14th century, was born at St. Albans, about 1300 ; and his fellow-townsmen long after set up a painted tablet, still to be seen in the nave of the Abbey, in which they claim for the town not only his birth but his burial.

" Lo in this Inn, of Travellers doth lie
    One rich in nothing but a memory :
    His name was Sir John Mandevill," etc.

But Weever, who notes the erection of an earlier tablet (1631), adds, " That he was born here in this town I cannot much deny; but I am sure that within these few years I saw his tomb in the city of Leege," and then gives the insc. and other particulars. There is no doubt that Mandeville died and was buried at Liège. Two of the most distinguished lawyers of the 17th century were natives of St. Albans. Sir John King, 1599—1637, Solicitor-General to James Duke of York, and Counsel in Ordinary to Charles II.; and Sir Francis Pemberton, 1625—1697, Chief Justice successively of the King's Bench and Common Pleas, and, after his removal from the Bench, a leading advocate for the Seven Bishops. Mr. Peter Cunningham, author of the ' Handbook of London,' and editor of Walpole's Letters, lived at St. Albans from 1860 till his death there, May 18th, 1869.

The Abbey † was founded, as we have

---

* Chauncy, Hertfordshire, vol. ii., p. 320.
† The history of St. Albans Abbey, from its foundation to the end of the 14th century, is told with singular fulness by the remarkable men who constituted what has been called "the historical school of St. Albans," especially by Matthew Paris

seen, in 793, by Offa, king of the Mercians, for an abbot and 100 Benedictine monks. Though for the time a splendid structure, by the middle of the 10th cent. the church had come to be looked upon as too small and mean for the monastery, and Abbot Ealdred began to collect materials for a new building. The task was continued by his successor Eadmer, who also rebuilt portions of the monastery. In 1077 Paul, a monk of Caen, was elected abbot by the influence of Abp. Lanfranc, whose kinsman he was, and whom he had accompanied to England. Finding at hand an ample store of materials, Abbot Paul set about the reconstruction of the abbey church. Aided by the favour of Lanfranc and his successor in the primacy, the work was so vigorously prosecuted that, according to Matthew Paris, the church was entirely rebuilt in eleven years. But it was not till 1116 that the new ch., the largest and one of the grandest yet built in England, was consecrated with great solemnity, in presence of the king and queen (Henry I. and Matilda), Godfrey, Abp. of Rouen, the Bps. of London, Durham, Lincoln, and Salisbury, and a great array of abbots, priests, and nobles. Before a century had well passed the monks began to think even this ch. not sufficiently splendid. In 1195 Abbot John de Cella, having received 100 marks which his predecessor had set apart as a building-fund, pulled down the W. end, and collected stones, columns, and timber for the rebuilding. But, says the chronicler, he had not heeded the warning suggested in the Gospel as to counting the cost before beginning to build.

in his *Vitæ Viginti Trium Abbatum S. Albani;* and the *Gesta Abbatum Monasterii Sancti Albani.* Also, *Chronica Monasterii S. Albani*, ed. H. T. Riley, 6 vols., 1862 (Rolls series), the 1st part of which is by Thos. Walsingham, the 2nd part by William Rishanger, and the 3rd by Trokelowe, Blaneforde, and anonymous writers ; Sir F. Madden's ed. of Matthew Paris's *Historia Minor*, 1866 ; and the vols. of the *Annales Monastici*, edited by H. R. Luard, 1864, etc. The architectural features of the abbey ch. are well shown in the large engravings published by the Soc. of Antiquaries in 1810, and clearly described in Buckler's Hist. of the Architecture of the Abbey Church of St. Alban, 8vo, 1847. Newcome's History of the Ancient and Royal Foundation called the Abbey of St. Alban (4to, 1794) is a prolix history of the abbey and abbots, compiled and frequently transcribed from the chroniclers (chiefly Matthew Paris), with a large admixture of irrelevant matter : honest but tedious.

His 100 marks, and many more, were expended before the new walls had been raised above the level of the floor. Covering them for the winter, the abbot purposed to resume operations in the spring if he could procure fresh funds ; but the rain and frost caused the new walls to split and crumble, and all that had been done was rendered useless. He began again, but was again unsuccessful. Disheartened, he turned from the church to improve the dwellings of the brethren. Chief of these works were a more spacious refectory and dormitory,—the monks for the 15 years they were in progress voluntarily foregoing their wine in order to forward the building. The rebuilding of the W. front and the W. end of the nave was left for Abbot William de Trumpington (1214-35), who also rebuilt St. Cuthbert's Chapel, W. of the transept, in a richer manner, and effected many other improvements. John of Hertford, his successor (1235-60), besides adding greatly to the splendour of the church, built a noble guest hall, with parlours and sleeping chambers for the use of strangers, and stables for 300 horses—a measure of the magnificent hospitality of the abbots of St. Alban. The next abbot, Roger de Norton (1260-90) gave rich vestments, jewels, and costly decorations to the church, and Buckler says added the 5 bays on the south side of the nave, west of those built by William Trumpington. But this is a mistake. No reference is made to any such undertaking in the account of Abbot Roger, in the Gesta Abbatum, and the style of the architecture is clearly later. In fact, as we know, this portion of the church gave way in 1323, and remained in a semi-ruinous condition for about 20 years, when Abbot Michel de Mentmore rebuilt it as we now see it. The Lady Chapel was the work of Abbot Hugh de Eversden (1308-26).

A century now passed without any considerable alteration in the church, except the erection of St. Cuthbert's Screen, and probably the elaborately decorated flat roof, by Abbot Thomas de la Mare (1349-96), but the work of reparation and decoration seems hardly ever to have ceased. Abbot John de Whethamstead (1440-60) placed " a fair large window " in the W. front, opened new windows in the N. side of the church, and adorned the Lady Chapel, and other parts of the ch. and convent, with paintings. Whethamstead also built a sepulchral chantry for himself on the S. side of the sanctuary; to correspond with which Abbot Ramryge (1492-1524) built a chantry for himself on the N. side. This was the latest work. Cardinal Wolsey was elected Abbot of St. Albans in 1526; held it *in commendam* with the archbishopric of York, and did nothing for church or monastery. Wolsey was abbot four years; his successor eight. The next and last abbot, Richard Boreman, elected 1538, surrendered the monastery to Henry VIII.'s visitors, December 5th, 1539.

St. Albans was one of the wealthiest abbeys in the kingdom. It had estates in almost every county in England. At the surrender its revenue was estimated at over £2500; * but, says Stevens, "if the old lands were united together" it would be "worth at this day, in all rents, profits, and revenues, about £200,000 a year, according to the approved rents at this day."† Commensurate with the wealth and dignity of the Abbey were the extent and grandeur of the buildings.

"The long slope of the hill, from the summit to the very edge of the little river, which washed the base of its outer wall, was covered to a wide extent with the quadrangles, the gateways, the chapter-house, the halls, the towers, the turrets, and every variety of form and feature suitable to the position and the destination they held in the systematic arrangement. Above all this goodly array of architecture rose, as its crowning feature, the stupendous church in its full proportions, with its three towers, the central one augmented in height and beauty of appearance by the lofty octagonal lantern and tapering pinnacles."‡

Of all the Abbey buildings only the ch. and a gatehouse are left. The unevenness of the ground between the ch. and the river rudely indicates that it may long since have been covered with such buildings—king's chambers, queen's rooms (the Queen being by special provision excepted from the rule which made it unlawful for any woman to lodge in the monastery), abbot's house, chapter house, library, scriptorium, larder, granary, refectory, dormi-

* Weever; Dugdale gives the net value £2102.
† Stevens, Additions to Dugdale, 1722, vol. i., p. 265.
‡ J. C. and C. A. Buckler, Hist. of the Architecture of the Abbey Church of St. Alban, p. 7.

tory, justice hall, audience chambers, cloisters, kitchens, long stables, etc.—as were required for conventual order and discipline and princely hospitality, but over all the grass grows green. In their general arrangement the buildings of St. Albans resembled those of every other Benedictine monastery, only differing in scale and splendour, and in necessary adaptation to the special duties of the abbot and the nature of the locality.

As it stands, the Abbey Church consists of nave with aisles, triforia, and clerestorey; choir, presbytery, and sanctuary; central tower and transept; and once more, after being severed from it for more than three centuries, the Lady Chapel may be spoken of as a part of the building.

Including the Lady Chapel, St. Albans is the longest church in the kingdom: its internal length being 535 ft., and exceeding that of Winchester Cathedral by 5 ft., Ely by 18, Canterbury by 21, and Westminster Abbey by 30 ft. The transepts are 176 ft. across. The internal width east of the tower is 76 ft. 8 in.; west of the tower, 74 ft. 2 in. The nave is 276 ft. long from the W. wall to the tower arch. The extreme length of the exterior, including the Lady Chapel, is 556 ft. The tower is 144 ft. high.

The great interest of the church consists in its being substantially the church built by Abbot Paul in 1077-88, and consequently one of the earliest Norman churches—perhaps the earliest on a large scale—remaining in this country. But beyond this, it comprises not only the early Norman plan and construction, but dated examples of each subsequent period of English ecclesiastical architecture. The walls and entire central portion of the present church—from the fifth bay of the nave on the N. (reckoning from the W. door) to the first bay of the sanctuary, and including the transepts and central tower —is a part, constructionally little injured by time or wear, of the Norman ch. The five western bays of the nave are E.E. (1214-35); the S. aisle and nave piers are of the early Dec. style; the Lady Chapel and portions of the E. end later Dec.; the windows on the N. of the nave, the W. window, and chantrys, Perp.,— some of it very late in date.

Matthew Paris says that Abbot Paul

built his church " of the stones and bricks (or tiles, *tegulæ*) of the old city of Verulamium," and the visitor may at once verify his testimony. The Norman portion is constructed throughout of bricks precisely similar to those which may be seen, by crossing the river, in the still remaining Roman walls. In this respect St. Albans is unique among our churches. But it is remarkable that, whilst the old Roman bricks were used as they were taken—and, as may be observed, the builders tried to imitate the Roman manner of construction by using the bricks as bonding courses with flints— there has not been found a single Roman shaft, capital, or carved stone worked up in any part of the building. Some rude banded shafts (as in the triforia of the transepts) are supposed to have been taken from Offa's Saxon ch., and used without alteration ;* but if any carved Roman stones were used—and we can hardly believe that there were not some among the *spolia* of Verulam—they must have been ruthlessly recut. The use of stone in the walls was, however, almost confined to the base of the central tower, where it occurs in massive blocks.

This peculiarity in the construction deserves the visitor's attention, as it greatly influenced the original character and will account for the present appearance of the edifice. The rude, rugged, as some would say *unfinished*, condition of the external walls is, for example, at once explained by the construction. The church was built of brick (with flint in the basement), but was meant to be covered, both inside and out, with cement, and the brickwork was left rough that the cement might adhere the better. Not only are the walls from base to summit, including the angles, constructed of Roman bricks, but the vouissoirs of the arches, the steps and newels of the stairs, the cores of the massive piers which support the triforia, and the string courses and mouldings are of the same material.

The bricks are laid with wide joints in a bed of mortar almost rivalling that of the Romans in tenacity. But almost every particle of cement has disappeared from the exterior, and the interior cement has been only partially renewed. Hence the Norman work has a deceptively rough and decayed aspect, though in truth the brick has lasted far better than the stone where that material was used. To restore in imagination the Norman ch., we must replace throughout the smooth cement, and suppose it to be lined in imitation of masonry wherever there was no pictorial decoration. This early use of imitative cement is rather opposed to ecclesiological notions, but there can be no doubt of the fact, and it is one suggestive in many ways. Further, it must be remembered that the present E. and W. ends, the screens and chantrys, are of more recent date than the main building. The original Norman church was 426 ft. long (the same length as Peterborough Cathedral); had a grand W. front flanked by square towers ; the central tower was crowned by a parapet, roof, and angle turrets. There were two apsidal chapels opening from the E. side of each transept ; and a very long presbytery with an apse at the E. end, in which the decoration of the interior culminated in rich metal-work, carvings, paintings of a Majesty, the Virgin, and several saints. All the Norman surface decoration has disappeared; there is no such forest of piers as arrests attention in the long vista of Winchester Cathedral ; and it must be admitted that in the first view of the Abbey the severe simplicity of its aspect is cheerless and disappointing. But this very simplicity, the grandeur of scale, and harmony of proportions, produce their impression if the building be lingered over. St. Albans Abbey is, in truth, one of those buildings which require to be studied to be understood and appreciated ; and it grows in estimation in proportion as it is studied.

The present entrance to the Abbey is on the S., and the visitor is generally led to the transept or chancel ; but to see the interior aright, he should pass at once to the W. door, and view the building in the way its authors meant it to be seen. Some day we hope the W. door will be again the ordinary entrance. The gene-

---

* Buckler, Architecture of the Abbey Church of St. Alban, p. 134.   Sir Gilbert Scott, after a minute comparison of these baluster columns with similar shafts in the Saxon churches at Castle Cliff, Dover, Jarrow-on-the-Tyne, and Monk Wearmouth, restored by him, expresses a very decided opinion that the St. Albans columns "formed portions of King Offa's church." (Report on St. Albans Church.)

The Abbey, St. Albans

Shooter's Hill (see p.554)

ral impression on looking at the *nave* is (or was before the tower arch was temporarily blocked up) that its length is excessive ; but it must be remembered that the original proportions have been somewhat altered : as the apparent height of the exterior has been reduced by the accumulation of some six feet of rubbish at the foot of the wall, so has that of the interior by raising the floor some three or four feet above the original pavement, and laying it with a gradual rise from the W. door to St. Cuthbert's Screen. The original pavement was formed of small tiles. A new one was laid down in the 14th cent. ; but the present pavement, of black and white marble, only dates from about 1738.

Whatever be the impression produced by the nave, there is felt to be a remarkable want of congruity in its architectural character. This, as is quickly seen, arises from the curious admixture of styles, and the direct way in which they are brought into juxtaposition. " Probably no other church," as Mr. Buckler remarks, " exhibits so many incongruous junctions with so much refined and stately architecture." Very striking examples of these incongruous junctions may be seen on the N. side of the nave, where the arch of the last E.E. bay springs from the Norman pier in the baldest possible fashion, and on the S. side at the junction of the E.E. and Dec. work of the fifth and sixth bays ; but others equally remarkable occur in the choir and sanctuary.

The W. end of the Norman church was demolished by Abbot John de Cella (1195-1214), with a view to its reconstruction on a more magnificent scale, and more in accordance with current taste. He failed, as we have seen, to accomplish his undertaking ; but the foundations and remaining fragments of the superstructure suffice to prove that his front, with its great flanking towers, noble entrance porch, and rich clustered columns of Purbeck marble, would have been a far grander and more beautiful front than that actually raised by his successor, William de Trumpington (1214-35). The present W. window of nine lights was inserted by Abbot Whethamstead in the middle of the 15th cent., and is only remarkable for its size.

Looking from the W. porch eastward, we see that while the western bays of the nave are E.E. in style, and the farther bays on the S. are of later date, the larger portion on the N. side is early Norman in character. In fact, the first five bays on the S. side, and the first four on the N. are, from floor to roof, E.E., the work no doubt of Abbot Trumpington. This portion of the ch. is very fine, free from all adventitious ornament, but noble in the mass, and exceedingly graceful in the details. For its construction the Norman walls were removed to the foot of the clerestorey ; but in rebuilding, the original piers being retained, the Norman proportions were adhered to in the arcades, though, as the pointed arches rose higher than circular arches, the triforia were necessarily higher, and the architect appears to have intended to substitute a groined roof in place of the original brick vaulting.* To form the clustered columns of the E.E. arcade, the massive Norman shafts were cut away, and the greatly diminished brick core cased with masonry. The arches of the triforia, instead of a single opening, as in the Norman, have within the outer arch, which is borne on elegant clustered shafts, two recessed arches with a central column of good design. The mouldings in the triforia are admirable, and the dog-tooth ornament is introduced with excellent effect. The clerestorey is merely a continuous series of narrow windows, the bays being marked by slender shafts. Mr. Buckler, from an examination of the foundations, arrived at the conclusion that the most western bay was intended to have been a pronaos or narthex.

The E.E. work terminates with the fourth bay on the N. side, though very curiously the clerestorey window of the fifth bay is E.E., probably from this portion of the Norman wall having fallen, or been materially injured, on the demolition of the adjoining portion. The remaining bays on this side are Norman of the severest plainness. The massive rectangular piers, very nearly as wide as the interspaces, are only relieved by a slight projection of the side faces and reveals, the arches are without mouldings or any constructional ornament, and plain pilaster shafts divide the several bays. Of the three stages the triforium is the lowest,

---

* Buckler, p. 103.

and suffers by juxtaposition with the lighter and loftier E.E. arcade. The Norman piers, as we have said, are of brick, covered with cement. During repairs in 1863, paintings executed in fresco or distemper were uncovered on the W. and S. face of each shaft—so placed as to face the congregation. When the limewash was first removed, some of them were in fair preservation; but though they were carefully oiled and varnished, the colours gradually changed, and in some instances the designs have almost disappeared. The paintings on the W. sides of the piers, and consequently facing the worshipper as he walked up the nave or looked eastward. represent Christ on the cross, with the Mother and St. John at its foot; the figures about 4 feet high. Each of the five differs, especially in the position of the Saviour. In all the flesh colours have become brown, in some nearly black. The form of the Saviour is generally meagre, but much more correctly drawn in some than in others. Under the first (the fourth pier from the W. door) is a bracket for a lamp. On the nave face of this pier is a colossal St. Christopher, with the child Saviour on his shoulder. On the southern faces of the other piers are figures of the Virgin and saints, a Martyrdom of St. Alban, and the infant Saviour with the fingers raised in the act of benediction. Mr. Buckler suggests that the fourth (first Norman) pier was probably spared when the first four bays were renewed by Abbot Trumpington from a feeling of reverence, an altar being attached to its western face.

The five eastern bays on the S. were rebuilt about the middle of the 14th cent., and are consequently of the best period of the Dec. style. In general character they agree with the earlier bays, the architect having evidently sought to make them accord, but the mouldings are of course fuller, enriched cuspings are introduced, and the whole has a richer and more florid character. We admire more the severe simplicity of the earlier bays, but these are very beautiful, and we agree with Mr. Buckler that "it would be difficult to name, in any church, an elevation which rivals in magnificence that of the ten bays which complete the range on the S. side of the nave, between the W. end and St. Cuthbert's screen."

This portion of the S. aisle is groined; the western half, and the entire N. aisle, have plain timber roofs.

Unfortunately, in the autumn of 1875, these bays showed such serious symptoms of failure, caused, no doubt, by the sinking eastward of the great tower (to be noticed presently), that it was deemed necessary to support them by strong shores, and they will consequently not again be properly seen till they have passed through the hand of the restorer.

The ceiling of the nave and choir has been attributed to Abbot John de Whethamstead (1420-40), but is more probably the work of Thomas de la Mare (1349-96). It is of oak or chesnut, flat, divided into four lines of panels, and painted with bright colours and scrolls, each panel having in old characters the monogram I.H.S. The effect is remarkable, and if not altogether pleasing, this may be owing to the coarse way in which, some generations ago, the whole was repainted "in imitation of the original." At any rate, the choir ceiling, which is decorated in a similar manner, but more elaborately, has had the modern paint removed and the old work restored with surprising benefit. Whether the ceiling was planned with a view to acoustic qualities we know not, but it is noteworthy that, divine service having been performed in the nave since the restoration of the tower and choir was commenced, notwithstanding the great length and height of the nave, the preacher can be distinctly heard in every part of it without raising his voice.

The nave is divided from the choir at the tenth bay by *St. Cuthbert's Screen.* The usual practice is for the choir to commence at the E. arch of the transept. But here, when the chapel of the patron saint was partitioned off, the eastern limit of the choir being abridged, the remaining space was insufficient for the requirements of the monks. The immense length of the nave allowed a portion of it to be taken without unduly encroaching on the ch. of the laity, and its four eastern bays were added to the existing choir. Abbot Richard d'Aubeney, near the close of the 11th cent., dedicated a chapel to St. Cuthbert, in commemoration of his withered arm being miraculously cured on occasion of the translation of St. Cuthbert' bones at Durham. This gave place to a more magnificent chapel and screen erected by Abbot Trumpington in the 13th cent. ; and this in its turn was removed on the completion of the eastern bays of the S. arcade, towards the middle of the 14th cent., and the present screen substituted. The screen is of Tottenhoe stone, solid and lofty, entirely shutting off the E. end of the ch. It has a centre of two tiers of niches with canopies, the upper tier, seven in number, being distinguished by greater size and enrichment. On either side is a doorway leading to the choir. A carved cornice and trefoil crest crown the screen, which no doubt bore in the centre a tall rood. In front stood the altar of the saint; unless, indeed, as is possible, the chapel of St. Cuthbert stood apart from the screen on the S., and the altar in front of the screen was that of the Holy Cross. The screen is of fair design and admirable workmanship; but it is much defaced, blocks the way, and is altogether very much out of place. In preparing the ch. for use as a cathedral, it is to be hoped that St. Cuthbert's screen will be removed to a side wall, where a suitable place may easily be found for it, and an open metal screen be substituted—if any screen is required W. of the transept.

The Choir extends from St. Cuthbert's screen to the tower, the four bays of which it is composed retaining the massive Norman piers and plain round arches up to the triforia and clerestoreys. The ceiling is a continuation of that of the nave, but more elaborately painted, and will soon reappear in its pristine brilliancy. In 12 of the panels angels are represented holding in one hand shields of arms of the early English kings, in the other scrolls with invocations to the Trinity. In the central panels are representations of the Saviour and the Virgin under canopies. The other 52 panels have angels bearing the arms of England, France, Castile, Portugal, etc. The choir is now being thoroughly restored, and in it Sir Gilbert Scott is colouring and reliéving the walls and shafts in accordance with portions of the old work which have been uncovered. *Obs.*, in the S. aisle, the low recessed canopied tomb, said by a modern inscription to be that of the hermits Roger and Sigar ; and beyond

it the "Abbot's Doorway," of carved oak.

The eastern extension of the choir, *The Sanctuary*, or *Presbytery*, was that part of the building in which its splendour culminated, and must in its palmy days have been of extraordinary magnificence. In the Norman ch. it extended unbroken eastwards, with aisles of the same width as those of the nave, and terminated probably in a spacious apse, within which stood the shrine of St. Alban. The Lady Chapel was on the S., and there were three other chapels, all apsidal in form.[*] But about the middle of the 13th cent., Abbot John de Hertford (1235-60) pulled down the whole eastern end of the ch., beyond the second bay from the tower, and rebuilt it in the lighter and richer manner which marks the transition from the E.E. to the Dec. style. The Lady Chapel was added to the eastern end by Abbot Hugh de Eversden in the first quarter of the 14th cent. The Sanctuary, as it now appears, is closed eastward by the lofty screen erected by Abbot William Wallingford (1476-84), nearly in the centre of the 2nd arch from the tower, and between the monuments of Abbots Whethamstead and Ramryge. The architecture of Hertford's building is light, graceful, and beautifully finished. Note the greater altitude of the arches, the narrower bays, the increased internal space obtained by the comparative thinness of the pillars and walls, and the elegance of the cusps and mouldings. The N. and S. doorways, after being closed on the conversion of the abbey into a parish ch., have been reopened, and the beautiful tabernacle work over them carefully restored.

The *Altar Screen* (or Wallingford's Screen, as it is frequently called,) bears a marked resemblance to that of Winchester Cathedral, which is of about the same date. It is a lofty and solid structure of Tettenhoe stone ; is in three compartments, a centre and two wings, and rises in three stages of the most elaborate carved work. The central compartment was filled by the high altar, with its rich dorsal wrought with the martyrdom of St. Alban. Over this is a tier of 13 canopied niches ; the central one filled, as is supposed (for all the statues are gone),

* Buckler, p. 47.

with a figure of the Saviour, the others with the Apostles. Above these is a cruciform space, once, doubtless, occupied by a crucifix. The wings have each a doorway leading to St. Alban's Chapel, with, on either side, richly canopied arches; above are two tiers of canopied niches, and the whole is crowned with a range of rich canopied work and perforated cornice. Shields with the arms of England and France and of Abbot Whethamstead, and a variety of devices, complete the design. The east front is less elaborate, but still very rich. A large part of the surface is panelled; the Abbey arms supported by angels, and the arms of Abbot Whethamstead, are conspicuous; and the crowning cornice is ornamented with delicately carved vine leaves, fruit, etc. In its way nothing can well exceed the richness and beauty of the carvings on the shrine, but with all its beauty it will, we fear, be a serious obstruction to the magnificent vista which would, but for it, be obtained when the Lady Chapel is opened to the body of the church.

St. Alban's Chapel extends E. of the Altar Screen to the Lady Chapel. Near the centre of the chapel stood the Shrine of St. Alban, on the beauty and splendour of which the chroniclers never tire of expatiating. At its W. foot, probably, stood the altar of St. Alban. On the N. side of the chapel, looking directly on the shrine, is the Watch Gallery, where night and day the shrine keeper and his assistants kept watch over the treasures of the shrine. On the opposite side is the monument of the good Duke Humphrey of Gloucester, and at its foot the vault in which he was interred. The eastern, or processional aisle, E. of the shrine, opened into the Lady Chapel by five tall pointed arches, three in the central span and one on each side. These arches were walled up in 1553, when the Lady Chapel was severed from the ch. and converted into a grammar-school.

From the Suppression, or shortly after, the *Shrine of St. Alban*, both platform and feretory, disappeared. Buckler, indeed, accepting the Cologne legend, states that "the treasure, the possession of which had for ages rendered the Abbey illustrious, was conveyed for security to Rome, and subsequently consigned to the care of the Theresian convent at Cologne, in whose

church of St. Mauritius in that city may still be visited the shrine of St. Alban of England."[*] This is, however, as mythical as the possession of the saint's bones by Ely or Owensee. The Cologne shrine belongs to St. Albinus—a very different person to the English Alban. The only vestiges of the shrine known in fact to exist, were the stone flags marking the place on which it stood, with hollows in them, worn, as you were told, by the knees of the pilgrims. But quite recently, not indeed the shrine, as is commonly asserted, but the platform or basement of it, has been brought to light in the most remarkable manner. Some 20 years ago, Dr. Nicholson, the rector of St. Albans, caused the central arches of the Lady Chapel to be opened, and among the bricks and flints and fragments of carved stones which had been employed for filling the arch, found numerous pieces of wrought Purbeck marble. The Cologne myth having been exploded, Dr. Nicholson thought these might be remnants of the shrine, and had them carefully preserved. Nothing further was done till Sir Gilbert Scott, in the course of the restorations at the Abbey, ordered the modern wall-casing of the S. aisle to be removed, Feb. 1872, when behind it was found an immense quantity of carved fragments of stone, many of which on comparison were found to agree with those discovered by Dr. Nicholson. The search was diligently prosecuted, the remaining western arches of the Lady Chapel were opened, the gabled panels of the ends and side arcades were found, and at length the marble work of the shrine was almost perfectly recovered. But it was in hundreds of little fragments, the zeal of the iconoclasts having led them to mutilate the idolatrous shrine, as they hoped, past remedy. The fragments were however found in such regular order that they almost explained their place in the design. As soon as the general plan was made out, the work of rebuilding was commenced, a work of enormous difficulty owing to the numberless small and shapeless pieces, and continued with amazing patience and ingenuity † till the whole

---

* Arch. of the Abbey Ch. of St. Alban, p. 168.
† The shrine was laboriously built up, and all the fragments fitted and fastened together with mastic cement by Mr. Jackson, a foreman mason.

was put together, as it now stands, in the site it occupied for centuries, and in a more perfect condition than even the more famous shrine of St. Edward at Westminster.

As reconstructed, the shrine is in two stages, nearly 9 ft. long, 4 ft. wide, and 8 ft. high. The lowest stage, which stands on two low steps, is tomb-shaped, the sides divided into four square panels, each ornamented with a vigorously moulded and cusped quatrefoil, at each end a similar panel. In three of these quatrefoils are lozenge-shaped openings, cut through the marble—two on one side, one on the other. Their purpose is not clear, but it appears most likely that they were intended to allow worshippers to look at the relics deposited within (and we know that besides the bones of St. Alban, which were in the feretory on the summit, there were relics of many other saints in the shrine), perhaps also to insert diseased limbs. The second stage consists of tall niches the width of the lower panels, elaborately groined and traceried within, and terminating in cusped arches and crocketed pediments, within which are beautifully carved floral ornaments. Above is a bold cornice and cresting. Within the tympana are carved at the W. end the Decollation of St. Alban, at the E. the Scourging of St. Amphibalus. In the spandrels and elsewhere are figures of angels with censers, kings, etc. Opposite the principal divisions have been detached buttresses, terminating in pinnacles, 14 in all, but of these only portions have been recovered. In the lowest step of the shrine, which had never been removed from its place, were 6 curious depressions, of old supposed to mark the places of the pillars on which the shrine rested, but which, contrary to expectation, were proved to be altogether outside the shrine. Fragments of a twisted shaft with a base that fits these hollows have been found, and little doubt remains that here were the candlesticks for the "6 wax lights" which "Abbot William appointed should be lighted" on feasts and principal days, and for which he made due provision by imposing a fine of a mark in money, to be received annually of the house at Ben-

ham. With the exception of the groining of the niches, which are of clunch, the whole of the recovered shrine is of Purbeck marble; and the carving, and especially that of the natural foliage, which is very beautiful, where not damaged by the puritanic hammer, is as crisp and sharp as the day it was finished. Respecting the date of its original erection there is some doubt. Walsingham says * that "the marble tomb as we now see it" was made by Abbot John Maryns, or de Marinis (1301-8); but the work looks somewhat later, and Sir Gilbert Scott, after a minute examination, is of opinion that though Abbot De Marinis "might have so far commenced it . . . as to have the credit of being its author, its execution must have been long delayed. I should attribute it," he adds, "to Eversden, who succeeded De Marinis, and held the abbacy till 1326, and I should suppose the work not to have been completed till close upon the last-named period." However this may be, the shrine as it stands is one of the most beautiful extant, and its resuscitation is one of the most wonderful romances of stone-work we know of.†

This fine work was however only the base which supported the actual shrine, or feretory, which contained the relics of the saint. "That elaborate, costly, and excellent work the feretory of St. Alban," as it was styled by Matthew Paris, who was in the habit of looking on it daily, was completed after many years' labour by "the incomparable artist" Anketil, goldsmith and monk of St. Albans, who had been moneyer to the King of Denmark. It was a glorious work, rich in gold and precious stones, and cunning workmanship. "On the sides were shown the story of the martyrdom of the saint, in raised work of silver and gold; at the west end was figured his decollation, so as to be seen by the celebrant; at the east end was the crucifix, with images of the blessed Mary and John, and many rich jewels were set in comely order. And on the W. front he set an image of the Blessed Virgin sitting on a throne, with the divine Infant on her lap. The story of the martyrdom was

We watched him at wor⁾ ᵃ ᵃᵃ d admired his rare tact and skill.

* Gesta Abbatum, vol. ii., p. 107.
† The Shrine of St. Alban, by J. T. Micklethwaite, F.S.A., with note by Sir G. G. Scott, R A., in Archæol. Journal, vol. xxix., pp. 201—211.

also represented on the sides of the ridged top of the shrine, which there rises into a cunningly wrought foliated cresting, with at the four corners open towers with marvellous bosses of crystals." This gorgeous work was only shown on high days or at special times, it being on other occasions covered with an operculum, which could be raised or lowered as required by means of cords and pulleys—the holes for which may still be seen in the roof directly over the shrine. Of the feretory not a vestige, so far as is known, remains.

Over against the shrine, the feretrarius and his companions kept constant watch. The *Watching Loft* stands on the N. side of the chapel, and is a handsome piece of carved oak work, with subjects from the legend of St. Alban in high relief round the frieze. The monks kept their vigil in a shallow chamber, reached by a few awkward narrow stairs. In the lower part are cupboards—" ambreys for the reliquaries, and presses for the sacred vestments."

On the S. side of the chapel, opposite the Watching Loft, is the *Monument of Humphrey, Duke of Gloucester*, a work for its time of unsurpassed beauty. The mont. has been attributed to Abbot Whethamstead, whose arms are carved upon it ; and though it has been objected that the Duke died in the abbacy of John Stoke, Whethamstead's successor, yet as Whethamstead resumed the abbacy in 1450, three years after the Duke's death, and remained abbot till his own death in 1460, it is probable that he did build this splendid mont., the Duke having been his great patron and Whethamstead thoroughly devoted to the Duke. The mont. is in two stages ; the lower has the chamber for the tomb—though neither tomb nor effigy is there. The lofty stone canopy has a groined roof of fan tracery and triple arches, left without intermediate supports so as not to intercept the view of the saint's shrine, the back being open, but protected by wrought iron work. On the sides are smaller arches, with arms and devices in the spandrels of England and France, the Duke of Gloucester, and Abbot Whethamstead. In the upper division are three tiers of canopied niches—those on the N. side empty, but those on the S. filled with 17 statuettes of English sovereigns, ancestors of Duke Humphrey.

The Duke was buried in a vault at the foot of his mont., and there his remains lay undisturbed till 1703, when the vault was accidentally broken into. Since then, till a very few years back, the vault was left open, and the Duke's bones, or what were said to be his bones, exposed to the rude handling of every visitor. In the S. aisle, behind the mont., is *Duke Humphrey's Chantry*, founded by Abbot Whethamstead, in which two priests did constant service. The ordinary entrance to the ch. was for the last century through this chantry, which suffered accordingly.

West of his patron's mont., occupying the last arch on the S. of the Sanctuary, is the less costly but very beautiful *Mont. of Abbot Whethamstead* himself, and prepared during his lifetime. His arms, the three wheat-ears, are of frequent occurrence, and there are numerous other quaint devices very charmingly cut. The lower chamber has a rich canopy with groined roof of fan tracery : the upper stage has quatrefoil panels filled with carved ornaments, and over all is an elaborate cornice. Abbot Whethamstead's effigy was once on the floor, but the brass was stolen, and now the brass of Abbot Thomas De la Mare, d. 1396, occupies its place. This, one of the finest brasses in the country, has often been engraved, and is well known. It is a Flemish brass, probably engraved during the life of the abbot, as the marginal insc. was left unfinished. It is 9 ft. 3½ in. long and 4 ft. 3½ in. wide. De la Mare is figured in full abbatal vestments, under a rich canopy. In the upper part are the effigies of Saints Peter, Paul, and Alban ; with King Offa as founder of the Abbey. Below are Saints John the Evangelist, James the Great, Andrew, Thomas, Bartholomew, and others.

Opposite Whethamstead's mont., and occupying the last arch on the N. side of the Sanctuary, is the *Monument of Abbot Thomas Ramryge*, d. 1524, a good late Perp. chantry, about 12 ft. by 6½ ft., internal measurement. The chamber, or chantry, is divided into 4 bays, has an elaborate canopy, with groined roof of fan tracery, and central pendants and bosses. The upper stage has canopied niches, tabernacle work, and rich cornice ; shields of arms, figures of animals, and various devices, the whole most delicately and skilfully carved. *Obs.* the abbot's arms with rebus supporters, rams bearing collars with the letters R Y G E ; and over the door the figures of ram, lion, dragon, etc.   The mutilated rilievo appears to represent the Martyrdom of St. Amphibalus. To make room for the monument, its architect cut recklessly into the last great Norman pier, and when in 1871 the tower showed signs of sinking, the mischief extended to Ramryge's mont., which cracked longitudinally and threatened to fall apart. Prompt measures were taken, the chantry was rendered secure, all necessary repairs were effected, and the incised slab on which was formerly the abbot's effigy, which had been broken and removed when the abbot's grave was converted into a "family vault," was found, pieced together, and replaced in the chantry.

The *Lady Chapel* was erected by Abbot Hugh de Eversden (1308-26) in the reign of Edward II.   In its best days a structure of exceeding beauty, it has suffered far greater injury than any other part of the building.   When the body of the ch. was sold to the townsmen for a parish ch., the Lady Chapel was separated by a wall and a public passage made through the ante-chapel, and it was not till some years afterwards, when it was already becoming a ruin, that it was appropriated to the use of the Grammar School.   Stripped of its stalls and other ornamental features, it continued to be so used for 300 years, only in the last years of its occupation, more convenient school-rooms having been provided, the chapel served as the boys' playground.   At length, in 1869, the Abbey Gate-House was purchased and appropriated for the school ; and in 1875 the restoration of the tower, transepts, and eastern end of the main building having been completed, and in prospect of the church being made episcopal, funds were raised by the ladies of Hertfordshire for restoring the Lady Chapel, and uniting it once more to the main building.   The work is now in progress under the supervision of Sir Gilbert Scott, and will be very complete.   The Lady Chapel comprises an ante-chapel nearly as wide as the sanctuary, and the chapel proper, 55 ft. long, 25 ft. wide (about the width of the opening between the great piers of the tower), and 30 ft. high, small, but a gem of wondrous loveliness.   The walls were originally lined with canopied stalls, and

decorated with niches, canopies, pinnacles, and other ornaments, and bell-flower and other mouldings.   The windows were of varied, and some of singularly beautiful design : *obs.* the charming effect of that newly restored at the end of the S. aisle of the sanctuary.   The 6 side windows have the central mullions enriched with figures in niches ; the E. window has an arch of unusual but good character, as will appear when the restoration is completed.   The roof is formed of wooden groins springing from niches in the piers, but hitherto has been seen with difficulty.

In the ante-chapel has been built up the core and a few fragments of the basement of the Shrine of Alban's fellow-martyr, St. Amphibalus.

Whether the saint, or, as Abp. Usher supposed, his name only, is mythical, is of little consequence now ; in any case, the discovery of his shrine is equally interesting.[*]   Along with the fragments of St. Alban's shrine, were mingled in the *débris* of the walls a great many fragments of the hard chalk, locally known as clunch, some of them exquisitely carved, others brightly coloured or gilt, and a few with a curious interlacing pattern of tracery, in which were old English letters.   The same skilful mason who pieced together the shrine of St. Alban, tried his hand on these unpromising vestigia ; and though there were numerous lacunæ, he was able to make out a large portion of the shrine-stand, and, curiously enough, put together sufficient of the tracery to complete the word Amphibalus.   Here was sufficient evidence that this was the veritable shrine, but if more were needed it was supplied by the monogram R.W., on the side-pieces—the initials of the sacrist Richard Whitcherche, who as we know placed the feretrum of St. Amphibalus on a basement of white stone.   When put together, the fragments will form a structure resembling that of St. Alban in shape, but much smaller, being only about 6 ft. long and 3 ft. wide.

We have still to look at the *Transepts* and *Tower*, which, with the Choir, form the great central portion of the Norman

[*] The " Invention " of St. Amphibalus occurred in 1178 ; in 1186 his relics were translated to the new shrine prepared for them ; and forty years later the shrine was removed to a more honourable position in the centre of the church.

building, and that in which the original character has been best preserved ; though the visitor must now make allowance, when viewing it, for recent restorations which, however admirably and conscientiously carried out, have greatly changed its aspect, and substituted a youthful and modern for the former venerable though battered appearance.

Internally the transepts are 176 ft. across and 32 ft. wide. Broadly the bays resemble the Norman bays of the nave ; but the triforia, which are much more highly wrought than those of the nave, have never received light from the exterior. In place of the small Norman windows at the ends and sides, new windows were inserted in the 15th cent., as the Abbey Chronicles expressly say, in order to give additional light. The E. window of the S. aisle is recent. The gables which so appropriately terminated the transept ends, and tall roofs, are gone. In both transept and tower the triforia have double arches, divided by the curious baluster shafts, which are generally regarded as Saxon, and which Messrs. Buckler and Sir Gilbert Scott are agreed in accepting as relics of the ch. of King Offa. These shafts are of stone, circular or octagonal, very rudely wrought, with various bands and mouldings. Being of different lengths, they have been fitted with Norman capitals, made taller or shorter as necessary to adapt them to the required heights.

The windows of the N. transept have been least altered. Internally, Sir G. Scott has removed the plaster to show the construction of the brick arches. In the floor of this transept has been laid every tile or fragment of tile found during the restoration of the ch., and among them are some of the finest in England. The S. transept and S. aisle were much altered and decorated by William de Trumpington, who also inserted two new windows. *Obs.* the aperture, like a small two-light Perp. window, in the great Norm. pier at the angle of the choir in the S. transept. It is the outlook from a *Watch Chamber*, about 16 ft. above the ground, an odd-shaped room some 6 ft. deep, cut out of the mass of the pier in the 15th cent.—a somewhat hazardous experiment, seeing that little more than a foot of the pier wall is left at the N.E. corner. This chamber, which is reached by a gallery

over the cloisters, may have been constructed, as is popularly supposed, to enable the abbot or one of the upper officers to overlook the proceedings in the Abbey ; or, as is more probable, for the purpose of watching the chapels and altars, with their reliquaries, which were so numerous in the S. transept and S.E. aisle.* Remains of some of the chapels may still be made out, but they are not of much interest.

A recent discovery by one of the altars is sufficiently curious to be noticed. It was known that when Abbot Roger de Norton died, "on the morrow of All Souls Day " (Nov. 3rd, 1290), his body, in remembrance of his great services to the Abbey, was interred in front of the high altar, but his heart was by his own desire buried at the foot of the Altar of Mary of the Four Tapers ; and on the lowest step of the altar, on a small stone, was placed the effigy of the Abbot.† This altar was in the S. aisle of the eastern group of altars, and whilst levelling the ground in front of it, in the course of the restorations, 1874, writes Sir Gilbert Scott, "we found a little cylindrical hole (perhaps a foot in diameter) worked in two blocks of freestone, and in this a wooden box-cover . . . . of apparently oriental character." ‡ The contents of the box could not be determined, but there could be little doubt that it was that which once contained the heart of Roger de Norton. Its oriental character may perhaps be accounted for by the interest which Norton took in the Crusades from the time when he attended " at the Council of Lyons where it was decided to support the cause of the ' Sacred Enterprise '—a decision which the monastery of St. Albans appears not to have acted up to," and where he may possibly have had the box given to him as a memorial of the East. Instances of heart-burial are not uncom-

* Newcome gives, from Amundesham's Annales, an account of these chapels, Hist. of Abbey of St. Alban, p. 318 ; but the subject is more fully treated by Mr. R. Lloyd. An Account of the Altars, Monuments, and Tombs existing in 1428 in St. Albans Abbey, 1873.

† Gesta Abbatum, vol. i., p. 485 ; Joh. Amundesham, Annales Mon. S. Alb., vol. i., p. 434 ; Newcome, Hist. of the Abbey of St. Alban, p. 314.

‡ Sir G. G. Scott, R.A., Notes upon the Burial of the Heart of Sir Roger de Norton in St. Albans Abbey, in Archæol. Journal, vol. xxxi., p. 293.

mon among knights, but rare in the case of ecclesiastics, while hardly another instance is recorded of a body being buried in one part of a church and the heart in a different part of the same church.

The *Tower*, so striking a feature in any general view of the town or abbey, is the most massive Norman tower in England. It is nearly 150 ft. high, and about 50 ft. square (at 100 ft. high, the tower is 48½ ft. by 46, the walls 7 ft. 4 in thick). Like the body of the Norman ch., it is constructed of Roman bricks, and rises in 4 storeys above the inner arches—triforium, clerestorey, ringing-floor, and belfry,—and was originally crowned by an octagonal lantern and angle turrets, long since removed. The tower is carried on 4 piers of vast thickness, additional support being obtained by thickening the abutments of the arches next the tower piers. In the lower stage is an inner gallery in the thickness of the wall, recessed, with 3 arches on each side, borne on brick shafts. The next stage has a gallery open towards the exterior, with rude stone shafts and capitals, forming the arcade which is so striking a feature in the outer view of the tower. The interior of the belfry-stage has never been covered with cement, and exhibits very clearly the construction of the walls, arches, lozenge-shaped apertures for the transmission of sound, and the substantial timber roofing erected in the 15th cent. for carrying a spire—which was only taken down in 1830. In passing up the narrow staircase, *obs.* the peculiar construction, entirely in Roman bricks, newel, steps, and wall, and how admirably the newel is wrought. The view from the summit is very extensive, and on a clear calm day will amply repay the trouble of the ascent. *Obs.* from it the great length of the nave roof—better appreciated from here than anywhere.

The immense tower looked as though it might set Time at defiance. After having stood 700 years, it seemed as solid as when the top stone was laid by Abbot Paul. Writing in 1846, the Messrs. Buckler state as the result of their prolonged professional examination, that "its integrity as to structure and design is complete, and that just as it now appears so it was left by the Norman builders," and they add that "the walls of the Tower remain perfectly sound and free from lacerations; the sub-

structure is far too solid and compact, and rests on too sure a foundation, to be the occasion of accidents of this kind."[*] Other architects long after expressed a similar opinion. But the rocking of the tower when the bells were rung, had about 1830 led to the prohibition of the practice; and though the caution of the authorities gave occasion to some mockery and many complaints, it probably saved the tower from destruction. In the summer of 1870, "lacerations" were noticed, and dust as of powdered mortar was observed to be continually falling. The fissures increased in magnitude; cracks appeared in the transept walls; the monuments showed signs of disturbance; the roof of Ramryge's chantry split;—it was plain, in short, that the tower was pressing bodily eastward. Under the direction of Sir Gilbert Scott, prompt measures were taken to arrest the mischief; the tower was shored up with huge balks of timber, arches were hastily bricked, and a complex apparatus of trusses erected; and though the delicate tests inserted in various parts continued for days and even weeks to show that the tower was still sinking, it was seen as the supports were strengthened that the movement was steadily decreasing, and at length stayed. The thorough examination which then became possible showed not only the extent but the sources of the danger. The failure of the tower, even after 700 years had passed, was not chargeable upon the Norman builders. The great piers on which the tower rested, and those which served as buttresses, had been recklessly hacked away and dug into at all times from the 13th to the 19th century, in some cases to the extent of destroying the wall bondings, and the foundations had been excavated for interments. But these things, however mischievous, were done in ignorance, not malice. Another, and the strangest of all, was clearly intentional. At the base of the S.E. pier, a sort of cavern, 5 or 6 ft. wide, had at some time been hollowed out, stout props being inserted as the work proceeded to secure the safety of the workmen, and thus enable a hole to be bored large enough for a man to crawl along nearly through the pier. Sir Gilbert Scott satisfied himself that the excavation

* Buckler, p. 117.

must have been made with the deliberate purpose of destroying the tower; the intention probably being to adopt the practice common in early siege works of setting fire to the timber supports after the mine was completed. The great central tower of Waltham Abbey ch. was destroyed in this way by "undermining" and burning the props. (*See* WALTHAM ABBEY.) Probably the mine was excavated, when the monastic buildings were destroyed, and when it may have been intended to demolish the church—an intention, if ever entertained, abandoned when the church was purchased by the townsmen.

The work of repairing and strengthening the grand old tower was carried out thoroughly. The foundations were made good and largely extended; an immense mass of cement concrete was inserted down to the native chalk the whole width of the aisle; the piers repaired, and where necessary, bit by bit, rebuilt; the upper stages constructionally restored, new bell-framings fixed, and the bells rehung; and, lastly, to the great improvement of its appearance, the remaining cement was stripped from the exterior, the mortar repointed, and the structural character fairly exposed to view.* The result of all is that the tower, as far as it is possible to judge, is as strong as ever, and capable of standing at least as many more centuries; whilst its appearance, if now somewhat prim and modern, will gain by the weathering of every winter. As we stood on the roof and watched the battlements, when for the first time for over 40 years the bells rang out a merry peal, it was pleasant to feel that though there was soon a decided movement, it did not, even when the ringers tested the strength of the tower by volley "firing," increase beyond a steady, measured, almost rhythmic beat.

All the structural parts of the Abbey, beyond St. Cuthbert's Shrine to the present eastern wall of the ch., have now been restored; the Lady Chapel is undergoing renovation, with a view to its reunion with the parent church; and funds are being raised for the restoration of the

* Statement made by Sir Gilbert Scott, and Paper read by Mr. J. Chapple, Clerk of the Works, at Meetings of the St. Albans Archæol. Soc., 1873-74; Builder, 1870-75.

nave and W. front—a costly and important undertaking, but urgently required, as is shown by the recent failure of the south-eastern bays. It will, no doubt, soon be taken in hand, and we may hope that whenever the church is handed over to the new bishop, St. Alban's Cathedral will be found not unworthy to rank among the older cathedral churches of England.

The *Abbey Gate House*, the only other relic left of the monastery, stands about 50 yards W. of the ch., and in old time was the entrance to the Great Court of the Abbey. Another but smaller gatehouse was on the opposite side of the Court, whence the road led to the Abbey Mill. The chief entrance to the Abbey precinct was by a gatehouse S.E. of the Abbey, on the road to Sopwell. The present gatehouse is a large sombre structure, with a low pointed archway and groined roof. Over the archway is the Great Chamber in which the abbot's steward held his courts of assize; the upper and possibly some lower rooms served as prison cells. It was erected in the last half of the 14th century by Abbot Thomas de la Mare (1349-96), when the old gatehouse having been blown down by a high wind, a new one was built from the "foundations, with its chambers, its prisons, and its vaults, and the roof was covered with lead." After the suppression of the monastery, the gatehouse became the prison of the borough and liberty of St. Albans, and the sessions business continued to be transacted in the great room till 1651, when the sessions were transferred to the Town Hall. The whole upper part of the building was then converted into a house of correction, and it continued to be so used till the erection of a new prison in 1869. It was then decided to adapt the gatehouse for the Grammar School; the building was accordingly restored externally, and remodelled inside, and is said to serve its new office very well. The large old house adjoining it is the Head Master's house. The new *Borough Gaol* is a large red brick building on Victoria Hill, close to the Midland Railway Station.

Sopwell Nunnery was founded in the meadows S.E. of the abbey and town by Abbot Geoffrey de Gorham about 1140, originally for two holy women who had dedicated themselves to a life of poverty, and whom he found dwelling there in a hovel they had made for themselves out of the roots and bark of trees, and having only bread and water for their food. Struck by their piety, the abbot founded this cell, and in memory of its first occupants having been accustomed to dip their crusts in the neighbouring spring, he gave it the name of Sopwell. He directed that the inmates should not exceed 13 in number ; should follow the rule of St. Benedict; should dwell under lock and key ; have chapel and cemetery, but in the latter neither man nor woman, neither cleric nor laity, nor any one not a member of the sisterhood, should on any account have a place.* The nunnery came to have many inmates of high rank, and one at least famous in literary history —Dame Juliana Berners, whose ' Boke of St. Alban's,' printed at the Abbey in 1486, and reprinted by Wynken de Worde, was the first, and long the only, treatise on hunting, hawking, and angling in the language. The nunnery seems to have had some difficulty, towards the end, in keeping up its numbers: it of course met the fate of all such establishments. The site was granted, with the manor of Sopwell, by Henry VIII. to Sir Richard Lee, from whom in the female line it descended to Thomas Saunders of Beechwood, who sold it to Sir Harbottle Grimston, Master of the Rolls, 1660, to whose descendant, the Earl of Verulam, it now belongs.

Of the nunnery not a fragment is left. The so-called Ruins of Sopwell Nunnery are really the remains of the mansion Sir Richard Lee built for himself on the site, and are not of much account. They comprise portions of the walls, which are of red brick with flint, the weather-mouldings of a window and doorway, fragments of carved stone, and a shield of arms, all imperfect, the crumbling walls and ground overgrown with ivy, brambles, and nettles, difficult of access, and not worth the trouble of exploration. A foolish tradition assigns this as the place where Anne Boleyn stayed whilst waiting for the verdict that condemned her to the block ; and another still more absurd says that she was privately married to Henry VIII. in the chapel of Sir Richard Lee's house.

Churches.—*St. Michael's*, rather more

* Gesta Abbatum Mon. S. Albani, vol. i., p. 80.

than ½ m. W. of the Abbey, is much the most interesting of the remaining churches both architecturally, and as Bacon's church and grave. It stands on the edge of the meadows on the road to Gorhambury. The ch. was thoroughly restored by Sir Gilbert Scott in 1867, when Elizabethan porches, ceilings, and fittings—that one felt strengthened the Baconian associations—were swept away, and new roofs, windows, mouldings, pavement, and seats substituted. The ch. looks modern and somewhat commonplace now, but is really among the most ancient we possess. It stands about the centre of Verulamium, and Sir Gilbert Scott is, we believe, of opinion that it was built on the foundations of a Roman basilica or temple. Roman bricks are largely used as bonding tiles, and worked up in the walls. A church was built here by Wulsin (Ulsinus) the 6th abbot, in the 10th cent. The walls of this early edifice remain in part the walls of the present ch., and Sir Gilbert Scott has had all the Saxon arches cleared of the cement which previously concealed them, pointed, and left open, so that the construction can be readily examined. The original ch. seems to have been a plain oblong, with solid walls pierced only by the doorway and small widely-splayed clerestorey windows. The rude semicircular arches have, however, been cut through by Norman, E.E., and all subsequent architects, the plan of the building altered at will, new windows inserted, a tower and porch added,—and now in general plan and appearance it differs little from the ordinary country ch. The tower is Perp., square, rough-cast, and contains a peal of 4 bells. *Obs.* the way in which the arch by it on the S. was blocked up with Roman tiles and flints when the doorway was shifted, and a stone porch erected a little farther E. Farther on, by the S. door of the chancel, *obs.* in the outer wall a low recessed (sepulchre) tomb, cusped arch above, and coffin-shaped stone with abbatal cross below, uncovered when the ch. was restored, and very properly left open and *in situ*.

Inside, the chief object must always be the mont. of BACON, which stands within a shallow arched recess on the N. side of the chancel, and was erected by his friend and secretary Sir Thos. Meautys.

"For my burial, I desire it may be in St.

Michael's church, near St. Albans: there was my mother buried; and it is the parish church of my mansion house at Gorhambury; as it is the only Christian church within the walls of old Verulam."[*]

The mont. is especially interesting as having a marble statue of Bacon, the resemblance of which is certified by Sir H. Wotton who wrote the insc., and Meautys who placed it here. " Sic sedebat," is engraved under it, and there is an air of verisimilitude about it that refutes objection. Bacon is represented seated in his tall arm-chair, as we may imagine him seated in his study—unless, indeed, the wearing his hat may render that locality questionable. His head leans on his left hand, the elbow on the arm of the chair, the right hand hanging droopingly over the opposite arm of the chair, the eyes gazing as on vacancy, the whole air and attitude that of one absorbed in philosophic musings. The name of the sculptor is unknown, as is that of the sculptor of the bust of Sir Nathaniel Bacon, at Culford, Suffolk, but both are evidently by the same hand. The Verulam Chapel, opposite the tomb, with its Elizabethan entrance, ceiling, and pews, had quite a Bacon character before the recent restoration, when all that was modern was swept away, and the chapel reduced to an ordinary chancel aisle. *Obs.* before leaving, the A.-S. doorway of Roman tiles laid open by Sir Gilbert Scott. Other monts. are of little interest, but there is a good 14th cent. *brass*, and one temp. Edward VI. The road W. from the church, is the private road to *Gorhambury*, but till about 1828 was the main road from London to Holyhead.

St. Peter's Church, at the N. end of St. Peter's Street, is for the most part late Perp., rough-cast, with a tall tower at the E. end of brick, rough-cast, with three pilaster buttresses and battlements, and containing a fine peal of 10 bells. The unusual position of the tower is due to the circumstance that the ch. was originally cruciform, but the partial fall of the tower in 1801 did so much damage to the body of the ch. that the transepts, tower, and chancel were taken down, and only the tower and chancel rebuilt, on a more contracted scale. Several of the windows are filled with painted glass. Three on the S. side, erected in 1867, are by J. B. Capronnier, of Brussels. The pulpit is a very fine specimen of modern Belgian carving. On the W. wall is a tablet with bust of Edward Strong, d. Feb. 1723, "master mason" of St. Paul's, "who equally with its ingenious Architect, Sir Christopher Wren, and its truly pious Diocesan, Bishop Compton, shared the felicity of seeing both the beginning and finishing of that stupendous fabric," which, as the work was over 35 years in progress, was a sufficiently remarkable circumstance to deserve commemoration. St. Peter's ch. being on the southern margin of Bernard's Heath, and not far from the Keyfield, "the church and churchyard were filled with the bodies of those slain in the two Battles" of St. Albans, including Sir Berten Entwyel, the Babthorpes father and son, and other distinguished partizans, to whom monuments were erected, now all, or nearly all, lost:

" Behold wheer two Ralph Babthorpes, both the
        Son and Father lie
    Under a stone of marble hard interr'd in this
        mould drie:
    To Henry Sixth the Father Squire, the Son he
        Sewer was,
    Both true to Prince, and for his sake they
        both their Life did passe," etc.

Dr. Cotton (d. 1788), author of the 'Visions in Verse,' the once popular 'Fireside,' and other poems, and keeper of the *College Insanorum*, in St. Peter's Street, of which the poet Cowper was for some time an inmate, lies in the ch.-yard. Cowper was under Dr. Cotton's care in his season of greatest mental depression, and the dawn of his recovery. He thus notes his departure: "On the 7th of June, 1765, having spent more than eighteen months at St. Albans, partly in bondage, partly in the liberty wherewith Christ had made me free, I took my leave of the place at four in the morning, and set out for Cambridge."[*]

St. Stephen's Church, about ½ m. S.W. of the town, and ¼ m. beyond the N.-W. Rly. Stat., at the parting of the roads to London by Elstree and to Watford, and on the line of the old Watling Street, was one of the three churches founded by Abbot Wulsin, in the middle of the 10th cent.; but little is left of the Saxon ch.

---

* Lord Bacon's Last Will.

* Southey, Life of Cowper, chap. vi.

beyond the foundation walls and Roman tiles and flints worked up in the older parts of the superstructure. On the N. is an altered Norm. arch ; some portions are of the 13th cent.; the remainder is Perp. of the 15th cent. The building comprises nave and S. aisle, chancel with S. chapel, and a wooden tower and spire rising from the W. gable. The whole was restored, and the chancel rather elaborately embellished, by Sir Gilbert Scott in 1861-2. The little chapel on the S. of the chancel has been called the Leper Chapel, from a tradition, or supposition, that it was built by Abbot Gorham for the use of the inmates of his Hospital of St. Julian. The chapel now opens to the chancel by an arch, but it is affirmed that there was originally only a hagioscope, or opening sufficiently large to admit a view of the altar. It is, however, very doubtful whether, even so guarded, lepers would have been admitted into such close proximity to the congregation, while there can be little doubt that a chapel was attached to the hospital.* In the amended articles of Abbot Michel, the superior is entitled Rector Capellæ Juliana. The eagle lectern, which will be noticed in the nave, was found about 1750 buried in the earth, apparently for concealment from some undesired visitors : it has inscribed on it the name of George Crichtoun, Bp. of Dunkeld. From cinerary urns, calcined bones, and other Roman remains having been dug up at different times in the ch.-yard, it would appear to have been the site of a cemetery of Verulamium.

The *Leper-House*, or *Hospital of St. Julian*, stood to the rt. of the Elstree Road, about ¼ mile from St. Stephen's Church. Abbot Geoffrey de Gorham, with the consent of the convent, founded and amply endowed it for the reception of persons afflicted with that loathsome malady, and appointed a number of priests to serve in it. He does not appear to have limited the number of inmates, but it is said there were never more than three at one time ; and in 1344 Abbot Michel de Mentmore revised the statutes, and limited the number of " leper brothers" to six, and appointed five priests to be always resident. Nothing remains of the buildings, but the site is marked by a farm-house.

* Gesta Abbatum, vol. i., pp. 77, 78.

Christ Church, in the Verulam Road, was commenced in 1848, by A. Raphael, Esq., M.P. for St. Albans, as part of a large Roman Catholic institution ; but dying before he could carry out his purpose, the building was purchased in 1856 by Mrs. Worley, of New Barns, and completed as a church of the Establishment— a district parish being assigned to it—in 1859. It is of white brick and stone, Lombardic in style, with a campanile at the W. end : light, airy, and convenient, but not otherwise remarkable.

VERULAM. — The site of the Roman Verulamium is still unbuilt upon except in one part, and its boundaries are easily traceable. The ground on which it stood rose gently southwards from the Ver, its northern boundary, immediately W. of the higher ground on the opposite side of the river on which stands the present town of St. Albans. To reach the ancient city take the path from the S. door of the Abbey, across the meadow, where stood the extensive monastic buildings, to the Silk Mill (the successor of the old Abbey Mill) seen below. Cross the foot-bridge and in the field just beyond you strike the N.E. angle of the wall of Verulamium. Here on your rt., within an enclosed field, are several blocks of the wall which encompassed the Roman city. Of late years they have been much reduced, and are slowly crumbling away, but they show as well as any we may visit the character of the old Roman wall. The outside is of flints, large and in regular layers, the core or hearting of rough rubble, set in a bedding of mortar of great tenacity, and held together by bonding-courses of two layers of bricks or tiles, the tiles and the bed of mortar between them being of about the same thickness. The bonding-courses are nearly 3 feet apart, and carried through the substance of the wall, which is about 12 feet thick, closely resembling the Roman wall of London. The bricks in the two walls are almost identical in size and character. Those of Verulam are from 14 to 16 in. long, 12 in. wide, and 1½ to 2 in. thick; their weight is from 20 to 22 lb.

From this N.E. angle the short line of wall northwards to the river is marked by uneven high ground and a row of firs.

Returning to the path from the Mill, a straight embankment marks the site of the wall, which extends before you in a south-westerly direction for about ½ m., and you soon enter on a pathway overhung with trees that would be attractive under any circumstances, but is especially so when you discover that you are on the outer edge of the wall of Verulam, with the mass of the wall on one hand, the fosse on the other. The fosse of Verulam is better preserved than that of any other Roman city in England. It appears to have varied in width according to circumstances, and here was probably 30 ft. across. It is overgrown with firs, maples, elms, and a few oaks, some of them trees of tolerable size, and an abundance of brambles and underwood. A path winds along the bottom, now of course dry. On the rt. of the walk the wall is frequently visible, and in some places well shown, but it is better seen from the other (or field) side, where it rises 10 or 12 ft. from the ground. It is for the most part overgrown with ivy, and shaded by tall trees, but there is now none of that "good liquorice," which, according to old Fuller, "groweth naturally out of the ruinous walls of Verulam."

At the end of this pretty walk the wall makes a sharp turn to the N.W., in which direction it continues for nearly ¾ of a mile. Quitting the path, turn to the rt. along the road to Gorhambury, and you will see in the field on your rt., running parallel with the road, the low wall and fosse, the latter, however, much filled up, and in places neither wall nor fosse visible. Enter the field by the first swing-gate, and a few yards will place you again on the top of the wall, where on the rt. (E.) will be noticed an abrupt termination of the fosse, which for some distance forwards has been pretty much filled in and ploughed over. Returning to the road, you may take the lane on rt.—the ancient road across the city—and a clap-gate a few yards down on the l., will put you again on the line of wall, a good fragment of which will be seen on the l. on entering the field, with the partially filled fosse below, now smooth grass, looking in autumn like a hollow in the South Downs. Beyond (on the other side of the footpath and enclosed) the fosse is deeper, the bottom thick with underwood, the sides bordered with oak, ash, and hazel. Cross

the fosse at the first gate and pass through the wall by a section, which well exhibits its structure. Onwards the line of wall is perfectly plain, but you can only occasionally make out a fragment of the masonry. The fosse, however, continues broad and deep, but overgrown with wood and brambles, and enclosed. Presently the line turns abruptly to the N., and you reach a great mass of the wall, marked by a full-grown oak, and locally known as *Gorhambury Block*. This is the end of the wall now, and is probably very nearly its original termination. A portion may have been destroyed in constructing the Gorhambury road, which passes directly N. of Gorhambury Block, but no trace of a wall has been found in the meadow below, along the farther side of which flows the Ver, and which once was plainly overflowed by it. Along the river side of the city, there was probably no wall of masonry, but only an earthen embankment to confine the waters, which here were made to form a large pool or lake. The river was a sufficient defence on this side of the city.

The wall which we have thus perambulated is about 1¼ m. in length, the river frontage ¾ m. The area enclosed is ovate, the smaller end of the ellipse being at the W., the length about ¾ of a mile; the greatest width nearly ½ a mile; the surface about 150 acres. This, as Roman cities were laid out, with large spaces set apart for the forum, temples, basilica, theatre, baths, and villas surrounded by their grounds and gardens, would not allow of a large population; but traders and the bulk of the poorer inhabitants would dwell in a suburb of wooden huts, outside the great wall, and defended from marauders by an earthen vallum—of which vestiges may yet be traced. A main street traversed the city from E. to W., and another crossed it from S. to N., running along the line of the Watling Street, the hollow lane now leading from St. Stephen's to St. Michael's ch. Newcome, writing in 1794, says that "but a few years since the ruins of that south gate were dug up;"* a portion of the road was laid bare and destroyed as late as 1826. The roads appear to have been from 24 ft. to 28 ft. wide. The site of Verulam is now occupied by

* Newcome, Hist. of St. Albans, p. 28

well-cultivated fields, except the short space from St. Michael's ch.—which stands near the centre of old Verulam, and according to some sanguine antiquaries marks the site of the Temple of Apollo—to the bridge over the Ver. Except the outer walls, no relic of the ancient city is visible, though a century and a half ago some ruins appear to have been standing.[*] The plough occasionally turns up a Roman coin, a few tesseræ, or a broken piece of pottery. When a deeper trench is made, walls of houses and pavements are met with, layers of burnt wood turned up, and sometimes the lines of streets are crossed; but no systematic or extended investigation has been made; and Verulam, for four hundred years the monument of Roman enterprise and power, and a centre of Roman civilisation, lies like another Nineveh, Troy, or Pompeii, awaiting a Layard or Schliemann to disinter its buried treasures. Probably, however, little of value would be discovered. For centuries the fallen city was used as a quarry by the Abbots of St. Albans for building the Abbey ch. and monastic buildings, and the churches they erected at the entrance to the town, and doubtless by the townspeople for their houses, and for years its ruins were strictly searched, and whatever would now be regarded as of especial value carried away or destroyed.

Matthew Paris relates with evident enjoyment the doings of Ealdred and Eadmer, the 8th and 9th Abbots of St. Albans. Minded to build a new and more worthy ch. of the martyr, in place of the plain structure which then served the purpose, and to improve the town, Ealdred caused extensive excavations to be made in the old city of *Verlamcestre* with a view to obtaining the necessary materials, and uprooted the subterranean vaults and solid arches which had come to be the common haunts of robbers, malefactors, fugitives from justice, and harlots. In doing so, his workmen found not only stones, bricks, paving tiles, and abundant materials of all kinds, but in digging deep trenches by the river, exhumed oaken planks covered with pitch, and with the

nails still in them, oars, anchors, and other maritime implements, as well as great quantities of shell-fish, and other manifest signs that the river had formerly been navigable up to the ancient city; and these places the people called Oyster-hill, Shellford, Anchorpool, and Fishpool (the first and last of which names, by the way, are still retained). But the most wonderful discovery was a deep cave which had formerly been the abode of a great dragon. Ealdred seemed indeed to be wholly absorbed in these researches; he collected a great store of materials, but he had done nothing towards building his ch. when he went the way of all flesh.

His successor, Eadmar, continued the work, and was rewarded by discoveries that would now be regarded as of priceless value. In overturning the foundations of a great palace, his workmen found in a recess hollowed out in a wall a treasure as precious, had it been preserved, as that found by Schliemann in the palace at Hissarlik—a collection of books and rolls. But as they related, or were supposed to relate, to idol worship, and especially to the rites of Apollo and Mercury— "called by the English *Woden*,"—Eadmar burned them all, sparing only one. This, a volume strongly bound in oak, with bands of silver, and an inscription in letters of gold, was written in a language that could not be deciphered till an aged priest, named Unwona, was found, who pronounced it to be a History of St. Alban written in the tongue of the ancient Britons. At the request of the Abbot, Unwona translated it into Latin, when, wonderful to relate, immediately he had completed his revision, the original crumbled into dust. Further, among the ruins Eadmar found many stone tablets, roofing tiles, columns, and other materials for building, which he reserved for his ch.; and in the foundations of houses and subterranean vaults great numbers of vases, amphoræ, and various other fictile and turned wares, as well as glass vessels containing the ashes of the dead. Also, under fallen temples he found altars and idols, and coins and medals of divers kinds, all of which, by order of the Abbot, were broken in pieces.[*]

Later abbots, as we may see by the

---

[*] Stukeley, Plan of the remaining Walls and City of Verolamium; Vetusta Monumenta of the Soc. of Ant., vol. i., plate i., 1721.

[*] Matthew Paris, Gesta Abbatum, pp. 24—28.

materials of the Abbey, and St. Michael's ch., continued to spoil the ancient buildings, but we have no detailed record of their proceedings. In recent years there have been found about St. Michael's and towards the Gorhambury Block, besides the tiles, tesseræ, and pottery already mentioned, foundation walls, mostly of small houses, with traces of fresco painting, floors of red and white tiles, vases, household pottery, and coins. But the most remarkable find, and one that shows how much may yet repay the careful excavator, was that of a theatre—the only Roman theatre found in England—which was discovered in 1847, by Mr. R. G. Lowe, in the field on the l. of the Gorhambury road, immediately W. of St. Michael's ch., from which it is about 300 yards distant. It is of the usual form, 193 ft. in diameter; the walls double, with a passage of about 9 ft. between them. The stage appears to have been only about 46 ft. wide and 9 ft. deep; the orchestra and præcinctio about 70 ft.; the auditorium contained about 20 rows of seats. The walls were lined with slabs of marble, and decorated with frescoes, the colours of which when exhumed were still bright and fresh. Among the ruins were found fragments of pottery, a brass fibula, and 170 coins, ranging from Tiberius to Gratian. Foundations of buildings were found on the other side of the street; but the land is valuable, and the excavations were very soon filled in. The theatre was reopened on occasion of the visit of the British Archæological Association in 1869, but closed when the visitors departed, and now wears once more the appearance of an ordinary corn-field.*

Bernard's Heath, the theatre of the second Battle of St. Albans, fought on Shrove Tuesday, the 17th of Feb., 1461, lies a little way N. of St. Peter's. Warwick, with whom was the king, Henry VI., had hastened from London with such forces as he could muster, and encamped on Bernard's Heath, in order to check the great army which Queen Margaret had collected in the north, and which was

advancing rapidly on London. Passing round the town, the Queen's troops came into contact with Warwick's men in the lane N. of St. Peter's ch., forced their way through, and deployed on the Heath. The two armies thus brought face to face fought fiercely, and the result was for long doubtful; but the northerners were strongest in numbers and elated with success, and Warwick's men were in the end utterly routed. "In this battle," writes Hall, "were slain 2300 men, and not above, of whom no noble man is remembered save Sir John Gray."

More than three centuries have since passed, and Bernard's Heath (No Man's Land was its synonym then) has been lessened in extent by enclosures, divided by roads, broken up for brick and tile works, and gravel pits, and otherwise encroached upon; but there is still a rough wild gorse-clad common, some half a mile across, pleasant and picturesque to ramble over, and where the historical student may test his skill in making out the course of that Shrove Tuesday fight.

At the northern end of Bernard's Heath, commencing about half a mile up the Harpenden road and running in a N.E. direction for over three-quarters of a mile to the Sandridge road, is the remarkable entrenchment known as *Beech Bottom*, some 30 to 40 ft. wide and 20 to 30 ft. deep, resembling roughly a great railway cutting, but now overgrown with trees, ferns, and underwood. A few years ago you could walk along it from end to end, but the southern half has been cleared and converted into a volunteer rifle range, and the northern end severed by the Midland Rly. being carried across it. The best way to reach the open part is to proceed along the Sandridge road to the lane on the St. Albans side of the railway bridge, where it can be readily examined.

Evidently an artificial work, the rampart formed of the excavated earth still in many places perfect, antiquaries were inclined to regard Beech Bottom as a portion of a Roman sunken road, its direction being towards Verulam. But an ingenious and more feasible explanation has been proposed by Mr. Samuel Sharpe,* who regards it as a portion of the defences—

* R. G. Lowe, Description of the Roman Theatre at Verulam: Proceedings of St. Albans Archit. and Archæol. Soc., 1848. For the Coins see J. Evans, F.S.A., Account of Coins found at Verulam, 1848.

* Archæol. Journal, vol. xxii., p. 299.

the outer wall and fosse mentioned by Cæsar—of the Oppidum of Cassivellaunus. Mr. Sharpe with much difficulty was able, as he believed, to make out the entire circumvallation; and, after carefully going over the ground, we believe his general conclusions to be well founded.

Starting from the Ver at Sopwell Mill, S.E. of St. Albans, the line of fosse and wall runs N.E. past Camp House and across the Hatfield road to Beaumont, where it turns N., and bending round, N.W., joins the northern end of Beech Bottom. From the southern end of Beech Bottom it can easily be traced for some distance westward, when it turns southward and joins the Ver midway between St. Michael's ch. and Gorhambury Block. No other portion is nearly so perfect as Beech Bottom; indeed nearly everywhere else, as Mr. Sharpe remarks, "the British ditch has very much been filled up and its space reclaimed for the purposes of agriculture; and the yearly ploughing has given it an appearance of a natural depression in the ground. But here and there we find traces of art sufficiently clear to enable us to follow the line on the map:" a statement we can corroborate. Mr. Sharpe supposes that besides this outer defence, "a bank was raised between the town and the river;" but we find no traces of it, and believe that the Oppidum being on high ground, the townsmen trusted, as Cæsar says, to the morasses of the Ver for their river-side defence.

The circumvallation as above traced is about 4½ miles in circuit, and encloses the town of St. Albans, Bernard's Heath, and several farms. The area enclosed is about 1800 acres. The extent of the area and character of the outworks quite accord with what Cæsar says of the Oppidum, with its admirable defences of fosse, vallum, and marshes, and the great quantities of cattle he found within; it being, in fact, not merely a fortified town, with scattered groups of houses, fields, and cattle within the enclosure, but also an entrenched stronghold in which the people of the surrounding country with their herds could take refuge on the approach of an enemy. And the great extent of wall and marsh explains how it was that Cæsar was unable to invest it, and how when his soldiers stormed it on two sides, the Britons were able to make their way

out by another.* If this speculation as to the site and defences of the Oppidum be well founded, we have in St. Albans the instance of the still existing fosse and vallum of a British as well as of a Roman town—each being unique in this country.

ST. ANNE'S HILL, SURREY (see ANNE'S HILL, ST.)

ST. GEORGE'S HILL, SURREY (see GEORGE'S HILL, ST.)

ST. MARGARET'S, HERTS (see STANSTEAD ST. MARGARET'S).

ST. MARY'S CRAY, KENT (see CRAY, ST. MARY'S).

ST. PAUL'S CRAY, KENT (see CRAY, ST. PAUL'S).

SANDERSTEAD, SURREY, a pretty secluded vill. on the road to Warlingham, 3½ m. S.E. from the E. Croydon Stat. of the L., B., and S. C. Rly., and 13 m. from London: pop. 267.

The village is charmingly situated on an outlyer of Thanet sand on the edge of the chalk Downs, 576 ft. above the sea level, in the midst of a varied and picturesque country, surrounded by extensive woods and broad downs, and reached by pleasant country lanes abounding in wild flowers and singing birds, and especially rich in nightingales. The manor was purchased of Richard Gresham in 1591 by John Ownsted, sergeant of the carriages to Queen Elizabeth. Dying without issue, he devised the manor to his cousin Harman Attwood and his two sisters. Attwood purchased his sisters' shares, and the property continued in his descendants till 1759, when John Atwood (the modernized mode of spelling the name) having no children, bequeathed it to a nephew, Thos. Wigsell. In 1807 it passed by bequest to Atwood Wigsell Taylor, who assumed the name and arms of Wigsell, and is now the property of his son Atwood Dalton Wigsell, Esq.

Sanderstead *Church* (All Saints) is a

---

* Cæsar, De Bell. Gall., lib. v., cap. xxi.

pretty little village ch. of flint and stone, mostly Perp. in style, but has been restored and embellished, and painted glass inserted in the windows. It consists of nave and aisles, chancel, and tower and shingled spire at the W. end. *Monts.* on N. Wall, John Ownsted, d. 1600, servant to Queen Elizabeth, and "Sergeant of her Majesties Carriages by ye space of 40 years;" white marble, with kneeling effigy in armour under an arch. On spandrel of nave arch, mural mont. with effigy of Joanna Ownsted, d. 1587. End of S. aisle, low altar tomb, with recumbent effigy of Mary Bedell, d. 1655, wife successively of Ralph Hawtrey and Lewis Audeley. In the ch.-yard is the grave (chosen by himself) of the Rt. Hon. Sir Francis Bond Head, Lieut.-Governor of Upper Canada, and Author of 'Rides across the Pampas,' and ' Bubbles from the Brunnen,' d. at Croydon 1875. Two large and some smaller old yew-trees are in the ch.-yard ; the lich-gate is recent. Close to the church is *Sanderstead Court*, the seat of A. D. Wigsell, Esq. *Obs.* the fine elms in the park. The stately castellated mansion N.E. of Sanderstead Court is *Selsdon*, in Croydon par. (*See* CROYDON.) *Purley*, which gave its second title to Horne Tooke's 'Πτεροεντα, or the Diversions of Purley,' 1½ m. W., is in Sanderstead par., but close to Caterham Junction, under which heading it is noticed.

SANDOWN PARK, ESHER,

SURREY, a piece of sloping ground of about 120 acres, enclosed and laid out as a racecourse, is situated on the l. of the L. and S.-W. Rly., a short distance past the Esher Stat.: the entrance is on the rt. of the road as you enter Esher village, 14 m. from London by road, 15 m. by rly.

Sandown (of old *Sandon*) manor was part of the endowment of the Hospital of St. Mary and All Saints, or Sandon, which stood E. of Sandown Park and near the rly. stat. (*See* ESHER, p. 203.) The ground forming Sandown Park has been laid out specially for horse-racing, but space is provided for polo, croquet, and other open-air pastimes. There are two courses, one for flat races, and the other for steeplechases. The Flat course affords a straight run of nearly a mile. Above it is a terrace on which are four Grand Stands —one for royal personages, one for subscribers, one for the public, and one for the press—a little beyond the last being the judge's seat. The steeplechase course has ten or twelve leaping-fences, and a water jump 14 ft. wide. Beyond the stands, the ground rises into a wooded knoll, on which are pleasant walks shaded by groves of beech, elm, and fir. The general direction of the ground is in the Sandown Park Club. The park was opened, and the first race meeting held, on April 22, 1875.

SANDRIDGE, HERTS, 2½ m.

N.E. of St. Albans, on the road to Whethampstead: pop. 820.

At the Dom. Survey *Sandrige* formed part of the demesne of St. Albans Abbey. It was said to have been given by King Egfrid to the monastery in 796, and was held by it till the Dissolution, Dec. 1539. A few months after, May 1540, the manor was given by Henry VIII. to Ralph Rowlet, on the death of whose son it passed to his sister, the wife of Ralph Jennings, in whose family it remained till, on the death of a later Ralph Jennings, it descended to his three daughters, of whom Sarah, the youngest, was the wife of Colonel Churchill, afterwards the great Duke of Marlborough. Churchill purchased the shares of the other sisters, and became possessed of the entire manor. It was from this manor he took his first title, Baron Churchill of Sandridge.

The vill. stands high, on a byroad through which there is a considerable local traffic ; consists of a few cottages, wheeler's and general shops ; two or three comfortable looking private houses ; a couple of inns, the Rose and Crown and Queen's Head ; a good schoolroom off the road on the l., and the old dingy looking ch. on the rt. The men are chiefly employed in agriculture ; straw-plaiting occupies many of the females.

The *Church* (St. Leonard) comprises nave, aisles, chancel, and battlemented tower at the W. end. The body of the ch. is rough-cast, the tower of flint and red brick ; commonplace in character and uninteresting. The interior is better. The nave is divided from the aisles by octagonal shafts with beak mouldings (recarved) and round arches, and the N. aisle has some good details. *Bernard's*

Heath, on which was fought the second battle of St. Albans, is in this parish. (*See* ST. ALBANS, p. 544.)

SARRATT, HERTS, on the Buckinghamshire border, 4 m. N.W. from Rickmansworth, which is the nearest rly. stat.: pop. 654.

The houses lie in widely separated groups, the largest collection being at *Sarratt's Green*, on the King's Langley side of the par., where the road widens into a broad green, on either side of which is a row of small shops, cottages, and homesteads, not too closely packed.

Sarratt, "so called," says Chauncy, "from Syret, a Saxon, who, I suppose, was an ancient possessor of it," belonged to the Abbey of St. Albans from the time of Edward II. to the Dissolution. Lying away from any main line of road, and from the rail, it retains its primitive rusticity unaltered; stands in a pleasant neighbourhood, and has an interesting old church. The field walk to the ch. from Sarratt's Green, about a mile, carries you along high ground with, on your rt., an open stretch of undulating country, bounded by fine old woods, and the little Chess river winding through the broken valley.

The *Church* (of the Holy Cross) is a small cruciform E.E. building, with a long chancel, and a W. tower, the upper part of which is of early brickwork, ending in a gable roof. It had fallen into bad condition, but in 1866 was thoroughly restored, both inside and out, under the direction of Sir G. G. Scott, R.A.; the transepts extended westwards so as to form aisles; nine new windows inserted; the plaster ceiling removed and the old timber roof exposed; new open oak seats added, and the E. window filled with painted glass, by Clayton and Bell, representing the Crucifixion and Ascension. In removing the whitewash from the transepts and over the chancel arch, remains of some 13th or early 14th cent. paintings in distemper, apparently of events in the life of Christ, were uncovered: the most perfect (on the W. wall of the S. transept) was preserved. All the walls had been coloured of a deep red, and decorated with flowers, fruit, and foliage. S. of the chancel are a large and a smaller piscina, and on the N.

an ambry. The pulpit is old and noteworthy. *Obs.* on S. wall the 17th cent. mont., with small kneeling effigies of William Kingesley, with three sons behind him, and opposite his wife and daughter. *Sarratt Hall* (R. Branton Day, Esq.), at Micklefield Green, 1 m. S.E. from the ch., is the chief seat.

SEAL, KENT, a village on the Westerham and Maidstone road, 2½ m. N.E. from Sevenoaks, and 1½ m. E. of the Sevenoaks (Bat and Ball) Stat. of the L. C. and D., and S.-E. Rlys.: pop. 1590.

Seal is beautifully situated, amidst woods, parks, villas, broad commons, hop gardens, green fields, and shady lanes. The pursuits are agricultural; hops, wheat, and peas are largely grown; and the many resident gentry add to the prosperity. Seal *Church* (St. Peter) is of rubble-stone, large and interesting. It consists of nave with aisles, chancel with aisles or chapels, tall battlemented W. tower with angle turret, and stone porch on S. A portion of the nave arcade on the S. is E.E.; but the rest of the nave, S. aisle, and chancel are Dec. The N. aisle was added in 1855. The tower and porch, over which is a niche and within a holy water stoup, are Perp. The interior was thoroughly restored and embellished, and a new open timber roof and open seats added, in 1855. *Obs.* piscina on S. The S. or Camden Chapel belongs to the family at Wildernesse Park; the N. chapel to the Grove—the two chief seats in Seal. The painted glass windows in the chancel and Camden Chapel are memorials of the last two Marquises Camden and the late Marchioness. In the Camden Chapel is a mont. of Charles Pratt, Earl Camden, the famous Lord Chief Justice and Lord Chancellor, d. 1794; also a tablet to his father, Sir John Pratt, Chief Justice of the King's Bench, d. 1724. *Obs.* by door of vestry an insc. (the effigy gone) to "John Tibold alias Theobauld," d. 1577. In the chancel is a good *brass* of Wm. de Bryene, d. 1395; effigy in armour, the joints not marked; under the head is a very early example of the tilting helmet with crest and mantling. At W. end of nave is a slab with indents of man and woman.

In a large and richly wooded park immediately S. of the village, is *Wildernesse,* the fine seat of the Marquis Camden, now tenanted by Sir Charles H. Mills, Bart. M.P. *The Grove* is the seat of the Ladies Pratt. Other seats are *Under River House* (Miss Wood); *Fawke House* (C. G. Hale, Esq.), etc.

At *Under River* is an elegant little E.E. church, consecrated in 1874. It was erected as a memorial of his mother by the late Rt. Hon. J. R. Davidson, Q.C., of Under River House, from the designs of Sir G. G. Scott, R.A.

SELSDON, Surrey (*see* Croydon).

SEVENOAKS, Kent, a market

town, 6 m. N.W. from Tunbridge, and 23 m. from London by road ; 20 m. by the S.-E. Rly. (Dunton Green Stat.), and 25 m. by the L. C. and D. Rly. (Tubb's Hill Stat.) Pop. of the town 4118; of the par. 5949, but this includes the eccl. districts of Sevenoaks Weald, 742, and Riverhead, 750. Inns, the *Royal Crown Hotel*, overlooking Kippington Park, a first-class house ; *Royal Oak*, opposite the entrance to Knole Park, also an excellent house ; *Rose and Crown Hotel*, High Street ; *Railway Hotel*, and *Sennocke Arms Hotel*, by the Tubb's Hill Rly. Stat.

The name (anc. *Seovenaca*) is said to be derived from 7 oaks which stood near the town. Tradition points out as their successors the trees opposite the White Hart Inn, on the Tunbridge Road, nearly 1 m. from Sevenoaks. Its history is nearly a blank. "I finde not in all historie," writes old Lambarde (whose mont. is in Sevenoaks ch.), "any memorable thing concerning it, save onely that in the time of King Henry the sixt, Jack Cade, and his mischievous meiny, discomforted there Sir Humfrey Stafford and his brother, two noble gentlemen, whom the King had sent to encounter them." * But if the town has no history, it has a pleasant locality. It stands on the northern brow of a greensand range of highland, has Knole Park on one side of it and Kippington Park on the other and the surrounding country is beautiful, fertile, and well cultivated. The town consists of two main streets, which meet near the church, are lined with respect-

able houses, market-place, well-built bank, new county court house, an old Grammar School, and by it the gates of Knole, with an attractive avenue running from them. All around are fine old seats and modern villas. The pursuits are in the main agricultural, Sevenoaks being the centre of a rich corn and hop country, but the town is largely dependent on the numerous resident gentry. A market for corn is held every Saturday, and a stock market monthly.

The *Church* (St. Nicholas) at the S. end of the town, is a large and handsome Perp. building, and comprises nave and aisles, chancel, and lofty W. tower, in which is a peal of 8 bells. Standing on elevated ground, the tower is a conspicuous object for a considerable distance. The *int.* of the church is not remarkable, and its appearance is not improved by the galleries at the sides and W. end ; in the latter, however, is a good organ. In the S. aisle is a marble mural slab to Wm. Lambarde (d. 1601). "The Perambulator of Kent and the Father of county historians," removed from Greenwich on the demolition of the old ch. There are also monts. to the Dorset, Amherst, Fermor, and Boswell families, but none of particular interest. Thomas Farnaby, equally famous in the reign of Charles I. as a scholar, schoolmaster, and the editor of Greek and Roman authors, d. 1647, was buried in the chancel. He removed his school to Sevenoaks in 1636, accumulated wealth by his labours, and purchased Kippington and other property in the neighbourhood.

St. John's ch., St. John's Hill, a chapel-of-ease to St. Nicholas, is a neat little early Dec. building, erected in 1858, from the designs of Messrs. Morphew and Green. Other noticeable eccl. buildings are a Gothic (Dec.) Congregational ch., erected in 1866, which is some day to have a tall spire ; and a Wesleyan chapel built in 1853.

The *Grammar School* was founded in 1418, by Sir William Sevenoake, or Sennocke, who, a foundling in the streets, was brought up by the charity of some of the inhabitants, and apprenticed to a grocer in London. There he came in time to be Lord Mayor, and in gratitude founded a free grammar school and hospital in the town, where he was found,

---

* Lambarde, Perambulation of Kent, p. 470.

nurtured, and named after. The school was remodelled and the endowments enlarged in the reign of Elizabeth, and entitled Queen Elizabeth's Grammar School. School and Hospital were rebuilt in 1727 ; and the school buildings have been restored and enlarged, and the school arrangements improved, within the last few years. It now bears a good name. and has several scholarships and exhibitions to Cambridge. George Grote, the historian of Greece, is the most illustrious of its scholars. Elijah Fenton, the friend of Pope, and his colleague in translating the Odyssey, was for a time an assistant in the school, and then " kept a school for himself at Sevenoaks, which he brought into reputation ; but was persuaded to leave it (1710), by Mr. St. John, with promises of a more honourable employment."*

Sevenoaks Hospital, or almshouse, adjoins the school, and affords lodging and an annuity of 6s. a week to 20 poor persons, and lodging without the gratuity to 12 more. There is another endowed free-school, now conducted on the national system, founded by Lady Margaret Boswell, wife of Sir William Boswell, ambassador from Charles I. at the Hague. A cottage hospital has been recently established in Holm Dale, St. John's Hill.

Knole, E. of the town, is described elsewhere (*see* KNOLE). *Kippington Park*, the seat of W. J. Thompson, Esq., is a good mansion, the park small but pleasant. Among the many other mansions around Sevenoaks are—*The Mount*, the fine seat of Lieut.-Col. W. Brook Northey ; *Ashgroves* (Kirkman D. Hodgson, Esq., M.P.), famous for its gardens; *Beechmont* (Multon Lambarde, Esq., D.L.) ; *Riverhill House* (J. Thornton Rogers, Esq.), noted for the extensive views obtained from both house and grounds ; *Shaw Well* (Percival Battiscombe, Esq.)

Sevenoaks Weald is an eccl. dist. formed out of Sevenoaks par. in 1861. The vill. is pleasantly situated, in the midst of hop-gardens, on the Penshurst road, about 2 m. S. of Sevenoaks. The pursuits are almost wholly agricultural. The little *ch.* (St. George), built in 1820, was enlarged in 1872 by the addition of a

* Johnson, Lives of the Poets : Fenton.

chancel—prettily finished, with windows of stained glass. Here are almshouses for 8 poor persons. *Riverhead*, the other eccl. dist. of Sevenoaks, has a separate notice. (*See* RIVERHEAD.)

SEVERNDROOG CASTLE, KENT (*see* SHOOTER'S HILL).

SEWARDSTONE, ESSEX, a hamlet of Waltham Abbey, on the W. border of Epping Forest, and the lower road from Chingford to Waltham Abbey, about midway (2½ m.) between those two places. It is a long, rambling, and loosely-connected district, including Sewardstone Street, Sewardstone Green, Sewardstone Bury, Sewardstone Mill, Sewardstone Wood, etc., stretching N. and S. from Waltham Abbey to Low Street, Chingford, and E. and W. from Sewardstone Wood and High Beech, in Epping Forest, to Sewardstone Mill on the Lea ; a varied and often picturesque tract, in parts thickly wooded, occasionally hilly, and affording wide prospects ; much of it out-of-the-way, primitive-looking, and little visited. The pursuits are agricultural, but there are large dye works at Sewardstone Mills, on the Lea. Near Sewardstone Mills is *Sewardstone Lodge* (W. Melles, Esq.), a good house with pretty grounds sloping to the Lea. Other seats are *The Grange* (P. Mills, Esq.) ; *Gilwell Park* (W. A. Gibbs, Esq.), a handsome house in a small park by Sewardstone Green ; and *Yardley House* (J. S. Davies, Esq.), near Low Street. Sewardstone has a tradition that it was once a distinct parish, named after one Seward, a great Saxon thane, and used to show a heap of broken ground as the site of the old church.

SHEEN, EAST, SURREY, a hamlet of Mortlake, lies on the road from Putney to Richmond, ¼ m. S. of the Mortlake Stat. of the L. and S.-W. Rly.

Sheen is charmingly situate on a gentle upland, with villas all around, standing amidst ample grounds, and abounding in noble trees, while a pleasant walk of about ½ m. leads through its still more sylvan satellite, *Upper Sheen*, to the Sheen Gate of Richmond Park. East Sheen *Church* (Christ Ch.), a chapel-of-ease to Mortlake, was built in 1863, from the designs of Mr. A. W. Blomfield, as a memorial of Edward Penrhyn, Esq., of East Sheen. It is a picturesque Dec. building of Bargate and Bath stone, has nave and S. aisle of 4 bays with gables, chancel, and tower; the interior is richly decorated, has shafts of marble, stone, and slate, and several memorial windows of painted glass. Among the many villas are—*Sheen House* (Col. Marcus Beresford, M.P.); *The Cedars* (E. H. L. Penrhyn, Esq.); *Palewell Lodge* (J. J. M'Andrew, Esq.) At *Upper Sheen* are—*The Observatory* (Lady Denison), noted for the grounds and views; *Halsteads* (Lord Radstock); *Temple Grove* (Ottiwel C. Waterfield, Esq.), in the 17th cent. the residence of Sir John Temple, Master of the Rolls in Ireland, and brother of the more celebrated Sir Wm. Temple. Sir John d. in 1674, and was buried in Mortlake ch. Temple Grove descended to his grandson, Henry, 1st Viscount Palmerston, who lived in it many years, and rebuilt the garden front. On the d. of the 2nd Viscount, it was sold to Thos. Bernard, Esq., who rebuilt the road front. It was afterwards occupied for some years as a superior boarding-school. *Uplands* is the residence of Sir Henry Taylor, the author of 'Philip Van Artevelde.' *Park Cottage*, of Edwin Chadwick, Esq., C.B. Immediately within the gate of Richmond Park is *Sheen Lodge*, since 1852 the residence of Prof. Owen.

SHEEN, WEST, SURREY.

Sheen was the original name of Richmond, and a royal palace stood on the W. side of the present Richmond Green, between it and the river. Henry V. founded in 1414 a convent of Carthusians, which he called the *House of Jesus of Bethlehem at Sheen*. The buildings, which were of great extent, stood about ¼ m. N.W. of the palace, and about them grew up a hamlet, which later was called *West Sheen*. The convent was richly endowed, and had several cells, or alien priories. Perkin Warbeck sought refuge in it; Cardinal Pole in early life spent two years "in studious retirement" in lodgings granted to him in the convent; Dean Colet, the founder of St. Paul's School, built a house within the precincts, spent his last years there, and there d. in 1519; and it was to the Convent of Sheen that the Earl of Surrey carried the body of James IV. of Scotland for interment,

after the fatal fight of Flodden. It is said, however, to have remained there unburied; and about 1552 Stow saw in a lumber-room of the convent a body wrapped in lead, which he was told was the body of the Scottish king: that it really was the body of James IV. is, however, very doubtful.[*]

At the Dissolution, the convent had a revenue of £777. The prior who made the surrender, Henry Man, was conformable, and somewhat later was made Dean of Chester and Bishop of Man. Queen Mary restored the convent in Jan. 1557, but it lasted hardly two years, being again suppressed at her decease. "The monks retired to Bruges in 1559; to Louvain in 1578; to Mechlin in 1591; their successors removed to Nieuport, in Flanders, in 1626, where they continued till 1783; there were then only three professed monks and two lay-brothers, being the only English convent of monks that had never been dispersed."[†] The history of the migrations and persistence of an English convent of nuns, the Sisters of Syon, is, however, even more remarkable. (*See* ISLEWORTH.)

Henry VIII. granted the priory to the Earl of Hertford, afterwards Duke of Somerset, on whose attainder in 1551 the priory estate was transferred to his rival, Henry Duke of Suffolk, father of Lady Jane Grey, on whose fall it reverted to the Crown. It was granted for life by Elizabeth to Sir Thomas Gorges and his wife, Helen, widow of William Parr, Marquis of Northampton; and by Charles I., in 1638, to James, Duke of Lenox. By the Parliamentary surveyors it was valued, as Crown land, at £92 per annum, and purchased by William Eaton. The survey described the priory church as standing, but very ruinous; the buildings comprised the Prior's Lodgings, of brick; the Monks' Hall, of stone; the Lady of St. John's Lodgings; the Anchorite's Cell; and a building called The Gallery.

Soon after his restoration, Charles II. granted a lease of The Priory for 60 years to Lord Lisle, who the next year sold it to Lord Bellasys, but continued for some

[*] Stow, Annals; Lysons, Environs, vol. i., p. 331.

[†] Lysons, vol. i., p. 352; Abbé Man, Account of English Convents on the Continent: Archæologia, vol. xiii., p. 254.

years to reside here. Bellasys in 1662 surrendered the lease to the Crown, and obtained a renewal of the grant for 60 years.

In 1675 a new lease was granted to trustees for Henry (afterwards Lord) Brouncker, and Sir William Temple. Brouncker occupied the mansion, Temple a house which he had for some years rented. Sir William had looked to his "little corner at Sheen" as his English home and haven during his long diplomatic residence at Brussels (1666 and onwards), his wife the greater part of the time living at Sheen; and in the midst of his political negotiations he wrote to Lord Lisle (Aug. 1667) that he was "contriving this summer how a succession of cherries may be compassed from May to Michaelmas, and how the riches of Sheen vines may be improved by half-a-dozen sorts which are not known there, and which I think much beyond any that are." *

Temple brought over his cherries, and he "had the honour," as he is careful to record in his famous Essay on Gardening, "of bringing over four sorts of vines into England," as well as "the Brussels apricock which grows a standard, and is one of the best fruits we have, and which I brought over among us;" and "I may truly say, that the French who have eaten my peaches and grapes at Sheen in no ill year, have generally concluded that the last are as good as any they have eaten in France on this side Fontainebleau, and the first as good as any they have eat in Gascony." Further, the 'Sheen plum' was one of the best of its kind. and his oranges as good as any he had seen in France, except at Fontainebleau, or in the Low Countries, except some very old trees in the Prince of Orange's gardens. Temple's Sheen garden became a great attraction. Evelyn visited the two houses after Lord Brouncker's death.

"24 *March*, 1688.—I went with Sir Charles Littleton to Sheen, an house and estate given by

* Sir William had been visiting the Bishop of Munster, who, as he relates in his Essay on Gardening, had no trees but cherries in a great garden he had made; the reason, as he told Temple, was that he found no other fruit would ripen well in that climate, and so he had limited his curiosity to cherries, "whereof he had so many as never to be without them from May to the end of September."—Miscellania, p. 119.

Lord Brouncker. . . . It is a pretty place, with fine gardens, and well planted, and given to one worthy of them, Sir Charles being an honest gentleman and soldier. . . . After dinner we went to see Sir William Temple's next to it: the most remarkable things are his orangery and gardens, where the wall fruit trees are most exquisitely nailed and trained, far better than I ever noted elsewhere. There are many good pictures, especially of Vandyck's, in both these houses, and some few statues and small busts in the latter."*

When Temple wrote his 'Essay upon the Gardens of Epicurus; or of Gardening in the Year 1685,' he was living at Sheen, fully recompensed, as he writes, by the sweetness and satisfaction of this retreat for having withdrawn from all public employments; and here, he adds, "I have passed five years without ever going once to Town." He gave up his Sheen house soon after to his son John, and went to live at Moor Park, Surrey, but the events of 1688 recalled him to the seat of government. About this time Jonathan Swift became a member of his household. Distant relation, half secretary, half amanuensis, it was a situation Swift did not like in after-years to refer to, but perhaps was not the least pleasant or profitable portion of his gloomy life. Intercourse with the old diplomatist opened to him new views of life; access to a splendid library helped to extend his present narrow store of learning; and teaching Hester Johnson was a pleasant relief from obsequious attendance upon one who never forgot what was due to his position. William III. had known Temple when in Holland, and, like all the statesmen of his day, entertained a high opinion of his abilities, and would gladly have secured his assistance in his new ministry. Temple refused all offers, and William, unable to change his resolution, used to come over frequently from Hampton Court or Kensington to consult the sage, or discuss the condition of Europe. William was as fond of gardens as Temple, and the Sheen garden was a revival of a Dutch paradise. When Temple was confined to his room by gout, Swift was deputed to attend the King in his walks round the garden; and it was here, and not at Moor Park, as is commonly said, that William instructed him in the Dutch mode of cooking and eating asparagus, and offered him

* Evelyn, Diary.

the captaincy of a troop of horse. Swift did not take orders till some years later. Temple left Sheen for good in 1689.

Little more need be told of West Sheen. About 1769 there remained a gateway of the priory; by it was the hamlet, which then consisted of 18 houses. A lane to the hamlet crossed the Lower Park. It was the time when George III. was bent on Kew and Richmond improvements, and he wished to sweep away whatever obstructed them. The necessary powers were obtained, the road was closed, the priory gate pulled down, the hamlet demolished, and the whole site laid down in turf. Not a vestige of West Sheen has since been visible, though it is said that in very dry summers traces of the buildings may be made out by the browner grass.

SHENFIELD, Essex, on the Chelmsford road, 1 m. N.E. of Brentwood, and ½ a mile W. of the Shenfield stat. of the Gt. E. Rly.; pop. 1232, of whom 248 are in the eccl. dist. of Christ Church.

The vill. lies along the turnpike road, and contains several of the ordinary small characterless Essex roadside cottages, a few of a better class, shops, and an inn. Part of Brentwood is in Shenfield par., and houses straggle on from the village to the town. The *Church* (St. Mary the Virgin) stands solitary, a field's length away from, but in sight of, the vill. It was restored in 1853, and bears marks of the restorer's hand in a coating of dark gray rough-cast and rechiselled mouldings and window tracery, but is still interesting. It consists of a nave and chancel, originally of E.E. date, with a narrow north aisle and chapel, added in the 15th cent., a tower and tall thin wooden spire, and a deep carved oak Perp. S. porch. The int. is plain, but *obs.* the remarkable solid oaken piers, carved to appear like clustered columns, which divide the nave and aisle and carry low wooden arches. Both piers and arches have been mutilated and mended, but should be examined, as they are almost unique. Of the original E.E. work little is left, though some remains are traceable, as in the wall-plate, with dog-tooth ornament at the E. end of the S. wall. The windows are all Perp., and some are filled with modern painted glass. *Obs.* The marble mont.,

N. of the altar, with recumbent effigy of Eliz. Robinson, d. 1652.*

N. of the ch. is *Shenfield Hall*, a many-gabled 15th cent. manor-house, now a farm-house. The manor passed in the 14th century to Thomas of Woodstock, 6th son of Edward III.; belonged in the next cent. to Humphrey Duke of Buckingham, on whose death, at the battle of Northampton, it was seized by Edward IV. and settled on his wife, Queen Elizabeth. It afterwards passed to the Lucas family, and in 1644 gave title to Baron Lucas of Shenfield, whose daughter carried it to the Duke of Kent, from whose family it went in the 18th century, by marriage, to the Earl of Hardwick. It now belongs to the Countess Cowper. A second manor-house, *Fitzwalters*, but locally known as the Round House, 1½ m. N.E. of the vill., was destroyed by fire some years back, and not rebuilt. *Middleton Hall*, on l. of the road near Brentwood, is the seat of the Countess Tasker. Other seats are *Shenfield Place* (E. Courage. Esq.), by the road S. of the ch.; *Park House* (W. G. Bartleet, Esq.)

SHENLEY, Herts, (Dom. *Scenlai*) 2 m. E.N.E. from Radlett Stat. of the Midland Rly., along a crooked but pleasant lane direct from the stat., and for the greater part of the way by Porters Park. The par., of 1380 inh. (of whom 382 belong to the eccl. dist. of Colney St. Peter), extends from Barnet to London Colney, nearly 6 miles. The par. ch. is ¾ m. N. of the village, which is clustered about the cross-way, S.E. of Porters. Inn, *Black Lion.*

At the Domesday Survey, Shenley belonged to the Abbot of St. Albans and Geoffry de Mandeville; the present lord of the manor is T. B. Myers, Esq. The *Church* (St. Botolph), which stands alone, a little rt. of the road to St. Albans, is of chalk faced with squared flints, with brick buttresses, and consists of nave and chancel, with a square wooden tower and tiled roof at the S.W. It is throughout Perp. in style, and the large 4-light E. and W. windows, as well as two or three others, are filled with memorial painted

---

* Shenfield ch. is engraved and described in Buckler's Twenty-two of the Churches of Essex, pp. 68—80.

glass. The ch. has been partially restored, but still looks fitting companion of the antique yews in the ch.-yard. Of these, one immense tree with hollow trunk, but green and bushy top, stands close to the E. end of the ch.; on the S.W. is another nearly as large; while 4 more, of smaller dimensions but of venerable years, are at the corners of the ch.-yard. On the S. side of the ch. is an old sundial. *Obs.* in ch.-yard, the mont. of Nicholas Hawksmoor, d. 1736, the architect of St. George's, Bloomsbury, St. Mary Woolnoth, Lombard Street, and other well-known London churches. Owing to the distance of the ch. from the bulk of the population, a neat chapel-of-ease has been built in the centre of the vill., in which the aft. and evening services are performed, the morning service being still held in the old church. *Porters* is now the residence of H. W. Eaton, Esq., M.P. Other seats are—*High Canons* (R. Durant, Esq.), on l. of the main road, 1½ m. S.E. from Shenley vill.; *Shenley Hill* (F. Alleyne McGeachy, Esq.); *Shenley Lodge* (H. E. Chetwynd Stapleton, Esq.)

SHEPHERD'S BUSH, MIDDX., a

hamlet and eccl. dist. of Hammersmith par., and a stat. of the Metr. Dist. Rly., on the Uxbridge road, 3 m. from the Marble Arch, and a short m. N. of Hammersmith Broadway: pop. 8733.

The old village, consisting of dwellings mostly small, shops, and an inn, was built about a triangular green, at the parting of the New Road (to Turnham Green) from the main Uxbridge road; but of late years new villas, cottages, and shops of the usual suburban type have extended along the roads, and new streets have been laid out in various directions. The place has little to interest any one. The green, a flat treeless common of 8½ acres, has been secured for public use, and is now under the charge of the Metropolitan Board of Works: it appears to be chiefly used by boys as a cricket ground. The dist. *Church* (St. Stephen's), in the Uxbridge road, W. of the Green, is a good stone building for 600 persons, erected at the cost of Bp. Blomfield in 1849-50, from the designs of Mr. A. Salvin. It consists of nave, aisles, and chancel, and a tower and spire at the N.W. 150 ft. high. The interior is roomy

and well fitted, and several of the windows have painted glass. Another ch., (St. Paul's), Gothic, like St. Stephen's, but of less costly character, has been recently erected in the Uxbridge road; and there are 3 or 4 chapels. *Wormholt Scrubs*—also in Hammersmith parish—is about a mile N.

SHEPPERTON or SHEPERTON,

MIDDX. (A.-S. *Sceapheardton* = Shepherd's Town: Dom. *Scepertone*), a vill. on the Thames, immediately above Halliford, and the terminus of the Shepperton br. of the L. and S.-W. Rly. Pop. of par. 1126. Inns, the *Anchor*, the *Crown; Railway*, by the stat.

Shepperton is a quiet little river-side vill., chiefly visited by anglers and boating-men, but having about it some good residences hidden away behind tall old elms. The Green has around it large elms and horse-chesnuts. The reaches of the river are very pretty; the surrounding country level, but green and pleasant. *Shepperton Deeps* are much resorted to for barbel, roach, perch, jack, and occasional trout fishing. The Upper Deep, 200 yards; the Old Deep, E. of the Creek rails, 240 yds.; and the Lower Deep, 200. Shepperton Creek is also available. Punts and boats may be hired, the Purdues and Rogersons are fishermen of old standing, and the Anchor and the Crown are reasonable anglers' inns. At the former used to be a portrait of a fish taken here, with the insc. under it, "Oct. 3, 1812, at Shepperton Deeps, Mr. G. Marshall, of Brewer Street, London, caught a salmon with a single gut, without a landing net, weighing 21¼ lb." Salmon are no longer caught here, but it is not unusual to take a trout from 7 to 10 or 12 lb. Punt and skiff building is now carried on to some extent. There is a ferry over the Thames from near Shepperton ch.

The *Church* (St. Nicholas) stands close by the river. It is small, cruciform, Perp. The body of flint and stone in squares, of the 16th cent., but partially rebuilt several years ago. The brick tower, at the W. end, was built in 1710, by the Rev. Lewis Atterbury, the rector, brother of the noted Bp. of Rochester. Wm. Grocyn, the friend and correspondent of Erasmus, and one of the earliest teachers of Greek at Oxford, was rector 1504-13.

The principal seats are—the *Manor House* (Wm. Schaw Lindsay, Esq.); *Shepperton Creek* (Sir P. Colquhoun, Q.C.) ; *Halliford House* (H. H. Blyth, Esq.)

Roman and other remains have on several occasions been found in this neighbourhood. A good vase was dug up in 1817 in a field S.W. of the vill. On the E., between Shepperton Field and Walton Bridge, appears to have been a Roman cemetery. In 1868, various remains, reported to be Saxon, were found at the junction of Shepperton Range and Littleton. (*See* HALLIFORD.)

SHIRLEY, SURREY, a hamlet of Croydon, 2 m. E. of the East Croydon Stat. of the L., B., and S. C. Rly., on the road to Addington and Wickham; pop. 683. Inns, *Sandrock Hotel ; Crown.*

The neighbourhood is exceedingly pleasant, and Shirley Common is still a broad, open, breezy tract, though circumscribed in extent of late years, and very different to what Hone described it in 1827,* when broom-making was extensively carried on here, the materials being obtained from the common and the adjacent woods and copses. Hone's "John Bennett, broom maker and wood dealer," is however still represented by descendants at Shirley, Wm. Bennett and Son, "wood brokers." Many villas and genteel cottages have been built at Upper and Lower Shirley, but the district is still rural. *Shirley House,* the fine seat of the Earl of Eldon (now tenanted by Fredk. Bambury, Esq.), lies on the Addiscombe side of Shirley; the grounds are rich and picturesque. Shirley was created an eccl. dist. in 1846. The *Church* (St. John the Evangelist), erected in 1856, is a pretty little building of black flint and stone, Dec. in style, with a richly ornamented chancel, stained glass E. window, and a good organ.

SHOOTER'S HILL, KENT, be- tween the 8th and 9th milestones on the Dover road; an isolated mass of London clay, rising to an elevation of 446 ft.

* Hone, Table Book, col. 449, etc.

above the Ordnance datum, famous for its prospect of London and the valley of the Thames, and of old a notorious haunt for highwaymen—whence indeed it is said to have derived its name.

"Shooter's Hill, so called for the thievery there practised, where travellers in elder times were so much infested with depredations and bloody mischiefs, that order was taken in the 6th year of Richard II., for the enlarging the highway, according to the statute made in the time of King Edward I., so that they venture still to rob here by prescription; and some have been so impudent to offer to engage the sun shining at mid-day, for the repayment of money called borrowed in a thievish way, to the great charge of the hundred that still was in the counter-bond : and King Henry IV. granted leave to Thomas Chapman to cut down, burn, and sell all the woods and underwoods, growing and confining to Shooter's Hill, on the S. side, and to bestow the money raised thereby, upon mending the highway." *

"Surely," continues old Philipott, "Prince Henry his son, and Sir John Falstaff his make sport, so merrily represented in Shakepeare's comedies, were now the surveyors." Whoever were the surveyors, the ways were not mended. A quarter of a century after Philipott, Oldham writes (1682),

"Oft we encounter midnight Padders here :

* * * *

Hither in flocks from *Shooter's Hill* they come,
To seek their prize and booty nearer home :
'Your purse !' they cry ; 'tis madness to resist,
Or strive, with a cock'd pistol at your breast." †

The road continued a steep and narrow way closed in by thick woods, a convenient harbour for highwaymen, till about 1733, when a "road of easier ascent and of great width was laid out at some distance from the old one ;"‡ but long after highwaymen lingered about it. For discouraging robbers the usual methods were adopted, and Shooter's Hill was seldom without the ornament of a gibbet.

"*April* 11*th*, 1661.— . . . Of all the journies I ever made this [from Dartford to London] was the merriest. . . . Among other things I got my lady to let her maid, Mrs. Anne, to ride all the way on horseback. . . . Mrs. Anne and I rode under the man that hangs upon Shooter's Hill, and a filthy sight it was to see how his flesh is shrunk to his bones." §

* Philipott, Vill. Cant., 1659, p. 135.
+ Oldham, A Satyr, in imitation of the Third of Juvenal : Works, ed. 1703, p. 449.
‡ Hasted, Hist. of Kent, vol. i., p. 60 ; Lysons, vol. i., p. 491.
§ Pepys, Diary, vol. i., p. 211.

The hill maintained its reputation long after the new road was made. Don Juan, it will be remembered, having alighted at Shooter's Hill to enjoy the prospect of London, was accosted by a minion of the moon with the usual demand, "Your money or your life"—and laid his assailant dead with a shot from his pocket pistol. Byron's description of the prospect from "the high hill, which looks with pride or scorn toward the great city," is characteristic:

"A mighty mass of brick, and smoke, and shipping,
Dirty and dusky, but as wide as eye
Could reach, with here and there a sail just skipping
In sight, then lost amidst the forestry
Of masts : a wilderness of steeples peeping
On tiptoe through their sea-coal canopy ;
A huge, dim cupola, like a foolscap crown
On a fool's head—and there is London Town !"*

But in the olden time the hill was renowned for shooting of another order. On May-day 1515, Henry VIII. and his Queen, accompanied by many lords and ladies, "rode to the high ground of Shooter's Hill to take the open air."

"And as they passed by the way, they espied a company of tall yomen, clothed all in grene with grene whodes and bowes and arrowes, to the number of iiC. Then one of them, which called him selfe Robyn Hood, came to the kyng, desyring him to se his men shoote, and the kyng was content. Then he whistled, and al the iiC. archers shot and losed at once, and then he whisteled agayne, and they likewyse shot agayne, their arrowes whisteled by crafte of the head, so that the noyes was strange and great, and much pleased the kynge and quene and all the company. All these archers were of the kynge's garde. . . . Then Robyn Hood desyred the kynge and quene to come into the grene wood and see how the outlawes lyve. The king demanded of yᵉ quene and her ladyes, if they durst adventure to go into the wood with so many outlawes? Then the quene sayde, that if it pleased him, she was content ; then the hornes blewe tyl they came to the wood under Shoters Hil, and there was an Arber made of boowes (boughs) with a hal, and a great chamber and an inner chamber, very well made and covered with floures and swete herbes, which the kyng much praysed. Then said Robyn Hood, 'Sir, Outlawes brekefastes is venyson, and therefore you must be content with such fare as we use.' Then the kynge and quene sate doune, and were served with venyson and wyne by Robyn Hood and his men to their contentacion. Then the kyng departed and hys company, and Robyn Hood and his men them conducted." †

Of the pageant that met them on their

* Don Juan, c. x., v. lxxxii.
† Hall, Chronicle, p. 582.

way back to Greenwich it does not belong to us to speak. There is a tradition that Queen Elizabeth was wont to come here sometimes a-maying, but no such pretty spectacle has ever again been seen on Shooter's Hill as that of King Henry's greeting by Robin Hood and his men.

Shooter's Hill is a sufficiently quiet place now. The woods have been cut down or enclosed ; the hill spotted over with genteel villas. The name has been appropriated to an eccl. dist. formed in 1865 out of the parishes of Eltham, Woolwich, and Lewisham, which numbered 461 inh. in 1871. A neat E.E. district church, *Christ Church*, was built on the W. slope of the hill in 1865, but proving inadequate to the growing requirements a new one (All Saints) has been recently erected in the Englefield road. Here too are the Cordwainers' and Bread Street Ward Schools.

On the summit of the hill, a short distance on the rt. of the road, is *Severndroog Castle*, erected in 1784 from the designs of Mr. Jupp, by Lady James, of Park Farm House, in commemoration of the gallantry of her husband, Sir Wm. James (d. 1783), " and in a peculiar manner to record the conquest of the Castle of Severn Droog, on the coast of Malabar, which fell to his superior valour and able conduct on the 2nd day of April, 1755." The Castle is a triangular brick tower, of three floors, about 45 ft. high, with taller turrets at the angles, and windows of unequal size and equal ugliness. Inside were placed armour, weapons, etc., captured at Severndroog. From the summit (482 ft. high) the prospect has always been celebrated. It is somewhat circumscribed now by the growth of the trees, and is seen to most advantage in early spring or at the end of autumn. The tower is now closed and much dilapidated, but admission can generally be obtained on proper application : and on a clear day it is worth obtaining.

Just beyond the castle a spacious semi-gothic red brick villa, *Castle Wood* (H. T. Jackson, Esq.), has been recently erected, which commands almost unbroken views. Close by is *Castle House* (Mrs. Harris). *Park Farm House* is now the residence of Col. G. Boothby. Other villas are *Denholm Lodge* (Gen. Fred. Aug. Yorke, R.E.) ; *The Shrubbery* (Col.

T. Close) ; *Elmhurst* (Col. R. Young Shipley); *Perrina Lodge* (Major H. Brackenbury), etc.

On the summit of the hill is a mineral spring, once of repute : William Godbid wrote an account of it in 1673, and Evelyn records that he "drank the Shooters Hill waters" in 1699. The tea-gardens of the Bull inn at the top of the hill were a favourite summer resort in the last century, and the house was noted for wedding dinners.

The *Herbert Hospital*, Kidbrooke Common, the hospital for the Woolwich garrison, is on the W. slope of Shooter's Hill, by the road to Eltham. It was erected in 1866 from designs prepared in the Engineers' department, under the direction of Capt. D. Galton. It is built of Suffolk brick and stone, on the pavilion system, and comprises 6 parallel blocks, in which are the hospital wards, providing 650 beds ; a central block containing the chapel, day-room, library, etc.; and at right angles to these, facing the Dover road, and presenting to it an ornamental front, the Administrative block. These are all detached buildings (standing 63 ft. apart), but connected by covered corridors. There are besides separate and contagious wards, offices, etc. The appliances are ample and complete, and the general arrangements much commended by professional men.

SHOREHAM, KENT, a vill. on the Darent, about 5 m. N. of Sevenoaks, through Otford, and a stat. on the Sevenoaks br. of the L. C. and D. Rly. Pop. 1300, of whom 89 are in the eccl. dist. of St. Mary Woodlands. Inns, *George*, by ch. ; *Crown*, at N. end of vill.

The vill. is picturesquely placed in a narrow valley, the Darent, here crossed by an old stone bridge of two arches, flowing through the village, fringed with willows, and having a large corn mill at one extremity and a larger paper mill at the other. The chalk hills, into which the river has here cut deeply, rise high on either hand, and afford fine views over a great extent of varied country, with the Valley of the Darent winding northward among the hills by Lullingstone and Farningham towards the Thames, and southwards expanding into the broad and pleasant Holmesdale. Be-

yond is the richly wooded Greensand range of Sevenoaks. The soil of Shoreham is chalk and loamy marl, and there are hop grounds, corn fields, and fruit gardens all around. These afford the chief employment, but the paper-mills of Mr. G. Wilmot at the N. end of the vill. employ many hands.

There are old manors, old families, and in the reign of Henry VIII. there were the ruins of an old castle at Shoreham ; but their history is of no general interest, and of the castle only the memory is preserved in the picturesque old Castle Farm.

The *Church* (St. Peter and St. Paul), on the E. side of the vill., is of flint, Kentish rag, and Bath-stone, the earlier part Dec., the later Perp.; comprises nave and N. aisle, short S. aisle or chapel, chancel, and low tower at the W. end, of flint and brick, with pinnacles at the angles, clock and peal of 6 bells. The *int.*, restored in 1865, and reseated with good oak benches, is wide and lofty, has an arcade of tall light columns and arches, a plain old open timber roof, and several painted glass windows. The nave is shut off from the chancel by a very perfect *rood screen*, restored, but in the main old, of carved oak, with doorway on the N. The stairs, and door opening on to the top of the screen, are still perfect. The font is old, but not otherwise remarkable. There are some showy and well-carved 18th cent. mural monts., to members of the Borrett family. Before leaving the ch.-yard, *obs.* on S.W. of ch. the picturesque old oak porch, covered with ivy, and the lich-gate at the entrance.

At *Shoreham Place*, the seat of H. St. John Mildmay, Esq.—a fine mansion in very picturesque grounds—is a small but choice collection of Dutch and Flemish pictures. Other good residences are *Water House* (S. Love, Esq.) ; *Dunstall Priory* (R. H. Borwick, Esq.); and *Darent Holme*, the pleasant abode of Prof. Prestwich, the distinguished geologist.

From Shoreham there is a charming walk along fields and the river to Lullingstone Castle. (*See* LULLINGSTONE.) Pass the Crown, and turn by the paper-mill into the field-path with the river on the rt.; proceed through hop-gardens (and at hop-picking time it is a lively scene along here), and by the Castle Farm, a picturesque old half-timber, overhanging, many gabled, and tall-roofed house, set off by heavy masses of elms, and looking out upon the willow-fringed river.

SHORTLANDS, KENT (*see* BECKENHAM).

SION HOUSE, MIDDX. (*see* SYON HOUSE).

SIDCUP, KENT, a hamlet and eccl.

dist. of Chiselhurst, and a station on the North Kent Loop-line of the S.-E. Rly., is situated on the Maidstone road, 11 m. from London, and 1 m. N.W. of Foot's Cray. Pop. 883. Inns, *Black Horse Hotel; Railway Tavern.*

The village stands in a pleasant country, on which, however, the builder is making inroads. Fruit is grown extensively. The *Church* (St. John the Evangelist), erected in 1844, and partly remodelled in 1874, is of brick and flint, Byzantine in style, with 2 towers at the W. end, and an apsidal chancel. The interior is richly fitted: *obs.* the carved oak pulpit (inscribed Antwerp, 1851) and reading desk, and the finely carved marble reredos. The painted glass windows are memorials of the late Lord Bexley, of Foot's Cray, and of Richard and Henry Berens of Sidcup, the principal contributors to the erection and endowment of the ch. The handsome almshouse was built and endowed by Mr. H. Berens for six unmarried ladies above the age of 45. The principal seats are—*Sidcup*, (H. Halse Berens, Esq.); *Sidcup Place* (J. Gooch Hepburn, Esq.); the *Manor House* (Misses Hoare); *Belmont House* (J. Gundry, Esq.)

SLOUGH, BUCKINGHAMSHIRE, a

long straggling town on the Bath road, 21 m. from London, 2½ m. N. of Windsor, and a stat. on the Grt. W. Rly., 18 m. Pop. 4509.

As a town Slough has little to arrest attention. Of late years it has greatly increased in extent and population. Many genteel houses have been built around it; and a new suburb of villas, Upton Park, has been formed, with reading and billiard rooms, and over 30 acres of pleasure-grounds. The streets of Slough are lined with good shops and dwellings, and there

are various offices and institutes. At the E. end of the town are the noted nurseries of Messrs. Turner—always worth visiting, but especially so in the rose season. A market, chiefly for cattle, is held on Tuesday.

Slough is for the most part in the parish of Upton-cum-Chalvey, and old Upton ch. was the only ch. for Slough till 1837, when a new ch. was erected in the High Street, and some time after made the parish ch. It is (1876) about to be replaced by a larger and more ecclesiastical structure. A new and rather elaborate ch. by Mr. G. E. Street was erected at Chalvey in 1861, and another has since been added to the number, whilst old Upton ch. has been restored, and is again used for divine service.

The *British Orphan Asylum*, by the Slough stat., was founded in 1827 "for the maintenance, clothing, and education of destitute orphans, from all parts of the British empire, whose parents were once in prosperous circumstances." The house was at Clapham Rise till 1865, when Mr. Edw. Mackenzie, of Fawley Court, Henley-on-Thames, purchased the large building known as the Queen's Hotel, by Slough stat., remodelled the interior, added a large dining-hall and school-room, and presented the house and grounds to the institution. The place, named after its donor *Mackenzie Park*, was formally opened by the Prince of Wales, Jan. 25, 1865. A new wing was added to the building in 1875, and it now contains about 250 children of both sexes.

A little way out of the town, on the l. of the Windsor road, stands a plain old red-brick dwelling, of old *Ivy House*, now called *Herschels*, memorable as for nearly 40 years the residence of Sir William Herschel. Here he constructed his Forty-foot Telescope, which he set up in the garden in 1786; made his numerous and most important discoveries, and here died in 1822. Here also lived and laboured, till Herschel's death, his sister, Caroline Herschel, with a success that added lustre to the name. Here too Sir J. F. W. Herschel was born; and here commenced, and till 1840 prosecuted, his great astronomical observations and researches.

The Forty-foot Telescope excited unbounded interest when first made, no instrument approaching it in size having up to that time been seen. Miss Caroline Herschel relates that before the optical parts were finished, the family assembled inside the vast tube, and "'God save the King' was sung in it by the whole company." Many visitors, she adds, "had the curiosity to walk through it, among the rest King George III.; and the Abp. of Canterbury, following the King, and finding it difficult to proceed, the King turned round to give him the hand, saying, 'Come, my Lord Bishop, I will show you the way to Heaven!'" [*]

When Sir John Herschel left Slough the telescope was laid in the garden, on three stone piers horizontally, the optical apparatus placed "inside of the tube and riveted up from all intruders; and all the polishing apparatus *fixed* on the spot." There the valued relic is religiously preserved. "The great mirror is now put up in the hall of the house—*Herschels*—by the present tenant, Mr. Montressor, who has spared no pains to do honour to the relics as well as to keep up the character of the old-fashioned 'habitation' which owes much to the taste and judgment he has bestowed on it." [†]

A short mile W. of the Slough Stat. on the Bath road, is *Salt Hill*, with the *Mons*, tumulus or hillock, the goal of the old Eton Montem. (*See* ETON.) Of old there were two or three hotels, but with the abolition of the Montem, and the loss of the posting business by the opening of the railway, their prosperity declined. There is however still a good hotel, the Windmill, but known as *Botham's Inn*, in favour alike with Etonians and families. The village is pleasant, quiet, and genteel.

SNARESBROOK, ESSEX, a hamlet of Wanstead, on the Woodford road, 6¾ m. from Whitechapel ch., and a stat. on the Ongar br. of the Grt. E. Rly. Inn, the *Eagle*.

Seated on the S.W. skirt of Epping Forest, and not far from Hainault, Snaresbrook was of old a very delightful spot. Fifty years ago, herds of deer roved freely about it. The great pond abounded with waders. The largest trees of the forest were in this neighbourhood. It was the

haunt of innumerable varieties of song birds. But for many years past enclosures have been made on every hand, and Snaresbrook has been severed from the mass of Epping Forest. Hainault Forest has been disafforested. Now only a few scrubby fragments of forest land remain about Snaresbrook. Still it is a pleasant locality, and it continues to be resorted to in summer by East-end holiday folk. For them a great attraction is the *Eagle*, a large and good inn with excellent gardens, and the great pond, or lake, as it is now called, in front. The old hamlet contains many good old-fashioned "country houses," of the type favoured by well-to-do citizens of the past generations, and numerous in all these eastern suburbs; smart new villas and cottages have sprung up on all sides, and a pretty Gothic ch., Christ Church, has been built by the Green, so as to serve for Snaresbrook as well as Wanstead.

Immediately S. of the lake—the grounds reaching down to it—is the *Infant Orphan Asylum*, founded by Dr. Andrew Reed in 1827, for children whose parents have occupied a respectable position. The building, a substantial and spacious Elizabethan structure, was erected in 1843 from the designs of Moffatt and Scott. The institution is carefully and well conducted, and has always been popular. The children are eligible for election at any age under 7, and may remain till 12. In the autumn of 1875 there were 340 boys and 260 girls in the Asylum. The office is 100, Fleet Street.

Close to the stat. is the *Merchant Seamen's Orphan Asylum*, another admirable institution, first established in 1817, in a street in St. George's-in-the-East—a seamen's haunt—and supported mainly by persons connected with the merchant service. Outgrowing the premises, it migrated to the Borough Road, and thence hither. The Prince Consort laid the first stone of the present building in 1861, and it was opened by Earl Russell two years later. It is a showy Gothic edifice of red brick, with black bands and Ancaster stone dressings. A conspicuous feature is the tall tower and spire, and porch, with Devonshire marble shafts in the base. The architect was Mr. G. C. Clarke. The elegant little chapel, on the l. of the main building, was presented to

---

[*] Mrs. J. Herschel, Memoir and Correspondence of Caroline Herschel, 1876, p. 309.
[†] *Ibid.*, p. 310, note

the institution by Lady Morrison. The great dining-hall is an addition: the first stone of it was laid by the Prince and Princess of Wales in June 1866. The building affords accommodation for 300 children; in November 1875 there were 270 resident. (Office—132, Leadenhall Street.)

SOUTHALL, MIDDX., on the

Uxbridge road, 9½ m. from London, and a stat. (at Southall Green, ¼ m. S. of the town) on the Grt. W. Rly., 9 m. from Paddington. Southall is an eccl. dist. of Hayes par.: pop. 993.

Southall is a busy but not an attractive place. The country is flat, and disfigured by extensive brickfields, though in some directions there are green fields, shady lanes, and pleasant walks. Farming is a leading occupation, and there are gas works, chemical works, and large steam flour mills. A great cattle market is held every Wednesday. The Grand Junction Canal runs between Southall and Norwood. Southall *Church* (St. John) is a plain but substantial stone building, erected about 1838. Close to Southall Stat. is the Marylebone District School, an immense structure, in which over 400 children are lodged, taught, and trained to industrial pursuits, and which is capable of accommodating 500.

The manor of Southall belonged to the Abp. of Canterbury, under whom it was held, in the 14th cent., by John Shore-dych. It then passed with the manor of Norwood to the Willys, Chesemans, and Chamberlaynes, and was about 1580 alienated to Gregory Fynes, Lord Dacre. On the death of his widow in 1595, it was sold to Francis Awsiter, in whose family it continued till 1756. It was then sold to Mrs. Agatha Child, and with the other estates passed by marriage to the Earl of Jersey. The manor is now held by Sir Charles Mills. *The Manor House* is the residence of Edward Weston, Esq. *Dorman's Well*, the seat of Lord Dacre, ¾ m. N.E. of Southall Street, is now a farmhouse. *Southall Park*, formerly the seat of Sir W. Ellis, a fine red-brick mansion, situated in beautiful grounds S. of the town, is now a private lunatic asylum. Another mansion, *The Shrubbery*, is similarly occupied.

SOUTHCOTE, SURREY (*see* ADDLESTONE).

SOUTHFLEET, KENT (Dom. *Sudfleta*), a pretty secluded vill., 2½ m. S. of Northfleet, and 3 m. S.W. of Gravesend: pop. 730.

The name is derived from the *fleot* which rising here entered the Thames at Northfleet. (*See* NORTHFLEET.) The vill. lies to the S. of the ancient Watling Street, and is supposed to occupy the site of the Roman station, Vagniacæ. Cinerary urns, fragments of pottery, coins, etc., found here indicate the existence of a Roman cemetery. Till the Dissolution, Southfleet belonged to the Priory of St. Andrew, Rochester, and the priors had charter of free warren. In the second half of the 17th cent. the manor was held by Sir Charles Sedley. The employments are agricultural: corn, hops, and fruit are largely grown.

The *Church* (St. Nicholas) of different dates, comprises nave and S. aisle, chancel, W. tower (in which is a peal of 6 bells), and porch. It was restored and reseated, several painted glass windows inserted, and the chancel paved with encaustic tiles in 1867. In the chancel are sedilia, piscina, and six old stalls. Among the *monts*. is an altar tomb to John Sedley, lord of the manor, and wife; and there are *brasses* to John Urban, d. 1420, and wife; and to John Tubney, Archdeacon of St. Asaph, chaplain to the bishop, and rector of Southfleet. The principal seats are *Joyce Hall* (Edward Colyer, Esq.); *Court Lodge* (J. Garland, Esq.); *Westwood House* (Walter Solomon, Esq.); and *Scadbury House* (Capt. Andrus).

Spring Head—tea-gardens and watercress beds—a popular resort of Gravesend visitors, is in Southfleet par., about 1½ m. N. of the village.

SOUTHGATE, MIDDX., a hamlet

and eccl. dist. of Edmonton, pop. 3743, so named as being the S. entrance or gate to Enfield Chase, is 8 m. N. from London, ¾ m. N.W. from the Palmer's Green Stat. of the Grt. N. Rly., Enfield line, and 1¼ m. N.E. from the Colney Hatch and Southgate Stat. of the Grt. N. Rly. main line, by a pleasant byroad lined with shady elms.

The village is quiet, sheltered, and flourishing ; one of the pleasantest looking and least changed round London. A long stretch of shops and residences, put in all sorts of shady nooks and corners; a broad green lined with great elms, and opposite it a modest and comfortable inn, the *Cherry Tree ;* a handsome modern church ; and all around numerous noble trees standing by the roadside or within spacious grounds, and revealing glimpses of stately mansions. Once Southgate boasted its patrician residents, but its aristocracy now consists of opulent citizens, with an occasional nabob.

Among the chief seats are *Arno's Grove,* by the Green (John Walker, Esq.), formerly *Arnolds,* the seat of Sir John Weld, who built the neighbouring chapel, 1615, and founded the family of the Welds of Lulworth Castle. The present house, erected from the designs of Sir R. Taylor by Sir Geo. Colebrooke about 1720, was enlarged about 1777 by Lord Newhaven, who gave it its present designation. *Minchenden,* in the last century the seat of the Duke of Chandos : in the grounds is a pollard oak of great celebrity ; "it covers the largest extent of ground of any tree in England, and has now (1873) a spread of 126 ft., having increased 8 ft. since 1820."* *Southgate House* (W. J. Armitage, Esq.) *Grovelands,* at the S. end of the vill., well known as *Culland's Grove,* when the abode of Ald. Sir William Curtis, M.P. for the City in the days of the Regency, who was raised to the baronetcy in 1802 as "of Culland's Grove, Southgate." In Sept. 1865 a pair of ospreys (or bald buzzards) frequented a sheet of water in the grounds, carrying the fish they captured to the masthead of a pleasure boat, where they devoured it. They continued here till they had been several times shot at.† *Broomfield Park* (R. D. Littler, Esq.), for three centuries the property of the Jacksons, a fine old mansion, having a grand entrance hall and staircase of carved oak, with walls and ceilings painted by Sir Jas. Thornhill, approached by a double avenue of elms, and standing in a well-timbered park of 75 acres. *Bowes Manor,* a little farther S., was the seat of Lord Truro (who died

there Nov. 11, 1855), and is now the residence of Ald. Sidney. *Osidge House,* N. of the village, is the pleasant seat of A. Bosanquet, Esq.

Southgate *Church* (Christ Ch.), W. of the village, occupies the site of the old Weld chapel. It is a handsome stone building, E.E. in style, erected by Sir G. G. Scott, R.A., in 1863, and consists of nave and aisles, with clerestorey, chancel, and tower, and octagonal stone spire at the N.W. The interior is light and lofty, with a tall well-proportioned chancel arch, borne on shafts of Devonshire marble. *Obs.* in E. window of 3 tall lancet lights, the painted glass by Clayton and Bell, and the saints and virtues, of severest pre-Raphaelite design, in small windows at the E. end of the N. aisle by Burne Jones, and at the W. end of the S. aisle by Rossetti. The ch.-yard is prettily laid out, and well kept.

Palmer's Green, a little gathering of houses on the road to Enfield, is a member of Southgate. The pleasantest way to it from Southgate is by the field-path l. of the Cherry Tree. After passing the great oak, take the lane to the l. by Grovelands. The rly. stat. is some little distance S.W. of the Green.

New Southgate.—A portion of Southgate district was in 1873 united with the hamlet of Colney Hatch in Friern Barnet par. to form the eccl. district of *New Southgate ;* and a handsome church (St. Paul), E.E. in style, designed by Sir Gilbert Scott, erected for its accommodation. (*See* COLNEY HATCH.) At *Bowes Manor,* the southern extremity of Southgate, towards Tottenham Wood, another new district church (St. Michael and All Angels) —a handsome and well-finished E.E. fabric—was erected in 1874 from the designs of Sir Gilbert Scott.

Leigh Hunt was born at Southgate, Oct. 1784.

SOUTH MIMMS, HERTS (*see* MIMMS, SOUTH).

SOUTH OCKENDON, ESSEX (*see* OCKENDON, SOUTH).

SOUTH WEALD, ESSEX (*see* WEALD, SOUTH).

SPRING GROVE, MIDDX., an eccl. dist. E. of Hounslow on the main

---

* Ford, Hist. of Enfield, p. 182.
† Harting, Birds of Middlesex, p. 3.

western road, 9 m. from Hyde Park Corner, and a stat. on the loop line of the L. and S.-W.Rly. Pop. of the eccl. dist. (formed in 1856 out of the pars. of Heston and Isleworth), 1657.

Spring Grove was the name of an estate at Smallbury Green, in Heston par., which belonged in 1645 to Sir John Offley. A descendant sold it in 1754 to Edward Biscoe, Esq., who built a new mansion. This about 1790 was leased, and in 1808 purchased, by Sir Joseph Banks, President of the Royal Society. Sir Joseph altered the house, improved the grounds, and built new conservatories, which he stored with the rarest plants, such as only his official position, fame as a botanist, and connections with collectors throughout the world, could have enabled him to obtain. He was in the habit of inviting distinguished men of science and letters, both foreign and native, and Spring Grove became celebrated.

"As the spring advanced he left his house in London to reside at a villa known as *Spring Grove*, near Hounslow, where he remained until the session of the Royal Society terminated. Here he dined daily at 4 o'clock, in order that his frequent visitors from London might have ample time to return in the evening. When the weather permitted his guests adjourned to have tea and coffee under the cedars in the garden. In the intermediate time is was not unusual to visit his hothouses and conservatories, under the auspices of his unmarried sister, Miss Banks; or the dairy, which was under the especial care of Lady Banks, who was proud of displaying a magnificent collection of old china-ware which was there deposited. The parties at Spring Grove were not the less agreeable because they generally consisted of a few persons, and everything was conducted in a simple and unostentatious manner."*

Sir Joseph Banks died at Spring Grove, June 19, 1820. Some years after the house was pulled down, and the ground let for building purposes, and Spring Grove became the nucleus of a village of villas, to which it bequeathed its name. Spring Grove has become a large district of good houses, and is daily growing in extent and population, but like most such districts it has little that is distinctive in its aspect.

The *Church* (St. Mary) stands on high ground between the road and Osterley Park; is a spacious, modern Dec. building of smoothed stone, comprising nave and aisles, chancel, and tall tower and

* Autobiography of the late Sir Benjamin Brodie, Bart., p. 74.

spire. The Saddlers' Company Almshouse for 8 poor persons is at Honnors House.

The *London International College*, on the site of the old Spring Grove, is a large collegiate Gothic brick and stone building, having a frontage 250 ft. long, and three storeys high, with a fourth storey in the high-pitched roof, a central tower with angle turrets and pyramidal roof, and slightly advanced wings. The building, designed by Messrs. Norton, and inaugurated by the Prince of Wales in July 1867, has accommodation for 150 pupils. The *Wellingtonia gigantea* on the lawn in front of the college was planted by the Prince of Wales on the day of opening the college.

STAINES, MIDDX., a market town

on the l. bank of the Thames, 17 m. from London, and a stat. at the junction of the Windsor and the Wokingham and Reading branches of the L. and S.-W. Rly. Pop. of the town 3469, of the par. 3659. Inns, *Angel and Crown Hotel*, High Street; *Railway*, by the stat.

The town stands at the confluence of the Colne with the Thames, on the site, as is believed, of the Roman station *Pontes*, and at the starting-point of the great Roman road which traversed Surrey to Silchester (*Segontiacum*). The name is derived from the A.-S. *stán*, a stone; so applied from the boundary stone which stood here, marking the western limit of the jurisdiction of the City of London over the Thames; but in considering this claim it must be remembered that the town bore the name of *Stanes* at the Dom. Survey. The London Stone, as it is called, still stands in a meadow near Staines Bridge, by one of the smaller arms of the Colne, and has inscribed on it "God preserve the City of London. A.D. 1285," with the names of various Lord Mayors, and the dates of their respective official visits to the stone. The stone was erected on its present pedestal "in the mayoralty of Sir Watkin Lewis, 1812." The last Mayor's name we find inscribed is John Johnson, 1846; while on the S. base is engraven "Conservators of the River Thames, 1857." In the regulations of the Thames Conservancy the City Stone at Staines is taken as the dividing-point between the Upper and the Lower Thames.

Staines Forest, the western extremity of the great Forest of Middlesex, was "unwarrened and disafforested for ever," by charter of Henry III., Aug. 18, 1227.

The manor of Staines was granted by Edward the Confessor to the Abbot of Westminster. At the Dissolution it became vested in the Crown, and was granted by James I. in 1613 to Thomas Lord Knyvet, and sold by Thomas Knyvet, Esq., in 1629, to Sir Francis Leigh. It was conveyed in 1669 to Sir William Drake, who sold it in 1678 to Richard Tayler, whose descendant Robert Gibbons Tayler, Esq., is the present lord of the manor.

After London Bridge, that of Staines was one of the earliest which crossed the Thames. "Three oaks out of Windsor Forest were granted for its repair in 1262," * and the charters for tolls, Acts of Parliament, and deeds referring to it are very numerous. Its recent history is somewhat remarkable. In 1791 an Act was passed appointing commissioners for the erection of a new bridge. One was accordingly constructed from the designs of Thomas Sandby, professor of architecture in the Royal Academy. It was of stone, of three arches, and was opened in March 1797; but within a few weeks sank so much that two of the arches had to be taken down. An attempt to rebuild it was unsuccessful, and it was resolved to substitute an iron bridge of a single arch of 180 ft. span. The engineer employed was Mr. James Wilson, the builder of the noted iron bridge over the Weir at Sunderland, but the design was said to be copied from one by the notorious Thomas Paine. Paine had erected an arch at Paddington in order to demonstrate the value of his system, and the materials were purchased and employed in the construction of that at Staines. However that may be, the bridge—begun in 1801 and completed in 1803—was no sooner opened than it showed symptoms of failure. It was closed, and the old wooden bridge, which had been left standing, was fitted up as a temporary bridge. A second iron bridge was then erected, and the old wooden bridge pulled down. But this too gave way, and as the engineers called in pronounced it essentially

weak, it was decided to remove it, and Mr. George Rennie was empowered to construct a new bridge somewhat higher up the river. This was commenced in the spring of 1829, and opened with much ceremony by William IV. and Queen Adelaide, on Easter Monday, April 24, 1832; and appears to be as stable now as when first opened. It is a handsome granite structure, of three elliptical arches, the centre of 74 ft., the side arches of 66 ft. span; two narrow arches over the towing-path, and six shore arches, serve for the passage of flood water. It remained a toll bridge till Feb. 21, 1871, when it was formally opened as a free bridge—the remission being the act of the Corporation of London.

The town consists of a main street—High Street and Church Street—above a mile long, clean, quiet, commonplace, lined with many good shops, old-fashioned private houses, inns, a great brewery, and, at the extreme W. end, the church, clean and commonplace as all the rest. For long years past this street has remained unaltered; but the bank has been lately rebuilt, and this innovation will no doubt lead to others. By the rly. stat., a new suburb, mostly of small houses, with a few more pretentious villas, has grown up, the business works have extended, and the population has, we are told, about doubled within the last 10 or 12 years.

Besides Messrs. Ashby's great brewery, there are the extensive mustard mills of Messrs. Finch and Rickman, papier-maché mills, linoleum works, etc. The neighbourhood is agricultural, and a market is held every Friday. The Thames here is favourable for boating and fishing, and Staines has consequently a great influx of summer visitants.

The *Church* (St. Mary) was erected in 1828, on the site of the old ch.—a much-patched Gothic building, with some lancet windows, and a Norm. doorway in the chancel—which fell down one Sunday morning. The present ch., designed by Mr. J. B. Watson, is of brick and stone, and Gothic of the year 1828; large, bald, and uninteresting; roomy and neat inside, with comfortable fittings and a painted glass E. window. The tower, the lower part of which was preserved from the old ch., was erected, as an insc. on it records, by Inigo Jones, in 1631; but the lower

* Lysons, Environs, vol. ii., p. 240.

part was repaired and the upper part added when the present ch. was built : it is of brick, square, quite plain, with plain buttresses at the angles, and its uncomeliness is partially veiled by ivy. In the tower is a peal of 8 bells. Besides the usual chapels, there is here a very old Quakers' Meeting-house : the Friends having always flourished in Staines. The town is now governed by a Local Board ; and has a Literary and Scientific Institute, by the bridge ; a Mechanics' Institute, in Church Street ; a boating club, cricket club, and the like.

STANFORD RIVERS, ESSEX, on the Ongar road, and 2¼ m. S.W. from that town ; 19 m. from London. Pop. 958 (including 120 persons in the Ongar Union-house, which is in Stanford Rivers par.) Inn, *White Bear*.

The vill. owes its name to a ford over the little river Roding, probably paved on account of the deep miry soil : the suffix was added—to distinguish it from Stanford-le-Hope, near Orsett—from the Rivers family to whom it belonged from 1213, when it became the property of Richard Rivers by his marriage with the heiress of the Lucys, till it passed to the Staffords. Previously it appears to have been called Stanford Parva, or Little Stanford.

Stanford Rivers is a quiet agric. vill., with its ch. standing apart among the fields, half a mile W. of the main road, along which stretch most of the few houses in very irregular order. The country is secluded and pretty ; there are green and sylvan lanes, broad well-tilled fields, woods and thickets, a gently undulating surface, and the little river meandering through the shallow valley. The old families have passed away, and now the farmers are the only resident gentry.

The *Church* (St. Margaret) is a plain village ch. of the Dec. period ; has nave, chancel, wooden tower, and shingled spire at the W., and wooden porch at the N. The interior is equally unadorned. There are two or three 16th cent. monts., but none of interest. S. of the nave is a mural brass to Anne, wife of Wm. Napper, gent., d. 1584, effigy kneeling, with 6 daughters behind. Haines mentions brasses of a man in armour, about 1450 ;

a child, Thos. Greville, 1492 ; and Robt. Barrow, 1503. There is also an insc. to Robert Green, 1535. The font is large, E.E., with panels on the sides, a thick central shaft, and slender shafts around. Richard Montague, author of 'A New Gag for an Old Goose,' and other High-Church pamphlets, which attracted much notice in the latter part of the reign of James I. and the early years of Charles I., was rector of Stanford Rivers from 1622. Montague was formally censured by the Parliament, whereupon Charles appointed him his chaplain, in order to screen him from the vote of the House of Commons, thus greatly embittering the strife. A late rector (1849-68) was Dr. Henry Tattam, the distinguished Oriental scholar.

In the ch.-yard, with "his wife and two daughters who preceded him," lies Isaac Taylor, d. 1865, author of the 'Natural History of Enthusiasm,' 'Ancient Christianity,' etc., who for 40 years (1825-65) pursued his literary labours in this sequestered village. His house, "a rambling old-fashioned farm-house," standing in a large garden, was on the rt. of the Ongar road, his study, the walls and doors "lined with patristic folios," overlooking the valley of the Roding and the woods beyond.[*]

STANMORE, STANMORE MAGNA, or GREAT STANMORE, MIDDX., so called to distinguish it from the adjoining par. of Stanmore Parva, is on the road to Watford, 2 m. N.W. from the Edgware Stat. of the Grt. N. Rly. ; 2¼ m. E. from the Pinner Stat., and a little farther from the Harrow Stat., of the L. and N.-W. Rly. Pop. 1355. Inns, *Crown ; Vine ; Abercorn Arms*.

Stanmore is on the border of Herts, whence probably the name (*Stanmere, Stanmera* in Dom.), from *Stán-mearc*, a boundary stone. The ground is high, much broken, picturesque, and abounds in fine views. The village is 284 feet above the sea-level ; on one hand the Heath, though much encroached on, affords many pretty bits of wild woodland, with distant prospects over Harrow

* Rev. Isaac Taylor, Family Pen, vol. i., p. 65 ; Josiah Gilbert, Autob. and Memorials of Mrs. Gilbert (Ann Taylor), vol. ii., p. 93.

and Londonwards, and on the other Stanmore Common is still a broad open space, glorious with gorse and heather, and overlooking a wide extent of country. " Some high trees on the common" were, according to the Ambulator (1792), "a land mark from the German Ocean," but we have not heard of their serving that purpose of late years.

The village is neat, clean, genteel. In and about it are many good houses, bordering it are large parks, and richly timbered grounds. Near the Common is the extensive brewery of Messrs. Clutterbuck. Dr. Parr opened a school at Stanmore on his removal from Harrow, 1771. The original church stood at some distance S. of the present structure or its predecessor. On account of its inconvenient site it was taken down, and a new ch. erected near the village by Sir John Wolstenholme, and consecrated by Bp. Laud in 1632. This, now known as the Old Church, is of brick, with a tower and porch designed by Nicholas Stone. As it stands, close embowered in ivy, it looks picturesque, but it is really a poor building. Its baldness and insufficiency caused its condemnation some 30 years back, and the erection of a new ch. close by it on the E., but on somewhat lower ground, the old ch. being allowed to stand, partly on account of the monts. it contained, but more, perhaps, on account of its picturesqueness. The foundation-stone of the new church (St. John the Evangelist) was laid by Queen Adelaide, her last appearance in public, shortly before her decease; it was consecrated Jan. 16, 1850. It is a spacious stone building, Dec. in style, and comprises nave with aisles, roomy chancel with S. aisle, tower with angle turret at the N.W., and S. porch. The E. window, by Willement, is a memorial of Queen Adelaide. The archt. was Mr. H. Clutton. In the tower is a peal of 6 bells, removed from Little Stanmore in 1720. In the old church are *monts.* with effigies of Sir John Wolstenholme, d. 1639, the founder of the ch., and of his grandson John Wolstenholme, Esq., and wife, Dorothy Vere; of John Burnell, citizen and merchant, d. 1605, and wife Barbara; Lord Henry Beauclerk, d. 1761; John Drummond, M.P., d. 1774; and other members of the families of Beauclerk and Drummond. In the ch.-yard was in-

terred Charles Hart, d. 1683, the celebrated tragic actor, " The Roscius of his age." He had a country house at Stanmore, where he was enrolled a copyholder in 1679, but there is no memorial of him in the ch. or ch.-yard.*

Bentley Priory, the fine seat of Sir John Kelk, Bart., is to the N. of Stanmore ch., the park stretching away from it for 1½ m. to Stanmore Heath. The house and upper part of the park are in Harrow par. The priory of Benethley, or Bentley, of which little is known, was suppressed, with the other smaller monasteries, in the early part of the reign of Henry VIII. The estate appears to have been transferred to the monks of St. Gregory at Canterbury, but was exchanged by Cranmer with Henry VIII., in 1543, for other lands. Henry granted the priory house and lands, in 1546, to Robert Needham, who, the following year, alienated them to Elizabeth Colte. After passing through various hands, the manor was, in 1788, purchased by the Marquis of Abercorn, who made great alterations in the park, and employed Sir John Soane to rebuild the house, which he fitted up with great magnificence, and filled with a fine collection of paintings and other works of art. Bentley Priory was a famous place whilst in Lord Abercorn's possession. The Prince Regent (afterwards George IV.) came here with the Emperor of Russia and King of Prussia to meet Louis XVIII. when he left Hartwell to return to France. In April 1807 Sir Walter Scott, when on a visit here, corrected the revises of 'Marmion,' and at Lord Abercorn's suggestion added the complimentary lines on Fox—

" For talents mourn untimely lost,
    When best employed, and wanted most," etc.

" I have heard, indeed," writes Lockhart, " that they came from the Marquis's own pen."† Shortly after the decease of William IV., Queen Adelaide rented Bentley Priory, which she made her principal residence—to the great benefit of the poorer inhabitants of Stanmore. She died here, Dec. 2nd, 1849. Bentley Priory was purchased in 1854 by Mr. (now Sir John) Kelk who has greatly altered the house, built large and costly conservatories, and otherwise added to

* Lysons, vol. ii., p. 668.
† Lockhart, Life of Scott, chap. xvi.

its magnificence. It is now a very stately and splended structure, and contains a good collection of modern paintings. Both house and park command extensive prospects. Harrow Hill forming a prominent feature in the landscape. The gardens and grounds about the house are celebrated among horticulturists, and the park is of great extent, varied in surface, in parts richly timbered, and very beautiful.

Stanmore Park, the seat of Lord Wolverton, lies to the S. of Bentley Priory and Stanmore ch. The estate, then known as *Belmont*, was purchased, about 1729, by Andrew Drummond, the founder of the great banking-house. When in the possession of Mr. G. H. Drummond, the house was enriched by a collection of English historical portraits, bequeathed to the Hon. Mrs. Drummond by the Duke of St. Albans. The estate was purchased by the Marquis of Abercorn in 1840, and the collection, which contained many works by Lely and Kneller, was sold by auction by Christie and Manson (June 27, 1840,) for what would now be regarded as very inadequate prices. The estate was afterwards purchased by George Carr Glyn, Esq., and is now the seat of his son, Geo. Grenfell Glyn, Lord Wolverton. The house is a good modern building. The park, though smaller than that of Bentley Priory, is very beautiful. It contains a handsome lake, and at the south-western extremity, approched by a good avenue, is the *Mount*, with a summer-house on the summit, famed for its prospects, from which the estate derived its original name.

Other good seats are—*Stanmore Manor* (the Hon. Mrs. Noel) ; *Pynacles* (Col. L. McQueen) ; *The Hall* (R. Holland, Esq.); *Warren House* (S. Keyser, Esq.) ; *Broomfield* (Capt. W. Greig), a good modern Gothic house, designed by Mr. Knowles, commanding from its lofty site an extensive prospect ; *The Elms* (James Gleig, Esq.), near the ch.

Great quantities of Roman coins, rings, fibulæ, pottery, etc., have at various times been found in Stanmore and the vicinity, from the site of Bentley Priory away E. to Brockley Hill, whence the rhyme quoted by Lysons,—

" No heart can think, nor tongue can tell,
What lies between Brockley Hill and Pennywell."

Pennywell (by Elstree) and Brockley are, however, both far away to the N.E. of Stanmore.

STANMORE PARVA, LITTLE

STANMORE, or WHITCHURCH, Midx., ½ m. W. of Edgware, 1 m. S.E. of Great Stanmore : pop. 818, including the W. side of Edgware, which is in Little Stanmore parish.

From the reign of Henry III. to the Dissolution, the manor belonged to the priory of St. Bartholomew, Smithfield. Under the name of Canons and Wimborough in Whitchurch, it was granted in 1544 to Sir Hugh Losse. In 1604 it was bought by Sir Thomas Lake, the amanuensis of Sir Francis Walsingham, and secretary to James I. About 1710, Mary, great-granddaughter of Sir Thomas Lake, carried it by marriage to James Brydges, Esq., afterwards Earl of Carnarvon and Duke of Chandos (the Timon of Pope's satire, the Grand Duke of the multitude). The old house of the Losse family Lysons supposed to be the " ancient house on the Whitchurch side of Edgware," then as now called the Chandos Arms. In one of the rooms were the Losse arms, with the initials R. L., and the date, 1577. The house, built by Thorpe for Sir Thos. Lake, and the palace of the Duke of Chandos, are noticed under CANONS.

Little Stanmore is a quiet agricultural parish, lying, except the Edgware portion, away from the main road ; the surface gently undulating, much of the land pasture, the lanes shaded by tall old trees, and varied northwards by the broad open slopes and avenues of *Canons* (Mrs. Begg).

To the visitor the chief object of interest is the *Church* (St. Lawrence), of old famous as the chapel of Canons. It stands amidst old trees, and the fields between it and Canons retain their park-like aspect. There was a private chapel at Canons, but the Grand Duke came in state on Sundays to the public service in the parish ch,, and he wished the ch. not to be behind the chapel in splendour. He accordingly pulled down the body of the ch. (then called Whitchurch), and raised the present structure in its place (1715-20). Tradition says that he would have rebuilt the tower also, but that the parishioners, anticipating his munificence, hastened to sell the bells (*see* STANMORE, GREAT), and he, in disgust at their cupidity, left the tower standing.

The building is comparatively plain outside—the " severely simple " classic of the early part of the 18th century—but within, stately, pompous, and uncommon. It consists of a nave, without aisles, and a small chancel raised by 3 steps from the nave, and separated from it by richly carved oak columns. At the W. end is the Chandos gallery. But what gives its peculiar character to the interior is the costly and unusual decoration. Walls and ceiling are alike resplendent with paintings and carved work. On the walls between the windows are figures in monochrome of the Evangelists and the Seven Cardinal Virtues. On the recess, behind the altar, are paintings by Bellucci of Moses Delivering the Law, and Christ Preaching the Gospel. On the sides of the organ are the Offering of the Magi and the Descent from the Cross. At the W. end, over the Chandos gallery, is a copy of Raphael's Ascension, by Bellucci. The ceiling of the chancel is painted azure and powdered with golden stars. In the panels of the nave ceiling are 8 paintings by Laguerre of events in the life of the Saviour.

" On painted ceilings you devoutly stare,
  Where sprawl the saints of Verrio and Laguerre."*

Pope, in denying that by Timon's Villa he meant Canons, says that "the paintings [at Canons Chapel] are not by Verrio and Laguerre, but Bellucci and Leeman."† Rhyme, and the desire to conceal the direct personality of his satire, would account for Pope using the former and well-known names rather than the latter and comparatively obscure. But Lysons, writing with the Vertue MSS. before him, says distinctly that " the ceilings and walls are painted by Laguerre, the Nativity (Adoration of the Magi) and a Dead Christ, on each side of the altar, by Belluchi." ‡ That Verrio could have had no hand in the Stanmore pictures is evident, as he was dead a dozen years

before they were begun, but about Laguerre's participation, there can be little doubt. But whoever the paintings are by, they are good specimens of their class. The carved work is ascribed to Grinling Gibbons, and if not actually carved by him was probably executed under his direction. That all might be in harmony, the Duke presented the ch. with a superb service of silver-gilt communion plate. This is displayed in part on communion Sundays, but the whole is set out on the altar only on the great festivals of Christmas, Easter, and Whit Sunday, and on Bishop's visitations.

The *Organ*, which stands in the chancel behind and just above the altar, is interesting as being that on which Handel played. Is was built by Jordans for the place it occupies, and is small, but of very sweet tone. An insc. on it, placed there in 1750, states that " Handel was organist of this church from the year 1718 to 1721, and composed the oratorio of Esther on this organ." As mentioned under Canons, Handel was chapel-master to the Duke of Chandos, and not only played on the organ, but composed some 20 anthems for the service ; the music for the morning and evening services being composed by Pepusch. As long as the Duke reigned at Canons the service was performed by a carefully selected vocal and instrumental choir. Handel is believed to have written his oratorio Esther for the opening of the ch., Aug. 20, 1720 : it was certainly performed here in that year— Dr. Randall of Cambridge, Bird, and Savage being among the vocalists.

On the N. side of the ch., and entered from it, is the Chandos Chapel, or Monument Room, in which the Duke of Chandos is buried. His mont. bears a long and pompous insc., and a statue of the Duke in Roman costume and flowing wig, supported by kneeling life-sized effigies of his first two wives : his third wife (married 1736, d. 1759) it may be remembered (as a fly in his pot of manna) was "often reproached with being bied up in Bur Street, Wapping."* The Duke's mont. having fallen into disrepair, was restored by the Duke of Buckingham in 1864-5. Several other monts. of members of the Brydges family are in the vault. Sir

---

* Pope, Epistle to the Earl of Burlington.
† Letter to Aaron Hill, Feb. 5, 1732.
‡ Lysons, Environs, vol. ii., p. 673.

* Mr. Pendarves to Swift, April 22, 1736.

Thomas Lake, King James's secretary, was buried in the church.

In the ch.-yard, E. of the ch., was a low wooden rail mont. having painted on one side " Sacred to the memory of William Powell, the HARMONIOUS BLACKSMITH, died Feb. 27, 1780, aged about 78," and on the other, " He was Parish Clerk at this Church many years, and during the Time the Immortal Handel resided much at Cannons with the Duke of Chandos. Erected by permission of the Rèv. G. Mutter free of expense, through the exertions of Rd. Clarke and Henry Wylde, 1835." But this humble rail was in 1868 displaced by a substantial stone bearing, in a sunk medallion, hammer, anvil, laurel-leaf, and a bar of music, and a somewhat modified insc., to the effect that " He was parish clerk during the time the immortal Handel was organist of this church." This is the Powell whose rhythmical beating on his forge—one form of the tradition says in accord with a tune he was singing or whistling, the other with the church bells then merrily pealing,— suggested to Handel his charming melody of the Harmonious Blacksmith.* The story is at least doubtful, and it seems certain that Handel did not himself give the air its popular title. But the natives cherish the belief, and Dr. Schalcher, who investigated the story with all the patient zeal of a German biographer, says that when he " made a pilgrimage to Edge-ware, a sort of square shed, standing in the middle of the great street was shown to him as being the veritable forge used by Powell."† The shed stood on the spare space between the road and footway, on the Whitchurch side of Edgware, but the tradition connecting it with Powell is, we fear, recent. Schalcher's conclusion is that the tradition that Handel derived the *tune* from the sound of Powell's hammer, " whether true or not, remains un-verified." ‡

Behind the ch. is a snug-looking alms-house, built by Dame Mary Lake, and augmented by Dame Essex Drax, executrix of Sir Lancelot Lake, 1693, for four poor men and three women, who, besides

* Clarke, Reminiscences of Handel, his Grace the Duke of Chandos, Powell, etc., fol., 1836.
† Schalcher, Life of Handel, 1859, p. 66.
‡ *Ibid.*, Appendix.

lodging, are supplied with coals and a small annuity. There is also an endowed school founded by Sir Lancelot Lake.

STANSTEAD ABBOTS, HERTS,

2½ m. S.E. from Ware, and a Stat. (at St. Margaret's) on the Grt. E. Rly. (Hert-ford and Ware br.) 22 m. from London : pop. 1057. Inn, the *Pied Bull.*

Stanstead (Dom. *Stansteda*) received the suffix of Abbots from Michael de Wanney having given the moiety of the manor to the Abbot of Waltham. The other moiety he sold to Henry II., who transferred it to the Abbot. The manor was held by the Abbots till the Dissolu-tion ; it afterwards passed through many hands, and is now the property of Thomas Fowell Buxton, Esq.

The *Village, Stanstead Street*, of old a town, extends from the Lea Navigation by St. Margaret's to the Ware road, where a branch of the Lea crosses it. The ch. is a mile distant, within Stansteadbury Park. Stanstead Street is a long, dirty, but busy-looking street, lined with houses of most irregular kind, some good and new, or if old, substantial ; others small, mean, and not a few dilapidated. Several cottages are of wood and plaster, and thatched. By the Lea are wharfs, mills, and malt-houses ; along the street many ' publics,' maltings, a brewery, large builders' yards, a shabbily picturesque smithy, and a heterogeneous variety of shops, some quite rustic in their varied business—that of W. Miller, for example, having over the front "Draper and Clothier, Family Grocer, and Butcher," and supplying also sweets and toys for children, and stationery and fancy articles for adults. There are besides chapels, a literary institute, a workmen's reading-room, almshouses, and a school.

Turning rt. from Stanstead Street to-wards Roydon you pass through a very pretty half-mile of road overhung with trees, till you reach Stansteadbury and Stanstead ch. But *obs.* at the parting of the roads, just before reaching the ch., the great oak, 18 ft. in girth at 4 ft. from the ground, and spreading wide over the road on either side.

The *Church* (St. James) stands on high ground within the pale of Stansteadbury, within sight of the Roydon Stat., and about ½ m. from it. The ch. is of flint and stone, the body roughcast; in the lower courses of the chancel some Roman tiles are worked up. It has nave, chancel with N. aisle or chapel, tower at the W. end, containing a peal of 4 old bells, and crowned with a short thin leaden spire of the usual Hertfordshire type. On the S.W. is an old oak porch. The ch. is in the main of the Dec. period, but Perp. windows have been inserted on the N. of the nave. The chapel on N. of chancel was built by Ralph Baesh. lord of the manor. in 1578. The tower has a Perp. doorway with good carving in the spandrels; Dec. upper windows; buttresses. battlements. and an angle turret; and is partly covered with ivy. The interior is that of an ordinary country ch., but the ch. was restored in 1866, and much altered both inside and out. In the chapel are several monts. to members of the Baesh family. *Obs.* small mural mont. to Edward Baesh, d. 1587, "General Surveyor of the Victuals for the Royal Navy,... under 4 princes of this land, viz. King Hen. VIII., King Edward VI., Queen Mary. and Queen Elizabeth:" kneeling effigies of himself, wife, and 2 children. Before leaving the ch.-yard, *obs.* the fine horse-chesnuts which surround it, and the extensive views along and over the valley of the Lea. A path nearly opposite the ch.-yard. by the great gravel-pit, leads across the Rye Meads to Rye House. *Obs.* at the entrance to this path, the great oak, almost as large as that noticed above, but hollow.

Stansteadbury (Capt. E. Spencer), the old manor-house, by the ch., is a large many gabled mansion, of late thoroughly "restored" (or transformed), and now a very ornate building. The grounds are extensive and pleasing. *Obs.* the large cedar on the lawn, in front of the house. Other good seats are *Easney Park* (Thos. Fowell Buxton. Esq.), and *Stanstead Hall* (D. E. Langham, Esq.)

STANSTEAD ST. MARGARET'S,

HERTS, on the Lea. opposite Stanstead Street (*see* STANSTEAD ABBOTS). with which it is united by a bridge, and a stat. on the Grt. E. Rly. Pop. 107. Inns, *Crown: Railway Tavern.*

St. Margaret's consists of a few scattered cottages—there were but 23 houses in the par. in 1871—the inn with a malt-house opposite it, and the ch.: hardly a village,

but rural, embowered in trees, and in summer leafy and pleasant ; the "willow-shaded Stanstead" of Scott of Amwell's verse. Heretofore, says Chauncy, called *Thele*, it had a college so named, "in old time founded of one custos and 4 chaplains to celebrate divine service for the souls of the founders thereof," which had to be reformed in the reign of Henry VI., in consequence of the negligence and misconduct of the custos, and was swept away at the Dissolution. The *Church* (St. Margaret) is a donative of small value, held by the Rev. Chas. Pratt, the lord of the manor : a plain little country ch. lying back from the road, half-hidden among trees. Of flint and stone, roughly plastered over, it consists of nave and chancel of the same pitch, with a little wooden bell-cote, rising from the W. end of the red-tiled roof. On the N. may be seen traces of an aisle removed at an early period, when small windows were inserted within the blocked arches. The windows on the S. are much larger. In the chancel is a good 5-light late Dec. window, with flowing tracery, and carved heads at the ends of the dripstone. S. of the chancel is a priest's door, closed. The interior is plain, filled with high pews, and has a gallery at the W. end. The monts. are of no interest. Hoole, the translator of Tasso, was for awhile resident here.

From St. Margaret's there is a pleasant walk of about ¾ of a mile, by the New River to *Amwell.* Take the path on l., nearly opposite the ch. street, and ascend the bank : the New River is on your l., a clear and fishful stream, the rly., and beyond it the open Lea valley on your rt. : the path is a good one all the way, and the opposite bank is throughout overhung with trees.

STANWELL, MIDDX., (Dom.

Stanwelle) an agril. vill., 2½ m. N.E. of Staines, on the road from Bedfont to Colnbrook, and on the Isleworth and King's rivers. Pop. of the par. 1955, but this includes 324 in St. Thomas. Colnbrook, and 242 in Staines Union Workhouse, which is situated about 1 m. from the vill. on the road to Staines.

Stanwell lies on the Buckinghamshire border, the Colne river being its western boundary, and dividing it from Horton, Colnbrook, and Iver. The country is flat, but green and pleasant, especially on the Bucks side. Stanwell is a secluded vill. of a few humble cottages, some better houses standing apart in well-sheltered grounds or pretty gardens. The little Green might tempt the sketcher or painter. In the centre stands a huge old elm, its lowest branches broken, but still vigorous, full of leaves, of good form, and fortunate in its accompaniments. Beyond it is the wheelwright's shop, with an occasional flare from the forge, and in front a wild array of broken carts, ploughs, trunks of trees. Close at hand is a rustic inn, the Five Bells. Over the ch.-yard yews and elms rises the village spire. Old men and children give life and colour to the foreground.

The *Church* (St. Mary) is of stone with some flints interspersed; and comprises large Perp. nave and N. aisle; S. aisle, longer than the N., and E.E.; deep chancel, lower than nave, Dec., with 4-light E. window, plastered, and supported by brick buttresses; small square tower, of flint and stone, in chequers, and tall octagonal shingled spire; small transepts with gable ends, and modern plate tracery in the windows; wooden porch on the N., and red-tiled roofs. The int. is large and airy, the nave wide, the aisles narrow. *Obs.* the arcades of octagonal piers and equilateral arches, and clerestory,—rebuilt when the ch. was restored in 1863,—timber roof, ceiled between the main beams, painted glass in chancel, and open oak seats. Near the N. door, removed from the chancel, is a canopied altar tomb, with matrices of effigies, the brasses lost, of Thomas Windsor, d. 1486 (father of Andrews, 1st Lord Windsor); interesting as illustrating the use in a par. ch. of a tomb as the Easter Sepulchre. By his last will, made 1479, Thomas Windsor directs that his body shall be buried on the N. side of the choir of Stanwell ch., "afor the ymage of our Lady, wher the sepultur of our Lord stondith." His tomb is to be a plain "tomb of marble of a competent height, to thentent that yt may ber (bear) the blessid body of our Lord, and the sepulture at the time of Estre, to stand upon the same," etc. Four tapers of wax, each weighing 10 lb., and 22 wax torches, each weighing 16 lb., are to be carried, lighted as well at "the time of my burying as at my monethes mynde,"

by 24 very poor men, who are to have 8*d.* apiece and a gown of frieze; the 4 tapers are then to be given to the ch., 2 of them to burn yearly, as long as they will endure, "before the sepultur of our Lord at Estre, and the other 2 to help the light that standeth upon the branch before the image of our Lady." Four of the torches are bequeathed to Stanwell ch., the others to 16 of the nearest parishes in Middlesex.* There are bequests to priests and poor persons. for 100 children, each within the age of 16 years, at his month's mind [monthly commemorative service], to say our Lady Psalter, etc.,—but the above is what relates to the Easter sepulchre.

A more showy tomb is that of Thomas Lord Knyvet, d. 1622, and Elizabeth his wife, N. of the chancel. The tomb is supported by Corinthian columns, and has life-sized kneeling effigies in the elaborate costume of the day. It was executed by Nicholas Stone, and cost £215. This Lord Knyvet founded and endowed the Stanwell Free School, on the Staines road. Bruno Ryves, author of the Mercurius Rusticus, was vicar of Stanwell at the great rebellion, was ejected, but restored on the return of Charles II., and retained the living till 1662.

Stanwell Place, the manor-house, N.W. of the ch., is a spacious modern mansion, formal and dull outside, commodious and richly fitted within. It stands in a park of moderate size, rich in timber, especially elms and chesnuts, with a branch of the Colne flowing through it and forming a lake, with swans and all desirable amenities, and approached through stately gates which indicate a former more magnificent mansion. Early in the 12th cent. the manor belonged to Walter Fitzother, and was inherited by his son William, who, being warden of Windsor Castle, assumed the name of Windsor. The manor continued in the Windsor family till 1543, when Henry VIII. forced Andrews, 1st Lord Windsor, much against his will, to exchange his ancestral estate for the manor of the suppressed Abbey of Bordesley in Worcestershire. The king's measures were prompt and peremptory. He sent Lord Windsor a message that he would dine with him at Stanwell on a certain day.

---

* Collins, Peerage. ed. 1779, vol. iv., p. 74; Lysons, vol. iii., p. 257.

"He accordingly came, when he was magnificently entertained. Whereupon the king told him he liked that place so well that he was resolved to have it; yet not without a more beneficial exchange. And the Lord Windsor answering, he hoped his highness was not in earnest; it having been the seat of his ancestors for many ages, and humbly begging he would not take it from him. The king with a stern countenance replied 'It must be,' commanding him on his allegiance, to go speedily to his Attorney General, who would more fully acquaint him with his reasons for it. . . . He repaired accordingly to the Attorney General, who showed him a draught ready made, of an exchange of his lordship of Stanwell . . . in lieu of Bordesley Abbey. Whereof being constrained to accept of this exchange, he was commanded to quit Stanwell, though he had then laid in his Christmas provisions for the keeping of his wonted hospitality. All which he left in the house, saying, 'They should not find it bare Stanwell.'"*

Leases were granted of the manor-house and lands by Henry VIII., Edward VI., and Elizabeth; and in 1603 James I. granted to Sir Thomas Knyvet the site of the manor and demesne lands. Knyvet was a favourite of James, who placed his daughter, the Lady Mary, under his care, and she died at Stanwell in 1607. In 1613 the king granted to him, being then Lord Knyvet, the estate, subject to a rent of £100. Lord Knyvet died in 1622, having settled the manor in moieties on his great-nephew, John Cary, and his great-niece, Elizabeth Leigh, grandchildren of his sisters. The family wished to maintain the manor intact by their marriage, and a decree was obtained in Chancery to that effect. But Elizabeth Leigh married Sir Humphrey Tracey; and in 1678 a deed of partition was executed by which John Cary became sole lord of Stanwell manor. Not deterred by the ill-success of marriage awards in his own case, Cary, by will dated 1686, bequeathed the manor to his great-niece, Elizabeth, only surviving daughter of Lord Willoughby of Parham, provided that within three years of his decease she should marry Lord Guildford, failing which condition the estate should go to the Falkland family. The lady, however, disapproved the selection, and married the Hon. James Bertie; but a judgment of the House of Lords preserved her life-interest in the manor, and gave the reversion to Lucius Henry Lord Falkland. Mrs. Bertie died in 1715; and Lord

Falkland sold the manor to John Earl of Dunmore, in 1720. Lord Dunmore died in 1752, and two years after his executors sold it to John Gibbons, afterwards Sir John Gibbons, Bart., K.B.,* in whose descendants it has since remained. It is now the property and seat of Sir John Gibbons, Bart.

West Bedfont, a hamlet ½ a mile E. of Stanwell, on the road to East Bedfont, was of old an independent manor, but has merged in that of Stanwell.

Poyle is another hamlet, 2½ m. N.W. of Stanwell, near Colnbrook, consisting of a few scattered houses, the Punch Bowl inn, a chapel, and the large paper-mill of Messrs. Ibetson and Sons.

Perry Oaks is another outlying irregular hamlet, about 1 m. N.E. from Stanwell, on the road to the Magpies.

That portion of *Colnbrook* which lies E. of the Colne, is in Stanwell parish. (*See* COLNBROOK.)

STAPLEFORD ABBOTS, ESSEX,

(pop. 511,) lies S. of the Ongar road and of the river Roding, 1½ m. E. of Lambourne. The ford from which it derives its name is between Stapleford Abbots and Stapleford Tawney. It owes the suffix *Abbots* to having been the property of the Abbots of Bury St. Edmund's. There is no vill.; the principal seat, ALBYNS, is described under its title. The *Church* (St. Mary), which is about 1 m. S. of Passingford Bridge, the old ford, was rebuilt 1861-2 (Mr. T. Jeckell, archt.), except the old brick tower at the W., and the Abdy pew or chapel on the N. The new building is of Kentish rag, Dec. in style, and consists of nave and chancel, with a porch of carved oak and stone on the S.W. The only noticeable mont. is one in the Abdy pew to Sir John Abdy of Albyns, which has a good medallion portrait. Over the door of this pew is fixed an Abdy helmet. Dr. Godfrey Goodman, afterwards Bp. of Gloucester, and author of the 'Memoirs of the Court of James I.,' held the living in 1606. Thomas Day, the author of 'Sandford and Merton,' lived here for awhile, and made one of his unsuccessful experiments in building.†

---

* Dugdale, "on the information of Thomas, Lord Weston:" Collins, Peerage, vol. iv., p. 82.

* Lysons, vol. iii., pp. 251—253.
† Memoirs of R. L. Edgeworth, p. 223.

STAPLEFORD TAWNEY, Essex,

(pop. 271,) lies chiefly on the N. of the Ongar road and the Roding river: the churches of the two Staplefords are 1¾ m. apart, in a direct line N. and S. Both parishes are agricultural. The country is undulating, well wooded, and pleasing. There is no village, no general shop, and the only inn is the *Talbot*, at Passingford Bridge, on the Ongar road. The *Church* (St. Mary) stands on high ground, and is a conspicuous landmark. It was restored, or rebuilt, in 1862. It is small, of flint and stone, with a wooden turret and spire; is E.E. in style, and consists of a nave, chancel, and S. porch. The interior is without interest. *Suttons* (Sir C. Cunliffe Smith, Bart.) stands in a fine park on the S. of the Ongar road.

STIFFORD, Essex, stands on

high ground, above the little Marditch brook, 2 m. N. from the Grays Stat. of the Southend Rly. Pop. 211. Inn, *Dog and Partridge*.

A quiet, secluded, agricultural village of clean thatched cottages, it affords a charming stroll from Grays. From the station take the path across the fields, between the two great chalk-pits; then a lane bordered by hornbeam hedges and hedgerow elms,—and here look back for occasional dips in the road which lead the eye to a broad reach of the Thames, spotted over with steamers and sailing craft, set in a woodland frame—take the field-path on l. past a disused chalk-pit, now overgrown with tangled trees and shrubs, through the farmyard of Sugar-loaf House, and straight to the ch.-yard.

The *Church* (St. Mary) looks well, standing apart in a quiet burial-ground surrounded by tall trees; but was deprived of its wonted air of hoar antiquity by restoration in 1865. It consists of nave and chancel, of flint, with iron-stone worked in irregularly, a south aisle of ironstone and conglomerate, and a low square ivy-clad tower with shingled spire, from the N. side of which projects a bell-cote covering a single bell. The S. aisle of the chancel is E.E.; the chancel and S. aisle of nave Dec.; the nave, of 2 bays, Perp. The N. doorway is plain Norman. The door itself is old, of oak, with good original scroll hinges. The interior is that of a neat well-kept village ch. *Obs.* the coloured pattern on last shaft and arch of S. arcade of nave; piscina and shelf above—new or rechiselled—in chancel; old heraldic shields in 2 windows S. of chancel, and large unornamented E.E. font. On floor N. of chancel are two *brasses* (half-length) of priests, Ralph Perchehay, quondam rector, of 14th cent., the other 15th cent., with the hands supporting a heart. On the wall are brasses of John Ardalle, gentylman, lord of Styfford, d. 1504, and wife; and of three members of the Latham family—Wm. Latham, gent., late lord of Stifford, d. 1622, and Susan his wife in rich robe and ruff; Ann Latham, 1627, in ruff and furred robe; and Eliz. Latham, 1630. The garden of the cheerful-looking, long, low, half-timber rectory opens into the ch.-yard. The vill. extends W. towards Stifford Bridge, and there is a pleasant field walk from it to South Ockendon. *Stifford Hall*, E. of the ch. (W. P. Beech, Esq.), and *Ford Place* (Charles Moss, Esq.), on the opposite side of the Marditch, are the principal seats. Of old the manor belonged to the De Crammavilles, and lately to the Broderers' Company, of whom it is now held on lease by R. B. Wingfield Baker, Esq.

STOKE D'ABERNON, Surrey,

on the l. bank of the Mole, 2½ m. N.W. from Leatherhead, 2 m. S.E. from Cobham; pop. 356. Stoke D'Abernon is secluded and somewhat inaccessible. The readiest way to reach it on foot is to take the lane on rt. after leaving Leatherhead Stat., go through Randall Park. and then along the lane, leaving Platsome Green to the rt., past Bullock's Farm; but a pleasanter and shorter route, in dry weather, is to turn to the l. on leaving Randall Park, cross the Mole, and by field paths to *Slyfield*, 1 m. W. (*see* Bookham, Great), when Stoke D'Abernon ch. will be seen about ½ m. N. There is no village proper. A few houses and cottages are dispersed along the road to Cobham; the church, the only thing a stranger is likely to visit Stoke D'Abernon for, is within the grounds of the Manor House.

Stoke (*Stoche* in Dom.) received its distinctive designation from the D'Abernon family, to whom it belonged early in the 13th cent., and who retained it till 1359, when it passed by the marriage of Elizabeth D'Abernon to Sir W. Crosier. For several generations the air of Stoke seemed to favour only heiresses. The heiress of the Crosiers carried the manor by marriage to Sir Henry Norbury, whose heiress conveyed it in like manner to Sir Richard Haleighwell; his daughter, Jane, conveyed it to her husband, Sir Edmund Bray, captain of the band of gentlemen pensioners to Henry VIII., who created him Baron Bray. Dying before his wife, she married for her second husband Sir Uriah Brereton. Leaving no son, her estates were on her death, 1559, divided among her 6 daughters. Stoke fell to the share of Frances, who married Thomas Lyfield, and died leaving only a daughter, Jane, who married Thomas Vincent, by whom the charm was broken. Vincent was knighted by Queen Elizabeth, who visited him at Stoke. In 1606 Sir Thomas Vincent was sued at Westminster by the Attorney-General for usurping liberty of court-leet and free-warren within his manors; but after a long inquiry Sir Thomas made good his title at all points. He died in 1613, and the manor descended in regular succession to Sir Francis Vincent, who d. in 1809, leaving two sons, minors, and shortly after the trustees sold the manor to Hugh Smith. It is now held by the Rev. F. P. Phillips. Sir Francis Vincent built, 1775, the first bridge here; previously the Mole had to be crossed by a ford, impassable in floods, and always more or less dangerous.

There was a church at Stoke when the Dom. Survey was made, and it is customary in architectural works to speak of the present ch. as containing "vestiges of Saxon architecture."* No vestige is visible now, nor has there been any for many years past. The chancel arch was semicircular, and was by some called Saxon, but it was taken down and a pointed arch substituted when the ch. was *restored* in 1854. The ch. was restored anew, in accordance with more advanced ecclesiastical tastes, in 1866, and in the course of the two restorations so much was taken down and rebuilt, so

much recast, remodelled, and rechiselled, so much old work replaced by new, and so much new work made to look like old, that it would now be unsafe to trust the apparent antiquity, or attempt to distinguish the relative ages of any parts of the fabric. Essentially no doubt it is E.E., but the superficial features have all been more or less renewed. The ch. comprises nave and N. aisle, chancel, chantry chapel erected by Sir John Norbury, about 1520; and small tower and shingled spire rising from the W. gable.

The interest of the church lies in the *brasses*, which are among the most remarkable we possess. On chancel floor, brass of Sir John D'Abernon, about 1277, the earliest and one of the largest brasses in England. It is 7 ft. 6 in. long, and very well engraved. The knight—full life-size—has his feet resting on a lion couchant, is habited in a suit of mail, basinet, and knee plates; has a long spear, two-handed sword, over his mail a surcoat cut open in front; on his left arm a shield with enamelled field, the azure enamel almost perfect.* By it is a brass of his son, Sir John D'Abernon, d. 1327. This is 6 ft. 4 in. long. The change in the armour in the half-century is remarkable. Plate is to a great extent substituted for mail, and where mail is employed it is of a very different pattern. The casque is different; the surcoat is entirely changed in form, and much more ornamented. Over the head of the younger knight is a canopy. Against pier, small brass, 12 in. long, with effigy in shroud, of Eliza, daughter of Sir Edmond May, d. 1316. *Monts.*—S. of chancel, altar-tomb with recumbent effigy of Sarah Lady Vincent, d. 1608; curious Elizabethan dress, large ruff, her hair spread out from under a great hood: on front of tomb, in relief, her 5 sons and 2 daughters, kneeling. In Norbury chapel, within niche, small kneeling effigy in armour of the founder, Sir John Norbury, executed at the cost of Sir Francis Vincent in 1633. N. side of this chapel, a costly altar tomb to Sir Thomas Vincent, d. 1613, and wife, Jane, d. 1619, with recumbent effigies, of the knight in armour leaning on his

* Bloxam, Principles of Gothic Eccl. Archit., 0th ed., p. 92; Glossary, vol. i., p. 329.

* The brass is engraved on a large scale, and coloured, in Messrs. Waller's Monumental Brasses.

elbow, the lady in elaborate costume, with hands raised in prayer.

Several of the window have painted glass. In the E. window are the arms of the families who have owned the manor from the D'Abernons downwards. In Oct. 1875, two windows received memorials of Bps. Sumner and Wilberforce. The pulpit is well carved in panels. Against the pier by it is a wrought-iron hour-glass stand, one of the very few remaining. Here too is still in use a substantial oak church-chest, of the E.E. period, one of the two oldest known,* and much finer than the other, which is at Climping ch., Sussex.

The *Manor House* is the residence of the Rev. F. P. Phillips ; *Woodlands Park*, of John Smith, Esq.

Ockshot (formerly Oxhot, probably a corruption of *Oaks-holt*, the oaks copse) is a sequestered hamlet on the western edge of Stoke Common, about 2 m. N.E. from Stoke D'Abernon ch. In it is a school for boys and girls, founded by the Duchess of Kent, and used on Sundays for divine service.

STOKE POGES, Bucks, Gray's

burial-place and the scene of his Elegy, is about 2½ m. N. of the Slough Stat. of the Grt. W. Rly.—a pleasant walk by shady lanes and field paths. Pop. 1850; but the par. is very large, comprising 3343 acres, and includes parts of the town of Slough and the hamlet of Salt Hill.

The manor of *Stoches* was held by William Fitz-Ausculf at the Dom. Survey. In the reign of Edward I., Amicia de Stoke conveyed it by marriage to Robert Pogeys, who was chosen knight of the shire in 1300. By the marriage of his granddaughter Egidia, it passed to Sir John Molins, treasurer to Edward III. Molins obtained a licence from the King to fortify and embattle his manor-houses at Stoke and Ditton, and to hold them exempt from the authority of the King's marshal. He was also empowered to hold a fair of six days' continuance, beginning on the feast of St. Giles, at Stoke. From the Molins it passed, by the marriage of Alianore, daughter of Sir Wm. Molins, to Sir Robert Hungerford, afterwards Lord

Hungerford and Molins, beheaded at Newcastle after the battle of Hexham. His son, Sir Thomas Hungerford, was beheaded at Salisbury, 1468, for taking an active part in the attempt to restore Henry VI. His daughter Mary married Edward afterwards Lord Hastings, who on the accession of Henry VII. was restored to the forfeited family estates. Henry Hastings, Earl of Huntingdon, rebuilt the house in the early part of the reign of Elizabeth. Shortly after the estate was seized by the Crown for a debt. Sir Edward Coke, the great lawyer, obtained a lease of the house, and here in 1601, being then Attorney-General, he entertained Queen Elizabeth.

" Now, I think, she (the Queen) be at the farthest for this year, and they say is driving back to Windsor ; where, at her last being, I forgot to tell you that she made a step to Mr. Attorney's at Stoke, where she was most sumptuously entertained, and presented with jewels and other gifts, to the amount of £1000, or £1200.*

Coke, then Lord Chief Justice, obtained a grant of the manor from James I.; † here spent in retirement his last years, and here died, Sept. 3, 1634 ; his house having been searched for seditious papers only three days before his death by Sir Francis Windebank, under an order in council, and all his legal MSS. carried off. On Coke's death the manor passed to his son-in-law Villiers, Visct. Purbeck, and in 1647 Charles I. was for a short time kept a prisoner here.

Stoke was sold to John Gayer in 1656, and on his decease in 1657 passed to his elder brother, Sir Robert Gayer. In 1723 it was bought by Edward Halsey, M.P., whose daughter and heiress, Anne, married Sir Richard Temple, afterwards

---

* Engraved in Parker's Glossary of Architecture, Plate 31.

* John Chamberlain to Dudley Carleton, Sept. 10, 1601; Nichols, Progresses of Q. Eliz., vol. iii., p. 568.

† Lysons, Magna Brit. : Buckinghamshire, says that King James I., "about the year 1621, granted the manor in fee to Lord Chief Justice Coke," and the same statement is made in other county histories and topographical works. But the date must be wrong ; the grant must have been made at least 5 years before. Coke was dismissed from the chief-justiceship in 1616, and was in disgrace in 1621, the asserted date of the grant. But what decides the matter is that on the marriage of Coke's daughter with Villiers in 1616, the reversion of the manor of Stoke was settled on them, and Villiers was in 1619 created a peer, with the title of Baron Villiers of Stoke Poges and Viscount Purbeck.

Visct. Cobham. Lady Cobham surviving her husband, retired to Stoke, and whilst residing at the manor-house gave occasion to Gray's famous 'Long Story.' Her executors sold the manor to Thomas Penn, son of William Penn, the founder of Pennsylvania. It remained in the Penn family till 1848, when it was purchased by the Rt. Hon. Henry Labouchere, created, 1859, Baron Taunton. On the death of Lord Taunton it was bought by its present owner, E. J. Coleman, Esq.

Stoke Manor House was rebuilt by Lord Huntingdon about 1560. It was a large rambling red-brick mansion with projecting wings and pointed gables, sunny bays and oriels, tall roofs and quaintly grouped stacks of carved brick chimney-shafts. Inside were large low rooms, long galleries, and capacious kitchens with huge fireplaces, emblems of the ancient hospitality ;

" Rich windows that exclude the light,
   And passages that lead to nothing."

Gray was living at Stoke with his mother, when he was surprised by a visit of Lady Cobham, who, admiring the Elegy, wished to make the author's acquaintance ; " and as the beginning of this acquaintance had some appearance of romance, he soon after gave a humorous account of it in the verses which he entitled a Long Story." * Gray describes the house and its associations very pleasantly, but he was misled by the tradition † that affirmed it to have belonged to " Huntingdons and Hattons," into telling how

" Full oft within the spacious walls,
   When he had fifty winters o'er him,
My grave Lord-Keeper led the brawls ;
   The seals and maces danced before him."

Wherever my grave Lord-Keeper led the brawls, it was not at Stoke Manor. The " ancient pile " was pulled down by John Penn in 1789, with the exception of a wing, which was left as a memorial. It stands but a short way from the ch., and is worth visiting. With its quaint gable and chimney shafts, and ivy mantling, it is a picturesque object. Inside are the great kitchen, with its wide fireplace, and

an upper floor with heraldic devices on the walls, and various sage mottoes, "Feare the Lord," " Obey the Prince," " Love thine Enmis," and the like.

The old house stood in a low sheltered position ; the present mansion occupies a higher site. It is one of the elder Wyatt's classic structures, of brick covered with stucco, cold, dignified, and spacious, with some excellent state-rooms : it has, however, been a good deal altered. The S. front has a colonnade of 12 columns, with a projecting tetrastyle Ionic portico. The N. front has ten columns of the Tuscan order. The park, of 570 acres, is well-wooded, and many of the oaks, beeches, and elms are of large size; well stored with deer ; gently undulating in surface, and varied by a streamlet being led through it, and forming in the midst a long lake. In the upper part of the park, towards the N.W., is a column, 68 ft. high, surmounted with a colossal statue of Sir Edward Coke, by Rossi. On the eastern side, close to Stoke ch., Mr. Penn erected, 1799, a cenotaph " in honour of Thomas Gray, among the scenes celebrated by that great Lyric and Elegiac Poet." It stands within an enclosure, open to the visitor. Stoke Manor was celebrated in Lord Taunton's time for the choice pictures in the house : the present owner has rendered it attractive to agriculturists by the successful scientific farming operations and extensive irrigation works carried out on the Home Farm.

Many churchyards have claimed the inspiration of Gray's Elegy. If " Written in a Country Churchyard " is to be rendered literally, it is to Stoke that the glory must be assigned. Tradition has been constant to this effect. Between 1741-58 Gray used to spend his summer vacations at Stoke in the house of his mother and aunt. Shortly before he wrote the Elegy, his aunt, to whom he was much attached, had been laid in the churchyard. Gray had hastened to console his mother, lonely and in feeble health, and he was already dreading that he might ere long have to lay her beside the sister she mourned. Church, churchyard, and surrounding scenery, correspond closely with the descriptions and imagery of the Elegy. And we have his own testimony that the poem was finished at Stoke :—

" I have been here at Stoke a few days (where I

---

* Mitford's Gray, p. 147.
† The only ground for the tradition seems to be the fact that Henry Lord Huntingdon mortgaged the house towards the end of the 16th cent.

Stoke Poges Church

The Gallery, Strawberry Hill (see p.587)

shall continue a good part of the summer); and having put an end to a thing, whose beginning you have seen long ago, I immediately send it to you. You will I hope look on it in the light of *a thing with an end to it ;* a merit that most of my writings have wanted, and are likely to want."*

That this "thing with an end to it" was the Elegy no one has ever doubted : and there is just as little reason to doubt that the ch. and ch.-yard are those of Stoke, if they are not a mere poetic fiction.

In the ch.-yard, immediately E. of the ch., is the plain tomb which the poet raised over the vault which contains the remains of his aunt, Mary Antrobus, d. 1749, and, "beside her friend and sister, . . . Dorothy Gray, widow ; the careful tender mother of many children, one of whom alone had the misfortune to survive her." She d. March 1753. Gray died in July 1771, and was laid in the same vault, but no friendly hand added an inscription to his memory : and though when the costly monument was erected 20 years later in the adjacent park, there was engraven on it that the great poet " lies unnoticed in the adjoining churchyard," it does not seem to have occurred to the builder that *he* might supply the omission with as little trouble or cost as record it. However, after another half-century had passed, a plain slab was fixed under the E. window of the ch., which points out the poet's burial-place.

Stoke *Church* (St. Giles) has nave and aisles, chancel with S. aisle, or Hastings Chapel, massive ivy-mantled tower and modern wooden spire at the E. end of the N. aisle, and a large and good oak porch on the S. Close to the porch are two venerable and wide-spreading yews. Church and ch.-yard are in aspect and feeling notably picturesque, sombre, solemn. The ch. is of various dates. The chancel is Norm., but the chancel arch was rebuilt in 1844. The original windows on the N. are blocked up, and the E. window is an insertion of the Perp. period. The nave arcades are late E.E., as are some of the double lancets within enclosing arches in the aisles, the others being Dec. The Hastings Chapel was built in 1557. The interior was partially restored in 1860, and refitted with an oak pulpit and seats. *Obs.* 3 sedilia on N. of chan-

* Gray to Horace Walpole, 12th June, 1750.

cel, piscina on S. In the chancel is a canopied tomb, without effigy or insc., supposed to be that of Sir John Molins, treasurer to Edward III. *Obs.* at W. end of N. aisle mural tablet by Flaxman to his friend Nathaniel Marchant, R.A., d. 1816, a distinguished gem engraver ; on upper part a line of medals, an emblematic female figure, and a medallion of George III. on horseback. Brass with effigies of Sir Wm. Molins, d. 1425, and wife. Two or three other brasses are of little value. In the cloisters, N. of the ch., are several pieces of painted glass, chiefly armorial, from old Stoke Manor House.

West End, the house in which Gray's mother lived, and he wrote much poetry and many letters, now called *Stoke Court* (J. Darby, Esq.), is about 1 m. N. of the ch. Gray described it as a " compact neat box of red brick, with sash windows, a grotto made of flints, a walnut-tree with three mole-hills under it," etc., but the house was rebuilt by Mr. Penn, about 1845, on a larger scale, and is now a gentlemanly villa. The room in which Gray wrote was, however, preserved unaltered, and forms a part of the present house. The walnut tree and grotto were retained, and the " basin of gold fishes " greatly enlarged. There is a charming walk of little more than a mile from West End to Burnham Common and Burnham Beeches, celebrated by Gray. (*See* BURNHAM BEECHES.)

Stoke Place, ½ m. S.E. of Stoke ch., was the seat of Field Marshal Sir G. Howard, d. 1796. It now belongs to Col. R. H. R. Howard Vyse. The park is celebrated for its lake and cedars. *Stoke Farm* (Lady Maria Molyneux), the property of Earl Sefton, stands in a small but very pretty park.

The manor of *Ditton* was possessed, along with that of Stoke, by Sir John de Molins, who obtained licence from Edward III. to embattle both manor-houses. A new house was built on the site of that at Ditton by Sir Ralph Winwood, Principal Secretary of State to James I. The manor passed by marriage to the Montagues, and was carried by the daughter of John Duke of Montagu to her husband, Lord Beaulieu, who bequeathed it to his niece, Elizabeth Duchess of Buccleuch. The house, when the residence of John Duke of Montagu, d. 1749, was celebrated for the hospitality maintained, and the gatherings of the wise and witty in it. The house was destroyed by fire April 28, 1812, and rebuilt in 1813 by the Duchess of Buccleuch. It is now the property and a residence of the Duke of Buccleuch. *Ditton Park* lies between Langley Marsh and Ditton, 3½ m. S.E. of Stoke ch. The house is large and stately, with something of a picturesque character from a tower and some other portions of the old house preserved from the fire having been worked up in it, and the moat being retained. The park contains much fine timber.

Baylis, the property of the Duke of Leeds, 1½ mile S. of Stoke ch., towards Salt Hill, is an old red-brick mansion, erected by Dr. Godolphin, Provost of Eton, 1695. It was the residence of Lord Chesterfield, of the Letters to his Son; and afterwards of Alexander Wedderburn, Earl of Rosslyn, who died in it, Jan. 1805. It has for many years been occupied as a Roman Catholic educational establishment. A chapel in it is open for public service. *Salt Hill*, noticed under Eton and Slough, is in this parish.

STONDON MASSEY, Essex, 2½

m. S.E. from Ongar Rly. Stat., pop. 285, is a quiet secluded place, hardly a village, comprising a couple of good mansions, a rectory, half a dozen scattered farms, and a church which stands alone at the angle of the road leading to *Stondon Hall*, once a manor, now a farm-house. The *Church* (St. Peter and St. Paul) is a plain little building ; the N. aisle Norm., the rest Perp.; restored in 1874. It consists of a nave and chancel, with a priest's door on the S. ; a wooden belfry, with 3 bells, and a shingled spire, rising from the red-tiled roof at the W., and a wooden porch at the S.W. The interior is of no interest. From the ch.-yard some wide views are obtained over a thickly wooded and fertile country. *Stondon Place* is the residence of F. E. Brace, Esq. ; *Stondon House* of Capt. Francis Baker.

STONE, Kent (Dom. *Estanes*),

on the Dover road, 1 m. W. of the Greenhithe Stat. of the S.-E. Rly. (North Kent line), 2½ m. W.N.W. of Dartford. Pop. of par. 1617, but this includes 176 in Greenhithe, 306 in the City Lunatic Asylum,

and 41 in the County Female Penitentiary, leaving 1094 in Stone proper.

The pop. is very scattered, and there is hardly anywhere what can be called a village. Agriculture is the chief employment. Corn and beans are much grown, and there are extensive fruit gardens. Chalk and gravel pits, Portland cement, lime, and whiting works, and a brewery employ many hands.

Stone was given, it is said, to the Bp. of Rochester in 995 ; and no doubt the manor belonged to the see from a very early date. The bishops had a house here, the distance making it a convenient resting-place between Rochester and London. The Ecclesiastical Commissioners now hold the manor. Here, too, as Philipott writes, was "formerly a castle which acknowledged the Northwoods for its founders." It dated from the reign of Edward III., "and although it now lies wrapped up in its own ruins, yet the shell or skeleton of it, within which Sir Richard Wiltshire laid the foundation of that fabric now extant, represents to the eye some symptoms of its former strength and magnificence." This was written more than two centuries ago, and of what was then left of the castle, a small tower alone remains. There is nothing of general interest in the history of the castle or in its descent. It stands to the S. of the Dover road, about a mile S.E. of Stone, in pleasant park-like grounds, and is the residence of W. Munro Ross, Esq. Other seats are *Stone Park* (Thomas Bevan, Esq.); *Barnsfield House* (W. O. White, Esq.)

The *Church* (St. Mary), architecturally one of the most interesting of the Kent churches, stands, with the rectory, almost alone, on the edge of the marsh, across which there is a path of about ½ m., with the Thames on your l., to Greenhithe. The ch. door is generally left open, but if closed the key may be obtained at the rectory. The building was restored throughout in 1860 by Mr. G. E. Street, R.A., and has a look of newness which somewhat detracts from the impression its age, position, and architectural beauty would otherwise produce: but the renewed portions are said to be careful reproductions of the originals. It is of flint and stone, and comprises nave and aisles, chancel, and low massive W. tower, with buttresses. A peculiar effect is produced by the chancel roof being higher than that of the nave, and nearly as high as the tower. In the main the ch. is late E. E. in character. Mr. Street says, "The chancel, nave, aisles, and western tower are E.E.; and were probably built during the episcopate of Laurence de St. Martin (Bp. of Rochester from 1251 to 1274). In the 14th cent. the vestry N. of the chancel was added, and the windows at the W. end of the nave and aisles were inserted. The tower piers were also altered at this time. In the 16th cent. the Wiltshire Chantry, forming the N. chancel aisle, was added." * *Obs.* doorway at W. end of the aisle with chevron moulding, which, however, Mr. Street thinks is " no doubt a curious instance of imitation of earlier work, rather than evidence of the doorway itself being earlier than the rest of the church."

The interior will repay close examination. The nave arcades, of 3 bays, have tall E. E. arches, borne on light clustered columns, thin shafts of Sussex marble intervening between the stouter stone shafts. The arches are well proportioned, and have deep mouldings with the dogtooth in the centre. The roof is of timber, ceiled. The chancel arch has around·it a band of foliage, with richly foliated quatrefoils in the spandrels. The chancel is still more ornate ; indeed, as Mr. Street observes, "the most remarkable feature in the design is the way in which the whole of the work gradually increases in richness of detail and in beauty from west to east." Around the walls of the chancel is an arcade with Sussex marble shafts, the spandrels filled with foliage of exceeding delicacy and beauty. The windows and groined roof are new, but " in strict accordance with the original design." Most of the windows are filled with painted glass. S. of the altar is a piscina. The floor is laid with encaustic tiles and coloured marble. Obs. *brasses* on floor of Lambarde, rector, 1408, small effigy in centre of a cross fleurée (very good); John Sorewell, rector, 1439. In the vestry is a good altar tomb, with matrix of brass effigy on Purbeck marble slab ;

* Street : Account of the Church of St. Mary, Stone, Kent, 1861 ; originally printed in the Archæologia Cantiana, vol. iii.

nameless, but said to be of Sir John Wilshyre, Controller of the town and marches of Calais under Henry VIII. On the wall of the N. aisle several paintings were uncovered when the ch. was restored: the best preserved is a Virgin and Child.

Stone ch. was built whilst the chief works were in progress at Westminster Abbey, and Mr. Street is of opinion—and on such a subject his opinion is of the highest value—that the two churches were the work of the same architect. He gives in detail the points of resemblance in design, materials, and workmanship. W. of the ch. is a yew-tree of good size and form.

On an elevated site by the Dover road is the *City of London Lunatic Asylum*, erected 1862-66, at a cost of £65.000, from the designs of Mr. Bunning, the City architect. The original building provided for 250 inmates, and a wing added in 1874 provides for 70 more. Without much architectural pretension the building is pleasing in appearance, commodious, and abundantly supplied with sanitary appliances. It stands in spacious grounds, from which good views are obtained of the river and surrounding country.

By the Brent, 2 m. from Dartford, is the *Kent County Female Penitentiary*, a good building, erected in 1866 for 50 inmates.

STRAND-ON-THE-GREEN,

MIDDX., an irregular line of houses stretching for about ½ m. along the Thames, from the foot of Kew Bridge towards Chiswick, to which par. it belongs. Here are extensive malt-houses, boat and barge building yards and wharves, a few good residences, many poor ones, and several inns.

Until the early part of the last century it consisted almost wholly of fishermen's hovels. A few houses of a better sort were then erected, and for a time it was in some favour. Joseph Miller, the comedian, better known by his Jest Book as ' Joe Miller,' died at his house here Aug. 15, 1738, and was buried in St. Clement's Dane burial-ground, Portugal Street, London. David Mallet, the poet, lived here ; his first wife (died 1742) is buried at Chiswick. John Zoffany, R.A., died at his house here in 1810, and was buried at Kew. Zoffany used the fishermen of Strand-on-the-Green or Brentford as models for his pictures. In a 'Last Supper,' which he painted as an altar-piece for Old Brentford ch., he copied the features of several of the fishermen with so much success, that they were afterwards commonly designated by their apostolical sobriquets—somewhat, it is said, to the disgust of the wife of Judas, surnamed Iscariot.

The peculiar wooden structure on the eyot, opposite Strand-on-the-Green, was built originally as a collecting-house for the tolls paid to the City by river craft. Here now are the Thames Conservancy Works. The iron bridge which here crosses the Thames, without adding to its beauty, belongs to the Richmond and Hammersmith branch of the L. and S.-W. Rly.

STRATFORD, or STRATFORD LANGTHORNE, ESSEX, extends from Bow Bridge for 1½ m. along the Romford road, and for a considerable distance along the roads to Low Leyton and Leytonstone. The Broadway is 3½ m. from Whitechapel ch. There are three stats. on the Grt. E. Rly., Stratford Central, Stratford Bridge, and Forest Gate. Stratford Langthorne is a ward of West Ham par., and had 23,286 inhab. in 1871—since greatly increased.

Stratford has become a considerable manufacturing district. Much of the land is low and marshy, and being well provided with rly. facilities, and the navigable Lea on one side of it affording ready access to the Thames and docks, it has become the home of many factories which find difficulty in obtaining sites so near to London. Besides the old-established cornmills, distilleries, breweries, chemical and dye-works by the Lea, there are now extensive engineering establishments, printworks, jute spinning mills, manufactories of vestas and matches, printing ink, aniline colour, varnish, soap and candle factories, oil, grease, creosote, bone-boiling, paraffin, coprolite, nitro-phosphate, guano, and other artificial manure and gas and tar works, and a variety more of an equally unfragrant character. But at the northern end of the town, from the Broadway, where the roads diverge, there are still green spaces, roads lined with trees, and good private residences. The town itself has little that is attractive, beyond the churches,

the Town Hall, and the factories for those who feel an interest in them. Of old, Stratford was regarded as a part of West Ham, but it has long outgrown the mother par., which lies on one side in quiet obscurity.

Stratford Langthorne Abbey, for monks of the Cistercian order, was founded in 1135 by William de Montfichet, and endowed with the manor of West Ham and other estates in the county. The abbey stood in the marshes, on a branch of the Lea known as the Abbey Creek, or Sea-river Channel, about ½ m. S. of Stratford Broadway, and in its early days suffered so much from floods, that the monks were compelled to migrate to a cell on their estate at Burghstead, near Billericay; but the buildings being "reedified by King Richard," the monks returned, and the abbey became a flourishing establishment. The abbot was summoned to Parliament in 1307. John de Bohun, Earl of Hereford and Essex, High Constable of England, was buried in the abbey in 1335. William Huddlestone, the last abbot, surrendered the abbey to Henry VIII. in March 1538; the net revenue was then estimated at £652. Henry, in 1539, granted the site to Sir Peter de Meautis, who had been his ambassador to the French court. At this time, Margaret Countess of Salisbury—the last in the direct line of the Plantagenets—was residing within the abbey precincts. Two years later, May 27, 1541, she was beheaded for high treason. Henry Meautis sold the abbey in 1633 to Sir John Nulls, whose son sold it in 1663 to Richard Knight; and in 1786 it was purchased of Richard Dudlas Knight by Mr. Thomas Holbrook.

Up to this time, many portions of the abbey appear to have been standing. But Mr. Holbrook destroyed nearly all that was left, dug up the foundations of the monastery, and, " after having built walls with some of the stones, has sold quantities of them to great advantage." * A gateway of the abbey was left " standing over the road from the mills ;" in a field were " the remains of one of the chapels, now used as a stable," a doorway, and various fragments in the garden of the Adam and Eve, a public-house which had been built

---

* Ambulator, 1792, p. 266; Lysons, vol. i., p. 728.

on a portion of the site. The Adam and Eve retains its old position, and a fragment of the doorway is still attached to it, but so imperfect and suspicious—having to all appearance been rebuilt—as not to be worth visiting. During Mr. Holbrook's operations, gravestones, leaden coffins, and coins were exhumed; but the only antiquity "worthy of note, was a small onyx seal, with the impress of a griffin, set in silver, on which is the following legend : *Nuncio vobis gaudium et salutem*," * the seal, no doubt, of one of the abbots. The abbey precincts, of about 16 acres, were surrounded by a moat. The Adam and Eve and the Abbey Mills are now considered to belong to West Ham, not Stratford. Close by is the Mid Level Pumping Station of the Metropolitan Main Drainage.

Stratford *Church* (St. John) was erected in 1834, from the designs of Mr. Blore, on what was the village Green, at the parting of the roads to Romford and Leytonstone. It is a large and commodious structure, of Suffolk brick and Bath stone, E.E. in style, with a tower and short spire. It cost £23,000, but has no great architectural merit. Originally a chapel-of-ease to West Ham, it was made a district ch. in 1844, and a parochial vicarage in 1868. In front of the ch. is a granite obelisk, 40 ft. high, with a drinking fountain, designed by Mr. J. Bell, erected in 1861, as a memorial of the late Samuel Gurney, by his fellow-parishioners.

Christ Church, in the High Street, close to the Main Drainage Works, is a respectable Dec. building, of hammered stone, with a good tower and spire, also of stone. *Obs.* near it the Local Board School, a cheerful looking and good building.

St. Paul, Maryland Road, is a rather fanciful fabric of various coloured bricks, erected in 1865 from the designs of Mr. E. B. Keeling. There are also churches at Forest Gate and Stratford New Town, but they do not call for particular notice.

Stratford New Town is a dense collection of small houses, by the rly. stat., originally called *Hudson Town*—the Railway King being then at the head of the Great Eastern Rly.; but on the fall of that potentate the name was changed.

The Roman Catholics have a chapel,

dedicated to St. Vincent de Paul, a neat Italian building erected in 1868, in Grove Crescent Road; and a Convent of Jesus Mary, Park House, in the Grove. The Congregational Church, Grove Crescent Road, is a large and costly classical Italian edifice, erected a few years since, from the designs of Mr. Rd. Plumbe. The front has a lofty portico of six composite columns with very ornate capitals, and pediment, and on the rt. a campanile tower.

The only secular building of note is the *Town Hall* (or Public Offices and Vestry Hall), erected in 1867-69, from the designs of Messrs. Giles and Angell. It is semi-classic in style, with two fronts, each of about 100 ft., that towards the Broadway of Portland stone, that in West Ham Lane of white brick and stone. The Broadway front has a portico of two stages with polished red granite shafts, and a tower 100 ft. high; and the building is surmounted with statues of Britannia, St. George, Science, Art, Commerce, Industry, Justice, Mercy, Fortitude, Prudence, and Temperance.

The Bridge which unites Stratford with Bow—the Stratford-atte-Bow of Chaucer and our old writers down to Will Kempe—occupies the place of that built at the beginning of the 12th cent. by Matilda, Queen of Henry I. The old bridge, which had been so often repaired as to leave little of the original recognisable, was taken down in 1835, and the present one erected on its site, from the designs of Messrs. Walker and Burges. It was formally opened Feb. 14, 1839. It is a substantial stone structure of a single elliptical arch, 66 ft. in span and of very flat curve. The old bridge was of three narrow arches, very wide piers with angular projections. The original width was only 13 ft. 6 in. between the parapets, widened to 21 ft. in 1741. On it was a chapel (long since removed) called St. Katherine's Chapel-upon-Bow-Bridge. When taken down, the piers of the old bridge showed neither settlement nor fracture. They were laid on gravel a few feet below the bed of the river, without piling of any kind.* Queen Matilda is said to have founded another bridge called Channel Sea Bridge, over an affluent of the Lea, for the service of Stratford Abbey.

STRAWBERRY HILL, TWICK-ENHAM, MIDDX.,

the famous "Gothic Castle" of Horace Walpole (Earl of Orford) and now the seat of Frances Countess of Waldegrave and Lord Carlingford, stands on a gentle elevation about 300 yards from and overlooking the Thames, immediately above Twickenham. The Strawberry Hill Stat. of the L. and S.-W. Rly. (New Kingston line), is a short distance W.

The history of Horace Walpole's Strawberry Hill is best told in his own words :

"Where the Gothic castle now stands, was originally a small tenement, built in 1698 [by the Earl of Bradford's coachman] and let as a lodging-house. Cibber once took it and wrote one of his plays here, 'The Refusal, or the Lady's Philosophy.' After him, Talbot, Bishop of Durham, had it for eight years ; then Henry Bridges, Marquis of Carnarvon, son of James Duke of Chandos, and since Duke himself. It was next hired by Mrs. Chenevix, the noted toy-woman, who, on the death of her husband, let it to Lord John Philip Sackville, second son of Lionel Duke of Dorset : he kept it about two years, and then Mr. Walpole took the remainder of Mrs. Chenevix's lease in May 1747, and the next year bought it by Act of Parliament, it being the property of three minors of the name of Mortimer." *

Walpole was fond of the locality and delighted with his acquisition. When a boy he had spent a summer with his tutor at Twickenham, and may have retained an early liking for it. At any rate he never tired of lauding the scenery and the associations of

"Twit'nam, the Muse's fav'rite seat."

The commencement of his occupancy was thus announced to his two most intimate friends :—

"I may retire to a little new farm that I have taken just out of Twickenham. The house is so small that I can send it you in a letter to look at. The prospect is as delightful as possible, commanding the river, the town, and Richmond Park ; and being situated on a hill, descends to the Thames through two or three little meadows, where I have some Turkish sheep and two cows, all studied in their colours for becoming the view. This little rural *bijou* was Mrs. Chenevix's, the toy woman *à la mode*, who in every dry season is to furnish me with the best rain water from Paris, and now and then with some Dresden-china cows, who are

to figure like wooden classics in a library : so I shall grow as much a shepherd as any swain in the Astræa." *

"Twickenham, June 8th, 1747.

"You perceive by my date that I am got into a new camp, and have left my tub at Windsor. It is a little plaything house that I got out of Mrs. Chenevix's shop, and is the prettiest bauble you ever saw. It is set in enamelled meadows with filigree hedges :

A small Euphrates through the piece is roll'd,
And little finches wave their wings in gold.

Two delightful roads, that you would call dusty, supply me continually with coaches and chaises ; barges as solemn as Barons of the Exchequer move under my window ; Richmond Hill and Ham walks bound my prospect ; but, thank God ! the Thames is between me and the Duchess of Queensberry. Dowagers as plenty as flounders inhabit all around, and Pope's ghost is just now skimming under my window by a most poetical moonlight." †

It was not till a year later, when he had completed the purchase, that the name was found which he was to make so famous.

"I am now returning to my villa, where I have been making some alterations : you shall hear from me from STRAWBERRY HILL, which I have found out in my lease is the old name of my house ; so pray, never call it Twickenham again. I like to be there better than I have liked being anywhere since I came to England." ‡

When Walpole rented Mrs. Chenevix's house, it was little more than a cottage, and the grounds were of narrow compass. As soon as he became its owner, he began to enlarge the house and extend the grounds. The cottage grew into a villa, the villa into a mansion. In this there was nothing uncommon ; the novelty consisted in his deliberately adopting the then proscribed *Gothic* style. As early as Jan. 1750, he writes to Sir Horace Mann that he is "going to build a little Gothic Castle at Strawberry Hill," and asks him to "pick me up any fragments of old painted glass, arms, anything," if there are any such things to be found among the old chateaus in Italy.§ For the grounds, he writes to the same correspondent somewhat earlier, "I have got four more acres, which makes my territory prodigious in a situation where land

* Walpole : A Description of the Villa of Mr. Horace Walpole, at Strawberry Hill, near Twickenham, p. 1.

* Horace Walpole to Sir Horace Mann, June 5, 1747 ; Letters, vol. ii., p. 85.
† Horace Walpole to the Hon. H. S. Conway ; Letters, vol. ii., p. 86.
‡ Walpole to Sir Horace Mann, June 7, 1748 ; Letters, vol. ii., p. 113.
§ Walpole's Letters, vol. ii., p. 190.

is so scarce, and villas as abundant as formerly at Tivoli and Baiæ. I have now about fourteen acres, and am making a terrace the whole breadth of my garden on the brow of a natural hill, with meadows at the foot, and commanding the river, the village, Richmond Hill, and the park, and part of Kingston." *

Having formed his plan, Walpole carried it out in a systematic though deliberate way. He was his own architect, and with Bentley as draughtsman, visited cathedrals, abbeys, castles, manor-houses, and colleges, and made copies of whatever would serve as a model or furnished a suggestion. Windows, doorways, groined roofs, cloisters, screens, tombs, were borrowed from Westminster or Durham, St. Albans, Lincoln, Salisbury or Winchester, Oxford or Cambridge, for like, or more often for unlike features at Strawberry.

By slow degrees the cottage grew into a castle; for many years its transformation seeming to be its master's most serious occupation—as in the succeeding years was the collection and arrangement of its rich and multifarious contents. The plan was sketched in 1750; but " the Castle was not entirely built from the ground, but formed at different times by alterations of and additions to the old small house. The library and refectory, or great parlour, were entirely new built in 1753 ; the gallery, round tower, great cloister, and cabinet in 1760 and 1761 ; the great north bed-chamber in 1770; and the Beauclerk tower with the hexagon closet in 1776." †

Walpole designated his house " a fantastic fabric," a "romance in lath and plaster." If the house and its contents are regarded as heterogeneous, he will not defend them by argument. " It was built to please my own taste, and in some degree to realize my own visions." He has observed the Gothic style not only in the architecture but in the fittings and furniture, but he did not mean to make his house " so Gothic as to exclude convenience, and modern refinements in luxury. The designs of the outside and inside are strictly ancient, but the decorations are modern." Could he " describe the gay but tranquil scene where it stands,

and add the beauty of the landscape to the romantic cast of the mansion . . . . at least the prospect would recall the good humour of those who might be disposed to condemn the fantastic fabric, and to think it a very proper habitation of, as it was the scene that inspired, the author of the *Castle of Otranto*."

There was some affectation in this humility. Walpole really believed his house would go far to effect an entire change in architectural taste ; and there can be little doubt that it did much to call attention to the long-neglected and comparatively despised wealth of Gothic architecture in the country, and to stimulate the investigation of its principles and peculiarities, and thus prepare the way for the remarkable Gothic revival by which our own time has been distinguished. But Walpole's work found ample recognition in his own day. Gothic houses were built in imitation of Strawberry Hill, and Strawberry Hill itself became the fashion.

" Some talk of Gunnersbury,
    For Syon some declare ;
And some say that with Chiswick House
    No villa can compare :
But all the beaux of Middlesex
    Who know the country well,
Say that Strawberry Hill, that Strawberry
    Doth bear away the bell." *

Not only beaux of Middlesex, and idlers about town, but people in every profession, lords and ladies, dukes and duchesses, came to see Strawberry Hill ; foreign ministers, and indeed most foreigners of distinction, made a point of visiting it, and an English tour was deemed incomplete if Strawberry Hill were not included in the programme. Walpole pretended to be annoyed : he had not, he declared, a quarter of an hour of peace in it ; his whole time was taken up in giving tickets for seeing it, and hiding himself while it was seen ; and he warns his friend never to build " a charming house for himself between London and Hampton Court : everybody will live in it but you."

But he relates the visits of the more distinguished sightseers with unmistakeable gratification. It is curious now to read how a grand party of this kind was received somewhat over a century ago.

* Walpole to Sir H. Mann, Dec. 26, 1748.
† Walpole, Description of the Villa, etc.: Introd.

Lord Bath's Stanzas to the old tune of Rowe's ballad on Dodington's Mrs. Strawbridge, 1755.

On a May morning in 1763 came the Comtesse de Boufflers, Madame Dusson, Lady Mary Coke, Lord and Lady Holdernesse, the Duke and Duchess of Grafton, Lord Hertford, Lord Villiers, Messieurs de Fleury, Duclos, and the afterwards too famous Chevalier D'Eon. They breakfast in "the great parlour," and the host has "filled the hall and large cloister by turns with French horns and clarionets." They are taken to see the printing-press which Walpole has set up in the garden, where some impromptu verses are struck off in honour of the French ladies, and "the Duchess of Grafton, who had never happened to be here before, perfectly entered into the air of enchantment and fairyism, which is the tone of the place, and was peculiarly so this day." *

At other times he records the visits of the Archduke and Archduchess, of the Princess Emily, of the Prince and Princess of Wales, and, as the crowning honour, of George III. and his Queen.

"The King and Queen have been here this week to see my castle, and stayed two hours. I was gone to London but a quarter of an hour before. They were exceedingly pleased with it, and the Queen so much that she said she would come again." +

The fêtes at Strawberry were so celebrated that, as we have described a breakfast, it may be well to give a companion picture of a dinner there:—

"Strawberry has been in great glory; I have given a festino there that will almost mortgage it. Last Tuesday all France dined there: Monsieur and Madame du Châtelet, the Duc de Liancourt, three more French ladies, whose names you will find in the enclosed paper, eight other Frenchmen, the Spanish and Portuguese ministers, the Holdernesse, Fitzroys, in short we were four-and-twenty. They arrived at two. At the gates of the castle I received them, dressed in the cravat of Gibbons' carving, and a pair of gloves embroidered up to the elbows that belonged to James I. The French servants stared, and firmly believed this was the dress of English country gentlemen. After taking a survey of the apartments, we went to the printing-house, where I had prepared the enclosed verses, with translations by Monsieur de Lille, one of the company. The moment they were printed off, I gave a private signal, and French horns and clarionets accompanied this compliment. We then went to see Pope's grotto and garden, and returned to a magnificent dinner in the refectory. In the evening we walked, had tea, coffee, and lemonade in the Gallery, which was illuminated with a thousand, or thirty candles, I forget which, and played at whisk and loo till midnight. Then there was a cold supper, and at one the company returned to town, saluted by fifty nightingales, who, as tenants of the manor, came to do honour to their lord." *

Strawberry Hill, when completed, was a Gothic building, but Gothic of no particular period, class, or style. Windows, doorways, and mouldings of the 13th cent., stood side by side with others of the 15th or 16th. Ecclesiastical were commingled with secular features, collegiate with baronial or military. Next to an abbey entrance, was the oriel of an Elizabethan manor-house, or the keep of a Norman castle, while battlements and machicolations frowned over wide bay-windows that opened on to the lawn. Gothic purists nowadays talk with devout horror of Strawberry Hill Gothic; but however heretical now, it was accepted as orthodox then. Twenty years after it was completed, we find a learned Oxford professor, in an elaborate dissertation on architecture, inviting the connoisseur to "contemplate all that is exquisite in the Palladian architecture" at Chiswick, and "all that is fascinating in the Gothic style at Strawberry Hill," and presently commending the latter as "the happiest attempt of the kind" yet produced.+

But the contents were even more remarkable than the house. As he looks through Walpole's 'Inventory of the Furniture, Pictures, Curiosities, etc.,' brightened as it is by his matchless manner of illustrating the pedigree of this or the other renowned article, adding a sly reference to the person represented, or story of some former owner, a collector of the present day may well be filled with envy or admiration. The number seems endless of articles that would now excite no gentle rivalry at Christie's. Pictures ascribed to Holbein and Mabuse and Vansomer, to Vandyck and Kneller, and Hogarth and Reynolds; antique sculpture, bronzes, cameos, gems; Oriental, Sèvres, Bristol, and Chelsea china; Majolica and other mediæval fayences, and modern porcelain; Limoges enamels,

* Walpole to George Montagu, May 17, 1763; Letters, vol. iv., p. 80.
+ Walpole to Sir Horace Mann, June 9, 1766; Letters, vol. iv., p. 504.

* Walpole to George Montagu, May 11, 1769; Letters, vol. v., p. 160.
+ Dallaway, Anecdotes of the Arts in England, 1800, p. 148.

and miniatures by Petitot, Zincke, and other famous masters, unequalled in number, beauty, and interest ; ivories, mosaics, illuminated missals, rare books, including vellum copies from the Strawberry Hill press ; choice engravings ; jewels, trinkets, relics, and a wide range of those " curiosities " that owe more than half their charm to the wonder how they came to be thought worth preserving : the fans with which Barbara Villiers or the Countess of Hamilton flirted ; Dr. Dee's spirit speculum—"the Devil's looking-glass, a stone ; " a locket with Mary Queen of Scot's hair ; Sir Julius Cæsar's travelling library ; the copy of Homer used by Pope when translating ; Sir Robert Walpole's standish ; Charles the Second's warming-pan ; the spurs worn by William III. at the Battle of the Boyne ; a toilette worked by Kitty Clive ; and the original sketch of Sarah Malcolm the murderess, made by Hogarth the night before her execution, " when she had put on red to look the better." Walpole was not only an insatiable collector, but turned his friends into collectors also. He haunted sales, was always accessible to those who had anything promising to dispose of, and absorbed into his own whole collections like that of Conyers Middleton.

Walpole drew an elaborate picture of his house for Sir Horace Mann, in 1753 ; but as he went on adding to it for 20 years longer, we must refer to his Description and Inventory, enriched with ground-plans and views, to see what it was like when he had completed it. " Entering by the great north gate," he writes, " the first object that presents itself is a small oratory enclosed with iron rails ; in front an altar, on which stands a saint in bronze ; open niches and stone basins for holy water. . . . On the right hand is a small garden parted off by an open screen taken from the tomb of Roger Niger, Bp. of London, in old St. Paul's. Passing on the left by a small cloister is the entrance to the house, the narrow front of which was designed by Richard Bentley, only son of Dr. Bentley, the learned master of Trinity College, Cambridge. Over the door are the three shields of Walpole, Shorter, and Robsart." But even before entering the house were to be seen some of those objects which made the place so remarkable. In this little cloister, for example, among other curiosities, on a pedestal stood the large blue and white china vase in which Walpole's cat was drowned, a catastrophe immortalized in Gray's ' Ode on the Death of a Cat.'

Looked at from the garden, the house is an irregular structure of three floors, battlemented throughout, with crocketed pinnacles at the angles, a large round tower at the western end, and by it a smaller turret crowned with a spire, and boldly projecting bays in the several fronts—a fantastic fabric, as its master designated it, of lath and plaster covered with roughcast. Entering by a small hall, rendered gloomy by painted windows, you passed through a vestibule to the *Refectory*, or *Great Parlour*, 34 ft. by 20, and 12 high, " hung with paper in imitation of stucco." Here were portraits of Walpole's father, family, and friends, a Conversation piece by Reynolds, Etruscan vases, China beakers, Sèvres bowls, a table of Sicilian jasper, and so forth. In the *Waiting Room* was the Interior of King's College, by Canaletti, busts of Dryden and Cibber—the latter coloured from the life, a gift from Cibber to the Clive,—and a choice collection of oriental, continental, and English porcelain.

The *China Room*, which came next in order, contained a far larger and more varied " collection of porcelain, earthenware, glass, and enamel on copper, of various ages and countries," all which Walpole describes and much of it gossips over after this fashion : " Two Saxon tankards, one with Chinese figures, the other with European. These tankards are extremely remarkable. Sir Robert Walpole drank ale ; the Duchess of Kendal, mistress of King George the First, gave him the former. A dozen or more years afterwards, the Countess of Yarmouth, mistress of King George the Second, without having seen the other, gave him the second ; and they match exactly in form and size." Further it will be enough here to say that many of the examples were from celebrated cabinets, of the rarest and choicest kinds, and such as in these days are highly prized and eagerly sought after. The *Little Parlour* had quarterings in the window, a chimney-piece " taken from the tomb of Thomas

Ruthall, Bp. of Durham, in Westminster," and ebony chairs bought at Lady Conyer's sale. In the *Yellow Bed Chamber*, or *Beauty Room*, were ebony tables, bronzes, China ware, and portraits of the Beauties of the court of Charles II., mostly copies, the loss of which has been infinitely over-balanced by the worthier Beauties of our own day with which its present owner has furnished the gallery of Strawberry Hill.

The visitor now passed by the Stair-case, where he was shown a view of Richmond Hill, by Henry Bunbury, a present from himself, to the Principal Floor, and entered the *Breakfast Room*, in which, besides such things as an inlaid writing-case by Langlois, flower pots, Cupids and vases of Sèvres china, terra cottas and marbles, were several frames of miniatures by Petitot, Zincke, and other masters of the art, many of them of personages of historical renown, a part of the then unrivalled collection of minia-tures of which Strawberry Hill was the shrine. The *Green Closet* contained some curious old glass in the windows, many objects of value or curiosity, bronzes, wax models, dram-bottles of old Venetian glass, from the collection of Mrs. Kennon, the virtuosa midwife, and the like, about the room ; and on the walls, Hogarth's portrait of Sarah Malcolm, and a large number of views and portraits, mostly drawings, not of much artistic value, perhaps, but interesting for the persons or places represented, and over which Walpole knew how to gossip agreeably. The *Blue Bed Chamber* and the *Red Bed Chamber* contained more China ware, more choice furniture and bijouterie, and a great many portraits ; but we turn to the Staircase, "adorned with antelopes (the Walpole supporters) bearing shields ; lean windows fattened with rich saints in painted glass . . . and niches full of trophies of old coats of mail, Indian shields made of rhinoceros' hides ; broad-swords, quivers, long-bows, arrows, and spears "—and, chief of all, the splendid armour of Francis I., his ebony lance and inlaid sword, which Walpole believed was the work of Benvenuto Cellini. This brings us to an open vestibule of three arches, the *Armoury*, in which is the chief collection of arms and armour.

Beyond this is the *Library*, an oblong room, 28 ft. by 17 ft. 6 in., very elaborately fitted and decorated, and which for its contents must have been one of the most interesting rooms in the building. The books, some 15,000 volumes, chiefly his-torical and antiquarian, were ranged within Gothic arches, "taken from a side door-case to Dugdale's St. Paul's." The chimneypiece was from a tomb at West-minster ; the stone-work from one at Canterbury ; the ceiling painted by Cler-mont from a design by Walpole himself ; the windows were filled with allegorical figures in painted glass. On the walls were portraits and landscapes ; about the room were various articles of taste and curiosity—one of the most conspicuous being a clock of silver-gilt richly chased, surmounted by a lion holding the arms of England, a present from Henry VIII. to Anne Boleyn ; given by Lady Elizabeth Germaine to Walpole, and now the pro-perty of the Queen. The main interest, however, was in the books, many of which were choice editions or of great rarity ; in the volumes and portfolios of prints and drawings, and in the " 25 most precious coins and medals in rosewood case," all rare and some unique.

Walpole's and the *Plaid Bed Chamber*, with their portraits and bric-à-brac, may be passed over. The *Star Chamber* claims a passing glance, with its great painted window, quaint furniture, and point-lace cushions, cabinets of Greek and Roman, and of English and foreign coins and medals, and Torrigiano's own model in stone for the bust of Henry VII. for that king's tomb at Westminster. In the *Holbein Chamber* were the historic por-traits traced by Vertue from Holbein's originals at Buckingham House ; many others copied from the same master by inferior hands, and a few drawings and paintings ascribed to Holbein himself. Among the curiosities in the room was Wolsey's red hat, which at the sale was secured by Edmund Kean, the actor, for 20 guineas.

The *Gallery*, " 56 ft. long, 17 high, and 13 wide, without the 5 recesses," was a room Walpole was very proud of. The ceiling, in fan-tracery groining, was "taken from one of the side aisles of Henry VII.'s chapel." The great door was a copy of the N. door of St. Albans Abbey. "The side with recesses, finished with a gold net-work over looking-glass," was imitated from Abp. Bourchier's tomb at Canterbury. The windows contained all the quarterings of the family. The carpet was made at Moorfields—where carpets are made no longer. The walls were lined with Walpole's best historical pictures—a prominent place being given to his favourite, the ' Marriage of Henry VII.'—and portraits of historical personages—that of Henry Carey Lord Falkland, in white, being, as he points out, the portrait that suggested "the idea of the picture walking out of its frame, in the Castle of Otranto." On tables and pedestals were bronze and marble busts, one, very choice, of the Emperor Vespasian, in basalt, and, on an antique sepulchral altar The Eagle "found in the gardens of Boccapadugli, within the precincts of Caracalla's Baths at Rome," in 1742 ; " one of the finest pieces of Greek sculpture in the world : " it was this eagle which suggested to Gray the magnificent figure of the eagle with " ruffled plumes and flagging wing " in his ' Ode on the Progress of Poesy.' In quaint old coffers were old family costumes still more quaint; and in a closet with glass doors was a collection, rich and rare, of antique China, which belonged to Catharine Lady Walpole.

The *Round Drawing Room*, 22 ft. in diameter, lit by a large bay-window charged with the arms of Robert Dudley Earl of Leicester, had an elaborate chimneypiece "taken from the tomb of Edward the Confessor, improved by Mr. Adam, and beautifully executed in white marble, inlaid with scagliola, by Richter," the exquisite workmanship of which may still be admired *in situ*. The room was hung with crimson Norwich damask, and very richly furnished, but was perhaps most remarkable as containing Vandyck's fine portrait of Mrs. Lemon, and that still finer of Lady Dorothy Percy, Countess of Leicester, and her sister Lady Lucy, the famous Countess of Carlisle—which Walpole gave 29 guineas for at the Penshurst sale ; at his own sale fetched £231, and would now assuredly bear a high premium.

In the *Tribune*, " a square with a semi-circular recess in the middle of each side," was the bulk of Walpole's miniatures, gems and smaller articles of worth. A cabinet of rosewood decorated with ivory statuettes and bas-reliefs, designed by Wal-

pole, contained the choicest of his miniatures and enamels, by Petitot, Liotard, Zincke (the head of Cowley being Zincke's " masterpiece and perhaps the finest piece of enamel in the world "), Old Lens, Isaac and Peter Oliver, Cooper, Hoskins, etc. A case of antique rings ; gems; snuff-boxes ; an exquisitely wrought silver bell, made for a pope, by Cellini, for the ceremony of exorcising caterpillars; antique lamps ; silver-gilt chalices and other church jewellery ; seals and trinkets of various kinds ; apostle spoons and other small silver articles ; bronzes ; china ornaments ; drawings and paintings ; King Henry VIII.'s dagger in Turkish work ; " one of the 7 mourning rings given at the funeral of Charles I.," having the king's head in miniature, behind it a death's head, and the motto, " Prepared be to follow me ;" and a "magnificent missal, with miniatures by Raphael and his scholars, set in gold enamelled, and adorned with rubies and turquoises," which belonged originally to Queen Claude the wife of Francis I. of France.

The *Great North Bed Chamber* must have been a most uncomfortable room to sleep in, for every spare inch of space seems to have been filled with Sèvres and other choice porcelain, pottery, Wedgwood ware, crystal tankards, Venetian glass, enamels, bronzes, silver caskets wrought by Cellini, snuff-boxes, agate ornaments, and all sorts of *curiosities* from King James I.'s gloves, and William III.'s spurs, to Dr. Dee's spirit speculum, and Van Tromp's tortoiseshell and silver tobacco-pipe case ; " a most capital portrait on board " of Henry VII.; Hogarth's original sketch of the Beggar's Opera, with portraits of Walker as Macheath, and Lavinia Fenton (Duchess of Bolton) as Polly. The *Beauclerk Closet*, built in 1776 " on purpose to receive seven incomparable drawings of Lady Diana Beau-clerk, for Mr. Walpole's tragedy of The Mysterious Mother," was nearly as full of rarities ; and there were other rooms, closets, and staircases which contained more than enough to have satisfied an ordinary collector.

But the house was not all. In the wood was a *Chapel* designed by Walpole, Bentley, and Chute, from portions of several cathedrals, the façade being copied from a tomb at Salisbury, and containing pictures, statues, shrines, and painted glass. In the flower garden was a Cottage, in which was a tea-room, hung with prints, and filled with Chantilly, Sèvres, German, old Delft, and Nankin China ; and the Little Library, in which, besides printed books and MSS., were antique marbles, bronzes, and paintings, Etruscan and Staffordshire vases, and much Oriental porcelain.

Walpole was in his 30th year when he took Strawberry Hill, and he spent fifty summers in it, improving the house, adding to his collections, and enjoying the lilacs and nightingales in his grounds.* He bequeathed Strawberry Hill to the Hon. Mrs. Damer, his residuary legatee, for her life. Mrs. Damer made Strawberry Hill her residence, and did her best to maintain its celebrity. She gave garden parties which were eminently attractive ; and theatrical performances at which, besides a distinguished fashionable circle, Mrs. Siddons and Mrs. Garrick were among the auditors. Mrs. Damer recited prologues written for the occasion by Joanna Baillie, and sometimes sustained a part in the comedy. She was especially successful as Lady Vapour in Miss Berry's comedy of 'The Fashionable Friends.' Of her ordinary occupations, Miss Berry writes (Sept. 12, 1799) from Strawberry Hill (where she was as much at home as in Walpole's lifetime), "Mrs. Damer chips away at her marble one half of the morning, and trots about the grounds the other half in all weathers, and is much the better for this variety of exercise."

Mrs. Damer continued at Strawberry Hill from the death of Walpole in 1797 till 1811, when she was induced to resign it to the Countess Dowager Waldegrave, who held the reversion. At this time everything was exactly as Walpole had left it. But the house was now allowed to get out of repair, and the collections were neglected. Eventually, when in the hands of the Earl of Waldegrave, the whole of the contents were sold by auction and dispersed—George Robins being the auctioneer, and the sale occupying 24

days, April 25 to May 21, 1842—and the house was shut up.

From its dismantled and semi-ruinous condition it was, however, rescued some years later by Frances Countess of Waldegrave, who restored the building, added to it a new wing, refitted the interior, and, having made it her summer residence, has reinstated Strawberry Hill in at least its primal splendour.

As it now stands Strawberry Hill is a renewal of Horace Walpole's house, with modern sumptuousness superadded. All the old rooms are there, though the uses of many have been changed. Walpole constructed an endless number of little rooms for the reception and display of his multifarious collections. Many of these have been converted into bed-chambers and the like. But the state rooms are state rooms still, and others on a larger scale have been added. Walpole's Gothic ornaments—the chimneypieces on which he spent so much trouble and cost, the fretted ceilings, arches, screens, the recesses copied from cathedral chapels and altar tombs—are for the most part intact, though somewhat brightened with gold and colour ; and a goodly number of the old pictures and ornaments have been recovered. His favourite 'Henry VII., his Queen and Family,' for example, Reynolds's masterwork, the Three Ladies Waldegrave, Ramsay's Laura, and Charlotte Walpole, and several of the older Walpole family portraits, views of Strawberry, and many others of more or less value and interest, may again be seen in the old rooms, if not exactly in their old places. No attempt has however been made to replace Walpole's "Gothic fittings and furniture." The upholstery is all in the richest modern taste.

The *Refectory* is now the *Study*, and lined with a large collection of books, in capital oak presses, which cover every available inch of wall-space. There are some pictures, but the room is a working room, with a pleasant outlook over the garden and river. The *Staircase* has been apparently rendered somewhat more commodious, lined with pictures in place of weapons, and, instead of the armour of Francis I., has, as its crowning ornament, a graceful marble statue (about half life-size) of Frances Countess of Waldegrave, by Noble.

---

* "I pass half the week at Strawberry, where my two passions, lilacs and nightingales, are in full bloom." Walpole to Geo. Montagu, May 5, 1761. The "two passions" of his later years at Strawberry were the Miss Berrys.

Walpole's "Breakfast Room, one pair of stairs," is now Lady Waldegrave's *Morning Room*, and contains views in the Holy Land, water-colours, by *Lear*, and other modern and some old pictures, and various articles of taste, and commands charming prospects from the 3 windows of the great bay.

The *Library* is most like what it was originally. As of old, the books are arranged in presses within the Gothic arches of pierced work, and look as though they might be of Walpole's selection. Above are portraits, some we believe the same as hung there in Walpole's day. The ceiling, "painted by Clermont, from Mr. Walpole's design drawn out by Mr. Bentley," retains all the shields, symbols, and devices which he has described with so much parental fondness.

The *Great North Bed Chamber* is now a Sitting Room, for which, being light, well proportioned, having a cheerful outlook, and handsomely furnished, it is far better adapted than for a bed-chamber. Its chief ornaments are portraits, among which are Walpole's favourite niece, the Duchess of Gloucester, by *Reynolds*, and hardly less favourite friend, Lady Di. Beauclerk, by *Powell*.

The *Gallery* is still, as it was when Walpole lived, the most remarkable room in the house, though the new drawing-room far exceeds it in size. The fan-tracery of the ceiling, and the Gothic recesses, are as then the notable features; but the recesses in their fret-work of white and gold, and the portraits that are cunningly fitted into them, are far more effective than they could have been when lined with looking-glass. The furniture is modern; the ornaments are modern; in place of the "carpet made at Moorfields," the floor is laid with parquetry. But the great change is in the decorations. It is in this room that are hung the bevy of fair ladies, sometimes named the Waldegrave Beauties, and forming, however entitled, an unrivalled collection of contemporary portraits of noble ladies. They are all by *James Sant, R.A.*, and include the Duchess of Sutherland, the Marchioness of Stafford, the Duchess of Westminster, the Marchioness of Northampton, the Marchioness of Clanricarde, the Countess of Clarendon, the Countess of Shaftesbury, the Countess Spencer, Lady

Selina Harcourt, the Baroness Alphonse de Rothschild, the Hon. Mrs. Stonor, Lady Augusta Sturt, and several more. Frances Countess of Waldegrave looks out of a bower of roses and hawthorns from over the fireplace in the centre of the right-hand wall. At the royal end of the room, in a sumptuous frame, sits Alexandra Princess of Wales, with the Prince of Wales standing behind and leaning slightly over her. Close by are the Duc and Duchesse d'Aumale, and M. Van der Weyer, also by *Sant*. Finally, to balance so much beauty and bright colour, there are portraits in more sombre style, by *Dickinson*, of Earl Russell, Earl Grey, Lord Lyndhurst, Lord Palmerston, Bp. Wilberforce, Mr. Gladstone, Lord Stratford de Redcliffe, and other contemporary statesmen and diplomatists.

The New or West Wing, added by the Countess of Waldegrave about 1860-62, agrees in general style with the rest of the building, but is more solidly constructed, and the rooms are larger and loftier. The *Large Dining Room* is a noble room, lit by 3 great windows by day, by sun-burners in the evening. The ceiling, as in all the new rooms, is of stucco-work, corresponding to those of Walpole's designing, and the great chimneypiece is of stone elaborately carved. Among the portraits on the walls are King James II., and James, 2nd Earl of Waldegrave, by *Reynolds*, and very fine.

The *Great Drawing Room* is a very large and splendid apartment. Its grand ornament is *Reynolds's* masterly group of the three Ladies Waldegrave, daughters of James, 2nd Earl, which excited such general admiration at the Second Exhibition of National Portraits, 1867. It was painted for Horace Walpole, and Reynolds was long in finishing it. When he got it home, Walpole wrote to Sir Horace Mann that it was "a charming picture," but he grumbled somewhat over it to Pinkerton. "Sir Joshua," he said, "gets avaricious in his old age. My picture of the young Ladies Waldegrave is doubtless very fine and graceful, but it cost me 800 guineas."[*] Under this picture is a gorgeous mediæval coffer, carved and gilt, with a long painting in the front panel that contrasts

---

[*] Walpoliana, p. 159.

curiously in its minute finish with the breadth and richness of the masterpiece above. On one side of this is *Magni's* charming marble statue of the Reading Girl, on the other a seated Bacchante with Tambourine. Among the portraits are Maria Walpole, wife of the 2nd Earl of Waldegrave, by *Reynolds*—a charming picture of a mother and child, exquisite in feeling, colour, and execution ; Martha and Theresa Blount, Gay's

> " Fair-haired Martha
> And Theresa Brown ; "

Sir Robert Walpole, 1st Earl of Orford ; Horace Walpole and Mrs. Damer ; Lady Mary Faulkner, by *Liotard* ; Laura and Charlotte Walpole, daughters of Sir Edward Walpole, by *Ramsay.*

The end of the *Billiard Room* is occupied by a composition by *Dickinson* of the Gladstone Ministry, with life-sized portraits of Gladstone seated on the rt., Lowe and Bright on the l. ; beyond them the Duke of Argyll, and standing behind him Lord Carlingford, the lord of Strawberry Hill, for whom the picture was painted. The other members of the Cabinet are in their several places, and all, as far as we recognized them, are faithful portraits. In this room are also at present (for most of them must be taken subject to removal elsewhere), portraits of Frances Countess of Waldegrave, by *Dubufe ;* Lord Carlingford, by *Tissot ;* Sir Robert Walpole, Earl of Orford, ½-length, standing, with coronet by side ; James II., by *Kneller ;* George I., etc.

In an adjoining reception room are portraits of Henry, 1st Lord Waldegrave, and of his wife Henrietta Churchill, both by *Kneller*, and favourable examples of his pencil. James, 2nd Lord and 1st Earl of Waldegrave, and companion picture of his wife, Mary Webbe. Catherine Shorter, wife of Sir Robert Walpole. Princess Amelia, by *Reynolds.* On the Staircase, a full-length of John Braham, in theatrical costume, by *Healy ;* and one of John James, 6th Earl of Waldegrave.

The grounds and gardens are as beautiful and attractive as of old, the trees as verdant, the rosary as bright, the lawns as green ; and in their season, Walpole's "two passions, lilacs and nightingales," in as "full bloom" and abundance as ever. And Strawberry's ancient fame for garden parties is amply maintained. The lawns and terraces are brightened now with as gay and brilliant assemblies as the bravest and brightest of the olden time. By way of illustration we may mention one in the summer of 1875. In a June afternoon the noble host and hostess received in their garden the Prince and Princess of Wales ; the Austrian, Italian, Spanish, American, Danish, Swedish, Brazilian, and Persian ministers ; princes and princesses, archbishops, dukes and duchesses—in short, as Walpole would say, there were 800 there, and all of high social or personal distinction. Walpole's "festino" pales beside the glory of such a gathering.

STREATHAM, Surrey (Dom. *Estreham*), a vill. of mansions, villas, and genteel residences, extends for 1½ m. along the Brighton road from Brixton Hill towards Croydon, and rt. and l. to Tooting and Norwood, 6 m. from Westminster Bridge. There are 4 stats. on the L. C. and D. Rly., and the L. and S.-W. Rly., —at Streatham vill., Streatham Hill, Streatham Common, and Streatham Road. Pop. 12,148, of whom however only 2187 were in the original or mother parish.

The name is probably derived from its position on the anc. Stane Street. At the Dom. Survey Streatham was divided into several manors. The chief, Totinges, which included the hamlet of Tooting, was held by the Abbot of St. Mary de Bec, and hence came to be known as *Tooting-Bec.* Later it seems to have been assigned to the prior of Okebourn, Wilts, a cell of Bec Abbey ; and reverted to the Crown with the estates of the other alien priories in the reign of Henry V., who granted the manor to his brother, John Plantagenet. On his death in 1435, a lease of it was granted by Henry VI. to John Arderne, and in 1441 the King assigned the manor to his newly founded college of Eton. It was, however, resumed by Edward IV., who conveyed it for his life to Lawrence, Bp. of Durham. On its reversion to the Crown, it was granted to the Guild of the Church of St. Mary Allhallows, Barking, with whom it remained till the suppression of these institutions. In 1553 it was sold to John Dudley, Earl of Warwick ; afterwards passed to the Pakenhams, and was purchased in 1600 by Sir Giles Howland.

Elizabeth, daughter and heiress of John Howland, conveyed the property, by marriage in 1695, to Wriothesley, Marquis of Tavistock, afterwards 3rd Duke of Bedford, and Baron Howland, of Streatham. The marriage was performed by Bp. Burnet, at Streatham House, Lord Wriothesley being only 15 years old. Francis, the 5th Duke, conveyed it to his brother, Lord William Russell, who was murdered by his Swiss valet. Lord William made the house his residence, but about the close of the 18th cent. sold it to Lord Deerhurst, afterwards 7th Earl Coventry, who pulled down the old house and converted some of the offices into a dwelling. The Manor House was a large and stately red-brick Elizabethan mansion, which had its tradition of having been visited by the great queen, but of this there is no authentic record. After Lady Coventry's death, the house was bought by Mr. J. Grey, and is now the residence of Mrs. Haigh. The manor has passed through many hands and been variously divided. *Tooting-Bec Common*, of 150 acres, has suffered from encroachments, but the portion left is now secured to public use.

The manor of *Leigham*, or *Leigham's Court*, belonged to Bermondsey Abbey till the Suppression, when it was given by Henry VIII. to Henry Dowes, clerk. It was several times transferred, and at length passed by marriage, in 1752, to George, 5th Duke of St. Albans, who in 1785 sold a portion, and in 1789 the remainder, of the manor to Lord Thurlow. On a portion of the manor the Lord Chancellor built himself a residence at *Knight's Hill*, which however he never occupied, and which has long been pulled down, and, with the grounds, built over. (*See* NORWOOD.) *Balham* (anc. *Balgham*), another manor in Streatham par., though locally an appendage to Clapham, belonged to the Abbey of Bec, passed to that of Bermondsey, and reverting to the Crown at the Suppression, was granted by Henry VIII. to John Symondes in 1542, and to Edward Williams by Queen Elizabeth. It afterwards passed to various persons, and since 1701 has belonged to the Du Cane family. It is now covered with genteel residences.

Streatham is a large rambling district, occupying for the most part high ground, with a good deal of open heath—Streatham Common of 66 acres, and Tooting-Bec of 150 acres—and affording from many parts wide and pleasant prospects, and has from an early date been a favourite place of abode for opulent citizens. It abounds consequently in mansions encompassed by well-wooded grounds, comfortable-looking old brick houses, and more fanciful modern villas and genteel cottages; has several churches, schools, and institutions, numerous good inns, and all the usual accompaniments of such a locality. In the 17th and far into the 18th century, it was celebrated for a mineral spring, discovered in 1660, the water of which was described in contemporary advertisements as "the best for purging in England,"* whilst "good entertainment" was provided "for Gentlemen and Ladies at the Wells House." As late as 1810 the water was "sent in considerable quantities to some of the hospitals in London." The well still exists, but its fame has departed. At the present time Streatham receives a considerable influx of undesirable visitors from the *races* which are held here four or five times a year.

Now Streatham perhaps derives most celebrity from Samuel Johnson's connexion with it. *Streatham Place*, also known as *Thrale Place*, and later as *Streatham Park*, was the residence of Henry Thrale, the opulent brewer of Southwark, when Johnson was introduced to him by his friend Murphy (1765), and during Thrale's life Streatham Place was to Johnson a second home. He had his own room; his established seat at the table and the fireside; the library was his sanctum, and the books in it were of his selection; his favourite strolling-place in the grounds was known as Dr. Johnson's Walk, and his resting-place there as Dr. Johnson's Summer-house. Johnson's conversation, Thrale's hospitality, and his wife's cleverness, management, and lively manners, attracted to Streatham Place the most distinguished members of the social and intellectual life of the time. Johnson left Streatham after Thrale's death with a prayer that he might, with humble and sincere thankfulness, remember the comforts and conveniences which he had enjoyed at this place; and that he might resign them with holy submission.† His

* Post Boy, May 28, 1717.
† Boswell, Life of Johnson, vol. viii., p. 144.

farewell to the kitchen and the church was said in Latin.

Streatham Place was, in Thrale's time, "a large white house" of three floors, having a slightly projecting centre and wings, with on the rt. a semicircular termination. It stood in well-timbered park-like grounds of about 100 acres. When Mrs. Thrale became Mrs. Piozzi the house continued to be her residence, but Piozzi made many alterations in house and grounds. Sir Joshua Reynolds, a frequent and favourite guest, was commissioned by Thrale to paint the portraits of the more remarkable of his visitors, and the Streatham Gallery, as it was called, became famous. The portraits, 24 in number, included Johnson, Goldsmith, Burke, Reynolds, Chambers, Garrick, Murphy, Baretti, Burney, Conversation Sharp, Lord Lyttelton, the Duke of Bedford, Mr. and Mrs. Thrale, etc. The portraits—some of them the best likenesses extant of the persons represented—were dispersed by auction in May 1816. The house was pulled down and the materials sold by auction in May 1863. Streatham Park was on the S. side of the lower common, between Streatham and Tooting. Nothing remains of the Streatham Place of Thrale and Johnson.

The present *Leigham Court* is the residence of J. Tredwell, Esq. *Park Hill House* (Augustus Smith, Esq.), Streatham Common, is a handsome modern mansion designed by J. B. Papworth, standing within fine grounds of over 50 acres: whilst the residence of the late Wm. Leaf, Esq., it contained a noted collection of modern paintings. On Streatham Common are also *Hill House* (J. N. Bullen, Esq.); *Spencer House* (Sir Kingmill Grove Key, Bart.); and other mansions.

Streatham *Church* (St. Leonard), near the centre of the vill., was built in 1831 on the site of an old 14th cent. ch., the tower and shingled spire of which was retained. The spire was struck by lightning during a storm on Sunday morning, January 3, 1841. The tower was restored and heightened and a new octagonal brick spire erected. The ch. has since been enlarged, and was in 1866 remodelled, but · cannot be greatly praised. In it are some monts. removed from the old ch. A mutilated effigy of an unknown knight in armour under a canopy is popularly called John of Gaunt's Tomb. Of more interest are the marble tablets with long Latin inscriptions by Johnson to Henry Thrale, d. 1781; and Mrs. Salusbury, d. 1773, the mother of Mrs. Thrale; also a relief in marble by Flaxman, commemorative of Mrs. H. M. Hoare, d. 1824, the third daughter of Mr. Thrale. In the ch.-yard is the conspicuous cenotaph, with marble cross, of Alexander Edw. Murray, 6th Earl of Dunmore, d. 1845. The rectory, one of the best in Surrey, was held by Dr. Benj. Hoadly, along with the bishopric of Bangor, 1715, Hereford, 1721, till his promotion to Salisbury in 1723. Herbert Hill, d. 1828, the affectionate uncle of Robert Southey; and Henry Blunt, d. 1843, author of much-esteemed 'Sermons' were rectors.

Christchurch, towards Brixton Hill, erected in 1841 from the designs of Mr. J. W. Wild, is a spacious and rather striking Lombardic fabric, with a lofty campanile on the S.W. Emmanuel Church, Streatham Common, is an E.E. building, erected in 1854. St. Stephen's, Grove Road, is a Gothic ch., erected in 1867. St. Peter's, Leigham Court Road, is an early Dec. ch. of coloured bricks and stone, erected in 1870 from the design of Mr. R. W. Drew.

Thrale's Almshouses, Streatham Road, were built and endowed in 1832 by the daughters of Mr. Thrale, for the maintenance of 4 poor widows.

The *Royal Asylum of St. Ann's Society*, at the Brixton end of Streatham Hill, was founded in 1709 by inhabitants of the Ward of Aldersgate-Within, London, for the education and maintenance of children of necessitous parents of any nation who had once been in prosperous circumstances. The funds of the institution having steadily increased, it was decided to remove the school to a healthier locality, and Streatham Hill was chosen. The present building was erected in 1829, and the Royal Albert Wing added in 1865. It is a spacious structure of three storeys, with a central Ionic portico and pediment; is well arranged and well fitted, and has extensive grounds. It has now on the establishment about 200 boys and 140 girls, who are admitted between the ages of 7 and 11, and receive an excellent general education.

The *Magdalen Hospital*, founded by

Jonas Hanway in St. George's Fields, 1758, was removed to a healthier site and more commodious building, erected for the purpose at Streatham, in 1869.

SUDBURY, MIDDX. (see HARROW-ON-THE-HILL).

SULLONIACÆ, MIDDX. (see EDG-WARE).

SUNBURY, MIDDX. (Dom. *Suneberie*),

a vill. on the left bank of the Thames, 15 m. from London and 1½ m. above Hampton. The Sudbury Stat. of the L. and S.-W. Rly. (Thames Valley line) is about 1 m. N. of the ch. Pop. 3368. Inns: *Flower Pot*, much resorted to by anglers and boating parties; *Magpie*, *Castle*, also anglers' inns : all three are in Thames Street, by the river-side.

The village lies along a pleasant reach of the Thames, and stretches back to Kenton or Kempton Park on the E., and for ½ m. towards the rly. stat. on the W. By the river are several fine old red-brick houses, standing within well-wooded grounds. The river, with the wiers, eyots, swans, and skiffs, has a bright and cheerful aspect, and is in especial favour with boating men and anglers. Here and on the opposite shore are the pumping works and filtering beds of two or three of the London Waterworks Companies. *Sunbury Deep*, as defined and maintained by the Thames Conservancy, extends for 683 yards from the weir, eastward to the E. end pile of the breakwater. There is excellent jack and barbel fishing, and occasionally trout of good size are taken. At Sunbury are the rearing-ponds of the Thames Angling Preservation Society.

Sunbury Manor was given by the Confessor to Westminster Abbey, but was ceded in 1222 to the Bp. of London. Three centuries later it was surrendered to the Crown. Leases were granted by Elizabeth, and the manor itself was conveyed by James I. to Robert Stratford in 1603. In 1676 it was the property of Francis Phelips, by whose executors it was conveyed to his son-in-law, Sir John Tyrwhit, Bart., in 1693. It was sold in 1702 to John Crosse, and afterwards passed in succession to the St. Eloys, Hudsons, Boehms, and Mitchisons. The *Manor House*, a noble red-brick mansion, is now the seat of Anthony Wm. Mitchison, Esq.

The manor of *Chenetone* (afterwards *Col* or *Cold Kenyngton, Cold Kenton*, now *Kempton*,) was held under the Conqueror by Robert Earl of Cornwall, and on the rebellion of his son was seized, with the rest of the Earl's estates, by Henry I. in 1104. The manor-house was made a royal residence; Edward II. dates a charter from it in 1309, and it is described in a survey made for Edward III. in 1331. Leases of the manor were granted on several occasions. In 1558 the manors of Col Kenyngton and Hanworth were demised to Anne Duchess of Somerset, widow of the Protector, for her life, and the two manors were united in succeeding grants, till in 1631 Kenyngton or Kempton was granted in fee to Sir Robert Killigrew. It has since been often transferred, and is now owned by Thomas Barnet, Esq. *Kempton Park* lies about ½ m. N.E. of the vill. The house is a good modern mansion. Of the palace no trace whatever exists, though towards the close of the last cent. the "traces of an ancient building" existed which were supposed "to have been the remains of a religious house."* The park, of about 300 acres, contains much fine timber, and is skirted by the little stream which falls into the Thames between Sunbury and Hampton.

Charlton (anc. *Cerdentone, Cherdyngton*) manor was given at an early period to Merton Abbey, and retained by it till the Suppression, 1538. It was granted to Sir John Mason in 1550, and has since been many times alienated. The hamlet of Charlton, a little out-of-the-way place, lies some distance N. of the Thames, about 2 m. N.W. of Sunbury, and much nearer Littleton.

The other manor, *Upper Halliford* (anc. *Haleghford*), is noticed under HALLI-FORD.

Sunbury *Church* (of the Virgin Mary), familiar from its position by the river-side to every one who has rowed along the Thames, was erected on the site of an older ch. in 1752, by Mr. Wright, clerk of the works at Hampton Court. It was a large ugly brick building; but has within the last few years been much altered. New windows have been in-

---

* Lysons, vol. iii., p. 271.

serted, and a semicircular chancel and very elaborate W. porch, of red and black bricks, with stone arcades at the sides and decorative carvings, added. The interior has been still more thoroughly transformed. Instead of a plain brick barn, it is now a glittering Byzantine temple. The tower, with its odd cupola, and the heavy flag-staff projecting diagonally from the parapet, remains unchanged. The tower has a good peal of 6 bells. The ch.-yard is crowded with tombs, but neither here nor inside is there any memorial of interest. On the river side of the ch. is a large yew-tree.

A rather pretty little E.E. Roman Catholic ch., of Kentish rag and Bathstone, designed by Mr. Chas. Buckler, was consecrated by Abp. (now Cardinal) Manning, May 23, 1869, the Duc de Nemours assisting at the ceremony.

SUNDRIDGE, Kent (Dom. *Sondresse*), a short mile E. of Brasted, on the road to Sevenoaks, from which town it is about 3 m. W. Pop. 1593, of whom 635 were in the eccl. dist. of Ide Hill, and 206 in the Sevenoaks Union Workhouse, which stands in this par. Inn, *White Horse*, by the ch., a good house.

Lying somewhat irregularly about the meeting of the ways, where the Westerham and Sevenoaks road is crossed by the byroad to Knockholt, in a varied and attractive country, and surrounded by richly-wooded parks, hills, corn-fields, hop-gardens, and broad green meadows, a pretty stream flowing through it, and in itself clean and well-kept, yet wearing an air of rustic antiquity, Sundridge is a very good example of the typical Kentish village. Its mainstay is husbandry, and there are well-tilled fields, capital farm-houses both old and new, good farm buildings, and stores of shapely ricks all around. On the river are also paper mills, which employ a great many hands.

"Sundrich," writes Philipott, "was the possession (as high as any light, collected from antiquity, can waft us to a discovery) of an ancient family called in Latin records *de Insula* and in English Isley."[*]

The Isleys kept the manor down to the reign of Mary, when Sir Henry Isley,

Sheriff of Kent, "being unhappily entangled" in the disastrous insurrection of Sir Thomas Wyatt, was attainted of high treason and executed at Sevenoaks, and his estates forfeited to the Crown. Elizabeth restored the manor to Sir Henry's son, John Isley; but he, not long after, disposed of it to one Brooker, who sold it to a Hide, and its subsequent alienations have been numerous. It now belongs to Earl Amherst. The old manor house, which stood S. of the ch., has long disappeared.

Brook Place was another manor held by the Isleys till the reign of Edward IV. *Hethenden*, or *Henden*, belonged to the Clares, Earls of Gloucester, and passing by marriage to the Staffords, was by the attainder of Edward Stafford Duke of Buckingham, in 1521, forfeited to the Crown, and in 1543 granted by Henry VIII. to Sir John Gresham. Its subsequent history is without interest. The manors are now united.

Combe Bank, the chief seat now in Sundridge, about ¾ m. N. of the ch., "did formerly relate to the Isleys," but having passed to the Ash family, was, about the middle of the 18th cent., purchased by Col. John Campbell, afterwards Duke of Argyll, and created, 1776, Baron Sundridge—the title by which the Duke of Argyll sits in the House of Lords. The Duke rebuilt Combe Bank, and made it a very charming, but, as would seem, not very convenient, place. When the residence of Lord Frederick Campbell, a portion of the house was destroyed by fire, June 25, 1807, and Lady Frederick Campbell burnt to death. Lady Campbell's first husband, from whom she was divorced on account of his violence, was the Earl Ferrers, who was hanged at Tyburn, May 5, 1761, for the murder of his steward. The house was less injured by the fire than is usually stated. Miss Berry, who stayed at Combe Bank on a short visit within three months of the fire (Sept. 9 and 10, 1807), says that Lady Campbell, "having been thus actually burnt to ashes in a house of which one single room alone was destroyed . . . can only be accounted for by her having fallen into a fit with her head in the candle." Only "about three or four feet of the floor just near the sitting-room door" were actually burnt, but the whole room "is perfectly

lack and scorched and shrivelled up
rith the effects of the fire." Of the house
tself Miss Berry writes, "I think it unites
very possible discomfort." It has been
ften and greatly altered since, and is
ow probably sufficiently commodious. It
s a spacious classical Italian villa, having
centre with projecting wings and towers,
nd stands in a park remarkable for
nagnificent trees, lake, and distant pros-
ects. By the terrace is a cedar of
igantic size. From the Campbells, Combe
3ank passed to W. Manning, Esq., M.P.
father of Cardinal Manning), Lord Tem-
lemore, and Rev. A. P. Clayton. It is
ow the property and residence of Wm.
5pottiswoode, Esq., F.R.S. Towards the
niddle of the 17th cent., "many Roman
.rns of an antique shape and figure"
vere dug up near Combe Bank.

Other seats are *Woodside* (R. R. Drabble,
Esq.), a finely situated modern Gothic
nansion; *Shootfield* (S. Copestake, Esq.),
nd *The Ferns* (T. R. Wheeler, Esq.)

In the main street and in the street by
he ch. are some half-timber and a few
ld tile-fronted cottages; and in the lane
eading to the ch. is a curious pargetted
able dwelling—the plasterwork some-
vhat obscured by yellow-wash, but still
vorth noting.

The *Church* (dedication unknown)
tands apart, about 1¼ m. S. of the Brasted
oad, in a singularly beautiful ch.-yard,
vhich you enter by a lich-gate, beyond
vhich are some fine yews. The two grand
ld ash-trees at the E. end of the ch.-yard
vere planted by Bp. Porteus, about a
entury ago. The larger (which measures
6 ft. 3 in. at 4 ft. from the ground) is
lead; the other (12 ft. 9 in. in girth) is
till vigorous. Porteus held the living
or awhile, and liked the place so well
hat when he became bishop he built
iimself a country house here; and, though
e died at Fulham, was by his own desire
uried in Sundridge ch.-yard, where is
iis tomb.

The ch. comprises nave with aisles;
:hancel with short aisles; S. porch, and
nassive W. tower, with tall octagonal
hingled spire, and square stair-turret
eaching to the belfry, in which is a peal
f 5 bells. The body of the ch. is E.E.,
ut all the windows are Perp., except
hose of the clerestorey, which are quatre-
oils. Church and tower are partly covered
with ivy. The interior has been thoroughly restored, and fitted with open
seats of carved oak. Some of the windows
have painted glass. In S. wall of chancel
is a double piscina. *Monts.*—Perp. altar
tomb, with stone effigies of civilian and
wife, probably of John Isley, justice of
the peace and sheriff of Kent, 14 Edward
IV., d. 1484, "as appears by an insc.
affixed to his mont., yet extant (notwithstanding the late general shipwreck of
the remains of antiquity) in Sundrich
church."[*] Tablets to several of the Campbells, some with busts by the Hon. Mrs.
Damer, that which she herself most valued
being of her mother, Caroline Campbell,
only daughter of John, 4th Duke of Argyll,
and wife of Horace Walpole's friend,
Field-Marshal Conway. Mrs. Damer, d.
May 1828, lies by her mother: by her
express desire her working apron, chisels,
hammers, and other sculptor's and modelling tools, were deposited in her coffin.
Tomb of Henry Mompesson, murdered
by robbers in 1723. *Brasses.*—Roger Isley,
d. 1429; another, name lost, but having
fragments of the Isley arms, with effigies of civilian and wife, 6 sons and 3
daughters.

SURBITON, SURREY (*see* KINGS-
TON-UPON-THAMES).

SUTTON, SURREY (Dom. *Sudtone*=
South Town), on the old road to Reigate,
where it is crossed by the road to Epsom,
11 m. from Westminster Bridge and 3 m.
S. of Mitcham; a junction stat. on the
Croydon and Epsom, South London, and
Epsom Downs lines of the L., B., and S. C.
Rly., 15 m. from London Bridge. Pop.
6558, of whom 1790 are in the eccl. dist.
of Benhilton, and 1297 in the South
Metropolitan District Schools. Inns: the
Cock; Greyhound; Angel; Station Hotel.

Sutton lies on the edge of the Downs;
Sutton Downs running into Banstead
Downs on the one hand and Epsom
Downs on the other, and being like them
famed for the mutton they produce. The
Cock at Sutton is on the Epsom Derby
Day the last place of baiting on the way
to the Course, and the first on the way
home. The medley of carriages on a fine

---

[*] Philipott, Vill. Cant., fol. 1659, p. 331.

day, with what the landlord calls the amount of business done, is a sight worth witnessing.

The manor was the property of Chertsey Abbey at the Conquest, and so remained till surrendered to Henry VIII., who in 1538 gave it to Sir Nicholas Carew, of Beddington. On his attainder the following year, it reverted to the Crown; but was restored by Queen Mary,* in 1554, to Francis Carew, only son of Sir Nicholas. On his death, Sutton passed to Sir Robert Darcy; and having become vested in the Crown, was granted by Charles II. in 1663 to Jerome Weston, Earl of Portland. In 1669 it was purchased by Sir Richard Mason (father of the notorious Countess of Macclesfield, whom Richard Savage claimed as his mother); passed by marriage to the Brownlowes; was sold in 1716 to Capt. Henry Cliffe; was conveyed by marriage to Thomas Hatch of Windsor; and in 1865 was bought by Philip Lovett, Esq., the present lord of the manor.

The old *Church* (St. Nicholas) of no architectural value, was pulled down in 1863, and a larger one erected on the site, from the designs of Mr. Edwin Nash. It is of flint and stone; early Dec. in style; and comprises nave, aisles, and chancel, with red tiled roofs of high pitch; large S. porch, and tall buttressed tower and shingled spire on the W. In the ch. is a good mural mont. to William Earl Talbot, d. 1782, son of Lord Chancellor Talbot, who lies under a large tomb in the ch.-yard. Other monts. are to Dame Dorothy Brownlowe, d. 1700, wife of Sir Wm. Brownlowe of Bolton, and daughter and coheiress of Sir Richard Mason; and to Isaac Littlebury, d. 1710, translator of Herodotus, and son of "Mr. Thomas Littlebury, the famous bookseller in Little Britain." The huge tomb W. of the ch. marks the family vault of James Gibson, merchant, d. 1777, which has to be opened and a sermon preached every 12th of August as a condition of the payment of certain charitable bequests.

Sutton has of late years grown largely in wealth and population. Its easy distance from London, the rly. facilities, the proximity of the Downs, the pleasant-

ness of the scenery, and its reported salubrity, have made it a favourite residence for City men, and houses have been built for their accommodation on every available site. Northwards a new district of villas has sprung up; and scattered houses, or groups of houses, have been built on all sides, with, of course, new shops, inns, schools, and so forth.

Benhilton, the district just referred to, occupies the elevation N.E. of the old vill., formerly known as *Bon Hill*, *Been Hill*, and *Ben Hill*, and stretches away westward over what was Sutton Common, but enclosed and divided in 1810. Benhilton was created an eccl. dist. in 1863, and had 1790 inh. in 1871, but is now much more populous. The *Church* (All Saints) was erected in 1864-6 from the designs of Mr. S. S. Teulon. It is of flint and stone in courses, elaborately irregular in outline; in style early Dec., and somewhat fanciful in the details as well as the general form. By it are schools and a parsonage correspondent in character, and together forming a rather striking group. The fine 5-light E. window of the ch. is filled with painted glass as a memorial of the late Thos. Alcock, Esq., M.P., who contributed £18,000 towards the building and endowment.

At Sutton, on rt. of the rly. stat., are the *South Metropolitan District Schools*, for pauper children from 17 parishes in the E. and S.E. of London, who are educated and trained for industrial pursuits. The buildings, a large and noticeable group, were opened in 1855, but enlarged in 1874 by the addition of a junior and infant department and a new chapel. They have cost, with the ground, over £90,000, and can accommodate 1800 children, the average number being about 1500. About 14,000 children have passed through the schools.

SUTTON-AT-HONE, KENT, on

the l. bank of the Darent, and on the road from Dartford to Farningham, 2½ m. S. of Dartford, and about ¾ m. N. of the Farningham Road Stat. of the L. C. and D. Rly. Pop. of the par. 1671, but of these 616 were in the eccl. dist. of Swanley, and 105 in that of Crocken Hill Inn. the *Ship*.

The manor of Sutton belonged to the

* By a slip of the pen, Elizabeth was written instead of Mary, under Beddington, p. 38, col. 1.

Knights of St. John of Jerusalem till the suppression of the order. In the 12th century they had a commandery here called St. John's ; and about the same time there existed a hospital.* Henry VIII. granted the manor to Sir Maurice Dennis. In the reign of Elizabeth it was divided, Sutton going to Sir Thomas Smith, St. John's to Thomas Cranfield, from whose family it passed to Hollis, to the Lethieulliers, and to the Mumfords. Sutton manor is now the property of Thos. Fleet, Esq. ; St. John's, of Mrs. Fleet.

Sutton Place, overlooking the river, ¼ m. N.E. of the ch., was built by Sir Maurice Dennis, and was regarded as "a magnificent and elegant pile." In the reign of Elizabeth it became the residence of Sir Thomas Smith, and was by him "extremely enlarged by the additions both of bulk and ornament." Sir Thomas Smith was one of the most remarkable among Elizabeth's courtiers. He was not only, as his mont. in Sutton ch. records, "Governor of the East Indian and other Companies, Treasurer of the Virginian Plantation, and sometime Ambassador to the Emperor and Great Duke of Russia and Muscovy," but also the prime mover and chief "undertaker (in the year 1612) of that noble design the Discovery of the North-West Passage." Purchas has a warm "commendation of Sir Thomas Smith," as "he at whose forge and anvil have been hammered so many irons for Neptune ;" specifying in a note the "East Indies, Virginia Summer Islands, North and North-West discoveries, Muscovia, etc." "At his house," he adds, "are kept the courts, consultations, etc. I also have been beholden to him in this work."* He was the chief promoter of the voyages of Hudson, and Bylot, and Baffin, and the latter gave the name of ' Sir Thomas Smith's Sound' to the northern extremity or north-western arm of Baffin's Bay. Smith died at Sutton Place in 1625, it is said of the plague, then prevalent in the neighbourhood. In the reign of Charles II. Sutton Place was the residence of the Countess of Leicester. It afterwards passed to Mr. Hollis, to the Lethieulliers

and Mumfords, and is now the residence of Thos. Ronaldson, Esq. The larger part of the original house has been pulled down or altered. The present house is in the main modern. *St. John's* (J. Russell, Esq.), lying in a meadow between the two arms of the Darent, ¼ m. S.E. of the ch., has also been modernised, but retains some portions of the old building. The best preserved fragment is now used as a scullery.

The *village* is a long straggling line of commonplace houses, built along the main road, at an easy height above the western arm of the Darent, and overlooking the valley between Darenth and South Darenth. The neighbourhood is varied and pleasant, comprising hill, valley, and woods, and abounding in cornfields, hop gardens, and cherry orchards.

The *Church* (St. John the Baptist). which stands W. of the vill., was seriously damaged by fire and rebuilt in 1615, but is in the main a late Dec. fabric. It is of flint and stone, and consists of nave with S. aisle, chancel, large S. porch, and battlemented W. tower, with circular stair turret. The windows have flowing, almost flamboyant, tracery ; but the ch. was restored in 1864, when a new E. window was inserted and the others remodelled. Several of the windows have memorial painted glass. S. of the chancel is the mont. of Sir Thomas Smith, of Sutton Place, d. 1625, with recumbent alabaster effigy ; the figure without colour, the arms and ornaments painted.

Hawley (anc. *Hagelei*, and called by Philipott *Haly Sawters*), on the Darent, 1 m. N. of Sutton ch., belonged at the Dom. Survey to Odo, Bp. of Bayeux ; in the reign of Edward III. to Lawrence de Hastings, Earl of Pembroke ; in that of Richard II. to Richard Fitz-Allen, Earl of Arundel ; then to the Earls of Abergavenny and Baron Beauchamp, and since to various undistinguished persons. *Hawley House* is now the residence of Richard Saunders, Esq. Below it are Mr. T. H. Saunders' extensive paper mills, a hamlet, and the Bull Inn.

Swanley, a hamlet on the road to the Crays, nearly 2 m. S.W. of Sutton, has grown into local importance since it has become the junction station of the Sevenoaks and main lines of the L. C. and D. Rly. Inn, the *Lullingstone Castle*.

---

* Tanner ; Dugdale, Monast., vol. vi., pp. 669, 804.
† Purchas his Pilgrimage, fol. 1614, p. 744.

In 1862 Swanley was made an eccl. dist. The *Church* (St. Paul) is a pretty little Gothic building, early Dec. in style; the interior ornamented with mural painting, an elaborate reredos, painted glass windows, and carved oak seats. Swanley is a great hop and fruit district. Here are *Parkwood House* (Major Fanning), and other good seats.

SWAKELEY, MIDDX. (*see* ICKENHAM).

SWANLEY, KENT (*see* SUTTON-AT-HONE).

SWANSCOMBE, KENT, about 1 m. S.W. of the Northfleet Stat. of the S.-E. Rly. (North Kent line). Pop. of the par. 3105; but this includes 1276 in Greenhithe (the chief part of that little town being in Swanscombe par.), and 175 on board the training ship Chichester; the pop. of Swanscombe proper was 1654.

In the Dom. Survey the name is written *Swinescamp*, and this favours the early and as would seem traditional derivation, that it was here Sweyn, the Danish king, landed and established his winter quarters.

"The tradition of the country is, that that valley which interposes between the hill which ascends up to Northfleet, and that which winds up to Swanscamp, was once covered with water, and being locked in on each side with hills, made a secure road for shipping, which invited the Dane to make it a winter station for his navy; and the same report will tell you likewise, of anchors which have been digged up about the utmost verge of that marsh, which is contiguous to the Thames, and certainly if we consider the position of this valley, which is nothing but a chain of Marshland interlaced with a stream called Ebbsfleet, which swells and sinks with the flux and reflux of the adjacent river, and the dimensions of their ships then at that time in use, which were not of any extraordinary bulk, this tradition is not improbable." *

Philipott says that in his day (1695) there were "dismantled ruins" at Swanscombe "which evidence and declare to us that there was once a fortress there;" and Mr. Taylor speaks of there still being barrows; but we know of none. Swanscombe has, however, a more cherished tradition than that of Sweyn and his camp. Here, ac-

---

* Philipott, Vill. Cant., p. 307; and comp. Taylor, Words and Places, p. 180, and n. 4.

cording to tradition and chronicle, when, after the Battle of Hastings, William I. was in full march upon London, Stigand, Abp. of Canterbury, and Egelsine, the Abbot of St. Augustine's, had summoned the men of Kent, and, having laid before them the danger of the country, called upon them to resist the invaders. Shouting assent, they elected the archbishop and abbot to be their leaders. Like good churchmen, the new captains resolved to try the effect of stratagem before resorting to force. Every man was ordered to cut a green bough and carry it over his head, so as to conceal himself as well as his weapons. They then marched forward towards the advancing army. When William and his officers saw this moving wood they were filled with amazement, whilst the soldiers gazed with feelings of terror, thinking it had been some miraculous forest coming towards them. Approaching within hearing, the men of Kent cast down their boughs, sounded their trumpets, and clashed their arms; and at the same time the Abp. sent forward a messenger proffering a free way if the king would engage to continue them in the possession of their ancient liberties and immunities. To this the Conqueror willingly assented, and thus from this gathering at Swanscombe it happened that the men of Kent gained those privileges which have ever since been their proudest heirloom.

Swanscombe was one of the many manors given by the Conqueror to Odo, Bp. of Bayeux. It was long the property of the Montchenseys, and was carried by a heiress to Hugh de Vere, who sat in the first Parliament of Edward II. as Baron of Swanscombe. On his death it passed in right of his wife, a niece of William de Montchensey, to William de Valence, Earl of Pembroke, and on the death without issue, 1323, of Aymer de Valence, went to his widow as her dowry, and then to his sister Isabel, wife of Lawrence de Hastings, who, in her right, was made Earl of Pembroke and Baron of Swanscombe. On his death, 1389, it passed to Richard Talbot, in whose descendants it remained till towards the end of the reign of Henry VI., when it was alienated to Sir Thomas Brown, whose son resigned it to Edward IV. in 1472. It remained the property of the Crown till Elizabeth, in the first year of her reign, granted it to Ralph Weldon. From the Weldons, who held it for several generations, it passed through various hands, till, about the middle of the 18th century, it was purchased by Robert Child, the eminent banker, with whose other estates it has descended to the Earl of Jersey, the present lord of the manor.

The village stands on high ground about a mile from the Thames, in the midst of a rich and pleasant country, from many parts of which there are fine views. N. of it are the Swanscombe woods, a favourite resort for picnic parties and holiday folk. Here is a noted cavern in the chalk known as *Clappernabber's Hole*, of which the old inhabitants have many stories to tell. The vill. consists of ordinary red brick, with a few old timber and plaster houses, and the venerable ch. standing amidst fine old elms, with a large yew-tree W. of it. All around are farms, corn-fields, hop gardens, and orchards. In the lower part of the parish are lime and cement works, but these belong rather to Greenhithe and Northfleet than to Swanscombe.

Swanscombe *Church* (St. Peter and St. Paul) is one of the most interesting village churches in Kent. Parts of the tower are asserted to be Saxon,* and Roman tiles have been largely worked up in the basement. The church had become very dilapidated ; indeed as we saw it, in the summer of 1873, with the walls stripped and propped by shores, it was difficult to understand how it could have held together so long ; but it has been thoroughly repaired and restored under the careful supervision of Mr. J. Bignall, at the cost of Prof. Erasmus Wilson, a native of Swanscombe, and though somewhat shorn of its picturesque attributes, bids fair to number a new series of centuries. It consists of nave with narrow aisles and clerestorey, chancel, N. porch, and massive square tower at the W. end, with tall shingled spire—a landmark for miles around. The nave, arcade, and chancel arch are late or transition Norm. The walls of the chancel (which, *obs.*, inclines towards the S.) are Norm., with 2 small Norm. and 2 lancet windows, the E. window, Dec.,

showing when the chancel was lengthened. The S. aisle and the clerestorey windows are Dec. ; the N. aisle Perp. The base of the tower appears to be Norm., the upper part E.E., and later. The spire is new. The interior is comparatively plain, but good. *Obs.* the fine E.E. arch opening from the tower to the nave. On the shafts supporting the chancel arch may be noticed the place of the rood loft and remains of the staircase by which it was reached. During the restoration several imperfect paintings, representations of the Virgin, St. James, etc., and ornamental pattern work, were found in and about the chancel. The lectern is old, and of excellent workmanship. There are several monts. to the Weldons and others, the most interesting being that to Sir Anthony Weldon, Clerk of the Kitchen to Queen Elizabeth and James I., and author of 'The Court of King James,'—"the treasonous book," as Pepys designates it, "worth reading, though ill intended," in which James is as ill-painted as was Sir Anthony himself when Sir Walter Scott drew him, in the 'Fortunes of Nigel,' as Sir Mungo Malagrowther. On the opposite wall is the mont. of Lady Weldon. Another is a sumptuous altar-tomb of marble with recumbent alabaster effigies of Sir Ralph Weldon, d. 1609, and his wife ; the knight being in full armour.

In early times the ch. was much visited, among others, by Canterbury pilgrims, on account of its possessing the shrine of a miracle-working Saint :—

"The ch. at Swanscombe was much haunted times past for *St. Hildeferthes* helpe (a Bishop by coniecture of his picture yet standing in the upper window of the S. ile, although his name is not read in all the Catalogue of the Saxons) to whom such as were distracted, ran for restitution of their wits, as thicke as men were wonte to saile to Anticyra for Heleborus." *

St. Hildeferth is unknown, but the saint worshipped here was no doubt Bp. Hildebert, who has a place in the calendar, May 27. Only a fragment of the picture of the saint mentioned by Lambarde is now left.

The *Manor House* (John Coveney, Esq.), the ancient seat of the Weldons, is an interesting building. There are also some good houses in the pleasant hamlet of *Knockholt*, on the high ground overlooking

---

* Bloxam, Gothic Architecture, 10th ed., p. 92; Glossary of Architecture, vol. i., p. 327.

* Lambarde, Perambulation of Kent, p. 434.

Greenhithe and the Thames, nearly 1 m. W. of Swanscombe.

SYDENHAM, KENT, a populous district, now in effect a London suburb, lying between Dulwich and Norwood, and Lewisham, to which last par. the larger part of it belongs, is about 8 m. from London, and 7 m. from Westminster Bridge by road. Sydenham comprises the eccl. dists. of St. Bartholomew, or *Upper Sydenham* (formed 1855). pop. 5201; Christ Church, *Forest Hill* (1855), pop. 5315; Holy Trinity, *Sydenham Park* (1866), pop. 2962; St. Saviour's, *Brockley Hill* (1867), pop. 3369; and St. Philip, *Sydenham Hill* (1869), pop. 2218; in all 19,065; but this does not include the Crystal Palace district, which though locally a part of Sydenham, belongs to Lambeth parish, and the county of Surrey. Rly. Stats.: L., B., and S. C., *Upper Sydenham*, and *Forest Hill*; S.-E., *Lower Sydenham*; L., C., and D. Rly. *Sydenham Hill*; and *Crystal Palace*.

Of old only known as a genteel hamlet of Lewisham, famed for sylvan retreats, charming prospects, and once for its medicinal waters, Sydenham, after the opening of the Croydon Rly., grew rapidly in favour as a place of residence, and still more rapidly after the opening of the Crystal Palace. It has grown into a district of villas, detached and semi-detached cottages, terraces, so-called parks, and streets; has some half-dozen churches, Free, Presbyterian, Wesleyan, and other chapels, many schools both public and private, three public halls, library and working-men's institutes, and hotels, inns, and shops of all grades, several local societies, and two weekly newspapers. But it has lost its rural character, and is assuming every day more the aspect of a suburb of London.

Churches.—St. Bartholomew's, Sydenham Common (a common enclosed and built over), a roomy and commodious ch., erected in 1830, and Gothic of that period. *Christ Church*, near the Forest Hill rly. station, a neat early Dec. building, consecrated in 1855, and recently completed by the erection of the chancel and tower. *Holy Trinity*, Sydenham Park, a Dec. building of pleasing design, erected in 1865. *St. Saviour's*, Brockley Hill, the north-eastern extremity of

Sydenham, a large stone fabric, Dec. in style, consecrated in May 1866. *St., Philip*, Wells Road, a cruciform building with apsidal chancel, E.E. in style, erected in 1866, from the designs of Mr. Edwin Nash. *St. Michael and All Angels*, Lower Sydenham, a common-place Perp. edifice, serves as a chapel-of-ease to St. Bartholomew's.

When mineral waters were in vogue, Sydenham was resorted to for the waters of a spring discovered in 1640 upon Sydenham Common, and called indifferently the Lewisham, Dulwich, or Sydenham Wells. The waters, which were " of a mild cathartic quality nearly resembling those of Epsom," according to one authority, "a purging spring," according to another, " which have performed great cures in scrofulous, scorbutic, paralytic, and other stubborn diseases;" whilst a third asserts that they are "a certain cure for every ill to which humanity is heir," were recommended in a 'Treatise on Lewisham Wells,' by John Peter, Physician, 1681; and in another by Dr. Allen in 1699. Evelyn, after visiting Dulwich College, Sept. 2, 1675, "came back by certain medicinal Spa waters, at a place called Sydnam Wells, in Lewisham parish, much frequented in summer." Their popularity waned with that of the other English medicinal waters, but the Wells House continued to attract as a place of summer entertainment, and it was the head-quarters of the St. George's Bowmen till the enclosure of Sydenham Common put an end to their archery practice. Till within our own memory, however, the Sydenham Wells were resorted to by scorbutic and paralytic patients. The wells would be sought for in vain now. The church of St. Philip (built 1865-6) covers their site; but there is a cottage in which, according to the local tradition, George III. once stayed best part of a day whilst he drank of the waters—an escort of the Life Guards forming a cordon around the cottage.

Sydenham has no history, and the poet Campbell is almost its only eminent resident. Campbell's house is on Peak Hill— the third on the rt. before reaching the Sydenham Stat. of a row of tall plain houses, the poet's house being distinguished by green jalousies at the windows. The house is unaltered, but the gardens upon which it looked are gone. The house next to Campbell's has long been occupied by Mr. J. B. Buckstone. Here, as he wrote after leaving it, Campbell spent his happiest years. He came to live here in 1804, after he had achieved fame by the publication of the 'Pleasures of Hope.' He wrote to his publisher,—

"I find myself obliged to remove a few months sooner than I expected to a new house of which I have taken a lease for 21 years. The trouble of this migration is very serious. . . . I have ventured on the faith of your support to purchase the fixtures of a very excellent house, and about £100 worth of furniture, which, being sold along with the fixtures, I get at broker's appraisement, i.e., half of prime cost. . . . If you come to London and drink to the health of Auld Reekie over my new mahogany table—if you take a walk round my garden and see my braw house, my court-yard, hens, geese, and turkeys, or view the lovely country in my neighbourhood, you will think this fixture and furniture money well bestowed. I shall indeed be nobly settled, and the devil is in it if I don't work as nobly for it." *

Campbell lived here for about 16 years. He wrote here 'Gertrude of Wyoming,' 'O'Connor's Child,' and 'The Battle of the Baltic,' but he gave up his "noble work" for magazine management, editing, and hack writing which did him no credit. He lived handsomely at Sydenham, was visited by Scott, Rogers, Moore, and other distinguished men, and formed about him a little social circle, including Hill, the original of Paul Pry, who lived close by, and other genial spirits; and their convivialities helped little to further the poet's studies or improve his circumstances. His convivialities were not confined to his house. Sir Charles Bell describes a visit to "Tom Campbell's at Sydenham," and how, after spending the evening indoors, he and the poet "rambled down the village and walked under the delightful trees in the moonlight;" then "adjourned to the inn and took an egg and plotty. Tom got glorious in pleasing gradation, until, etc. . . . His wife received him at home, not drunk, but in excellent spirits. After breakfast we wandered over the forest; not a soul to be seen in all Norwood."† Bell would find the place strangely altered now:

* Thos. Campbell to Archibald Constable, Nov. 10, 1804; Constable and his Literary Correspondents, vol. i., p. 169.
† Letters of Sir Charles Bell, 1870, p. 75.

there are still trees in the village, but "the forest" is gone, and he would look far for solitude. Campbell's Sydenham housekeeping would have been sorely hampered but for the pension of £200 a year granted him in 1806.

Two years before Campbell settled at Sydenham, a more unfortunate poet, Thomas Dermody, died there (July 15, 1802), in abject misery, in a wretched lodging at Perry Slough, now called Perry Vale, on the opposite side of the railway, almost within sight of Campbell's front window. The house has long been removed. Dermody was buried in Lewisham ch.-yard.

The CRYSTAL PALACE, though not in Sydenham, is always considered to belong to it, and may be briefly noticed here. It occupies the summit of the high ground to the S.W. of Sydenham. The land over which the palace grounds, of about 200 acres, stretch, falls rapidly away to the E., and from the terrace in front of the palace a prospect is obtained of surpassing beauty over richly wooded and undulating plains to the distant hills of Kent and Surrey. A finer site could hardly be desired, for the building, and the grounds, and gardens increase in beauty every year. The handsome house a little N. of the palace, and overlooking the grounds is *Rockhill*, from 1852 the residence of Sir Joseph Paxton, the most fortunate of gardeners, the designer of the Crystal Palace, the Exhibition building of 1851, of Chatsworth conservatory and gardens, and of ducal Edensor, who died at Rockhill, June 8, 1865.

The palace, we need hardly repeat, was constructed on the plan and from the materials of the Great Exhibition of 1851, but with many modifications of form and details. The lofty towers at the extremities were designed by Brunel. The first column of the main structure was raised on the 5th of August, 1852; the building was formally opened on the 10th of June, 1854, the Queen, the Prince Consort, the King of Portugal, and other distinguished personages being present at the ceremony. The larger portion of the northern wing, including the tropical department and the Assyrian court, was destroyed by fire, Dec. 30, 1866, and has only been partially rebuilt — much to the injury of the symmetry of the edifice. The building is, too well known to require description. For its varied contents, artistic, archæological, ethnological, industrial, and ornamental, we must refer the visitor to the 'Guide to the Palace and Park,' and the Handbooks to the various Courts, published by the company, and obtainable at the palace. The building, though it has hardly fulfilled the anticipations of its projectors that it would inaugurate a "new order" of architecture, and prove a "structure capable of enduring longer than the oldest marble or stone architectural monuments of antiquity,"—seeing that it has already required repairs to an extent that has severely tried the company's resources, has shown itself peculiarly vulnerable to storm and fire, and that despite of every effort it has not been made rain-proof,—is a structure of its kind without a rival; and has, during the quarter of a century it has been in existence, provided the means of instruction and wholesome recreation to a far greater number of persons (it has had over forty million visitors) than any other private establishment in twice that time; and with judicious management there is no reason to apprehend any abatement of popularity or patronage.

It is needless to particularise the rly. facilities. The Crystal Palace is now in connection with nearly all the metropolitan lines.

SYON (or SION) HOUSE, ISLE-
WORTH, MIDDX., the seat of the Duke of Northumberland, stands in a small but very pretty park which stretches from Brentford to Isleworth along the l. bank of the Thames, opposite Kew Gardens. The chief entrance is by the Lion Gate on the Hounslow road, ¼ m. beyond Brentford, but a narrow lane at Brentford End, a short distance E. of the gate, leads to a public footpath which crosses the park to Isleworth, and affords a good view of the house.

Syon House occupies the site of Syon Monastery, the history of which is given under ISLEWORTH (p. 378, etc.) The house and appurtenances were granted by Edward VI., in the first year of his reign, to his uncle, the Duke of Somerset, Lord Protector, who at once began to build a stately palace on the site. As barely four years elapsed before his at-

tainder and execution, it is probable that he left the house unfinished, but Somerset's house is believed to be the shell of the present mansion. Having reverted to the Crown by Somerset's attainder, Syon was given by Edward VI. in 1553 to John Duke of Northumberland, and here were held the preliminary meetings at which it was arranged to offer the crown to Lady Jane Grey, who was then staying at Syon House with her husband, Lord Dudley; and it was from Syon House that she proceeded in state to the Tower.

By Northumberland's execution Syon reverted to the Crown; and Mary, as mentioned under Isleworth, restored it to the displaced Abbess and nuns. But they held it only to the accession of Elizabeth, when Sir Francis Knowles was appointed keeper for life, with reversion to his son. In 1604 James I. granted Syon to Henry Percy Earl of Northumberland, who had previously secured the leases of the demesne lands granted by Elizabeth. But the Earl fell into disfavour, and was eventually arrested on suspicion of complicity in the Gunpowder Plot, and sent to the Tower. After lying there some years, he was deprived of his offices, and by a decree of the Star Chamber amerced in a penalty of £30,000. In his distress he petitioned the King (1613) for mercy, and begged him in lieu of the fine to accept of Syon, "the only land I can put away, the rest being entailed." He had spent upon Syon, he tells the King, "partly upon the house, partly upon the gardens, almost £9,000;" and, he concludes, "if any man, the best husband in building, should raise such another in the same place, £20,000 would not do it; so as according to the works it may be reckoned at these rates, £31,000; and as it may be sold and pulled in pieces, £19,000, or thereabout." But the King valued money more than house and land, and the unfortunate nobleman lay 6 years longer in prison (15 in all), when he was released on payment of £11,000, and returned to spend his latter years at peace in Syon.

His son, Algernon Percy, 10th Earl of Northumberland, enlarged and greatly altered Syon House, employing Inigo Jones as his architect. In 1647, the plague being then in London, the Dukes of York and Gloucester and the Princess Elizabeth were sent by the Parliament to

Syon, and allowed to visit their father, Charles I., freely at Hampton Court. (*See* HAMPTON COURT.) By the marriage, in 1682, of Lady Elizabeth Percy, Syon was conveyed to Charles Seymour (the Proud) Duke of Somerset—(he being her third husband, and she just 15). Whilst in his possession Syon House became the temporary residence of the Princess (afterwards Queen) Anne, who here gave birth to a son, April 16, 1692, who, however, only lived an hour.

Shortly after the death of Charles Duke of Somerset, 1748, his son and successor, Algernon, gave Syon to his daughter Elizabeth, and her husband, Sir Hugh Smithson, who was afterwards created Duke of Northumberland, and in whose descendants the title and estates have since continued. It is to this Duke that Syon House owes its present form, and the gardens much of their beauty. Calling in to his aid Robert Adam, the most popular architect of the day, he entirely remodelled the exterior, and altered and fitted the interior in a style of great magnificence. Adam was very proud of his work, and Horace Walpole claimed a share in the internal arrangements:

"I have been this evening to Syon, which is becoming another Mount Palatine. Adam has displayed great taste and the Earl matches it with magnificence. The Gallery is converting into a museum in the style of a columbarium, according to an idea that I proposed to my Lord Northumberland." *

The Duke's improvements, which extended over many years, were not confined to the house, gardens, and conservatories. The well-known and much criticised Lion Gate was one of the works Adam devised for him.

"Mr. Adam has published the first number of his Architecture. In it is a magnificent gateway and screen for the Duke of Northumberland at Syon, which I see erecting every time I pass. It is all lace and embroidery, and as croquant as his frames for tables; consequently most improper to be exposed in the high road to Brentford. From Kent's mahogany we are dwindled to Adam's filigree. Grandeur and simplicity are not yet a fashion." †

Times change, and tastes change with them. Whatever may be thought of its grandeur, or want of it, Adam's filigree, if compared with recent work, would be pronounced simplicity itself.

Syon House is a large quadrangular

building, with a square tower at each angle, faced with Bath stone, three storeys high (including the ground floor), and crowned with an embattled parapet. In the centre of the W. front is an embattled portico, which affords a covered way for carriages, and serves as the grand entrance, a flight of steps leading from it to the great hall. From this front a broad lawn extends to the footpath to Isleworth, flanked on either hand by an embattled square stone lodge. The E. or river front has an arcade extending the entire length of the ground floor, between the towers; a projecting central bay carried the whole height of the building, and crowned, Sept. 30, 1874, with the well-known lion mounted on his old arched pedestal, which, till its demolition, graced the Strand front of Northumberland House. This front, with the surrounding trees, is seen to great advantage from the Thames, and has certainly gained in dignity and picturesqueness by the addition of the lion, which aptly breaks the hard line of battlements. From this front the view is very charming, the lawns bordered by noble trees sloping down to the Thames, which, as the boundary-wall is sunk and concealed, appears to flow through the grounds, Kew Gardens on the opposite bank forming in semblance a part of the domain.

The *Great Hall* is a noble room, 66 ft. by 31, and 34 ft. high. The floor is of black and white marble; along the sides are antique statues. It leads to the *Vestibule*, always regarded as one of the richest and most effective of Adam's apartments. It is about 34 ft. by 30, and 21 ft. high; has 12 Ionic columns of verd antique (found in the Tiber, and bought by the Duke of Northumberland for £1000 each), 16 pilasters of the same costly material, rilievi on the walls, and a floor of scagliola worked in patterns. The *Drawing Room*, 44 ft. by 21, and 21 ft. high, is the most sumptuous room in the house. The fittings, furniture, and decorations are of the richest and most costly kind; and the elaborately ornamented ceiling, chimney-pieces, and Mosaic tables, Roman antiques found in the Baths of Titus, deserve attention as works of art as well as ornament. Here, also; are a few good portraits.

In the *Dining Room*, a fine apartment, 62 ft. by 21, and about 22 ft. high, the

* Walpole to the Earl of Hertford, Aug. 27, 1764.
† H. Walpole to Rev. Wm. Mason, July 29, 1773; Letters, vol. v., p. 489.

walls relieved by marble pilasters, are some good portraits of Dukes and Duchesses of Northumberland, by Reynolds, Barry, Lawrence, etc.; a portrait of Queen Charlotte, by Reynolds, and a few more. In an adjoining room are portraits, by Ward, of the favourite chargers of Bonaparte and Wellington; Landseer's Deer-Stalkers; and a Boar Hunt, by Snyders. In the corridors and smaller rooms are portraits by Albert Dürer (of his Father), Schoreel, Schaüffelein, Bernard Van Orley, and other early German masters; and one or two by Hans Holbein. The other pictures include works of various degrees of merit by Garofalo, Luca Giordano, Salvator Rosa, Both, Gaspar Poussin, D. Teniers, Weenix, and other masters of the various schools, but recent and prospective changes render it undesirable to go further into details. The *Gallery*, of which Horace Walpole claimed to have given the idea, extends the entire length of the eastern front, and is 135 ft. long, 14 ft. wide, and 14 ft. high. The walls and ceiling are decorated with stucco-work and paintings in chiaroscuro. It is arranged as a combined museum and library, and contains, besides a fine collection of books, numerous objects of antiquity, and a splendid vase of Irish crystal mounted in gold which was presented by the ladies of Ireland to a late Duchess of Northumberland when leaving Ireland at the close of the Duke's Lord Lieutenancy.

The grounds, though level, are charming. They were laid out by Brown, but have since been much altered. The lawns are wide and smooth, the trees and shrubs of unusual variety, size, and beauty. There are magnificent cedars, the largest stone-pines in England, silver firs of surprising height, as well as many other varieties of the fir tribe, spruces, poplars, Turkey oaks,

copper beeches, Judas trees, tulip trees, magnolias, catalpas, large groups of acacias, giant Portugal laurels, and most of the ordinary park trees.

The gardens of Syon are of great extent and beauty, and have always been celebrated. The Protector Somerset, the builder of the first house, formed a "botanic garden" here, one of the first formed in England. It is twice noticed in the Herbal (1568) of Dr. Turner—who was Somerset's physician, and may have been his adviser in gardening. The Earl of Northumberland too, as we have seen, spent large sums on the Syon gardens (1616). It has since been several times remodelled, its present form being in the main due to the late Richard Forrest. It is especially famous for its fine collection of hardy exotics. The flower gardens are brilliant, and the fruit and kitchen gardens, some acres in extent, are models of good order and productiveness. The plant and forcing houses are very large, and much admired by horticulturists for their arrangements. The Great Conservatory, designed by Fowler, is in the form of a wide crescent, with pavilions at the extremities, and a lofty central dome. The centre, 100 feet long, is a tropical house, and is said to contain the finest collection of tropical plants in any private establishment in England. It is noteworthy that here only in this country has the cocoanut palm fully ripened; and the Victoria regia blossoms more freely and successfully than elsewhere. The stone vases on the pedestals of the terrace in front of the conservatory were carved by Grinling Gibbons.

In the outbuilding are some fragments of Syon Monastery, and tradition affirms that the ancient mulberry trees—now kept alive with difficulty—belonged to the convent gardens.

TADWORTH, Surrey (*see* Kingswood).

TALWORTH, Surrey (*see* Ditton, Long).

TANDRIDGE, Surrey (Dom. *Tenrige*), 1½ m. E. of Godstone, 2¼ m. N.E.

of Godstone Road Stat. of the S.-E. Rly.: pop. 623, of whom 168 were in the eccl. dist. of Blindley Heath, and 30 in that of Felbridge.

The village stands in a pretty sequestered district, away from any main line of road. The pursuits are agricultural; the fields mostly of corn and roots, with a few hop-gardens. An Augustinian priory, or hospital, for 3 priests and several poor brethren, was founded here in the reign of Richard I. Never rich, it yet continued to the Dissolution, when its revenue was valued at £78 16s. 6¾d. It stood at the foot of the chalk hills, but no vestige is left of the buildings. Near the site is a house called The Priory. Encaustic tiles have often been turned up by plough or spade.

The *Church* (St. Peter) stands on high ground, E. of the vill. It is small, though more than once enlarged. Originally Norman, it has had Dec. windows inserted; in 1836 a N. transept was added; in 1844 a S. aisle; and in 1874 a N. aisle, Sir Gilbert Scott being the architect. The large Dec. W. window was inserted and filled with painted glass as a memorial of Lord Chancellor Cottenham, d. 1851. Several other windows have memorial glass. The ch. has a tower and spire, with a peal of 5 bells. In the ch.-yard is the grave, marked by a plain coffin tombstone with a cross at the head, of Sir J. Cosmo Melvill, K.C.B., of the India Office. A more elaborate tomb is that of Mrs. Turner, wife of C. H. Turner, Esq., at whose cost the N. aisle of the ch. was built. W. of the ch. is the gigantic trunk of a yew, which still puts forth abundant leaves, though the trunk is quite hollow.

Tandridge Court, E. of the ch., is the seat of the Earl of Cottenham. *Rook's Nest*, a stately semi-classical mansion, with Ionic portico, on the way to Godstone, belongs to F. M. H. Turner, Esq., and is now the residence of Mrs. Bonsor. Other seats are *Tandridge Hall* (Henry Göschen, Esq.), a fine late 16th cent. mansion, but much altered; and *Southlands* (W. Dickenson, Esq.), a good modern house.

TATSFIELD, SURREY, on the

eastern border of the county, adjoining Westerham, Kent, from which town Tatsfield ch. is about 2½ m. N.W. Pop. 187.

Tatelefelle, at the Dom. Survey, was held by Anchetel de Ros of Bp. Odo. Early in the 14th cent. the manor belonged to Richard Fitz-Griffin, and remained with his descendants till about 1367. It then passed to the Uvedales, by whom it was held till alienated by Sir Wm. Uvedale to Sir John Gresham about 1634. By his marriage with Catherine Maria, daughter and heiress of Sir John Gresham, in 1804, it passed to W. Leveson Gower, Esq., and is now the property of G. W. G. Leveson Gower, Esq. Tatsfield Court Lodge, the old manor-house, stood near the ch., but was pulled down by the last Sir John Gresham. A new house was built at the foot of the hill, on the road to Westerham; but there is no gentleman's seat now occupied in the parish.

The *Church* (dedication unknown) is a plain old village ch., of flint and stone, standing on the summit of the chalk ridge which runs E. and W. through the par. It comprises nave, chancel, and W. tower. The walls, of great thickness, are in part E.E. (*obs.* the two lancets high up on the N., and their splays inside), but the windows are Dec. The tower and porch are modern (1838) and poor. E. of the ch. is a yew of great size, but formed of several stems. The views from the ch.-yard are extensive and fine. Along the S. slope of the hill the ancient Pilgrims' Road runs into Kent.

TEDDINGTON, MIDDX., on the l.

bank of the Thames, and on the main road from Richmond to Bushey Park and Hampton Court, midway, 1½ m., between Kingston-upon-Thames and Twickenham, 12 m. from London by road, and a stat. on the L. and S.-W. Rly. (New Kingston line). Pop. 4063. Inns: *Clarence Hotel*, Park Road; *Anglers'; Royal Oak; King's Head* (anglers' houses).

It is a favourite legend at Teddington, and one adopted by the Emperor Napoleon III. in his 'César,' that the place owes its name to the tide being arrested here—*Tide-end-town*. But the tide is stayed by a lock—the lowest on the Thames—and locks are a comparatively recent invention. In early times, before the construction of bridges, locks, and other obstructions, there can be no doubt the tide ascended much higher. But the fatal objection to the popular etymology is the spelling of the name, in the oldest records, *Totyngton*, *Todynton*, which points pretty conclusively to a patronymic, *Toding*, as in Totingas, Tooting, or *Tœting*, as in Taddington, Gloucestershire.

The tide now flows but feebly some way below Teddington: high-water at Teddington Lock is 1 h. 25 m. later than at London Bridge, the distance being 19½ m. The old, lumbering, but picturesque Teddington Lock has given place to a more solid and convenient structure of masonry, with a siding for the quicker passage of skiffs and pleasure-boats. There is good fishing on the Thames here, though no established deep. The Anglers' is the head-quarters for fishermen, and a favourite house of call with boating men. The Kemps are old-established fishermen. Teddington Lock is the limit below which, by Act of Parliament (1852-3), no water can be taken from the Thames for the supply of London.

Teddington manor, originally an appurtenance of Staines, belonged to Westminster Abbey till the Dissolution. Leases were granted to various persons by the Crown, till James I., in 1603, gave the reversion of the manor in fee farm to James Hill. It has since been several times alienated, but has had no owners of mark.

The village extends from the river-side, where is the ch., on the one hand towards Twickenham, on the other, in a very irregular way, to the gates of Bushey Park. Several of the old mansions for which Teddington was once celebrated have been removed, but a few remain, and a large number of villas and genteel dwellings have been built within the last years, the proximity of the river, Bushey Park, and Hampton Court rendering it an attractive place of residence now that the railway has made it readily accessible. A new village has sprung up about the stat., *Upper Teddington*, which already has ch., schools, hotel, and shops of a more showy description than those of the mother village.

The *Church* (St. Mary), close by the river, is a mean brick building ; the S. aisle, the oldest part, of the 16th cent., the N. aisle built in 1753, chiefly at the expense of Dr. Stephen Hales, who also built the tower in the following year. The chancel, of Suffolk brick and Dec. in style, is a recent addition. The interior is as poor as the exterior, but has some monts. of interest. The earliest is to Sir Orlando Bridgman, d. June 1674, commissioner for Charles I. at the treaty of Uxbridge, and after the Restoration successively Chief Baron of the Exchequer, Chief Justice of the Common Pleas, and

Lord Keeper of the Great Seal, from which office he was, however, dismissed in 1672 for refusing to sign the Declaration of Indulgence. E. wall of N. aisle, tablet to "Margaret Woffington, spinster," d. March 28, 1760, the once famous actress Peg Woffington. In the vestry, tablet to "Stephen Hales, D.D., clerk of the closet to the Princess of Wales, who was minister of this parish 51 years," d. Jan. 4, 1761, author of 'Vegetable Statics,' 'Statical Essays,' and other valuable books and papers in natural history and physiology, and inventor of a system of ventilation which was successfully applied in hospitals, prisons, ships, and other close and crowded places. He was buried under the tower which he had erected. Tablet to John Walter, founder and principal proprietor of the Times, the first of three distinguished bearers of that name : he had a residence at Teddington, where he died, Nov. 16, 1812. At the W. end of the ch. is the mont. of Henry Flitcroft, architect of the churches of St. Giles in the Fields, and St. Olave, Tooley Street. The body of Paul Whitehead, the poet, of dubious fame, d. Dec. 30, 1774, was buried in Teddington ch.-yard, but his heart, by his own desire, was placed in a marble urn, and deposited, with various heathenish ceremonies, in the mausoleum of his patron, Lord Le Despencer, at West Wycombe ; from which, after being exhibited to visitors for 60 years, it was stolen in 1839. Whitehead has no memorial at Teddington. His residence was on Twickenham Common. At Teddington also was buried Richard Bentley, d. 1782, the son of the great Greek scholar, author of 'Patriotism,' and other forgotten poems, sometime friend of Horace Walpole, his adviser and draughtsman in the erection and decoration of Strawberry Hill, and illustrator of some of the volumes issued from the Strawberry Hill press. Hales' successor in the curacy of Teddington was John Cosens, D.D., who published 'The Tears of Twickenham,' 'Œconomics of Beauty,' and other poems, and some volumes of sermons.

The *Church* of St. Peter and St. Paul, *Upper Teddington*, a large and handsome E.E. building of yellow brick with red brick mouldings and cornices, was partly erected in 1866, and completed (except the tower and spire) in 1873, from the designs of Mr. G. E. Street, R.A. By it is a spacious school-house, corresponding in architectural character, erected in 1874.

The *Manor House* was built by Lord Buckhurst early in the 17th cent. In the 18th cent. it was for several years the residence of Visct. Dudley and Ward, who altered the house and remodelled the grounds, where among other things he constructed, if we may trust his neighbour Horace Walpole, "an obelisk *below* a hedge, a canal at right angles with the Thames, and a sham bridge no wider than that of a violin." * His widow married a Capt. Smith, who swept away all these puerilities, and "nearly rebuilt" the house. It is now the residence of George Vatcher, Esq.

Among the more eminent inhabitants of Teddington are Q. Elizabeth's Earl of Leicester, who resided here in 1570; and the celebrated William Penn, who dated the letter, in which he rebutted the charge of being a Papist, from Teddington, Oct. 1688. Francis Manning dates the Preface of his translation of Theodosius from Teddington, and he continued to live here for many years afterwards.† Whilst still an outlaw, John Wilkes, during a surreptitious visit to England, had "an out-of-the-way lodging in the second turning past Teddington Church."‡ John O'Keefe, the dramatic author, was resident at Teddington in 1794 whilst he delivered his 'Works,' in 4 volumes, to his subscribers.

THAMES DITTON, SURREY (*see* DITTON).

THEOBALDS, a manor and the

site of a royal palace and park, in the par. of CHESHUNT, HERTS. Under CHESHUNT an account has been given of the manor. The palace was built, 1560 and following years, by Elizabeth's famous minister, William Cecil, afterwards Lord Burleigh, who had purchased the manor of Mr. Wm. Goring. Cecil began his house, as he writes (Aug. 1585), "with a mean measure, but

increased on occasion of her Majesty's often comyng." Elizabeth, in fact, came often, and did not come alone. She loved to witness the hunting of a hart, and Theobalds was close at hand to Enfield Chase or Waltham Forest. From 1564 she made a visit of some duration every summer, and her host was bound to adapt his house to her requirements. In the contemporary Life of Lord Burleigh it is said,—

"Her Majestie sometimes had strangers and ambassadors come to her at Theobalds; where she hath byn sene in as great royalty, and served as bountifully and magnificently as at any other time or place, all at his Lordship's chardg : with rich shows, pleasant devices, and all manner of sports could be devised, to the great delight of her Majestie and her whole traine." *

Cecil entertained the Queen 12 times, and each visit of his imperious mistress cost him "from £2000 to £3000," — a large sum in those days. At other times considerable state was maintained at Theobalds:—

"His Lordship's hall was ever well furnished with men, served with meate and kept in good order. For his steward kept a standing table for gentlemen; besides two other long tables (many times twice set) one for the clerk of the kitchen, the other for yeomen. And, whether his Lordship were absent or present, all men, both retainers and others, resorted continually to meat and meale at their pleasures. . . . . His Lordship was served with men of qualitie and habilitie. . . . Insomuch as I have nombred in his house, attending on the table, 20 gentlemen of his retainers of £1000 per annum a peace in possession or reversion. And of his ordinary men as manie. Some worth £1000; some worth 3, 5, 10, yea £20,000, daiely attending his Lordship's service. . . . . He also greatly delighted in making gardens, fountains, and walks, which at Theobalds were perfected most costly, bewtyfully, and pleasantly; where one might walk two mile in the Walks before he came to their ends." † His greatest delight was to "lye a day or two at his little lodge at Theobaldes, retired from business. . . Riding in his garden and walks upon his little mule was his greatest disport." ‡

Cecil's house was a stately structure of brick with stone dressings, comprising a central entrance gate-house, and two quadrangles with smaller courts, in style something between Hatfield and Knole. The first quadrangle, 86 ft. square, called the Fountain Court, from a fountain supported by 4 pillars of black marble, between which was a group of Venus and

---

* Walpole to the Earl of Strafford, July 28, 1787; Letters, vol. ix., p. 102.

† Lysons, vol. ii., p. 736.

‡ Entry in Sir Joshua Reynolds's Pocket-book, Aug. 28, 1766 : quoted in Leslie and Taylor's Life of Sir J. Reynolds, vol. i., p. 258.

---

* The Compleat Statesman, chap. xviii. Peck, Desiderata Curiosa, lib. i., p. 33.

† *Ibid.*, pp. 31—34. ‡ *Ibid.*, p. 50.

Cupid in white marble, contained the state rooms. On the ground floor was the Great Hall, paved with Purbeck marble, and having a roof of " carved timber of curious workmanship." The Presence Chamber was lined with carved wainscot, and had a " ceiling full of gilded pendants hanging down, setting forth the room with great splendor." On the first floor were the Presence Chamber, a Privy Chamber, richly ornamented, Withdrawing Chamber, King's Bed-chamber and a Gallery 123 ft. long and 21 wide, "wainscotted with oak, and paintings over the same of divers cities rarely painted and set forth with a frett seelinge, with divers pendants roses and flower-de-luces, painted and gilded with gold." Numerous other chambers and galleries were of corresponding splendour. The Middle Court was a quadrangle 110 ft. sq., containing the Queen's Chapel, Privy Chamber, and other apartments, the Prince's Lodgings, the Duke's Lodgings, the Queen's Gallery, 109 ft. by 14 ft., all of great splendour. S. of the house was, what may be regarded as a particular exemplification of Cecil's personal taste, " a large open cloister, built upon several large faire pillars of stone, arched over with 7 arches, with a fair rayle and balisters, well painted with the Kinges and Queenes of England, and the pedigree of the old Ld. Burleigh, and divers other ancient families ; with paintings of many castles and battailes, with divers subscriptions on the walls."* The gardens, which were very large, and considered the finest in England, were laid out in the taste of the age, with lakes, canals, bridges, fountains, labyrinths, knots, terraces, and summer-houses, and adorned with marble statues and busts, "and columns and pyramids of wood up and down the garden."†

The first Earl of Salisbury, Burleigh's youngest son, succeeded to Theobalds, and entertained James I. here for four days (May 1603), on his way from Scotland to take possession of the English throne, and here James received the homage of the Lords of the Council, and created his first batch of 28 English knights. Three years later James was again here with his

father-in-law, Christian, King of Denmark.* So delighted was James with the place that he persuaded the Earl to exchange it with him for Hatfield—the present seat of the Marquis of Salisbury, the lineal descendant of the owner of Theobalds. (See HATFIELD HOUSE.) An Act (4 and 5 Jas. I.) was passed for the transfer of Hatfield, and the King received possession of Theobalds, May 22, 1607.

" In purchasing of Theobald's House . . . . . the king did desire to gratify Salisbury, and surely the House was not so fit for a subject. It is very large, well contrived, very stately, a very sweet wholesome place ; but had neither lordship nor tenants, nor so much as provision of fuel : only a Park for pleasure and no more. Now seeing the king had houses about London on every side : in Kent he had Greenwich and Eltham ; in Essex, Havering ; in Middlesex, Hampton Court ; in Surrey, Nonsuch and Richmond and Oatlands ; therefore in the northern side towards Scotland he desired to have one house ; and in his time he made more use of it than of any other. Besides it was near to Waltham Forest, which is the nearest forest to London, and no doubt but he had an advantageous change.†

Ben Jonson wrote his ' Entertainment of the Two Kings of Great Britain and Denmark at Theobald's for the reception of Christian IV. in 1606.' When, the following year, Theobalds was about to be formally transferred by Cecil to the King, Jonson was again called in to furnish matter for the royal feast. He prepared the masque entitled ' Entertainment of King James and Queen Anne at Theobald's in 1607,' and in it he makes the Genius of the House, when Lord Salisbury delivers possession to the Queen, exchange sorrow for the loss of such a master for joy at the acquisition of so incomparable a mistress.

James greatly extended the park by taking in a portion of Enfield Chase, and Northaw and Cheshunt commons, and he surrounded it with a wall 10 miles in circumference. " At the distance of every mile there was fixed in the wall a square stone, with the date of the year and the number of miles."‡ When Lysons wrote

---

* Parliamentary Survey, 1650, quoted in Lysons, vol. i., p. 773, etc. ; Nichols, Progresses of Queen Elizabeth ; Compleat Statesman, etc.

* See the description in Paul Hentzner's Journey to England in 1598, Walpole's trans., p. 52.

* A glowing account of their reception was given in ' The King of Denmark's Welcome,' 4to, 1606.

† Bishop Goodman, Court of King James, vol. i., p. 174 : the bishop wrote in reply to Sir Anthony Weldon, who of course gives a different colour to the purchase.

‡ Lysons, vol i., p. 776, n. 33.

(1810), "one of these, with the figure VIII. and the date 1621," still remained "in a part of the old wall which forms the boundary of Mr. Russell's garden at Aldbury." James spent most of his leisure at Theobalds. The New River was carried through the park, and James took great interest in its construction. But it was nearly proving fatal to him. Riding in the park with Prince Charles on a winter afternoon, when the New River was thinly frozen over, the King's horse stumbled, and the King was thrown forward and disappeared under the ice. Sir Richard Young plunged into the water, seized the King by his boots, the only parts visible, and dragged him ashore, little the worse for his immersion. James was at Theobalds in March 1625, when he was attacked by tertian ague, and after nearly a month of irregular medical treatment and much suffering, he died there, March 27, 1625.

Charles I. visited Theobalds occasionally. Henry Cary Lord Falkland lost his life from breaking his leg on a stand in the park, September 1633. It was from Theobalds that Charles set out to put himself at the head of his army, Feb. 1642. In 1650 the Parliamentary Commissioners made a survey of the palace and park: they reported that the palace was an excellent building, in good repair, and by no means fit to be demolished. It was however dismantled, and the greater part razed, the proceeds of the materials being appropriated to the army. The park they state was 2508 acres in extent, and they value the timber in it at £7259, exclusive of 15,608 trees set apart for the navy and others which had already been cut down.

Immediately after the Restoration, Charles II. made a grant of Theobalds to George Monk, Earl of Albemarle, on the death of whose son, without male issue, in 1687, it reverted to the Crown. William III. granted the *palace and park* to his favourite Bentinck, Earl of Portland, whose grandson, the Duke of Portland, sold it in 1762 to Mr. George Prescott for £75,000, exclusive of the timber. The *manor* of Theobalds passed to Ralph Duke of Montagu, who married the Duke of Albemarle's widow. It was sold by John Duke of Montagu to Mrs. Letitia Thornhill, from whom it passed by marriage to the Cromwell family, and was held at his

death in 1821 by Oliver Cromwell, the last male descendant of the great Protector. It is now held by the executors of Thos. A. Russell, Esq.

The last vestiges of the palace were destroyed by Mr. Prescott in 1765, and the present *Theobalds Square* erected on the site. At that time there remained, among others, the room in which James was said to have died. The *Stables*, "which stood near the road leading from Waltham Cross to Cheshunt," included " on the W. side of the road a *camel* stable, 63 ft. in length ; * and on the E. side two stables, each 119 ft., and a barn 163 ft. in length."† Adjoining them was an almshouse, also erected by Lord Burleigh, for " aged and over-worn captains, gentlemen by birth and calling," which was left standing till 1812.

The present *Theobalds Park* is the seat of Alderman James Cotton, M.P. (Lord Mayor, 1875-6). The house—a good red-brick mansion—was built by George Prescott, Esq., 1765-70. It stands on rising ground about 1½ m. S.W. of the palace of Lord Burleigh and King James. The park proper is only about 200 acres, but the enclosed estate is very extensive ; there are roads and walks through it from Enfield Chase to Cheshunt ch., and also from Waltham Cross. Southey, writing in 1818,‡ says, " There still exists, though in decay, the moss walk, which formerly made part of the gardens of Theobalds. . . . About 30 years ago, and before the storm had made a breach through the old elms by which it was overshadowed, we remember this singular walk in its beauty ;—the only remains of all which rendered Theobalds the favourite palace of two succeeding sovereigns." In Gough's day there were left " a walk of abeles, between two walls, a circular summer-house, and traces of the park-wall." Dr. Isaac Watts resided for some years in the house of Sir Thomas Abney at Theobalds (before Sir Thomas removed

---

* The naturalization of the camel was a favourite notion of the age. James also sought to rear silk-worms here : in the Exchequer Accounts is an order for the payment of £50, Jan. 23, 1618, to " Munten Jenings, keeper of his Majesty's house and gardens at Theobalds . . . . for making a place for his Majesty's silk worms, and for making provision of mulberry leaves for them."

† Lysons.

‡ Quarterly Review, vol. xix., p. 18.

to Abney Park, Stoke Newington). The moss-walk and overhanging elms (even then the chief relics of Burleigh's famous grounds) came close to Sir Thos. Abney's garden, and within a few yards of the entrance to the walk was a "summer-house, which, 50 years after Watts's death, was shown as the place in which he had composed many of his works." The exterior of Theobalds is engraved in the Gentleman's Magazine, Feb. 1836; and at Hinton St. George (the seat of Earl Poulett) is a view of the interior by Poelemberg. The house was no doubt a conspicuous object. Izaak Walton makes *Auceps* say, "I shall by your favour bear you company as far as Theobalds;" and Piscator ends his discourse, "I must in manners break off, for I see Theobald's House." *

THEYDON, Essex, (pron. *Thoy-don,*) the name of three adjoining parishes lying on the S. and E. of Epping, between it and the Ongar road. In A.-S. charters the name is *Thegndun* (Thane's Hill), in Domesday (the manors being still undivided) it is *Taindena.* It is a pleasant district, undulating, well wooded, well cultivated, drained by the little river Roding and its runnels, and thinly populated.

THEYDON BOIS (pr. *Thoydon Boys*), the smallest of the three parishes, is about 2 m. S. by E. of Epping: the Theydon Stat. of the Grt. E. Rly. (Ongar branch), 15¾ m. from Liverpool Street, is at Theydon Gate, ½ m. E. of the ch. It is a scattered agric. par. of 798 inh., partly within the precincts of Epping Forest, whence the distinctive name, *Bois. They-don Gate* indicates the entrance to the forest.

Theydon manor belonged to Waltham Abbey from the reign of Henry III. to the Dissolution. It has since been held by private persons, and has no history. The vill., such as it is, lies for the most part about a broad pleasant green, with a long avenue on the l., and oak-bordered lanes running from it on all sides. W. of *Theydon Green* is the *Church* (St. Mary), a plain, commonplace, red-brick and stone building, E.E. in style, erected here in 1852, as a more convenient

site than that of the old ch. It is prettily situated, and, standing on high ground, its octagonal tower and slate spire form a good landmark for the village. The *old ch.* was about 1 m. S., at the corner of a farm-road, on the rt. of the lane to Abridge: the gables and chimneys of the large old-fashioned, red-brick farmhouse by the ch.-yard will guide the stranger to the spot. Not a trace of the ch. is left; the neglected ch.-yard is overgrown with nettles; the tombs and gravestones are covered with lichens, broken and ruinous. *Theydon Hall* is the seat of R. H. C. Pallett, Esq.

THEYDON GERNON (pr. *Thoydon Garnon*). adjoining Theydon Bois on the N. and E., owes its distinctive name to having belonged to the Norman Gernons. Pop. 1346; but of these 638 were in the eccl. dist. of Coopersale, and 135 in the Epping Union workhouse.

The old manor-house, ½ m. N. by W. of the ch., now a farm-house, is known as *Garnish Hall,* a corruption no doubt of Gernon's Hall. The *Church* (All Saints) is in the S. part of the par., near *Hobb's Cross,* on the Abridge and Epping road. To reach it from Theydon Stat., turn S. and take the first lane on the l., a charming walk of a mile along green and woody lanes. Passing *Theydon Place* (an old-fashioned, low, red-brick house, set amidst tall trees, the greenest of smooth-shaven lawns, and brightest of flowers), on the l. is a long, narrow lime avenue leading to the ch. door. The ch. is mostly of the Perp. period, but restored in 1863, when several new windows were inserted. The tall, sturdy, battlemented brick tower, with angle turret, was, according to a now illegible insc. on it, erected 1520. by means of a bequest of Ald. Sir John Crosby, of Crosby Hall, Bishopsgate Street. Rt. and l. of the altar are corresponding *monts.*, with small brasses and labels (or the places where they have been). On l., Sir Wm. Fitzwilliam (d. 1570) and wife Anne, *brass* with kneeling effigies of the knight in armour, girt with sword and spurs, and attended by 2 sons, and the lady (a daughter of Sir Wm. Sidney of Penshurst) kneeling, arms and label, with 3 daughters. Over this is a small *brass* of Alleyn, wife of John Branch, cit. and merchant of London, d. 1567. N. of the chancel is a *brass*, now mural, in good condition and very well engraved, of Wm. Ryrkeby, rector of the par., circ. 1458. In the upper part of the E. window is some painted glass. *Obs.* in the *ch.-yard* a picturesque half-timber cottage with pargetted plaster. Robert Fabyan, the chronicler, had a house here. In his will, dated 11th June, 1511, he directs that if he died " at my mansion called *Halstedys*, my corpse [shall be] buried atwene my pewe and the high awter within the qwere of the parisshe churche of Alhalowen of Theydon Gardon." No place named Halsteds is now known here, nor is any mentioned in Morant; and in 1810 Sir Henry Ellis could discover no tradition of any plot of ground bearing the name, nor in the parish registers, rent rolls, or muniments, any reference to a family named Fabyan. The old chronicler was buried in St. Michael's ch., Cornhill; but his mont. was already " gone" when Stow wrote his Survey of London at the close of the 16th cent.

At *Coopersale* hamlet, 2 m. N., is a district ch. (St. Alban's) built, with the adjacent parsonage, by Miss A. Houblon. *Coopersale*—a corruption, it has been suggested, of Cooper's Hall— the large mansion now better known as *Coopersale House* (Mrs. Houblon), at the N. end of the par., has been altered and modernized, but retains some of the old painted ceilings. *Coopersale Hall* (Wm. Willett, Esq.), 1 m. N.W. of the ch; *Gaynes Park* (T. C. Marsh, Esq.), 2 m. N., and *Theydon Place* (J. H. Smee, Esq.), are the other seats.

THEYDON MOUNT (pop. 184) lies E. of Theydon Gernon, between it and Stapleford Tawney. It is a pleasant country, but there is no village, not even a " public." The only thing to notice is *Hill Hall*, the property of Sir W. Bowyer Smijth, Bart., and now the residence of J. Fleming, Esq. Hill Hall was commenced by Elizabeth's famous secretary, Sir Thomas Smith, who came into possession of the estate by his marriage with Philippa, relict of Sir John Hampden, its former owner. Sir Thomas left the house unfinished at his death, 1576, but made provision in his will for its completion. It is a large quadrangular edifice, of the classic style then coming into vogue; red brick with stone dressings; engaged columns

and pediment in principal front, and a balustered parapet running all round. Some of the rooms are large; the spacious hall has a gallery on one side, and an ornamental stucco ceiling, and is hung with arms, armour, and family portraits. The great staircase is also noteworthy. In one of the bedrooms is a recess like a very large cupboard, which tradition (of recent growth) says was a hiding-place. It .was discovered some 40 years since, and is curious as retaining on the wall the original " water-work," like that Falstaff commended to Hostess Quickly (King Henry IV., part ii., act ii., sc. 2). This, as a label informs you, represents " the Destruction of Sennacherib and his Host." Some of the other rooms retain their old " fly-bitten tapestries." Hill Hall stands on high ground, whence it was named by Sir Thomas Smith, *Mount Hall*. The park is large, finely timbered, and broken by deep dells. Theydon Mount *Church* (St. Michael's) stands in the park ¼ m. S.E. of the hall. It is small, of brick, with tower and short spire, and was built by the first Sir William Smith (d. 1626) in place of the old ch. injured by lightning. It contains many memorials of the Smith or Smijth family, including those of Sir Thomas, the secretary, who is represented under an arched canopy, and belauded in a long Latin insc.; and Sir William, the builder of the ch.

THORNDON HALL (*see* HORNDON, Essex).

THORPE, SURREY (Dom. *Torp*), an agric. vill., midway, about 2 m., between Egham and Chertsey: pop. 590.

Lying in the meadows at the N. foot of St. Anne's Hill, with the heights terminating in Cooper's Hill on the W. and N., the Thames bounding it on the E., a streamlet flowing through the fields, expanding into the *Flete Pool* (a favourite resort of water-fowl and abounding in fish) and turning two mills, with broad green meads on every side, it is just the quiet, sylvan spot the naturalist, angler, or artist would delight to spend a brief holiday in.

The manor belonged to Chertsey Abbey from its foundation to its suppression. It was then retained by the Crown till 1590, when Elizabeth granted it to Sir John Wolley, her Latin secretary. For the past century it has belonged to the Bennetts. The *Church*, St. Mary, is cruciform, of flint and chalk ; Dec., except the ivy-clad tower, which is 16th cent. brick. It was carefully restored in 1854, and a wooden screen added. The chancel window has good Dec. tracery ; most of the windows are filled with modern painted glass. In the chancel are a piscina, credence, and sedilia. *Obs.* the very curious late *brass*, within marble frame, on S. wall of chancel, of William Denham, goldsmith, of London, d. 1583, his wife and 13 children, 4 sons and 9 daughters. [Was he grandfather, or any connection, of the author of Cooper's Hill ? The poet's father, as well as himself, lived at Egham.] Of the older brasses which were in the transept only fragments remain. There are several mural monts., chiefly to the Bennetts ; one has on it the verses written by Sterne, when "apprehensive" of the loss of a "dear friend" Eliza or Lady James),* and commencing, "Columns and laboured urns but vainly show.'

Thorpe Place (Rev. H. Leigh Bennett), built about 1800, on the site of the old manor-house, stands in a small but good park. The other seats are *Thorpe Lee* (J. C. Blackett, Esq.), at the Egham end of the par. ; *Thorpe House* (Hon. Mrs. Scott) ; and *Eastley End* (H. Ritchie, Esq.) Sir Edw. Nicholas, Secretary of State to Charles I., had a house at Thorpe, to which, in a letter dated Aug. 31, 1641, he begs the King's permission to remove on account of "ye sickness and small pox very rife in London."

THURROCK, GRAYS, Essex (*see* GRAYS).

THURROCK, LITTLE, Essex,

on the l. bank of the Thames, and on the road to West Tilbury, 1 m. E. of the Grays Stat. of the L. and Southend Rly. Pop. 321.

The village stands on elevated ground overlooking Thurrock and Chadwell Marshes, and from many parts there are

good views over the Thames. The vill itself has little to interest. The occupations are agricultural ; there are considerable arable farms ; the marshes afford pasture ; and vegetables, and especially peas, are largely grown for the London market. There are also extensive brick fields and chalk pits. Here, at Chadwell, and at East Tilbury, are the chalk shafts and caverns known as Cunobeline's Gold Mines and Daneholes, and described under CHADWELL ST. MARY, p. 80. Little Thurrock ch. (St. Mary) is a plain little village ch., comprising nave and chancel under one roof, much altered, and of no marked character or interest.

THURROCK, WEST, Essex, on

the l. bank of the Thames, 1½ m. W. from the Grays Stat., 3 m. E. from the Purfleet Stat. of the Tilbury and Southend line, Grt. E. Rly., 19 m. from London. Pop., exclusive of Purfleet garrison and Cornwall Reformatory ship, 546.

The vill. consists of a few cottages, some wooden, all poor, clustered by the vicarage and the Old Ship inn, or scattered along the road from Grays to Purfleet. Standing apart are several well-to-do farms. The ch. will be noticed by every traveller on the rly., seated solitary by the river-side, half a mile from the vill., the way to it being across a dreary marsh —in summer a tolerable walk, but in winter the very picture of desolation. It was not, however, always so lonely. By it was a religious house, traces of which have been found, and also, we are informed, flint foundations of ordinary dwellings.

Here, by the ch., was the last gathering-place of the pilgrims to Canterbury from the eastern counties, previous to crossing by the ferry into Kent. The *Church* (St. Clement) stands on a bed of gravel : it was formerly surrounded by a stout flint wall, but flints becoming very dear some five-and-thirty years ago, the churchwarden pulled down the wall, sold the flints, and put up instead a flimsy fence. The ch. is built of flint and chalk. A tablet on the front of the tower is said to bear the date 1040, but it is too much weatherworn to be now decipherable from below. If the date be correctly given, it would seem to carry back the building to before the Conquest (and this

---

* See his Letter to his Daughter, April 9, 1767.

would be of farther interest as illustrating the date of the river wall, which must have been constructed before the church). But no carving is left of Norman date, and the oldest part of the building appears to be E.E. The ch. consists of a nave and S. aisle, chancel, with an ugly modern south chapel, and a massive W. tower, chiefly of chalk and flint in regular courses, but with a modern upper storey of brick.

The church has been patched and disfigured both inside and out, yet suffered to become almost ruinous. The nave has been repaired and the whitewash removed, but the walls show cracks, the mortar is crumbling away, and the whole looks as though it would fall down before one of the gales which sweep with such force across the river here. Till lately the interior afforded a curious illustration of churchwardens' taste. Walls, arches, and pillars were all covered thickly with whitewash, and, by way of relieving the monotony, the capitals and mouldings of the columns were washed over with lampblack. There is a tradition that it was first done by way of putting the church into mourning for the Princess Charlotte, but if so it was not removed when the occasion was past. In 1865 the nave columns were purified, but those of the chancel remain untouched, and have a most absurd effect. Once the capitals were otherwise decorated. On carefully removing the white and black washes, it was found that they had been covered with gilding—perhaps by pilgrims. Traces of paintings were also found on the walls, but no figure could be made out. S. of the chancel is a good double piscina. The E. window is early Dec. of rather peculiar and very good tracery, but sadly weatherworn outside. The communion table appears to be the original one, of oak. No mont. now remains in the ch., but on the floor of the N. chapel lie the life-sized alabaster effigies of a knight in armour (16th cent.) and his wife : supposed to be of the Desborough family. They are in wonderful preservation considering the perils to which they have been exposed. The mont. itself being destroyed, a local magnate thought the two effigies would be more serviceable as ornaments to his house than in the ch. They were taken away, therefore, and for years formed the supporters of the gateway of High House (2 m. nearer Purfleet). Some years ago they were restored to the ch. The brass of Humphrey Heies, 1584, mentioned by Haines as lost, and that of his son Humphrey, 1585, being loose, were removed to the vicarage for safety. That of Heies's daughter, Kath. Redinge, 1591, is lost. By the altar is a stone with the place of a half effigy of a priest, and below it a very elegant cross, but the brasses are gone.

TILBURY, EAST, Essex, on the

l. bank of the Thames, about 3 m. below Tilbury Fort, and 1½ S.E. from the Low Street Stat. (24 m. from London) of the Southend Rly., which is in this par. Pop. 650. Inn, *Ship*.

East Tilbury is curiously out-of-the-way and old-world like. It lies on a projecting point of land which divides the Gravesend and Lower Hope reaches of the Thames, and overlooks the Tilbury Marshes. The ch. stands at the extremity of the street, which leads only to the river wall and fort, lonely and exposed to the keen winds sweeping over these dreary marshes. Of old the town—for so it was styled in the 14th cent.—was exposed to worse foes than the winter's winds. Thus in 1402, Henry IV., "considering the great losses, damages, and destructions which have happened in times past to the same town, by the arrival of French and other enemies there; and dreading that greater may happen in process of time, if no remedy be applied, both there and in the neighbourhood—especially as there is no other landing place on that side for a great space,"—grants to his "beloved lieges, the men of the town of East Tilbury in the county of Essex," permission to "fortify the said town " by means of a sea wall of earth and other works, " that our enemies sailing before the said town, when they shall have knowledge of the said fortification, may henceforth more fear and avoid entering the waters of the Thames in warlike manner." * This is the earliest mention of a fortification at East Tilbury.

---

* Rymer, Fœdera, vol. viii., p. 271 ; Cruden, Hist. of Gravesend, p. 122.

It has never since been without one, but as then as late as the reign of Charles II. the Dutch, the last enemy who sailed up the Thames with warlike intent, battered down the tower of East Tilbury ch., but did little harm to the town or fortress. It was on their second ascent up the Thames, July 1667, that the Dutch destroyed the ch. tower, as on the first they did not reach higher than Shellhaven, 5 m. below East Tilbury. In place of the old block-house a more regular battery was then built, but for many years little attention was given to it. Now, however, a new and much larger fort has been constructed at Coalhouse Point, as part of a comprehensive system of works for the defence of the Thames. The other forts and outworks are at Tilbury Fort and West Tilbury, on this side of the river, and at Hope Point, Cliff Creek, Shorne Mead, and Milton, on the opposite shore. The forts will be of great strength, and provided with guns of immense power, which will have the most approved appliances for working, and act in connection with a carefully arranged scheme of submarine mines, or torpedoes. The works at Coalhouse Point are not completed, but the guns are in position.

It is commonly said that it was at East Tilbury St. Cedd, the apostle of the East Saxons, founded a religious house and built a church, but West Tilbury is the more probable site. (*See* TILBURY, WEST; CHADWELL.) East Tilbury *Church* (St. Margaret) is a rude Dec. building, much patched, and the river-side wall strangely worn by exposure to storms. It comprises nave, north aisle, and chancel, with a makeshift tower, and possesses no feature of interest.

Near East Tilbury are some of the caverns in the chalk, known as Daneholes, of which other and more remarkable examples occur in the neighbouring parishes of Little and West Thurrock and Chadwell, and in the chalk districts on the other side of the Thames, and which are described under CHADWELL. Gervase of Tilbury (temp. Henry II. and John), Marshal of the kingdom of Arles, and author of the 'Otia Imperialia,' written for the amusement of the Emperor Otho, was a native of Tilbury, but whether of East or West Tilbury is not known, but it may well have been the former, as we have seen that East Tilbury was at an early date a town of some consequence.

TILBURY FORT, ESSEX, on the

Thames opposite Gravesend, and in West Tilbury and Chadwell parishes, is the chief of the river forts referred to under TILBURY, EAST. W. of the fort is the Tilbury Stat. of the London and Southend Rly. (22¼ m.), connected with which is a steamboat pier, whence there is a half-hourly steamboat ferry to Gravesend.

The earliest fortification "by the Thames side at Tilburye," was erected by Henry VIII. in 1539, and known as the Hermitage Bulwark ("Thermitage Bullwerk"). It was "furnished with ordenaunce and artillery"—a demi-cannon (30-pounder), "a French cut-nose saker," a falconet of brass, a mortar and other pieces of iron, 16 in all—with iron, lead, and stone shot, "bowes of yough," sheaves of livery arrows, Moorish pikes and black bills, the garrison being a captain, deputy, porter, 2 "souldeors," and 4 gunners. When the Armada threatened invasion, Tilbury Blockhouse was found to be sadly out of order. Under Federico Giambelli, a Mantuan engineer, who had already won fame at the siege of Antwerp, and had been taken into the service of Elizabeth, the works were hastily repaired. As soon as the danger was past, Giambelli was commissioned to rebuild the fort on the most approved principles—his salary being 6s. 8d. a day. The new fort was a pentagonal or star fort, with spreading bastions, rampart, glacis, moat, and counterscarp, in which Henry's fort was enclosed as the citadel.* Giambelli's fort served as the basis for all subsequent works till the recent remodelling.

The most important modification took place after the panic caused by the Dutch sailing up the Thames in 1667. The Dutch Admiral did not reach Tilbury Fort, but he would have met little resistance if he had. From a survey made in 1632, and a memorial of the commander, it appeared that through neglect the fort had fallen into disrepair, the counterscarp had been demolished, and

---

* A copy of the original plan by Giambelli (there called Genibelli) is in the Report on Arrangements for Internal Defence of Great Britain when Spain projected its Invasion, 8vo, 1798.

the moat filled up, and in consequence "the beasts and cattle from the adjoining common do frequently come into the fortifications and do exceedingly annoy the same." The reconstruction of the fort was entrusted to a foreigner, Sir Bernard de Gomme, under Sir Martin Beckman as engineer-in-chief, who submitted as alternative plans a parallelogram and a pentagon, when the latter was adopted, perhaps as requiring less interference with the existing works. The work did not, however, advance very rapidly. Evelyn in 1672 "went over to see the new-begun fort of Tilbury," and he regarded it as "a royal work indeede, and such as will one day bridle a greate Citty to the purpose before they are aware."[*] The date on the well-known gateway by the river is 1682, but the works were not finished in 1687, as we learn from various orders issued by the Master-General of the Ordnance in that year for the facing of ravelins and the completion of the North redout and other works. With subsequent extensions and modifications, these works remained to our own day. One of the most noteworthy of the outer defences, evidently imitated from the procedure of the Dutch engineers, was the formation of a system of sluices, by which the level country around the fort could be laid under water at the will of the commander.

The recent works, which will make this probably the strongest fortress of its class in the country, were taken in hand in 1867, in pursuance of a recommendation of the Fortification Committee, and according to a plan of Col. Jervois, drawn up under the direction of General Sir J. F. Burgoyne. But the rapid progress in the construction of heavy artillery on the one hand, and armour-plated ships on the other, has led to important modifications. As now being carried out, Tilbury Fort will certainly retain its old eminence. And under the new scheme for the Mobilization of the Army (Dec. 1875), it will be not merely as now the head-quarters for the river defences, but the seat of command for the garrison corps for this district—having behind it the magazines of Purfleet and the arsenals of Woolwich, whilst West Tilbury will be the camp of the Metropolitan Volunteers.

* Evelyn, Diary, 21 March, 1672.

The chapel in Tilbury Fort, erected in the reign of Elizabeth, but which for 150 years had been desecrated—its last use being as a reading and billiard room—was restored by the War Office, and re-opened by the Bp. of Rochester in Oct. 1870.

Since the opening of the rly. stat., many houses have been built about it, and a regular half-hour ferry is maintained with Gravesend. It was by Tilbury Fort that the author of 'Robinson Crusoe' established a pantile factory, he himself living in a house by the river. He was unsuccessful, and one of the scurrilous parodies on 'The True Born Englishman' asserts that

" Justices forc'd him to pay his slaves,
　Who, subjects to a worse than Pharaoh's law,
　Made bricks without due food instead of straw."

But De Foe, whilst complaining bitterly of his failure, by which he says he lost £3000, maintains his integrity, and claims credit for introducing into the country a new, and what but for the opposition he met with would have been a most serviceable, manufacture. " Before violence, injury, and barbarous treatment demolished him and his undertaking, he employed," he says, " a hundred poor people in making pantiles—a manufacture before always bought in Holland."[*]

TILBURY, WEST, Essex, 1¾ m.
N. of Tilbury Fort, about 2 m. N.W. of East Tilbury. and ¾ m. W. of the Low Street Stat. of the Southend Rly. Pop. 322. Inn, *King's Head.*

West Tilbury is a quiet, rustic, and not unpicturesque little agricultural village, on the low ridge of chalk hills overlooking Tilbury Marsh. The *Church* (St. James), the only building of consequence, is a small weather-beaten E.E. fabric, consisting of nave and chancel, and low square W. tower and spire, in which is a peal of 5 bells. Laud, when D.D., held the living of West Tilbury.[†]

This no doubt is the " Tilaburg . . . in ripa Tamensis " at which St. Cedd, the apostle of the East Saxons, founded one of his two religious houses, dwelt and

* True Born Huguenot, 1703, p. 14; Defoe's Review, No. 9: quoted in Rambles by Rivers; the Thames, vol. ii., p. 237.
† Hook, Lives of the Abps. of Canterbury, vol. vi., p. 14.

taught, in conjunction with his brother St. Ceadda or Chad.* (*See* CHADWELL ST. MARY.) Before his time, however, there was a Roman settlement here, as various remains of that people have at different times been exhumed, and in carrying the railway across here a cemetery was cut through which was pronounced to be Roman. Near the ch. are traces of a camp, which some consider Roman, though others regard them as vestiges of the camp of Elizabeth.

The troops collected from the eastern counties in anticipation of the arrival of the Armada were certainly encamped on the vantage-ground about the ch., whence they would have a wide outlook seaward, and are so shown on the contemporary chart copied for the Report on the Measures of Defence adopted in 1588, published by the Government in 1798. The camp was formed towards the end of July 1588, under the Earl of Leicester as general-in-chief. On the 8th of August Elizabeth landed, under all military honours, at Tilbury Fort, and was escorted to the camp by 1000 horse and 2000 foot, and a great array of nobles and gentlemen. Next morning, "mounted on a stately steed," truncheon in hand, and attended only by her lieutenant and chamberlain, she reviewed her troops, and addressed them in the spirit-stirring speech with which every reader of English history is familiar. Then, having dined in the camp, she returned to her palace. News having arrived of the final dispersion of the Armada, the camp was broken up on the 17th of August, little more than a week after the Queen's visit. Should another invasion be threatened, this historic ground is the appointed site for the Camp of the Metropolitan Volunteers. (*See* TILBURY FORT.)

TITSEY, SURREY (Dom. *Ticesey*), a secluded agricultural vill. near the eastern extremity of the Surrey Downs, S.W. of Tatsfield, on the road from Croydon to Westerham, from which last town it is about 3 m. N.W. Pop. 225.

Ticheseye, or Titsey, like Tatsfield, was owned by the Uvedales in the 14th century; was alienated to the Greshams, and from them went by marriage to the

Gowers. The present lord of the manor is G. W. G. Leveson Gower, Esq. The old manor-house, as well as the old ch., was taken down, towards the close of the 18th cent., by the last Sir John Gresham, who erected the present house, *Titsey Place* (G. W. Gresham Leveson Gower, Esq.), on the site. It has since been greatly altered and added to, and is now a spacious and stately edifice. In the library is a fine portrait by Sir Anthony More of Sir Thomas Gresham, the founder of the Royal Exchange. There also are some other good pictures, wood carvings from the old house, and various antiquities dug up on the estate.

Nearly opposite Titsey Place is the *Church* (St. James). The old ch. pulled down by Sir John Gresham stood some 200 yards distant, and close to the house. Gresham's ch., a mean brick building, was removed, and the present large and handsome ch. erected by Mr. Gower in 1861, from the designs of Mr. Pearson. The new ch. is of Bath stone; early Dec. in style, and cruciform. The S. transept is carried up as a tower to a height of 75 ft., and crowned with a stone spire of equal height. The N. transept serves as a mortuary chapel, and contain the monuments of the Gresham and Gower families, removed from the earlier churches. The ch. is admirably finished and furnished. From its elevated site and lofty spire, Titsey ch. is a landmark for miles around.

TITTENHANGER, HERTS (*see* LONDON COLNEY).

TONWELL, HERTS (*see* BENGEO).

TOOTING, LOWER TOOTING, or TOOTING GRAVENEY, SURREY, on the Epsom road, between Streatham and Mitcham, 7 m. from Westminster Bridge, and a junction stat. of the Tooting, Merton, and Wimbledon Rly., in connection with the L. and S.-W. Rly., L. B. and S. C. Rly., and L. C. and D. Rly. Pop. 2327.

Early topographers were puzzled by the name (Dom. *Totinges*). It is no doubt due to the settlement here of a branch of the Saxon or Teutonic family of the Totingas.* In legal documents the place

---

* Bede, Hist. Ecc., lib. iii., c. 22.

* Kemble, Cod. Dipl. Ævi Sax., Nos. 363, 785. Comp. Maine, Early Hist. of Institutions, Lect. iii., p. 82; and Freeman, Comp. Politics.

is designated Tooting Graveney (properly Gravenell), the addition being derived from a family of that name who held the manor, with other property, under the Abbot of Chertsey, in the 12th and 13th cents. The manor was afterwards held by the Castellos, Ladelowes, and Dymocks. In 1593 it was alienated to James Harrington, and by him transferred to Sir Henry Maynard, secretary to Lord Burleigh. William, the eldest son, was advanced to the peerage, but did not inherit Tooting, which was conveyed to the second son, Sir John Maynard (*not*, as sometimes stated, the famous lawyer and member of the Long Parliament, who lived to serve in the Convention 1689, whereas this Sir John Maynard died 40 years before). From the Maynards the manor passed by marriage to Sir Edward Honeywood; afterwards to Whichcote, Bateman, Lewis, Rice, Platt, Pole, Baring, Thomas, and is now held by W. J. Thompson, Esq.

Tooting is a region of villas and nursery gardens, very pleasant, and, except the Common, very commonplace. *Tooting Graveney Common*, of 63 acres, runs into *Tooting-Bec Common* of 155 acres, and that adjoins Streatham Common of 66 acres, making together a broad open space that is a great delight to London holiday-makers, as well as to the inhabitants of Tooting and Streatham. The Lower Common is overgrown with gorse, and in parts somewhat moist. The Upper Common affords fine views. The whole was in 1875 dedicated to public use, and placed under the control of the Metropolitan Board of Works.

Around the Common are several good old mansions with noble trees in the grounds; but the greater part of the houses are modern. Here for a time Sir Richard Blackmore, the City physician and bard, had his country house:

" Blackmore himself, for any grand effort
Would drink and doze at Tooting or Earl's
Court."*

Tooting *Church* (St. Nicholas) was erected in 1822, from the designs of Mr. Atkinson, and altered and re-consecrated in 1833. The ch. which it displaced was a small building with a low circular tower. The present building is of white brick, Perp. of a poor type, and has a W.

* Pope ; and see Hughes's Letters, vol. i., p. 224.

tower of 3 stages with buttresses and pinnacles. It was enlarged in 1873 by the addition of a transept and larger chancel. In it are some monts. removed from the old ch. The most noteworthy is of Sir John Hepdon, d. 1670, twice envoy to the Emperor of Russia, and frequently employed in negotiations for Charles I. and Charles II., " for whose interest he spared neither purse nor person, though to the prejudice of his own." In the ch.-yard are the tombs of Sir John Maynard, K.B., d. 1658, and of his only son, Sir John Maynard, Knt., d. 1664. The Independent Meeting is said to have been founded by Daniel Defoe, who, early in the reign of William III., formed the first body of members into a church. Dr. Oldfield was the first minister. Dr. Henry Miles, F.R.S., distinguished in his day by his attainments in natural philosophy, was pastor from 1726 till his death in 1763.

UPPER TOOTING, N.W. of Lower Tooting, on the W. of Tooting-Bec Common, belongs to Streatham par. (See notice of Tooting-Bec manor under STREATHAM.) It was formed into an eccl. dist. in 1855. The *Church*, of the Holy Trinity, is a neat Gothic building erected in 1854. Here was an alien priory, or cell. Upper Tooting contains several mansions and numerous villas. The large red brick Elizabethan structure in Burntwood Lane, on the edge of Wandsworth Common, is the *Surrey County Lunatic Asylum*, erected in 1840 from the designs of Mr. W. Moseley. It has accommodation for nearly 1000 inmates.

TOTTENHAM, or TOTTENHAM

HIGH CROSS, MIDDX. (Dom. *Toteham*), lies between Stamford Hill and Edmonton, on the Ware and Hertford road, 4½ m. from Shoreditch ch. Rly. Stats., Grt. E. Rly., *Tottenham*, High Cross Lane, and *Park Lane*, on the Cambridge line; *Seven Sisters*, *Bruce Grove*, and *White Hart Lane*, on the Enfield branch : Grt. N. Rly., *Wood Green;* Midland (South Tottenham and Hampstead br.), *South Tottenham*. Pop. of par. 22,809 (since greatly increased), but this includes the eccl. districts of Holy Trinity, Tottenham Green (and within the town), 7356 ; St. Paul's, Park Lane (at the N. end of the town), 3487 ; St. Ann's, Hanger Lane (now St.

Ann's Road), 4724, and St. Michael's, Wood Green, 5011.

The parish is of great size, extending for 2½ m. along the highroad, and being nearly 16 m. in circuit. The river Lea forms its eastern boundary, and divides it from Essex. The New River winds along its western side, and the little Muswell brook—the Mouse, Mose, or, as it is now called, the Moselle river—crosses the par. from W. to E., dividing it into two unequal portions. The legal division of the par. is into 4 *wards*—the Lower Ward, the Middle Ward, High Cross Ward, and Wood Green Ward.

The etymology of Tottenham has been much discussed. It is probably a patronymic, *Toting*, or *Toding*, with the suffix *ham*, home; but it may be from *tot*, an elevation, the site being a ridge of high ground overlooking the marshes which border the Lea.

The adjunct *High Cross*, of old more commonly used than now, was given from the Cross which, from an unknown antiquity, has stood on the E. of the road near the centre of the town. It has been commonly assumed that it was an Eleanor cross (*see* WALTHAM CROSS), but Tottenham was not one of the places where the corpse of Queen Eleanor rested, and the cross was probably merely one of the wayside crosses once common in the towns and villages of England: there is no mention of a market at Tottenham, and it was not therefore a market-cross. About 1580 it was merely a column of wood capped with a square sheet of lead to shoot the water off every way. Norden, ten years later, terms it a wooden cross lately raised on a little mound of earth. But both cross and name were of much more remote date. About 1600, the cross being decayed, Dean Wood, who lived in a house on the E. of it, had it taken down, and erected in its place one of brick, octagonal at the base, square above, with a sundial on one of the faces, and crowned with a crocketed terminal and weathercock. This was the *Tottenham High Cross* to which the Piscator of Izaak Walton's 'Complete Angler' bids his honest scholar Venator "Welcome." Over against it then stood the "sweet shady arbour, which nature herself has woven with her own fine fingers,—a contexture of woodbines, sweetbrier, jessamine, and myrtle, and so interwoven as will secure us both from the sun's violent heat and from the approaching shower." Tradition is constant that the arbour was in the garden of the Swan Inn, and that the Swan was Walton's usual resting-place when he came hither to fish. The Swan remains, but there is no such arbour there now, and none of that "drink like nectar" of which master and scholar partook, and pronounced "too good indeed for anybody but us anglers." *

Dean Wood's cross lasted for over two centuries, when, getting much out of order, the inhabitants had it repaired, covered with stucco, and "decorated with Gothic ornaments," as it now appears.

"Several alterations have taken place in this part of the country since you left it. . . . . *Tottenham Cross* has been cased with a composition resembling stone, and surrounded with an iron railing; it makes a very handsome appearance."†

Bedwell, the learned vicar of Tottenham, and one of the translators of the Bible, in his curious 'Briefe Description of the Towne of Tottenham High Crosse,' 1631,—one of the earliest topographies published, — arranging the "memorable things" in ternaries, says the "second ternary for antiquity are the Crosse, the Hermitage, and the Altar of Saint Loy. These are all in the great rode, all within lesse than half a mile. . . . The Crosse standeth as it were in the middest between the forementioned cell and the hermitage."‡ When he wrote, "the Offertory of St. Loy" was "a poor house situate on the W. side of the (high) rode, a little off from the bridge." The well was a deep pit near the highway, always full of excellent water. The Hermitage and Chapel of St. Anne was a small square building, with a little slip of ground attached to it, running along the highroad, a little N. of the Seven Sisters—where now stands the *Bull* inn. The building was standing within the memory of persons living at Tottenham when Bedwell was made vicar, 1607.

Tottenham has few historical associa-

* Complete Angler, b. i., chap. 21.
† Memoir of the Early Life of Rt. Hon. Sir W. H. Maule, by his Niece, Emma Leathley: Letter to Maule from his brother, dated Edmonton, July 26, 1809. Maule was a native of Edmonton.
‡ Bedwell, Briefe Desc. of Tottenham High-Crosse, 1631, b. ii., chap. 2.

tions, but the story of the manor is interesting on account of its owners. In the reign of the Confessor it belonged to Earl Waltheof, son of Siward, Earl of Northumberland, who defeated Macbeth of Scotland. Waltheof married, 1069, Judith, niece of the Conqueror, and was created, 1072, Earl of Northumberland, Huntingdon, and Northampton; but some years after, being charged with treasonable designs, was beheaded at Winchester. After the death of Waltheof's widow, the manor passed to their eldest daughter, Maud, who married, 1st, Simon de St. Liz, a Norman baron, and 2ndly, David, son of Malcolm III., King of Scotland. Henry I. granted to David the earldom of Huntingdon, with possession of all the lands held by Earl Waltheof; and the lands and title continued in his descendants for several generations, being held, among others, by Malcolm IV., King of Scotland, and William the Lion. In 1184, William, King of Scotland, gave the manor to his brother David, Earl of Angus and Galloway, to whom it was confirmed, with the earldom of Huntingdon, by King John, in 1199. The Earl of Angus married Maud, daughter and heiress of Hugh Earl of Chester, and their only son John became Earl of Chester and Huntingdon, and married Helen, daughter of Llewellin, Prince of Wales, by whom he is said to have been poisoned in 1237. Shortly after his death his widow married Robert de Quincy, a younger brother of Roger, the last Earl of Winchelsea of that family. She retained possession of the manor till 1254, when extent was taken of the lands of "Helen, formerly the wife of John Earl of Chester, to the intent that they might be divided between Robert de Brus, John de Baliol, and Henry de Hastings, as co-heirs of the said Earl"—Brus having married the Earl's sister Isabel, Baliol the daughter of his sister Margaret, and Hastings his sister Ada.

The manor of Tottenham was now divided into three distinct manors, each bearing the name of its owner. Sub-manors were subsequently formed from them, but with these we have no immediate concern.

The portion assigned to Robert de Brus has ever since been designated *Brus* or *Bruce Manor*. Robert de Brus is the Robert Bruce who was competitor with John Baliol for the throne of Scotland, when Edward I. as arbitrator, decided, 1292, in favour of Baliol. Brus gave the manor for life to his younger son Richard, who died 1287, before his father. Robert Earl of Annandale, and Carrick, the elder son, had accompanied Edward I. to the Holy Land in 1269, and settled in England on his return. To him the manor passed on the death of his brother, and he is believed to have made the manor-house, thence called Brus or Bruce Castle, his residence. On his death in 1303, his son Robert—*the* Bruce of Scottish history —succeeded as his heir. Three years later Bruce was crowned King of Scotland. Edward I. at once seized his English estates, and the connection of Tottenham with the Bruses terminated.

The manor of Bruses remained in the Crown, leases for life of parts, or of the whole, being granted to various persons, till 1376, when it was granted in fee to Edmund de Cheshunte, one of the King's falconers, he having already (1374) received a lease of it for life. It was sold in 1400, by his son, Robert de Cheshunte, alias Fauconer, to John Walden, on the death of whose widow, Idonea, in 1429, it passed to John Gedeney, alderman of London, by whom all the manors were reunited.

The manor of *Baliol* was seized by Edward I. on the renunciation of feudal homage by John Baliol, King of Scotland, 1295, and granted to John Duke of Brittany and Earl of Cornwall. Reverting to the Crown on his death, or shortly after, it was given, in 1337, by Edward III. to William Dawbeney, and came to be known as *Dawbeney's Manor*. In 1377 it was held by John Cavendish; in 1391 by John Northampton; in 1409 it passed to William Cumberton; and in 1449 Ald. Gedeney died seised of this with the other Tottenham manors.

Hastings Manor, the third portion of the original manor of Tottenham, descended to Lawrence de Hastings, who in 1339 was declared heir to the earldom of Pembroke, and the manor received from him the name of *Pembrokes*. On the death of Joanna, widow of his grandson, in 1401, the manor passed to Roger Walden, Bp. of London and Lord Treasurer; and from him to Ald. Gedeney.

The manors thus reunited have since remained in the same hands, but the ownership has been many times transferred. On the death of Ald. Gedeney's widow in 1462, they passed to her son, by a former husband, John Turnant, whose daughter, Thomasina, carried them by marriage to Sir John Risley, on whose death without heirs they escheated to the Crown. Henry VIII., in 1514, granted them to Sir Wm. Compton, whose heir, Lord Compton, mortgaged them in 1600; and in 1605 they were purchased of the mortgagee by Thomas Earl of Dorset. They were transferred in 1625 by Edward Earl of Dorset to Hugh and Thomas Audley, who the next year sold them to Hugh Lord Colerane. They remained in the Colerane family till the death of Henry Lord Colerane, the antiquary and collector, in 1749.[*] Having no issue male, Lord Colerane bequeathed the manors to his daughter Henrietta, born in Italy in 1745 of Mrs. Duplessis, on her reaching the age of 21. She being an alien, the manors escheated to the Crown, but they were restored to her on her marriage with James Townsend, alderman of London. Their son, Henry Hare Townsend, sold them in 1792 to Thomas Smith of Gray's Inn, and he in 1805 to Sir Wm. Curtis, Bart. The present lord is Wm. Curtis, Esq.[†]

Lands in these manors descend to the youngest son. In default of male issue the daughters are coheirs.

Mockings was a sub-manor formed out of Bruses, lying N. of the highroad, and S. of Marsh Lane. Granted to Richard Spigurnell, it was sold by him to John Mocking, who died seised of it in 1347; as did John Mocking the younger in 1360. It afterwards passed to the Legets, and was reunited to the other manors by Ald. Gedeney. The moated manor-house stood on the S. side of Marsh Lane, about ¼ m. from the highroad. Norden describes it as "an auncient house of the Lord

Compton's," but it was not here, as is sometimes said, but at Bruce Castle, that Lord Compton entertained Q. Elizabeth. With the principal manor, Mockings was bought in 1792 by Mr. T. Smith, who sold it in 1803 to Mr. Cooper, by whom the house was pulled down.

Ducketts, or Dovecot's, manor, in what was a green lane, on the rt. of the road to Southgate, belonged rather to Hornsey than Tottenham, though usually placed under the latter par. The old moated manor-house was long a farm-house. In the reign of Elizabeth it was held by Cecil. The estate is now divided.

Willoughby's, another moated manorhouse, was partly in Edmonton. The house has long been pulled down, and its site is uncertain. The present *Willoughby House* (W. Conolly, Esq.), a very commonplace modern building, stands S. of the old manor-house, in Tottenham parish.

Twyford Manor was so called of John Twyford, who held it in the reign of Henry V. It has long merged in the chief manor. The name of *Stoneleys* is retained, though no longer as a manor, and the estate is charged with an annuity to the occupants of Sanchez' almshouses.

Bruce Castle occupies the site of the ancient manor-house of Bruses, the probable residence of the father of Robert Bruce. Sir William Compton, on acquiring the manor, built himself a sufficient mansion, in which he received Henry VIII. and his sister Margaret Queen of Scots, on the Saturday after Ascension Day, 1516. Sixty years later (May 1578), his grandson, Henry Lord Compton, entertained Queen Elizabeth here. The house appears to have been new fronted whilst held by the Hare family. In the 17th century it became the residence of the Lord Coleranes, and towards the end of the century Henry Lord Colerane repaired and greatly altered it. A new E. wing was added to it by Alderman Townsend. Alderman Townsend figured somewhat prominently in the political circles of his day. He was a friend of Lord Shelburne, who writes to Lord Chatham from Bruce Castle, Feb. 25, 1771, while on a visit to Ald. Townsend, and Chatham in his reply speaks of "our worthy warm friend your landlord." Shortly after Mr. Smith purchased the manor, he sold

* A good half-length portrait of Henry Lord Colerane is in the collection of the Society of Antiquaries at Burlington House.

† The above sketch is little more than an abridgment of Lysons' full account of the descent of the manors, Environs, vol. ii., p. 746, etc. Robinson, Hist. and Antiq. of Tottenham, vol. i., p. 161, etc., repeats Lysons verbally, but adds some extracts respecting the liberties and customs of the manors from documents supplied him by Sir Wm. Curtis.

the house to Mr. Ayrton Lee. It was afterwards the property and residence of John Eardley Wilmot, Esq., Master in Chancery ; then of Mr. John Ede, who pulled down the W. wing. In 1827, the house, with 15 acres of grounds, was bought by Messrs. Rowland, Edwin, and Frederick Hill, who converted the house into a school as a " branch establishment of Hazelwood School, Birmingham," conducted by Thomas Wright Hill, and then in great repute as a middle-class boarding-school. Bruce Castle School soon acquired equal celebrity. Mr. Rowland Hill withdrew from the school in 1833, engaged in public life, and attained popularity and distinction as the inventor of the Penny Postage, and Secretary to the Post Office. Messrs. Edwin and Frederick Hill likewise left the school for the public service, in which they rose to high posts. Bruce Castle School was continued with great success by Mr. Arthur Hill, and is now conducted by Mr. Birckbeck Hill. The house has been so often and so much altered for school purposes, as to retain little of its ancient character or appearance. The detached tower by the W. wing, a fragment of the older house, is still standing, but completely covered with ivy.

It was of old the custom, when a member of the family died at Bruce Castle, not to convey the corpse through the gate, but to break an opening in the outer wall nearest the ch. The last breach in the wall was made in 1789, for the passage of the corpse of Alderman James Townsend.* *Bruce Grove* marks the site of an avenue of grand old elms, which led from the highroad to the house.

Nearly all the other old mansions have been removed. On the E. of the highroad, opposite White Hart Lane, was *The Black House*, once of great note. It was a large red brick and stone Tudor mansion which local tradition assigned to Henry VIII., but which is more reasonably supposed to have been the residence of that king's favourite servant, George Hynningham, who founded an almshouse here and was buried in the ch., where his portraiture was preserved on a brass till stolen a few years back. Henry is said to have often visited and slept at his servant's, as an

inscription in the royal chamber testified when Bedwell wrote (1631). The king's horses and men found lodging at an inn called The Horns, a short distance beyond. The Black House was afterwards for some time the seat of Sir Hugh Smithson,—a great benefactor of the poor of Tottenham, and ancestor of the Dukes of Northumberland. The house was pulled down in 1740.

Reynardson's, on the N. side of Tottenham Green, was a many-gabled red brick mansion, built in 1590, and was in the middle of the 17th century the seat of Alderman Sir Abraham Reynardson, Lord Mayor of London 1649, who for refusing to proclaim the Act abolishing the kingly power, was dismissed from his mayoralty by the Parliament, fined £2000, committed prisoner to the Tower for two months, and declared incapable of holding the office of alderman or mayor in future. He died at his house at Tottenham Oct. 4, 1661, and after lying in state at Merchant Taylors' Hall, was buried with great pomp in the ch. of St. Martin Outwich. After serving for many years as a boarding-school " for sons of Friends " (Quakers), the house was taken down in 1810.

Grove House, a plain quadrangular structure, with a semicircular bay at one angle, was for several years the residence of Sir Michael Foster, Justice of the King's Bench, 1745-63, an eminent lawyer and the " Old Foster just " of Churchill. He was a native of Tottenham, where his family had long been settled as solicitors. Grove House was afterwards the residence of Mr. Ardesoif, noted for his wealth and extravagance. Passionately addicted to cock-fighting, he backed his favourite bird, which had hitherto won every match, for a heavy sum. The bird was beaten, when Ardesoif, half-drunk, and furious at his loss, thrust the bird into the fire. His excitement continued, and three days later he died at Grove House in the furor of delirium tremens (1798).

White Hall, on the S. side of White Hart Lane, the seat of the Barkhams, Beauchamps, and Proctors, the site now marked by Whitehall Terrace ; *Page Green*, built by Repton ; *De la Haze's*, and other goodly mansions, were the abodes of citizens of credit and renown in their day, but now forgotten ; and the

* Robinson, Hist. of Tottennam, vol. ., p. 218.

houses, like their occupants, have for the most part ceased to exist, or passed into obscurity. Sir Julius Cæsar, the eminent civilian and Master of the Rolls, was a native of Tottenham, and resided there in 1593. His son, Sir Charles Cæsar, also Master of the Rolls, was resident at Tottenham in 1634-39, in which years the baptism of his three sons is registered. Nothing is known of their seat.

Bedwell printed "a ternary of proverbs" relating to Tottenham, which from the references made to them by other writers must have had a wide popularity.

"Tottenham is turned French" occurs also in Heywood, where referring to disappointed expectations he says,—

" A man might espye the change in his cheekes,
　Both of this poor wretch, and his wife, poore
　　wench,
　Their faces told toyes, that Tottenham was
　　turn'd French."

Fuller's explanation is, that "about the beginning of the reign of King Henry VIII., French mechanics swarmed in England, to the great prejudice of English artizans, which caused the insurrection in London, on ill May-day, A.D. 1517." The infection spread to "country villages for four miles about," and Tottenham took it. The application of the proverb is palpable.

Both the others referred to Tottenham Wood—a then existent fragment (314 acres) of the old Forest of Middlesex, lying about 2 m. W. of the town. One referring to things not likely to be accomplished, ran—" You shall as easily remove Tottenham Wood." The other was

" When Tottenham Wood is all on fire
　Then Tottenham Steet is nought but mire."

Which the worthy Vicar of Tottenham thus expoundeth — "When Tottenham Wood. . . . on the top of a high hill in the W. end of the parish, hath a foggy mist hanging and hovering over it, in manner of a smoke, then generally foul weather followeth; so that it serveth the inhabitants instead of a prognostication." Whereon old Fuller comments, "I am confident there is as much mire now as formerly in Tottenham street, but question whether so much wood now as anciently on Tottenham Hill." The wood has long been removed, and the land brought under the plough or built over,

and certainly the street has lost much of its mire.

With the ternary of Tottenham proverbs may be placed the curious alliterative poem of the 'Tournament of Tottenham,' first printed by Bedwell in his description of the town, from a MS. the use of which he obtained "by the means of the worthy and my much honoured good friend M. George Wither," the poet, who "much commended" the versification. Bedwell was inclined to carry back its origin to the early part of the 14th cent. ; while Warton assigns it to "some part of the reign of Henry VIII."* An entry in the MS.,† however, bears the date 34 Henry VI., and with that the phraseology and versification agree.

The 'Tournament of Tottenham' is a clever burlesque of the more serious tournaments still in vogue, though somewhat declining in popular favour. Bedwell supposes it to be the narrative of an actual occurrence ; and Warton allows that "it might originate in a real event," whilst Robinson states that "Randall the reve lived in the reign of Edward II ; " but it is more probable that it is altogether the invention of the poet. Be that as it may, it relates the pretended occurrence in a very circumstantial manner. The tournay was proclaimed by "Rondell the refe," who fixed the day on which it was to be held "at Totenham. . . . be the hyeway." The prize he offered was Tybbe his daughter, the weapon a flail :

" He that berys him best in the Turnament,
　He shall be granted the gre by the comyn
　　assent,
　For to wynne my doghter with dughtynesse
　　of dent ;
　And Coppul my brode hen that was broght
　　out of Kent,
　And my donned cow :
　For no spence will I spare
　For no catel will I care :
　　He shall haue my gray mare
　And my spotted sowe."

To the Tourney came

　　" alle the men of that contray
　Of Hisselton, of Hy-gate, and of Hakenay,"

while "all the wyues of Totenham came to see the sight." The bachelors came in

---

* Hist. of English Poetry, vol. iii., p. 98. Versions of the poem varying somewhat from Bedwell's have been printed by Percy, Ritson, Wright, and Robinson : our quotations are from the last."
† Harl. MSS., 5396.

full array, "with flayles and harnys, and trumpis mayde of tre." "Theire baner was ful bright," the "chefe was a ploo-mell," or plough-hammer. Their surcoat was of sheep-skin, and for armour "a baskett or a panyer before on thaire brest," and each had "a blac hatte in stidde of a crest." Tybbe herself was there, seated aloft on the gray mare, wearing a "gay girdle borrowed for the nones," with "a garland on head full of ruell bones," and carrying the brood hen in her lap. All the preliminaries were gone through in due form, and the several knights were paraded and made their vows. Then the fighting commenced, and

> " I vow it was no childer gamme, when thei
>   togeder mett."

The result of the fray, which lasted till evening, was that Perkyn the Potter was the victor, and carried off to church "that dere Tybbe that he shall wedde," all the vanquished who were able joining in the procession. On the morrow was the wedding feast, which

> " served was in rich array . . . .
> And so they sate in iolite [jollity], al the long day."

A supplementary poem gives further particulars of the feast, but it is apparently of later date and by an inferior hand.

The town stretches as an irregular line of houses, with scarcely a breach of continuity, for nearly 2 m. along the highroad, from the N. side of Stamford Hill till it loses itself in Upper Edmonton. Here and there blank walls with overhanging trees mark a house that is, or has been, a place of consequence; but generally the houses are of moderate size, while many are small and some very wretched. Some old houses remain with good wrought-iron gateways in front, relics of better days; but the most part are commonplace. The bye-streets and lower parts too often look damp and depressing. A noteworthy feature is the number of almshouses and benevolent institutions; some, like the Drapers', of exceptional size, schools, reading-rooms, temperance halls, and the like.

Tottenham is situated on the London clay, a stiff heavy soil; and of old the occupations were chiefly agricultural. There are still many outlying farms, and much of the land is under the plough. The broad marshes afford good grazing,

and heavy grass-crops. Of late years the growth of flowers, for sale in roots, but much more largely cut, for the London market, has become an important branch of industry.

Once Tottenham was noted for its greens. Several are greens no longer; but two will be observed in passing through the main street, Page Green on the rt., at its commencement, where stood the Seven Sisters, and Tottenham Green on the l., near the centre, a well-kept green, with the new ch. at its farther end, bordered by trees and good houses, one of which, at the S.W. corner of High-Cross Lane, when the residence of the late Mr. Benj. Godfrey Windus, was famous as containing one of the finest collections of water-colour drawings in England—Turner's drawings alone numbering over 200, Wilkie's sketches 600. From the highroad, streets and lanes run off on the one side to fields and uplands, on the other to the Lea and the marshes along it, lined mostly with scattered houses, but opening at others, as at Northumberland Park, into what are almost villages of modern villas and genteel cottages. The old roadside inns, once so numerous, have nearly all disappeared or been modernized. Izaak Walton's inn, the Swan, has been already mentioned. The next most noted inn was the *George and Vulture.* The large rambling old house had the arms of Q. Elizabeth over the entrance, and dated from the reign of the Virgin Queen. According to tradition it was originally the mansion of Balthasar Sanchez—to be spoken of presently. In the 17th and 18th cents. it was a favourite summer resort of the citizens, and belonged to the class of tea-gardens noticed under Hampstead, Isleworth, etc. It had spacious grounds in which were covered walks and arbours, a canal well stocked with fish, and a large banqueting hall and music-room. The George and Vulture is referred to in the ' Search after Claret,' 1691, and often advertised in the newspapers of a somewhat later date. One rhyming advertisement notifies that

> " The kind landlord glad attends
>   To welcome all his City friends ; "

has "a larder stored for every taste," the best of wines, and honest punch; and has so provided that

"The cautious Fair may sip with glee
　The freshest Coffee, finest Tea,"

whilst

"The spacious Garden, verdant Field
　Pleasures beyond expression yield,
　The Angler here to sport inclined
　In his canal may pastime find."

Early in the 19th cent. the inn was closed. In 1807 it was occupied as a boarding-school, and continued to be so occupied for some 20 years. It was pulled down in 1829, and several small houses built on the site. During its demolition many silver coins of Elizabeth, James, and the Charleses were found. The present George and Vulture is but a degenerate descendant of the old tavern.

The *Seven Sisters* mentioned above, one of the memorabilia of Tottenham, were 7 elm-trees growing in a circle by the roadside at Page Green. According to an obscure tradition they were planted by seven sisters when about to separate. In their midst grew of old a walnut-tree, which Bedwell includes in his "ternary of wonders" of the parish. This tree, he says, had stood there for many years, and regularly bore leaves, and yet it was observed that it grew neither greater nor higher. It was affirmed by old people that one was burned there for professing the Gospel, but his name the vicar could not learn. When Robinson wrote (1840) the elms were "considered to be upwards of 500 years old." They were then "fast going to decay." Thirty years later their lifeless trunks were standing; now all traces of them are gone. We knew them both green and leafless, and feel sure they could not have numbered more than half the years Robinson assigned them. Their memory is preserved by 7 young trees planted on the green a little E. of the old seven. The road opposite them bears their name. The Seven Sisters Road was constructed in 1831-33, and joins the Camden Road at Holloway, thus opening a direct communication with the Regent's Park and the West-end of London, the only road to which was till then through Islington.

Tottenham *Church* (All Hallows) stands about ¼ m. W. of the highroad, in the rear of Bruce Castle. The ch. was given by David King of Scotland, about 1125, to the canons of the ch. of the Holy Trinity in London, a religious house founded by his sister, Queen Matilda. It was held by them till the Dissolution, when the living was granted first to the Lord Howard of Effingham, and on his attainder to the Dean and Chapter of St. Paul's. The existing ch. is of much later date than King David, to whom some have ascribed its erection. It is a much-patched and altered fabric, of many dates and various materials. The older part, including the nave and S. aisle, is of flint and stone, and of the Perp. period. The N. aisle, which is of brick, was built in 1816. The tower, of flint and stone, thickly covered with ivy, appears to be older than the rest of the ch., but the W. window, doorway, and battlements are of the year 1846. The large brick porch, on the S.W., with a room over it, is of the beginning of the 16th cent.* A curious semicircular structure at the E. end of the N. aisle (removed in the summer of 1875) was built and endowed by Lord Colerane in 1697, as a vestry and entrance to the family crypt beneath. Lastly, completing the incongruity, a chancel, vestry, and organ chamber, of bright red brick and stone, Dec. in style, designed by Mr. Butterfield in the latest phase of ecclesiastical fashion, was carried out from the old ch. in the autumn of 1875, and completed in 1876. The interior has participated in most of these alterations, and has also undergone many churchwarden's additions and beautifications of its own, and is in process of undergoing more. The nave, of 4 bays, and the aisles are of equal width; the roof of plain timber and ceiled. At the E. end is some good 14th cent. painted glass, at the W. a representation of Christ blessing little children, modern and poor. *Monts.*—On rt. of old chancel was an elaborate memorial of Maria Wilcocks, d. 1644, wife of Sir Robert Barkham, with their half-length effigies in marble, the knight in armour, the lady in lace stomacher and veil, her hand resting on a skull : beneath 3 sons and 7 daughters ; above arms, etc. The sculptor, Edward Marshal, has engraved his name over the busts. On l. Richard Candeler, d. 1602 ; his wife, Eliza,

---

* The room over the porch was long appropriated as the residence of some poor pensioner. The last occupant was Elizabeth Fleming, who lived in this room 40 years, and died in it, about 1790, in her 100th year (Lysons ; Robinson).

d. 1622; their son-in-law, Sir Ferdinando Heyborne, gentlemen of the privy chamber to Queen Elizabeth and James I., d. 1618, and his wife Anne, d. 1615: of veined marble, with kneeling effigies of the deceased, fully coloured, under arches, with obelisks, shields of arms, and long laudatory inscriptions. S. aisle, mural, of coloured marbles, of Sir John Melton, d. 1640, keeper of the great seal for the north of England, with effigies, coloured, of the knight in armour and a lady kneeling, before faldstools: Sir John was thrice married, his first wife being Elizabeth, widow of Sir Ferdinando Heyborne, but which wife is represented on the mont. is not told,—probably the third, Margaret, relict of Samuel Alderley, who survived him. Hugh Hare, Lord Colerane, d. 1685, and Lucy, daughter of Henry Earl of Manchester, and wife of Hugh Lord Colerane, d. 1681. On the floor a black marble slab to James Paget, Baron of the Exchequer, d. 1638. There are also numerous memorials of wealthy residents, and one to "Mr. Wm. Bedwell, sometime vicar of this church, and one of King James' translators of the Bible, and for the Easterne tongues as learned a man, as most lived in these moderne times," d. 1632, the author of the ' Briefe Description of the Towne of Tottenham,' several times cited. Formerly there were numerous brasses in the ch., among others, to George Hynningham, "sometime servant and greatly favoured of King Henry VIII., who founded here an hospetal or almeshouse for 3 poore widdowes," d. 1536; Thomas Hynningham, d. 1499; William Hynningham, d. 1603, and other members of the family; Umfray Povy, d. 1510; and an interesting small brass, often engraved, of a priest, Walter Hunt (1419), holding a book and chalice;—but all have been stolen, some since 1840, when the 2nd ed. of ' Robinson's History of Tottenham,' in which several of them are engraved, was published.

The churchyard contains numerous tombs mostly of local magnates. On the N. side of the ch., close under the W. end of the N. aisle, is a mont., within railings, to "Margaret Lydia, wife of James Samuel, C.E., and daughter of the Ettrick Shepherd, who died 28 Feb., 1847, aged 22 years." Opposite the porch is a moderate-sized yew-tree and E. of it another.

Holy Trinity Church, on the N. side of Tottenham Green, was erected 1828-30, from the designs of Mr. J. Savage, as a chapel-of-ease, but was made an eccl. dist. ch. in 1844. It is a chapel-like brick building with buttresses and pinnacles, in style E.E. of impure character. Nor is the eccl. dist. ch. of St. Paul, Park Lane, 1859, a much better example of modern architecture. Far superior is St. Ann's ch., Hanger Lane (or, as it is now called, St. Ann's Road—a change that destroys the local signification, hanger = a meadow or enclosure by a wood). St. Ann's ch., with the adjacent parsonage, was built in 1861 at the cost of F. Newsam, Esq., from the designs of Mr. Talbot Bury. It is of Kentish rag and Bath stone; cruciform, with an octagonal apse, and a tower and spire, 127 ft. high, on the S.W.; is Dec. in style; very picturesque externally, and finished with unusual care and elegance inside. St. Michael's, Wood Green, is another dist. ch., erected in 1865, from the designs of Mr. H. Curzon, on the site of an old chapel. The chancel, tower, and spire were added in 1874.

Dissenters' places of worship are numerous, though few are of architectural value. The Roman Catholics have a chapel, the Congregationalists 2, Baptists 3, Presbyterians 2, Wesleyans 2, other Methodists 4 or 5, and there are several ' Mission halls,' and ' Gospel rooms.' Friends as well as Nonconformists have long flourished in Tottenham. The Friends' Meeting-house was built in 1714, and has been more than once enlarged.

When Dr. Robinson wrote, there were about 60 families of Friends in Tottenham, and here have been several of their chief boarding-schools. Bernard Barton, the Quaker poet, who was of a Tottenham family, and spent his childhood in Tottenham, gives a characteristic sketch of one of these solid old Quaker mansions, with its sedate, but not ungenial master—house and master now alike things of the past:

" My most delightful recollections of boyhood are connected with the fine old country house in a green lane diverging from the highroad which runs through Tottenham. . . . . It was a large house, with an iron palisade and a pair of iron gates in front, and a huge stone eagle on each pier. Leading up to the steps by which you went up to the hall door was a wide gravel walk, bordered in summer time by huge tubs, in which were orange and lemon trees, and in the centre of the grass-plot stood a tub yet huger, holding an enormous aloe. The hall itself, to my fancy then, lofty and wide as a cathedral would seem now, was a famous place for battledore and shuttlecock, and behind was a garden equal to that of old Alcinous himself. My favourite walk was one of turf by a long straight pond, bordered with lime trees. But the whole demesne was the fairy ground of my childhood, and its presiding genius was grandpapa. He must have been a handsome man in his youth, for I remember him at nearly eighty, a very fine-looking one. . . . In the morning a velvet cap ; by dinner a flaxen wig ; and features always expressive of benignity and placid cheerfulness. When he walked out into the garden, his cocked hat and amber-headed cane completed the costume." *

Thomas Shillitoe, one of the sect who in our day most resembled in fiery zeal the original Quakers, whilst in unceasing advocacy of every benevolent object he rivalled the meekest of their successors, lived for nearly 60 years at Tottenham, 1778—1836.†

To Tottenham Nonconformists belongs one of the greatest of Protestant missionaries, John Williams, the apostle and martyr of Polynesia, and author of ‘A Narrative of Missionary Enterprises,’ who was born at Tottenham 1796, and killed at Erromanga 1839.

In the Highroad, not far from the Cross, is the *Free Grammar School*, founded in 1686 by Sarah, Duchess Dowager of Somerset, and wife of Henry Lord Colerane. a foundation which is set forth as the first of her claims to remembrance on her mont. in Westminster Abbey. The school has never acquired celebrity, and it boasts of no distinguished scholars. The most eminent of the masters was William Baxter, nephew of Richard Baxter, the famous Puritan divine, editor of Horace and Anacreon, and author of a Dictionary of British Antiquities (‘Glossarium Antiquitatum veteris Britanniæ,’etc.,8vo,1719,) on which he spent 20 years. He quitted Tottenham. about 1700, for the mastership of the Mercers’ School, London, which he retained till shortly before his death in 1723. The school-house is now in a very dilapidated condition, one wing being closed and propped up with wooden struts.

The parochial almshouses have some interest from their founders. The oldest,

probably was that known as *Pound's*, in the Highroad, near the Manor Pound. the foundation of which is usually ascribed to Jasper Phesaunt, but which was in all probability the almshouse for 3 poor men and 3 poor women referred to in the insc. on the brass of George Hynningham (1536) cited above. The inmates are now 4 of each sex.

Sanchez' Almshouses, for "4 poor aged men and 4 women, widows and widowers. inhabitants of Tottenham," were founded by Balthasar Sanchez by his will dated 1599. The queer low range of tenements stands on the E. of the Highroad, by Scotland Green. Balthasar Sanchez, wrote his contemporary Bedwell (named in the will a trustee for the charity) "was a Spanyard borne (but a free denyzen of England) confectioner or comfit-maker, and grand-master of all that professe that trade in this kingdom." He came to England as comfit-maker in the train of King Philip, settled here, died in 1602, and was buried at St. Mary Woolnoth. In King Henry IV. (Part i., act iii., sc. 1) Hotspur says to his wife—

"Heart, you swear like a comfit-maker's wife !
. . . . Swear me, Kate, like a lady as thou art,
A good mouth-filling oath ; and leave in sooth,
And such protest of pepper-gingerbread,
To velvet-guards and Sunday-citizens."

King Henry IV. was entered at Stationers' Hall in 1597, and, as Mr. E. Ford, who called our attention to the passage, observes, it appears difficult to resist the conclusion that Shakspeare's "comfit-maker's wife," was Mrs. Sanchez. Velvet guards were then distinctive of the wives of aldermen and wealthy citizens, and Sanchez was "grand-master" of his trade. Shakspeare, it may be added, gives the unusual name of Balthasar to four different characters. What more likely than that he had seen and made a note of the flourishing and perhaps somewhat ostentatious, Spanyard-citizen Balthasar Sanchez?

Reynardson's Almshouse. — Nicholas Reynardson (son of the loyalist Lord Mayor noticed above) bequeathed the manor of Netherhall, in 1685, for the founding of an almshouse for 6 poor men and 6 women, and the instruction of 20 poor children. The bequest was not available till after the decease of the testator's wife in 1727, and the almshouse was

---

* Poems and Letters by Bernard Barton, with Memoir by his Daughter, p. xii.

† His story is told in a curious book—Journal of the Life, Labours, and Travels of Thomas Shillitoe, in the Service of the Gospel of Jesus Christ, 2 vols. 8vo, 1839.

not erected till 1737 ; and then for only 8 instead of 12 persons. The building stands near the High Cross, and in accordance with the founder's will provides "a lower and an upper room" for each pensioner, with "a convenient chapel in the middle of the building for the reading of prayers every forenoon." Besides lodging and coals, each person receives about £14 annually.

Besides the parochial almshouses, there are the *Sailmakers' Almshouses* in Bruce Grove ; *Alderman Staines' Almshouses* in Church Road ; the *Drapers' College*, a large collegiate Gothic pile, forming three sides of a quadrangle, and containing class rooms and dormitories for 100 boys, masters' houses, etc., erected in 1861 from the designs of Mr. Herbert Williams, for the education of the sons of freemen of the company ; the *Drapers Company's Female Orphan Asylum*, Lordship Lane ; and the *Drapers' Almshouses*, Bruce Grove, for 24 aged and decayed members of the company, a neat and cheerful group of new houses about a large lawn, with a grove of old elms in front—together a magnificent charity. Other institutions of a like kind are in Wood Green, etc.

In a large old mansion on the E. of the Green is the *Evangelical Protestant Deaconesses Institute and Training Hospital*, which besides training young women for nurses, receives about 300 patients annually. There are Dispensaries in the Highroad and St. Ann's Road ; a *Girls' Industrial Orphan Home*, established 1836, with accommodation for 120 orphans ; and various other benevolent institutions.

The first Savings Bank in England of a public kind, was founded at Tottenham, Jan. 1804, under the name of the *Charitable Bank*, by Mrs. Priscilla Wakefield—authoress of many once popular books for the young. The same benevolent Friend also established here in 1791 a 'Charity for Lying-in Women,' which is said to have been the earliest of its kind.

Tottenham Hale is a hamlet lying to the E. of the High Cross, and now united to the town : here is the Tottenham Stat. on the Cambridge line of the Gt. E. Rly. The road to Essex passes through it, and the name of the Hale is continued to the Lea, which was of old crossed by a ferry. The ferry has long been supplanted by a bridge, but its memory is preserved in the sign of the inn at its foot, the *Ferry Boat* a fishing inn and boating house, with large tea-gardens on the opposite side of the road, much resorted to in summer. On the opposite side of the Lea are the extensive reservoirs and filtering-beds of the East London Waterworks Company, commonly known as the *Tottenham Reservoirs*, but really in WALTHAMSTOW.

Wood Green is a large and growing hamlet, built about what was a green on the Southgate road, 2 m. W. of Tottenham, and stretching on the E. up Lordship Lane and on the W. towards the Alexandra Palace, the grounds of which are partly in Tottenham par. Wood Green was made an eccl. dist. in 1866, and had 5011 inhab. in 1871, a number since largely increased. The ch. (St. Michael) on the W. side of the Green, has been already noticed. Just beyond it is the *Printers' Pension Society Asylum*, a handsome Tudor building erected in 1850, and enlarged by the addition of wings in 1871. It provides comfortable apartments for 24 persons, and the corporation gives also home pensions to about 100 printers and printers' widows. Immediately beyond it is the *Asylum for Aged Fishmongers and Poulterers*, a capacious structure, in which 12 married couples are maintained. The institution also provides 12 home pensions of £15 a year. *Fuller's Almshouses*, Nightingale Lane, is a cheerful looking semi-Gothic building, erected in 1865 from the designs of Mr. C. A. Long.

In Lordship Lane, a short distance from Wood Green on the l.. is the *Royal Masonic Institution for Boys*, an old institution on a small scale, but greatly extended and improved when removed to Wood Green in 1865. The building, designed by Mr. E. Pearce, is large and of pleasing appearance, Collegiate Gothic in style, of white brick with stone dressings. It comprises a centre with bold bay window, wings, and tall turrets at the extremities. On one side is a chapel, on the other a large school-room : 200 boys are lodged, clothed, and maintained, and receive a thorough commercial education.

TOTTERIDGE, HERTS, a vill. at

the S.E. angle of the county, between Whetstone and Highwood Hill, Middx, 1. m. W. of the Great North Road, where is the Totteridge and Whetstone Stat. of the Gt. N. Rly. (High Barnet line): pop. 474. *Inn :* Orange Tree.

The name is derived probably from the A.-S. root *Tot*, a height, an elevation (*toten*, to elevate, as in Toot Hill, Tothill), and *ridge ;* but Taylor thinks such places as Tot Hill and the like "may possibly have been seats of Celtic worship," the names coming from the Celtic deity, *Taith*, the Teutates of Lucan.* Totteridge occupies the summit (437 ft. above the Ordnance datum) of the line of high land which stretches westward from Whetstone to Highwood Hill (402 ft. high), and thence N.W. to Elstree. The country is varied and agreeable, richly wooded, and affords extensive views, and Totteridge is as yet little defaced by the builder. About the Green are some good old houses, standing in the midst of fine grounds. The ch. is picturesquely placed on the highest point of the hill. From an early period Totteridge was united with Hatfield, and held by the Bp. of Ely, till surrendered to Queen Elizabeth for an annuity of £1500, to be paid out of the Exchequer to the Bps. of that see. The living of Totteridge is still held with that of Hatfield, forming together one of the two richest livings in the county ; † it is in the gift of the Marquis of Salisbury. Elizabeth gave the manor in 1590 to John Cage, from whom it passed to Peacock, then to Sir Paul Whichcote, who sold it in 1720 to James Brydges, Duke of Chandos. By Henry, 2nd Duke of Chandos, it was sold to Sir Wm. Lee, Lord Chief Justice of the King's Bench. It is now held by the trustees of the late John Lee, LL.D.

The *Church* (St. Andrew), on the rt. of the road from Whetstone, is a plain brick building erected in 1790, but enlarged in 1869 by the addition of an apsidal chancel and transept (organ chamber and vestry), and rendered more accordant with current ecclesiastical taste. Painted windows were at the same time inserted as a memorial of Lord Cottenham. The only mont. of interest is a tablet by Bacon to John Puget, Esq., d. 1805. Opposite the W. door of the ch. is a magnificent yew,

26 ft. in girth at 3 ft. from the ground, and 25 ft. at 4½ ft. Under the shadow of the great yew is the tomb of Charles Christopher Pepys, 1st Lord Cottenham, Lord Chancellor 1836-41, and 1846-50, d. April 29, 1851 ; also of Lady Cottenham.

Totteridge Park, a short distance W. of the ch., occupies the site of the old manor-house, and its successor, a hunting box erected by Lord Bateman, and afterwards sold by him to Sir Wm. Lee. The present house, a large bald brick edifice, was erected by John Jennings, Esq., early in the present cent. It stands in a finely wooded park of about 100 acres. Baron Bunsen lived here in 1848-49. During his residence he entertained many distinguished men here, and greatly enjoyed the grounds with their "grand trees, those lofty firs the pride of Totteridge, the fine terrace, the charming garden," etc. " O how thankful," he wrote, " I am for this Totteridge ! Could I but describe the groups of fine trees, the turf, the terrace walks ; " and to the last he loved to refer to its quiet and beauty.* Later, the house was occupied by Lord Cottenham. It is now a first-class boys' school.

Pointer's Grove, S. of the ch., belonged in 1652 to Lady Gurney, widow of Sir Richard Gurney, Lord Mayor, who died a prisoner in the Tower in 1647. It afterwards belonged successively to Sir John Aubrey, Sir Thos. Aleyne, Sir Peter Meyer, Sir John Sheffield, and the late John Hey Puget, Esq. The grounds were laid out by Brown.

Copped Hall (Mrs. Kirby), on the way to Hendon, is a fine house, remodelled a few years back by Mr. Kendall : the dining-room is lined with Gobelin tapestry. The grounds, of about 80 acres, were laid out by Repton.

When Lysons wrote, "Wm. Manning, Esq., M.P., one of the directors of the Bank of England," had " a handsome seat at Totteridge, with extensive gardens," and is noted as having presented a picture to the ch., and contributed liberally to the parochial charities. It was in this house that his son, Cardinal Manning, was born in 1809.

Lady Rachel Russell retired to Totteridge for a time after the execution of her

* Taylor, Words and Places, p. 326.
† Totteridge with Hatfield is valued at £2097 ; Hadham, Much and Little, at £2200.

* Lady Bunsen, Memoirs of Baron Bunsen, vol. ii.

husband, William Lord Russell, 1683. Richard Baxter, the eminent Nonconformist divine, after his release from imprisonment under the Conventicle Act, lived in retirement for several years at Totteridge, 1665-72. John Corbet, author of various theological tracts, found an asylum at his house. From an entry in the parish register made by " Mr. Liptrott, late curate of Totteridge," and quoted by Lysons *—" Mem. Ld Mohun, who was killed in a duel by the Duke of Hamilton and Brandon (who was likewise killed,) Nov. 15, 1712, is supposed to have been buried in that part called Sr Robert Atkyns's Chapel "—it has been assumed that " the wicked Lord " was buried at Totteridge. But Mr. Liptrott was mistaken or misinformed, notwithstanding that he adduces in confirmation of his belief the fact that in 1770, in the place indicated, there " was discovered a large leaden coffin, but the wooden one entirely decayed." Lord Mohun was buried at St. Martin's-in-the-Fields,† and according to the register, on the 25th of Nov., 1712. Thomas Whincop, " poet and lodger at Mr. Porker's," author of ' Scanderberg,' a tragedy, was buried at Totteridge 1730, and his widow 52 years afterwards. Among the entries of burials is " March 2d, 1802, Elizabeth King, widow, for 46 years clerk of this parish."

TURNHAM GREEN, MIDDX., on

the main western road between Hammersmith and Brentford, 4½ m. from Hyde Park Corner; a stat. on the Hammersmith and Richmond br. of the L. and S.-W. Rly., and ½ m. W. of the Hammersmith Stat. of the N. Lond. Rly. It is a hamlet of Chiswick, but was in 1845 created an eccl. dist. Pop. 3434.

The Green is enclosed ; around it are private houses and shops ; in the centre a church, E.E. in style, with a tower and tall spire, erected in 1843. Some of the houses are favourable examples of the comfortable brick suburban mansions of the last century, but on the whole the place has a modern look, though, from its situation, a roadside hamlet must have grown up here at an early period. The Pack

Horse (where Horace Walpole used to turn aside to bait, and still in use) is mentioned in an advertisement of the year 1697 ; * and another old sign, The King of Bohemia's Head, might be seen here a few years back.

Stukeley mentions the finding of a Roman urn, filled with silver coins, at Turnham Green in 1731, but there is no other evidence of its having been a Roman station. Prince Rupert encamped on the Green in 1642; and on the day of Brentford Fight (Nov. 12) there was skirmishing here till dusk, when, according to a pamphlet of the time, the prince drew off to the enclosed ground on the rt., leaving 600 of his cavaliers dead on the field. Another pamphlet narrates a less fatal but sufficiently serious encounter. ' Great and Bloody News from Turnham Green, or a Relation of a sharp Encounter between the Earl of Pembroke [Henry, 7th Earl] and his Company, with the Constable and Watch belonging to the parish of Chiswick, in which conflict one Mr. Smecthe, a gentleman, and one Mr. Halfpenny, a constable, were mortally wounded,' etc., fol. 1680. The "narrow and winding lane leading from the landing-place on the north of the river to Turnham Green," was the spot fixed on by the conspirators in what was known as "Barclay's Plot." for the assassination of William III. on his return from hunting in Richmond Park on the afternoon of Saturday, the 15th of Feb., 1696. The discovery of the plot, with the arrest and trial of the chief conspirators, is told at length by Macaulay.†

Sir John Chardin, the traveller, resided till his death at Turnham Green :

"1705. *May* 18.—I went to see Sir John Chardin at Turnham Green : the gardens very fine and exceeding well planted with fruit." ‡

In a house by the ch., now pulled down, Lord Lovat was resident before his arrest. It was purchased in 1789 by Lord Heathfield, the hero of Gibraltar, who lived here till his death the following year. The gardens were laid out by Aiton, and greatly admired.

TWICKENHAM, MIDDX., on the l.

bank of the Thames. between Teddington

---

* Environs, vol. i., p. 781.
† Cunningham, Hand-book of London, art. St. Martin's-in-the-Fields.

* London Gazette, No. 3387.
+ History of England, chap. xxi.
‡ Evelyn, Diary.

and Isleworth, and a little above Richmond ; 10 m. from Hyde Park Corner by road, and a stat. on the Loop line of the L. and S.-W. Rly. Pop. 10,533. Inns : *King's Head*, King Street ; *Albany Hotel*, Rly. Stat. ; *Railway Hotel*.

The village is beautifully placed on the Thames between the higher ground of Strawberry Hill and the pleasant Twickenham meadows, with Ham Walks and Petersham, backed by Richmond Hill and Park on the opposite side of the river. It has always been a favourite residence, and boasts consequently a larger number of noted houses and eminent inhabitants than almost any other village on the Thames. Many of these houses have disappeared, but several are left ; and though it has, like most of the villages round London, lost much of its rural seclusion by the advent of the railway and the progress of the builder, it is still sylvan, and by the river-side nearly as attractive as ever.

Speculation on the name has been even more than commonly unprofitable. Norden thought it was called Twickenham either because the Thames seems to be divided into two rivers by the islands (eyots) here ; or else of two brooks which near this town enter the Thames. Ironside is more recondite, and not unamusing in his absurdity : " The word *ken* signifies to look ; so that *Twy-ken-ham* may signify a village with two views, as it hath a view of Kingston one way, and Isleworth, as also Richmond, the other way." If this be not approved, he offers an alternative derivation from *twygen*, twigs ; and as willows grew abundantly by the river here, he thinks " we may say *Twickenham*, *Twygenham*, signifies a village among willows." * Unluckily for these suggestions, the earliest forms of the name are *Twittanham* (791,948) and *Twitham* (840). It is not mentioned in the Dom. Survey. *Twittenham* survived down almost to the present generation in popular usage, and in the last century it was a customary form among the best-educated inhabitants. Pope, who has made Twickenham poetic ground, invariably spells it *Twittenham*, and Horace Walpole, who has done little less to render the name imperishable, at

least in his earlier years, wrote *Twitenham* or *Twit'nam*.

> " Where silver Thames round Twit'nam meads
> His winding current sweetly leads ;
> Twit'nam the Muses' fav'rite seat,
> Twit'nam the Graces' loved retreat." *

Thomson, an inhabitant of Richmond, wrote,—

> " Here let us trace the matchless vale of Thames
> Far winding up to where the Muses haunt,
> To Twitnam's bowers."

And again a later and humbler Richmond bard—

> " Twit'nam ! so dearly loved, so often sung,
> Theme of each raptured heart and glowing
> tongue." †

Twickenham is one of those happy places which is not burdened with a history. A grave topographer did indeed write and publish the ' History and Antiquities of Twickenham,' but he despatched both the history and antiquities almost as summarily as a more learned predecessor did the reptiles in a famous chapter on serpents.

> " On the strictest enquiry I cannot find that there have ever been any discoveries made, any curious remains of antiquity found, or that any remarkable circumstances happened, or any synods, parliaments, or other meetings, civil or religious, were held in this parish."‡

Originally Twickenham was accounted a hamlet of Isleworth. Part of it was held from before the Conquest by the Brethren of the Holy Trinity at Hounslow ; the other and chief part by the monks of Christ Church, Canterbury. On the suppression of religious houses their property reverted to the Crown, and Twickenham was annexed to the Honour of Hampton Court. Charles I. settled it for life on his queen, Henrietta Maria, as a portion of her jointure. With other Crown lands it was seized by the Parliament, but resumed by the Queen Dowager at the Restoration. Charles II. settled it on his queen, Catherine of Portugal, in 1670, but granted a reversionary lease to the Earl of Rochester. This lease passed to Lord Bolingbroke, and upon his attainder, 1715, reverted to the Crown. Later leases are of no interest.

---

* Hist. and Antiq. of Twickenham, 4to, 1797, p. 3 ; in Bib. Top. Brit., vol. x.

* Walpole, Parish Register of Twickenham.
† Richmond Hall, a Poem, 1807, by the Rev. T. Maurice—better known by his ' Indian Antiquities.'
‡ Ironside, Hist. and Antiq. of Twickenham, p. 71.

"Twittenham," wrote Defoe in 1722, "a village remarkable for abundance of curious seats, of which that of Boucher, the famous gamester, would pass in Italy for a delicate palace. The Earl of Marr, the Earl of Strafford, the Earl of Bradford, the Lord Brook, the Lord Sunderland, the Lady Falkland, have each their pretty villas in this parish; but I think tnat of Secretary Johnstone, for the elegancy and largeness of the gardens, his terrace on the river, and the situation of his house, makes much the brightest figure here. "*

Walpole wrote of it in a similar strain some 30 years later, when, however, the array of names was less aristocratic though not less remarkable :—

"Nothing is equal to the fashion of this village : Mr. Muntz says we have more coaches here than there are in half France.   Mrs. Pritchard has bought Ragman's Castle, for which my Lord Lichfield could not agree.   We shall be as celebrated as Baiæ or Tivoli ; and if we have not such sonorous names as they boast, we have very famous people : Clive and Pritchard actresses ; Scott and Hudson painters ; my Lady Suffolk, famous in her time ; Mr. H——† the impudent lawyer, that Tom Harvey wrote against ; Whitehead the poet, and Cambridge the everything." ‡

One remarkable peculiarity Twickenham—if we may trust its chronicler—possessed in those days : "There is not so untittletattling a village as Twickenham in the island ; and if Mr. Cambridge did not gallop the roads for intelligence, I believe the grass would grow in our ears"—and this when Twickenham was, in his own words, "a colony of dowagers," and he himself was importing into our literature from this very village more tittletattle than any other man ever collected.

The *Manor House*, a large red-brick mansion, stands opposite the N. side of the ch.   An earlier house, which occupied the site, was, according to an unsupported tradition, the house to which Queen Katherine of Aragon retired after her divorce from Henry VIII.   In the early part of the 17th cent. the Manor House was the seat of Sir John Walter, Lord Chief Baron of the Exchequer (d. 1630).   Samuel Scott, the painter of river scenery (d. 1772) lived

* De Foe, A Journey through England, 8vo, 1722, vol. i., p. 63.
† This was Joseph Hickey, the "most blunt honest creature" of Goldsmith's 'Retaliation,' whose "one only fault," in Oliver's estimation—though "that was a thumper"—was that he was a "special attorney."
‡ Horace Walpole to Bentley, July 5, 1755 ; Letters, vol. ii., p. 447.

here for some time ; as did afterwards his pupil, Wm. Marlow, F.S.A.   The greater part of the house was taken down some years back.

Orleans House.—" A messuage parcel of the Manor of Twickenham," was in 1567 leased for 22 years to Sir Thomas Newenham.   In 1622 Andrew Pitcairne, groom of the bed-chamber, had a lease of it for 30 years.   In the Parliamentary Survey, 1650, it is described as " a pleasant and delightful tenement, about 20 poles from the river, built partly with brick, and partly with timber, and Flemish wall, with comely chambers."   It had 16 acres of cherry gardens ; and not only were the gardens " rare for pleasure, but exceedingly profitable, being planted with cabbages, turnips, carrots, and many other such like creatures."   The estate was sold to Richard Ell, but resumed by the Crown at the Restoration.   In 1671 a short lease was granted to Mrs. Jane Davies, who obtained several renewals of it.   She lent her house in 1694—refusing to accept any rental—to the Princess (afterwards Queen) Anne, her son the Duke of Gloucester requiring change of air.   Early in the 18th century Mrs. Davies made over her interest in the property to James Johnstone, Esq., Secretary of State for Scotland, who greatly improved the house, built the Octagon Room against a visit he received from Queen Caroline, and continued to reside here till his death, at the age of 90, in 1737.   Secretary Johnstone's house was famous.   De Foe, we have seen, thought it made " much the brightest figure here."   His further account of it is curious :—

"Secretary Johnstone's house may be more properly called a plantation, being in the middle betwixt his pasture, his kitchen-garden, his fruit-garden, and his pleasure garden and wilderness. The house is exactly after the model of the country seats in Lombardy, being of two galleries, with rooms going off on each side.   His gallery on the ground-floor makes a hall, fronting the pleasure-garden, and a parlour fronting the pasture ; which, when the doors are open, gives you a delicious prospect of the whole : and on each side are 5 rooms more, adorned with a very good collection of pictures ; and in the division betwixt the hall and parlour on each side, is a stair-case that leads you up to the gallery above, containing the same number of rooms.   His fine Octagon for the entertainment of his friends, at the end of his greenhouse, I think is too high for his house, and I think very much spoils the symmetry of it. . . . . He has the best collection of fruit of all sorts, of most gentlemen in England.   His slopes for his vines, of which he makes some hogsheads a year are very particular ; and Dr. Bradley, of the Royal Society, who hath wrote so much about gardening, ranks him amongst the first-rate gardeners in England." *

On Secretary Johnstone's death the lease was bought by George Morton Pitt, formerly Governor of Fort St. George. It was afterwards the property and residence of Lord Brownlow Bertie, and then of Sir George Pococke, who made many alterations in the house and grounds, and connected the octagon room with the main building by a long corridor.

The next occupant of mark introduces a new and foreign source of interest, as well for Twickenham as for the mansion. In 1800, Louis Philippe, then Duc d'Orléans, and his brothers, the Duc de Montpensier and the Comte de Beaujolois, after many adventures and vicissitudes in various parts of the world, met together in London for the first time since their exile from France in 1793 ; and shortly after the Duke took Mr. Pococke's house at Twickenham as a residence for himself and his brothers. Here they continued to live till the death of the Duc de Montpensier, Jan. 1807, when the health of Comte de Beaujolois showing like symptoms of decline, the Duke carried him to Malta, where he died in 1808. The Duke then removed to Palermo, where he remained till he obtained permission to return to France in 1814. The following year he was again an exile, when he rejoined his family at Twickenham, where he continued till he was recalled to France in 1817. The house, thenceforth to be known as *Orleans House*, became some years later the residence of the Earl of Kilmorey, who, in 1846, purchased the Crown interest in it for £8590. Once more an exile in England, and the apparently firm seat of Napoleon III. on the French throne rendering his early recall to France hopeless, Louis Philippe yearned after his old home at Twickenham, and in 1852 he succeeded in purchasing it of Lord Kilmorey for £23,000. The ex-king was comfortably housed at Claremont, and Orleans House became the residence of his son the Duc d'Aumale, who during his long occupancy—1852-71 —improved the building, erected a spacious

* De Foe, A Journey through England, 8vo, 1722, vol. i., p. 63.

picture gallery, remodelled the interior, and filled it with a noble collection of ancient and modern pictures, drawings, miniatures, enamels, MSS., and choice printed books and articles of taste. Other members of the Orleans family settled around Orleans House—the Comte de Paris at York House, the Prince de Joinville at Mount Lebanon, and the Duc de Nemours at Bushey Park, and many of their friends in the vicinity ; and thus for some years Twickenham was the great Orleans centre towards which the attention of their adherents was at all times directed. The house is a large and stately brick mansion with an oriel centre, and a long wing carried to the octagon tower at the W. The grounds are richly timbered, and contain some splendid cedars. Orleans House has, it is announced (May 1876), been taken for a residence by Don Carlos of Spain.

York House (originally York Place) stands directly E. of the ch., with its principal front facing the Thames, in charming and finely timbered grounds of nearly 7 acres. The house is of brick, with a high-pitched roof, of about the end of the 16th century, but it has been altered and enlarged, and during the occupancy of the Comte de Paris was fitted up in a style befitting a royal abode. It appears to have been given to Lord Chancellor Clarendon on the public announcement of his daughter's marriage with James Duke of York. Clarendon made it his summer residence, and whilst attending the King at Hampton Court, he mentions that he was in the habit of coming home every night to his house at Twickenham. It was also an occasional residence of the Duke of York, or retreat of the Duchess, as here the Princess (afterwards Queen) Anne was born, Feb. 1664 : a large room on the first floor retains the name of Queen Anne's Room. On Lord Clarendon's death, York House passed to his second son, Lawrence Hyde, Earl of Rochester. In 1740 it was sold to James Whitchurch, and on his death to Lieut.-Col. Webber. About the end of the cent. it became the property and residence of Prince Stahremberg, the Austrian minister, who made it gay with plays and festivals. In 1817 it was purchased by Mrs. Damer, who removed hither her sculptor's tools, marbles, and models, and built for herself a studio at the E. end of the house, in which she chipped away during the summer months, removing to Park Lane in the winter. She had numerous friends about her, and the Queen used occasionally to call and watch her at work. Her studio is the conservatory of the present York House. Mrs. Damer bequeathed the house to her niece, Lady Johnstone (widow of Sir Patrick Johnstone), and the house had among others the Duchess Dowager of Roxburgh and Lord Lonsdale for tenants. It was purchased of the Misses Johnstone, August 1864, by the Duc d'Aumale, for his nephew, the Comte de Paris, who made it his residence till he returned to France, with the other Orleans princes, in 1871. The house underwent many alterations for the Comte de Paris. The state or reception rooms comprised a great saloon 34 ft. 6 in. by 26 ft., a dining room 30 ft. by 21 ft., three drawing rooms opening into each other and to the conservatory, two libraries, etc. Since the Prince's return to France, York House has been unoccupied.

Mount Lebanon, late the residence of the Prince de Joinville, is a handsome modern mansion facing the river, between York House and Orleans House. The original house was that in which lived Dr. William Fuller, Pepys's "dear friend," who during the Commonwealth period kept a school at Twickenham; after the Restoration was made Dean of St. Patrick's, Bp. of Limerick, 1663, ànd Bp. of Lincoln, 1667. The house was bought by Thomas Earl of Strafford in 1701, and on the death of the 2nd Earl (Horace Wâlpole's correspondent) it became the property of his sister, Lady Anne Conolly, who pulled down the old house and built the present mansion on its site. On her decease it passed to her daughter, the Viscountess Howe. It then became the residence of the Miss Byngs, and after the death of Miss Fanny Byng, of the Duchess Dowager of Northumberland, who bestowed on it the name of Mount Lebanon, perhaps from the cedars which form so remarkable a feature in the grounds. She died in 1866, and the house became shortly after the residence of the Prince de Joinville, and so continued till 1871. Like York House, Mount Lebanon is unoccupied, and "the lease to be sold," (May 1876).

Twickenham Park, at the junction of the par. with Isleworth, below Richmond Bridge, laid claim to the highest antiquity among the Twickenham demesnes. The Conqueror himself, it was asserted, had a residence there. According to the larger Ordnance Map, it was in Twickenham Park, and not in Isleworth, as generally supposed, the Barons encamped in 1263. Here in 1415 was founded the Bridgetine convent of Syon, removed some years later to the larger house at Isleworth (*see* p. 378). Henry VIII., one authority avers, "had an occasional residence" at Twickenham Park. What is certain is that there was a mansion here in the 16th century, and that the Bacon family had a lease of it as early as 1574. Francis Bacon was dwelling at Twickenham Park in 1592, when he received a visit from Queen Elizabeth, and, whilst disclaiming any pretension to the title of poet, presented Her Majesty with a sonnet in commendation of the Earl of Essex. It has been said that Twickenham was given to Bacon by Essex; but the property, as already noted, had been for some time held by the family. Bacon obtained a renewal ⊕f the lease to himself in 1595, and the fee-simple the following year. He greatly enjoyed the beauty and quiet of his Thames-side estate—"that wholesome pleasant lodge and finely designed garden," as he terms it in writing to his brother Anthony,[*]—but his pecuniary needs were pressing, and he sold it, not long after he became its owner, for what even then must have been the inadequate price of £1800.[†] His thoughts however reverted to Twickenham with a feeling of regret even in his latest years. Thus in his MS. Instructions to Thomas Bushell[‡] respecting the project for a corporation for exploring deserted mineral works, he writes, "Let Twitnam Park, which I sold in my younger days, be purchased, if possible, for a residence for such deserving persons to study in, since I experimentally found the situation of that place much convenient for the trial of my philosophical conclusions."

Leases were afterwards granted to various persons, but the first name to

---

[*] Bacon Papers, vol. i., p. 486.
[†] Cobbett, Memorials of Twickenham, p. 232.
[‡] Quoted by Lysons, vol. ii., p. 775.

arrest attention is that of Lucy Countess of Bedford, the patroness of Ben Jonson, Donne, Daniel, and most worthy wits and poets of her time. She lived here till 1618, when she gave Twickenham Park to Sir William Harrington, who, three years after, sold it to Mary Countess of Home. The remainder of the lease was alienated in 1640 to Sir Thomas Nott ; by him in 1659 to Henry Murray, who, in 1668, transferred it to John Lord Berkeley of Stratton—so named from Stratton Fight, and who gave his name to Berkeley Square and Berkeley Street, and Stratton Street, Piccadilly. Lord Berkeley died here in 1678, and was buried in Twickenham ch. His widow, 20 years later, was laid beside her husband. Twickenham Park was sold in 1685 to the Earl of Cardigan, and by him in 1698 to the Earl of Albemarle, who in 1702 transferred it to Thomas Vernon, secretary to the Duke of Monmouth. It was bought in 1743 by the Earl of Monteath, whose widow, in 1766, bequeathed the use of it in succession to the Duchess of Montrose and the Duchess of Newcastle, with reversion to Lord Frederick Cavendish, and remainder to Sir Wm. Abdy. It curiously illustrates the insecure condition of the vicinity of London less than a century ago, that Horace Walpole in visiting the Duchess of Montrose with Lady Browne, Oct. 5, 1781, had his carriage stopped at the gate of Twickenham Park by a highwayman at 7 o'clock in the evening, and was robbed of his purse and 9 guineas. Lady Browne lost her purse also, but her's was a purse with only " bad money, which she carried on purpose."* Nor did Twickenham speedily become more secure. Just a year later he wrote, " I cannot now stir a mile from my own house [Strawberry Hill] after sunset without one or two servants with blunderbusses."†

Lord Frederick Cavendish was owner and occupant of the house when Angus's view of it was published, Jan. 1, 1795. From this it appears to have been a very large and stately structure of red brick and stone ; the principal front, facing the W., of 3 storeys above the ground floor, with 11 windows in each, the centre having a portico and pediment, and that and the wings being slightly advanced. It contained " several handsome apartments, with a noble staircase, painted in a similar manner to that at Windsor Castle." It also contained " some good pictures." On the death of Lord Frederick Cavendish the estate passed to Sir Wm. Abdy, by whom it was, in 1805, divided into lots and sold, the greater part being purchased by F. Gostling, Esq. Shortly after the house was taken down ; villas were built ; and the process has gone on until Twickenham Park has become a village of villas and genteel residences.

In the meadows between Twickenham Park and Orleans House are several houses of mark. *Cambridge House*, the first from the bridge foot, was built by Sir Humphry Lynd—a noted controversialist—early in the 17th cent. It was next the residence of Joyce Countess of Totness, who died in it in 1636 ; afterwards became the property and seat of Sir Joseph Aske ; and was in 1751 purchased by Richard Owen Cambridge, author of the ' Scribleriad.' Mr. Cambridge was a man of unusual accomplishments and social charm, and his Twickenham villa was a favourite resort of the most distinguished among his contemporaries. Boswell refers with unusual warmth to his " beautiful villa on the banks of the Thames," his " numerous and excellent library," his " extensive circle of friends and acquaintance distinguished by rank, fashion, and genius," and his " colloquial talents rarely to be found ; " and one of the pleasantest chapters in his book is that in which he relates his ride with Johnson to Mr. Cambridge's villa, where the doctor was " solaced with an elegant entertainment, a very accomplished family, and much good company"—as may very well be believed, Sir Joshua Reynolds, Gibbon the historian, and Hermes Harris being of the number.* Mr. Cambridge lived to enjoy his villa and the society of his friends for more than a quarter of a century after Johnson's visit, dying there in his 86th year, in Sept. 1802. It was afterwards for awhile the residence of his son, Achdeacon Cambridge, who, how-

---

* Walpole to Lady Ossory, Oct. 7, 1781.
† Walpole to the Earl of Strafford, Oct. 3, 1782.

* Boswell, Life of Johnson, 1775, vol. v., p. 08, etc., ed. 1835.

ever, built for himself a smaller house somewhat to the S. Cambridge House then became the residence of Lord Mount-Edgcumbe. Later it was purchased by Henry Bevan, Esq., who, with Mr. Vulliamy as his architect, remodelled the house, and enriched the grounds. Cambridge House is now the seat of his daughter, Lady Chichester, relict of Lord John Chichester. *Meadowbank*, erected by Archdeacon Cambridge, is now the residence of George Bishop, Esq., whose private observatory has acquired universal celebrity on account of the important observations and discoveries made in it under its distinguished superintendent, John Russell Hind, F.R.S., who resides at *Meadow Lodge*. On the meadows, in Owen Cambridge's day all open, has sprung up, as in Twickenham Park, a nest of villas, which has received the name of *Cambridge Park*, and a handsome church has been built within it for the service of the two parks.

Four or five hundred yards W. of Meadowbank, and a very conspicuous object from the Thames, is *Marble Hill*, "a house," as Swift writes, "built by Mrs. Howard, then of the bed-chamber, now Countess of Suffolk, and groom of the stole to the Queen. . . . Mr. Pope was the contriver of the gardens, Lord Herbert (Earl of Pembroke) the architect, and the Dean of St. Patrick's (Swift) chief butler and keeper of the ice-house." The house was built for Mrs. Howard by the king, George II., at a cost of £12,000; but, never liberal in money matters, he was possibly behindhand in his advances, as Swift in his 'Pastoral Dialogue between Richmond Lodge and Marble Hill,' written in June 1727, makes the lady's villa predict that its mistress will be ruined by the outlay; the house is unfinished, her pockets are empty.

"And now she will not have a shilling
  To raise the stairs, or build the ceiling."

The house will have to be sold to "some South-sea broker from the City," who will lay all the fine plantations waste, and

"No more the Dean, that grave divine,
  Shall keep the key of my (no) wine;
  My ice-house rob as heretofore,
  And steal my artichokes no more;
  Nor Patty Blunt no more be seen
  Bedraggled in my walks so green;
  Plump Johnny Gay will now elope;
  And here no more will dangle Pope.'

However, the house was finished in course of time, and Mrs. Howard, now Countess of Suffolk, quitted the Court in 1735, "married Mr. George Berkeley and outlived him," and for the remainder of her days spent her summers at Marble Hill, "living very retired both there and in London."* On her death, July 1767, Marble Hill became the property and residence of the Earl of Buckinghamshire, who bequeathed it to Miss Hotham. From her it was rented by Mrs. Fitzherbert, whose irregular marriage ceremony with the Prince of Wales, afterwards George IV., it has been said was performed here; but her relative and confidential friend, Lord Stourton, states that it occurred "in her own drawing-room in her house in town,"† *i. e.*, in Park Lane, 1785. She was at Marble Hill at the time of the Prince's marriage with the Princess Caroline. 1795. Marble Hill next became the residence of Lady Bath; then of Mr. C. A. Tulk; and afterwards of the Marquis of Wellesley, who left it about 1824. It was shortly after purchased by Col., now the Rt. Hon. Lieut.-General J. Peel, whose seat it now is.

A short distance E. was a cottage known as *Little Marble Hill*, which was occupied by Mrs. Clive until she removed to Little Strawberry Hill. On its site a much more pretentious mansion was built by Mr. Daniel Giles, when it appears to have been known as Twickenham Meadows. Afterwards, as *Spencer Grove*, it became the residence of Lady Diana Beauclerk, when it became celebrated alike on account of the elegance with which she fitted it up and the parties she assembled there. Several of the rooms were decorated by her ladyship's own pencil, and Horace Walpole never tired of applauding the taste and skill she displayed. One room particularly delighted him : "It is nothing but a row of lilacs in festoons on green paper, but executed in as great a style as Michael Angelo would have done for a Pope's villa."‡ Spencer Grove was afterwards the residence of Lady Tollemache and of Miss Hotham. It was then purchased by Sir John Lubbock; was for a time a residence of the Duke of Mon-

* H. Walpole, Reminiscences of the Courts of George I. and II., chap viii.
+ Langdale, Memoirs of Mrs. Fitzherbert, p. 43.
‡ H. Walpole to Rev. W. Mason, Aug. 4, 1782.

trose ; then of Mr. Kirby, and has since been unoccupied.

West of Marble Hill was another noted villakin, *Ragman's Castle*, which had been the residence successively of Lady Falkland (1635), John Duke of Montague, and the Dowager Lady Pembroke, when it was purchased in 1755 by Mrs. Pritchard, the famous actress, who spent a great deal of money in its improvement and decoration. After her decease, 1758, it was occupied by the Earl of Cholmondeley, Lady Lane, and Sir C. Warwick Bamfield. In 1783 it became the residence of George Hardinge, author of 'Letters to Burke,' and a man well known in social and political circles. To him succeeded, 1810, Jeremiah Dyson, Mr. H. Cole, Major Jelf Sharp. The house, in its latter days known as *Lawn Cottage*, was taken down by Lord Kilmorey in 1850, and the garden thrown into the grounds of Orleans House.

Continuing along the river, and passing Orleans House, York House, and the church, we come to *Richmond House*, or as it appears to have been called originally Richmonds, a good-sized mansion with its front to the Thames, opposite the W. end of Eel Pie Island. It was for many years the residence of Francis Newport, 2nd Earl of Bradford, a prominent politician in the reigns of Charles II. and James II., who died here in 1708, when it passed, with the fine collection of pictures which he had formed in it, to his second son, Lord Torrington. It was sold in 1740, by Lord Torrington's widow, to Anthony Viscount Montague, who four years later sold it to Anthony Keck. In 1766 it was purchased by Mary Countess Dowager of Shelburne, who bequeathed it to her second son, the Hon. Thomas Fitzmaurice. Subsequent owners were Mr. John Symmons, 1791 ; Mrs. Allanson, 1792 ; the Countess Dowager of Elgin, who died in it in 1810 ; and Lady De Crespigny. The old house was then taken down, and a new one built on its site, in 1816, for Mrs. Lionel Dawson Damer, the cousin of Mrs. Damer the sculptor. It was enlarged and brought to its present size and appearance in 1829, for the Countess Dowager of Roxburgh and her husband, the Hon. John Tollemache. Later it was the residence of Lord Lowth, Sir Henry Willock, Lady Ann Murray,

Sir Edward Blakeney, and is now the seat of George Gordon Mackintosh, Esq.

Poulet Lodge, immediately beyond Richmond House, occupies the site of the villa of M. Chauvigny, the French ambassador, which was burnt down in June 1734. The present house, of very formal aspect, was built by Dr. Batty, a physician of eminence in his day. After his death it became the property and residence of Vere, 3rd Earl of Poulet ; on the decease of whose widow it became the residence of Walpole's "horror," Mrs. Osbaldeston ; then successively of Lord Cardigan, Col. Webb, another Countess Poulet, and after her death, in 1838, of various undistinguished persons. It is now the residence of W. H. Punchard, Esq., who has greatly improved it. The long low back front lies open to the road at Cross Deep, a little N. of Pope's Villa.

Riversdale, the next house, the property of Lord Clifden, was in 1808 leased by Lady Monson, who greatly enlarged it ; afterwards by G. H. Drummond, Esq., Lord Uxbridge, and Lord Cawdor. It is now the residence of the Misses Young.

POPE'S VILLA.—We are thus brought, at length, to the residence of the poet who has made Twickenham famous wherever English literature has reached. Pope's Villa stood about 200 yards beyond Riversdale ; the entrance was in the road from Twickenham to Teddington. Pope took a lease of the house, with about 5 acres of ground, shortly after his father's death in 1717, and lived here till his own death in 1744. The villa, or villakin, as Swift called it, was much smaller when Pope took it than he left it. In 1717 it comprised only a central hall, with two small parlours on each side, and corresponding rooms above. He left it a brick centre of 4 floors, with wings of 3 floors—each storey with a single light towards the Thames.

Of the contents of the house some idea may be obtained. There were at least two portraits of Lord Bolingbroke (one by Richardson) ; three drawings of statues in monochrome by Kneller of the Hercules Farnese, the Venus de' Medici, and the Apollo Belvedere ; marble busts of Homer by Bernini ; of Sir Isaac Newton by Guelfi ; and four of Spenser, Shakspeare, Milton, and Dryden, a present to Pope from Frederick Prince of Wales, and now at Hagley, having been bequeathed to Lord Lyttelton by the poet.

The space between the river and the house was occupied by a lawn, fenced and concealed from a tanner's yard on one side, from the low houses on the other by a hedge and background of trees. The hedge on the London side was curved towards the river, decorated with terminal busts, and with an alcove commanding a view up the river, and of the gentle scenery of Surrey towards Kingston and Esher. Over against the alcove, on the other side, stood a large willow—the second weeping willow planted in England. Beneath the house and the highroad to Teddington, the poet constructed a tunnel as a means of communication between the lawn and the garden, which was on the other side of the road, lined it with " spars, minerals, and marbles," and made it for ever famous as

> " The Aegerian grot
> Where, nobly pensive, St. John sat and thought ;
> Where British sighs from dying Wyndham stole,
> And the bright flame was shot through March-
> mont's soul."

A small obelisk with an inscription to his mother—" Matrem optima, Mulierum amantissima"—terminated the garden vista.

Pope was fond of his garden and proud of it; and not without reason. Though of small size, like that of Alcinous, and of awkward shape, he contrived with the aid of Bridgman and Kent, the great professional gardeners, and Lord Peterborough and other eminent amateurs, to twist and twirl it into one of the prettiest gardens in England. He was the first to break through the Dutch formality of Hampton Court, and to revert to a more natural style. Gardening, he says, is more antique and nearer to God's own work than poetry. He worked and planned, and got his friends to work with him. His letters and his verses are full of his gardening and his grotto-making.

> " I am as busy in three inches of gardening as any man can be in three-score acres. I fancy myself like the fellow that spent his life in cutting the twelve apostles in a cherry stone. I have a Theatre, an Arcade, a Bowling-green, a Grove, and what not? in a bit of ground that would have been but a plate of sallet to Nebuchadnezzar the first day he was turned to graze." *

---

* Pope to Lord Strafford, Oct. 5, 1725.

> " I have turfed a little Bridgmannick theatre myself. It was done by a detachment of his [Bridgman's] workmen for the Princes' visit, all at a stroke, and it is yet unpaid for, but that is nothing with a poetical genius." *

> " And he † whose lightning pierc'd th' Iberian lines,
> Now forms my quincunx, and now ranks my vines ;
> Or tames the genius of the stubborn plain,
> Almost as quickly as he conquer'd Spain." ‡

> " Mr. Pope undoubtedly contributed to form his [Kent's] taste. The design of the Prince of Wales's garden at Carlton House, was evidently borrowed from the poet's at Twickenham. There was a little of affected modesty in the latter, when he said, of all his works he was most proud of his garden. And yet it was a singular effort of art and taste to impress so much variety and scenery on a spot of five acres. The passing through the gloom from the Grotto to the opening day, the retiring and again assembling shades, the dusky groves, the larger lawn, and the solemnity of the termination of the cypresses that led up to his mother's tomb, are managed with exquisite judgment; and though Lord Peterborough assisted him

> " To form his quincunx and to rank his vines,"

> those were not the most pleasing ingredients of his little perspective." §

Pope's success in landscape gardening was not due to a happy chance. The arrangement of his lawns, hedges, trees, and avenues was with him a serious occupation, as is evident from many passages in his letters. He explained his principles most distinctly perhaps to Spence :

> " The lights and shades in gardening are managed by disposing the thick grove work, the thin, and the openings, in a proper manner : of which the eye is generally the properest judge.—Those clumps of trees are like the groups in pictures (speaking of some in his own garden).—You may distance things by darkening them and by narrowing the plantation more and more towards the end, in the same manner as they do in painting, and as 'tis executed in the little cypress walk to that obelisk." ‖

The *Grotto* which figures so largely in the Letters and Poems was formed by lining the tunnel under the Teddington road with shells, spars, and minerals, which were liberally furnished for this purpose by his friends. The most lavish contributor was Borlase the Cornish antiquary, who was indefatigable in searching

---

* Pope to Lord Oxford, 22 March, 1726.
† Lord Peterborough.
‡ Pope, Satires and Epistles, Sat. i.
§ Horace Walpole (On Modern Gardening), Anecdotes, vol. iv., p. 295.
‖ Spence, Anecdotes, Singer's ed., p. 209.

out and forwarding the choicest marbles, serpentines, and stalactites, spars and crystals to be found in Cornwall ; and Pope showed his gratitude by setting up his friend's name in large gold letters in a conspicuous part of the grotto—much to the bewilderment of visitors. The Duchess of Cleveland was also a large contributor, and Sir Hans Sloane offered freely of the stores in his museum. Pope's description of the grotto is well known, but a portion of it must be given :—

"I have put the last hand to my works of this kind, in happily finishing the subterraneous way and grotto : I there found a spring of the clearest water, which falls in a perpetual rill, that echoes thro' the cavern day and night. From the river Thames, you see thro' my arch up a walk of the wilderness, to a kind of open Temple, wholly compos'd of shells in the rustic manner ; and from that distance under the temple you look down thro' a sloping arcade of trees, and see the sails on the river passing suddenly and vanishing, as thro' a perspective glass. When you shut the doors of this grotto, it becomes on the instant, from a luminous room, a *Camera obscura* ; on the walls of which all the objects of the river, hills, woods, and boats, are forming a moving picture in their visible radiations ; and when you have a mind to light it up, it affords you a very different scene ; it is finished with shells interspersed with pieces of looking-glass in angular forms ; and in the cieling is a star of the same material, at which when a lamp (of an orbicular figure of thin alabaster) is hung in the middle, a thousand pointed rays glitter and are reflected over the place. There are connected to this grotto by a narrower passage two porches, one towards the river of smooth stones full of light, and open ; the other toward the Garden shadow'd with trees, rough with shells, flints, and iron-ore. The bottom is paved with simple pebble, as is also the adjoining walk up the wilderness to the temple, in the natural taste, agreeing not ill with the little dripping murmur, and the aquatic idea of the whole place. It wants nothing to compleat it but a good statue with an inscription, like that beautiful antique one which you know I am so fond of." *

"The improving and finishing his Grotto," writes Warburton, in a note to Pope's verses ' On his Grotto at Twickenham,' "was the favourite amusement of his declining years ; and the beauty of his poetic genius, in the disposition and ornaments of this romantic recess, appears to as much advantage as in his best contrived poems." Be that as it may, and few are likely to accept the bishop's dictum, the poet lived to finish his grotto, and to experience a feeling of vacuity when it was finished.

"*Spence.* I pity you, Sir, because you have

* Pope to Edw. Blount, June 2, 1725.

[1743] completed everything belonging to your garden.—*Pope.* Why, I really shall be at a loss for the diversion I used to take in laying out and finishing things. I have now nothing left me to do, but to add a little ornament or two at the line to the Thames." *

Pope spent some £5000 on his improvements. He was only a tenant, and he had some thoughts of becoming the owner when the property was for sale, but he looked about in vain for a friend to whom he might leave it, who would be likely to live in it and preserve it unchanged. If Ruffhead may be trusted, he thought of bequeathing it to Mr. Murray, afterwards Lord Mansfield ; "but when he found by the growing fame and rising reputation of his friend, that it was never likely to be of any use to him, he laid aside that purpose."†

"My landlady, Mrs. Vernon being dead, the house and garden are offered to me in sale ; and I believe (together with the cottages on each side my grass plot next the Thames) will come at about a £1000. If I thought any very particular friend would be pleased to live in it after my death (for as it is it serves all my purposes as well during life) I would purchase it ; and more particularly could I hope two things : that the friend who should like it, was so much younger and healthier than myself, as to have a prospect of its continuing his some years longer than I am of its continuing mine. But most of those I love are travelling out of the world not into it ; and unless I have such a view given me, I have no vanity nor pleasure that does not stop short of the grave."‡

"As to my *mines* and my *treasures* they must go together to God knows who ! A sugar-broker or a brewer may have the house and garden, and a booby that chanced to be my heir at law the other : except I happen to dispose it to the poor in my own time."§

After Pope's death (1744) his villa was sold to Sir Wm. Stanhope, brother to the Earl of Chesterfield, who added wings to the house, and enlarged and improved the garden—greatly to the disgust of Walpole :—

"I must tell you a private woe that has happened to me in my neighbourhood—Sir William Stanhope bought Pope's house and garden. The former was so small and bad, one could not avoid pardoning his hollowing out that fragment of the rock Parnassus into habitable chambers—but would you believe it, he has cut down the sacred groves themselves ! In short, it was a little bit of ground of five acres, enclosed with three lanes, and seeing nothing. Pope had twisted and twirled, and

* Spence, Anecdotes, p. 273.
† Ruffhead, Life of Pope, 1769, p. 402.
‡ Pope to Bethel, March 20, 1743.
§ Pope to Allen, n.d., Ruffhead's Life of Pope, p. 199.

Pope's House, Twickenham

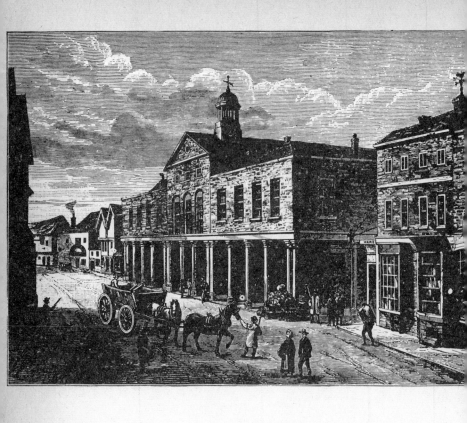

Market House, Uxbridge (see p.647)

rhymed and harmonised this, till it appeared two or three sweet little lawns opening and opening beyond one another, and the whole surrounded with thick impenetrable woods. Sir William, by advice of his son-in-law, Mr. Ellis, has hacked and hewed these groves, wriggled a winding gravel walk through them with an edging of shrubs, in what they call the modern taste, and in short, has desired the three lanes to walk in again—and now is forced to shut them out again by a wall, for there was not a Muse could walk there but she was spied by every country fellow that went by with a pipe in his mouth." *

Mr. Welbore Ellis (afterwards Lord Mendip) came into possession of the house after Sir Wm. Stanhope's death, and made it his residence, priding himself on preserving whatever was left of Pope's unaltered. The loss of the famous willow, which died in 1801, was his chief trouble that way. Cuttings of it had been sent to St. Petersburg in 1789, at the request of the Empress of Russia; and now the dead trunk was converted into Popeian relics. At Lord Mendip's death, the property was sold by auction to Sir John Briscoe, and on his death in 1807 to the Baroness Howe.

The Baroness was the daughter of Admiral Lord Howe, the hero of "the glorious 1st of June," and inherited his title. Widow of the Hon. P. A. Curzon, she took for her second husband the court oculist, Dr. Phipps, who was made a baronet, and on his promotion emerged from his plebeian chrysalis as Sir Wathen Waller. The lady knew not Pope, and was annoyed by his admirers coming to her place to ask after his house and gardens. She razed the house, therefore, stubbed up the trees, and destroyed whatever was his. "We went into Pope's back garden," wrote Miss Berry in her journal, Nov. 21, 1807, "and saw the devastation going on upon his quincunx by its now possessor Baroness Howe. The anger and ill-humour expressed against her for pulling down his abode and destroying his grounds, much greater than one would have imagined." The Baroness built herself a new house, not on the site of the poet's, but a hundred yards to the N. of it, absorbing in the process the house in which Hudson the painter, Sir Joshua Reynolds's master, used to live. The Baroness gave lawn-parties which were very attractive, and on the 1st of June a silver cup to be

rowed for in honour of her father's victory, when Sir Wathen Waller used to be exhibited on the lawn decorated with all the Admiral's stars and medals.* They in their turn passed away, and in the beginning of 1840 "Pope's Villa"—though Pope's Villa had long ceased to exist—was announced for sale. But no one would buy the counterfeit, and shortly after the "building materials" were disposed of by auction. A portion of the Baroness's house was however saved, and turned into two small dwellings.

Pope feared his house and garden might pass to "some sugar-broker or brewer;" the new owner was a tea-merchant, Mr. Thos. Young, who first proposed to reinstate the poet's house by building a facsimile of it; but changing his mind erected the present grotesque structure—distinguishable by its odd Chinese-Gothic tower —which if it bears no resemblance to the poet's house, at least preserves the name of Pope's Villa. It does not stand quite on the site of Pope's house, but is nearer to it than was the Baroness Howe's. The Grotto remains, or rather the tunnel, for it has been despoiled of all its rare marbles, spars, and ores, and is a mere damp subway.

The house next to Pope's was the residence of the Hon. George Shipley, and was known as *Spite Hall*, from its having been built for the purpose of intercepting the view of the Thames from Shipley's opposite neighbour:—

"The people here have christened Mr. Shipley's new house *Spite Hall.* It is dismal to think that one may live to 77, and go out of the world doing as ill-natured an act as possible."†

Radnor House, by the river, midway between Pope's Villa and Strawberry Hill, was built by the last Earl of Radnor, of the Robarts family. It was in Lord Radnor's garden that Pope first met Warburton, 1740—a meeting of no little consequence to both of them. The house, an ungainly attempt at Gothic, and the grounds, chiefly notable for their whimsical jumble of statues, obelisks, Chinese temples, and the like, formed a constant butt for the sarcasms of Horace Walpole, whose cant name for them was *Mabland*.

---

* Horace Walpole to Sir Horace Mann, June 20, 1760: Letters, vol. iii., p. 318.

* Cobbett, Memorials of Twickenham, p. 289.
+ H. Walpole to the Earl of Strafford, Sept. 9, 1780; Letters, vol. vii., p. 438.

After Lord Radnor's death the house was successively the property and residence of J. A. Hindley, one of the tellers of the Exchequer ; Sir Francis Basset ; the Ladies Murray ; Charles Marsh, F.S.A. ; and now of A. C. Stearns, Esq. *Cross Deep House*, the pleasant-looking mansion on the opposite side of the Teddington road, has been successively the abode of J. Ivat Briscoe, Esq., M.P., C. J. Freake, Esq., W. Vernon Harcourt, M.P., and now of Robert Morley, Esq.

STRAWBERRY HILL, a little farther S., Horace Walpole's famous Gothic castle, is described under its proper title. Farther on, the last house in Twickenham, on the lower Teddington road, is *Little Strawberry*,

> " Where lived the laughter-loving dame
> A matchless actress, Clive her name,"—

Walpole, to whom it belonged, having good-naturedly given her the use of it for life, and christened it *Cliveden*. She spent her last years here, liked by everybody, but having her small troubles.

> " Have you not heard of the adventures of your poor Pivey," she writes to Garrick, June 10, 1776; " I have been rob'd and murder'd coming from Kingston. Jimey [her brother, Raftor] and I in a post-chey at half-past nine, Just by Teddington church was stopt. I only lost a little silver and my senses, for one of them come into the carriage with a great horse pistol to search for my watch, but I had it not with me." *

This in a populous road, on a Midsummer evening, just a century ago ! Kitty died in 1785. In 1791, Walpole let the house, on the same easy terms, to the Miss Berrys (his Strawberrys) and their father ; and later bequeathed it to them for their lives. Here for a long series of years they held the quiet little afternoon parties at which the most distinguished people delighted to meet.

> " When London began to fill, and the season was at its height, the Miss Berrys used to retire to a pretty villa at Twickenham, where they received their friends to luncheon, and strawberries and cream, and very delightful these visits were in fine spring weather. I recollect once, after dining there, to have been fortunate enough to give a place in my carriage to Lord Macaulay, and those who remember his charming and brilliant conversation will understand how short the drive to London appeared." †

After Walpole's death the visits of the Miss Berrys to the Continent were more frequent, or their stay lengthened, and they let Little Strawberry by the year furnished, first to Prebendary Bell of Westminster, afterwards (1813) for a term of 7 years to Alderman Wood. At the end of his tenancy it was let to Admiral Bowen, who complained bitterly of " the ruinous condition in which the alderman had made it over to him." * The house has subsequently had no occupant of note, and none at all for some years. Now the house looks very dilapidated, and Horace Walpole's and Kitty Clive's favourite walk, " Drury-lane," is sadly out of order.

Towards the town, at the corner of the Teddington road, the site marked by Messrs. Corbin's coach factory, was a noble old red-brick mansion, *Grove House*, attributed to the inventive genius of Inigo Jones, and for a time the residence of the poetical and profligate Philip Duke of Wharton. Afterwards it was the seat of James Craggs, the friend of Pope, and to whom Addison, whom he succeeded as Secretary of State, dedicated his Collected Works. The house was pulled down in 1836.

On the l. of the Heath Road, E. of the rly. bridge, is *Saville House* (Col. T. G. Gardiner), a fine old red-brick mansion with tall roof, where for several years lived Lady Mary Wortley Montague, who came here to be near Pope—fast friends then, too soon to be bitter foes. To her succeeded Lady Saville, who left her name to the house, though she changed her own by marrying Dr. Charles Morton, principal librarian of the British Museum.

Next to it, and nearer the rly. bridge, is another old red brick mansion, very similar in style to Saville House, *Twickenham House*, for many years the residence of Sir John Hawkins, author of a voluminous History of Music, and executor of Dr. Johnson, of whom he wrote a Life as dull as Boswell's is brilliant. It was afterwards the residence and property of Paul Vaillant, the bookseller of the Strand ; and is now in the occupation of Dr. Hugh M. Diamond (known alike by his professional writings and researches in photography) as a first-class private lunatic asylum.

---

* Walpole's Letters, vol. ix., p. 525.
† Personal Recollections of Mary Somerville, by her Daughter, 1873, p. 222.

* Miss Berry's Journal and Correspondence (Journal, Oct. 17, 1818).

In Back Lane stand the entrance gates and outbuildings, all that is left, of *Copt Hall*, the residence of John, 11th Earl of Mar, of Admiral Fox, and of Lady Conolly. Not far from it stood an old-fashioned wooden house, which according to the local tradition was that occupied by Henry Fielding. Here it is said he wrote 'Tom Jones;' but the date of its publication makes this doubtful. What is certain is that his first son by his second wife was baptized at Twickenham ch. in 1747, and that Fielding left Twickenham in 1748.* The house has been long pulled down.

On the N. side of Twickenham Common is *Colne Lodge*, a good "Italian villa," in which lived and died (1774) Paul Whitehead, poet and satirist. (*See* TEDDINGTON.) It was afterwards the residence of the Countess of Dunmore, and of Miss Virginia Murray, and is now the seat of E. H. Donnithorne, Esq., J.P. In an old mansion which formerly stood on the Common, Bp. Corbet is said to have lived. His father had a nursery at Whitton, a hamlet of Twickenham. (*See* WHITTON.) Bp. Corbet's Poems were edited in 1807 by Octavius Gilchrist, a native of Twickenham.

In the Richmond Road, on the other side of the town, opposite Montpelier Row, is *North End House* (H. G. Bohn, Esq.), celebrated for the collections of pictures, rare books, and mediæval antiquities—somewhat thinned, however, by recent sales. In Montpelier Row, at what was then called *Chapel House*, now Holyrood House, lived (1850) Alfred Tennyson: his son Hallam was baptized at Twickenham ch. in 1852.

We have now come back nearly to our starting-point, and may end these notices of remarkable houses with one, in some respects, not the least remarkable among them. Somewhat to the N.E. of North End Lodge, on the l. of the Isleworth Road, leading from Richmond Bridge, opposite the farther entrance lodge to Twickenham Park, in a narrow lane leading to the Richmond Road, is *Sandycombe Lodge* (Miss Beaumont), the house which Turner, our great landscape painter, then rapidly rising in fame, built for himself in 1813, from his own designs. Turner at

first called it *Solus Lodge*—perhaps from its then standing in a somewhat solitary spot—but altered the name the following year to Sandycombe.* It is a small house with small rooms, and not very beautiful, but has been altered somewhat. It has a narrow centre, with balcony over a closed entrance porch, and lower and narrower wings, but before the Cambridge Park villas were built had an outlook over the river from the garden front. Turner lived here 12 years—the 12 years in which his genius was most rapidly ripening. Ruskin rather flouts "Twickenham classicisms," and perhaps with reason. But Turner learnt something better at Twickenham. He kept a boat, and spent day after day on the river, sketching and studying the water,—surface, colour, and reflections,—the ever-shifting cloud-forms, and the morning and evening mists. Here and in this way it was he learnt, as no painter had learnt before, the mysteries of cloud and vapour. The grand landscape in the National Gallery, 'Crossing the Brook,' was one of the early fruits of his Twickenham studies, as the 'View from Richmond Hill' was one of the latest.

Some other famous names remain to be mentioned among the eminent inhabitants of Twickenham. Sir Godfrey Kneller lived in the par., but his house was at Whitton, and will be noticed under that heading. John Lenthall, the Speaker of the Long Parliament, had a house here. So it is said had Robert Boyle, the great natural philosopher. Lord Bute lived here in 1748. Lady Fanny Shirley, "Fanny blooming fair," lived at Heath Lane Lodge. Nicholas Amherst, the author of 'The Craftsman,' died here in poverty, 1742, and was buried at the expense of Horace Walpole's printer, Franklin. Daniel Waterland, D.D., the eminent divine, was sometime Vicar of Twickenham. Lætitia Hawkins, author of some works more tedious and pompous than even her father's History of Music, and of some equally dull and more flippant Anecdotes of Dr. Johnson, which are still occasionally quoted, lived, after her father's death till her own, in Sion Row.

In one of the Ailsa Park villas, N.W. of Twickenham Park, lived, in 1838, Charles Dickens, and there Mr. Forster records,

---

with Talfourd, Thackeray, Douglas Jerrold, Sir Edwin Landseer, Stanfield, and Maclise, "we had many friendly days." * Sir Francis Chantrey, the sculptor, was married at Twickenham ch. to Mary Ann Wale, Nov. 23, 1809.

In a little cottage on the Staines Road, pulled down about 1866, lived and taught one who was in her day a very remarkable personage—Joanna Southcott, the prophetess. Here for some time her followers flocked to listen to her marvellous promises; and more than 50 years after her death (1814), Mr. Cobbett, in the course of his duties as curate of Twickenham, "found traces of attachment to her." †

Of Twickenham town there is little to be said. It is quiet, has an air of prosperity, and still lingering about it something of the savour of old-world gentility. Large old-fashioned houses, and low dark little shops, line the narrow streets, small private dwellings mingling with both; and there are occasional glimpses of the pleasant river. The ch. stands at the W. end of the town, by the river-side, and opposite to it is the large Twickenham eyot, the well-known Eel-pie Island. Church Street runs westward into the broader King Street, the chief street of the town, which at the farther end divides into the Teddington Road, running by the river, and the Heath Road turning inland. At the eastern extremity of Twickenham, as already mentioned, is the new district of villas, Cambridge and Twickenham Parks, with Ailsa Park running into St. Margaret's, Isleworth; while on the extreme W. is a corresponding, though less ambitious, new district growing up about Twickenham Common, Twickenham Heath, and Strawberry Vale. The numerous seats standing in grounds famous for the size, variety, and beauty of their trees, impart a distinctive and attractive character to the village and its vicinity, and the river all along here is beautiful. Inland the country is flat and tame. But though level, it has the reputation of being healthy and favourable to longevity. There are no manufactures proper. Nursery and fruit gardens are on an extensive scale.

Twickenham *Church* (of the Virgin

Mary) has a brick body and stone tower. The body of the old ch. fell down in the night of April 9, 1713. The present ch., erected (1713-18) in its place, Sir Godfrey Kneller being churchwarden and John James the architect, is a roomy red-brick structure, the style a so-called Tuscan, strangely out of keeping with the old battlemented Perp. tower on to which it was joined. The interior is as little interesting architecturally as the outside. What historic value it had as a church of the last years of Anne and the first of George, the ch. of Kneller and Walpole, of Kitty Clive and Lady Mary Wortley Montague, was destroyed by the transformation of the interior in 1859 and 1871, when the stately old galleries were lowered and re-arranged, the tall pews swept away, and "the whole area uniformly reseated with open benches;" the pulpit altered, the walls decorated, "a chorus cantorum in lieu of a chancel" constructed, the E. windows and the windows under the gallery darkened with modern mediæval glass, and the whole as far as possible brought into conformity with the current ecclesiastical fashion.

Probably the ch. has been improved for parochial purposes; but for the visitor the only interest the interior now possesses lies in its monuments, and those they commemorate. That which will first attract attention is one of marble on the E. wall, over the gallery, erected by Pope to his father (d. 1717, æt. 75) and mother (d. 1733, the insc. says æt. 93, but she was really only 90). On this, by his own direction, was added an insc. to himself:—

"As to my body, my will is, that it be buried near the monument of my dear parents at Twickenham, with the addition, after the words *filius fecit* —of these only, *et sibi : Qui obiit anno* 17—*aetatis* —[1744 æt. 57]—: and that it be carried to the grave by six of the poorest men of the parish, to each of whom I order a suit of grey coarse cloth as mourning." *

The insc. was accordingly added, but in 1761 Bp. Warburton erected another mont. with a medallion portrait of the poet on the N. wall, and placed on it, with more than questionable taste, Pope's somewhat incoherent lines. "For one who would not be buried in Wescminster Abbey."

"Heroes and kings your distance keep,
In peace let one poor poet sleep," etc.

---

* Forster, Life of Charles Dickens, vol. i., p. 157.
† Memorials of Twickenham, p. 345.

* Pope's Last Will (at end of Works).

When Sir Godfrey Kneller was buried in Twickenham ch. (1723), Lady Kneller claimed of Pope the fulfilment of a promise she asserted he had given to Sir Godfrey on his death-bed, to take down his father's monument, that she might erect one, 8 ft. wide and 14 ft. high, to her husband, "for it was the best place in the ch. to be seen at a distance"! "This," writes Pope, "surprised me quite. I hesitated, and said, I feared it would be indecent, and that my mother must be asked as well as I." She fell crying, and Pope was induced to say he would do all that he could do with decency. On consideration, Pope naturally refused to remove the monument. The Lady tried her influence with the parochial authorities— Kneller had been churchwarden of Twickenham—but they, of course, could not help her ; then commenced a suit against the poet, and failed ; and so Sir Godfrey lies in Twickenham ch. without any memorial. The mont. was erected in Westminster Abbey, and Pope wrote the epitaph for it.

Pope was buried in a vault in the middle aisle, "under the second pew from the E. end." Mr. Howett [*] states that during some repairs of the ch. the vault was opened, and Pope's head abstracted from his coffin, to enrich the museum of a phrenologist named Holm. But this is positively denied by Mr. Cobbett on the authority of the then Vicar of Tottenham. The coffin having been broken during the repairs, "a cast of the skull was taken," but nothing was abstracted. The skull was reverently restored to its place, and Mr. Fletcher, the curate, who watched the whole of the proceedings, remained "until the whole was restored and built up." [*] Whether it should have been disturbed at all may admit of question ; but removing the skull to take a cast from it, and at once restoring it to its place, and abstracting it altogether, are very different things.

In the chancel is a mural mont., with effigies in terra-cotta, coloured, of Francis Poulton, d. 1642, and wife. The urn, of veined marble, to Lady Frances Whitmore, d. 1692, with, on the pedestal, the fine lines by Dryden, commencing,

"Fair, kind and true ! a treasure each alone,
A wife, a mistress, and a friend in one,"

which formerly stood in the chancel, was, at the transformation of the interior, removed to the top landing of the N. staircase.

On E. wall of the S. gallery, corresponding in place to Pope's mont. to his parents, is a tomb, with long insc. in prose and verse, to John Lord Berkeley of Stratton (d. 1678), the hero of Stratton Fight, and "sprung from Danish kings of brightest fame," who has already been mentioned as owner of Twickenham Park. Mont. to Sir Joseph Ashe, Bart., d. 1682. On S. wall, over the gallery, mural mont. to Nathaniel Pigott, Barrister at Law, d. 1737. He was a Roman Catholic, and Pope wrote the epitaph, in which he states that "possessed of the highest character by his learning, judgment, experience, integrity," he was "deprived of the highest stations only by his conscience and religion." On same wall one to Sir Richard Perryn, d. 1803, for 23 years one of the Barons of the Exchequer. Mural, by Bacon, to George Gostling, Esq., d. 1799. Admiral Sir Chaloner Ogle, Commander of the Fleet, d. 1750. Under the mont. to Pope and his parents is a slab to Richard Owen Cambridge, d. 1802. S. aisle, tablet to Lætitia Matilda Hawkins, d. 1835. N. aisle, large slab to Louisa Viscountess Clifden, d. 1802, and her daughter, the Hon. Caroline Anne Agar Ellis, d. 1814. Tablet by Westmacott to Lady Margaret Wildman, d. 1825.

On the outer wall are tablets to Pope's nurse and to Kitty Clive. The first was erected by the poet.

"To the Memory of Mary Beach, who died Nov. 25, 1725, aged 78. Alex. Pope, whom she nursed in his infancy, and constantly attended for twenty-eight years, in gratitude to a faithful old servant erected this stone."

The mont. to Mrs. Catherine Clive (d. 1758, æt. 75) was erected by Miss Pope, the actress, and has a long poetical insc. by her :—

"Clive's blameless life this tablet shall proclaim,
Her moral virtues and her well-earn'd fame."

The ch.-yard abounds in tombs, including those of Selina Countess Dowager Ferrers, d. 1762 ; Lieut.-Gen. William Tryon, Governor of the Province of New York, d. 1788, and other persons of note in their day, but forgotten now. Admiral

---

* Homes and Haunts of the Poets, p. 115.
† Cobbett, Memorials of Twickenham, p. 279.

Byron (d. 1786), whose 'Narrative of the Loss of the Wager' is so well known, was buried here, but has no mont. Charles Morton, M.D., F.R.S., Principal Librarian of the British Museum, and Edward Ironside, the historian of Twickenham, d. 1813, lie in the new burial-ground.

There are two other churches in Twickenham, and one at Whitton. The district ch. of Holy Trinity, on the Green, is an early Dec. building of white brick and stone, erected by Mr. Basevi 1839-41, but enlarged under the direction of Mr. Dolman in 1863, by the addition of transepts and an apsidal chancel. In the ch. are several memorial windows, and tablets to the memory of Sir Wm. Clay, M.P., and Lady Clay, late of Fulwell Lodge, on the Hanworth road.

St. Stephen, Cambridge Park, is a good ch. of Kentish rag and Bath stone, the body E.E. with a large Dec. W. window. The first stone was laid Sept. 28, 1874, by the Duchess of Teck, the Patriarch of Antioch and the Bp. of Jerusalem being present at the ceremony. It was consecrated Dec. 1, 1875; but the chancel and spire remain to be added at a future day.

Among the institutions may be noticed the *Almshouses of the Carpenters' Company*, on the Hampton road, a neat and cheerful looking range of 10 dwellings with a large garden in front. The *Metropolitan and City of London Police Orphanage* is an excellent and well-managed school, supported almost wholly by the members of the force. The buildings can accommodate about 200; at present about 150 orphans are maintained.

The large islet opposite Twickenham ch. is *Twickenham Eyot*, but is best known as *Eel Pie Island*. The islet, 530 yards long and about 2 acres in area, has from time immemorial been a favourite resort of Thames anglers, boat parties, and excursionists, for whose accommodation a little inn was early established on the eyot, and in time acquired celebrity for the dainties which have given the place its vernacular title. The old *Eel Pie House*, a very unassuming but popular little barn, was pulled down in 1830, and the present *Eel Pie Tavern* erected. It is a much better house, and much in favour with anglers and boating men: but Eel Pie Island seems to have lost its old power of attraction for excursionists.

The river from Twickenham Eyot to the W. end of the lawn of Pope's villa, 410 yards, forms the *Twickenham Deep*, and is strictly preserved under the superintendence of the Thames Angling Preservation Society. It is a popular deep, affords excellent fishing, and belonging to it are half a dozen regular fishermen, who may be heard of at the King's Head and George Inns, or the Eel Pie Tavern.

The row of modern villas higher up the river, by Little Strawberry Hill, marks the western extremity of Twickenham. The farthest house is a landmark familiar to boating men as the *Bachelors*.

TWYFORD, or WEST TWYFORD, MIDDX. (Dom. *Tveverde*) is situated upon the river Brent and the Paddington Canal, 2 m. W. of Willesden Junction Stat. of the L. and N.-W. and the N. London Rlys., 1¾ m. N. by E. of the Ealing Stat. of the Gt. W. Rly. The country is level, but Twyford is charmingly placed among green lanes and broad meadows on the winding Brent, is in some respects unique among the parishes around London, and is well worth visiting. There is a pleasant walk from Acton or Ealing to the *Fox and Goose*, Hanger Hill (opposite which, notice, growing in the roadway, a large wild pear tree, a mass of blossom every spring). Rt. of the inn, the entrance by a lodge, the avenue which leads to Twyford ch. and Abbey.

The name indicates the existence of two fords over the Brent, here a very tortuous stream. The prefix *West* was adopted to distinguish it from the hamlet of East Twyford in Willesden par. It is frequently called *Twyford Abbey* (and is so written in the census returns) from the manor-house which is so named. Twyford is a secluded and till recently was a solitary and curiously unprogressive place. Of old it was an extra-parochial chapelry, but has long been deemed a parish. In 1251 the parish, of 275 acres, contained 12 houses. In the reign of Elizabeth the only house was the manor-house. This continued to be the case till "Thos. Willan, Esq., of Marybone Park," purchased the manor, in 1806, and shortly after pulled down the manor-house, then occupied as a farm, and built the present

Abbey and a farm-house at a little distance. At the census of 1861 there were only 2 houses and 18 inhab.—the smallest population of any parish around London. In 1871, however, the number of houses had increased to 8, and the pop. to 47—considerably outnumbering, therefore, the adjoining par. of Perivale, which had only 7 houses and 33 inhabitants.

Twyford Abbey is commonly said to occupy the site of an ancient abbey, but there is no record of any religious establishment having existed here. Still, as the manor was held under the canons of St. Paul's, and there was from very early times a chapel, with, in 1251, two altars outside the choir, it is possible there may have been a cell, or house, for the priests who served at the altars.

The old manor-house was moated. The present manor-house, *Twyford Abbey*—the property of Douglas Willan, Esq., but now unoccupied and undergoing repairs—was built about 1808, from the designs of Mr. Atkinson. It is a " castellated mansion," the principal front having the centre advanced and octagonal turrets at the extremities. It stands in wooded grounds of about 15 acres, through which winds the Brent. Before the house sweeps an ample lawn, and by it are lordly elms and grand old cedars.

Twyford *Church* stands immediately W. of the house, the ch.-yard and grounds running deviously into each other, only the few old and mossy gravestones marking the consecrated ground—all seeming a part of the manorial establishment. This, of course, the ch. was so long as

Twyford Abbey was the only house and the lord of the manor was resident ; and even now it is so in a measure. There is no incumbent, and when the Abbey was to let recently, it was stipulated that the tenant should be a member of the Church of England, and " provide a clergyman for at least six Sundays in the year." Service is not actually so limited, however. In 1875 it was announced that there would be every Sunday " In summer, Service at 3 o'clock, except the First Sunday, when it will be at 11 in the morning."

The church is a small brick barn, which was Gothicized nearly half a century ago by the addition of a porch, crocketed pinnacles, and a covering of stucco. It was hideous, but happily a luxuriant growth of ivy has spread over it, and made the little pile almost beautiful. The int. has been recently refurbished. *Obs.* mural monts. of Robert Moyle, of the Inner Temple, Prothonotary of the Common Pleas, d. 1638 (bust in black cap and gown) ; Walter Moyle, d. 1660 (bust) ; tablet to Henry Bold, author of ' Virgil Travestie,' and other poems, d. 1683 ; Fabian, son of Fabian Philipps, d. 1658. Fabian Philipps, the father, d. 1690, was buried at Twyford, but there is no memorial of him. An ardent and fearless loyalist, two days before the execution of Charles I., he wrote, printed, and actively circulated a protest against the execution ; and in 1660 defended the King's memory in ' Veritas Inconcussa' (a most certain truth), asserting that King Charles I. was no Man of Blood, but a Martyr for his People.

UPMINSTER, Essex, 3¾ m. E.S.E. from Romford Rly. Stat., through Hornchurch ; a secluded agricultural vill., lying E. of the Ingrebourn brook, in a green upland country, from many parts of which there are wide prospects. Pop. 1329.

Until the Dissolution the manor belonged to the monks of Waltham, and *Upminster Hall*, 1 m. N. of the ch., was their hunting seat. Part of the old half-timber house remains, but the greater part is modern. The *Church*, St. Lawrence, which stands by the crossing of

the Hornchurch and Aveley roads (or, as they say in these parts, by the four-wont way), was rebuilt in 1861-62, and is a commonplace Dec. building, comprising nave, S. aisle and porch, chancel, and W. tower, in which are 3 bells. Inside are some monts., rescued from the old ch., of persons who have held property in the par., and among them one to Geerard D'Ewes, raised by his grandson, Sir Simonds D'Ewes, the noted antiquary. Also a brass to Nicholas Wayte, citizen and mercer, d. 1545, and wife Ellen. But there is no memorial to the most distinguished resident at Upminster, William Derham, who was rector from 1689 to his death, April 5, 1735. Dr. Derham lived at *High House*, there wrote his two great works, the 'Physico-Theology,' and 'Astro-Theology,' and there carried out the experiments by which he determined the velocity of sound, as related in his paper 'On Experiments and Observations on the Motion of Sound.' * There also he made his notes 'On the Spots of the Sun from 1703 to 1711,' and prepared his valuable 'Tables of the Eclipses of Jupiter's Satellites from 1700 to 1727' (the 6th and 7th satellites were discovered by him), 'Meteorological Tables,' 'Notes on the Migrations of Birds,' etc. His astronomical observations were chiefly made from Upminster ch. tower.

The scenery is rural and pleasing; there are several good seats in grounds famous for their trees, especially cedars, of which there are several magnificent examples. *Great Gaines* (H. Joslin, Esq.) stands in a pretty little park, ½ m. S. of the ch. *Gaines* was for many years the residence of the Rev. John Clayton ("old John Clayton," of the Weighhouse Chapel), and afterwards of his son, the Rev. George Clayton, of Walworth, in their day popular ministers of the Independent Connection.† *Clock House*, ¼ m. E. of the ch. (J. Cory Havers, Esq.) ; *Oak Place* (John Rogers, Esq.)

Beyond Great Gaines, 1 m. S. of the ch., is the little rustic hamlet of *Corbet's Tey*, a hamlet of a dozen cottages, two or three farm-houses, a wheeler's and smithy, and a country inn, the Huntsman and Hounds.

UPTON (in official documents UPTON-CUM-CHALVEY), Bucks,

lies to the E. of the Slough and Windsor road, 1 m. S.E. of the Slough Stat. of the Gt. W. Rly. Pop. of the par. 5940, but this includes the town of Slough and portions of the hamlet of Salt Hill and the eccl. dist. of Gerrard's Cross, 173 inmates of the British Orphan Asylum, and 240 of the union workhouse.

Upton adjoins Slough on the E., the whole of Slough being within this extensive par. The country is verdant and sylvan, gently upland and slightly undulating. From its quiet semi-rural character and proximity to Eton and Windsor, Upton is a favourite place of residence. Numerous moderate-sized houses have been built, and Upton Park enclosed, and laid out as a select colony of villas. (*See* SLOUGH.)

The *Church* (St. Lawrence), a small Norm. building, injured by ruthless hands, winter, and foul weather, but still picturesque, and venerable for its antiquity —the "ivy-mantled tower" of Gray's Elegy, as commonly asserted, though that, as we have shown, is a mistake (*see* STOKE POGES)—was abandoned on the erection of the ch. at Slough in 1837, and suffered to go to ruin. But when the increase of the population rendered a second ch. necessary, it was suggested that the old ch. might be restored, and in 1851 this was accomplished under the direction of Mr. B. Ferrey, F.S.A. The old ch. consisted of a nave and chancel with a tower between them. In restoring the ch. the tower was lowered and a new aisle added. At the W. end is a good Norm. doorway with chevron moulding. The tower arches between the nave and chancel are Norm., and the chancel has a plain groined roof, reconstructed when the ch. was restored, but on the old lines. Between the nave and aisle is an arcade, the piers and arches of which are Norm., of course new, but an imitation of the old work. Some of the old Norm. and E.E. windows have been preserved. In the old ch. the chancel and tower were separated from the nave by three nearly unique E.E. arches of wood, with the dog-tooth moulding. These have been removed, without disturbing their arrangement, to the E. end of the aisle. Some of the windows have painted glass. The font is plain Norm. Against one of the tower piers is a tablet with long Latin insc. to Sir Wm. Herschel, d. Aug. 25, 1822, and buried here. In the chancel are *brasses* to the Bulstrode family : *obs.* Edward Bulstrode, Esquyer for the body to King Henry VII. and King Henry VIII., d. 1517, and Mary, Elyn, and Margaret his wyfs ; effigy in plate armour with skirt of mail, one wife on rt., two on l., 12 children below the insc. Edward Bulstrode, d. 1595, and wife Cecill; effigies of knight in plate armour, wife with

---

* Philosophical Transactions, No. 313.
† Aveling, Memorials of the Clayton Family.

winged head-dress, quilted ruff and plaited stomacher.

Near the ch. is *Upton Court*, the property of the Earl of Harewood, the old manor-house, now the manor farm. The walks along byroads and field-paths to Stoke on the one hand, and Eton, Black Potts, and Datchet on the other, are very pleasant.

The hamlet of *Chalvey* is about 1 m. from Upton, on the W. of the Windsor road. Chalvey Green and Chalvey Grove are outlying portions, the whole a bright semi-rural district. A Gothic ch., small but good, was erected at Chalvey, as a chapel-of-ease to Upton, in 1861, from the designs of Mr. G. E. Street, R.A.

UPTON, ESSEX (*see* WEST HAM).

UXBRIDGE, MIDDX., an "ancient borough" and market-town, on the Oxford road, 15 m. from London, about 1 m. N.W. of Hillingdon (in which par. it is situated), and the terminus of the Uxbridge br. of the Gt. W. Rly. Pop. of the township 3364. Inns: *Chequers* Hotel; *George*, commercial; *King's Arms*, etc.

The town is washed by two branches of the Colne, the Colne proper at the extreme W., and an arm of it which crosses the High Street some way to the E. The name points to a very early bridge, instead of a ford, as was then more usual, over the river here. The oldest known form of the name (about 1100) is *Wxebruge* or *Oxbruge;* the borough of *Woxebrigge*, *Woxebrygge*, is spoken of in 1328 and 1335; *Woxbruge*, in 1354; and *Woxebrugge*, alias *Uxbridge*, in 1397,* from which time the modern form has been commonly employed. Though from an early period the borough (later the town) of Uxbridge was separated from the rest of Hillingdon par. by well-defined boundaries, "encompassed by a borough ditch," and was governed by officers of its own election, it remained a hamlet or chapelry of Hillingdon, and the ch. was only a chapel-of-ease to the mother ch., till 1842, when it was created an eccl. district and the living a vicarage.

Uxbridge, like too many other towns, witnessed the burning of heretics in the reign of Mary. Several persons were prosecuted, three or four were burned, the place of execution being Lynch Green, by the Windsor road. The accused were examined by Bp. Bonner at his London house, but remitted to Uxbridge to undergo their sentence. John Denley, of Maidstone, Kent, and Robert Smith, a clerk in the college at Windsor, given to poetry and painting, were burnt on the 8th of August, 1555; Pathrick Packingham on the 28th. It was at the burning of Denley that Dr. Storey, to " mar an old song,"—the hymn which the martyr was singing at the stake,—hurled a faggot which struck him in the face, an act Storey, in a speech in the debate on the Supremacy Bill, Feb. 14, 1559, admitted and gloried in: " I threw a faggot in the face of an earwig at the stake at Uxbridge, and set a bushel of thorns at his feet, and see nothing to be ashamed of or sorry for " ! *

The Commissioners of Charles I. and the Parliament appointed to negotiate a Treaty for Peace, met at Uxbridge at the end of January 1654. Sixteen commissioners were named on each side, who were to confer together and endeavour to arrive at an agreement on the subject of Religion (or the Church), the Militia, and Ireland, " which three points being well settled, the other differences would be with more ease composed." The discussion was strictly limited to 20 days. Uxbridge was in the hands of the Parliament, and the arrangements for the meeting were necessarily left to their agents. They were, says Clarendon, who was one of the King's Commissioners, and has left the best account of the Treaty, " very civil in the distribution [of lodgings], and left one entire side of the town to the King's Commissioners, one house only excepted, which was given to the Earl of Pembroke."

"There was a good house at the end of the town, which was provided for the treaty, where was a fair room in the middle of the house, handsomely dressed up for the commissioners to sit in ; a large square table being placed in the middle with seats for the commissioners, one side being sufficient for those of either party ; and a rail for others

---

* Redford and Riches, Hist. of the Ancient Town and Borough of Uxbridge, p. 5 ; Lysons, vol. iii., p. 175.

* Strype's Annals, part i., p. 115, quoted by Froude, Hist. of England, vol. vii., p. 53 ; Foxe, Acts and Monuments.

who should be thought necessary to be present, which went round. There were many other rooms on either side of this great room, for the commissioners on either side to retire to, when they thought fit to consult by themselves, and to return again to the public debate; and there being good stairs at either end of the house, they never went through each other's quarters; nor met, but in the great room."*

The King's Commissioners lodged at the Crown, those of the Parliament at the George, " being two great inns which served very well to that purpose." Each party " eat always together ; " and at first frequent visits were paid from one side to the other among " old friends, whom they loved better than their new," though they had taken opposite sides, both parties " professing great desire and hope that the treaty would produce a good peace." But this hope grew fainter as the debate went on, and when the 20 days expired, the Commissioners separated at their last conference, a little before break of day, without agreement on a single point. On the next morning they " performed their mutual visits," parting from this formal leave-taking "with such coolness towards each other as if they scarce hoped to meet again."

The " fair-house " at which the conference was held had been a seat of the Bennets, " lately of Sir John Bennet," (ancestor of the Earls of Tankerville,) but then of Mr. Carr. It became the property of Wentworth Gurneys in 1689 ; in 1724 passed to C. Gostlin, having shortly before been the residence of Sir Christopher Abdy, as it was afterwards for many years of Dr. Thorold. Its fortunes now declined. It was partitioned and let out in tenements; divided, part pulled down, and part converted into an inn, and the highroad was diverted through the midst of the large garden in which it originally stood.

The house, long known as the *Treaty House,* or so much as remains of it, will be found on the l. of the road at the western extremity of the town, between the bridges over the river and the canal. It is still partly let in tenements, the rest forms the Crown and Treaty House inn.

A good late Elizabethan or Jacobean brick mansion with bays and gables, it has been much mutilated and covered with

* Clarendon, Hist. of the Rebellion, b. viii., Oxf. ed., 1720, vol. ii., p. 577.

stucco, and the exterior presents a very different aspect to what it did when the Commissioners met within, and the townsfolk gathered outside wondering what were the mysterious proceedings going on there day after day. Inside, however, somewhat more is retained of the original. The great room, where the Commissioners sat about the large square table, remains tolerably perfect, with its old and nearly black carved oak panelling. An adjoining room, known as the Presence Chamber, has still more elaborately carved old oak wainscoting, with quaint pilasters, cornices, and fireplace. Another room used to be called King Charles's Bedroom—from a long-cherished tradition that Charles (who was all the time at Oxford) slept in the one, and signed the treaty (which was never executed) in the other.* The lodge shown in the old engravings of the Treaty House was pulled down many years ago.

The Crown and George inns, in which the Commissioners lodged, were near the market-house, and nearly opposite each other. The Crown, the Royal Commissioners' inn, ceased to be an inn and was partly pulled down many years ago, the part left being converted into private houses. The George has at various times been reduced in size, the outer staircase in the great yard removed, and the front refaced and covered with stucco : but it still remains an inn, and retains something of its antique appearance. The interior has been even more altered than the outside. The Commissioners' sitting-room is still shown, but is sadly changed. Perhaps from the Commissioners having first held their religious services in it, the room was long used as a dissenting place of worship; afterwards for meetings of the County Court ; but for at least half a century its local celebrity has been due to the " harmonic meetings" of the Uxbridge Harmonic Society being held in it. The oak panelling was stripped from the walls several years back.

Leland writing in the reign of Henry VIII. says that Uxbridge has " but one

* In the Gentleman's Magazine for Aug. 1789, p. 685, is an article on the subject, with an engraving of 'The House in which Charles 1st signed the Treaty of Uxbridge,' and we have seen a like statement in later publications : with such authority in print, the innkeepers may be forgiven if they adhere to the tradition of their predecessors.

long street, but that, for timber, well builded;" and broadly this might be said of it now. It consists of a long main street, but has a few very short streets running from it, and a thickly populated suburb, St. John's. The main street is wide, clean, and lined with good dwelling houses and shops, some of the former large with good trees and gardens; and many of the latter handsome and well stocked. But all looks modern: a few old houses remain, but they have been altered and modernized, though one or two are said to retain the old oak panelling inside. Near the centre of the High Street, on the l., is the Market House, with the Corn Exchange over it, and behind it the ch. Inns still appear redundant, but there were thrice as many when the population was much smaller. Of old there were 53, now there are under 20 in the town proper. The town has a large local trade, but no manufacture properly so called. On the Colne are several corn mills, some of considerable size; on the Grand Junction Canal are timber, coal, and slate wharves, and saw and planing mills; and there are several breweries, and an iron foundry.

In 1294 Henry de Lacy, Earl of Lincoln, procured for Uxbridge the grant of a weekly market and an annual fair. A market for corn is now held in the Corn Exchange, and for cattle in the yard of the Chequers hotel, every Thursday, and a general market on Saturdays. Fairs are held on March 25 and July 31; a wool fair August 1, and statute fairs September 29 and October 11. Two newspapers are published weekly.

The *Church* (St. Margaret) occupies an out-of-the-way position behind the Market House, and is not remarkable for beauty or antiquity. Newcourt says it was built in 1447, and it has been frequently altered. It is a late Perp. fabric of flint and stone, and consists of nave and double N. aisle, short chancel, and tower at the N. W., in which is a peal of 6 bells. The doorway and windows are poor in character, but were somewhat improved when the ch. was repaired a few years back. The int. is of little interest; the aisle arcades have octagonal piers; the roofs are ceiled; the E. window has memorial painted glass. *Obs.* the original Perp. font, octagonal with quatrefoils and Tudor roses. *Mont.*

by chancel, with recumbent effigy, pediment with arms, etc., supported on Tuscan columns, at the base the window of a charnel-house, of Dame Leonora Bennet, d. 1638, daughter of Adrian Vierendeels of Antwerp, and wife of Sir John Bennet (he was her third husband), Judge of the Prerogative Court and Chancellor to Anne of Denmark, Queen of James I. In connection with the ch. of St. Margaret, a guild or fraternity, consisting of a warden, brethren, and sisters, was founded by Robert Oliver and others in 1447, in honour of the Virgin Mary and St. Margaret; and a few years later a chantry by Sir Wm. Shiryngton, Chancellor of the Duchy of Lancaster, which was endowed by his executors in 1459. Sir Wm. C. Ross, R.A., the eminent miniature painter, was born in a house by the ch., 1794.

The *Market House* is a large plain brick building, erected in 1788, 140 ft. long, the lower part open, the upper part being supported on 51 wooden columns. The roof was removed in 1860, a trussed lantern substituted, side windows inserted, and a Corn Exchange formed over the Market House—a spacious room 109 ft. by 25; archt., Mr. Shoppee. There are besides Public Rooms where the County Courts and Sessions are held, lecture halls, banks, etc.; but Uxbridge has as yet no public buildings noteworthy for their architectural character.

At Uxbridge Moor is the dist. ch. of St. John, a plain brick barn. Just beyond the W. end of the town is the large and handsome ch. of St. Andrew, designed by Sir G. G. Scott, 1864; but that is a dist. ch. of Hillingdon. (*See* HILLINGDON.) On this side of Uxbridge, along the Colne, by Chiltern, and about Uxbridge Common, the scenery is very pleasing, and the Colne affords good fishing. The mill on the rt. beyond the Treaty House and bridge, with the trees, rustic inn, broad water, and little island, has a quiet charm which even the showy brick dwelling, almost a mansion, recently erected, has not materially injured.

The Manor of Uxbridge was originally a part of the manor of Colham in Hillingdon; but was in 1669 separated from it. In 1695 the manor, with the tolls of the market, was sold by its then owner, George Pitt, Esq., to certain inhabitants of Uxbridge, the survivors of whom in

1729 conveyed to trustees, inhabitants and housekeepers in the town, "all that manor and burrough of Woxbridge alias Uxbridge," with all their rights, privileges, and property, to appropriate the proceeds to charitable purposes, "for the benefit and advantage of the town of Uxbridge only." These trustees, at present 7 in number, are styled "Lords in Trust of the Manor and Borough."

VALENTINES, Essex (see ILFORD, GREAT).

VERULAM, Herts (see ST. ALBANS).

VIRGINIA WATER occupies the north-western corner of SURREY, the upper part of the lake and grounds extending into BERKSHIRE; is nearly 5 m. S. of Windsor Castle, and 1½ m. W. of the Virginia Water Stat. of the L. and S.-W. Rly. (Staines and Reading br. 23 m.; Chertsey and Virginia Water br. 24¾ m.) Virginia Water is royal property, and enclosed, but visitors are admitted by the lodges; from the rly. stat. admission may be obtained through the pleasant grounds of the Wheatsheaf Hotel—a well-managed house, noted for luncheons and dinners, and for beds.

Virginia Water is the creation of William Duke of Cumberland, the hero of Culloden, who, having been appointed ranger of Windsor Great Park, came in 1746 to reside in what is now known as Cumberland Lodge. Lying at the southern end of the Great Park was this tract, then a marshy waste in Windsor Forest, through which a lazy streamlet made its way towards the Thames at Chertsey. This the Duke, partly for amusement, partly to furnish employment for labourers of the district, resolved to drain and plant. Paul Sandby, the water-colour painter, was the Duke's adviser in all such matters, and he designed the great landscape features of Virginia Water: the name was a forecast of the forest wilds, the broad waters, and tranquil solitudes that were to be called forth by the waving of the magician's wand.

, Sandby drained the swamp, enlarged and deepened the natural basin, threw a dam across the lower end, and diverted into it the lesser streamlets of the district. To give the utmost apparent extent to the *Great Lake*, the grand feature of his design, Sandby varied the outline and planted the borders, so that the boundaries might nowhere reveal themselves. It is said to be one of the largest artificial lakes in England, and till the formation of the Kingsbury Reservoir was by far the largest lake near London—as it is still the most beautiful. It is about 1¼ m. long, and one-third of a mile across where widest.

The dam gave way in 1768, and much injury was done by the consequent flooding of the lower lands. It was, however, rebuilt in a more substantial manner, and Sandby then constructed the *Waterfall*, thus adding an attractive feature to the landscape, and a tolerably efficient means of carrying off the surplus water. The Waterfall has been laughed at as a toy and plaything; but, though it cannot be compared with the natural waterfalls of Wales or Cumberland, now that the growth of a century has covered the artificial angles of the stones with thick layers of moss, and ferns, and plants have sprung up from every crevice, he must be captious who does not see beauty as the summer rill sparkles over it in the bright sunshine, or when a full turbid stream pours down in the late autumn.

The *Cavern*, immediately S. of the Waterfall, was constructed of great sarsen stones, dug up at Bagshot Heath, vestiges of some supposed Druidic structure.

The Duke of Cumberland formed some other elaborate toys, the Chinese Island and Pavilion, Belvedere Fort (a fort of Uncle Toby's order, but affording a capital outlook), and some fantastic lodges; but the costlier follies of the Fishing Temple, the Ruined Temple, etc., were added by George IV., who during the last years of his life, whilst living in seclusion in the Royal Lodge, spent much of his time here. The miniature frigate was placed on the lake by William IV. Her Majesty has recently rebuilt the fishing temple in a less grotesque style, and placed on the lake (Nov. 1875) a handsome state barge, built for the purpose by Burgoines of Kingston.

The *Ruins*, a short distance N. of the Waterfall, though put in a moist and sheltered dell, where a recluse might have fixed his hermitage, but where a Greek would certainly not have placed a temple, are really antique columns, capitals, entablatures, etc., with some fragments of sculpture, vestiges of several temples, and of quite incongruous orders, brought from Greece and the neighbourhood of Tunis. For a long time they had lain unregarded in the courtyard of the British Museum, when George IV., fancying that a ruined temple would grace his grounds, had them removed and set up where they now stand—a bridge which carries the Blackness and Windsor road, cutting the temple in twain. *Obs.* when here the stately beech and unusually fine firs, which group often very happily with one or other of the architectural fragments. From the height above the ruins, and from Belvedere Fort, a splendid view is obtained of Windsor Castle.

Virginia Water is a delightful place for a summer holiday. The embellishments may be too evidently artificial and in questionable taste, but the effect of a century of growth has been to change formal plantations into woods of noble trees, which make endless rich landscapes with the different reaches of the lake; the lawns are of the smoothest turf and finest green; there is ample shade; still lakes and falling water gratify alike the senses of seeing and hearing; while broad prospects are within easy reach; and charming strolls abound on every hand, outside as well as within the royal grounds.

When in England in 1873 the Shah of Persia was taken to see Virginia Water, and his account of it is interesting as showing the impression produced on the oriental mind by a favourite English landscape:—

"The avenues, the lawns, the trees (of Windsor Great Park) were interminable. We drove two leagues, and passed along another avenue resembling paradise, both sides of the avenue being a mass of tall trees (or shrubs), all in bloom with large light-blue, red, and other coloured flowers, of the oleander family (rhododendrons). So charming was this, that nothing superior can be imagined. We came to a lake of water of some extent, around which were multitudes of women and maidens. We crossed the lake to a small palace, very pretty, the property of the Sovereign. There we alighted and partook of some fruit. All our princes and suite came there also, and then went off to the station. We got into a boat and went about. On the other side of the water there was a crowd of women and men. After remaining on the water a little while, we went to a small model of a man-of-war, that has been constructed and armed with twenty-four guns about the size of swivels. We went on board, saw all over her, returned to our boat, and in her to the palace, where we again got into our carriage and drove to Windsor by a different road that was still all avenues, lawns, and numerous antelopes." [*]

At the S.W. extremity of the lake, just outside the lodge, is the pretty little hamlet of *Blackness*. The large and costly Gothic building seen near the Virginia Water Station is the Sanatorium, for persons of the middle class suffering from mental disease. It was erected 1874–76, at the sole cost of Thomas Holloway, Esq., from the designs of Mr. Crossland, and is a noble structure, its lofty and elaborate tower forming a striking feature for miles. The neat Gothic district ch., Christ Church, Virginia Water, was built in 1838, from the designs of Mr. W. F. Pocock, and endowed by Miss Irvine of Luddington House.

WADDON, Surrey (*see* Croydon.)

WALHAM GREEN, Middx., an eccl. dist. in Fulham parish; pop. 6174; on the Fulham road, 1½ m. N. of Fulham church. The Chelsea Stat. of the W. Lond. Junction Rly., which is in connection with most of the metropolitan lines, is at Walham Green, just off the main road, on the E.

Walham Green takes its name from the manor, which appears successively in

---

[*] Diary of the Shah of Persia during his Tour through Europe in 1873 (trans. by J. W. Redhouse), p. 150.

early court-rolls as Wendon Green, (1449) Wandon, Wansdon, Wansdowne, (1595) Wandham, and in 1693 for the first time as Walham Green, but is still occasionally written "Wansdon or Walham Green." The village, if it can be called a village, lies along the Fulham Road, and about the triangular space which was once the village green. Virtually it is now an outskirt of the metropolis, and has nothing distinctive in its appearance. Once, however, it was noted for its old houses, but of these only two or three dilapidated specimens remain ; and as late as 1749 a local bard (and nursery-man), Mr. B. Rocque, thus sang its charms :

" Hail, happy isle, and happier Walham Green,
   Where all that's fair and beautiful are seen !
   Where wanton zephyrs court the ambient air,
   And sweets ambrosial banish every care," etc.*

Walham Green *Church* (St. John's) occupies the site of the old village pond, in the centre of the green (its memory is still preserved by Pond Lane, on the W. of the ch.) It is an unassuming white-brick Gothic building of the year 1828, erected by Mr. Taylor at a cost of £10,000. At the W. end is a tall tower, with pinnacles at the angles. Here, too, is the extensive Swan Brewery of Messrs. Stansfeld, and by it the Swan Inn. Immediately beyond Walham Green, on the l. of the road, going to Fulham, is *Ravensworth House*, the seat of the Earl of Ravensworth. (*See* FULHAM.) *Beaufort House*, North End Road, is the headquarters of the South Middlesex Volunteers, and the meeting-place for exercise and races of the Athletic Club.

WALLINGTON, SURREY (Dom.

Waleton), a hamlet of Beddington, created an eccl. dist. in 1867, lies between Beddington and Carshalton, 2½ m. W. of Croydon, and a stat. on the Croydon, Epsom, and Dorking br. of the L., B., and S. C. Rly. Pop. of the hamlet 1335, of the eccl. dist. 842.

Though never of much importance, Wallington is a place of great antiquity, and gives its name to the hundred. At Woodcote extensive Roman remains have been found, whence Camden was led to place here the station *Noviomagus*, now

assigned to Keston. (*See* KESTON.) At the Dom. Survey the manor belonged to the King. By Henry II. it was granted to Maurice de Creon, whose daughter carried it to Guy de la Val, by whom it was forfeited to the Crown. King John gave it to Eustace de Courtenay ; it next passed to the Lyndes and Lodelawes, and in 1394 to Sir John Dymock. It was sold, 1593, by Sir Edward Dymock, to James Harrington, who transferred it, 1596, to Sir Francis Carew of Beddington. Towards the close of the 17th cent. it was purchased by Wm. Bridges, Esq., Surveyor-General of the Ordnance, and is now held by Nathaniel Bridges, Esq.

Wallington stretches from the chalk hills by the rly. stat. across the Epsom road to the Wandle. This is a great herb district, and at Wallington large quantities of lavender and fragrant herbs are grown. On the Wandle are paper and leather mills, and a tannery ; about Hackbridge (where is a second rly. stat.) are other factories. Of late many villa and cottage residences have been built. Holy Trinity district ch. is a neat E.E. building, erected in 1867 at the cost of N. Bridges, Esq.

WALTHAM ABBEY, or WALTHAM HOLY CROSS, ESSEX, a market

town, and the seat of the Royal Gunpowder Factory, on the river Lea, 12 m. N. by E. from Shoreditch ch., and ¾ m. E. of the Waltham Stat. of the Grt. E. Rly. (Cambridge line). The par., which has an area of 11,670 acres, is divided into 4 wards—Township, Holyfield, Sewardstone, and Upshire. The pop. in 1871 was 5197, but this included 535 in the eccl. dist. of High Beech. Inns: *King's Arms ; Cock ; New Inn.*

The Lea flows through the town in several channels ; for the river here "not only parteth Hertfordshire from Essex, but also seven times parteth from itself, whose septemfluous stream, in coming to the town, is crossed again with so many bridges." * The town lies low and looks damp ; the streets are narrow and crooked ; the houses mostly small, commonplace, and many very poor. But the church is one of the oldest in the kingdom, and one of the most interesting,

* London Magazine, June 1749.

* Thos. Fuller, Hist. of Waltham Abbey, B. i.

the scenery around is varied and pleasing, and Waltham itself has many historical and personal associations.

Waltham (the *weald*, or forest *ham*, or home) dates its origin from Tovi, or Tofig, the Proud, a powerful Danish thane, the royal standard bearer, at whose wedding feast Hardicnut died. Here Tovi built himself a hunting seat, " the place having plenty of deer," and he being a mighty hunter. It was on the edge of the great Forest of Essex, afterwards to be known as the Forest of Waltham. As late as the middle of the 17th cent., Thomas Fuller, who lived here many years, wrote : " On the one side the town itself hath large and fruitful meadows . . . . on the other side a spacious forest spreads itself, where fourteen years since (1640) one might have seen whole herds of red and fallow deer." Epping Forest, the diminished vestige of Waltham Forest, has receded farther from the town, but what is left of it crowns the heights on the east.

A wondrous cross was found in Tovi's land at Lutegarsbury, in Somersetshire, on the top of the peaked hill from which the place came to be afterwards called Montacute (*Mons acutus*). The cross was laid in a cart to be carried to Glastonbury, but the oxen refused to stir. Canterbury was named, but the oxen were still obstinate. At last Tovi bethought him of Waltham, and the oxen went cheerfully on their way. So Tovi built a church for its reception at Waltham, and called it the Church of the Holy Cross ; appointed two canons to administer in the ch., and placed there 66 persons who had been cured by its means in honour of the holy cross and devotion and service to the church.*

Tovi's son, Athelstan, forfeited the estate to King Edward (the Confessor), who gave it to his brother-in-law, Harold, and he pulled down Tovi's ch., and built a larger and more magnificent one on the site. But besides enlarging the ch., Harold greatly extended its functions. He increased the number of the clergy from two to twelve, who were to be secular

canons, and placed a dean at their head ; made the instruction of the young an important part of the college duties, and that it might be efficiently carried out, obtained the services of Adelhard of Lüttich, a very distinguished teacher, as chancellor and " childmaster." Harold's church was consecrated in 1060, Edward the King, the Queen Eadyth, the Earl Harold, and many bishops, priests, and nobles being present. Harold never ceased to watch over his ch. and college, and to add to its endowments. It is even said, and Mr. Freeman seems to adopt the story, that when about to march to Hastings to meet William of Normandy, he went first to Waltham, to pray in his ch. there, and to offer up relics on the altar. The legend adds that, as he prostrated himself before the holy rood, and prayed, the face of the holy image, which had before looked upwards, bent forwards and regarded the King as he lay : and thenceforward the head of the image was ever bowed towards the ground. Harold's battle-cry on the fatal field, it will be remembered, was " The Holy Cross," a reference, there can be little doubt, to the cross which was the great treasure and glory of his church at Waltham.

The body of Harold was, according to the local tradition, and the statement of chroniclers,* brought for interment in the chancel of his great ch. The fact of his burial at Waltham has been questioned, but the balance of evidence inclines in its favour.† Fuller gives a very particular account " from the pen of Master Thomas Smith of Sewardstone, in the parish of Waltham Abbey, a discreet person, not long since deceased," of the opening of a tomb towards the latter end of the reign of Elizabeth, which was believed to be that of Harold. It stood about 120 ft. E. of the present ch., in front of the site of the high altar of the ancient minster. The tomb was of hewn stone, the cover a slab of fair grey marble, " with what seemed a *cross florée* . . . upon the same, supported with pillarets, one pedestal whereof I have in my house." When the cover was " removed

---

* Prof. Stubbs' ed. of the tract De Inventione Sanctæ Crucis Walthamensis ; Fuller, Hist. of Waltham Abbey ; Freeman, Norman Conquest, vol. ii.

* See Annales Monasterii de Bermundesia, in Annales Monast. by Luard (Rolls ed.), vol. iii., p. 424, and Annals of Winchester (Ann. de Wintona), *ib.*, vol. ii., p. 27.

† Freeman, Norman Conquest, vol. iii., ch. 15.

from off the tomb . . . there appeared to the view . . . the anatomy of a man lying in the tomb abovesaid, only the bones remaining—bone to his bone, not one bone dislocated." There was plainly no distinct evidence that this was the skeleton or even the tomb of Harold, but there is nothing inconsistent with its being so in either the site or the character of the tomb. Fuller refuses to give the " reported epitaph " (Hic jacet Haroldus infelix) " because not attested in my apprehension with sufficient authority." *

William I. deprived the house of much of its plate and valuables, but spared the foundation. The secular college was suppressed by Henry II., professedly on account of the immoral lives of the canons; but the King rebuilt the monastery on a larger scale, placed in it an abbot and 24 regulars of the Augustinian order, and made the Abbey free from episcopal jurisdiction. From subsequent monarchs and benefactors the Abbey received many additional privileges and special gifts; the Abbot was mitred; and at the Dissolution the revenue of the Abbey was 15th in value among the abbeys of England. Little is told of the history of the Abbey in this long interval, but one occurrence is too remarkable to be passed over. When the corpse of Edward I. was brought from Cumberland (1307) to Westminster for interment, it rested in the ch. of Waltham Abbey. "For a while the two heroes lay side by side—the last and the first of English kings, between whom none deserved the English name, or could claim honour or gratitude of the English nation. . . . In the whole course of English history we hardly come across a scene which speaks more deeply to the heart, than when the first founder of our later greatness was laid by the side of the last kingly champion of our earliest freedom." †

If we were to believe the royal visitors, and traditional stories, the monks in the latter years of the Abbey were not remarkable for continence. Fuller tells of "a coltish trick served upon the monks of Waltham," whereby some of them in returning from a visit to Cheshunt nunnery one dark night, were trapped in a buckstall (wherewith deer used to be taken in the forest), and the next morning presented to the King, Henry VIII., " who had often seen sweeter, but never fatter, venison." * But he does not give any authority for the story, and it was probably one of the loose tales about Bluff King Harry which he found current when curate of Waltham.

Henry VIII. seems to have been a frequent visitor to Waltham—doubtless from its convenience for hunting. It was whilst staying here, at the house of a Mr. Cressy, that he heard of Cranmer's proposal for solving the difficulty of his divorce from Queen Katherine, to which he had been unable to obtain the assent of the Pope. Cranmer was then living at Waltham as tutor to two of Mr. Cressy's sons. He was summoned to the King's presence; satisfied the King's doubts; and though we can hardly venture to say, as our Waltham historian does, " the first seeds of the Reformation were sown here," there can be no question that the interview of Henry and Cranmer at Waltham Abbey was fraught with mighty consequences.

The site of the Abbey, and much of the Abbey land, was given by Henry VIII. to Sir Anthony Denny, privy councillor, and one of the executors of the King's will. The original grant was for 31 years, but shortly after Sir Anthony's death his widow obtained of Edward VI. the reversion in fee. Sir Edward Denny, grandson of Sir Anthony, was by James I. created Baron of Waltham, and by Charles I. Earl of Norwich. His daughter, Honora, carried the estate by marriage to the Earl of Carlisle. It passed by sale towards the end of the 17th century to Sir Samuel Jones of Northampton, and later by marriage to the Wakes, and is now the property of Sir C. Wake.

The present *Church* of Waltham Abbey is only the nave of the ancient abbey ch. The rest was demolished when the church was made parochial, the two easternmost bays of the nave being converted into a chancel. Some years back there was a rather warm discussion as to the age of the ch., Mr. Freeman very decidedly claiming that it is the actual building

---

* Hist. of Waltham Abbey ; Worthies of England : Essex.

† Freeman, Norman Conquest, vol. iii.

* Fuller, Church Hist., B. v., ch. 3.

erected by his hero, Harold; whilst on the other side it was as positively averred to be not earlier than the reign of Henry I., or Stephen. That it is essentially Norman in character is admitted on all hands. Sir Gilbert Scott, who has a larger and more intimate acquaintance with our early churches than most men, says of it, "there is clearly a difference between the eastern bay and the remainder," but he does "not think it is such as of necessity implies difference of date." On the "actual age of the nave," he "offers no opinion." Mr. Burges, who restored the ch., is not more decided. Whether it is Norman of the middle of the 11th or first half of the 12th century, must, therefore, be left undetermined.

In its original condition the church must have been a magnificent fabric. It was cruciform, and had a massive square tower rising from the intersection of the cross. Of the tower only the western supports remain. Of the choir and transepts no vestige is left. Probably the choir was apsidal, and we know from the site of Harold's tomb that it extended more than 120 ft. beyond the present E. wall. Mr. Burges supposes that it had chevets and a Lady Chapel at the E. end. The present ch., which, as has been said, was the nave of the abbey ch., is 108 ft. long and 54 ft. wide. Six massive piers divide the aisles from the nave, and support a triforium and clerestorey. The S. aisle is 12 ft. 4 in. wide, the N. aisle 11 ft. 8 in.; both aisles are of the full height of the two lower stages. Two of the great piers are carved with zigzag lines, two have deeply-cut spiral lines, the remainder are plain. The arches throughout have chevron mouldings. The triforium is open to the aisles, and consists of bold single arches, but Mr. Burges supposes that within these were triplets of smaller arches like those in the clerestorey, and as indeed is the most common arrangement in Norman minsters, though there are not wanting examples of single open arches like those of the Waltham triforium. On the S. side of the ch. is a Lady Chapel of the end of the reign of Edward II. or beginning of that of Edward III. It has some good Dec. work, and is worth examining. Below it is a fine crypt, of old used as a charnel-house, "the fairest," writes old Fuller, "that ever I saw."

In 1556 it was found necessary to remove what was left of the central tower and piers. This was done by "undermining," the "coles" used for the purpose costing the parish 2 shillings. [This will help to explain the procedure in excavating at the base of the tower of St. Albans Abbey. *See* p. 537-8.] A new tower, the present fabric, was then erected at the W. end of the ch. by the parishioners, from the old materials, the cost being defrayed partly from their "stock in the church box," partly by voluntary contributions. It was completed in three years; is 15 ft. square and 86 ft. high, "from the foundation to the battlements, each foot whereof (besides the materials pre-provided) costing 33s. 4d. the building," but the last "33 feet on the top (difficulty and danger of climbing made it dearer) cost 40s. a foot, as appeareth by the churchwardens' accounts, *anno* 1563."* To finish the tower "the parish was forced to sell their bells, hanging before in a wooden frame in the churchyard." To cover the tower the lead was stript from the Lady Chapel, which was now roofed with tiles. Waltham remained bell-less for 240 years; the present peal of 8 bells having been cast for the parish by Briant of Hertford in 1806. From the tower leads a fine view is obtained of the surrounding country. The entrance to the ch. from the tower is by a good Dec. doorway.

Having fallen into a very dirty and dilapidated condition, Waltham Abbey church was in 1859 handed over to Mr. W. Burges to restore internally, and the work was done thoroughly. To the exterior nothing was done beyond needful repairs, and its aspect is still somewhat that of a ruin. The E. end of the ch. is, except the main work, entirely new, and in style much later than the body of the ch. Within the great arch are three lancets and a rose window of early French character. The greatest innovation made in the process of restoration was, however, in the decoration. In the circular E. window are figured the seven days of creation, each in a separate circle; the large circle in the centre containing a representation of Him by whom all things were made. Below the eastern lancets

---

* Fuller, Hist. of Waltham Abbey, B. vi.

and spandrels are subjects from Æsop's Fables. The new flat roof which was placed over the nave is divided into lozenges, in which are painted the signs of the zodiac down the centre, and personifications of the months, alternating with geometrical patterns on the sides. The effect is novel, but crude, from the contrast of the strong colours with the cold hue of the heavy stone-work below; and though precedent may be found for the subjects, and probably for the mode of treatment, they are hardly accordant with modern religious feeling.

The ch. contains some interesting *Monts.* At the E. end of S. aisle, a much injured but sumptuous mont. of Sir Anthony Denny, to whom Henry VIII. granted the Abbey at the Suppression, has recumbent alabaster effigies of Sir Anthony and his wife, under a canopy, figures in relief of their children below, and on one side a larger effigy of a lady. Near this are mural brasses of Edward Stacey, d. 1555, and wife Katherine, d. 1565; Thomas Colte, d. 1559, and wife Magdalen, d. 1591. The regent Duke of Bedford in his will directed that he should be buried in Waltham Abbey ch. if he died in England: he died at Rouen, and was buried there.

Bishop Hall was for 22 years (1612, etc.) curate of Waltham; and "three degrees from him in succession," came the witty Thomas Fuller, who was curate from 1648 to 1658, and here wrote his ' Church History,' and brief ' History of Waltham Abbey,' and collected the materials and laid the keel of the ' British Worthies.' Some say it was at Waltham Abbey that Foxe, the martyrologist, wrote his ' Acts and Monuments.'

A gateway, known as the *Abbey Gate*, by a low bridge which crosses the Corn Mill Stream, a branch of the Lea, near the Abbey Mills and a short distance N.W. of the ch., is one of the few fragments left of the Abbey buildings. The gateway, which has two good pointed arches, a larger and a smaller, led into the court of the convent. The bridge has a ribbed arch, and is sometimes called Harold's Bridge. The Mill occupies the site of the ancient abbey mill. A small vaulted chamber known as the Potato-house, in the Abbot's garden, now a market-garden attached to the house in

the ch.-yard immediately behind the ch., is the only other relic of the Abbey left, except a few fragments of wall and some drains, which the local belief has transformed into "subterraneous passages" leading to Cheshunt Nunnery, and one hardly knows where besides—except these, nothing is left of the once extensive and splendid Abbey buildings. The Abbey House, which Sir Anthony Denny and his successors made their residence, the last complete portion of the ancient Abbey, was pulled down in 1770. Fragments of sculpture, figured tiles, metal-work, etc., are occasionally exhumed on the site or in the neighbourhood of the Abbey. Considerable quantities of pilgrims' jettons or groats have been found in the town. The Holy Cross doubtless attracted numerous pilgrims to Waltham. A few years ago a stone mould was dug up in Coleman Street, London, from which metal casts were taken, to be worn by Waltham pilgrims as the badges or insignia of their pilgrimage. The mould was cruciform, with a figure of a cross in the centre, surrounded by the legend, " *Signum Sancte Crucis de Waltham.*" [*]

Henry III., a frequent visitor and liberal benefactor to the Abbey, granted to the Abbot the right of holding a weekly market and an annual fair of 7 days' continuance. The demands of the Abbot for *stallage* at the fair, early led to disputes with the citizens of London, and peace was only made, 1256, after the Londoners had refused to resort to Waltham fair for three years and more, upon the Abbot agreeing to refund all distresses, and "granting to the Londoners acquittance of all such stallage for ever." [†]

The market is still held every Tuesday, and fairs in May and September. The old Elizabethan Market-house was taken down in 1852. In it the writer remembers to have seen a "pair of stocks," curious as being much carved, and bearing the date 1598. They were said to have been taken in charge by the police authorities, but on inquiring recently no trace of them could be found. The market-place is a large square, surrounded

---

[*] It is figured in the Proceedings of the Archæol. Association for 1873, p. 421.

[†] Fitz Thedmar, Chron. of London, 1108—1274; Maitland, Hist. of London, p. 52.

by small houses, by what was the entrance to the Abbey. The square is called the *Bramblings*—a corruption of *Romelands*, the name it bore when Fuller lived here, and given to it, he says, because " the rents peculiarly belonged to the Church of Rome." But the open spaces in front of the abbeys of St. Alban's and St. Edmund's Bury were also called Romelands, and Mr. Walcott thinks they were so called " from *rome*, roomy, as in Romney, Romsey, etc.,"* but this seems very doubtful. It was in the Romelands, according to Fuller, that Henry VIII. had the " pleasure-house " which other writers place in " the meadows at Waltham."

The chief modern establishment in Waltham, is the *Royal Gunpowder Factory*, the only factory of the kind the Government has, and where the modern " pebble " and " cube " as well as the old grain gunpowder is made. The establishment includes works for refining saltpetre, and the preparation of sulphur and charcoal. The works have been greatly extended of late years, and now occupy an area of nearly 200 acres. The houses, detached and isolated, for mixing the ingredients, pressing, granulating, drying, dusting, and barreling the gunpowder, stretch along the banks of the Lea and the islets formed by its dividing streams, for a distance of more than three miles. All the processes are carried out here; the powder, when packed in barrels, being first placed in the Grand Magazine, and then carried by the Lea and the Thames to the magazines at Purfleet. From 28,000 to 30,000 tons of gunpowder are now made at Waltham annually.

Since the destruction of the works at Stowmarket the manufacture of *gun-cotton* by the wet process has been exsively carried on at Waltham in a specially constructed factory, and so far with entire safety. The most stringent precautions are taken at the Waltham works to prevent accident, and no serious explosion has occurred for many years. By an Act passed in 1875, the regulations adopted at Waltham are made compulsory in all gunpowder factories and magazines. From January 1, 1876, such establishments are placed under Government supervision. Gunpowder mills had been " of late erected " here, when Fuller wrote (about 1660) " the mills in my parish have been five times blown up within seven years " —we have improved in this matter since then. The entrance to the Royal Gunpowder Factory is near the centre of Highbridge Street : the entrance gates are on both sides of the street.

In and around the town are flour mills, malt kilns, and a brewery, and at Farm Hill a manufactory of percussion caps. Watercresses are largely grown, and there are extensive market gardens. The County Court (erected 1849) occupies the site of an old silk-printing mill. Waltham Abbey has its weekly newspaper, literary institutes and reading-rooms, two or three cricket clubs, and a fishery.

The hamlets of HIGH BEECH and SEWARDSTONE are noticed under those headings. *Holyfield* and *Upshire* are little scattered agricultural hamlets lying 2 m. N. and 1½ m. E. of Waltham Abbey.

WALTHAM CROSS, HERTS, a

hamlet of Cheshunt, on the Ware and Hertford road, 11½ m. from London, 1 m. W. of Waltham Abbey, and ¼ m. W. of the Waltham Abbey Stat. of the Grt. E. Rly. (Cambridge line). Pop. of the eccl. dist. (formed in 1855), 3104.

Waltham Cross received its name from the cross erected here by Edward I. in memory of his wife Eleanor—but with funds, as would seem, provided by the Queen for the purpose.* Edward, it will be remembered, built a cross at each of the places where the corpse of his Queen rested on its way from the neighbourhood of Grantham, where she died (Nov. 28, 1291), to her burial-place at Westminster. Of these beautiful structures only this at Waltham and two others—one at Geddington, the other at Northampton—remain. This is by far the finest. It was the work of Alexander of Abingdon (called also Alexander de Imagineur), Domenic de Leger (written Dymenge de Legere) of Rheims, and Roger de Crundale, and was completed in 1294.

---

* M. E. C. Walcott, Church and Conventual Arrangement, p. 112.

* Thomas of Huntingdon, Chronicle, vol. i. ; Rev. J. Hunter, in Archæologia, vol. xxix. ; Archæol. Journal, vol. xvii.

The stone was brought from Caen, and the total cost was £95.* It had fallen into a terribly dilapidated condition, and seemed hastening to ruin when its restoration was undertaken in 1833 by Mr. W. B. Clarke. He executed the restoration with great care and skill, but unhappily deemed it necessary to rechisel and renew so much of the old sculpture and carving that it is even now difficult, and in a few years will be impossible, to distinguish the original work from the copy. As an example of the art of the time of Edward I., its value is irretrievably destroyed.

The Cross is hexagonal in plan, of three diminishing stages, with buttresses at the angles. The lowest stage, which is raised on a stepped platform, is of rich panelled tracery, under crocketed pediments, each side being divided into two compartments, in which are pendent shields charged with the arms of England, Castile and Leon, and Ponthieu. The second storey has canopied niches, within which are statues of Queen Eleanor. The third stage, which is of solid masonry, comparatively plain, is surmounted with a thin finial and cross. The outline and proportions are exceedingly graceful, and the carving is admirable.

It stands on the E. of the main road, close against the *Falcon Inn*, and at the corner of the road to Waltham Abbey. At the opposite corner is another and larger inn, the *Four Swans*, formerly a well-known posting-house. In it, according to the local legend, the body of Eleanor remained for the night preceding its solemn entry into London. A lagre signboard, supported on tall posts placed on the opposite sides of the way, swings across the road, and on it is inscribed " Ye Old Four Swannes Hostelrie, 1260." It is an old inn, (and a good one —Charles Lamb patronized it,) but some centuries later than 1260.

There is little besides the Cross to interest the stranger. He will, however, do well to visit Mr. W. Paul's famous Rose Nursery, a short distance past the Cross on the rt. The district ch. of the Holy Trinity is a plain brick building, Gothic of 1832, but improved in 1872.

* Manners and Household Expenses in England, printed for the Roxburgh Club, pp. 104—120; Archæol., **xxix.**, p. 184.

WALTHAMSTOW, Essex, lies between Leyton and Chingford, on the road to Waltham Abbey, 6 m. from Whitechapel and Shoreditch churches. There are four rly. stats. on the Chingford br. of the Grt. E. Rly.— St. James's Street, Hoe Street, Wood Street, and Hale End. Pop. of the par. 11,092: thus divided — district of mother-ch., 5717 ; eccl. districts, formed 1844, St. James, 2323 ; St. John, 1915 ; St. Peter, 1137.

The par. is large (4470 acres), extending for 3 m. along the highroad, and reaching back from the Lea at Tottenham to Woodford and Snaresbrook. Lying on the western edge of Epping Forest, at an easy distance from town, it early became a favourite residence with opulent citizens. Sir Wm. Batten, Commissioner of the Navy, Pepys's friend and colleague, had his country seat at Walthamstow, and thither Pepys often accompanied him. One of his visits gives a curious little picture of suburban life in the 17th century :—

"1661. *April* 13th.—Sir W. Batten this day gone with his lady to keep Easter. . . . .

"*April* 18th.—About nine o'clock took horse with both the Sir Williams (Batten and Penn), for Walthamstow, and there we found my Lady and her daughters all ; and a pleasant day it was, and all things else, but my Lady was in a bad moode, which we were troubled at, and had she been noble, she would not have been so with her servants, when we come together. . . . . After dinner, we all went to the Church-stile, and there eate and drank, and I was as merry as I could counterfeit myself to be."

Six years later (Oct. 12, 1667), Pepys records that " Sir W. Batten's body was to-day carried from hence, with a hundred or two of coaches, to Walthamstow, and there buried." But Sir Wm. Batten's was not the only house Pepys visited at Walthamstow. Among others, we find him on " the King's birth-day " (May 29th, 1661) taking coach with Sir W. Penn, having first " put six spoons and a porringer of silver " in his pocket, and " (the weather and the way being foule) went to Walthamstowe." There they heard the vicar, " Mr. Radcliffe, my former schoolfellow at St. Paul's, (who is yet a merry boy)," preach a " very simple " sermon ; then " back to dinner at Sir W. Batten's ; and then, after a walk in the fine gardens, we went to Mrs. Browne's, where Sir W. Pen and I were godfathers, and Mrs.

Jordan and Shipman godmothers to her boy. . . . I did give the midwife 10*s.* and the nurse 5*s.*, and the maid of the house 2*s.* But forasmuch as I expected to give the name to the childe, but did not (it being called John,) I forbore then to give my plate till another time, after a little more advice." However three months after (August 1st), "This morning Sir Williams both, and my wife and I, and Mrs. Margarett Pen went by coach to Walthamstowe, a-gossiping to Mrs. Browne, where I did give her six silver spoons for her boy "—but kept the porringer.

Many of these 17th and 18th century mansions remain ; old-fashioned, quaint, roomy, embowered in trees, the type and embodiment of quiet and substantial home-comfort and respectability. Their number is however steadily diminishing, whilst more obtrusive and pretentious villas are rising on every side.

Walthamstow is sometimes called a town, but the houses collected about the ch. scarcely form a village, the bulk of the houses being in outlying hamlets, or streets and ends, as they are for the most part named ; Marsh Street, Hoe Street, Wood Street, Clay Street, Sharnhall Street, St. James Street, Chapel End, Hale End, Higham End, Whip's Cross, and Woodford Side. The country on the forest side is varied and sylvan ; marshy by the Lea, and rising into low hills towards Chapel End and Chingford.

The manor of Walthamstow was in the reign of the Confessor a part of the large possessions of Waltheof Earl of Northumberland, and at the Domesday Survey belonged to his widow, the Countess Judith, niece of the Conqueror. Their daughter carried it by marriage to Ralph de Toni, son of Toni the standard-bearer to William I., in whose descendants it continued till 1309, when it went by marriage to Guy de Beauchamp, Earl of Warwick. About the middle of the 15th cent. the manor passed by marriage to the Ross family ; early in the following cent. to Sir Thomas Lake, who sold it to Sir George Rodney, and he in 1639 disposed of it to William Lord Maynard, in whose family it remains. There are sub-manors, but their history is complicated, and of no general interest.

The *Church* (of the Virgin Mary) is mainly of brick, the body covered with cement, and of no architectural merit. I comprises nave, aisles, chancel, and tower with turret, at the W. end. The S. aisle was built in 1535 by Robert Thorne, a famous merchant of London and Bristol, founder of the Grammar School, Bristol, and a scholarship in Merchant Taylors' School, London. The chapel at the E. end of the N. aisle, and the tower, were built about the same time by Sir George Monox. In the tower is a peal of 6 bells.

The interior is not more beautiful than the outside, and the pews and galleries do not add to its attractiveness. But the *monts.* are interesting. In the Monox Chapel is the tomb of the founder, Sir George Monox, some time Lord Mayor of London, d. 1543, and wife Ann, d. 1500. On the wall are *brasses* with effigies of Sir George and his lady, and shield of arms of the Drapers' Company : the insc. lost. Lady Lucy Stanley, daughter and coheir of Thomas Earl of Northumberland, and wife of Sir Edward Stanley ; with life-size kneeling effigy under an arch. Four of her daughters are buried with her under this mont. ; 3 survived her, one of whom was Venetia, wife of Sir Kenelm Digby, of whose beauty so much has been written.

In the chancel, an elaborate mont. of Elizabeth, wife of Sir Thomas Merry, d. 1632, with their busts in marble, and below their 4 children in high relief. It was executed by Nicholas Stone, who received £50 for it. In the Thorne Chapel, at the E. end of the S. aisle, are monts. to Sir Gerard Conyers, Lord Mayor of London, d. 1737, and other members of the Conyers family ; and a brass of George Johnson, minister of the Gospel, d. 1576. with effigy in pulpit. At the W. end of the aisle, mont. with life-size effigies of Sigismond Trafford, of Dunton Hall, Lincoln, d. 1723, and wife, Susannah, d. 1689. There are also monts. to other members of the Trafford family ;—to the Maynards, Lowthers, Coles, Bonnells, etc.,— and a small brass to — Hale, d. 1588, and wife, the effigy of the latter mutilated.

The ch.-yard abounds in tombs ; the most noticeable perhaps is one E. of the ch. to Thomas Turner, d. 1714 ; it is surrounded by a railing, and has a yew tree at each corner. It is kept in repair out of a sum of money left for the purpose. *Obs.* the great elm by the N. entrance to the ch.-yard.

N. of the ch.-yard are a Grammar School and a range of low almshouses, founded and endowed by Ald. Sir George Monox, whose mont. we have just seen. In the almshouses are 13 pensioners. Almshouses founded by Mary Squire provide for 6 more.

There are three district churches— St. James, Marsh Street ; St. John, Chapel End ; and St. Peter, Forest Side—to be commended rather for their usefulness than beauty. St. Saviour's Church, Markhouse Road, erected in 1874 at the cost of Messrs. R. Foster and J. Knowles (who also provided the endowment and built the parsonage), claims notice as an elegant and well-finished structure. It is of Kentish rag ; early Dec. in style ; and was designed by Mr. T. F. Dolman.

The Monox Grammar School has been mentioned. More important is the *Forest School*, Forest Side, near Snaresbrook, founded 1834 in connection with King's College, which is a large and flourishing institution. Here are besides a *School for Daughters of Missionaries,* and a Roman Catholic Home for Orphan Boys. *Sherne Hall* (G. A. Grimwood, Esq.) was for several years the residence of Cardinal Wiseman. Benjamin Disraeli was educated at Mr. Logan's academy, Higham Hill.

George Gascoigne, the Elizabethan poet, is said to have been a native of Walthamstow ; in his maturer years it was his usual residence : he dates the dedication of his ' Complaynt of Philomeal' from his "pore house at Walthamstow the sixteenth of April 1575." Guillim, the herald, was resident at Walthamstow when he wrote the account of Queen Elizabeth's funeral published in the ' Monumenta Vetusta.'

The Walthamstow Marshes in the valley of the Lea have within the last eight or ten years opened a new and rich field of interesting inquiry. Till about a century ago Epping Forest extended down to the Lea, and it was only in 1777 that this district was disafforested. It has since been for the most part pasture land ; but a few years back the East London Waterworks Company commenced the construction of two vast reservoirs, capable of storing 500 million gallons of water, extending for considerably more than a mile along the Lea, and covering an area of about 120 acres. The average depth excavated was about 10 feet, but the trenches made for the retaining or ' puddle ' walls, were from 20 to 24 ft. deep. The excavations were all in posttertiary deposits—loam, peat clays, sands, and sub-angular and rolled gravels—but the remains brought to light proved to be of unexpected value. An old bed of the Lea was passed through ; and a submerged forest tract was laid bare,—a tract which naturalists and geologists concurred in believing had been flooded by beaverdams, and in which the remains of beavers were abundant, along with the remains of the elk (the most southerly locality in which they have yet been found), reddeer, roe-buck, moose, and reindeer ; ox (*Bos primigenius, B. longifrons,* and another) ; horse (*Equus caballus*), elephant (*E. primigenius*), wolf, fox, wild-boar, together with a great variety of land and fresh-water shells, and, what was not least interesting, a considerable number of works of man's industry—flint implements, bronze spear and arrow heads, knives, a sword, and a few fragments of pottery— but we believe no remains of man himself. The vegetable remains were, as may be supposed, very abundant. In the beds above the sandy marl, trees were brought to light "with their spreading roots *in situ*, but in most instances converted into lignite and coated with bog-iron ore." Oak and alder appeared to be the most common trees, hazel nuts were abundant. The peat bed was in places over 3 ft. thick.*

WALTON-ON-THE-HILL,

SURREY, so called from its position, and to distinguish it from Walton-on-Thames. occupies an outlying patch of Thanet Sand on the southern side of the Epsom Downs. and is 2½ m. N. of the Betchworth Stat. of the S.-E. Rly. (Dorking and Guildford branch), and 4½ S. by E. of Epsom. Pop. 543. Inn, the *Chequers.*

Away from a main road, on a height overlooking the broad furze-clad Walton Heath, Walton-on-the-Hill is a pleasant and not unpicturesque village of comfortable commonplace dwellings climbing

---

* H. Woodward, F.R.S., on ' Freshwater Deposits of the Valley of the Lea near Walthamstow, Essex,' in Geol. Mag., Sept. 1869 ; Notes made during the excavations.

the hill-side, and clustering about the ch., on the summit, an old manor-house and abundant trees. Beyond, stretching miles away, are the breezy, health-inspiring heath, and smooth chalk downs. The occupations are agricultural, and there is a race-horse and training establishment.

The manor, which had belonged at the end of the 13th cent. to John de Lovetot, one of the King's judges; afterwards to John de Drokensford, Keeper of the Great Seal, and Bp. of Bath and Wells; the Earl de Warren, Sir John Arundel, and others, passed at length to the Crown, and was assigned by Henry VI. to his newly founded college of Eton. But the grant was cancelled by Edward IV., who settled the manor on his Queen, Elizabeth Woodville. By Henry VIII. it was given to his consort Katherine of Aragon. In 1533 he granted it to Sir Nicholas Carew of Beddington, and it followed the fate of the Beddington property. (*See* BEDDINGTON.) It now belongs to E. Studd, Esq.

The old manor-house, *Walton Place*, was long used as a farm-house, but is now the residence of C. H. Cumberland, Esq. It stands near the ch., has thick walls, stout buttresses, and curious old chimney-pieces, and is surrounded by a moat. It is one of the many houses assigned as the dwelling-place of Anne of Cleves after her divorce, and may in part be as old as her time, but the larger part is much more modern. A chapel, in which was a stone pulpit, existed as part of the house as late as 1780. Other seats are the *Hermitage* (Mrs. Rostock); *The Oaks* (T. H. Fischer, Esq.); *Frith Park* (A. Holford, Esq.); *Peeble Combe* (T. H. Perks, Esq.)

The *Church* (St. Peter) was almost entirely rebuilt, in very tasteless fashion, in 1822. The most noticeable feature is the elaborate though by no means beautiful octagonal tower, of 3 stages, of flint and stone, with buttresses and tall pinnacles. Inside, the only thing worth notice is a richly ornamented circular leaden font of late Norman date. Around it is an arcade of 9 arches, within each of which is the seated figure of a bishop or a saint. Only one or two other examples are known.

Remains of a Roman villa, and among the *débris* a bronze statuette of Æsculapius, were found on Walton Heath in 1772; and in 1802 further vestiges of what was supposed to have been "the pretorium of a Roman station" were uncovered. There is a delightful walk across Walton Heath to Betchworth Clump; and thence, with ever-varying and beautiful prospects, along the chalk ridge to Box Hill, or in the opposite direction towards Reigate. Nor less exhilirating are the walks or rides over the Downs to Epsom and Banstead.

WALTON-UPON-THAMES,

SURREY, on the rt. bank of the Thames, about midway (4 m.) between Chertsey and Hampton; 17 m. from London by road, and 1 m. N. from the Walton Stat. of the L. and S.-W. Rly. Pop. of the town dist. 2036, of the par. 5383, but this includes the eccl. districts of Oatlands and Hersham. Inn, *Duke's Head.*

Walton (*Wáltún*, or *Wealtún—Waltone* in Dom.—a walled or fortified place) no doubt derived its name from having been at a very early period an enclosed military town or outpost. Remains of important earthworks are still extant in the vicinity, a rampart or boundary dyke extended from it to St. George's Hill, and a strongly fortified ford crossed the Thames just above where it is now crossed by Walton Bridge. (*See* St. GEORGE'S HILL, p. 229, and COWEY STAKES, p. 119.)

Walton is a large village, or small town, stretching back from the Thames and running out into many irregular streets. The church is on the London side of the village; beyond it broad meadows border the Thames; away from the river stretches the wide sandy heath called Walton Common, covered with gorse and ling, and bordered with fir woods; and southward are the large and finely timbered parks of Oatlands, Ashley, and Burwood. The Thames affords good fishing and boating, besides adding life and beauty to the scenery. Altogether a desirable locality, as is shown by the numerous villas, Italian and Gothic, of every variety of type, which have been built, or are building, wherever land could be obtained.

When the Conqueror took inventory of the soil, the manor of Walton belonged to Edward of Salisbury, whose daughter Maud carried it by marriage to a relative of the King, Humphrey de Bohun, whose son was created Earl of Hereford. The manor remained in the Bohun family till 1373, when on failure of heirs male it passed by marriage to Henry of Bolingbroke, who assumed the Bohun's title of Earl of Hereford, and on the deposition of Richard II. ascended the throne as Henry IV. As part of the personal estate of Henry VI., Walton was vested by parliamentary enactment in Edward IV. Leases of the estate were, with certain reservations, granted by Henry VIII. and succeeding monarchs down to Charles I., who in 1630 granted the manor in fee, at a quit rent, to Sir William Russell. This rent was conveyed in 1650 to William Lilly, the astrologer. The manor passed to Francis Drake (1678), Phillips, and many more, till at the close of the 18th cent. it was bought by the Duke of York, who then held Oatlands. From him it was purchased by Edward Hughes Ball Hughes, and is now the property of J. E. Paine, Esq. The manor of *Walton-Leigh* was also bought by the Duke of York, and has since passed with the superior manor. *Apps Court* is noticed under that heading.

The chief object of interest in Walton is the *Church* (St. Mary). It is large and old, but so much patched and altered as to be externally far from handsome and hardly picturesque. It is of flint, rough stone, and hard chalk, but mended with brick, and in parts covered with plaster. It has nave with aisles, deep chancel, and heavy W. tower, in which is a peal of 6 bells. The piers of the nave arcade are late Norman, the outer walls and windows of various dates, some being quite recent insertions, whilst those which are old have been defaced. The interior of the ch. has been partially restored, and the E. window filled with painted glass. The organ is by Father Schmidt. A pier near the pulpit bears deeply engraven the verses attributed to Queen Elizabeth—

" Christ was the Worde and spake it :
    He took the Bread and brake it ;
    And what the Worde doth make it,
    That I believe, and take it."

Some of the monts. are noteworthy. In the N. aisle the large and costly mont., by *Roubiliac*, of Field-Marshal Richard Boyle, 2nd (and last) Lord Shannon, d. 1740, erected by his only daughter, Grace Countess of Middlesex. On a lofty base-

ment of grey marble is a pedestal of black marble, upon which is the life-size statue of Lord Shannon in full military costume, and holding a marshal's baton in his hand. Immediately behind him is a lowered flag, behind and above which is a military tent. On either side are cannon, kettle-drums, flags, and other military insignia. At the foot of the pedestal is a statue of Lady Shannon, kneeling and looking upwards. The whole forms one of Roubiliac's most characteristic works, executed in his best manner. *Chantrey's* mourning female on the mont. of Christopher D'Oyley, d. 1795, and wife Sarah. d. 1833, looks but feeble after that of Lady Shannon. In the chancel is a marble mont. by *Gott*, of Rome, to Mary, wife of Sir Thomas Williams, of Burwood House, d. 1824, with figures in high relief representing Faith consoling Grief. Others are to Sir Henry Fletcher of Ashley Park, d. 1807 ; Thomas Kirby, S.T.P., d. 1721, with Ionic pilasters supporting a cornice, on which are small figures of " Genii, one extinguishing a torch, the other sounding a trumpet," and a much more modest tablet over the vestry door to Henry Skrine. LL.B., d. at Walton, 1803, the author of ' A General Account of all the Rivers of note in Great Britain.' This, which is by the younger Bacon, has a rilievo of a large oak *skrineing* (screening, protecting,) some saplings—in allusion to his generous care of his relatives.

A " fair black marble stone" on the floor in front of the S. entrance to the chancel, records the burial here, 1681. of William Lilly, " Astrologi peritissimi,"—

" Who not far from hence did dwell
    That cunning man hight Sidrophel."

Lilly was buried on " the left side of the communion table," and this stone was placed over his grave to mark the spot by Elias Ashmole—costing him, as he notes, £6 4s. 6d.,—but removed to its present unmeaning position several years back. By the altar is a slab to Jerome Weston, Earl of Portland, d. 1662.

Screwed on to a board in an oaken frame on the N. wall of the chancel, by the entrance to the vestry, are 4 small *brasses*, which were long left loose in the vestry. They represent John Selwyn, d. 1587, his wife, and their 5 sons and 6 daughters. Selwyn was " keeper of her

Ma'ties Parke of Otelande," and one of the brasses represents him on the back of a stag, into the neck of which he is thrusting his hunting knife. The traditional explanation is that Selwyn, who was an accomplished rider, at a grand stag-hunt at Oatlands, at which Elizabeth was present, in the heat of the chase threw himself from his horse on to the back of the stag, and seizing its horns, by them and his conteau guided the terrified animal towards the Queen, and when he came near her, plunged his knife into the creature's throat so that it fell dead at Her Majesty's feet. A somewhat different version of the event is engraved on the reverse of the brass, but cannot of course be seen, since it has been screwed to the board. The principal difference is that on the back Selwyn is represented grasping one of the antlers with his left hand, bare-headed and spurred.

In the vestry is still preserved a *brank*, scold's bit, or gossip's bridle. It consists of a horizontal circlet of iron, that goes round the face, and another with hinges at right angles to it which goes over the head, fixes a thin projecting piece of iron in the mouth so as to hold down the tongue, and is then secured by a padlock. The scold or gossip with this apparatus on her head was led through the town by the beadle, or exposed in the market-place. The Walton bridle has on it the date 1633, and the following inscription (now, however, illegible) :—

> " Chester presents Walton with a Bridle
> To curb Women's tongues that talk too idle."

The tradition is that the donor having suffered grievously—some say lost an estate—by the idle talk of a gossiping woman, took this means of avenging himself upon the sex.

In the churchyard are many tombs to persons of local consequence, but none of wider interest. Here lies, but without a memorial, Wm. Maginn, LL.D., the Ensign O'Doherty of ' Blackwood,' the satirist and Homeric ballad writer of ' Fraser,' who died at Walton, in a house opposite the Bear Inn, Aug. 20, 1842.

At the back of Church Street, on the rt. towards the river (the lane by the Old Manor House Inn leads to it) is the *House of President Bradshaw*. It consists of a long low centre with deep tiled roof,

between slightly projecting gabled wings and is formed of a very solid timber framing, bricks, and plaster. It was a plain half-timber mansion of the reign of James I., but from long neglect has become terribly dilapidated, dirty, squalid, and unwholesome ; and is divided into 6 or 7 tenements, the occupants of which are miserably poor. In the ground floor of the W. wing is a panelled room which has a chimneypiece of carved oak, with coupled columns, cornice, etc., but much defaced and covered with whitewash. The massive beam which crosses the ceiling is also elaborately carved. Traditions that Charles I.'s death warrant was signed in this room ; that there was a subterraneous passage from the house under the Thames ; and that the ghost of its regicide master haunted the old rooms, used of old to linger about the house, but now all seem to be lost. Whilst Bradshaw lived here, Charles occasionally kept his court at Oatlands—how little the neighbours could have imagined the relation in which before long they would stand to each other !

A short distance S.W. of Walton ch., on the rt. of the road to the rly. stat., is *Ashley Park* (Mrs. Sassoon). The house, a large, red-brick Elizabethan mansion, is locally said to have been built by Wolsey, and occupied by Henry VIII. and Oliver Cromwell. For this there is no better foundation than the fact of Henry VIII. having purchased the estate in order to throw it into his honour of Hampton Court. Edward VI., Mary, and Elizabeth granted leases of Ashley, and James I. gave it in fee to Christopher Villiers Earl of Anglesea, a younger brother of the favourite, Buckingham. In 1668 Ashley was held by Henry Lord Arundel ; afterwards by Sir Walter Clarges ; by Sir Richard Pyne Lord Chief Justice of Ireland ; and in 1718 was purchased by Richard Boyle, Lord Shannon, who altered and enlarged the house, and added greatly to the park. Lord Shannon died at Ashley Park in 1740, and was buried in Walton ch., where is Roubiliac's splendid mont. to his memory. Ashley Park passed to his daughter Grace, Countess of Middlesex, who bequeathed it to her cousin, Colonel John Stephenson. On his death it passed to a nephew of the Countess of Middlesex, Sir Henry Fletcher, in whose family it remained till purchased by the late S. D. Sassoon, Esq., about 1864. The house has a long front with projecting wings, bays, and gables, evidently of the reign of Elizabeth or James, but much altered long subsequently. It contains some good apartments, but the chief features of the interior are the Great Hall, which occupies the entire height of the building, and the Gallery, which extends the whole length of one side of the house, 100 ft. The park, of about 300 acres, is varied, picturesque, and richly wooded. The Scotch firs are remarkably fine, and there are noble elms, oaks, limes, aspens, and cedars.

Adjoining Ashley Park on the W. is *Oatlands*, but this will be more conveniently noticed under WEYBRIDGE.

Burwood Park, on the opposite side of Walton Common, the residence till his decease of the late Sir Richard Frederick, Bart., but now unoccupied and for sale, is a low and poor stucco-fronted pile with central portico of 4 columns built by Sir John Frederick at the end of the 18th cent. It stands in the midst of a park of nearly 400 acres, within a belt of fir trees, level in surface, but falling towards the S. It has many fine and picturesque old oaks and pines, ancient thorns, and tall beeches, abundant fern and underwood. S. of the house is a chain of ponds.

S. of Burwood is *Burhill* (F. T. Bircham, Esq.), a good house which belonged to Peter De la Porte, a director of the South Sea Company, who was fined £10,000 for his share in the company's proceedings. Mr. De la Porte bequeathed Burhill to General Johnson, in whose family (his son having assumed the name of Tynte) it remained till within the last few years.

Burwood House, some way farther S., was the property and seat of Admiral Sir Thomas Williams, on whose death, in 1841, it was purchased by Lord Francis Egerton, afterwards Earl of Ellesmere, and is now the residence of the Countess Dowager Ellesmere. The house stands within very beautiful grounds which adjoin the Countess's fine estate, ST. GEORGE'S HILL. (See that heading.)

S. of St. George's Hill is *Silvermere* (Chas. E. Smith, Esq.), a handsome and convenient house, designed by George Atkinson, the architect, for his own residence. The grounds, taken from the waste, are large, command extensive views, and have a natural lake 10 acres in area. *Pain's Hill*, farther S., is noticed under COBHAM.

Mount Felix (Mrs. Ingram), on the Thames, at the foot of Walton Bridge, is an elegant Italian villa, built, or remodelled from an older house, by Mr. (afterwards Sir) Charles Barry, in 1837-39, for Charles 5th Earl of Tankerville. The house is noteworthy as the first attempt to introduce the true Italian villa, with the Italian roofs and campanile, into England. It was sold on the death of Lord Tankerville, and has been much altered by subsequent possessors. It is now more capacious and more splendid, but has lost much of its original elegance, refinement, and charm. The grounds are very fine, celebrated for the great variety of beautiful trees and shrubs, and especially the magnificent cedars and silver firs. Other seats are the *Manor House* (Fred. Lee Bevan, Esq.); and *Brokenhurst House* (E. H. Lushington, Esq.) *Holme Lodge* is the residence of the distinguished painter of oriental scenery and character, John F. Lewis, R.A.

The Thames at Walton is very attractive. From the bridge there are lovely reaches both up and down the stream. One of Turner's most charming home landscapes is his Walton Bridge—a comparatively early work. The present Walton Bridge is less picturesque than that Turner painted, but the river is no less lovely, and the banks are even more richly wooded. This part of the stream is also in great favour with anglers. From Mount Felix, for 250 yards eastward, is *Walton Sale*, the Thames Conservancy preserve, famous for pike, which are taken here up to 20 lb. weight. Trout are not uncommon; and there is good bottom-fishing for roach, dace, chub, and barbel. For boating, the river here is most enjoyable.

A bridge was constructed over the Thames from Cowey Hill, by Mount Felix, Walton, to Shepperton, on the Middlesex shore, at the cost of Mr. Samuel Decker, in 1747-50, the architect being a Mr. W. Etheridge. It was a very peculiar structure, the main fabric being of oak, very strongly put together, the centre arch 132 ft. in span, and rising 26 ft. above floodwater level, with side arches of 44 ft., and others of diminishing span towards the shore, the shore arches on each bank being of brick. Mr. Decker was sanguine that his bridge would last for 200 years without any repairs ; but before 30 had passed the bridge had become unsafe. For the 3 central arches, 4 of stone were now substituted, the rest of the wooden fabric being replaced with brick. The architect was James Paine, the builder of Chertsey and Kew bridges, and the most distinguished bridge-builder of his day. It had a somewhat longer life than its predecessor, but was equally unfortunate. In 1859 the central arch suddenly fell, and the other arches were found to be insecure. A new bridge was constructed of lattice girders of iron on brick piers, very similar to that at Hampton Court, and by the same engineer, Mr. E. F. Murray, and opened in 1863. If less picturesque than the old bridge, it is more convenient, being far less steep, and affording a clearer water-way. The main bridge is joined to the Surrey roadway by a second bridge of 15 brick arches, thrown across the hollow of a long meadow which is flooded in winter. The bridge was made free of toll in 1870.

A short distance above Walton Bridge is the site of Cowey Stakes, where Cæsar is supposed to have crossed the Thames. (*See* COWEY STAKES.) Bronze swords and other early remains have at different times been found in the Thames near Walton Bridge, and quite recently an ancient British gold coin was dredged up.

The hamlet of *Hersham* (anc. *Heversham, Heverisham*, from the Hevers family, who had property and a residence here) lies to the E. of Burwood Park, about 1½ m. S. of Walton, across the Common, and ½ m. S.E. from Walton Station. Hersham was made an eccl. dist. in 1851, and had 2090 inhab. in 1871. A pleasant and healthy little village, it has, since the opening of the rly., become encompassed with a belt of good villa residences. The church (of the Holy Trinity) is a neat chapel-like structure, of Suffolk brick and stone, Norman in style, with a shallow tower at the W. end, terminating in an open bell turret; it was erected in 1839, from the designs of Mr. Thos. Bellamy. Hersham was the residence of Lilly, the astrologer. He had a house here as early as 1636, but he only gave up his London dwelling and settled in Hersham in 1665.

In the interval he had acquired a good deal of property in the neighbourhood, and he lived here as a person of consideration. He died at Hersham in June 1681, and, as already mentioned, was buried in the chancel of Walton ch.

Oatlands, St. Mary, is another eccl. dist. in Walton par., created 1869 ; pop. 2090 in 1871. It is of quite recent growth, having arisen from the erection of a number of villa residences on the southern side of Oatlands Park, and partly on land enclosed from Walton Common. A street or two of shops and cottages followed, and in 1862 a pretty little church was built from the designs of Messrs. Francis, facing the Common and Burwood Park. It is of Kentish rag and Bath-stone, early Dec. in style, has an apsidal chancel, bell turret, and glazed S. porch. A N. aisle was added in 1873. It stands in a prettily planted and well-kept piece of ground on the edge of the Common, with a dark background of thick fir plantations.

The long flat red-brick building by the railway and facing the Common, between Oatlands and Hersham, is the home of the *Metropolitan Convalescent Institution*, founded in 1854, to provide a temporary asylum for poor convalescent patients leaving the London hospitals. The building was erected in 1854, from the designs of Mr. J. Clarke, and though not to be commended for its exterior is said to be well adapted to its purpose. The situation, at least, is as good as could have been found. The chapel in the grounds was built in 1870, and the home enlarged. It now provides beds for 280 adults ; whilst the branch at Kingston Hill affords accommodation for 150 children. Each patient remains about 4 weeks in the homes—more than 3000 convalescents thus obtaining annually benefit of change of scene and a breath of country air before returning to their ordinary occupations. More could be done if the funds were more abundant. Office, 32, Sackville Street, Piccadilly.

WANDSWORTH, SURREY, on the river Wandle at its confluence with the Thames, 5½ m. from Westminster Bridge, on the road to Kingston. The L. and S.-W., and the L., C., and D. Rlys. have stations at Wandsworth. Pop. of the par. 19,783 ; but this includes the vicarage of St. Anne's Hill, 10,116, and the eccl. dist. of St. Mary, Summer's Town, 1435, and 1853 in St. John's, Union Road, Battersea.

The name, Dom. *Wandelesorde* and *Wandesore*, in early records *Wandlesworth*, is plainly derived from its situation: it is the *worth*, or village (*i.e.* enclosed place), on the river Wandle.

From the increase of London, Wandsworth has become virtually a suburb. It is a busy place, has extensive manufactures and a large trade, and is continuously increasing in population. On the Wandle, the entrance from South Street, are the Royal Paper Mills of Mr. M'Murray, a very large establishment; and there are extensive corn mills, distilleries (Messrs. Watney's), breweries, maltings, dye-works, chemical works, colour factories, cloth printing and bolting mills, match factories, artificial manure works, and so forth; and the creek at the mouth of the Wandle forms a dock for lighters, with coal wharfs and stores. By the Thames the ways are narrow and dirty, but away from the river are broader streets lined with good shops; outside is a vast number of genteel dwellings, and about the Common, and on East and West Hills, are many good houses. The Common has suffered greatly from encroachments and defacements; but it remains a common still, wide, open, and pleasant; connected, on the one hand, with Putney Heath, on the other with Clapham Common, and running back to Tooting and Streatham Commons.

Aubrey relates that before his time there had been established at Wandsworth a manufacture of "brass plates for kettles, skellets, frying-pans, etc., by Dutchmen, who keep it a mystery." The houses in which the mystery was carried on were long known as the Frying-pan Houses. Dye works were in operation here at least as early. Towards the close of the 17th cent., many of the French Protestants who sought refuge in England upon the revocation of the Edict of Nantes, settled in Wandsworth, and engaged in silk dyeing, hat making, etc. For their worship they rented and enlarged the old Presbyterian chapel in the High Street, and in it service was performed in French for over a century. Gradually the French element became absorbed in the surrounding population, but Wandsworth was long famous for hat making. At the parting of the roads to Clapham and Vauxhall is a small burial-ground—the *Huguenots' Cemetery*—where many old gravestones of Frenchmen remain, some almost illegible. From the many English names on the later gravestones it appears to have been used as the ordinary burial-ground for that end of the parish when the Huguenot population began to die out.

A very different French refugee made Wandsworth for some time his abode. On Voltaire's release from his second imprisonment in the Bastille, he was ordered to leave France, and he came to England. For two years, 1726-7, he lived at Wandsworth, the guest of Sir Everard Fawkener, to whom he dedicated 'Zaïre.' He was in bad health, but he occupied himself in studying English books, and picked up a sufficient acquaintance with the language to write in it tolerably for the rest of his life.

Wandsworth Bridge. — In 1873 was completed a new iron lattice girder bridge of five spans, connecting York Road, Wandsworth, with King's Road, Fulham. It is described more fully under FULHAM, p. 227.

Wandsworth has five churches. The old church (All Saints), in the High Street, near the bridge over the Wandle, is a plain square brick fabric, erected in 1780, except the tower at the W. end, which was built in 1630, but recased in 1841, and raised by the addition of a belfry storey for the reception of a peal of 8 bells, cast by Mears of Whitechapel.

The interior is not more beautiful than the outside, but contains a few interesting *monts.* from the older ch. On the E. wall, S. of the chancel, mural mont. of Alderman Henry Smith, died 1627, with his effigy, in gown and ruff, kneeling at a desk, under an entablature borne on Ionic columns. Beneath is a tablet with an insc. setting forth his numerous benefactions. Ald. Smith was a native of Wandsworth, of humble lineage; acquired what was for the time a large fortune by business in the City; married, but was left a widower without children, and in 1620, being then 72 years of age, made over his estates, both real and personal, to trustees for charitable purposes, reserving to himself an annuity from them of £500 a year for his maintenance. His benefactions embraced every town and almost every parish in Surrey, the object being not merely to afford "reliefe of the poore," but the "setting them a-worke." Smith gave primarily and chiefly to his native county, but his charity was not limited to it. Among other bequests he left £1000 to purchase lands, in order to provide a fund for "redeeming poor captives and prisoners from the Turkish tyranie;" £10,000 to "buy impropriations for godly preachers;" £150 to found a fellowship at Cambridge for his own kindred, etc. The statement on the insc.—"*here* lyeth," repeated in a Latin insc. on a gravestone below, is inaccurate: there is no trace of interment under the grave-stone; that and the mont. were removed from the older ch., and Smith's burial-place is unknown.

By Smith's is another mural mont., with small kneeling effigy of Susanna Powell, d. 1630, benefactress to this parish, widow of John Powell, servant to Queen Elizabeth, and daughter of Thomas Hayward, yeoman of the guard to Henry VIII., Edward VI., and the queens Mary and Elizabeth. N. of chancel, mont. to Sir Thomas Brodrick, died 1641, and wife, Katherine, d. 1678, with their busts in marble. Sir Alan Brodrick, Surveyor-General of Ireland, d. 1680; Alan Brodrick, 1st Viscount Middleton, d. 1747; George Brodrick, 2nd Viscount Middleton, d. 1765, and other members of the family were also buried here. Their house was at Garrett. The register records the burial, April 1635, of " Sarah, daughter of Praise Barbone," supposed to be the " Praise-God Barebone," the Puritan leather-seller of Fleet Street, who gave his name to Cromwell's first or "little" Parliament.

Griffith Clerke, vicar of Wandsworth, his chaplain, his servant, and Friar Ware, were hanged and quartered, at St. Thomas Waterings (by the Old Kent Road, then the usual place of execution for this part of Surrey), on the 8th of July, 1539, for denying the royal supremacy.

St. Anne's Church, St. Anne's Hill, made a district ch. in 1847, was erected in 1822-24 from the designs of Sir Robert Smirke, R.A. It is a Grecian temple, 100 ft. by 70, with a hexastyle Ionic portico and pediment at the W. end.

The body of the ch. is of brick with stone dressings, the portico and pediment are of stone. From the roof rises a circular tower in two stages, with engaged columns, and crowned with a cupola and cross: a ch. worth noting as a characteristic example of a past phase of fashion in ecclesiastical architecture.

St. Mary, Summer's Town, Garrett, was made an eccl. dist. ch. in 1845. The ch. is very poor E.E., and consists of nave, S. aisle, and bell turret. St. Paul's, on St. John's Hill, a chapel-of-ease, belongs as much to Battersea as to Wandsworth. It is a good Gothic building of stone, with tower and spire, and apsidal chancel. Holy Trinity, by Wimbledon Park, another chapel-of-ease, is a substantial stone structure; Gothic, and cruciform; erected in 1860, and enlarged in 1870.

There are many dissenting places of worship, one for Friends, and one for Roman Catholics. It should be noted that the first Presbyterian Church in England was founded at Wandsworth in 1572: their principles of church government and rules of worship were set forth in a publication called 'The Orders of Wandsworth.' *

The secular buildings include a County Court, Police Court, offices of the District Board of Works, banks, large schools, mechanics' institutes, etc., but none of any architectural interest.

Wandsworth has many almhouses and charitable institutions, and the open country outside has been chosen as the site for several large establishments unconnected with the locality. On the Common, near the Clapham Station, is the *Royal Patriotic Asylum*, founded and endowed from the surplus funds of the Crimean Patriotic Fund of 1854, for the nurture and education of orphan children of soldiers, sailors, and marines. The first stone of the asylum for girls was laid by the Queen, July 11, 1857. The building, intended for the accommodation of 300 children, was designed by Mr. Rhode Hawkins, as a free imitation—with some important deviations and the omission of the ornamental details—of Heriot's Hospital, Edinburgh. At a short distance is a correspondent asylum for boys; but

* Neale, Hist. of the Puritans, vol. i., p. 243; Lysons, vol. i., p. 383.

the establishments are quite distinct. The large quaint-looking red brick Gothic building, with great central clock-tower, and overhanging watch towers at the angles, seen above the railway cutting, is the *Freemasons' Female Orphan Asylum*, erected, 1852, from the designs of Mr. Philip Hardwick. In Spanish Road, Wandsworth Common, is the *Friendless Boys' Home*, a valuable refuge for boys from 10 to 16 years of age, "who have lost character, or are in danger of losing it." It is said that of the lads who pass through the school about 75 per cent. are reclaimed. About 200 are now in training. At East Hill is *St. Peter's Hospital*, the Almshouse of the Fishmongers' Company, a spacious, solid, and comfortable looking range of buildings, occupying 3 sides of a quadrangle, with a chapel in the centre, erected 1849-51. The *Royal Hospital for Incurables*, West Hill, is noticed under PUTNEY.

On the Common will also be observed two enormous piles of buildings, the Surrey Lunatic Asylum and the County Prison. The former, erected in 1840, from the designs of Mr. Wm. Moseley, is a late Tudor structure, consisting of centre and advanced wings, 535 ft. long, and provides accommodation for 950 inmates. The Surrey House of Correction, an equally huge group of brick and stone buildings, erected in 1851, makes provision for 1000 convicted criminals, with all appliances for labour, instruction, and sickness. The Union Workhouse, East Hill, is another vast brick pile, affording accommodation for 850 paupers, with a large infirmary attached.

Garrett is a hamlet of Wandsworth, about 2 m. S. on the road to Tooting. United with Summer's Town, it was made an eccl. dist. in 1845. The name appears to be derived from a mansion which some 3 cents. since was known as *The Garretts*, and was the seat of the Brodrick family, of whom there are many memorials in Wandsworth ch. The place has little in itself to attract attention; but in the last cent. it acquired notoriety as the scene of a mock election, which appears to have been always exceedingly popular with the London mob, who flocked to it in prodigious crowds, and it obtained general celebrity from Foote having dramatised the incidents of the election in one of the most

popular of his comedies, 'The Mayor of Garrett,' produced at Drury Lane in 1764. Various attempts have been made to explain the origin of the election, but none worth repeating. All that is really known is that the custom had grown up, on the occurrence of a general election, to elect a Mayor of Garrett, who in course of time came also to be constituted Knight and M. P. The candidates were usually conspicuous by some personal deformity or peculiarity, and a fluent tongue. The electors were the mob, the electoral oath being administered on a brickbat. There were processions from town of the candidates, a hustings and speeches, charing of the elected, tumult and debauchery. " The publicans at Wandsworth, Tooting, Battersea, Clapham, and Vauxhall [the line of the procession], made a purse," writes Sir Richard Phillips, " to give it character." Its character was at best a bad one. But it is easy to see why the publicans upheld it.

"None but those who have seen a London mob on any great holiday can form a just idea of these elections. On several occasions a hundred thousand persons, half of them in carts, in hackney coaches, and on horse and ass-back, covered the various roads from London, and choked up all the approaches to the place of election. At the two last elections, I was told, that the road within a mile of Wandsworth was so blocked up by vehicles, that none could move backward or forward during many hours; and that the candidates dressed like chimney-sweepers on May-day, or in the mock fashion of the period, were brought to the hustings in the carriages of peers, drawn by six horses, the owners themselves condescending to become their drivers." [*]

If peers escorted and drove the candidates, Foote, Garrick, and Wilkes, according to the same chronicler, wrote some of their addresses. Becoming at length insufferable, the election was suppressed in 1796. An attempt was made to resuscitate it in 1826, but the authorities intervened, and the election for Garrett belongs as much to the past as an election for Gatton or Old Sarum. The proposed election of 1826 induced Hone to visit Garrett and collect whatever traditional information yet lingered there. He gave the result in his 'Every-day Book,' (vol. ii., col. 819—866) accompanied with much additional matter, engravings of the last two mayors, Sir Henry Dimsdale, M.P.

* Sir Richard Phillips, A Morning's Walk to Kew, 1817, p. 81.

Wandsworth

Westerham (see p.685)

and muffin-seller, and Sir Jeffry Dunstan, M.P. and itinerant dealer in old wigs, and some characteristic "reminiscences of Sir Jeffry Dunstan," contributed by Charles Lamb.

Dr. John Jebb, Bp. of Limerick, died at West Hill in 1833. Mulberry Cottage, Wandsworth Common, was the residence of Francis Grose, the antiquary.

WANSTEAD, ESSEX, lies on the rt. of the Chigwell road, between it and the river Roding, about 3 m. beyond Stratford, and 6 m. from Whitechapel ch. by road; ½ m. S.E. of the Snaresbrook Stat. of the Grt. E. Rly. (Ongar line). Pop. 5119, but this includes the hamlet of Snaresbrook, and 647 persons in the Infant Orphan Asylum, 209 in the Merchant Seamen's Orphanage, and 74 in Woodhouse Asylum. Inns, *George; Nightingale.*

The little rambling village is very pleasantly situated towards the southern extremity of Epping Forest, only the long level waste, known as Wanstead Flats, lying beyond it. W. of it is Leytonstone, N. Woodford.

The name (Dom. *Waenstede*) seems to be derived, says Lysons, "from the Saxon words *wan* and *stede*, signifying the white place, or mansion." * This, however, is very improbable, and more recent authorities prefer to suppose it a corruption of *Wodens stede*, or place,—implying the existence here of a mound, or other erection, dedicated to the widespread worship of Woden. † Wanstead appears to have been a Roman station. In 1715, in digging holes to plant an avenue in Wanstead Park, the workmen came upon a Roman pavement, which they traced about 20 ft. from N. to S. and 16 ft. from E. to W. It was formed of small square coloured tesseræ, had in the centre a figure of a man on horseback, and a border of scroll-work, about 1 ft. wide. ‡ At other times foundations of buildings, fragments of pottery, silver and brass coins, etc., have been found.

The manor of Wanstead was given by

* Lysons, Environs, vol. i., p. 716.
† Kemble, Saxons in England, vol. i., p. 312; Taylor, Words and Places, p. 322.
‡ S. Lethieullier, Archæologia, vol. i., p. 56 and p. 73.

Ælfric to the monks of Westminster, and the grant was confirmed by the Confessor; but it shortly after passed, probably by exchange, to the Bp. of London, under whom it was held by Ralph FitzBrien when the Dom. Survey was made. It afterwards passed to the Hodings, Huntercombes, Tattersalls, and Hastings; and in the reign of Henry VIII. belonged to Sir John Heron, by the attainder of whose son, Sir Giles Heron, it was forfeited to the Crown. Edward VI. granted it in 1549 to Robert Lord Rich, whose son sold it in 1577 to Robert Dudley, Elizabeth's Earl of Leicester. His widow, to whom Wanstead was bequeathed, married Sir Christopher Blount, and Wanstead was conveyed to Charles Blount, Earl of Devonshire. It was then alienated to George Marquis· of Buckingham, who sold it, 1619, to Sir Henry Mildmay, Master of the Jewel Office under James I. Having escheated to the Crown in consequence of Sir. W. Mildmay's share in the trial of Charles I., it was given by Charles II. to his brother, James Duke of York, who transferred it to Sir Robert Brookes. He falling into difficulties, sold it in 1667 to Sir Josiah Child, the great merchant and banker, and governor and autocrat of the East India Company, whose son Richard was created Viscount Castlemaine in 1718, and Earl Tylney in 1732. On the death without issue of John Earl Tylney, in 1784, this manor, with other large estates, devolved to Sir James Tylney Long, whose daughter and heiress, Katherine, married the Hon. Wm. Wellesley Pole, who assumed the name of Wm. Pole-Tylney-Long-Wellesley, and succeeded, 1845, to the title of Earl of Mornington. The manor is now the property of Earl Cowley.

The original manor-house, said to have been called Naked Hall Hawe, was taken down and rebuilt by Lord Chancellor Rich, who made it his summer residence. Queen Mary stayed in it some days between her accession to the throne and her coronation, and Elizabeth visited the Chancellor here in July 1561. The Earl of Leicester enlarged and improved the house, and in May 1578 entertained Queen Elizabeth for some days. For the occasion, Sir Philip Sidney wrote a dramatic interlude, printed at the end of the 'Arcadia,' which was played before the

Queen in Wanstead Garden, and in which the May-Ladie, mistress of "this place and this time," does homage "to the beautifullest Lady these woods have ever received," and craves her judgment between her two lovers. In the following September, Elizabeth again visited the Earl at Wanstead; and almost immediately after her departure, the 20th of September, 1578, Leicester was married at Wanstead House to the widow of Walter Devereux, Earl of Essex. From the inventory of his property, taken at Leicester's death, Wanstead House would not seem to have been very splendidly furnished, the entire furniture, stock, etc., being valued at only £1119 6s. 6d. But the prices of the several articles were hardly such as they would be appraised at now. The pictures in the gallery, including three portraits of Henry VIII., and others of Queen Mary and Queen Elizabeth, in all 43 in number, were rated at £11 13s. 4d.—an average of something under 5s. 6d. each! The Earl's library—consisting of an old Bible; Foxe's Acts and Monuments, old and torn; seven psalters, and a service-book—were valued at 13s. 8d. The horses at Wanstead were valued at £316. In June 1603 the Earl of Mountjoy, on returning from Ireland with Hugh O'Neil, Earl of Tyrone, lodged at Wanstead for a season before they were received at Court. James I. stayed here in Sept. 1607, on his return from a western progress. Of the old fabric there is a view, on a small scale, in the background of a portrait of Queen Elizabeth, by De Heere, at Welbeck. A small print of it was published in 1649 by Stent. Whilst the residence of Sir Robert Brookes it was visited by Pepys, who thus records his impression of it :

"May 14th, 1665.—I took coach to Wanstead, the house where Sir H. Mildmay died, and now Sir Robert Brookes lives, having bought it of the Duke of York, it being forfeited to him : a fine seat, but an old-fashioned house, and, being not full of people, looks flatly." *

When Sir Josiah Child bought the manor, and made Wanstead his residence, he spent large sums in improving the gardens, planting trees, laying out avenues, and forming a lake and canals. In the spring of 1683, Evelyn went to look at his improvements :

* Pepys, Diary.

"16 March, 1683.—I went to see Sir Josiah Child's prodigious cost in planting walnut trees about his seate, and making fish-ponds, many miles in circuit, in Epping Forest, in a barren spot, as oftentimes these suddenly monied men for the most part seate themselves. He, from a merchant's apprentice, and management of the East India Company's stock, being arrived to an estate ('tis said) of £200,000 ; and lately married his daughter to the eldest son of the Duke of Beaufort, late Marques of Worcester, with £50,000 portional present, and various expectations." *

The old house was taken down, and a new one begun, about 1715, by the 1st Earl Tylney, then Sir Richard Child. Colin Campbell was the architect employed, and Wanstead House, when completed, though without the wings which Campbell designed, was generally considered the best of his works. Its sumptuousness greatly impressed contemporary critics, who pronounced it "one of the noblest houses, not only in England, but in Europe." It was of Portland stone, 260 feet long and 70 deep. In the centre was a stately portico of six Corinthian columns, and a pediment with the Childs' arms on the tympanum, the approach being by a double flight of steps. The Great Hall, 53 ft. by 45, had the ceiling decorated with paintings of Morning, Noon, Evening, and Night; the walls were hung with paintings, and antique statues and statues of the Arts were ranged on pedestals. The Dining Room and the Drawing Room were each 27 ft. square. The State Dining Room, 27 ft. square, had the ceiling painted with the Seasons ; the corresponding Drawing Room, 30 ft. by 25, had on the ceiling the story of Jupiter and Semele. The Great Dining Room was 40 ft. by 27, and the adjacent Drawing Room 27 ft. square. A Saloon 30 ft. square was adorned with sculpture. The Ball Room, 70 ft. by 27, was fitted up in the utmost splendour of the time. There were besides a Common Dining Parlour, 40 ft. by 35 (making four in all), and a Breakfast Room, 32 ft. by 25, and no fewer than four large state bedrooms, and many secondary chambers.† All the rooms were hung with pictures, and the furniture was of the richest description. If Walpole is not hypercritical,

* Evelyn, Memoirs.
+ Campbell has given elevations, sections, and ground plans of Wanstead House in the Vitruvius Britannicus, vol. i., pl. 21—27.

much of it was, however, in questionable taste :—

"I dined yesterday at Wanstead : many years have passed since I saw it. The disposition of the house and the prospect are better than I expected, and very fine : the garden, which they tell you cost as much as the house, that is, £100,000 (don't tell Mr. Muntz) is wretched ; the furniture fine, but totally without taste : such continencies and incontinencies of Scipio and Alexander, by I don't know whom ! such flame-coloured gods and goddesses by Kent! such family-pieces, by—I believe the great Earl himself, for they are as ugly as the children that he really begot ! The whole great apartment is of oak, finely carved, unpainted, and has a charming effect." *

A very different and perhaps fairer critic wrote—

"Wanstead upon the whole is one of the noblest houses in England. The magnificence of having four state bedchambers, with complete apartments to them, and the ball-room, are superior to anything of the kind in Houghton, Holkam, Blenheim, and Wilton. But each of these houses is superior to this in other particulars ; and to form a complete palace, something must be taken from all. In respect of elegance of architecture, Wanstead is second to Holkam. But what a building would it be, were the wings added according to the first design." †

Sir J. Tylney Long died in 1794, and his only son, an infant, shortly after. For many years, during the minority of the heiress, Miss Tylney Long, Wanstead was the residence of the Prince de Condé (father of the unfortunate Duc d'Enghien), and the occasional residence of Louis XVIII., and other exiled members of the Bourbon family.

The competition for the hand of "the rich heiress," as she was styled, was keen, even royalty, it was said, taking part in it. The prize was won by the least worthy. The Hon. W. Pole Tylney-Long Wellesley entered into possession, and by reckless and profligate expenditure soon dissipated the heiress's wealth, and encumbered the estates ; and in June 1822 the contents of Wanstead were sold by George Robins. The auction lasted 32 days, and produced £41,000. Finally, no one being found willing to purchase it as it stood, the house was pulled down, and the materials sold piecemeal.

Now, not a vestige of the palace remains, and of the ornaments of the grounds only the dismantled grotto. The lake and

canals are left, the heronry is still kept up, some of the avenues remain, and a few old trees are standing, but all available timber was long ago converted into cash. At the sale of the contents of the house, the family portraits were reserved ; but later (Feb. 8, 1851) these too were dispersed by Christie and Manson, "in consequence," as the catalogue states, "of the non-payment for expenses for warehousing room." A more complete wreck was hardly ever witnessed. The rich heiress died Sept. 1825—three years after the sale of her goods and destruction of her house.

Within the park stands Wanstead *Church* (of the Virgin Mary), built 1787-90, at the cost of Sir James Tylney-Long in place of the old parish ch., which was small, inconvenient, and dilapidated. The new ch., which was designed by Thomas Hardwick, is of Portland stone, a plain rectangular cube, with, at the W. end, a tetrastyle Doric portico, and a small cupola-crowned Ionic turret. The interior is in like manner coldly classic, as classic architecture was then understood. But it is well and even elegantly finished ; the nave is separated from the aisles by Corinthian columns, and the E. window is filled with painted glass. The great feature of the int. is however the sumptuous mont. of Sir Josiah Child (d. 1699), removed here from the old ch. A statue of Sir Josiah, the size of life, is on a pedestal, under a pediment. Beneath are semi-recumbent statues of his son, Sir Richard, and his wife. A mourning female is seated on each side of the pedestal ; boys, angels, and emblematic figures are variously disposed ; and from a canopy which is suspended over all, depends a falling curtain.

Dr. James Pound, distinguished in his day as a naturalist and astronomer, was rector of Wanstead from 1707 till his death in 1724. Pound wrote several papers which were printed in the 'Philosophical Transactions,' but his most enduring claim to remembrance is that he supplied Newton with many observations, which are acknowledged in the 'Principia,' and taught his more famous nephew, James Bradley, how to observe. James Bradley resided for some time with his uncle as his curate. After his uncle's death he erected, 1727, a zenith sector in the house of his aunt ; with it made the observations which

---

* Horace Walpole to Richard Bentley, July 17, 1755 ; Letters, vol. ii., p. 451.

† Arthur Young, Six Weeks' Tour in the South of England, 1768.

confirmed those made by him at Kew, and continuing his investigations here, arrived at his great discovery of aberration—one of the most important in the history of astronomy. The house was pulled down long ago, and the site is forgotten.

To Pound's house, or for his use, was brought the famous May-pole of the Strand.

"The May-pole, commonly called the May-pole in the Strand, above 100 feet in height, being grown old and decayed, was April 1717, obtained by Sir Isaac Newton, Knt., of the parish ; and being taken down, was carried away through the City in a carriage of timber, unto *Wansted* in Essex. And by the leave of Sir Richard Child, Bar. Lord Castlemain, granted to the Rev. Mr. Pound, rector of that parish, was reared up and placed in his park there ; the use whereof is for the raising of a telescope the largest in the world, given by a French gentleman [M. Hugon] to the Royal Society : he being a member thereof. It had not long been set up there, but these witty verses were fashioned upon it by an unknown Hand.

'Once I adorn'd the Strand,
 But now have found
 My way to *Pound*,
 In Baron Newton's Land,' " etc.*

John Saltmarsh, a noted Puritan divine and controversialist, lived at Wanstead, and was buried in the ch.-yard, 1647. The famous citizen, Sir William Curtis, M.P. (d. 1829), and Joseph Wilton, the sculptor (d. 1803), were also buried here. Sir Wm. Penn, Pepys's friend and colleague in the Navy Office, and father of the founder of Pennsylvania, was for some years a resident, and at one time gave out that he was about to buy Wanstead House of Sir Robert Brookes ; but " I dare be hanged," wrote Pepys, " if ever he could mean to buy that great house, that knows not how to furnish one that is not the tenth part so big." †

On the W. of Wanstead Park, divided from it by the road to Snaresbrook, remains what looks like a wild bit of the Forest, but having avenues across it, the chief nearly a mile long—no doubt relics of the old avenues of Sir Josiah Child's planting. The larger avenue, known as *The Avenue*, is a favourite resort of East-end holiday-makers and school parties, who come here during the summer months in vans and other vehicles in prodigious numbers, and amuse themselves with swings, donkey and pony races, and a variety of sports. Some of the trees are large, but the best timber trees have been felled. *Obs.* on the rt., on entering from the park, a magnificent oak, partly hollow and decaying, but the head still verdant, and the whole picturesque. Between the Avenue and the Park is *Park Gate*, the pleasant seat and grounds of Alderman T. Quested Finnis ; and *Park House* (Mrs. Venables).

A little S., within a bank-and-hedge enclosure, stood *Lake House*, of old an outlying banqueting hall belonging to Wanstead House, now pulled down. Of Lake House, Thomas Hood took a lease in the spring of 1831, and made it his residence till driven away, sorely against his will, by increasing pecuniary difficulties, in 1835. Whilst here he wrote ' Tylney Hall,' the title, at least, suggested by the story of Wanstead House, as many of the descriptions were by the scenery of the neighbourhood.

The broad level space S. of Wanstead Park is *Wanstead Flats*—in the Ordnance Map marked *Epping Lower Forest*, a name unrecognized in the locality. About 400 acres in area, it was, only a few years back, a bright breezy expanse of furze and bramble, heath and fern, with a few trees, mostly hornbeams, scattered irregularly about it. But it has been much encroached on and defaced. The trees have been felled, farms laid out, brick-fields opened, gravel dug, and it is now a mere waste, rough and uninviting. From beyond memory it has been a great resort of gipseys,* and the tribes who have adopted gipsey habits and a wandering life, hawking mats and brooms and the like, telling fortunes to servant girls, picking up unconsidered trifles, and dwelling in caravans, many of which may be seen at almost any time about the edge of Wanstead Flats.

On these flats, in 1806, George III. reviewed a force of 10,000 men. The Duke of Wellington is said to have strongly recommended their being obtained as a place on which to exercise large bodies of

---

* J. Styrpe, Stow's Survey of London, ed. 1720, b. iv., ch. 7, vol. ii., p. 104. From what is said in another place (p. 112) there would seem to have been only about 20 ft. of the May-pole left when Sir Isaac Newton obtained leave to remove it.

† Pepys, Diary, April 14th, 1667.

* Borrow, Romano Lavo-Lil, p. 273, etc.

troops. His advice was at the time unheeded, but in June 1874 Wanstead Flats were secured by the Government for military drill and exercise.

The village lies N. of Wanstead Park, about the Green and Grove, and the lanes running off towards Barking Side, Snaresbrook, and Woodford. New houses have been built wherever land could be obtained, some large and good, but the greater part of moderate size, and many small. The country, though much altered, is still rural, sylvan, and in places almost forestal. On the N. side of the Green a new *church* (Christ Church) was built in 1861, and enlarged and a new tower and spire added in 1871. It is a very good village ch., of stone with slated roofs; early Dec. in style, with plate tracery to the nave windows; comprises nave with wide aisles, chancel, tower at the N.W., with octagonal stone spire, and S. porch. The E. and W. windows are filled with painted glass.

At *Woodside* is the *Princess Louise Home for Young Girls*, for the reclamation and protection of young women, and preparing them for service. There are (May 1876) 92 girls in the home; 1201 have been admitted since the opening, of whom 915 have been sent to service, 176 restored to friends. At *New Wanstead* are the Almshouses of the Weavers' Company, a well-built, roomy, and comfortable pile.

The hamlet of SNARESBROOK, with the Infant Orphan Asylum, and the Merchant Seamen's Orphan Asylum, is noticed under that heading.

WARE, HERTS, a market town, on the left bank of the river Lea, 2 m. N.E. of Hertford, 21 m. from London by road, 24 m. by the Ware and Hertford branch of the Grt. E. Rly. Pop. of the town 4917; of the par. (including 202 in the Union Workhouse) 5403. Inns: *Railway Tavern; Saracen's Head; French Horn; White Lion.*

The town consists now, as a century and a half ago, of "one fair street in length, with divers back streets and lanes, full of houses and famous for inns"— famous, that is, for number, for Ware inns are anything but famous for goodness. The High Street runs E. and W. by the river, two broad streets run from it northward, and at the E. end the main street turns sharply, and crosses the Lea by a wide iron bridge erected in 1845. The fine old ch. stands in an open space on the rt. of the High Street, near the centre of the town, of which it is the chief ornament. The old houses are few, but there are two or three with timber frame-work, carved: as the Bull's Head Inn, opposite the lane to Ware Park. Ware has a Town Hall and a Corn Exchange, a branch bank, and the like, but none of its buildings besides the ch. are of architectural value. The malt-houses form the most conspicuous feature, both of the town and its suburbs. Ware is the largest malting town in England. The malt-tax collected in it amounts to a quarter of a million annually. There are also several breweries; large corn mills; brick-fields; the timber trade is considerable, and the corn market, held on Tuesday, is one of the largest in the county. The Corn Exchange, Church Street, is a substantial building, erected in 1867; behind it is the Cattle Market. Over the bridge, Ware has a southern suburb, of which *Amwell End* may be considered a part. (*See* AMWELL.)

In 896 the Danes towed their ships up the Lea, constructed a fortress on that river 20 miles above London, and there wintered. In the summer the Londoners, with such help as they could obtain, attacked them in their encampment, but were repulsed, compelled to retreat, and four of the king's thanes were slain. Alfred now placed his army so as to enable the Londoners to secure their harvest unmolested, made a careful survey of the Lea river, and ascertained where the watercourse might be so dealt with that the Danes would be unable to bring out their ships. There he accordingly constructed fortifications on the opposite banks, and set his men to work. The Danes, when they found that they could not float their ships down the river, abandoned them, broke up their camp, and marched across the country towards Cambridge.

The locality of the Danish camp is uncertain; but it is believed to be somewhere between Ware and Hertford. Nor does the Saxon Chronicle state clearly the nature of the operation by which Alfred rendered it impracticable for the Danes to take their ships down the river. It is supposed that he effected his purpose by making several new cuts about Waltham Abbey and lower down the stream, and thus diverting the water from the natural channel. The notion that he made a weir for the purpose of obstructing the navigation seems hardly feasible, and least of all that Ware was " the place at which Alfred constructed his weir across the river Lea in order to cut off the retreat of the Danes."* If the Danes were encamped on the Lea only 20 miles from London, they must have been at the farthest at Hertford, and they would hardly have allowed Alfred to build his two fortresses within sight of their camp, and carry out his works, whatever they were, unopposed. It is indeed clear from the Chronicle that the works took the Danes by surprise, and could not therefore have been carried on in their immediate vicinity. From Camden downwards it has however been usual to ascribe the name of the town (*Waras* in Dom.) to a weir (A.-S. *wær*) constructed across the Lea at the Danish inroad, but the more common opinion is that the weir was made by the Danes to form a secure haven for their ships during the winter.

" Some say this town was built, An. 914, by order of King Edward, the son of King Alfred," † but the burh built by him is expressly stated to have been at Hertford, and " on the S. of the Lea," whereas Ware is on the N. of that river. (*See* HERTFORD, p. 338.) At the Dom. Survey Ware was a small place of about 130 inhabitants. There were a village reeve and a priest, and probably therefore a church, 38 villans, 27 bordarii, 12 cottars, and 9 bondmen; also 2 Frenchmen and 3 Englishmen, with 32 serfs, villans, and bordarii under them. There were 2 mills, the rent of which was four-and-twenty shillings and 400 eels save 25. The other vassals had 3 mills paying ten shillings of rent yearly. Meadows; pannage for 400 hogs; a park of wild animals (parcus bestiorum silvaticarum), and 4 arpents of vineyard newly planted—perhaps by the Frenchmen. The whole value was £45; when received £50: the same as in King Edward's time.

At this time the manor belonged to Hugh de Grentemaisnil, and it was held

by his descendants till towards the end of the 12th cent., when a heiress, Petronill, carried it by marriage to Robert Blanchmaines, Earl of Leicester. It afterwards passed to Saier De Quincy, Earl of Winchester, who " by his great power " broke down the iron chain which locked up the passage over the bridge, and succeeded in freeing the town from the toll paid to the corporation of Hertford, by all who passed over the bridge or through the town; and " by this means, the great road was turned from Hertford through this town, where inns and houses have been since erected by degrees, for the receipt of travellers; so that from a small vill., it is now become a great and populous town."* In 1254 Robert De Quincy obtained of Henry III. a grant for a market and fair. In 1262 the manor passed by marriage to Baldwin Wake; in the reign of Edward III., to Sir Thomas Holland, afterwards Earl of Kent, in whose family it remained notwithstanding the execution and attainder of his heir, Thomas Duke of Surrey, in 1400, till carried by a heiress, 1409, to Thomas de Montacute, Earl of Salisbury. It afterwards passed to the King-maker Earl of Warwick; then to Richard Duke of Gloucester, afterwards King; and upon his death at Bosworth was settled by Henry VII. upon his mother, the Countess of Richmond. On her death it was granted to the Lady Margaret Pole, Countess of Salisbury, mother of the Cardinal, and upon her execution reverted to the Crown. Queen Mary, on her accession, restored the manor to Katherine Countess of Huntingdon, granddaughter of the Countess of Salisbury, who about 1570 sold it to Thomas Fanshawe, remembrancer in the Exchequer, an office held by five successive generations of the family, from Elizabeth to Anne. The manor was sold about 1700 to Sir Thomas Byde, a brewer of London, in whose family it remained till 1846, when it was alienated to James Cudden. In 1853 it was purchased by Daniel De Castro, and in 1869 by George Rastrick, Esq. †

The manor-house stands on the W. side of *Ware Park*, about 1 m. W. of Ware. The house, a spacious and comfortable but commonplace mansion, was built by

---

* Taylor, Words and Places, p. 304.
† Chauncy, Hertfordshire, vol. i., p. 394.

* Chauncy, vol. i., p. 397.
† Chauncy; Clutterbuck; Cussans.

Sir Thomas Byde, on the site of the ancient seat of the Fanshawes. Happily, Sir Thomas, while pulling down the house, spared the ancestral trees, many of which are now of magnificent proportions. The avenue, above half a mile long, through which there is a public way from Ware to Bengeo, is particularly fine. One noble oak in it measures nearly 20 ft. in girth at 4 ft. from the ground, and has a grand head and immense roots spreading far above-ground. This avenue, and the great oaks and elms which so happily adorn the park, are said to have been planted by Sir Henry Fanshawe, who, according to his friend Sir Henry Wotton, was an incomparable gardener.

"Though other countries have more benefit of sun than we, and thereby more properly tyed to contemplate this delight [a garden]; yet have I seen in our own, a delicate and diligent curiosity, surely without parallel among foreign nations: namely, in the Garden of Sir Henry Fanshawe, at his seat in *Ware Park;* where, I well remember, he did so precisely examine the tinctures and seasons of his flowers, that in their settings, the inwardest of which that were to come up at the same time, should be always a little darker than the utmost, and so serve them for a kind of gentle shadow, like a piece, not of Nature, but of Art: which mention (incident to this place) I have willingly made of his name, for the dear friendship that was long between us." *

The visitor to Ware should not fail to visit Ware Park : it lies immediately W. of the town. High and undulating, sloping on the W. steeply to the Lea, it affords capital views of the valley of the Lea, the towns of Ware and Hertford, and the country beyond. Ware Park is now the seat of John Gwyn-Jeffreys, Esq., LL.D., D.L.

The other manors need not detain us. But the manor-house of Blakesware—"a fair seat" old Chauncy terms it, "about three miles distant from the town on the east," the seat of the Featherstones, Leventhorpes, Clutterbucks, and Plumers, has won a lasting place in our literature. It is the *Blakesmoor Hall* of Charles Lamb's delightful essay, 'Blakesmoor in H——shire.' Of the fine old mansion, which stood directly opposite the road from the neighbouring village of Widford, not a vestige is left. It was pulled down in 1822 by Mrs. Plumer, then lady of the

* Sir H. Wotton, Elements of Architecture, Reliquiæ Wottonianæ, 4th ed., 1685, p. 64.

manor. Close by it stood the cottage in which dwelt Lamb's Rosamund Gray. This too has been swept away.

A priory was founded on the W. side of the town, beyond the ch., according to Chauncy, "about the 18th year of the reign of King Henry III., by Margaret, Countess of Leicester," but it was more probably of earlier foundation, and enriched and enlarged by her. It was for friars of the order of St. Francis, who held it till the Dissolution. The estate was given by Henry VIII. to Thomas Byrch; has since frequently changed hands; and now belongs to Clement Morgan, Esq., who purchased it in 1868. Only a few fragments of the conventual buildings remain. The mansion built on the site is known as *The Priory.*

Ware *Church* (St. Mary) is a large and handsome cruciform building of flint and stone, with a lofty embattled tower of 5 floors and short thin spire. The body of the ch. is Dec., the chancel and tower are Perp. In the tower is a peal of 8 bells. The interior is roomy and striking. It has a wide nave of 5 bays, with a good open timber roof. The chancel arch is large and well moulded, and a lofty arch opens into the tower and displays the W. window. In the large E. window is a representation of the Crucifixion. A Lady Chapel on the S. is divided from the chancel by an arch with a slender central clustered column of polished Purbeck marble, and from the S. transept by a screen of carved oak. The large window in this transept is recent, and foreign in character to the rest of the building. The ch. was restored throughout, the interior thoroughly, a few years back, when the mouldings and tracery were for the most part rechiselled, and much new work inserted. *Obs.* the font, of the reign of Henry IV., and good. It is octagonal, and has on the panels figures in high relief of the Virgin, St. Gabriel, St. John the Baptist, St. Christopher carrying the Saviour, St. George, St. Margaret, St. Catherine, and St. Thomas. In the Lady Chapel are a piscina, sedilia, and ambreys.

When the ch. was restored, many of the monts. were removed and lost, or set up in other places. The only one left of any interest is a mural marble mont. removed from the Lady Chapel—of old the manor chapel of Ware Park—to the S. transept, of Sir Richard Fanshawe, d. at Madrid, 1666, translator of Guarini's Pastor Fido, the Luciad of Camoens, etc., ambassador from Charles II. to the Courts of Portugal and Spain, and husband of Anne Lady Fanshawe, authoress of the 'Memoirs of the Fanshawe Family,' which throw so attractive a light on the last years of Charles I. There are other monts. to Fanshawes, Dickinsons, etc. An altar tomb in the N. transept had some good *brasses*, which were stolen several years ago by the parish clerk. Several of the brasses on the floors were lost at the restoration of the ch., but two or three are left. The most curious is that in the S. transept to Wm. Pyrry, d. 1470, and his wives Agnes and Alice, by each of whom he had 5 sons and 5 daughters. Elen, wife of Wm. Warbulton, 1454; and a female without name of somewhat late date.

In the ch.-yard, S. of the ch., is the tomb of Dr. William Mead, d. 1652, "aged 148 years, 9 months, 3 weeks, and 4 days;" but the inscription is only of about the year 1850, and the age, enough to startle Mr. Thoms from his propriety, is probably due to the mason employed to recut the insc., which had become illegible,*—or to his employer.

Christ Church, in the New Road, is a handsome building of Kentish rag and Bath stone, E.E. in style, erected in 1858, at the cost of Robert Hanbury, Esq., of Poles, from the designs of Mr. W. E. Stevens. It has nave, aisles, porches, and a tower and spire at the S.E.

There are the usual chapels, all commonplace as buildings. It was as minister of the Independent Chapel, Ware, that William Godwin, the author of 'Political Justice,' and 'Caleb Williams,' commenced his unconformable career. Among the natives must be placed William of Ware, the teacher of Duns Scotus, since, as Fuller has it, he was "born in that thoroughfare town," though nothing is said of any later connection with it.

Roman remains have been found at different times on the N.W. of the town, and in the lower ground by the Lea. They include weapons, a brass steelyard, coins of Severus, etc. Some stone coffins have also been found in what was probably a cemetery of the priory.

The most noted of the local antiquities, though now lost to the town, is the *Great Bed of Ware*, already famous in Shakspeare's time :

"*Sir Toby Belch.*—Go write it in a martial hand; be curst and brief; it is no matter how witty, so it be eloquent and full of invention . . . . and as many lies as will lie in thy sheet of paper, although the sheet were big enough for the Bed of Ware in England, set 'em down."*

Allusions to the "Bed of Ware" are not unfrequent in our literature. Chauncy † noticing the "large bed which is twelve foot square," observes that "the strangeness of this unusual size oftentimes invited the curious traveller to view the same," and he adds a not very decent story of six citizens and their wives who came from London in a frolic, which probably Byron had in his memory when he wrote that

"All (except Mahometans) forbear To make the nuptial couch a *Bed of Ware*."‡

The great bed, or rather bedstead, is said to have belonged to Ware Park, but of this there is no evidence. It was kept at the Crown until that inn was taken down in 1765, when it was transferred to the Bull. It was afterwards removed to the Saracen's Head, where it was placed in a large room on the second floor, with other old furniture. Later the requirements of the inn led the landlord to divide the room into two, and the great bed was shortened some 3 ft. to adapt it to the lessened room. The bedstead is of very dark oak : the end posts have massive pedestals about 2 ft. high, on which rest 4 thin pillars bearing arches, above which are circular posts about 4 ft. high, very elaborately carved. The canopy and head-board are also elaborately carved, the latter having panels separated by human figures, and decorated with heraldic and symbolic devices, roses interlaced and coloured, and renaissance ornaments. The total height is about 12 ft. In its last years at the Saracen's Head, it looked sadly dilapidated, and bore marks of having been much hacked and damaged by visitors. On it was painted the date

---

* J. E. Cussans, Hist. of Hertfordshire, fol. 1870, p. 151.

* Twelfth Night, Act iii., sc. 2.
† Hist. Antiq. of Hertfordshire, vol. i., p. 414.
‡ Don Juan, Canto vi., 12.

1463, but this was palpably modern. From the style of the carving it appeared to be of the reign of Elizabeth. It was put up for sale by auction in 1862, but the purchase was not completed, and it remained at the Saracen's Head till 1869, when it was bought by the proprietor of the Rye House, where it is now shown in a room prepared for its reception. (*See* RYE HOUSE, p. 518.)*

In a meadow S. of the Lea, on the rt. of the road to Hertford, ¾ m. from Ware bridge, is *Chadswell*, the head spring of the New River. The site of the principal spring is marked by a stone erected by the New River Company, an insc. on which states that it was opened in 1608, and that the water is conveyed a distance of 40 miles. From the spring the water flows into a circular basin, and thence into a channel, which, having been swelled by some cuts from the Lea, and by large additions from the Amwell springs (*see* AMWELL), runs for several miles parallel to the Lea. The vale of the Lea, from Ware nearly to Tottenham, is the scene of the 'Complete Angler,' the neighbourhood of Ware, Ware Park, and Amwell being particularly favoured by Walton; but the disciple of honest Izaak who makes a pilgrimage along the meadows he describes so lovingly, must not look to find them so " chequered with water-lilies and lady-smocks," or in any way so inviting as they were when Piscator and his scholar rambled and gossiped along them.

Ware Side is a hamlet about 2 m. N.E. of Ware, and an eccl. dist. of 738 inh., formed in 1844, with the addition of a small portion of Thundridge par. It is a quiet little place, with a small semi-Norman ch. (Holy Trinity) erected in 1841, and an old Grammar School, which has been resuscitated of late years, and is now in a tolerably flourishing state.

Wade's Mill, 2 m. N. of Ware, gave rise to a local proverb, "Ware and Wades Mill are worth all London," which, says Thomas Fuller, " is, I assure you, a master-piece of the vulgar wits in this county, wherewith they endeavour to amuse travellers, as if Ware, a thoroughfare market, and Wade's Mill (part of a village

lying 2 m. N. thereof) were so prodigiously rich as to countervail the wealth of London. The fallacy lieth in the homonymy of *Ware*, here not taken for that town so named, but for all vendible commodities." *

WARLEY, GREAT,—WEST WARLEY, or WARLEY ABBESS, ESSEX,

3 m. S. of the Brentwood Stat. of the Grt. E. Rly. (Colchester line), on the road to Grays. Pop. 1416, but of these 1004 were in the eccl. dist. of Great Warley Christ Church, the northern portion of the parish. Inn, *Headley Arms.*

The names Great and West Warley were given to distinguish it from the adjacent par. of Little Warley, which lies immediately E. of it. It was called Warley Abbess, from the manor having belonged to the Abbess of Barking down to the Dissolution. It is a pleasant undulating country famed for farming and hunting. Wheat and barley, beans and peas, are largely grown; there are still considerable woodlands, but that part of Warley Common which belongs to this par. is enclosed and cultivated. The inhabitants are widely scattered, the houses extending from the old ch. northwards nearly to Brentwood station, Warley Street being about midway. There are many good seats, especially towards the Brentwood end.

Great Warley *Church* (St. Mary the Virgin) stands in a treeless ch.-yard, far away from the village, its only neighbour a farm-house. It is modern, the nave red brick, the chancel, the newest portion, yellow brick with stone dressings. But in 1860 the building was rendered more ecclesiastical by the insertion of French Dec. windows, the addition of an open belfry and short tiled spire to the tower, and the transformation of the interior by various alterations, the substitution of open seats for pews, laying down a pavement of encaustic tiles, and placing painted glass in the E. window. On the N. of the chancel is a mural mont. with bust.

Christ Church, erected 1854, to supply the eccl. dist. formed in 1855 from the northern part of the par., with the addition of small portions of South Weald and Shenfield parishes, is a neat brick and

---

* The bedstead is engraved in Clutterbuck's Hist. of Hertfordshire, vol. iii. ; Shaw's Ancient Furniture ; and Knight's Pictorial Shakspeare, Notes to Twelfth Night.

* Worthies : Hertfordshire.

stone building, E.E. in style, with a tall battlemented tower.

The *Manor House* stood close by the ch., but has been long taken down. *Warley Place* (Anthony G. Robinson, Esq.) is a good old red-brick embattled mansion modernized. It stands within pleasant grounds a little N. of Warley Street, and 2 m. from the old ch. Other good seats are— *Coombe Lodge* (Edward Ind, Esq.) ; *The Lea* (E. M. Daldy, Esq.); *Brookland House* (Col. Legge); *Goldings* (W. T. Graves, Esq.); *Warley House* (Rev. J. F. H. English, LL.D.)

WARLEY, LITTLE, Essex, lies

immediately E. of Great Warley, from which it is divided by the stream that rises in the northern part of the parish, flows through Bulphan Fen and Stifford, and falls into the Thames at Purfleet. Pop. 1367, but this includes 1196 in Warley Barracks, leaving only 171 civilian inhabitants. Inn, the *Greyhound*.

Warley stands on high ground, and from various parts there are extensive prospects; that from Warley Gap is particularly fine. There is no village proper. Like that of Great Warley, Little Warley church stands apart, its only neighbour a farm-house, but it has the advantage in being surrounded by fine old elms. The *Church* (St. Peter) is chiefly of brick, the nave of red brick, the chancel more recent, yellow stock, with a plain lancet triplet. At the W. end is a tall square brick tower, bearing the date 1778. The interior is very plain; but there are two monts. in the chancel worth noticing. On the S. is a good marble recumbent effigy of a lady. On the N. the recessed tomb of Sir Denner Strutt and wife, with their effigies in alabaster, the costume temp. Charles I., very carefully made out. This mont. has been twice restored of late years by the descendants of the knight, and lost something of its antiquarian value in the process.

At *Warley Common*, 2 m. N.W. from Little Warley ch., and nearer Brentwood, camps of militia, volunteers, and regulars were formed on a large scale during the wars with France and when the country was stirred by threats of invasion. George III. and Queen Charlotte visited Warley Camp and reviewed the troops, Oct. 20, 1778, on which occasion

their Majesties were guests of Lord Petre at Thorndon Hall, 2 m. E. (*See* HORNDON, WEST.) There are two fine views of Warley Camp and Common, painted by De Loutherbourg, in the Corridor of Windsor Castle : one of them was exhibited at the Royal Academy in 1780. Dr. Johnson spent a week at the camp, the guest of his friend Bennet Langton, who was stationed there as captain in the Lincolnshire Militia. Johnson slept in a tent lent him by an officer, attended a court-martial, and "notwithstanding a great degree of ill-health," took great pains to make himself acquainted with military topics and the occupations and accommodation of the men.

"It was in the summer of the year 1778 that he complied with my invitation to come down to the camp at Warley, and he staid with me about a week. . . . . He sate, with a patient degree of attention, to observe the proceedings of a regimental court-martial, that happened to be called in the time of his stay with us ; and one night, as late as eleven o'clock, he accompanied the major of the regiment in going what are styled the *rounds*, where he might observe the forms of visiting the guards, for the seeing that they and their sentries are ready in their duty on their several posts. . . . . On one occasion, when the regiment were going through their exercise, he went quite close to the men at one of the extremities of it, and watched all their practices attentively." [*]

On the S. side of the Common are the extensive *Warley Barracks*. They were originally erected by the East India Company as a depôt for recruits ; purchased by the Government in 1842 for £17,000 for a depôt for the Royal Artillery, and are now an establishment for the Infantry, with accommodation for 1500 men. To fit them for their present purpose they have been much altered and added to, the sanitary arrangements improved, and a roomy and handsome chapel, Byzantine in style, erected from the designs of Mr. M. D. Wyatt.

WARLINGHAM, SURREY, 5 m.

S.E. of Croydon, on the road to Titsey and Limpsfield, and a stat. on the Caterham branch of the S.-E. Rly. Pop. 773.

Warlingham Stat. is in the Caterham Valley, 1½ m. from the vill., by a pleasant uphill walk. To reach the vill., pass under the bridge of the abandoned Surrey and Sussex Rly., and take the steep path

[*] Langton in Boswell's Johnson, vol. vii., p. 224.

up the hill-side, through the copse and by the large farm-house, E. by N.; or the lane, hardly less steep, a little farther on the Caterham road, where is the outer lodge to Marden Park, but turning sharp to the l.

A few humble cottages gathered about a broad Green, two or three sleepy shops, a smithy, a Methodist chapel, and a couple of little inns, the *Leather Bottle*, and the *White Lion*—the latter also a general shop—with a farm-house or two, and a dismanted windmill, constitute the village. The church stands apart in a lonely-looking field, ¼ m. N.

Warlingham was a settlement of the Saxon *Wearlingas*.* The church and manor belonged in the 12th cent. to the monks of Bermondsey, and was held by them until the suppression of monasteries. They were granted by Henry VIII. in 1545 to Sir John Gresham. In 1591, Richard Gresham sold Warlingham, with Sanderstead, to John Ownstead; who, dying without issue in 1600, bequeathed his Surrey estates to his cousin, Harman Attwood, and his two sisters. Their shares were purchased by Mr. Attwood, from whom the whole descended, like Sanderstead, to the present lord of the manor, Atwood Dalton Wigsell, Esq. (*See* SANDERSTEAD, p. 545.)

The *Church* (All Saints) is small; consisting of a nave and chancel, of flint and stone, roughcast, with a wooden bell-turret at the W. end. The frame of the fabric is E.E., and several lancets remain; but a late Dec. E. window, and several of Perp. character in the nave, have been inserted. The ch. was partially restored and the W. doorway renewed in 1866. There are no monts. W. of the ch. is a very fine yew, and on the S. one still larger, but decaying.

The wide heath, redolent of purple ling and golden gorse, known as *Warlingham Common*, which formed the chief charm of Warlingham, one of the loveliest spots round London, was enclosed in 1864-5, and is now cultivated, of the 300 acres 5 acres being reserved as a "recreation ground." But though the Common is lost, there is still a fine open country, the air is invigorating, and the neighbourhood healthy and picturesque. Warlingham

* Kemble, Saxons in England.

is one of the "five places on the hills." (*See* CHELSHAM.)

Godstone Road, in Caterham Valley, a little collection of modern dwellings, two or three shops, and the *White Leaf* tavern, is a detached portion of Warlingham parish.

WATFORD, HERTS, a market-town on the Aylesbury road, 15 m. from London, and a stat. on the L. and N.-W. Rly., 17¾ m. Branch rlys. diverge from the main line at Watford to St. Albans, 7 m., and to Rickmansworth, 4 m. Pop. of the town (Local Board dist., including 200 in Bushey par.) 7461; of the parish, which has an area of 10,792 acres, 12,071, but of these 2374 were in public institutions. Inns: *Clarendon Hotel*, by Rly. stat., a first-class house; *Essex Arms Hotel*, by the market-place; *Rose and Crown*, *George*, etc., High Street.

Watford Manor belonged to the Abbey of St. Albans down to the Dissolution. Retained by the Crown till 1609, it was then granted by James I. to Thomas Lord Ellesmere, Lord Chancellor of England. From him it descended to the Earls of Bridgewater, in whom it remained until purchased in 1767 by William, 4th Earl of Essex, the lord of Cassiobury. The present lord of the manors of Watford and Cassiobury is Arthur Algernon Capel, 6th Earl of Essex. The history of CASSIOBURY manor is told under that heading. The other manors are of no general interest.

Watford town stands on moderately high ground, being built on a ridge of gravel overlying the chalk, above the rt. bank of the river Colne. The Colne crosses the lower part of the town, dividing it from Bushey—now a kind of southern suburb of Watford. The town runs up from the river northwards, in a single main street, for about 1½ m. to Nascott, beyond the entrance gates to Cassiobury Park. The passages which diverge on either hand are little else than courts and byways. The High Street is broad in the upper part, lined with good houses and shops, and clean throughout; but the byways and back passages are poor and squalid, though much has been done for their improvement of late years by the Local Board of Health, and some new thoroughfares have let in a little useful ventilation. The market-place is near the centre of the town on the W., and by it is the church. The L. and N.-W. Rly. Stat. is outside the town, at its north-eastern extremity. For the southern part of Watford the Bushey Stat. is most used. The Rickmansworth line has a station near the centre of the High Street.

The Market Place is the nucleus of the town; but neither the Market House, nor any of the buildings about it, except the church, possesses any claims on the attention of the antiquary or student of architecture. The newer buildings include a Post Office; a County Court and Sessions House, King Street; a Public Library and School of Science and Art, a showy Gothic building with a good lecture hall, erected 1874, in the Queen's Road; an Agricultural Hall; a Masonic Hall, at the back of the Essex Arms; and a Branch Bank. The town has also a Literary Institute, an active Natural-history Society, and supports a weekly newspaper. The local trade is large, and there are corn-mills, paper-mills, a silk-mill, large breweries, maltings, iron and engineering works, etc. Within the last few years many good villa residences have been built about Nascot, and around the rly. stat. a new and rapidly extending district has grown up.

The *Church* (St. Mary) is a spacious and handsome building, comprising nave with broad aisles, chapels (the St. Katherine Chapel on the N., the Essex on the S.), chancel, a lofty tower at the W. end, with buttresses and battlements, and two porches. It is of the Perp. period, but was thoroughly restored in 1870-71, under the direction of Mr. Christopher of Watford, when the S. aisle, and St. Katherine chapel and porches, were taken down and rebuilt, the exterior refaced with flints and Bath-stone, new windows inserted nearly throughout, those left of the old ones being repaired and rechiselled,—the whole, indeed, (except the Essex chapel) being made "as good as new." The interior restoration was also complete; and a new reredos, pulpit, font, and organ were erected. For the antiquary the chief interest consists now in the *Monts.*, and especially those in the Essex or Morrison chapel, erected at the cost of Bridget Countess of Bedford, in 1595, and happily

undisturbed by the restorer. Strictly a monumental chapel, stately tombs with marble effigies line the walls and occupy the floors, and present a striking—to the casual visitor, it must be owned, somewhat tantalizing—aspect. For though the panelling of the screens which shut off the chapel from the chancel and aisles is glazed, and through it the monts. may be seen, the chapel can only be entered by special permission: the door is locked, and the key kept at Cassiobury.

In the centre of the chapel is an altar tomb of coloured marbles, with recumbent effigy in countess's robes and coronet, between two knights in complete armour, of Lady Bridget, Countess Dowager of Bedford, the founder of the chapel, d. 1600, "in great favour with her Prince, and generally reputed one of the noblest matrons of England, for her wisdom and judgment." A long insc. sets forth in full her great virtues and family connections. Her first husband was Sir Richard Morrison; her second, Edward Manners, Earl of Rutland; and Francis Russell, Earl of Bedford, her third. Beyond this is another altar tomb, with 6 marble Tuscan columns, supporting a recumbent effigy of the Rt. Hon. Lady, Dame Elizabeth Russell, wife of Sir William Russell, Lord Russell of Thornaugh, d. 164-.

Against the S. side of the chapel is a lofty architectural mont., in which, beneath a canopy supported on tall Corinthian columns, is the semi-recumbent effigy in armour of Sir Charles Morrison the elder, d. 1619. Angels with trumpets, shields of arms, and other enrichments adorn the mont., whilst on a pedestal outside the tomb, at the knight's head, is a life-sized kneeling effigy of his son, and at his feet a corresponding figure of his daughter, Bridget Countess of Sussex. This elaborate mont. was the work of old Nicholas Stone, whose pocket-book, so happily saved by Vertue, tells what he was paid for it:—

"1619.—A bargain made with Sir Charles Morison of Cashioberry, in Hartfordshire, for a tomb of alabaster and touchstone onely. One pictor of white marble for his father, and his own, and his sister the Countess of Sesex, as great as the life of alabaster, for the which I had well payed £260, and 4 pieces given me to drink." *

---

* Walpole, Anecdotes, vol. ii., p. 43.

Opposite to this, against the N. wall, is a mont., equally large and elaborate, to Sir Charles Morrison the younger, with his effigy in armour, leaning on his right elbow, his hand on a skull; beneath him the effigy of his lady; at his feet his two sons kneeling; at his head, his daughter. This was also executed by Nicholas Stone, who covenanted that it should be a "faire and straightly tomb or monument," to be made of "white marble, touchstone and allabaster, and containe in the whole 14 foote in breadth and 16 foote in height from the ground." The "statue or picture" of Sir Charles is "to be royally and artificially carved, polished, glazed, and made of good and pure white marble in complete armour," etc., "according to the life, to consist of 6 foote in length of one entire stone." The statue of the worthy lady his wife is also to be royally carved, etc., and to be 6 feet in length; the statues of the daughters are "to be 4 foote in height, kneeling: the sons to be, the eldest 3 foote in height kneeling," the youngest 2 feet. For this and completing the work he is to receive £400.* Also on the N. wall, mont. "To the Memory of the vertuous Lady Katherine Rotheram, late wife to Sir John Rotheram; first espoused to Sir John Hampson, Knt. and Alderman of London," d. 1625, with her effigy in short cloak and surcingle, kneeling on a cushion, under a canopy borne on 4 marble columns. At W. end, square brass, with effigies in cloaks of Henry Dixon, d. 1610, George Miller, d. 1613, and Anthony Cooper, "late servants to Sir Charles Morryson, Knt., and after retayned in service with Dorothy, Lady Morryson, his wife, and Sir Charles Morryson, Knt. and Bart., their son, by the space of 40 years, in Memory of them the said Dorothy Lady Morryson hath vouchsafed this stone and inscription over their heads." There are also tablets to Admiral John Forbes, d. 1796, and Lady Mary Forbes, d. 1782.

In the St. Katherine Chapel are brasses to Hugo de Holes, quondam justiciaris, d. 1415, large but injured, and one to his wife Margaretta, d. 1416, insc. lost. Here and in the chancel are monts. to the Heydons, Attewells, Roberts, Carpenters, Whites, and other persons of local consequence, but none that we have observed of wider interest.

In the ch.-yard, on the family altar tomb, is an insc. to Robert Clutterbuck, author of the 'History and Antiquities of the County of Hertford,' who d. 1831, in his 59th year. By the ch. are almshouses for 8 poor women, founded by Francis Russell, 2nd Earl of Bedford in 1580.

A cemetery, with neat little mortuary chapels, has been constructed at Colney Butts, S.W. of the town, and here were laid, July 2, 1870, the remains of George, 4th Earl of Clarendon, the distinguished Foreign Minister.

St. Andrew's District Church, *New Watford*, the district by the rly. stat., is a neat E.E. ch. of flint and stone, with tower on the N.E., erected from the designs of Mr. Teulon in 1857, and enlarged by the addition of a S. aisle in 1865. A little W. of the ch. stands the *Almshouses of the Salters' Company*, a spacious and attractive group of buildings, erected in 1864, for 6 men and 12 women. They are of red brick and stone, Domestic Gothic in style, and comprise a centre, with bold bay window, projecting but detached wings, and an embattled tower. The houses are set well back from the road; the space in front forms a garden of 2 acres, prettily laid out in lawns and flower-beds, and each house has its own little garden.

The very striking group of buildings close to the rly. stat. is the *London Orphan Asylum*. Founded in 1813 by Dr. Andrew Reed, it has grown gradually to be the great institution we see. From 1813 the children were kept in a building at Clapton, until it was decided to remove them to the present healthier site. The first stone of the new buildings was laid by the Prince and Princess of Wales. July 13, 1869; the asylum was partially inaugurated in 1871, and the seventh house for boys formally opened by the Duke and Duchess of Edinburgh, May 20, 1875. When the eighth house is completed there will be accommodation for 600 children, 400 boys and 200 girls: there are now 550 in the aslylum. The buildings form a series of partially connected blocks, with a central dining hall and administration offices, chapel, infirmary, and tall

* Covenant in possession of the Earl of Essex, printed by Clutterbuck, Hist. and Ant. of Hertf., vol. i., p. 262.

clock tower. and occupy an area of about 15 acres. They are Domestic Gothic in style, of Suffolk brick picked out with red bricks and stone, and form an effective and well-distributed group. The architect was Mr. H. Dawson. Each house provides for 50 children. The cost of one for boys (£3000) was defrayed by the Grocers' Company; and the natives of Hertfordshire subscribed a similar sum, "as a welcome to the county," to build another. The very elegant Chapel was built, at a cost of about £5000, by a lady who was brought up in the asylum, and afterwards served as its head mistress.

Leavesden is a hamlet of Watford, from which it is about 3 m. N. on the road to King's Langley; which is 1½ m. farther. Leavesden was made an eccl. dist. in 1853, and has a neat E.E. ch. of flint and stone, consecrated in 1852. On an elevated site in Leavesden stands the Metropolitan District Asylum for Imbeciles—a vast structure of stock brick, almost a counterpart to that at Caterham. The wards are built in detached blocks, but connected by corridors. The male and female wards are on opposite sides of the ground, and between them are the central administrative block, chapel, infirmary, kitchens, workshops, houses of officials, etc. There is no superfluous ornament, but the buildings are far from gloomy in aspect, and the sanitary arrangements have been carefully studied, and liberally provided. The buildings occupy an area of about 18 acres, and 67 acres are under culture by the inmates. The cost has been about £150,000. At *Woodside*, Leavesden, is another large pauper establishment — the *Industrial Schools* for the parish of St. Pancras.

Oxhey is a hamlet on the Colne, 1½ m. S. of Watford, quiet, rural, with cornmills and silk-mills varying the level meadows. *Oxhey Place*, the seat of the Heydon family in the reign of Elizabeth, was taken down in 1668 by Sir Wm. Bucknall, who built himself a new and more commodious mansion on the site. This was demolished in 1799 by the Hon. Wm. Bucknall. Both the Bucknalls, however, left standing the Jacobean chapel built by Sir James Altham in 1612. This remains, and serves as a chapel-of-ease to Watford. On the S. wall of the chapel is the mont. of its founder, Sir James Altham, d. 1616, with his effigy in judge's robe, kneeling, between pillars which support a canopy. Behind him is the effigy of his lady. Here also is the mont., with figure of a mourning female leaning on an urn, of John Askell Bucknall, d. 1796. The house stood a little W. of the chapel.

WEALD BASSETT, NORTH,

ESSEX, (Dom. *Welda,*) 3 m. N.E. from Epping on the road to Ongar, and a stat. on the Epping and Ongar branch of the Grt. E. Rly., 20 m. from London. Pop. 984.

North Weald was so called to distinguish it from South Weald, which lies some 8 m. to the S. The suffix, Bassett, is derived from the noble family of that name to whom the manor belonged in the 13th cent. By the marriage of Aliva, daughter of Philip Bassett, with Hugh le Despencer, it passed to that family, and was forfeited to the Crown. Edward II. granted it to his brother, Edmund Plantagenet, Earl of Kent, to hold by the yearly fine of a sparrowhawk. On his decapitation, 1330, the manor was given to Bartholomew Burghersh for life, but resumed and granted to John Plantagenet, son of Edmund, and on his death to his sister Joan, the Fair Maid of Kent. It afterwards passed to the Montacutes; to Warwick the King-maker; the Duke of Clarence; Margaret Pole, Countess of Salisbury; to the Rich family; and since through many hands. The present lord of the manor is A. G. Puller, Esq.

North Weald is a rambling place with a very scattered population. The pursuits are agricultural; the village rural; outside it are green lanes, with abundant hedgerow elms, and pleasant field-paths.

The *Church* (St. Andrew) is old, but much altered; commonplace, and uninteresting. It comprises nave and S. aisle, chancel, and brick tower and spire. In the tower is a peal of 6 bells. The ch. was repaired and a new roof added to the nave in 1865. The interior had been re-seated some years before.

WEALD, SOUTH, ESSEX, about

2 m. W.N.W. from the Brentwood Stat. of the Gt. E. Rly. Pop. 2994, but this includes 767 in the Essex County Lunatic Asylum.

On leaving the stat., turn l., cross the High St., Brentwood, take the road immediately opposite, and follow its windings to the l., for the most part up-hill, but increasing in beauty the whole way, till you reach the village. It stands on a richly wooded height, picturesque in itself, and commanding wide views across a bright and fertile tract of country. The vill. contains only a few dwellings; but the church, schools, almshouses, the hall, and park, are all above the average merit, and altogether a visit to South Weald will well repay the drive or walk.

South Weald *Church* (St. Peter), with rather a dilapidated air, was one of the most interesting and picturesque churches in this part of Essex, and has always been a favourite with the county historians. Unfortunately, when it was desired to restore it a few years back it was found that decay had gone too far, and there was no help but to pull the old ch. down. The new ch. is built on the old lines, but on a securer foundation, the old architects having contented themselves with little more than levelling the ground. The old church comprised nave with N. aisle wider than the nave, and chapel at the E. end; chancel; a lofty stone tower at the W. end, with a good angle turret; and a wooden porch on the S. The nave and chancel were E.E. in style, with on the S. double lancet windows, and a triplet at the E. The N. aisle was Perp. The new ch. differs considerably in appearance and arrangements. The old Perp. windows have been copied in the nave and chancel; the aisle windows have early Dec. tracery. Both nave and aisle are covered with new wooden roofs, but the old columns and arches have been re-erected. Most of the old monts. have been relegated to the tower, but a few have been replaced in the chancel and chapel: none were of much interest. The brasses (all imperfect) have been taken away, (except the inscription of Sir Anthony Brown's, d. 1567,) and the slabs used for paving-stones, outside the ch.

The int. of the new ch. is handsome and cheerful; the exterior, of flint and stone, more picturesque than new churches usually are. The lower portion of the noble old tower is retained, only the uppermost storey being new. The small and often engraved late Norman door-way, with characteristic shafts, chevron mouldings, and reticulated pediment and spandrels, has been re-erected in its original place in the S. wall, and the stones *not* rechiselled. A new S. porch, and a lich-gate, both good examples of modern carpentry, have been substituted for the old ones. The new ch. was consecrated Dec. 22, 1868: its archt. was Mr. Teulon, from whose designs were also erected the handsome Elizabethan almshouses (1858) for 12 inmates, founded and endowed by Sir Anthony Brown, 1558, and the school, 1860.

Immediately beyond the ch. is *South Weald Hall* (C. J. Hume Tower, Esq.), a spacious brick building, with stuccoed and stone centre, comprising 6 attached Ionic columns and a pediment, reaching the whole height of the house. The older part is of the 16th century, but much of it is more recent. Of the int. the chief feature is the great hall, which was thoroughly restored and renovated in 1869-70. In contains some interesting pictures, including a Lioness and Cubs, by *Rubens;* the Port of Rhiæ, by Castro; portraits of Charles II. and James II., and others assigned to Raphael, Correggio, Titian, Ruysdael, Wouvermans, and Vandyck; a bust of Napoleon I. by Canova; a fine collection of china, and other articles of taste: but they can only be seen by special permission. On an elevation between the house and the church is a tower called the Belvedere, which affords an extensive prospect. The park is undulating, has broad sheets of water, ragged old oaks and tall elms, and is altogether unusually picturesque. It used to be open, but strangers are now restricted to the public path across it from the village towards Coxtie Green. The manor belonged to Waltham Abbey; was transferred by Henry VIII., in 1540, to Sir Brian Tuke; passed from him to Sir Richard Riche; next to Sir Anthony Brown (who founded the almshouses here, and the Grammar School at Brentwood); was sold in 1661 to Chief Justice Scroggs, who retired to the hall after his removal from office, and died there in 1683. His son sold the house and manor to Alderman Erasmus Smith, and in 1759 it was purchased by C. Tower, Esq., in whose descendant it remains.

Rotchetts, divided from South Weald

by the lane leading to Bentley, is another good house standing in a small but charming park ; was the favourite residence of Earl St. Vincents, who died there in 1823 : and is now the seat of Octavius E. Coope, Esq., M.P.   *How Hatch* (Osgood Hanbury, Esq.), at St. Vincents Hamlet, N.W. of Rotchetts, is noteworthy for the splendid elms in front of the house. Other . seats are *Pilgrims' Hall* (Sir Fredk. Arrow), Pilgrims' Hatch, 2 m. N. ; *Oakhurst* (Hon. Fredk. Petre) ; and *Ditchley's* (Collison Hall, Esq.)   *Great Ropers* (F. Hotham Hirst, Esq.), and *Boyles Court* (J. F. Lescher, Esq.), on the other side of the Brentwood road, are the seats of sub-manors in this parish. Brentwood itself is a manor of South Weald. (*See* BRENTWOOD.)

As the name impleis, South Weald was a clearing in the great Forest of Essex, and though the forest has long disappeared there are still numerous trees, old enough to have been at least saplings when the land was disafforested. The hamlet of *Pilgrims' Hatch*, 1 m. N. by E. from South Weald ch. (following the park), tells of the *hatch*, or forest gate, through which the pilgrims passed on their way to the chapel of St. Thomas the Martyr at Brentwood. The County Lunatic Asylum, noticed under BRENTWOOD, is in South Weald parish.

WELLING, KENT, a hamlet by

the 10th mile-stone on the Dover road, at the eastern foot of Shooter's Hill, and extending towards Bexley Heath. The northern site of the village is in East Wickham par., the southern in Bexley.

The name had, according to the topographers, a curious origin. It was called *Well-end*, says Hasted, "from the safe arrival of the traveller at it after having escaped the danger of robbers through the hazardous road from Shooter's Hill." Rather perhaps from *half* the dangerous way having been passed, as Bexley Heath must have been nearly as hazardous as Shooter's Hill. Really the name is shown by the suffix *ing* to be an ordinary Saxon patronymic.

Welling consists of the usual roadside habitations, a few respectable shops, a couple of good roadside inns, *Guy Earl of Warwick*, and the *Nag's Head*—the former the best,—a temporary church,

schools, etc. The extensive grounds seen on the rt. in entering and passing out of the village are a part of *Danson Park.* The house, a stately semi-classic structure, of Portland stone, regular in plan—a centre with wings—and having some handsome rooms, was built, about 1770, for Sir John Boyd, Bart., from the designs of Sir Robert Taylor. The park was laid out about the same time by Capability Brown. It is extensive, undulating, richly timbered, and has a large sheet of ornamental water.

WEMBLEY, MIDDX., a hamlet of

Harrow-upon-the-Hill, from which town it is 2½ m. S.E., and ½ m. N.E. from the Sudbury Stat. of the L. and N.-W. Rly., was created an eccl. dist. in 1846, and had 1195 inhab. in 1871.

The farm manor of Wembley, or Wymbley, belonged to the Priory of Kilburn down to the Dissolution. It was granted by Henry VIII. in 1543 to Andrewes and Chamberlayne, who conveyed it the same year to Richard Page, in whose descendants it continued till 1802, when it was sold by another Richard Page to John Gray, Esq. It is now the property of the Rev. John Edw. Gray, whose seat, *Wembley Park*, is the manor-house. The park extends E. of the hamlet towards Kingsbury, is large, varied in surface, abundantly timbered, and watered by a branch of the Brent.   Other seats are *Wembley House* (J. T. Woolley, Esq.) ; *Oakington Park* (Col. the Hon. Wellington Talbot) ; *Hill House* (Thos. Nicoll, Esq.)

Wembley Hill is celebrated for the prospects from the summit, though the distant country westward is cut off by the heights of Harrow. The *Green Man*, with its gardens, on the top of the hill, is much frequented by holiday parties and for trade dinners. The walks by the lanes from Wembley Hill to Kingsbury,. the Hyde, and Hendon or Whitchurch, are very pleasant.

The district church, St. John the Baptist, by the Sudbury Rly. Stat., is a good early Dec. building, with bell-cote over the W. gable, and deep chancel, erected in 1846, from the designs of Sir Gilbert Scott, to supply the united districts of Wembley, Sudbury, Appleton, and Preston. About the ch. has grown up a little colony of villas and cottages, with a cottage-hospital, a district school, a workmen's hall, and a young men's institute.

WENNINGTON, Essex, a village on the road to Grays, midway (2 m.) between the Rainham and Purfleet Stats. of the Lond., Tilbury, and Southend Rly., and 14 m. from London by road. Pop. 199. Inn: *Lennard Arms.*

The village lies along the low upland which overlooks the marshes bordering the Thames. Wennington Marsh runs out 2 m. from the vill., forming what is known as Great Coalharbour Point, directly opposite Erith. The occupations are agricultural, and there is a small india-rubber factory. Large quantities of peas are grown for the London market. There are no resident gentry. *Wennington Hall,* the old manor-house, on the Rainham side of the vill., is now a farm-house.

The *Church* (St. Mary the Virgin and St. Peter) is a venerable looking structure, comprising nave and N. aisle, chancel, and tall weather-beaten W. spire. The staple of the fabric is E.E., but it has been much altered. The chancel is of transition character; a small door on the S. has the circular arch and dog-tooth moulding. The chancel arch and windows are E.E.

WEST DRAYTON, Middx. (*see* Drayton, West).

WEST HAM, Essex, a village lying to the E. of Stratford on the road to Plaistow, and about ¾ m. from the Stratford Stat. of the Grt. E. Rly. The parish of West Ham is of great extent, stretching N. and S. from Wanstead and Leyton to the Thames, and E. and W. from East Ham to the river Lea. The par. is divided into three wards, Church Street, Stratford-Langthorne, and Plaistow: the latter are treated under PLAISTOW and STRATFORD; the former, or West Ham proper, remains to be noticed here. The pop. of the par. was 62,919 in 1871; that or West Ham proper, 7928.

A century ago West Ham was a favourite residence of merchants and wealthy citizens, who in those days seem to have had quite a Dutch taste for low, moist, level districts. In the returns of the King's surveyor of houses and win-

dows, 1762, the number of houses in West Ham par. was stated to be 700, of which "455 are mansions and 245 cottages." Whatever definition be given to mansions, this seems too liberal a proportion; but five or six years later, Morant, the historian of Essex, described West Ham as "the residence of several considerable merchants, dealers, and industrious artists."[*] Now the wealthier merchants have their houses elsewhere, and the old mansions have for the most part been pulled down, divided, or diverted to other uses. West Ham is not now an attractive place. It has become the home of manufactures which have been driven from London and its immediate boundary, and the buildings and their surroundings, especially such as are to be found about the marshes, the railway, and the many branches of the Lea, are pleasing to none of the senses. Chemical works, varnish manufactories, match mills, candle factories, manure works, cocoa-nut fibre and leather-cloth factories, and distilleries, are on a large scale.

West Ham had a market, procured in 1253 by Richard de Montfichet, but it has not been kept for many years. An annual fair of 4 days' continuance was granted at the same time.

West Ham *Church* (All Saints) stands in the midst of the village, in a sort of broadway, two main streets running rt. and l. of the wide ch.-yard. It is a large building, the basis ancient, but much of the fabric modern, and as a whole a poor patchwork-looking pile. It comprises an early nave, to which a common builder's brick aisle, with round-arched windows, has been added on the S., the Perp. N. aisle remaining of stone; a modern chancel of red brick, and a good old Perp. W. tower, 74 ft. high, in 3 stages, square, with a tall angle turret, and battlemented. The tower has a large W. window of good Perp. details, and contains a peal of 10 bells.

The interior of the ch. was renovated in 1866, when above the arcade, which is of the Dec. period, was found a transition Norman clerestorey. At the same time was uncovered a curious painting, first brought to light on scraping the walls in 1844, but after a brief exposure again

---

* Morant, Hist. of Essex, vol. i., p. 16.

covered with limewash and irretrievably damaged. It is described as an oil painting on rough plaster, but may have been in distemper ; of the latter part of the 15th century, elaborately executed, but without much artistic skill, and about 8 feet by 5 in size. It occupied the eastern end of the N. clerestorey wall. The subject was the Resurrection of the Righteous, and comprised figures of a king, a cardinal, bishops, priests, and a crowd of souls of the saved, with angels leading them to the gates of the Heavenly Jerusalem. Angels playing musical instruments and female figures filled the angles, and above and behind were arches, niches, tabernacle work, etc. On the outer edge were falling fiends. The painting was too much defaced to be made out except from a scaffold, and it was not considered desirable to save it, as the rest of the plaster was being removed for pointing. On the opposite wall—on the left hand of the Judge, who, no doubt, was represented on the eastern wall—was, probably, a corresponding painting of the Condemnation of the Wicked, but no trace of it could be found.*

There are numerous *monts.*, though few of interest. Altar tomb for Robert Rook, 1485. N. wall of chancel, Sir Thomas Foot, Knt. and Bart., Lord Mayor 1650, d. 1688, æt. 96, with effigy standing in Lord Mayor's robes, wife in dress richly ornamented with lace. James Cooper, 1743, life-size marble statue. In S. aisle of chancel, William Fawcet, d. 1631, with recumbent effigies of Fawcet and his wife; her second husband, Wm. Toppesfield, who erected the mont., kneeling at a faldstool. Showy marble mont. to Sir James Smyth, sometime Lord Mayor of London, d. 1706, and wife ; and Sir James Smyth, Bart., d. 1717, and wife Mirabella. On the floor are slabs to three Sir Robert Smyths.

In the ch.-yard—tombstone to James Anderson, LL.D., editor of the *Bee*, and author of a great number of works on agricultural and industrial subjects. George Edwards, F.R.S., eminent as a naturalist, and the friend of Linnæus, a native of West Ham, born at Stratford 1693, d. at Plaistow 1773. Dr. Samuel Jebb, a

* Trans. of Essex Archæol. Soc., vol. iv., p. 47 ; Archæological Journal, vol xxiii., p. 63.

physician of eminence, and author of several professional works, a Latin Life of Mary Queen of Scots, and editor of Aristotle and Bacon, lived at Stratford ; and in West Ham ch. was baptized, 1729, his more famous son, Richard, made a baronet by George III., and physician in ordinary to the king. In leaving, *obs.* the long covered way from the S. door of the ch. to doorway in the ch.-yard wall, a relic of the days when West Ham was a village of mansions, and the congregation came in carriages.

A short distance from the ch. are almshouses for 20 inmates, and in Gift Lane are others for 6 poor persons. Mrs. Bonnell's Endowed School for Poor Girls, was a well-meant charity, but has been ill-administered. It has of late been improved, and now educates about 100 girls. Other schools—primary, model, and industrial—are numerous.

The pretty rural hamlet of *Upton* is a little more than a mile N.E. of West Ham ch., towards the Romford road, along which extends *Upton Place*, the northern end of the hamlet. *Upton Manor House* is a good red-brick Jacobean mansion, recently restored. More widely known was *Ham House* and Park, lying between Ham Lane and Upton Lane. Ham House was for many years, and till his death, the residence of Samuel Gurney, and the centre of the great philanthropic measures in which he and Mrs. Fry (who lived in a house in Upton Lane close by) were the prime movers. The house, which was only interesting from its associations and the many eminent persons, foreign as well as native, who visited it during Mr. Gurney's life, was taken down some few years after his decease, and an offer was made to purchase the park for building on. Happily it was proposed to secure it as a public park for the crowded poor of West Ham. Mr. John Gurney met the proposal by offering it at the sum the building society had bid for it, £25,000—towards which the Gurney family would contribute £10,000. Local efforts could only raise £5000, when the Corporation of the City of London generously voted the other £10,000, and undertook to keep the park in order. It was accordingly purchased, vested in the Corporation, and formally opened for public use by the Lord Mayor, on the 20th of July, 1874.

West Ham Park has an area of about 80 acres. The surface is nearly level, but richly and variously timbered, it having been famed in Mr. Gurney's time for its ornamental trees, among which were many rare American and Australian varieties, as well as for the ordinary park trees and larger shrubs. The plantations on the south-eastern side are particularly rich, and many of the trees are old and large. There are wide open lawns and meadows, of which a portion is set apart for cricket and play grounds ; broad terraces, and ample gardens formed on the site of the house and its immediate grounds, with good old-fashioned shady walks—altogether a cheerful and pleasant place, and a great boon to the inhabitants of West Ham and Plaistow. West Ham Park is a very short distance from the Plaistow Rly. Stat. (*See* PLAISTOW.)

Near the Park is a country inn, the *Spotted Dog*, with large grounds and gardens, much resorted to by East-end holiday folk. In Upton Lane is an Ursuline convent.

Forest Gate is a hamlet lying to the N. of Upton and the Romford road, at the edge of Wanstead Flats, the southern extremity of Epping Forest, to which this was the entrance (gate). Forest Gate, with Upton and part of East Ham par., was made an eccl. district in 1852 : pop. 7127. At Forest Gate is a stat. on the Grt. E. Rly. (main Colchester line). By it is the *Eagle and Child*, tea-gardens and holiday resort. Emmanuel district ch. is a neat little Gothic building at the corner of Upton Lane. In Woodgrange Road is the *Pawnbrokers' Charitable Institute*, a cheerful group of 5 almshouses. Here is the West Ham Cemetery. Also, in Cemetery Road, the Jews' Cemetery, in which is the stately mausoleum of the Rothschild family, erected, 1867, from the designs of Mr. Digby Wyatt.

The outlying districts, with their various industries, which have grown up in West Ham Marshes and towards the Thames, are noticed under PLAISTOW. Those on the other side, including West Ham Abbey, are spoken of under STRATFORD.

The Northern Main Sewer of the Metropolitan Main Drainage system traverses the parish, entering at the Lea on the W. from Old Ford, passing along the West Ham Marshes, as a grass-covered embankment, crossing the main street of Plaistow, and quitting the par. at East Ham. Along here the drain is a brick tunnel 10 ft. high. At the Abbey Mills is the chief Pumping Station on the N. of the Thames. By it the sewage of the Low-level drain, which has flowed thus far by gravitation, is lifted from the pumping wells and forced through iron cylinders 10 ft. 6 in. in diameter, into the outfall sewer, which discharges itself by gravitation into the receiving tanks at Barking Creek. The works are of great extent and capacity, and will repay examination. There are six steam engines, each of 112 nominal horse-power. The pumps, 16 in number, are each 3 ft. 10½ in. in diameter, with a stroke of 4 ft. 6 in. ; and are together capable of lifting 15,000 cubic feet of sewage per minute. The buildings, which are of an ornamental character, occupy an area of 7 acres. The two octagonal chimney-shafts, which form a conspicuous landmark for miles, are each 209 ft. high and 8 ft. in diameter. The interior of the building is kept scrupulously clean, the machinery in admirable order, and, considering the nature of the operations, there is a surprising absence of offensive odour.

WEST SHEEN, SURREY (*see* SHEEN, WEST).

WEST THURROCK, ESSEX (*see* THURROCK, WEST).

WEST TILBURY, ESSEX (*see* TILBURY, WEST).

WEST TWYFORD, MIDDX. (*see* TWYFORD).

WEST WICKHAM, KENT (*see* WICKHAM, WEST).

WESTERHAM, KENT, a small market town on the road from Godstone to Sevenoaks, 1½ m. W. of Brasted. The nearest rly. stats. are Edenbridge (L. and S.-E. Rly.), 4 m. S., and Sevenoaks (L., C., and D., and L. and S.-E. lines), 5 m. E. Pop. 2283, of whom 514 were in the eccl. dist. of Crockham Hill. Inns : *King's Arms*, a good house ; *George and Dragon*.

The little town is pleasantly situated in Holmesdale, at the foot of the chalk downs, near the source of the Darent, where Kent and Surrey meet, and in the midst of scenery which is charmingly characteristic of both counties. It is built on a slope, the church crowning the height at the eastern end. At the lower end are the finely timbered grounds of Squerryes; at the upper those of Valence, or Park Hill. A long straggling place, roomy for its population, and the houses far from crowded; rural, quiet, perhaps a little dull. More than once it has been disappointed in the expectation of having a railway brought to it, but it has not lost heart. Population has not materially increased, and no new source of prosperity has been opened; but the little town has extended westward, built itself a new Public Hall, improved the shops, established a literary institute, erected almshouses and a cottage hospital, and continues to hold its market every Wednesday at the King's Arms Hotel. Outside the town, the pursuits are chiefly agricultural. The growth of hops has been considerably extended; there are nurseries, breweries, and maltings.

The *Church* (St. Mary) is large, comprising a wide nave with aisles, chancel and aisles, tall tower with short shingled spire at the W. end, and porch on the S. The building is in the main late Perp., but some portions have been rebuilt, the interior restored, and open oak seats substituted for the old pews. The E. window of the S. aisle is late Dec. *Obs.* the piers of the nave arcade, which are of Godstone firestone. Several of the windows have painted glass. In the E. wall of the S. chancel are a piscina and ambrey. In this chancel is a mural *mont.* with small kneeling effigies, coloured, of Thomas Potter, of Well Street, d. 1611, and wife. On the E. wall are *brasses*, removed there when the ch. was restored. Richard Potter, 1563, who by his wives Elizabeth, Ann, and Alice, had 20 children—of whom 3 sons and 10 daughters were left alive at his decease; the effigies of the other 7 are engraven on the brass. Richard Hayward, 1590, effigy in merchant's robe. Several other brasses were in the ch., but they appear to have been lost or removed. Over the S. entrance to the ch. is a marble tablet raised by the townsmen to GENERAL WOLFE, "born in this parish, January 2nd, 1727, and died in America, Sept. 19th, 1759, Conqueror of Quebec.

" Whilst George in sorrow bows his laurelled head,
   And bids the artist grace the soldier dead ;
   We raise no sculptured trophy to thy name.
 *   *   *   *   *
With humble grief inscribe our artless stone,
And from thy matchless honours date our own."

Wolfe was buried, it will be remembered, at Greenwich (*see* p. 262). *Quebec House*, a gabled house a little beyond the ch., is usually pointed out as General Wolfe's birthplace. But it is an error. He was born in the Vicarage. The room in which he was born was that with the three-light window facing the ch.-yard, now blocked. A short time after his birth, his father took the house now called Quebec House, and there the future hero spent his early years. After Wolfe's death it was rented as a school by some ladies, who gave it its present name. The lines on the tablet in Westerham ch. are attributed to General Warde of Squerryes, who erected another memorial to Wolfe in Squerryes Park.

Besides Wolfe, Westerham claims as natives, Fryth, the colleague of Tyndale and teacher of Cranmer; and a divine of somewhat different temperament, Benjamin Hoadly, Bp. of Winchester.

Squerryes (Lieut.-Col. G. Warde), S.E. of Westerham, is a good 17th century red-brick mansion, standing, amidst grand ancestral trees, in a small but very beautiful park. It was in the grounds of Squerryes that Wolfe received his commission; here a column has been erected to his memory, and in the house are his portrait and various personal relics. The Darent rises in Squerryes Park, not far from the house.

Valence, at the other end of the town, was in the last century noted as *Hill Park*, the seat of the Cotton family. The house is spacious and substantial, and contains some good rooms. In the grounds are noble cedars, firs, and pines; and the park is rich in oak and beech, many of magnificent proportions, affords from the higher parts very extensive views, and is diversified by a streamlet, lakes, and cascades. Valence has been for some years the seat of the Earl of Norbury, but is at present unoccupied.

The rather peculiar Gothic mansion, the tall square tower of which is so conspicuous an object in the town, is *Dunsdale*, erected in 1863 for Joseph Kitchin, Esq., by Prof. Kerr. The grounds are laid out with great taste; and on the estate is a very complete model farm. *Chart's Edge* (Mrs. Streatfield), a modern Gothic villa on the hill-top, is noted for its views. Other seats are *Springfield*, (Major J. Board); *Mariners* (Mrs. Whittaker).

Crockham Hill, 2 m. S. of the town, a hamlet and eccl. dist., should be visited for the famous view over the Weald of Kent, Surrey, and Sussex, obtained from Crockham Gap. The way to it over Westerham Common, or by Chart, is very beautiful. Crockham church is a neat little modern Gothic building of the year 1841. The beauty of the neighbourhood has led to the erection of several good residences. The principal seats are— *Lewin's* (T. C. Donnie, Esq.); *Chartwell* (Rev. J. E. Campbell-Colquhoun); *Mapleton Lodge* (Alderman Sir Benj. S. Phillips); *Redland* (G. M. Tracy, Esq.); *Crockham House* (A. H. Shand, Esq.)

WEYBRIDGE, Surrey, the site

of a royal palace, and the burial-place of Louis Philippe, King of the French, a village lying between Oatlands Park and the river Wey at its confluence with the Thames, 2½ m. S.W. of Walton-upon-Thames, and 3 m. S.E. of Chertsey. The Weybridge Stat. of the L. and S.-W. Rly. is about a mile S. of the vill. Pop. 2604. Inns, *Hand and Spear*, by rly. stat.; *Oatlands Park Hotel*; *Mitre*.

At the Dom. Survey *Webrige* was a manor held by the Abbot of Chertsey: its value was 20 shillings. It passed to the Crown with the other property of the abbey, was annexed by Henry VIII. to the honour of Hampton Court, and was thenceforth generally held, under leases from the Crown, by the possessors of Oatlands.

An estate called Oatlands, in Weybridge, was purchased of Humphrey Ruggeley and wife in 1500 by John and Bartholomew Rede and others. When Henry VIII. was forming his chase of Hampton he sought to obtain this estate, which was then held by William Rede, offering in exchange for it lands belonging

to the suppressed priory of Tandridge. Whilst negotiations were in progress Rede died, leaving his son John, a child, his heir. The king took a short way to remove the difficulty this made to his obtaining the estate. He constituted Sir Thomas (afterwards Lord) Cromwell guardian of the boy, and he in that capacity conveyed the estate to the king, Jan. 1538. Oatlands was an old hunting ground of the king. He was there in the autumn of 1514, and in the meadows was killing of stags, "holden in for the purpose," one after another all the afternoon.[*] Henry lost no time in commencing the erection of a palace on his new estate. Almost before he could have obtained legal possession, his builders were at work. Materials were found in the ruined monasteries. Stone was brought from Chertsey and Bisham; marble for pavements from Abingdon. The good red bricks which formed the walls were made at Woking (the accountants spell it *Okyng*, much as the natives still pronounce it). For the "hasty expedycion of the same," hard-hewers were kept at work in the fore-court, and carpenters upon the chapel, the lodging adjoining, the lodging over the pastry, the king's lodging, the great parlour, and elsewhere, by night as well as by day. Why the king was in so great a hurry is not clear, but he seldom loitered over a resolve; and having resolved to have a hunting lodge at Oatlands he was probably impatient till he possessed it.

The main building was completed in two or three years; but the decorations, the furnishing of the house, and laying out and planting the grounds, occupied a longer time. For his orchards the king found provision of apple trees, pear trees, and cherry trees in the gardens of Chertsey Abbey. The furniture was of the most sumptuous kind. Velvet and cloth of gold covered the chairs, the walls were hung with the finest tapestries of France and Flanders, and on the floors were laid "carpets of Turque." It was for his expected bride, Anne of Cleves, that the new palace was in a special manner designed and the fittings ordered. But before the building was ready the

---

[*] Sir Philip Draycot, in Lodge's Illustrations of Brit. Hist., vol. i., p. 6.

bride had come, proved unacceptable, been divorced, and a new one found. And with a new wife Henry had sought a new palace. He was now busy in the preparation of the still costlier and more superb Nonsuch, and Oatlands seems to have been comparatively neglected. It was consigned to the keeping of Sir Anthony Brown, and it was the occasional residence of the Princess Mary, but the references to it are few during the last years of Henry's reign.

The Palace of Oatlands appears, from the drawings of it formerly in the possession of Mr. Gough,* and in the Bodleian at Oxford, to have been a structure of great extent and complexity. The foundations are said to have been traced over an area of 14 acres. The palace stood in the meadow by the Thames, now known as Oatlands Palace Gardens, on the western side of the present Oatlands Park. It was built of red brick, with stone quoins and dressings, gables, bays, and ornamental chimney shafts, somewhat after the fashion of Hampton Court. From the outer gate you entered the Fore Court, on either side of which was a range of low buildings, apparently stables. Before you stretched the broad many-gabled principal front, with a turreted central gate-house, as at Hampton Court or St. James's. Through this you passed to an oblong Inner Court, or quadrangle, lined with hall or chapel and state apartments. A taller gate-house occupied the centre of the farther side, and led to a numerous cluster of buildings arranged within an irregular triangle, about several small courts. In the centre of this triangle was a lofty circular tower, having a projecting upper storey with windows all around. apparently for affording an outlook over the surrounding country ; whilst from the apex of the triangle projected towards the river a range of buildings which terminated in a tall stern rectangular castellated edifice, the meaning of which is not very evident. Terraces, flower gardens, orchards, fountains, fish ponds, detached summer-houses, and paddock, formed the pleasance around the house, and beyond was the deer-park, fenced about with a quickset hedge of hawthorn.

* Engraved in Manning and Bray's Surrey, and in Nichols's Progresses of Queen Elizabeth, vol. iii.

Edward VI. kept court at Oatlands, in 1548, with Somerset as Lord Protector. On the 3rd of February, 1555, Philip and Mary removed for a few days from Hampton Court to Oatlands. "On the way Mary received consolation from a poor man who met her on crutches and was cured of his lameness by looking on her."* Henry VIII. had made a private way, "with hanging gates," from Hampton Court to Oatlands, probably the river road past his manor of App's Court, and it was no doubt along this Philip and Mary travelled.

Elizabeth was here often in the early part of her reign, in the summer of 1599, and again in 1602. She loved to hunt the tall deer, and is said to have shot at them with the cross-bow as they were driven past her stand in the paddock. Near where we may suppose her stand was placed are a couple of yew trees, known as *Queen Elizabeth's bow-shot*— but tradition knows nothing of the cross-bow. The trees stand 60 yards apart, and mark the queen's shot when she practised with the long-bow. Another memorial of Elizabeth's hunting (or watching the hunt) at Oatlands, may be seen in the brass in Walton church of John Selwyn, "keeper of her Majesty's park of Otelande." (*See* WALTON-UPON-THAMES, p. 660.)

James I. was often at Oatlands; but the house is more spoken of as the favourite residence of his consort, Anne of Denmark, who here entertained with great ceremony the Venetian ambassador Busano. She made many alterations in the place, built a silkworm house—the rearing of silkworms, it will be remembered, was a favourite project of the king's,— and employed, as is believed, Inigo Jones to erect the arched gateway, which was standing till within the last few years. Prince Henry "kept house" at Oatlands in 1603.

Oatlands was settled by Charles I. on his queen, Henrietta Maria, and here in 1640 their youngest son, Henry of Oatlands, was born. When discord was abroad, the queen on one occasion, whilst the king was in Scotland, is said to have armed her household and such friends as she could hastily muster, and kept them

* Froude, History of England, vol. vi., p. 363.

watching through the night in the park, ready to repel an attempt she suspected was about to be made to carry off the young princes by force. Charles was here for the last time in August 1647, before his removal to Hampton Court. After his death Oatlands was dismantled and razed, the deer sold, the trees serviceable for the navy felled, and the land disparked.

On the Restoration, Oatlands was returned to the Queen Dowager. Some detached buildings were converted into a lodge. A lease for 40 years, if the Queen should live so long, was granted in 1661 to Henry Jermyn, Earl of St. Albans, Henrietta's second husband. She died in 1669, and the lease was renewed to the Earl for the remainder of the term at a rental of 20s. He sold his interest in it to Chief Justice Sir Edward Herbert, who procured from James II. a reversionary lease for 76 years from the expiry of the existing lease. Herbert, involved in the fatal measures of James II., fled the country on the King's fall, was attainted, and his estates forfeited. But in 1696, William III. granted Oatlands in fee-simple to Herbert's elder brother, Arthur Earl of Torrington, who bequeathed it to Henry Fiennes Clinton, 7th Earl of Lincoln. The fragment left of the palace was not suitable for a residence, and the Earl about 1725 began a new mansion on higher ground and nearer the centre of the park. His grandson, Henry Clinton, Duke of Newcastle, enlarged the house, remodelled the grounds, formed the great lake, and constructed the grotto, long one of the glories of the modern Oatlands. Walpole visited Oatlands in the latter years of the Duke of Newcastle's ownership, and "was disappointed."

"Oatlands, that my memory had taken it into its head was the centre of Paradise, is not half so Elysian as I used to think. The Grotto, a magnificent structure of shell-work, is a square, regular, and, which never happened to grotto before, lives up one pair of stairs, and yet only looks on a basin of dirty water: in short, I am returned to my own Thames with delight, and envy none of the princes of the earth."[*]

The *Grotto* still remains, and, though shorn of much of its splendour, is worth visiting as an illustration of the taste of the times and an example of misapplied

ingenuity. It was constructed for the Duke of Newcastle by an Italian and his two sons, who were occupied over 20 years upon it. In the early accounts it is said to have cost £12,000 or £13,000, a sum since magnified to £40,000. The Grotto is a building of three or four chambers on the ground floor, connected by low dark passages, and a large room above. The exterior is formed of tufa curiously put together; the rooms and passages are a mosaic of minerals, marbles, spars of various kinds, and shells, worked into a multitude of quaint devices with infinite patience and skill. The ceilings are of stalactites and satin spars. In the bath-room is a copy of the Venus de' Medici; painted glass obscures the light. The upper room, reached by an outer staircase, has an elaborate cupola of artificial stalactites of satin-spar; the walls a more complex repetition of the mosaic of the lower chambers. In this room George IV., when Prince of Wales, gave a splendid supper to the Emperor of Russia, the King of Prussia, and the princes and generals in their train, on their visit to England after the battle of Waterloo. The chamber for the occasion was lighted by cut-glass chandeliers; the chairs and sofas had satin cushions embroidered by the Duchess of York. In visiting the Grotto notice the many fine specimens of minerals still left, especially the various quartz crystals; also the ammonites and other fossil as well as recent shells.

Oatlands was purchased by the Duke of York, about 1790, for £45,000. The house was in great part destroyed by fire, June 6th, 1794, whilst the Duchess of York was residing in it. A new mansion was shortly after commenced on a grander scale, avowedly from the designs of Holland, the architect of Drury Lane Theatre (destroyed by fire in 1806), but John Carter (more favourably known by his etchings of Gothic buildings), who superintended its erection, claimed to be also its designer.[*] The house did little credit to the taste of either architect. It was a long, low, rambling structure; the style a meagre variety of Strawberry Hill Gothic, battlemented throughout. It had, however, some noble rooms with ample

* Walpole to Countess of Ossory, July 9, 1788: Letters, vol. ix., p. 132.

* Brayley, Hist. of Surrey, vol. ii., p. 387.

bays. Of the residence of the Duke of York here more than enough will be found in Greville's Memoirs; but it is best remembered as the residence of the Duchess of York, who lived here, much alone, from 1790 to her death at Oatlands in 1820, and endeared herself to all classes in Weybridge. Amidst many peculiarities of habit, she was never forgetful of her poorer neighbours, to whom she was an untiring benefactor, and by them her memory, now little more than a tradition, is still reverently cherished. Walpole gives a lively account of one of her early parties :—

"The Duchess of York gave a great entertainment at Oatlands on her Duke's birthday; sent to his tradesmen in town to come to it, and allowed two guineas a piece to each for their carriage; gave them a dance, and opened the ball herself with the Prince of Wales. A company of strollers came to Weybridge to act in a barn : she was solicited to go to it, and did out of charity, and carried all her servants with her. Next day a Methodist teacher came to preach a charity sermon in the same theatre, and she consented to hear it on the same motive; but her servants desired to be excused, on not understanding English. 'Oh,' said the Duchess, 'but you went to the comedy, which you understood less, and you shall go to the sermon;' to which she gave handsomely, and for them. I like this." *

A party nearly 20 years later, given on occasion of her own birthday, May 1810, illustrates even better her liveliness and goodnature. The king and queen, with the princes and princesses, arrived at Oatlands by two o'clock; the king wearng the Windsor uniform, the queen and princesses in plain white. The Duke and Duchess of York were in waiting at the bottom of the steps to receive their illustrious guests, whom they conducted to the grand saloon. The improvements in the house were admired, the gardens visited, and then a sumptuous banquet was served on gilt plate. The king, queen, and princesses departed about 8 o'clock; the princes remained. The park gates were set wide open, and the whole population of Weybridge and "the neighbouring peasantry" streamed in. There was no exclusion. Tables were laid in all the lower rooms, piled with hot fowls, veal and ham, beef and mutton. Strong ale and porter took the place of the wines that had flowed at the upper tables; and

as soon as the viands were despatched a great bowl of punch was placed on each table. Then all were summoned by music to the library and a dance. The Duchess led off the ball with Col. Upton in the Labyrinth, and it afforded the royal party no little amusement to watch the embarrassment of the rustics when in going down the dance they had to make their bow to the heir-apparent. The dance was kept up till 2 in the morning, when the music ceased and all retired. It is not surprising that the Duchess was popular at Weybridge.

One passage of somewhat later date will suffice to show the private life of the Duke of York at Oatlands :—

"*August 4th*, 1818.—I went to Oatlands on Saturday. There was a very large party. . . . We played at whist till four in the morning. On Sunday we amused ourselves with eating fruit in the garden, and shooting at a mark with pistols, and playing with the monkeys. I bathed in the cold bath in the grotto, which is as clear as crystal, and as cold as ice. Oatlands is the worst managed establishment in England : there are a great many servants and nobody waits on you; a great number of horses and none to ride or drive.—The parties at Oatlands take place every Saturday, and the guests go away on Monday morning. These parties begin as soon as the Duchess leaves London, and last till the October meetings. . . . We dine at 8 and sit at table till 11. In about a quarter of an hour after we leave the dining room the Duke sits down to play at whist, and never stirs from the table as long as anybody will play with him. He is equally well amused whether the play is high or low, but the stake he prefers is fives and ponies." * [£5 points and £25 on the rubber.]

The Duchess, says the Diarist, "dresses and breakfasts at 3 o'clock, afterwards walks out with all her dogs [of which she has at least 40 of different kinds], and seldom appears before dinner time."†

Fondness for animals was strongly developed in the Duchess. She protected the wild song birds, and would not allow a rook to be shot; the cows and pigs on the farm would run to her sure of a choice morsel; whilst for dogs her partiality was excessive, and to her visitors annoying; but doubtless she found, as she says in one of her shapeless rhymes, their

"frolic play
Enlivened oft the lonesome hours."

She did not neglect them even when dead. Around the margin of a circular basin for

---

* Walpole to Hon. H. S. Conway, August 31, 1792.

* Greville, Memoirs, 1874, vol. i., p. 4.
† *Ibid.*

gold fish (now drained), she formed a cemetery for her pets, burying each in turn with care, strewing its grave with flowers, and placing over it a little stone with the animal's name, date of decease, and, if its merit was remarkable, a tribute in verse from her own pen.* Sixty or seventy of these stones still fringe the margin of the hollow; and when the Queen visited Oatlands in 1871, noticing that the tombstones were out of order, she, with her usual kindliness, gave orders for their restoration. They now look quite fresh, and four or five have been added for dogs recently deceased.

An Act was passed in 1804, by which the King was enabled to grant to the Duke of York the inheritance in fee-simple of Oatlands; and on the enclosure of Walton and Weybridge Commons in 1800, the Duke had obtained an addition of 1000 acres to his estate, to which he further added by the purchase of several neighbouring properties. But he was too heavily in debt to allow the property to be kept together. Oatlands was sold to E. Hughes Ball Hughes, Esq. (the Golden Ball); and was for some years the residence of Lord Francis Egerton, afterwards Earl of Ellesmere. About 1856 the estate was bought by a company for the purpose of converting the house into an hotel. A large portion of the Duke of York's house was taken down by Mr. Hughes; the remaining portion was now remodelled; and with large additions made by Mr. Wyatt, was in 1858 opened as the *Oatlands Park Hotel*. In appearance it is a stately Italian mansion, contains handsome suites of apartments, stands on a lofty terrace, and commands splendid views along the valley of the Thames from Kingston to Windsor. Just below the terrace is the great lake, Broadwater, very commonly mistaken for a reach of the Thames. The park has been much abridged, but is still extensive, and contains many noble trees and abundant evergreen and other shrubs. The severed portion of the park has been divided, and built over with first-class villas.

West of Oatlands, the Wey flowing through the grounds, was another house possessing a sort of historic celebrity, *Ham House*, or *Ham Farm* as it was at one time called, was built by the Duke of Norfolk in the reign of Charles II.

" *23 Aug.* 1678.—Upon Sir Robert Reading's importunity I went to visite the Duke of Norfolk at his new palace at Weybridge, where he has laid out in building neere £10,000, on a copyhold, and in a miserable barren, sandy place, by the street side; never in my life had I seene such expense to so small purpose. The roomes are wainscotted, and some of them parquetted with cedar, yew, cypresse, &c. There are some good pictures, especially that incomparable painting of Holbein's where the Duke of Norfolk, Charles Brandon, and Henry VIII. are dauncing with the three ladies, with most amorous countenances and sprightly motion exquisitely expressed. . . . My Lord leading me about the house made no scruple of shewing me all the hiding places for the Popish priests, and where they said masse, for he was no bigotted Papist." *

After the Duke's death, Ham House was sold to Catherine Sedley, Countess of Dorchester, the more witty than beautiful mistress of James II., who spent a good deal of money in improving the house and grounds. Her royal lover is said to have been a frequent visitor; and the chapel which the Duke of Norfolk showed Evelyn was pointed out as that in which James used to have mass said when he visited Ham; the priests' hiding-places (Bray called them cupboards) being, according to the local tradition, the barracks in which he lodged his guards.† The Countess married David Collyear, 1st Earl of Portmore, and the house remained the family seat till the time of the last Earl, when, owing to family quarrels, it was deserted, suffered to go to ruin, and left a prey to the villagers, who carried off the furniture and used the house as a quarry, till what remained of it was finally taken down, seven or eight years before the last Earl's death (1835). The massive gateway, and some magnificent cedars by the river, are the only vestiges left of its ancient splendour. It was a stately brick mansion, with a terrace

---

* There is some doubt as to the authorship of these verses. Macaulay who visited the graves and " was disgusted by this exceeding folly," supposed them to be " the mature efforts of Monk Lewis's genius," but was told by Lady Dufferin that they were " the childish productions of herself and her sister," Mrs. Norton. (Trevelyan, Life of Lord Macaulay, vol. ii., p. 405.) The dates and character of the epitaphs hardly allow the claim to be admitted without qualification, and the explanation which follows as to the number of the graves is unnecessary and certainly inaccurate.

* Evelyn, Diary.
† Manning and Bray, Hist. of Surrey, vol. ii. p. 789.

which commanded fine views of the Thames and Wey. The grounds E. of the Wey formed the home park; the meadows on the other side, of about 350 acres, being kept as paddocks.

The village is quiet, respectable, seemingly somewhat overawed by the predominance of the grand residences on every side of it. The houses are a good deal dispersed, but most thickly congregated by the church and green. Trees abound; the roads and lanes are pleasant, and there are some charming reaches of level river scenery along the meadows by the Wey. The Common is an untiring resource. Walton and St. George's Hill are within an easy distance.

The column on the Green is of popular and poetic fame. It was of old the central column of Seven Dials :—

" Where fam'd St. Giles's ancient limits spread,
An inrail'd Column rears its lofty head ;
Here to seven streets seven dials count the day
And from each other catch the circling ray." *

When the column was removed from Seven Dials in 1773, it was taken to Sayes Court, but never erected. It lay neglected there, till, on the death of the Duchess of York, the inhabitants of Weybridge conceived the design of commemorating her by a memorial, when some one recollected the fallen pillar, and suggested that it would exactly serve their purpose. It was accordingly purchased ; a pedestal with appropriate inscriptions erected on the Green, and the column placed upon it. But instead of the old dials, it was crowned with a royal coronet, and " inrailed " as of yore. The deposed stone of the seven dials was utilized as a horseblock at a roadside inn ; but it has been removed, and may now be seen on the edge of the Green opposite the column. It is sadly battered, however, and the directions on its six (not seven) faces are no longer legible. A large house on the Green, now the boys' boarding school of the Rev. Thos. Spyers, D.D., is known as *Holstein House*, " from its having been once inhabited by a duke or prince of Holstein when sojourning in England."†

The *Church* (St. James) was erected on the site of the semi-ruinous old ch. in 1848, and enlarged in 1864 (archt., Mr.

J. L. Pearson). It is early Dec. in style, and consists of nave with aisles, and stone porches, chancel, W. tower and spire 150 ft. high. It has a good peal of 8 bells, the gift of a lady. The interior is spacious, roomy, and light : the peculiarity of effect observed on entering arises from there being a second, and narrower, S. aisle. There are some monts. of interest preserved from the old ch. Vice-Admiral Sir Thomas Hopson, d. 1717, who forced the boom that lay across the Bay of Vigo, " whereby he made way for the whole Confederate fleet, under the command of Sir George Rooke, to enter, take, and destroy all the enemy's ships of war and galleys ; which was the last of 42 engagements he had been in, in some of which he received many honourable wounds for the service of his country." Memorial to the sisters Katherine and Mary Horneck, the Little Comedy and Jessamy Bride of Oliver Goldsmith's ' Verses in Reply to an Invitation to Dinner.' Katherine married Henry Wm., youngest son of Sir Wm. Bunbury, Bart., and d. 1799. Mary (the Jessamy Bride) married General Sir F. E. Gwyn, and survived till 1840. She it was who had the lid removed from the poet's coffin, that she might secure a lock of his hair, and who, "upwards of 40 years later, was still talking of her favourite Dr. Goldsmith, with recollection and affection unabated by time."* It was with the Miss Hornecks and their mother that Goldsmith in 1769 made the excursion to Paris, of which he wrote so characteristic an account to Sir Joshua Reynolds.

On the S. wall of the tower (it occupied a more honourable position in the old ch., but gratitude seldom outlives its generation) is a marble mont., with kneeling portrait by Chantrey, life-size, and in high relief, of Frederica Charlotte Ulrica Katherine, Duchess of York, died at Oatlands, August 6th, 1820. Tomb of David Collyear, 1st Earl of Portmore, Commander of the army in Portugal, and Governor of Gibraltar, d. Jan. 1730 ; and of his wife, Catherine Sedley, Countess of Dorchester (daughter of Sir Charles Sedley and mistress of James II.), who died at Bath, Oct. 1717, and was brought here for interment. On the floor of the tower is a *brass* of John Wylde, gent., d. 1598, and

---

* Gay, Trivia, Book ii., l. 73—76.
† Brayley, vol. ii., p. 398.

* Forster, Life of Goldsmith.

his two wives, Audrey and Elizabeth, one on the rt. with 5 children, the other on l. with 7 ; 3 shields of arms remain, a fourth has gone. Another brass is to Thomas Inwood, d. 1586 ; in long robe kneeling, with 3 wives and 5 children kneeling before him :

" In perfect fayth he lyved and dyed, of life sincere and puir,
Whose godly fame and memory for ever will endure."

In the old church were small brasses with that favourite mediæval legend of mortality the Three Deaths.

A new church, St. Michael and All Angels, was built in the Prince's Road in 1874, from the designs of Mr. Butterfield. It is of red brick, stern and deterrent outside, but pleasanter within. The tall spire seen a short distance from it belongs to the Congregational Ch., a good stone structure erected in 1865, from the designs of Mr. Tarring, and since enlarged.

Facing the Common, opposite a group of fine old fir trees, is the little *Roman Catholic Chapel of St. Charles Borromeo*, memorable as the mausoleum of the family of Louis Philippe. The chapel, a Greek cross, with a cupola over the centre, and a tower on one side, stands within the grounds of Waterloo Cottage. It was erected in 1836 by Jas. Molyneux Taylor, Esq., who constructed beneath it a vault for deceased members of his family ; and in it he and his family (now extinct) repose. On the death of Louis Philippe at Claremont, Aug. 26, 1850, this was selected as his temporary resting-place. His tomb, an unadorned but massive sarcophagus, stands on a broad basement of two steps, partly within an arched recess ; and here his remains are deposited " donec in patriam, avitos inter cineres, Deo adjuvante, transferantur." By his side lie the remains of his queen, Marie Amelie. d. March 24, 1866 ; the Duchesse d'Orléans, d. May 13, 1858 ; the Duchesse de Nemours, and five of his grandchildren. On the death of the young Prince de Condé in Australia, May 24, 1866, his body was brought to England, and a vault and tomb constructed for its reception contiguous to that of his grandfather ; and in it, Dec. 1869, the body of his mother, the Duchesse d'Aumale, was laid beside that of her beloved son. Pious hands continue to adorn the vault with vases of fresh flowers, and place upon the tombs wreaths of immortelles—among these being some placed there by Queen Victoria, the Princess Louise, and other members of our royal family.

*** Since the above was in type the royal remains have been removed to France ; but we leave the account unaltered, thinking the reader may like to have a description of the crypt as it was while still the Orleans mausoleum. Except that of the Duchesse de Nemours, all the bodies were taken away, and reinterred in the mausoleum of the Orleans family at Dreux on the 9th of June, 1876.

WHETSTONE, MIDDX., a hamlet of Friern Barnet, and a village on the Great Northern Road, 2 m. S. of Barnet and 1 m. W. of Totteridge. The Totteridge and Whetstone Stat. on the High Barnet br. of the Grt. N. Rly. is on the W. of Whetstone village. The eccl. dist. of Whetstone, formed in 1836 out of the parishes of Finchley and Friern Barnet, had 2356 inh. in 1871.

The village straggles for a considerable distance in disconnected rows and groups of houses, sometimes on one side of the highroad, sometimes on the other ; the houses, mostly small, some old-fashioned, many poor ; with several roadside waggoners' inns and publics, a veterinary forge, a little church, 2 or 3 chapels, a school, and a police station. Away from the road, and towards Totteridge, collections of genteel villas, Oakleigh Park and the like, have grown up within the last few years, and there has been a large increase of population. But the place itself is quite devoid of interest. The walks towards Totteridge on the one side, and Southgate and Friern Barnet on the other, are green and pleasant.

The *Church* (St. John), on the W. of the road at the London end of the vill., is a little chapel-like brick structure, with pinnacles at the angles : a feeble attempt at Gothic of the pre-Gothic era.

WHITCHURCH, MIDDX. (*see* STANMORE PARVA).

WHITTON, MIDDX., a hamlet of Twickenham, created in 1862 an eccl.

dist.; pop. 893; lies on the edge of Hounslow Heath, about midway between Hounslow and Twickenham, 10 m. from Hyde Park Corner by road, and ½ m. S. of the Hounslow and Whitton Stat. of the L. and S.-W. Rly. (Loop line).

Whitton is noteworthy for its seats, and cedars, nursery and fruit gardens, and memories of Sir Godfrey Kneller and the Duke of Argyll. The little Crane brook winds deviously through it—a pretty brook which the otters that once haunted its banks have not wholly abandoned, a pair having been seen, and hunted, in the autumn of 1875. The market gardens are very extensive and celebrated. Large quantities of strawberries are grown. Vincent Corbet, father of Bp. Corbet, had a nursery at Whitton, and dying in 1619, was buried in Twickenham ch. Ben Jonson wrote his epitaph:

> "His mind as pure and neatly kept
> As were his nurseries, and swept
> So of uncleanness or offence
> That never came ill odour thence."

He was a contributor to Sir Hugh Platt's 'Garden of Eden.' (*See* EWELL.) Sir John Suckling, the poet, was born at Whitton in 1609. It was to an old farmhouse at Whitton that Dr. Dodd (hanged for forgery June 27th, 1777), was tracked and there arrested.

Whitton Place was built by Archibald Earl of Islay, afterwards Duke of Argyll. The grounds, which were very extensive, were partly taken from Hounslow Heath, in virtue of a grant obtained from the Crown. Lord Islay spent large sums in planting them with cedars (raised from seed in 1725), Scotch firs, and exotics. According to Walpole, we are principally indebted to him for "the introduction of foreign trees and plants" that have "contributed essentially to the richness of modern landscape." His aboriculture did not, however, escape criticism. An 'Epigram on Lord Islay's Garden,' by the Rev. James Bramston (author of 'The Man of Taste'), particularly diverted Walpole.

> "Old Islay, to show his fine delicate taste
>   In improving his gardens purloin'd from the waste,
> Bade his gard'ner one day to open his views,
> By cutting a couple of grand avenues:
> No particular prospect his lordship intended,
> But left it to chance how his walks should be ended.

> With transport and joy he beheld his first view end
> In a favourite prospect—a church that was ruin'd:*
> But alas! what a sight did the next cut exhibit!
> At the end of a walk hung a rogue on a gibbet!

> He beheld it and wept, for it caused him to muse on
> Full many a Campbell that died with his shoes on.
> All amazed and aghast at the ominous scene,
> He order'd it quick to be clos'd up again
> With a clump of Scotch firs, that serv'd for a screen."

After his death the house changed hands more than once, and the trees and plants were mostly removed, with the exception of the firs and cedars: the choicest were transplanted to Kew Gardens about 1762. At length the property was purchased by Mr. Gostling, who divided the grounds into two parts, reserving one in which was the Grand Conservatory, which he converted into a villa, for himself; the other, with the Duke's house, he sold to Sir William Chambers.

Whitton Place in the hands of Chambers underwent many alterations. He converted the house into an Italian villa, which was greatly admired at the time; the grounds he filled with statues, ruins, and temples—among the latter being one to Æsculapius raised in honour of Dr. Willis. In the house he formed a collection of antique statues, pictures, and a splendid library of works on architecture. After Chambers's death the property was repurchased by the Gostling family, and was for a while the residence of Sir Benj. Hobhouse, M.P. After Hobhouse vacated it, Whitton Place was taken down, and the grounds united with those of Whitton Park.

Nothing is left of Chambers's house. That which was built on the site and partly out of the Duke of Argyll's conservatory is now the mansion of *Whitton Park*, and is the seat of Miss Gostling. The books, marbles, etc., collected by Chambers are preserved. The park is large and fairly wooded. In it are two good sheets of water, and a tower or observatory. The firs and cedars, now 150 years old, are magnificent.

Knellex Hall.—About ½ a mile E. of Whitton Place, Sir Godfrey Kneller, the

---

* The body of Twickenham ch. had recently fallen down, leaving the tower standing. (*See* TWICKENHAM, p. 640.)

famous painter, built himself a house, 1709-1711, made it his summer residence, in it spent his last years, and died, 1723. It was of red brick, stately, had good rooms and a grand staircase, which, according to the fashion of the time, was painted by Laguerre. Kneller intended to employ Sir James Thornhill, but hearing that he was engaged on a portrait of Sir Isaac Newton, said no portrait painter should paint his house, and called in Laguerre. Kneller, the most fortunate of portrait painters, had painted ten monarchs, and been celebrated in verse by Dryden, Prior, Pope, Addison, Steele, and Tickell. He was very wealthy, lived here in great state, was a justice of the peace, and, having no distrust of his own judgment, was apt to decide, as Walpole says, by equity rather than by law. Pope's lines are said to have been occasioned by an actual occurrence,—Kneller having dismissed a man who stole a joint of meat, and reprimanded the owner for putting temptation in the poor man's way.

" I think Sir Godfrey should decide the suit,
Who sent the thief, that stole the cash, away,
And punish'd him that put it in his way."

After the death of Kneller's widow the house became the residence of Sir Samuel Prime. Later it was purchased by Mr. Calvert, who had the house enlarged and remodelled under the superintendence of Mr. Philip Hardwick, R.A. *Kneller Hall*, as the house was now called, was purchased in 1847 by the Council of Education, and converted into a Training School for Schoolmasters of Workhouse Schools, the first master being Dr. Fredk. Temple, subsequently Master of Rugby, and now Bishop of Exeter. To fit it for a training school, the house was in a measure transformed; but in 1856 it was still further altered on being transferred to the War Department, and converted into a school for the education of bandmasters and musicians for the army. The *Royal Military School of Music* provides a thorough course of practical and theoretical instruction, under a competent staff of teachers. Little is now left of Kneller's house. The grounds are about 34 acres in extent.

A pretty little *Church* (St. Philip and St. James) was erected at the parting of the roads, E. of Whitton Park, in 1862, from the designs of Mr. F. H. Pownall.

It is E.E. in style; the exterior Kentish rag, the interior brick; and has several of the windows filled with painted glass.

WICKHAM, EAST, KENT, 10 m.

from London, 2 m. S.E. from Woolwich Arsenal, and 1½ m. S. from Abbey Wood Stat. of the S.-E. Rly. (N. Kent Branch); pop. 942.

East Wickham derives its name from its situation by what was of old the highroad to Dover (*wic*, road or way; *ham*, a dwelling), with the prefix East to distinguish it from WEST WICKHAM. The Dover road now passes nearly a mile S. of the village. East Wickham is pleasantly situated, but contains nothing besides the ch. to interest a stranger. The pursuits are agricultural, and a great quantity of fruit is grown; but many of the inhabitants are employed in Woolwich dockyard and arsenal.

The *Church* (St. Michael) stands away from the houses on the E. side of the lane. It is small and humble, and a good deal out of repair, but picturesque and interesting. It is of flint and stone, patched, and strengthened with brick buttresses, and was probably built by Robert Burnell, Bishop of Bath and Wells, who held three-fourths of the manor from 1284 to his death in 1292. It consists of a nave and chancel, with a small wooden bell turret (containing two old bells) at the W. end. The N. wall has two original lancet windows, deeply splayed inside. The chancel has a small 3-light Perp. window. The S. wall and west end are modern. The *interior* has tall pews, a plastered ceiling, and whitewashed walls; but under the whitewash are ten or a dozen 13th cent. *frescoes*, chiefly of events in the life of the Saviour. In the chancel is a *brass* (14th cent., much mutilated), with half effigies within the head of a cusped cross, of John de Bradigdone and wife Maud—noteworthy for her costume. On the N. wall is another in good condition, with effigies of William Payn, yeoman of the guard, d. 1568, and two of his wives, the third wife and her son being lost. In the ch.-yard *obs.*, from S. of the ch., the fine view between the hills N.E. towards Plumstead and Woolwich. *East Wickham House* (R. Jones, Esq.) is a good mansion a little W. of the ch. WELLING, on the Dover road, is partly in this parish.

WICKHAM, WEST, KENT (Dom. *Wicheham*). lies N. of Addington, Surrey, and W. of Hayes, Kent, 2½ m. S. of the Beckenham Stat. of the S.-E. and L. C. and D. Rlys. Pop. 884. Inn, *Swan*, a good country house.

West Wickham—the West prefixed to distinguish it from two other Kentish Wickhams, East Wickham, near Plumstead, and Wickham Breaux, near Canterbury—is situated in the midst of a pleasant and beautiful country, at present not greatly disfigured by the builder. The par. is large, the surface and soil varied; chalk, clay, sand, and gravel occur in different parts, and there are woods, hills, deep hollows, or "bottoms," rich in ferns and wild flowers, and long, winding, umbrageous lanes, but commonless, though close to Hayes Common.

The manor belonged in the reign of the Confessor to one Godrick; by William I. was given to Odo, Bp. of Bayeux; during the 14th cent. belonged to the Huntingfields; then passed to the Coppledikes, Squerreys, Trevalians, and Scropes. About 1470 it became the property of Sir Henry Heydon, in whose family it remained for a century, when it was sold by Sir William Heydon to John Lennard, Esq. The present lord of West Wickham manor is Col. J. Farnaby Lennard.

West Wickham Court, the seat of Col. J. F. Lennard, occupies the site of the ancient manor-house, and is itself a building of respectable antiquity. There are subterraneous passages, and a dungeon under the N.W. turret, which may have belonged to the mediæval castellated mansion. The present house is in the main the "right fair manor place" which Sir Henry Heydon built in the reign of Henry VII. It is of red brick, has octagonal turrets at the angles, was surrounded by a moat, and clearly had originally somewhat the character of a fortress, being strong enough to withstand a marauding attack, if not to sustain a siege. The house has been often altered, added to, and modernized, but retains much of its antique character, and is very interesting. Besides a fine old manorial hall with a gallery, the interior contains some good rooms, and interesting family and other pictures.

At a house in West Wickham, but not at Wickham Court, as is commonly stated,

resided, from 1729 till his death, 1751, Gilbert West, the translator of Pindar, author of some original poetry which gained him a place among Johnson's Poets, and of 'Observations on the Resurrection,' and other religious pieces. West "was very often visited by Lyttelton and Pitt, who, when they were weary of faction and debates, used at Wickham to find books and quiet, a decent table, and literary conversation. There is at Wickham a walk made by Pitt: and, what is of far more importance, at Wickham Lyttelton received that conviction which produced his 'Dissertation on St. Paul.'"[*] Among the eminent friends who visited West at Wickham was Glover, the author of 'Leonidas.' Glover was subject to strange fits of absence of mind. One morning, as Lord Lyttelton looked from his dressing-room window, he saw Glover in the garden below, pacing to and fro with a whip in his hand, and gesticulating vehemently, as though in a fit of poetic ardour. It was in the days when tulips were the rage. Mrs. West was a zealous florist, and she had a bed of choice tulips ready to blow, just then her peculiar care. By these Glover was declaiming, when, to his dismay, Lyttelton beheld him suddenly apply his whip vigorously to their stalks, and "before there was time to awaken him from his reverie," the unlucky tulips were levelled with the ground. So entirely unconscious was he, that when the devastation was pointed out to him he could with difficulty be brought to believe he had committed it.

William Pitt, Earl of Chatham, had a house, *South Lodge*, in West Wickham village, before his removal to Hayes. *Monk's Orchard* (Lewis Lloyd, Esq.) is a spacious castellated mansion, erected in 1860, on the site of West Wickham Park. *West Wickham House* is a large and picturesque mansion, very pleasantly situated, erected in 1871, in the revived Queen Anne's style, from the designs of Mr. Norman Shaw, A.R.A. Other seats are *Wickham Hall* (J. S. Forbes, Esq.); *Ravenswood* (Misses Hall), etc.

The *Church* (St. John the Baptist) occupies an elevated site near Wickham Court, the ch.-yard looking down into

---

[*] Johnson, Lives of the Poets, vol. iii.: Gilbert West.

deep hollows on nearly all sides; all around are great elms, and the grouped chimneys and ivy-covered turrets of Wickham Court strengthen the character and charm of the scene. At the entrance to the ch.-yard is an old oak lich-gate with a tiled roof. The church was rebuilt in the reign of Henry VII. by Sir Henry Heydon, the builder of Wickham Court. Though in the main late Perp. in style, some fragments of the older ch. seem to have been retained or inserted. It is of flint and stone, in part covered with plaster, and comprises nave, chancel, and N. aisle, and low square entrance tower on the S.W., with heavy double buttresses at the angles, and a peal of 5 bells inside. The int. was restored in 1844, and is in good condition. In the windows is some good 16th cent. painted glass, figures of St. Anne, St. Christopher with the Child Saviour, St. Catherine, etc. *Monts.* in N. aisle to Sir Samuel Lennard, 1618; and others to members of the Lennard family. In the chancel are a piscina and ambrey; in the E. end of the N. aisle a second piscina. *Brasses*, small, to Wm. Thorpe, rector, 1407; Sir John Stokton, priest, 1515; and mutilated effigy of a priest. On the floor are many fragments of encaustic tiles, apparently from the older church.

The village, *Wickham Street*, is nearly a mile N. of the church. It is a pleasant quiet cluster of country cottages about a green, and along the road to Croydon. Note at the parting of the roads the grand old village elm, with seats beneath it, and opposite it the comfortable-looking village inn, the Swan. The walks hence, along *Wickham Bottom* to Addington, and in the opposite direction to Beckenham, or eastward to Hayes Common, are very beautiful.

WIDMORE, Kent (*see* Bromley).

WILLESDEN, or WILSDON,
Middx. (Dom. *Wellesdone*), a semi-suburban vill., lying to the W. of the Edgware road, about 4½ m. from Hyde Park Corner. The L. and N.-W. Rly. runs along the western side of the par., and has a stat. near Harlesden, the Willesden Junction Stat., which serves also for the N. London line. The Midland Rly. has a stat. at Dudding Hill, about ½ m. N.E. of Willesden ch., and another by the Harrow road for the new district called Stonebridge Park. Pop. of Willesden par. 15,869. Inns: *White Horse; White Hart,* Church End.

A very few years ago Willesden was a quiet, retired, thoroughly rural village, a favourite haunt of the holiday-maker, summer rambler, botanist, and sketcher, who reckoned on the White Horse for a substantial country lunch or dinner. Now London has reached its outskirts. The builder has invaded the once tranquil meadows; field-paths (and fields also) are disappearing; and the lanes are for the most part green no longer. As late as 1861, though the irruption had made great progress, the pop. of the parish was under 4000; in 1871 it was nearly 16,000 (more exactly, 3879 and 15,869). The chief increase of course was at the London end, those parts of Kilburn (Holy Trinity) and Kensal Green which are in Willesden par., and which contained respectively 10,399 and 2138 inh. Since 1871 the increase has been commensurate and continuous. Still the more distant parts towards Wembly, Neasdon, Kingsbury, and Twyford remain comparatively rural.

The manors of Willesden and Harlesden were held by the Canons of St. Paul's at the Domesday Survey—the original grant was by King Athelstan—and have been held by them ever since. But in the course of the 12th cent. they were divided, and appropriated to prebendaries,—*Willesden*, in the southern and eastern half of the par., into Willesden, Brandsbury, or as it is now called Brondesbury, Mapesbury, and Chambers, or Chamberlain's Wood; *Harlesden (Herulvestune)*, the western and northern portion, into Harlesden, East Twyford, Neasdon, and Oxgate: there are thus no fewer than 8 prebendal manors in the parish.

The *Church* (St. Mary) is interesting. Previous to 1850 it consisted of a nave and chancel, S. aisle, tower at the W. end of the aisle, and S. porch. It had suffered from alterations, was partially covered with stucco, and was much out of order, but had a venerable and picturesque aspect, and was in great favour with artists and sketchers. Several engravings of it exist, but that which best exhibits its picturesque character is a spirited etching made by George Cooke in 1828. In 1851 it was enlarged and repaired, substantially, but with some artistic loss. In 1872 it was carefully restored throughout under the direction of Mr. Edw. J. Tarver; a N. aisle, chapel or transept, and entrance porch added; the cement cleared from the exterior; the tower opened to the interior; and the ground floor of the tower converted into a baptistery.

The body of the fabric is of different dates. The arcade of the S. aisle, of 3 bays with circular piers, is E.E., and the oldest part of the ch.; but in the recent restoration, some fragments of the earlier Norm. ch., including the round arches of two narrow windows, were discovered in removing the N. wall. The chancel, S. aisle, and tower are Perp. The new chapel or transept at the end of the N. aisle is E.E. in style. The N. arcade has been constructed to correspond with that of the S. aisle, on the bases of an ancient arcade found *in situ*, the first pier being formed of the old stones exhumed in clearing the ground. The tower rests on arches, has buttresses at the angles, a wide stair-turret terminating at the belfry, battle-mented parapet, and low pyramidal roof, and contains a peal of 6 bells. The eastern bay of the S. aisle forms a chantry open-ing to the aisle and chancel by arches, and a similar arrangement has been adopted in the N. aisle. In the E. window is a representation of the Crucifixion; some of the windows in the aisles have painted glass; that in the W. window of the nave, by Halliday, was inserted in 1875. The piscina in the S. wall of the chancel was found during the recent restoration, and removed to its present position. The sedilia, reredos, and pavement of encaustic tiles in the sacrarium are new. The late Norm. font, no doubt that of the earlier ch., has a large square black marble bowl, with sharp carvings at the angles, sup-ported on a thick central stem and 4 corner shafts. In the N. wall of the chancel is a recessed or Easter sepulchre, and another is in the S. wall of the E. chantry. The old pews have been re-moved, and open seats substituted—with a single exception, the proprietor of one tall pew sturdily insisting on the main-tenance of his legal rights.

The monts. include a tablet to Richard Paine, d. 1606, æt. 95, J.P., and gentle-man pensioner to Henry VIII., Edward VI., Q. Mary, Q. Elizabeth, and James I. John Barne, 1615; Sir John Francklyn, 1647; several to the Roberts family, and a gravestone to General Charles Ottway, d. 1764. *Brasses:* Bartholomew Willes-den, 1492, and wives; Mary Robert and children, 1505; Edmund Robert and wives, 1585; Jane Barne, 1609; also William Lichfield, vicar, in cope and amice, 1517.

The wooden house in the ch.-yard shown in Cooke's etching, and all the other old buildings, have been pulled down, and the ch.-yard enlarged.

The scene of some of Jack Shepherd the ubiquitous highwayman's exploits is laid by his romancing biographer at Willesden; Cruikshank has drawn him picking pockets at Willesden ch.; and equally trustworthy tradition has buried him in Willesden ch.-yard: but he is un-recorded on church register or memorial stone.

An inventory of the church furniture of the middle of the 13th cent. contains entries of a scarlet banner with a repre-sentation of the Virgin Mary of cloth of gold; and of two large carved images of the Virgin. These probably had reference, or may have given rise, to the pilgrimage to *Our Lady of Willesden*, a popular pilgrimage resembling the more famous one to Our Lady of Walsingham. The object of adoration at Walsingham was a wooden shrine of St. Mary, in the form of the Holy House of Nazareth. There may have been a shrine, there was certainly an image, asserted to be miraculous, of St. Mary in Willesden ch., and to it the Londoners of both sexes flocked in great numbers, it being in the 15th cent. their most favourite resort. But the pilgrims were, at least in the later years of the pilgrimage, often persons of immoral character; and the pilgrimage itself was the occasion of much scandal. "Ye men of London," said the Scottish friar, Father Donald, in a sermon he preached at St. Paul's Cross, not long before the sup-pression of the pilgrimage, "gang you yourselves with your wives to Willesden, in the Devyl's name, or else keep them at home with you with sorrow." The pil-grimage was suppressed, and the miracu-lous image of Our Lady of Willesden was destroyed at Chelsea, along with the shrine of Our Lady of Walsingham, in 1548.

Willesden is made up of many parts. There are a few houses about the ch., at what is called Church End; more at Willesden Green, 1 m. E. of the ch., formerly a picturesque collection of old houses about a village green, removed to make way for rows of mean brick cottages; Queen's Town, of modern growth, midway between Church End and the Green; the outlying hamlets of Neasdon, Harlesden, Sherrick Green, Dollis Hill, Stonebridge Park, and Brondesbury, but most thickly of all at the London end of the par., Kilburn and Kensal Green. There are a few good seats, but no buildings of importance. The institutions—all on a small scale—include a Working Men's Institute; Workmen's Hall; Good Templars and Temperance Orphanage; Horticultural Association, etc.

In Willesden Lane is a Jewish cemetery, consecrated Oct. 1873, and in which were interred Baron Mayer de Rothschild, Feb. 1874, and Sir Anthony de Rothschild, Jan. 1876. The grounds are prettily laid out and planted, and there are three carefully finished buildings of Kentish rag and Bath stone, with shafts of red Mansfield stone, Dec. in style, designed by Mr. N. S. Joseph, in which the various burial rites are performed. The larger building in the centre is that in which the coffin is deposited, and the preliminary prayers recited. The others are for special ceremonial observances.

Harlesden Green, somewhat over 1 m. S. of Willesden Church End, and ½ m. N. of Willesden Junction Stat., was a quiet rustic hamlet, but has been utterly spoiled by the builder. Here are a small chapel-of-ease, dissenting chapels, and several public-houses. *Harlesden House* (T. Nixon Kerr, Esq.) is a good mansion standing in grounds noted for horticultural and floricultural displays.

Brondesbury, nearly 2 m. S. of Church End, near the Edgware road and Kilburn Wells, is a new district of genteel villas. With the adjacent hamlet of *Mapesbury* it forms the eccl. dist. of Brondesbury Christ Church, which in 1871 had a pop. of 1094—since much increased. The Church, erected in 1866 from the designs of Mr. R. B. King, is a spacious stone structure, E.E. in style, and cruciform,

with tower and tall spire. *Brondesbury Park*, the seat of Thos. Brandon, Esq., stands in large grounds W. of the ch.

Cricklewood, N.W. of Brondesbury and Mapeswood, is a hamlet of Willesden on the Edgware road, the pretty rural tract so named stretching away to Child's Hill, Golder's Green, and Hampstead. The Midland Rly. runs through it, and has a stat., which serves for both Child's Hill and Cricklewood.

Neasdon, ¾ m. N. of Church End, in the most rural part of Willesden, has a separate notice. Half a mile W. of it, in the lane leading to the Edgware road, is the pretty little hamlet of *Dollis Hill*, in an elevated, well wooded, and picturesque district.

Sherrick Green, midway between Dollis Green and Church End, lies in a hollow on a little feeder of the Brent away from the main road, and looks pleasant, peaceful, and secluded.

Stonebridge Park, by the 5 m. stone on the Harrow road, about ¾ m. S.W. of Church End, is a cluster of 60 or 80 smart new villas for City men, with a large inn, the Stonebridge Park Hotel, and a station on the Midland Rly.

WILMINGTON, KENT, on the l. bank of the Darent, 1½ m. S. of Dartford, on the road to Sevenoaks. Pop. 1105.

Standing chiefly on the side of a hill which slopes down to the Darent, the situation is naturally pleasant, and there are from many points good views over the adjacent country; but the gunpowder mills prevent free access to the river, and on the Dartford side the builder is encroaching. The village cottages on the roadside are in straight rows, and not attractive. But away from road and river-mills, more of rusticity is preserved. There are broad well-cultivated fields, good farms, orchards, and gardens. Fruit is largely grown, and the neighbourhood is noted for its cherry orchards: a church path, S. of the ch., runs through one, and will enable the visitor to observe the system of culture. The trees are kept well pruned, and currants are planted in the spaces between them. Very pretty they look in April, when in blossom; very tempting three or four months later, when in fruit.

The *Church* (St. Michael) stands on the

brow of the hill. It has nave and chancel of equal height, a short N. aisle ; and at the W. end a wooden belfry and short octagonal spire. It is of flint and stone ; Dec. in style, the windows small, except the E. window, which is a Perp. insertion. The ch. was restored throughout in 1868. The interior is neat, but uninteresting. It has open seats, a W. gallery, and a good carved pulpit of the reign of James I. About the ch.-yard are several large elms; but a row of 9 of noble proportions, which skirted the northern side of the ch.-yard, rendered it uncommonly picturesque from below, and served as a screen from the N. and N.E. blasts, was cut down in April 1867, and ch. and ch.-yard suffer not a little from the Vandalism.

Wilmington Manor House, by the village, now ruinous, occupies the site of a residence of the King-maker Warwick. Later the manor belonged to Margaret Plantagenet, Countess of Salisbury, and mother of Cardinal Pole. *Wilmington House* (F. Talbot Tasker, Esq.), and *Mount Pleasant* (E. Lewis, Esq.), are some distance S. and S.W. Other seats are *Hulse Wood* (T. Dunster, Esq.), and *Monks' Orchard* (J. C. Hayward, Esq.)

Wilmington Common stretches S.W. from the ch. A mile or so farther W. is *Joyden's Wood*, also in this parish, where are traces of early works and buildings, the age and purpose of which are not clearly determined.

WIMBLEDON, Surrey, a vill.

on the south-eastern edge of Wimbledon Common, 3 m. S. of Putney, and 7 m. from Hyde Park Corner. The Wimbledon Stat. of the L. and S.-W. Rly. is ½ m. S.E. of the vill., and 7¼ m. from the Waterloo Stat. Lines diverge here to Mitcham, Tooting, the Crystal Palace, Croydon, and Epsom. Pop. 9087.

The received derivation of Wimbledon, anciently written *Wymbaldon, Wymbeldon*, and *Wimbeldon*, is from "some Saxon proprietor Wymbald, and *dun* or *dune*, a hill in the Saxon language." * But the earliest form is *Wibban-dune*,† and suggests *Worms Hill*, or *Worms*

* Brayley, Hist. of Surrey, vol. iii., p. 499; Lysons, Environs, vol. i., p. 391.
† A.-S. Chronicle, An. 568 ; Ethelwerd has *Uubbandune*; Florence of Worcester, *Wibbandune*; Henry of Huntingdon, *Wipandune*.

Down, rather than *Wymbald's Hill*, as the radical : *Wibba*, a worm ; *dun*, a hill or down ; though Wibba may have been a proper name.

A battle was fought at Wibbandune in the year 568 between Ceawlin, King of Wessex, and Æthelbriht, King of Kent, when the latter was defeated and driven back into Kent, and two of his ealdermen, Oslaf and Cnebba, were slain. The great entrenchment now known as Cæsar's Camp—to be noticed presently—shows that Wimbledon had been the scene of military operations at an earlier period ; and it may have been to gain possession of this fortress that Ceawlin and Æthelbriht fought.

Wimbledon is not mentioned in the Domesday record, no doubt because it then formed a part of the Abp. of Canterbury's great manor of Mortlake. It appears to have been a grange or farm, and was held with the manor till that was alienated by Cranmer to Henry VIII. in exchange for other lands. Henry granted Wimbledon to Thomas Cromwell, and after his attainder settled it upon Queen Catherine Parr for her life. It was given by Queen Mary to Cardinal Pole. In 1576 Queen Elizabeth granted the manor-house to Sir Christopher Hatton, who sold it the same year to Sir Thos. Cecil (afterwards Earl of Exeter), to whom, 14 years later, Elizabeth transferred the manor in exchange for an estate in Lincolnshire. Cecil bequeathed the estate to his 3rd son, Sir Edward Cecil, created by Charles I. Viscount Wimbledon and Baron Putney; on whose decease in 1638 it was sold to Queen Henrietta Maria. Seized by the Parliament as Crown land, it was valued by their surveyors at £386 19s. 8d. a year, and sold to Adam Baynes, of Knowstrop, Yorkshire, at 18 years' purchase. He shortly after parted with it to General Lambert, who was lord of the manor in 1656. On the return of Charles II. it was restored to the Queen-Dowager, and sold by her in 1661 to George Digby, Earl of Bristol. On his death in 1676 it was sold by his widow to the Lord Treasurer Danby, created, 1694, Duke of Leeds. He died in 1712, and in 1717 Wimbledon was sold under a decree in Chancery to Sir Theodore Jansen, Bart. He was one of the directors of the South Sea Company, and when that bubble burst,

Wimbledon was put up for sale, and purchased by Sarah Duchess of Marlborough for £15,000. She demised it to John Spencer, M.P., youngest son of Charles Earl of Sunderland, by her Grace's second daughter, Lady Anne Churchill. On his death it devolved on his only son John, created Earl Spencer and Viscount Althorp in 1765, from whom it descended to John, 5th Earl Spencer, who sold his manorial rights in 1871.

Under the archbishops, some curious manorial customs had to be observed by the tenants. When a new abp. came for the first time to Wimbledon, each customary tenant must present him with " a gyfte called *saddle silver*," of the value of 5 marks. Every tenant of two-yard-lands, or 30 acres, was liable to serve the office of beadle ; of three-yard-lands, that of reeve or provost. On the death of a freeholder, the lord was entitled to " his best horse, saddyl, brydell, spere, sworde, boots, spores, and armure, if he any should have." * Lands descend to the youngest son.

Whilst still only lessee of the manorhouse, Sir Thomas Cecil built himself in 1588, " the year of the Armada," a magnificent mansion, long famous as *Wimbledon House*. " A daring structure," Thomas Fuller called it, comparable with the royal palace of Nonsuch. The architect was John Thorpe, among whose designs in the Soane Museum is one of " Wymbleton an howse standing on the edg of an hie hill." Here Sir Thomas, then Lord Burghley, entertained Queen Elizabeth for three days in the early part of 1599. In June 1616, and again in June 1619, James I. was here at banquet and hunting. Gondomar, the Spanish ambassador, was also magnificently feasted at Wimbledon, and in return initiated its owner in the mysteries of the Spanish olio.

"The old Earl [of Exeter] was very fond of him [Lord Ross], and for his sake began to comply with Count Gondomar, the Spanish ambassador, and as I take it feasted him at his house at Wimbledon ; and I was once at dinner with the Earl of Exeter, when the Ambassador sent him a Spanish olio, a pie consisting of many ingredients, out of which pie I did eat bacon, pheasant, partridge, chesnuts, pease, and many other things." †

When Wimbledon House became the property of Queen Henrietta Maria, she enriched it with a fine collection of paintings and works of art. Charles I. was often there, took much interest in the gardens, and only a few days before his trial ordered some seeds of Spanish melons to be "planted in his garden at Wimbledon." The Parliamentary General Lambert, who succeeded Charles and his Queen in the occupancy of Wimbledon House, was as fond as the King of the gardens and pictures. At Wimbledon House, Lambert "turned florist, and had the finest tulips and gilliflowers that could be had for love or money." * He was as fond of painting flowers as growing them, and when dispossessed of the house at the Restoration, a mocking pamphlet, that professed to be ' The Humble Petition of the Lord Lambert,' makes him beg that the Parliament "would let him see once again Wimbledon House and the Queen's pictures." Several pictures of his painting are said to have been long preserved in Wimbledon House.

The Queen-Dowager, as we have seen, sold Wimbledon to the Earl of Bristol, who spent a considerable sum in repairs and alterations.

"3 *February*, 1662.—I went with my Lord of Bristol to see his house at Wimbledon, newly bought of the Queene Mother, to help contrive the garden after the moderne. It is a delicious place for prospect and the thicketts, but the soile cold and weeping clay." †

Here occurred the curious scene of the Earl of Bristol's public renunciation of Catholicism, recorded by the Comte de Comminges, the French ambassador, who professes great indignation that such an act is allowed to pass unpunished.

"Last Sunday the Earl of Bristol appeared in the parish church of Oulmilton, about 2 leagues from London, with a notary and witnesses, and made a public declaration that he was a Protestant, and that from his heart he renounced the Catholic religion. After that he took the minister and other gentlemen to dine with him, for the house belonged to him, he having purchased it of the Queen Mother. The dinner ended he mounted his horse with 4 gentlemen and rode away. The act is insolent and daring, and leads one to suppose he will present himself to take his seat as soon as the Parliament opens." ‡

* Records of Manor, quoted by Lysons, vol. i., p. 393 ; Bartlett, Hist. and Ant. of Wimbledon, p. 60.
† Bp. Goodman, Court of King James, vol. i., p. 194.

* Coke's Detection, p. 400.
† Evelyn, Diary.
‡ Comminges, Au Roi (Louis XIV.), Jan. 25—Fev. 4, 1663-4, quoted in App. to Pepys, vol. v., p. 436.

Bristol was at this time busy intriguing against the Lord Chancellor Clarendon, and the King tried without success to reconcile them. Somewhat later Pepys is told that "the King is offended at my Lord of Bristol," and "sent a guard and a herald last night to have taken him at Wimbleton, where he was in the morning, but could not find him; at which the King was and is still mightily concerned, and runs up and down to and fro from the Chancellor's like a boy: and it seems would make Bristol's articles against the Chancellor to be treasonable reflections against his Majesty. . . . God knows what will come of it." [*] Nothing came of it; the business, as Pepys notes, was "hushed up," and the Earl died in quiet possession of Wimbledon, in 1676.

Wimbledon House suffered severely whilst in the occupation of Sir Edward Cecil Viscount Wimbledon, by an explosion of gunpowder, 1628; and very curiously his stately London mansion on the N. side of the Strand was the day after destroyed by fire. Wimbledon House was quickly repaired, and redecorated, and the exterior painted in fresco by Francis Cleyn.[†] The Parliamentary Survey, made in 1649,[‡] and the two large views, of the principal front and the garden front, engraved by "Henry Winstanley at Littlebury in Essex," 1678, give a tolerably clear notion of Cecil's house. It occupied an elevated site on the hill-side, and was approached from the outer gate by no fewer than "5 several ascents," each a stately flight, and in all "consisting of three score and ten steps." In the Lower Court was a fair fountain; the Upper formed the approach to the house. The house consisted of a centre and deep projecting wings, with square turrets at the inner angles, capped by tall pyramidal roofs. The fabric was of "an excellent good brick . . . . the angles, window stanchions and jambs all of ashler stone." The grand central entrance porch had "columns of free-stone very well wrought." The garden front, though less varied, was stately and ornate; the side fronts rose from broad terraces, overlooking sunk gardens, an arrangement that reminds one of Hatfield House, which it will be

remembered had been completed by Cecil's father only 10 or 12 years before the erection of Wimbledon House.

The interior contained on the ground floor "a room called the Stone Gallery, 108 foote long, seeled over head, pillored and arched with grey marble." Like the gallery at Hatfield, it was lined with oak wainscot, but this was garnished with green and spotted with stars of gold, and "benched all along the sides and angles." In the middle of the gallery was a grotto, "wrought in the arch and sides thereof with sundry sorts of shells, of great lustre and ornament, formed into the shapes of men, lions, serpents, antick formes, and other rare devices," with in the centre a jet of water. Opposite to the doors of this room are "fortie sights of seeing glass sett together in one frame, much adorning and setting forth the splendour of the roome." A great table "of one entire piece of wood, 21 feet long and 6 inches thick," stood in the middle of the gallery. Around the room was "a border or fret having set therein 11 pictures of very good workmanship." The ceiling was of fretwork with a well-wrought landscape in the centre, and 7 others in surrounding panels. The floor was of black and white marble. Outside a balcony extended the whole length of the gallery. An Organ Room had "a fayre and rich payre of organs." The Chapel had "a quadrate arched roof," painted with landscapes; as were also the walls above the oak wainscoting. The pavement was of black and white marble, polished. The Lower Parlour; the Balcony Room; the King's Chamber, the Queen's Chamber, Withdrawing Rooms, Bath Rooms, and other principal rooms on this floor, had all richly fretted and decorated ceiling, were lined with oak, and variously adorned. A stone gallery 62 feet long, had on the walls "many sententious sentences"—for the edification, perhaps, of suitors pacing its length whilst waiting an audience.

Staircases in the turrets led to the upper floor. The walls of both were lined with paintings—"landskipps of battles, anticks, heaven and hell"—whilst at the head of one hung a great picture of Henry IV. of France on horseback. Under the stairs was "a little compleate roome, called the 'Den of Lyons,' painted round with

* Pepys, Diary, 14th March, 1664.
† Walpole, Anecdotes, vol. ii., p. 227.
‡ Archæologia, vol. x.

lyons and leopards." The Great Gallery on the upper floor, 109 ft. 8 in. long and 21 ft. wide, was "floored with cedar boards, casting a pleasant smell," and lined with oak wainscot to the height of nearly 14 ft.; the pilasters and panels bossed with stars and crosses and fillets of gold, the ceiling delicately wrought in fretwork, very well lighted, and having in the midst a fair large chimneypiece "of black and white marble, engraved with coats of arms, adorned with several curious and well-gilded statues of alabaster, with a foot-pace of black and white marble." Contiguous to this was the Summer Chamber, and on the same floor were the Duke's Chamber, the Duchess's Chamber, and various others.

Around the house were gardens filled, besides flowers, with over a thousand fruit trees, orangeries, alleys, mazes, wildernesses, etc., whilst from the ascent in front of the house was "a way cut forth of the park," lined with elms and other great trees "in very decent order, extending itself in a direct line, 231 perches from thence, quite through the park northward unto Putney Common."

Sir Theodore Jansen had begun to pull down Wimbledon House—"the finest house round London," as Swift called it—in order to build another on the site, when it passed from his hands to those of the Duchess of Marlborough—who continued and completed the work of demolition. Her Grace desired a snugger dwelling, and one to which she should not have to go up any steps, and the Earl of Pembroke undertook to build her one. It was completed in 1735:

"Her Grace the Duchess Dowager of Marlborough has finished her fine house at Wimbledon : her Grace designing to reside there this summer." [*]

When she saw it, she told the Earl it looked "as though it were making a curtsey"! "But it was the whimsical old woman's own fault," wrote Horace Walpole. She desired him not to make her go up any steps, "and so he dug a saucer to put it in, and levelled the first floor with the ground."[†]

The house was destroyed by fire on Easter Monday 1785. Earl Spencer converted some offices which had escaped the

* Daily Courant, May 10, 1735.
† Walpole to Geo. Montagu, July 22, 1751.

fire into an occasional residence ; and in 1801 a new mansion, designed by Holland, was completed somewhat to the N.W. of the former. The new house, now called *Wimbledon Park House*, was from about 1827 the residence of the Duke of Somerset; "and here it was that Sir Joseph Paxton began life as under-gardener to his brother, then head-gardener in these grounds."[*] *Wimbledon Park House*, with about 7 acres of the grounds, is now the property of Mrs. Bertram Evans.

Wimbledon Park, which Earl Spencer had increased by the purchase of land on the Wandsworth side to about 1200 acres, was in 1836 severed from the Spencer estates, and sold by Lord Althorp, to redeem the property from a heavy debt.

Handsome houses have been built on the ridge by H. C. Forde, Esq., — Hardman, Esq., — Mortimer, Esq., etc.; but the central portion, including a fine lake of over 30 acres, is still unsold, open, and very pleasant. The surface is diversified : there are hill and dell, trees numerous, large, and flourishing, the broad lake, wide prospects, and nightingales and other singing-birds abound.

Wimbledon *Church* (St. Mary) adjoins Wimbledon Park and the site of the old manor-house, but is some distance from the village. It stands high, and is seen far. The old ch. was taken down, except the chancel, in 1788, and rebuilt in the manner of a Methodist meeting. That fashion went out of favour, and in 1833-4, after lasting just half a century, the barn gave place to a Gothic church erected by Messrs. Scott and Moffatt. In 1843 the ch. was enlarged ; in 1860 the old chancel, which had been retained, was rebuilt. The church is of black flint and stone ; Perp.; and comprises nave, aisles, chancel, and tall W. tower, with thin slated spire, conspicuous for miles around. The interior is well fitted and in good order. Several of the windows have memorial and heraldic glass. S. of the chancel is the Wimbledon Chapel, erected, *temp.* James I., by Viscount Wimbledon as a family mausoleum. In the centre is the black marble altar tomb, with long insc., of " Sir Edward Cecill, Knight, Lo. Cecill and Baron of Putney, Viscount Wimbledon of Wimbledon," who "followed the

* Bartlett, Hist. of Wimbledon, p. 70.

Warres in the Netherlands five and thirty years," and commanded at Cadiz : d. 1638. Over the tomb is suspended an earl's coronet; around are his helmet and pieces of armour ; on the walls and floor inscriptions to other members of the family, and to Betensons, etc. On the wall of S. aisle, *obs.* marble tablet, erected by the Fox Club, with relief by Westmacott, of James Perry, d. 1821, for many years proprietor and editor of the ' Morning Chronicle.' On wall of N. aisle tablet to Sir Jas. Allan Park, d. 1838, one of the judges of the Common Pleas. On the chancel floor is the gravestone of Sir Richard Wynne, d. 1649, gentleman of the Privy Chamber to Charles I.: Wynne accompanied Charles when Prince of Wales on his romantic journey to Spain.

In the ch.-yard are many pompous tombs, the most noticeable perhaps being the *columbarium*, erected by Benj. Bond Hopkins, of Pains Hill and Wimbledon House, d. 1794, as a family burial-place. Near the gate is the vault of John Hopkins, d. 1732, " whose rapacity obtained him the name of *Vulture Hopkins*. He lived worthless, but died worth three hundred thousand pounds," and has been immortalized by Pope.* The pyramidal structure is to Gerard de Visme, d. 1797. Margaret, Countess of Lucan, 1814, has an urn on an Ionic column. Altar tomb on N. of Field-Marshal Thomas Grosvenor, d. 1851. Altar tomb of Sir Theodore Jansen, d. 1748, and Sir Abraham Jansen, d. 1763. Comparatively inconspicuous is the mont. on N.W. of ch.-yard of that excellent painter Gilbert Stuart Newton, R.A., d. 1835.

Three other churches have been built in Wimbledon. *Holy Trinity*, in the Merton Road, is a neat early Dec. building, with a bell turret, erected in 1862 from the designs of Mr. J. Johnson. In 1875 a window of painted glass, the Transfiguration by Mayer of Munich, was erected by Madame Lind Goldschmidt (of Oak Lea, Wimbledon), as a memorial of Bp. Wilberforce.

Christ Church, on the Ridgeway, is a good building of Kentish rag and Bathstone, early Dec. in style, erected in 1859 from the designs of Mr. S. S. Teulon. The large red-brick building with high-

pitched roofs and peaked dormer windows, a little E. of Christ Church, and a conspicuous object from the S.-W. Rly., is *Wimbledon School*, a proprietary grammar school, established in 1859. St. John the Baptist, Spencer Hill, and Immanuel, Copse Hill, are chapels of recent erection.

The old *village* is a little distance S.W. of the ch. and Wimbledon Park, on the hill-top and skirting the south-eastern side of the Common ; but it has extended its borders wherever practicable along the Ridgeway on the road to Kingston and down the hill towards the Rly. Stat., whilst an outlying suburb, New Wimbledon, has grown up on the road to Merton. Not only in Wimbledon Park, but wherever land was to be had, villa and cottage residences have been built, and occupied as soon as finished. Many of these are large and good houses, and stand in ornamental grounds. But the old red-brick mansions with their tall elms and stately surroundings, and large richly-wrought iron garden gates, are fast disappearing. The old village too has ceased to be rural as the place has become populous—and the population very nearly doubled between 1861 and 1871. Wimbledon has no manufactures ; and the trade is local. The village has its village *Club and reading rooms ;* many and good schools ; on Copse Hill a *Cottage Hospital* erected in 1860, and the Morley *Convalescent Hospital*, remodelled in 1874, for the reception of convalescent patients from St. George's Hospital. Wimbledon is the head-quarters of the 11th Surrey Rifles. The London Scottish Golf Club have their head-quarters at the Iron-house on the common, and may often be seen there engaged in their national sport. And on the rt. of the rly. a little beyond the station is the All-England Croquet Club ground—where on any great day may be seen at once the best croquet lawns and croquet players.

The glory of Wimbledon is its *Common*, a broad, open, gorse-covered heath of 1,000 acres, stretching westward from Wimbledon Park to Putney Heath, and including portions of the parishes of Putney and Wandsworth. It is the widest and most picturesque of the commons immediately contiguous to London, and happily by the Wimbledon and

* Mo1 al Essays, Epistle iii., l. 85 and 291.

A Military Review, Wimbledon Common

Windsor Castle (see p.710)

Putney Commons Act of 1871 has been saved from enclosure and placed under satisfactory control. Wimbledon Common was in duelling days a noted place for hostile meetings. Here in May 1789 the Duke of York and Lieut.-Col. Lennox fought, the Colonel's bullet grazing the Duke's hair. Hardly less noise was made by the duels between Sir Francis Burdett and James Paull, May 1807, in which both were hurt; that between Mr. Clarke and Mr. George Payne, Sept. 1809, in which the latter was mortally wounded; and the later ones between the Marquis of Londonderry and Henry Grattan, June 13, 1839; and the Earl of Cardigan and Capt. H. Tuckett, Sept. 21, 1840, which led to the trial of Lord Cardigan in the House of Lords, and did much to bring the practice of duelling into disrepute. The usual meeting-place was by the Windmill, of old so picturesque a feature of the Common,—now the head-quarters of the Rifle Association. The duels between Pitt and Tierney, and Castlereagh and Canning, though commonly assigned to Wimbledon Common, were fought on Putney Heath. (*See* PUTNEY, p. 478.)

Wimbledon Common was also a notorious resort of highwaymen; and on it one of the most famous of the fraternity, Jerry Abershawe, was hanged in chains, having been first hanged in the ordinary way on Kennington Common. (*See* p. 116.)

In the last century Wimbledon Common was several times used for reviews. Here on July 4, 1799, George III. held a grand review of the Surrey Volunteers. Now every July witnesses a much grander gathering of volunteers on Wimbledon Common, at the annual meeting of the *National Rifle Association*, which has made the name of Wimbledon a household word wherever a volunteer dwells, wherever indeed rifle shooting is practised or cared for. The camp is formed in July, but the butts are permanent, and at certain butts rifle practice goes on every week-day except Wednesday all the year round.

At the south-western extremity of Wimbledon Common, and about 1 m. W. of the village, are the remains of an ancient earthwork called *Cæsar's Camp*, but known to the natives for many years

past as *The Rounds*. It was nearly circular, the only deviation being caused by the rapid fall of the ground on the N. The extreme diameter was 950 ft.; within the vallum about 750 ft., enclosing an area of about 10 acres.* It was surrounded by a fosse, from 12 to 15 ft. wide, and of an average depth of 12 ft., and a vallum from 12 to 20 ft. above the ground immediately beyond it. There are still traces of an outer vallum, and some years ago there were traces of outworks on the southern side. Vestiges of hut-circles have also been described, but none have been discoverable for many years past. Very different ages have been assigned to the camp. It has been called British, Roman, Saxon, Danish. Camden, who visited it, says that it was then called *Bensbury*, and suggests that it might take its name from Cnebben (Cnebba), the ealderman and general of Æthelbreht, who was slain at Webbandune in the fight with Ceawlin, in 568. Nothing has been found within the entrenchment to identify its makers; but the form and general character were those of a British work, though it may not improbably have been occupied by the Romans, the position being in a military point of view of great value.†

This very interesting work—the finest and most perfect in the vicinity of London—after being for years threatened, has been let for building on, and in spite of the energetic opposition of residents and archæologists, has been wholly destroyed by the owner, a Mr. Grosvenor Drax. The vallum has been levelled, the fosse filled, and building materials placed on the ground. The outline of the camp can only be made out by a few trees as yet unfelled which grew in the trench. Happily, the threatened building has been for the present stayed, the Master of the Rolls having (Dec. 1875), on appeal, made perpetual an injunction restraining the builder from using the road over the Common to the Camp for any other than agricultural purposes—and there is no

* All the old accounts make the area 7 acres; Mr. Tregelles says, "the true area of the enclosure is about 14 acres:" but *within the vallum* it is certainly under 10 acres.
† W. H. Tregelles, in Archæol. Journal, vol. xxiv., p. 261 *et seq.*, the best account of the Camp, with a good plan of it.

45

other access. There are wide views from the Camp; Combe Warren forms a picturesque object, and towards the N. W. was a charming bit of purple heathland. There is a way across the Camp towards Kingston, but the passenger is now warned against "trespassing" on either side.

Douglas describes 23 *barrows* on Wimbledon Common, "on the left of the highroad from London to Kingston." The largest were about 27 ft. in diameter. He opened some in 1786, but found nothing in them except a "small vessel of dark brown-greyish earth," about 3 inches high. Most of the barrows had, however, been already opened. They were all afterwards "remorselessly swept away to clear the roads."[*]

On the borders of the Common are several good houses. The most remarkable is *Wimbledon House*, in the last cent. the seat of Ald. Sir Henry Bankes. It was then for some time the residence of Benjamin Bond Hopkins, whose tomb is conspicuous in Wimbledon ch.-yard. From him it was purchased, in 1791, by M. Calonne, Comptroller-General of the Finances, and Minister of State to Louis XIV., who sold it, 1792, for £15,000 to Earl Gower, afterwards Marquis of Stafford. From him it was purchased, 1798, by Sir Stephen Lushington. From 1810 to 1814 it was the residence of the Prince de Condé. In 1815 it was purchased by Joseph Marryat, Esq., M.P. (father of the novelist), and after his death, 1824, was for several years the residence of his widow, who made the grounds famous for rare plants and flowers. It is now the property of Sir H. W. Peek, Bart., M.P., who has built handsome conservatories, and has restored the house and gardens to their former splendour. The house opposite to it was for several years the residence of Sir Wm. Congreve, of rocket celebrity.

In a large red-brick mansion of William III.'s time which stood in the rear of the Crooked Billet, lived for several years, and here died, July 1, 1782, the minister Lord Rockingham. The following year, whilst Secretary of State, Charles James Fox was its occupant. Shortly after the house was taken down. A modern villa, *Belve-*

* Douglas, Nenia Britannica, fol., 1793, p. 93; Brayley, Hist. of Surrey, vol. iii., p. 509.

dere, supplies its place, but Rockingham's house stood more to the W.

Wimbledon Lodge (Miss Murray) on the S. side of the Common, facing the Green, was built by Gerard de Visme, Esq., and after his death became the property of his daughter, during whose minority it was the residence of Earl Bathurst. Miss De Visme married General the Hon. Sir Henry Murray; and Wimbledon Lodge was their seat as long as they lived.

In the house W. of Lady Murray's, on the S. of the Common, lived in the last half of the 18th cent. William Wilberforce, whose namesake, nephew, and ward, the afterwards eminent abolitionist, came in his 9th year to live with his uncle, and attend school at Wimbledon. On his uncle's death, in 1777, the greater William Wilberforce inherited the mansion, and for the next ten years made it his residence. Pitt and Wilberforce were at this time close friends, and Pitt used to be a frequent visitor at Wimbledon, often riding down to sleep there—sometimes for the month together—and having rooms set apart to occupy whenever convenient. Wilberforce's Journal contains frequent entries of these visits, which the statesman enjoyed as a schoolboy would a holiday. "One morning," writes Wilberforce, "we found the fruits of Pitt's earlier rising in the careful sowing of the garden-beds with the fragments of a dress-hat with which Ryder had come down from the Opera." In later years the house was occupied by Wm. Van Mildert, Bp. of Durham.

The house on the other side of Lady Murray's was the residence of Sir Francis Burdett at the time of his duel with Mr. Paull, 1807.

At *West Side*, facing the Green, the house now occupied by the Hon. Charles A. Gore, Lyde Brown, an eminent merchant and Bank Director, formed a very celebrated collection of antique sculpture, which he sold to the Empress of Russia, in 1787, for £22,000. Unfortunately his agent failed, and he lost the larger part of the money, and the news being abruptly conveyed to him caused an apoplectic fit of which he died almost immediately. The house was afterwards occupied by Robert, 2nd Viscount Melville; and later by Lord Lyndhurst.

Henry Dundas, 1st Viscount Melville, who played so prominent a part in politics at the close of the last and in the early years of the present century, the friend of Pitt, Wilberforce, and Scott, lived in the next house northward, now called *Cannizaro ;* but during his impeachment and following years retired to a smaller house which he called *Dunira Cottage,* now pulled down. The Duke of Cannizaro was a subsequent occupant, and it has since borne his name. It is now the residence of J. Boustead, Esq.

In the corner house immediately S. of Mr. Gore's, Horne Tooke spent the last 20 years of his life, and there died, March 1812. He gave Sunday parties—dinner at 4 in the parlour looking on to the Common—and collected many of the remarkable, and some of the less reputable, men of the day around his board. Tooke prepared a tomb in his garden, in which he desired to be interred ; but his executors disregarded his injunctions, and buried him in the ch.-yard at Ealing. (*See* p. 158.)

The farthest house of the row in which Horne Tooke's stands, as you turn round to the Camp, now known as *The Keir,* was the residence of Benson, who supplanted Wren as surveyor-general and architect of St. Paul's, erected the mont. to Milton in Westminster Abbey and inscribed his own name on it, and was pilloried by Pope.

At *Gothic House,* in the hollow on the way to Christ Ch. and Kingston, and nearly opposite Lord Melville's Dunira Cottage, lived for awhile Lady Bernard, the authoress of 'Auld Robin Gray.' Later it was rented by Captain Marryat the novelist. In a cottage facing the Common, near Mr. Gore's, lived William Gifford, the translator of Juvenal and editor of the 'Quarterly Review,' not far from the house of his friend John Murray, the publisher of the Review, and correspondent of Byron. At *Wood Hayes* (J. Russell Reeves, Esq.), the S.W. extremity of the Common, lived Thomas Tooke, the author of the standard 'History of Prices,' and other valued works in political economy. Farther W., beyond Christ Ch., where is now the Morley-Atkinson Convalescent Hospital, stood a large house which was occupied in succession by John Lambton, 1st Earl of Durham, one of the framers of the Reform Act, and Governor-General of Canada, and Lord

Chancellor Cottenham. On Lord Cottenham's decease the property was sold for building purposes, and the house pulled down.

Wimbledon is now a district of villas— *Elmsley House,* Park Side (Earl Beauchamp) ; *Wressell Lodge* (Sir Bartle Frere) ; *Somerset Lodge* (Baroness Dimsdale) ; *Newstead* (John Murray, Esq.) ; *The Grange* (H. W. Elphinstone, Esq.) ; *Ridgeway* (Sir Edw. Pearson, F.R.S.) In the Park, *Edgcombe Hall* (Ald. Sir Thomas Gabriel, Bart.) ; near the cross-roads, *Park Lodge* (W. R. Greg, Esq.) ; and a hundred more.

WINCHMORE HILL, MIDDX., a

district of about 400 houses (there were "40 or 50" in 1819 [*]) straggling over the eminence from which it derives its name, and the neighbouring Bush Hill, is situated midway between Southgate and Edmonton, 8 m. from London ; and a stat. on the Enfield br. of the Grt. N. Rly. Pop. 1780. Inn, *King's Head,* by the Green.

The country hereabouts is undulating, abundantly wooded, and agreeable, and it has long been a favourite residence with City men, whose comfortable houses are seen on every hand. Winchmore Hill was created an eccl. dist. of Edmonton par. in 1851. The *Church* (St. Paul) is a chapel-like Perp. building, of white brick and stone, erected in the early days of the Gothic revival. The E. window represents, in 12 medallions, the leading events in the life of St. Paul. Nearly opposite to the ch. is a small plain brick Friends' Meeting House ; in the burial-ground adjoining which lies John Fothergill, the celebrated Quaker physician (d. 1780).

The chief seat is *Bush Hill Park,* on the road to Enfield—a large brick house standing in a spacious and well-timbered park, through which the New River winds deviously. The grounds are said to have been originally laid out by Le Nôtre. It was the seat of the Sambrooke family ; afterwards of Wm. Mellish, M.P. for Middlesex ; and lately of J. Moorat, Esq. In the hall is the "large carving in wood of St. Stephen Stoned," by Grinling Gibbons, which, as Walpole records, was "long

* Robinson, Hist. and Antiq. of Edmonton p. 33.

preserved in the sculptor's own house, and afterwards purchased and placed by the Duke of Chandos at Canons."* This, he adds, was the piece which Evelyn found Gibbons engaged upon, and admired so greatly that he obtained permission to introduce the artist and his work to the king, Charles II. But in this he is mistaken. That piece was a "Crucifix of Tintoret."†

Bush Hill is said to have received its name from the hawthorn, sweet briar, and bramble bushes with which it was once thickly covered. On it was formerly held the fair known as *Beggars' Bush Fair*. Sir Hugh Myddleton had a house at Red Bridge, on the Enfield side of Bush Hill, for the convenience of superintending the New River works. The New River was here carried across the dell in a wooden aqueduct, 660 ft. long, which was regarded as an engineering marvel, and the memory of which is perpetuated in more than one engraving. It gave place in 1784-85 to an earthen embankment.

Sharon Turner, the historian, and Thomas Hood ('Song of a Shirt') resided for some years at Winchmore Hill.

WINDSOR, BERKS, (in official documents NEW WINDSOR, to distinguish it from *Old Windsor*, the subject of the next article,) is a market town and municipal and parliamentary borough on the rt. bank of the Thames, 22 m. from London by road, 21 m. by the Grt. W. Rly., which has its stat. near the centre of the town : the Stat. of the L. and S.-W. Rly. is in Datchet Lane, at the N.E. end of the town. Pop. of the mun. borough, 11,769 ; of the parl. borough, 17,281 ; of the parish, 7814. Inns, *White Hart, Castle ;* both good houses.

Windsor, the most famous place within the environs of London, owes all its fame, as it owed its origin, to the royal Castle which towers so proudly over it. Apart from the Castle, the town is of little interest. "Windsor," wrote Swift to Stella, "is a delicious situation, but the town is scoundrel." If this were true in the reign of Anne, it is not true in the reign of Victoria. But if not scoundrel

it is commonplace. Ancient, but retaining few relics of antiquity ; wealthy, but with no public building of consequence ; of late years improved in aspect, and still steadily improving, though with loss of its old-fashioned picturesqueness, commonplace respectability is its essential attribute.

Of its origin nothing is told. It grew up unheeded under the shadow of the Castle to which the Norman kings repaired for hunting, or occasionally kept court. When they were absent the castle was still a military stronghold, and had its governor and garrison, and an outside population would be sure to find protection and support, and steadily increase in number and importance. From being a chapelry of Clewer, Windsor was constituted a distinct parish. Edward I. in 1276 made it a free borough, granted it a market, and in 1302 called upon it to send representatives to Parliament. This last was but an occasional requirement ; but from the reign of Henry VI. (1447) Windsor continued to send two members to the House of Commons, till 1867, when the number was reduced to one. Edward IV. gave the borough a charter of incorporation, and Windsor has since been governed by its mayor, aldermen, and councillors.

The town consists of a main street (Church Street, High Street, and Thames Street), which stretches from the Castle gates to the Thames opposite Eton, with which town it is united by a bridge, the High Street of Eton being in effect a continuation of that of Windsor. On the right of this are the church, town hall, and castle, the latter being now brought into full view by the removal of the mean houses that stood at the edge of the castle ditch. On the left diverge a main thoroughfare, Peascod Street, and several smaller streets. Of the public buildings, the oldest is the *Town Hall*, erected in 1686 by Sir Christopher Wren, and renovated and partially remodelled in 1852 by Mr. Philip Hardwick. Not much is to be said for its architectural merits ; and the statues of Queen Anne and her consort, Prince George of Denmark, which adorn the opposite ends of the building, are still less to be commended. The lower part of the building forms a market-place ; the upper is the court-

---

* Anecdotes, vol. iii., p. 151.
† Evelyn, Diary, Jan. 18, 1671.

room, in which are portraits of the kings and queens of England from Charles I. to Victoria, the Prince Consort, and various prelates, statesmen, and local magnates who have found favour in the eyes of the corporation. In the Council Chamber is the memorial bust, by *Durham*, of Charles Knight, who was born in the town, and is interred in the Old Burial Ground—the Gothic gateway to which was also raised to his memory.

The parish *Church* (St. John the Baptist) was erected in 1822 from the designs of Mr. C. Hollis. It is Gothic (Perp.) of the time; large, light, and commodious; and comprises nave and aisles, chancel, and tall W. tower, in which is a good peal of 10 bells. The interior was remodelled by Mr. Teulon in 1869. New windows were inserted, and several of them filled with painted glass. Some monts. from the old ch. may be noticed. Edward Jobson, d. 15—, with effigies, in relief, of himself, wife Eleanor, and their 10 children. Chief Justice Reeve, d. 1735, with busts of himself and wife, and various symbolic figures. John Dugdale, d. 1670, son of Sir William Dugdale.

Holy Trinity dist. church, Clarence Crescent, is a neat Gothic building, designed by Mr. Blore, the first stone of which was laid by the Prince Consort in April 1842. All Saints Church, Francis Road, is an early Dec. building of brick and stone, designed by Mr. A. W. Blomfield—the first stone laid by the Princess Royal in Nov. 1863.

The Roman Catholic ch. of St. Edward the Confessor, in the Alma Road, erected in 1868 from the designs of Mr. C. A. Buckler, is a good transition E.E. building.

Windsor has Royal Free and Industrial Schools, with endowments for apprenticing boys and providing marriage rewards for girls; almshouses; and a variety of benevolent institutions. The school and the large Elizabethan almshouse by Bachelors' Acre are among the best of the recent additions to the borough architecture. There is a comfortable little *Theatre;* but it is not "that smallest of playhouses," the Theatre Royal of Windsor, where "Majesty," in the person of George III. and his family, "oft delighted to recreate itself with hearty laughs at the comic stars of sixty years

since." * The present house holds about 500 people. The *Bachelors' Acre* is a meadow on the W. side of the town, between Peascod Street and Sheet Street, vested in the corporation, but reserved under the Inclosure Act free to the inhabitants for playing thereon at all sports and pastimes. The Bachelors hold an annual revel there on the 17th of August, when prizes are given in various athletic exercises, and the sports are said to be of a less boisterous description than in the olden times. The Obelisk on the Acre was erected to commemorate the visit of Queen Charlotte at the Bachelors' entertainment on occasion of the Jubilee on the completion of the 50th year of George III.'s reign.

For a town of such antiquity, Windsor has remarkably few old houses, and the few there are have mostly been modernized. Not long ago there was a good old red brick house behind the ch., which local fame ascribed to Inigo Jones. The Free School, the Bank, and a house near the bridge are by the same authority assigned to Sir Christopher Wren, and some old carved work inside the last to Grinling Gibbons.† Some houses in the main street and Peascod Street may be of the 17th cent., but all are more or less altered. An old inn, the Duke's Head, near the bottom of Peascod Street, is said to have been the residence of Villiers Duke of Buckingham.

The inns of Windsor are a feature of the town, and appear to have always been so. The town records show that in 1650 there were no fewer than 70 in the town, although the licences of some had been suspended. The number is even larger now, if all classes of public-houses be included, and is out of all proportion to the population. The excess has been attributed to the superior attractiveness of Windsor ale; it is no doubt mainly due to the large military element in the population, and the unusual proportion of male servants of residents and visitors.

One inn of fame—patronized by Samuel Pepys as well as Sir John Falstaff—*The Garter*, has long ceased to exist. It

* Charles Knight, Passage of a Working Life, vol. i., p. 45.
† Stoughton, History of Windsor, Tighe and Davis, Annals of Windsor.

stood close to its rival the White Hart, by the top of Peascod Street, and was in its palmy days the chief inn of the town. Mine host of the Garter was a man of mark, not merely with the personages of the 'Merry Wives of Windsor,' but in the eyes of his townsmen generally. One host, Richard Gallis, was thrice mayor of Windsor town, and in 1562 M.P. for the borough; and though there is no later instance of one being elected to Parliament, there are many of the landlords of both the White Hart and the Garter being chosen mayor. The Garter is gone, and Ford's and Page's houses have gone too. We may indeed feel a doubt whether they were ever more than airy nothings to which the poet gave a local habitation and a name : but the townsmen have no doubt of their objective actuality. Among the houses swept away at the clearance of the Castle Ditch, and almost directly opposite the site of the Garter, was a half-timber tenement occupied by Mr. Woolridge, chemist, which was pointed out as Master Ford's house, or as standing on its site; whilst one at the foot of the Hundred Steps, demolished in 1860, was said to be Mistress Page's.*

WINDSOR CASTLE is the oldest and beyond comparison the noblest of our royal palaces. It is equally unrivalled in affluence of associations. For more than seven hundred years it has been the residence of the sovereign. It has been the meeting-place of regal and national councils; the scene of many splendid pageants and courtly assemblies, of illustrious events and great crimes. Seen near at hand or from a distance, its appearance is very striking. Seated on an eminence which overlooks the broad valley of the Thames, with the town at its base, the massive proportions of the castle—its

proud keep and long array of turrets, walls, and battlements—display themselves to great advantage, whilst from towers, windows, and terraces stretches far away " that incomparable prospect," as it was designated two centuries ago, which fills every one with wonder and delight when gazed upon for the first time, and which no familiarity renders wearisome.

The erection of the first castle is commonly attributed to the Conqueror, who obtained the manor by exchange from the Abbot of Westminster (see WINDSOR, OLD), and made Windsor a residence. But there is no evidence that his works were more than additions to already existing buildings. No masonry of his time has been observed in any part of the fabric; and we learn from the Domesday record that he took possession of a castle which Earl Harold had rented from the Confessor. William, we may assume, recognized its value as a military position, as we know he did its convenience as a lodge for hunting in the neighbouring forest. He no doubt added to the buildings and strengthened the defences, but his works are not likely to have been of a very solid description. However that may be, its importance as a stronghold is shown by his appointing Walter Fitz-Other to be the Constable of Windsor Castle—an office that has lasted down to the present day.

William Rufus made Windsor Castle a prison as well as a palace, by confining the Earl of Northumberland and several of his adherents in it—and the precedent was only too faithfully followed by succeeding kings. Henry I., "having overcome his enemies, and settled the affairs of Normandy after his own pleasure . . . crowned with victory, and then for the first time firmly established as king, held his court at Easter (1106) at Windsor, at which the nobles of England as well as those of Normandy were present in fear and trembling." * In subsequent years he often kept court here, and in a chapel which he built he married, 1122, his second wife, Adeleis, or Alice the Fair, daughter of Geoffrey of Louvain. Henry probably built or rebuilt the castle in a

---

* Tighe and Davis, Annals of Windsor ; Stoughton. The tradition, or belief, we suspect, is of very modern growth. Mr. Charles Knight, who spent all his early years in Windsor, and was curious about every Shakspearian association, makes no reference to it. Speaking of his boyhood, he says, "I then knew an old house at the corner of Sheet Street (alas ! it is pulled down) where Mr. and Mrs. Ford once dwelt, and whence Falstaff was carried in the buck-basket to Datchet Mead." (Passages, vol. i., p. 51.) Elsewhere he places, conjecturally, Ford's house in Thames Street and Page's "in the High Street a little to the N. of the present Town Hall": see Local Illustrations to his editions of the 'Merry Wives of Windsor.'

* Capgrave, Book of the Illustrious Henries, by Rev. F. C. Hengeston, p. 56.

solider manner, the oldest parts of it now remaining being of his time. At the Christmas of 1126 Henry summoned a great council of the prelates and nobles of the realm and the chief tenants of the Crown, at which it was decreed that Henry's only daughter, Matilda, Empress Dowager of Germany, should succeed him as Queen of England. David King of Scotland, who was present, was the first to take the oath of allegiance, and he was followed by Stephen Earl of Boulogne, and all the nobles of England, every one engaging to maintain her succession. Stephen became king, and held the castle —the military importance of which was recognized in the treaty of Wallingford as second only to that of the Tower of London. Henry II. lived much here, repaired the old and added new buildings, and, as the Treasury records testify, spent much money on the vineyards. Here, in those last gloomy years when his sons were in open rebellion, he found a grim solace according to Fabyan—a somewhat late authority—in having painted on the walls of his chamber the figures of an old eagle with three young ones scratching at its body, and a fourth pecking at its eyes; and when one asked him what the parable might signify, the King replied, " The old eagle is myself; the young birds betoken my four sons which cease not to pursue my death, and especially my youngest son John." When John was king, Windsor Castle more than once changed masters. It was from Windsor Castle that John set out on the 15th of June, 1215, to meet the Barons assembled at Runnimede ; and to it he returned after signing the Great Charter.

In the first year of Henry III. (1217) the Barons besieged Windsor Castle, but failed to take it. Many years later (1263) it had to surrender, but was soon recaptured by Prince Edward. Henry III. was a man of decided artistic tastes, and throughout his long reign he appears to have been occupied in repairing or embellishing Windsor Castle or in adding new buildings. Among these were a stately chapel, a great hall, and sundry royal chambers. But he was always hampered by want of money ; was even reduced to pawn the best image of the Virgin Mary in the New Chapel Royal to meet the current expenses, and was at last compelled to bring

the works to an abrupt close. He made it, however, a very different place to what it had been hitherto ; and a contemporary chronicler, Matthew of Westminster, declares that Windsor Castle was the most splendid royal dwelling in Europe.

Both Edward I. and ˙Edward II. were often at Windsor Castle : held courts and counsels there ; gave solemn audiences ; proclaimed jousts and tournaments ; had children born and die there. But it was in the reign of Edward III. that Windsor Castle attained its greatest splendour. It was his birthplace—whence his title, Edward of Windsor, frequently used by our older historians—and he never ceased to regard it with affection. Much of his time when in England was spent at Windsor, holding courts or tourneys, or engaged in the chase. or the pastime he liked still better of hawking. His youngest son, William, was born there ; there Edward the Black Prince was married, 1361, to Joan the Fair Maid of Kent ; and there, 1369, the Good Queen Philippa died. Very early, Edward, as we are told by Froissart, who had been in the service and confidence, first of Queen Philippa and then of the King himself, resolved to rebuild the Castle of Windsor, which of old had been founded by King Arthur, and to revive in it an order of Loyal Knights such as Arthur had gathered about his Round Table. And this double purpose he in a great measure accomplished. If he did not wholly rebuild the castle, he made magnificent additions to it, and left it, in its majestic outline, nearly as we possess it. Before his time the building was confined to what has since been known as the Lower Ward. He built the Round Tower, the great central feature of the castle, and formed the Upper Ward as the royal dwelling. The Rose Tower and other towers of inferior fame, are also of his time. He enlarged and enriched, if he did not rebuild, the chapel founded by Henry III., and he built arcades and cloisters, a deanery, treasury, chapter-house, halls, and the like. John Peynton, Richard de Rotheley, and Robert de Burnham were successively his surveyors or clerks of the works at Windsor, but from 1356 to 1362 the direction of the works was entrusted to William of Wykeham. William de Mulso was Wykeham's deputy from 1358, and succeeded him as chief warden and surveyor in 1362. The more important works in the castle appear to have been executed between 1359 and 1374, and it must remain doubtful therefore to what extent they were influenced by the genius of Wykeham, or were due to his successor. The warrants to the surveyors gave them ample powers to seize wherever they might find suitable stone, wood, timber, coal, lead, glass, iron, or other materials, and to impress masons, hard-hewers, and other artificers, necessary for the royal works.

The Lower Ward Edward appropriated chiefly to his splendid acclesiastical foundation, the Chapel, or College, of St. George, with its canons, clerks, choristers, and poor knights, and for which he craved special privileges from the Pope because he had established it in the place of his birth. The Upper Ward he created for the royal dwelling. The Round Tower or Middle Ward was devoted to knightly acts, and thus associated with both Upper and Lower Wards.

The Round Tower was among Edward's earliest works. Having matured the scheme of his Round Table, he, in 1343, ordered the Round Tower in which it should be held to be constructed with all possible rapidity. It was made ready in about ten months, and on Jan. 19, 1344, Edward III. held the Round Table at which was inaugurated the newly-founded *Order of the Garter.* To the festival, not only the flower of the English chivalry, but knights from every part of Europe, were invited, free passes being sent for all. Jousts and tourneys were held, the King himself taking part, and the whole nobility of the land being witnesses. Then followed huntings and hawkings, banquets and dances, and whatever could grace the court, or do honour to the visitors. Similar festivals are recorded in 1347, 1348, etc., but as yet they are not strictly the festivals of St. George, and though the Round Table and the 26 knights are there, no mention is made of the garter. But a few years later the festival is held on St. George's Day, and at that of 1351 the knights are all clad in mantles of blue cloth, powdered over with garters, and wear the great collar of the order. The knights, with the King at their head, proceed to the chapel where the rites of installation

are performed. Then they assemble about the Round Table, for the reception of which the Tower has been built, and hold solemn conference and banquet. Froissart's narratives of these gatherings are among the brightest of his vivid pages.

The pride and power of Edward were shown differently, but even more distinctly, when some years later he had as his captives in Windsor Castle, John King of France, and his son, Prince Philip, and David King of Scotland. Stow relates as a tradition that it was a remark made by one of the captive kings that led to the eastward extension of the buildings. The three kings were walking on this higher ground, when the strangers, commending the situation, judged that the Castle would have been better built in that place than where it was, " as it would be more open to see, and be seen afar off." Edward approved their judgment, and added pleasantly that " it should so be, and that he would bring his castle thither, that is to say, enlarge it so far with two other wards, the charges whereof should be *borne with their ransoms* : as after it came to pass." Unluckily for the story, the Exchequer accounts show that the works had been in progress many years before the three kings could have so conversed together, and were carried on but a short time after (the ransom notwithstanding), owing to exhaustion of funds.

Richard II. kept his first regal Christmas at Windsor, and was often there afterwards, especially at the Festival of St. George, the keeping of which at Windsor had now become an established custom. It was at Windsor that Henry Duke of Hereford (afterwards Henry IV.) and the Duke of Norfolk made before the King (April 1398) mutual appeal of treason, and were assigned trial of arms at Coventry—a scene which Shakspeare has dramatized so effectively in the opening of his play of King Richard the Second. Geoffrey Chaucer was appointed by Richard II. clerk of the works at Windsor, his chief duty being to superintend the repairs of St. George's Chapel, and his engagement lasting from 1390 to 1393.

During the best part of the reign of Henry V., King James I. of Scotland was captive here. He was in his 20th year when brought to Windsor, an age when enforced confinement is perhaps most irksome, but the years he spent at Windsor were the happiest in his long captivity. He was treated with all respect and kindness; intermingled freely with the noblest of the land; engaged in jousts and royal pastimes; spent his solitary hours in studying Gower and Chaucer, and imping his own wings for a poetic flight; and, what contributed most of all to sweeten his later prison hours, as he looked from his window one May morning, "to see the world and folk that went forby," and listened to "the little sweete nightingale," singing loud and clear from the green branches in the garden, casting his eye down again, he saw, walking under the tower,

" The fairest or the freshest younge flower
That ever I saw methought before that hour."

The effect of this vision, the hopes and fears it aroused, he has told in not unmelodious measure in his ' King's Quhair.' Here it will be enough to say that the lady, Jane, daughter of the Duke of Beaufort, a woman who was all her royal lover described her, became in good time his wife, shared the honours and the toils of his throne, strove in vain, though at the peril of her life, to arrest the hands of his assassins, and lived long to mourn his untimely death. The Round Tower is commonly said to be James's prison, and Washington Irving, in his pleasant essay, ('A Royal Poet,') not only adopts the tradition, but sees in the garden "in what was the moat of the keep," the very garden "sheltered blooming and retired" of the days of James. Not, however, the Round Tower, but the Earl Marshal's, or Devil's Tower, at the south-eastern angle of the Upper Ward, was the state prison, and doubtless that in which the Scotch King was lodged.

Henry VI. was born and buried at Windsor; and it was for awhile the prison of his widow. Edward IV. was partial to the place; built St. George's Chapel—the finest ecclesiastical building of its time—and enlarged and enriched the College of St. George, in which it was his desire to merge the recent foundation of Eton College. By his express directions he was buried in his chapel, and beside him, as she prayed, was laid, in 1492, his queen, Elizabeth Woodville. Beside him

also was laid, perhaps in mockery, the body (with the head, as Sir Thomas More has it) of his favourite Lord Hastings (beheaded June 1483). Henry VII. added the rich groined roof and choir to St. George's Chapel; and liking the place, removed the chapel of Henry III. in order to construct a sumptuous tomb for himself, for which he engaged the artists and collected the materials, but afterwards changed his mind and transferred them to Westminster. Here, in 1506, he entertained with great pomp Philip of Castile. The two kings concluded a treaty of peace and amity, which they swore before the high altar duly to observe, "kissing the very cross"—i.e., a cross much prized at Windsor as having enclosed within it a piece of the true cross.

In his earlier years, Henry VIII. made the castle gay with feats of arms and stately shows, with " active games of nimbleness and strength," and " cry of hounds and merry blasts between" chasing "the fearful hart of force." He completed the works about St. George's Chapel, and built the great gateway to the Lower Ward. Charles V. of Spain was entertained by him, in June 1522, with huntings, plays, masques, and banquets. On Sept. 1, 1522, the Consecrated Golden Rose was delivered to Henry as Defender of the Faith with great state and solemnity at Windsor Castle, by the legate of Pope Clement VII. In the summer of 1546, Henry Howard, Earl of Surrey, was imprisoned in Windsor Castle. In early youth he had been here as an honoured guest, the friend and companion of the Duke of Richmond, natural son of Henry VIII.; and the contrast was excessively galling to his proud spirit.

" So cruel prison how could betide, alas !
    As proud Windsor, where I in lust and joy,
    With a Kinges son, my childish years did pass,
    In greater feast than Priam's sons of Troy.
    Where each sweet place returns a taste full sour.
    The large green courts where we were wont to
        hove,
    With eyes cast up into the Maiden's tower,
    And easy sighs, such as folk draw in love." *

He was not long prisoned at Windsor; but hardly was he set at liberty when he was again arrested, sent to the Tower of London, and thence to the block (Jan. 21,

* Surrey, Prisoned in Windsor, he recounteth his pleasure there passed : Poems, p. 17.

1547). Within a week the king died, and was laid, according to the directions in his will, in the choir of St. George's Chapel, "midway between the stalls and the high altar."

Edward VI. was hurried for safety to Windsor Castle from Hampton Court, (*see* HAMPTON COURT, p. 299,) Oct. 6, 1549, by the Protector Somerset, and a few days after Somerset was arrested and consigned to the Beauchamp Tower, preparatory to the Tower of London and the block. Mary came to Windsor Castle upon the suppression of Wyatt's insurrection. Bishops Cranmer, Ridley, and Latimer were summoned here in the following April, to the mock disputations which were to clear their path to the stake. A few months later, August 1554, Mary celebrated with banquets and pageantry her hapless marriage with Philip of Spain, and Philip's installation as a Knight of the Garter.

Elizabeth has associated her name more agreeably with Windsor Castle. She greatly delighted in the place, built the new gallery and banqueting-house, laid out gardens and pleasance, of which all trace has been lost, and constructed the North Terrace, which has ever since been a perennial source of enjoyment. In her New Gallery there is reason to believe was played, 1593, the new comedy, devised at Her Majesty's desire, of the 'Merry Wives of Windsor,' Shakspeare himself superintending the performance. During this visit the Queen employed her spare hours in translating Boethius' 'de Consolatione Philosophiæ.' She began it on the 10th of Oct., and finished it on the 5th of November, 1593: or as Her Majesty's Keeper of the Records calculated, omitting Sundays and other holy days, and days on which she "rode abroad to take the air, and on those days did forbear to translate," she was only employed 12 days, and on these only two hours in translating, so that "the computation falleth out, that in fowre-and-twenty houres your Majestie began and ended your translation." *

James I. fortunately employed John Norden early in his reign to make a survey of the Honour of Windsor. For it

Norden received £200 in 1608-9, did his work very carefully, and has left a bird's-eye view of the castle, a map of the forest, and 15 plans of the park and "rayles lying within." These are drawn on vellum, and enable any one to obtain a tolerably clear conception of the general character of the castle and grounds at the beginning of the 17th cent.* The castle was then, as Norden writes, "divided (as it were) into 2 partes, whereof the Upper part belongeth only to y^r Matie and the Lower for the most part to the ecclesiastical governors and almes knights." James is described as spending most of his time at Windsor in the fields and parks; but he had some ceremonial festivities, as on the entertainment of his brother-in-law, Christian IV. of Denmark, in 1606, the installation of Prince Henry as Knight of the Garter, three years earlier, and the reception of the Spanish ambassador in 1622. In September 1621, Ben Jonson's 'Masque of the Metamorphosed Gypsies' was "presented to King James" for the third time : "at Burley, Bever, and now last at Windsor." Charles I. was at Windsor soon after his accession, and several times subsequently. He purposed repairing some of the old and adding new buildings, but troublous times interposed. He came here from Hampton Court in January 1642, as being, says Clarendon, "more secure from any sudden popular attempt," but left in February—not again to visit it as a free agent. The castle was taken possession of by the Parliament in Oct. 1642 without opposition, and an attempt to seize it made shortly after by Prince Rupert was unsuccessful. The castle was made one of the headquarters of the Parliamentary generals; St. George's chapel was stript of its rich plate, and images, vestments, and fittings were destroyed; and the soldiers killed large numbers of the deer in the park and forest. Charles I. was brought here a prisoner from Hatfield, July 1, 1647, and remained till Aug. 16, when he was removed to Oatlands. After his execution, his body was ordered to be buried in Windsor Castle, "in a decent manner,"

---

* Richard Bowyer, quoted by Nichols, Prog. of Queen Elizabeth, vol. iii., p. 564, n.

* The originals are in the British Museum, Harleian MSS., No. 3749. The bird's-eye view of the castle and one or two of the maps are copied in facsimile in Tighe and Davis's Annals of Windsor.

the whole expense "not to exceed £500." It was brought in a hearse, Feb. 8, 1649, and the next day, in a bitter snowstorm, was carried from the great hall, where the unfortunate monarch had so often presided in state, to St. George's Chapel, and there, without any religious ceremony —the Governor of the castle refusing to allow Bishop Juxon to read the Burial Service of the Prayer Book—deposited in the vault of Henry VIII. On descending into the vault a large coffin was found which was assumed to be that of Henry, and on its left side the smaller coffin, as was supposed, of Jane Seymour. On the right was a vacant space just sufficient to receive the coffin of Charles. After the Restoration, Parliament voted a sum of £70,000 for the removal of the corpse of the king to a fitting mausoleum which was to be erected to receive it. Charles II. took the money, but nothing more was heard of the erection of the tomb or the removal of the body. It was said that the vault was searched for, but could not be found, and that the proposal to build the tomb was consequently abandoned : but Evelyn states distinctly enough the locality,* and when the Prince Regent (George IV.) wished the body to be examined, it was found without difficulty.

Very soon after his restoration, Charles II. formed the design of renovating the castle and rebuilding the state rooms in the modern taste. He seems to have actually commenced the works in 1663, but they proceeded fitfully on account of deficiency of funds. The nominal architect was Sir John Denham, the poet, who held the office of surveyor-general, while the works were really designed and erected by Sir Christopher Wren, first as Denham's assistant, and then as his successor. Chief among the additions made by Charles II. was the Star Building, so called from a large figure of the star of the order of the Garter on the N. front. It extends for 170 ft. along the Terrace, and had on the principal floor a suite of 17 state rooms, adorned by Verrio in his most exuberant style. He also renovated and Verrio decorated St. George's Chapel; but all that was done there has been happily swept away. The restoration of St. George's Hall was also commenced,

but left for completion in a later reign. Evelyn visited Windsor in 1670, had some talk with the King, and learnt that the castle, that is the older part, was "now going to be repaired, being exceedingly ragged and ruinous." Already "Prince Rupert, the Constable, had begun to trim up the keepe, or high round tower." Whilst Evelyn was at Windsor "the King passed most of his time in hunting the stag, and walking in the parke, which he was now planting with rows of trees."* Besides erecting new buildings and restoring the old, Charles completed the terrace begun by Elizabeth by continuing it around the E. and S. fronts. Outside the castle he built Cumberland and Cranborne Lodges, besides minor structures. To Verrio he was a munificent patron. For his performances at Windsor the fortunate painter received £7000 in money, the place of master-gardener, and a lodge in the park (afterwards known as Carlton House), where he lived in great state. To adorn the walls of his royal apartments the King commissioned Sir Peter Lely to paint the Gallery of Windsor Beauties— now consigned to Hampton Court. Wissing's pencil was also much employed at Windsor.

It was at Windsor Castle that James II. received with ostentatious pomp and ceremony Abp. Adda, the Papal Envoy, July 3, 1687. He fitted up Wolsey's Tomb House as a Roman Catholic Chapel, and in a more splendid manner the private chapel next St. George's Hall. There Evelyn "went to heare a Frenchman preach before the King and Queen;" but "their Majesties going to masse," he "withdrew to consider the stupendous paintings of the Hall, which both in the art and invention deserve the inscription in honour of the painter, Signor Verrio."†

A little later (Dec. 17, 1688), and the Prince of Orange was sitting with the Peers in deliberation on the misguided King's fate, and sending him recommendations where to remove. William III. was little at Windsor. He preferred Hampton Court as a residence, and only came to Windsor occasionally. But he continued and completed the planting begun by Charles II., and he laid out the

---

* Diary, June 8, 1654.

* Evelyn, Diary, August 28, 1670.
† Ibid., Sunday, Sept. 6, 1685.

famous Long Walk. He also contemplated remodelling the castle, and converting it with Wren's assistance into a regular edifice in the modern taste. Wren proposed to remove part of the S. side of the Upper Ward, and to raise on the site a palatial structure having a façade 200 feet long, with a great gateway in the centre, precisely where George IV.'s Gateway has since been placed.* Happily the work was never executed, but the designs are in the library of All Souls' College, Oxford.

Queen Anne made Windsor her summer residence, and employed Sir James Thornhill to complete the decorations on ceilings and staircases begun by Verrio. Herself she employed in the manner described by Swift, "hunting in a chaise with one horse, which she drives furiously like Jehu." In Dec. 1703 she entertained the Archduke Charles, the so-called Charles III. of Spain, at Windsor. Anne was popular, and the Corporation (1706) set up her effigy, at a cost of £40, at the N. end of their new Town Hall, a corresponding statue of her consort, Prince George of Denmark, being placed at the S. end (1713) by Sir Christopher Wren.

The next two monarchs lived chiefly at Hampton Court, and Windsor was neglected. In the reign of George II. the royal rooms were let as lodgings "during the absence of the royal family."† When George III. decided to reside at Windsor it was found that the castle was so much out of repair and so inconvenient an abode for a family that it seemed preferable to keep it for show and build a plain comfortable dwelling adjacent. The Queen's Lodge was accordingly erected (1778), near where are now the Royal Stables ; and there, as long as he retained health and reason, the King and his family lived in a singularly homely, unostentatious manner, within daily view of the townspeople, seen by all and knowing every one. Madame D'Arblay has described minutely the royal life at Windsor ; and Mrs. Delany, who lived in a house close by, where the King would drop in unpremeditatedly at any hour, has added many supplementary touches. On Sunday after-

noons the Court used to assemble on the Terrace, where a couple of military bands played, and politicians, church dignitaries, naval and military officers, and expectant placemen collected in the hope of a chance word, or at least a nod of recognition from the good-humoured monarch, who with his queen, children, and royal *cortége*, "moved up and down amidst the double line of his subjects duteously bowing or curtseying"—for no one decently dressed was excluded from the Terrace or the presence of royalty, and none were too great to mingle with the throng. Mr. Knight records having (1804) seen Pitt, when at the summit of power and popularity, "waiting among the crowd till the time when the King and Queen should come forth from a small side-door, and descend the steps which led to the level of the Eastern Terrace."* George III. employed James Wyatt to restore and Benjamin West to decorate St. George's Chapel ; but their performances, though costly, were very unsatisfactory, and have all been swept away. Wyatt also made various alterations in the castle, and gothicised after his fashion the north side of the inner quadrangle, the Star Chamber, the staircase, etc.; but most of his work was removed in the next reign.

George IV. dwelt in seclusion at Windsor, but to him is due the restoration of the castle to something like its ancient architectural eminence. Externally the castle had become a mass of incongruities, whilst the apartments were small, inconvenient, ill-connected, and quite inadequate to the requirements of a royal establishment. The King having in 1823 signified his desire to make Windsor Castle a suitable residence for himself and his successors, the Parliament voted a sum of £300,000 for the proposed improvements, and Mr. Jeffry Wyatt (afterwards knighted as Sir Jeffry Wyattville†) was appointed to carry them out. Wyattville took up his abode in the castle, devoted the rest of his life

---

* Poynter, Essay prefixed to Sir Jeffry Wyattville's Illustrations of Windsor Castle.
† Pole, Hist. of Windsor Castle, p. 19.

* C. Knight, Passages of a Working Life, vol. i., p. 42.
† Dec. 1828. The architect's elevation and change of name called forth the following epigram :—

    " Let George, whose restlessness leaves nothing
        quiet,
      Change, if he will, the good old name of *Wyatt* :
      But let us hope that their united skill,
      May not make *Windsor Castle—Wyattville !*"

to superintending the works, and died in the Wykeham Tower in 1840. The private apartments were completed, and occupied by the King in 1828 ; but the operations were continued till what was virtually the reconstruction of the eastern half of the building was effected. The enlargement of the superficial area was "made principally within the quadrangle, on the exterior facing the North Terrace, to which the Brunswick Tower has been added, and by converting what were two open courts in that northern mass of building, viz. the Brick Court and Horn Court, into the State Staircase and the Waterloo Gallery." * Rooms were united and made of sufficient size for all domestic and ceremonial purposes, and a stately corridor 450 ft. long was constructed giving separate access to the rooms which had previously been all "thoroughfare" rooms ; additional state and private rooms were built ; St. George's Hall was enlarged by adding the royal chapel to it, and the Waterloo Hall formed. The exterior was remodelled and rendered uniform in character ; the Round Tower was doubled in height, and made the central feature of the composition ; other old towers were raised, and several new towers and a new state entrance erected. When George IV. died the works were not nearly finished, but they were continued under William IV. till Wyatville's scheme was in the main completed. To effect this Parliament had liberally furnished funds as called upon, and before all had been accomplished upwards of a million had been expended.

In the present reign the improvement of the castle has been carried still farther. The Prince Consort took great interest in the building, and most of the recent works were suggested by him. Chief of these has been the restoration of the Lower Ward. The old walls and towers have been cleared of incongruous modern additions, and under the direction of Mr. Salvin have put on a uniform and somewhat stern mediæval aspect. As already mentioned, the houses at the foot of the castle have been cleared away, and the vast pile is revealed in all its sombre majesty. St. George's Chapel has been thoroughly restored; the Wolsey Chapel,

or Tomb-house, gorgeously refitted as a memorial of the Prince Consort ; and the other buildings mostly renewed.

In the Upper Ward, the Entrance Hall and State Staircase have been rebuilt, many of the Royal Apartments renewed or embellished, and alterations of various kinds made. Regret may perhaps be felt at the extent of some of the alterations, and objections be taken to the propriety of some of the 'restorations,' but having regard to the use of the castle as one of the principal residences of the sovereign, and the theatre of state banquets and ceremonials, the transformation of the interior must be accepted as a work of necessity ; and there can be no question that externally, as a whole, the fabric has gained immensely in dignity, grandeur, and picturesqueness.

The *buildings* which constitute Windsor Castle stretch for nearly 1500 feet from E. to W. along the summit of a spur of high land, which is cut at its western extremity by a great bend of the Thames. The site commands a wide extent of country, and was at a very early period made a fortified post. With works at Old Windsor, it served to watch and control the highway of the Thames for a considerable distance. The early works consisted of embankment, fosse, and mound. Within and on these the Saxon or early English occupants erected their improved though still rude dwellings and defences. These gave way to the more advanced Norman works. Earl Harold made it his residence. How from these rude beginnings the castle grew up has been told.

Windsor Castle consists of three wards or courts: the Upper Ward, the eastern portion, occupied by the royal apartments; the Lower Ward, the western portion, in which are St. George's Chapel, the Deanery, and the Cloisters; and the Middle Ward, chiefly occupied by the Round Tower.

The *Lower Ward* is the oldest part of the existing castle. It is entered from the town by King Henry VIII.'s Gateway. The area is divided by St. George's Chapel, which, with the Prince Consort's Memorial Chapel and the Dean's Cloister, extends along the central line from E. to W. It is well defended by a wall and several towers. None of the masonry is of Norman date ; but a subterraneous passage,

* Wyatville.

rudely hewn through the solid chalk from an entrance 15 ft. below the surface to a postern in the outer fosse 30 ft. below the upper surface, has a Norman doorway at each end, and the vault of the passage as far as the buildings above extend is late Norm. carried on chalk walls. The earliest masonry, as in the Clewer (or as it is now called Bell or Cæsar) Tower, at the S.W. angle, and the Garter Tower, the largest of these early towers, is of the reign of Henry III. The Garter Tower has been ably restored by Mr. Salvin, and a wide and well-formed arch displayed. In the base of the Clewer or Bell Tower the prison chamber is still perfect, with a window and door opening to the fosse. It is generally said that there is a subterraneous prison beneath this tower, but search was made whilst the recent works were in progress, and none could be found. The other towers in the Lower Ward are those known as the Wardrobe Tower, nearly opposite the Deanery; the Salisbury Tower, the official residence of the Chancellor of the Order of the Garter; and the Wykeham or Winchester Tower, at the W. end of the North Terrace, the work of William of Wykeham.

By the Clewer Tower was the King's Hall of Henry III. It has been at various times altered and modernized, and is now the College Library. It has a fine open timber roof, of the 15th cent., when probably the Hall and continuous Horse-shoe cloister were partially rebuilt. Beyond this was the Royal Kitchen. Still farther, N. of St. George's Chapel, and following the line of the N. wall, were the King's Chambers, completing the Domus Regis of Henry III. All but a few fragments of these were removed some years ago. Of this time are the S. ambulatory of the Dean's Cloister, which has some good shafts and mouldings, the Galilee porch at the W. end of the Memorial Chapel, and a doorway leading from the cloister.

St. George's Chapel, erected by Edward IV., is one of the finest ecclesiastical buildings of the Perp. period extant. Some details of an earlier ch. at the E. end excepted, the building is throughout of one date, and bears the impress of one mind. It was, however, at first covered with a wooden roof, but that was removed by Henry VII., and the present elaborate groined roof of stone substituted. Ex-

ternally, from the chapel adjoining other buildings, only the S. front is properly displayed, but that is impressive though simple in character. The plan of the chapel should be observed. It is cruciform, the short transepts, near the middle of the building, consisting of little more than octagonal bays or chantrys, with two storeys of windows. Similar but smaller projections are at the angles of the building : all these are divided from the body of the church by screens, and serve as monumental chapels.

The interior is very striking. The walls are panelled throughout, the windows and doors forming parts of the design; the columns spread out into fan-like tracery and groining, of admirable proportions and studied richness. The roof is decorated with Edward IV.'s cognisance, the rose en soleil, and the arms of the Knights of the Garter fully emblazoned. The Choir, divided from the nave by a screen, is rich, with dark carved oak stalls of the knights, their helmets, banners, and mantles, suspended overhead, and all that could be devised to give dignity to the place where the ceremonies of installation are performed of the noblest order of knighthood in Europe. Brass plates at the back of the stalls bear the names of the knights who formerly occupied them, and include a remarkable list of foreign princes and illustrious Englishmen. On a stone in the centre of the choir is inscribed the names of those interred in the Royal Vault beneath : King Henry VIII. ; Queen Jane Seymour ; Charles I. Nearer the altar is the entrance to the vault in which are buried George III., George IV., William IV., Queens Charlotte and Adelaide, the Princess Charlotte, the Princess Amelia, the Duke of Kent, the Duke of York, and the Princess Augusta.

The great W. window occupies the entire end of the nave above the door ; is of 16 lights in 5 stages, presenting a pierced panelling corresponding in style to the panelling of the walls. It is filled with fine old painted glass, and produces a surpassingly rich effect when the western sun streams through it. The great E. window was of similar character, but in 1787-90 the mullions, transoms, and tracery were partially removed to allow of the insertion of a transparent painting of the Resurrection by Benjamin West. At the same time an oil painting by him of the Last Supper was placed over the altar. These have, however, been removed ; a reredos, designed by Sir Gilbert Scott, substituted for the oil painting; the window frame and tracery restored, and mediæval glass painted by Clayton and Bell, as a memorial of the Prince Consort, inserted. The new window represents in the lowest tier subjects from the life of the late Prince; in that above it the Adoration of the Kings as the central picture, with on one side Old Testament Kings and Prophets, on the other Saints from the New Testament. The third tier upwards has the Resurrection in the centre, on one side Patriarchs and Prophets, on the other Apostles ; whilst above is the Lord in Glory with the heavenly hierarchy laying their crowns before the throne.

The *Queen's Gallery* (usually called the *Queen's Closet*), on the N. of the altar, was originally erected for ladies and distinguished persons admitted to witness the installation of Knights of the Garter, and is now occupied by the Queen when she attends the service in the chapel. It is lighted by two fine oriel windows. Under this gallery is the tomb of Edward IV., despoiled of its royal surcoat and coat of mail, and defaced by the Parliamentary soldiers in 1643, and now only remarkable for the admirable Gothic iron *screen*. This has been usually ascribed to Quentin Matsys, the famous painter-smith of Antwerp, but is now with better reason believed to be the work of the King's smith, John Tresilan. The names of " Edward IV. and his Queen Elizabeth Wydvill " are inscribed on a slab within the tomb, and on the opposite side of the choir a plain slab bears the name of the rival King, Henry VI., who was buried on the S. side of the choir. A little W. is a black marble slab inscribed Charles Brandon, d. 1545. This was the Brandon Duke of Suffolk who married Mary, widow of Louis XII. of France, and sister of Henry VIII.

The chantry chapels beginning from the E. are—

The *Lincoln Chapel*, on the S., contains the magnificent altar tomb of Edward Earl of Lincoln, Lord High Admiral, and distinguished as a statesman, in the reign of Elizabeth, d. 1584. It was erected by his widow ; is of alabaster, with shafts of porphyry, and has recumbent statues of the Earl and Countess, with on the sides of the tomb the effigies in relief of their 5 sons and 3 daughters. On the W. of the chapel are the Lincoln arms carved in alabaster and richly emblazoned. Here also was buried Richard Beauchamp, Bp. of Salisbury and first Chancellor of the Order of the Garter. On the centre of the arch above are figures of Edward IV. and the Bp. kneeling on opposite sides of a crucifix. In a recess opposite the tomb is chained a black-letter Bible, which has taken the place of a breviary the Bp. directed to be placed there to assist " priestis and ministers of Godis Church, seying therein theyr divyne servyce, and for all other that lysten to sey thereby theyr devocyon," in return for which he asketh that they will say for him the " comune oryson." Here also was brought by Bp. Beauchamp, from North Marston, Bucks, the remains and shrine of Sir John Shorne, 1290, whose power over demons was celebrated in painted windows.

Opposite to this on the N. is the *Hastings Chapel*, dedicated to St. Stephen by Elizabeth, widow of William Lord Hastings, chamberlain to Edward IV., beheaded by Richard III. 1483, but permitted to be buried beside the tomb of his master. The chapel has a groined roof and some good carving.

Farther on the S. is the small *Oxenbridge Chapel*, founded 1522, by a canon of that name, and dedicated to St. John the Baptist. In it is a curious painting in three divisions of the Preaching of St. John ; his Decollation ; and Herodias' Daughter presenting his head to Herod—the persons being represented in the costume of the 16th century. Corresponding to this on the N. is the elegant little *Aldworth Chapel*, so called from several members of the Aldworth family being buried in it, but which is believed to have been founded by Oliver King, Bp. of Exeter 1492, and of Bath and Wells 1495, and Registrar of the Order of the Garter, the builder of Bath Abbey. Several members of the King family are interred here.

The S. transept is known as the *Bray Chapel*, it having been founded by Sir Reginald Bray, to whom is ascribed the beautiful groined roof of the choir, and who was buried in this chapel, 1502.

without a mont. In the centre of the chapel is a curious old font. Several monts. are worth noting. Dr. Brideoak, Bp. of Chichester, d. 1678, effigy in episcopal robes and mitre; crozier by side. Giles Thompson, Bp. of Gloucester, d. 1682; coloured bust. Sir Richard Wortley, d. 1603, mont. with some good carving. Tablets to Dr. Jones, Bp. of Kildare, d. 1804; Baron Clotworthy, Lord Langford, d. 1825; Henry Emlyn, F.S.A., architect, d. 1815. Beneath a black marble slab is interred the learned theologian and controversialist, Daniel Waterland, D.D., d. 1740.

The N. transept, called the *Rutland Chapel*, was founded by Sir Thomas Syllinger (St. Leger) to contain the remains and tomb of his wife. Anne Duchess of Exeter, sister of Edward IV.; their effigies, kneeling before a crucifix, are on a brass on the wall. Mont. with recumbent effigies of Sir George Manners, Lord Ros, d. 1513, and wife Anne, daughter of Sir Thomas and Lady Syllinger, and niece to Edward IV. *Brass* of Robert Honeywood, Canon of Windsor, d. 1522, effigy kneeling before the Virgin and Infant Saviour; St. Catherine standing by. Marble tablets to Dr. Theodore Aylward, d. 1801, organist of St. George's Chapel, Gresham Professor of Music, and of some note as a composer; Major R. C. Packe, killed at the Battle of Waterloo.

At the S.W. angle is what has hitherto been known as the *Beaufort Chapel*, from its containing the tombs of Charles Somerset, Earl of Worcester, 1526, who founded the chapel, and Henry, 1st Duke of Beaufort, 1699; but these were removed in 1874 and placed with the other family monuments in Badminton church. The Beaufort Chapel has been converted by the Queen into a memorial chapel of her father, Edward Duke of Kent. The tomb, designed by Sir G. G. Scott, is a sarcophagus of alabaster resting on a broad base of dark-coloured marbles, and surmounted with a recumbent effigy of the Duke by Mr. J. E. Boehm.

The corresponding chapel at the N.W. angle, of old the *Urswick Chapel*, is the memorial chapel of the Princess Charlotte, d. 1817. In it is the costly but unsatisfactory mont. to the Princess, raised by public subscription, and executed by Matthew Cotes Wyatt. On a bier, at the corners of which are weeping attendants, lies the body of the Princess, whose beatified spirit is represented rising in a golden light heavenwards, led by two angels, one of whom bears her infant. The intention is good, the chiselling skilful, but the sentiment and treatment border too closely on the dramatic, and the mont. is at best but a feeble reflex of the sorrow of a mourning nation.

Near the cenotaph of the Princess Charlotte is a memorial of her husband, Leopold I., King of the Belgians, erected by the Queen. The recumbent statue of Leopold is from the chisel of Miss Durant, and is esteemed an excellent likeness; a merit which was allowed to the portrait of the Princess Charlotte in the ascending figure in her mont. But the mont. of Leopold has an air of calm dignity and propriety, which cannot be ascribed to that of the Princess.

Near the Aldworth Chapel is a graceful memorial " erected by Queen Victoria as a tribute of respect and affection to her beloved aunt, Mary Duchess of Gloucester, A.D. 1859." The Duke of Gloucester and members of his family are also commemorated. The tomb is of white marble and serpentine, designed by Sir G. G. Scott, and decorated with bas-reliefs by *Theed*, representing the Acts of Charity—'Clothing the Naked,' 'Giving Bread to the Hungry,' 'Relieving the Wanderer,' 'Visiting the Sick.' In the choir is a tablet to Princess Louisa of Saxe Weimar, niece of Queen Adelaide, who died at Windsor in 1817.

On the S., nearly opposite the Chapter Room, is a colossal marble statue by *Sevier* of Field-Marshal Earl Harcourt, d. 1830, who is habited in field-marshal's uniform, and the robe he wore at the Coronation of George IV., as the verger carefully informs visitors. Near this is a tablet to Lieut.-General Elley, K.C.B., and M.P. for Windsor, d. 1839. a good and gallant soldier, who rose from the ranks to one of the chief places in the service.

St. George's Chapel is open to visitors every week-day from 12 till 4: entrance by the S. door. " The officers of the chapel are forbidden to demand any gratuity."

Immediately E. of St. George's Chapel is the *Albert Memorial Chapel*, known till recently as the *Wolsey Chapel*, or.

Tomb House. The chapel was built, or rebuilt, on the lines of an earlier chapel, by Henry VII., with a view to its being a burial-place for himself and his successors; but, as already mentioned, he changed his mind, erected instead the splendid chapel at Westminster, and left this incomplete. In the next reign Wolsey obtained a grant of it, completed the chapel, and commenced the erection in it of a magnificent tomb for himself or his master—it is not quite clear which. His fall put a stop to the works, and during the Long Parliament the chapel was dismantled, the statues on the tomb broken for the metal, and the contents sold for £600. The only vestige of the tomb left was the massive black marble sarcophagus, which lay neglected till 1805, when it was appropriated as the tomb of Nelson. Charles I. was to have been reinterred in this chapel, which was to have been his memorial; but nothing was done towards carrying out the proposal. By James II. it was converted into a Roman Catholic chapel, and a mob demolished the windows and decorations. From his abdication it was unused, except for awhile in the reign of George II., when the Free School was kept in it. George III. caused a crypt to be constructed beneath the chapel as a burial-place for himself and family, and the chapel was now designated the Tomb House. But the entrance to the vault was made in St. George's Chapel, and the Tomb House was left as before, empty and unadorned, and only used as a robing room at the installation of a Knight of the Garter. Thus it remained until Her Majesty selected it for restoration and decoration by herself and her children as their tribute to the memory of the lamented Prince Consort.

To Sir Gilbert Scott was entrusted the restoration of the chapel and the general direction of the works, the Baron Triqueti, acting in conjunction with the architect, having charge of the decorations. After having been over ten years on hand, the chapel was completed in 1875, nothing that care and thought and the most liberal expenditure could supply having been left undone to render it worthy of its purpose. Every portion of the interior is covered with sculpture, mosaic, or other artistic decoration in some rich and costly material, and it is undoubtedly the most sumptuous work of the kind in England, if not in Europe. The chapel is comparatively small, but lofty, and has an apsidal chancel. The style is of course Perp. The nave is of 5 bays; and there are windows in the chancel—all filled with painted glass by Clayton and Bell. The groined roof, which is new, is entirely covered with mosaics executed by Salviati from designs by Clayton and Bell, those over the apse being symbolical of the Passion, those over the nave referring to characteristics of the Prince. The floor is a rich mosaic of coloured marbles. The windows of the apse, each of 4 lights, and divided by transoms into 3 stages, contain Scriptural subjects classed under 'The Garden of Eden,' 'The Garden of Gethsemane,' 'The Passion' (this is the central window), 'The Garden of St. Joseph,' 'The Garden of the Blessed.' The nave windows illustrate the genealogy of the Prince Consort by portraits and heraldic bearings. The blank window at the W. end is filled with mosaics, by Salviati, of the sovereigns and more distinguished persons who have borne a leading part in the history of Windsor Castle.

The most original decorative feature is the series of pictorial tablets, by Baron Triqueti, which fill the panels or wall spaces beneath the windows. These are 15 in number, the larger about 11 ft. wide and 9 ft. high, and are executed by inlaying variously coloured marbles and spars upon a slab of white Sicilian marble, coloured and dark cements being employed where deemed necessary to give firmness to the outline or depth to the shadows. The process, the invention of Baron Triqueti, is a revival and extension of the old Florentine tarsia work, and as thus developed gives much of the fullness, variety, and breadth of painting, while it promises to be as lasting as the walls on which it is executed. The tablets are set in a frame of mosaic, with illustrative rilievi, and over each tablet is a medallion, executed by Miss Durant, of the Prince or Princess by whom the tablet was presented. The tablets in the nave represent subjects from the Old Testament, chosen as illustrative of excellences or attributes of the Prince; those in the apse depict the Passion of the Saviour.

The tablets on the S. side of the nave, beginning at the W. end, represent—

46

'Daniel in the Lion's Den,' with the motto, "Fortitude;" 'Moses blessing the Children of Israel,' the motto, "Steadfastness and Truth;" 'Return of Abraham with Isaac from the Offering,' motto, "Duty and Obedience;" 'Joseph made Viceroy over Egypt;' 'Jacob on his Death-bed Blessing his Children.' On the N. wall, commencing at the W., are—'Nathaniel in his Garden, Praying,' the motto, "Sincerity;" 'David in the House of the Lord,' harp in hand amidst the musicians he is instructing, motto, "Eloquence and Harmony;" 'Solomon in all his Glory,' receiving gifts from the kings of the earth, motto, "Wisdom and Science;" 'Jehoshaphat sending Teachers to Judah;' 'Jerusalem Mourning over Josiah.' Between the tablets are marble rilievi of prophets and teachers.

The tarsia tablets in the apse depict the Entombment. In the centre is a costly reredos, designed by Sir Gilbert Scott and executed by Baron Triqueti. On a base of coloured marbles and alabaster are three panels with bas-reliefs in Sicilian marble of the Resurrection; above, are elaborately carved canopies; and over all, a large Greek cross, studded with agates and malachite.*

The sarcophagus of the Prince, the central object of the chapel, stands in the midst of the nave, close to the steps of the apse. It is of the usual altar-tomb form, and bears a recumbent statue of the Prince Consort, habited in a full suit of armour, with the insignia of the Order of the Garter. The slab on which the statue rests is supported by angels; in niches on the sides are statues of the Virtues, at the ends are Mourners. Around is the insc. : "Albert Prince Consort: born August xxvi., MDCCCXIX : died December xiv., MDCCCLXI. Buried in the Royal Mausoleum at Frogmore. I have fought the good fight, I have finished my course." And thus we read that this splendid tomb is an unreality : the sarcophagus an empty show.

Visitors are allowed to see the Chapel on Wednesdays, Thursdays, and Fridays, from 12 *till* 3 *o'clock. Admission is by tickets only, which can be obtained at the office of the Clerk of the Works at Windsor Castle.* "No more than 200 tickets will be issued for each day." The entrance to the chapel is in the covered way leading to the Cloisters, at the E. end of St. George's Chapel.

On the N. of the Albert Memorial Chapel are the *Dean's* or *Great Cloisters*, a work of much beauty, built for Edward III. by Robert of Burnham, before William of Wykeham was appointed Clerk of the Works. The arches are particularly fine. The S. wall is interesting as the only fragment left of Henry III.'s Chapel. On this wall is a portrait of Henry III. wearing his crown, executed, as an Exchequer record shows, by the monk William of Westminster in 1248. It was discovered on clearing away the plaster in 1859. The lower part of the figure was destroyed, but the head is tolerably perfect. In these cloisters are several tablets to the memory of Military Knights.

The large building E. of the Dean's Cloisters is the *Deanery*, erected by Dean Urswick in 1500, and bearing on the front his name and arms. It contains several handsome rooms. The Garter Room, in which Knights of the Garter robe at installations, contains a curious old screen, on which are emblazoned the arms of Edward III., and a large array of subsequent knights. Behind the Deanery is the Winchester Tower, built by William of Wykeham, and for a time his residence. The inscription, *Hoc fecit Wykeham*, was cut by direction of Sir Jeffry Wyattville.

A passage at the N.W. corner of the Dean's Cloisters leads to the *Canons'* or *Inner Cloisters*, of much less interest. Here are the Canons' residences and Library. A narrow passage on the N. leads to the castle wall, and by a flight of stone steps to a formidable looking postern gate, which opens on to the famous *Hundred Steps*, the delight of all Windsor boys. The steps, really 122 in number, wind round the slope of the hill to Thames Street, and are the shortest way between the interior of the castle and the L. and S.-W. Rly. Stat. They are closed at sunset. A passage on the l. leads by a good E.E. doorway to the N. of St. George's Chapel, where on the outside of

---

* The tablets are well illustrated in 'The Triqueti marbles in the Albert Memorial Chapel, Windsor : a series of (117) photographs executed by the Misses Davidson and dedicated by express permission to the Queen,' folio, 1876.

one of the canon's houses may be seen the few remaining traces of the Domus Regis of Henry III. mentioned above.

The *Middle Ward* lies E. of the Lower Ward, and between it and the Upper Ward. It is almost filled by the *Round Tower*, built by Edward III. to contain the Round Table. The mound on which it stands is entirely artificial, being formed of carried chalk, and was probably the mound of the original British or Roman fortress. That it was older than the tower, and that the tower was adapted to it, is evident, the tower being, not a perfect circle, but flattened on the E. side where the mound is flat : its greatest diameter is 102 ft., the smallest only 93. Further, as Mr. Parker has pointed out, whilst the rolls contain the weekly accounts of expenditure for building the tower, there is no entry for digging the moat or forming the mound.

Though commonly spoken of as the Keep of the Castle, the Round Tower was not, as we have seen, built for defensive purposes, and it may be doubted if it was at any time strong enough to withstand a determined assault. It was built in great haste, of hard chalk obtained from the royal quarries at Marlow and Bisham, faced with a better stone from Wheatley (Oxon), some stone which the Dean of St. Paul's had collected for his own building operations, but was persuaded to give up to the King, and three ship-loads brought direct from Caen. So impatient was the King, that he sent out Warrants to all parts of the country to impress masons and skilful artificers, and for a while several hundred workmen were actually employed. Edward's Round Tower was low and dumpy, its height being less than half its diameter. Wyattville nearly doubled its height, and added the Watch Tower or Flag Turret—an alteration that has greatly improved the picturesque character of the castle, and rendered it much more conspicuous and imposing as a distant object. Wyattville found the old foundations to be too rotten, and the walls too weak, to bear the additional height ; he therefore laid down a new foundation of solid concrete, upon which he raised a brick wall *within* the original stone wall, and upon that carried up the additional storey, which is quite unsupported by the old tower. New

part and old, he faced alike with flints, so that the whole, though of such different character and dates, looks to be the work of one hand. The Round Tower is now 80 ft. high from the top of the mound ; the Watch Tower 25 ft. higher : from the level of the Quadrangle the total height is 148 ft. From it a view of vast extent is obtained, embracing, it is asserted, 12 counties. But wide as it is, wanting the contrast of the neighbouring trees, the prospect is far less beautiful than that from the Terrace. But from no other spot can so good an idea of the *plan* of the castle, and the character and connection of the several buildings, be obtained. When the Queen is at Windsor, the Royal standard floats over the Round Tower—a flag 36 ft. long and 27 wide, but dwarfed by the huge structure. *Permission to ascend the Tower may be obtained on application on the days the State Apartments are open.*

The Round Tower is usually assumed to be the same as the Rose Tower, and is so described by the authors of the Annals of Windsor. But they were clearly different structures. The Rose Tower, there can be little doubt, was the octagonal tower at the S.W. angle of the Quadrangle of the Upper Ward—S.E. of the Round Tower, and between it and George IV.'s Gateway. The name, La Rose, was given from its decoration with Edward's badge, the rose en soleil. The tower was so much altered by Wyattville as to retain little of its original character ; but the rose is still conspicuous on the central bosses of the vaulting in the two lower chambers—the only rooms left of the original fabric. The tower was an important portion of the Royal apartments, and against one of the great festivals, 1366, the exterior was made resplendent with colours and gold. The exact nature of the decoration is not told, but the painter, William Burdon, was with his assistants at work upon it for 123½ days, and consumed 67 lb. of white lead, 18 lb. of red lead, 12 lb. of green paints, 28 lb. of vermilion, and 1400 leaves of gold, besides oil and varnish. This was the Maiden's Tower of Surrey's days.

The entrance from the Middle to the Upper Ward is by what is miscalled the *Norman Gateway* on the N. of the Round Tower, but which is really the work of

William of Wykeham (1356-62). A passage on the l. leads to the Terrace.

The *Upper Ward*, the eastern division of the castle, comprises the site added by Edward III., and contains the royal apartments—the private as well as the state rooms—which are built about three sides of a great quadrangle, the Round Tower with its outworks occupying the fourth, whilst the Terrace is carried round the three outer sides of the royal buildings. Broadly speaking, the State Apartments occupy the northern side of the Quadrangle, the Queen's Private Apartments, including the royal drawing, dining, reception, and throne rooms, picture galleries, private chapel, and the like, the eastern side; and the more strictly private apartments, the rooms of the officials, etc., the southern side. On the S. side, between the York and Lancaster Towers, is the principal entrance to the Quadrangle, *George IV.'s Gateway*, which opens upon the Long Walk, and commands a full view of it from end to end. Directly facing this on the N. side of the Quadrangle is the *State Entrance* to the royal apartments, a boldly projecting carriage porch, which opens into a spacious vestibule. the new state staircase (designed by Mr. Salvin), and N. corridor. The Queen's Private Entrance is a projecting porch, under the Oak Breakfast Room, at the S.E. angle of the quadrangle. In the centre of the quadrangle formerly stood the equestrian statue of Charles II., which "Toby Rustate, a page of the back stairs . . . a very simple, ignorant, but honest and loyal creature,"* presented to his royal master. It was removed by George IV. to its present position at the W. end of the quadrangle. The statue was the work of Josias Ibach Stada, who has put his name on the horse's hoof; the pedestal was carved by Grinling Gibbons. "The fruit, fish, implements of shipping, are all exquisite; the man and horse may serve for a sign to draw a passenger's eye to the pedestal."† The statue cost Rustate £1000. The quadrangle is not open to the public, but it may be very well seen from the passage behind Rustate's statue. The quadrangle and the whole exterior of the buildings of the Upper Ward were

remodelled and raised a storey by Wyattville, and now present a tolerably uniform architectural character. Objections may be raised to the style as a whole, to the intermixture of leading features and details of widely different periods and purpose; but with all its faults the royal ward proclaims its palatial character, and possesses a breadth and majesty which none of our other palaces approach.

The *State Apartments*, situate in the Stuart Building, the Star Building of Charles II., *are open gratuitously to the public on Mondays, Tuesdays, Thursdays, and Fridays, when Her Majesty is not in residence. Visitors may obtain tickets in Windsor at the Lord Chamberlain's Office near the Winchester Tower, at the head of the Lower Ward of the Castle, or of Mr. W. F. Taylor, bookseller, 13, High Street. These tickets are only available for the day on which they are issued. The hours for admission are from 11 to 4 from April to October, and from 11 to 3 from Nov. 1 to the end of March. Tickets may also be obtained in London from Messrs. Colnaghi, 14, Pall Mall East; Mr. Mitchell, 33, Old Bond Street; and Mr. Wright, 60, Pall Mall. These tickets are available for a week; and, like those obtained at Mr. Taylor's, admit the visitor two hours earlier than those issued at the Lord Chamberlain's Office.* The Queen's Private Apartments can only be seen in the absence of the Court, by a special order from the Lord Chamberlain. The State Apartments are entered by a Gothic porch at the N.W. corner of the Quadrangle, before you to the rt. on passing through the Norman Gateway. The apartments are approached by a narrow staircase, and are shown in the following order:—

1. The *Queen's Audience Chamber*. The ceiling, painted by *Verrio*, exhibits Catharine of Braganza, as Britannia, seated in a car and attended by Ceres, Flora, and other goddesses, proceeding to the Temple of Virtue: other ceilings we shall come to are about equal to this in intelligence. The walls on three sides are hung with rich Gobelin tapestry, illustrating the life of Esther. Portraits, of little value, but in exquisitely carved frames by *Gibbons*, of—Mary Queen of Scots, *Fr. Clouet*, her execution represented in the background. The father and grandfather of William

---

* Evelyn, Diary, July 24, 1680.
† Walpole, Anecdotes, vol. iii., p. 151.

III., Frederick and William, Princes of Orange, both full-length, by *Honthorst*.

2. The *Vandyck Room*. This, to the lover of pictures, is the most attractive of the rooms shown to the public. The portraits by *Vandyck* are more in number and finer than are brought together in any other room in Europe. There are no fewer than 22 of them, and several are of historical value, whilst others are admirable examples of his style. They are—1. Henri, Comte de Berg; half-length, oval; baton in hand. 2. Charles I. seated in robes of state, l. hand on table, on which are crown and sceptre; Queen seated on his l., Prince Charles standing on rt. A large and famous picture, and worthy of its fame, but somewhat injured by the restorer. 3. Mary Duchess of Richmond, only daughter of George Villiers, 1st Duke of Buckingham; full-l., as St. Agnes, with the lamb and palm-branch. From the collection of Charles I. 4. William Killigrew and Thomas Carew, poets; dated 1638, the year before Carew's death; half-length, seated figures. Carew reading; a good head; Killigrew looks a debauchee. 5. Henrietta Maria, Queen of Charles I.; full-l., in low white satin dress; countenance elegant, sensuous, intellectual; crown on table on rt. This picture hung in Charles I.'s bedroom. 6. Lady Venetia Digby, whom Clarendon describes as "a lady of extraordinary beauty, and of as extraordinary fame;" full-l., seated; Cupids holding a wreath over her head; Calumny bound at her feet: a picture in Vandyck's most grandiose style, and painted with more dash and vigour than usual. 7. George and Francis Villiers, sons of the 1st Duke of Buckingham; brilliantly painted; belonged to James II. 8. Thomas Prince of Carignan; ¾-l., in armour, with commander's baton: a duplicate at Berlin. 9. Queen Henrietta Maria; half-l., profile: painted for the sculptor Bernini to model from at Rome; formerly in the collection of James II. 10. Beatrice de Cusance, Princess of Cantecroix; full-l., charmingly painted. 11. Children of Charles I. One of Vandyck's great works; signed and dated 1637; a copy is in the Museum, Berlin. In centre Prince Charles with his hand on the head of a great mastiff; on his right are the Princesses Elizabeth and Mary; on his left the Princess Anne.

Prince James is sitting on a stool, only partially dressed. This picture hung in Charles I.'s breakfast-room at Whitehall. 12. The head of Charles I., three times on one canvas—front face, profile, three-quarters—painted for the guidance of Bernini the sculptor, in executing his bust for Whitehall: the melancholy head which is stamped on the memory as that of the unfortunate king. 13. Queen Henrietta Maria; full face, painted for Bernini to model from. 14. Lucy Countess of Carlisle; full-l. 15. Sir Kenelm Digby, seated by table on which is his sphere; rt. hand on breast. 16. Charles II. at the age of 11; in armour, pistol in rt. hand. Belonged to James II. 17. Vandyck; painted when young; very fine. 18. Q. Henrietta Maria; full-length and very fine. 19. Prince Charles (afterwards Charles II.), at the age of 9, the Duke of York (James II.), and the Princess Mary; full-l., standing, with two spaniels on the floor; dated 1638. 20. Mary Countess of Dorset; seated on a bank, rt. hand on lamb. 21. Charles I. on a grey horse, in armour, with broad falling ruff; l. hand resting on a truncheon. The Duc d'Epernon, Master of the Horse, is looking up to the King, whose helmet he is holding. The King sits his horse with consummate ease and dignity; and the horse is painted with great spirit. The picture, 12 ft. by 9 ft., one of Vandyck's most important works, was painted in the maturity of the artist's powers, and is executed in his best manner. A duplicate or copy, of somewhat smaller dimensions, is at Hampton Court, and there are repetitions at Warwick Castle and Lamport Hall. This copy was sold in the Commonwealth time to Remée van Leemput, the painter, for £200, but recovered through a lawsuit by Charles II. 22. Portrait; ¾-length; said to be of Jan Snellinck, a friend of Vandyck, but this more than doubtful.

3. The *Queen's State Drawing Room*; also known as the *Zuccarelli Room*, from its containing 9 large scenic landscapes by that painter. It also contains portraits of the first three Georges; Henry Duke of Gloucester, youngest son of Charles I.; and Frederick Prince of Wales.

4. The *State Ante-Room* is chiefly remarkable for the beautiful carvings of fish, fruit, flowers, and birds by *Grinling*

Gibbons. The ceiling is decorated with a Banquet of the Gods by *Verrio*.

5. The *Grand Staircase* forms, with the vestibule, recently remodelled by Mr. Salvin, a splendid and effective feature of the palace. *Obs.* in the recess on the first landing *Chantrey's* colossal marble statue of George IV.

The *Grand Vestibule* is a noble hall, 47 ft. long, 28 ft. wide, and 45 ft. high, lit by an octagonal lantern. It contains some pieces of sculpture, and several suits of 16th and 17th cent. armour, and military trophies and weapons decorate the walls. Here too is *Boehm's* fine statue of the Queen with her favourite collie by her side.

6. The *Waterloo Chamber*, a magnificent room, 98 ft. long, 47 ft. broad, and 45 ft. high, used for state banquets. By day the room is lighted by a lantern of ground glass, at night by a range of sunlights. On the walls are portraits of the sovereigns, statesmen, and generals who bore a prominent part in the war which terminated in the victory of Waterloo. The portraits, 38 in number, were (with the exceptions named) painted by *Sir Thomas Lawrence*, by command of George IV. Taking them in their order, they are— 1. Duc de Richelieu ; 2. General Overoff ; 3. Duke of Cambridge; 4. Earl of Liverpool ; 5. William IV. (by *Sir D. Wilkie*) ; 6. George III. (*Sir W. Beechey*); 7. George IV.; 8. Visct. Castlereagh ; 9. Duke of York ; 10. Baron Humboldt; 11. George Canning ; 12. Earl Bathurst ; 13. Count Münster ; 14. Cardinal Gonsalvi ; 15. Prince Hardenberg ; 16. William III. of Prussia; 17. Francis I. of Austria ; 18. Alexander I. of Russia ; 19. Count Nesselrode ; 20. Pope Pius VII. ; 21. Count Capo d'Istrias ; 22. Prince Metternich; 23. Visct. Hill (*H. W. Pickersgill*) ; 24. Charles X. of France ; 25. Prince Schwartzenberg ; 26. Archduke Charles of Austria ; 27. Sir Thos. Picton ; 28. Duc d'Angoulême ; 29. Duke of Brunswick ; 30. Leopold I., King of the Belgians ; 31. Sir James Kemp (*Pickersgill*) ; 32. Count Platoff ; 33. Duke of Wellington ; 34. Prince von Blucher ; 35. Count Alten (*Reichmann*) ; 36. Marquis of Anglesca ; 37. Count Czernitshoff ; 38. William Prince of Orange. *Obs.* the carvings by *Gibbons*.

7. The *Presence Chamber*, or *Grand*

Ball Room, a very stately apartment, 94 ft. long and 34 wide, fitted in the style of Louis XIV. On the walls are six magnificent specimens of Gobelin tapestry, a present to George IV. from Charles X., representing the legend of Jason and the Golden Fleece. Here are also the two elaborately wrought granite vases presented by Frederick III. of Prussia to William IV.; and the great malachite vase, the gift of the Emperor Nicholas to Her Majesty.

8. *St. George's Hall*, a spacious gallery fitted by Wyattville especially for festivals of the Order of the Garter, but used also for state banquets when on a large scale. The room is 200 ft. long, but only 34 wide and 32 high. On one side is a range of 13 lofty windows, which look into the great quadrangle ; on the other are portraits of the sovereigns of England from James I. to George IV. Trophies of arms and armour are hung between the pictures. On 24 shields behind the throne are the arms of the Sovereigns of the Order from Edward III. to William IV. The panels of the roof are emblazoned with the arms of all the knights from the foundation of the Order, the numbers on them corresponding to the names of their respective owners, painted between the panels of the windows. Galleries of dark oak, for musicians, are at each end. The portraits of James I. and Charles I. are by *Vandyck ;* Charles II. and James II. by *Lely ;* Mary II., William III., Anne, and George I. by *Kneller ;* George II. by *Zeeman ;* George III. by *Dupont ;* George IV. by *Lawrence.*

9. The *Guard Chamber*, a great Gothic room of somewhat irregular form, being 78 ft. long, 26 ft. wide at one end and 21 at the other, with a groined ceiling (of plaster), is filled with a rich collection of armour. Life-sized figures display the suits of the Duke of Brunswick (1530) ; Lord Howard of Effingham (1588); the Earl of Essex (1596); Henry Prince of Wales (1612); Charles Prince of Wales (1620) ; and Prince Rupert (1635) ; and suits of armour, breastplates, helmets, shields, and a great variety of weapons are ranged on the walls. At the end of the room, on a pedestal formed by a portion of the mast of the *Victory* perforated by a cannon ball, is a colossal bust of Nelson by *Chantrey*. Rt. and l.

of the great admiral are busts of Marlborough, a copy by *Sevier* from Rysbrack, and Wellington by *Chantrey ;* over them being suspended the small banners presented by their representatives to the sovereign on the anniversaries of Blenheim and Waterloo, in satisfaction of the tenure of the estates of Blenheim and Strathfieldsaye. Various military trophies occupy places on the floor, and within a glass case over the chimneypiece is the matchless shield by *Benvenuto Cellini*, presented by Francis I. to Henry VIII. on the Field of the Cloth of Gold.

10. The *Queen's Presence Chamber* has one of Verrio's refulgent ceilings, representing Catherine, Queen of Charles II., as the central figure, surrounded by all the Virtues, "Fame proclaiming the happiness of the country," and Justice driving away Envy, Hatred, and Discord. On the walls are four large specimens of Gobelin tapestry, setting forth the history of Queen Esther. The portraits are, the Princesses Elizabeth and Dorothea of Brunswick, by *Mytens*, and Henrietta Duchess of Orleans, youngest daughter of Charles I., by *Mignard*.

These are all the State Rooms now shown to the public. Five or six others which used to be shown, and in which is the general collection of pictures, are now included in the *Queen's Private Apartments*, and can only be seen, in the absence of the Court, by *an express order from the Lord Chamberlain*.

The *Queen's Closet*, a pretty room overlooking the North Terrace, contains a number of fine pictures, mostly of cabinet size, including the popular 'Misers' (or 'Money Changers') of *Quentin Matsys*, and several heads attributed with more or less probability to *Holbein*. Of these, that of Sir Henry Guildford, a gross yellow-visaged personage, is undoubtedly from the master's own pencil. So also, though not so good a picture, is Thomas Howard, 3rd Duke of Norfolk, father of the poet. Others are more open to question, and one or more (as the Edward VI.) seem irreconcileable with the dates of Holbein's decease. The portrait of Erasmus by *Pens* is full of character and well painted, whether an original likeness, or, as said, a copy from Holbein. Small landscapes by *Claude Lorraine*, interiors by *Teniers*, and others ascribed to *L. da Vinci, Titian, Rembrandt, Rubens, Honthorst, B. Van Orley*, etc., fill the room.

The *King's Closet*. St. Catharine, *Domenichino :* a characteristic example. Portraits of the Emperor Charles V., and of the Duke of Alva, *Sir Antonio Moro*. 'Holy Family,' *Tintoretto*, admirably painted. 'Mary Magdalen anointing the Feet of the Saviour,' *Rubens*, brilliant and characteristic. Portrait of the artist and his wife, *J. Van Cleef*, a very good example of a painter whose name seldom occurs in catalogues. Interior, *Jan Steen ;* 'The Woman of Samaria,' *Guercino ;* two or three roadside groups by *Wouvermans ;* a Prison by *Steenwyck ;* Landscapes by *Gaspar Poussin*, and a couple of Views of Windsor Castle, 1674, by *Jan Vostermann*, will repay examination.

The *King's Drawing Room*, best known as the *Rubens' Room*, from the pictures in it being entirely by that master, is a magnificent room alike from its appearance, contents, and the grand view obtained from the great oriel at the end, overhanging the best part of the North Terrace. The chief paintings are—Portrait of Rubens, the picture, so well known by the engravings, of the painter in a broad hat and gold chain, painted for Charles I.; an inimitable work, to which there is here an equally admirable and famous companion, the Portrait of Helena Fourment, his second wife. The large group of Rubens' friend Sir Balthasar Gerbier and his Family is now usually attributed to Vandyck, but it is very much in Rubens' manner. St. Martin dividing his Cloak with the Beggar, a large and vigorous work, in Rubens' broadest style. Holy Family, with St. Francis of Assisi, a masterly production. Philip IV. of Spain on horseback, Victory awarding him the palm—a court picture ; as is also, though a more remarkable work, the equestrian portrait of the Archduke Albert of Austria as Governor of the Netherlands. Two large landscapes (7 ft. 7 in. wide, by 5 ft. high), called respectively Winter and Summer, painted by Rubens to decorate his own house at Antwerp, and purchased with the rest of his Antwerp collection by George Villiers Duke of Buckingham, are brilliant pictures, quite unlike the landscapes of any other painter, and full of power. The broad expanse of low level country is wonderfully well rendered in the Summer (more correctly 'Going to Market'), but the scene is marred by an ungainly group of cattle in the foreground.

The *Council Chamber.*—' St. John,' in a landscape, *Correggio.* A Sibyl, *Guercino.* 'Silence : Virgin and Child, St. John Approaching,' *A. Carracci*, the well-known picture. Magdalen, *C. Dolce.* Two Interiors of Churches, by *Peter Neefs.* Duke of Marlborough, *Kneller.* Duke of Cumberland, *Reynolds.* Prince Rupert, *Lely.*

The *Throne Room*, a superbly decorated apartment, has some remarkably fine carvings by *Gibbons*, and full-length portraits of George III. by *Gainsborough ;* George IV. by *Lawrence;* and William IV. by *Shee.*

The remainder of the rooms on the N. side of the castle, and those on the E. of the quadrangle—the Private State Rooms proper—are right royal rooms, large, stately, sumptuously fitted and furnished, and withal have a thoroughly comfortable aspect. The *Corridor*, which gives access to them, and affords an indoor promenade (with the North Corridor) 520 ft. long, is lined with busts of sovereigns, nobles, statesmen, warriors, writers, and other distinguished persons ; statues, the most important being the group of the Queen and the Prince Consort by *Theed ;* portraits by *Lawrence* and other eminent artists ; views of Venice by *Canaletto ;* of London, Windsor, etc., by *Zuccarelli* and others ; and numerous beautiful cabinets, including one which belonged to Wolsey. The *North Corridor* has been fitted in a particular manner with arms and armour of exceptional rarity and value; the swords of remarkable personages—among others those of Columbus and of Sobieski, that carried by Charles I. at Naseby, and that worn by Hampden at Chalgrove Field ; the footstool of Tippoo Saib's throne, a tiger's head of gold with teeth of crystal, and the peacock set with precious stones which decked the same potentate's state umbrella ; various costly oriental objects, presents chiefly from Eastern Princes ; and several richly wrought mediæval shields and weapons. The *Great* or *Crimson Drawing Room* is very splendid, but chiefly remarkable for its hangings and furniture of red silk. The names of the *White* and the *Green Drawing Rooms* bespeak their respective characteristics.

The *Queen's Drawing Room* is the room in which George IV. and William IV. died. The *Private Drawing Room* is noted for its mirrors, the gilded tracery of its walls and ceilings, and as containing the large and elegantly wrought silver-gilt wine-cooler designed by *Flaxman* for George IV.

But to see what treasures in plate the Castle possesses, a *special order for the Plate Room must be obtained of the Lord Steward*—which is not often granted. Windsor is famous for its gold (or silver-gilt) plate, which embraces an almost endless variety of articles, and is probably in extent and richness unequalled. Many of the cups, vases, salvers, candelabra, and shields are of extreme beauty ; others are equally remarkable for massiveness or quaintness. When the dinner-service is laid out at a state banquet, and the buffets are loaded with the larger and choicer objects, the effect is described as surpassingly fine. In point of art the highest places are assigned to the Nautilus Cup of *Benvenuto Cellini*, some 16th century cups of exquisitely carved ivory mounted in gold, and the Achilles Shield of *Flaxman.* Greatly prized is the silver fountain designed by the Prince Consort, and made by Messrs. Garrard. For their rarity, or associations, are pointed out the silver wine fountain taken from the Spanish Armada ; a cup made of Spanish dollars captured at Havannah in 1702 ; Nell Gwynne's golden bellows : a salver with the arms of Elizabeth of Bohemia ; the St. George candelabrum of silver, 4 ft. high ; and an almost endless variety of objects equally rich and rare.

The *Royal Library* is exceedingly interesting. George IV. having given (or sold) the royal collection of books to the British Museum, William IV. determined to found a new Royal Library at Windsor. The more valuable books remaining in the several palaces; MSS., including the Stuart Papers ; the Royal Miniatures ; and the magnificent collection of drawings by the great masters, were brought together and deposited in the Castle.

The library as thus formed was of great value and extent, but incomplete and ill-arranged ; and the Prince Consort devoted himself with rare ardour to remedy its deficiencies, and to render its stores available. He was not spared to accomplish all he purposed, but his plans have been faithfully followed, and the library reconstructed as he designed it. The printed books now number some 40,000 volumes, are comprehensive in range, include choice editions and rare old copies, and many are of great interest to the bibliographer and lover of binding. But the glory of the library is the almost unrivalled Collection of Drawings. Curiously enough, the foundation of the collection was laid by Charles II., who was persuaded by Sir Peter Lely to purchase at the sale of Lord Arundel's collection in Holland the drawings and MSS. of Leonardo da Vinci and Holbein, with many by Michel Angelo, Raphael, and other great Italian masters. They seem, however, to have been little regarded, were laid aside, and after a time forgotten, and only in the reign of George II. were they by accident discovered packed away in a bureau at Kensington Palace. About the same time Frederick Prince of Wales bought the extensive collection of Italian and French drawings and miniatures formed by Dr. Mead; and with these two collections as the basis, George III. formed the Royal Collection as it now exists at Windsor. By his agents on the Continent, and in England, George III. purchased very largely, though not always with judgment, and the collection as he left it contained no fewer than 15,000 drawings. They were in a chaotic condition when deposited in the library at Windsor, but, following the directions of the Prince Consort, they have been reduced to order, their relative place and value as far as practicable determined, and every important drawing remounted so as to display it to the best advantage, and preserve it from injury. In this process of examining and remounting, many precious works were discovered. Unknown treasures were brought to light in looking through portfolios; and often in removing drawings from their mounts, sketches, studies, variations of figures, or parts of figures, were disclosed.*

The drawings by *Leonardo da Vinci,* originally mounted in 3 volumes, form a

* E. B. Woodward, F.S.A., Librarian to the Queen and Keeper of the Royal Prints and Drawings, Papers on the Drawings in Windsor Castle, in the Fine Arts Quarterly Review, and in Gent. Mag. 1866; Waagen, Treasures of Art in Great Britain, vol. ii.; MS. Notes.

collection only rivalled by that of the Grand Duke of Tuscany, and that in the Ambrosian Library, Milan. The range of subjects is extraordinary, and not less so the power and grandeur of some of the drawings, and the delicacy and refinement of others. *Michel Angelo's* drawings, with some miscellaneous Italian drawings, also filled 3 volumes. Many of those attributed to him are certainly not by the mighty Florentine, but enough are indubitable to make the series of great value. Several are studies for the frescoes in the Sistine Chapel, and other important works. To Raphael 53 drawings are attributed, but Passavant admits only 19 as genuine.

The *Raphael Cabinet,* a handsome piece of furniture in the Print Room, well exemplifies the Prince Consort's anxiety to make the royal collections subserve thoroughness in the study of art. The object was to see how far it would be possible to illustrate the life and works— the mental processes and modes of operation—of a great artist, and Raphael was selected for the first experiment. In order to procure "the best possible representation of every picture or other work of the master," copies were obtained of every engraving of value of the several works; and where no sufficient engraving existed, or was obtainable, a photograph was, if possible, secured. With this was arranged whatever of value could be brought together respecting the particular work. The sketches and studies for each composition, and for every group and separate figure in it, were collected and placed with the representation of the finished work, photographs being for this purpose procured of nearly all the known drawings by Raphael in the public museums and private collections throughout Europe. Then prints, drawings, or photographs, were obtained, and duly arranged, of all the earlier works which may be supposed to have influenced the master in the composition, or suggested any incident, attitude, or figure. A somewhat similar but supplementary series follows of subsequent works of accepted value, which appear to have been suggested by, or are imitations of, Raphael's work. Finally, there is a complete collection of the portraits of Raphael—photographs and engravings. The several specimens were uniformly mounted, and the Raphael Cabinet was designed and made by Mr. Crace for the reception of this unique collection—which will eventually, it is assumed, form 50 great volumes. Similar illustrations of Michel Angelo and Da Vinci, and probably of other great artists, were to have followed, but for the Prince's too early death.*

There are many drawings by Fra Bartolommeo, Correggio, Parmigiano, Luca Signorelli, Fra Filippo Lippi, a large number by Guercino and Domenichino, and others by Guido, Andrea del Sarto, and other of the chief Italian painters. There is also an exceedingly interesting series (part of Dr. Mead's collection) of over 1500 beautifully finished antiquarian drawings by *Sandro Bartoli*, embracing, among other things, drawings of 900 antique bas-reliefs, then in Rome, and accurate representations, many coloured, of all the ancient paintings and mosaics which had been discovered in Rome before the end of the 17th century.

Of drawings by *Holbein* there is a magnificent collection, numbering 87 examples, many of them heads drawn from the life, of eminent historical personages. Like the Raphael drawings, these have been photographed, and are familiar to the art-student. Many drawings by Albert Dürer, Lucas Cranach, and other famous masters of the early German school, as well as a large number by Nicolo Poussin, Claude Lorraine, and the leading masters of the half-Italian early French school.

The collection of Prints has been greatly augmented and entirely rearranged since the accession of Her Majesty, and is now one of the finest in the kingdom, rich alike in the works of the great early engravers and of the more eminent moderns. The classification of the collection of engraved historical portraits was one of the first steps taken by the Prince Consort in the reconstruction of the Royal Library.

Before quitting the Castle, the *Terrace*, some 2500 ft. long, which surrounds it on the N., E., and S. sides, should be visited. The North Terrace is open every day; the East Terrace only on Saturday and Sunday afternoons, from half-past one to sunset,

during summer : on the Sunday evenings military bands play. The formation of the Terrace has been told, and how George III. walked his hour daily along it, to the great delight of his subjects, as Elizabeth, Charles I., and Charles II. had done before him, and as Cromwell used to do whilst he dwelt in Windsor Castle. The North Terrace affords the finest views. The prospect may not be, as Evelyn asserted, one of the finest in the world, but it would be difficult to find one in this country to surpass it.

"Where is there any worse land in the world than some parts of Windsor Forest?—whereas I myself have spoken with Italians upon the Terrace at Windsor, who looking about and seeing all the country did compare it to Lombardy." *

From the East Terrace, the prospect, wanting "Eton, the meandering Thames, and the sweet meadows" through which it flows, cannot compare with that from the North Terrace ; but it commands a wide stretch of sylvan scenery, the Home and Great Parks, Windsor Forest, and Virginia Water, and is only bounded by the hazy Surrey hills. Below the Terrace are the *Queen's Private Garden* and the carefully tended *Slopes*, running gently into the level meadows of the Home Park. At the foot of the Slopes was the Tournament Ground of the early Festivals of St. George, and there Edward III. challenged all comers, his shield bearing his cognizance of the White Swan, with the motto—

"Hay, Hay, the white swan ;
By Goddes Soul I am thy Man."

South of the Castle, the entrance from Castle Hill, are the *Royal Stables*, erected in 1840 at a cost of about £70,000. They are built about several open courts, and are "castellated so as to accord in style with the castle," but are of little architectural value. They are, however, said to be well adapted to their purpose, and are of course fitted with the most approved appliances. Stabling is provided in them for over 100 horses, and there are coach, harness, and saddle departments, veterinary houses, etc. The *Riding House*, near the centre of the stables, is 170 ft. long, 52 wide, and 40 high, and has at one end a

---

* Becker and Ruland (Librarians to the Prince Consort), On the Raphael Collection at Windsor, in Fine Arts, Quart. Rev., vol. i.

* Bishop Goodman, Court of King James, vol. i., p. 169.

Royal Gallery, whence the exercises may be witnessed. *The Stables and Riding House may be visited on application any week-day between 1 and 3 o'clock.* A small gratuity is expected by the person showing them. The grooms are not allowed to uncover the horses.

The *Home Park* (formerly known as the *Little Park*) lies E. and N. of the Castle, with the Thames as its outer boundary.* The area is about 500 acres, the circuit somewhat over 4 miles. It is for the most part level, but contains many noble trees standing singly, in groups, and in long and stately avenues of the times of Charles II. and William III., and now at their fullest growth. The Home Park has been much altered of late years, and is now a strictly private park; the road and paths across it having been diverted, and the park closed to the public. It was in the Home Park, about Frogmore, that Shakspeare laid many of the scenes of his 'Merry Wives of Windsor.'

Herne's Oak. — A tall, withered, and barkless tree stood till lately within a railing in the line of the avenue of elms, near the park wall, and not far from the footpath to Frogmore, which, under the name of *Herne's Oak*, had a wide renown from the belief that it was the veritable " oak with great ragg'd horns " which Herne the hunter all the winter time at still midnight walked round about, and under which Sir John Falstaff was so unmercifully handled. The tree, which had long leant over, fell on the 31st of August, 1863. A young oak has been planted to mark the site. But the tree was of more than doubtful verity. Neither in size nor appearance did it correspond to the tree described by Mrs. Page, and it was not known as Herne's Oak in the beginning of the present century. That name was then and long before given to a larger oak some 30 yards distant, which had " great ragg'd horns," and which was cut down by order of George III., along with some other decayed and " unsightly

trees," the King not knowing when he gave the order that Herne's Oak was of the number.*

Frogmore House and grounds were granted (47 Geo. III., cap. 45) on lease for 99 years, at a nominal rent, to Queen Charlotte, who lived here, and here had a private press, with which she amused herself by printing some poetry. It was afterwards the residence of the Princess Augusta, and later of the Duchess of Kent. It is now held by the Queen; and here is the *Royal Garden*, of about 30 acres, famous for its fruits and flowers. The *Royal Dairy* is a daintily ornamented little model dairy, but like all else at Frogmore strictly private.

On an artificial mound by the Ornamental Water at Frogmore is the *Mausoleum of the Duchess of Kent* (d. 1861). The building, a circular temple of Portland stone, with a cupola of copper, is surrounded by 16 Ionic columns, the shafts of polished grey granite, the bases and capitals of bronze. The frieze beneath the dome, the doorway, and door are also of bronze. The interior has a lower chamber in which is the sarcophagus, of polished granite, containing the remains of the Duchess of Kent, and an upper chamber in which is her effigy by *Theed*. The architect was Mr. A. J. Humbert. A marble bust, by *Theed*, of her daughter the Princess of Hohenlohe-Langenberg, was placed " beside the tomb of the Mother, lamented by both, by her only sister, Victoria R.," 1873.

Not far from the above, and within sight of Windsor Castle, stands the *Royal Mausoleum*, erected by the Queen, 1862-70, to contain the remains of the Prince Consort. The building, designed by Mr. A. J. Humbert, is cruciform in plan, the limbs of the cross being of equal length, and small chapels filling the interspaces. The centre rises as an octagonal lantern, and is surmounted by a large gilded cross.

---

* The name Home Park is sometimes confined to "the low ground between the N. side of the Castle and the river, in contradistinction to the *Little Park*," which includes the rest of the tract included under the name of the Home Park ; but no such distinction was formerly made. (See Tighe and Davis, Annals of Windsor, vol. i., p. 31, n.)

* Mr. C. Knight, Local Illustrations to 'Merry Wives of Windsor,' has discussed the subject with the advantage of early local knowledge, and has given engravings of both the trees. The question is also fully examined in Tighe and Davis's Annals of Windsor, vol. ii. ; and see Gilpin, Remarks on Forest Scenery ; Gent. Mag., April 1841, and Jan. —April 1868. Mr. Jesse in the 2nd series of his Gleanings, 1834, and Mr. Perry in a Treatise on the Identity of Herne's Oak, 1867, maintain the authority of the tree that fell in 1863.

At the E. end is an entrance porch. The external dimensions are 80 ft. by 70; the height to the top of the lantern 83 feet. The walls are of Portland stone, with polished granite columns on a basement of granite. The interior decorations, designed by Prof. Grüner, in the Italian Cinque-Cento style, are of exceeding richness. The walls are lined with a great variety of coloured marbles; the columns, cornices, etc., are of white statuary marble, with bases, capitals, and other ornamental features of bronze gilt. Arabesques occupy the interspaces. The pendentives of the lantern are filled with pictures executed by Salviati in mosaic. Along the vaulting ribs of the lantern are gilded statues of angels. In the chapels are large paintings—that over the entrance being by the Princess Royal (the Princess Imperial of Germany). Statues of prophets, frescoes of the Evangelists, mosaics, and elaborate ornaments in gilt bronze, fill every remaining portion of wall space. The windows have Munich painted glass. The pavement is a mosaic of coloured marbles. In the centre, under the lantern, on a base of polished black marble, stands the massive sarcophagus, wrought from a block of grey Aberdeen granite—the largest ever quarried. At the angles are bronze statues of kneeling angels. On the lid of the sarcophagus is a recumbent statue of the Prince Consort in white marble, from the chisel of Marochetti. On the W. is an altar of marble and mosaic, and above it a large painting of the Resurrection. (These monuments are not accessible to the public.)

Windsor Great Park stretches away for 4 or 5 miles southward of the town, castle, and Home Park. Norden in 1607 estimated it at 3650 acres, and the Parliamentary Survey of 1649 at 3670 acres. William III. threw into it 390 acres of the Moat Park. But on the death of the Duke of Cumberland, ranger of Windsor Park, in 1791, George III. took the management into his own hands; disparked all but 1800 acres of the Great Park, and converted the larger half into farms. The area of park land has since been somewhat extended by annexing a portion of the disafforested Windsor Forest. The Great Park abounds in rich sylvan and wild forest-like scenery;

pleasant walks and drives extend in every direction, and large herds of deer wander at will over the broad heathy slopes and ferny dells. A recent parliamentary return shows that the number of deer kept in Windsor Great Park, on an average of the last 10 years, is 1658; the number killed annually is 128; the number required for the Royal Hunt, 16.

From the castle the Great Park is traversed by the famous avenue known as the *Long Walk*, begun by Charles II. and completed by William III. The Long Walk is a perfectly straight road, nearly 3 miles long, with on each side a double row of noble elms, now somewhat past their prime. Many of the elms are decaying, and several have fallen, but every care is taken to preserve them, and to maintain as far as practicable the matchless avenue. On Snow Hill, at the end of the Long Walk, is a colossal equestrian statue, by Sir Richard Westmacott, of George III. in a Roman habit. From it there are fine views of the castle, and close at hand some beautiful forest walks.

On the W. of the Long Walk, stretching from Hudson's Gate at the bottom of Sheet Street to the southern boundary of the park, is a still longer single avenue of elms, called *Queen Anne's Ride*, from having been planted by Q. Anne in 1707.

About a mile S. of the Long Walk is *Cumberland Lodge*, built originally by Charles II., but which received its present name from having been for many years the residence of the Duke of Cumberland, the hero of Culloden, when ranger of the parks. The lodge was nearly destroyed by fire, Nov. 14, 1869, but has been rebuilt, and is now the residence of the Prince and Princess Christian of Schleswig-Holstein.

Between Cumberland Lodge and the statue is the *Royal Lodge*, known as the *King's Cottage* in the days of George IV., who built it, and spent his last years secluded in it. After his death the larger part was pulled down; but it has been partially restored and fitted for the occasional residence of the Prince of Wales. Near it is a pretty little Gothic Chapel, rebuilt in 1866.

Cranborne Lodge, on the W. side of the park, one of the lodges built by Charles II., and the residence of Lord Ranelagh, afterwards of the Duke of St. Albans, the Duke of York, the Duke of Gloucester, for awhile of the Princess Charlotte, and later of Nash the architect. It was some years since pulled down, except a sort of tower, but it has recently been refitted as a royal resting-place on occasional excursions from Windsor Castle. It is pleasantly placed on a moderate elevation, and commands extensive prospects. The vicinity is famous for its oaks. One great tree is known as *William the Conqueror's Oak.* Within a clearing in the wood, on the other side of the Winkfield road, is a splendid oak, the trunk rising straight and clean for some 50 ft. before the branches spread out into a stately head. On the trunk is a brass plate inscribed *Queen Victoria's Tree.* From it there is a charming wild walk for nearly two miles along the sides of a steep ravine.

On the eastern side of the park by Bishopsgate are some delightful woodland solitudes. "In the summer of 1815, after a tour along the southern coast of Devonshire, and a visit to Clifton," Shelley rented a house on Bishopsgate Heath ; "spent his days under the oak shades of Windsor Great Park," and found in "the magnificent woodland a fitting study to inspire the various descriptions of forest scenery we find in the poem" of Alastor which he there composed. And now, as then, one who wanders there will find that

> " Silence and Twilight here, twin sisters, keep
> Their noonday watch."

By *Sandpit-gate,* famous for its beeches, is a noted heronry, "a noble appendage to the park," Mr. Jesse truly terms it, "and any monarch might well be proud of it, as well as of the trees on which the nests are built." *Blackness* is hardly less rich in noble trees and lovely scenery, and all the way thence is beautiful to Virginia Water.

Windsor Forest, the chase of the Conqueror, and other mighty hunters of the ages past—

> " A dreary desert and a gloomy waste
> To savage beasts and savage laws a prey,
> And kings more furious and severe than they "*—

extended far beyond the precincts of the

Great Park to the W. and S.; but it may be doubted whether in the Norman times there was any division into park and forest, the whole district being the royal hunting-ground. The circuit of the Norman forest is stated to have been over 180 miles. In Norden's Survey of the forest, 1607, the circuit is given as 77½ miles. In Rocque's Map it is reckoned at 56 miles. As time went on enclosures were made and cultivation advanced, but the forest was still a broad open tract of woodland heath and waste, the home of a wild and reckless race, who gained a precarious livelihood by poaching and other lawless practices, and were the terror of their more quiet and industrious neighbours. At length, in 1806, a parliamentary commission was appointed to inquire into the condition of the forest, and during the following years, 1807-10, they made several reports. From these it appeared that in 1790 the forest was reputed to contain 59,600 acres, of which 24,628 acres were open forest and waste. Deer killing was rampant, and in 1806 only 318 deer were left in the forest. At this time the forest included the whole of 11 parishes and parts of 6 others.

In 1813 an Act was passed for enclosing Windsor Forest, by which all the lands within the parishes and liberties of Windsor Forest were declared to be disafforested and all forestal rights abolished from the 1st of July, 1814. Of the open land 6665 acres were allotted to the Crown. Of these about 3000 acres were enclosed and planted with oak, fir, and larch ; the rest was for the most part brought under the plough. Eight years later (Oct. 1822) the radical Cobbett found little to admire in its aspect. " On leaving Oakingham for London, you get upon what is called *Windsor Forest ;* that is to say, upon as bleak, as barren, and as villainous a heath as ever man set his eyes on. However, here are *new enclosures* without end. And here are *houses* too, here and there, over the whole of this execrable tract of country."* The forest soon disappeared as a forest. With the exception of the irreclaimable heath, the Crown enclosures, now a sea of firs, and some few fragments of woodland left open on the skirts of the Great Park. the district is everywhere en-

---

* Pope, Windsor Forest.

* Cobbett, Rural Rides, p. 59.

closed and cultivated, Pope's ' Windsor Forest' would not now serve as a pocket guide. All that is beautiful or characteristic of the ancient Forest of Windsor now lies within the Great Park or close upon its borders.

WINDSOR, OLD, BERKS, a

village on the rt. bank of the Thames, 2 m. S.E. from the town and castle of Windsor, and 3 m. N.W. of Egham. Pop. of par. 2112, but this includes 619 in the eccl. dist. of Holy Trinity, Sunningdale, formed in 1841, and 23 in that of St. Peter, Cranborne ; 252 in the Union Workhouse, and 170 in Beaumont College. Inn, the *Bells of Ouseley*.

As the name implies, Old Windsor is the parent of the neighbouring town, New Windsor. *Windlesora*,[*]—according to some authorities the winding shore, from A.-S. *windel*, to wind, and *or*, a shore, in allusion to the serpentine course of the Thames here,—was the seat of a royal residence in A.-S. times. In May 1061, Æthelsige was consecrated Abbot of St. Augustine's, Canterbury, by the Archbishop Stigand, at the royal house at Windsor. Edward the Confessor kept court here occasionally. At a banquet given by him is said by some to have occurred the death of Earl Godwin, but the better reading of the legend gives Winchester as the place. On another occasion the quarrel between Harold and his brother Tostig, in 1064, is placed in the royal hall at *Windleshores*.[†] Edward gave the manor to the Abbot of Westminster, but it was resumed, in exchange for other lands, by William I., who liked the place on account of its proximity to the river and to the great Forest of Windsor, to which he desired to resort for hunting. But he disliked the low and exposed situation of the house, and built for himself a castle on the high ground within the Forest where now stands Windsor Castle: or it may be only appropriated and extended one, which had belonged to Harold there. (*See* WINDSOR.)

The old palace continued to be used as a residence till the castle was com-

pleted — occasionally perhaps till the reign of Henry I. Its site is uncertain, but " a farm, which till recently stood W. of the ch., and near the river, surrounded by a moat," has been pointed out by the local historians as " the probable site " of the Confessor's residence.[*] Moat and mounds are still traceable, and it is quite possible that they may mark the site of the early English palace, which is not likely to have been a very substantial structure, but would no doubt have a moat and some defensive works. The place has no subsequent independent history.

Old Windsor is now a pretty, secluded, scattered and thinly populated place, with the Thames, here very beautiful, on one side of it, and on the other the grand old trees of Windsor Park, and rising high above them the towers of Windsor Castle. On every hand are stately houses and gay villas, with wide and well-planted grounds.

The *Church* (St. Peter) is of the 13th cent., but has been much altered. The original building consisted of a nave and chancel of equal width, and a tower at the W. end. In 1864 it underwent a complete renovation, and partial transformation, at the hands of Sir Gilbert Scott. The tower and original E.E. windows were retained, but all else was altered. A chancel aisle was added on the N., and a new porch on the S. Inside a new solid oak roof was erected; the old pews were removed, and open oak seats substituted, and several of the windows were filled with painted glass, by O'Connor.

There are no monts. calling for notice within the building. In the ch.-yard, *obs.* at the N.E. end, the altar tomb, overhung by a yew-tree and fir, of Mrs. Mary Robinson, d. 1800, æt. 43, the celebrated and unfortunate actress who, as Perdita, in the ' Winter's Tale,' won the heart of the Prince of Wales, afterwards George IV. At the W. end of the ch.-yard a flat cross marks the grave of Charles Brinsley Sheridan, d. 1843, second son of Richard Brinsley Sheridan. On the S. side of the ch.-yard is a very fine yew-tree.

Among the old mansions the most conspicuous was *Beaumont*, on high ground, overlooking the Thames, ¾ m. S. of the village, which was in the last century the

---

* A.-S. Chron., An. 1061; Kemble, Cod. Dip. Ævi Sax., vol. iv., pp. 178, 209, etc.

† Henry of Huntingdon, Hist. Angl., Lib. vi. ; Mon. Hist. Brit., p. 761.

* Tighe and Davis, Annals of Windsor, vol. i., p. 10.

seat of Warren Hastings. It has been remodelled and added to, and is now the Roman Catholic *College of St. Stanislaus*, for young gentlemen.

Other seats are *The Friary* (F. Ricardo, Esq.); *Runnimede House* (Rev. W. Kitching); *The Priory* (G. Romain, Esq.)

In 1865 two Roman tombs were discovered in the course of some drainage operations at a farm called Tyleshod. Both contained charred bones, and in one was found a glass bottle of elegant shape, but broken; in the other a well-shaped cinerary urn 14 inches high.

WOBURN FARM; WOBURN PARK, SURREY (*see* ADDLESTONE).

WOLDINGHAM, SURREY, a settlement of the *Wealdingas* (Kemble), Dom. *Wallingham*, a secluded little village 3 m. N.E. of Godstone, 2 m. E. of the Caterham Rly. Stat. To reach Woldingham from Caterham take the path up the hill, nearly opposite the stat., to *Tillingdown Farm* (which leave on rt.); then cross the bottom (where is the rifle ground—look out for the red flag), and go past the barn, and at the end of the field take the path which *caters* (as they say hereabouts) to the rt., and cross the Deer Park (the N. end of Marden Park—*see* GODSTONE), a wild-looking place, half forest skirt, half common, and very picturesque—through Nether Court Farm Yard, and to the rt. by the *Hop Pole*;—but some of these ways may be stopped; they are stopping many of the field-paths in this neighbourhood just now.

By the Hop Pole are the houses—scarcely a village. The whole parish in 1861 contained only 8 houses and 67 inh., but these had increased in 1871 to 13 houses and 82 inh., so that the population is not stationary; in 1811 there were only 58 inhabitants.

The *Church* (dedication unknown) is ½ a mile S. of the Hop Pole, in a field on the rt. of the road, and far away from any house. When John Evelyn was here, just two centuries ago, with Sir Robert Clayton, then owner of the property, he says, "I earnestly suggested to him the repairing of an old desolate dilapidated Church, standing on the hill above the

house, which I left him in good disposition to do, and endow it better; there not being above foure or five houses in the parish besides that of this prodigious rich scrivener." * But the good disposition went where many other good dispositions of prodigious rich scriveners have gone, and the ch. remained desolate and dilapidated. It was only a room, without tower, bell-cote, or bell, about 30 ft. long and 17 wide, divided by a screen into nave and chancel. At last, about 1830, getting too dilapidated, it was taken down, and the present unsightly structure substituted. It is of flint and brick, a mere oblong room, capable of holding between 30 and 40 people, without ornament outside, except a porch, and inside, without even the screen to mark off a chancel. In the ch.-yard is a grand old yew-tree, and fronting the porch is an ash of great size and still handsome, though it has lost some of its upper limbs.

From the brow of the hill beyond the church—the best point is at the turn of the road, somewhat less than ½ a mile S. of the ch.—is a wide and splendid view over the Weald of Surrey, Kent, and Sussex. The walks from Woldingham, E. along the ridge of the hill, or S. and E. by Oxted and Limpsfield, are very beautiful.

Aubrey records the finding, early in the 17th cent., of a coin of Constantine at Woldingham; and on the Upper Court Lodge Farm, the farm nearest the ch., and of old the manor-house, several iron arrow heads, celts, and two bronze fibulæ were found in the early part of the present century. Other remains have been found in the neighbourhood. A rental of Upper Court Lodge Farm, of 1402, mentions a place there as "quondam Campes," and it again occurs as "Campis" in a survey of 1577. No vestiges of camp or barrow appear to have escaped the plough, but there are two fields on Upper Court Lodge Farm called respectively the "Great" and the "Little Barrow Leys," names which seem to imply the former existence of one or other—perhaps of both.† Barrow Green and Botley Hill—very suggestive names—are not far off.

---

* Evelyn, Diary, 12 Oct., 1677.

† Aubrey, Surrey, vol. iii., p. 6; Manning and Bray, Hist. of Surrey, vol. ii., p. 416; Brayley, Hist. of Surrey, vol. iv., p. 213; Proc. of Soc. of Antiquaries, vol. vi., p. 395.

WOOD GREEN, Middx. (*see* Tottenham).

WOODFORD, Essex (Dom. *Wodeford*), a district of citizens' villas, on the Epping road, 7½ m. from London by road, 8½ m. by the George Lane Stat. (for Church End), 9½ m. by the Woodford Stat. (for Woodford Green and Woodford Bridge), of the Epping and Ongar branch of the Grt. E. Rly. Pop. 4609, of whom 1188 were in the eccl. dist. of St. Paul Woodford Bridge, and 106 in public institutions. Inns: *White Hart, George,* Church End ; *Castle Hotel,* Woodford Green ; *Horse at Well,* Woodford Wells.

Woodford, so named from the ford over the Roding, at what is now known as Woodford Bridge, lay wholly within the Forest of Waltham. It was one of the manors given by Harold to his abbey of Waltham Holy Cross, and amidst all changes was held by the abbey till the Dissolution. Granted to John Lyon in 1546, it was resumed by Edward VI. in exchange for other lands, and given to Edward Lord Clinton and Say, who in 1553 sold it to Robert Whetstone. In 1640 it was alienated to Sir Thomas Roe or Rowe, Queen Elizabeth's celebrated ambassador. On the death of Roe's widow in 1675 it was sold to Sir Benj. Thorowgood, and by his son sold to Sir Richard Child, afterwards Earl Tylney. It is now the property of Earl Cowley. (*See* Wanstead.) Borough English prevails within the manor.

The parish is of great extent. There is no village proper, but instead are four distinct and widely separated clusters of houses — Woodford, or Church End, Woodford Green, Woodford Wells, and Woodford Bridge.

Woodford Church End consists of little more than a dozen commonplace houses by the ch., with a few great houses standing apart in elm-bordered grounds. Many new houses have, however, been built lately within the ch. district, but to the W. of the highroad. The *Church,* St. Mary, is a very poor specimen of the Gothic of 1817. It is of brick covered with stucco, and consists of nave, aisles, and short chancel, S. porch, and tall battlemented W. tower. The interior has galleries and pews, a wretched painted glass E. window, and is nearly as ugly, though not quite as mean, as the exterior. There are several monumental tablets, but none of much interest. Sir Thomas Roe, who has been mentioned as lord of the manor, and who was born in the neighbouring parish of Leyton, was buried in the chancel, Nov. 8, 1644, but has no memorial. At the S.W. corner of the ch.-yard is a conspicuous tall Corinthian column of veined yellow marble, with a disproportioned capital bearing an urn. On the pedestal is a long insc. commemorating " the ancient and knightly family of Godfrey, which flourished many years in the county of Kent," and " of whom the most distinguished character" was Sir Edmund Bury Godfrey, Knt., " descended according to tradition from Godfrey le Fauconer, son of William Fitz Balderic, to whom Henry II. granted the manor of Herst and other lands in Kent ;" but the column is raised to the particular honour of Peter Godfrey, Esq., M.P. for the City of London, d. 1742. Sir Thos. St. George, Principal Garter King of Arms, d. 1703, has a tomb ; the others are mostly to local magnates. S. of the ch. is a yew-tree, the trunk of which is over 14 ft. in girth at 3 ft. from the ground.

Immediately N. of the ch., with a doorway from the grounds into the ch.-yard, is *Woodford Hall,* a large brick mansion standing high, like the ch., in pleasant grounds, and having a cheerful outlook. Of old the seat of Wm. Hickman, Esq., ancestor of the Earl of Plymouth, of Sir N. H. Hickman, and afterwards of the Maitlands, and having grounds of much greater extent, it is now *Mrs. Gladstone's Convalescent Home.* About 80 inmates, chiefly though not exclusively from the East of London, are received from the hospital or sick room ; admission is free ; and the management is praised alike by visitors and inmates. Like most similar institutions, the great difficulty is that of raising sufficient funds. (Office, 30, Clarges Street, W.)

At *Woodford Green,* ½ m. N. of the ch., are the best shops, many of them large and well-stocked, with good plate-glass fronts, ranged about two sides of a very large green ; on the farther side is the Castle Hotel, a large and good house. Bordering the green are several mansions standing within elm-lined grounds. On the N.E. is an early Dec. church, with a tall tower and shingled spire; and the rapid increase of the population is shown by the fact that though the ch. is almost new, it is being enlarged (May 1876) by the addition of a N. aisle. Not far from it is a large and handsome Congregational ch., of stone, E.E. in style, cruciform, with a tower and spire 145 ft. high. The noticeable Byzantine building of coloured bricks, on the opposite side of the Green, is a Methodist Free Church.

Woodford Wells, about ½ a mile N. of Woodford Green, and connected with it by modern cottage and villa residences, owes its name to medicinal springs formerly in repute for many diseases, but which were a century ago already neglected.[*] The hamlet, which has a cheerful, old-fashioned, country aspect, lies at the foot of Buckhurst and Chigwell Hills, and the southern edge of the open part of Epping Forest; and though the wells are neglected, an ornamental drinking fountain, with a tall roof of enamelled tiles, on the Green, by the Horse at the Well inn, serves to recall their memory. At Woodford Wells is the Rescue Society's Home for Girls.

Woodford Bridge, on the Ongar road, 1½ m. E. of Woodford Green, and 2 m. N.E. of Woodford ch., is an outlying hamlet, which was created an eccl. dist. in 1854, and had 1188 inhab. in 1871. The houses line the road up the slope of the hill, N. of the bridge over the Roding, from which the place takes its name. The *Church* (St. Paul) lies off the road, on the rt., by the 9 m.-stone, on the edge of Wilcox Green. It is a plain early Dec. building of stone, erected in 1854, and comprises nave, deep chancel of a lower pitch, and tower and short spire at the N.W. The Woodford Rly. Stat. is midway between Woodford Green and Woodford Bridge.

Hearts, or *Harts*, N. of Woodford Green (J. Spicer, Esq.), is a good old house, built in 1617 by Sir Humphrey Handforth, Master of the Wardrobe to James I. When hunting in the forest, James was on several occasions entertained here by Sir Humphrey. Hearts was afterwards the seat of Foot Onslow,

father of the Speaker. Later it was the seat of Richard Warner, who made the grounds famous by his publication, 'Plantæ Woodfordiensis,' 1771, to which Forster published 'Additions' in 1784. Warner was also distinguished as a Book-collector, for his critical knowledge of Shakspeare, and by translations from Plautus; and did what he could to advance and perpetuate after his death the tastes he cultivated in life, by bequeathing his fine library to Wadham College, Oxford, and a sum of money for founding a botanical lectureship.

Ray House, Snake's Lane, W. of Woodford Bridge (G. T. Benton, Esq.), was the seat of the Clevelands and Hannots, and was purchased in 1770 by Sir James Wright, Bart., Governor of Virginia, and afterwards minister at Venice, who, "at a great expense," established here a manufactory of artificial slates, by a process he had learned at Venice. The slates were light and fireproof, and the manufacture excited much interest, but was commercially unsuccessful, and after several years' perseverance was abandoned.

Grove House, W. of the ch., was another interesting old house. Tradition said it was a hunting lodge of Robert Devereux, Earl of Essex, but there is no other authority for the assertion. It was spacious and some of the rooms were large and curiously fitted. One, known as the ball-room, had on the walls 12 paintings in tempera of landscapes and subjects of rural life—the "water-work" for the walls Falstaff recommends to Mrs. Quickly as a substitute for her tapestry. The house was taken down in 1832, and the site and grounds built over.

Higham Court (F. Puckridge, Esq.) is a large square brick mansion, with wings, built in the last cent. by Anthony Bacon, and sold by him to Governor Hornby. The house stands high, the grounds are extensive and well planted, and the prospects much admired. *Monkhams* (H. F. Barclay, Esq.), on the slope of Buckhurst Hill, is another mansion noted for its site, prospects, and grounds. Other good seats are *Knighton House* (Edw. North Buxton, Esq.); *Claybury Hall*, S. of Woodford Bridge; *Elmshurst* (Harrison Smith, Esq.); *The Manor House*, Woodford Wells (Thos. Read, Esq.); *The Shrubbery* (Barclay Reynolds, Esq.)

[*] Morant, Hist. of Essex, 1768, vol. i., p. 39.

Among the eminent inhabitants of Woodford, Holy George Herbert is assigned a prominent place; but he was a visitor rather than inhabitant :—

"About the year 1629, and the 34th of his age, Mr. Herbert was seized with a sharp quotidian ague, and thought to remove it by a change of air; to which end he went to Woodford in Essex, led out thither more chiefly to enjoy the company of his beloved brother, Sir Henry Herbert, and other friends then of that family. In his house he remained about twelve months and there became his own physician." *

William Master, rector of Woodford 1660-84, was author of 'Drops of Myrrhe,' and of a volume of Moral and Theological essays. Nicholas Lockyer, who succeeded Rous as Provost of Eton, and was ejected at the Restoration for nonconformity, spent his last years at Woodford, where he died in 1685. James Greenwood, author of a collection of poems entitled 'The Virgin Muse,' and of other works, was a schoolmaster at Woodford. The Rev. Thomas Maurice, the learned author of 'Indian Antiquities,' translator of the 'Œdipus Tyrannus,' and assistant librarian at the British Museum, was for several years curate of Woodford. The Rev. Sydney Smith was born at Woodford in 1771.

WOODMANSTERNE, SURREY,

(Dom. *Odemerestor;* anc. *Wodemere-thorne, Wodemerston,* and *Woodmanston,*) a secluded little village on the Surrey Downs, 1½ m. E. from Banstead vill., and 2½ m. E. from the Banstead Stat. of the Epsom Downs branch of the L., Br., and S. C. Rly., 16 m. from London by road. Pop. 276.

The little village is on the highest part of the Banstead Downs. Local authorities say that the floor of the Rectory is on a level with the cross of St. Paul's. The Downs are delightful—whether for a stroll or a gallop—and afford views of great extent and some variety. The vill. lies quite away from any main road. The occupations are agricultural and pastoral. The *Church* (St. Peter) is small, plain, and unassuming. Old, but much altered, and the exterior covered with plaster, and splashed to imitate granite, it hardly looked the model village ch., but within the last few years it has been repaired

and somewhat improved in appearance. It comprises nave and chancel, with wooden bell-cote and short shingled spire. The interior is neat, has open benches, and the Perp. windows have painted glass —some of it old.

Among the seats, one is a house of fame —*The Oaks,* which gave its name to the Ladies' Stakes at Epsom. The house was originally built as a club and meeting-house during the hunting season by "the Hunters' Club." It was afterwards occupied by Sir Thomas Gosling, the banker, and then by Lieut.-General Burgoyne, who enlarged the house, improved the grounds, and built a dining hall that excited much admiration. Burgoyne transferred the lease to his father-in-law, Edward, 11th Earl of Derby, whose parties made the house famous. Of these the most celebrated was the *Fête Champêtre* —the first in England under that name— given in June 1774, in honour of the approaching nuptials of Lord Stanley, grandson of the Earl, with the only daughter of the Duke of Hamilton and Brandon.

"The Duke of Devonshire and Georgiana Spencer were married on Sunday: and this month Lord Stanley marries Lady Betty Hamilton. He gives her a most splendid entertainment to-morrow at his villa [The Oaks] in Surrey, and calls it a *Fête champêtre.* It will cost £5000. Everybody is to go in masquerade but not in mask. He has bought all the orange-trees round London, and the haycocks, I suppose, are to be made of straw-coloured satin." *

The fête was very splendid and very successful. A large proportion of the fashionable world was there. Besides the minuets and country dances of the visitors, a corps of ballet dancers was brought down from the Opera House with the ballet master as director; and General Burgoyne wrote for the occasion a Sylvan Masque, in honour of the bride-elect, entitled, 'The Maid of the Oaks.' The rooms were splendidly illuminated, and the trees in the grounds and gardens hung with festoons of flowers, and myriads of coloured lamps, some thousands of persons being admitted as spectators of the festival. Nor was the public curiosity sated with the display. Garrick reproduced General Burgoyne's masque as an operatic drama at Drury Lane, with a

---

* Isaac Walton, Life of George Herbert.

* H. Walpole to Sir Horace Mann, June 8, 1774; Letters, vol. vi., p. 88.

brilliant representation of the scene at
The Oaks, and the piece had a great
run ; the 'Gentleman's Magazine' gave an
elaborate account of the proceedings, and
large and costly engravings were published
by Grignion and Caldwell of the interiors
of the ball and supper rooms. But
the ending was hardly so happy. The
Maid of the Oaks died on the 14th of
March, 1797, and the Earl of Derby
married, as his second wife, Miss Farren,
the actress, on the following 1st of May.

The Earl of Derby continued The Oaks
as a sporting seat; kept there a pack of
stag-hounds ; and maintained great hospitality, holding more than 50 bed-chambers at the service of his guests.

"*May 27th*, 1833.—I went to the Oaks on Wednesday, where Lord Derby kept house, for the first
and probably (as the house is for sale) for the last
time. It is a very agreeable place, with an odd
sort of house built at different times and by different people ; but the outside is covered with ivy
and creepers, which is pretty, and there are two
good living rooms in it. Besides this there is an
abundance of grass and shade ; it has been for
thirty or forty years the resort of all our old jockeys
and is now occupied by the sporting portion of the
Government. We had Lord Grey and his daughter,
Duke and Duchess of Richmond, Lord and Lady
Errol, Althorp, Graham, Uxbridge, Charles Grey,
Duke of Grafton, Lichfield and Stanley's brothers.
It passed off very well—racing all the morning, an
excellent dinner, and whist and blind hookey in
the evening." *

The Earl of Derby died Oct. 21, 1834,
and the estate was transferred to Sir
Charles Grey. In 1842 it was sold to
Joseph Smith and John Jones, Esq.,
brothers-in-law, who made it their joint
residence. It is now the property of
Joseph Smith, Esq., lord of the manor of
Woodmansterne, but is at present (May
1876) advertised for sale.

The name of The Oaks is said to have
been taken from a grove of ancient oaks
called *Lambert's Oaks*, after the Lambert
family who owned the estate. The Lam-
berts were said to have lived and held property in Woodmansterne "in regular
descent ever since the Conquest." Mrs.
Lambert, the last of the name, resided in
the house by the ch. within the last 20
years.

Other good seats are—the *Manor House*
(H. A. Wedd, Esq.), a quaint old mansion
by the church ; *Court Hawe* (Mrs. Mildred) ; *Stagbury* (Rev. T. Walpole) ; and
Fairlawn House (Fredk. Chapman, Esq.)

* Greville' Journal, vol. ii., p. 374.

WOOLWICH, KENT, (A.-S.
Wulewic, Dom. *Hulviz**), a garrison town,
the seat of the Royal Arsenal, and a
member of the Parliamentary borough of
Greenwich, is situated on the rt. bank of
the Thames, 8 m. from London by road,
10 m. by water. The Mid-Kent line of
the S.-E. Rly. has Stats. at the Dockyard
and Arsenal. The Grt. E., N. London,
and L. and N.-W. Rlys. run trains to
North Woolwich, and thence steam-ferries
to Woolwich Pier ; and steamboats run
regularly through the day from the Westminster and City piers to Woolwich. Pop.
of the Parl. borough 34,162 ; of the parish
35,557, of whom 4110 were military. Inns,
Crown and Anchor, High Street ; *Royal
Mortar*, by the Arsenal gates, Beresford Square ; *King's Arms*, near the
Barracks ; *Cambridge*, by the Dockyard
Station.

Nearly half the area of Woolwich par.
is on the Essex side of the Thames, con-
stituting what is now the eccl. dist. of
NORTH WOOLWICH ; whence arose the
local proverb or witticism, " More wealth
passes through Woolwich than any other
town (or parish) in the world," referring
to the ships that sail along the Thames
between the two halves of the par.
Woolwich is commonly spoken of as
having been at no very remote period
merely "a small fishing village," but from
an early date Woolwich had a weekly
market, which by an Act of 1807 was
made to be held twice a week, Wednesdays
and Saturdays. Apart from the Dockyard
and Arsenal, the history of the town is a
blank. The parish is held to be within
the royal manor of Eltham, but the sub-
manor of Southall in Woolwich was early

* Mr. Taylor (Words and Places, p. 164), assign-
ing the name to the Danes, explains it—" Woolwich, *the hill reach*, so called apparently from its
being overhung by the conspicuous landmark of
Shooter's Hill." This may be correct, but when he
adds in a note, "The etymology is confirmed by
the fact that Woolwich is written *Hulviz* in Domesday," we feel that he is on unsafe ground. A
comparison of the names in Domesday with the
earlier A.-S. forms shows that in a large number
of instances the Domesday spelling—at first sight
often very startling—is merely the attempt of a
Norman clerk to represent the, to him, strange
English pronunciation. The English called Woolwich, *Wulewic* (which we are afraid will not help
Mr. Taylor's etymology); this the Norman scribe represented by *Hulviz*, just as in the 17th cent. we
find a French ambassador writing *Oulmulton* for
Wimbledon (see p. 701).

alienated, and has passed through a great number of undistinguished hands.

The Town owes its growth and importance to the foundation and progress of the Royal Dockyard and Arsenal. Apart from these, it is singularly uninteresting. It extends for over two miles along the Thames, but for nearly all the way the Dockyard and Arsenal are between it and the river, and where they are not the streets are low, narrow, and dirty. The High Street, and the streets which diverge from it, are alike narrow, irregular, and lined with mean brick dwellings and small shabby shops. Larger shops are intermingled with the small ones, but hardly in sufficient numbers or close enough together to relieve the dull monotony. The public buildings are few and mean; the churches poor; there are literary and other institutes, but they occupy inconspicuous buildings; the banks make no show; the theatre looks dirty and degraded; and though there are many inns and some hotels, none are even moderately good. Outside the town there are, however, good houses, and about Woolwich Common some noteworthy buildings. Two newspapers are published weekly. The Town Hall and Police Court stand together in Wellington Street. The open Market-place is in the High Street.

The parish *Church* (St. Mary Magdalen) stands on Church Hill, the highest ground by the river, midway between the Arsenal and Dockyard, and is conspicuous from the river as well as from many parts of the town. It is of brick, quite devoid of ornament or distinctive feature, except the ugly square W. tower. It was built in 1733-40, as one of the fifty new churches erected in pursuance of the Act 9 and 10 of Queen Anne: the old ch. stood a few yards N. of the present building. It has nave, aisles, and chancel; the interior "is fitted up in the Grecian style," with galleries supported on pillars of the Ionic order. There are no monts. of interest. In the northern part of the ch.-yard lies Andrew Schalch, from 1716 to his death in 1776 director of the gun foundry, whose name is intimately associated with the early history of the Royal Arsenal; and near him is buried Henry Maudslay, d. 1831, the engineer, who was a native of Woolwich, and began life as a powder boy in the Arsenal. The most conspicuous

mont. in the ch. part of the burial-ground (E. of the ch.)—marked by a colossal lion resting his fore-paw on an urn—is that of Thomas Cribb, b. 1781, d. May 8, 1848. This was the "Tom Cribb, the champion" of the pugilistic ring. "A great man," as Byron wrote of him, "and converses well . . . very facetious though somewhat prolix."[*] He began life as a coal-heaver, was a sailor and in actions at sea, turned pugilist and publican, and I fear, adds Byron, sinner, and died at Woolwich, "the respectable and respected" proprietor of a baker's shop in the High Street.

Holy Trinity Church, Beresford Street, by the entrance gates of the Royal Arsenal, is a bald semi-classic white brick building, with Ionic portico, erected about 1834. It serves as a chapel-of-ease to the mother ch. St. John's, Wellington Street, is a district ch., E.E. of the year 1847. St. Thomas, Maryon Road, New Charlton, is also a district ch.; and of a better type of Gothic. There are besides St. George's, Garrison ch., Woolwich Common, to be further noticed presently; the Dockyard ch., built by Sir Gilbert Scott in 1859 —the best Gothic building in the town; and the Arsenal and the Ordnance chapels. Denominational places of worship are very numerous, but they are almost without exception devoid of architectural character or historical interest.

The *Royal Dockyard*, extending along the Thames for about a mile on the W. side of Woolwich, like that at Deptford (*see* p. 141), was founded early in the reign of Henry VIII. There has been some question as to which was the first dockyard and naval station, but they were called into existence by the same circumstances, and seem to have been as nearly contemporaneous in their beginning as they were in their close. It is certain, however, that the great 'Harry-grace-a-Dieu,' which has been assigned both to Erith and Deptford, was really built at Woolwich, payments for "shippwrights, and other officers working upon the Kinges great shippe called the Harry-grace-a-Dieu at Wolwiche," and for the materials used in its construction, being regularly entered, from the 4th December, 1512, in a book kept for the purpose, and now deposited in the Record Office. The

---

[*] Moore, Life of Byron, vol. ii., p. 277.

" summa totalis of this Boke " amounts to £6472 8s. 0¾d., but timber is not charged for, that being supplied by various monasteries and other corporate bodies, and noblemen and bishops, whose names, with the particulars of their several gifts, are duly specified. The King often visited the ship whilst it was building, and John Wodowse, "steward in the Henry-grace-a-Dieu" is paid 16d. for "creme by him purveied at sundry tymes for the Kinges grace " when he came to Woolwich. The great ship was launched in Oct. 1515, in presence of the King and Queen, and "well nigh all the lords and prelates of the kingdom, and all dined on board at the Kinges charge." The Great Harry, as she was called, was of 1500 tons burden, and when launched it took 400 men 4 days to work her to Barking. Before the launch took place we find (April 1515) entries of charges for bringing the Sovereign "from Erith to Woolwich and so into her Dock," and in 1521 it is reported that "the Sovereign, being of the portage of 800 tons, lyeth in a Dock at Woolwich." Clearly, therefore, Woolwich was by this time established as a naval dockyard as well as a building-yard. The progress of the royal yard was probably slow, but in 1546 the King purchased of Sir Edward Boughton two parcels of land called Boughton's Docks, and two other parcels called Our Lady Hill and Sand Hill, for its extension. Queen Elizabeth witnessed, May 3rd, 1559, the launch of a great ship which had been built at Woolwich, and to which she gave her name. The Royal Sovereign, a splendidly decorated vessel of 1637 tons, and pierced for 116 guns, which distinguished itself so much under the Parliamentary captains as to win from the Dutch the name of 'The Golden Devil,' was built here in the reign of Charles I., and launched Oct. 7, 1637.

In Charles II.'s time there was a great deal of work done at Woolwich Dockyard, which included also a Victualling and Rope-yard. Pepys as Clerk of the Acts of the Navy, with the regulation of the Dockyards devolving upon him, was often at Woolwich, examining the houses, stores, and ships, and doing there "a great deal of business," though he at first found the stores "in very great confusion for want of store-houses."

The Rope-yard greatly interested him, and appears to have been even then of considerable extent. He looked carefully into the various processes, and the modes of "working and experiments of the strength, and the charge in the dressing of every sort," which he was able to bring "to so great a certainty" as to "have done the King some service in it," but comes to the sorrowful conclusion—"I see it is impossible for the King to have things done so cheap as other men"—very much as dockyard experience in our own day teaches.

When the Dutch threatened the Thames, 9 large ships with their loads on board were hurriedly sunk "in the river off Woolwich to prevent their coming up higher if they should attempt it," and batteries were thrown up, "which, indeed, are good works to command the River below the ships that are sunk, but not above them. It is a sad sight to see so many good ships there sunk in the River, while we would be thought masters of the sea." *

Prince Rupert was placed in command at Woolwich, and constructed a battery of 60 guns. The passage in the rear of it, where is now the Control Wharf, was long known as Prince Rupert's Walk. The Prince was probably much at Woolwich, and the building on the W. side of the Arsenal, now used as the Laboratory Museum, is said to have been erected by him, and used as his residence. It is more probable that it was built for the use of Charles II. and the Duke of York on their frequent visits to the Dockyard. By it was a lofty tower or observatory, known as Prince Rupert's Tower, demolished in 1786.

Great additions were made to the works in the latter part of the 18th cent., and new building slips, docks, and mast ponds were constructed. But the protraction of hostilities created an ever-growing demand for ships of war and warlike stores, and Woolwich Dockyard was in the early part of the 19th cent. again greatly enlarged and improved. The skill of the Rennies (father and sons) was called into requisition; new granite wharfs and docks, and immense ranges of workshops and warehouses, were constructed, and the dockyard

* Pepys, Diary, vol. iv., p. 87.

became one of the most extensive and complete in existence. Then came steam and iron, and the docks and workshops were again remodelled under Sir John Rennie, a great steam reserve basin, two building slips for first-rates, mast slip, and river wall were constructed at a cost of £300,000, and powerful machinery erected. Woolwich Dockyard was as much a model establishment for building and fitting the giant iron war-steamer as it had been for the wooden first-rate. It could not, however, keep pace with the growth of the armour-clad ships. Vessels of such enormous tonnage could not, without increasing risk and difficulty, be launched in so shallow and crowded a river, and economy and convenience alike pointed to the importance of concentrating as much as possible our great naval yards. A Parliamentary Committee (1864) recommended that the dockyards at Deptford and Woolwich should be closed. Their recommendation was adopted, and, the works on hand being completed, Deptford was closed as a dockyard in May 1869, and Woolwich on the 17th of Sept., 1869. A small portion of the yard has been sold; the rest has been transferred to the War Department of the Government, and is used for stores,—building slips, basins, and factories, as well as warehouses being adapted to the purpose. The torpedo stores, including the multiform cases, insulating wire, and all the varied apparatus, are now deposited here. Occasionally a dock is lent for the repair or temporary housing of a vessel, where private yards are not available, as in the case of the Brazilian war-steamer injured in the unsuccessful attempt to launch, and a recently launched Turkish man-of-war.

The ROYAL ARSENAL stretches for a mile along the Thames E. of the Dockyard. It is the only arsenal in the kingdom; the smaller establishments at the other dockyards are called *gun-wharfs*, and receive their supplies from Woolwich. To see the Arsenal is usually the chief object of a visit to Woolwich, and few establishments are better worth a visit. *It is necessary*, however, *that an order be first obtained from the War Office, Pall Mall. On either the written or personal application of a British subject* (a foreigner must apply through the consul or representative of his country), *a card will be given for*

admission any Tuesday or Thursday within 14 days from the day of issue. The hours of admission are from 10 till ½-past 11 in the forenoon, and from 2 till ½-past 4 in the afternoon: but the visitor who may find the morning hours too short—as he assuredly will if he makes even a cursory examination of the principal works—may, by mentioning his intention when he gives up his card on leaving the Arsenal, return at 2 o'clock, and continue his studies till ½-past 4 or 5. And this he will find his best course. A day industriously employed will be only too short for an intelligent examination of the marvels of the Arsenal. There is no official guide to the Arsenal; the best substitute is Mr. W. T. Vincent's 'Warlike Woolwich: a History and Guide,' 1875.

Until questioned recently by Lieut. Grover,[*] a somewhat romantic legend was generally accepted as to the foundation of the Royal Arsenal at Woolwich. On the 10th of May, 1716, there was to be a great casting of cannon at Mr. Bagley's foundry, Moorfields, the Master-General of the Ordnance having directed that the cannon taken by the Duke of Marlborough should be recast. The principal officers of the Ordnance and a numerous assembly were present. Among the visitors was a young German, Andrew Schalch, of Schaffhausen, a journeyman founder, travelling according to the custom of his country prior to working as master. Schalch, observing that the inside of the mould was damp, called the attention of Col. Armstrong, the Surveyor-General, to it, and warned him that if the metal were poured into it while in that state an explosion would inevitably occur. No notice was taken of the warning; Schalch withdrew; and the explosion happened as he had predicted. The master-founder and his son, the Clerk of the Ordnance, and 14 other persons were killed, or so much burnt that they died shortly afterwards. General Borgard was among the injured, but recovered. Inquiry was made for the young German, but he could not be found. Advertisements were then issued requesting the "young foreigner" to call on Col. Armstrong, "as the interview might be for his

[*] Historical Notes on the Royal Arsenal at Woolwich. By Lieut. G. E. Grover, R.E. (Proc. of R.A. Institution), 1869.

advantage." He did call; inquiries respecting his capacity and character were satisfactory; he was appointed. master founder, and directed to choose a spot within 12 miles of London suitable for a new foundry and gun factory. He selected the Warren at Woolwich, on account of the abundance of loam in the neighbourhood suitable for making the moulds, and its proximity to the river affording facilities for transport. The selection was approved. Vanbrugh designed the foundry, and the works were speedily brought into operation. This, it is added, was the origin of the Royal Arsenal.

It is a pretty story, but it is not true. The explosion undoubtedly happened as stated, but neither in General Borgard's account of the accident, the official minute book, or the notices in the newspapers, does Schalch's name occur in connection with it; nor has the most diligent search brought to light the advertisement so specifically described. The earliest version of the story that has been discovered in which Schalch plays any part was printed in 1802.

In fact the Arsenal, though under another name, was in existence long before the explosion at Moorfields. Lysons, writing from official information, says "the Gun-Wharf at Woolwich is of very ancient date; it formerly occupied what is now the site of the market-place. When removed to the Warren, where it now is, it was for some time called by that name, but is now called the Arsenal, or Royal Arsenal." Its name in the 17th cent. was the Tower Place. Between 1668 and 1695 the guns and artillery stores were removed to it from Deptford and the Tower of London; a laboratory and workshops were erected; and proofing parapets and butts for artillery practice formed. A plan of the Royal Warren, made by General Borgard in 1701, and now in the Royal Military Repository, shows laboratory, powder house, "firework barne," carriage yards, shot yards, shot piles, gun and mortar "for experiments," proof parapets and butts, master-gunner's and storekeeper's houses, smiths' shops, and the various other requisites of an arsenal. The gun-foundry was established at Woolwich after the Moorfield's explosion, but it was in consequence of "the most experienced

officers" being of opinion that "the Government ought to have a foundry of their own," and the Tower Place, Woolwich. was fixed on because of the vicinity of the gun-wharf and proofing butts.

The site having been chosen, and the gun-foundry commenced, an advertisement was inserted in the 'London Gazette' of July 10, 1716, notifying that "all founders as are desirous to cast Brass Ordnance are to give in their proposals forthwith," etc. To this advertisement Schalch replied, his testimonials and references proved satisfactory, and he was appointed master-founder at a salary of £5 a week. This post he held for 60 years; he died at Charlton in 1776, æt. 84, and was buried, as we have seen, in Woolwich ch.-yard.

It is unnecessary to follow the progress of the Arsenal. During the French wars of the last and the first 15 years of the present century, it grew to be a place of great extent and importance; but the tools and processes were comparatively primitive, and it is only since the introduction of machinery that any great advance has been made. Indeed the most remarkable development has taken place within the last 25 years, and has been a consequence of the rapid improvement in artillery and the materials of war, and in armour plates and the means of defence.

Without including the powder magazines in Woolwich Marshes, the Arsenal as now constituted occupies an area of 333 acres, about half of which is in Plumstead parish. Within the Arsenal are made the heavy artillery for our land and sea service, the carriages on which they are borne, the shot, shell, and cartridges with which they are fed, the ammunition for our small arms, the torpedoes that are to protect our coasts, and whatever, in fact, is included under the name of material of war. It is also the great repository and storehouse, as well as manufactory, of guns and warlike materials. Usually about 10,000 workpeople are employed in the Arsenal, but in "busy times," as during the Crimean war, the number reaches 14,000.

As now arranged, the Royal Arsenal comprises four departments: the *Laboratory*; the *Gun Factories*; the *Carriage*

Department; the Stores, or Control Department. These we proceed to notice, of necessity briefly, but sufficiently to indicate their extent and distinctive features. The buildings, erected at different times for manufacturing and warehousing purposes, make no pretensiod to architectural style or symmetry, but without any very scientific grouping, appear to have arranged themselves in a tolerably convenient manner. Broadly it may be said that the Laboratory occupies the W. side of the Arsenal, the Gun Factories the E., the Carriage Department the S., and the Store or Control Department the N., whilst there is some intermingling of the first three in the centre : one great section of the Laboratory Department, the *Composition Establishment*, where the explosive compositions are prepared, and caps, shells, and cartridges filled, is placed altogether apart from and E. of the Arsenal proper, with which we are at present concerned. A *Narrow-guage Tramway* traverses every part of the Arsenal, and is carried to the Cannon Cartridge Factory and Powder Magazines far away in the Marshes. It has a gauge of only 18 inches, and the little locomotive, with its goods trucks or passenger cars, turns the sharpest curve easily, safely, and silently. The whole is formed of solid slabs of wrought iron, with grooves for the wheels of the engine and carriages to run in. Projecting rails would have been not only inconvenient but dangerous in the level ways of an establishment like the Arsenal. The grooves offer no impediment, and they are equally available for hand and horse trucks. The saving of labour effected by the tramway is enormous. It is said to have repaid the cost of construction and material in a year. It was wholly made within the Arsenal.

The *Laboratory*, which lies before you to the l. after passing through the entrance gates, may be conveniently visited first. To reach it you pass the old Brass Gun Foundry, Vanbrugh's original building, but of course much altered. Brass guns are no longer made, but the old foundry, with its odd cannon-shaped chimneys and great furnace, is preserved as a relic. The Laboratory Workshop is generally visited first, but it is better to begin with the *Laboratory Pattern Room*, or *Museum*, which contains patterns, duplicates, or models of all the objects made by the department. Here are the old bar and chain shot, grape shot, and shells of obsolete patterns side by side with the formidable Palliser shot and shell, broken, to show the remarkable alteration which the metal undergoes in the process of chilling, and the destructive shrapnel, the construction of which is made clear by sections. Cartridges and fuzes whole and in section, and not least noticeable the great sack-like cartridges, nearly 4 ft. high and 250 lb. weight, that feed the monster 81-ton gun. The 'grains' of powder in these are cubes of 1·5, 1·7, or 2 inch s each, about the bulk of a moderate potato. A great variety of torpedoes, with buoys and connected apparatus. Models of rockets and rocket-apparatus, alike for saving and destroying life. The very curious Boxer parachute light shell, a section of which exhibits the ingenious way in which the parachute is packed into the upper half of a spherical shell, while the light-giving composition fills the lower. When discharged, the time-fuze ignites the composition ; this causes the outer halves of the shell to fall away; the parachute expands, and the apparatus floats in the air, casting a brilliant light over the enemy's quarters. An example of the shell in this state, with the parachute fully expanded, is suspended from the ceiling. The Gatling, an improved mitrailleuse of great power, adapted by the military authorities for special service, will be observed with interest. There is besides a great number and variety of modern as well as obsolete warlike appliances, and descriptive labels enable even the uninitiated civilian to appreciate their peculiarities.

The *Laboratory Workshop*, or *Main Factory*, is, however, the chief attraction in this department. It is situated between the Brass Gun Factory and the Pattern Museum, and is said to be the largest workshop under one roof in existence. It will at once remind the visitor of the great 'Action Room' at the Enfield Small Arms Factory (*see* p. 183), but is larger, though, as it seemed to us, not so wide as that remarkable room. It is hard to say in which the extent, complexity, and ingenuity of the machines, and the orderly working of the whole, are the more admirable. Here there are said to be over

500 machines of various kinds in operation, most of them to a great extent automatic, motion being given to them by some 4000 feet of revolving shafts overhead.

The Martini-Henry bullet is made in this shop at the rate of a million a week, but the machines are capable of turning out thrice that number. After leaving the furnace, the molten metal, a mixture of lead and tin, is driven by hydraulic pressure through an aperture in the top of the *lead-squirting machine*, and issues in the form of an endless rod the thickness of the bullet. This is coiled as it issues, and conveyed to the *bullet machine*, which cuts off a piece of the proper length, compresses one end into a cone and hollows the other, and drops it into a box below a perfectly formed bullet. A second machine. of like simplicity and rapidity of action, makes the grooves, or cannelures, round the bullet, and completes it. The various solid parts of rockets, fuzes, discs for cartridges, and many other articles, are wrought here by the aid of machines of more or less ingenuity and beauty; and as all the parts of every instrument are interchangeable, all have to undergo a system of gauging which, however various, is in every instance simple and rapid in application, and as interesting to watch as the motions of the machines.

Close by is the *Cap Factory*, where percussion caps required for the cartridges are made with marvellous celerity. Ribbons of copper pass swiftly through a machine which at one blow punches out circular discs, and shapes them into straight-sided caps, the ribbon emerging in the semblance of a Jacquard card, the caps falling into a box below. Each machine produces 30,000 caps an hour. At other machines boys feed with both hands these caps, the closed end downwards, into suitable receptacles, a punch descends upon them, forms the projecting lip, and delivers them as finished caps: with a nimble-fingered feeder, each machine completes 60,000 caps a day. Paper discs for the cartridges are made by machines like those which make the metal discs. Other machines make the plugs of compressed clay now fitted to the base of the bullets. Others, again, make the anvils and cups which fit into the caps.

The finished caps must be *exactly* of the same size, and are rapidly gauged. The gauger has a brass plate pierced with 1000 holes of the right size ; this he drives into a box of caps, and with a turn of the wrist, the holes are at once filled, and all with caps of the right calibre. The plate is turned to the light, and any defective cap instantly detected ; and thus, in a hardly appreciable space of time, 1000 caps are gauged and counted.

The *Rifle Shot and Shell Factory* belongs to this department, though situated some distance E. of the other laboratory buildings. It is a large and rather ornamental structure, and will be distinguished by the great chimney-shaft of its furnaces, which rises 220 ft. high in the rear of the main building. Here, whilst the furnaces, and the easy nonchalant way in which the molten iron is carried about in buckets, will most astonish those unaccustomed to visit great foundries, the feature of greatest interest is the casting of the Palliser shells. These shells are intended to pierce the thickest armour plates ; the point therefore has to be of the intensest hardness, the body at once hard and brittle, so that after piercing the plate it may break up into a shower of fragments. To attain this double quality the point of the mould is an "iron chill," the body of sand, the object being that the point shall cool rapidly, the body more slowly. The moulds are arranged vertically in circles ; by means of a crane and cradle the molten iron is poured in ; the holes for the studs are made by a special mechanism ; and after standing till the metal is set, the moulds are carried to the cooling ground, and buried for two days to ensure the gradual cooling necessary to the perfection of the implement. The shells being now too hard to be smoothed or brought to gauge by even the most powerful lathes, grindstones of enormous size, and of course worked by steam, are employed. Other machines test them ; steam them preparatory to japanning the insides ; drive in and trim the bronze studs which fit into the rifle grooves of the great guns, and do apparently all that is necessary to prepare the shells to receive their deadly charge.

The *Saw Mills*, with their wonderful array of circular, vertical. and horizontal saws ; and the Carpenters' shop, with its planing and dovetailing machines ; the Coopers' Shop and the Tinmans', however interesting to the mechanic, will probably be passed over by the visitor. One shop just by (Shed 45) he would probably like to look into, when told that there the Whitehead fish, or some other mysterious torpedo, is in process of incubation : but the door is hermetically closed against a stranger ; the most he can hope for is to be in the way at the right moment to catch a glimpse of the monster as emerging from his lurking-place, he makes his hasty way (by rail) to his "run" in the marshes.

The *Gun Factories* are usually the first places to which an Emperor of Germany or Russia, a Shah of Persia, or other mighty potentate is conducted when he visits Woolwich. In them are carried out all the processes of making our field and naval artillery, from the light mountain gun, 200 lb. in weight, to the giant of 81 tons. The guns on which attention is at present most fixed are those known emphatically as *the Woolwich Guns*, the 38-ton gun, the favourite for general service, which, with a charge of 130 lb., will discharge a Palliser shell of 800 lb. with an "initial velocity" of 1425 ft. per second, or a force sufficient to carry it through an armour plate 14 inches thick, with all its wood and iron backing ; and the 81-ton gun, which, with a charge of 300 lb., will send a shot of 1460 lb. with an initial velocity of 1540 ft. per second ; and when enlarged, as it is to be, to a calibre of 16 inches, will with the full charge send a projectile of 1650 lb. at a muzzle velocity of 1470 ft., sufficient to pierce, at 1000 yards' distance, armour-plated vessels of 22 inches thickness. The 81-ton gun is 26 ft. 9 in. long, has a calibre of 15 inches (to be increased to 16 inches); takes a charge of 310 lb. of gunpowder; and throws a shot of 1466 lb. (to be increased eventually to 1650 lb.)

The Woolwich Gun consists of a tube of toughened steel ending in a massive solid iron breech-piece, surrounded by two or more coils of wrought iron, and a jacket-piece which encloses the breech end of the tube, and carries the trunnions. The cost of the Woolwich Gun is about £70 a ton ; the 81-ton gun is at present exceptional.

Visitors are usually taken first to the

Coiling Mills, and the coil is so distinctive and essential a feature of the Woolwich Gun, that it is well to begin with it. A furnace, 200 or 250 ft. long, extends the whole length of the shop. In this a bar of iron of the requisite length and thickness (150 to 250 ft. long, 4 in. or 7 in. thick) is heated to a white heat; the end is then fastened to a catch on the side of a huge mandril which revolves in front of the furnace door, and the bar winds round it without hitch or hindrance till the whole lies coiled round the core like a colossal armlet. Rolling and welding the iron into these monster bars, preparatory to the coiling, may be seen in other shops, and are interesting as showing how entirely these great masses of molten and red-hot metal are under control, and the certainty and order with which the successive operations are conducted. By the coiling furnace is a huge pair of shears, which clips off a piece of the 7-inch bar as glibly and noiselessly as a tailor's shears cuts through a piece of cloth.

Following the great coil, the next stage brings us to the *Great Furnace* and the *Forty-Ton Hammer*. These are in a large building of corrugated iron, the hammer being near the centre, the furnaces near the ends. The great furnace, as big as a moderate-sized dwelling-house, has a doorway through which an omnibus might be driven. The door, of fire-bricks in an iron frame, weighs 7 tons, but slides open—it is lifted by steam and hydraulic pressure —seemingly with as much ease as an ordinary door, or, what it more resembles, an iron shutter. In order to bring the coil to welding heat, it remains in the furnace, heated many times more than Nebuchadnezzar's, from one to three days, the "jacket-piece" which carries the trunnions requiring an exposure of 60 hours.

Let us turn now to the Forty-Ton Hammer. The name is given to it because the hammer, or falling portion, weighs within a few pounds of 40 tons ; but that as little represents the force of the blow as the weight of an ordinary hammer would the force of a blow from it when wielded by a stalwart smith. The actual or "striking fall" of the great hammer is 15 ft. ; but by the injection of steam into the cylinder above, it is driven down with immensely increased force, the impact being then equal to what it would be if the hammer fell of itself from a height of 80 ft. To sustain this ponderous mass aloft, with all the connected apparatus, requires an enormous framework. This takes the form of two immense iron piers, which at about 10 ft. from the ground bend over to form an imperfect arch, open in the centre for the rise and fall of the hammer, and bearing the open turret-like frame and apparatus. The whole height is 45 ft.; the base covers an area of 120 ft. square; and the entire structure weighs 550 tons. But to support this structure, the anvil, and the tremendous thumps of the great hammer, requires a still bulkier mass below, and foundations of unusual magnitude. An area 30 ft. square was obtained by driving 100 foot-square piles 18 ft. into the ground, at a depth of 15 ft. from the surface. Concrete was poured all round them, making a solid bed 42 ft. square. Upon the piles were placed three cast-iron plates, weighing together 115 tons; upon these planks of rock elm, then oak baulks, again plates of cast iron, and so by stages—liquid grouting being poured between plates and timber, and concrete all around—it was built up to receive the anvil-block, an enormous mass which weighs 103 tons, and when cast took six months to cool. The anvil itself, which rests on this block, weighs 60 tons. The entire weight of iron in the underground foundation is about 660 tons. The hammer was manufactured by Messrs. Nasmyth, the patentees, and cost altogether about £50,000. On either side of it is a correspondingly Titanic steam crane, worked by friction gearing throughout, which can lift 100 tons, and slew round with it with perfect ease.

When the coil is sufficiently heated, an enormous pair of tongs—they weigh some 50 or 60 tons, and take several men to manœuvre—is, with the aid of the ever-ready crane overhead, brought in front of the furnace. The door moves slowly up, and the interior of the furnace stands revealed in all its terrible majesty. An Oriental prince to whom it was lately shown, said, " It is the very gate of Hell;" and the spectacle is indeed awe-inspiring. But the workmen move about unconcernedly, regardless of the sight, and not mastered by the heat, which at their distance would seem to be unbearable. The tongs are thrust into the midst of the fire,

the arms opened and brought together; there is a backward movement; from the centre streams out a fiercer and more vivid glare, at first utterly intolerable to the eye, but presently allowing you to see the giant coil, an intense, glowing, upright mass, slowly gliding forth from the midst of the burning fiery furnace, and then gently guided to its place on the anvil. After two or three partial movements, like the preliminary swayings of a' smith, the hammer slowly descends, and the coil settles into form. The hammer is raised, driven down, again and again, with increasing impetus. the vast coil visibly shrinking, and sending forth showers of sparks and flame, at every blow. When the process has been carried far enough, the tongs again clip hold of it, now a red-hot cylinder rather than a coil, lift it tenderly on to three blocks, give it a slight trip, and lay it at length on its back, as readily and softly as a Westmoreland wrestler does his rival champion at a fell-side gathering. But here the prone giant is not left to recover himself. He is rolled to the centre, and his ribs unmercifully thumped. Again set upright under the hammer, an enormous punch, a gauge, as it were, of the interior, is driven into and through the centre of the coil, and with a few more parting taps the cylinder is completed. Twenty-four large boilers furnish steam for the great hammer, cranes, and rolling mills.

In other shops may be seen the *boring* of the toughened steel tube which forms the lining of the great gun; the *rifling* of the tube, of all the operations that, perhaps, which requires the most skill and watchfulness; the cutting and fitting the screws to the breech pieces, the lapping, gauging, testing, and a great many other processes.

The *Turnery*, close by the boring shop, should on no account be left unvisited. In it are 4 of the largest and finest turning lathes yet made. At one, revolving as easily between the centres as a hand-rail in a wood-turner's lathe, is seen perhaps the tube or breech-piece of a 38-ton gun, or it may be the great gun itself, shavings of the rough iron three or four inches wide and $\frac{1}{4}$ of an inch thick peeling off as readily as though they were wood shavings. But delicate turnings are more common, and as effective, as these coarse ones; and all are executed with a degree of accuracy of which the ordinary turner has no conception.

Turned, tempered, gauged, and tested, the parts have to be fitted, by *shrinking on* the outer coil upon the toughened tube or inner cylinder. This with the great guns is performed in the open air. The outer coil, the bore of which is smaller than the outer diameter of that it has to enclose, is made red-hot, expands, and is lifted by the great hydraulic crane, and dropped upon the inner cylinder and set to cool—the process being hastened by copious jets of water. The pressure exerted by the shrinking mass in cooling is so great that the inner cylinder would be crushed out of shape but that it is kept cool by a jet of water constantly playing inside it.

The great operations, such as the rolling, coiling, welding, and shrinking on, of the several portions of the 81-ton gun are of course of comparatively infrequent occurrence, and, as the presence of a crowd of spectators is inconvenient, no announcement is made of the hours at which they are to take place, and the visitor must not reckon on witnessing them. But he will see the machines, and in or outside the shops he will see the various parts of the great gun in their several stages, and be able to form a tolerably clear conception of the different processes. But in other shops and forges he may see the various processes themselves, though on a smaller scale. Thus in the *West* or *Old Forge* are two great hammers, one of 12 tons, the other of 14 tons, at which the operation of welding the coils may frequently and conveniently be witnessed. In the *Rifled Ordnance Factory* all the operations of boring and rifling the steel tube, turning, and the like, are constantly in progress, and every variety of the smaller ordnance of the service made. The fittings are made in the upper rooms. In the *Uniting Furnaces*, the short coils used for lining old smooth-bore guns, and converting them into rifled guns on the Palliser system, are united, shrunk, and toughened, by plunging at a regulated temperature into a vertical bath of oil, where they remain till cold.

After the guns are built up, bored, and rifled, they are taken to the *Sighting*

Room, where they are fitted with the sighting apparatus, go through the several finishing processes, and leave the room ready for service or store.

Having thus seen all the stages of making a gun, the *Pattern Room* will be visited with great interest. In this "sealed patterns"—that is, exact duplicates—are exhibited of every kind of gun made in the Arsenal, from the elegant little 7-pounder mountain gun to the giant of $12\frac{1}{2}$ or 20 tons. The Woolwich Infant, 38 ton, and 81 ton guns, are not yet in duplicate here, but there are beautiful sectional models showing their construction.

Further, as he has seen the gun in its germ, growth, and maturity, so he may if he please visit what in the Arsenal is designated its cemetery, an enclosure N. of the Pattern Room and Proof Square, overshadowed by a grove of elms. Here in regular rows are deposited the remains of the guns burst in testing and experimenting, and over the worthiest are inscriptions setting forth their age, conditions of service (number of rounds fired), and the circumstances under which their existence terminated.

The *Royal Carriage Department* is hardly less interesting than either of the preceding departments. In it are made all the gun carriages, limber equipments, and the like required in the sea and land services. It employs some thousand hands, and has perhaps a greater variety of automatic machinery than any other department. The several parts of the carriage may be traced here through the successive stages of manufacture, in the same manner as the gun, by one who has time and attention to spare. We can glance at but one or two of the salient features. The large field will be noticed. A great variety of woods lie there, and more down on the marsh. But of late years in one and another division iron has been supplanting timber, and thus far it is believed with great advantage as to cost and wear.

The *Saw Mills* contain some very ingenious tools. The great cross-cut saw, 7 ft. in diameter, which rises from the floor, slices off the rough end of a log of timber in a trice, and then quietly sinks out of sight, and the vertical saws, that cut the log into planks, are curious; but the visitor will be more struck with the endless band and ribbon saws, and oscillating platforms, in the *Machine Shop* adjoining, where those marvellous implements adapt themselves to any line, and cut wood, as in another room we may see one of tougher fibre cut iron, into any shape required. Other machines in this shop for shaping, planing, boring, and the like, are somewhat similar in plan and purpose to those used for shaping rifle butts and stocks at Enfield (*see* p. 183); but here they are in greater variety. Among the machines that particularly deserve notice are the lathes, which are of great excellence, and the very ingenious riveting machines.

In the *West Forge* will be seen some very pretty forging and stamping operations under the steam hammer, the variety of articles made being so great that it is said the number of stamping tools exceeds that in any other shop in the kingdom. Nut and bolt forging by machinery may also be witnessed. The finishing is carried on in the room adjoining. The *Main Forge* is, however, the more remarkable. It contains steam hammers, 60 forges, 3 furnaces, a powerful travelling crane, several large forging machines, duplex and other planing machines, boring machines, radial drilling and slotting machines, a great variety of lathes, and a very clever machine for fastening the brackets of gun-carriages; but the most novel and attractive of all are De Bergue's shears, a cutting and punching machine which slices or punches holes through, or pieces out of, plates of iron 2 inches thick with the greatest ease and celerity. Here also may be seen Moncrieff's gun carriage and hydro-pneumatic apparatus, in which the heaviest gun after discharging has the recoil brought perfectly under control, and the gun, after gliding with a stately measured motion up the incline platform, returns of itself, slowly and almost gracefully, to its normal position.

The *Wheel Factory*, in which wheels are manufactured almost wholly by automatic machinery, is the most generally attractive section of the carriage department. In it, from rude blocks of wood, the spokes, naves, and felloes are shaped by means of steel guides (as rifle butts and stocks are fashioned at Enfield), smoothed, the tongues cut, and every part finished by self-acting machines, and turned out so exactly to gauge, that if at any time a part is injured it may be removed and another at once substituted. The finished parts are taken to what is called the *Shoeing Pit*, and fitted rudely together on a circular iron plate over a tank. The tire is brought from a furnace close by, and by a dexterous turn flattened on the iron pavement. It is then lifted, still red-hot, dropped over the wheel, and by a few brisk blows driven into its place, when the wheel with its tire sinks bodily into the tank. The sudden plunge into cold water causes the iron to contract with such irresistible force as to compress the tire irremovably upon the felloes, and the whole together as though made of a single piece.

In the *Pattern Room*, as in the Pattern Rooms of the previous departments, are finished duplicates of all the articles manufactured in the shops.

The *Stores*, or *Control Department*, comprises a very extensive range of buildings extending along the greater part of the river front of the Arsenal, with others on the East Wharf and in the Marshes. In them are stored, ready for immediate use, war material of every kind, from guns and gun-carriages, shot and shell, tents and military equipage, to pails, brushes, and stable fittings. The supply is constantly being drawn upon, and as constantly replenished. In illustration of the character of the department, the more important visitor is usually conducted through the *Harness Stores*, in which is a seemingly inexhaustible display of saddles, bridles, collars, traces, bits, curbs, and stirrups, all in perfect order, and arranged with no little taste—the stirrups, for example, being stacked in shining columns, the bits and bridles pendent from the ceiling in endless festoons. From these stores 10,000 troops could be at any moment supplied.

The *Wharf* extends for about a mile along the river, and is at times a very busy place. Here troops land and embark, and stores are shipped, the Shipping or T Pier being opposite the central offices of the Control Department. A new iron pier has been constructed about 250 yds. farther E., especially for embarking heavy guns. Along the wharf are numerous hydraulic cranes, some of them for lifting the heaviest weights. The various houses seen along here are the Engine-House, for furnishing power to the hydraulic machinery, the Chain Cable Testing House, etc. Before quitting this part of the Arsenal may be noticed the Russian and Chinese bronze guns and mortars—some of the latter beautiful examples of metal casting, and the statue—not exactly Phideian in execution—of the Duke of Wellington.

East of the departments we have visited, and shut off from them by walls or canals, is the *East Laboratory*, a series of detached and to a certain extent isolated buildings, in which cartridge cases are made, the various explosive compositions mixed, and percussion-caps, fuzes, and small-arm cartridges, etc., filled. Girls and boys are largely employed in these operations, but a rigorous supervision is exercised, and every provision made against accidents. The rocket and detonating sheds are beyond the canal; the shell sheds, cannon-cartridge factory, and gun-cotton sheds are in the marshes farther down the river. In these marshes too are the practice ranges for small-arms and ordnance, and the great Butt, at which such monsters as the 38 or 81-ton guns send their quarter or half-ton shots. Here also the gun-cotton and torpedo experiments are carried out. The fish torpedo's "run" is the long canal immediately E. of the East Laboratory.

The *Garrison Buildings* are mostly grouped about or near the Common. Between the Dockyard and the Common are the Red or *Royal Engineer Barracks*, a very extensive range, in large part of recent erection and well planned. The *Royal Artillery Barracks* are however the more important, as the head-quarters of the Military Staff at Woolwich, and the most imposing building in the town. The building has a frontage of over 1200 ft., facing the Common, and, in four divisions, has an equal depth. In it are included administrative offices, and the mess and club rooms—perhaps the finest attached to any barracks in the kingdom, as in them are received and entertained royal personages and distinguished foreign officers on occasions of reviews on the Common or visits to the Arsenal. Opposite the centre of the façade is the *Crimean Memorial*, "erected by their Comrades, to the Memory of the Officers, Non-Commissioned

Officers, and Men of the Royal Regiment of Artillery, who fell during the War with Russia," 1854-56. The memorial is a bronze statue, by John Bell, of Victory, holding the laurel crown, on a lofty granite pedestal, on the front and back of which are bronze shields bearing the inscriptions. Close to the Memorial is a remarkable bronze gun, captured at Bhurtpore in 1828, and given by George IV. to the officers of the Royal Artillery. The gun is 16 ft. 4 in. long, has a calibre of 8 in., and weighs nearly 18 tons. The view from the front of the barracks is very fine. The *Royal Horse Artillery Barracks* and the *Grand Depôt* form a part of the establishment; as do also the *Riding School*, 150 ft. by 63 ft., and the *Ménage*, where the soldiers practise their sword exercise. Connected with the barracks, but in a distinct building, E. of the main building, is the *Royal Artillery Institution*, with its library, museum, reading rooms, lecture theatre, studios, and laboratory, magnetic and meteorological observatory, etc.; an admirable institution, and one in which much good work has been done. For the instruction and amusement of the men, there have been provided well fitted and furnished *Recreation Rooms*, and a *Theatre* for amateur performances. St. George's Church, the garrison chapel, erected in 1863, the richest specimen of ecclesiastical architecture in Woolwich, faces the end of the Artillery Barracks. It is large and lofty, of coloured bricks with stone dressings; the style, as described by the architects, Messrs. T. H. and Digby Wyatt, "an adaptation of Lombardic architecture to the materials and processes in use in the 19th century;" but it suffers externally from the absence of a campanile, a necessary adjunct to a church in that style. The interior is more striking from its space and loftiness, the area being unimpeded save by the light iron columns which carry the gallery and the arches of the clerestorey. Coloured decoration is freely employed, and most of the windows are filled with memorial painted glass.

On the W. side of the Barrack Field, beyond the Battery, and enclosed within a line of field-works, is the *Royal Military Repository*, where all artillery officers have to pass through a course of instruction, and the soldiers are taught to mount, serve, and dismount heavy guns, the use of pontoons and whatever is required in field service. The grounds are extensive, much broken, laid out with earth-works, have large sheets of water for pontooning, and are provided with all requisite military and mechanical appliances.

The Repository is of course not open to visitors, but within its boundaries, in the building known as the *Rotunda*, is the *Royal Artillery Museum*, which is *open to the public every week-day without tickets, from 10 till 12.45 in the morning, and from 2 to 4, 5, or 6, according to the season, in the afternoon.*

The building will be recognised by its unusual appearance: the walls a polygon of 24 sides; the roof a circular tent. It was originally designed by Nash and erected by George IV. (then Prince Regent), in the grounds of Carlton House, as a supper-room, for an entertainment given to the Allied Sovereigns in 1814: it was applied to its present purpose in 1820. As a temporary expedient, it may have been suitable enough; but the museum has outgrown its capabilities. The articles cannot be properly arranged, and the light is insufficient.

The Museum is no longer a mere "collection of naval and military models" and miscellaneous curiosities; but aims to be, and in a great measure is, a comprehensive museum of military arms and appliances, ancient and modern. It comprises a large and valuable, though incomplete, collection of early arms and armour, including such things as a complete suit of armour, said to have belonged to the mirror of knighthood, Bayard, and which good judges have pronounced to be certainly of his time; a large number of tilting helmets, salades, basinets, vamplates (some of them unique), shirts and sleeves of mail, and the other equipments of the knights of the middle ages. The arms and armour of the Cavaliers and Roundheads of the 17th. cent. are also very fairly illustrated. There is a good collection of early swords, and a collection, not less complete, of rapiers and modern dress swords. But it is, as might be expected, —the museum being essentially an artillery museum,—in gunnery that it is exceptionally rich. Here, for example, is the earliest English gun known. It is believed to be of about the middle of the

14th cent., a short thick mortar-like weapon, strengthened with rings, and made to throw stone balls; it was found in the moat of Bodiam Castle, Sussex, and was doubtless intended for its defence. Of nearly equal antiquity are several guns found, with their ammunition of stone balls, in the sands of the island of Walney, Lancashire: long ungainly instruments made of bars or plates of wrought iron, bound together and strengthened by iron hoops. There are also several very curious and very interesting hand-mortars, fire-arrows, and hand-grenades.

But the most interesting, just now, are the early breech-loading and rifled guns, in which, however rudely, almost every modern contrivance seems to have been anticipated—at least in principle. One of the most remarkable is an English breech-loader of the 15th century, very rudely forged, and as would seem a very wild shooter; but the breech arrangement is simple (something after the Krupp principle), and it is noteworthy that in this, as in some other early examples, a duplicate breech-piece was provided to save time in loading. A smooth-bore arquebus, dated 1537, and said to have belonged to Henry VIII., is remarkable for the resemblance of the breech mechanism to that of the Snider breech-loader of the present day.[*] Some of the early Italian breech-loaders are very superior implements. A French double-barrel breech-loading wall-piece, of about 1690, is particularly noteworthy. The barrels are placed one above another, and each rifled with 12 rectangular grooves. The barrel is formed of an inner rifled tube and outer coating, and the muzzles are ornamented with brass heads of animals. There are also German and French breech-loading wall-plate and rampart guns of the 17th cent.; Chinese bronze breech-loading swivel-guns with their tripod stands; various Indian bronze breech-loading guns; and, indeed, a surprisingly large variety of breech-loaders of widely different countries and times. Contrasting with these are the Armstrong breech-loaders of our own day and service, a handsomely finished Krupp's 12-pounder, and the breech arrangement of his 100-pounder in its latest form.

---

[*] Brig.-General Lefroy, R.A., in Archæol. Journal, vol. xxiv., p. 71.

Rifling is equally well illustrated. Here is a rifle with the barrel dated 1547, being the earliest *dated* rifle barrel known, and 42 years earlier than the next in order of time, one in the Paris collection dated 1589. It has seven grooves, and one turn in 22 inches. From these the progress of rifling, both in ordnance and small-arms, may be followed pretty closely in examples from various countries. The rifle was adopted in the English army in 1792, and here are several of the arms used, clumsy instruments with flint locks which continued in use, with few altera-tions, till 1839. Of subsequent kinds, down to the Enfield, Snider, and Martini-Henry, there is a complete series; as well as the needle-guns of the German, and Austrian armies, and the Chassepôts of the French.

The ordinary service arm may be here traced downward from the wheel-lock arquebuses, of which there is a large number, and some highly enriched and in various ways remarkable dated speci-mens by Kotter, Seffler, and other noted German gunsmiths; carbines, petronels, matchlocks, and so on, down to our once familiar, but now discarded, Brown Bess. Of pistols there is of course a large and wide variety. As an example, *obs.* in central glass-case the pair of Spanish holster-pistols, elaborately wrought in silver; but these, rich as they are, are far surpassed by several Oriental examples. Of modern work, revolvers, repeaters, and the like, the specimens are numerous.

As illustrating foreshadowings of recent inventions and processes, *obs.* the two early Chinese cannon of which there are longitudinal sections. One 9 ft. long consists of a tube of wrought iron about $2\frac{1}{4}$ in. thick, with a bore of $5\frac{1}{2}$ in., sur-rounded by an outer casing of bronze 4 in. thick. The tube has been wrought on a mandril, but the welding is imper-fect, the bore very irregular, and the firing consequently must have been very wild. The other is a bronze howitzer, with an inner iron tube which the section shows to have been in like manner rudely wrought on a mandril, but it has the peculiarity that whilst the bore for the shot is 9.2 in. in diameter, the powder chamber (which is 28 in. long) is con-tracted to a diameter of only 4.5 in.

Another division displays shot and shell

of all times, concluding with sections showing the form and composition of most recent varieties of shells used in the British service, as well as models, sec-tions, etc., illustrating their penetrative and destructive effect. Rockets may be traced from Congreve to Hale; their value for warlike purposes and for saving the shipwrecked is variously illustrated; and there are models of rocket trains and rocket apparatus.

Among the almost endless military models, notice the Russian Field Battery presented to the Duke of Wellington by the Emperor Nicholas in 1834. It com-prises 22 guns, each drawn by 16 horses —the whole finished with minute accuracy.

Another noticeable feature is the collec-tion of models of English, colonial, and foreign dockyards, harbours, fortresses, and military works, some executed on a large scale. The most remarkable perhaps is that of Gibraltar, 36 ft. long, the scale 1 in. to 100 ft., a work of great labour and minutely correct.

War trophies from China and Abys-synia; South African and American Indian war implements; pre-historic stone in-struments; the guns and shot raised from the wreck of the 'Mary Rose' (1545), and the ' Royal George;' " infernal machines" of various sorts; the cinder that represents the 56,000,000 one-pound notes burnt when recalled from issue; the trophy of relics —guns, bayonets, swords, etc., curiously molten and intertwisted—from the great fire at the Tower of London, Oct. 1841, and hundreds of other "curiosities," serve as popular counterfoils to the more strictly scientific and antiquarian portion of the Museum. An excellent Official Catalogue may be had at the Rotunda, but as it is sold at the unusual price of 3*s.* 6*d.*, few visitors purchase it : the Museum is so interesting and instructive, if intelligently examined—and to do this a good cata-logue is indispensable—that it is to be hoped the authorities will soon issue a de-scriptive catalogue—even though it be less elaborate than the present—at a moderate price.

Outside is an open-air collection of armour plate targets which have been subjected to the blows of shot and shell, each hole or dent having its record of the occasion, size of shot, etc.; Palisser and other shot and shell as fractured by impact; Chinese and other remarkable guns, and gun-carriages; and relics from the 'Mary Rose' and 'Royal George.'

On the opposite side of the Common, about a mile S.E. from the Rotunda, is the *Royal Military Academy*, which originated in a grant of £1000 by George II., April 30, and Nov. 18, 1741, for the military education of gentlemen cadets. The original school was the house known as Prince Rupert's, within 'Woolwich Warren,' now the Laboratory Museum. The present building was erected in 1804, at a cost of £150,000, from the designs of Sir Jeffry Wyattville. The façade towards the Common consists of a square castellated centre, with cupola-crowned turrets at the angles and wings, united with the centre by corridors, and enclosing an inner quadrangle. The style was described by the architect as partly E.E., partly Elizabethan; and if not very pure, is, like most of Wyattville's work, fairly picturesque. On the 1st of Feb., 1873, the central portion was destroyed by fire, and some damage done to other parts of the building; but the whole has been restored, and additions made to the main structure. The instruction in the Woolwich Academy is preparatory for the Royal Artillery and Royal Engineers: the scientific corps of the British army, and the staff of professors and officers is large, and particularly strong on the scientific side. Students are admitted between the ages of 16 and 18, after a preliminary examination conducted by the Civil Service Commissioners, in which, besides ancient and modern languages, "a thorough knowledge of each of the four branches of mathematics" is required. In April 1876 there were 205 gentlemen cadets in the Academy. The Duke of Connaught, and the Prince Imperial of France, it will be remembered, completed their military education, as Queen's scholars, at the Royal Military Academy.

Woolwich Common is about a mile across; the area 185 acres, of which 60 acres are in Woolwich, and 125 in Charlton parish. It is the property of the Government, the manorial rights having been purchased early in the present century, and is used for exercising the troops and reviews; but there is an open road across it, and the public have free

access to it, except when any part is required for military purposes.

Herbert's Hospital, the noble Garrison Hospital on the western slope of Shooter's Hill, faces the south-western end of the Common: it is noticed more fully under SHOOTER'S HILL (p. 554).

On the Thames, W. of the Dockyard, off Charlton Pier, was moored the old man-of-war 'Warspite,' the training ship of the Royal Marine Society. It was destroyed by fire on the morning of Monday, the 3rd of Jan., 1876, only 11 days after the burning of the 'Goliath' training ship at Grays (*see* p. 245), which was burnt on the 23rd of Dec., 1875. Both ships will be replaced by larger vessels. The new 'Warspite,' formerly the 'Conqueror,' is now at her moorings.

WOOLWICH, NORTH, KENT,

a modern vill. in Woolwich parish, but on the l. bank of the Thames, opposite Woolwich, and the terminus of the Victoria Docks and N. Woolwich br. of the Gt. E. Rly. over which the N. London Rly. also runs trains. Pop. 1455. Inn: *Royal Hotel.*

Though a detached portion of Kent, North Woolwich is locally within the county of Essex. The village is of quite recent growth. A very few years ago there were only a few cottages and the Old Barge House, whence the ferry boats crossed to Woolwich. The formation of the railway and pier, and the establishment of a regular steam-ferry to Woolwich, the construction of the Victoria Docks, and the opening of extensive manufacturing establishments in the immediate vicinity, caused the influx of a large number of working men, and of necessity the building of houses for their accommodation; and whilst the greater number settled in the district known as London over the Border, on the London side of the Victoria Docks, a little town sprang up at North Woolwich. A portion of the great Beckton Works of the Gaslight and Coke Company is in North Woolwich, and there are extensive Electric Telegraph and Submarine Cable, American Leather, Creosote, and other works. North Woolwich is a part of the eccl. dist. of St. Mary, Victoria Docks, for which a spacious Gothic church has been erected.

The *North Woolwich Gardens*, attached

to the Royal Hotel, are a popular place of summer resort.

WORCESTER PARK, SURREY (see MALDEN).

WORMHOLT (popularly WORM-WOOD) SCRUBS, MIDDX.,

celebrated for duels, rifle ranges, and pigeon shooting, is about ¾ m. N. by W. of Shepherd's Bush ; there is a stat. on the N. London and N.-W. Junction Rly.

Wormholt Barns, a sub-manor of Fulham, was leased by Bp. Bonner, in 1549, "on the eve of his first deprivation," to Edward Duke of Somerset, for a term of 200 years. On Somerset's attainder, it became vested in the Crown, and was granted by Queen Elizabeth, in 1559, to Simon Willis. It afterwards passed to George Penruddock and others, and on the termination of the lease was divided into two parts, which have since been leased to private persons.

The waste called *Wormholt Scrubs* was formerly a wood (*holt*) of over 200 acres ; Old Oak Common (*see* ACTON) being an extension of it. Along its N. border runs the G. Western Rly. and the Grand Junction Canal. At the commencement of the present century about 140 acres remained unenclosed, and was used by commoners for pasturage ; by the Government for military exercises, and occasionally for militia encampments ; and by duellists and highwaymen for less innocent purposes. Now it is nearly all enclosed, though not built over. Some sections have been appropriated for the rifle ranges of the Queen's and other volunteer corps ; a portion is occupied as the pigeon shooting ground of the Gun Club ; and the remainder is reserved by the Government for drilling grounds. A large convict prison was erected in 1875, on Wormholt Scrubs, in place of Millbank Prison.

WORMLEY, HERTS (Dom. *Wermelai*),

a vill. on the Ware road, 1½ m. beyond Cheshunt, and 1 m. S. by W. from Broxbourne Stat. of the Gt. E. Rly. Pop. 692. Inn : *White Horse.*

Wormley belonged to the Canons of Waltham Holy Cross from before the Conquest till the Dissolution. The manor was given by Henry VIII. to Edward North, has since passed through a suc-

cession of private hands, and is now the property of Mrs. Grant. The vill. consists mostly of small houses placed irregularly along the highroad. The church stands by the manor-house, ¾ m. W. of the village. The occupations are agricultural : vegetables are largely raised for the London market.

The *Church* (St. Lawrence) is small but interesting, and very prettily placed. It consists of an ancient nave and chancel, and a S. aisle of recent erection. The old walls are low, covered with rough-cast, and have tall tiled roofs ; the aisle is of flint and stone. Above the W. gable is a bell-cote containing two small bells ; on the S.W. a wooden porch. The chancel has 2 original lancets on each side, but the triplet at the E. end was inserted at the recent enlargement of the ch. The nave windows are insertions of Perp. date. At the N.W. is a small plain Norman doorway. The interior has a W. gallery and pews. The font is Norman, and worth examination. Over the altar is a painting of the Last Supper, attributed to Palma. *Monts.*—Marble tomb with recumbent alabaster effigies of Wm. Purvey, d. 1617, auditor of the Duchy of Lancaster, and Dorothy his wife. *Brasses.* —John Cleve, rector, d. 1424 ; Richard Rufton, rector, d. 1457. Brass on tomb in chancel of man, wife, and 12 children, insc. lost. Tablet on S. wall to Richard Gough, the famous antiquary, who d. at his house, Enfield, Feb. 20, 1809, and was buried by his own desire in Wormley ch.-yard. On the N. wall of nave, tablet, with relief of kneeling female, by Westmacott, to Charles Lord Farnborough, d. 1838, and his wife, Amelia Lady Farnborough, d. 1837. Also tablet to Sir Abraham Hume, Bart., of Wormley Bury, d. March 24, 1838, in his 90th year. *Obs.* in the ch.-yard, the large yew-tree opposite the N.W. door, and a smaller one E. of the ch. Also the great elm at the entrance to the ch.-yard.

The manor-house, *Wormleybury* (Mrs. Grant), E. of the ch. is a large brick mansion of three storeys, with, in the centre, a tetrastyle Ionic portico and pediment reaching to the roof. It stands in a small but pleasant park, with a little stream flowing along the bottom, which, opposite the house, expands into a broad sheet of water. W. of the ch. is an attractive country district. *West Lea* is the seat of G. Boulnois Ireland, Esq.; *Wormley House* of J. F. Johnson, Esq.

WROTHAM PARK, MIDDX. (*see* MIMMS, SOUTH).

WYRARDISBURY, BUCKS, pronounced, and now commonly written, WRAYSBURY (Dom. *Werecesberie*), lies in the meadows, ½ m. from the l. bank of the Thames, and a little to the W. of the Colne; 1½ m. S.W. from Horton, and 3 m. N.W. from Staines; a vill. and a stat. on the Windsor branch of the L. and S.-W. Rly. Pop. 731. Inn: *The George.*

The vill. is a long straggling collection of small houses, with a few of a better description, and two or three good seats. The pursuits are mainly agricultural, but there are paper and millboard mills by the Colne, and the vill. is in some favour with anglers. The country is level, but green, pleasant, well-watered (in winter subject to floods), abounds in trees, and has Cooper's Hill and the towers of Windsor Castle near enough to form important features in the landscape. Charter or Magna Charta Island lies off Wraysbury, and Runnimede is on the opposite bank of the Thames.

Wyrardisbury *Church* (St. Andrew) was rebuilt in 1862, under the direction of Mr. Raphael Brandon, only the chancel and the nave arcades of the old ch. being retained. The tower and spire were added in 1871. It is of square hammered Kentish rag and Bath stone. The nave has E.E. windows; the chancel Dec.; the vestry, on the N., Perp. The doorway in the N. aisle is a copy of that of the old ch. The interior has a good open-timber roof, painted glass in the windows, and low open seats. Obs. *brass* of a youth, — Stonor, 1512, in a kind of academical habit; said to be of an Eton boy, but this is doubtful: nothing on the brass supports the belief; the college rolls for the period are imperfect, but no such name occurs on them. There are mural monts. to the Stonor, Hassel, Harcourt,

and Gyll families, but none of general interest.

In the ch.-yard, W. of the ch., are the tombs of the Harcourt family. On the W. is a good-sized yew-tree. The entrance is by a 17th cent. lich-gate.[*]

Remingham House is the seat of G. W. J. Gyll, Esq., lord of the manor of Remingham and Cow (holding it on lease of the Dean and Canons of Windsor), and author of the 'History of Wraysbury' (4to, 1862). *Place Farm*, on the road to Datchet, the picturesque old grange popularly known as *King John's Hunting Lodge*, is noticed under DATCHET (p. 138). It is the property of Mr. Gyll, and carefully preserved by him. *Ankerwyke House* and the great yew-tree are described under ANKERWYKE (p. 13).

Charter Island, or *Magna Charta Island*, is an eyot of about 2½ acres, lying off the upper end of the grounds of Ankerwyke House. In Aubrey's day the tradition ran that the treaty between John and the Barons was made "in an eight (eyot) over against Yard-Mead, which is Runny-Mead, and the Great Charter sealed there." Accepting the tradition, Mr. G. Simon Harcourt, then lord of the manor, erected in 1834 a Gothic cottage on the island, fitted it with old carved oak wainscoting, and adorned windows and walls with a portrait of John and the arms of the associated Barons. In the centre of the room, set in a massive oak frame, he placed a stone inscribed "Be it remembered that on this island, in June 1215, John, King of England, signed the Magna Charta": but as to that see RUNNIMEDE (p. 516); where also is noticed a later treaty which was signed on the island. Charter Island is united with the mainland by a causeway at the upper end.

YEADING, MIDDX. (*see* HAYES).

YIEWSLEY, MIDDX. (*see* HILLINGDON).

---

[*] It is engraved in Lipscomb's Hist. of Buckinghamshire, vol. iv., p. 612.

INDEX.

The date within brackets is that of death, unless otherwise indicated.

772 INDEX.

GUNDULF.   HAWKINS.

Locket, George, residence, 432.
Lock's Bottom, 213.
Lockyer, Nicholas, ejected Provost of Eton, died (1685), 738.
Lodge, The, Hampton Court, residence of Ranger, 69.
Lodge, The, Morden, 438.
Lodge, Thomas, poet (1695), lived, 419.
London, Bishops of, Palace at Fulham, 222 : royal visitors, 223 ; portraits, 222 ; tombs, 221 ; ancient seat, 362.
Londonderry, Robert Stewart Lord Castlereagh and Marquis of. *See* Castlereagh.
London Orphan Asylum, 679.
London Stone, Staines, boundary of City jurisdiction, and dividing mark of Upper and Lower Thames, 561.
Long, C. A., building by, 625.
Long, Colonel S., residence, 418.
Long Cross, 92.
Long, Sir J. Tylney (1794), mont., 669.
Longden, Major-Gen., residence, 215.
Longford, 320.
Longland, John, Bp. of Lincoln (1547), mont., 210.
Longley, Archbp. (1868), buried, 6.
Longman, Thos., residence, 354 ; died (1797), 291.
Longmore, Philip, residence, 339.
Lonsdale, Earl of, residence, 27.
Lothian, Marquis of, lived, 502.
Lotto, Lorenzo, painting by, 307.
Loudwater House, 509.
Loudwater Paper Mills, 509
Louis Philippe, King of the French (1850), at Claremont, 206 ; at Twickenham, 630 ; burial-place, 693.
Louis XIV., portrait, 310.
Louis XVIII., lived, 669.
Louisa, Princess (of Saxe Weimar), d. 1817, mont., 720.
Loutherbourg, Philip James de, R.A. (1812), lived, 277 ; his mesmeric cures, 278 ; mob break his windows, 278 ; mont., 107 ; painting by, 256.
Lovat, Simon Fraser Lord, lived before arrest, 627.
Love, S., residence, 556.
Lovekyn, Edward (1305), founds Grammar School, 402.
Lovell, Gregory, cofferer to Queen Elizabeth (1597), mont., 427.
Lovelace, Colonel, the poet (1658), portrait, 155.
Lovelace, Earl of, owns manor, 148.
Lovibond, Edward, poet (1775), scholar at, 402.
Lowe, Rt. Hon. Robert, M.P., residence, 78.
Lowen, John, one of Shakspeare's 'Fellows,' lived, 57.
Lower Cheam Park, 86.
Lowth, Robert, Bp. of London (1787), portrait, 222 ; mont., 221.

Lowther, Hon. Barbara (1805), mont. by Flaxman, 503.
Loyd, Jones, residence, 3.
Lubbock, F., residence, 449.
Lubbock, Sir John, M.P., seat, 154.
Lubbock, Sir J. W. (1865), lived, 436.
Lucan, Earl of, seat, 410.
Lucan, Margaret Countess of (1814), mont., 704.
Lucas, statue by, 318.
Luch, Mrs. C. C., residence, 289.
Lullingstone Castle, 423.
Lumley, John Lord (1609), the great book collector, mont., 86.
Lunatic Asylum : county of Essex, 60 ; Middlesex 115, 312 ; City of London, 577 ; County of Surrey, 615.
Lupton, Provost of Eton, chapel and tomb., 210.
Lushington, E. H., residence, 662.
Lushington, Mary (1797), mont. by Flaxman, 417.
Lushington, Sir Stephen, lived, 706.
Lusk, Ald. Sir A., Bart., M.P., residence, 422.
Luti, B., portrait by, 310.
Lyall, G., residence, 336, 510.
Lynd, Sir Humphry, builds Cambridge House, 632.
Lyndhurst, Lord (1863), lived, 706 buried, 349 ; portrait, 587.
Lyne, 92.
Lyne Grove, 92.
Lyon, John (1592), founder of Harrow School, brass, 322.
Lyonsdown, Barnet, 31.
Lyttleton, George, 1st Lord (1773), 'Conversion of St. Paul,' at Wickham, 696.
Lyttleton, Thomas, 2nd Lord (the Bad), died 1779, 199.
Lytton, Lord. *See* Bulwer, Sir Edward Lytton.

MABUSE (Van Gossaert), pictures by, 309, 310.
M'Adam, John Loudon (1836), the road-maker, lived, 359.
Macandrew, J., residence, 431.
Macandrew, J. J., residence, 550.
MacAndrew, Mrs., residence, 382
MacArdell, James (1765), engraver, buried, 286.
Macartney, George Earl of (1806), 'Embassy to Spain,' residence, 110 ; buried, 107.
MacCalmont, R., seat, 227.
Macclesfield, Thomas Parker, 1st Earl of, Lord Chancellor (1732), lived, 288.
M'Dowell, P. sculpture by, 256.
M'Geachy, F. Alleyne, residence, 553.
Macintosh, D., residence, 333.
Mackenzie, Ed., gift to British Orphan Asylum, 557.
Mackintosh, George Gordon, seat, 634.
Mackintosh, Sir James (1832), tomb, 285.

M'Lean, James, the gentleman highwayman, executed at Tyburn, 1750, at Putney, 479.
MacLeary, G., residence, 52.
M'Murray, W., residence, 509.
M'Niven, C., residence, 463.
Macpherson, Jas. (1796, Ossian), lived, 478.
M'Queen, Colonel L., residence, 565.
Maes, N., painting by, 229.
Magdalen Hospital, 591.
Maginn, W., LL.D. (1842), buried, 661.
Magna Charta, signed, 516.
Magna Charta Island, 516, 755.
Magni, statue of the Reading Girl, 588.
Main Drainage, Southern Outfall Stat., 2 ; Northern Outfall Stat., 23 ; Crossness, 202, 474 ; Pumping Stat., 579 ; Northern Main Sewer, 685.
Mall, Chiswick, 105.
Mall, Hammersmith, 273, 277.
Mallet, David (1765), lived, 577.
Mallet du Pan, Jacques (1800), buried, 504
Malthus, Thomas Robert, political economist (1834), birthplace, 152.
Mammalian remains, Thames Valley, 377 ; Valley of the Lea, 658.
Manchester, Duchess of, lived, 382.
Mandeville, Sir John (1300), birthplace, 525.
Mandey, Venturus, learned bricklayer (1701), mont., 383.
Manning, Cardinal, born, 626.
Manning, Francis, translator of Theodosius, lived, 605.
Manor House, Abbot's Langley, 3 ; Barnet, 32 ; Little Bookham, 54 ; Bushey, 69 ; Crayford, 123 ; Ealing, 160 ; Claremont, 207 ; Fawkham, 215 ; Finchley, 217 ; Hadley, 267 ; Heston, 342 ; High Beech, 343 ; Petersham, 470 ; Pinner, 470 ; Shepperton, 554 ; Sidcup, 557 ; Southall, 559 ; Stoke d'Abernon, 573 ; Stoke Poges, 574 ; Streatham, 589 ; Sunbury, 591 ; Swanscombe, 597 ; Teddington, 605 ; Walton-on-Thames, 662 ; Woodford, 737 ; Woodmansterne, 739.
Mansfield, Earls of, family monts., 337.
Mansfield, William Murray Earl of, Lord Chief Justice (1793), purchases and enlarges Caen Wood, 71 ; relics from fire of library ; portrait, 71, 265.
Mansfield, W., 3rd Earl of (1840), mont., 395.
Mantegna, Andrea, cartoons by, 310.
Manuscript, French, from Barking Abbey, 21.
Mapesburg, 699.
Maplescombe, 396.
Mapleton Lodge, 687.

CORRECTIONS.

Page 2, col. 2, for Lord *Abbot*, read Lord *Raymond*.
,, 6 ,, 1, l. 35, for 1848, read 1845.
,, 8 ,, 1, l. 13, for *Payne*, read *Paine*.
,, 10 ,, 1, l. 38, for *division*, read *brigade*.
,, 15 ,, 2, last line, for 1644, read 1664.
,, 17 ,, 2, l. 21, for 1736, read 1733.
,, 19 ,, 2, . 33, for *Maudesley*, read *Maudslay*.
,, 27 ,, 2, l. 22, for 1712, read 1727.
,, 29 ,, 1, The restoration of Barnet church was completed, and the church re-opened, May 25, 1875.
,, 38 ,, 1, l. 42, for *Elizabeth*, read *Queen Mary*.
,, 57 ,, 1, l. 43, for *Poole*, read *Peele*.
,, 73 ,, 2, l. 45, for *Earl* of Abercorn, read *Duke*.
,, 74 ,, 1, l. 30, for 1747, read 1744.
,, 77 ,, 2, l. 34, for *Gibbon*, read *Gibbons*.
,, 92 ,, 1, l. 29, for *Payne*, read *Paine*.
,, 106 ,, 1, l. 31, for 1*st* Earl, read 4*th*.
,, 128 ,, 1, Croydon pleasure fair was prohibited October 1875.
,, 148 ,, 2, l. 42, Lord St. Leonards died Jan. 29, 1875.
,, 150 ,, 2, l. 51, for *Mason Good*, read *John Mason*.
,, 166 ,, 2, l. 20, for 1437, read 1347.
,, 174 ,, 1, l. 31, for Hatfield *Hall*, read Hatfield *House*.
,, 245 ,, 1, l. 22, The Goliath Training Ship was destroyed by fire, December 23, 1875, but has been replaced by a larger ship, The Exmouth.
,, 278 ,, 1, l. 25, for Sir *Christopher*, read Sir *Clifton*.
,, 337 ,, 2, l. 41, for Sir *John*, read Sir *Joseph*.
,, 407 ,, 2, last line but one, for 4*th* Duke, read 3*rd*.
,, 427 ,, 2, l. 18, for *George* Lovell, read *Gregory*.
,, 451 ,, 2, l. 6, for 1710, read 1707.
,, 508 ,, 2, l. 14, for *Rospigliari*, read *Rospigliosi*.
,, 639 ,, 2, l. 34, for *John*, read *William*.
,, 641 ,, 2, l. 47, for 1758, read 1785.
,, 648 ,, 1, l. 37, for *Paul* Sandby, read *Thomas*.
,, 714 ,, 1, l. 1, for 1547, read 1457.
,, 732 ,, 1, l. 49, dele "*in* 1791."